HT 361 URB

Urban Space in the Middle Ages and the Early Modern Age

# Fundamentals of Medieval and Early Modern Culture

Edited by
Albrecht Classen and Marilyn Sandidge

4

Walter de Gruyter · Berlin · New York

# Urban Space in the Middle Ages and the Early Modern Age

Edited by
Albrecht Classen

Walter de Gruyter · Berlin · New York

# QM LIBRARY
# (MILE END)

∞ Printed on acid-free paper which falls within the guidelines
of the ANSI to ensure permanence and durability.

*Library of Congress Cataloging-in-Publication Data*

Urban space in the middle ages and the early modern age / edited by
Albrecht Classen.
    p. cm. − (Fundamentals of medieval and early modern culture ; 4)
Chiefly in English with three contributions in German.
Includes index.
ISBN 978-3-11-022389-7 (alk. paper)
    1. Urbanization − History.    2. Cities and towns − Growth − History.
I. Classen, Albrecht.
    HT361.U718   2009
    307.7609−dc22

                                       2009027975

ISBN 978-3-11-022389-7
ISSN 1864-3396

*Bibliographic information published by the Deutsche Nationalbibliothek*

The Deutsche Nationalbibliothek lists this publication in the Deutsche
Nationalbibliografie; detailed bibliographic data are available in the Internet
at http://dnb.d-nb.de.

Printed in Germany
Cover design: Christopher Schneider, Laufen
Printing and binding: Hubert & Co., Göttingen

# Table of Contents

Albrecht Classen

(University of Arizona)

# Urban Space in the Middle Ages and the Early Modern Age: Historical, Mental, Cultural, and Social-Economic Investigations[1]

## Investigative Queries: The Starting Point, Where Have We Come From, Where Are We, Where Are We Going?

When did urban space gain relevance in the Middle Ages, or when was it perceived as a separate and significant entity where human affairs were negotiated and decided, where power structures manifested themselves, and where the real economic center rested, in contrast to the world of the rural population? What did the city really mean for medieval or early-modern people, as far as we can trust the countless literary and historiographical documents from that time period? The contrast between the urban world of the Roman Empire and that of the early Middle Ages with its almost exclusive focus on agriculture as its economic base is more or less self-evident. Although many cities had originally been founded by the Romans throughout Europe, they continued to exist, even if many had to wait many centuries until they experienced a solid flourishing again in terms of population, wealth, the arts, architecture, and the economy.[2]

---

[1] I would like to express my gratitude to Marilyn Sandidge, Westfield State College, Westfield, MA, for her critical reading of this introduction and great support in many other ways. All remaining mistakes are, of course, my own. My colleague Fabian Alfie, University of Arizona, read through many of the contributions and alerted me to a number of small errors, for which I am very thankful.

[2] John Rich, *The City in Late Antiquity*. Leicester-Nottingham Studies in Ancient Society, 3 (London and New York: Routledge, 1992); *Towns in Transition: Urban Evolution in Late Antiquity and the Early Middle Ages*, ed. Neil Christie and S. T. Loseby (Aldershot, Hants, England, and Brookfield, VT: Scolar Press, 1996); Bertrand Lançon, *Rome in Late Antiquity: Everyday Life and Urban Change, AD 312–609* (New York: Routledge, 2000); Yizhar Hirschfeld, "Habitat," *Interpreting Late Antiquity: Essays on the Postclassical World*, ed. G. W. Bowersock, Peter Brown, and Oleg Grabar (Cambridge,

If a medieval or early-modern writer mentioned a town or a city, did s/he really mean the same as we do today when we refer to such a place? And if a town/city is mentioned, what value or meaning was attached to it? When and how did medieval artists reflect upon urban space, and why did they do so, when normally ecclesiastic space and courts seem to have dominated public imagination most of the time? How did medieval people view and respond to the ancient urban civilization, which continued to be present far beyond the fall of Rome in the fifth century both in the form of numerous cities established by the Romans and in literary works predicated on Roman models dealing with urban space?[3] Was the ancient Roman city a challenge, or model, or a base upon which medieval people built their own society within an urban setting?

Undoubtedly, urban space certainly meant something quite different to people in the Middle Ages and the early modern age than to those who still lived with the Roman culture in mind or drew their values and inspiration from that ancient world. We can probably assert that the same kind of difference exists between, on the one hand, our modern attitude to and relationship with urban space, and that held by people in the premodern era, on the other. At any rate, however, both then and today urban space constitutes a focal point for many different societies, perhaps more in the postmodern age than in the premodern age, but even then towns and cities proved to be some of the most critical nodes in the larger network of a whole country or people.[4]

The modern Italian novelist Italo Calvino expressed it perhaps best in his fictional travel narrative, *Le città invisibile*, an imaginary account by Marco Polo writing to the Mongol ruler Kublai Khan, describing, for instance, the city Zaira:

---

[3]  MA, and London: The Belknap Press of Harvard University Press, 2001), 258–72. See the various contributions to: *La Fin de la cité antique et le début de la cité médiévale: de la fin du IIIe siècle à l'avènement de Charlemagne. Actes du colloque tenu à l'Université de Paris X-Nanterre les 1, 2 et 3 avril 1993*, réunis par Claude Lepelley. Munera. Studi storici sulla tarda antichità, 8 (Bari: Edipuglia, 1996). For comprehensive and most updated scholarship on this large topic, see the entries dealing with city, city laws, urban divinities, urban law, and urban architecture in *Der neue Pauly: Enzyklopädie der Antike*, ed. Hubert Cancik and Helmuth Schneider. Vol. 11 (Stuttgart and Weimar: Metzler, 2001), 890–912.

[4]  There are whole bookshelves full of studies on urban space today; see, for instance, Allan B. Jacobs, *Great Streets* (Cambridge, MA, and London: The Hit Press, 1993); Martin M. Pegler, *Streetscapes* (New York: Retail Reporting Corporation, 1998); David Pinder, *Visions of the City: Utopianism, Power and Politics in Twentieth-Century* Urbanism (Edinburgh: Edinburgh University Press 2005); Urban Space. No. 5: Featuring Green Design Strategies, ed. John Morris Dixon. Designed by Veronika Levin (New York: Visual Reference Publications, 2007). As urban architects commonly express also nowadays, the question of what constitutes urban space and how to design it constitutes a critical question for society at large because of all people involved, the management and maintenance, safety, and the need to offer functionality and aesthetic appeal at the same time; see Sarah Gaventa, *New Public Spaces* (London: Mitchell Beazley, 2006).

The city does not consist of this [how many steps make up the streets rising like stairways, ibid.], but of relationships between the measurements of its space and the events of its past: the height of a lamppost and the distance from the ground of a hanged usurper's swaying feet; the line strung from the lamppost to the railing opposite and the festoons that decorate the course of the queen's nuptial procession; the height of that railing and the leap of the adulterer who climbed over it at dawn . . . . A description of Zaira as it is today should contain all Zaira's past. The city, however, does not tell its past, but contains it like the lines of a hand, written in the corners of the streets, the gratings of the windows, the banisters of the steps . . ., every segment marked in turn with scratches, indentations, scrolls.[5]

Calvino composed his novel directly drawing from Marco Polo's *Milione*, but whereas the Venetian traveler was mostly determined by mercantile interests and the curiosity about the foreign world in its physical manifestation, Calvino explored the mental stage of urban spaces.[6]

## Cities in the Transitional Phase from the Late Roman Empire to the Early Middle Ages

One point regarding towns and cities in the Middle Ages needs to be stated right from the beginning, which will hopefully deconstruct one of the many myths about that period as a time of alleged primitivism, barbarism, and lack of civilization. Although we tend to identify towns or cities and complementary urban life with the early modern age, more narrowly defined as the Renaissance, many cities already dotted the early medieval landscape, though in most cases considerably smaller in size and physical extent than those centuries later. And depending on the specific region in Europe, urban culture extensively influenced medieval society as early as the eleventh and twelfth centuries, and this even in face of the fact that a vast majority of the population continued to live in the

---

[5]    Italo Calvino, *Invisible Cities*, trans. from the Italian William Weaver (1972; New York and London: Harcourt Brace Jovanovich, 1974), 10–11; see also the contributions to *Medieval Practices of Space*, ed. Barbara A. Hanawalt and Michal Kobialka. Medieval Cultures, 23 (Minneapolis and London: University of Minnesota Press, 2000), especially Michael Camille, "Signs of the Cith: Place, Power, and Public Fantasy in Medieval Paris" (1–36).

[6]    Marina Zancan, "*Le città invisibili* di Calvino," *Letteratura italiana: Le opera*, vol. 4: *L Novecento*, part 2: *La ricerca letteraria*, ed. Alberto Asor Rosa (Turin: Einaudi-Gallimard, 1996), 828–930; Martin McLaughlin, "Calvino's Rewriting of Marco Polo: From the 1960 Screenplay to *Invisible Cities*," *Marco Polo and the Encounter of East and West*, ed. Suzanne Concklin Akbari and Amilcare Iannuci (Toronto, Buffalo, and London: University of Toronto Press, 2008), 182–200.

countryside and that the aristocracy still held on to its leading role as inherited from the early Middle Ages at least until the fifteenth century.[7]

Urban space and urban culture then had most likely a different character than during the Renaissance, yet not necessarily without significant similarities in social and economic terms, and definitely regarding civic pride and identity. This phenomenon has been studied many times, yet it continues to vex us deeply, and requires ever new approaches drawing from different source material, whether historical, art-historical, literary, or social-economic. In addition, the meaning of urban space changes from area to area, from country to country, and so also from language region to language region. Surprisingly, however, common elements can be discovered everywhere, as I will discuss below, whether we investigate the treatment of towns/cities and their cultural manifestation in eighth-century Iberia or in thirteenth-century Norway.[8]

We have to take general statements about medieval urbanism really with a grain of salt, as when Kathryn L. Reyerson claims, trying to summarize the state of art in her field: "One of the most dramatic instances of retrenchment and shrinkage that distinguishes the ancient world from the medieval is to be found in the medieval town. The civilizations of the Greeks and the Romans were essentially urban . . . . In contrast, the barbarians and their institutions were not, in general, associated with towns, although there certainly existed fortified enclosures, oppida, in Gaul and in Germany . . . . The contrasts between towns of the Roman period and those of the early Middle Ages were profound. From a complex juridical vocabulary associated with towns in antiquity one passes in Merovingian times to a simplified system of classification. Three terms were used by the Merovingians to describe urban forms: civitas, castrum, and *vicus*."[9] She primarily subscribes to the ideas developed by Henri Pirenne regarding the loss of

---

[7]    This finds remarkable expression in the vast corpus of Books of Hours in which the world of agriculture provides the essential basis for the calendar because of the cycle of seasons could be best observed in nature, Teresa Pérez Higuera, *Medieval Calendars* (1997; London: Weidenfeld & Nicolson, 1998), 128–32. However, at closer examination there are also numerous, though very small references to urban life emerging in the distant background. An excellent example following the same model, though not a Book of Hours, proves to be the pictorial cycle in the Castello del Buonconsiglio in Trento, ibid., 181–83. Here an aristocratic company enjoys itself with throwing snowballs at each other, while hunters stand by in the background, next to the mighty city and castle.

[8]    See the contributions to *The Comparative History of Urban Origins in Non-Roman Europe: Ireland, Wales, Denmark, Germany, Poland, and Russia from the Ninth to the Thirteenth Century*, ed. Howard B. Clark and Anngret Simms. BAR International Series, 255 (Oxford: B.A.R., 1985). For a specific case study for the western, non-Romanized world, see *Dublin*. Part 1: *To 1610*, ed. H. B. Clark, Anngret Simms, and Raymond Gillespie. Irish Historic Towns Atlas, 11 (Dublin: Royal Irish Academy, 2002).

[9]    Kathryn L. Reyerson, "Urbanism, Western Europe," *Dictionary of the Middle Ages*, ed. Joseph R. Strayer. Vol. 12 (New York: Charles Scribner's Sons, 1989), 311–20; here 311–12.

importance of the town for the early Middle Ages (313), but then she adduces actually considerable evidence that seems to point toward a different direction, emphasizing the role of Emperor Charlemagne, and of the Church at large to dedicate much new energy to the development of urban space. She concludes this section, however, with the negative summary: "the return to the town initiated by Charlemagne failed because it was linked to a political effort that did not endure" (314).

The size of cities does not really matter for the exploration of urban culture and urban space in the premodern world, especially not in the time shortly after the Roman period, as long as we can recognize that urban space continued to dominate social, economic, and political life. Historians and archeologists have disagreed, however, over the definition of what constitutes a city in concrete terms. Would an administrative seat, or an economic center be sufficiently significant to talk about a city in the early Middle Ages? As so often has been the case, simplistic answers do not serve us well; instead we need a *Kriterienbündel* (a bundle of criteria), as established by Edith Ennen, including 1. defense; 2. street planning; 3. market(s); 4. a mint; 5. legal autonomy; 6. a role as a central place; 7. a relatively large population; 8. economic diversification; 9. urban types of houses not specifically geared for agricultural living and production; 10. social differentiation; 11. a complex religious organization; and 12. judicial functions.[10]

But again, as scholars have repeatedly warned, we have to accept remarkable differences between urban settlements north of the Alps and south of them, if we can untangle the thorny issue of what makes up a town and what a city.[11] Political and military developments in medieval England also led to a considerably different development of cities compared to those on the continent because a long period of internal peace had made the city wall mostly unnecessary for defense purposes at least since the thirteenth or fourteenth century, and it maintained only

---

[10] Edith Ennen, *Die europäische Stadt des Mittelalters*. 3rd, rev. and expanded ed. (1972; Göttingen: Vandenhoeck & Ruprecht, 1979); Engl. trans. as *The Medieval Town*, trans. Natalie Fryde. Europe in the Middle Ages, 5 (Amsterdam and New York: North-Holland Pub., 1979).

[11] Chris Wickham, *Framing the Early Middle Ages: Europe and the Mediterranean 400–800* (Oxford and New York: Oxford University Press, 2005), 591–96. This model was essentially put together by Martin Biddle, "Towns," *The Archeology of Anglo-Saxon England*, ed. David M. Wilson (London: Methuen, 1976), 99–150; here 100. See also Wolf Liebeschütz, "Cities, Taxes, and the Accommodation of the Barbarians," *From Roman Provinces to Medieval Kingdoms*, ed. Thomas F. X. Noble. Rewriting Histories (London and New York: Routledge, 2006), 309–23. For a nice overview of the social, economic, military, religious, and literary aspects determining the transition from late antiquity to the early Middle Ages, though without taking urbanism into consideration, see William R. Cook and Ronald B. Herzman, *The Medieval World View: An Introduction*. Sec. ed. (1983; New York and Oxford: Oxford University Press, 2004), 90–128. But they discuss, rather superficially, the rise of the city since the tenth century on pp. 178–84.

the role as a customs barrier, protecting the merchant class inside and allowing the city to levy tolls on all goods imported by outside traders.[12]

Curiously, however, as Chris Wickham alerts us, already in the late Roman Empire the general appeal of living in the city had declined, especially because of the growing militarization of Roman society and the new focus on landed estates for the elite. Concomitantly, as he observes, "cities changed too. Their own identities shifted, as they became less the stage of all significant civil aristocratic activity, less the focus for an autonomous, inward-looking, public politics. Public space became more religious, for example, as bishops became more important (the smaller the city, by and large, the more religious its public space became—in the *civitas* of northern Francia (France) and England which kept their bishops but lost their urban economic features, religious ceremonial was all that was left)."[13]

One of the key reasons seems to have been the switch of a taxation system controlled by local governments to a taxation system organized by the central government in most cases far away, undermining some of the crucial motivating factors that had traditionally supported the urban elite—the end of the *curia*, both in cities in the eastern and in the western Empire, which subsequently led to the "physical decay of the forum/agora and its associated civic buildings at the centre of cities, which . . . could happen at the same time as the building or repair of rich private houses and privately founded churches elsewhere in town."[14]

Nevertheless, cities did not simply disappear in the wake of extensive military problems and political crises during the post-Roman period, but the aristocratic elite found it less and less attractive to live there, which was to become the clear harbinger of the early-medieval world where "participation in the political retinue of a count could be done from either an urban or a rural base; and counts might not have so much authority that social leaders needed to be in their retinues at all."[15]

This could lead to a general disintegration of the urban community, but not necessarily so, which forces us to be extremely careful in the assessment of urban history at that early stage in the Middle Ages. As Pablo C. Díaz puts it, "If until the

---

[12] A. E. J. Morris, *History of Urban Form Before the Industrial Revolutions*. Third ed. (1972; New York: Longman Scientific & Technical, 1994), 97–99.
[13] Chris Wickham, *Framing the Early Middle Ages*, 595.
[14] Chris Wickham, *Framing the Early Middle Ages*, 598; Timothy W. Potter, *Towns in Late Antiquity: Iol Caesarea and Its Context*. Occasional Publication, Ian Sanders Memorial Fund, 2 (Sheffield: Ian Sanders Memorial Fund, 1995), 63–102. See also *Towns and Their Territories Between Late Antiquity and the Early Middle Ages*, ed. Gian Pietro Brogiolo. The Transformation of the Roman World, 9 (Leiden, Boston, and Cologne: Brill, 2000); *Towns in Transition: Urban Evolution in Late Antiquity and the Early Middle Ages*, ed. Neil Christie and S. T. Loseby (Aldershot: Ashgate, 1998); Giacomo Gonella, *The History of Early Medieval Towns of North and Central Italy: the Contributions of Archaeological Evidence* (Oxford: Archeopress, 2008).
[15] Chris Wickham, *Framing the Early Middle Ages*, 602.

beginning of the fourth century *possessor* and *decurio* were considered synonymous, by the end of that century and in the fifth we find that the members of the *curia* belonged to a genuinely urban middle class, especially small landowners and merchants or artisans not connected with landowning."[16]

After all, the many examples of significant and even growing cities speak a loud and distinct language. In some regions the aristocracy notably lived in cities, such as in post-sixth-century Italy, but even there the number of important aristocrats residing in the countryside was also not negligible. In Merovingian France the majority of nobles lived outside of the cities, but again, this did not necessarily affect urban growth negatively after ca. 550 C.E. Chris Wickham provides the valuable summary: "In 700–50, say, Egypt, Italy, and Syria-Palestine are clearly the regions with the most urbanized aristocrats. Next come southern Spain and southern Gaul, perhaps the Marmara sub-region close to Constantinople, and maybe Africa, where cities were not the only locations for aristocratic living, but important ones all the same."[17]

## The High Middle Ages

As soon as we turn our attention to the tenth and eleventh centuries, the situation changes remarkably, and becomes much more complex. As Joseph and Frances Gies emphasize with regard to early-medieval Milan, for instance, it "boasted a hundred towers in the tenth century. Its prosperity had derived originally from its fertile countryside and the road and river network of which it was the hub. But during the tenth and eleventh centuries it became the chief workshop of Europe. Its smiths and amorers turned out swords, helmets, and chain mail for the knights of Italy, Provence, Germany, and even more distant lands, while its mint struck over twenty thousand silver pennies a year."[18] They point out the intricate relationship between advanced agricultural productivity, such as wine growing,

[16] Pablo C. Díaz, "City and Territory in Hispania in Late Antiquity," *Towns and Their Territories Between Late Antiquity and the Early Middle Ages*, 2000, 1–35; here 7. He offers the most insightful conclusion that the fundamental transformation of the Roman city to the post-Roman city was triggered by the "alteration of the scheme of relationships and reciprocal influences that defined the former with respect to the latter. In practice, city/country unity broke dwn, the *territoria* became independent from the control of the city, and the State functionaries acted from the city on a rural area which, despite administrative schemes, was regulated by its own mechanisms. The country acquired its own morphology and in the end the city remained as a consuming appendix unable to exist without the country, but which the country could well afford to ignore" (34–35).
[17] Chris Wickham, *Framing the Early Middle Ages*, 608–09; he emphasizes the exceptional situation of early-medieval England (with hardly any urbanism until ca. 700), and the Rhineland with its significant economic prosperity focused on urban economies.
[18] Joseph and Frances Gier, *Life in a Medieval City* (New York: Harper & Row, 1981), 11.

and sophisticated craftsmanship production methods, which led to the development of major markets, the central points within a city. In other words, technological developments had a direct bearing on improvements in agriculture, craftsmanship, and merchandising/trade, which all in turn supported and strengthened the development and growth of cities much earlier in the Middle Ages than commonly assumed.

Nevertheless, both in our investigation of this period and later ones we have to be careful not to confuse general trends with specific cases, and also not to fall prey to global assumptions about the steady growth of medieval cities far into the early-modern world, as if history could be described as a progressive, linear process. As for Italy, for instance, the period from 550 to 750 is commonly described as a time of urban crisis and wide-spread decline in economic and cultural activities, whereas the period from 750 to 950 is mostly seen as a time of noteworthy revival and new growth.[19]

Using the French city of Troyes as an example, Joseph and Frances Gies underscore: "All had abbeys and monasteries, as well as many churches—most of timber, a few of stone with timber roofs. A feature of many cities, including Troyes, was the palace of a secular prince. There were still empty spaces in these municipalities—swampy land along a river, or an unexploited meadow. Most cities ranged in area from a hundred acres to half a square mile, in population from two or three thousand to between ten and twenty thousand. Many had built timber bridges on stone piers, and in London a stone-arch bridge had actually been constructed."[20] Considering the extensive privileges and freedoms that citizens enjoyed, in contrast to the rural population living within the framework of highly restrictive feudalism, the lure of the city already in the early Middle Ages was considerable.

Not surprisingly, many medieval poets, even when focusing primarily on the life at court and the courtly protagonists, projected, at least in the background, or on the sideline of the major events, cities, citizens, and the power of urban communities in producing money, products of craftsmanship, food, clothing, and all kinds of the nice amenities of a more sophisticated lifestyle. I will provide below a number of examples from the twelfth through the fifteenth centuries when urban life increasingly gained in economic, political, and military importance, and so also became attractive for literary projections.

Remarkably, despite countless military attacks during the age of migration and beyond, late-antique and early-medieval cities were not simply abandoned or

[19]  *Towns and Their Territories Between Late Antiquity and the Early Middle Ages*, ed. Gian P. Brogiolo, 2000; *Città, castelli, campagne nei territori di frontiera: 5. Seminario sul Tardoantico e l'Altomedioevo in Italia Centrosettentrionale, Monte Barro - Galbiate (Lecco), 9 - 10 giugno 1994*, ed. Gian P. Brogiolo. Documenti di archeologia, 6 (Mantua: Ed. S.A.P., Soc. Archeologica Padana, 1995).
[20]  Joseph and Frances Gies, *Life in a Medieval City*, 15.

allowed to decline because of the attacks by Germanic peoples, often rather falsely identified as 'barbarians.' Even when cities were besieged and destroyed, most were rebuilt and then might even have flourished more than ever before. Only when a city lost its position as a relevant nodule in the international network of trade could it happen that it was abandoned. Consequently, the sheer numbers of cities and their growth in medieval Europe proves to be remarkable even from an early time.

According to some statistics, there were ca. twenty major cities at around 900 C.E. in central Europe; by ca. 1150 the number had grown to ca. 200, and by ca. 1250 C.E. the medieval landscape was dotted by ca. 1500 cities. In fact, 90% of all cities still in existence today in that large geographic area were founded between 1100 and 1350. In eleventh-century Germany, about 40 out of 120 towns that can be identified today were sites of bishops' seats, and 20 were near monasteries, and about 60 developed around royal foundations. Nevertheless, the significance of the "specific location on an important long-distance trade route, as well as [ ] he existence of a stronghold providing protection for the growing merchant community" must not be overlooked, nor the extensive impact of the colonization process extending into central, eastern, and northern Europe at least since the twelfth century. Even Ireland experienced a strong urbanization process as a result of its colonization by the Anglo-Normans beginning in the eleventh century.[21]

This does not mean that those early cities could pride themselves on a large number of inhabitants. In Cologne, for instance, only a few thousand people lived during the tenth century, whereas London (Lundenwic) housed between five and ten thousand people.[22] In the eleventh and twelfth centuries the population of Paris is estimated to have been between 80,000 and 200,000; Florence, Venice, and Milan boasted of up to 100,000 people by the year 1300, whereas Flemish towns normally did not exceed 50,000 people. Of course, we have to be careful in trusting any of those figures since they are all estimates and depend very much on the selection of criteria, hence the vast range for Paris, for example.[23] But cities south of the Alps with their long-standing Mediterranean culture stand out because of their extensive population, sometimes reaching up to ninety-thousand people even in the middle category, such as Cordoba, Spain, whereas Rome and Athens, for

---

[21]  Anngret Simms, "The Early Origins and Morphological Inheritance of European Towns," *Urban Landscapes: International Perspectives*, ed. J. W. R. Whitehand and P. J. Larkham (London and New York: Routledge, 1992), 23–42; here 27; and N. J. Baker and T. R. Slater, "Morphological Regions in English Medieval Towns," ibid., 43–68. See also A. E. J. Morris, *History of Urban Form*, 94–95 (some of his perspectives, however, are very much based on older research, but he provides an excellent survey with good visual material, maps, and graphs.

[22]  Felix Barker and Peter Jackson, *London: 2000 Years of a City and Its People* (London: Cassell, 1974), 15–44, with excellent illustrative material.

[23]  Kathryn L. Reyerson, "Urbanism," 315–16.

instance, represent cities of a more individual status that would need particular treatment for which there is no room here.[24]

We can be certain now that many of the Roman cities, even those founded outside of Italy and even those north of the Alps, continued to exist long after the fall of the Roman Empire, though they experienced tremendous changes, both economically and architecturally, and successfully competed with new city foundations, ultimately and to a large degree surviving until today.[25] After all, administrative and judicial services continued to be of supreme importance, even for the new colonizers and rulers who took over the lands where the Romans had dominated before, such as on the Iberian Peninsula.[26] This does not imply at all that the ancient Roman cities did not undergo tremendous change, but they did not simply disappear.

As Adela Cepas notes with regard to the city of Clunia in Northern Hispania, "Clunia's archeological story is a familiar one: a fast urban development in the early empire followed by a late Roman period marked by the change of function and/or abandonment of most of its structures . . . . By the late empire, though, most of the public buildings had lost their former function. The abundant material culture unearthed by Palol since 1958 is in sharp contrast with the use people made of the city's buildings . . . . After the fifth century Clunia, to be sure, did not look much like the standard Roman city it had once been."[27]

Similar developments can be observed in other areas of the former Roman Empire, where we also discover plenty of evidence regarding the reasons for the survival and then growth of urban centers. After all, as Grenville Astill

---

[24]  H. Steuer, "Stadt: Kulturgeschichtlich," *Reallexikon der Germanischen Altertumskunde*. Sec., completely revised and expanded ed. by Heinrich Beck, Dieter Geuenich, and Heiko Steuer. Vol. 29 (Berlin and New York: de Gruyter, 2005), 447–72; here 451–53. This article also provides an extensive bibliography.

[25]  Steuer, "Stadt: Kulturgeschichtlich," 458–61, emphasizes that there were hardly any construction activities in Gallic and Italian cities until the seventh century, but between 650 and 700 this changed remarkably, probably because of renewed trade and commerce, parallel to the emergence of an urban network along the coast of the North Sea. He insists that we have been deluded by the traditional historiographical perspective of a rural world north of the Alps and an urban world in the Mediterranean region during the late antiquity and the early Middle Ages: "Mit gewissen Unterschieden, die auch nicht übersehen werden sollten, entwickelten sich überall nach Bedarf zentrale Orte—die einen in einer urspr., von Stämmen bewohnten Landschaft, die anderen auf der verwandelten Grundlage des ehemaligen Röm. Reiches" (461).

[26]  See, for instance, J. Arce, "Los gobernadores de la Diocesis Hispaniarum (ss. IV–V d. C.) y la continuidad de las estructuras administrativas romanas en la Península Ibérica," *Antiquité Tardive* 7 (1999): 73–83.

[27]  Adela Cepas, "The Ending of the Roman City: The Case of Clunia in the Northern Plateau of Spain," *People and Space in the Middle Ages, 300–1300*, ed. Wendy Davies, Guy Halsall, and Andrew Reynolds. Studies in the Early Middle Ages, 15 (Turnhout: Brepols, 2006), 187–207; here 191–92. Specialized research on her topic can be found there.

emphasizes, "urbanization continued to be stimulated and dominated by aristocratic production and consumption until at least the late eleventh/early twelfth century, when there are signs that some of the urban population had achieved sufficient economic and political power to achieve a degree of independence. This trend had considerably accelerated by the later twelfth century, when there is extensive evidence for the increased commercialization of the countryside and a greater involvement of a large part of the population in the market."[28]

Of course, there was no city just like any other, and yet we cannot ignore the fundamental identity of the most critical features. However, on a political level, some were dominated by the bishop and his cathedral; others were controlled by a feudal lord who had his residence in the city or nearby; others again enjoyed considerable freedom from local lords and achieved a degree of independence that was unprecedented even in antiquity, only subordinated under the king or emperor, particularly in the later centuries. As Joseph and Frances Gies summarize: "Medieval cities enjoy a great deal of individual liberty, varying degrees of self-government, and little democracy. Their charters, many of which were written in the twelfth century, are principally grants of freedom from feudal obligations—the head tax, the labor service, the tax at will, the marriage tax—in return for payment of a cash impost. Limits are set for their military service, they are allowed to operate their own law courts for lesser crimes ('low justice') and, usually, they are permitted a mayor and council."[29]

## Urban Space as an Epistemological Challenge

As countless studies have already demonstrated, the particular focus on individual cities allows for in-depth investigations of specific aspects of each culture, whether we consider religious groups and their conflicts with each other, economic aspects concerning individual social classes (merchants and bankers versus crafts-men/artisans and journeymen), gender relationships, age differences, cultural and linguistic groups (Florentines in London, Germans in Venice, Flemish in Cologne, etc.),[30] or the world of sexuality (prostitution, brothels, pimps, rape, adultery,

---

[28] Grenville Astill, "Community, Identity and the Later Anglo-Saxon Town: The Case of Southern England," *People and Space in the Middle Ages*, 233–54; here 234.
[29] Ibid., 199.
[30] For a study of early-modern immigrants in cities since the seventeenth century, see Alexander Cowan, "Foreigners and the City: The Case of the Immigrant Merchant," *Mediterranean Urban Culture 1400–1700*, ed. id. (Exeter: University of Exeter Press, 2000), 45–55.

marriage, etc.).[31] The city was regularly the site where major tensions developed and were fought out most intensively, as seen when we think of the pogroms that were directed against Jewish populations in Rhenish cities during the First Crusade (1096),[32] or in the wake of the Black Death in 1348–1350, and subsequently far into the late fifteenth century, such as in Nuremberg. On a more mundane level, considering everyday life, we might want to follow Arsenio Frugoni's lively, but probably also very accurate description, taking exception only in details or considering local variants here and there:

> The medieval city, after the eleventh century, had so much fervent life and confidence that we can readily recognize characteristics of our own modern world in it. But it is also extraordinarily different in many ways, and we need to emphasize that as well as we follow medieval people through an average day. Between the evening twilight and the grayness before dawn one can hardly make out the walls of the houses for there is no lighting in the medieval city as we said. At evening curfew the women cover the coals in the hearth with ash to reduce the fire hazard and keep them alive until next morning. The houses are built with beams of oak and every one is a potential tinderbox waiting to blaze up so at night the only flames left burning are the candles before the holy images. Why would the streets need to be lit anyway? In the evening the entrances to the dangerous neighborhoods are barred, chains are stretched across the river to prevent a surprise attack from barbarian raiders coming upstream, and the city gates are locked tight. The city is like one big household, with everything well secured.[33]

---

[31]   Alice Beardwood, *Alien Merchants in England 1350 to 1377: Their Legal and Economic Position* (Cambridge, MA The Medieval Academy of America, 1931); Grethe Jacobsen, "Guilds in Medieval Denmark: the Social and Economic Role of Merchants and Artisans," Ph.D. diss. University of Wisconsin, Madison, 1980; Timothy O'Neill, *Merchants and Mariners in Medieval Ireland* (Dublin: Irish Academic Press, 1987). For specific examples of the role of merchants in a medieval city, see John Edwards, *Christian Córdoba: The City and Its Region in the Late Middle Ages*. Cambridge Iberian and Latin American Studies (Cambridge, London, et al.: Cambridge University Press, 1982); Peter Spufford, *Power and Profit: the Merchant in Medieval Europe*. 5th ed. (2002; New York: Thames & Hudson, 2003). See also the contribution to the present volume by Fabian Alfie. As to sexuality in medieval cities, that is, primarily prostitution, see Ruth Mazo Karras, "Prostitution in Medieval Europe," *Handbook of Medieval Sexuality*, ed. Vern L. Bullough and James A. Brundage (New York and London: Garland, 1996), 243–60. See also some of the contributions to *Sexuality: in the Middle Ages and the Early Modern Age*, ed. Albrecht Classen. Fundamentals of Medieval and Early Modern Culture, 3 (Berlin and New York: de Gruyter, 2008), especially Gertrud Blaschitz's study on brothels and prostitutes (715–50).

[32]   These tragic events have already been richly documented and analyzed, and for a good anthology also of primary texts dealing with the desperate actions taken by the Jews in the Rhenish cities, see Robert Chazan, *European Jewry and the First Crusade* (Berkeley, Los Angeles, and London: University of California Press, 1987).

[33]   Robert Arsenio Frugoni, "Introduction," Chiara Frugoni, *A Day in a Medieval City*, trans. William McCuaig (Chicago and London: The University of Chicago Press, 2005), 1–13; here 6.

Pursuing this approach further, we can also study the design of the street patterns, of the houses, the interior spaces, the work spaces, the churches, the public buildings and squares, the city wall, the gates, the storage houses, the market stalls and shops, administrative offices, churches, schools, and libraries.[34] The city life was determined both by economic aspects and religious perspectives. In fact, even if not necessarily present in everybody's mind, St. Augustine's concept of the city of God as the spiritual ideal for the earthly city as its natural counterpart represented the fundamental paradigm for medieval urban dwellers.[35] Consequently the need arose for countless ecclesiastic buildings, altars, relics, chapels, confessionals, and so the need for the respective priests and other clerics was supreme, transforming the earthly city often into the location for the individual's quest for a spiritual home.

Whatever city we might want to use as an illustrative example, in virtually every case the citizens expressed great pride in their social environment, whether in the city walls or the facades of their own homes, their churches or the piazza/city square, as wonderfully illustrated by the late-medieval artist Neroccio di Bartolomeo di Benedetto de' Landi, whose "The Virgin Commends Siena to Jesus from 1480 (Siena, Archivio di Stato) shows the kneeling Virgin holding a small model of the city standing on three marble columns of different hue, presenting it to Christ hovering above. The model's three columns represent the fundamental Christian virtues of faith, hope, and charity, as reflected by their individual colors.[36]

But there was no reason for any urban community to trust in its own self-assurance and confidence, as countless examples of destroyed, burnt-down, and razed cities demonstrate, all victims of innumerable wars, feuds, fires, and natural catastrophes. The worship of saints, the dedication of churches and cathedrals to the Virgin Mary and also to martyrs as helpers in emergencies, military or natural, found enormous and most impressive expression in wall paintings, and sculptures, and in naming of ecclesiastic buildings in medieval and early-modern cities. Not surprisingly, St. Christopher, the giant who carried the baby Jesus across a river without knowing his true identity, was one of the most popular saints in medieval urban art for very good reasons.[37]

---

[34]   For recent examinations of the architectural design and social function of urban houses, see the contributions to *Medieval Domesticity: Home, Housing and Household in Medieval England*, ed. Maryanne Kowaleski and P. J. P. Goldberg (Cambridge: Cambridge University Press, 2008), especially by Felicity Riddy, Mark Gardiner, Sarah Rees Jones, and Jane Grenville.

[35]   Frugoni, "Introduction, 9–10.

[36]   Chiara Frugoni, *A Day in a Medieval City*, 21–23; the illustration is on p. 22..

[37]   Frugoni, *A Day in a Medieval City*, 27–31. See also Carol Armstrong, *Lives and Legends of the Saints: With Paintings from the Great Art Museums in the World* (New York: Simon and Schuster, 1995)—though for young readers, still useful for the illustrations.

## Everyday Life in a Medieval City

Both birth and death took place in the city, the first requiring extensive medical care and health service, the other requiring considerable efforts to bury the deceased appropriately. As the contributors to *Death in Towns* suggest, life in a city could be precarious, considering infectious diseases (Keith Manchester). Burial practices determined medieval urban culture quite significantly (Alan Morton); and hospitals that provided the last resting place for the dying were of great importance for the urban population (Roberta Gilchrist). Far into the late Middle Ages the cemeteries were centrally located, right next to the parish church, hence in the middle of the city (Julia Barrow). Finally, the funeral processions and memorial cult and services played an important part in urban life (Clare Gittings; Malcolm Norris).[38] Only by the fifteenth century did cemeteries finally disappear from the city center because space became limited, and the city governments realized the health hazards resulting from the burying of the dead so near the water supply of the urban population.[39]

Urban space, however, cannot be identified as a collective image equally relevant and identifiable for each inhabitant. As M. Gottdiener and Alexandros Ph. Lagopoulos observe, though from a modern perspective: "The image of the city in cognitive maps is not the city itself, nor is it some reflection of fundamental innate processes of spatial perception, because we know that most of the ways in which people perceive space are socially learned and experientially based. The cognitive map is so much a product of social interaction that even individuals living near each other in the very same neighborhood will hold different conceptions of their area as a product of separate social networks . . . . In sum, cognitive geography locates the production of spatial meaning within the minds of individuals."[40]

---

[38]   *Death in Towns: Urban Responses to the Dying and the Dead, 100–1600*, ed. Steven Bassett (1992; London and New York: Leicester University Press, 1995). See also Colin Platt, *King Death: The Black Death and Its Aftermath in Late-Medieval England* (Toronto and Buffalo: University of Toronto Press, 1996), 19–31.

[39]   Anja Tietz, "Der Gottesacker der Stadt Eisleben: Martin Luthers Einfluss auf das Begräbniswesen," *Martin Luther und Eisleben*, ed. Rosemarie Knape. Schriften der Stiftung Luthergedenkstätten in Sachsen-Anhalt, 8 (Leipzig: Evangelische Verlagsanstalt, 2007), 189–205. For an older, yet still valuable study of this topic, see Herbert Derwein, *Geschichte des christlichen Friedhofs in Deutschland* (Frankfurt a. M.: Franzmathes, 1931).

[40]   M. Gottdiener and Alexandros Ph. Lagopoulos, "Introduction," *The City and the Sign: An Introduction to Urban Semiotics*, ed. id. (New York: Columbia University Press, 1986), 11.

In other words, there is a certain type of social grammar that allows the individual to perceive the urban space in the first place, and to determine that space from a social perspective in the second place: "Urban semiotics then becomes the study of spatial structures derived from internalized grammars of patterns and designs which become externalized through semiosis."[41] These theoretical approaches laid the foundation for the cultural-historical analysis of urban space also in the premodern times where towns and cities began to grow or continued their expansion since Roman times. There are countless signs in a city to interpret, and in a way these very signs make up the urban space; concomitantly, both the urban space and its semiotics are constantly subject to historical change because the social subject perceives, interprets, and creates the signs differently at any given moment.[42] However, this is not to ignore the tremendous impact that social determinants had on the individual and the social group, whether we think of the Church, the guild, or the family, which also shade and influence the perspective of and the modeling of urban space, and this both in the Middle Ages and today.

As Roland Barthes notes, though again from a modern perspective, but still pertinent to our topic, "the city center is always felt as the space where subversive forces, forces of rupture, ludic forces act and meet. Play is a subject very often emphasized in the surveys on the center . . . . In contrast, all that is not the center is precisely that which is not ludic space, everything which is not otherness: family, residence, identity."[43]

Some of the major literary protagonists in the Middle Ages, such as Alexander the Great and Apollonius of Tyre, clearly operate in cities and utilize cities for their global strategies, and this at a time when most medieval cities were still a far-cry from the model provided by ancient cities and when most audiences would not have been familiar with the concept of true urban living space as antiquity.[44]

---

[41]   Gottdiener and Lagopoulos, "Introduction," 15.

[42]   Umberto Eco, "Function and Sign: Semiotics of Architecture," *The City and the Sign*, 55–86; here 69: "So, in the course of history, both primary and secondary functions might be found undergoing losses, recoveries, and substitutions of various kinds. These losses, recoveries, and substitutions are common to the life of forms in general, and constitute the norm in the course of the reading of works of art proper."

[43]   Roland Barthes, "Semiology and the Urban," *The City and the Sign*, 87–98; here 96.

[44]   Rolf Bräuer, "Alexander der Große: Der Mythos vom unbesiegbaren Eroberer der Welt als Vorbild, Warnung und pejoratives Exempel," *Herrscher, Helden, Heilige*, ed. Ulrich Müller and Werner Wunderlich. Mittelalter-Mythen, 1 (St. Gallen: UVK. Fachverlag für Wissenschaft und Studium, 1996), 3–19. See also the contributions to *Alexanderdichtung im Mittelalter: Kulturelle Selbstbestimmung im Kontext literarischer Beziehungen*, ed. Jan Cölln, Susanne Friede, and Hartmut Wulfram. Veröffentlichungen aus dem Göttinger Sonderforschungsbereich 529 "Internationalität nationaler Literaturen." Serie A, 1 (Göttingen: Wallstein, 2000).

Certainly, medieval knights, as reflected by courtly poets, roam the forests, meadows, and fields; they visit castles and leave again for new adventures, as if the world of burghers, merchants, bankers, and craftsmen did not matter or did not even exist. In other words, most, if not all, medieval courtly romances tend to refrain from discussing urban life, cities as such, and the class of burghers, although the history of medieval cities begins very early and gains in considerable significance at least by the eleventh or twelfth century.

These observations raise the questions of when did medieval mentality take note of the city as a significant separate entity on the horizon of most people's minds? And when did people realize the remarkable difference between urbanite dwellers, the rural population, and members of the aristocratic courts? Can we properly use the rise of the city, or of the central urban space, as the benchmark for the transition from the Middle Ages to the Renaissance, or at least to the Early Modern period? Or looking backwards, can we draw from the history of urban centers in late antiquity to identify more specifically when the ancient world really came to an end, giving rise to the medieval period?

All these transitions were certainly fluid and took a long time, but if we talk about paradigm shifts in urban history, we can clearly recognize the importance of cities as stakes in the long-term shift from one period to another. Urban life did not simply disappear with the end of the Roman Empire, though there was, over the centuries, a remarkable decline in economic activities and artistic production in those urban centers along with a refocus on agricultural production.[45] In early medieval Tuscany, for instance, that is, during the sixth to the eighth centuries, we can observe the trend toward the establishment of "concentrated rural population, within which it is difficult, if not impossible, to discern archeological data that points to social differentiation . . . . Inside these villages the process of creating the material settlement structures on an 'urban' model paralleled the establishment of rural aristocracies, and started only in the mid-eighth century."[46]

The slow but steady disappearance of public Roman buildings, for instance, and the use of the amphitheaters and colloseums as quarries for private buildings signal a fundamental shift in interest and orientation among the local population, although the economic production in those old Roman centers did not disappear. On the contrary, as Joachim Henning underscores, "specialized craft production flourished in Merovingian times. Gregory of Tour's sixth-century Paris was a

[45]   Chris Wickham, "Rethinking the Structure of the Early Medieval Economy," *The Long Morning of Medieval Europe: New Directions in Early Medieval Studies*, ed. Jennifer R. Davis and Michael McCormick (Aldershot, Hampshire, and Burlington, VT: Ashgate, 2008), 19–31; here 27–29.

[46]   Riccardo Francovich, "The Beginnings of Hilltop Villages in Early Medieval Tucscany," *The Long Morning of Medieval Europe*, 55–82; here 68.

living city with workshops and markets."[47] Turning to Cologne, the author now corroborates that the ruralization process did not occur, that there was no major hiatus between the ancient Roman world and the early Middle Ages as far as urban life was concerned. "Instead, the Merovingian period saw flourishing craft production, including highly specialized installations such as glass ovens. When production activities next picked up is still in dispute but it seems to be about the tenth century at the latest."[48]

But absolute continuity was never a given, and the destiny of medieval cities often depended on global developments in economic, military, and social terms. Some urban centers experienced dramatic declines, others witnessed a rebirth, and others again simply continued their steady growth. In this regard, the focus on urban space allows, though not pursued here in further detail, an excellent insight into larger issues pertaining to empire building under the Merovingians and Carolingians, long-term famines, economic restructuring processes, and military conflicts.[49]

## The Church and the City

Concomitantly, the role of ecclesiastical buildings within medieval cities, especially of cathedrals and parish churches, abbeys and convents, cannot be underestimated with regards to attracting new settlements around them and providing both more security and culture.[50] Moreover, churches, monasteries, priories, chapels, and other ecclesiastical buildings represented focal points for urban growth and development throughout the entire Middle Ages and far beyond, such as in the case of the city of Mainz on the Rhine, today west of Frankfurt, as a major ecclesiastical center, as the local of major economic production and trade, and as a significant "transit point for the shipment of goods brought across the Alps,

---

[47] Joachim Henning, "Strong Rulers – Weak Economy? Rome, the Carolingians and the Archeology of Slavery in the First Millennium AD," *The Long Morning of Medieval Europe*, 33–53; here 50.

[48] Henning, "Strong Rulers," 50–51.

[49] Henning, "Strong Rulers," 51–53, with further literature on this topic.

[50] In a series of short articles Bernd Fuhrmann discusses the following aspects: urban space in late antiquity and the early Middle Ages; urban space in the high and late Middle Ages; urban building methods, urban living culture; urban procurement of food and other supplies, along with handling of waste products; and urban social topography, in: *Enzyklopädie des Mittelalters*, ed. Gert Melville and Martial Staub, vol. II (Darmstadt: Wissenschaftliche Buchgesellschaft, 2008), 256–79; for a bibliography, see 478–79. As in most other cases in this encyclopedia, these entries provide nice surveys, with a lot of concrete data, but the critical, academic, approach is lacking, not surprising (and also not necessarily to be expected) for an encyclopedia. See my review, forthcoming in *Mediaevistik*.

including spices from the east, and was visited by Muslims and Jewish traders."[51]
The same applies to Lucca, Italy, which boasted of over 50 churches before the
tenth century; hence it was a major ecclesiastical center of great urban significance,
although, or particularly because, it maintained close connection with its rural
*hinterland*.[52] Even the aristocracy tended to settle in the city, the site of the
archbishop's seat.

In these early medieval cities people could find their only reliable refuge in the
case of an emergency because there they found the only buildings out of stone
available anywhere, hence could resist fire or flooding, and here the enemy could
not easily achieve the desired goals and cause havoc. The belfries served
exceedingly well as watch towers, and the neutrality of a public space invited
administrators, rulers, and representatives of larger urban groups to meet there for
negotiations, councils, or debates. But many cities north of the Alps, particularly
in Scandinavia, the Baltics, and Ireland, such as York, England, or Dublin, were
mostly built out of wood, even if close to 10,000 people could live there at the end
of the tenth century.[53]

Not surprisingly, the church proved to be the ideal location to deposit important
legal and political documents; and the city governments liked to store their
privileges, seals, measures, and weights in churches. In other words, the parish
church, and so the cathedral in larger cities, emerged as the central point for urban
administration and information, which also led to the foundation of important
libraries right there (see, for instance, Heidelberg). Finally, churches were the first
buildings in medieval cities with mechanical clocks, and the bells structured the
lives of all people living in a city, at least since ca. 1370–1380.[54] But what does all
this mean for the creation and further development of urban space in the Middle
Ages and the early modern age? And how do we understand space in the first
place, certainly a most complex semiotic phenomenon where the private and the
public intersect, communication channels operate or not, community is
established, and law and order practiced?

---

[51]   Julia M. H. Smith, *Europe after Rome: A New Cultural History 500–1000* (Oxford, New York, et al:
       Oxford University Press, 2005), 192.
[52]   Lynette Olson, *The Early Middle Ages: The Birth of Europe* (Houndmills, Basingstoke, Hampshire,
       and New York: Palgrave Macmillan, 2007), 134–35.
[53]   Olson, *The Early Middle Ages*, 137.
[54]   Jan Kuys, "Weltliche Funktionen spätmittelalterlicher Pfarrkirchen in den nördlichen
       Niederlanden," *The Use and Abuse of Sacred Places in Late Medieval Towns*, ed. by Paul Trio and
       Marjan De Smet. Mediaevalia Lovaniensia. Series I / Studia XXXVIII (Leuven: Leuven University
       Press, 2006), 27–45; see also Gabriela Signori, "Sakral oder Profan? Der Kommunikationsraum
       Kirche," ibid., 117–34.

## Critical Approaches to the Medieval City

All these inquiries are, of course, only based on rhetorical questions that cannot be answered easily; otherwise the present volume would not have been necessary or even possible in the first place. We know that the emergence of the city as a separate topographic and architectural entity dramatically and unavoidably changed the topography and mentality of the Middle Ages and then deeply influenced and determined the early-modern world. As the contributors to a symposium held in Trient, November 9–11, 2000, indicate, the phenomenon of the medieval city fundamentally triggered the creation of a new type of consciousness, the rise of an urban class, an urban culture, and an urban identity.[55] And as early-modern historians and historians of mentality have often confirmed, those urban centers all over Europe increasingly attracted a growing amount of wealth, even effectively competing against the traditional power players, especially the Church and the nobility, though it would have to be a matter of further and intensive debate as to the role which territorial dukes played, and how much the royal courts could maintain their cultural, military, and political supremacy even when located outside of city walls.

But the critical function of towns and cities — for the purpose of this study I will not draw a particular distinction between both terms, though statistically and economically the city would have to be defined as a much larger, much denser, and much more important entity than a town — in the network of production and consumption, trade and markets, already so central in the world of antiquity, also continued to play the most important role ever since, whether a city was an episcopal, ducal, royal property or not.[56]

---

[55] *Aspetti e componenti dell'identità urbana in Italia e in Germania (secoli XIV–XVI)*, a cura di Girogio Chittolini and Peter Johanek. Annali dell'Istituto storico italo-germanico in Trento, 12 (Bologna and Berlin: Il Mulino-Dunker and Humbolt, 2003); see also the review by Elena Di Venosa, in *Studi medievali* 49, 1 (2008): 436–44. Chittolini correctly emphasizes: "Il periodo proposto è stato quello dei secoli XIII–XVI; un'età in cui la città da un lato ha maturato, sia in Italia che in Germania, una forte 'coscienza civica', dal punto di vista politico; e in cui, nello stesso tempo, deve fronteggiare altre forze politiche esterne, come signori, principi e 'dominanti', ed è quindi sollecitata a riflettere e a esprimere in forme particolari la propria identità" (8). Bernd Roeck emphasizes, on the other hand, the need to analyze the fundamental transition from the imaginary city, as borrowed either from antiquity or from the autochthone examples, as reflected on seals or frescoes, to the realistically identifiable city vastly expanded beyond the traditional castle and the narrow range of houses shadowed by the tall church towers and the city wall: "Die Stadt wird zur Neuzeit hin immer entschiedener in ihrer spezifischen optisch greifbaren Individualität gefaßt, und sie begegnet schließlich als Gegenstand autonomer Darstellung" (ibid., 12).

[56] H. van Werveke, "The Rise of the Towns," *The Cambridge Economic History of Europe*. Vol. III: *Economic Organization and Policies in the Middle Ages*, ed. M. M. Postan, E. F. Rich, and Edward Miller (Cambridge: At the University Press, 1963), 3–41; here 22–24.

The modern world is, as we all know, increasingly dominated by urban culture, and less and less of the world population is living in the country, which is a strong trend that continues to impact our modern lives both in the Western and in the Eastern world.[57] Modern urban spaces are being designed, and artificially created for political, economic, social, and cultural purposes.[58] The opposite was normally the case in premodern times, and yet the root of the explosive development of cities all over the European landscape rests in the eleventh and twelfth centuries, if not earlier, as I have discussed above. It would really take until the eighteenth, and especially the nineteenth centuries for cities of the size of a megapolis to emerge, though truly urban space existed already in the Middle Ages, even if only in a microscopic dimension compared to what we experience today.

The historical exploration of the medieval city has a long tradition, obviously because urban centers have represented the nodes of an ever growing network deeply influencing medieval society. Constitutional historians have treated the phenomenon of the city from many different perspectives, especially with regard to urban privileges and freedoms that made life in a city so different from living in the country within rural communities where feudal structures continued to dominate far into the eighteenth and nineteenth centuries. Fritz Rörig, for instance, examined the rise of the medieval city in the wake of the crusades, the development of an urban landscape in central and eastern Europe during the so-called eastern Colonization, the new relationship between city and state since the late Middle Ages, the considerable growth of the urban population and the establishment of urban power all over medieval Europe. He identified as the major causes for this tremendous phenomenon the establishment of independent city governments (not everywhere, but often enough), the role of the guilds, an urban education systems, and hence the rise of literacy, the economic power of cities, and many times urban naval power both along major rivers and the coastlines of the various seas, apart from military power and their defense systems.

In most cases the newly established urban pride and identity found its best expression in the city halls, or town halls, always very representative buildings,

---

[57]   *Encyclopedia of Urban Cultures: Cities and Cultures Around the World*, ed. Melvin Ember and Carol R. Ember. 4 vols. (Danbury, CT: Grolier, 2002); Chris Jenks, *Urban Culture: Critical Concepts in Literary and Cultural Studies*. 4 vols. (London and New York: Routledge, 2004); Alan C. Turley, *Urban Culture: Exploring Cities and Cultures* (Upper Saddle River, NJ: Pearson/Prentice Hall, 2005). The literature on modern urban space is actually legion and does not need to be discussed or listed here in detail.

[58]   The number of relevant studies that have appeared only recently is almost uncountable; see, for instance, *Urban Design*, ed. Alex Krieger and William S. Saunders. Architecture/Urban Studies (Minneapolis: University of Minnesota Press, 2008); John R. Short, *Alabaster Cities: Urban U.S. since 1950*. Space, Place, and Society (Syracuse, NY: Syracuse University Press, 2006); *A Companion to Urban Economics*, ed. Richard Arnott and Daniel P. McMillen. Blackwell Companions to Contemporary Economics, 4 (Malden, MA, and Oxford: Blackwell, 2006).

though differences between English and French cities, on the one hand, and German cities on the other, depending on the political framework, not to speak of Italian and Spanish cities, continued to be remarkable.[59] Jean-Denis G. G. Lepage calls this unparalleled development "urban emancipation," and comments:

> In spite of the authorities' resistance, the burghers were gradually admitted into society and obtained their freedom. As early as 1032 the burghers of Venice proclaimed their freedom and bound themselves by oath to defend it. The same happened in Milan in 1067 and Lucca in 1068. In 1070, the city of Le Mans in France was in rebellion, followed by Cambrai in 1077 and then by the northern Italian cities of Lombardy and Genoa. In the 12th century large-scale city emancipation began in all the areas between the Seine and Meuse rivers, as well as in Thuringia, Saxony and Bavaria.[60]

But extensive differences between Western and Southern, between Northern and Eastern Europe always need to be taken into consideration, especially as far as efforts toward urban independence and economic influences are concerned. Nevertheless, most economic trade, but then also the creation of art, the flowering of schools and universities, and to some extent also the production of literature relied heavily, if not exclusively, on cities with their markets, craftsmanship, political power, and military security. In fact, as historians have observed only very recently, cities were very difficult to conquer, and many sieges had to be abandoned "if there was real resistance. Scale was a very big issue because armies were rarely very large. Tortona, attacked by Barbarossa on his way to Rome, was a small place, but it held out from February to April 1155. He besieged Crema from July 1159 to January 1160 and Milan, for the second time after the failure in August/September 1158, from May 1161 to March 1162."[61] John France states it very clearly: "a city with a will to resist was so formidable that many sieges failed. By contrast castles were usually smaller and sometimes weaker targets."[62]

---

[59]  Fritz Rörig, *The Medieval Town*, trans. J. A. Matthew (1932; Berkeley and Los Angeles: University of California Press, 1967); see also the contributions to *The English Medieval Town: A Reader in English Urban History 1200–1540*, ed. Richard Holt and Gervase Rosser. Readers in Urban History (London and New York: Longman, 1990); R. H. Hilton, *English and French Towns in Feudal Society: A Comparative Study*. Past and Present Publications (Cambridge, New York, et al.: Cambridge University Press, 1992); *Villes et sociétés urbaines au moyen âge: Hommage à M. le Professeur Jacques Heers*. Cultures et civilisations médiévales, XI (Paris: Presses de l'Université de Paris-Sorbonne, 1994).

[60]  Jean-Denis G. G. Lepage, *Castles and Fortified Cities of Medieval Europe: An Illustrated History* (Jefferson, NC, and London: McFarland & Company, 2002), 251.

[61]  John France, "Siege Conventions in Western Europe and the Latin East," *War and Peace in Ancient and Medieval History*, ed. Philip de Souza and John France (Cambridge, New York, et al.: Cambridge University Press, 2008), 158–72; here 163.

[62]  France, " Siege Conventions," 163.

However, each city faced different challenges and enjoyed different opportunities, whether there was an overbearing overlord or the lack of a unifying system on a global level, such as in Germany, at least since the end of the Hohenstaufen dynasty. Cities faced conflicts with Muslim neighbors on the Iberian peninsula, conflicts with nobles, such as in England, above all, and struggles with the German emperor, such as in Italy.[63] Each medieval and early-modern city was different in its historical roots, its economic and political conditions, and the context of its cultural, geographical, and religious conditions. At the same time, we can group many cities into the same categories with regard to their origins, developments, structures, and cultural and economic emphases.

Historians have regularly divided medieval European cities into three geographical zones, first the inner, or southern zone comprising the territory of the former western Roman Empire, centered on the Mediterranean. The northern zone consisted of those cities located in the area north of the Alps, mostly situated on the banks of the rivers Rhine and Danube. The third zone comprised the region where Roman culture and civilization had exerted either very little or no influence, such as Scotland, Ireland, Scandinavia, and the Slavic countries where economic and cultural aspects did not attract the colonizers' interests.[64]

But then there were new foundations, relocations, merging of smaller settlements, granting of privileges that triggered the creation of markets and hence of cities. New cities were not only planned and realized at one swoop in the early-modern age, say, in the late Renaissance, but already in the high, or late, Middle Ages, such as Aigues-Mortes. As Georges Zarnecki observes, "This large enterprise is a precious example of a town built practically anew in the thirteenth century, and was not finished until the next reign, that of Philip the Bold (1270–1285)." Contrary to many modern assumptions, this was not the only case in medieval Europe.[65]

---

[63] Lepage, *Castles and Fortified Cities*, 252–53.

[64] The classical study of this phenomenon is Edith Ennen's *Frühgeschichte der europäischen Stadt*. Veröffentlichung des Instituts für Geschichtliche Landeskunde der Rheinlande an der Universität Bonn (Bonn: L. Rörscheid, 1953). Now see also Joachim Herrmann, "Siedlungsgeschichtliche Grundlagen und geschichtliche Voraussetzungen für die Entwicklung Berlins," *Frühgeschichte der europäischen Stadt*, ed. Hans-Jürgen Brachmann and id. Schriften zur Ur- und Frühgeschichte, 44 (Berlin: Akademie Verlag, 1991), 7–18. For a focus on the Russian world, see *The City in Russian History*, ed. Michael F. Hamm (Lexington: University Press of Kentucky, 1976); for a focus on Scotland, see *Edinburgh: The Making of a Capital City*, ed. Brian Edwards and Paul Jenkins (Edinburgh: Edinburgh University Press, 2005). For an archeological approach to this topic, see John Schofield and Alan Vince, *Medieval Towns: The Archeology of British Towns in Their European Setting* (London and New York: Continuum, 2003), 21–26. See also Edith Ennen, *Die europäische Stadt des Mittelalters*. 2nd expanded and improved ed. Sammlung Vandenhoeck (1972; Göttingen: Vandenhoeck & Ruprecht, 1975).

[65] Georges Zarnecki, *Art of the Medieval World: Architecture, Sculpture, Painting, The Sacred Arts*. Library of Art History (New York: Harry N. Abrams, 1975), 395.

Over and over again, it deserves to be emphasized that the variety of medieval and early-modern cities was considerable, whether we think of a bishop's seat, a castle of a nobleman, an imperial palace or estate, a juncture of major trading routes, etc., around which then emerged the earliest urban settlement and then developed over time. Not surprisingly, then, urban growth did not proceed lineally and systematically, and there were many set-backs and failures at specific times and periods, especially when we think of the deep impact of the so-called Black Death, not to speak of wars, famines, economic crises, and other factors.[66] Details cannot be examined and discussed here, which would only repeat what has often been stated elsewhere; hence it will suffice for our purposes just to keep in mind that the history of medieval and early-modern cities differed considerably from region to region, from country to country, and also from culture to culture.

In other words, despite a seemingly uniform history of medieval cities, varieties and differences dominated considerably, the result of which still can be observed today. The differences are as remarkable as the similarities, and much depended on economic prosperity, political fortune, religious appeal, and growth of the population. Consequently, the range of topics covered by scholars in this area cannot even be exhaustively defined. To gain just a taste of the enormous potentials for research into medieval and early-modern city life, and to grasp the wealth of critical insights into this field, following I will list a few random examples of more recent publications.

Paul Trio, like many other historians, has worked intensively on medieval confraternities, focusing on Ghent.[67] John Henderson had preceded him with a comparable studies on the confraternities in medieval Florence.[68] Marjan De Smet investigated, together with Paul Trio, the relationship between Church and town in the late-medieval Low Countries.[69] Poverty and the hospital in late-medieval

---

[66]   Joseph P. Byrne, *The Black Death*. Greenwood Guides to Historic Events of the Medieval World (Westport, CT, and London: Greenwood Press, 2004), 57–72; Jürgen Strothmann, "Der 'Schwarze Tod' – Politische Folgen und die 'Krise' des Spätmittelalters," *Pest: Die Geschichte eines Menschheitstraumas*, ed. Mischa Meier (Stuttgart: J. G. Cotta'sche Buchhandlung, 2005), 179–98.

[67]   Paul Trio, *Volksreligie als spiegel van een stedelijke samenleving: de broederschappen te Gent in de late middeleeuwen*. Symbolae Facultatis Litterarum et Philosophiae Lovaniensis. Series B, 11 (Leuven: Universitaire Pers Leuven, 1993); id., "Confraternities in the Low Countries and the Increase in Written Source Material in the Middle Ages," *Frühmittelalter-Studien* 38 (2004): 415–26.

[68]   John Henderson, *Confraternities and the Church in Late Medieval Florence* (Oxford: Basil Blackwell, 1986).

[69]   Marjan De Smet and Paul Trio, "De verhouding tussen Kerk en stad in de Nederlanden in de late Middeleeuwen, onderzocht aan de hand van het interdict," *Jaarboek voor middeleeuwse geschiedenis* 5 (2002): 247–74. See also her article "The Involvement of the Late Medieval Urban Authorities in the Low Countries with Regard to the Introduction of the Franciscan Observance," *Revue d'histoire ecclésiastique* 101, 1 (2006): 37–88.

urban society constitute the research interest of Sheila Sweetinburgh,[70] but we also need to mention the seminal study by Michel Mollat from 1978 focusing on the poor at large.[71] The contributors to *Armut und Armenfürsorge* (2006) examine the public discourse about the poor within the context of the monastic orders, the role of hospitals and other charitable institutions, the points of contacts between Jews and Christians in the area of charity for the poor, and the variety of perspectives on the poor in texts and images from the fourteenth through the sixteenth centuries.[72] Cities were deeply affected by war and by natural consequences,[73] but their steady rise from the early Middle Ages to the Renaissance and beyond could not be stopped, and despite our common assumption that the medieval world was dominated by chivalry and knighthood, along with the Church, whereas the vast majority of peasant population was simply downtrodden, holds true only for certain periods and certain areas, and even there we would have to differentiate considerably.[74]

Moreover, it would be erroneous to assume that urban life in the premodern period was tranquil and stable, with most people only busily working hard to make a living as craftsmen and artists. The history of urban uprisings and revolts extends over centuries and indicates how much these urban communities were in constant flux and underwent regular changes according to political, economic, religious, and social transformations.[75] In fact, the dense living conditions in a city,

---

[70]  Sheila Sweetinburgh, *The Role of the Hospital in Medieval England* (Dublin: Four Courts, 2004); eadem, "Clothing the Naked in Late Medieval East Kent," *Clothing Culture, 1300–1600*, ed. C. T. Richardson (Burlington, VT: Ashgate, 2004), 109–21.

[71]  Michel Mollat, *The Poor in the Middle Ages: An Essay in Social History*, trans. Arthur Goldhammer (1978; New Haven: Yale University Press, 1986)

[72]  *Armut und Armenfürsorge in der italienischen Stadtkultur zwischen [dem] 13. und 16. Jahrhundert: Bilder, Texte und soziale Praktiken*, ed. Philine Helas and Gerhard Wolf. Inklusion/Exklusion: Studien zu Fremdheit und Armut von der Antike bis zur Gegenwart, 2 (Frankfurt a. M., Berlin, et al.: Peter Lang, 2006). For recent studies on marginalized people in the Middle Ages, see *Living Dangerously: On the Margins in Medieval and Early Modern Europe*, ed. Barbara A. Hanawalt and Anna Grotans (Notre Dame, IN: University of Notre Dame Press, 2007). But the urban context does not play any significant role in the contributions.

[73]  See, for instance, Gerhard Fouquet, "Für eine Kulturgeschichte der Naturkatastrophen: Erdbeben in Basel 1365 und Großfeuer in Frankenberg 1476," *Städte aus Trümmern: Katastrophenbewältigung zwischen Antike und Moderne*, ed. Andreas Ranft and Stephan Selzer (Göttingen: Vandenhoeck & Ruprecht, 2004), 101–31.

[74]  See, for instance, the contributions to *Art and Politics in Late Medieval and Early Renaissance Italy, 1250–1500*, ed. Charles M. Rosenberg. Notre Dame Conferences in Medieval Studies, 2 (Notre Dame: University of Notre Dame Press, 1990).

[75]  Jelle Haemers, "A Moody Community? Emotion and Ritual in Late Medieval Urban Revolts," *Emotions in the Heart of the City (14th–16th Century)*, ed. Elodie Lecuppre-Desjardin and Anne-Laure Van Bruaene. Studies in European Urban History (1100–1800), V (Turnhout: Brepols, 2005), 63–81; Aurelio Espinosa, *The Empire of the Cities: Emperor Charles V, the Comunero Revolt, and the Transformation of the Spanish System*. Studies in Medieval and Reformation Traditions, 137 (Boston:

where the various social classes—and by the same token also the two genders—had to interact with each other on a daily basis repeatedly resulted in conflicts and tensions, some of which erupted into riots and military confrontations. But many uprisings were, as I have mentioned above, specifically directed against the city's overlord, a bishop or a secular ruler, whether we think of Milan (1035–1037, 1042–1045), Cambrai (1077–1227), Laon (1107–1112 and 1128), Cologne (1073 and 1074), Bruges (1127–1128), Rome (1143–1155), London (1191–1216), and many others throughout time far into the sixteenth century.[76]

After all, as even Dante Alighieri confirmed in his *Divina Commedia* (*Paradiso*), people are social beings and need to live together in order to prosper and grow:

> Ond' elli ancora: "Or dì: sarebbe il peggio
> per l'omo in terra, se non fosse cive?"
> "Sì" rispuos' io; "e qui ragion non cheggio."[77]
>
> [And he continued: 'Now tell me, would it be worse
> for man on earth if he were not a social being?'
> 'Yes,' I agreed, 'and here I ask no proof.']

Following Claire E. Honess, it deserves to be noted that Dante strongly embraced the notion of the civic community forming the essential framework for productive human life. She comments, "Dante states very explicitly that the individual is worse off in this life if he is not a citizen, a point of view clearly illustrated by the exchange . . . between the pilgrim and Charles Martel [Par. VIII, 115–17]."[78] In this regard we might even consider Dante to be already far removed from traditional medieval ideology: "Dante's notion of citizenship . . . represents a rethinking, though not necessarily a rejection, of many of the most common medieval ideas on the role of the Christian within political society, put forward, above all, by St

---

[76]  Brill, 2008). See also the contribution to the present volume by Lia B. Ross.
Knut Schulz, "Denn sie lieben die Freiheit so sehr . . .: *Kommunale Aufstände und Entstehung des europäischen Bürgertums im Hochmittelalter* (Darmstadt: Wissenschaftliche Buchgesellschaft, 1992). See also Gerd Schwerhoff, "Öffentliche Räume und politische Kultur in der frühneuzeitlichen Stadt: Eine Skizze am Beispiel der Reichsstadt Köln," *Interaktion und Herrschaft: Die Politik der frühneuzeitlichen Stadt*, ed. Rudolf Schlögl. Historische Kulturwissenschaft, 5 (Constance: UVK Verlagsgesellschaft, 2004), 113–36.

[77]  Dante Alighieri, *Paradiso*. A verse translation by Robert and Jean Hollander. Introduction and Notes by Robert Hollander (New York, London, et al.: Doubleday, 2006); see the commentary at 199. Cf. also Claire E. Honess, *From Florence to the Heavenly City: The Poetry of Citizenship in Dante*. Italian Perspective (London: Modern Humanities Research Association and Maney Publishing, 2006), 37: "Following Aristotle, Dante maintains that, socially, human beings incline naturally towards that which they believe to be good—the 'vita felice'—an aim which individuals alone can never hope to achieve without the help of their fellow human beings within the community." I would like to express my thanks to my colleague Fabian Alfie, University of Arizona, for pointing out this passage in Dante and the study by Honess.

[78]  Honess, *From Florence to the Heavenly City*, 38.

Augustine."[79] In other words, an individual's identification with urban space and the urban community might be considered a critical benchmark to differentiate social, mental, and ideological differences between two global periods, the Middle Ages and the early modern age (not necessarily the Renaissance).

Some medieval cities grew out of ancient Roman settlements; others were the product of early-medieval foundations of monasteries and bishoprics; others again developed out of small rural settlements or around castles where craftsmen were constantly needed, apart from the servants and farmhands. There are, ultimately, many diverse explanations for the establishment and growth of cities, so suffice here to observe that it would be utterly erroneous to regard premodern cities as negligible entities within the context of feudal society, even though medieval poets tend to ignore the merchants or regard them as dubious, untrustworthy, unstable, and often simply not as reliable and honorable characters.[80] As H. van Werveke concludes,

> The towns, once they had acquired their own constitution and had become independent political entities, often tried through their town privilege to consolidate their prosperity and their preponderance over the surrounding countryside, which had originally resulted from the free interplay of economic forces. In the same way, within the towns, the ruling class, whose ascendancy was originally founded on wealth alone, tended to transform itself into a politically privileged patriciate, capable for that reason of modifying to its own advantage the conditions of material life. On the other hand, in those places where, about 1300 or later, the lower class was able to assure itself even a modest participation in the management of public affairs, it also exercised an influence on economic life by striving for regulation, with the object no longer of higher productivity but of a socially more equitable distribution of existing sources of wealth.[81]

Some of the most important areas in Europe where cities sprang up and flourished throughout the centuries were: southern England, Flanders, northern France,

---

[79]   Honess, *From Florence to the Heavenly City*, 39.

[80]   Wolfram von Eschenbach, however, particularly in his *Willehalm* (ca. 1220), casts quite a different picture of the admirable, highly ethical and courteous merchant; see Danielle Buschinger, "L'Image du marchand chez Wolfram von Eschenbach," *Guillaume et Willehalm: Les Epopees françaises et l'œuvre de Wolfram von Eschenbach*, ed. eadem. Göppinger Arbeiten zur Germanistik, 421 (Göppingen: Kümmerle, 1985), 7–13. For *Willehalm*, see Wolfram von Eschenbach, *Willehalm: Nach der Handschrift 857 der Stiftsbibliothek St. Gallen*. Mittelhochdeutscher Text, Übersetzung, Kommentar, ed. Joachim Heinzle. Mit den Miniaturen aus der Wolfenbütteler Handschrift und einem Aufsatz von Peter und Dorothea Diemer. Bibliothek des Mittelalters, 9 (Frankfurt a. M.: Deutscher Klassiker Verlag, 1991).

[81]   H. van Werveke, "The Rise of the Towns," 41; see also the various contributions to *The Cambridge Economic History of Europe*. Vol. II: *Trade and Industry in the Middle Ages*, ed. M. M. Postan and Edward Miller (1952; Cambridge, London, et al.: Cambridge University Press, 1987).

southern and western Germany, northern and central Italy, and eastern Spain.[82] But significant cities could also be found in Scotland, Scandinavia, in the Baltic countries, and Russia.[83] The difficulties for urban communities, or communes, throughout medieval and early-modern Europe to establish themselves, to fend off regional or local lords, and to find their own identities were legion, and although many succeeded to establish more or less their freedom and independence, others ultimately failed and were totally dominated by a noble lord, a bishop, or the emperor himself, as Jean-Denis G. G. Lepage confirms:

> Some cities obtained only privileges but remained under the direct tutelage of the local lord, prelate, bishop or archbishop. Other cities were submitted to the authority of a prince, king or emperor. Still other urban communities became totally independent. Called communes in northern Europe and municipalities in the South, free-towns became collective powers, autonomous laic republics, or independent principalities. According to the charter, free cities had the right to maintain a permanent army, build fortifications, make war, and conclude alliances and peace treatises.[84]

Not surprisingly, a whole sleuth of relevant documents in urban archives and elsewhere confirm the profound impact of urban life on medieval and early-modern society in every possible meaning of the word, though most importantly with regard to politics and economics. Nevertheless, from a mental-historical perspective, the city as such does not seem to have played a major role in public discourse, or rather, it emerged on the mental horizon very late. At least this is the general impression that needs to be critically analyzed in holistic and specialized terms.

## New Approaches to the Study of Urban Space

The purpose of the present Introduction and the numerous contributions cannot be to study the history of medieval and early-modern cities in Europe and the neighboring world regions at large, though all those aspects will come into play in various contributions to this volume. After all, the number of relevant studies on cities in their historical and social-economic context is legion, either focusing on global aspects or on specific themes relevant for individual cities in particular

---

82   For the Low Countries, see the contributions to *The Use and Abuse of Sacred Spaces*, 2006.
83   Jean-Pierre Leguay et al., "Stadt," *Lexikon des Mittelalters*, Vol. VII (Munich: Lexma Verlag, 1993), 2169–2208; see also Clive Foss, "Urbanism, Byzantine" (304–07); A. L. Udovitch, "Urbanism, Islamic" (307–311); Kathryn L. Reyerson, "Urbanism, Western European" (311–20), *Dictionary of the Middle Ages*, ed. Joseph R. Strayer. Vol. 12 (New York: Charles Scribner's Sons, 1989).
84   Lepage, *Castles and Fortified Cities*, 256. See also Olson, *The Early Middle Ages*, 186–89.

regions.[85] Similarly, the interest in particular aspects of urban culture has also been intense because its examination sheds important light on the development of medieval and early-modern society.[86] This does not mean, however, that the characteristics of urban culture, or medieval and early-modern life within the urban space, have been adequately and satisfactorily analyzed and discussed. A vast corpus of relevant source materials is available to examine further and to a much greater depth about the physical environment and social services, civic religion, the urban economy, social organization and tensions, including riots, uprisings, general protests, and mob activities, and the political structures (guilds and the patriciate).[87] These include urban chronicles and altar pieces, liturgical plays, secular plays, letters, musical pieces, sculptures, and so also urban architecture. Surprisingly, many of so-called *Stadtbücher*, containing a wide range of documents mirroring all kinds of social, legal, economic, religious, and political activities in the city, still await their thorough examination. Every person who wanted to gain the privilege to join the civic community had to apply and wait for

---

[85]   See, for instance, *Das Leben in der Stadt des Spätmittelalters: Internationaler Kongress Krems an der Donau 20. bis 23. September 1976*. Österreichische Akademie der Wissenschaften. Philosophisch-historische Klasse, Sitzungsberichte, 325. Veröffentlichungen des Instituts für Mittelalterliche Realienkunde Österreichs, 2 (Vienna: Verlag der österreichischen Akademie der Wissenschaften, 1980); *L'evoluzione delle città italiane nell'XI secolo*, a cura di Renato Bordone e Jörg Jarnut. Annali dell'Istituto storico italo-germanico, 25 (Bologna: Società editrice il Mulino, 1988); Brigitte Streich, *Zwischen Reiseherrschaft und Residenzbildung: Der Wettinische Hof im späten Mittelalter* (Cologne and Vienna: Böhlau Verlag, 1989); Knut Schulz, *"Denn sie lieben die Freiheit so sehr . . ."*; Evamaria Engel, *Die deutsche Stadt des Mittelalters*. Beck's Historische Bibliothek (Munich: C. H. Beck, 1993); Heike Bierschwale and Jacqueline van Leeuwen, *Wie man eine Stadt regieren soll: Deutsche und niederländische Stadtregimentslehren des Mittelalters*. Medieval to Early Modern Culture, 8 (Frankfurt a. M., Berlin, et al.: Peter Lang, 2005).

[86]   See, for instance, Penelope Davis, *Town Life in the Middle Ages* (London: Wayland, 1972); *Crossroads of Medieval Civilization: The City of Regensburg and Its Intellectual Milieu*, ed. Edelgard E. DuBruck and Karl Heinz Göller. Medieval and Renaissance Monograph Series, V (Detroit: Michigan Consortium for Medieval and Early Modern Studies, 1984); *Towns in Transition: Urban Evolution in Late Antiquity and the Early Middle Ages*, ed. Neil Christie and S. T. Loseby (Aldershot, Hants, England, and Brookfield, VT: Scolar Press, 1996): David Nicholas, *The Growth of the Medieval City: From Late Antiquity to the Early Fourteenth Century* (London and New York: Longman, 1997); *Stadt und Literatur im deutschen Sprachraum der Frühen Neuzeit*, ed. Klaus Garber, Stefan Anders, and Thomas Elsmann. 2 vols. (Tübingen: Niemeyer, 1998); see especially Garber's contribution "Stadt und Literatur im alten deutschen Sprachraum" (3–89). Adrian J. Boas, *Jerusalem in the Time of the Crusades* (London: Routledge, 2001).

[87]   These are the subheadings in the anthology of relevant documents for the history of Italian cities in *The Towns of Italy in the Later Middle Ages*, trans. and annotated by Trevor Dean. Manchester Medieval Sources Series (Manchester and New York: Manchester University Press, 2000). See also Gerd Schwerhoff, "Öffentliche Räume und politische Kultur in der frühneuzeitlichen Stadt: Eine Skizze am Beispiel der Reichsstadt Köln," *Interaktion und Herrschaft: Die Politik der frühneuzeitlichen Stadt*, ed. Rudolf Schlögl. Historische Kulturwissenschaft, 5 (Constance: UVK Verlagsgesellschaft, 2004), 113–36.

official approval, which was then recorded. Guilds had regulations, which were jotted down in such city books, or chronicles,[88] and judicial conflicts were also documented. In other words, a careful examination of the relevant sources allows us to gain far-reaching insights into the basic structure and development of an urban community over time, and sheds significant light on the city's topography, economic position within the global European network of trade, the relationship between the Christian majority and the Jewish minority (never the other way around!), and the conditions of everyday life within the families.[89]

To study medieval cities and their urban space both in economic and social, and so in cultural and intellectual terms requires a highly complex approach, taking into view a kaleidoscope of various social classes, physical aspects, economic interests and concerns, legal criteria, and religious factors.[90] The interest of the present collection, however, though touching upon many or all of these aspects, lies in mental-historical investigations that find, for instance, remarkable source material in such things as the so-called family books (*Haus-* and *Familienbücher*; see also below). These were normally composed by members of an individual family who were deeply concerned with their own identity and that of their family both past and present, reflecting upon personal, dynastic, and communal interests, and drawing from a wide variety of specific urban sources.[91]

But how did medieval and early-modern people really perceive the city as a material object versus an idea and utopian concept? How did outsiders, often making up the vast majority of the population, that is, the peasants, and then also noblemen, respond to the rise and constant growth of cities? What did urban space mean for the traveler, the churchman, the widow, the student, the poet, the artist, the lawyer, or the craftsman? Some answers can be provided easily because of the

---

[88]   See the extraordinarily valuable series of city chronicles, *Chroniken der deutschen Städte vom 14. bis ins 16. Jahrhundert* (1862–1968; Göttingen: Vandenhoeck & Ruprecht, 1961–1969).

[89]   A great example prove to be the Weimar city books, see *Die Weimarer Stadtbücher des späten Mittelalters: Edition und Kommentar*, ed. Henning Steinführer. Veröffentlichungen der Historischen Kommission für Thüringen. Große Reihe,11 (Cologne, Weimar, and Vienna: Böhlau Verlag, 2005). See also *Das älteste Rostocker Stadtbuch (etwa. 1254–1273)*, ed. Hildegard Thierfelder mit Beiträgen zur Geschichte Rostocks im 13. Jahrhundert (Göttingen: Vandenhoeck & Ruprecht, 1967). There are many similar examples for other areas of medieval Europe; see, for instance, *Epistolari de la València medieval*, ed. d'Agustín Rubio Vela; pròleg d'Antoni Ferrando. 2 vols. (València Spain: Institut Interuniversitari de Filologia Valenciana; Barcelona: Publicacions de l'Abadia de Montserrat, 1998–2003); *Medieval Gloucester, 1066–1547*, an extract from the Victoria History of the County of Gloucester. Vol. IV: *the City of Gloucester*, ed. Nicholas Herbert (1988; Gloucester : Gloucestershire Record Office, 1993).

[90]   Evamaria Engel and Frank-Dietrich Jacob, *Städtisches Leben im Mittelalter: Schriftquellen und Bildzeugnisse* (Cologne, Weimar, and Vienna: Böhlau Verlag, 2006).

[91]   Birgit Studt, "Einführung," *Haus- und Familienbücher in der städtischen Gesellschaft des Spätmittelalters und der frühen Neuzeit*, ed. eadem (Cologne, Weimar, and Vienna, 2007), 1–31.

excellent availability of critical archival and literary documents, but many
questions will remain because we still do not know enough about people's real
attitudes, ideas, and values concerning the city and urban life in the Middle Ages
and the early-modern age.

,It is clear that burghers generally displayed a strong sense of identity with their
home city, as powerfully reflected by festivals, public rituals, coats of arms,
donations, legal practices, the city government itself, and the local arts.[92] The best
evidence for this not so surprising phenomenon consists of the cathedrals and
other churches erected in medieval and early-modern cities, monuments in stone
of communal efforts extending over many generations to prove to the outside
world the glory, wealth, and power of an urban community, but especially to
display its dedication to God and to illustrate God's obvious favor granted to the
city.[93]

Both the pictorial program in stone (sculptures) on the facades and the
individual portals, and then the ideological program in images, such as the
frescoes and the stained glass, explicitly address urban values and ideals within
a religious framework, that is, civic pride in the best possible representation of the
city in its ecclesiastical architecture and art program.[94] After all, many chapels,
sculptures, altar pieces, and other elements in medieval and early-modern cities
were donated and commissioned by well-to-do citizens who wanted to represent
their wealth, their piety, and their social-political status within a religious context.

Critical investigations of the history of mentality have not yet adequately
incorporated 'urban space,' though topics such as 'man and nature' and 'the
experience of space' have certainly attracted considerable attention.[95] But Henri
Lefebvre has alerted us to the fact "that an already produced space can be

[92] See the contributions by Pietro Corrao (97–122), Roberto Bizzochi (123–34), Paola Ventrone
(155–91) and others to *Aspetti e componenti dell'identità urbana.*
[93] See the contributions to *Der gotische Dom in Köln,* ed. Arnold Wolff (Cologne: Vista Point Verlag,
1986); Robert A. Scott, *The Gothic Enterprise: A Guide to Understanding the Gothic Cathedrals*
(Berkeley: University of California Press, 2003); Günther Binding, *Als die Kathedralen in den Himmel
wuchsen: Bauen im Mittelalter* (Darmstadt: Primus Verlag, 2006).
[94] Ulrich Meier, *Mensch und Bürger: Die Stadt im Denken spätmittelalterlicher Theologen, Philosophen und
Juristen* (Munich: R. Oldenbourg, 1994); id., "Burgerlich vereynung: Herrschende, beherrschte und
'mittlere' Bürger in Politiktheorie, chronikalischer Überlieferung und städtischen Quellen des
Spätmittelalters," *Bürgerschaft: Rezeption und Innovation der Begrifflichkeit vom Hohen Mittelalter bis
ins 19. Jahrhundert,* ed. Reinhart Koselleck and Klaus Schreiner. Sprache und Geschichte, 22
(Stuttgart: Klett-Cotta, 1994), 43–89.
[95] See the relevant contributions to "Natur/Umwelt" and "Raum" in *Europäische Mentalitätsgeschichte:
Hauptthemen in Einzeldarstellungen,* ed. Peter Dinzelbacher. Kröners Taschenausgabe, 469
(Stuttgart: Alfred Kröner, 1993); the 2nd rev. and expanded edition appeared just recently
(Stuttgart: Kröner, 2008). He points out, however, how much air pollution in cities was met with
severe protests by the urban population, such as in Bruges, Lyon, London, Arles, and elsewhere
(652–53).

decoded, can be *read*. Such a space implies a process of signification."[96] This specific, culturally and economically defined space proves to be characteristic of each individual society: "every society —and hence every mode of production with its suvariants [sic], i.e. all those societies which exemplify the general concept—produces a space, its own space."[97]

Studying space properly requires one, according to Lefebvre, to embrace three concepts, that is, spatial practice, representations of space, and representational space.[98] In addition, all historical events and activities produce space: "the forces of production (nature; labour and the organization of labour; technology and knowledge) and, naturally, the relations of production play a part . . . in the production of space."[99] Examining medieval cities, for instance, in comparison with cities in the early modern age, will force us to consider novel use and production of space. To quote Lefebvre again:

> 'people'—inhabitants, builders, politicians—stopped going from urban messages to the code in order to decipher reality, to decode town and country, and began instead to go from code to messages, so as to produce a discourse and a reality adequate to the code. This code thus has a history, a history determined, in the West, by the entire history of cities. Eventually it would allow the organization of the cities, which had been several times overturned, to become knowledge and power—to become, in other words, an *institution*. This development heralded the decline and fall of the autonomy of the towns and urban systems in their historical reality.[100]

Concretely, this meant that in the course of time the actual configuration of urban space was changed to meet the needs for public representation and government, leading to the emergence of the early-modern, or Baroque, city: "façades were harmonized to create perspectives; entrances and exits, doors and windows, were subordinated to façades—and hence also to perspectives; streets and squares were arranged in concord with the public buildings and palaces of political leaders and institutions."[101]

Lefebvre offers a most insightful analysis of the profound changes affecting the urban space in the transition from the early to the high Middle Ages with its invention of the magnificent Gothic cathedrals. Whereas the previous period, or rather the Church of that period, had primarily focused on the crypt, as the sacred space of its cult of the dead, the development of tall Gothic buildings with their spires leaping into vertical space inverted the concept of space. In his own words,

---

[96]   Henri Lefebvre, *The Production of Space*, trans. Donald Nicholson-Smith (1974; Oxford: Basil Blackwell, 1991), 17.
[97]   Lefebvre, *The Production of Space*, 31.
[98]   Lefebvre, *The Production of Space*, 38–39.
[99]   Lefebvre, *The Production of Space*, 46.
[100]  Lefebvre, *The Production of Space*, 47.
[101]  Ibid.

"They [the cathedrals] 'decrypt' in a vigorous . . . sense of the word: they are an emancipation from the crypt and from cryptic space. The new space did not merely 'decipher' the old, for, in deciphering it, it surmounted it; by freeing itself it achieved illumination and elevation."[102]

Of course, we have to take Lefebvre's observations with a grain of salt and distinguish further in the detail, particularly because he ignores the history of Romanesque churches, many of which had already explored and conquered open space in a majestic fashion, such as the cathedral of Mainz. But we can certainly subscribe to his general approach insofar as the medieval city very often established itself around the church or cathedral, and soon enough, if not parallel to it, around the market, the central hub of an economic network that liberated the urban population from the agricultural production and laid the foundation for "a space of exchange and communications, and therefore of networks."[103] He recommends, however, and quite rightly so, not to limit our understanding of urban space to the economic aspect since there was also space for political representation, private space, and space of education and learning.[104] This does not mean, however, that the urban world was completely divested from agriculture and typically rural occupations, considering the extensive gardens, house animals, and also the transfer of rural production of beer, for example, into the city.[105] Scholars continue to debate how much the rural world spilled over into the cities, as reflected, for instance, by specific building designs that for a long time shared many similarities with those houses characteristic of a rural settlement with its

---

[102]  Lefebvre, *The Production of Space*, 256–57. He relies heavily on Erwin Panofsky, *Gothic Architecture and Scholasticism* (1951; New York: New American Library, 1976), 58, who had coined the crucial term "visual logic" for the new Church-dominated space.

[103]  Lefebvre, *The Production of Space*, 266.

[104]  Here I break off the discussion of Lefebvre's marvelous, though sometimes also deceptively glossy explanations based on radical abstractions and generalizations; for further comments on his work, see Sheila Sweetinburgh, "Mayor-Making and Other Ceremonies: Shared Uses of Sacred Space Among the Kentish Cinque Ports," *The Use and Abuse of Sacred Places*, 165–87; here 167–70. Felice Riddy, "'Burgeis' Domesticity in Late-Medieval England," *Medieval Domesticity: Home, Housing and Household in Medieval England*, ed. Maryanne Kowaleski and P. J. Goldberg (Cambridge: Cambridge University Press, 2008), 14–36, convincingly questions some of the fundamental notions propounded by Philippe Ariès that until ca. 1700 there was no concept of privacy, not even in urban houses. Much depends, as Riddy observes, on the social class and the time, as the wealthy inhabitants increasingly created their own private rooms, and this already by the fourteenth and the fifteenth centuries. The best evidence for this development can be found in late-medieval Dutch genre paintings.

[105]  Richard W. Unger, *Beer in the Middle Ages and the Renaissance* (Philadelphia: University of Pennsylvania Press, 2004), 40–43. He emphasizes, for instance, "By 1300, making beer was a viable occupation in towns in northern Europe. Not everyone could be a brewer since there were requirements of skill at making beer, at organizing a business enterprise, and of access to capital. Still, many individuals did take up the trade, not just to supply domestic needs but as a commercial venture" (43).

specific needs to accommodate husbandry with living space for the farmer and his family.[106]

Social historians have examined many specific aspects, such as particular markers in a city reflecting power and control wielded by families, individuals, and political groups; linguistic features determining urban geography; space for legal arbitration; staging of spirituality in prayers, meditation, and liturgical rituals; and space for penalties and executions.[107]

## The City and the Courtly World

As has often been emphasized, in a rather stark contrast to our previous observations, the knightly protagonist in medieval literature normally traverses only the countryside and forests, and returns, after having accomplished his task and having overcome his challenges, to King Arthur's court, which again consists only of a small setting, perhaps a camp with tents, or at times a castle. This observation applies both to German and English, French and Italian, Spanish and Portuguese courtly romances or verse narratives, whether the audience was truly aristocratic only, or also included urban readers/listeners. Despite the city's growing importance at least since the eleventh century, medieval poets do not seem to have incorporated urban space as truly significant for their individual protagonists, or for their audiences.[108] Both heroic epics and courtly romances,

---

[106]   This was the central thesis advocated by W. A. Pantin, "Medieval English Town-House Plans," *Medieval Archaeology* 6–7 (1964, for 1962–1963): 202–39); this is now challenged by Sarah Pearson, "Rural and Urban Houses 1100–1500: 'Urban Adaptation' Reconsidered," *Town and Country in the Middle Ages: Contrasts, Contacts and Interconnections, 1100–1500*, ed. Katherine Giles and Christopher Dyer (Leeds: Maney, 2005), 43-63. As Jane Grenville, "Urban and Rural Houses and Households in the Late Middle Ages: A Case Study from Yorkshire," *Medieval Domesticity: Home, Housing and Household in Medieval England*, 92–123; here 95, demonstrates (so her thesis): "some buildings seem to depend on the direct and explicit relationship between town and country while others emphatically do not, but rather represent a distinctively urban type." She rightly concludes, 123: "In the development of the medieval town, the forces of conservatism were continuously pitched against the spirit of entrepreneurship. Material culture was used to signal these tensions . . . ."

[107]   *Medieval Practices of Space*, ed. Barbara A. Hanawalt and Michal Kobialka, 2000; Joyce E. Salisbury, *The Medieval World*. The Greenwood Encyclopedia of Daily Life, a Tour Through History from Ancient Times to the Present, 2 (Westport, CT, and London: Greenwood Press, 2004). Whereas the first volume falls short of providing concrete examples, the second addresses mainly a non-academic audience.

[108]   Uta Störmer-Caysa, *Grundstrukturen mittelalterlicher Erzählungen: Raum und Zeit im höfischen Roman*. de Gruyter Studienbuch (Berlin and New York: de Gruyter, 2007). She heavily relies on Bakthinian theories for her analysis of the essential structures pertaining to space and time in the courtly romance. If we follow her conclusions, the world of the courts, as reflected in the literary discourse, knew nothing of urban space. Indeed, despite some fleeting references here and there,

didactic texts and lyric poetry hardly ever mention cities, to an astonishing degree ignoring a major phenomenon that was going to change the entire world of the Middle Ages, or rather accompanied the feudal structure from early on, ultimately even superseding the agriculture-based society with a society in which craftsmanship and early forms of industrial production dominated within an urban context.

One interesting example would be the Middle High German *Diu Crône* (The Crown) by the Styrian poet Heinrich von dem Türlin, composed sometime between 1210 and 1240, offering an amazing panoply of Arthurian themes and meta-literary references and reflections, with Gawein emerging as the main protagonist who not only accomplishes many chivalric goals, outdoing even Parzival in his quest for the Grail. Most uncannily, Gawein witnesses many scenes obviously drawn from an infernal fantasy, or from the Day of Judgment, which deeply astonish and frighten him and the audience as well, without anyone being able to get involved because they represent imaginary settings or quotes from previous literary texts. Overall, however, as J. W. Thomas insightfully comments, "The court reappears at intervals throughout the work as something of great value that must be preserved at any cost from the dangers that threaten it from within and without. For it is not merely a community of Sybarites but also a source of aid for the oppressed in the surrounding lands."[109] Indeed, people in the countryside receive help, whereas those living in cities are barely mentioned.

At one point Gawein enters a chapel to pray, which some maidens observe with great curiosity. While they all wonder who these impressive knights might be, one of them sarcastically speculates: "They are two wily merchants who are transporting much goods and treasure and are pretending to be knights in order to save themselves from robbery; they think this will protect them. Their bags are

---

neither the Arthurian romance nor the literary manifestations of Tristan and Isolde are predicated in any clear sense on city life. A good example would be Tristan in Gottfried von Strassburg's eponymous romance (ca. 1210) where the badly wounded protagonist arrives in Dublin under the pretense of being a merchant who has been severely wounded by pirates and now seeks help in Ireland. After having been pulled in from the water outside of the harbor, Tristan is quickly whisked from the city of Dublin to the court of the Irish queen Isolde, and we never hear of Dublin again. Gottfried von Straßburg, *Tristan*. Nach dem Text von Friedrich Ranke neu herausgegeben, ins Neuhochdeutsche übersetzt, mit einem Stellenkommentar und einem Nachwort von Rüdiger Krohn. Universal-Bibliothek, 4471 (Stuttgart: Reclam, 1980), 7362–766. A priest learns of Tristan's miraculous skills, and quickly leaves the city of Dublin, turns to the castle, and reports to the queen what he has learned about this stranger.

[109] Heinrich von dem Türlin, *The Crown: A Tale of Sir Gawein and King Arthur's Court*, trans. and with an introd. by J. W. Thomas (Lincoln and London: University of Nebraska Press, 1989), xiii. For a good summary of the relevant research, see Markus Wennerhold, *Späte mittelhochdeutsche Artusromane: 'Lanzelet', 'Wigalois', 'Daniel von dem Blühenden Tal', 'Diu Crône'. Bilanz der Forschung 1960–2000*. Würzburger Beiträge zur deutschen Philologie, 27 (Würzburg: Königshausen & Neumann, 2005), 182–253.

bulging, and I can see from their appearance that they are full of treasure; a child would know that they don't hold hauberks, for these would rattle."[110] Gawein seems to hear her words as he looks up to the window, but then he simply mounts his horse and enters the city to find quarters for himself and his companion. But the merchant was already a specific figure at that time, however mostly regarded with suspicion by the aristocracy, especially because he quickly gained economical preponderance and could challenge the traditional political and social role played by the nobility.[111]

Here is another occasion for the author to add some really brief remarks on a town in the immediate vicinity of a castle: "They wandered about only a short time before finding quarters with a worthy merchant, who furnished everything needed for their comfort. The man was so honest, respected, and wealthy that his like could not be found in the entire town; he was also brave. His house stood below the palace but was so tall that anyone who was curious could see from it all that went on in the palace" (200). Is this really a modest merchant, or a pre-capitalist super-rich international trades person? Apparently, his tower hovers even above the royal palace, and his wealth certainly equals that of a royal person, a narrative motif that finds some reflections in contemporary literature, such as Wolfram von Eschenbach's *Parzival* (ca. 1205) and Rudolf von Ems's *Der guote Gerhard*.[112] More interestingly, prior to this brief description, the author has included a scant reference to a town where, strangely enough, the entire male population is missing: "Gawein found there a town that was large and stately but lacked one thing: neither in it nor in all the country around was there a single man" (196). And later Heinrich mentions another town, but only because "a host of knights whom I cannot name" (204) has assembled there, preparing itself for a tournament: "When the time came the following morning for every man to get ready for the tournament, many were plainly concerned with the contests ahead" (205).

Apparently, then, at closer scrutiny urban space certainly figured on the mental horizon, but for romance authors only as negligible location where knights

---

[110] Heinrich von dem Türlin, *The Crown*, 200.

[111] Jenny Kermode, *Medieval Merchants: York, Beverly and Hull in the Later Middle Ages.* Cambridge Studies in Medieval Life and Thought, Ser. 4, 38 (Cambridge: Cambridge University Press, 1998); Richard K. Marshall, *The Local Merchants of Prato: Small Entrepreneurs in the Late Medieval Economy.* The Johns Hopkins University Studies in Historical and Political Science, 117th series, 1 (Baltimore: Johns Hopkins University Press, 1999).

[112] Rudolf von Ems, *Der gute Gerhard*, ed. Moriz Haupt. Rpt. (1840; Hildesheim: Weidmann, 1988); see also id., *Der guote Gerhart*, ed. John A. Asher. 2nd rev. ed. Altdeutsche Textbibliothek, 56 (1962; Tübingen: Niemeyer, 1971); for a comprehensive analysis, see Sonja Zöllner, *Kaiser, Kaufmann und die Macht des Geldes: Gerhard Unmaze von Köln als Finanzier der Reichspolitik und der "Gute Gerhard" des Rudolf von Ems.* Forschungen zur Geschichte der älteren deutschen Literatur, 16 (Munich: Fink, 1993).

sometimes spend a night to get some rest (Wolfram von Eschenbach's *Willehalm*), where they find new equipment (Hartmann von Aue's *Erec*),[113] or are bothered by the guardsmen who do not properly recognize who they really are (Wolfram von Eschenbach's *Willehalm*).

Exceptions to the rule confirm our general conclusions as to urban space in the Middle Ages and beyond, such as when we think of the three holy cities, Jerusalem, Rome, and Santiago de Compostela, all of them evoking a specific imagery as to an ideal city supported by God or the Holy Ghost.[114] But a visit to any of them always represented a most unusual situation, and the reports about the pilgrimage sites were normally determined by the religious perspective, focusing on churches, tombs, altars, and the clergy, not, however, on urban life and urban space on the microscopic level.[115]

When Margery Kempe (ca. 1373–ca. 1440), for instance, stays in Rome during her pilgrimage, she only comments on her usual prayers and crying, and the conflicts

[113]   Hartmann von Aue, *Erec*. Mit einem Abdruck der neuen Wolfenbütteler und Zwettler Erec-Fragmente, ed. Albert Leitzmann, continued by Ludwig Wolff. 7th. ed. Kurt Gärtner. Altdeutsche Textbibliothek, 39 (Tübingen: Niemeyer, 2006). When Erec arrives at the castle where the tournament is to take place, he avoids the castle and turns his horse toward the town below it: "ein market underm hûse lac" (222) and: "nû vant er an dem wege / von den liuten grôzen schal. / diu hiuser wâren über al / beherberget vaste" (228–34). Chrétien de Troyes, *The Complete Romances*, trans. with an introd. by David Staines (Bloomington and Indianapolis: Indiana University Press, 1990), by contrast, offers a considerably more detailed impression of life within the city/town, but we have to be careful in our assessment of the details: "Erec continued his pursuit of the armed knight and the dwarf . . . until they reached a well-situated town, which was both beautiful and fortified, where they immediately entered through the gateway. In the town there was jubilation among the knights and among the maidens, for many beautiful maidens were there. Along the streets, some people were feeding molting falcons and sparrowhawks; others were bringing tercels outside, along with sorrel-hooded goshawks. Elsewhere, other people were playing games, some at dice or another game of chance, others intent on chess and backgammon. In front of the stables the grooms were rubbing down and currying the horses" (5). Although we are led to believe that Erec has entered a town, the description rather insinuates that it is the courtyard of a big castle.
[114]   Bianca Kühnel, *From the Earthly to the Heavenly Jerusalem: Representations of the Holy City in Christian Art of the First Millenium* (Rome: 1987); *La Gerusalemme celeste*: catalogo della mostra, Milano, Università Cattolica del S. Cuore, 20 maggio –5 giugno 1983, ed. Maria Luisa Gatti Perer (Milano: Vita e Pensiero, 1983); Claus Bernet, "Das himmlische Jerusalem im Mittelalter: Mikrohistorische Idealvorstellungen und utopischer Umsetzungsversuch," *Mediaevistik* 20 (2007): 9–35.
[115]   Nine Robijntje Miedema, *Die 'Mirabilia Romae': Untersuchungen zu ihrer Überlieferung mit Edition der deutschen und niederländischen Texte*. Münchener Texte und Untersuchungen zur deutschen Literatur des Mittelalters, 108 (Tübingen: Max Niemeyer, 1996); see also Christian K. Zacher, *Curiosity and Pilgrimage: The Literature of Discovery in Fourteenth-Century England* (Baltimore: The Johns Hopkins University Press, 1976); Zachary Karabell, *Peace Be Upon You: The Story of Muslim, Christian, and Jewish Coexistence* (New York: Alfred A. Knopf, 2007). Many other scholars have commented on these major cities; see, for instance, E. Baldwin Smith, *Architectural Symbolism of Imperial Rome and the Middle Ages* (Princeton: Princeton University Press, 1955); Richard Krautheimer, *Rome, Profile of a City: 312–1308* (Princeton: Princeton University Press, 1980).

with her social environment: "Then this creature was taken in at the Hospital of St. Thomas of Canterbury in Rome, and there she received communion every Sunday with great weeping, violent sobbing and loud crying, and was highly beloved by the Master of the Hospital and all his brethren."[116] For her, the experience of establishing spiritual friendship with a German priest who did not even understand English was more important than anything else in the entire eternal city: "Another time, while this creature was at the church of St. John Lateran, before the altar, hearing mass, she thought that the priest who said mass seemed a good and devout man" (118). In fact, for Margery Rome serves only as a backdrop for her own mystical visions, or at least her attempts to establish those: "Another time while she was in Rome, a little before Christmas, our Lord Jesus Christ commanded her to go to her confessor, Wenslawe by name, and ask him to give her leave to wear her white clothes once again . . ." (128).

Remarkably, we can identify, despite the lack of concrete references to cities in Arthurian romances, more literary texts and art works from the Middle Ages and the early modern age that actually focus on urban space and the city as a unique entity than traditionally assumed. Whereas a historical approach to the topic at stake has certainly shed much light on the issue, we still need to investigate how people in premodern times perceived the city as an innovative, challenging, and, most importantly, as a promising and exciting site for a community to establish itself, proffering economic prosperity, security, culture, education, and religion. Keith D. Lilley offers this intriguing perspective:

> In the same way that ancient Roman cities were viewed as microcosms of a wider Roman cosmology, the social and spatial ordering of the medieval townscape acted as a mirror of a broader medieval cosmology. In particular, there was a belief that what was good in the world was situated at the centre, while that what was 'other' or different occupied the 'edge', the spatial margins. . . . This 'core-periphery' / 'inside-outside' idea is also reflected in ninth- and tenth-century depictions of the holy Jerusalem descending from Heaven.[117]

---

[116]  *The Book of Margery Kempe*, trans. B. A. Windeatt (London: Penguin, 1985), 116. For a comprehensive discussion of her work, now see Albrecht Classen, *The Power of a Woman's Voice in Medieval and Early Modern Literature: New Approaches to German and European Women Writers and to Violence Against Women in Premodern Times*. Fundamentals of Medieval and Early Modern Culture, 1 (Berlin and New York: Walter de Gruyter, 2007), 271–308.

[117]  Keith D. Lilley, *Urban Life in the Middle Ages 1000–1450*. European Culture and Society (Houndmills, Basingstoke, Hampshire, and New York: Palgrave, 2002), 242. His focus rests on the following topics: urban legacies; institutional urbanism; geographies of urban law; lordship and urbanization; urban landscapes; urban property and landholding; and townspeople and townscapes.

Before I examine some of the basic aspects of medieval and early-modern urban history, with an emphasis on the history of mentality, let us take into view some literary examples with important references to the city as a significant site for a character's individual development.

Throughout the entire Middle Ages and far beyond, the anonymous novel from late antiquity, the *Historia Apollonia Tyrus*, attracted enormous attention and enjoyed far-reaching popularity. This might come as a surprise because both the geographical setting—the eastern Mediterranean—and the value system codified in the text seem to be far removed from medieval and early-modern culture. The protagonist operates as an ideal, but certainly absolute ruler, only subject to God and fortune. Travel takes place by means of ships, and pirates are a steady threat. Christianity is not yet present, and the sense of man's destiny being subject to fortune, very much in the sense of Boethian teaching, irrespective of the slightly anachronistic problem, constitutes a central concern. Moreover, and this is the most significant observation in our context, the narrator and the numerous subsequent translators focus intensively on the city as the critical stage where people interact with each other and also experience some of their worst and happiest moments in life.

   Although the earliest surviving manuscripts date from the ninth century, sixth-century Venantius Fortunatus already refers to the *Historia Apollonia Tyrus* in one of his poems, describing himself as being sadder than the protagonist Apollonius. Throughout the following centuries poets continued to cite the *Historia* and comment on its importance. Library catalogues all over Europe contain listings for this text since the ninth century, and the number of actually existing Latin manuscripts is about one hundred. Then there are countless translations into the various vernaculars and creative adaptations, which often incorporated new material and pursued different agendas. As Elizabeth Archibald confirms,

> By the fifteenth century the story of Apollonius was being retold in a great number of vernaculars; its wide appeal is demonstrated by texts from hitherto silent areas. These include a Czech version with biblical and folklore colouring [V19]; three German prose versions [V25 and 26], not particularly innovative, but in the case of Steinhöwel's *Volksbuch* very popular; a heavily Christianized Greek version, the *Diegesis Apolloniou* [27]; and two exemplary Spanish versions, based respectively on the *Gesta Romanorum* and the *Confessio Amantis* [V28 and 29].[118]

Once the printing press had been invented, the *Historia* achieved renewed fame and popularity in many different languages, and it was also translated into a

---

[118]   Elizabeth Archibald, *Apollonius of Tyre: Medieval and Renaissance Themes and Variations.* Including the text of the *Historia Apollonii Regis Tyri* with an English translation (Woodbridge, Suffolk: Boydell & Brewer, 1991), 48–49.

dramatic version by Shakespeare with his *Pericles* (1609). Following Archibald again, "By the fifteenth and sixteenth centuries a great variety of versions existed: some stressed chivalric values, others Christian morality; some medievalized heavily, others reintroduced classical details."[119] We might go so far as to claim that the *Historia* truly represents a world classic, and this until today. Particularly medieval audiences, however, seem to have enjoyed this text, despite, or perhaps just because of, its almost Oriental, that is, certainly exotic, setting. Surprisingly, throughout the novel, the city emerges as the central location where most of the significant events take place. As the very first line in the Latin text indicates: "In the city of Antioch there was a king called Antiochus, from whom the city itself took the name Antioch" (113).

This rapist father is very much concerned with preserving the air of a good ruler who cares for his people, the citizens of Antioch: "He presented himself deceitfully to his citizens as a devoted parent" (115). His opponent, young Apollonius, is similarly identified with his city and its citizens who are worried about him after his return home and want to pay their respect to him. But he has already left again, having realized that he had actually solved the riddle presented by Antiochus and might face serious danger of being killed.

Significantly, the entire population in the city laments and grieves his disappearance, casting the city into mourning. We receive a short glimpse of the actual urban life of a Roman city, basically unheard of in any medieval text: "So great was his people's love for him that for a long time the barbers were deprived of clients, the shows were cancelled and the baths were closed" (117). Most important for our investigation, the poet here allows a deep glance into the interior of the city, referring to the entertainment and service industry, and the healthcare system.[120] After all, dense city life brought together masses of people from all strata of society, and a certain percentage were always trying to make a living from artistic performances and other types of services, some legal, other illegal, as would be the case today as well. "Games of sleight of hand, trained animals, and songs and little concerts were habitual spectacles, especially when the arrival of

---

[119]   Archibald, *Apollonius*, 51. For the German print history of this novel, see Bodo Gotzkowsky, *"Volksbücher": Prosaromane, Renaissancenovellen, Versdichtungen und Schwankbücher. Bibliographie der deutschen Drucke*. Part I: *Drucke des 15. und 16. Jahrhunderts*. Bibliotheca Bibliographica Aureliana, CXXV (Baden-Baden: Verlag Valentin Koerner, 1991), 184–91.

[120]   Gertrud Blaschitz, "Das Freudenhaus im Mittelalter: *In der stat was gesessen / ain unrainer pulian . . .*," *History of Sexuality in the Middle Ages and the Early Modern Age*, ed. Albrecht Classen. Fundamentals of Medieval and Early Modern Culture, 3 (Berlin and New York: de Gruyter, 2008), 715–50.

one of the religious holidays made it likely that a numerous public would turn up for these tempting attractions."[121]

Moreover, the entire urban community demonstrates its close-knit relationship when they all turn to mourning over the disappearance of their lord, as we learn from a boy's response to the assassin Taliarchus's inquiry about the curious situation in the city: "'What a shameless man! He knows perfectly well and yet he asks! Who does not know that this city is in mourning for this reason, because the prince of this country, Apollonius, came back from Antioch and then suddenly disappeared'" (117).

Apollonius, on the other hand, has reached another city in the meantime, Tarsus, where famine threatens without hope for a reprieve. The young king intervenes, however, and, speaking on a platform in the forum to the entire populace, he assures them that he would save them, granting them all the grain they need, without taking any money for it because he does not want to appear as a merchant. The citizens, in their thankfulness, "decided to erect a bronze statue to him, and they place it in the forum" (121). Whereas in most other medieval narratives the focus rests on the court in a castle or palace, without any sense of an urban environment, here the city community comes forward and expresses its thankfulness collectively.[122]

Although the narrative focuses on a protagonist, he does not operate in a vacuum and has to deal with the people living in the city as a whole. Apollonius's stage of operation proves to be the city, which finds it confirmation already in the next scene after he has left Tarsus and almost drowns on the high sea during a mighty storm that makes his ship sink. Albeit he is a shipwreck, Apollonius quickly regains his good fortune in the city of Pentapolis where he ingratiates himself with the king and his daughter whom he eventually marries. Here once again the urban context emerges in the background, even though only fleetingly, when a young boy announces to the public that the gymnasium has been opened: "'Listen, citizens, listen, foreigners, freemen and slaves: the gymnasium is open!'" (125).

From here on the events that take place are limited to the court, whereas the city itself fades away into the background. The reason for this development simply consists of the growing love that the princess feels for this amazing foreigner, yet

---

[121]   Chiara Frugoni, *A Day in a Medieval City*, 85. She observes that in many cases the city governments even paid for those entertaining spectacles in order to appease the population and to keep it under control, 190, note 77: "Quod . . . camerarius comunis de ipsius comunis pecunia det et solvat istis tubatoribus, menestreriis et ioculatoribus qui venerunt et honoraverunt festum sanctorum Floridi et Amantii istas pecunias."

[122]  Albrecht Classen, "Reading and Deciphering in *Apollonius of Tyre* and the *Historia von den sieben weisen Meistern*: Medieval Epistemology within a Literary Context," *Studi Medievali* 49 (2008): 161–88.

we can be certain that the city itself remains a constant element both here and later. And each time, despite the prominent role played by the respective kings, we gain a clear sense of the urban population playing its own important part. For instance, when Apollonius marries Archistrates's daughter, the celebrations do not only take place in the palace; instead they also involve the entire city: "There was great rejoicing throughout the city; citizens, foreigners and guests revelled" (137). The same occurs in other cities, such as Mytilene, where Apollonius's daughter Tarsia is taken as a slave and prostitute much later. The urban public is always present and participates in the events that are located in the center of the city: "She was landed among the other slaves and put up for sale in the market place" (149). Once she is transferred to the brothel, we gain another insight into the urban space filled with people: "Tarsia was taken to the brothel, preceded by a crowd and musicians" (151). Later, when her father happens to arrive at Mytilene, the citizens are celebrating the "feast of Neptune" (157), and Apollonius allows his crew to participate in the happening, which opens up a noteworthy narrative background with considerable urban space crowded with people.

Of course, the crucial encounters between Athenagoras, the prince of the city, and Apollonius takes place in the bow of the ship where the latter spends his time mourning. Once the prince has learned of the other man's suffering, he sends Tarsia to the ship to lighten up the poor man's sorrow, which she manages successfully, indeed, which leads to their mutual recognition. But for our purpose the narrative involves two stages here, the ship at the beach, or rather in the harbor, and the actual city in the background, ever present because of the brothel there, the local festivities, and the extensive festivities.

Once Apollonius has learned of his daughter's destiny at the hand of the pimp, he expresses his intention to exact his revenge and to destroy the city. Atenagoras immediately announces this terrible news to the entire city population, which underscores, once again, the considerable depth of perception upon which this novel is predicated: "When prince Athenagoras heard this, he began to call out in the streets, in the forum, in the senate house, saying: 'Hurry, citizens and nobles, or the city will be destroyed'" (169). The response is, of course, enormous, which indicates how much the urban population enjoyed its own weight on the political stage as described here: "An enormous crowd gathered, and there was such an uproar among the people that absolutely no one, man or woman, remained at home" (169).

Not surprisingly, everything concludes, like in a fairy tale, with a happy ending, but the narrator hastens to add a brief comment on Apollonius's realm, which is marked by cities, not by countries, or by fields, forests, and other types of land: "He ruled Antioch and Tyre and Cyrene as his kingdom, and led a peaceful and happy life with his wife" (179). As a confirmation for this, Apollonius's actions in Tarsus underscore the importance of the city in the life of all people: "So

Apollonius added to the public rejoicing in return for this: he restored public works, he rebuilt the public baths, the city walls, and the towers on the walls" (177). This focus on individual cities as the space of tragic events and political developments characterizes the entire text, which subsequent translators and adaptors did not change substantially.[123]

In the goliardic epic *Herzog Ernst*, composed in Middle High German first in ca. 1170 (ms. A), but fully available only in two much later manuscripts (ms. a and b from 1441 and late in the 15th century respectively) that are based on copies from the early thirteenth century (reconstructed ms. B), the male protagonist struggles for a long time against his evil father-in-law, Emperor Otte, because an envious advisor had maligned the young duke, claiming that he intended to usurp the throne.[124] The military conflict rages for a long time, but eventually, no longer able to resist the pressure, the duke has to leave his country and he goes on a pilgrimage to the Holy Land. On his way there he stops at Constantinople and is warmly welcomed by the Byzantine emperor and his court. The narrator does not comment on the city at all; instead he focuses on the personal relationship between these two leaders who display great respect for each other.

After some time Ernst receives a well equipped ship and embarks on his next journey, accompanied by a whole flotilla of Greek ships. But after five days a mighty storm arises and almost everyone drowns, except Ernst and his men. Nevertheless, three months pass without them reaching firm land, and they begin

[123] For the German tradition, particularly with regard to Heinrich von Neustadt's *Apollonius von Tyrland*, see Simone Schultz-Balluff, *Dispositio picta – Dispositio imaginum: Zum Zusammenhang von Bild, Text, Struktur und 'Sinn' in den Überlieferungsträgern von Heinrichs von Neustadt "Apollonius von Tyrland"*. Deutsche Literatur von den Anfängen bis 1700, 45 (Bern, Berlin, et al.: Peter Lang, 2006), 136–53. The pictorial program is consistently, even if not always, predicated on cityscapes in the background or looming large on the horizon. See now also Giovanni Garbugino, *Enigmi della Historia Apollonii Regis Tyri*. Testi e manuali per l'insegnamento universitario del latino, 82 (Bologna: Patròn, 2004); G. A. A. Kortekaas, *Commentary on the Historia Apollonii Tyri*. Mnemosyne, Bibliotheca Classica Batava, Supplementum, 284 (Leiden and Boston: Brill, 2007).

[124] *Herzog Ernst: Ein mittelalterliches Abenteuerbuch,* herausgegeben, übersetzt, mit Anmerkungen und einem Nachwort versehen von Bernhard Sowinski (1974; Stuttgart: Reclam, 1979). For further studies, see Albrecht Classen, "Medieval Travel into an Exotic Orient: The *Spielmannsepos Herzog Ernst* as a Travel into the Medieval Subconsciousness,"*Lesarten. New Methodologies and Old Texts*, ed. Alexander Schwarz, Tausch, 2 (Frankfurt a. M., New York, and Paris: Lang, 1990), 103–24; id., "Multiculturalism in the German Middle Ages? The Rediscovery of a Modern Concept in the Past: The Case of *Herzog Ernst*," *Multiculturalism and Representation. Selected Essays*, ed. John Rieder and Larry E. Smith (Honolulu: University of Hawaii Press, 1996), 198–219; see also the introduction to *Gesta Ernesti ducis: Die Erfurter Prosa-Fassung der Sage von den Kämpfen und Abenteuern des Herzogs Ernst*, ed. Peter Christian Jacobsen and Peter Orth. Erlanger Forschungen. Reihe A: Geisteswissenschaften, 82 (Erlangen: Universitäts-Bibliothek, 1997), 1–83; Odo von Magdeburg, *Ernestus*, ed. and commentary Thomas A.-P. Klein. Spolia Berolinensia, 1 (Hildesheim: Weidmannsche Verlagsbuchhandlung, 2000), IX–LXII.

to fear dying from hunger and thirst. In the last moment, so to speak, they finally reach the country Grippia where they hope to restock their supplies. The sailors release the anchor and the knights approach the city itself which unexpectedly emerges as a miraculous phenomenon in architectural and aesthetic terms.

Grippia proves to be the first extensive description of a major city in medieval vernacular literature, if we ignore the numerous references to classical Troy, Carthage, and Rome, the three monumental stages in Aeneas's career, fleeing from burning Troy via Carthage to Italy where he founds, upon the gods' commands, the new city, imperial Rome.[125]

The goliardic poet of this Middle High German tale had referred to several cities before, such as those occupied by Duke Ernst and the Emperor respectively. In those cases each city was treated as a fortress that the enemy besieges, such as Nuremberg (878), which can resist Otte's army and proves to be impenetrable to the hostile forces. Insofar as the emperor does not easily achieve his goal to squash the young duke, he calls for an imperial diet in Speyer, but that city is hardly given any profile, and the description seems to be entirely limited to the court where the emperor resides (1243–44).

In a highly bold move, Ernst secretly enters the palace to assassinate the emperor, who manages, however, to escape in the last minute, whereas his evil advisor, the Count of the Palatinate, is decapitated. Ernst and his men make their way out of the camp safely, and disappear in the distance, as if there had not been any city walls, guards, streets, market squares, and other typical elements of a fortified medieval city.

---

[125] See, for instance, Adolf Emile Cohen, *De visie op Troje van de westerse middeleeuwse geschiedschrijvers tot 1160*. Van Gorcum's historische bibliotheek, XXV (Assen: Van Gorcum, 1941); C. David Benson, *The History of Troy in Middle English Literature: Guido delle Colonne's Historia Destructionis Troiae in Medieval England* (Woodbridge, Suffolk: D. S. Brewer, and Totowa, NJ: Rowman & Littlefield, 1980); Gert Melville, *Troja: die integrative Wiege europäischer Mächte im ausgehenden Mittelalter* (Stuttgart: Klett-Cotta, 1986); *Entre fiction et histoire : Troie et Rome au moyen âge*, ed. Emmanuèle Baumgartner and Laurence Harf-Lancner (Paris: Presses de la Sourbonne Nouvelle, 1997); *Fantasies of Troy: Classical Tales and the Social Imaginary in Medieval and Early Modern Europe*, ed. Alan Shepard and Stephen D. Powell. Essays and Studies, 5 (Toronto: Centre for Reformation and Renaissance Studies, 2004). This short selection of relevant studies clearly demonstrates how much the myth of Troy has determined Western Europe throughout the centuries, though the focus has not necessarily rested on Troy as a city in its architectural dimensions. See also Sylvia Federico, *New Troy: Fantasies of Empire in the Late Middle Ages*. Medieval Cultures, 36 (Minneapolis: University of Minnesota Press, 2003); Bettany Hughes, *Helen of Troy: Goddess, Princess, Whore* (New York: A. Knopf, 2005); Wolfram A. Keller, *Selves & Nations: the Troy Story from Sicily to England in the Middle Ages* (Heidelberg: Winter, 2008). For solid studies of the role of Troy in medieval German literature, see Manfred Kern, *Agamemnon weint, oder, arthurische Metamorphose und trojanische Destruktion im "Göttweiger Trojanerkrieg"* Erlanger Studien, 104 (Erlangen: Palm & Enke, 1995); Elisabeth Lienert, *Geschichte und Erzählen: Studien zu Konrads von Würzburg "Trojanerkrieg"*. Wissensliteratur im Mittelalter, 22 (Wiesbaden: L. Reichert, 1996).

When the emperor later strikes back, he attacks the castles and cities in Ernst's dukedom of Bavaria, though he faces stiff resistance, particularly by the citizens of Regensburg, who give up their fight only after five years of bitter fighting.

During that time of siege, both sides make every possible attempt to thwart the opponent's military operations, but at the end the emperor carries the day because of his better resources. The narrator provides only fleeting descriptions of the entire city, emphasizing the city gates (1467), the towers and other parts of the fortification system (1531), and the moat (1547), and he also refers to the citizens as the defenders (1521), but overall he conceives of Regensburg as a "burg," or castle (1570), although he also resorts to the term "stat," or city (1556).[126]

The situation in Grippia is entirely different. We might really doubt whether Nuremberg or Regensburg as described here fleetingly represents a city in the ancient or in the modern sense of the word, considering that the narrative focus there rests almost entirely on the fortification system. By contrast, Grippia consists of fully-developed urban space, with streets, palaces, squares, a city wall, towers, and a park, in its most splendid design representing almost a medieval urban utopia. A sophisticated defense system with a strong wall, gates, and a moat is present as well, but the wall, for instance, is brilliantly decorated, consisting of marble stones glowing brightly in many different colors (2215–29). Moreover, almost undermining the basic function of the wall to defend the city, many sculptures have been attached that strongly reflect the light (2224–29), as if they serve only decorative purposes. The narrator's eyes carefully wander over all the details, such as the merlons and crenels, covered with gold and gems (2233–39), as if they did not have any military and architectural function. Nevertheless, the poet still emphasizes that this was a castle ("burc," 2240) that could not be conquered.

For our purpose of exploring the mental-historical construct and perception of urban space in the Middle Ages and the early modern age as part of the wider mental history, the narrative presentation of Grippia deserves greater attention.[127] The radius of the entire city is extensive, and the foreigners can hardly find their way into it without getting lost (2510). Many valuable sculptures decorate the city, and so do numerous palaces, giving a real of sense of a complex architectural ensemble. Grippia is located next to the sea, making it impossible for potential

---

[126]   Jean-Denis G. G. Lepage, *Castles and Fortified Cities of Medieval Europe: An Illustrated History* (Jefferson, NC, and London: McFarland, 2002), offers an excellent and detailed encyclopedic overview of medieval cities.

[127]   Hartmut Kugler, *Die Vorstellung der Stadt in der Literatur des deutschen Mittelalters*. Münchener Texte und Untersuchungen zur deutschen Literatur des Mittelalters, 88 (Munich: Artemis, 1986), 19, 133; Albrecht Classen, "Confrontation with the Foreign World of the East: Saracen Princesses in Medieval German Narratives," *Orbis Litterarum* 53 (1998): 277–95; Richard Spuler, "The Orientreise of Herzog Ernst," *Neophilologus* 67.3 (1983): 410–18.

attackers to surround the entire city from all sides (2553–56). An animal park, like a zoo, constitutes the heart of the city, but the royal palace dominates everything, covered with gold and green emeralds. The individual rooms dazzle the observer with all their gems in the walls (2565–67). One of them impresses above all, obviously a king's private chamber (2570–2644). The narrator is careful to add interior space to his overall description of the city, thereby providing depth to the urban tableau.

Once Ernst and his advisor Wetzel have left the building again, they enter a large yard in which many cedar trees have been planted. To their delight, there is also a bath house where warm and cold water flows into the tubs depending on the user's desires (2670–78).[128] Once the water has run through the tubs, it exits them again and pours out onto the street where it can serve as a cleaning agent. The entire set-up proves to be most efficient and impressive, as if Grippia were an eighteenth-century city with an extensive and sophisticated canalization and sewer system:

> daz geschach mit sinne.
> die strâzen dar inne
> beide grôz und kleine
> wârn von marmelsteine,
> sumlîche grüene als ein gras.
> so in der burc erhaben was
> und man dâ schône wolde hân,
> sô liez man daz wazzer sân
> über al die burc gên.
> sô mohte dâ niht bestên
> weder daz hor noch der mist.
> in einer vil kurzen frist
> sô wart diu burc vil reine.
> ich wæne burc deheine
> ûf erden ie sô rîch gestê:
> ir strâzen glizzen sô der snê.          (2682–98)

[This was arranged deliberately.
All the streets in the city,
both the great and the small ones,
were built out of marble stones,

---

[128] For the history of baths and bathing in the Middle Ages, see Gertrud Wagner, *Das Gewerbe der Bader und Barbiere im deutschen Mittelalter* (Zell i. W.: F. Buar, 1917); Hans-Jürgen Sarholz, *Heilbäder im Mittelalter: die Anfänge der Kur in Mitteleuropa*. Bad Emser Hefte, 155 (Bad Ems: VDGL, 1996); see also Georges Vigarello, *Concepts of Cleanliness: Changing Attitudes in France since the Middle Ages*, trans. Jean Birrell (1985; Cambridge and New York: Cambridge University Press; Paris: Maison de Sciences de l'Homme, 1988).

some as green as grass.
When people woke up in the city (castle)
and desired it to be clean,
they let the water immediately run out
throughout the entire place.
Nothing of all the dirt and dust
could then stay behind.
Very quickly the city
was very clean.
I believe there is no other city
in the world like this one:
its streets gleam like snow.]

The contemporary audience would have agreed, and even within the narrative context we can confirm the remarkable difference between those cities located in Western Europe, such as Nuremberg and Regensburg, and Grippia somewhere in the exotic Orient. Generally speaking, neither large public spaces nor hygiene in the modern sense of the word was fully available or of major significance in medieval cities,[129] though they quickly emerged in the late Middle Ages and the Renaissance, along with major public buildings, such as town halls, guild houses, court buildings, etc.[130] As Philippe Contamine notes:

> Perhaps the most striking feature of the medieval city was the scarcity of public places and buildings. Streets and squares were under the jurisdiction of the municipal, seigneurial, or royal authorities, and the right of eminent domain was not unknown. Nevertheless, one has the impression that the public sphere was limited and residual; worse still, it was constantly threatened by private encroachment.[131]

Nevertheless, we must not forget that "[p]eople in the Middle Ages spent a lot of time together, in the streets with their neighbors . . . . Dealers and artisans for the most part had their shops in the houses they lived in, on the ground floor, and displayed their products in the street on counters made of wood, or built into the

---

[129]  See the contributions to *Medieval Practices of Space*, ed. Barbara A. Hanawalt and Michal Kobialka. Medieval Cultures, 23 (Minneapolis and London: University of Minnesota Press, 2000). As Hanawalt and Kobialka emphasize in their introduction, "By focusing on the practices within a heterogeneous space, it becomes apparent that space is thoroughly imbued with quantities and qualities marking the presence of bodies, signs, and thoughts that had disappeared from view or a discourse in the topography of the medieval landscape." (xi)

[130]  Georges Zarnicki, *Art of the Medieval World*, 395–97.

[131]  Philippe Contamine, "Peasant Hearth to Papal Palace: The Fourteenth and Fifteenth Centuries," *Revelations of the Medieval World*, ed. Georges Duby, trans. Arthur Goldhammer. A History of Private Life, II (1985; Cambridge, MA, and London: The Belknap Press of Harvard University Press, 1988), 425–505; here 438. See also the entertaining and well informed study by Daniel Furrer, *Wasserthron und Donnerbalken: Eine kleine Kulturgeschichte des stillen Örtchens* (Darmstadt: Primus Verlag, 2004), 38–55. He also discusses the history of medieval baths.

wall of the house."[132] Only by the late Middle Ages did this situation begin to change, and both concerns for public hygiene and the improvement of public life were voiced repeatedly, which led to more distinct separations of private and public spaces. Antonio of Beatis commented, for instance, on Mecheln in Belgium: "Superb city, very large and highly fortified. Nowhere have we seen streets more spacious or more elegant. They are paved with small stones, and the sides slope down slightly, so that water and mud never remain standing."[133]

Returning to the Middle High German goliardic poem, not surprisingly, Grippia with its almost modern looking canalization system would have to be regarded as an extraordinary exception, perhaps almost like an architectural ideal. Medieval cities certainly did not look like that, and the comments about Regensburg and Nuremberg do not indicate at all any similarities with Grippia. Of course, the poet projects an ideal setting, almost an urban utopia, but he only glorifies the building elements, whereas the people populating that city quickly turn out to be members of a monstrous race, half human and half crane. As to be expected, hardly have Ernst and Wetzel finished taking a bath and put on their armor again when the Grippians return from a war campaign during which they have killed the king of India and his wife, and have kidnapped their beautiful daughter. The Grippian king wants to marry her, but when a servant discovers the two travelers hiding in a dark corner, they believe that some of the princess's servants have followed, so they stab her to death with their beaks, which then forces the heroes to rush forward and kill everyone in their way, hacking a way through the throngs to the city gate where they are eventually rescued by their own people. Outside they unexpectedly face an army of Grippians, and they can barely fight their way to the ships, losing many of their own men.

Once Ernst and his companions have left Grippia behind, they encounter numerous other adventures, but they never come across a city like the one built by those crane people, although they spend a long time with other monstrous peoples in the mysterious East. Surprisingly, not even Jerusalem is deemed important enough to receive any particular attention later in the narrative. We only learn that Duke Ernst eventually reached the goal of his pilgrimage/crusade

---

[132]   Chiara Frugoni, *A Day in a Medieval City*, 49–50. She refers to literary and art-historical evidence, such as a novella by Franco Sacchetti and a miniature in a manuscript from ca. 1470. Turning from the public to the private space, she emphasizes: "The shortage of space in the interiors drove people out of doors; the streets became ever more narrow, even as they became more animated, because men and women stopped in front of the counters to buy, to make contracts, to chat, perhaps with a member of the household . . . . Women liked to be at the window or on the balcony . . ." (51). "Men liked to be in the streets and the piazzas, doing business, making purchases, talking and arguing about things" (58). Whether this strict gender differentiation regarding public and private space in a medieval city can be upheld remains to be examined more carefully. See the contribution to this volume by Lia B. Ross.

[133]   Cited from Contamine, "Peasant Hearth," 441.

and fought for a long time against the infidels, acquiring a great reputation. Once he has been secretly informed that his father-in-law, the German emperor, has changed his mind and would welcome him back home, Ernst departs from Jerusalem and travels to Europe, paying on his way west a visit to Rome, of course. But again, here the narrative focus does not rest on the urban space; instead we only hear that the duke was led to Saint Peter and donated valuable cloths (5800–24).

Only Grippia emerges as a veritable city in the modern sense of the word, but it seems more like an exotic entity than an ideal model, despite all its beauty and cleanliness. And once Ernst has reached Germany again, all personal encounters take place at court and in a cathedral, which leaves out the urban space entirely.

Although medieval society was mostly determined by feudalism—for an exception, see Iceland—and the dominance of the rural population at least in statistical terms, it would be incorrect to ignore the deep and growing impact of cities and city life, as we have observed repeatedly. Historians have paid great attention to this phenomenon, and we would carry proverbial owls to Athens if we wanted to review and rewrite the history of medieval cities.[134] Individual scholars have also discussed how the city was presented and projected in medieval literature. Hartmut Kugler, for instance, examines the *laudes urbium*, the literary images of Carthage and Rome, the metaphor of the celestial city of Jerusalem and its concrete function in the historical context, and finally the city as the center of a region determined by human activities, implying the *situs urbis* as the central location of a complex communal system.[135] But as our discussion of the goliardic epic poem *Herzog Ernst* has indicated, we also need to approach the topic of urban space from a mental-historical perspective.

How might the various audiences of this most popular tale have reacted to the stunning description of Grippia? Did it represent a literary dream or a warning against excessive development of the urban space which could only be found in the exotic East? After all, Ernst takes too much time enjoying the urban privileges, wandering around in amazement and then taking a bath, where he is caught by surprise when the Grippians finally return and begin with their wedding

---

[134]  See, for instance, Norman Pounds, *The Medieval City*. Greenwood Guides to Historic Events of the Medieval World (Westport, CT, and London: Greenwood, 2005). He discusses the following topics: origins; the urban plan; the urban way of life; the Church in the city; city government; urban crafts and trade; health, wealth, and welfare. He correctly concludes that the city became "the fastest growing and the wealthiest of any division of society, and it was quick to make its influence felt at least in western and central Europe" (153). Reviewing the architectural, artistic, intellectual, religious, and political inheritance from the Middle Ages, all attributable to the city, he notes: "The artistic and cultural achievement of western civilization, like its political legacy, was by and large the achievement of its cities and towns" (163).

[135]  Kugler, *Die Vorstellung*.

festivities. On the one hand the protagonist proves to be a victim of his own curiosity and temptability, awe-struck by the beauty and wealth of the urban architecture. On the other, his entire journey represents a rite of passage for him, ultimately leading to a form of rebirth once he and his men have traveled through a mountain on a little raft during their next major adventure.[136]

This would imply that Grippia represents the first of many challenges for him, though the city itself would not constitute a threat to his character or morality. Instead, he is seriously concerned with and erotically interested in rescuing the Indian princess, though he underestimates the military prowess and strength of the crane people. In fact, he and his companion Wetzel would have died at the end had not his comrades arrived in time to free them from the deadly conflict within the city, forcing their way through the gate to the inside.

One could also not really blame Duke Ernst for his desire to visit the city a second time and then to take a bath in the most sophisticated bathhouse — apparently an exotic rarity for him and his advisor. Nevertheless, the city itself represents otherness and the danger of the mysterious Orient for the Christian warrior on his pilgrimage to Jerusalem.[137] Despite all its luxuriousness, splendor, size, and wealth, Grippia would not be a place where Ernst could exist, or just rest, and at the end he must literally hack his way out of the city, barely surviving the onslaught by the Grippian army outside. This does not mean, however, that the anonymous poet of *Herzog Ernst* would cast this city as a site of sinfulness, debauchery, and decadence, perhaps as a new Sodom and Gomorrah. In fact, the protagonist deeply admires the urban architecture and enjoys the unheard of amenities that this city offers its uninvited guests.

Admittedly, the crane people are not described in positive terms: they carry out a brutal and unjustified warfare against India, and they immediately stab the kidnapped princess to death when they think that some Indian soldiers are hiding in the palace. But they behave like most other medieval people would have, and their king could easily be compared to any other European ruler, considering the vast corpus of bridal-quest narratives.

The goliardic poem contains elements of criticism of and admiration for this new type of city; it offers a most appealing image of such an architectural marvel to the

---

[136]  David Malcolm Blamires, *Herzog Ernst and the Otherworld Voyage: A Comparative Study.* Publications of the Faculty of Arts of the University of Manchester, 24 (Manchester: Manchester University Press, 1979); Albrecht Classen, "Medieval Travel into an Exotic Orient: The *Spielmannsepos Herzog Ernst* as a Travel into the Medieval Subconsciousness," *Lesarten: New Methodologies and Old Texts,* ed. Alexander Schwarz. Tausch, 2 (Frankfurt a. M., New York, and Paris: Peter Lang, 1990), 103–24.

[137]  For further reflections upon this phenomenon, see the contributions to *Diesseits- und Jenseitsreisen im Mittelalter: Voyages dans l'ici-bas et dans l'au-delà au moyen âge,* ed. Wolf-Dieter Lange. Studium Universale, 14 (Bonn and Berlin: Bouvier Verlag, 1992).

general audience and yet also warns them not to identify too closely with this kind of city because the inhabitants belong to the monstrous races, which associates their urban space also with a sense of the dangerous exotic.

In all likelihood the poet reflected upon the new experiences that the Christian crusaders had in the Holy Land where they encountered a superior and highly advanced urban culture which was soon to influence western civilization as well in terms of urban space.

Yet this was only one of a myriad of perspectives toward the medieval city in East and West, and we also would have to consider the most important world of learning and schooling at least since the twelfth century that emerged in urban centers when the traditional cathedral schools lost esteem and had to cede much of their influence and authority to new institutions of higher learning.[138] After all, with the twelfth century, universities sprang up everywhere in Europe, all of them located in cities and drawing specifically from urban life, whether in Paris, Oxford, Cambridge, Bologna, Salamanca, Salerno, or in Montpellier, Toledo, and ultimately also north of the Alps in Prague, Heidelberg, Cracow, and Vienna. The life and career of Peter Abelard (1079–1142), one of the most famous medieval philosophers, was intimately and significantly predicated and dependent on urban space, despite his various attempts to withdraw into an isolated monastic community far away from Paris.[139] In fact, as any survey of medieval literature will

---

[138]  C. Stephen Jaeger, *The Envy of Angels: Cathedrals Schools and Social Ideals in Medieval Europe, 950–1200*. Middle Ages Series (Philadelphia: University of Pennsylvania Press, 1994); Alan Balfour, *The Medieval Universities: Their Development and Organization* (London: Methuen, 1975); *Universities and Schooling in Medieval Society*, ed William J. Courtenay. Education and Society in the Middle Ages and Renaissance, 10 (Leiden: Brill, 2000); Vern L. Bullough, *Universities, Medicine and Science in the Medieval West*. Variorum Collected Studies Series, 781 (Aldershot: Ashgate Variorum, 2004); Rainer Christoph Schwinges, *Studenten und Gelehrte: Studien zur Sozial- und Kulturgeschichte deutscher Universitäten im Mittelalter*. Education and Society in the Middle Ages and Renaissance, 32 (Leiden: Brill, 2008). There is a legion of further detailed research on medieval and early-modern learning and schooling. Now see Hunt Janin, *The University in Medieval Life, 1179–1499* (Jefferson, NC, and London: McFarland, 2008), though his study is marred by numerous mistakes and a rather superficial treatment of his topic. Particularly his explicit criticism of allegedly hair-splitting scholarship in this context is rather ironic and amusing. The most seminal study proves to be *A History of the Universities in Europe*, ed. Hilde de Ridder-Symoens. Vol. 1: *Universities in the Middle Ages* (Cambridge and New York: Cambridge University Press, 2003).

[139]  Now see *Letters of Peter Abelard, Beyond the Personal*, trans. Jan M. Ziolkowski. Medieval Texts in Translation (Washington, D.C.: The Catholic University of America Press, 2008), which offers an excellent overview of Abelard's biography and the most critical positions of modern research focused on his work and relationship with his social environment. The most comprehensive study of medieval universities continues to be *Universities in the Middle Ages*, ed. Hilde de Ridder-Symoens History of the University in Europe, 1 (Cambridge and New York: Cambridge University Press, 1992).

demonstrate, by the thirteenth century the focus of literary productivity moved away from the courts to the urban centers, reflecting a profound transformation process even in terms of mental history.[140] Nevertheless, the universities increasingly became the intellectual centers of late-medieval towns, and there were numerous economic consequences for the urban population as well, whether we think of room and board for scholars and students, book production, the erection of special university buildings, and arts and entertainment.[141]

Turning to the late Middle Ages, increasingly cityscapes dot the imaginary landscape of poets and writers. One of the most influential French poets, Christine de Pizan (ca. 1364–1430), went even so far as to utilize the metaphor of the city for her ruminations on women's freedom and equality.[142] In her *City of Ladies* (1405) she creates one of the most remarkable manifestoes for women's rights and women's power in the Middle Ages, drawing, for instance, from Aristotle's *Politics* and Augustine's *City of God*, both times being inspired by their philosophical-religious metaphor of the city as the central site of human history.[143] All these

[140] Ursula Peters, *Literatur in der Stadt: Studien zu den sozialen Voraussetzungen und kulturellen Organisationsformen städtischer Literatur im 13. und 14. Jahrhundert*. Studien und Texte zur Sozialgeschichte der Literatur, 7 (Tübingen: Niemeyer, 1983); *Über Bürger, Stadt und städtische Literatur im Spätmittelalter : Bericht über Kolloquien der Kommission zur Erforschung der Kultur des Spätmittelalters 1975–1977*, ed. Josef Fleckstein and Karl Stackmann. Abhandlungen der Akademie der Wissenschaften in Göttingen.; Philologisch-Historische Klasse, 3. Folge, 121 (Göttingen: Vandenhoeck & Ruprecht, 1980); Heinz Schilling, *Die Stadt in der frühen Neuzeit*. Enzyklopädie deutscher Geschichte, 24 (Munich: Oldenbourg, 1993). For a recent survey of literature composed in late-medieval cities, see Graeme Dunphy, "Literary Transitions, 1300–1500: From Late Medieval to Early Modern," *Early Modern German Literature: 1350–1700*, ed. Max Reinhart. The Camden House History of German Literature, 4 (Rochester, NY, and Woodbridge, Suffolk: Boydell & Brewer, 2007), 43–87; here 62–74.

[141] Francsisco Bertelloni, "Nähe und Distanz zu Aristoteles: Die neue Bedeutung von civitas im politischen Denken des 13. bis 15. Jahrhunderts: Zwischen Thomas von Aquin und Nikolas von Kues," *University, Council, City: Intellectual Culture on the Rhine (1300–1550): Acts of the XIIth International Colloquium of the Société Internationale pour l'Étude de la Philosophie Médiévale, Freiburg im Breisgau, 27–29 October 2004*, ed. Laurent Cesalli, Nadja Germann, and M. J. F. M. Hoenen. Recontres de Philosophie médiévale, 13 (Turnhout: Brepols, 2007), 323–47.

[142] The number of older and more recent studies on this text is legion; suffice it here to refer to a short selection: For a sympathetic, brief though concise introduction to Christine, see Elisa Narin van Court, "Christine de Pizan," *Encyclopedia of Medieval Literature*, ed. Jay Ruud (New York: Facts on File, 2006), 135–38. See also Bärbel Zühlke, *Christine de Pizan in Text und Bild: Zur Selbstdarstellung einer frühhumanistischen Intellektuellen*. Ergebnisse der Frauenforschung, 36 (Stuttgart and Weimar: J. B. Metzler, 1994); Sister Prudence Allen, R.S.M., *The Concept of Woman*. Vol. 2: *The Early Humanist Reformation, 1250–1500* (Grand Rapids, MI, and Cambridge: William B. Eerdmans, 2002), 610–54.

[143] Lori J. Walters, "La Réécriture de Saint Augustin par Christine de Pizan: De La Cité de Dieu à la Cité des dames," *Au Champs des escripture: IIIe. Colloque international sur Christine de Pizan*, ed. Erick Hicks, Diego Gonzalez, and Philippe Simon. Études christiniennes, 6 (Paris: Champion, 2000), 195–215.

details do not need to be discussed here further since they have been explored many times before, whereas the metaphor itself deserves greater attention than it has enjoyed so far.[144]

Three allegorical ladies appear to the author-narrator who represent fundamental virtues that any woman can or should subscribe to, if not any person: reason, rectitude, and justice. They challenge Christine to build a city where all women can properly reside because it would be built upon those values and ideals by which all people could live honorably. Whereas a city normally represented, in concrete, material terms, a location where a maximum of protection was available to the citizens, these allegorical figures imply considerably more: "so that from now on, ladies and all valiant women may have a refuge and defense against the various assailants, whose ladies who have been abandoned for so long, exposed like a field without a surrounding hedge . . . ."[145]

Lady Reason even goes into further details why Christine should build a city for all women: "you will draw fresh waters from us from clear fountains, and we will bring you sufficient building stone, stronger and more durable than any marble with cement could be. Thus your City will be extremely beautiful, without equal, and of perpetual duration in the world" (177). On the one hand, the metaphor of the city serves well as an expression of strength for women in a hostile world; on the other it indicates that women can have a place of their own, being proud of their own beauty and inner strength. Comparing the city of the Amazons with the one to be erected by Christine, Lady Reason insists that the latter will last longer than the former because of its better and more solid foundation and defense mechanisms: "[it] will be far stronger, and for its founding I was commissioned, in the course of our common deliberations, to supply you with durable and pure mortar to lay the sturdy foundations and to raise the lofty walls all around, high and thick, with mighty towers and strong bastions, surrounded by moats with firm block-houses, just as is fitting for a city with a strong and lasting defense" (178).

Whereas in *Historia Apollonius* there is a clear sense of a veritable city with a complex population, here Christine resorts to standard images of the city basically constituted by its defense structures. The actual city as a site for a close-knit

---

[144]  See, for instance, Judith L. Kellog, "*Le Livre de la cité des dames*: Reconfiguring Knowledge and Reimagining Gendered Space," *Christine de Pizan: A Casebook*, ed. Barbara K. Altmann, Debora L. McGrady, with a foreword by Charity Cannon Willard. Routledge Medieval Casebooks, 34 (New York and London: Routledge, 2003), 129–46; Betsy McCormick, "Building the Ideal City: Female Memorial Praxis in Christine de Pizan's *Cité des Dames*," *Studies in Literary Imagination* 36, 1 (2003): 149–71.

[145]  *The Writings of Christine de Pizan*. Selected and ed. by Charity Cannon Willard (New York: Persea Books, 1994), 176. See also Christine de Pizan, *The Book of the City of Ladies*, trans. and with an introduction and notes by Rosalind Brown-Grant (London: Penguin, 1999).

population, or community, with countless social groups and classes that all collaborate, in a way, to make the urban identity possible, however, does not actually surface in the text. Only Lady Rectitude offers meaningful reflections upon the actual urban space, when she remarks: "All things are measured by this ruler, for its powers are infinite. It will serve you to measure the edifice of the City which you have been commissioned to build, and you will need it for constructing the façade, for erecting the high temples, for measuring the palaces, houses, and all public buildings, the streets and squares, and all things proper to help populate the City" (179).[146]

Lady Justice, finally, in her comments about what her meaning might be in the construction of the allegorical city, mentions further architectural elements: "my job will be to construct the high roofs of the towers and of the lofty mansions and inns which will all be made of fine shining gold. Then I will populate the City for you with worth ladies and the mighty Queen whom I will bring to you" (180).

Only some of the illustrated manuscripts containing Christine's text also provide imagery of an actual city. Ms. Harley 4431, British Library, London, however, proves to be an excellent exception where on fol. 323 Droitture (Rectitude) leads the sibyls into the city. We clearly recognize the city gate and wall, a large number of houses with various rooftops, and one house that is still in the process of being erected, with beams for the roof already set up but not yet covered by tiles. The artist even included chimneys, reflecting on the need for comfort within the living spaces.[147]

A similar scene, providing fascinating details of carpenters' work on the roofs, can be found in the splendid illumination in the manuscript housed in Munich, Bayerische Staatsbibliothek, Codex gall. 8, fol. 90v.[148] Ms. Ffr. 1177 in the Bibliothèque National, Paris, on the other hand, shows very little interest in depicting concrete urban space. On fol. 45r, for instance, we see Justice, who leads the sibyls into the city, with a door to the immediate right opening up rather unexpectedly because the actual city gate with its two tall towers rises in the

---

[146] Maureen Quilligan, *The Allegory of Female Authority: Christine de Pizan's Cité des Dames* (Ithaca and London: Cornell University Press, 1991), 104–17.

[147] Quilligan, *The Allegory*, 106. She also observes, "Droitture's emphasis on the sibyls continues the subtle critique of Rome begun in section one by Reason and reinforced by her emphasis on an alternate tradition of female civilization with its very different set of cities, Carthage and Babylon" (108).

[148] See plate 1 (following p . 42) in Susan Groag Bell, *The Lost Tapestries of the City of Ladies: Christine de Pizan's Renaissance Legacy* (Berkeley, Los Angeles, and London: University of California Press, 2004). Other illuminations go far back in thematic design prior to the erection of the utopian city, such as the miniature in the Belgian manuscript of *Le Livre de la cité des dames*, Royal Library of Belgium, Brussels, MS 9235, fol. 10v; see the plate viii in Groag Bell's *The Lost Tapestries*.

background. There is no real sense of a city here obviously because the artistic focus rests on the group of sibyls and their highly stylish fashion.[149]

Subsequently, returning to Christine's text, there is not much talk about the city as such anymore because the allegorical imagery has fulfilled its purpose. Nevertheless, overall Christine explicitly indicates how much the city had emerged as a crucial metaphor for all aspects in human life, and that a strong and reliable human existence crucially needs the relevant support within a city, at least for the non-aristocratic classes. For her, and many people among her audiences that tended to support and even adore her, the defense of women against male attacks both in physical and metaphorical terms could be fully achieved only by hiding behind city walls, at least in imaginary terms, not however, behind those of a castle, probably because Christine identified with the city as women's true and only safe haven.

At the same time, as fleeting references in Christine's texts indicate, those freedoms of the urban culture were not necessarily stable and could be easily lost.[150] But this city, in its literary and subsequently also visual manifestation, provided a significant medium for the female readers and viewers to identify with their own community. The city becomes, in Christine's terms, the location of memory and utopia as well where women can find refuge and a safe existence dominated by virtues and ethical and moral ideals.[151] In a subtle, but certainly significant way Dante had also outlined this concept in his *Paradiso* where women, primarily as mothers and wives, were regarded as the essential members of the urban community who kept the memory of the glorious past alive and passed it on to their children. As Honess now observes, "the image of the Florentine women put forward in *Paradiso* XV serves as a very clear illustration that, for the poet, both men and women function as citizens, and that both are able to function as

---

[149] Quilligan, *The Allegory*, 127. The illustration of Carthage where Dido commits suicide in Ms. Royal C V 20, London, British Library, fol. 65r, seems rather odd. The group of three men witnessing Dido's death to their right stands behind a low wall, and the actual cities rises behind them, with oriental looking towers in the distance, whereas a series of connected houses constitute the actual city; see Quilligan, *The Allegory*, 172. See also Sandra L. Hindman, "With Ink and Mortar: Christine de Pizan's *Cité des Dames* (An Art Essay)," *Feminist Studies* 10 (1984): 457–77; eadem, *Christine de Pizan's "Epistre Othéa": Painting and Politics at the Court of Charles VI* (Toronto: Pontifical Institute of Mediaeval Studies, 1986); Rosalind Brown-Grant, "Illumination as Reception: Jean Miélot's Reworking of the 'Epistre Othea'," *The City of Scholars: New Approaches to Christine de Pizan*, ed. Margarete Zimmermann and Dina De Rentiis. European Cultures, 2 (Berlin and New York: de Gruyter, 1994), 260–71.

[150] Diane Wolfthal, "'Douleur sur toutres autres': Revisualizing the Rape Script in the *Epistre Othea* and the *Cité des dames*," *Christine de Pizan and the Categories of Difference*, ed. Marilynn Desmond. Medieval Cultures, 14 (Minneapolis and London: University of Minnesota Press, 1998), 41–70.

[151] Margarete Zimmermann, "Christine de Pizan: Memory's Architect," *Christine de Pizan: A Casebook*, ed. Barbara K. Altmann and Deborah L. McGrady. Routledge Medieval Casebooks (New York and London: Routledge, 2003), 57–77; here 66–71.

examples, conveying a fundamental lesson about the relationship between individual and community."[152]

Globally speaking, living in the city still meant that the individual could enjoy vast advantages over the people living in the countryside. Lady Rectitude indicates how important a city was for everyone who could enjoy the privilege of living there. More importantly, though, she provides a deep glance into the actual structure of a late-medieval city with its highly diversified topography: "our construction is quite well advanced, for the houses of the City of Ladies stand completed all along the wide streets, its royal palaces are well constructed, and its towers and defense turrets have been raised so high and straight that one can see them from far away" (191–92). This idyllic, perhaps utopian, city signals how much urban life was aspired to by everyone who could afford to live there: "How happy will be the citizens of our edifice, for they will not need to fear or worry about being evicted by foreign armies, for this work has the special property that its owners cannot be expelled" (192).

This city houses only most intelligent and dignified ladies: "they shall all be women of integrity, of great beauty and authority, for there could be no fairer populace nor any greater adornment in the City than women of good character" (192). Despite the obvious idealization, Christine powerfully circumscribes the late-medieval value system according to which the best place for a person's residence would be the city because here the highest goals of ethics, morality, justice, rectitude, and reason can be achieved by the residents.

However, she immediately forces us also to discriminate between the ideal image of an urban space where people with a noble spirit live, and the often harsh and excruciating conditions for married women who suffer from brutal and ignorant husbands and many other male perpetrators—in the city, especially if the women did not enjoy male protection from a father or a husband: "How many harsh beatings—without cause and without reason—how many injuries, how many cruelties, insults, humiliations, and outrages have so many upright women suffered, none of whom cried out for help. And consider all the women who die of hunger and grief with a home full of children, while their husbands carouse dissolutely or go on binges in every tavern all over town, and still the poor women are beaten by their husbands when they return, and *that* is their supper" (193).

Christine vocally challenges husbands' abuse of their wives, particularly within the urban setting, though she knows of no other realistic recourse but to withdraw into the metaphorical City of Ladies, a literary dream world where the urban space

---

[152]    Honess, *From Florence to the Heavenly City*, 51; see also Jacques Goudert, *Dante et la politique* (Paris: Aubier-Montaigne, 1969), 139.

turns into a safe haven for women against their violent and brutal husbands.[153] She
is realistic enough, however, to recognize and admit publicly that the urban space,
as a most familiar site of late-medieval society according to her own experience
and that of her audience, proves to be a site where men of all classes, ages, and
political statuses can also roam freely and abuse women, where taverns invite
people to come in and drink, where vices and sinfulness flower freely, and where
the physically weaker members of society can become victims of those with more
power.

Of course, and not truly expected, Christine does not have a real answer for how
to deal with male violence, both within marriage and outside—in fact, no one in
the late Middle Ages had any pragmatic suggestion or solution, except to
recommend to women that they submit to their destiny and to pray to God—but
she dreams of a city where upright and virtuous women can live freely from all
that abuse and dedicated to the fundamental virtues and values in human life:
"Now we have come back to our City, thank God, with all the noble company of
fair and upright women whom we will lodge there" (194).

Similarly, Lady Justice also offers her advice and makes a contribution to the
City of Ladies, again in metaphorical terms, and emphasizes at the end: "it seems
to me that I have acquitted myself well of my office in completing the high roofs
of your City and in populating it for you with outstanding ladies, just as I
promised" (205). The city emerges both as a metaphor of women's very own space
free of male persecutions, and as a site where they have to accept their earthly
blight. As Christine comments herself, this unique city houses "ladies from the
past as well as from the present and future, for it has been built and established for
every honorable lady" (205). It is a city of "virtue, so resplendent that you may see
yourselves mirrored in it, especially in the roofs built in the last part as well as in
the other parts which concern you" (206).

Christine continues with a discussion of marriage, especially with an evil or
cruel husband, and appeals to her female readers to be patient and humble. For
her, this audience consists of women from all social classes, "whether noble,
bourgeois, or lower-class" (207), which signals that she perceives the city as a
cosmos of the entire society. She strongly suggests that her female audience flee
the evil city of their present existence and seek refuge, parallel to Augustine's *City
of Good*, in the city of virtuous and glorified ladies: "And so may it please you, my
most respected ladies, to cultivate virtue, to flee vice, to increase and multiply our
City, and to rejoice and act well" (207).

---

[153]  Albrecht Classen, *The Power of a Woman's Voice in Medieval and Early Modern Literature*.
Fundamentals of Medieval and Early Modern Culture, 1 (Berlin and New York: de Gruyter, 2007),
181–84.

For Christine and her contemporaries the city had obviously already emerged as the central icon of their time, a key metaphor with multiple connotations.[154] As Rosalind Brown-Grant now suggests, "Christine's use of the symbol of the city underpins one of the central arguments of her text, namely that women have contributed to the moral and spiritual development of civilization as epitomized by the urban community."[155] Of course, the moral symbolism alluding to the desired protection of women's chastity within this city cannot be overlooked, and has been discussed numerous times. But the fact that Christine resorts to the imagery of the urban space in the first place also indicates the considerable interest in the city as the locus of late-medieval culture and civilization, replacing the court, the palace, and the church, despite the poet's great concern to appeal to her most important patrons, the higher echelons of French aristocracy, hence the courtly audience.

For Christine, the city proves to be the location where virtues can bloom and find the necessary protection, if, and this is a big caveat, this city can be properly built and constructed appropriately for women's needs and desires.[156]

It was a literary imagination, yet it was also predicated, by default, on a very concrete concept of the city in its complex structure and properties. Discussing the city in her context, Christine reaffirms the fundamental significance of the city as the new and all important central location of social, economic, and cultural-religious activities, even though she projects virtually nothing but a fantasy concept. This is not to deny the permeability of the city wall, and the openness of the urban space in its metaphorical connotation, to the outside world, especially in intellectual terms, insofar as the author allows the numerous references to outstanding women from the past, whether princesses or martyrs, to enter the female space, thereby opening a extensive communication system in which the city serves as the central hub.[157]

---

[154]   Sandra L. Hindman, "With Ink and Mortar: Christine de Pizan's *Cité des Dames*: An Art Essay," *Feminist Studies* 10 (1984): 457–84.

[155]   Christine de Pizan, *The Book of the City of Ladies*, trans. and with an introd. and notes by Rosalind Brown-Grant (London: Penguin, 1999), xxix–xxx. See also Brown-Grant, *Reading Beyond Gender: Christine de Pizan and the Moral Defence of Women* (Cambridge: Cambridge University Press, 1999).

[156]   Douglas Kelly, *Christine de Pizan's Changing Opinion: A Quest for Certainty in the Midst of Chaos.* Gallica (Woodbridge, Suffolk, and Rochester, NY: Boydell & Brewer, 2007), 84–85. He emphasizes how much Christine knew how to discriminate among virtuous and sinful women as burghers in her new city: "Women, like men, can be good or bad. The *Cité* acknowledges this by admitting only the former within its walls. Hence, some outsiders will fit the misogynists' stereotypes as Christine understands them . . ." (97).

[157]   Here I draw from a paper by Federica Anichini, "Christine de Pizan's *City of Ladies*: Excavating Prejudice, Building Knowledge," delivered at the *44th International Congress on Medieval Studies, May 7–10, 2009,* Kalamazoo, MI, at the Western Michigan University. See also the contributions to *The City of Scholars: New Approaches to Christine de Pizan,* ed. Margarete Zimmermann and Dina De Rentiis. European Cultures, 2 (Berlin and New York: Walter de Gruyter, 1993).

This finds intriguing confirmation in the poetic works of her contemporary, Thomas Hoccleve, who worked as a scribe in London, being first cited in Chancery rolls from shortly prior to June 21, 1387 to May 8, 1426, a posthumous note.[158] He was born around 1367 and began his career as an apprentice clerk in the Privy Seal, serving as underclerk to Guy de Roucliff. Shortly before 1408 he had achieved such a rank that he was assigned an assistant clerk, John Welde. He retired in 1426 and died soon after.[159] Hoccleve has suffered for a long time being regarded as a secondary poet in the long shadow cast by Geoffrey Chaucer, but recent research has recognized his most idiosyncratic approaches, styles, themes, and images.[160] He might actually be comparable to François Villon and Oswald von Wolkenstein because of his strong interest in autobiographical self-reflections in his poems and the rebellious, satirical, sometimes almost grotesque verses.[161] In his *La Male Regle*, for instance, written in 1405, he "presents himself . . . as an apostate to the god Helthe. He has for twenty years been a glutton and a fool, eating and drinking until he can't get out of bed in the morning, and spending all his little money to buy the flattering words of boatmen on the Thames and of 'Venus femel lusty children deere.' The poem shows Chaucer's influence in the comic presentation of Hoccleve's past misdeeds, but it is quite un-Chaucerian in its detailed imagination of clerkly life in early fifteenth-century London."[162]

Hoccleve regularly refers to himself and his life in the city of London, providing not systematic, but most interesting insights into how an early fifteenth-century

---

[158] A. C. Reeves, "Thomas Hoccleve, Bureaucrat," *Mediaevalia et Humanistica* n.s. 5 (1974): 201–14; see also T. F. Tout, "Literature and Learning in the English Civil Service in the Fourteenth Century," *Speculum* 4 (1929): 365–89; Ethan Knapp, *The Bureaucratic Muse: Thomas Hoccleve and the Literature of Late Medieval England* (University Park, PA: The Pennsylvania State University Press, 2001), 20–43, et passim. See also Günter Hagel, *Thomas Hoccleve: Leben und Werk eines Schriftstellers im England des Spätmittelalters.* Europäische Hochschulschriften. Reihe 14: Angelsächsische Sprache und Literatur, 130 (Frankfurt am Main, Bern, et al.: Peter Lang, 1984).

[159] *Selections from Hoccleve*, ed. M. C. Seymour (Oxford: Clarendon Press, 1981), xi–xxxiii.

[160] Though addressing a major text in Hoccleve's œuvre that does not necessarily shed light on our topic, Nicholas Perkins, *Hoccleve's Regiment of Princes: Counsel and Constraint* (Woodbridge, Suffolk: D. S. Brewer, 2001), sheds important light on Hoccleve's position in the history of Middle English literature. See also Thomas Hoccleve, *The Regiment of Princes*, ed. Charles R. Blyth. Middle English Texts (Kalamazoo, MI: Medieval Institute Publications, 1999).

[161] Albrecht Classen, *Die autobiographische Lyrik des europäischen Spätmittelalters: Studien zu Hugo von Montfort, Oswald von Wolkenstein, Antonio Pucci, Charles d'Orléans, Thomas Hoccleve, Michel Beheim, Hans Rosenplüt und Alfonso Alvarez de Villasandino.* Amsterdamer Publikationen zur Sprache und Literatur, 91 (Amsterdam and Atlanta: Editions Rodopi, 1991).

[162] Knapp, *The Bureaucratic Muse*, 37. See also A. C. Spearing, *Medieval to Renaissance in English Poetry* (Cambridge: Cambridge University Press, 1985), 110–20; Eva M. Thornley, "The Middle English Penitential Lyric and Hoccleve's Autobiographical Poetry," *Neuphilologische Mitteilungen* 68 (1967): 295–321; Albrecht Classen, "Hoccleve's Independence from Chaucer: A Study of Poetic Emancipation," *Fifteenth-Century Studies* 15 (1990): 59–81; id., "The Autobiographical Voice of Thomas Hoccleve," *Archiv für das Studium der neueren Sprachen und Literaturen* 228 (1991): 299–310.

poet perceived and reacted to the urban space upon which his own existence was predicated. In his *La Male Regle*, for instance, Hoccleve comments in general about the moral decline of his time, of which he is just as guilty, wasting his money with drinking, partying, and enjoying life to excess. Repeatedly he mentions his life in the taverns: "Of him þat hauntith tauerne of custume, / At shorte wordes, the profyt is this:" (161–62).[163] Satirically he casts himself as the best known man in the entire area around Westminster, clearly signaling the relevance of the urban space in that quarter for his personal debaucheries:

> Wher was a gretter maistir eek than Y,
> Or bet aqweyntid at Westmynstre yate,
> Among the tauerneres namely
> And cookes, whan I cam eerly or late?
> I pynchid nat at hem in myn acate,
> But paied hem as þat they axe wolde,
> Wherfore I was the welcomer algate
> And for a verray gentilman yholde.         (77–84)

Moreover, he specifically outlines his way from the tavern home to the Privy Seal, providing us with a true sense of a dense city life with many streets, spaces, bars, bridges, people, traffic, and so forth (185–92). Yet, warning his audience about the negative example that he himself had offered as a rowdy character, he also reveals interesting aspects about the social life of the lower classes, if not of the poor people and the workers, in London: "And ther the bootmen took vpon me keep, / For they my riot kneewen fern ago. / With hem I was itugged to and fro, / So wel was him þat I with wolde fare, / For riot paieth largely eueremo" (195–99). Subsequently he turns to extensive moralization about the dangers of deceptive and flattering words uttered by servants to their lords, about the consequences of a violent life in public, especially in taverns, then about lying, and the problem with money: "A, nay, my poore purs and peynes stronge / Han artid [compelled] me speke as I spoken haue" (395–96), ending with an appeal to his patron to reward him monetarily (445–48).

Hoccleve certainly follows many traditional medieval tropes and themes in this and other poems, but he does not shy away from positioning himself in the midst of all of these ruminations, thereby granting the audience important insight into the concrete living conditions of a clerical poet in the big city of London.[164] Additional confirmation for this new perspective can be found in his *Complaint* from November 1421 where he sorrowfully reflects upon his tragic suffering from

---

[163]    'My Compleinte' and Other Poems, ed. Roger Ellis. Exeter Medieval Texts and Studies (Exeter: University of Exeter Press, 2001), 68.

[164]    Katherine C. Little, *Confession and Resistance: Defining the Self in Late Medieval England* (Notre Dame, IN: University of Notre Dame Press, 2006).

mental illness. As the narrator emphasizes: "For ofte whanne I in Westmynstir Halle / And eke in Londoun amonge the prees went, / I sy the chere abaten and apalle / Of hem þat weren wonte me for to calle / To companie . . . " (72–76).[165] Everyone flees from him, afraid of his bout of lunacy, comparing him to a vessel lost at sea (81) or a wild ox (120). The narrator then seeks refuge at home where he stares into the mirror to find out who he really is: "And in my chaumbre at home whanne þat I was, / Mysilfe aloone I in þis wise wrou₃t. / I streite vnto my mirrour and my glas / To loke howe þat me of my chere þou₃t" (155–58), thereby signaling the two sides of the coin living in a city, that is, the public and the private.[166] But he bitterly complains that people subsequently mistook him as still being ill and a victim of lunacy, although he had recovered years earlier: "Man bi hise dedis and not by hise lookes / Shal knowen be, as it is writen in bookes" (202–03).

Naturally, Hoccleve ultimately focuses primarily on philosophical, ethical, and moral concerns, asking his audience to reflect upon a reasonable approach to the recognition and identification of an individual and also how a person should live properly in this worldly existence. But even within this framework we clearly recognize a sense of the urban space populated by the poet, his friends, and many other people, all of them gazing at each other with curiosity, fear, suspicion, interest, and other emotions, and all this here indicated through the autobiographical lens:

Many a saute made I to this mirrour,
Thinking if þat I looke in þis manere
Amonge folke as I nowe do, noon errour
Of suspecte look may in my face appere.
This countinaunce, I am sure, and þis chere

If I it forthe vse is no thing repreuable
To hem þat han conceitis resonable          (162–68).

Although Hoccleve does not discuss the city as such, it noticeably constitutes the crucial social framework for his entire existence, both considering his partying and trouble-making in taverns and elsewhere, and his walking to and from his work, finally spending time at home and examining his face, and hence his identity.

## The City as a Theme and Motif in Mental-Historical Terms

[165] Quoted from *Selections from Hoccleve*, 77; see also Seymour's comments, 122–35. Cf. the notes by Roger Ellis in his anthology, *'My Compleinte'*, 128–30.
[166] D. M. Palliser, T. R. Slater, and E. Patricia Dennison, "The Topography of Towns 600–1300," *The Cambridge Urban History of Britain*. Vol. 1: *600–1540*, ed. D. M. Palliser (Cambridge: Cambridge University Press, 2000), 153–86; here 175–78.

Significantly, by the late Middle Ages, a growing number of individual citizens, belonging to both the upper class (merchants) and to the aristocracy, realized that they needed to take stock of their lives and to reflect upon their families in a larger context, leading to the creation of a fairly large corpus of so-called *Haus- und Familienbücher* (House and Family Books), as mentioned above.[167] These memorial books shed important light on the social network within the respective city, on the social and economic structure, and the intellectual development, that is, the educational level that the individual authors had achieved. Mostly serving private purposes, these fairly compendious volumes contain a vast variety of information relevant for many different social and age groups, containing data about the family business, the marriage relationships, births and deaths, offices, gifts, income, property; hence they lend themselves extremely well to an in-depth analysis of late-medieval urban everyday life, mental structures, religious attitudes, gender, and economic and political issues.[168]

As we have learned through much recent research, these family books served not only the purpose of memorializing the preceding and present generations. They were also commonly composed by members of individual families who had either experienced a dramatic rise in power or suddenly faced a major decline in their family fortune, if not simply the disappearance of the entire family through

[167] *Haus- und Familienbücher, in der städtischen Gesellschaft des Spätmittelalters und der frühen Neuzeit,* ed. Birgit Studt. Städteforschung. Reihe A: Darstellungen, 69 (Cologne, Weimar, and Vienna: Böhlau, 2007).

[168] See, for instance, Pierre Monnet, "La Mémoire des élites urbaines dans l'Empire à la fin du Moyen Âge entre écriture de soi et histoire de la cité," *Memoria, communitas, civitas: Mémoire et conscience urbaines en occident à la fin du Moyen Âge,* ed. Hanno Brand, Pierre Monnet, and Martial Staub. Beihefte der Francia, 55 (Ostfildern: Thorbecke, 2003), 49–70; Heinrich Schmidt, *Die deutschen Städtechroniken als Spiegel des bürgerlichen Selbstbewußtseins im Spätmittelalter.* Schriftenreihe der Historischen Kommission bei der Bayerischen Akademie der Wissenschaften, 3 (Göttingen: Vandenhoeck & Ruprecht, 1958). The interest in these urban documents of autobiographical nature has been intense in recent years; see the contributions to *Das dargestellte Ich: Studien zu Selbstzeugnissen des späteren Mittelalters und der frühen Neuzeit,* ed. Sabine Schmolinsky, Klaus Arnold, and Urs Martin Zahnd. Selbstzeugnisse des Mittelalters und der frühen Neuzeit, 1 (Bochum: Winkler, 1999); Gabriele Jancke, *Autobiographie als soziale Praxis: Beziehungskonzepte in Selbstzeugnissen des 15. und 16. Jahrhunderts im deutschsprachigen Raum.* Selbstzeugnisse der Neuzeit, 10 (Cologne, Weimar, and Vienna: Böhlau, 2002). For further bibliographical information, see Birgit Studt, "Erinnerung und Identität: Die Repräsentation städtischer Eliten in spätmittelalterlichen Haus- und Familienbüchern," *Haus- und Familienbücher,* 1–31. See also Gabriele Hofner-Kulenkamp, *Das Bild des Künstlers mit Familie : Porträts des 16. und 17. Jahrhunderts.* Selbstzeugnisse des Mittelalters und der beginnenden Neuzeit, 2 (Bochum: Winkler, 2002); Sünje Prühlen, *"Alse sunst hir gebruchlich is": eine Annäherung an das spätmittelalterliche und frühneuzeitliche Alltags- und Familienleben anhand der Selbstzeugnisse der Familien Brandis in Hildesheim und Moller in Hamburg.* Selbstzeugnisse des Mittelalters und der beginnenden Neuzeit, 3 (Bochum: Winkler, 2005).

death or lack of heirs.[169] After all, urban centers were the site of intensive social struggles despite the rather rigid class structures, separating, for instance, particularly the craftsmen from the merchant class, commonly identified as the patriciate.[170]

For the time being, it might be enough to reflect upon the emerging early-modern city where a limited degree of liberty dominated and where individual writers of so-called family and house books created individualized and yet most insightful reflections upon their own history and that of their cities. This stands in remarkable contrast to some contemporary late-medieval and early-modern book illustrations where the city itself does not seem to exist in mental-historical terms. In one of the most spectacular manuscript copies of the thirteenth-century *Roman de la rose*, composed by Guillaume de Lorris ca. 1237, then continued and vastly expanded by Jean de Meun ca. 1264/1274,[171] dedicated to the French King Francis I (1515–1547) probably shortly after his famous victory over the Swiss army defending the duchy of Milan against him in September 1515, we come across a most remarkable example of how urban space and the city itself continued to

---

169   Studt, "Erinnerung und Identität," 9; see also Valentin Groebner, "Ratsinteressen, Familieninteressen: Patrizische Konflikte in Nürnberg um 1500," *Stadtregiment und Bürgerfreiheit: Handlungsspielräume in deutschen und italienischen Städten des Späten Mittelalters und der Frühen Neuzeit*, ed. Klaus Schreiner and Ulrich Meier. Bürgertum: Beiträge zur europäischen Gesellschaftsgeschichte, 7 (Göttingen: Vandenhoeck & Ruprecht, 1994), 278–308; Pierre Monnet, "Reale und ideale Stadt: Die oberdeutschen Städte im Spiegel autobiographischer Zeugnisse des Spätmittelalters," *Von der dargestellten Person zum erinnerten Ich: Europäische Selbstzeugnisse als historische Quelle (1500–1850)*, ed. Kaspar von Greyerz, Heinz Medick, and Patrice Veit. Selbstzeugnisse der Neuzeit, 9 (Cologne, Weimar, and Vienna: Böhlau, 2001), 395–430; id., "Particularismes urbains et patriotisme locale dans une ville allemande de la fin du Moyen Âge: Francfort et ses chroniques," *Identité régionale et conscience nationale en France et en Allemagne du Moyen Âge à l'epoque moderne. Actes du colloque organisé par l'Université Paris XII-Val de Marne, l'Institut universitaire de France et l'Institut historique allemand à l'Université Paris XII et à la Fondation Singer-Polignac, les 6, 7 et 8 octobre 1993*, ed. Rainer Babel and Jean-Marie Moeglin. Beihefte der Francia, 39 (Sigmaringen: J. Thorbecke, 1997), 389–400.

170   This topic has been discussed many times with the focus on many different cities in late-medieval and early-modern Europe; see, for instance, Alexander Cowan, *The Urban Patriciate: Lübeck and Venice, 1580–1700*. Quellen und Darstellungen zur hansischen Geschichte, neue Folge, 30 (Cologne: Böhlau, 1986); see also the contributions to *Towns in Societies: Essays in Economic History and Historical Sociology*, ed. Philips Abrams and E. A. Wrigley. Past and Present Publications (Cambridge and New York: Cambridge University Press, 1978); and to *Florentine Tuscany: Structures and Practices of Power*, ed. William J. Connell and Andrea Zorzi. Cambridge Studies in Italian History and Culture (Cambridge and New York: Cambridge University Press, 2000).

171   Albrecht Classen, "Guillaume de Lorris" (285–86), "Jean de Meun" (345–47), "Roman de la Rose" (548–49), *Encyclopedia of Medieval Literature*, ed. Jay Ruud (New York: Facts on File, 2006).

hover in the background of late-medieval mentality, and yet also demanded new attention.[172]

Typically for that time and the royal culture, the dedication illumination focuses on the court, with the king in the center, receiving the volume. The spectator's gaze travels into the background through a loggia, which opens up to a vast landscape with some building on a hill to the left (4r). As to be expected, many of the illustrations show garden structures with a high wall around the area and a mighty gated tower (e.g., fol. 12r). Occasionally we see, again in the background, a kind of city surrounding a palace, but the buildings before that, such as in fol. 21r, are dilapidated or seem to be simple wooden constructions. At other times, profiles of an extensive fortress emerge in the background (fol. 25r), or the lover is shown approaching a palace (fol. 29r), whereas urban space, or city life, does not seem to figure at all. If there is any realistic background, then it consists of landscapes, regularly with a blue mountain rising up in the distance (fol. 57v and fol. 58r). When other types of buildings dot the landscape, they belong to a rural setting, or might represent a country estate (fol. fol. 61r). On fol. 104r we observe a group of courtiers in front of a imaginary city, which consists of several tall buildings and towers, while a specific city as such is not truly recognizable.

The absence of true urban space in favor of park-like nature scenes with individual buildings in the background, some of which seem to form part of a farm, whereas others represent both the old castle on top of a mountain and the new palace at its foot (fol. 147v), speaks volumes, especially in comparison with contemporary printed books, such as Hartmann Schedel's *Nuremberg Chronicle*, which already belongs to a new world, the German Renaissance (see below).[173]

Only one time has the illuminator made an effort to provide the sight of a city with a solid wall (fol. 202v). Because the city is ablaze in fire, the citizens are fleeing through the city gate, while flames engulf the tall towers and high-rising

---

[172]  See the commentary of the facsimile edition by Margareta Friesen, *Der Rosenroman für François I*. New York, Pierpont Morgan Library, M. 948 (Graz: Akademische Druck- und Verlagsanstalt, 1993; Vollständige Faksimile-Ausgabe des Rosenromans für François I. M. 948 aus dem Besitz der Pierpont Morgan Library in New York. Codices Selecti, XCVII (New York: The Pierpont Morgan Library; Graz: Akademische Druck- und Verlagsanstalt; Lyon: Les Sillons du Temps, 1993). She emphasizes, 120: "Schwere Rundtürme, Festungsruinen, strohgedeckte Fachwerkhäuser und mächtige Renaissancepaläste bestimmen die Hintergrundsgestaltung. Ihre Anordnung im Bildfeld wird immer neu komponiert. Zwar sind es die gleichen Grundtypen von Bauwerken, die sich wiederholen, doch führt ihre abwechslungsreiche Variierung in jeder Miniatur zu einem anderen Ergebnis. Wenn auch die Paläste (fol. 29r, 50v, 79v oder 84v) im Stil der Renaissance wiedergegeben werden, so wird doch der Forderung der italienischen Renaissancebaukunst nach Symmetrie, Gleichmaß und Harmonie keine Rechnung getragen. Immer schieben sich die Baumassen von einer Seite ins Bild und unterlaufen jeglichen Versuch, Pilaster, Gesimse und Bauornamente symmetrisch angeordnet darzustellen" (120–21).

[173]  See the contribution to this volume by Albrecht Classen.

buildings. The large number of frightened citizens indicates that the walls hide a fairly large urban space, but that space is not visible, nor does it evoke any interest for the artist or the audience. After all, this famous allegorical romance represents one of the masterpieces of the Middle Ages, and this particular copy in the Pierpont Morgan Library in New York was composed for and dedicated to the French King Francis I. It does not come as a surprise that such a royal artwork and piece of literature is far removed from the early-modern awareness about and interest in urban space in countless other contexts.[174]

## The Social Discourse About Urban Space and Identity

Overall, we face a fascinating and intricate combination or competition of various discourses by the individual power players in late-medieval and early-modern society. Whereas the nobility tried hard to maintain its traditional status as long as possible, both the city as such and the wealthiest burghers struggled with all their options available to carve out a niche in public life for themselves, to gain recognition, and to determine the nature of the contemporary culture with the help of their own means, often openly competing with the members of the aristocracy serving at courts situated in cities, such as Vienna and Salzburg.[175] We cannot expect, of course, to find necessarily representations of the different social classes and groups within the same text genres or artworks, though we still would have to agree with the general observation that an amalgamation process in the late Middle Ages brought nobility and urban patriciate significantly close to each other.[176]

Moreover, even within the traditional medieval city, a profound discrimination process took place, increasingly excluding the craftsmen and the poorer members

---

[174]   Ulrich Müller, "Burg," *Burgen, Länder, Orte*, ed. id. and Werner Wunderlich. Mittelalter-Mythen, 5 (Constance: UVK Verlagsgesellschaft, 2008), 143–60. For the role of castles in late-medieval German literature and woodcuts from the perspective of mental history, see Albrecht Classen, "Die Burg als Motiv in der Literatur des deutschen Spätmittelalters," to appear in *Die Burg im Mittelalter*, ed. Peter Dinzelbacher.

[175]   Christian Schneider, *Hovezuht: Literarische Hofkultur und höfisches Lebensideal um Herzog Albrecht III. von Österreich und Erzbischof Pilgrim II. von Salzburg (1365–1396)*. Beiträge zur älteren Literaturgeschichte (Heidelberg: Universitätsverlag Winter, 2008), 50–63.

[176]   Wolfgang Herborn, "Bürgerliches Selbstverständnis im spätmittelalterlichen Köln. Bemerkungen zu zwei Hausbüchern aus der ersten Hälfte des 15. Jahrhunderts," *Die Stadt in der europäischen Geschichte: Festschrift für Edith Ennen*, ed. Werner Besch et al. (Bonn: L. Röhrscheid, 1972), 490–520; Horst Wenzel, "Aristokratisches Selbstverständnis im städtischen Patriziat von Köln, dargestellt an der Kölner Chronik Gottfried Hagens," *Literatur, Publikum, historischer Kontext*, ed. Gert Kaiser. Beiträge zur Älteren Deutschen Literaturgeschichte, 1 (Bern, Frankfurt a. M., and Las Vegas: Peter Lang, 1977), 9–28.

of the urban society from the city government. As George Huppert observes regarding Frankfurt am Main: "Frankfurt's élite consisted of some 45 families, less than 1 percent of the population. This small group retained exclusive control of the 15 top offices from the fourteenth to the eighteenth centuries and it invented elaborate associations to safeguard its position in the city."[177] At the same time, this urban elite endeavored hard to climb even higher and to join the nobility, if the necessary criteria for this move could be met: "The standard test of nobility, by the late sixteenth century, was the demonstration that a family had lived nobly—that is, without working—for three generations. This standard was easily met by the members of urban élites, but it did not satisfy the feudal nobility, from whose perspective nobility was an inherited quality residing in the blood and tested on the battlefield."[178]

Nevertheless, the urban centers attracted a growing number of people from different backgrounds and social classes, and with different educational levels and individual interests. Major councils met in cities, such as Constance (1414–1418) and Basel (1431–1449).[179] Trade and banking were centrally located in cities, and so were the educational system, health care, craftsmanship, and the arts. Musical entertainment and the literary process were intimately associated with the city, as the countless songbooks indicate.[180] Scholarship has amply investigated the kaleidoscopic range of characteristic features of late-medieval and early-modern city life, whether we consider the areas of legal practice, food, religion, arms for the burghers, exterior and interior architecture, keeping of animals, fashion, the availability of mills, and, most critically, of good drinking water.[181] Beer, for

---

[177] George Huppert, *After the Black Death: A Social History of Early Modern Europe*. Sec. ed. Interdisciplinary Studies in History (1986; Bloomington and Indianapolis: Indiana University Press, 1998), 45.

[178] Huppert, *After the Black Death*, 50.

[179] Christopher M. Belitto, *The General Councils: a History of the Twenty-One General Councils from Nicaea to Vatican II* (New York: Paulist Press, 2002); *The Church, the Councils, and Reform: the Legacy of the Fifteenth Century*, ed. Gerald Christianson, Thomas M. Izbicki, and Christopher M. Belitto (Washington, DC: Catholic University of America Press, 2008).

[180] Albrecht Classen, *Deutsche Liederbücher des 15. und 16. Jahrhunderts*. Volksliedstudien, 1 (Münster: Waxmann, 2001); id., Georg Forsters Liederbücher im 16. Jahrhunderts: Letzte Blüte und Ausklang einer Epoche. Rezeptionsgeschichtliche Untersuchungen zur Gattung des spätmit-telalterlichen Liedes," *Lied und populäre Kultur. Jahrbuch des Deutschen Volksliedarchivs* 48 (2003): 11–47; see also the various contributions to *Stadt und Literatur im deutschen Sprachraum*.

[181] See the contributions to *Das Leben in der Stadt*; Keith D. Lilley, *Urban Life in the Middle Ages*; Norman Pounds, *The Medieval City*; Roberta Magnusson, "Public and Private Urban Hydrology: Water Management in Medieval London" (171–87), and Thomas F. Glick and Luis Pablo Martinez, "Mills and Millers in Medieval Valencia" (189–234), *Wind and Water in the Middle Ages: Fluid Technologies from Antiquity to the Renaissance*, ed. Steven A. Walton. Medieval and Renaissance Texts and Studies, 322. Penn State Medieval Studies, 2 (Tempe: Arizona Center for Medieval and Renaissance Studies, 2006).

instance, a major beverage in medieval urban culture, deeply determined the social and economic fabric of cities, whether we think of the breweries themselves, the purchase of basic ingredients, the varying types of fuel for the brewing process, trade, taxation, the impact of brewing on the labor market, and property rights.[182] Only the urban market with a large pool of customers made possible the development of considerable differentiation in the brewing process, creating specialists and competition among breweries. But many town governments imposed strict regulations and tax systems, which illustrates nicely to what extent the production of beer had a deep impact on urban life at large.[183]

Practically every aspect of human life was intimately connected with urban space, as Hartmut Boockmann's comprehensive survey indicates. He discusses the following topics: walls, gates, towers, and weapons; urban houses; interior space; hygiene and health; trade and traffic; craftsmanship; city halls; law and order; urban struggles for superiority among the various social classes; the city as a site for the ducal residence; funerals and memorials; urban churches and monasteries; hospitals; pilgrimage to cities; piety, superstition, and heresy; Jews in cities; guilds and confraternities; children; schools and education.[184]

## Late-Medieval Urban Life in Art

Although the growth of medieval cities was a ubiquitous, though certainly not an automatic, progressive, and linear, phenomenon, the perception of cities differed widely, particularly because so many different people congregated within cities. However, those who lived within the city walls certainly identified with the city and regarded their own existence as considerably more secure than that in the countryside. As Chiara Frugoni comments: "In the following centuries [since the thirteenth century — A.C.], down to the Renaissance, this awareness of a contrast, denoted by the walls, between order and chaos, organized space and savage nature, grows more acute; as a result every violent death, every event that disturbs the peaceful unfolding of a life regulated by laws—like the executions that, the

---

[182]  Richard W. Unger, *Beer in the Middle Ages and the Renaissance*, 38, emphasizes: "The source of the urban brewing industry was not the presence of brew-houses in monasteries or episcopal households, regardless of the technical influence such establishments could and did have. It was rather the transfer of traditional brewing practice from the countryside to the cities by rural migrants, the people who formed the population of European towns in the twelfth and thirteenth centuries."

[183]  Unger, *Beer in the Middle Ages*, 43–50. He underscores that in the end "[t]he tax system and regulation in general hindered small-scale brewing and promoted the development of an urban industry increasingly dominated by professional brewers."

[184]  Hartmut Boockmann, *Die Stadt im späten Mittelalter*. 2nd ed. (1986; Munich: Beck, 1987). His book is richly illustrated, whereas the bibliography proves to be somewhat thin.

statutes tell us, did in fact take place 'outside' — is ordinarily represented occurring in the open."[185]

Even though medieval artists continued to create idealistic images of cities, commonly following the model of the Holy Jerusalem, hence treating the city basically as a symbol and not as a realistic space,[186] by the late Middle Ages the city became the object of intensive critical analysis because local governments emerged that felt increasingly independent and wanted to express this new sentiment of civic pride and identity in public art works, such as Ambrogio Lorenzetti's "Sala della Pace" in the Palazzo Pubblico of Siena (1338–1339).[187] Michel Feuillet has recently described the urban network visible in Lorenzetti's frescoes as follows:

> L'artiste a serré les unes contre les autres de nombreuses maisons, hautes et confortables, colorées, percées de multiples fenêtres, surplombant en encorbellement les rues et les places et s'ouvrant pour davantage d'agrément sur d'élégantes *logge*. Comme signe supplémentaire de cette croissance de l'habitat urbain, l'artiste représente un chantier de construction ou s'affaire une équipe de maçons juchés sur des échafaudages.[188]

> [The artist has pressed the houses tightly together, tall and comfortable, colored, pierced open by many windows, extending in cantilevers out on to the streets and squares, opening up onto elegant loggias to enhance the charm of the scene. As a supplementary sign of the interlacing of the urban habitat

---

[185] Chiara Frugoni, *A Distant City: Images of Urban Experience in the Middle Ages*, trans. William McCuaig (1983; Princeton, NJ: Princeton University Press, 1991), 11.

[186] Frugoni, *A Distant City*, 108–09; see also Kugler, *Die Vorstellung der Stadt*, 79–141.

[187] Frugoni, *A Distant City*, 118–88. See also George Rowley, *Ambrogio Lorenzetti*. 2 vols. (Princeton, NJ: Princeton University Press, 1958); Chiara Frugoni, *Pietro and Ambrogio Lorenzetti* ([Bergenfield, NJ, ?, and New York ?]: Scala Books, 1988); Randolph Starn, *Ambrogio Lorenzetti: The Palazzo Pubblico, Siena* (New York: George Braziller, 1994); Max Seidel, *Dolce Vita: Ambrogio Lorenzettis Porträt des Sieneser Staates* (Basel: Schwabe & Co., 1999); *"La pace è allegrezza": L'ordinamento di una città operosa sull'esempio dell'affresco "Il Buon Governo" di Ambrogio Lorenzetti da Siena*, a cura di A. Luisa Haring and Erich Kaufer (Siena: Edizioni Il Leccio, 2002); *Ambrogio Lorenzetti: La vita del trecento in Siena e nel contado senese nelle committenze istoriate pubbliche e private. Guida al Buon Governo*, a cura di Alberto Colli. Introduzione di Mario Ascheri (Siena: Arti Grafiche Nencini - Poggibonsi, 2004); Luciano Bellosi and Giovanna Ragionieri, *Giotto e la sua eredità: Filippo Rusuti, Pietro Cavallini, Duccio, Giovanni da Rimini, Neri da Rimini, Pietro da Rimini, Simone Martini, Pietro Lorenzetti, Ambrogio Lorenzetti, Matteo Giovannetti, Masso di Banco, Puccio Capanna, Taddeo Gaddi, Giovanni da Milano, Giottino, Giusto de'Menabuoi, Altichiero, Jacopo Avanzi, Jean Pucelle, i fratelli Limbourg* (Florence: Il Sole 24 Ore, 2007). Likewise, Chiara Frugoni, *A Day in a Medieval City*, intensively draws from this pictorial evidence for her mental-historical investigation of late-medieval life in the city.

[188] Michel Feuillet, "La Fresque des *Effets du Bon Gouvernement* d'Ambrogio Lorenzetti dans le Palazzo Pubblico de Sienne: une mise en image de la dialectique ville-campagne à la fin du Moyen Âge," *Ville habitée, ville fantasmée: Actes du colloque "La ville dans et hors les murs"* . . . , ed. Georges Frédéric Manche (Paris: L'Harmattan, 2006), 79–92; here 80.

the artist shows a construction site where a team of masons perched on scaffolding is busily at work.

Simultaneously, the concern grew everywhere regarding the proper government of cities, as reflected by a large corpus of corresponding critical poems and treatises about good and bad urban governments ("Stadtregimentslehren"). Particularly those texts that contain also general didactic concepts were widely disseminated, such as the *Antwerpse school* and the stanzas "Hoemen ene stat regeren sal" and "Von gûtten râtten," especially because they were not focused on one individual city and could be applied everywhere. But the entire genre enjoyed considerable popularity between 1300 and 1500, when the interest in them seems to have declined, although with some major exceptions far into the seventeenth century.[189]

Late-medieval art, especially from the Flemish area, demonstrates the enormous fascination exerted by the new urbanism. As James Snyder comments, for instance, regarding the painting "Madonna with the Chancellor Nicolas Rolin" by Jan van Eyck (ca. 1435), "The background landscape in the Rolin Madonna has been identified as Bruges, Autun, Liège, Maastricht, and Geneva. But as with his architectural interiors, Van Eyck is his own architect and city planner here, fashioning a convincing setting that at the same time serves as a symbolic backdrop for the figures. The city on the right bank, behind Mary, is filled with countless churches including one huge cathedral, all of which are proper attributes of Notre Dame once again . . . ."[190]

Significantly, we can also discover a remarkable depiction of urban space in the famous English *Luttrell Psalter* from the first half of the fourteenth century which provides much information about daily life both in the countryside and, to some extent, also at court (scenes of games, jousting, hunting, etc.). Although this heavy tome, consisting of 309 leaves, written by one single scribe, focuses, in its pictorial program, mostly on rural aspects of farm work, created by at least five different illuminators, we also discover one spectacular image of a walled medieval town (fol. 164v). Janet Backhouse offers the following description and comment:

> The townscape (41) is thus of special interest, not so much for its dancers and musicians as for the substantial variety of the buildings crammed within its walls. The central feature is a cruciform church with a tower and steeple. It appears to be roofed

---

[189]   Heike Bierschwale and Jacqueline van Leeuwen, *Wie man eine Stadt regieren soll*, 145, summarize their finding as follows: "Die Sprüche erinnerten Amtsträger in abbreviierter Form an ihre amtlichen und moralischen Pflichten, gleichzeitig vermittelten sie ein Bewußtsein von der herausgehobenen gesellschaftlichen Position der Ratsherren, womit ihnen in diesem Sinne auch repräsentative Funktionen eigneten."

[190]   James Snyder, *Northern Renaissance Art: Painting, Sculpture, the Graphic Arts from 1350 to 1575* (New York: Harry N. Abrams, 1985), 109.

with lead and the steeple is crowned with a weathercock. The city walls are strongly constructed of dressed stone, with suitable traces of fortification [crenellation, A.C.]. Between the two is a varied collection of houses, some roofed with tiles and others with thatch. While the majority are timber framed, some seem to be of stone, a couple even possibly of brick. Various forms of window and door are discernible. The third house from the left in the uper row is jettied out over the square. Several buildings have highly decorative pierced chimneys and the grandest of the houses, in the lower right-hand corner, boasts a row of decorative crests along its ridge. This house has a shield of arms hanging from a pole on the face which fronts the square. The jettied house and the house nearest to the city gate are both apparently identifiable as inns because they carry the sign of a bush on a pole.[191]

The artist here obviously deviated from the traditional townscape characterized by a cluster of houses densely packed together behind tall city walls, profiled mostly by church towers and spires, normally giving us no sense of a market or any other open space. Here, by contrast, we witness a strong interest in the urban setting, people's living conditions, diverse architecture, and also in the opening up of the city to the outside, as reflected by a row of dancers, all but one with their back to the viewer, leaving the city gate on the left. Michael Camille identified the dance performance as the procession associated with the Rogation Day (Christianization of the ancient May festival).[192] A group of women assembled on top of the gate gazes down upon them.

At another occasion, one of the artists also included the image of a castle (of love) besieged by knights, on fol. 75v, placed at the bottom of the page, but this clearly serves allegorical purposes because the defenders are women throwing flowers down upon the attackers, men.[193] Since the cityscape on fol. 164v proves to be the only one in the entire psalter, and since it consists of so many innovative elements, it deserves to be regarded as a unique, but most important signal of the

---

[191]  Janet Backhouse, *Medieval Rural Life in the Luttrell Psalter* (Toronto and Buffalo: University of Toronto Press, 2000), 50–51. See also Eric George Millar, *The Luttrell Psalter: two Plates in Colour and Eighty-Three in Monochrome from the Additional Manuscript 42130 in the British Museum* (London: Printed for the Trustees, 1932); Michael Camille, *Mirror in Parchment: The Luttrell Psalter and the Making of Medieval England* (Chicago: University of Chicago Press, 1998). For a stunning facsimile, now see *The Luttrell Psalter: A Facsimile,* commentary by Michelle P. Brown (London: The British Library, 2006). The image reproduction in Backhouse's book is considerably larger than in the facsimile and allows us to study even minute details without any difficulties.

[192]  Michael Camille, *Mirror in Parchment,* 274–75; see also the commentary by Michelle P. Brown, 45. She claims that the musicians' trumpets bear the arms of Luttrel and Sutton, ibid., but the enlarged image in Backhouse does not confirm that.

[193]  See Brown's commentary, 39.

emergence of the city as a major focus of public attention, even among the landed gentry.[194]

---

[194] As Backhouse, *Medieval Rural Life*, 51–52, comments, "Medieval stone houses which would have been known to Sir Geoffrey Luttrell survive both within the city of Lincoln and at Boothby Pagnell, only a few miles north of his Irnham home. Timber framed houses are, however, more susceptible to decay and to alteration and are correspondingly less easy to pinpoint. A surviving early fourteenth-century cityscape of the type offered by this miniature would indeed be a rarity, though the houses of which it is composed can be compared with known buildings."

Figure 1: *Luttrell Psalter*, fol. 164 verso

This growing and profound interest in urban space as the new pictorial background becomes almost ever-present in fifteenth-century Flemish art, even if the viewer's eye is directed primarily on the foreground, mostly an interior setting, such as in Robert Campin's "Salting Madonna" from ca. 1430 (National Gallery, London). The window in the top left is set far in the background, and opens only a small space looking onto the city, the details of which are hard to recognize. Nevertheless, because of the darkness in the room, except for the brightly illuminated Madonna nursing the Infant, and also for the Bible lying open on the lectionary, the viewer's attention is almost equally divided between the religious scene and the urban world nicely framed in the depth of the pictorial space.[195] Hans Memling was certainly a master of this motif and included many elaborate details of urban space in his altarpieces, such as in the left panel of the "Altarpiece of the Virgin with Saints and Angels" from 1479 (Hospital of Saint John, Bruges), where numerous buildings in a city fill the background. But even the center piece, though focusing on the Virgin with the Child, surrounded by shepherds and angels, is predicated on the idea that all important events in human existence take place within the framework of a city.[196]

In simultaneous altarpieces, such as Lucas Moser's "Magdalen Altarpiece" (exterior) from 1431 (Church, Tiefenbronn), we recognize, at the same time, a harbor setting, an interior space, and a public scene under a tower.[197] Other artists who followed the same strategy and design model were Johann Koerebecke and Derik Baegert, and finally also Michael Pacher, to name some more names of those who confirm the general interest in the city as a pictorial motif.[198]

Albrecht Dürer might well have offered one of the most intriguing examples of the intensive fascination with urban development when he created his oil painting "The Feast of the Rose Garlands (The Brotherhood of the Rosary)" in 1506, today housed in the Národni Galerie in Prague.[199] The German colony of merchants in

---

[195] See James Snyder, *Northern Renaissance Art*, 123, no. 119. See also a very similar set-up and design in Dieric Bouts's "Madonna and Child" from ca. 1465 (National Gallery, London; here 145, no. 142.

[196] Snyder, *Northern Renaissance Art*, 197, color plate 31. See also Gerard David's "Altarpiece of the Baptism of Christ" from ca. 1502–1507 (Groeningemuseum, Bruges; here 198, color plate 33, and Michael Wolgemut's (attributed) "Resurrection" from the Hofer Altarpiece, ca. 1485 (Alte Pinakothek, Munich); here 204, color plate 40.

[197] Snyder, *Northern Renaissance*, 221, no. 212.

[198] Snyder, *Northern Renaissance*, 232–37. See also the comprehensive studies by Frederick Hartt, *History of Italian Renaissance Art: Painting, Sculpture, Architecture* (Englewood Cliffs, NJ: Prentice-Hall, and New York: Harry N. Abrams, n.d. [1969]); and André Chastel, *The Studios and Styles of the Renaissance: Italy 1460–1500*, trans. Jonathan Griffin (1965; London: Thames and Hudson, 1966).

[199] For a wonderfully large-size digital version, see the copy online at: http://i.blog.empas.com/pia212/33660574_750x638.jpg; or at: http://www.wga.hu/frames-e.html?/html/d/durer/1/05/03rose.html; alternatively, see the site: http://www.booksplendour.com.au/gallery/classics/Durer/durer_The%20Altarpiece%20of%20

Venice, housed in the Fondaco dei Tedeschi, had commissioned him to paint this panel for their chapel in the parish church of San Bartolomeo, which shows the enthroned Virgin Mary, holding the infant Jesus on her lap, while Pope Julius II (?) and the designate Holy Roman Emperor Maximilian I kneel to both her sides, the latter already crowned with a garland of roses by the Virgin, whereas Jesus is just about to crown the Pope. A group of people, none of whom can be easily or positively be identified, throng around the throne, which allowed Dürer to include himself in the background on the right-hand side standing next to a tree. Left to his head, in the far distance, emerges a splendid city with wonderful towers, walls, urban residences, and houses, all before a mighty mountainous landscape. The lower part of the city extends into a sun-flooded lower section of the city, enriched with an elegant bridge and gate tower, not to mention many other details only faintly recognizable.

Whether Dürer here portrayed a really existing city, or created an ideal, does not concern us here, but he made sure to give the viewer the sense of the spectacular nature of urban space as the ultimate resource in which the individual can find a home and also an identity. So it might be Nuremberg, but it could be any other city, a proud representation of the early-modern urban space.[200] The painting itself later became a crown jewel of Emperor and Czech King Rudolph II's collection, who bought this masterpiece for the exorbitant price of 900 gold ducats.[201] There are striking parallels to the image of Nuremberg in Hartmann Schedel's famous world chronicle.

## The City in Late-Medieval Literature

For those who were not members of the civic communities, the urban space represented a source of tremendous attraction and also suspicion. Throughout the Middle Ages we observe how both peasants and aristocrats, both goliards and scholars, musicians and medical doctors invested much energy and resources to join an urban community, that is, to gain legal status as a citizen. Even craftsmen faced a hard time achieving that status if there were not sufficient positions open as masters in the specific professions. It was a privilege, not a right one was

<hr>

[200] the%20Rose%20Gardens.jpeg (last accessed on Dec. 9, 2008). For a detail of this city scene, see Peter Strieder, *The Hidden Dürer* (1976; Rushcutters Bay, NSW, Australia: Bay Books Pty, 1978), 94–5.

[201] *Albrecht Dürer: The Feast of the Rose Garlands 1506–2006*, ed. Olga Kotková (Prague: Národni galerie v Praze 2006): Catalog of an exhibition held at National Gallery in Prague, Collection of Old Masters, Wallenstein Riding School, June 21–Oct. 1, 2006; for a review, see Jeffrey Chipps Smith, in *Sehepunkte* 7 (2007), No. 2 at:
http://www.sehepunkte.de/2007/02/12411.html (last accessed on Dec. 9, 2008).

necessarily born with, as we know from many craftsmen who strove with all their might to marry either a craftsman's daughter or his widow because only in that case were they allowed to settle in the town, then to rise in rank, and to gain the status as master who could run a workshop in the city.[202]

Primarily in urban centers money changed hands, and the cost of living was very high, but there were also many forms of entertainment and learning. In the cities customers could find all kinds of specialized services, including that of sex workers, i.e., prostitutes. Brothels were strategically located at the city gates to help reduce the problem with sexual violence, and prostitutes actually sometimes played a rather significant role in diplomatic affairs, officially welcoming a dignitary outside of the city gates.[203] But prostitutes were always regarded and treated as outsiders, and their social existence was not enviable, very much actually like today. Nevertheless, they constituted a noticeable social group within late-medieval urban life, attracting numerous customers and also triggering sharp criticism by the clerics, although their profession was mostly regarded like most others despite its morally negative association.

---

[202] There is a legion of relevant scholarship; see for instance John Harvey, *Mediaeval Craftsmen* (London: Batsford, 1975); *Deutsches Handwerk in Spätmittelalter und früher Neuzeigt: Sozialgeschichte – Volkskunde –Literaturgeschichte*, ed. Rainer S. Elkar. Göttinger Beiträge zur Wirtschafts- und Sozialgeschichte, 9 (Göttingen: Schwartz, 1983); Heather Swanson, *Medieval Artisans: An Urban Class in Late Medieval England* (Oxford: Basil Blackwell, 1989); Steven A. Epstein, *Wage Labor and Guilds in Medieval Europe* (Chapel Hill: University of North Carolina Press, 1991); *Artisans in Europe, 1300–1914*, ed. James R. Farr. New Approaches to European History, 19 (Cambridge: Cambridge University Press, 2000); Ingeborg Seltmann, *Handwerker, Henker, Heilige: Bilder erzählen vom Leben im Mittelalter* (Ostfildern: Thorbecke, 2005); Günther Binding, *Wanderung von Werkmeistern und Handwerkern im frühen und hohen Mittelalter*. Sitzungsberichte der Wissenschaftlichen Gesellschaft an der Johann Wolfgang Goethe-Universität Frankfurt am Main, 43.1 (Stuttgart: Steiner, 2005). See also the *Hausbücher der Nürnberger Zwölfbrüderstiftungen*, online at: http://www.nuernberger-hausbuecher.de (last accessed on Dec. 8, 2008).

[203] Gertrud Blaschitz, "Das Freudenhaus im Mittelalter," 715–50. See also Leah Lydia Otis, *Prostitution in Medieval Society: The History of an Urban Institution in Languedoc* (Chicago and London: The University of Chicago Press, 1985); Beate Schuster, "Frauenhandel und Frauenhäuser im 15. und 16. Jahrhundert," *Vierteljahrsschrift für Sozial- und Wirtschaftsgeschichte* 78, 2 (1991): 172–89; Peter Schuster, *Das Frauenhaus: Städtische Bordelle in Deutschland (1350–1600)* (Paderborn, München, Wien und Zürich: Ferdinand Schöningh, 1992); Beate Schuster, *Die freien Frauen. Dirnen und Frauenhäuser im 15. und 16. Jahrhundert* (Frankfurt und New York: Campus, 1995); Ruth Mazo Karras, "Prostitution," *Women in the Middle Ages: An Encyclopedia*, ed. Katharina M. Wilson and Nadia Margolis (Westport, CT, and London: Greenwood Press, 2004), vol. II: 770–75. See also Ruth Mazo Karras, "The Regulation of Brothels in Later Medieval England," *Sisters and Workers in the Middle Ages*, ed. Judith M. Bennett, Elizabeth A. Clark, Jean F. O'Barr, B. Anne Vilen, and Sarah Westphal-Wihl (1976; Chicago and London: The University of Chicago Press, 1989), 100–34; eadem, *Common Women: Prostitution and Sexuality in Medieval England*. Studies in the History of Sexuality (1996; New York and Oxford: Oxford University Press, 1998); Fernando Bruquetas de Castro, *Historia de los burdeles en España: de lupanares, puteríos reales y otras mancebías* (Madrid : Esfera de los Libros, 2006).

Significantly, prostitutes were simply one social group in a kaleidoscope of urban dwellers, though their unusual profession makes them stand out in our investigations, whereas the historical sources do not necessarily confirm that.[204] Customers could be criticized harshly because of their original vow of chastity (clerics), or they could be ridiculed because they had become victims of their own lustfulness and ignorance, especially when they became victims of the manipulations of go-betweens and pimps.[205]

One late-medieval German poet, Oswald von Wolkenstein (1376/1377–1445), whose castle was located in modern-day South Tyrol (now in Italy), but who was privileged enough to travel throughout Europe in many different functions, reflected repeatedly on his experiences with prostitutes and also discussed his observations in various cities, some pleasant, others disagreeable. The last few decades have witnessed an ever-growing interest in this most fascinating poet whose works place him oddly between the Middle Ages and the Renaissance. He produced incredibly detailed autobiographical poetry, yet he also relied heavily on topical language and imagery. His life can be traced in greatest detail both through historical documents (ca. 1000 are still available today) and his song-poetry. Oswald traveled extensively all over Europe, and he was intensively involved in local and national politics. Musicologists and philologists have likewise expressed great respect for his work, though he heavily copied melodies and probably also many topics, motifs, images, metaphors, and expressions from contemporary French, Flemish, and Italian poets.[206]

---

[204] See Sarah McDougall, "The Prosecution of Sex in Late Medieval Troyes," *Sexuality in the Middle Ages and Early Modern Times*, 691–714.

[205] Gretchen Mieszkowski, *Medieval Go-Betweens and Chaucer's Pandarus*. The New Middle Ages (New York: Palgrave Macmillan, 2006); see also her contribution "Old Age and Medieval Misogyny: The Old Woman" (299–19) to *Old Age in the Middle Ages and the Renaissance: Interdisciplinary Approaches to a Neglected Topic*, ed. Albrecht Classen. Fundamentals of Medieval and Early Modern Culture, 2 (Berlin and New York: Walter de Gruyter, 2007), along with the parallel, but certainly not identical contribution by Karen Pratt, "*De vetula*: the Figure of the Old Woman in Old French Literature" (321–42), ibid. Intriguingly, although both rely on much of the same material, they reach rather different conclusions.

[206] Die *Lieder* Oswalds von Wolkenstein, ed. Karl Kurt Klein. 3rd newly revised and expanded ed. by Hans Moser, Norbert Richard Wolf, and Notburga Wolf. Altdeutsche Textbibliothek 55 (1962; Tübingen: Niemeyer, 1987); Werner Marold, *Kommentar zu den Liedern Oswalds*, revised and ed. by Alan Robertshaw. Innsbrucker Beiträge zur Kulturwissenschaft. Germanistische Reihe, 52 (1926; Innsbruck: Institut für Germanistik, 1995); Johannes Spicker, *Oswald von Wolkenstein: Die Lieder*. Klassiker-Lektüren, 10 (Berlin: Schmidt, 2007); for Oswald's borrowing from Italian poetry, see Albrecht Classen, *Zur Rezeption norditalienischer Kultur des Trecento im Werk Oswalds von Wolkenstein (1376/77-1445)*. Göppinger Arbeiten zur Germanistik, 471 (Göppingen: Kümmerle, 1987); for the best historical biography, see Anton Schwob, *Oswald von Wolkenstein: Eine Biographie*. Schriftenreihe des Südtiroler Kulturinstitutes, 4 (1977; Bozen: Verlagsanstalt Athesia, 1989); see also Albrecht Classen, "Oswald von Wolkenstein," *German Writers of the Renaissance and Reformation 1280–1580*, Dictionary of Literary Biographies, 179, ed. James Hardin and Max

Oswald proves to be an extraordinary literary source for many different aspects in the history of late-medieval mentality, whether we want to probe gender relationships, religious sentiments, legal concepts, political issues, travel experiences, pilgrimage, the enjoyment of languages, sexuality, marriage, and the relationship between landed gentry and peasantry, not to forget Oswald's conflictual interaction with the territorial duke of Tyrol, Frederick IV.[207] Interestingly, Oswald also drew from his personal experiences in various south-German cities for some of his autobiographical poems, offering intriguing insight into how an aristocratic singer-poet who worked in the diplomatic service of Emperor Sigismund, the Tyrolean Duke Frederick IV, and the Bishop of Neustift near Brixen operated in the urban space of Constance and Überlingen.

For instance, in his song Kl. 45 "Wer machen well" he mockingly discusses the experience of foreigners in the city of Überlingen on the Lake Constance where hyperinflation has caused the visitors to suffer badly from their inn-keepers and others who provide services. In fact, Oswald is surprisingly detailed as to the specific prices, the currency used, and then as to the customers' complaints as to the high costs of all goods: "fleisch lützel, krut ain gross geschrai; / auss klainer schüssel gat der rai / von mangem lai" (9–11; They serve little meat, but any amount of cabbage; / the row of many people / eats from a small bowl).[208]

---

Reinhart (Detroit, Washington, DC, and London: Gale Research, 1997), 198–205; Alan Robertshaw, *Oswald von Wolkenstein: The Myth and the Man*. Göppinger Arbeiten zur Germanistik, 178 (Göppingen: Kümmerle, 1977). See also *Die Lebenszeugnisse Oswalds von Wolkenstein: Edition und Kommentar*, ed. Anton Schwob. 3 vols. (Vienna, Cologne, and Weimar: Böhlau, 1999–2004) (ultimately 5 vols. in total). See now Albrecht Classen, *The Poems of Oswald von Wolkenstein: An English Translation of the Complete Works (1376/77–1445)*. The New Middle Ages (New York: Palgrave Macmillan, 2008).

[207] See, for instance, Albrecht Classen, "Onomatopoesie in der Lyrik von Jehan Vaillant, Oswald von Wolkenstein und Niccolò Soldanieri," *Zeitschrift für deutsche Philologie* 108, 3 (1989): 357–77; id., "Der Bauern in der Lyrik Oswalds von Wolkenstein," *Euphorion* 82, 2 (1988): 150–67; *Die autobiographische Lyrik des europäischen Spätmittelaltlers: Studien zu Hugo von Montfort, Oswald von Wolkenstein, Antonio Pucci, Charles d'Orléans, Thomas Hoccleve, Michel Beheim, Hans Rosenplüt und Alfonso Alvarez de Villasandino*, Amsterdamer Publikationen zur Sprache und Literatur, 91 (Amsterdam and Atlanta, GA: Editions Rodopi, 1991); id., "To Fear or not to Fear, that is the Question: Oswald von Wolkenstein Facing Death and Enjoying Life. Fifteenth-Century *Mentalitätsgeschichte* Reflected in Lyric Poetry," *Fear and Its Representations in the Middle Ages and Renaissance*, ed. Anne Scott and Cynthia Kosso. Arizona Studies in the Middle Ages and the Renaissance, 6 (Turnhout, Belgium: Brepols, 2002), 274–91; Sieglinde Hartmann, *Altersdichtung und Selbstdarstellung bei Oswald von Wolkenstein*. Göppinger Arbeiten zur Germanistik, 288 (Göppingen: Kümmerle, 1980); see also the contributions to *Oswald von Wolkenstein: Beiträge der philologisch-musikwissenschaftlichen Tagung in Neustift bei Brixen 1973*, ed. Egon Kühebacher. Innsbrucker Beiträge zur Kulturwissenschaft,. Germanistische Reihe, 1 (Innsbruck: Institut für deutsche Philologie der Universität, 1974).

[208] The translation is mine, borrowed from my translation of Oswald's complete works (New York: Palgrave, 2008).

Significantly, Oswald does not really relate details about the city itself, or the urban space. Instead, his poem basically reflects his highly subjective perspective and perception, focusing on eating and drinking, payment, housing, entertainment, such as: "Zwar güter kurzweil sicht man vil / da mitten auf dem blatze, / mit tanzen, springen, saitenspil / von ainer rauhen katze" (43–46; Truly, you can observe there in the middle of the square much entertainment, like dancing, jumping, and play with the fiddle, presented by an unkempt cat). The characteristically self-centered poet Oswald casts an image of himself as a man who rambunctiously partakes of all the pleasures that a city can offer, constantly referring to sexual enticements and joys, though he then also indicates, in a strongly ironic, if not sarcastic, manner how much he had to suffer in the city because of his personal poverty and inability to see through the various strategies of the prostitutes, his own inn-keeper, food providers, and others to rob him of his money: "Mein wiert, der was beschaiden zwar, / er schied das gold von leder; / das nam ich an der bettstat war, / zwelf pfenning gulten ain feder" (52–55; My inn-keeper knew his business: he took the gold out of [my] leather bag. I noticed that at the price for a bed: One feather mattress cost twelve ducats!).

In this sense the parallels to his contemporary, Margery Kempe, among many other late-medieval travelers, are rather striking, though she pursued primarily religious goals when she visited Rome. Oswald addresses a specific audience, probably his companions in Überlingen, or his family and friends back home in rural Tyrol, none of whom had a clear sense of what the city truly meant, being only dazzled, if not dumbfounded, by the splendor, noise, crowds, sexual attractions, music, and food. In a way, Oswald's poem can be read as the typical reflection of an ignorant tourist who only perceives the most glaring aspects of a site or city, either deeply intrigued by the glitter and sham, or disgusted by the abuse of the foreigners at the hand of the urban merchants and other service providers, including pimps and prostitutes.

For our purposes it does not matter whether Oswald created this poem during his participation in the Council of Constance as a diplomat or translator, or at some other time later in the service of Emperor Sigismund, in 1430, who had taken quarters there instead of in Constance because of civic unrest in that city.[209] Instead, we can observe how much the poet focuses on his personal experiences in a highly idiosyncratic fashion, almost satirizing city life as a place for entertainment, struggle, and strife, not, however, as a site with which a landed aristocrat like Oswald, irrespective of his cosmopolitanism and polyglot skills,

---

[209] See the comments by Burghart Wachinger in Oswald von Wolkenstein, *Lieder: Frühneuhochdeutsch / Neuhochdeutsch*. Ausgewählte Texte herausgegeben, übersetzt und kommentiert von Burghart Wachinger. Melodien und Tonsätze herausgegeben und kommentiert von Horst Brunner (Stuttgart: Reclam, 2007), 376–77.

would have fully identified. Otherwise he would not have mocked, for instance, the poor quality of the local wine, which he sarcastically contrasts with those that he can find in his home region: "Vasst süsser wein als slehen tranck, / der reuhet mir die kel so kranck, / das sich veierrt mein hels gesangk, / dick gen Traminn stet mein gedanck; / sein herter twangk / pringt scharpfen ungelimpfen" (31–36; Really sweet wine, like juice of the black thorn, made my throat very scratchy and made my song get stuck deep in there. In my thoughts I'd rather turn to the Traminer wine. Its harsh grip causes considerable discomfort).

However, we can never fully trust that Oswald is formulating his true opinion because he always demonstrates an enormous degree of an actor's attitude, constantly performing in changing roles and with shifting masks, which applies even in his autobiographical poetry, though we should not underestimate his full concern with creating his literary self-portrait.[210] This finds its confirmation in his poetic encomium on Constance, Kl. 98 "O wunnikliches paradis," where the singer is suddenly full of praise for the wonderful and most pleasing atmosphere in the city, which has nothing to do with the shift from Überlingen to Constance, closely situated to each other. On the contrary, Oswald simply shifts to a different register in his poetic treatment of city life, one underscoring all its positive features, then ridiculing the abuse committed by inn-keepers and prostitutes who traditionally suffered from a bad reputation.[211]

In "O wunnikliches Paradis" he also turns his full attention to the ladies in the city,[212] praising them for their beauty which pleases him mightily (9–16), particularly because of their elegant comportment, sophisticated speech, and educated manners (17–19). However, the city itself does not really enter his literary horizon; instead he only emphasizes the extraordinary opportunity to enjoy the dance with the ladies in the city dance hall (28), who impress him as much as courtly ladies have always done in traditional courtly poetry: "Und der ich nicht

---

[210] Albrecht Classen, *Die autobiographische Lyrik des europäischen Spätmittelalters*, 1991; Johannes Spicker, *Literarische Stilisierung und artistische Kompetenz bei Oswald von Wolkenstein* (Stuttgart and Leipzig: Hirzel, 1993); Sieglinde Hartmann, "Oswald von Wolkenstein et la Méditerranée: espace de vie, espace de poésie," *Jahrbuch der Oswald von Wolkenstein Gesellschaft* 8 (1994/95): 289–320. Johannes Spicker, *Oswald von Wolkenstein: Die Lieder*. Klassiker-Lektüren, 10 (Berlin: Erich Schmidt, 2007), 38–51, takes a much too extreme counter position and questions virtually all autobiographical comments in the poet's work as authentic. See my review, forthcoming in *Neuphilologische Mitteilungen*. For Oswald's metapoetic reflections about himself, see Albrecht Classen, "Sangeskunst und moderne Selbstverwirklichung im Werk Oswalds von Wolkenstein (1376/77–1445), *in hôhem prîse: A Festschrift in Honor of Ernst Dick*, ed. by Winder McConnell. Göppinger Arbeiten zur Germanistik, 480 (Göppingen: Kümmerle, 1989), 11–29.
[211] Richard W. Unger, *Beer in the Middle Ages*, 50–51; 180–81; 218–19, et passim.
[212] Marold/Robertshaw, *Kommentar*, 241, identifies "Paradis" (Paradise) as a suburb northwest of Constance, located outside of the city wall which was used, at least in the Middle Ages, as a site for tournaments and festivals.

vergessen wil; / das macht ir minniklich gestalt. / mit eren lustichlich freuden spil / vindt man zu Costnitz manigvalt" (29–32; I cannot forget them at all because of their delightful appearance. Polite, delightful entertainment of all kinds you can find in Constance). But if we search for any specific reference to the city itself, we come up empty-handed, except for the brief mention of the dance hall "der Katzen" (28).[213]

Of course, and this is rather significant for our overall investigation, this should not really surprise us because the poet does not perceive himself as part of the urban community and only discusses Constance as one point during his many travels and diplomatic missions. In fact, the city itself does not matter to him per se, and he reacts to the various urban experiences only insofar as they had either a negative or a positive impact on him.

After all, in Kl. 123 "Der seines laids ergeczt well sein" Oswald harbored quite different feelings regarding Constance, now returning to the same register that he had used in his Überlingen song Kl. 45. Again, he sarcastically reports the women's abuse of the outside guests, robbing them of all their money, though he probably only means the local prostitutes:

> Der seines laids ergeczt well sein
> und ungeneczt beschoren fein,
> der ziech gen Costnitz an den Rein,
> ob im die raiss wol füge.
> Darinn so wont mang freulin zart,
> die kunnen grasen in dem part,
> ob sich kain har darinn verschart,
> daz er nit geren truge.                    (Kl. 123, 1–8)

> [He who wants to be free of his worries
> and would like to be shorn dry clean,
> ought to travel to Constance on the Rhine,[214]
> if this trip fits into his plans.
> Many fine women live there
> who know well how to scratch gently the beard,
> looking to see whether a hair might be hiding in it
> that might bother him.]

Not surprisingly, Oswald biographers have touched upon those passages only fleetingly because they realize only too well that the poet does not demonstrate any remarkable interest in the city as such and treated it only as a backdrop for his

---

[213] Marold/Robertshaw, *Kommentar*, 242, identifies "in der Katzen" as the old guild building for the city aristocracy and the patriciate.
[214] Technically, this is correct since the Rhine, originating from Switzerland, is flowing through Lake Constance, while Constance is situated on the northwest side.

reflections upon his personal sentiments and experiences.[215] Contemporary chroniclers such as Ulrich von Richental regularly projected the very opposite perspective of the city because the latter, at least, lived in Constance and so was naturally inclined to paint a very positive picture of his home city. George F. Jones adds the unusual but certainly correct angle that the high prices in Constance were really reasonable considering the economic circumstances. Moreover, "the city fathers of Constance broke with medieval monopolistic practice by permitting tradesmen and artisans from outside to open shop in the city for the duration of the council."[216] And as to Oswald's satirical description of the ugly women in the city, Jones adds: "Oswald's parodistic description of the housemaid is typical of the times, for he presents exactly the opposite of the stylized ideal of feminine beauty."[217]

Concluding his song with some reflections upon his overall experience in the city, Oswald finally states:

> wenn ich von Costnitz schaiden sol,
> des emphind ich an der seitten.
> Ich preiss den edlen, guldin Schlegel,
> zu dem so ker ich meinen segel,
>
> ett wo ich in der welt hin ker,
> des lob ich selden meide.                                    (75–80)

> [When I have to leave Constance,
> I will notice it at the side.[218]

---

[215]  Anton Schwob, *Oswald von Wolkenstein*, 107–08. He correctly comments, 107: "Seine Konstanzer Lieder berichten vornehmlich von Lustbarkeiten am Rande des Konzils, von Trinkgelagen, Tanzveranstaltungen, der Geschäftstüchtigkeit der Konstanzer *"freulin"* und den Wucherpreisen der Wirte" (His Constance songs report primarily of entertainment at the margin of the council, of drinking bouts, dance events, of the economic skills of the Constance "ladies" and of the usurious prices). Subsequently he adds the insightful characterization, 109: "Während Oswalds Lieder den Anschein erwecken, als ob er nichts anderes zu tun gehabt hätte, als seinen Zechgenossen die ernüchternden Erlebnisse eines amüsierfreudigen Provinzlers in der Bodenseestadt vorzutragen, überstürzten sich die politischen Ereignisse" (While Oswald's songs evoke the impression as if he had nothing else to do but to present the sobering experiences of a man from the province interested in finding some fun [in the city], the political events [that he mentions] come quickly one after the other).

[216]  George F. Jones, *Oswald von Wolkenstein*. Twayne's World Authors Series, 236 (New York: Twayne Publishers, 1973), 52.

[217]  Jones, *Oswald von Wolkenstein*, 52. For the rhetorical register of old women, see Gretchen Mieszkowski, "Old Age and Medieval Misogyny: The Old Woman," *Old Age in the Middle Ages*, 299–319. See also Karen Pratt, *"De vetula*: the Figure of the Old Woman in Medieval French Literature," ibid., 321–42.

[218]  Meaning: I will not have any money left; my bag on the left side will be empty.

I praise the noble, golden truncheon,[219]
in the direction of which I turn my sail;
wherever I might get in the world,
I will never withhold my praise for it.]

However much Oswald turned his attention to individual cities—and he also discusses Nuremberg (Kl. 99), and Augsburg (Kl. 122)—in reality this aristocratic poet could not identify with urban centers and included them only as curious sites where he as a visitor had both pleasant and uncomfortable experiences, where the food prices were excessive and the prostitutes unfriendly to him.[220] Not surprisingly, whenever he found an opportunity to ridicule and decry the new class of rich merchants, such as in his song "Ain burgher und ain hofman" (Kl. 25), Oswald made full use of this, though without thereby idealizing the aristocracy altogether. Instead, his criticism against those who make a living as courtiers is characterized by ridicule and wrath.[221]

Everything depends on the individual viewpoints, of course, and while Oswald, as a landed gentry, only passed through a number of German and other European cities, reflecting upon them fleetingly as it fit his own personal agenda, his contemporary Swiss author Heinrich Wittenwiler argued vehemently in favor of cities that knew how to assess their individual situation in contrast to foolish peasants and erratic aristocrats. In his highly satirical-didactic allegorical poem *Der Ring* (ca. 1400) he primarily paints a deftly critical image of the world of the stupid peasants who are utterly subject to their emotions, lack rationality, and cannot learn from any serious teaching. The verse narrative focuses on a young peasant couple that intends to get married, though they face a number of obstacles that they have to overcome until they can finally join in a wedding. But then violence breaks out, and this quickly erupts into a full-blown war in which the entire village where the groom had originated from is wiped out. Only the protagonist survives, but he does not demonstrate that he has learned anything from the catastrophe,

---

[219]   Either the name of an inn, then it would be "Schlegel," or an ironic reference to some beating that he received there; see Wernfried Hofmeister, in Oswald von Wolkenstein, *Sämtliche Lieder und Gedichte*. Ins Neuhochdeutsche übersetzt von Wernfried Hofmeister. Göppinger Arbeiten zur Germanistik, 511 (Göppingen: Kümmerle, 1989), 352.

[220]   Wachinger, in Oswald von Wolkenstein, *Lieder*, 376: "Immer geht es Oswald dabei nicht um die Städte als solche, sondern um die Stilisierung von Erfahrungen bei geselligen Gelegenheiten. Insofern stehen diese Lieder mit dem Interesse an Stadtbeschreibungen und Städtelob, das sich im 15. Jahrhundert entfaltete . . . , nur in sehr entferntem Zusammenhang" (Oswald is never truly interested in the cities as such; instead he is concerned with the stylization of experiences at social gatherings. In this sense these songs are only remotely connected with the interest in describing cities and singing the praise of cities, which developed in the fifteenth century).

[221]   See also the sonnet "E merchatanti della mia Fiorenza" composed by the Florentine wool-beater Burchiello in 1457, studied in this volume by Fabian Alfie.

and naively withdraws into the Black Forest, spending the rest of his life as an hermit.[222]

As part of their war preparations, the Lappenhausen farmers deliberate in their council whom they could approach as allies, and they first send messengers to the cities asking for their help. The narrator, however, first tries to provide his audience with an understanding of the urban world as every well-educated person should know it, and develops a lengthy list of the major cities all over Europe, beginning with Rome, Venice, and Bruges, then turning to the Spanish cities of Santiago de Compostela, Pamplona, Barcelona, Sevilla, and so forth, covering also those in France, Italy, Cyprus, Tyrol, Savoy, Flanders, Germany, Switzerland, Bohemia, Poland, and Austria. He mentions Constantinople, above all, but his knowledge begins to fade when he turns to Prussia and neighboring countries (7608–86). The number of cities cited here amounts to 72, a highly symbolic number often used in learned, encyclopedic works, if we consider, for instance, the 72 disciples whom Christ sent out to the world (Luke 10:1) and the common assumption in the Middle Ages that there were only 72 languages spoken,[223] which implies that Wittenwiler regarded the network of cities that spans the globe indeed as the most important aspect of public life where all trade, administration, banking, and education took place and also where the most intelligent and cultured people live, an explicit slap against the rural population.[224]

Wittenwiler does not specifically express an interest in the urban space per se, a topic that would not have been appropriate for his narrative focus of satirizing foolish peasants. But he projects the representatives of the various cities as extraordinarily wise, circumspect, careful, diplomatic, and peace-oriented, all in clear contrast to the hot-headed members of Lappenhausen, the country bumpkins, ever ready to start fighting inconsiderately and disregarding all risks and implications. As the Roman senator underscores:

---

[222]   Horst Brunner, *Heinrich Wittenwiler: Der Ring. Frühneuhochdeutsch / Neuhochdeutsch.* Nach dem Text von Edmund Wießner ins Neuhochdeutsche übersetzt und herausgegeben. Universal-Bibliothek, 8749 (Stuttgart: Reclam, 1991); Christoph Gruchot, *Heinrich Wittenwilers "Ring": Konzept und Konstruktion eines Lehrbuches.* Göppinger Arbeiten zur Germanistik, 475 (Göppingen: Kümmerle, 1988); Eckhart Conrad Lutz, *Spiritualis fornicatio: Heinrich Wittenwiler, seine Welt und sein 'Ring'.* Konstanzer Geschichts- und Rechtsquellen, XXXII (Sigmaringen: Thorbecke, 1990); Ortrun Riha, *Die Forschung zu Heinrich Wittenwilers "Ring" 1851–1988.* Würzburger Beiträge zur deutschen Philologie, 4 (Würzburg: Königshausen & Neumann, 1990); Albrecht Classen, *Verzweiflung und Hoffnung. Die Suche nach der kommunikativen Gemeinschaft in der deutschen Literatur des Mittelalters.* Beihefte zur Mediaevistik, 1 (Frankfurt a.M., Berlin, Bern, et al.: Peter Lang, 2002), 401–35.

[223]   Arno Borst, *Der Turmbau von Babel: Geschichte der Meinungen über Ursprung und Vielfalt der Sprachen und Völker.* Vol. 1 (Stuttgart: A. Hiersemann, 1975), 674–75; Bernhard Sowinski in: Heinrich Wittenwiler, *"Der Ring"*, herausgegeben, übersetzt und kommentiert von Bernhard Sowinski. Helfant Texte, T 9 (Stuttgart: helfant edition, 1988), 476–77.

[224]   Sowinski, Heinrich Wittenwiler, *"Der Ring"*, 477.

"Lamparter sein weis genuog.
Die von Franchreich sunder chluog,
Teutscher man ist auch gelert;
Dar umb sei in die er beschert:
Was der priol von Florentz
Und der amman von Costentz,
Von Pareis der haubtman
Sprechent, daz sei alz getan!'                    (7695–702)

['The Lombards are smart enough,
Those from France are particularly clever,
The Germans are also learned;
therefore the following deserve the honor:
What the Prior of Florence
and the magistrate of Constance,
and the governor of Paris
say (recommend), that shall be accepted!']

Particularly the Constance magistrate is given extra space to formulate his theoretical concepts about how to give council to friends and foes and how to approach the request by the Lappenhausen peasants in a most pragmatic manner.[225] He emphasizes, for instance:

Ze schirmen sein wir alle gpunden
Einen cristan ze den stunden,
So man im vil unrecht tuot
An leib, an er als an dem guot;
Doch geschech das in der mass,
Daz man allermänchleich lass
Ungeschlagen und -gestochen:
Won daz würd an uns gerochen,
Ob der so geschlagen man
Wär eins andern undertan.                         (7781–90)

[We are all obligated to protect
a Christian at any time
when he suffers from injustice
to his body, his honor, and to his property.
This protection ought to be done in such a manner
that one stays away at all cost
from beating and stabbing him.

---

[225] Some scholars have tried to read a sarcastic, parodistic tone into Wittenwiler's description of this magistrate; see, for instance, Lutz, *Spiritualis fornicatio*, 212, but this would not do justice to the undisputably positive characterization of the *amman*; see Riha, *Die Forschung zu Heinrich Wittenwilers "Ring"*, 15 and 169.

That would be avenged against us,
if this beaten man
were the subject of another lord.]

After short further deliberations, the council of cities decides to accept this and the previous recommendations and to abstain from taking sides in this conflict among the peasants. Not surprisingly, the war-hungry people of Lappenhausen therefore turn to the neighboring villages where they find many strange fellows and obscure creatures willing to join them, though at the end everyone will be slain. By contrast, though not further discussed in the text, the cities stay out of the fight and continue to thrive and to prosper, a clear swipe at the foolish people living in the countryside, and a powerful, even if somewhat elusive, praise upon the intelligent and cultured burghers.

Searching for further evidence of the growing, if not central, significance of late-medieval and early-modern cities in public and private life, we could easily refer to the rich entertaining literature of short, hilarious tales, such as the *fabliaux*, *mæren*, *novelli*, and *fazetie*. Both Boccaccio and Chaucer, both Heinrich Kaufringer and the anonymous composer/s of the *Novellino* (also known as *Libro di novelle e di bel parlar gentile*), then the famous, also notorious, Poggio Bracciolini and Giovanni Straparola have, among many others, richly contributed to this genre and have amply drawn from their own experiences in urban settings. We can safely assume that their audiences were also constituted of city dwellers, that is, the urban intelligentsia that could fully enjoy the social parodies, witticism, and specific allusions to the intricacies and complexities of the compact living conditions within a city. Whereas traditional courtly literature (romance and love poetry) is commonly predicated on life at court, these short didactic and entertaining narratives are usually set in cities.[226]

One at first sight rather innocuous, yet still meaningful example would be the first tale of the second day in Boccaccio's *Decameron* where the setting is Treviso:

---

[226]  Robert J. Clements and Joseph Gibaldi, *Anatomy of the Novella: The European Tale Collection from Boccaccio and Chaucer to Cervantes* (New York: New York University Press, 1977); Klaus Grubmüller, *Die Ordnung, der Witz und das Chaos: Eine Geschichte der europäischen Novellistik im Mittelalter: Fablaiau – Märe – Novelle* (Tübingen: Niemeyer, 2006). Concerning Boccaccio, he observes that a majority of his narratives take place in cities such as Genoa (I 8 and II 9), Bologna (I 10, VII 7, X 4), Treviso (II, 1), Naples (II, 5, III 6, VI 2, et al.), Pistoia (III, 5), Venice (IV, 2), Brescia (III, 6), Salerno (IV, 10), Rome (V 3 and X 8), and so forth. Moreover, Boccaccio has also set his eyes on major cities outside of Italy, such as London, Bruges, Paris, and Alexandria (272–73). For a brief introduction into the genre of German *mæren* and the related late-medieval narratives, see *Erotic Tales of Medieval Germany*. Selected and trans. Albrecht Classen; with a contribution by Maurice Sprague; and with an edition of Froben Christoph von Zimmern's "Der enttäuschte Liebhaber." Medieval & Renaissance Texts & Studies, 328 (Tempe: Arizona Center for Medieval and Renaissance Studies, 2007).

Era, non è ancora lungo tempo passato, un tedesco a Trivigi chiamato Arrigo, il quale, povero uomo essendo, di portare pesi a prezzo serviva chi il richiedeva; e, con questo, uomo di santissima vita e di buona era tenuto da tutti. Per la qual cosa, o vero o non vero che si fosse, morendo egli adivenne, secondo che I trivigiani affermavano, che nell'ora della sua morte le campane della maggior chiesa di Trivigi tutte, senza essere da alcun tirate, cominciarono a sonare.[227]

[Not long ago there lived in Treviso a German named Arrigo. He was very poor, and hired himself out as a porter. But he was a man of most holy life and everyone thought him a good man. Whether this was so or not, the people of Treviso say that when he was dying the bells in the largest church of Treviso began to ring miraculously, untouched by human hand.[228]]

The information provided is not essential for the further plot development, except that it clearly signals where the events take place. However, as we can clearly perceive, the city always represents a dense urban space with crowds of people of all kinds of social classes, from the rich and mighty to the old and sick, with an intensive religious life embracing all, but also a place where individuals suffer from poverty and have to make a meager living by doing simple menial jobs.[229] In other words, Boccaccio's narrator sheds light on religious, sociological, economic, and urban-political aspects.[230]

Surprisingly, however, the rich corpus of fourteenth- and fifteenth-century illustrated Boccaccio manuscripts offers hardly any specific references to urban life and offers only tiny indications of urban settings.[231] Whereas here one person alone

---

[227] *Giovanni Boccaccio*, scelta a introduzione di Nino Borsellino. Cento Libri Per Mille Anni, ed. Walter Pedullà (Rome: Istituto Poligrafico e Zecca dello Stato, 1995), 322.

[228] Giovanni Boccaccio, *The Decameron*, trans. Richard Aldington (1930; New York: Dell Publishing, 1970), 83. For an excellent analysis of many of Boccaccio's rhetorical strategies, see Marilyn Migiel, *A Rhetoric of the Decameron* (Toronto, Buffalo, and London: University of Toronto Press, 2003).

[229] Chiara Frugoni, *A Day in a Medieval City*, 69–80, offers good illustrations and draws from a variety of literary and historical documents.

[230] See, for instance, Mario Baratto, *Realtà e stile nel Decameron* (1970; Vicenza: Neri Pozza Editore, 1974); Vittore Branca, *Boccaccio: The Man and His Works*, trans. Richard Monges. Cotrans. and ed. Dennis J. McAuliffe. Foreword by Robert C. Clements (New York: New York University Press, 1976), 56–85; Francesco Bruni, *Boccaccio: L'invenzione della letteratura mezzana* (Bologna: Società editrice il Mulino, 1990).

[231] *Boccaccio visualizzato: Narrare per parole e per immagini fra Medioevo e Rinascimento*, a cura di Vittore Branca, vol. 3: *Opere d'arte d'origine francese, fiamminga, inglese, spagnola, tedesca* (Turin: Giulio Einaudi editore, 1999). There are commonly some city walls, individual houses, towers, interior settings, and palaces. But see the remarkable exception of an elongated street perspective drawing the viewer's gaze deep into the background: *De cas des nobles hommes et femmes*, Munich, Bayrische Staatsbibliothek, ms Gall. 6, from Paris or Tours, 1458, here 127, no. 185. Interestingly, the artist allows us first to look onto a scholar's study on the left where Boccaccio himself is seated at his desk writing his text, observed by all the figures in his narrative, before the eye turns toward the major scene in the foreground where the book is offered to Mainardo de' Cavalcanti, before the long line of houses making up the sides of a densely populated street with people walking and

attracts the attention of the entire city because of his alleged sanctity, many other contemporary accounts and chronicle reports underline the relevance of the religious life within the city in which the entire community participated. Beguines, for instance, to draw from a non-literary example, experienced both criticism and suspicion and also enjoyed great respect and authority because of their chaste (or not so chaste) life in their urban settlements.[232] But they created their own spaces within the urban world, withdrawing into their Beguinage, such as the one in Bruges. At the same time they intensively partook in the church life of the city, attending church masses, confessing, praying, participating in the regular performances and rituals, altogether creating a kind of "street mysticism," as Ulrike Wiethaus has called it regarding the Viennese Begune Agnes Blannbekin.[233]

Of course, with Boccaccio, a fourteenth-century Florentine, we would not expect much else, yet it still deserves to be emphasized how much he locates most of the events in his accounts in cities and largely favors the urban space as the ideal setting for the events that characterize his tales. Not that he focuses on cities for their own sake, but for him, as for many other authors of short narratives, the human interactions in cities provide enough of provocative and satirical material to achieve the goal of teaching and entertaining his audience at the same time, such as in the seventh tale of the third day where Emilia explains her choice of story with: "A me piace nella nostra città ritornare, donde alle due passate piacque di dipartirsi, e come un nostro cittadino la sua donna perduta racquistasse mostrarvi" (458; "It pleases me to return to our city, whereas the last two tale-

---

riding on horseback extend behind it. Whereas Branca characterizes the interior space as Italian, he believes that the street scene reflects French urban architecture (126, note to fol. 10r where the miniature is located). Another interesting example proves to be a miniature illuminating Boccaccio's *Teseida*, Vienna, Österreichische Nationalbibliothek, ms 2617, fol. 39r, from ca. 1457–1461 and 1470–1471, here no. 362. Although the city itself does not come into full focus, we observe urban space fully because the public in Athens throngs around a triumphal carriage transporting the protagonist Theseus and two ladies, while five grieving widows sit on the side. All the windows are filled with curious onlookers. The masses behind the carriage slowly disappear in the winding streets in the background.

[232]  Ernest W. McDonnell, *The Beguines and Beghards in Medieval Culture: With Special Emphasis on the Belgian Scene* (1954; New York: Octagon Books, 1969); Saskia Murk-Jansen, *Brides in the Desert: The Spirituality of the Beguines* (Maryknowll, NY: Oaks Books, 1998); Walter Simons, *Cities of Ladies: Beguine Communities in the Medieval Low Countries, 1200–1565*. The Middle Ages Series (Philadelphia: University of Pennsylvania Press, 2001); Helga Unger, *Die Begine: eine Geschichte von Aufbruch und Unterdrückung der Frau*. Herder Spektrum, 5643 (Freiburg i.Br.: Herder, 2005).

[233]  Ulrike Wiethaus, "Spatiality and the Sacred in Agnes Blannbekin's *Life and Revelations*," *Agnes Blannbekin, Viennese Beguine: Life and Revelations*, trans. from the Latin with Introd., Notes and Interpretive Essay by eadem. Library of Medieval Women (Cambridge: D. S. Brewer, 2002), 163–76; here 170. She is, of course, heavily obligated to Peter Dinzelbacher and Renate Vogeler, *Leben und Offenbarungen der Wiener Begine Agnes Blannbekin († 1315): Edition und Übersetzung*. Göppinger Arbeiten zur Germanistik, 419 (Göppingen: Kümmerle, 1994).

tellers were pleased to depart from it," 207). Not surprisingly, she has her account begin in Florence:

> Fu adunque in Firenze un nobile giovane il cui nome fu Tedaldo degli Elisei, il quale d'una donna, monna Ermellina, chiamata e moglie d'uno Aldobrandino Palermini, innamorato oltre misura per li suoi laudevoli costumi, meritò di godere del suo disiderio. (458)

> [In Florence there lived a noble young man, named Tedaldo degli Elisei, deeply in love with a lady named Monna Ermellina, the wife of Aldobrandino Palermini; and on account of his eminent virtues he fully deserved to enjoy his desires, 208]

But poets such as François Villon (1431–1463), who was deeply impacted by his life in Paris and deftly used it as the foil and background for his poetry,[234] deliberately did not shy away from drawing freely from the urban setting, but then in a very different, much more intimate, approach compared to that of Oswald von Wolkenstein:

> Item, I add on to the stick
> The house sign of Saint Antoine Street
> Or else a club for driving balls,
> And daily a potful from the Seine
> To those 'pigeons' who're badly off
> All locked up in the 'aviary,'
> My fine mirror, just what they need,
> And the smiles of the jailer's wife.[235]

As fragmentary as this impressionistic allusion might be, it certainly indicates the extent to which this poet lived in and with the city and its citizens, as is also nicely illustrated by a stanza in his *Le Testament*:

> Item, I give my barber, called
> Colin Galerne, who lives quite close
> To Angelot the herbalist,
> A big ice block (From where? The Marne),
> To spend the winter comfortably.
> Let him keep it near his stomach; then,
> So treating himself all winter long,
> Next summer he'll be warm enough.          (154)

---

[234] Albrecht Classen, "Villon, François," *Encyclopedia of Medieval Literature*, 663–65.
[235] François Villon, "The Legacy," stanza 29, or C23, quoted from François Villon, *Complete Poems*, ed. with English trans. and commentary by Barbara N. Sargent-Baur (Toronto, Buffalo, and London: University of Toronto Press, 1994). Because this is a bilingual edition, I refrain from copying the Old French original as well.

As Michael Camille commented: "Examples like this suggest that in thinking about the place that was the medieval city we have to enlarge our conception of public space to include this shared system of signs. . . . There was a taste in the fifteenth century for fantasies made up from street names and house signs . . . . the medieval city was peopled by signs . . . ."[236] As David A. Fein confirms, Villon differs remarkably from most of his French predecessors in his utilization of "more graphic imagery."[237] He goes so far as to underscore: "Filled with images of familiar individuals, sites, shared experiences, the *Testament* draws the intended reader into a poetic world in which he finds constant reflections of his own world."[238] Nevertheless, Villon does not paint completely realistic images of late-medieval life in the city; instead, as in the case of most other contemporary poets, he transformed the urban setting for his own purposes, both to entertain the audience and to reflect upon his own position within fifteenth-century society. Living within the urban context, however, also seems to have forced him to box his way through the throng, metaphorically speaking, as a fairly little recognized, often rather maligned, poet struggling to achieve public fame for his satirical verses.[239] But he was both a product of the city and also influenced the culture in the city with his poems, offering fascinating comments on the world he lived in, deftly reflecting on its kaleidoscopic nature.

We find confirmation for this observation not only in literary documents, but also in a wealth of late-medieval and early modern art, as I have noted already above. It might be important, however, also to consider the rich source of fifteenth- and sixteenth-century miniatures, such as those contained in Books of Hours—small-sized collections of texts, almost like psalters, but for private purposes, and usually richly illustrated—and countless other didactic, and religious manuscripts. The wealth of realistic details proves to be overwhelming, almost bursting out of the seams, or the frame, of the images. The range of specific details concerning people's lives, housing conditions, but then also street scenes,

---

[236]  Michael Camille, "Signs of the City: Place, Power, and Public Fantasy in Medieval Paris," *Medieval Practices of Space*, ed. Barbara A. Hanawalt and Michal Kobialka., 2000, 1–36; here 17.

[237]  David A. Fein, *François Villon and His Reader* (Detroit: Wayne State University Press, 1989), 29. See also id., *François Villon Revisited*. Twayne's World Authors Series, 864 (New York: Twayne Publishers; London, Mexico City, et al.: Prentice Hall International, 1997). See also John Fox, *The Poetry of Villon* (London, Edinburgh, et al.: Thomas Nelson and Sons, 1962), and David Mus, *La Poétique de François Villon* (Paris: Champ Vallon, 1967), for solid introductions to this poet.

[238]  Fein, *François Villon*, 41.

[239]  Jane H. M. Taylor, *The Poetry of François Villon: Text and Context*. Cambridge Studies in French (Cambridge: Cambridge University Press, 2001), 117–18; she specifically emphasizes: "As he invites us to look and feel via his perceiving consciousness, his urgent self, he makes indifference impossible . . . . Villon's passionate personal and ideological engagement—with an issue as seemingly anodyne as the relative merits of the city and the riverbank—is one of the most potent weapons in his poetic armoury" (138).

everyday life settings, palaces, markets, interiors of churches, bedrooms, construction sites, altarpieces, etc. seems inexhaustible.

Obviously, by the end of the Middle Ages artists all over Europe felt deeply fascinated by the new opportunities to explore the reality of their world, although they were still required to connect it with the spiritual dimension aimed for by the genre of the book of hours, among many others where the miniature assumed central position.[240] Space as a topic gained supreme importance, whether the open landscape, farmland, or the urban environment. As Maurits Smeyers observes, "People, objects, and nature were all represented in the greatest detail. The varied clothing was painted with all of its folds, clasps, buttons, and decorative elements. Miniaturists showed how all of the individual components of furniture and implements were fastened to one another and embellished, in addition to conveying the distinctive qualities of the materials. The interiors were minutely observed."[241]

## Urban Space, Social Conflicts, and the History of Emotions

At the same time, urban space became increasingly the critical setting for people's emotions to be acted out, performed, ritualized, and staged, both in the streets where the individuals actually interacted with each other, and, concomitantly, on the late-medieval stage where Shrovetide plays and many different religious plays (Christmas, Passion, Easter, etc.) provided a medium for communicating with the citizens regarding their religious values and morality.[242]

---

[240] Maurits Smeyers, *Flemish Miniatures from the 8th to the Mid–16th Century: The Medieval World on Parchment* (Leuven: Brepols, 1999), chapters VI–VIII.

[241] Smeyers, *Flemish Miniatures*, 422. See also Roger S. Wieck, *Painted Prayers: The Book of Hours in Medieval and Renaissance Art* (New York: George Braziller, 1997); Gregory Clark, *The Spitz Master: A Parisian Book of Hours*. Getty Museum Studies on Art (Los Angeles: J. Paul Getty Museum, 2003); *Libro de horas de Juana I de Castilla, Juana I de Castilla* (Barcelona: M. Moleiro, 2005); Albrecht Classen, "The Book of Hours in the Middle Ages," *Futhark: Revista de Investigación y Cultura* 2 (2007): 111–29.

[242] See the contributions by Valerie M. Wilhite (203–222), Eve-Marie Halba (223–42), Dirk Coigneau (243–56), and Stijn Bussels (257–69) in *Emotions in the Heart of the City*; Jody Enders, *The Medieval Theater of Cruelty: Rhetoric, Memory, Violence* (Ithaca and London: Cornell University Press, 1999); eadem, *Death by Drama and Other Medieval Urban Legends* (Chicago and London: University of Chicago Press, 2002); Mitchell B. Merback, *The Thief, the Cross and the Wheel: Pain and the Spectacle of Punishment in Medieval and Renaissance Europe* (Chicago and London: The University of Chicago Press, 1998); Johan Nowé, "Wir wellen haben ein spil": Zur Geschichte des Dramas im deutschen Mittelalter. Darstellung und Anthologie (Leuven and Amersfoort: Acco, 1997); Eckehard Simon, *Die Anfänge des weltlichen deutschen Schauspiels 1370–1530: Untersuchung und Dokumentation.* Münchener Texte und Untersuchungen zur deutschen Literatur des Mittelalters, 124 (Tübingen: Niemeyer, 2003).

All this was important because in the late fifteenth century urban life underwent, it seems, a fundamental paradigm shift, liberating it finally and definitively from the countryside as the main source of income. As Henri Lefebvre observes:

> The historical mediation between medieval (or feudal) space and the capitalist space which was to result from accumulation was located in urban space — the space of those 'urban systems' which established themselves during the transition. In this period the town separated from the countryside that it had long dominated and administered, exploited and protected. No absolute rift between the two occurred, however, and their unity, though riven with conflict, survived . . . . The urbanites located themselves by reference to the peasants, but in terms of a distantiation from them: there was therefore duality in unity, a perceived distance and a conceived unity.[243]

If we consider, for instance, the constant ridiculing of the peasant in late-medieval Shrovetide plays, as composed by the Nuremberg Mastersinger Hans Sachs (1494–1576), this observation gains strong support from literary history. But Sachs, like many of his contemporaries, did not simply make a fool of his peasant figures. In "Der farendt Schuler im Paradeiß," for instance (1550), both wife and husband prove to be ridiculous and ignorant, but not because they are peasants. They represent, basically, common people's lack of intelligence, discrimination, foresightedness, and smartness. The wife dislikes her second husband and grieves the loss of the first, who seems to have been much kinder and more generous than the second. When a student arrives and begs for food, he tries to impress her with the reference to Paris where he had studied until recently. She does not seem to know anything about Paris; instead she is only familiar with the term 'paradise,' which she now confuses with the actual city. Immediately she inquires about the well-being of her husband there and has to learn, to her great chagrin, that he is suffering from severe poverty and cannot even eat and drink to his satisfaction as everyone else. The peasant woman thus decides to utilize the ideal opportunity and gets clothing, food, and money from her hiding places, asking the student to take them to her deceased husband. The student is more than delighted with his good luck, takes everything and disappears as quickly as possible.

As soon as the second husband returns home, he learns from his wife what has happened, and realizes how badly she had been duped. Pretending to be worried that she might not have given the student enough money for her first husband, he rushes after the young man, who recognizes him early enough to hide all gifts. When the farmer arrives at the spot, he is so rash and impatient that he does not realize who is standing in front of him. Consequently, upon the student's advice he runs over a swampy field on foot, trying to catch the 'thief.' Foolishly, he had asked the student to hold the horse in the meantime because the ground of that field would be too soft. The young man chuckles over so much foolishness, and

---

[243]   Lefebvre, *The Production of Space*, 268–69.

then rides away, knowing full well that he has now cheated both the ignoramus wife and her husband. The peasant learns of this soon enough and harshly blames himself, but then he also begins to understand how stupid he has performed himself. Deeply embarrassed he refrains from blaming his wife and continues to play his previous role, hoping that all this will remain a secret. Unfortunately, however, his wife has already spread the word everywhere in the village, making both of them the public laughing stock. This provides the peasant with his final lesson because he perceives now that although married life is fraught with many difficulties, misunderstandings, and disagreements, mostly both partners have to be blamed for any conflicts and disagreements. Hence, a good marriage would be based on mutual respect, tolerance, and love, that is, above all, the ability to overlook failings, if they are not too egregious, and to accept the other with all his/her shortcomings as long as love bonds them together because the one who criticizes might easily prove to be just as foolish or ignorant as the other.[244]

Despite the rural setting, there is no doubt that Sachs intended this Shrovetide play for an urban audience but used a peasant couple as the major protagonists so as to avoid directly criticizing his urban audience. The basic message addresses the basic principles of happy marital life, and in this he specifically targeted married people in Nuremberg and other cities, wherever the play was performed, whereas it seems most unlikely that it ever might have reached a village audience.[245] Although Sachs projected the world of peasants, which was certainly easier to do than to present an urban, perhaps a merchant or patrician, couple fighting with each other, he had no intention, as all the context and common practice of the urban theater indicate, of dealing with the lives of peasants. After all, the critical point of his play targeted one of the most important aspects in the lives of burghers in the early-modern cities: marriage.[246] But for the playwright Sachs, the humorous lesson could be more easily conveyed to his audience if the point of criticism were not too direct. Laughing about silly people living in the countryside was highly common and regularly appealed to the urban audience, providing them with a strong sense of cultural superiority. Sachs's true literary strength, however, rested in his ability to project a substitute world, populated by farmers

---

[244] Cited from: Hans Sachs, *Meisterlieder, Spruchgedichte, Fastnachtspiele: Auswahl*. Eingeleitet und erläutert von Hartmut Kugler. Universal-Bibliothek, 18288 (Stuttgart: Reclam, 2003), 87–102.

[245] Albrecht Classen, "Women, Wives, and Marriage in the World of Hans Sachs," *Daphnis* 32, 3–4 (2003): 491–521.

[246] Albrecht Classen, "Love, Marriage, and Transgression in Medieval and Early Modern Literature: Discourse, Communication, and Social Interaction," *Discourse on Love, Marriage, and Transgression in Medieval and Early Modern Literature*, ed. Albrecht Classen. Medieval and Renaissance Texts and Studies, 278 (Tempe, AZ: Arizona Center for Medieval and Renaissance Studies, 2004 [appeared in 2005]), 1–42; id., *Der Liebes- und Ehediskurs vom hohen Mittelalter bis zum frühen 17. Jahrhundert*. Volksliedstudien, 5 (Münster, New York, Munich, and Berlin: Waxmann, 2005). See also my contribution to the present volume on Hans Sachs's urban encomia poems.

and their wives, which nevertheless intriguingly served as a poignant mirror of people's lives within the urban framework.

## Late-Medieval Development of Urban Space

Ultimately, then, in this context also following Lefebvre, the early modern town or city created its own identity and its own history, resulting in considerable conflicts with the royal and papal powers all over Europe. "Together with its territory, the Renaissance town perceived itself as a harmonious whole, as an organic mediation between earth and heaven."[247] This also had tremendous implications for urban planning and urban architecture because a systematic design and strategy increasingly determined the further development of urban growth: "The Renaissance town ceased to evolve 'after the fashion of a continuous narrative', adding one building after another, an extension to a street, or another square to those already in existence. From now on each building, each addition, was politically conceived; each innovation modified the whole, and each 'object'—as though it had hitherto been somehow external—came to affect the entire fabric."[248]

Remarkably, already in the late thirteenth century, apart from new cities that were strategically planned and built to serve specific military and political purposes, such as Aigues-Mortes in southern France (see above), many different cities in Tuscany,[249] or Kells in Ireland,[250] individual city administrators decided

---

[247]   Lefebvre, *The Production of Space*, 271.

[248]   Lefebvre, *The Production of Space*, 272; here Lefebvre relies strongly on Manfredo Tafuri, *Teorie e storia dell'architettura* (Rome and Bari: Laterza Figli, 1968); see also Chiara Frugoni, *A Distant City*; and *The Towns of Italy in the Later Middle Ages*; Oscar Schneider, *Nürnbergs grosse Zeit: reichsstädtische Renaissance, europäischer Humanismus* (Cadolzburg: Ars vivendi, 2000); Naomi Miller, *Mapping the City: the Language and Culture of Cartography in the Renaissance* (London and New York: Continuum, 2003); Patricia Fortini Brown, *Private Lives in Renaissance Venice: Art, Architecture, and the Family* (New Haven and London: Yale University Press, 2004); Manfredo Tafuri, *Interpreting the Renaissance: Princes, Cities, and Architects.* Harvard University Graduate School of Design Series (New Haven: Yale University Press; Cambridge, MA: In association with Harvard University Graduate School of Design, 2006).

[249]   David Friedman, *Florentine New Towns: Urban Design in the Late Middle Ages* (New York: Architectural History Foundation; Cambridge, MA: MIT Press, 1988).

[250]   Georges Zarnecki, *Art of the Medieval World*, 395; Georges Jehel, *Aigues-Mortes, un port pour un roi: les Capétiens et la Méditerranée* (Roanne Le Coteau: Horvath, 1985); Michel-Édouard Bellet and Patrick Florençon, *Die Festungsstadt Aigues-Mortes.* Itinéraires du patrimoine (Paris: Onum, Éd. du Patrimoine, 2001). For the degree to which medieval towns were actually planned, see Anngret Simms, "The Early Origins," *Urban Landscapes*, 1992, 30: "Kells is typical of other monastic sites which appear to have been designed in conformity with a planned arrangement, in which the round tower usually stands to the west of the church. The entrance to the enclosure was generally

to improve the condition of the streets, which obviously also involved the sewer system. As we know of some Italian cities, for instance, in "1290, it was decided to brick over all the streets of Siena because the side streets, which were unbricked, were spilling filth and mud into the thoroughfares, which were already 'paved'(with bricks, that is, not stones). In the portion of Lorenzetti's fresco *Il Buo Governo. Gli Effetti del Buon Governo in campagna* (Good Government. The Effects in the Countryside), we see wide and well-kept roads dividing fields and hills into a sinuous checkerboard, exactly the way the magistracy for the roads of Siena and the surrounding district prescribed that they should."[251]

In other words, modern assumptions that urban efforts to work toward the improvement of public streets, hygiene, and the sewer system did not begin before the eighteenth or nineteenth century have to be seriously questioned, considering that much depends on a city's size, the availability of flowing water, the planting of gardens, and the city's geographical location, and the percentage of people continuing with farming and gardening inside of the city walls.[252] How cities truly dealt with waste products, however, still escapes our full understanding, though we can be certain that this was regularly regarded as a problem that required public attention. In fact, the growth of cities throughout times created ever new difficulties and new solutions, so practical approaches pursued in, say, the eighteenth century, were certainly different than in the Middle Ages, yet the issue

---

located to the east and was marked by a special cross, a boundary cross, around which market functions developed." Other cities, such as Rostock on the Baltic Sea, developed only in stages and experienced a number of devastating setbacks throughout time (37–39).

[251] Chiara Frugoni, *A Day in a Medieval City*, 38; Duccio Balestracci and Gabriella Piccinni, *Siena nel Trecento: Assetto urbano e strutture edilizie* (Firenze: Clusf, 1977), 41; for further source material regarding the innovative urban renovation, see Zdekauer, *La vita pubblica dei Senesi nel Dugento* (Siena: I. Lazzeri, 1897), 104; see also W. Braunfels, *Mittelalterliche Stadtbaukunst in der Toskana* (Berlin: G. Mann, 1959); Cesare Brandi, *Pittura a Siena nel Trecento*, a cura di Michele Cordaro (Turin: Giulio Einaudi, 1991). Cf. Keith D. Llilley, "Mapping the Medieval City: Plan Analysis and Urban History," *Urban History* 27 (2000): 5–30.

[252] Citing L. Mumford (*The City in History* [1961; Harmondsworth, Middlesex: Penguin, 1992]), A. E. J. Morris, *History of Urban Form*, 100, emphasizes: "Sanitary conditions are closely related to density. Although medieval towns had only rudimentary refuse disposal arrangements and water supply was a continual problem—particularly in hill towns—it must not be assumed that disease was necessarily an everyday accompaniment to urban life." See also the contribution to the present volume by Britt C. L. Rothauser. Allison P. Coudert, also in this volume, argues differently, and her evidence is very solid as well, which indicates that here we are dealing with long-term problems in the development of medieval and early-modern cities that were not fully addressed or even solved perhaps until the late nineteenth and twentieth centuries. For the significance of water and hygiene throughout times in the various cultures, see *The Nature and Function of Water, Baths, Bathing and Hygiene from Antiquity through the Renaissance*, ed. Cynthia Kosso and Anne Scott. Technology and Change in History, 11 (Leiden and Boston: Brill, 2009).

remained the same.[253] But there are many other issues characterizing the early-modern city that continue to challenge modern historiography, which do not need to be discussed here in greater detail, though we have to be aware of the wider implications for the global approach taken in the present volume.[254] We must recognize, however, that altogether the medieval and early-modern city, here disregarding the myriad of differences, did not simply develop in a chaotic, irregular, and unsystematic fashion. Both town plans and distinct lay-outs of street patterns, neighborhoods, open spaces, etc. signal that many cities grew so well over time because their administrators or lords (bishops, princes, or the patriciate [i.e., the upper-ranking governing class]) had great interest in seeing to the promotion and furthering of urban development, and this even in the early Middle Ages.[255]

Satirical and ironic authors, such as Giovanni Boccaccio (*Decameron*), Franco Sacchetti (*Cento Novelle*), Poggio Bracciolini (*Facetie*), Hermen Bote (authorship still somewhat uncertain; *Till Eulenspiegel*), Hans Wilhelm Kirchhof (*Wendunmuth*), Martin Montanus (*Wegkürzer*), Michael Lindener (*Rastbuechlein* and *Katzipori*), and Marguerite de Navarre (*Heptaméron*), hence writers from all over Europe, describe in a number of their short prose narratives how people encounter conflicts and are thrown into the privies, fall into a sewer canal, or come into most unpleasant contact with human feces in other ways while operating in the city, aiming for a love affair or being victimized by cheaters and criminals. The same applies to the vast corpus of fourteenth- through fifteenth-centuries German short verse narratives, the *mæren*, perhaps best represented by Heinrich Kaufringer (ca. 1400).[256]

But the figure of Till Eulenspiegel demonstrates also how much a protagonist, who operates most cunningly within urban culture to pull everyone's leg, to reveal the underside of polite society, and to ridicule pretenses, hypocrisy, arrogance,

---

[253] See the contribution to this volume by Allison P. Coudert. For further details and images, see Jacob Blume, *Von Donnerbalken und innerer Einkehr: eine Klo-Kulturgeschichte* (Göttingen: Verlag Die Werkstatt, 2002); Daniel Furrer, *Wasserthron und Donnerbalken: eine kleine Kulturgeschichte des stillen Örtchens* (Darmstadt: Primus, 2004).

[254] Raymond Williams, *The Country and the City* (New York: Oxford University Press, 1973); Jan de Vries, *European Urbanisation, 1500–1800* (London: Methuen, 1984); Christopher R. Friedrichs, *The Early Modern City, 1450–1750. A History of Urban Society in Europe* (London: Longman, 1995); Alexander Francis Cowan, *Urban Europe 1500–1700* (London: Arnolds, 1998); David Nicholas, *The Later Medieval City, 1300–1500. A History of Urban Society in Europe* (London: Longman, 1997); *Country and the City: Wymondham, Norwich and Eaton in the 16th and 17th Centuries*, ed. John Wilson. Norfolk Record Society, 70 (Norfolk: Norfolk Record Society, 2006); Jaroslav Miller, *Urban Societies in East-Central Europe: 1500–1700*. Historical Urban Studies Series (Aldershot and Burlington, VT: Ashgate, 2007).

[255] Anngret Simms, "The Early Origins," *Urban Landscapes*, 1992.

[256] *Erotic Tales of Medieval Germany*. Selected and trans. Albrecht Classen, 2007.

false claims, and false pride, utilizes feces in many different situations, both creating general disgust and public laughter.[257]

Whereas medieval authors virtually never turn their attention to this topic, especially not when they allow the urban space to enter their discourse, which is rare enough, the situation had changed considerably by the sixteenth century. In Kirchhof's short jest narrative "Von einem studenten und bauren" ("Of a Student and a Peasant," *Wendunmuth*, 1563, vol. 1, no. 141) we hear of a student who has his apartment with a window toward the backyard in the city of Leipzig. The local farmers who regularly come to the market and sell their products, apparently do not have a chance to use any public toilets, which is especially difficult for them after they have drunk a beer or two in celebration of having made a good business deal and having paid off some of their debt to a rich merchant. They have, however, discovered that the backyard where the student happens to live provides the needed opportunity, which causes an intensive stench and badly bothers the student, who expressively voices his serious protest against their habit without bringing about any change in their behavior because they simply follow the call of nature and disregard his complaints.[258]

Finally the student hits upon a brilliant idea and uses animal blood which he shoots, by means of a contraption, onto one of them who is just about to do his business underneath his window. The poor fellow believes to have been fatally shot, regarding the massive amount of blood on his body, and he faints. His friends come to his rescue and take him to the doctor, who realizes, however, that there is only the old, well known hole, and no actual wound, as the narrator emphasizes. Realizing that the peasant is only a victim of the student's strategy, he laughs about the situation, does not charge his patient, and instead encourages him to return to drinking, since nothing else could be done (W 1, S. 172).[259] Altogether, the student is the winner in this case because the fooled peasants realize that the backyard can no longer be used as a toilet and avoid the location from then on.

Even though we cannot be certain whether the narrative indicates that urban authorities were seriously concerned with creating public toilets and building a sewer system, we know for sure that the humor in this tale is predicated on the

[257] Albrecht Classen, "*Till Eulenspiegel*: Laughter as the Ultimate Epistemological Vehicle in the Hands of Till Eulenspiegel," *Neophilologus* 92 (2008): 471–489; id., "Transgression and Laughter, the Scatological and the Epistemological: New Insights into the Pranks of Till Eulenspiegel," *Medievalia et Humanistica* 33 (2007): 41–61.
[258] For further examinations of how early-modern city dwellers perceived and how the authorities dealt with stench, see *The City and the Senses: Urban Culture since 1500*, ed. Alexander Cowan and Jill Steward. Historical Urban Studies (Aldershot, England, and Burlington, VT: Ashgate, 2007).
[259] Hans Wilhelm Kirchhof, *Wendunmuth*. Vol. 1, ed. Hermann Österley. Bibliothek des Litterarischen Vereins in Stuttgart, IC (1869; Hildesheim and New York: Olms, 1980).

realization that human feces is disgusting and must be taken care of hygienically. The satire is aimed at the peasants who have no access to toilets, which might indicate that the situation for urban dwellers, including the student, is very different. Without providing us with specific information about the availability of toilets in the city of Leipzig, Kirchhof still indicates clearly that the public was seriously concerned about it as he invited his audience to scoff at the ignorant and foolish peasants who simply use the backyard to relieve themselves.

Without going into further details, we can draw from this one narrative, and certainly many other examples, how much urban space truly occupied medieval and early modern mentality and also reflected specific aspects of urban culture.[260] A careful analysis of literary examples indicates how much information we can cull from literary and art-historical material regarding human interaction in medieval and early-modern city life, the relationship of people within an urban setting. Taking all the evidence together, we can be certain that the Roman city did not simply disappear, that the awareness of the significance of urban culture continued to dominate public opinion throughout the Middle Ages, that economic, political, and cultural life focused on cities from surprisingly early periods onwards and only continued to grow far into the early modern age and then until today. Undoubtedly, medieval culture is primarily concerned with the court, but an attentive reading of a wide variety of medieval narratives and paintings indicates that the city itself, despite a sometimes rather dramatic downturn after the end of the Roman Empire, flourished again and attracted most of the economic resources, cultural activities, and political power found in any given society, at least in western medieval and early-modern Europe.

## Urban Space from an Interdisciplinary Perspective

To do justice to this vast topic, we would have to draw from the wide range of disciplines in the humanities, including architecture, archeology, musicology, ethnology, anthropology, and history. The contributors to this volume can only represent some of the research areas because there are natural limitations in all such scholarly efforts. Nevertheless, the ideal of an interdisciplinary approach still

---

[260] There is a wealth of relevant research literature on this topic; see, for instance, Christopher R. Friedrich, *The Early Modern City, 1450–1750*. History of Urban Society in Europe (Harlow, England, London, New York, et al.: Longman, 1995); David Nicholas, *The Later Medieval City 1300–1500*. A History of Urban Society in Europe (London and New York: Longman, 1997); *Shaping Urban Identity in Late Medieval Europe*, ed. Marc Boone and Peter Stabel. Studies in Urban, Social, Economic and Political History of the Medieval and Early Modern Low Countries, 11 (Leuven-Appeldorn: Garant, 2000); *The Cambridge Urban History of Britain*. Vol. 1: *600–1540*, ed. D. M. Palliser (Cambridge: Cambridge University Press, 2000).

can be realized to some extent by having at least a group of medievalists and early-modernists from different faculties talk to each other. This goal was realized at the Fifth International Symposium on Medieval and Early Modern Studies at the University of Arizona, Tucson, May 2008. Not every contributor was able to participate in this volume, but the papers assembled here present a wide range of views regarding urban space and its relevance for poets, musical composers, artists, and chronologists.

There was no specific attempt to discuss 'the' medieval or early-modern city, neither in pragmatic nor in idealistic terms. Simply put, such a city has never existed. We can observe many parallels with and similarities between Spanish and English, French and Italian, Dutch and German cities, but at the end each urban space constitutes an entity fairly much on its own. People and ideas shape those spaces as much as social, economic, geological, climatic, political, and religious conditions. But within those spaces people interact with each other most intensively, and we might say that our understanding of everyday life in the Middle Ages and the early modern age is best viewed through the lens of urban space. Not exclusively, but certainly dominantly we can identify most clearly how people viewed childhood and old age, how the gender relationships developed, what value love, marriage, and sexuality enjoyed, how citizens responded to the Church, how Christians reacted to Jews,[261] how the private person regarded the members of the royal houses and other authority figures, what people thought about life and death, how they accumulated wealth, what entertainment and health care they looked out for, how they defended themselves, how they were clothed and what they did in their free time.

In fact, although medieval literature seems to be mostly determined by courtly ideals and values, this gave quickly way to new and yet old, that is, antique-Roman, concepts centered on urban living. Simply by default, whenever classical-ancient literature experienced its revival or reception in the post-Roman period, the focus turned toward urban space. Admittedly, the merchant did not appear

---

[261]   See, for example, Donatella Calabi, "The Jews and the City in the Mediterranean Area," *Mediterranean Urban Culture 1400–1700*, ed. Alexander Cowan, 56–68; *Convivencia: Jews, Muslims, and Christians in Medieval Spain*, ed. Vivian B. Mann, Thomas F. Glick, and Jerrilynn Denise Dodds (New York: G. Braziller in association with the Jewish Museum, 1992). See also the excellent studies on urban space and urban life in the late Middle Ages and the early modern world, and so also on the cohabitation of Jews and Christians, by Alfred Haverkamp, *Gemeinden, Gemeinschaften und Kommunikationsformen im hohen und späten Mittelalter: Festgabe zur Vollendung des 65. Lebensjahres*, ed. Friedhelm Burgard, Lukas Clemans and Michael Matheus (Trier: Kliomedia, 2002). Most important in this regard prove to be the research results by Elisheva Baumgarten, *Mothers and Children: Jewish Family Life in Medieval Europe*, trans. from the Hebrew. Jews, Christians, and Muslims from the Ancient to the Modern World (Princeton: Princeton University Press, 2004). See also Bernard Lewis, *Cultures in Conflict: Christians, Jews, and Muslims in the Age of Discovery* (New York: Oxford University Press, 1995).

early on the literary stage, but by the end of the Middle Ages he was a stable figure, especially since the world of the urban setting gained tremendously in importance.                                      As the rich corpus of letters (ca. 140,000), ledger books, account books, deeds of partnership, insurance policies and bills of lading, bills of exchange and cheques, either written by or addressed to the Prato merchant Francesco di Marco Datini (ca. 1335–1410) indicate, commerce was, already at that time, one of the most profitable businesses and brought in extraordinary wealth for those who knew how to practice their trade well. Merchants like Datini established a communication network all over Europe and beyond, by means of an intensive correspondence, and they also emerged, because of their wealth, as major art donors and patrons. Iris Origo characterizes him as follows:

> His life was not a serene one. 'Destiny has ordained', he wrote to his wife at the age of over sixty, 'that from the day of my birth I should never know a whole happy day.' The canker which ate all joy away, both in youth and old age, and which is revealed by almost every line of this correspondence, was anxiety. It is this, perhaps, that makes Datini seem so akin to us, so much the precursor of businessmen of our own time. He was an astute and successful merchant; but he was, above all, an uneasy man. Each of his was a constant source of anxiety: he mistrusted his partners, his managers, and the captains whose ships carried his merchandise; and he went in constant fear, too, of all the misfortunes that might overtake these ships—shipwreck, piracy, over-loading, or an outbreak of plague among the crew. And when his great fortune was made at last, fresh anxieties sprang up; he worried about his investments, his taxes, and his fines. He trusted his bailiffs and servants at home no better than those abroad. He lived in daily apprehension, according to Mazzei, of being defrauded, 'even of the shoe-buckle of the wench that serves your slave'.[262]

Moreover, the rich correspondence also sheds important light on Francesco Datini's marital life with Margherita with whom, unfortunately, he had no

---

[262]   Iris Origo, *The Merchant of Prato* (1957; London: The Folio Society, 1984), 6–7. In fact, merchants have left many testimonies about their trade, their lives, their contacts, and also about their personal relationships. For further examples of late-medieval merchants, see *Le lettere di Gilio de Amoruso, mercante marchigiano del primo Quattrocento*. Edizione, commento linguistico e glossario a cura di Andrea Bocchi. Beihefte zur Zeitschrift für Romanische Philologie, 237 (Tübingen: Niemeyer, 1991); Elisabeth Barile, Paula C. Clarke, and Girogia Nordio, *Cittadini veneziani del Quattrocento: I due giovanni Marcanova, il mercante e l'umanista*. Memorie. Classe di Scienze Morali, Lettere ed Arti, CXVII (Venice: Istituto Veneto di Scienze, Lettere ed Arti, 2006). For a Renaissance perspective, see F. Ruiz Martín, *Lettres marchandes échangées entre Florence et Medina del Campo*. École Pratqique des Hautes Études. — Vie Section Centre de Recherches Historiques. Affaires et Gens d'Affaires, XXVII (Paris: S. E. V. P. E. N., 1965). See also Gunther Hirschfelder, *Die Kölner Handelsbeziehungen im Spätmittelalter*. Veröffentlichungen des Kölnischen Stadtmuseums, X (Cologne: Kölnisches Stadtmuseum, 1994); Carolin Wirtz, *Köln und Venedig: Wirtschaftliche und kulturelle Beziehungen im 15. und 16. Jahrhundert*. Beihefte zum Archiv für Kulturgeschichte, 57 (Cologne, Weimar, and Vienna: Böhlau, 2006).

children, which ultimately caused much grief and unhappiness. In other words, the wealth of testimonies from the world of the merchant class allows us to gain deep insight into the everyday life of city dwellers.[263]

Globally speaking, all this does not mean that the court as a central administrative and cultural institution lost in importance; in fact, the opposite seems to have been the case at least since the sixteenth century in the wake of the massive territorialization process and the growth of the Renaissance and then the Baroque court.[264] But the city did not fall into the court's shadow; instead it experienced its own economic, political, and cultural development, as reflected in early-modern literature, music, and the visual arts.

But we would be wrong to pursue a polarity between the city and the court since the fifteenth and sixteenth centuries. Instead, as art history convincingly teaches us, both social worlds competed with and complemented each other. Princes continued to have their separate residences and palaces standing all by themselves in the countryside, but they also ventured into the cities where they established themselves increasingly since the late sixteenth century. As Thomas DaCosta Kaufmann comments, "Innovations in urban architecture were often either directly initiated by or else came in response to aristocrats. Residential towns came increasingly under the sway of their lords, who desired to control their commerce; the position of many of the castles rebuilt or constructed in this period, dominating the towns, expresses quite well the relationship."[265] Many times towns that had burnt down were rebuilt by the princes who then directed the architects to model the urban space according to their own needs for urban representation of the lord's power, such as the town of Zamość that was refounded by the *hetman* Jan Zamoyski, with a centralized plan according to an ideal model actually seldom realized even in Italy where this new model of the early-modern city had first been developed. In order to realize this plan, Zamoyski called in the Italian artist

---

[263]   Origo, *The Merchant of Prato*, 157–77.

[264]   *Princes, Patronage, and the Nobility: the Court at the Beginning of the Modern Age, c.1450–1650*, ed. Ronald G. Ash and Adolf M. Birke. Studies of the German Historical Institute, London (London: German Historical Institute; New York: Oxford University Press, 1991); *Ein zweigeteilter Ort: Hof und Stadt in der Frühen Neuzeit*, ed. Susanne Claudine Pils and Jan Paul Niederkorn. Forschungen und Beiträge zur Wiener Stadtgeschichte, 44 (Innsbruck: StudienVerlag, 2005); *Der Hof und die Stadt: Konfrontation, Koexistenz und Integration in Spätmittelalter und Früher Neuzeit: 9. Symposium der Residenzen-Kommission der Akademie der Wissenschaften zu Göttingen, veranstaltet in Zusammenarbeit mit der Historischen Kommission für Sachsen-Anhalt, dem Institut für Geschichte der Martin-Luther-Universität Halle-Wittenberg und dem Deutschen Historischen Institut Paris, Halle an der Saale, 25.–28. September 2004*, ed. Werner Paravicini and Jörg Wettlaufer. Residenzenforschung, 20 (Ostfildern: Thorbecke, 2006).

[265]   Thomas DaCosta Kaufmann, *Court, Cloister, and City: The Art and Culture of Central Europe, 1450–1800* (Chicago: The University of Chicago Press, 1995), 159.

Bernardo Morando from Padua who strove hard and successfully to design this new city as an earthly mirror of the divine universe, reflecting specifically on the lord's central power invested in him, as presumed, by God.

The other model of the early-modern city was the free city, only subject to the emperor or king, who often enjoyed demonstrating his power through a pompous entry into the city, accompanied by astounding art work, musical performances, drawings, poems, and the like, perhaps best represented by Charles V's entry into Nuremberg.[266] Here "the structures erected by townsmen can be seen as a response to a more general fashion, in which certain architectural elements become the desired mode."[267] However, both models could find expression combined in one building, such as the town hall of Poznań, Poland, reconstructed from 1557 to 1567 by the North-Italian architect Giovanni Battista Quadro of Lugano. On the one hand the building's overall design indicates the civic pride and independence-minded attitude of the citizens; on the other the crenellated parapet on the top evokes the image of an aristocratic urban palace. The formerly attached portraits of kings on the exterior expressed explicit opposition to the power of local lords and the desire to associate with the central government, which certainly provided the city with considerably more independence. Moreover, the numerous medallions show heads of wise men from antiquity, underscoring the civic pride that found its excellent expression in this Renaissance building with its three-storey loggia.[268]

In Germany, by contrast, many town halls were designed in the late-medieval Gothic style far into the sixteenth century, mostly influenced by Netherlandish architects, and this in areas mostly further to the north and away from the Italian influence, generally reflecting more patrician and burgher values and also the rise

---

[266] Albrecht Kircher, *Deutsche Kaiser in Nürnberg: Eine Studie zur Geschichte des öffentlichen Lebens der Reichsstadt Nürnberg von 1500–1612*. Freie Schriftenfolge der Gesellschaft für Familienforschung in Franken, 7 (Nuremberg: Die Egge, 1955); Roy C. Strong, *Art and Power: Renaissance Festivals, 1450–1650* (Berkeley and Los Angeles: University of California Press, 1984); Bonner Mitchell, *The Majesty of the State: Triumphal Progresses of Foreign Sovereigns in Renaissance Italy (1494–1600)*. Biblioteca dell' "Archivum Romanicum," 203 (Florence: Olschki, 1986); Klaus Tenfelde, "Adventus: Zur historischen Ikonologie des Festzugs," *Historische Zeitschrift* 235 (1982): 45–84; Arthur Groos, "The City as Text: The Entry of Charles V into Nuremberg (1541)," *The Construction of Textual Authority in German Literature of the Medieval and Early Modern Periods*, ed. James F. Poag and Claire Baldwin. University of North Carolina Studies in the Germanic Languages and Literatures, 123 (Chapel Hill and London: The University of North Carolina Press, 2001), 135–56.

[267] DaCosta Kaufmann, *Court, Cloister, and City*, 160.

[268] Teresa Jakimowicz, *Ratusz poznański* (Warsaw: Sport i Turystyka, 1979), 36; Teresa Jakimowicz, *Dzieje Poznania* [History of Poznań], ed. Jerzy Topolski, vol. 1 (Warsaw and Poznań: Pańnstwowe Wydawnictwo Naukow, 1988), 575–86; Jan Skuratowicz, *Ratusz poznański* (Poznań: Wydawnictwo Miejskie, 2003), 122.

in urban wealth, first observable in the Low Countries.[269] Most important, however, medieval city halls clearly expressed civic pride, the strong sense of a burgeoning independence, and a new emphasis on political urban identity.[270] Naturally, the architects had to fend with a variety of social, political, and economic interests, so the history of building designs north of the Alps does not necessarily tell us the full story about the early-modern city in its position as an independent entity or as a major pawn in the hand of a local lord or of the king because the same architectural style could serve for very different political purposes, unless we combine the study of specific designs with an examination of the concrete interests and motifs determining the patrons and other supporters, including the entire urban community.[271]

Carefully considered, urban space proves to be a most complex issue that cannot be analyzed simply from one perspective or in light of one disciplinary approach. Architectural history must be taken into account as much as art history, literary history, religious history, social-economic history, political history, and a smattering of other fields of investigation. The obvious reason for this consists of the simple fact that urban communities have always consisted of a conglomerate of different types of people with a variety of social, economic, intellectual, and religious backgrounds. The different ages had to live together as much as the two

---

[269] Peter Kurmann, "Late Gothic Architecture in France and the Netherlands," *The Art of Gothic: Architecture, Sculpture, Painting*, ed. Rolf Toman (Cologne: Könemann, 1998), 156–87; here 182–87, with beautiful full-page illustrations.

[270] Stephan Albrecht, *Das Bremer Rathaus im Zeichen städtischer Selbstdarstellung vor dem 30-jährigen Krieg*. Materialien zur Kunst- und Kulturgeschichte in Nord- und Westdeutschland, 7 (Marburg: Jonas, 1993); id., *Mittelalterliche Rathäuser in Deutschland: Architektur und Funktion* (Darmstadt: Wissenschaftliche Buchgesellschaft, 2004). See also Kristine Greßhöner, "Rathausbau im späten Mittelalter: Repräsentation und Raumbedarf – Forschungsüberblick und Bibliographie," *Mediaevistik* 23, forthcoming.

[271] DaCosta Kaufmann, *Court, Cloister, and City*, 160–65. He provides many examples and shows how the competing architectural models influenced or complemented each other. He shies away, however, from drawing specific conclusions as to a city's political and economic position within its historical and geographical context. Architecture represents, after all, people's lives, ideas, emotions, and political interest. To examine the history of architecture allows us to reach a deep understanding of urban space, that is, space of people's culture and how they perceived their social, religious, and cultural environment. After all, the arrangement of specific buildings, of urban spaces (markets, parks, etc.), the building of a city wall, the erection of a city hall, and of other public buildings, not to speak of aristocratic and patrician residences, and the establishment of specific quarters for the various guilds, parishes, and also religious communities (Jewish ghettos), deeply influenced people's attitudes toward urban space as the framework of the social and religious community.

Figure 2: Poznań City Hall

genders, and collaboration, even on the most mundane level, was of prime importance for everyone involved. In fact, the differences between the aristocracy and the leading bourgeois families, at least since the late Middle Ages, were not as dramatic as we might think today.[272]

As we have seen above, the history of urban life can be beautifully employed to gain a deeper understanding of the paradigm shift from the late Roman Empire to the early Middle Ages, and so also of the paradigm shift from the early to the high, then late Middle Ages, and, considering the next major step, from the late Middle Ages to the Renaissance and the age of the Reformation. Of course, urban history will always face the danger of remaining fragmentary because just too many factors are involved in shaping the lives of the many individuals within a city. This very shortcoming, however, also proves to be one of the greatest advantages in focusing thematically on urban space because here we grasp both the lives of ordinary people and of the social and economic elite. Outsiders, such as wandering scholars and landed gentry—a curious but certainly not inappropriate coupling of these two groups—viewed the city with awe and disrespect, with admiration and fear, with jealousy and anger.

Poets expressed their sentiments about cities as much as musicians and painters did. Chroniclers such as Hartmann Schedel indicated their great pride in their home city, and craftsmen poets such as Hans Sachs went so far as to project their identity in light of the urban space. Italian and Spanish merchants emerged as major representatives of their own urban communities, and so also medical doctors, international trades people, architects, composers, and scholars. After all, already in the Middle Ages, but above all since the fifteenth and sixteenth centuries the city had turned into the crucible of culture in the widest sense of the word, although, concomitantly, aristocratic courts outside of urban centers also emerged as crucial centers of political power and cultural developments.

Hartmann Schedel's famous world chronicle, his *Liber chronicarum*, indeed nicely illustrates the supreme importance of the chronicle for our topic, urban space in the premodern world. This chronicle, known under its full title as *Liber chronicarum cum figuris et ymaginibus ab inicio mundi*, was printed on July 12, 1493, by the highly respected and extraordinarily successful Anton Koberger in Nuremberg, probably the most productive and esteemed book printer and seller in all of Germany, and hence in late-medieval Europe.[273] A German translation followed on December 23,

---

[272]  See the contribution to this volume by Jan Hirschbiegel and Gabriel Zeilinger.

[273]  Here I am relying on the facsimile edition: *The Nuremberg Chronicle: A Facsimile of Hartmann Schedel's Buch der Chroniken: Printed by Anton Koberger in 1493* (New York: Landmark Press, 1979); see also Elisabeth Rücker, *Hartmann Schdels Weltchronik: Das größte Buchunternehmen der Dürer-Zeit. Mit einem Katalog der Städteansichten* (Munich: Prestel, 1988). Now see also Hartmann Schedel, *Weltchronik: Nachdruck [der] kolorierten Gesamtausgabe von 1493*. Einleitung und Kommentar von

1493. The chronicle contains altogether 1,809 woodcuts from 645 woodblocks and thus was, at its time, the one printed book in the entire world with the most illustrations.[274] The drawings were created by Michael Wolgemut, Albrecht Dürer's teacher, and his son-in-law, Wilhelm Pleydenwurff. The Nuremberg bankers and merchants Sebald Schreyer and his brother-in-law Sebastian Kammermeister funded the entire project, which had actually originated as early as 1471, so it took more than two decades to reach its completion.

Schedel was in close contact with many Nuremberg humanists to assist him in special details, such as the famous medical doctor Hieronymus Münzer, who helped him, based on his own travel experiences, to create a two-page map of Germany and to cover, for the purpose of a chronicle, the most recent events on the Iberian Peninsula, where Münzer had traveled between 1494 and 1495, focusing mostly on the individual Spanish and Portuguese cities and offering, as one of the first, always global views over the entire urban space perceived from an elevated point, such as church towers.[275]

Indeed, the global paradigm shift found powerful expression in Germany (but also in other parts of Europe) where increasingly the imperial power faded in its influence, giving way to growing territorial princes and also mighty and independent cities for which chronicles gained a new significance as a medium to reflect the individual concerns, disadvantaging universal history.[276]

Most interestingly, Schedel paid great attention to cities and offered detailed descriptions. Thirty-two of the urban vedute are apparently done based on personal observations. Most important, on leaf 100 the author included the cityscape of Nuremberg, a triumphant visual encomium on this imperial city, the

---

[274] Stephan Füssel (Augsburg: Weltbild, 2004). For a completely digitized version of the chronicle, see http://www.obrasraras.usp.br/; and http://mdz1.bib-bvb.de/~mdz/kurzauswahl.html?url=http://mdz1.bib-bvb.de/cocoon/bsbink/Exemplar_S-199,1.html (both last accessed on Sept. 29, 2008).

[275] *Europäische Reiseberichte des späten Mittelalters: Eine analytische Bibliographie*, ed. Werner Paravicini. Part 1: *Deutsche Reiseberichte*, ed. Christian Halm. 2nd, revised and expanded ed. with an appendix. Kieler Werkstücke. Reihe D: Beiträge zur europäischen Geschichte des späten Mittelalters, 5 (1993; Frankfurt a. M., Berlin, et al.: Peter Lang, 2001); Albrecht Classen, "Die Iberische Halbinsel aus der Sicht eines humanistischen Nürnberger Gelehrten Hieronymus Münzer: *Itinerarium Hispanicum* (1494–1495)," *Mitteilungen des Instituts für Österreichische Geschichtsforschung* 111, 3–4 (2003): 317–40; id., "Südwesteuropäische Grenzüberschreitungen aus deutscher Perspektive: Fremdbegegnung zwischen deutschsprachigen Reisenden und der iberischen Welt im Spätmittelalter," *Mitteilungen des Instituts für Österreichische Geschichtsforschung* 116, 1–2 (2008): 34–47.

[276] Leopold Hellmuth, "Geschichtsepik und Reimchronistik," *Von der Handschrift zum Buchdruck: Spätmittelalter, Reformation, Humanismus: 1320–1572*, ed. Ingrid Bennewitz and Ulrich Müller. Deutsche Literatur: Eine Sozialgeschichte, 2 (Reinbek bei Hamburg: Rowohlt, 1991), 140–48; here 146–47.

center of German economic power, craftsmanship, and the arts.[277] (fig. 9) Some of
the churches are identified by name, and we can more or less trust the artist for
having portrayed the city in a rather realistic manner, showing us the double wall,
the city gates, bridges, and, most outstandingly, the castle towering above the city.
But the humanist perspective finds its reflection here as well since the eye is
invited to wander into the far distance, to linger on hills with some buildings, then
to move back to the river flowing around the city, and to some building
constructions outside, such as the paper mill, then to the gallows, and fences as
part of the forward defense system. In this regard Schedel was not at all the only
one to perceive his world in different terms, as contemporary vernacular and Latin
literature that focused heavily on city encomia indicates, but his richly illustrated
chronicle provides some of the most impressive evidence for the fundamental
paradigm shift that affected views of urban space.[278]

In fifteenth- and sixteenth-century Germany and Italy new wealth was
accumulated, and the early-modern banking industry can be traced to the late-
medieval cities, especially in Lombardia/Italy, but also in Flanders, England, and
Southern Germany. Not surprisingly, this also led to considerable criticism and
opposition by those social groups that could not participate in this new economy.

> The enmity which the middle class earned from the practice of changing and lending
> money—inevitably in what was rapidly becoming an international credit-based
> economy—can be best understood by their most common caricatures, Avarice and
> Usury . . . . Whereas previously transactions tended to be based either on barter or on
> faith—the direct exchange of goods in kind or the promise of such an exchange—now
> the faith exchange was replaced by money.[279]

The hatred that had often developed over the abuse of the common man at the
hand of priests and monks who hoarded considerable wealth and used it to their
advantage against impoverished farmers or those in sudden need because of crop
failure, etc., now turned against merchants and bankers.[280]
    Concomitantly, the new wealth produced in the cities also facilitated enormous
architectural programs, lavish decorations with sculptures and frescoes, making
life in the city incredibly attractive, even if the public display of power and wealth

---

[277] Klaus Arnold, "Bilder und Texte: Stadtbeschreibung und Städtelob bei Hartmann Schedel," *Acta Conventus Neo-Latini Hafniensis*, ed. Rhoda Schnur et al. (Binghampton, NY: Medieval & Renaissance Texts & Studies, 1994), 121–32.
[278] Hartmut Kugler, *Die Vorstellung der Stadt in der Literatur des deutschen Mittelalters*. Münchener Texte und Untersuchungen zur deutschen Literatur des Mittelalters, 88 (Munich: Artemis, 1986), 103, 105, 164, 179–80.
[279] Alick McLean, "Medieval Cities," *The Art of Gothic*, 262–65; here 262.
[280] See also the contribution to this volume by Fabian Alfie.

often represented more aspiration than reality.[281] The common goal was to compete with, to adapt to, and to adopt noble values, aristocratic status, and political rank comparable to that of the landed gentry. Of course, much depended on the origin of a city, whether from a Roman settlement/city or from a bishop's seat, from a simple trading post or from a harbor, which had tremendous implications for the respective architecture, political and economic structure, and social-cultural conditions, making it rather difficult to compare medieval and early-modern cities according to a roster of just a few categories.[282]

Concomitantly, some of the wealthiest bankers, or usurers, such as Enrico Scrovegni in Padua, hired the best artists and architects of their time, such as Giotto, to create private chapels for the use of their families only where the iconographic program provided visual aids for confession and contrition on part of the usurer. Of course, this famous Scrovegni Chapel also allowed him to display his extraordinary wealth and power that had made it possible for him to hire such a famous artist as Giotto and Giovanni Pisano to decorate the interior space. But as he stated in his own document regarding the endowment of the chapel, it was built, to draw from Anna Derbes's and Mark Sandona's words, for the glory of the Virgin and the city of Padua, and for the salvation of his own soul and those of his predecessors. More specifically, in Enrico's own words, found in his last will, composed only a few months before his death in 1336, the chapel was to serve as his burial site. Most revealingly, the usurer commands that "all of my ill-gotten gains . . . ought to be restored and paid with any expenses incurred at the time, to all petitioners without any lawsuit, controversy, trial, condition, or pact."[283]

We know that the question regarding the proper government of a city, whether by a bishop, a secular lord, or by the urban patriciate and the guilds became a topic of great intensity in the late Middle Ages and the early-modern age.[284] The sixteenth-century jest prose writer Hans Wilhelm Kirchhof confirms this through his narrative "Dreyerley herrschafft in einer statt" contained in his collection of

---

[281] McLean, "Medieval Cities," 263: "the medieval bourgeoisie invested considerable amounts of money in developing alternative ways of representing themselves. Their story is inscribed in their urban architecture just as much as in their literature, portraits, and family houses. The streets, squares, and buildings of the emerging medieval middle class are not, however, just records of their success, but rather expressions of their aspirations . . . . Instead, they aspired to being either noble or holy, generally both."
[282] McLean, "Medieval Cities," 264–65.
[283] Anne Derbes and Mark Sandona, *The Usurer's Heart: Giotto, Enrico Scrovegni, and the Arena Chapel in Padua* (University Park: The Pennsylvania State University Press, 2008), 35–36.
[284] Heike Bierschwale and Jacqueline van Leeuwen, *Wie man eine Stadt regieren soll*, 2005, provide a solid overview of the didactic literature treating this topic from German and Dutch cities in the Middle Ages and the early modern age (until the early sixteenth century).

prose jest narratives, *Wendunmuth* (1561). In a bishopric town a burgher and a foreigner debate the question of what would be the best government for the urban community. For the burgher there is no alternative but to recognize and acknowledge the bishop out of a deep sense of tradition and loyalty: "wie von alters her und noch" (118). But the foreigner points out that the countless evils and sexual deprivations of the entire clergy, including the bishop, would make the latter unfit to serve as ruler over a city. Although he also recognizes the unchanging nature of the present political structure ("de jure et de facto," 118), he warns his opponent of the dangers for all women in the city who are regularly exposed to erotic temptations to sleep with the priests and monks. This would open all floodgates for the devil to enter the civic community and to destroy its ethical and moral foundation (ibid.).[285]

Kirchhof does not pursue this topic further in this short narrative, but this one tale alone with its insightful debate, despite its primary focus on the traditional anti-clerical sentiment, clearly indicates how much even within ordinary discussions or in satirical narratives the issue could surface as to which was the most appropriate form of urban government in the sixteenth century.

Although we tend to identify the emergence of urban space with the rise of the Renaissance, and this certainly for many good reasons, we can also draw extensively from medieval sources which examine the city and its specific culture and social framework in order to gain important insights into the mental history of that world. Significantly, the focus on urban space allows for very rich investigations taking us from late antiquity through the Middle Ages and then far into the early modern age. Differences are clearly noticeable, and yet there are also many remarkable similarities and commonalities among the plethora of premodern cities. Tracing the development of a city from its earliest foundation to its expansion and steady, if not explosive, growth in the seventeenth and eighteenth centuries would facilitate the projection of a far-reaching and profound cultural history, combining the physical world of the city architecture and the public spaces with the images of urban space as projected by writers, painters, sculptures, carvers, and also composers.

But such a project really requires the collaboration of many scholars from different disciplines, as indicated above. Critics will probably, and rightly so, point out, however, that this goal has been achieved only partially because the exploration of the city in premodern times would require many more perspectives than even this collection of articles could assemble. Architectural historians,

---

[285] Hans Wilhelm Kirchhof, *Wendunmuth*, Vol. II, 2/3. Ed. Hermann Oesterley. Bibliothek des litterarischen Vereins in Stuttgart, XCVI (1869; Hildesheim and New York: Georg Olms, 1980), No. 74, 118–19.

musicologists, religious scholars, and others have not joined us. Still, the breadth of perspectives included here promises to provide us with a solid range of concepts regarding the meaning of urban space. And I also hope that this introduction has covered much ground of scholarship in many different disciplines. Recently, Maryanna Kowaleski edited an excellent textbook dedicated to *Medieval Towns*, which contains, as Ben R. McRee comments, a wealth of material that illustrates the daily lives and concerns of medieval urban people."[286] But, as McRee also observes, there is "not much in the collection that deals with urban topography or the uses of urban space." Hopefully, the present volume will address this desideratum more comprehensively and extensively, focusing on mental-historical aspects, modes of perception, social and economic conditions, and on the interaction of various social groups within the urban community.

Following I will offer brief summaries of the individual contributions to this volume, which will be, as I hope, a fitting addition to our book series "Fundamentals of Medieval and Early Modern Culture."


Whereas most medieval city descriptions take pains to focus both on the architecture and the living culture, that is, the people, in the case of Rome the situation tended to be remarkably different. C. David Benson explores how medieval English descriptions of Rome (both in English and Latin) seem to perceive only a city of ruins and relics, reflecting a glorious past. In his paper he uses, after having outlined the textual history of the major branches of Rome descriptions, as his critical sources particularly a verse account of Rome inserted in the *Metrical Version of Mandeville's Travels* and the Augustinian friar John Capgrave's *Solace of Pilgrims*, composed shortly after his return from Rome in 1450, along with a handful of other important travel reports, such as the one by Master Gregorius.

Instead of providing information about church services, processions, the church structure in contemporary Rome, the medieval authors prefer to ruminate on the history of the churches in Rome and their supreme importance for the pilgrim in the present, and on the ruins from classical times. This is the more surprising considering that most other city encomia emphasize the current population, the economy, and politics, hence present the city in its present stage as a community and actual conviviality. Although occasionally there are references to Roman senators, or to inhabitants in Rome who told the narrator something about the history of the city, the focus predominantly rests on the ruins, hence on the empty, hollowed out urban center of the Roman empire. The interest is directed at the

---

[286] *Medieval Towns: A Reader*, ed. Maryanne Kowaleski (Peterborough, Ontario: Broadview Press, 2006), review by Ben R. McRee in *The Medieval Review* 09.01.09.

ashes and sarcophagi of former emperors and at sculptures and monuments dedicated to the dead who suffered their fate for their Christian faith.

Roman glory in its physical manifestation, however, often finds critical commentators who condemn major public buildings, such as the Colosseum, as pagan temples, clearly in ignorance of the true purpose of those monumental buildings. The authors explicitly voiced their desire to see such un-Christian architecture destroyed and removed, particularly because they appeared to be too attractive and alluring, distracting the Rome visitors from the true purposes of their journey, attending church, seeking indulgence, and asking for absolution from their sins.

At the other end of the discourse about Rome we find Master Gregorius who in his *Narracio de Mirabilibus Urbis Romae* (late twelfth or early thirteenth century) extols the beauty and brilliance of the ancient statues and buildings. However, the majority of voices leaned the other way and highlighted the experience of death in that city, that is, on the one hand, the death of Christian martyrs and saints, and of the mighty and powerful in the past on the other. This historical perspective, almost by default, depopulates Rome within the medieval narratives and gives absolute preference to the significance of Rome serving as the site of remembrance and memory. Hence the great emphasis in these narratives on the relics and bodies of martyrs, which might well be characteristic, as Benson observes, not of travelogues or encomia intended as guides for the actual traveler or pilgrim; but instead of religious reading material for those who stay behind—religious armchair readers, if you like.[287]

In other words, the English encomia on Rome did not simply ignore people's lives, but chose primarily to talk, first, about martyrs, hence about those who had died in Rome for their faith and whose relics could provide new, spiritual life to the faithful visitors to the ancient city, granting indulgences and pardons, hence paving the way to the readers' salvation. Curiously, the number of years promised by the individual churches and sites of worship quickly reached inflationary dimensions, but this typified the common, late-medieval interest in Rome as one of the holiest pilgrimage centers, next to Jerusalem and Santiago de Compostela. Second, they also focused on antiquity that had survived only in its ruins.

Even though the descriptions of Rome are mostly void of comments about contemporary life there, they allow the past to speak through numerous stories

---

[287] This is very much the same case in the German pilgrimage account written by Felix Fabri for a female audience, after he had published an actual travelogue in Latin, see his *Die Sionpilger*, ed. Wieland Carls. Texte des späten Mittelalters und der frühen Neuzeit, 39 (Berlin: Schmidt, 1999); see Albrecht Classen, "Imaginary Experience of the Divine: Felix Fabri's *Sionspilger* Late-Medieval Pilgrimage Literature as a Window into Religious Mentality," *Studies in Spirituality* 15 (2005): 109–28. Now see also Suzanne Yeager, *Jerusalem in Medieval Narratives*. Cambridge Studies in Medieval Literature (Cambridge: Cambridge University Press, 2008).

told about individual buildings or sculptures that commemorate a martyr or a saint. They particularly refer to churches that commemorate a martyr or saint, or, much more commonly, to churches that owned a relic, even if they were not named for it. By the same token, the ancient sculptures and monuments were of interest as well because they were dedicated to pagan figures from ancient Rome.

The less these medieval writers reflect upon contemporary life in Rome, the more they allow the past life, that of the Christian role models in late antiquity, to surface in their texts who promise, so to speak, new, spiritual life. For them, dead Rome is the foundation for a new Rome, the future, heavenly Jerusalem.

Whereas medieval theologians and preachers commonly referred to the concept of the City of God as conceived of by St. Augustine, we must not overlook, as Kisha Tracy reminds us, of the considerable significance of medieval cities as the location where death occurred and death was celebrated as the crucial transitory stage to the afterlife. Cemeteries were moved out of cities only by the late Middle Ages, hence the presence of death was deeply felt and even celebrated in medieval life. In fact, it enjoyed a pervasive role. Tombs of deceased secular rulers or bishops, heads of households, and other influential personalities dotted the urban landscape, both within the precincts of the churches and convents, but also elsewhere on sacred ground. There was a specific architecture for the dead, and the dead continued to influence urban life for decades and even centuries.

Medieval poets explicitly reflected upon this phenomenon, emphasizing, for instance, the importance of individual rulers as founders of cities, such as in Layamon's chronicle, in the early thirteenth-century *Brut*, and in the mid-twelfth-century Old French *Roman d'Enéas*. The death and burial of an admired person could lead to the naming of the city after him or her, which finds most vivid expression in the discussion of how London got its name, according to Layamon. The kings' resting places are situated on elevated locations, making them visible to all as constant reminders of the past heroes and their actions, benefitting the city, similar to epitaphs dedicated to the dead.[288] As Tracy comments with regard to the burial of Camille in the Old French *Roman*, the deceased queen continues to protect the city by means of a mirror placed on top of her tomb.

The literary accounts find remarkable confirmation in actual medieval architecture and funeral art, allowing the surviving family members and the larger urban community to commemorate the dead and to draw spiritual strength from the deceased founders and rulers. All this clearly signals an awareness of the

---

[288] A similar approach can be observed in the almost timeless narrative of *Apollonius of Tyre*, see Albrecht Classen, "Reading and Deciphering in *Apollonius of Tyre* and the *Historia von den sieben weisen Meistern*: Medieval Epistemology within a Literary Context," *Studi Medievali* 49 (2008): 161–88.

intimate correlation between death and life within medieval mentality, particularly within the urban setting.[289] But urban societies also experienced a troublesome disruption in the family traditions because of people's constant migration from the countryside to the city. The wealthier citizens therefore turned to the priests and paid for masses to be read for the dead, creating a whole religious memorial business, upon which William Langland comments rather sardonically in his *Piers Plowman* (B-text), criticizing priests for seeking positions in cities because of the much higher income there resulting from the funeral services and the countless ramifications, all leading to specific income for the clerics.

Intriguingly, as Tracy outlines as well, the importance of the dead in their past life could strongly contribute to a city's political, military, and economic stance, as illustrated by the conditions of eleventh-century Cambrai or early-medieval Venice, both heavily drawing from long-dead founding bishops or saints in order to gain public reputation and importance in direct confrontation with neighboring cities (such as Aquileia).

In her study, Tracy illustrates this phenomenon particularly with regard to late fourteenth-century Middle English poem *Saint Erkenwald* where the discovery of the bones of the early-medieval bishop saint underneath St. Paul's provided significant impetus for the city in the fourteenth century to regard itself as divinely blessed and as the capital of the entire country. More specifically, rulers of medieval cities deliberately utilized the cult of the dead, the memory of the past, and the reappearance of the remains of saints and other virtuous people who had died in the very early history of those cities for the aggrandizement of the respective urban community, powerfully interlacing the past with the present and the future, underscoring the relevance of the dead for the survival and prospering of a city far into the future.

Since late antiquity, Jerusalem has been a linchpin in the global relationship among Christians, Jews, and Muslims. As a holy city, Jerusalem has been central and iconic for Western and Eastern cultures and religions, so it does not come as a surprise that many wars have been fought over it; but sadly major world conflicts continue to focus on this city for more or less the same reasons. Even though the Western Christians lost in their 'bid' for the Holy Land with the fall of the last fortress, Acre, in 1291, European fantasies and desires continued to focus on

---

[289]   Peter Dinzelbacher, *Europa im Hochmittelalter 1050–1250: Eine Kultur- und Mentalitätsgeschichte.* Kultur und Mentalität (Darmstadt: Primus, 2003), 96–99; ibid., "Eschatology," *Handbook of Medieval Studies,* ed. Albrecht Classen (Berlin and New York: de Gruyter, forthcoming). See also the contributions on "Sterben/Tod" to *Europäische Mentalitätsgeschichte: Hauptthemen in Einzeldarstellungen,* ed. Peter Dinzelbacher. Kröners Taschenausgabe, 469 (1993; Stuttgart: Kröner, 2008), 265–313 (antiquity: Christian Böhme; Middle Ages: Peter Dinzelbacher; early modern age: Karl Vocelka).

Jerusalem, above all, and for centuries beyond that specific date. This finds an impressive reflection in the continuous stream of pilgrims and tourists who went to Palestine throughout time, many of whom composed a variety of travelogues.[290]

But we can never forget the crucial period of the early Crusades as a critical moment in history when the future destiny of Jerusalem was deeply shaped by the religious-military conflict, which has lasted until today, both because Christian knights conquered it in 1099, and then because the Muslims, under the leadership of Saladin, recaptured it in 1187, and this, of course, to the great chagrin of the European Christians.

Although modern fantasies of medieval chivalry and knighthood convey a beautiful image of an impressive age long gone, the brutal reality of medieval warfare was quite different, as Alan V. Murray demonstrates in his insightful, detail-oriented, and rather painful study on how the respective conquering armies dealt with the civil population.[291] Every army has to rely, if it wants to be effective and successful in achieving its goals, on the best possible logistics for supplies and people, and on solidifying its conquests and fortifications as quickly as possible. But the crusaders were only a small and rather amorphous force compared with the fairly large Muslim and Jewish population in Jerusalem and elsewhere in the Holy Land in 1099, not to mention the large hostile military forces threatening them.

When the Arabs under 'Umar had reconquered Jerusalem in 638 C.E., they forced most of the surviving Christian intelligentsia to leave the city. Nevertheless, this was not at all comparable to what happened in 1099, when the crusaders found themselves in a difficult situation as a small military entity facing a large non-Christian population. There is no doubt that the crusaders immediately began with massive slaughter within the city, carrying out what we would call today 'ethnic cleansing.' The surviving Christian sources clearly signal that this massacre was explained away through references to relevant passages in the Bible, notably

---

[290]  Christian Halm, *Deutsche Reiseberichte*. Europäische Reiseberichte des späten Mittelalters, 1. Kieler Werkstücke. Reihe D: Beiträge zur europäischen Geschichte des späten Mittelalters, 5 (Frankfurt a. M., Berlin, et al.: Peter Lang, 2001); Suzanne M. Yeager, *Jerusalem in Medieval Narrative*. Cambridge Studies in Medieval Literature (Cambridge: Cambridge University Press, 2008). For the crusades, see Christopher Tyerman, *God's War: A New History of the Crusades* (Cambridge, MA: Belknap Press of Harvard University Press, 2006); for a modern political-historical perspective, see Dore Gold, *The Fight for Jerusalem: Radical Islam, the West, and the Future of the Holy City* (Washington, DC: Regnery Publ., 2007).
[291]  For a general introduction and critical analysis, see Maurice Hugh Keen, *Medieval Warfare: A History* (Oxford and New York: Oxford University Press, 1999); see also the contributions to *Violence in Medieval Courtly Literature: A Casebook*, ed. Albrecht Classen. Routledge Medieval Casebooks (New York and London: Routledge, 2004). Further, see Jonathan Riley-Smith, *The Crusades: A History*. 2nd ed. (1987; London and New York: Continuum, 2005); Helen J. Nicholson, *Medieval Warfare: Theory and Practice of War in Europe, 1300–1500* (Houndmills, Basingstoke, Hampshire, and New York: Palgrave Macmillan, 2004).

the *Apocalypse*. Nevertheless, in simple terms, the crusaders slaughtered hundreds and quite possibly thousands of people in order to get rid of a potentially dangerous non-Christian population.

Murray alerts us, however, to the complexity of the concrete situation in Jerusalem after the conquest, which was by no means stable and unequivocal for the crusaders who chose to settle there. Having conquered a major city with a solidly hostile population it does not come as a shock that the first major steps taken were directed at the dangerous Muslims, civil and military. To secure Jerusalem against hostile elements both within and outside of the city represented a major challenge, which helps us to understand—though it certainly does not excuse the situation—the most violent treatment of the civil population.

It took decades until the Christian rulers decided to let Syrian Christians to settle in the city, which underscores the problematic nature of population control in the case of such a disputed city. They also expelled Greek Orthodox clerics and established numerous Catholic churches to meet their own religious demands. But many areas or quarters in the city continued to be unoccupied for decades, as a direct result of the crusaders' massacre immediately after their conquest.

By contrast, when Saladin took control of Jerusalem in 1187, he pursued a rather different strategy, expelling instead of slaughtering the major portion of the Western Christian population. There was a considerable risk that a huge number of Muslim prisoners held captive inside the city might be slaughtered in response to an attack, and Saladin obviously believed that it would be more effective to allow the Frankish population to pay for its freedom than to slaughter it. Not only did this provide him with a huge profit and free the city of enemy population, but it also swelled up the few remaining Christian-held cities with a civilian population that would make them more difficult to defend against the Muslims.

Saladin encouraged Muslims to settle in Jerusalem, and allowed Jews and eastern Christians to return because these people helped him to gain economic profit. But the entire Frankish population was removed, transforming Jerusalem from an exclusively Christian, and largely Western city, into a totally Eastern city of plural faiths. All this strongly suggests that in the battle for this place sacred to three religions, the removal or, in the thinking of the crusaders, the elimination of an enemy population was regarded as a necessity. The Muslim approach was, however, much more complex, but we also have to keep in mind that Saladin and other Islamic rulers enjoyed much better logistic conditions and could afford to pursue more flexible approaches.

Murray's focus on Jerusalem dramatically illuminates the military significance of cities in the Middle Ages, the dangers the civil population often faced in wars, and also how rulers believed that manipulation of the different social and religious groups that inhabited them were an essential tool in the establishment of their regimes.

We can gain a good understanding of the basic character and essence of a city and its social structure within its historical context when we pursue many different approaches, which is the primary purpose of this volume. One of them concerns legal conditions and the work of notaries, the topic of Andreas Meyer's contribution to this volume. From early on notaries played a significant role in late-medieval Italian cities, because they were highly instrumental in helping people handling inheritances issues and property transfer. Meyer underscores the significant change of keeping records by the notaries since the twelfth century in Northern Italy when notaries began to keep centralized registers on the basis of which individual documents could be created for specific legal purposes. This ultimately reduced the costs for everyone involved considerably. Basically, the notary became an archivist for his entire neighborhood and thus helped the urban community to have much better and easier control over the relevant documents pertaining to property or legal matters. At the same time, the registers that the notaries actually owned became a good and long-term source of income for him and his family. Only by the fifteenth century did city administrators force the notaries to hand over their registers to public archives, which truly centralized the entire legal process and record keeping.

In this long-term process notary registers were increasingly collected by fewer and fewer notaries who mostly inherited them from deceased colleagues. This often meant, however, that when one of these archives was destroyed or damaged the loss of documents was highly dramatic for an entire neighborhood. The contemporaries already realized the subsequent grave dangers for the entire community and the legal system, trying their best to counteract numerous risk factors, but mostly to no avail. A notable exception to the rule was the case of Genoa where the city organized from early on in the fourteenth century centralized communal depots for the notary registers. Nevertheless, the repeated attempts to enforce this policy to collect all registers there and the possibility for notaries related to those who had deceased to fetch the registers and to store them at home again signals how difficult it was, despite the best efforts, to upkeep and maintain the centralization process. At the same time, the Genoese vaults contained numerous other types of legal documents, often private in nature, so by the end of the fifteenth century they were privatized altogether.

Tragically for modern historians, since the fourteenth century many of the registers and documents of private nature from earlier periods were sold as wrapping material or for other purposes, and large contingents are simply lost to us today for very mundane reasons. However, there were also major space problems, and since older registers had considerable less value for the contemporaries, it is not surprising that a large quantity of them disappeared and made room for new ones since the legal process continued continuously.

Although Meyer's investigation focuses on a specialized textual genre, it powerfully illustrates the degree to which internal legal structures had a tremendous impact on the growth and development of towns and cities in northern Italy since the thirteenth century, and, by analogy, probably in other parts of Europe, where Roman Law was to be effective, as well.

Many of the major cities in antiquity and the Middle Ages were founded and settled near waterways, the most important means of transportation of large goods and a crucial source of drinking water. When medieval poets reflect upon urban space, they commonly also discuss the rivers or the coast nearby as major characteristic markers for the urban identity formation.[292] Larger bodies of water served at least three fundamental purposes in the relevant urban encomia or descriptions of cities in medieval literature, as Britt C. L. Rothauser outlines in her contribution to this volume: 1) as a defining element; 2) a protective barrier; and 3) as a cleansing agent. But water was also an important source of energy in industrial production or craftsmanship, which she touches on only in passing.

Whereas the historical significance of water for urban development in the Middle Ages and beyond has been commented on already in previous research focused on urban history, Rothauser investigates how various Middle English poets perceived the physical, the real city and its environment, regularly separated from the countryside through water, beginning with Fitz Stephen's twelfth-century *Descriptio nobilissimæ civitatis Londoniæ*. For him, the countryside was of no particular relevance, mostly depopulated and serving only for providing the necessary nourishment of the city. Nevertheless, by way of discussing the Thames, Fitz Stephens clearly indicates the demarcation of the city's parameters, and also signals the crucial venues for the burghers to do commerce internationally, and also to enjoy free time in gardens outside of the city.

In remarkable contrast, the fourteenth-century anonymous poet of the allegorical *Pearl* poem identifies the river as the defining boundary that separates the New Jerusalem from the earthly realm, thereby granting waterways a much more powerful significance in keeping the Christian, here the dreamer, outside of the holy city until the Day of Judgment — and this in important parallel to the river Styx that separates the netherworld from the earthly existence, such as in Dante's *Divina Commedia*, and then, of course, also in classical-antique literature. Whereas in Fitz Stephan's Latin encomium the water of the river Thames is also used for keeping the city clean, the *Pearl* poet specifies the function of the heavenly river as one to represent the divine will, or God's civilization, as reflected by the paving of the riverbed and the embankment, an architectural achievement only possible, it seems, by the Lord Himself. But it also indicates how much late-medieval people

---

[292] Now see the contributions to *The Nature and Function of Water, Baths, Bathing, and Hygiene from Antiquity through the Renaissance,* ed. Cynthia Kosso and Anne Scott, 2009.

desired to improve the living conditions in their cities and imagined urban space
where even the riverbed is paved with gems as a reflection of the heavenly, ideal
city.[293]

Turning to John Gower's *Vox Clamantis* and his *Mirour de l'Omme*, however,
Rothauser identifies a very different perspective on rivers and other waterways
because Gower projects them as potentially highly dangerous and threatening to
the well-being of the city. For Gower, the river served as a metaphor of the
relationship between city and country insofar as the Peasants' Revolt in 1381
brought much devastation and misery to the city. According to the poet, the
swelling of the river and subsequent flooding of urban space represent the unruly
peasant class that requires control and channeling at the hand of the urban, hence
also royal government. As long as the countryside fulfilled its function to produce
food for the city, the social hierarchy was stable and harmonious, but the city still
needed walls to protect itself against the dangerous riotous peasants or,
metaphorically speaking, the rising river.

Rothauser then turns to the question how much rivers could really protect a
city, and whether they might not have constituted additional dangers to the
defenders, as Gower also expresses in his texts, whereas for the *Pearl* poet the
situation was radically different because of the religious function of the waterway,
which, together with the city wall, fully kept all besiegers out of the holy place.
This also finds confirmation in the fourteenth-century alliterative *Legend of Saint
Erkenwald* where a lake substitutes for a river but achieves the same constructive
goal.

Finally, the author examines the cleansing function of the river Thames, as
clearly outlined, for instance, in the *Letter-Book A* of 1275, or in John Lydgate's
description of New Troy in his *Troy Book*, written in 1420. The ability to harness the
natural flow of the river to sweep away all detritus and debris from the city
represents, as these late-medieval writers emphasize, a high level of civilization
and urban architecture, otherwise rarely seen or described.[294] The cleanliness of a
city could become a symbol of the cleanliness of the human soul inhabiting such
a divine city. Nevertheless, by outlining this aspect, Gower, for instance, also
indicates the constant liability of losing this degree of virtue because vice was
powerful enough to seep into every corner or crevice, and hence also into the
fissures of the soul, to stay in the image (*Vox Clamantis*). As Rothauser reminds us,
of course, the metaphors of water, its flow, of baptism, and cleansing of dirty
streets served powerfully for allegorical interpretations as well. As much as the

---

[293]   See the contribution to this volume by Allison P. Coudert. After all, serious complaints about dirty
        city streets and places and the lack of functioning sewer systems were continuously voiced
        throughout the centuries.
[294]   A remarkable exception proves to be the anonymous twelfth- and early thirteenth-century
        goliardic Middle High German epic *Herzog Ernst*, see above in the early part of my Introduction.

earthly city could reflect the heavenly city, the New Jerusalem, so rivers, waterways, and water at large could symbolize the tension between virtues and vices in a Christian, but also very dangerous world where the social hierarchy was not an absolute guarantee.

Urban space means, of course, not only building and physical extensions, but very much also living space, hence people and their interaction with each other. One of the most burning questions concerning this aspect pertains to the cohabitation of Christians and Jews in the Middle Ages and beyond. Birgit Wiedl offers penetrating perspectives regarding this situation mostly in Austrian cities, investigating concrete historical and art-historical documents which often shed a different light on the issue than what the specific laws and rules by both the Church and the secular authorities stipulated. In fact, on the level of everyday-life activities, there were numerous contacts, and in many cities both groups cooperated in a variety of ways, which Wiedl's careful investigation demonstrates convincingly. Particularly complaints by the Church on several occasions against the violation of its rules against such contacts indicate how much Jews and Christians actually lived together as neighbors, and not as religious enemies, despite much public polemic to the contrary. Interior house decorations (wall paintings) or book illustrations commissioned by Jewish owners indicate the extent to which both groups shared the same cultural values and enjoyed the same aesthetic ideals.

Nevertheless, Jews experienced a variety of legal conditions in medieval Austria, with the regional rulers continuing for a long time to hold power over the Jewish communities, even though city governments regularly tried to wrest that privilege from them. The rulers were even so powerful that only they could grant the right to erect any public building for the Jewish community, such as a synagogue in the individual cities. For a long time Christians lived as much among, or next to, the Jews as the latter lived among Christians, and we have plenty of evidence that both groups provided service to each other against payment, including women acting as wet-nurses. Under certain circumstances the synagogue could also function as the site for legal proceedings involving Jews and (!) Christians. In the judicial world we also encounter many Jews who served as witnesses and arbiters, and Jews could turn to a Christian judge appointed for their own concerns, both signaling an astonishing degree of mutual acceptance and collaboration particularly within the urban space of late-medieval cities small and large.

The many protests, particularly raised by the Church, against these common practices prove the point of intense exchange in late-medieval Austrian cities, at least until the thirteenth century. However, once the city governments gained new independence from regional or territorial rulers, they tried hard to utilize their legal rights to control the Jewish population, to impose new taxes, but also to integrate them more in the urban defense system. Interestingly, Wiedl provides even evidence that Jews were entitled to get a share of the public markets, though they were not allowed to assume public offices.

A real conflict emerged when Jews were also involved in the crafts and competed with their Christian neighbors, such as in the area of butchering and selling meat. Soon enough, they and their meat were maligned or excluded from the public spaces, a convenient strategy to come to terms with this problem from the perspective of the majority. This, in turn, created the basis for religious arguments to emerge, quickly leading to blood libel and accusations of alleged host wafer desecrations, the latter of which make up the majority of accusations raised against Austrian Jews. Despite the overwhelming evidence of intense exchanges and even cohabitation of both religious groups far into the early fourteenth century, by the end of the next century expulsions and banning of Jews also from Austrian cities became the norm for a wide variety of reasons. Most significantly, however, as Wiedl concludes, we would badly misconstrue the medieval and late-medieval history of Christian-Jewish contacts if we perceived them only through the lens of the crusade mentality with its subsequent persecution obsession directed against the Jewish population who, after all, contributed significantly to the country's history. Of course, Austria was not a safe haven for Jews, particularly not in the late Middle Ages, but there were strong traditions of remarkable forms of cohabitation and cooperation especially within urban communities.

Whereas Wiedl discusses the issue of cohabitation of Jews and Christians in late-medieval Austria, Rosa Alvarez Perez investigates the same topic with regard to contemporary France. There, however, the situation was rather more dangerous and ultimately catastrophic because the Jews were repeatedly expelled, for the last and final time in 1394. Nevertheless, the focus on urban space invites a more careful and detailed investigation because it was here where actual contacts took place and where the representatives of the two religions encountered each other. Perez concentrates on northern French Jewish communities because there conflicts gained in intensity only later, and relatively peaceful coexistence seems to have been more pronounced in earlier times (especially from the ninth to the eleventh century). Whereas other scholars have already discussed the larger issues at stake, here the role of Jewish women gains a new profile, particularly because they appear to have exercised some degree of agency within their communities and society at large.

During the high Middle Ages, urbanization in northern France, similarly to many other areas north of the Alps, experienced dramatic growth rates, which also led to a significant increase of the Jewish population in the cities where many economic opportunities awaited them. We can measure this, for instance, by means of the number of Rabbinic schools. Ironically, royal decrees soon enough forbade Jews to live in rural areas and small towns, forcing them instead to settle in the larger urban centers, perhaps in order to control them better and to gain more financial profits because they were the 'king's servants.' Similarly as in other parts of Europe, however, soon enough Jews functioned as catalysts for general sentiments of fear and insecurity.

As Perez discovers, despite numerous decrees targeting Jews, forcing them to live in specific areas and wearing particular badges (especially since the Fourth Lateran Council in 1215), in many cases Jews still enjoyed some freedom to settle in various parts of a city and could easily interact with their Christian neighbors. Nevertheless, the ghettoizing process took place everywhere as well, forcing Jews to live in cramped, often unhealthy spaces, whereas Christians had more of a chance to expand. One of the difficulties the Jewish populations faced was the constantly shifting political climate, with some rulers pursuing a very hostile policy, at times culminating in expulsions, while others allowed them to return to their previous urban settlements, such as in Paris, though they had then to content themselves with non-central locations there. To be sure, economic and political reasons often played a much bigger role in the expulsions than religious convictions.

Although Jews were generally banned from traditional crafts, some still could pursue that kind of work for internal needs, as surviving records with specific names indicate. But money-lending (and usury) was, as everywhere else in medieval Europe, a privilege for Jews, and here we even come across a number of Jewish women who were also active in this field. In fact, as research has demonstrated, female money lenders were much more common than previously assumed, but they focused on smaller amounts and relied on pledges as guarantees instead on costly notaries. But Perez also observes that the close proximity of these two religious and economic communities in late-medieval northern French cities tended to lead to violence on a small scale, even involving a significant number of women, as legal court documents inform us.

As the many examples adduced by Perez indicate, despite these constant conflicts, Jews and Christians collaborated in many instances, and there are more reports of erotic relationships among them than expected, as the repeated legal stipulations and law cases confirm. Albeit the Church expressed abhorrence at the idea of Christians mingling sexually with Jews, the very fact that such statements exist confirms the existence of such affairs, and this even long after the official and final expulsion of all Jews from France in 1394. As we learn from various literary and legal documents, it appears that Jewish women were more loath to religious conversion than Jewish men, but this issue still requires further investigation. Moreover, Perez sheds light on Jewish representation in contemporary literature through a close reading of *Li Roumans de Berte aus Grans pies* (late thirteenth century), where many of the traditional stereotypes raised against Jews are fully represented.

Despite the severe problems and threats late-medieval French Jews had to suffer from, their existence in the northern urban centers was of significance for the entire population, as Perez can solidly confirm. We must be careful in our evaluation of the manuscript evidence because it tends to highlight the criminal, legal, and procedural aspects, and blinds us at times to the everyday-life experience of Jews and Christians living for a long time in surprisingly close proximity to each other.

One of the most famous image of urban space ever developed in the entire Middle Ages—at least in allegorical terms—(if not prior to it) was Augustine's (354–430 C.E.) concept of the Heavenly city in his *De civitate dei* (*City of God*). Only those Christians worthy to enter God's divine realm were guaranteed the salvation of their souls, whereas those who stayed behind and contented themselves with their existence in the earthly city could not even think of hope. But not everyone subscribed to Augustine's teaching regarding the vainness and uselessness of the worldly city in its metaphorical dimension. The late-medieval English mystic Julian Norwich (1342/1343–ca. 1416) pursued, as Jeanette Zissell argues, quite a different approach, drawing much inspiration from her mystical interpretation of the symbolic hazelnut. Julian perceived God's love to be so profuse that it also extended to the earthly city because it could not be contained only in the heavenly city. The former proves to be not much larger than a hazelnut, and yet it is entirely embraced by God's love. The heavenly city, however, the one Augustine had talked about, is located, according to Julian, within herself, in her heart. In specific contradistinction to the theological tradition, then, the mystic argues that God's salvific power extends to both cities and offers much more hope than the Church had assumed in the past. In other words, according to this English mystic, there is very good reason to be optimistic about the afterlife because even the material city, where people live in their human existence, can be redeemed.

Zissell suggests that Julian deliberately deviated from the Augustinian tradition, or rather, reinterpreted it in order to come to terms with the concept of global love extended by God to both cities within creation, the heavenly and the earthly. Whereas Augustine focused on how people love each other, which determines whether they can transition from the earthly to the heavenly dimension, Julian primarily looks at God's love for people, which implies that both dimensions are embraced by Him equally.

Augustine did not foresee universal salvation, as Origen (ca. 185–254 C.E.) had suggested, and instead projected a city for the select few. By contrast, Julian believed the opposite and argued that God's love is much larger than the Church Father could have imagined, allowing it to extend also to the material existence, the earthly city. Salvation, for Julian, was not limited to those who had been lucky enough to escape the dangers of this world, but it actually extended to the entire universe, or creation, because of God's unlimited love, which also includes the earthly city, as long as the individual inhabitant of this city proves to be a believer. In other words, God's love can already be experienced in human life, here within this urban space.

More specifically, the earthly city, the hazelnut, represents the human soul where God resides, in fact, and the heavenly city is the source of all divine love. In this sense, the metaphor of the city served Julian exceedingly well to describe in poetic terms the ethereal union of the human soul with the Godhead, which takes place within the mystic's, or any other person's, heart, a merging of both urban spaces because of the infinite power of God's love. As much as the believer's spiritual city is enclosed in his heart, the earthly city is enclosed in the believer's hand, as represented by the hazelnut. Although the earthly city does not guarantee spiritual protection and restfulness, but it clearly indicates, as Julian formulates it, the extent to which God's love of man and of the human world is present and assured for everyone who returns this love.

Zissell uncovers a significant epistemological-theological level of meaning in Julian's use of the hazelnut metaphor and demonstrates how much urban space, even within the mystical discourse, was of great metaphorical signification because it constituted the meeting space of the human soul with the Godhead. In this sense, as Zissell suggests, Julian could be identified as a follower of the ideas developed by Origen, in almost explicit opposition to Augustine. In our context, however, we can draw the important conclusion that urban space, here cast in the image of a hazelnut, emerged as a powerful metaphor for profound theological interpretations concerning human existence and the meaning of salvation.

Urban space in the Middle Ages was not simply limited by the city walls; instead the city's authority regularly extended far beyond, sometimes even to other cities, or whole regions. To what extent, however, could a city government bring to trial a person who had commissioned men to commit a crime in a different city? What constituted urban and legal authority, and what made up urban space in this context, especially when it was contested from the outside? To explore these complex issues, Patricia Turning investigates such a case in fourteenth-century Toulouse involving two men whose business relationship had gone sour, then had turned to legal means, though in vein. Finally the outsider resorted to hiring a band of assassins who were charged with disfiguring the opponent in his face. Significantly, this dangerous plot had been planned for months, and it was carried out in the vicinity of the city hall, deliberately provoking the city councilors to pursue legal actions. Turning employs recent space theory (Bordieu et al.) to illuminate how much urban space was actually territory in competition and the battle ground for various social groups both within and outside the city's boundaries. The attack on the lawyer in Toulouse was only one indicator of a much larger context concerning the true authority within a medieval city, as countless pageants, tournaments, processions, etc. also served to stake out areas of control exerted by individuals and special interest groups. Even public executions, with all their gory details of torture and slow dismemberment, also served, apart from its prosecutory intentions, the purpose of demonstrating urban authority and power within a clearly demarcated urban space. Nevertheless, there were everywhere competing jurisdictions, and worldly and ecclesiastic authorities jealously guarded their own domains within that limited space.

Significantly, throughout the Middle Ages, and so also in Toulouse, the city authorities had to negotiate on a regular basis with the ducal or royal powers the extent to which they could exert their own jurisdiction, hence could claim political, legal, and military independence.[295] The physical attack on the Toulouse lawyer Bernardus de Bosto was motivated, of course, by his opponent's desire for revenge, but it also expressed explicitly the defiance of an outsider who disregarded the honor of the urban community represented by this lawyer. His facial disfigurement was, metaphorically speaking, a slap in the face of the urban authorities. Hence, as Turning argues, the city had to endeavor massive public court proceedings and to bring the opponent, Stephanus Saletas, to trial. However, the authorities of his home city, Villamuro, balked at that idea, and the entire affair entered into a public struggle for dominance among these cities, quickly spilling into the neighboring space outside of the respective city walls. Ultimately, Saletas was handed over and thrown into prison, questioned, and tortured, but the sources do not reveal the outcome of the trial. Nevertheless, the entire case clearly indicates how much urban space and individual space could easily enter into competition, not to forget the many other forces involved, both on a smaller and a larger scale, which all indicates the true extent to which a medieval city was at the crossroads of numerous political, social, religious, and cultural groups and organizations.

As Jean E. Jost reminds us in her penetrating analysis of Chaucer's *The Knight's Tale*, space within a city constitutes more than just a physical entity; instead, it also provides identity for the individual protagonists. Some spaces are protective, others are perilous, and some are a mixture of both for the urban environment, as it had developed by the late Middle Ages, offered, as it still does today, a plethora of different possibilities for individuals to pursue their interests and to lead their ordinary lives. Chaucer, for instance, includes both Thebes and Athens where he has his characters operate on different stages, which powerfully allow the further development of the narrative, providing depth and distance, interior and exterior

---

[295]  See also the contribution to this volume by Lia B. Ross. The difficulties even for the most powerful cities came most clearly to the fore in the case of sixteenth-century Nuremberg, as the Mastersinger and cobbler poet Hans Sachs reflects in his urban encomia. See the contribution to this volume by Albrecht Classen.

sites. But even more interesting proves to be the liminal space of the city's edges where travelers arrive and depart, where major events take place, and where decisions are being made. After all, the *Canterbury Tales* are predicated on a pilgrimage, which traverses many different spaces, both rural and urban, hence the significance of the border areas as the major transition points. As Jost illustrates, Chaucer strategically operates with a multiplicity of spaces within the city and at its edges, and forces his protagonists to explore the various options in each one of them for their own purposes. Although the city is regularly surrounded by a wall, the interior space does not guarantee full protection, harmony, and happiness, as is the case in Athens in Chaucer's narrative, especially when Duke Theseus encounters the lamenting widows at the outskirts and gets off his horse, which blatantly blurs the social difference between them.

On another level, love blooms also at the city's edges because the male gaze can espy the lovely lady in the garden from a window in the prison tower. The orchard, which carries multiple symbolic meanings, specifically serves to promote the love story, made problematic by the physical and social barrier separating the two knights and their lady—they are prisoners, she is a princess. Architectural elements and ornamental designs strongly contribute to the narrative development of *The Knight's Tale*, injecting a discourse on vices and virtues represented in images and buildings. Even Theseus's palace proves to be a most important staging ground for the individual characters, and the narrator clearly signals how much space itself represents the critical framework for the key elements in Chaucer's text. In fact, there seems to be a city within the city, and the individual spaces begin to communicate with each other, no doubt, in a typically Chaucerian fashion.

The irony of *The Knight's Tale* proves to be, as Jost convincingly argues, the storyteller's great interest in limited space, especially urban, although he himself has traversed the entire known world in search of chivalric adventures. But the critical point might well be, as Jost concludes, that the narrative really focuses on interior spaces for the development of emotions and desires. Those spaces, however, clearly reflect also the exterior spaces within an urban environment. In other words, the Knight tells us his story with its great emphasis on the urban world because within the city and at its liminal edges the fundamental human conflicts find most powerful expressions. In this sense, as Chaucer perceives it, the city offered agonal space to live out interior tensions and feelings, and it was not necessarily exclusively a site of community and harmonious collaboration.

Curiously, the growing pains of late-medieval cities seem to have been quite similar to those that modern cities are going through under comparable circumstances. This was the case of Paris as much as London, the latter of which finds good reflection in a number of literary texts, such as Geoffrey Chaucer's *Canterbury Tales*. Even in some of his shortest tales, the poet took pains to allude to urban life and to utilize the social framework of the city in order to address specific social problems and concerns characteristic of late-medieval London. Daniel F. Pigg here examines the way how Chaucer reflects upon urban society and the tensions within the city as reflected in *The Cook's Tale*, where the central conflict concerns the relationship between a foot-loose apprentice, Perkyn Revelour, and the class of guildsmen. This young man served Chaucer exceedingly well to explore the meaning of masculinity within late-medieval urban society where traditional power structures easily collided with the interests of migrant workers from the countryside and especially the young generation (apprentices) who challenged the authority of the craftsmen and struggled hard to establish their own masculinity. In this regard the story itself, despite its external fragmentary character, proves to be basically complete because the fundamental message concerning the social conflicts predicated on the idea of masculinity, especially its formation process within the urban setting, is clearly formulated.

Pigg sets out with a global discussion of the rise of guilds as constitutive institutions in late-medieval cities that heavily relied on a strong regulation system for all its members, especially apprentices who were commonly kept under close control and had to submit under their master, almost substituting their own father. The guildsmen were most concerned with preventing their apprentices from having sexual relations and from marrying. In other words, the relationship between apprentice and master proved to be the central intersection where the male individual explored masculinity and tried to establish his own sexual identity.

The cook's position in late-medieval urban society proved to be rather unstable, easily subject to public ridicule and contempt, which makes the entire narrative framework even more problematical regarding the young man's quest for masculinity. Butchering and food preparation could easily carry strong political, ideological, and economic implications, as the study by Birgit Wiedl in this volume regarding the position of Jews in late-medieval Austrian cities demonstrates, considering their need to prepare their own meat according to specific religious rituals. Moreover, as Pigg now indicates, cooking also evoked strong sexual connotations, which powerfully reflects on the cook as narrator, who finds himself in a rather uncomfortable position vis-à-vis the host who, as an inn-keeper, naturally regarded cooks, if working independently, as strong competitors.

Curiously, the apprentice Perkyn in the *Cook's Tale* does not conform to the moral standards expected from young men like him, enjoying the city's night-life to the fullest, but not quite in the traditional male role. Instead, as Pigg observes, the narrator casts him almost in a feminized role, dancing and singing, performing as an entertainer himself, yet also as a thief taking money from his master. We might even identify Perkyn as a prostitute, or at least as a completely unproductive member of his society, which finally expels him, disgusted with his lack of masculinity and disregard for traditional *mores*.

Since he proves to be unproductive, the urban society, based on crafts and guilds, disassociates itself from this young man, which then also allows the narrator to break off his tale, whether this leaves the tale as a fragment or not. Insofar as the apprentice does not embrace masculinity as expected from him, and insofar as he disregards the traditional strictures of late-medieval urban society that heavily relied on production, service, and the crafts and guilds as the organizational framework, there is only one choice for the master but to let him go. As Pigg suggests, unproductive masculinity was simply not tolerated in medieval cities, which sheds important light on the deep-seated tensions and anxieties in late-fourteenth-century urban society, especially after the Black Death.

Contrary to common assumptions about urban women's roles in the late Middle Ages and in the early modern period, they were not, as a collective, simply forced to spend all their time within the domestic sphere of the house under the control of a husband, or a father, limited to their typical roles as daughters, mothers, wives, and widowers. We have already known for a long time that such generalizing concepts have more to do with ideological projections than with socio-historical reality that differ remarkably from each other from period to period, and from region to region. We cannot even claim any longer that the year 1500 was a clear watershed between a time in which urban women still enjoyed considerable freedom to participate in the city's public economic life, and then, after 1500, a time in which the economic crisis forcefully removed them from the public sphere into total domestic work and marginal, low-paying jobs since the guilds blocked most women from working as crafts persons. Certainly, there is strong evidence that women increasingly lost status and influence in the early-modern market economy, such as in Cologne after 1550 or so, and also in Ghent, but this was not tantamount to the establishment of an absolutely patriarchal system.[296] Nor do the deteriorating conditions for women in the sixteenth century

---

[296]     Martha C. Howell, *Women, Production, and Patriarchy in Late Medieval Cities*. Women in Culture and Society (Chicago and London: The University of Chicago Press, 1986); Heide Wunder, *"Er ist die Sonn', sie ist der Mond": Frauen in der Frühen Neuzeit* (Munich: Beck, 1992); Albrecht Classen, "Frauen als Buchdruckerinnen im deutschen Sprachraum des 16. und 17. Jahrhunderts," *Gutenberg-Jahrbuch* 75 (2000): 181–95; id., "Frauen im Buchdruckergewerbe des 17. Jahrhunderts. Fortsetzung einer spätmittelalterlichen Tradition und Widerlegung eines alten Mythos. Methodische Vorüberlegungen zur Erhellung der Rolle von Buchdruckerinnen," *Gutenberg-Jahrbuch* (2001): 220–36; see also the contributions to *Connecting Spheres: European Women in a Globalizing world, 1500 to the Present*, ed. Marilyn J. Boxer and Jean H. Quataert. 2nd ed. (1987; New York: Oxford University Press, 2000); Janine Marie Lanza, *From Wives to Widows in Early Modern Paris: Gender, Economy, and Law*. Women and Gender in the Early Modern World (Aldershot, England, and Burlington, VT: Ashgate, 2007); Rachel Leah Greenberg, "Transforming Women's Labor in Early Modern Literature: Sex, Gender, Class, Identity," Ph.D. diss. State University of New York at Buffalo, 2008.

simply allow us to draw analogies regarding the situation during the fourteenth or fifteenth centuries.

To probe this issue further, Shennan Hutton here investigates the situation for women in fourteenth-century Ghent where the extensive wool-cloth industry had brought many profits for the city and where some markets existed where women could carve out a rather significant niche for themselves. This did not mean the undermining of patriarchal rule, on the contrary, but all indicators point to a remarkably mixed situation, allowing women traders and even bankers to operate fairly freely and to their considerable advantage.

Focusing on Ghent, which was one of the most powerful, influential, and economically most prosperous cities in the northwestern part of Europe, Hutton's research promises to shed light on more global conditions for women within the wider network of wool traders who focused on high-end quality products.

One important observation presented here concerns the differences in roles and spaces occupied by men and women within the urban community. Nevertheless, women had middling positions even in some the most important markets and could pursue their own trading business there, though undoubtedly only on a smaller scale, and not in the whole-sale business which was, by specific city regulations, dominated by male representatives of the wealthiest families. Nevertheless, as Hutton underscores, they had a good chance in the middle position and energetically and effectively pursued their business there. Because of the smaller size of trade carried out by them, they did not really compete with the big cloth whole-sellers, hence they could occupy a female space, significant by itself, but not threatening to the male counterparts.

There is even concrete indication that many of the stalls held by women were passed on to other women over generations, supporting the observation that there were specific female spaces in the urban markets, whether these supported female status within the city or challenged male prerogatives. In other words, within urban society there were areas privileged for women, and others for men. Or, women could hold on to their own, even if they were not entitled to rise to the top level within the trading business of specific products.

The situation for women within the world of butchers, for instance, was very different because the male butchers had gained solid control over their profession and had excluded women from entering that field above all. In the corn market women fared even worse because there they were excluded entirely, both as merchants and as customers. If they dared to enter, they were regarded as prostitutes and fallen women, and they could not even think of opening their own stalls there. Women were also excluded from the group of hostellers who were poised to earn the largest profits from the international trade by offering room and board. This does not mean, however, that women were not employed there, at least in the background, both as cleaning personnel and cooks, as prostitutes and laundresses.

Hutton, however, also alerts us to alternative markets, such as the *Friday Market*, where women could certainly become active as merchants and play a significant role in the spice trade, for instance, or as mercers, and this both as customers and sellers. It all depends on the specific situation, on the product sold on the markets, and on the traditional gender roles in the particular trade. Of course, there were gender markers and gender lines, and of course patriarchy held on to its traditional power base wherever possible. But as the situation in Ghent indicates, gender was not the only and all-pervasive criterion allowing or denying women entrance to the profession of traders. Space could be negotiated, and some women in the wealthy city of Ghent knew rather well how to navigate their passage in the complex web of trade relations, in traditionally gender-privileged spaces in the particular markets, and in the economic framework at large. In other words, in Ghent, as in many other late-medieval cities, the gender discourse found some of its best expression in the distribution of spaces in the markets, some of which were exclusively preserved for men, whereas others allowed women to occupy a specific vacuum and to assume the position of middle-level merchants.

Contrary to certain assumptions about late-medieval towns and cities as harmonious, law-abiding, and peaceful communities where craftsmen and merchants collaborated most productively, we have to recognize that urban communities could become quite easily hotbeds of social unrest, class conflicts, and violence by individuals or the mob. Multiple interests easily collided with each other, whether economic, religious, political, or artistic, and often the various social groups, opposed to each other along the dividing line of individual crafts, fought for specific political goals that could become intermingled with concerns related to the king's position or that of the most powerful members of the royal family. [297]

One of those conflicts, the *cabochien* revolt in Paris in 1413, is the topic of Lia B. Ross's contribution to this volume. Her interest is focused on the ambiguous nature of this revolt, partly urban insurrection and partly courtly coup, and the relationship that developed between the popular and aristocratic parties. Drawing both from the abundant contemporary sources and from modern sociological insights, Ross suggests that this revolt might have been the result of external political manipulations and secret strategies that did not pursue goals specific to

---

[297] See the various contributions to *Emotions in the Heart of the City (14th–16th Century)*, ed. Elodie Lecuppre-Desjardin and Anne-Laure Van Bruaene, 2005 (loc. cit.); Ernst Piper, *Der Aufstand der Ciompi: über den Tumult, den die "Wollarbeiter" im Florenz der Frührenaissance anzettelten.* Wagenbachs Taschenbücherei, 49 (Berlin: Wagenbach, 1978; with many reprints); Alessandro Stella, *La Révolte des Ciompi: les Hommes, les lieux, le travail* (Paris: Editions de l'Ecole des hautes études en sciences sociales, 1993).

urban affairs; instead these were developed by the major power players in France who used the Parisian streets as the staging ground for their political interests.

While the wider motivation behind this revolt finds its explanation in larger "national" tensions among the ruling houses in France, their most poignant expression is in the urban conflict within Paris, probably the most effective stage for the struggle for national superiority. In 1407, for instance, this city witnessed the murder of Louis Duke of Orléans by assassins at the pay of his opponent, Duke John the Fearless of Burgundy. John was brazen enough to defend himself immediately afterwards with a reference to the danger to the king's life resulting from Louis's violent political maneuvers. The populace was rather willing to accept this explanation because the victim seems to have been hated far and wide for his association with courtly waste and corruption. But this was only one of many violent events inside and outside of Paris during those years, the details of which Ross outlines in admirable clarity.

Once the mob took to the streets, there was no stopping its fury, very much as seen in more recent times whenever mass movements take control of a city. Nevertheless, as Ross argues, the mob was not acting entirely on its own, but somehow followed more or less subtle directives from the outside, and was manipulated by ducal interests that had nothing to do with urban concerns in the narrow sense of the word. One is left to wonder whether the butchers of Paris, the strongest force behind the *cabochien* revolt, really understood how much they were used for larger purposes only relevant for the rival ducal houses. And in contrast to modern historical events where urban revolts have been known to spark regional and national revolutions,[298] the *cabochien* revolt was quickly dispatched by the mere threat of princely armies.

Apart from lack of physical resources to stand up to the nobility, as Ross sensitively observes, the urban population seems also to have been rather handicapped by an abstract identification with the royal house and hence did not pursue any kind of reformist goals during its brief success. Rather, as Ross concludes, the insurgents explicitly strove for the maintenance of traditional privileges and rules, and regarded themselves as the protectors of the royal house, much to the dismay of the latter, perhaps except for the mad king himself. This attitude might have been more typical of Paris than of other cities, such as in Flanders and Northern Italy, where urban revolts were directed much more specifically against local power structures, and was shared (perhaps to a lesser extent) by the Londoners, who also revealed a strong sense of identification with the royal court and hence could not truly succeed in any kind of uprisings during the late Middle Ages.

---

[298]   See, for example, Dennis E. Gale, *Understanding Urban Unrest* (London: Sage, 1996).

The *cabochien* revolt powerfully illustrates the highly complex nature of late-medieval urban structures, the conflictual web of interests amongst various groups, the newfound power of the mob, and yet also its openness to political manipulations by higher forces, such as the mighty French barons and dukes. In fact, rapidly switching to modern times, we can actually confirm that many major revolutions started within cities, that is, centers of great population aggregates, so the analysis of late-medieval urban unrest can shed important light on contemporary concerns as well.[299]

Late-medieval urban life is intimately associated with the merchant class. In fact, mercantile interests and activities have always characterized, if not dominated, cities throughout time and in most cultures, which still might be true today. Since the fifteenth century we also observe representatives of the merchant class turning to the arts, writing poetry (such as the *Meistersinger* in Germany), composing music, collecting songs, books, and involving themselves in the arts as major patrons, eagerly competing with the traditional aristocracy.[300]

Fabian Alfie here investigates the work of the Florentine poet-barber of the Calimala district, Domenico di Giovanni, nicknamed il Burchiello (b. ca. 1390–1400; d. ca. 1448) who created rather bizarre poetry, but enjoyed considerable popularity at his time, although modern scholarship has mostly disregarded him as trivial or irrelevant, yet probably not for really convincing reasons. Significantly, many other poets followed Burchiello's model, and he might actually be identified as the initiator of a whole movement of fifteenth-century Italian comic poetry. His œuvre focuses specifically on the ordinary life in the city, which makes his texts so significant for the exploration of the larger topic pursued in this volume, urban space in its cultural and mental-historical framework.

In one sonnet, probably composed by one of Burchiello's many imitators, "E merchatanti della mia Fiorenza" (1457), which Alfie now makes finally available in a critical edition, all the ambivalence in late-medieval urban society in Italy toward the merchant class and the considerable influence of huge capital gains

[299] Ulrich Meier, "*Molte rivoluzioni, molte novità:* Gesellschaftlicher Wandel im Spiegel der politischen Philosophie und im Urteil von städtischen Chronisten des späten Mittelalters," *Sozialer Wandel im Mittelalter: Wahrnehmungsformen, Erklärungsmuster, Regelungsmechanismen,* ed. Jürgen Miethke and Klaus Schreiner (Sigmaringen: Thorbecke, 1994), 119–76.

[300] Horst Brunner, *Die alten Meister: Studien zu Überlieferung und Rezeption der mittelhochdeutschen Sangspruchdichter im Spätmittelalter und in der frühen Neuzeit.* Münchener Texte und Untersuchungen zur deutschen Literatur des Mittelalters, 54 (Munich: Beck, 1975); Fritz Langensiepen, *Tradition und Vermittlung: literaturgeschichtliche und didaktische Untersuchungen zu Hans Folz.* Philologische Studien und Quellen, 102 (Berlin: Schmidt, 1980); Winfried Frey, "The Intimate Other: Hans Folz' Dialogue Between 'Christian and Jew'," *Meeting the Foreign in the Middle Ages,* ed. Albrecht Classen (New York and London: Routledge, 2002), 249–67.

newly acquired, especially also by the bankers, come to the fore and form the basis for the specific poetic humor and ideological criticism pursued by Burchiello.

Although at first sight the sonnet seems to belong to poetry composed on the street for coarse entertainment, Alfie's careful philological and literary-historical analysis indicates that the poet, assuming the first-person voice of a wool-beater, certainly alluded to the notorious Ciompi riots of 1387 and underscored how much power the urban masses still held against the merchant class. Moreover, there are sufficient signals and allusions in the text to confirm Burchiello's high level of familiarity with the history of Florentine literature. After all, Dante, to whom he refers explicitly, had already railed against the potentially evil nature of merchants in his *Inferno*, and other poets had also drawn from this topos, so Burchiello's sonnet continues a long-standing tradition within the urban discourse.[301]

It might actually be possible that the text was intended to appeal to the nobility because they were particularly threatened by the economic rise of the merchant class, and the narrative voice consistently suggests that the aristocratic world was in danger of being undermined by these nouveaux riches.[302] Also, the rich web of intertextual allusions to older and contemporary Italian poets who had voiced similar concerns and hence had also relied on the trope of invectives against the uncanny surge of capitalistic power by means of trade with goods, confirms this impression.

Alfie points out the significant parallel between the invectives against the merchants in pseudo-Burchiello's sonnet on the one hand, and the rich tradition of invectives against old women (the *vituperatio vetulae* topos), both aggressively associated with pervasive sinful lifestyles. The most curious element, however, of the sonnet consists of the ambivalent social position the wool-beater assigns to himself. Although wool-beaters belonged to some of the lowest classes in late-medieval Florence, the poet voice strongly suggests this association with the nobility in his stark opposition against the merchants, perhaps using the figure of the wool-beater only as a mask for his true identity, thereby successfully pretending to be Burchiello. This would also explain why the poetic I idealizes the value of the traditional class structure, even to the practical disadvantage of the

---

[301]   There might well be significant parallels to the poetry by Oswald von Wolkenstein who pursued similar arguments against the mercantile class, see his poem "Ain burgher und ain hofman" (Kl. 25), cited above.

[302]   This phenomenon has been studied already for a long time; see the by now classical study by Erich Maschke, "La Mentalité des marchands européens au moyen âge," *Revue d'histoire économique et sociale* 42 (1962): 457–84; Jacques le Goff, *Marchands et banquiers du moyen âge*. Que sais-je!, 699 (1956; Paris: Presses Universitaires de France, 1962). See now also Kathryn L. Reyerson, "The Merchants of the Mediterranean: Merchants as Strangers," *The Stranger in Medieval Society*, ed. F. R. P. Akehurst and Stephanie Cain Van D'Elden. Medieval Cultures, 12 (Minneapolis and London: University of Minnesota Press, 1997), 1–13; Jennifer Kermode, *Medieval Merchants: York, Beverly, and Hull in the Later Middle Ages*, 1998.

wool-beaters to which he allegedly belonged. At any rate, this sonnet provides excellent insight into the social discourse within early-Renaissance poetic discourse which poignantly took aim at the changes in the class structure because of the unstoppable rise of the merchant class based on their monetary power.[303]

Medieval and early-modern cities prove to be highly fascinating entities, certainly much more complex in their constitutive political, social, economic, and religious components than commonly assumed. More specifically, they do not represent, as we are wont to think, localities for the burgher class alone, almost like bulwarks against the external rural world still dominated by medieval feudal structures and forces. Instead, as Jan Hirschbiegel and Gabriel Zeilinger demonstrate, we can also observe intricate and multi-layered exchanges between the nobility and the burghers at large. Scholarship has, however, mostly focused on the clear separation of courtly and civic cultures, regularly studying either the one or the other only, although the evidence actually points toward the other direction. In fact, by the late Middle Ages we can observe a steadily growing merging of the two social spheres, embraced by the urban framework where life simply proved to be much more amenable, exciting, and enriching than in a castle or a rural residence, such as a manor house.[304] By the same token, rich burghers, especially bankers, tried hard to imitate the aristocratic lifestyle, at times even buying old castles and moving into those establishments,[305] but this is not the topic of Hirschbiegel's and Zeilinger's investigation. Instead, they focus on events in smaller towns where both social classes seem to have met quite regularly and shared many experiences. The two authors cogently argue that small towns were distinctly characteristic of the urban structures of the Holy Roman Empire and were consequently quite influential with regard to the global politics as well either because they were the very location of the prince's or bishop's residence, or were situated in close proximity to his residence.

The best expression of the shared culture can be found in public festivities, processions, and ceremonies, when representatives of both social groups closely cooperated in the ritual processes, or public performances. One of these, the Council of Constance (1414–1418), proved to be a unique and highly meaningful

---

[303]  Peter Sufford, *Power and Profit: The Merchant in Medieval Europe* (New York: Thames & Hudson, 2003).

[304]  For earlier efforts in this regard, see Hartmut Boockmann, *Die Stadt im späten Mittelalter*. 2nd ed. (1986; Munich: C. H. Beck, 1987); id., *Fürsten, Bürger, Edelleute: Lebensbilder aus dem späten Mittelalter* (Munich: C. H. Beck, 1994).

[305]  I have discussed this phenomenon already in a different context to illustrate the growing economic, political, and cultural exchanges between Germany and Italy in the late Middle Ages, *Zur Rezeption norditalienischer Kultur des Trecento im Werk Oswalds von Wolkenstein (1376/77–1445)*. Göppinger Arbeiten zur Germanistik, 471 (Göppingen: Kümmerle, 1987), 33-58. Older social-historical research literature is listed there.

long-term event, as almost the entire medieval world seems to have gathered there, where major decisions were reached regarding the malaise of the Church in local and also global terms, and where territorial and imperial policies were established and then enacted. Poets and artists met in Constance, public entertainment was of highest value, and diplomats and lawyers from many different parties and groups met and debated major issues. The chronicler Ulrich Richental provided an in-depth report about the most important events at the Council, which were also reflected in numerous other accounts, including some poems by the South-Tyrolean poet, landed gentry, and statesman *in spe* Oswald von Wolkenstein (1376/1377–1445).

King Sigismund's entry into the city in December 1414, the celebratory *introitus*, required extensive preparations involving the entire urban community and others and led to most splendid ceremonies serving to display, on the one hand, the king's esteem and power, and, on the other, the burghers' wealth and political independence. The lengthy process proved to be an ideal occasion, or challenge, for burghers and aristocrats alike, voluntarily or involuntarily, to share the same urban space, both metaphorically and literally, considering, for instance, the tremendous need to find housing for the throngs of people attending the entry and then the council itself. Richental's chronicle proves to be truly remarkable both for its detailed account of the events and for the rich illustration program. This source, among others, allows Hirschbiegel and Zeilinger to analyze the specific aspects of this ceremonial entry into Constance and to focus on the individual media strategies employed to enhance the public-theatrical character of this procession.

Although the spectacular event seems to have been highly exceptional, bringing the everyday-life experience to a halt, almost the opposite can be observed to some extent, as the two authors confirm. Of course, the exceptional situation cannot be doubted, but the various chronicles outline very specifically the enhancing and profiling effect of the *introitus*, shedding intensive light on the normal conditions in the city where, as Hirschbiegel and Zeilinger conclude, the courtly and the civic met much more commonly and shared a considerable degree of interests and values.[306]

---

[306]  Thomas Zotz, "Adel in der Stadt des deutschen Spätmittelalters: Erscheinungsformen und Verhaltensweisen," *Zeitschrift für die Geschichte des Oberrheins* 141 (1993): 22-50; Pierre Monnet, "Doit-on encore parler de patriciat dans les villes allemandes de la fin du Moyen Âge?," *Bulletin de la Mission Historique française en Allemagne* 32 (1996): 54-66; Martin Aurell, "Western Nobility in the Late Middle Ages," *Nobles and Nobility in Medieval Europe: Concepts, Origins, Transformations*, ed. Anne J. Duggan (Woodbridge, Suffolk, and Rochester, NY: Boydell, 2000), 263–73; Edward Coleman, "Cities and Communes," *Italy in the Central Middle Ages 1000–1300*, ed. David Abulafia. The Short Oxford History of Italy (Oxford: Oxford University Press, 2004), 27–57, 255–57; Birgit Studt, "Erinnerung und Identität: Die Repräsentation städtischer Eliten in spätmittelalterlichen Haus- und Familienbüchern," *Haus- und Familienbücher in der städtischen Gesellschaft des Spätmittelalters und der Frühen Neuzeit*, ed. eadem (Cologne, Weimar, and Vienna: Böhlau, 2007),

As towns and cities grew over time and reached unforeseen dimensions in the late Middle Ages, urban space also became increasingly the site for public entertainment, primarily in the form of plays, often religious in nature, but then also Shrovetide plays and other secular plays. Klaus Amann and Max Siller focus on the area of Tyrol (today split between Austria and Italy) and examine the rich tradition of plays composed and performed in the Tyrolean urban centers. These plays came into being parallel to a veritable explosion of popular songs that circulated far and wide and soon made their way into often voluminous song collections, mostly commissioned by wealthy burghers or patricians.[307] One of the best known love songs, "Isbruck, ich mus dich lassen," enjoyed great popularity far into the modern age and powerfully reflects the strong attraction of urban centers as the site for new types of an identification process. Other songs, such as the "Glurns song," referred to military and political conflicts closely associated with towns, and were probably produced by members of the respective community.

Amann and Siller, however, focus especially on dramas, particularly those collected and staged by Benedikt Debs and Vigil Raber. These shed important light on sociological and ideological aspects within the city, such as the gender relationships, class structures, ethical and moral issues, then on political and economic conditions, and finally they also illustrate, of course, powerful religious themes and topics publicly debated and here performed on the stage. As the two authors observe, the passion plays were regularly acted out by male representatives of the upper social classes, whereas women were absent, and so aristocrats even though they had their representatives in the Bozen city council, for instance. Moreover, the clergy is entirely missing, indicating that the plays served primarily as a mode of self-identification for the upper-rank lay population. Not surprisingly, some of the plays also include subtle and not so subtle criticism of chivalry and hence of the aristocratic class. Nevertheless, this does not mean that none of the secular plays included traditional themes or motifs borrowed from medieval heroic epics, for example, which allowed the actors to demonstrate their fencing skills. Tournaments and jousts obviously appealed to urban audiences as well, despite the attempts by the cities to distance themselves from the traditional

---

1–31; here 3–5, offers an excellent overview of the relevant research literature. Now see also Paul Oldfield, *City and Community in Norman Italy* (Cambridge Studies in Medieval Life and Thought. Fourth Series (Cambridge, New York, et al.: Cambridge University Press, 2009), 184–225. He offers plenty of evidence pertaining to the special region in Southern Italy, which can also be used in support of the claim made here with regard to the intermingling of the social classes in Constance and other Southern German cities.

[307] Albrecht Classen, *Deutsche Liederbücher des 15. und 16. Jahrhunderts*. Volksliedstudien, 1 (Münster, New York, et al.: Waxmann, 2001).

nobility.[308] Overall, however, as Amann and Siller conclude, the rather popular plays in late-medieval and early-modern Tyrolean cities reflect a growing sense of urban culture and urban identity, irrespective of many traditional elements that still dominated the stage.

Not only did city life considerably expand in the late Middle Ages, both artists and writers also drew increasingly from the daily experience and living conditions in cities, as I have observed several times above. Jean E. Jost, in her contribution to this volume, demonstrated how much Chaucer utilized urban space, encompassing both interior and exterior locations, central locations and liminal areas, for the development of his narratives. Connie Scarborough extends this observation through her careful reading of the Spanish *Comedia de Calisto y Melibea* by Fernando Roja, first printed in 1499 and published ca. three years later in a considerably expanded version as *Tragicomedia de Calisto y Melibea*. Indeed, here all the major moves by the individual protagonists throughout the city underscore the relevance of urban space as the new setting where all central aspects of life are carried out. But the city also provided the framework for crimes and all kinds of violence; hence venturing out of the house could be highly dangerous, especially for those seeking erotic adventures.[309] Although a night-watch or guardians patrol the streets, the *Tragicomedia* indicates how much people actually feared the lawlessness of the night in the city.[310]

Another major characteristic of late-medieval urban life proves to be a clear sense of time, determined by public clocks. Of course, time measurement had been practiced throughout the Middle Ages, especially in monasteries, but in Roja's early-modern text we observe a new emphasis on time pressure and time sensitivity, structured by a mechanical device, the clock.[311] Scarborough also identifies the significance of the *plaza*, the major central market place where criminals are punished in the presence of the entire population as witnesses and

---

[308]  See, for instance, Waltraud Hörsch, "Adel im Bannkreis Österreichs: Strukturen der Herrschaftsnähe im Raum Aargau – Luzern," Guy P. Marchal, *Sempach 1386: Von den Anfängen des Territorialstaates Luzern. Beiträge zur Frühgeschichte des Kantons Luzern* (Basel: Helbing & Lichtenhahn, 1986), 353–403; Arend Mindermann, *Adel in der Stadt des Spätmittelalters: Göttingen und Stade 1300 bis 1600*. Veröffentlichungen des Instituts für historische Landesforschung der Universität Göttingen, 35 (Bielefeld: Verlag für Regionalgeschichte, 1996); *Der Hof und die Stadt: Konfrontation, Koexistenz und Integration in Spätmittelalter und Früher Neuzeit. Halle a. d. Saale, 25–28. September 2004*, ed. Werner Paravicini. Residenzforschung, 20 (Ostfildern: Thorbecke, 2006).

[309]  See also the contribution to this volume by Patricia Turning.

[310]  Jean Verdon, *Night in the Middle Ages*, trans. George Holoch (1994; Notre Dame: University of Notre Dame Press, 2002); Tzotcho Boiadjiev, *Die Nacht im Mittelalter*, trans. from the Bulgarian into German by Barbara Müller (2000; Würzburg: Königshausen & Neumann, 2003).

[311]  For a critical survey of time and measurement in the Middle Ages, see Camarin M. Porter, "Time Measurement and Chronology in Medieval Studies," *Handbook of Medieval Studies*, ed. Albrecht Classen (Berlin and New York: de Gruyter, forthcoming).

audience. Nevertheless, urban space is also determined by private spaces, such as houses with their living quarters and bedrooms, and, above all, gardens, where lovers meet, for instance (see also Jost's observations in this regard). For the narrative development of the *Tragicomedia,* and apparently in direct reflection of late-medieval urban life at least in Spain, walls and doors constitute major markers or dividers, indicating the complexity of urban space both outside and inside. Similarly as in Italian cities, towers also figure prominently in this urban landscape (see the frescoes by Ambrogio Lorenzetti, as discussed above).

Nevertheless, despite all efforts by the upper class to separate itself from the lower class by means of architecture (walls, towers, gardens, etc.), in the *Tragicomedia* urban space becomes the location where both meet and mingle, interact, and struggle to cope with each other in this dense living quarters. However, Celestina's house, basically a brothel, is generally regarded with disrespect, as prostitution in general was viewed with very mixed feelings, although it played an important role in late-medieval cities and was certainly much more tolerated than in later centuries. But even Celestina was forced to move her house from the center of the city to its outskirts and to live at that liminal space where traditional ethics and morals were not so strictly pursued.

Other typical aspects of urban life reflected in Roja's work concern labor, the role of servants, money and payment, class distinctions based on one's individual wealth, and hence also the conflict between older aristocratic circles and the new urban class drawing its income from capitalistic enterprises. In other words, as Scarborough concludes, the *Tragicomedia* powerfully reflects the social transformation taking place in the late-medieval city where old and new forces clash with each other and yet have to learn how to deal with each other.

As Albrecht Classen reconfirms in his contribution, cities in the late Middle Ages and the early modern time emerged as the crucial centers of economic, political, artistic, intellectual, cultural, and religious developments. One of the best representations of this global paradigm shift can be found in the world chronicle by the Nuremberg medical doctor and humanist Hartmann Schedel, the *Liber chronicarum* (1495), to which major artists of his time, such as Albrecht Dürer, contributed significant and outstanding woodcuts depicting individual cities, such as Nuremberg, placed right in the center of this chronicle. Schedel's work stands out, above all, because of its large number of highly detailed and most impressive cityscapes, or vedute, from all over Europe and even the Levant, including Constantinople and Jerusalem. These scenes show a change from earlier views of medieval cities, limited by their city wall, allowing the viewer just to observe the fortification system, the city gates, and perhaps some church towers and a castle. On the contrary, the artists whose works Schedel assembled made great efforts to situate the city always in its context, opening many perspectives on the environs, signaling the importance of the hinterland and the travel routes connecting a city with the entire country.

But Classen's focus rests not only on Schedel's work. Instead he aims for a broadly conceived comparative perspective, taking into view also the elaborate and variegated city encomia composed by the Nuremberg cobbler poet, Hans Sachs (1494–1576). These might not rank among the best vernacular sixteenth-century poetry, but in our context they serve exceedingly well to illustrate the considerable interest in the city as the central location for a growing number of people who certainly preferred living within an urban community rather than in the countryside. Sachs owned a copy of Schedel's chronicle, and in his *Lobspruch der statt Nürnberg* from 1530 he developed an intriguingly complex perspective on this city which enjoyed some of the highest reputation as an urban center all over Germany due to the crafts, arts, humanistic endeavors, and politics practiced there, and also due to its outstanding architecture and urban spaces.

Moreover, the *Lobspruch* also proves to be an important vehicle in Sachs's political maneuvers to convince the city government to lift its ban on his publications that had become too political for the well-being of Nuremberg in a dangerous military climate. Hence, Sachs sings a song of praise on the whole city, and in this context also provides most detailed information about specific characteristics of this imperial center.

Although this encomium explicitly served to meet a political goal, it also reveals the extent to which the poet deeply identified with Nuremberg and wanted to paint a glorious picture of all the various social groups, the government, the crafts, and the urban architecture. The operative word here is "vatterland" (198, 37; fatherland), but Sachs went one step further and described in his other city encomia additional locations situated along his own travel route through the German speaking lands during his time as a young journeyman, where a similar civic pride could be observed. At times the poet even pursued historical perspectives, as if he had culled that information from Schedel's chronicle, or comparable works. Not content with focusing on the essential elements that make up a city, Sachs also incorporated comments about urban spaces, such as in his encomium on Munich (1565), and on economic events, such as major mercantile fairs as in his encomium on Frankfurt (1568).

Another intriguing feature in Sachs's encomia proves to be the discussion of the roads that lead to and from the various cities, then of bridges, ports, and markets, and then also of specific products sold by individual city merchants. That is, the emphasis naturally also rests on the economic importance of the respective cities. On the other hand, there are also encomia, such as the one on Hamburg (1569), that limit themselves almost entirely to the historical background and dimension. And in the case of Salzburg (1549), Sachs even mentions the profession of book printers—certainly representing one of the most important new professions in early-modern cities.

Even though often ridiculed by modern scholarship for certain perceived shortcomings, Sachs emerges, especially because of his encomia, as a remarkable spokesperson of urban culture and urban identity, very much in the vein of Hartmann Schedel's world chronicle. Whether we could identify either one of them with the Renaissance in the narrow sense remains questionable, or at least vague. Nevertheless, both provided most impressive documentation for the supreme importance of the city for early-modern culture, mentality, politics, and, above all, individual identity. In a certain way Sachs followed the pictorial model developed in Schedel's chronicle, and we might certainly argue that the chronicle provided a good framework for the poet to create his city encomia.

We rarely hear from women what they thought about the city where they lived in and about the urban society during the Middle Ages and the early-modern time at large. A remarkable exception proves to be Isabella Whitney's "Wyll and Testament" from 1573 in which she reflects with astounding clarity and perception on London and the social ills that affect its community, deeply determined by excessive monetary values and a lack of ethical ideals. In fact, as Marilyn Sandidge illustrates in her contribution to this volume, Whitney emerges as a quite vocal critic of her world, exposing the extensive poverty and squalor in sixteenth-century London. But she was not, as earlier critics have assumed, a member of the lowest social classes; instead we may safely argue that Whitney belonged to the middle class that also suffered badly from economic woes, as autobiographical references in her text, but then especially the concrete criticism against the behavior of the upper class indicate. Considering what she published and whom she selected as her printers, we can be certain that Whitney belonged to a small but dedicated and active group of early-modern English urban literati. In this regard we might well compare her with Christine de Pizan (d. 1432), as a more or less independent and intellectual writer of her time who prospered because of her individual skill as a writer and because of her topics, focusing, especially in her "Wyll and Testament," on social problems in the city.

The author addresses London in poetic terms as her own lover, but she laments how much the city has abandoned her, and so thousands of other people as well who cannot survive in the city due to lack of money and jobs. In contrast to traditional city encomia, Whitney mostly ignores any church structures or institutions; instead she directs our attention to public spaces and streets populated by crowds of ordinary people. Although she emphasizes the richness and complexity of the city as such, she also complains about pollution, noise, crammed living conditions, and so, altogether, views London rather negatively.

In her "Wyll and Testament" Whitney also outlines in remarkable detail the economic structure of London, specifying where the various types of food are being sold, where the specific craftsmen have their workshops, and then also where physicians and apothecaries can be found helping people in their medical needs. Here the author embarks, as Sandidge observes, on an increasingly critical strategy, revealing the social woes that badly beset early-modern London, and she does not neglect to mention the prostitutes and bath houses, clearly profiling the strong contrasts between the poor and the wealthy, between social misery and aristocratic luxury, underscoring the injustice and inequality characteristic of sixteenth-century urban society. This finds its most impressive expression in her discussion of the prisons that were filled to a large extent with people who simply could not pay their debts and did not get a 'bail-out' as in modern society during the current global economic crisis (2009). Poor relief came trickling in only sparingly, and the economic and social suffering was great, as Whitney saw it.

The final comments in "Wyll and Testament" concern the legal system and the Inns of Court situated far outside of the city center, safely protected from the squalor and poverty that dominated the heart of London. It might well be, as Sandidge speculates, that Whitney intended this last section of her text as an appeal to the young law students to pursue justice and to provide legal help in the future to those who languish away in prisons because of their inability to pay back their debts. To be sure, this text addresses the middle class and tries to lay the foundation for a discourse among the literary minded intellectuals and readers on the well-being of the urban community and on the dangers for London resulting from bad financial conditions, poverty, illness, and subsequent criminality. Although Whitney does not seem to have pursued an aggressive agenda in her social commentary, she certainly appealed to her audience to reach out to those in need, both financially and medically, thus aiming for a global improvement of the life in the metropolitan city in explicitly social terms.

Whereas most of the contributions to this volume concentrate on urban space and cities that developed in central, southern, or western Europe during the Middle Ages and beyond (but see Pınar Kayaalp's article), Michael E. Bonine takes us to the Middle East where urban culture had already played a significant role since the time of the ancient Greek and Roman civilizations. However, with the coming of the Islamic religion, many aspects of urban culture changed considerably, deeply determined by *shari'a* (Islamic law) and the local customary law (*urf*). One of the most important central points in the Muslim city was *waqf*, or religiously endowed property, which can be discovered in many different countries wherever the Islamic religion dominated. As Bonine illustrates, *waqf* emerged as the crucial social institution offering a wide range of social services for the urban population in the Islamic world. Contrary to traditional viewpoints regarding the usual structure of *waqf*, existing within unchanging traditional patterns, Bonine shows that *waqf* experienced tremendous organic changes throughout time and depending on the specific context. In other words, his essay offers important information about the economic and social structures, developments, and functions of a pivotal social institution within the urban context of the Middle East, extending to many different countries wherever Islam dominated.

As Bonine emphasizes, *waqf* assumed both secular, economic and political, and also spiritual-ritual functions, perhaps somewhat similar to the countless cathedrals in medieval Europe, though the social obligations to the under classes seem to have been stronger in the East than in the West throughout times. We might even want to go so far as to correlate the *waqf* to the space outside of the Christian church in medieval cities, although the practical functions were rather different after all. In particular, *waqf* provided rental income for the religious institution within the city, even though it was also subject to rather specific requirements, laws, and rents. But *waqf* could also turn into private property and hence then be subject to rather fluid economic forces and stipulations. Most commonly, as Bonine illustrates, *waqf* owned commercial property and provided it with the necessary means to carry out its social functions, such as to support a mosque, to maintain public fountains, or to provide welfare for the needy. Because of its peculiar character, *waqf* could be flexible under specific circumstances, even circumventing Islamic law (*shari'a*). In some cases this institution could also pursue goals very different from those initially associated with the endowment, which had often been established by members of the ruling houses.

After having laid down the principles of *waqf*, Bonine turns to a wide range of individual case studies, including Constantinople/Istanbul, Ottoman Aleppo and Cairo, Damascus, Jaffa, Safavid Isfahan, Balk (Afghanistan), Qajar Tabriz (Iran), and even Jerusalem. Whether the *waqf* contributed to the growing density of city buildings, or whether its establishment affected the opposite depends on the various contexts, so both phenomena can actually be observed. Sometimes rural property served for the financial support of the urban *waqf*, sometimes urban space was cleared to erect new buildings for *waqf*, and sometimes *waqf* initiated the establishment of a cemetery. As Bonine concludes, in many cases *waqf* truly contributed to the growing density of the *medina*, but in other instances *waqf* property led to dilapidation and hence a decline in the urban density.

At any rate, Bonine's article allows us to understand in great detail the essence of urban space within the Islamic world from the late Middle Ages to the early modern world from a socio-religious, economic, and political perspective, combined with insights into urban planning according to Muslim principles and ideals.

Despite the bitter military and religious conflicts between Christian Europe and the Ottoman Empire, there is no doubt that we must equally integrate the Islamic world into our global investigations for a full understanding of the culture and history of the sixteenth and seventeenth centuries. Urban development in architectural, economic, and cultural terms took place also, and very much so, in the regions of the eastern Mediterranean. In fact, in her contribution to this volume

Pınar Kayaalp urges us to keep in mind that Istanbul was one of the largest European cities by the middle of the sixteenth century. She focuses on a new construction project, the Mihrümah's mosque complex (*külliye*) in the district of Üsküdar, across the Bosphorus, in 1543, as an example of early-modern city planning, involving public and private buildings, imperial constructions and religious ones, primarily mosques. Whereas before Üsküdar had only been an army and trading post, it now transformed into a truly urban center of great significance, shedding important light on how city planning took place in the Ottoman Empire during a time we would already identify as the Renaissance. Both the members of the imperial house as well as rich merchants, not to forget representatives of the religious communities, recognized the foundation of the Mihrümah's mosque complex as a most convenient and appealing new urban avenue where they could withdraw from the bustling city across the Bosphorus and enjoy the serene coastal shore. Many mosques were erected there as well, so Kayaalp's investigation allows for excellent insight into the profound impact that the establishment of mosques could have for the urban development at large. The topographic challenges were regularly met with ingenious architectural design, which allows the author to offer a detailed case study of the way how strategically pursued urban growth was realized and then continued over centuries to come.

But Üsküdar was not only a site for the concentration of mosques and palaces. Over time, schools, stables, barracks, and other public building were added on. Most importantly, however, Kayaalp can convincingly demonstrate how much deliberate planning determined the growth of this new urban center in an aesthetically most pleasing and also pragmatically effective way, actually not far removed from late-medieval and Renaissance urban planning in the rest of Europe. Charitable institutions complemented the growth of neighborhoods for private residents, who in turn relied on the availability of stores and shops, which altogether truly led to the emergence of a modern city, centrally designed, almost as a forerunner of a Baroque city. Moreover, Üsküdar continued to serve as a central location for caravansaries, allowing large contingents of foreign merchants to rest, to prepare for the next journeys, and also to sell their wares.

Overall, as Kayaalp underscores, the careful planning and designing of this new city supported many different purposes, bringing together the administrative, religious, educational, mercantile, military, and charitable functions in one site. By investigating how Üsküdar was founded and then developed over centuries, she can outline in impressive detail how an Ottoman city emerged and was then organically constructed in the course of time, a most intriguing test case for the history of the early-modern city.

We commonly read that early-modern European women experienced a considerable decline in public status and were increasingly forced to retire within their domestic sphere because of male, specifically patriarchal, pressure. For instance, the year 1500 is normally regarded as the crucial watershed for patriarchal power-structures gaining in preponderance, as reflected by the growth of capitalistic production modes that were less and less anchored in the family, hence mostly excluding women. We have, however, already seen in Shennan Hutton's paper in this volume how much a careful analysis of local conditions in Ghent, for instance, can force us to modify this perception and to treat this whole complex of issues with much greater care and an open mind.

Martha Moffitt Peacock takes the next bold step in examining how seventeenth-century Dutch artists depicted women, which quickly offers a strong contrast to the prescriptive and moralizing language used by contemporary didactic authors, such as Jacob Cats. Peacock suggests that a sensible art-historical approach might actually undermine our reliance on Cats and others in the evaluation of early-modern women's economic and political roles in Netherlandish cities. For example, guilds were not particularly loathe to allow women to join the ranks of the guilds, and we can find numerous confirmations of women's active participation in the economic sphere, both as producers and sellers, and also as shoppers. In other words, the extensive corpus of seventeenth-century Dutch paintings focusing on market scenes, provides solid evidence that public life was not simply dominated by men. On the contrary, as Peacock underscores, in many of these genre paintings the men stand or sit in the background, portrayed as passive and even helpless, whereas the individual women are presented as active, energetic, self-reliant, and dominant, without attracting the painters' scorn or derision for this seemingly topsy-turvydom in gender roles.

The Netherlands might have been the exception to the rule with regard to women's influence in their society as numerous travelers report with astonishment that they observed how much the Dutch women exerted extensive influence on their civic communities. This is best reflected in their involvement in the market activities, where they even operated very successfully on their own as shopkeepers and traders, both in close and equal partnership with their husbands, or alone, either as widows or as unmarried women. This finds confirmation in various social factors and legal traditions that appear to have benefitted women's independence and power in this culture. In addition, much of this unique development is related to the rise in urbanization and the enormous economic boom which the Netherlands enjoyed during the seventeenth century.

Most of this circumstantial evidence points to the realistic character of the market scenes in seventeenth-century Dutch paintings that highlight most dramatically women's renewed or recently gained strength in all walks of life within the city. Not surprisingly, we also come across a number of paintings portraying women as regents who here emerge as powerful and independent individuals. This also finds explicit expression in the artistic representation of a plethora of women as shoppers, or buyers, hence as a social group they dominate the urban commerce most markedly, at least according to the art-historical evidence. After all, here we see women who control the money, hand it out, collect it, or distribute it, commanding the economic life-line of the city's market in global terms. As Peacock emphasizes, the images not only show ordinary women as consumers; many times the artists depict elegantly dressed women shopping that thereby reflect the overall growth in wealth in seventeenth-century Dutch urban society.

Moreover, when inflation hit the markets, women knew how to exert their muscles, as recorded in the various histories regarding revolts. Thus, it is likely that Dutch artists primarily created their works for female customers, who obviously felt great pride in their independence and economic and political power. The triumph of the city thus also created the groundwork for women to overcome ancient patriarchal stereotypes and prejudices, and the disrespect and disadvantages that accompanied those old traditions.

When did urban dwellers in medieval and early-modern Europe begin to find the pollution of their cities and the uncontrolled depositing of waste products and excrement in the streets and open spaces not only obnoxious, but also disgusting and intolerable? Above in this Introduction, I have already discussed the strategy employed by a student against peasants who regularly relieve themselves in the backyard right under the student's window, as described in a jest narrative (*Schwank*) by Hans Wilhelm Kirchhof (ca. 1560). For him, being constantly confronted with the excremental smell, the situation soon becomes unbearable, which forces him to take energetic steps to scare the peasants and chase them away. In other words, there was a clear sense already at that time that defiling the city, wherever it might be, constituted an insult to human senses and was not really acceptable. And Britt C. L. Rothauser, in her contribution to this volume, focusing on fourteenth- and early fifteenth-century English texts, finds plenty of evidence already pointing into that direction.[312] But as Allison P. Coudert can

---

[312] In her review of Susan Signe Morrison's *Excrement in the Late Middle Ages* (2008), Valerie Allen correctly points out that it might be somewhat misleading to subscribe to the generalizing notion that by the late Middle Ages urban authorities increasingly dealt with human excrement as dirt and as despicable matter that had to be removed out of sight and smell. Certainly, excrement was dirt, but the negative or positive (!) connotation of dirt depends very much on its practical use (such as fertilizer) or uselessness, and also on the location where it is deposited. In particular, she refers to Toft Green in fifteenth- and sixteenth-century York that "was the only wide-open space positioned inside the city walls, in the south- west, beside Micklegate Bar. It was there that cattle-markets and weekly horse-markets were held (yielding plenty of manure), and the site also boasted a large midden for the dumping of city refuse and offal, providing fertilizer for soil and crops" (*The Medieval Review*, online, 09.03.08). See also Angelo Raine, *Mediaeval York: A Topographical Survey Based on Original Sources* (London: John Murray, 1955), 244–45. Allen then goes on to plead for much more interdisciplinary research in this regard: "It is perhaps time for literary studies of the scatological to merge their appreciation of the symbolic and cultural significance of excrement with the scientific findings of archaeology, chemical soil analysis, and

demonstrate, the fundamental problem, i.e., the lack of appropriate toilets and a functioning sewer system, did not find an easy solution, and it took a veritable paradigm shift in the eighteenth century to make people react with real vehemence and radical protests to the soiling of urban space with human excrements. Whereas in earlier times dirt was regarded as a mundane problem, which could easily be interpreted in a metaphorical fashion, in the eighteenth century a scientific revolution concerning olfactory sensation took place that subsequently led to the strict condemnation of foul smells and all kinds of waste products as unacceptable for fine society. This even went so far as to affect the purification of the French language, for instance, which was deliberately cleaned of any words associated with excrements.

As Coudert observes, after the great fire of London in 1666, profound changes took affect concerning public hygiene, expressed in new building codes especially concerning the treatment of waste products. Writers such as Swift and Defoe and artists such as Hogarth took clear note of the disgusting appearance of Dublin or London and satirized both the urban population and the government in their witty criticism concerning wide-spread depositing of dirt. But continental writers such as Johann Wolfgang Goethe also observed with disgust the extent to which cities were soiled everywhere. For Pierre Chauvet Paris was the "center of stench," obviously echoing a large public sentiment.

Most significantly, Coudert attributes this changing attitude toward dirt and refuse to the development of a new hypersensitivity to foul odors especially among the upper classes, and explains this as a reaction to new scientific discoveries regarding the highly heterogenous composition of air at large which could easily carry dangerous germs (miasma theory). Commonly people voiced great concern about all kinds of fissures out of which could emerge evil smells, which was no longer naively associated with suffumigation coming from Hell, but instead with dangerous gases exiting from the earth. Modern science had entered the world of hygiene, and suddenly the upper social classes, especially in cities, tried hard to distinguish themselves from the lower classes also in terms of smell. By way of the nose the rich and powerful knew how to separate themselves from the poor and downtrodden, and so the smells in eighteenth- and nineteenth-century cities provided a critical instrument for the differentiation among the social classes.

This does not mean, however, as Coudert underscores, that these elites could simply eliminate all the dirt and bad smell around them, as efforts to install modern sewer systems were slow and not as effective as desired. But the derogatory comments and the general ridicule of those whose hygiene did not meet newly defined social standards provided the upper classes a strategy to close

environmental studies."

their eyes to the reality of human life, hence of the actual hygienic conditions of
their time. Nevertheless, for them body odor, or rather lack thereof, had suddenly
become a major marker of social class attribution.[313]

As the contributions to this volume demonstrate, and as countless new research
projects, book publications, and conference activities indicate, the world of
medieval and early-modern urban space proves to be a most fascinating and
productive topic that invites ever new analysis. By studying urban culture and
urban populations, by examining the literary and art-historical evidence reflecting
medieval cities, we are quickly put into a most powerful position to gain further
insights into a plethora of diverse aspects relevant for economic, political, cultural,
religious, and artistic history. As Paul Oldfield now comments regarding cities in
twelfth-century Norman, or South, Italy, "The cities were active participants in,
not the supine victims of, wider, volatile events. . . . South Italian urban
communities were constantly in a position to make choices, and choices brought
a voice and power . . . . At the same time there is a greater evidence of the fluidity
of the social ordering of urban communities, while the notion of citizenship and
civic identity acquired greater articulation."[314] He rightly warns us not to equate
modern notions of "a poverty-stricken South" with the actual urban conditions in
the Middle Ages when the citizens were considerably more capable to express
their political opinion and to establish a certain degree of freedom and
independence than we might assume today.[315] The contributors to a volume with
proceedings resulting from an international conference on a similar topic held at
Nájera, Spain, in 2006, mostly confirm these observations, but concentrate
primarily on the situation on the Iberian Peninsula.[316]

---

[313] For a somewhat different viewpoint, see Ulrich Rosseaux, *Städte in der Frühen Neuzeit.* Geschichte
kompakt (Darmstadt: Wissenschaftliche Buchgesellschaft, 2006), who warns us from projecting
too quickly from general laments about poor hygienic conditions in nineteenth-century cities to
those in the Middle Ages and the early modern time. See also Bea Lundt, *Europas Aufbruch in die
Neuzeit 1500–1800: Eine Kultur- und Mentalitätsgeschichte.* Kultur und Mentalität (Darmstadt:
Wissenschaftliche Buchgesellschaft, 2009), 40–41. But Coudert's evidence still holds because she
deals with the impact of the miasma theory on attitudes toward stench and filth at large, and on
the attitude toward waste products within early-modern urban life.
[314] Paul Oldfield, *City and Community in Norman Italy,* 264.
[315] Oldfield, *City and Community,* 265. See also Bea Lundt, *Europas Aufbruch in die Neuzeit 1500–1800),*
39–52.
[316] *La ciudad medieval y su influencia territorial: Nájera. Encuentros internacionales del Medievo 2006,* ed.
Beatriz Arízaga Bolomburu and Jesús Ángel Solórzano Telechea (Logroño: Instituto de Estudios
Riojanos, 2007).

In this regard, the studies assembled here promise, as I hope, to shed further light on fundamental aspects of medieval and early-modern culture, the hallmark of our book series. I would like to express my gratitude, once again, to all contributors for their marvelous research, their incredible patience with me as their nagging editor, and for their collaboration in revising all and every piece included here many times until they met all expectations. My thanks also go out to the wonderful staff at Walter de Gruyter in Berlin, especially to Mr. Florian Ruppenstein, and then, most importantly, Dr. Heiko Hartmann, editor-in-chief, who had invited me several years ago to launch this book series. A whole sequence of future volumes is already in preparation. I owe also an expression of gratitude to my dear colleague Marilyn Sandidge for excellent assistance in reviewing and revising some of the contributions.

C. David Benson

(University of Connecticut)

# The Dead and the Living: Some Medieval Descriptions of the Ruins and Relics of Rome Known to the English

The formal description of cities is part of a long tradition of epideictic rhetoric stretching back to antiquity that continued in the Middle Ages as a recognizable genre, in prose and poetry, of urban praise: the *encomium civis* or *laus civis*.[1] Medieval examples survive from as early as the eighth century and were especially prominent in Italy where they expressed the growing sense of civic pride of such centers as Milan and Verona. These works celebrate the material splendor of cities (*laudes urbium*)—their sites and such architectural features as walls, towers, and churches—and also the vibrancy of civic life (*laudes civitatum*)—their cultivation of the arts and sciences as well as the wealth and charity of their citizens.[2] In this, as in so many other things, Rome was different. Medieval descriptions of Rome do not so much laud the current city and its citizens, but instead take the form of another, more backward-looking kind of praise (*elegiae urbium*), an elegiac meditation on the ancient remains of the city, its pagan monuments and bodies of Christian saints: the physical traces of what had been.[3]

---

[1]   See, especially, Ernst Robert Curtius, *European Literature and the Latin Middle Ages*, trans. Willard R. Trask (1948; 1953; Princeton: Princeton University Press, 1973), 155–57; J. K. Hyde, "Medieval Descriptions of Cities," *Bulletin of the John Rylands Library* 48 (1965–1966): 308–340; John Scattergood, "Misrepresenting the City: Genre, Intertextuality and FitzStephen's *Description of London* (c. 1173)," *Reading the Past: Essays on Medieval and Renaissance Literature* (Dublin: Four Courts Press, 1996), 15–36; and Paolo Zanna, "'Descriptiones urbium' and Elegy in Latin and Vernaculars, in the Early Middle Ages," *Studi Medievali*, 3rd series (1991): 523–96.

[2]   For this distinction and the idea of the *elegiae urbium* that follows, see Zanna,"*Descriptiones urbium*"; cf. also Curtius, *European Literature*; more recently, Claire E. Honess, *From Florence to the Heavenly City: The Poetry of Citizenship in Dante*. Italian Perspectives, 13 (London: Legenda, 2006).

[3]   I shall, however, refer to all of these medieval depictions of ancient Rome, despite their elegiac

The medieval descriptions of Rome portray a city that appears largely empty of living people and is instead populated by inert fragments from the distant past—a world-famous ghost town. The eternal city, Golden Rome, once the arena of empire, marvels, and glorious martyrdoms, is now a depository of relics and ruins, the debris of death. There are signs of life in the medieval descriptions of Rome, but they tend not to be found in the present city or in the civic, religious, and commercial activities of its citizens, but rather in the responses of individual writers, often visitors, as they try to interpret the inanimate objects they observe.

In addition to editions of the primary texts in Latin and English and bibliographical manuals, previous scholarly work on the medieval descriptions of Rome, from which I have greatly profited, tend to concentrate on single texts or on a particular subgroup of texts, such as those that discuss the pagan remains in the city or those that discuss the ancient churches and their holy relics. Much of this work has been broadly historical or antiquarian and attempts to assess the accuracy of these descriptions, which are often found wanting, as well as identifying possible sources. Some of the best studies are commentaries to editions and English translations, which will be cited when they are discussed below. My aim in this essay is less to establish the truth content or the origins of individual texts than to trace a particular, paradoxical theme (the relationship of death and life) across the spectrum of these rich materials. Perhaps the most ambitious previous attempt to consider several of these descriptions (including the more obviously literary work of Chaucer) is the essay by Jennifer Summit, though her primary interest is the ways these texts handle the transformation from paganism to Christianity, which is only one part of my own interest in the varieties of life found in the inert remains of the ancient city. I concentrate on the English knowledge of these accounts of Rome, and especially on texts in the vernacular, and I pay particular attention to two neglected works: a verse account of Rome inserted in the *Metrical Version of Mandeville's Travels* and John Capgrave's vast *Solace of Pilgrims*.

There were two different, if overlapping, classes of medieval descriptions of Rome. The first, which includes the *Mirabilia* and its subsequent versions, Master Gregorius's *Narracio*, and the beginning of Capgrave's *Solace*, focuses primarily on the classical remains of the city, though the individual writers also mention the ancient Christian catacombs, comment on the Christian destruction or rededication of ancient monuments, or, in passing, note the present name of a structure. By far the most popular example of this kind of description is generally known after the

---

tone, by the more neutral term "descriptions." These descriptions are sometimes called guides to Rome, even though (despite a general resemblance to some aspects of modern guides and the probability they were sometimes used this way) this is an incomplete designation of works often more accurately identified as catalogues, memoirs, or reports to friends and patrons.

title of its twelfth-century Latin original, *Mirabilia Urbis Romae (The Marvels of Rome)*, which was probably first put in the shape known to us about 1143.[4] The *Mirabilia* contains three different kinds of description: first the author or compiler provides a catalogue, little more than a list of names, of the different types of ancient structures in Rome, such as its walls, gates, baths, arches, and columns; secondly, he tells stories associated with some prominent monuments, such as the bronze equestrian rider we know as Marcus Aurelius, the oversized statues of two naked men and their horses we know as the Dioscuri (Castor and Pollux), and the Pantheon; finally, he traces an itinerary through the streets of Rome with its variety of ancient sites beginning at the Vatican, crossing the Tiber, traversing the center of the city, and ending back across the river in Trastevere.

I shall refer to the general tradition of the *Mirabilia* under that title, unless otherwise noted, but no single title or form adequately represents the protean variety of this extraordinarily plastic work, which is a prime example of a medieval "multi-text," to use a term coined for *Mandeville's Travels*."[5] The original version of the *Mirabilia*— itself a compilation of older texts, information current in Rome, and personal observation— was transformed, with passages both added and subtracted, as it was adapted into multiple forms and languages throughout Europe well into the fifteenth-century.[6] Versions of the Latin *Mirabilia* would have been available to English visitors to Rome, where it was a best seller into the age of print; examples were also copied into manuscripts produced for English readers.[7] But the most popular form of the *Mirabilia* in England seems to have been the slightly later twelfth-century Latin version known as the *Graphia Aureae Urbis* (ca. 1155), one of whose most common routes of dissemination was as a reduced version near the beginning of the influential thirteenth-century *Chronicon*

---

[4]  For recent discussions of the *Mirabilia*, see, especially, Nine Robijntje Miedema, *Die 'Mirabilia Romae': Untersuchungen zu ihrer Überlieferung mit Edition der deutschen und niederländischen Texte*. Münchener Texte und Untersuchungen zur deutschen Literatur des Mittelalters, 108 (Tübingen: Niemeyer, 1996); *I 'Mirabilia Urbis Romae,'* ed. Maria Accame and Emy Dell'Oro (Rome: Tored, 2004); and Dale Kinney, "Fact and Fiction in the *Mirabilia urbis Romae*," *Roma Felix—Formation and Reflections of Medieval Rome*, ed. Éamonn Ó Carragáin and Carol Neuman de Vegvar. Church, Faith and Culture in the Medieval West (Aldershot and Burlington, VT: Ashgate, 2007), 235–52.

[5]  Iain Higgins, *Writing East: The 'Travels' of Sir John Mandeville*. The Middle Ages Series (Philadelphia: University of Pennsylvania Press, 1997), viii.

[6]  For editions of some of the later versions of the *Mirabilia*, see *Codex Urbis Romae Topographicus*, ed. Carl Ludwig Urlichs (Würzburg: Stachelianis, 1871), 113–69. For a recent discussion and editions of some of these texts, see Cesare D'Onofrio, *Visitiamo Roma Mille Anni Fa: La Città dei Mirabilia*. Studi e testi per la storia della città di Roma, 8 (Rome: Romana Società Editrice, 1988).

[7]  See the list of manuscripts of various forms of the *Mirabilia* (and of the *Stationes* and *Indulgentiae* of Rome to be discussed below), classified by language, in Miedema, *Die 'Mirabilia Romae'* In addition to manuscripts whose provenance are definitely identified as English, others suggest that they too were produced for an English audience by their inclusion of works of English history.

*Pontificum et Imperatorum* by Martinus Polonus (Martin of Troppau).[8] In addition
to the various Latin texts of the *Mirabilia* tradition accessible to English readers, at
least two, much abbreviated versions of its material were produced in Middle
English. The most significant of these is a 400-line addition in lively rhymed
couplets inserted near the beginning of the fifteenth-century *Metrical Version of
Mandeville's Travels*.[9] The lines are based on Martinus Polonus's redaction of the
*Graphia* supplemented by details from local British history, such as an account of
how Julius Caesar defeated the British king "Cassiblian" (Cassivelaunus in
Geoffrey of Monmouth) and built the Tower of London (371–80).

The end of the twelfth-century or beginning of the thirteenth saw another, more
idiosyncratic Latin description of the Roman antiquities, the *Narracio de Mirabilibus
Urbis Romae* by a certain Master Gregorius. The *Narracio* does not attempt to
provide a comprehensive catalogue of the city's ancient structures like the
*Mirabilia*, but instead reports, ostensibly to some of his fellow clerks studying
Scripture, the marvels that most impressed and delighted Gregorius on his first
trip to Rome.[10] Gregorius was most attracted to the artistic remains of Rome,
broadly considered, not only to the splendor of so many structures but also to
images of all kinds, such as the narrative reliefs on triumphal arches and, in
particular, the numerous bronze and marble statues whose skill he constantly

8    The *Graphia* both adds some material to the original *Mirabilia* (especially a preliminary history of
     Rome that emphasizes its Trojan origin, which would have been of special interest to English
     readers who also claimed Trojan ancestors) and omits other material. These additions are often
     marked in the original edition of Francis Morgan Nichols's translation of the *Mirabilia* (*Mirabilia
     Romae: The Marvels of Rome or a Picture of the Golden City* [London: Ellis and Elvey, 1889]). These
     additions are not indicated in the second edition of Nichols used and cited below. References to
     the Latin *Graphia* are to the edition of Roberto Valentini and Giuseppe Zucchetti in their *Codice
     Topografico della Città di Roma*, vol. 3. Fonti per la storia d'Italia, pub. dal R. Istituto storico italiano
     per il medio evo. Scrittori. Secoli I–XV, 90 (Roma: Tipografia del Senato, 1946), 67–110. For the
     influence of Martin Polonus, see Wolfgang-Valentin Ikas, "Martinus Polonus' Chronicle of the
     Popes and Emperors: a Medieval Best-Seller and Its Neglected Influence on Medieval English
     Chroniclers," *English Historical Review* 116 (2001): 327–41. The most recent edition of Martin's work
     is *Martini Oppaviensis Chronicon*, ed. Ludwig Weiland. Monumenta *Germaniae Historia*, Scriptorum
     22 (1872; New York: Kraus, 1963), 37–482.
9    All quotations of this text are from *The Metrical Version of Mandeville's Travels*, ed. M. C. Seymour.
     Early English Society, OS 269 (London: Oxford University Press, 1973); they are cited by line
     number and the spelling is slightly modernized. There is also a seventy-line verse fragment that
     contains *Mirabilia* material edited by John Scattergood, "An Unpublished Middle English Poem,"
     *Archiv für das Studium der neueren Sprachen und Literaturen* 203 (1967): 277–82.
10   Quotations of Gregorius's *Narracio* are from the Latin edition of *Magister Gregorius: Narracio de
     Mirabilibus Urbis Romae*, ed. R. B. C. Huygens. Textus minors, 44 (Leiden: E. J. Brill, 1970) and the
     English translations, slightly modified, from John Osborne, *Master Gregorius: The Marvels of Rome*
     (Toronto: Pontifical Institute of Medieval Studies, 1987). All further citations will be included in
     the text and will refer first to the page and line number of the Latin original and then to the page
     number of the Osborne translation.

praises and whose destruction, along with that of other monuments, he blames on Churchmen, particularly Saint Gregory, the avarice of the Roman people, and the simple ravages of time. Nothing is definitely known about Magister Gregorius to whom the *Narracio* is attributed in its prefatory incipit, but he is generally assumed with some reason to have been an English cleric.[11] The text of the *Narracio*, in a copy that is not the original and apparently is somewhat truncated, survives in a single manuscript now in Cambridge, and it reached a wide English audience, learned and vernacular, because of its use by Ralph Higden in his popular early fourteenth-century Latin *Polychronicon*, still extant in some 135 complete manuscripts, which itself was twice translated into Middle English, most significantly by John Trevisa in the late fourteenth century; fourteen manuscripts of Trevisa's translation also survive.[12]

The second class of medieval descriptions of Rome known to the English was addressed to devout pilgrims, not antiquarians, though its subject is likewise the Roman past. More like a guide than the *Mirabilia* and also extant in many forms, it enumerates the remains of early martyrs and other relics contained in the city's many churches as well as the pardon from sin these objects offer to the devout visitor.[13] Many Latin manuscript copies of this brief guide are still extant in English libraries, and its material appeared in Middle English in the fifteenth century, usually in undistinguished verse of under a thousand lines with many variants from text to text (there is also one prose version).[14] The work is collectively known in English as *The Stations of Rome*, though this is a somewhat misleading title. In fact, *Stationes* properly were medieval Latin calendars that identified the particular church in Rome at which, on any day, but especially during Lent, the principal mass of the city was celebrated by the pope or his representative.[15] The Middle

---

[11]   See Osborne, *Master Gregorius*, 12–15.

[12]   See, for example, John Taylor, *The "Universal Chronicle" of Ranulf Higden* (Oxford: Clarendon Press, 1966); David C. Fowler, *John Trevisa*. Authors of the Middle Ages, 2 (Aldershot: Variorum, 1993); A. S. G. Edwards, "John Trevisa," *A Companion to Middle English Prose*, ed. id. (Cambridge: Brewer, 2004), 117–26.

[13]   For an account of these descriptions, based primarily on Latin examples in the British Library, see James Hulbert, "Some Medieval Advertisements of Rome," *Modern Phililogy* 20 (1923): 403–24. For a brief account of the history of indulgences (pardons), see Robert W. Shaffern, "The Medieval Theology of Indulgences," *Promisary Notes on the Treasury of Merits: Indulgences in Late Medieval Europe*, ed. R. N. Swanson (Leiden: Brill, 2006), 11–36, and, now, Robert W. Shaffern, *The Penitents' Treasury: Indulgences in Latin Christianity, 1175–1375* (Scanton and London: University of Scanton Press, 2007).

[14]   Hulbert, "Some Medieval Advertisements," notes that there are variations in the Latin texts he studied in the British Museum. For the extant Middle English versions of the *Stations of Rome*, see, *A New Index of Middle English Verse*, ed. Julia Boffey and A. S. G. Edwards (London: British Library, 2005), item 1172.

[15]   This usually involved a procession to the stational church and a mass there. See John F. Baldovin, S. J., *The Urban Character of Christian Worship: The Origins, Development, and Meaning of Stational*

English *Stations*, despite their name, are actually versions of a related type of Latin work, known as *Indulgentiae*, which catalogues the relics and pardons in Roman churches. *Stationes* and *Indulgentiae*, as complimentary guides to what Roman churches had to offer pilgrims, are sometimes found together in medieval manuscripts.[16] Material from both the *Stationes* and *Indulgentiae*, prefaced by a version of the *Mirabilia*, is included in the most ambitious description of Rome in Middle English, *The Solace of Pilgrimes* by the Augustinian friar John Capgrave, which was written after his journey to Rome in about 1450 and survives in a single incomplete manuscript.[17] After an opening account of the ancient monuments, the *Solace* declares that it will, in its second part (which ultimately is expanded to a third part), "tretith of the cherchis in Rome and of the spirituale tresour conteined in hem" (60). This the *Solace* does by first describing the seven principal Roman basilicas before continuing with the stational churches for each day in Lent and concluding with accounts of other significant churches.

These medieval descriptions of Rome, whether their primary attention is on the ancient pagan or Christian city, are alike in finding its glorious past accessible only by means of its few remaining physical fragments. The capital of the once great Roman Empire has shrunk to some ravaged monuments. Likewise, the holiness and heroism of the martyrs who conquered that empire survive in the tokens of their broken bodies. These accounts of the past show little curiosity about the residents or activities of present-day Rome. Master Gregorius occasionally mentions the cardinals as a reliable source of information about the city's past, but neither the *Narracio* nor any of our other descriptions has anything to say about the arcane workings of the modern papal court, the reason for so many English trips to Rome on ecclesiastic business. Similarly, we are not shown the elaborate religious processions that often wound through the city's streets, such as the one that annually paraded a miraculous portrait of Christ from the Lateran to S. Maria Maggiore to reunite the image of the Son with an equally wonder-working portrait of his Mother.[18]

---

*Liturgy*. Orientalia Christiana Analecta, 228 (Rome: Pont. Institutum Studiorum Orientalium, 1987). The original purpose of the Roman stations may have been a papal attempt to unite the various parishes and regions of Rome, but it also offered a program (and perhaps an opportunity to rest) for pilgrims touring the city's churches.

[16]  See Miedema, *Mirabilia Romae*.

[17]  John Capgrave, *The Solace of Pilgrimes*, ed. C. A. Mills (London: Oxford University Press, 1911). All quotations, with the spelling somewhat modernized, will be from this edition and cited by page number in the text.

[18]  Herbert L. Kessler and Johanna Zacharias, *Rome 1300: On the Path of the Pilgrim* (New Haven and London: Yale University Press, 2000), chapter 3. Capgrave does mention the "solempne procession" held at the Lateran on Psalm Sunday, but then instead of giving a full account of this procession, he discusses the history of Psalm Sunday commemorations throughout the Church from the time of the Apostles to Charlemagne (146–47). In referring to Roman saints and their

Capgrave says the most about contemporary Rome, though even he provides little more than brief glimpses, such as noting in passing that a passion play is held before S. Croce on Good Friday (79) or his speculation that women were not allowed into the chapel of relics at the same church either because the well-known tendency of female pilgrims "to touch and kisse every holy relik" might slow things down or because the press of the crowd would have been dangerous for the health of sick or pregnant women (77). Although the *Solace* lists the stational churches at which papal masses were said during Lent, it says almost nothing about these special liturgies, though Capgrave does, in his account of the last station, report a slight difference in the saying of the *agnus dei* from the English custom ("as we do"), which he heard at "divers masses" (155). This unusual moment in the *Solace* emphasizes how little we are otherwise told about the actual religious life of medieval Rome in these descriptions. Amid accounts of both pagan and Christian remains, the contemporary city is not shown as an active, functioning community, but instead it resembles an abandoned film set whose actors and technicians have long since departed, leaving only the residue of their stale dramas—a few scattered props and sagging backdrops—for the solitary visitor to contemplate.

Contrast these accounts of the ruins and relics of ancient Rome with a civic description written in the same century as the *Mirabilia* and *Graphia* (and perhaps the same century as Master Gregorius's *Narracio*) portraying a city much closer to home for the English reader: the Latin *encomium* of London with which William Fitzstephen prefaces his life of Saint Thomas à Becket, the *Descriptio Nobilissimae Civitatis Londonaiae* (1173–1175).[19] Like the *Mirabilia* and *Graphia*, Fitzstephen's *Descriptio* mentions some of the notable topographic features of London, but its primary attention is on the communal life of the present city rather than on its past monuments. Fitzstephen announces at the end of his prologue that his account of London will consider two aspects of the city: its physical situation (*situm*) and its

---

churches, I have used the modern Italian forms of their names except for the most common examples, such as Peter and Lawrence, which, for clarity, I give as English names.

19   Quotations from the Latin *Descriptio* are from *Materials for the History of Thomas Becket, Archbishop of Canterbury: (Canonized by Pope Alexander III., A. D. 1173*, ed. James Craigie Robertson. Rolls Series. Rerum Britannicarum Medii Aevi Scriptores, 67 (London: Her Majesty's Stationery Office, 1877; rpt. [Nendeln, Liechtenstein:] Kraus 1965), 3.2–13. I also use the translation by H. E. Butler, with some modifications, in *Norman London* (New York: Italica Press, 1990). All further citations will be included in the text and will refer first to the page number of the Latin original and then to the page numbers of the Butler translation. See the discussion of the work in Scattergood, "Misrepresenting." Fitzstephen's work helped to shape the English conception of London through the seventeenth-century. It survives in several Latin manuscripts, was included in the important fourteenth-century register of London documents, the *Liber Custumarum*, and parts of it also appeared in another municipal collection, the *Liber Albus*. At the very end of the sixteenth century it both inspired and was first printed as an appendix to John Stow's *Survey of London*.

public life (*rem publicam*) (2, trans. 48), but his emphasis is very much on the latter. The *Descriptio* celebrates the citizens and social activities of London, instead of its architectural monuments or holy shrines, making it a *laus civitatis* rather than a *laus urbis*. The city's walls and gates, which begin the *Mirabilia*, are noted by Fitzstephen (3, trans. 49), but the length of the former is not measured nor are the latter named; instead these structures are shown in use, not as defensive ramparts but as recreational passages through which crowds of Londoners (especially young Londoners) eagerly pass to reach the pleasures of the countryside beyond, whether taking the air at suburban wells in the summer (3–4, trans. 50) or, more ambitiously, skating on the Moorfields to the north of the city in the winter (11–12, trans. 58–59). Within the walls of London, the building given the most attention is not a great church or palace (St. Paul's is mentioned only briefly and not described in any detail), but a modest "public cook-shop" (*publica coquina*) by the Thames (5, trans. 52). This seemingly humble canteen is praised by Fitzstephen because it is useful to much of the city and "pertaining to the art of civic life" (*Haec equidem publica coquina est et civitati pluriumum expediens et ad civilitatem pertinens*), being open day and night to serve food to all levels of society—the rich and the poor—and especially convenient to residents if unexpected guests should arrive (6, trans. 52).[20] Fitzstephen presents a current social practice rather than an account of the past. His London, in contrast to Rome in the medieval descriptions, is dynamic with the everyday urban activities of contemporary life: tradesmen and laborers going each morning to their special districts in the city, public displays of schoolboy wit and learning; horse fairs in Smithfield.[21]

My comparison of London to Rome is not gratuitous, for Fitzstephen throughout both explicitly and implicitly contrasts the two cities, and although the English borough conspicuously lacks both the pagan monuments and Christian saints of its ancient rival, the *Descriptio* is insistent that it is the more vital of the two, as seen especially in the extended emphasis given to the boisterous, competitive games that are played in different parts of London throughout the year by youths (male youths, Fitzstephen's inclusiveness has it limits). The vigor of these games animates the entire city, as Fitzstephen makes clear in a detailed account of the ball games at Carnival played by both students and young tradesmen. The games are observed by the elders of the town, and because of them they feel rejuvenated. Their natural spirits are rekindled by the violent action they see before them, and "by their partaking in the joys of untrammeled youth"

---

[20]  Despite the singular, the reference here may be to a row of cook-shops rather than to a single establishment by the Thames, whose dignity is enhanced by Fitzstephen's citation of Plato on the art of cooking that immediately follows.

[21]  Of course this is a selective portrait of the city, with no mention of the poor or hospitals, for example, as Scattergood recognized ("Misrepresenting," 19).

(*participatione gaudiorum adolescentiae liberioris*) they feel young again (9, trans. 56–57). London is as communal and convivial as any Bakhtinian could wish.

The bustling public activity of Fitzstephen's London is absent from the medieval descriptions of Rome. The *Mirabilia* and the *Narracio* of Master Gregorius and their vernacular redactions do not mention the commercial life of Rome or the recreations of its citizens because their attention is on the physical remains of the classical city. And yet even these material objects are not fully present—much has disappeared or is only in fragments. The *Mirabilia* begins confidently by listing what Rome "has" (*habet*), such as its wall, and the structures that "are" (*sunt*) there, such as its gates and arches (17.1 and 5, trans. 4, 5), but the narratives in the middle section are set in the remote past, "in the times of the senators and consuls" (*temporibus consulum et senatorum*), when Rome was still golden (34.1, trans. 21).[22] The perambulation through the city in the final section again and again records what was there but is no longer, such as the many temples that "as far as I can remember" (*quae ad memoriam ducere possum*) had once been on the Capitol (51.7, trans. 38).

Many of the most active and ingenious of the marvels of Rome had now vanished. The *Mirabilia* and at greater length Gregorius's *Narracio* tell of a magical system of statues with bells around their necks representing each province under Rome's sway (*Mirabilia* 34.3–9, trans. 21; *Narracio* 18.214–19.239, trans. 24). If a province became rebellious, the bell on the appropriate image would instantly ring and thus the authorities were alerted to a threat that needed attention. But these statues and bells have vanished like the empire they were meant to protect. All that is left, according to Master Gregorius, are portions of the walls of the building in which the statues were and a "stark and inaccessible" (*horride et inaccessibiles*) crypt (18.222, trans. 24). Even those ancient marvels that have not completely disappeared from medieval Rome are often broken, useless except to gaze upon. Although Master Gregorius begins his *Narracio* with the stirring panorama of his first sight of Rome, the towers and palace he saw looking down from the hills, a closer examination of the city reveals, in a verse he quotes from Hildebert of Lavardin, a Rome that is "almost a total ruin" (*prope tota ruina*) and shattered (12.40, trans. 18). Although Gregorius promptly draws the consoling moral that Rome's decline teaches us the impermanence of all temporal things, his *Narracio* is a record of his growing indignation about this destruction.

---

[22] Quotations from the original *Mirabilia* are from the edition by RobertoValentini and Giuseppe Zucchetti in their *Codice Topografico della Città di Roma*, vol. 3 (Roma: Tipografia del Senato, 1946), 3–65. I also use, with some modifications, the translation of the *Mirabilia* (conflated with later versions) by Francis Morgan Nichols, *The Marvels of Rome*, 2nd ed. (1st ed.,1889; New York: Italica Press, 1986). All citations will be included in the text and refer first to the page and line number of the Latin original and then to the page number of the Nichols translation.

If the structures of ancient Rome are decayed or vanished in these medieval descriptions, its present inhabitants are largely invisible: the conclusion of the *Mirabilia* lists as one of its sources the stories he was told by old timers (65.4, trans. 46), and Master Gregorius occasionally refers to cardinals and clerks, but none of these figures makes an actual appearance in either narrative. Classical Romans are even less on the scene, of course, because they are long dead, and funeral monuments are given particular attention in the *Mirabilia*, as in the beginning of its perambulation, which describes the supposed sepulcher (*sepulchrum*) of Romulus (45.6, trans. 35), the elaborate temple of the Emperor Hadrian (now Castel Sant' Angelo) containing his sarcophagus (46.5–47.3, trans. 35–36) [Figure no. 1] and the castle built by Augustus to entomb Rome's emperors (47.8, trans. 36). Perhaps the most revealing example of a supposed monument to the dead, however, is that containing the remains of one of the empire's greatest rulers: Julius Caesar. The *Mirabilia*, Master Gregorius, and Capgrave each recount the legend that Caesar's ashes were in a small round container at the top of the Egyptian obelisk that is today in the center of St. Peter's Square and was nearby in the Middle Ages (*Mirabilia*, 43.7–44.8, trans. 33–34; *Narracio*, 28.513–29.548, trans. 34–35; *Solace* 22–24) [Figure no. 2]. These accounts of Caesar's pillar (or "needle" [*agulia*]) comment on its remarkable construction from a single stone and some discuss the emperor's life (including his bloody assassination) and accomplishments. The *Mirabilia* and Capgrave draw special attention to the suitability and irony of his resting place, for just as he was ruler over all men, now all still remain below his final perch, but the contrast between Caesar living and Caesar dead is stark and poignant:

> Caesar, you were once as great as is the world,
> But now you are enclosed in a small cave.
>
> Caesar, tantus eras quantus et orbis,
> Sed nunc in modico clauderis antro.
>
> [*Mirabilia*, 44.5–6, trans. 33]

Caesar, like Rome, is a much diminished thing, there are only fragments of ashes, enclosed in a "litil den" according to Capgrave (24), to testify to what once was alive.

In addition to actual tombs, some of the most prominent classical statues described in these works are said to have been designed as memorials, intended to preserve the fame if not the bodies of their subjects after death. The gilded bronze statue of the mounted equestrian (now recognized as Marcuse Aurelius) was especially admired by the writer of the *Mirabilia* and by Master Gregorius, as it has been ever since by so many others (*Mirabilia*, 32.3–33.22, trans. 19–21;

*Narracio* 13.56–16.163, trans. 19–22).[23] In the Middle Ages the statue was placed before the Lateran complex, as depicted in a fifteenth-century fresco by Filippino Lippi in the church of S. Maria sopra Minerva, perhaps in the mistaken belief that it represented the first Christian Emperor Constantine [Figure no. 3]. In the sixteenth-century the figure was moved to the plaza on top of the Capitoline Hill, where a copy stands today, with the original indoors nearby, protected from the elements [Figure no. 4]. Our authors give somewhat different stories about the identity of the horseman (Gregorius offers a choice of two), but, as with another monumental image of two men and their horses, now known as the Dioscuri, the equestrian statute is said to have been specifically intended as a remembrance: "a memoriall in minde for evermore" as Trevisa's translation of the *Polychronicon*'s puts it (231).[24] Even before telling of the deed that earns the horseman this monument, he is already imagined as dead and gone. An alternative explanation of the statue by Master Gregorius even more explicitly associates the horseman with death: when no one else is willing to sacrifice himself by riding into a chasm that had brought a fatal plague to Rome, the leader of the republic does so himself and thereby saves the city by his own destruction.

In addition to many that contain or represent the dead (and others that were adapted to other purposes), the classical structures and statues in the medieval descriptions of Rome were often subjected to deliberate acts of annihilation. These monuments became ruins not only because of the inevitable decay of time, but also, like the English monasteries under Henry VIII, their "dissolution" is shown to be the result of a policy of extermination by the new religion. A later version of the *Mirabilia* adds a detailed account of the Colosseum, then as now an example of both Rome's glory and its decline, which is only mentioned in passing in the original version [Figure no. 5]. Not understanding the true function of this immense structure, the fourteenth- or fifteenth-century writer calls it a temple and declares there was a gigantic statue of the sun in a hall containing a model of the firmament with functioning sun and moon that produced actual thunder and rain.[25] An especially dramatic account of this temple and its statue (and their fate)

---

[23]   For a brief account of the history of this statue, see the commentary by Osborne to his translation of *Master Gregorius* cited above, 43–48.

[24]   Quotations from John Trevisa's English translation of Ralph Higden's *Polychronicon* are from the first volume of the Rolls edition, ed. Churchill Babington (London: Longman, 1865), and will be cited in the text by page number.

[25]   The account of the Colosseum in this later version of the *Mirabilia* is edited by Urlichs, *Codex*, "Quarta Classis," 136, cf. also 160; it is translated in Nichols's *Marvels*, 28–29. This passage is full of information rejected by modern scholars but reflecting medieval views: the great statue referred to was probably erected by Nero and was later placed outside the Colosseum, which, of course, was not a temple. The head and hand said to be from this statue are probably from another statue of an emperor and are now displayed in the Capitoline Museum. See the notes to Seymour's edition of the *Metrical Version of Mandeville*, 91, and Osborne's commentary to *Master Gregorius*,

is given in the description of Rome inserted into the *Metrical Version of Mandeville's Travels* (385–412). The poet begins by praising the Colosseum as the "moost mervailous temple of alle" with high walls, towers, and "peinted alle with riche coloures" (386–92), and he describes its similacrum of the heavens with awe:

> The rooff was made verament
> Evenliche unto the firmament,
> With sonne and moone and sterris brighte
> That shined bothe daye and nighte.
> Thundir and lightenenge, hayle and rain,
> Whenever they wolde in certain,
> Thai shewed it in dede apertly.

[393–299]

But admiration for such ingenuity is tempered by damningly attributing it to the "crafft of sorcery" (400), perhaps because what was produced seemed too much like an imitation of God's creation. The giant bejeweled statue in the center of the temple with a sphere in its hand is described as correspondingly presumptuous in its claim of earthly predominance: "And in his honde a golden balle / In tokene that Rome was chieff cite / Of alle this worlde" (410–12) [Figure no. 6]. This assertion of pagan Rome's control of the heavens and the earth cannot stand if the city is to become Christian. And so we are told that Pope Sylvester, the first pontiff given temporal power over Rome according to the legend of the Donation of Constantine, demolished ("fordid") the idol ("that riche mamette") despite its magnificence (415). He further "distroyed that temple of lim and stone / And other templis ful many oone" (417–18) and in their place builds churches that offer eternal, Christian riches: "ful grete pardoun" (421).

The later medieval version of the Latin *Mirabilia* already cited, which seems to be the source of this material, makes it clear that such temples as the Colosseum must cease to exist precisely because they are so marvelous: Pope Sylvester eradicated the pagan temples so that visitors to Rome would not be able to visit such "profane buildings" (*edificia profana*), but instead go devoutly to Christian churches.[26] The *Metrical Mandeville*, in a passage immediately following its account of the Colosseum, is explicit that some structures of pagan Rome had to be destroyed not because they were dilapidated but rather because they were all too alive and fascinating. The poet says that "holye men" destroyed these places of worship because pilgrims to the city had more "devocioun / To seen the mervailis in that stage [place] / Than to fulfillen thaire pilgrimage" (431–34). The wonders of Rome's pagan temples proved more attractive to Christians than all the promise

26  48–53.
Urlichs, *Codex*, "Quarta Classis," 136, Nichols's translation of *Miracles of Rome*, 29.

of future pardon and so they are terminated (with extreme prejudice). The later version of the *Mirabilia* describes the treatment of the colossal statue of the Sun almost as if there were an execution: Sylvester orders the head and hand of the idol (*caput vero et manus praedicti ydoli*) to be placed in front of his palace.[27] Dismembered like a captured enemy or condemned criminal, the bronze remains are displayed before the pope's palace at the Lateran as if they were a trophy of Christian conquest and triumph.

In many medieval descriptions of Rome, in English and in Latin, pagan monuments are shown to have to 'die' in order that the new religion may live. The most famous dissenter from that position among our writers is Master Gregorius. Enraptured by Rome's past architectural glory from his first sight of it from the hills above the city, he repeatedly criticizes the loss of such a rich classical heritage, which must have appeared especially remarkable and precious to one whose native experience seems to have been of British art and architecture.

Gregorius deplores anything that diminishes the original splendor of those monuments. For all his admiration of the bronze equestrian statue, he notes it was once even more magnificent, blaming Roman avarice (*Romana . . . avaricia*) for having stripped the gold that once had lavishly gilded it and *beatus Gregorius* (Pope Gregory the Great) for having taken down the statue from its original location on the Capitol in order to remove the four columns on which it stood to use in the papal church of St. John Lateran (13.63–68, trans. 19). Despoiling and reuse are bad enough in Master Gregorius's view, but he prefaces his account of the most beautiful statue he encountered in Rome, the Venus discussed below, by suggesting that his namesake (and elsewhere a special hero to the English because of his role in the conversion of the island, the same "blessed Gregory") was something like a mass murderer against the marble statuary of Rome: "almost all of which were destroyed or toppled by blessed Gregory" (*que pene omnes a beato Gregorio aut delete aut deturpate sunt*) (20.277–78, trans. 26).[28]

That ancient Christian Rome as well as ancient pagan Rome is a city of death in the medieval descriptions is even easier to demonstrate. If the *Mirabilia* tradition and especially Master Gregorius are haunted by the ruin that time has wrought—Rome's ancient empire vanished, its heroes confined to mausoleums or statues, its religion exterminated, its marvelous creations stilled and broken—death is at the very center of Christian accounts of the city and shown to

---

[27]  Ibid.

[28]  In a later English guide to Rome (c. 1470), William Brewyn judges hacking off the heads and limbs of the pagan images by St. Gregory as a triumph of "ecclesiastical truth" (*A XVth Century Guide-Book to the Principal Churches of Rome*, trans. C. Eveleigh Woodruff [London: Marshall Press, 1933], 14). In fact, these accusations of iconoclasm against St. Gregory, though widespread in the Middle Ages, seem to have been unfounded: see Tilmann Buddensieg, "Gregory the Great, the Destroyer of Pagan Idols," *Journal of the Warburg and Courtlaud Institutes* 28 (1965): 44–65.

be the source of its preeminence. Works such as the Middle English *Stations of Rome* and the second and third parts of John Capgrave's *Solace of Pilgrimes* extol the martyrdoms that baptized the city and made it holy, and the former is principally a catalogue of the bodies of saints in Roman churches. Death did not overthrow or diminish Christian Rome; it created it. The city's special spiritual authority comes directly from the famous martyrs who were executed there—Peter and Paul, most important of all, who, according to the *Stations*, redeemed the city with "heore flesch and with heore blode" (14), but also many others from the heroic first age of the Church, such as Agnes, Lawrence, Cecilia, and Sebastian, as well as thousands of anonymous victims[29] [Figure no. 7]. In the prologue to the second part of his *Solace*, Capgrave considers why the Church at Rome should have "swech grete privilege" as the "principal moder and norcherer of oure feith" (60); the last of the reasons he gives is that of "the multitude of martires whech spilt her blood in confirmacioun of our feith in that same place" (61). Even the *Mirabilia*, primarily concerned with classical monuments, has a chapter on the locations of Roman martyrdoms (chapter 8 in the Latin) and another on its Christian catacombs (chapter 10).

The lifelessness of these remains is emphasized not only by reference to the saints' violent deaths but also by calling attention to their broken bodies. The *Stations of Rome* is a guide to where these "holy bones" (a frequently repeated phrase) are to be found in Rome, such as at the church of St. Sebastian, where such bones "lay under grounde / An hundred yer er they weore founde" (161–64). The numbers of the ancient sacred dead are sometimes staggering. We are told that "mony is that holy bone" under the altar of the chapel of Scala Coeli (no less than the remains of 10,000 martyrs) at the abbey now known as Tre Fontane (123–25), while at the church of S. Pudenziana the bodies of 40,000 martyrs rest according to the Vernon text (542), though other versions put the number at a more modest, but still impressive, 3,000 (Cotton, 666). Not only are these relics regularly referred to as little more than bones, but even the best preserved examples are often in pieces. The church of St. Julian is said to contain that saint's "chin with his teth" (450), and, of special interest to English readers, St. Thomas à Becket's arm and "a parti of the brayn" is in Santa Maria Maggiore (497–99).The bodies of Peter and

---

[29] My quotations from the *Stations of Rome* are taken from two fifteenth-century verse forms of the work, the Cotton version, as edited by Frederick J. Furnivall in *Political, Religious, and Love Poems*. Early English Text Society, OS 15, second edition (London: Kegan Paul, 1903), 143–73, and the Vernon version, edited by Furnivall in *The Stacions of Rome*. Early English Text Society, OS 25 (London: N. Trübner, 1867), 1–33, with the Vernon Prologue subsequently edited by Furnivall in *The Minor Poems of the Vernon MS*. Early English Text Society, OS 117 (London: Kegan Paul,1901), 2.609–11. All citations are by line number and will be given in my text; they are from Vernon unless otherwise indicated.

Paul lie in their respective basilicas, but their heads, kept over the high altar of the Lateran, were displayed during the week before Easter, and Capgrave reports the sight in the *Solace of Pilgrimes*: "The hed of Petir is a brood face with mech her on his berd and that is of grey colour betwix whit and blak. The hed of Paule is a long face balled with red her, both berd and hed" (73). The non-human relics which were so famous and abundant in Rome are also often associated with death and mutilation, not surprisingly for a faith whose primary sign is the cross. These include the pillar on which Christ was scourged by Pilate at S. Prassede and the wood and nails from the cross itself at S. Croce.

Once again, as with the medieval descriptions that emphasize the remains of classical Rome, the Christian *Stations of Rome* and even the second and third parts of Capgrave's *Solace* say little about contemporary Rome and its social activities, residents, or visitors. Capgrave offers the most information of this kind, but only in brief, unsystematic glimpses, as previously noted, though he does report, with strong disapproval, a local Spring contest involving attacking pigs as they run down Mt. Testaccio, resulting in death and injury to men and animals alike: "a ful onlikly game me thoutgh [sic]" (50–51). When Capgrave mentions the exhibition of the heads of Peter and Paul at the Lateran, he says nothing about any ceremony associated with this display nor about the response of others; instead he offers only his own personal observation. The city appears even more deserted and inanimate in the *Stations of Rome*. The generous pardon that these texts announce was available in many Roman churches and obviously attracted large crowds, but we almost never see them, certainly not in any detail. A rare mention of pilgrims in general notes that Pope Silvester offered pardon "to pilgrimes / That thider cometh" (103–04); yet even here it is the past not the present that is evoked by citing such an early pope, and the word "pilgrimes" may be used as much for its rhyme as anything else. Current liturgical services in Rome also go unmentioned in the *Stations*, though reference is occasionally made to those of long ago. For example, St. Gregory is told by an angel of the holy bones buried at St. Sebastian "as he song masse" at the high altar there (149–52).[30]

The underlying argument of the *Stations* (the reader should visit Rome rather than other holy sites for pardon) is implicitly made to all Christians, but it is often, though not always, expressed in the second person singular: "*Thou* shalt have as muche pardoun / As *thou* to Seint Jame [Compostella] went and com" (91–92, my emphasis). Indeed, the *Stations* often seems to be conducting a private tour for the reader. The notation of specific distances between churches, such as "two myle is holde betwene" (95), and even, as in one especially vivid moment at the tomb of Lawrence and Stephen, its instruction about how to act, "Putte in thy heed or thy

---

[30]    The Vernon also notes the "great solempnite" (167), also in the distant past, when the buried bones were recovered at S. Sebastian's.

honde, / And thou shalt fele a swete gronde / A swete smelle of bodyes that ther be" (Cotton 528–30), may have been intended less as a practical guide for an actual traveler to Rome than as a prompt for a mental pilgrimage by the solitary reader back in England.

But if medieval Rome in these various descriptions known to the English is permeated by death, there are also some signs of life among the ancient ruins and relics. Not present-day communal life as in Fitzstephen's *Descriptio*, but past or future life accessible to the individual observer (and reader) who can imaginatively or devoutly respond to the remains of Rome. Just as death is even more obvious in the *Stations of Rome* than in the *Mirabilia* tradition, so is life, and both are a result of the most prominent feature of these texts: the bodies of martyrs and other relics in Rome's churches. The life these objects promise is, of course, beyond this present world, and yet the saints' bodies and relics have not been wholly immobile even on earth. Although in accordance with ancient custom, most of the original Roman martyrs were killed and then buried outside the city walls, not all remained in their catacombs. Whereas early Christians journeyed beyond the city limits to worship at the extramural cemeteries that contained the most famous burial sites (such as those of Saints Peter and Lawrence, which were eventually enclosed by basilicas), later popes, once they were free to do so, brought the bones of these martyrs into the heart of Rome, as their numbers at such central churches as S. Prassede and Santa Pudenziana, already mentioned, testify. Other bodies were moved to Rome from farther away, such as that of St. Jerome: "From the cite of Damas [Damascus] / He was brought into that plas" (481–82). Non-human relics were brought all the way from the Holy Land, such as the table used for the Last Supper (305–08) and Aaron's rod (321), among many others at the Lateran, not to mention "a fot of Marie Magdaleyn" (664) at S. Cecilia.

More important than the illusion of animation implied by their urban or international movement, the bodies of the saints in Roman churches, far different from the cold ashes of Caesar on his pillar, were still active and capable of giving the gift of future life to others: the abundant, blissful life of heaven rather than the torments of hell.[31] The unique Prologue to the Vernon version of the *Stations* promises to teach the reader who finds "his soule in sinne bounde" (Prologue, 9) and fears that he will suffer "the fuir of helle, / Wher-of the peynes no mon con telle" (Prologue, 15–16) how he may obtain the medicine of pardon at "grete Rome" (Prologue, 17), thereby insuring that "Nedes to hevene moste he wende /

---

[31]    See R. N. Swanson, *Indulgences in Late Medieval England: Passports to Paradise?* (Cambridge: Cambridge University Press, 2007), and Robert W. Shaffern, *The Penitents' Treasury.*

Withouten peyne lasse or more" (Prologue, 26–27).[32] The *Stations* provides a list of
the many Roman churches that offer this medicine and in what amount, for
without such pardon from deadly sin, "may thy soule not live" (179). Present
existence is less important than what the Roman St. Cecilia in Chaucer's *Second
Nun's Tale* calls "bettre lif in oother place,"[33] and thus we are told of martyrs who
"suffrede deth alle in Rome / Heore soules in hevene for to come" (127–28; cf.
199–200).

The *Stations* does not require such ultimate sacrifice from the pilgrim (or reader),
but instead explains how he may avoid the future tortures of Hell and even obtain
release from the pains of Purgatory. In addition to securing one's own life in
heaven, Rome permits one to procure it for others, even after their deaths: "Ther
men may helpe quike and dede / As the clerkes in bokes rede" (129–30).
Attendance at the church of St. Lawrence every Wednesday for a year, for
example, allows you to free someone already in Purgatory: "A soule to drawe
from Purgatory fer" (412). More generously, the Cotton version says that at the
church of S. Giovanni a Porta Latina, in addition to the everyday personal pardon
of five hundred years (Cotton, 272–73), if you are in attendance on the festival day
of the saint, "a sowle fro Pugratorye winne thou may" (Cotton, 271). At least one
Roman site seems to guarantee a place in heaven, with no mention of reform,
simply for being interred there. Near the end of the Cotton version of the *Stations*,
we are told that St. Gregory "purchased syche grace" at the church of St. Andrew
that whoever is buried there ("man or woman") will be saved from hell as long as
the person has faith in God and the Church regardless of past behavior: "If he
beleve in God & Holy Chyrche also, / He shall not be dampned *for nought that he
hathe doo*" (Cotton, 898–901, my emphasis). The narrator insists that this blanket
pardon, for all its apparent unorthodoxy, is "the sothe that I the tell," though he
acknowledges that some readers may not believe him and offers as proof that it is
explicitly written down there: "on the chyrche-dore thou mayst hit see" (Cotton,
903–05). Such faith in the written word.

In contrast to the narrow span of human existence, the *Stations* repeatedly speaks
of the vast expanse of years to come when the reader will be free from the
penalties of Purgatory to enjoy the blissful life of heaven. Like a series of spiritual
ATM machines that reward all who use them regardless of funds on deposit, the
churches of Rome pay off in multiples of years. Originally indulgences were
granted by the popes only to Crusaders, and when, apparently in response to

---

[32]   The Prologue stresses that anyone desiring pardon must be "in love and charite" with others and
       keep himself "clene to his ende" (23–25), though in the body of *Stations* pardons seem more
       automatically available without the reminder of the receiver's responsibility.

[33]   *The Riverside Chaucer*, ed. Larry D. Benson et al., third edition (Boston: Houghton Mifflin, 1987),
       VIII, 323.

public demand, they were later made more generally available to pilgrims, an effort was made to restrict the years of the pardon, forty years being the limit that individual bishops could grant, for example.[34]

But the hopeful expectations of visitors to Rome soon inflated this currency as surely as that of Weimar Germany. For example, the church of St. Clement granted "two thousand yer" (704) of pardon and that of St. Julian "eighte thousand yere" (452). In the theology of indulgences, it was never made clear just how these years were determined, who was keeping the accounts, or exactly how much time the sinner might actually need. At times the amounts listed in popular texts like the *Stations*, whether or not officially approved, are thrown around like so much Monopoly money, with multiples of a thousand the most common denomination, though sometimes the figures are fussily precise: thus one church promised 1030 years (662) and another 4384 (720–24). The time of year can increase the numbers dramatically: at the high altar of St. Peter's the usual pardon is 28 years, but from Holy Thursday to Lammas it shoots up to 14,000 (48–54). The difficulty of the journey also affects the amount: when the Vernicle of St. Veronica (the cloth with the imprint of Christ's face) is displayed at St. Peter' there are 3,000 years of pardon for a resident (4,000 in Cotton, 83), 9,000 for a non-resident, and 12,000 for a pilgrim who has made a sea-journey (indicating, despite the lack of attention to them, implicit recognition of the many natives and visitors in Rome), plus the forgiveness of a third of one's sins—and all these numbers are doubled during Lent (59–70).[35] The bones and relics of Rome are not only material witnesses of ancient death and suffering in the city, but they are also the means by which the pilgrim can achieve the heavenly life to come.[36]

Whereas it is the future life that concerns the *Stations of Rome*, in the *Mirabilia* tradition, Master Gregorius, and even Capgrave, it is the past that is brought to life. Perhaps the most memorable examples of a sympathetic observer finding life in the inert ruins of Rome are Master Gregorius's encounters with ancient statues. The first statue he mentions, a bronze bull like the one that Jupiter used to deceive Europa, is not described in any real detail but we are told that it was so skillfully made that it appears to viewers as if it were about to "bellow and move" (*mugituro et moturo*) like a living creature (13.54, trans. 19). Gregorius often makes clear that the animation of these images results not only from the skill of the creator but also from the careful attention of the observer: thus to one looking intently (*attencius inspexerit*), the bronze head of the Colossus appears to be "moving and speaking"

---

[34] See Shaffern, "The Medieval Theology of Indulgences."
[35] Often the *Stations* goes beyond precise numbers and simply mentions that a particular site offers a plenary indulgence for all sins.
[36] Given the indulgences available at Rome, the *Stations* tells us, there is no need to travel as far as the Holy Land, for at Rome "pardoun ther is withouten ende" (285–93).

(*moturo et locuturo*) because of the care and expense with which it was made
(17.204–18.205, trans. 23). These responses have been seen as proto-Humanist,
though Gregorius is attracted more by the ingenuity and even emotional appeal
of these works than by purely aesthetic appreciation, as is clearest in Gregorius's
most dramatic account of such an experience, his repeated visits to view a marble
statue of Venus that some have identified with the "Capitoline Venus"[37] [Figure
no. 8]. As will be true for many subsequent travelers to Rome, Gregorius finds a
presence in the cold marble that affects him viscerally, perhaps even erotically. As
with the bronze bull, Gregorius first associates the Venus with an ancient legend,
the Judgment of Paris, before abruptly moving from myth to the object before him.
This Venus, he insists, was made with such wonderful, even inexplicable art (*miro
et inexplicabili perfecta est artificio*) that it seems more like a living person (*viva
creatura*) than a statue; he even imagines he can see it blush and declares that those
who look closely (*comminus aspicientibus*) can see the blood flow in her snowy
complexion (*in niveo ore ymaginis sanguinem natare*), which caused him (perhaps as
the result of a magic spell) to be drawn to revisit it three time even though it was
distant from his lodgings (20.286–293, trans. 26).

Higden's *Polychronicon* and its Middle English translations make Gregorius's
accounts of these statues less personal to accord with their more objective style of
history, but they do retain his claims for the life-like appearance of the images.
Thus Trevisa says the bull "semed lowinge and startlinge" (225), the mouth of the
Colossus "as they [though] it were spekinge" (235), and, most vividly, the Venus
"so craftliche made that in the mouthe and lippes, that were as white as eny snow,
semede fresche blood and newe" (225). The extraordinary effect of the Venus on
Gregorius suggests the tale of Pygmalion, but we should note that in his telling,
not to mention in the less fervent English versions, there is a significant difference.
Although Gregorius does suggest supernatural forces behind the statue's appeal
to him, his lady does not step off her pedestal and go off with her admirer. Venus

---

[37]   Gordon Rushforth, "Magister Gregorius *De Mirabilibus Urbis Romae*: A New Description of Rome
in the Twelfth Century," *Journal of Roman Studies* 9 (1919): 14–58; here 25, made the identification
of Gregorius's Venus with the famous one now in the Capitoline Museum, and this was accepted
by Osborne, *Master Gregorius*, 59, but Dale Kinney, "*Mirabilia Urbis Romae*," *The Classics in the
Middle Ages*, ed. Aldo S. Bernardo and Saul Levin (Binghamton: Medieval and Renaissance Texts
and Studies, 1990), calls this identification "neither likely . . . nor necessary" (214). It may,
however, well have been a statue similar to the Capitoline Venus.
   For Gregorius as a proto-humanist, see, for example, James Bruce Ross, "A Study of Twelfth-
Century Interest in the Antiquities of Rome," *Medieval and Historiographical Essays in Honor of James
Westfall Thompson*, ed. James L. Cate and Eugene N. Anderson (Chicago: University of Chicago
Press, 1938), 302–31; here 320, and Cristina Nardella, "La Roma dei visitatori colti: dalla mentalità
umanistica di Maestro Gregorio (XII–XIII Secolo) a quella medioevale di John Capgrave (XV
Secolo)," *Archivio della Società Romana di Storia Patria* 119 (1996): 49–64; here, 52. Compare Kinney's
more skeptical view of the nature of Gregorius's appreciation ("Mirabilia," 214–19).

remains an ancient marble. But even if the observer is not able to find actual life in the marble, he can recapture the illusion of it first created by the anonymous artist long ago. Gregorius's intense scrutiny has made a connection across the centuries to a once thriving world.

The writers of the medieval descriptions of Rome know, as Odysseus and Aeneas discover in the underworld, that it is impossible to physically embrace the dead, but their shades can be evoked and recognized. Gregorius does this most dramatically during his encounter with the statue of Venus, but the most common method these texts use to make the past come alive is by means of stories. In addition to the sense of animal and human presence that Gregorius experiences from some Roman statues, he more often uses the ancient images he finds as prompts to recreate the true narratives of the past he assumes (almost always incorrectly) they tell. Thus in his rather lengthy account of the triumphal arch near the Pantheon said to honor Augustus's victory at Actium, Gregorius first mentions what he claims are its statues of the battle's military commanders, especially a skillful portrait of Augustus himself, before turning to the reliefs on the arch, which, he says, when looked at closely (*cum intencius aspicias*), makes you imagine that you are seeing the very struggle of Actium itself (*vera bella videre existimes*), as Augustus pursues Cleopatra (24.406–07, trans. 30).[38] Gregorius's characteristic attention to the reliefs inspires him to portray the battle as if it were happening before his eyes (while also allowing the reader to visualize it), as in this breathless account of the marble's representation of Cleopatra being captured, applying the asps to her breasts, and going pale in death: "*Cleopatra subducitur et appositis aspidibus mammis suis in Pario marmore superba mulier moritura pallescit*" (24.410–12, trans. 30).[39]

A number of especially prominent ancient statues saved from the ruins of Rome inspire our writers to go beyond cataloguing and objective description and attempt to bring to life the real human beings behind the monuments by giving them back their voices and actions. Of course these stories are largely legends, though they were undoubtedly widely believed in medieval Rome. The middle section of the *Mirabilia* includes several such narratives. Thus the bronze equestrian rider, already mentioned, whom we know to be Marcus Aurelius, is given a long narrative complete with the character's thought, intentions, speech, and dramatic action (32.3–33.22, trans. 19–21) [Figure no. 9]. At the request of the daring squire

---

[38]   None of the arches known to have been built for Augustus fit the description here; a single arch, not a multiple one, commemorating the battle of Actium was built in the Forum (not near the Pantheon as here) and appears to have been demolished in 19BC, see Osborne's commentary to his *Master Gregorius*, 79–89.

[39]   The *Polychronicon* briefly notes Augustus's arch with, in Trevisa's words, "his dedes descryved" (215), but does not, in fact, identify Actium as one of those deeds or describe its events.

who is our hero, the senate promises both money and a memorial statue if he can
rid them of a king's army besieging Rome. The squire had noticed that the king
was in the habit of relieving himself at a certain tree every night. Therefore,
disguised as a groom, he approaches the tree, and though warned away by royal
attendants, boldly seizes the king and carries him back into the city, telling the
Romans to attack the now leaderless army, which they do successfully. Neither the
statue nor the story appears in the *Metrical Mandeville's Travels*, but Capgrave tells
a version in the opening section of the *Solace* that is even livelier than that in the
*Mirabilia*. He changes the latter's indirect statement that the attendants told the
disguised squire to get away from the king, *coeperunt clamare, ut ipse auferret se de
via ante regem* (33.8–9, trans. 20), into convincingly blustering speech: "Be war, carl,
what thou do. Come not so ny the kyng. Thou schal be hangid and thou touch
him" (32).

Master Gregorius provides not one but two different long narratives about the
real-life actions that inspired this equestrian monument (chapters 4 and 5). The
first is a version of the *Mirabilia*'s story with some changes in detail (the king less
comically goes out at night to practice magic, not to relieve himself), and the
second tells of Quintus Quirinus, a ruler of the republic who gave his life for the
common good by riding into a fiery chasm because only by this sacrifice would
that earthly fault, whose fumes were causing a terrible plague in Rome, be closed.[40]
The Latin *Polychronicon*, which often shortens Gregorius, gives both stories in some
detail and both also appear in its two Middle English translations (228–33). The
figures represented by the statue are allowed to exist again, at least textually, as
active, speaking humans.

John Capgrave, perhaps inspired by the classical stories from the *Mirabilia* that
he retells in the first part of his *Solace of Pilgrimes*, recreates the religious as well as
secular past of Rome with narratives that are far more extensive than the brief
biographical notices found occasionally in the Middle English *Stations of Rome*.[41]
He is more interested in the lives of the saints than their physical remains, and he
repeatedly moves from perfunctory descriptions of a church and its relics, with
only occasional notation of available pardons, to extended accounts of what the
saints did while alive, at the same time reporting their martyrdoms and their
miracles for believers after death. For example, the church of SS. Giovanni and
Paolo itself is identified in a few sentences: Capgrave tells the date during Lent of

---

[40]  There is a much shorter version of this second story in the *Mirabilia* (56.1–5, trans. 41).
[41]  Most saints in the *Stations* are simply mentioned by name; it is after all the power of their sacred
bones that the pilgrim seeks for pardon. A few episodes, not full biographies, from the lives of
some important saints are briefly told, especially the curing of Constantine's leprosy by Pope
Sylvester and the emperor's conversion (241–76), and St. Peter's encounter with Christ outside
Rome that sends him back into the city and to his martyrdom (201–10).

its station mass, its location "fast by the monastery of Seynt Andrew," the "certein thingis whech thei selle there" on the day of the station, the "fair place" that belongs to a cardinal on one side, and the ruined palace on the other (89–90). Then, after noting the "ful grete indulgens that day" for visitors to the church, but without specifying exactly its extent or giving any account of the relics there, Capgrave devotes the vast majority of his chapter (perhaps 75 percent) not to the physical church and its contents, but to stories of the two saints for whom it is named. As a preface to this, Capgrave explains his general method to the reader: after reference to the pardon as a result of the holy bones of Giovanni and Paolo, he declares, "but we think best at this time to telle sumwhat of the lif of these seyntes and why thei wer dede," an emphasis on narrative fullness and particularly the human "lif" of the saints that he says he will follow throughout: "as we cast us for to do of alle othir" (90).

Human stories such as these do indeed dominate the second and third parts of the *Solace of Pilgrimes*, in contrast to the repetitive lists of objects and pardons that make up so much of the *Stations of Rome*. Capgrave's holy legends, in the manner of the *exempla* in clerical homilies, seem more interested in providing his readers with inspirational models for living on earth than in simply promising future rewards in heaven. Specific relics of Rome inspire Capgrave to tell stories from the medieval period as well as from the ancient past. For example, he says that he saw a "memoriale" in the church of S. Sabina on the Aventine concerning Saint Dominic and how when he was praying at that church for the confirmation of his order, he so angered the Devil that the fiend "threw a grete ston as mech or more than a mannes hed" trying to kill the saint, but by a "grete miracle" it missed and only broke a piece of marble (87). Capgrave even quotes the Latin inscription about the incident and gives its "sentens" in English, both of which are somewhat less detailed and dramatic than the version he has just told. What gives this story immediacy is not only the energy of its narration but also the physical proof that Capgrave notes remains in the church: both the chipped marble and, "a grete evidens of the truth" (87), the very stone that was thrown by the Devil (which is still displayed in S. Sabina today) [Figure no. 10]. This is hardly a story of death and suffering, but one about the triumph of an exemplary Christian, and its still available material sign (the stone) promises the visitor not pardon but inspiration for his/her own earthly trials.

Other stories in Capgrave's *Solace* show the power of Christian faith as alive in the present as it was in the heroic past. His initial chapter on the ancient and magnificent church of S. Maria in Trastevere does not describe the structure's appearance at all, but instead tells how, at a time when the location was a refuge for the soldiers of the Roman Empire, two wells of oil (*fons olei*) suddenly sprang forth on the day Christ was born (111) [Figure no. 11]. This popular story evokes the pre-Christian history of the site, but Capgrave makes the ancient miracle relevant to contemporary Christians by arguing, with many Biblical examples, that clerks say that the wells ran with oil rather than another liquid because oil "signifieth mercy" and Christ's coming meant the establishment of "a lawe ful of mercy" (111). In contrast to the specific years of indulgence promised to visitors at specific churches in the *Stations*, this is a general (and more theologically sound) "pardon" available at all times and everywhere: "The name of Jhesus is oile largely spred abrood in hevene, spred in erde, spred in helle" (112).

As this manifestation at ancient Rome of the birth of Christ suggests, the medieval city is often presented in these descriptions not as an absolute break from the pagan past but as a continuation.[42] Some of these texts, as we have seen, do report with satisfaction the destruction of false idols, but others show Rome's greatest leaders endorsing the coming of the new way, the new truth, and the new life. This is clearly noticeable in the story of the vision of Emperor Octavian (Augustus) at S. Maria in Aracoeli, which appears in both the *Mirabilia* (but not in the *Metrical Mandeville*) and in Capgrave, though it is absent from Master Gregorius, who includes an analogous story concerning Romulus that is also in the *Mirabilia* and *Metrical Mandeville*. I shall retell Capgrave's expanded version of Octavian's vision, though without most of his added learning and lessons [Figure no. 12]. Because of Octavian's great beauty and many accomplishments, the Roman Senate wants to deify him: "we alle with on assent are thus acordid to worchip thy persone as a god" (39). But Octavian, knowing that he is mortal, hesitates and seeks the advice of the Sybil, proving, according to Capgrave, that there were "ful goode and holy creatures" among the Roman heathens as among the early Jews (40). The Sybil, after fasting and praying, brings prophetic verses to the emperor that say, among other things (in English translation), "Jesus Crist, the son of God, our saviour" (40). Once these verses are expounded, Octavian is granted a vision (apparently because of his goodness and holiness) of an altar in the sky on which was "a fair maide standing and in hir arme a child" (40), while a heavenly voice declares, "This is the auter of God; to this, loke thou do worchep" (40), in response to which Octavian falls down in reverence. He then returns to the senators and relates the "gret merveilis which he had seyn," and, refusing their devotion, "seide he wold be servaunt onto this child evyr while he may live" (41). Pagan Rome has become a part of providential history and shown to be already preparing itself to be the holy city because its greatest emperor is able to glimpse

---

[42]  On this point, see Osborne's suggestion in the introduction to *Master Gregorius* that the *Mirabilia* attempts "to construct a series of bridges between the pagan past and the Christian present" (10). Jennifer Summit, "Topology as Historiography: Petrarch, Chaucer, and the Making of Medieval Rome," *Journal of Medieval and Early Modern Studies* 30 (2000): 211–46; 225 argues that the *Mirabilia* "overarching project" is to reconcile two ancient pasts and from its ruins find "the significance of Rome's historical transformation from pagan to Christian city."

and accept the Christian future. The vision certainly heralds the death of old Rome, but, like the fall of Troy, this permits the birth and future life of the new Rome.

The medieval descriptions of Rome discussed here are of limited help to modern topographers, even though, amid the fantastic legends, there is genuine information about the old city. But these works tell us less about ancient Rome than they do about the medieval perception of it. As such they are irreplaceable testimony to the fascination that the remains of Rome, pagan and Christian, exerted on the Middle Ages. Medieval Rome was a city whose grand imperial monuments were now in decay or adapted for modern uses and whose holy martyrs survived as bones. The descriptions of Rome discussed here are, in one sense, a catalogue of death and loss: both the empire and the early church that replaced it were no more, and the greatest leaders of both, including Julius Caesar and Peter and Paul, were in their tombs. But if no longer golden, Rome remains eternal for these writers, who find life of all kinds in these inert remains. The most triumphant and certain life, to be sure, is that promised by God through the intercession of the saints; the abundant pardons of Rome offer the pilgrim a place in the heavenly Jerusalem. But Capgrave, for one, also finds a more quotidian story in these holy martyrs: in addition to their deaths, he chronicles the exemplary faith, hope, and charity they displayed while residents of the earthly Rome. He also records Christian manifestations in the city throughout its history, whether in a vision to the pagan Octavian or the protection of St. Dominic from stoning by the devil. Furthermore, Rome, then as now, is shown to contain the memory of other kinds of life, as least for those willing to respond to it. The ingenious, even magical devices that once operated in the city fascinate these writers, even if some finally reject their energy as diabolical. And Master Gregorius even realizes the ultimate antiquarian's dream of making the past come alive, if only for a moment and only in his imagination, when he connects with the spark of animation first created by the original sculptor of the Venus. The subjects of these medieval descriptions of Rome are dead ruins and relics, but their writers attempt to make them live again.

Figure 1: Castel S. Angelo (Hadrian's Sepulchre)

C. David Benson

Figure 2: Obelisk at St. Peter's (Caesar's Pillar or Needle)

Figure 3: Fresco of Equestrian Statue before Lateran (by Filippino Lippi at
S. Maria sopra Minerva)

Figure 4: Copy of Equestrian Statue (Marcus Aurelius) on Capitoline Hill

Figure 5: Colosseum

Figure 6: Head, Hand, and Sphere of Emperor (Idol of Sun)

Figure 7: Tomb of Saints Lawrence and Stephen (under high altar of
Saint Lawrence)

Figure 8: Capitoline Venus

Figure 9: Original Equestrian Statue (Marcus Aurelius)

C. David Benson

Figure 10: Stone Thrown at St. Dominic by Devil (S. Sabina)

Figure 11: Site of Well of Oil at Christ's Birth (S. Maria Trastevere)

Figure 12: Altar in Octavian's Vision (S. Maria in Aracoeli)

Kisha G. Tracy
(University of Connecticut)

# Defining the Medieval City through Death:
# A Case Study

Given the words "city" and "death," those familiar with medieval imagery would, more than likely, particularly as a result of the work of St. Augustine, immediately think of the heavenly city populated by the souls who once lived devout or virtuous lives. Texts such as the Middle English Gawain-poet's *Pearl*, Dante's *Divine Comedy*, and a variety of medieval sermons vividly illustrate the nature of this urban afterlife and the requirements for becoming one of its citizens.[1] While the presence of death is, given the path a soul must take in order to go through the gates, understood to be an essential feature in discussions of this ethereal city, the significance of death's role in perceptions of the earthly city is not as well-recognized, yet examinations of historical documents, art, and literary texts reveal

---

[1] See *Envisaging* Heaven *in the Middle Ages*, ed. Carolyn Muessig and Ad Putter. Routledge Studies in Medieval Religion and Culture 6 (London: Routledge, 2007); *Heavenly Realms and Earthly Realities in Late Antique Religions*, ed. Ra'anan S. Boustan and Annette Yoshiko Reed (Cambridge: Cambridge University Press, 2004); John Howe, "Creating Symbolic Landscapes: Medieval Development of Sacred Space," *Inventing Medieval Landscapes: Senses of Place in Western Europe*, ed. John Howe and Michael Wolfe (Gainesville: University Press of Florida, 2002), 208–23; *Imagining Heaven in the Middle Ages: A Book of Essays*, ed. Jan Swango Emerson and Hugh Feiss, Garland Medieval Casebooks 27 (New York: Garland, 2000); E. Ruth Harvey, "Constructing Bliss: Heaven in the *Pearl*," *The Middle Ages in the North-West: Papers presented at an International Conference sponsored by the Centres of Medieval Studies of the Universities of Liverpool and Toronto*, ed. Tom Scott and Pat Starkey (Oxford: Leopard's Head Press, 1995), 203–19; and Sarah Stanbury, "The Body and the City in *Pearl*," *Representations* 47 (1994): 271–85. For discussion of heaven in art, see *The Iconography of Heaven*, ed. Clifford Davidson. Early Drama, Art, and Music Monograph Series, 21 (Kalamazoo, MI: Medieval Institute Publications, 1994); Joan E. Barclay Lloyd, "Heaven and Hell in Medieval Italian Art," *Spunti e ricerche: Rivista d'italianistica* 11 (1995), 18–34; Nicola Coldstream, "The Kingdom of Heaven: Its Architectural Setting," *Age of Chivalry: Art in Plantagenet England 1200–1400*, ed. Jonathan Alexander and Paul Binski (London: Royal Academy of Arts in association with Weidenfeld and Nicolson, 1987), 92–97; and *Homo, Memento Finis: The Iconography of Just Judgment in Medieval Art and Drama*, ed. David Bevington. Early Drama, Art and Music Monograph Series, 6 (Kalamazoo, MI: Medieval Institute Publications, 1985).

that images of the medieval city are frequently juxtaposed with images of death. Death and dead bodies are often necessary in defining the identity of the city. This definition sometimes includes emphasizing a city's unique individuality, validating accounts of foundation or power structures, or establishing a new, emerging urban character. Historical texts disclose instances of public performances in which death plays a prominent role; they also emphasize the value of cemeteries and tombs as memorial devices in city settings.[2] Simultaneously, literary texts from wide geographic, chronologic, and stylistic ranges—including such examples as the Old English poem *The Ruin*; the Middle English *St. Erkenwald* and *Piers Plowman* as well as the works of Hoccleve and Lydgate; the Old French *Roman de Thèbes* and the *Roman d'Enéas*; Heinrich von Veldeke's Middle High German *Eneit*; the Spanish *Cantar del mio Cid*; Giovanni Boccaccio's *Decameron*; and the chronicles of Geoffrey of Monmouth, Wace, and Layamon—use the metaphor of death or depict images of death in conjunction with their particular needs regarding the narrative construction of their respective cities. Considered together, historical and literary analysis paints a dramatic picture of how death, far from being a simply static idea, is indeed a dynamic part of medieval urban space, confirming—not denying—the vigorous energy and historical significance of the city.

Consistently throughout the Middle Ages, the dead were an important aspect of everyday life, a common physical presence as well as a common topic for thought.[3] As Patrick Geary remarks in *Living with the Dead in the Middle Ages*:

---

[2]    One valuable reference concerning this concept is *Death in Towns: Urban Responses to the Dying and the Dead, 100–1600*, ed. Steven Bassett (London, New York: Leicester University Press, 1995). This collection of essays is mostly based in archaeological and anthropological studies of burial sites and mortality patterns. Also see Colin Platt, *King Death: The Black Death and Its Aftermath in Late-Medieval England* (Toronto: University of Toronto Press, 1996); *Der Tod des Mächtigen: Kult und Kultur des Todes spätmittelalterlicher Herrscher*, ed. Lothar Kolmer (Paderborn, Munich, et al.: Ferdinand Schöningh, 1997); *Tod im Mittelalter*, ed. Arno Borst, Konstanzer Bibliothek, 20 (Constance: Universitätsverlag Konstanz, 1993); Edward L. Bell, *Vestiges of Mortality & Remembrance: A Bibliography on the Historical Archaeology of Cemeteries* (Metuchen, NJ: Scarecrow Press, 1994); and *Mortality and Immortality: The Archaeology and Anthropology of Death*, ed. S. C. Humphreys and Helen King (London: Academic Press, 1981).

[3]    For valuable studies on medieval death, see Paul Binski, *Medieval Death: Ritual and Representation* (Ithaca: Cornell University Press, 1996); Howard Williams, *Death and Memory in Early Medieval Britain* (Cambridge: Cambridge University Press, 2006); Patrick J. Geary, *Living with the Dead in the Middle Ages* (Ithaca: Cornell University Press, 1994); *Last Things: Death and the Apocalypse in the Middle Ages*, ed. Caroline Walker-Bynum and Paul Freedman. *Middle Ages Series* (Philadelphia: University of Pennsylvania Press, 2000); Christopher Daniell, *Death and Burial in Medieval England, 1066–1550* (London: Routledge, 1997); Victoria Thompson, *Dying and Death in Later Anglo-Saxon England* (Woodbridge: Boydell Press, 2004); *The Place of the Dead: Death and Remembrance in Late Medieval and Early Modern Europe*, ed. Bruce Gordon and Peter Marshall (Cambridge: Cambridge University Press, 2000); Craig Koslofsky, *The Reformation of the Dead: Death and Ritual in Early Modern Germany, 1450–1700* (New York: St. Martin's Press, 2000); *Death and Dying in the Middle*

Death marked a transition, a change in status, but not an end . . . The dead were present among the living through liturgical commemoration, in dreams and visions, and in their physical remains, especially the tombs and relics of the saints. Omnipresent, they were drawn into every aspect of life. They played vital roles in social, economic, political, and cultural spheres.[4]

Geary characterizes death as infiltrating the cultural and social practices of the living, emphasizing how fundamental the relationship was. This interaction with the dead speaks to a connection with the past, to the individuals who left a mark on their societies either in the memories of those who came after them or through physical and material legacies. The people of the Middle Ages envisioned an energetic and significant position for the deceased, brought on, at least partially, by the insistence of the Christian Church that its followers contemplate on death in order to avoid sin in life.[5] Given this pervasiveness of the dead, it is, then, not surprising that they should have a place in the environment of the city, both in its historical and fictional manifestations. It remains, however, to see how this conceptual bond reveals itself and what it can tell us about the employment of the dead in city contexts. In my research, I have found several different avenues of evidence supporting the concept of juxtaposing the city and death—for instance, the location and geography of cemeteries within cities or the anthropological study of how relocation to cities changed how one approached death in the face of new "relationship frameworks," in the phrase employed by Jean-Claude Schmitt.[6] In this article, through a series of representative case studies from both well-known and more obscure literary and historical examples, I will attempt to explicate a few of these conceptual relationships including: the space for death in cities, especially physical and social spaces, and how the dead played into urban politics.

---

*Ages*, eds. Edelgard E. DuBruck and Barbara I. Gusick (New York: Peter Lang, 1999); Frederick S. Paxton, *Christianizing Death: The Creation of a Ritual Process in Early Medieval Europe* (Ithaca: Cornell University Press, 1990); *Dies Illa. Death in the Middle Ages: Proceedings of the 1983 Manchester Colloquium*, ed. by Jane H. M. Taylor. Vinaver Studies in French, 1 (Liverpool: Francis Cairns, 1984); *Death in the Middle Ages*, ed. Herman Braet and Werner Verbeke (Leuven: Leuven University Press, 1983); and T. S. R. Boase, *Death in the Middle Age: Mortality, Judgment, and Remembrance* (New York: McGraw-Hill, 1972).

[4] Geary, *Living with the Dead in the Middle Ages*, 2.

[5] See Daniell, *Death and Burial in Medieval England*, 1–2: "The time on earth was transitory and infinitesimal to the life of the soul after death, but the eternal fate of the soul was determined by its actions whilst in the mortal body. To save the soul from sin the Church consistently reminded people about sin, death and the eternal afterlife by encouraging medication upon death." D.L. D'Avray, *Death and the Prince* (Oxford: Clarendon, 1994), remarks that "liturgy created real communities in which the living and the dead were drawn together" (1) and that "memorial preaching in the period is about life as well as death" (68).

[6] Jean-Claude Schmitt, *Ghosts in the Middle Ages: The Living and the Dead in Medieval Society* (Chicago: University of Chicago Press, 1998), 126.

Whereas previous studies tend to focus on one aspect of medieval culture or on one geographical area, this discussion will synthesize various representations, revealing how the architects behind different types of documents and artistic endeavors manipulated and applied the influential concept of death within urban environments and made the concept of death both a real, physical presence as well as a device for community interaction. This study explores the intersection of historical reality, literary construction, and artistic expression.

## The Space for Death: Physical and Social

The pervading presence of the dead in cities manifests itself in different ways, occupying spaces both physical and intangible. Literary texts are a rich source of material for considering how authors are able to use the dead in depicting the parameters of the various cities important to their texts and how they further their own particular agendas. Here, I will examine the use of dead kings to mark urban foundations, particularly that of London, in Layamon's chronicle, the early thirteenth-century *Brut*, and the dead as urban protectors in the mid-twelfth-century Old French *Roman d'Enéas*. These literary instances of how the dead are integrated into city spaces are paralleled by artistic and historical representations of the dead in urban settings, particularly through monuments, such as the Eleanor of Castile crosses.[7] While these images speak to how death has a significant physical space in cities, others, including the fourteenth-century Middle English *Piers Plowman* by William Langland, reveal the role of death in influencing how and why people relocated to cities and how this migration changed community networks. Anthropological and sociological evidence has documented the way in which urban development altered social frameworks. Literary authors frequently explore the consequences of this evolving social landscape. Passages in *Piers Plowman*, for instance, demonstrates how death in cities significantly affected the religious life of more rural areas.

---

[7] Another article in this volume, C. David Benson's "The Dead and the Living: Some Medieval Descriptions of the Ruins and Relics of Rome Known to the English," argues that the medieval texts which explore the faded glories of Rome, particularly its ruins and relics, are more than simply descriptions of a dead city, but are, rather, an attempt to bring the metropolis back to life through composition.. This study demonstrates both how prominent monuments to the dead were in Rome and how authors attempted to reinvigorate ancient urban spaces.

## The Dead as Urban Foundation: *Layamon's* Brut

To begin a discussion of the physical space of the dead, I would first like to turn to the concept of urban foundational myths through a look at Layamon's *Brut*, a chronicle of the Britons.[8] As Lesley Johnson has noted:

> The *Brut*, according to its own introduction, is the fulfilment [sic] of Laȝamon's desire to tell of the noble men who were first in the land 'of Engle' (7—the name which supersedes that of Britain according to Laȝamon's text) and tells of the foundation of human society on the island, of the ancestors of the inhabitants of the island, and of the key political events in the reigns of subsequent rulers.[9]

One of the aspects of British society that Layamon and his sources, Geoffrey of Monmouth and Wace, are interested in exploring is the construction of cities, from the ones that Brutus either encounters or founds as he journeys to his new kingdom to the ones that spring up in Britain. With respect to this study, however, what is particularly interesting is that these stories are often accompanied by an image of burial. Indeed, often, it is a death which leads to the naming of a city or which identifies one of its defining features, and, furthermore, the bodies of the dead are frequently buried within these cities. For example, one of the first to exhibit this relationship is Tours in France. When one of Brutus's most devoted followers and kinsman, Turnus, is killed in battle, his body is returned to the fortress the Trojans recently built and buried there. This act is responsible for the naming of the city it would one day become:

> Brutus hine funde dead and into þane castle dude
> and þerinne biburiȝede bi ane stan walle.
> Þuru þan ilka Turnus Turs wes ihaten,
> Turuine al þat lond þurh Turnus deaðe.          (865–68)[10]

> [Brutus found him dead and took him into the fortress, and buried him within it beside a stone wall. Because of that Turnus it was called Tours; the whole region was called Touraine because of the death of Turnus.]

---

[8]   The passages that I will point out here are almost exactly the same as the parallel passages in Layamon's twelfth-century source, Wace's *Roman de Brut*.

[9]   Lesley Johnson, "Reading the Past in Laȝamon's *Brut*," *The Text and Tradition of La amon's Brut*, ed. Françoise Le Saux (Woodbridge, Suffolk: D. S. Brewer, 1994), 141–60; here142. For a broader study of chronicle writing in England, see Chris Given-Wilson, *Chronicles: The Writing of History in Medieval England* (London and New York: Hambledon and London, 2004).

[10]  All quotations from and translations of Layamon taken from *Laȝamon's Brut or Hystoria Brutonum*, ed. and trans. W. R. J. Barron and C. S. Weinberg (New York: Longman, 1995).

The very foundation of this urban center is built around the warrior's dead body. He is physically connected to Tours in that he is interred within its walls, and he is also inserted into the legendary space of the city.[11]

As Layamon's text is concerned mostly with the history of Britain, the city of London is central to its story, including its founding and the evolution of how its name changed from New Troy, designated by Brutus, to London. Throughout this retelling, it is clear that it is not just the kings who lived in this city who are significant, but also those kings who died and were buried there. Indeed, their burials indicate both the love of their people as well as the significance of the city itself. Three figures, in particular, illustrate these concepts: Brutus, Belin, and Lud. Brutus, the namesake of the text and London's founder, is interred within the city by his sons:

> Þa heora fader wes dead alle heo nomen enne read
> and hine biburien in New Troye þere burh₃e
> þat heora fader hefde imaked mid muchelere blisse.   (1049–51)

[When their father was dead they agreed unanimously to bury him in the city of New Troy which their father had founded with great joy.]

Much like Turnus is buried within Tours, Brutus is placed in the city he founded, once again connecting his dead body with the urban myth and giving him a ubiquitous presence within London's walls. The exact location of his burial is not noted, creating a sense that Brutus is at the heart of the city, almost as if London is built around him.

On the other hand, the tombs of the two other kings I wish to point out, Belin and Lud, are given specific locations. Belin, as a beloved ruler, is placed at the top of a tower above a gate, called Billingsgate, which he himself had ordered to be constructed:

> Þe king leouede longe þat hit com touward his ende,
> þat i Lundene he wes dæd—sari wes his du₃eðe;
> wa wes heom on liue for þæs kinges dæðe.
> Heo ferden to his horde and nome þer muche deal goldes;
> heo makeden ane tunne of golde and of ₃imme;
> þene king heo duden þerinne, þat wes here louerd Belin,
> vp heo hine duden he₃e an ufenmeste þan turre
> þat me mihte hine bihalden wide ₃eon þeon londe.   (3027–34)

---

[11]   For a discussion of other proper names besides those of cities in Layamon's text, see J.D. Bruce, "Some Proper Names in Layamon's *Brut* Not Represented in Wace or Geoffrey of Monmouth," *Modern Language Notes* 26.3 (1911): 65–9.

[The king lives long until his end came, and he lay dead in London—his subjects were sad; because of the king's death they were sorry to be alive. They went to his treasury and took from it a great quantity of gold; they made a vessel of gold and of gems, put the king, who was their lord Belin, in it, placed him high up in the topmost part of the tower so that he could be seen far and wide across the land. They did that out of their great love, because he was their beloved lord.]

One of the most important aspects of this scene, beyond the fact of the king's burial within the city, is the description of his interment. Situated in the tower, "so that he could be seen far and wide across the land," Belin's body almost becomes a symbol of the city, both visible and omnipresent. Lud, a later king, is similarly buried next to a gate that he had constructed, named Port Lud:

> Þa gon þis lond wenden þat com þis kinges ende.
> Lud king iwarð dæd—in Lundene me hine leide.
> Þer weoren eorles swiðe whæte, and leiden þene king bi ane $_3$ate
> þat $_3$et me cleopeð fuliwis Port Lud a Bruttisce.

(3555–59)

[And so this land fared well until the king's life came to an end. King Lud died—he was buried in London. The bravest nobles were present, and they buried the king beside a gate which is, indeed, still called Port Lud in the British language.]

Whereas Brutus is the founder of the city, Lud is the king who built a wall around London and changed the name to Kaer Lud to reflect his own. This renaming establishes him as a sort of secondary founder. Burying him next to the gate, which was part of the fortified wall he constructed, equates the king's body with the stability of the city.[12]

Marie-Françoise Alamichel remarks that, in Layamon's work, "[c]ities, for example, protect themselves behind stockades or ramparts. However, any protection is nothing but an illusion. Just like rivers, towns become symbols of death. Besieged cities are usually totally destroyed—except for those that surrender." While Alamichel's assertion may work for those cities which are depicted as being besieged, I would argue that, in the case of Lud and his burial beside its protective wall, death is not a form of destruction, but rather a reinforcement of permanence. In these three instances, the bodies of dead kings become, respectively, synonymous with the foundation of London, with its prominence, and with its boundaries, defining both mythical and physical urban space.

---

[12] Marie-Françoise Alamichel, "Space in the *Brut*," *The Text and Tradition of Laȝamon's* Brut, ed. Françoise Le Saux (Woodbridge, Suffolk: D. S. Brewer, 1994), 183–92; here 188.

## *Camille: Urban Protector in the* Roman d'Enéas

The mid-twelfth-century *Roman d'Enéas*, a romance retelling of Virgil's *Aeneid*, provides an interesting parallel to the images we see in Layamon's work. Unlike its primary source, this *Roman* does not depict the famous scene of Aeneas descending into the underworld, the realm of the dead, where he is told that he and his lineage are destined to found the great city of Rome. Indeed, this work has very little concern for the foundation of Rome; rather, it transforms Virgil's interest in the veneration of the history of his city into an interest in making Enéas into a chivalric knight, successful both in love and war.[13] Given this renovation of the story, it seems logical to suppose that the author would have no real need for the dead with respect to any urban considerations. However, this is not the case. One particular figure is worthy of examination in this context—that of Camille, queen of Vulcane. A warrior woman described as both queen *and* king, Camille arrives to aid Turnus in his war against Enéas for the hand of Lavine and, thus, the right to govern Laurente, the city of Latinus. Rather than the few lines accorded her by Virgil, the *Roman* author spends quite a bit of time describing her appearance, her dedication to chivalry, and even, at one point, her horse, and it is clear in the text that she is accorded the esteem of an equal combatant by her allies, if not always by her enemies. Her relationship with Turnus, in particular, is one of mutual respect as it is to her he turns for help when he decides to set up an ambush against Enéas.

It is after Camille has died in battle that we see how death plays into the image of the city and how the dead function as guardians in this romance context. Following the account of the entire army, especially of Turnus, and the citizens of Laurente grieving, there is a description of how her body is transported in a great procession through the streets and then how it is taken to her own city. Once there, she is interred in a magnificent shrine. The interesting aspect of this scene lies in the fact that a large mirror is placed at the top of this unusual tomb, a mirror that serves to protect the city. The text reads:

> de desore ot .I. miroior :
> illuec pooit bien l'en veoir
> quant l'en s'i vendroit asseoir,
> ou fust par mer ou fust par terre,

---

[13]   See Helen C. Laurie, "Eneas and the Doctrine of Courtly Love," *Modern Language Review* 64 (1969): 283–94 and Howard R. Bloch, "Enéas before the Walls of Carthage: The Beginnings of the City and Romance in the Suburbs," *Beginnings in French Literature*, ed. Freeman G. Henry (New York: Rodopi, 2002), 1–27. For a broader study of chansons de geste and death, see Sarah Kay, "The Life of the Dead Body: Death and the Sacred in the *Chansons de geste*," *Yale French Studies* 86 (1994): 94–108.

jamais ne fust conquis par guerre.
Bien verroient au miroior
qui ert assiz en son la tor
lor anemis vers euz venire,
dont se povoient bien garnir,
appareillier a euz deffendre ;
n'erent pas legier a sorprendre. (7670–80)[14]

[Over that was a mirror, in which they could see very well when someone was coming to attack them, whether by sea or by land. They would never be conquered in war; whoever was seated at the foot of the tower could see in the mirror their enemies coming toward them. Thus they could supply themselves well and prepare themselves for defense; they would not be easy to surprise.][15]

Camille continues to fulfill her duty as defender of Vulcane; even though she herself was killed in war, her body and the tomb that venerates it averts the same fate for her people. Furthermore, her demise prevents the potential destruction of Laurente itself. When the text turns away from the digression concerning her tomb back to the war, Turnus immediately gives the speech in which he decides to face Enéas in hand to hand combat rather than continuing the devastation of open battle. In Virgil's version, Turnus's decision is rendered in a succinct, anger-driven monologue. In the *Roman*, the tone of his speech is sad and resigned, and one cannot help but feel that his grief at the death of Camille has brought about his resolution. As a result, Laurente avoids potential destruction, such as that found in the near-contemporaneous text, the *Roman de Thèbes*, in which the title city is razed to the ground in the aftermath of a bloody civil war. Thus, by placing such emphasis upon the protective power of the deceased Camille, both for her own city and for Laurente, the author of the *Enéas* is able to explore an emotional aspect of Turnus that is unnecessary in the epic original.

## The Art of Death: Monuments, Tombs, and the Eleanor Crosses

The representation of the physicality of dead bodies within urban settings in the *Brut* and the *Enéas* is not only a fictional device. Historical and archaeological evidence reveals that the dead were present everywhere, especially through monuments, tombs, and graveyards. Family members would often commission artwork, such as gravestones, stained glass windows, plaques, or columns, to

---

14  Quotation taken from *Roman d'Enéas*, Livre de Poche (Paris: Lettres Gothiques, 1997).
15  Translation of *Roman d'Enéas* taken from *Eneas: A Twelfth-Century French Romance*, trans. John A. Yunck. Records of Civilization: Sources and Studies, 93 (New York: Columbia University Press, 1974), 204–05.

commemorate their relatives, thereby hoping to ensure that they would be remembered; wealthier urban families, especially, chose to order works of this nature.[16] Those attending church would be surrounded by memorials of those who had passed on, creating areas in which the dead were visually and symbolically present to the living. Royal figures, particularly in capital cities, were frequently memorialized and idealized with effigies and public burial spaces.[17] In addition, most cities supported a large number of graveyards, which is not surprising given the amount of people within these environments and urban mortality rates. Vanessa Harding has noted, for instance, that there were 107 churches plus St. Paul's and many religious houses within London prior to the Reformation, all of which were responsible for interring the London dead.[18] Monuments and cemeteries, within and outside of cities, were a means of creating a bridge between the living and the deceased. With respect to cemeteries, Jean-Claude Schmitt remarks:

---

[16] A literary example of this commemoration can be found in the Apollonius of Tyre texts, in which a significant monument is raised, effecting the development of both the story and the characters. For basic discussions of the transmission of the Apollonius story, see Elizabeth Archibald, *Apollonius of Tyre: Medieval and Renaissance Themes and Variations, Including the Text of the* Historia Apolloni Regis Tyri *with an English Translation* (Cambridge: D. S. Brewer, 1991). Also see Albrecht Classen, "Reading and Deciphering in Apollonius of Tyre and the 'Historia' von den sieben weisen Meitern: Medieval Epistemology within a Literary Context," *Studi Medievali* 49.1 (2008): 161–89.

[17] For discussions pertaining to the "art of death," see Mark Duffy, *Royal Tombs of Medieval England* (Gloucestershire, U K: Tempus Publishing, 2003); Ann Marie Yasin, "Funerary Monuments and Collective Identity: From Roman Family to Christian Community," *Art Bulletin* 87.3 (2005): 433–57; Karl S. Guthke, *The Gender of Death: A Cultural History in Art and Literature* (Cambridge and New York: Cambridge University Press, 1999); Howard Colvin, *Architecture and the After-life* (New Haven: Yale University Press, 1991); Nigel Llewellyn, *The Art of Death: Visual Culture in the English Death Ritual, c.1500–c.1800* (London: Reaktion Books, 1991); and James Clark, *The Dance of Death in the Middle Ages and the Renaissance*, reprinted in *Death and the Visual Arts* (New York: Arno Press, 1977). The *Dance of Death* is a particularly interesting subject in that it crosses visual and literary culture as representations appeared in churches, such as in Paris, and in the works of such authors as John Lydgate, mainly in the fifteenth century after the ravages of the plague. These images depicted the universality of death.

[18] Vanessa Harding, "Burial Choice and Burial Location in Later Medieval London," *Death in Towns: Urban Responses to the Dying and the Dead, 100–1600*, ed. Steven Bassett (London and New York: Leicester University Press, 1995), 119–35; here 120. Also see Vanessa Harding, *The Dead and the Living in Paris and London, 1500–1670* (Cambridge: Cambridge University Press, 2002). For an overall discussion of the history of cemeteries in England, see Daniell, *Death and Burial in Medieval England*, 145–74. For a similar discussion of burials in Flanders and Tuscany around the time of the Black Death, see Samuel K. Cohn, Jr., "The Place of the Dead in Flanders and Tuscany: Towards a Comparative History of the Black Death," *The Place of the Dead: Death and Remembrance in Late Medieval and Early Modern Europe*, eds. Bruce Gordon and Peter Marshall (Cambridge: Cambridge University Press, 2000), 17–43.

In the center [of many European villages] is found the parish church, and then crowded around it are the tombs of the cemetery . . . The cemetery was enclosed by a wall . . . Between the church and the village, the cemetery was therefore an intermediary place, and it played a mediating role: the living had to go through it constantly, not only when they went to church or returned from church but also when they went from one end of the village to the other or, in town, from one quarter to another.[19]

Monuments too played a similar role in that they were intended to keep the dead in the minds and memory of the living.[20]

There are many examples of monuments and tombs in medieval urban settings, particularly in city cathedrals and churches. However, the Eleanor crosses are interesting specifically because they mark one of the most elaborate collections of royal monuments in the history of England. Erected along the funerary procession route to London of Eleanor of Castile, queen of Edward I, who died in 1290,[21] the series of twelve crosses were constructed by the order of Edward and were finished in the years following the procession to commemorate each stop that Eleanor's body made as it was taken from Harby, where she died, back to Westminster Abbey.[22] There have been many theories as to Edward's reason for

[19] Schmitt, *Ghosts in the Middle Ages*, 183.

[20] See Elizabeth Valdez del Alamo and Carol Stamatis Pendergast, "Introduction," *Memory and the Medieval Tomb*, eds. Elizabeth Valdez del Alamo and Carol Stamatis Pendergast (Aldershot, United Kingdom and Brookfield, VT: Ashgate, 2000), 1–15; here 1: "Monuments designed for the purpose of commemoration utilize many devices to trigger memory: vivid images that are both marvelous and active; strategically placed figurations or inscription which contextualize the site; and a kinetic relationship between the funerary monument and its visitors, often manifested in ritual acts involving movement around or in the monument. These memorial strategies established a dialogue between the living and the dead and articulated mutual benefits for both parties."

[21] For studies on Eleanor of Castile or her death, see John Carmi Parsons, *Eleanor of Castile: Queen and Society in Thirteenth-Century England* (New York: St. Martin's, 1995); John Carmi Parsons, *The Court and Household of Eleanor of Castile in 1290* (Toronto: Pontifical Institute of Mediaeval Studies, 1977); Anne Crawford, "The Queen's Council in the Middle Ages," *English Historical Review* 116.469 (2001): 1193–211; and David Crook, "The Last Days of Eleanor of Castile: The Death of a Queen in Nottinghamshire, November 1290, At House of Richard de Weston in Harby," *Transactions of the Thoroton Society of Nottinghamshire* 94 (1990): 17–28. For a discussion of her burial in relationship to other queens of the time period, see John Carmi Parsons, "'Never was a body buried in England with such solemnity and honour': The Burials and Posthumous Commemorations of English Queens to 1500," *Queens and Queenship in Medieval Europe: Proceedings of a Conference Held at King's College London, April 1995*, ed. Anne J. Duggan (Woodbridge, Suffolk: Boydell & Brewer, 1997), 317–37.

[22] For a brief history of the crosses, see Doreen Shakesby, "The Crosses of Queen Eleanor," *Medieval History* 3 (1993): 26–29, and *Eleanor of Castile 1290–1990: Essays to Commemorate the 700th Anniversary of Her Death: 28 November 1290*, ed. David Parsons (Stamford: Paul Watkins, 1991). Most of these monuments were destroyed during the English Civil War. In addition to the crosses, there were also three tombs built for Eleanor in Lincoln Cathedral, the Dominican Blackfriars

commissioning these memorials, but most seem to agree that it was out of devotion to his wife. Doreen Shakesby states that Edward "certainly went to extraordinary lengths to mark the route taken to his queen's final resting place, presumably in the mistaken belief that the memorials he erected would stand as a perpetual visible testimony to his melancholy journey back to Westminster."[23] There have been some scholars, such as Nicola Coldstream, who suggest that Edward intended the crosses to encourage a view of royal splendor and power.[24]

Not only are these crosses exceptional as examples of monuments intended to commemorate royal death, they are also distinctly urban in their character, both in location and in the circumstances of their construction. The crosses were built in the following places: Lincoln, Grantham, Stamford, Geddington, Northampton, Stony Stratford, Woburn, Dunstable, St. Albans, Waltham, West Cheap, and Charing. These sites were, by and large, towns at the time the crosses were constructed, while West Cheap and Charing were located within the boundaries of London. Most of these monuments were built in the squares or at the crossroads in the town centers, prominently displayed for all travelers to see, including those following the same path that the procession took into London. Furthermore, the two within the metropolitan area, West Cheap and Charing, were the most elaborate and the most famous, costing £226 and £700 respectively as opposed to the average of £100 at which the others have been estimated. Indeed, the work for all of the crosses originated in London and was overseen by one of the city's master-masons, Richard of Crundale.[25] These monuments marked the route of a royal funeral procession back into an urban center, and they became the defining symbols of the other smaller towns and cities along the way, illustrating the ubiquitous presence of such death markers.

## Death and Social Space in Urban Settings: Masses for the Dead

It is well-documented that, with the rise of cities, the geographic location of populations shifted as people migrated into these areas. These changes affected how individuals responded to their own deaths and to that of others. Samuel K. Cohn remarks, based on the research of Jacques Chiffoleau, that "urbanisation, commercialisation and migration uprooted the individual from families, neighbors and lineages, particularly in cities, as early as the thirteenth century"; this "loss of

church, and Westminster Abbey.

[23] Shakesby, "The Crosses of Queen Eleanor," 29.

[24] Nicola Coldstream, "The Commissioning and Design of the Eleanor Crosses," *Eleanor of Castile 1290–1990*, ed. David Parsons (Stamford: Paul Watkins, 1991), 55–67; here 65.

[25] Coldstream, "The Commissioning and Design of the Eleanor Crosses," 59.

family and ties to the ancestors led to new levels of fear feeding the growth in the
territory of Purgatory and with it the need for ever-increasing numbers of masses
and intercessors for the soul."[26] Instead of depending upon one's family to perform
the necessary rites after death, this separation from ancestral lines forced people
in urban environments to develop other means of ensuring the continued prayers
for their souls after they died. As a result, the business of performing masses for
the dead flourished in cities as individuals began giving money to religious houses
to ensure their place in the afterlife through posthumous prayer.[27] The examples
of this practice are numerous. For instance, urban guilds, which were wealthier
than their more rural counterparts, were able to pay priests to perform masses for
their dead members.[28] In literature, this custom generally elicited scorn. For
example, in the B-text of William Langland's *Piers Plowman*, there is a concern that
priests were abandoning their villages in favor of London in order to enjoy the
ease and wealth which resulted from this occupation:

> Persons and parisshe preestes pleyned hem to the bisshop
> That hire parisshes weren povere sith the pestilence tyme,
> To have a licence and leve at London to dwelle,
> And syngen ther for symonie, for silver is swete.
>
> (B.Prologue.83–86)[29]

This migration of priests left parishioners without anyone to see to their spiritual
needs, which is, of course, a problem that they, and Langland, criticize. The
performance of the masses for the dead, while not unique to cities, became a
popular trade within them, influencing religious practices and the shape of
communities as inhabitants were forced to seek out networks beyond their families
and affecting relocation of priests to urban areas.

---

[26]   Samuel K. Cohn, Jr., "The Place of the Dead in Flanders and Tuscany," 19, 20.
[27]   For a study of the early development of the rites of death, see Paxton, *Christianizing Death*.
[28]   Daniell, *Death and Burial in Medieval England*, 19–20.
[29]   Quotation from the B-text of *Piers Plowman* taken from *The Vision of Piers Plowman*, ed. A.V.C.
       Schmidt (New York: Everyman, 1995). Simony does, of course, include other acts besides
       accepting payment for performing masses for the dead; however, it is generally considered by
       scholars of the poem that this passage is referring to this act specifically. For studies on simony
       in *Piers* in general, see Russell A. Peck, "Social Conscience and the Poets," *Social Unrest in the Late
       Middle Ages: Papers of the Fifteenth Annual Conference of the Center for Medieval and Early Renaissance
       Studies*, ed. Francis X. Newman (Binghamton, NY: Medieval and Renaissance Texts and Studies,
       1986), 113–48; M. Teresa Tavormina, "*Piers Plowman* and the Liturgy of St. Lawrence: Composition
       and Revision in Langland's Poetry," *Studies in Philology* 84 (1987): 245–71; Alan J. Fletcher, "A
       Simoniacal Moment in *Piers Plowman*," *Yearbook of Langland Studies* 4 (1990): 135–38; and Joseph
       H. Lynch, "Simoniacal Entry into Religious Life from 1000 to 1260: A Social, Economic, and Legal
       Study" (Columbus: Ohio State University Press, 1976). Also, for the Wycliffite view on the subject,
       see John Wyclif, *On Simony*, trans. Terrence A. McVeigh (New York: Fordham University Press,
       1992).

## Political Roles of the Urban Dead

Katherine Verdery, in a study on the dead in postsocialist cultures, remarks that
"[d]ead bodies have enjoyed political life the world over and since far back in
time."[30] This assessment is appropriate for the dead in medieval cities for they
were very much a part of the political atmosphere. Depending on how they were
manipulated, they could either solidify authority already in place or escalate
contention, serve as a city's symbol or its protector. The bodies of those who had
already passed on, particularly those who had some sort of power or position in
life, were as much a part of political negotiations and operations as were the living.
To illustrate the possibilities of this concept, I will briefly examine two historical
cases; the first, from eleventh-century Cambrai, demonstrates how the dead are
employed within a city's internal affairs and the second, concerning the ninth-
century rise of Venice, associates death with the development of external political
affiliations and identity. While these are only two illustrations, they do reveal how
the physical presence of bodies, whether of saints, holy figures, or members of the
community, is significant, even necessary, in defining political urban character.
The dead can be employed, as in the case of the celebration at Cambrai, to create
the appearance of civic unity, or, as with St. Mark and Venice, to provide a means
for amplifying the power base of a city. Furthermore, this historical evidence for
the prevalence of the political ramifications of death imagery in cities is matched
in its literary counterparts. As with historical references, the sheer amount of
useful material in this context is widespread and almost limitless; here, however,
I will explore the late fourteenth-century Middle English poem *Saint Erkenwald* as
it is a text with both overt urban concerns and clear images of death.

## Cambrai, Bishop Gerard, and St. Géry

In reading a relatively recent article by Robert Stein entitled "Sacred Authority and
Secular Power: The Historical Argument of the *Gesta Episcoporum Cameracensis*,"[31]
I was introduced to a text called "The Deeds of the Bishops of Cambrai," the
composition of which was commissioned around 1024 by Bishop Gerard I; it is a
three-volume work that details the succession of the city's bishops, recounting the
foundation of Cambrai, and its affiliations with neighboring monasteries and

---

[30]   Katherine Verdery, *The Political Lives of Dead Bodies: Reburial and Postsocialist Change* (New York:
       Columbia University Press, 1999), 1.

[31]   Robert M. Stein, "Sacred Authority and Secular Power: The Historical Argument of the *Gesta
       Episcoporum Cameracensis*," *Sacred and Secular in Medieval and Early Modern Cultures: New Essays*,
       ed. Lawrence Besserman (New York: Palgrave, 2006), 149–65.

religious houses.[32] The final section is concerned with Gerard's own life and the restoration of the Cathedral of Notre Dame. The scene in the *Gesta* that is of particular interest for this study is one that Stein also refers to in his article, although for a different purpose. In November of 1030, Bishop Gerard, at the completion of the work on the Cathedral, organized a special ceremony to dedicate the church, an occasion that brought together all the people of the city and the surrounding area. The text's author describes how the body of St. Géry, or St. Gaugericus in the Latin, is brought into the Cathedral. Géry is considered to be the founding bishop of Cambrai, living from the latter half of the sixth century to the beginning of the seventh. Gerard has the saint set on the "cathedra pontificali" ("the pontifical seat"); notably, the text then says that he was seated there "sicut ante fuerat" (III.49.30; just as he had been before). The image here is that of the revered body of a dead holy man accorded the same courtesy and the same respect that he would have been given during his lifetime. Furthermore, Saint Géry is not the only deceased figure in attendance. The bodies of other Cambraian bishops—Aubert and Vindicien of the seventh century and Hadulf of the eighth century—are allowed space at the event. They are even placed so as to appear as if they are helping in the rituals at the altar as they did during their time in office; as the text states, "ipsi eiusdem altaris comministri fuerant" (III.49.30; they themselves had ministered to the same altars). Arranged with these holy individuals of the past are also others from the bishopric, the city of Cambrai; the bodies of "martires confessores ac virgines" (III.49.30; martyrs, confessors, and virgins), are all arranged according to their social stations.

All in all, in this scene of the *Gesta*, as Robert Stein observes, the dead seem "to join the living members of the congregation in the holy ceremony."[33] Indeed, it is characterized in just such a fashion as the author remarks, "sanctorum corpora nostrae dioceseos cum plebe et clero in unum congregata . . . commixtos" (III.49.42–43; the bodies of the saints were mixed together with the people and clerics of our diocese in a single congregation). The image promoted by the *Gesta*, whether or not it was true in reality, is of a gathering of the citizens of Cambrai, both past and present, in a unified celebration. In a study of Gerard of Cambrai, Diane Reilly recognizes the Bishop's awareness of his position as a political entity: "As a defender of the ecclesiastical status quo, Gerard of Cambrai sought not just to preserve the ancient rights of bishops, but also with them the divinely

---

[32]  All quotations from the *Gesta Episcoporum Cameracensis* taken from *Gesta pontificum Cameracensium*, http://mdz10.bib-bvb.de/~db/bsb00001080/images/index.html?seite=403), *Monumenta Germaniae Historia, Scriptores 7*, ed. Ludwig Bethmann (1846; New York: Kraus, 1963). An online version of this text can be found at the digital *Monumenta Germaniae Historia* (http://www.dmgh.de/). Translations are the author's (both websites last accessed on Feb. 7, 2009).

[33]  Stein, "Sacred Authority and Secular Power," 150.

sanctioned rights of kings . . . . As the product of the imperial patronage system for bishops, he was intimately familiar with the workings of court politics and his potential to act as a religious powerbroker."[34] By displaying the bodies of the city's ecclesiastical past and merging them so seamlessly with the living members of the diocese, Gerard's purpose seems to have been to emphasize the historic power of the bishopric and the newly completed cathedral and to bring the city together under this authority.[35]

## St. Mark and the Rise of Venice

Next, I would like to turn to an example drawn from the history of Venice; this particularly famous case illustrates the political and cultural value of saints' tombs and monuments, particularly those found in urban areas. To give some quick historical background, the city of Venice itself was founded in the early fifth century, with various stories and myths surrounding its origin. It remained a somewhat minor area for the first three centuries of its existence. Then, in 775, the eastern island of Olivolo received a bishopric, and a cathedral was built. By 805, after a series of political and martial upheavals and despite internal, divided loyalties between pro-Byzantium factions and pro-Frankish ones, Venice paid homage to Charlemagne; however, in 810, in a display of unity, the Venetians repelled a Frankish army led by Pepin of Italy. When the Frankish and Byzantine Empires reached a treaty in 811, the effect on Venice was to free the city from Charlemagne's control and, while still retaining status as a Byzantine province, to allow it to become, for all intents and purposes, autonomous.[36]

---

[34]  Diane J. Reilly, *The Art of Reform in Eleventh-Century Flanders: Gerard of Cambrai, Richard of Saint-Vanne and the Saint-Vaast Bible (Leiden: Brill, 2006)*, 141. Besides serving the general intention of providing vivid, physical evidence of authority, the ceremony also was aimed at reinforcing Gerard's control over the nearby abbey of Saint-Vaast, as he enters the procession with Richard, the monastery's abbot. See Reilly, *The Art of Reform*, 111–14.

[35]  Another excellent example of the dead reinforcing urban episcopal authority is the thirteenth-century episcopal pantheon in Léon Cathedral. For a study, see Rocío Sánchez Ameijeiras, "*Monumenta et memoriae*: The Thirteenth-Century Episcopal Pantheon of Léon Cathedral," *Memory and the Medieval Tomb*, ed. Elizabeth Valdez del Alamo and Carol Stamatis Pendergast (Aldershot, England, and Brookfield, VT: Ashgate, 2000), 269–86. Also, the manipulation of the life and death of St. Helen of Athyra in the political struggles between the cathedral and the city of Troyes in the thirteenth century is useful as well. See Geary, *Living with the Dead in the Middle Ages*, 221–40, as well as Elizabeth Chapin, *Les Villes de foires de Champagne des origines au début du XIVe siècle* (Paris: Champion, 1937), 32–4.

[36]  For a thorough history of Venice, see John Julius Norwich, *A History of Venice* (New York: Alfred A. Knopf, 1982).

It is into this environment that St. Mark is brought in 828. Stolen from Alexandria by Venetian merchants in a dramatic, covert maneuver, the Evangelist's body was installed in the doge's private palace chapel. Prior to his appearance in Venice, the acknowledged ecclesiastical power in the province was Aquileia, an older city that allegedly claimed Mark had ordained its first patriarch. The year before Mark's remains were translated, in 827, Aquileia's official rights were affirmed at the Synod of Mantua. When the saint's body was secured, however, a new legend was circulated, stating that Mark had been forced, by a storm, to put into port in what would become part of the Venetian lagoon; during his stay, he reportedly had a dream in which he was told to "be at rest," a vision that was subsequently interpreted, as a way of rationalizing the theft, to mean that his body was destined to belong in Venice. The physical presence of the Evangelist achieved a number of objectives for the city. Religious authority shifted away from the neighboring Aquileia since possessing the body of the saint trumped simple myth. As Gary Wills remarks, "Venice . . . managed what Otto Demus calls a 'coup d'état,' wrenching from Aquileia the original basis of its authority, the connection with Mark."[37] Furthermore, it allowed Venice to separate itself even further from both Byzantium and Rome. In St. Mark becoming the city's patron, Byzantine saint Theodore, the previous patron, was replaced, distancing Venice from the Empire. Also, by claiming an Apostolic heritage, Venice could assert a "spiritual level second only to Rome itself, with a claim to ecclesiastical autonomy . . . unparalleled in Latin Christendom."[38]

As I mentioned previously, the body of the Evangelist was placed, not in the cathedral at Olivolo, as might be expected, but in Doge Giustiniano's palace, a move that allowed him, a secular figure, control over Mark's remains, including the right to appoint chaplains charged with the care of the relics. This decision deposed the authority of the bishops, who were literally pushed to the edges of sacral importance in that they were housed at the outlying cathedral. The presence of Mark in the palace chapel incorporated the saint into every aspect of Venetian political life. In the following centuries, the symbol of Mark, the lion, would spread throughout the city, and Venice's martial successes, as well as their progress in

---

[37] Garry Wills, *Venice: Lion City — The Religion of Empire* (New York: Simon & Schuster, 2001), 29. Also see Elisabeth Crouzet-Pavan, *Venice Triumphant: The Horizons of a Myth*, trans. Lydia G. Cochrane (Baltimore: The Johns Hopkins University Press, 2002), 53: "Venice thus placed itself under the protection of a patron saint and privileged intercessor who permitted it to proclaim its originality and the growing strength of the world of the lagoon in the face of Aquileia and the mainland but also to state its will for independence from Byzantium."

[38] Norwich, *A History of Venice*, 29.

maritime ventures, would be attributed to the Evangelist's protection.[39] Thomas
Dale has observed that "[t]he saint's tomb was a nexus of political and
ecclesiastical power in the medieval city. Beyond perpetuating his *praesentia* or
physical presence as a focus of communal intercession, the tomb could evoke a
sacred past to legitimize current civic institutions."[40] He continues by commenting
that Mark's translation was "tangible evidence for a newly invented sacred past."[41]
This invention, predicated on the body of the saint, was an important factor that
allowed Venice to solidify its independent identity and to achieve a rise to civic
and ecclesiastical power.

## Establishing London as "mayster-toun" in Saint Erkenwald

Next, let us turn to the Middle English *Saint Erkenwald*, the tale of a pagan judge's
body found beneath St. Paul's cathedral as it was being rebuilt in the seventh
century by the titular bishop. This work has long been acknowledged as a text
intimately tied to the city in which it is set. Ruth Nisse, for instance, calls it "a work
manifestly about London and its citizens."[42] The poem's opening prologue sets the
text firmly within the English city, describing it as the "metropol" and the
"mayster-toun," "the chief city" (26).[43] It is clear from the beginning that the author
is concerned with the conversion of England to Christianity, specifically as it is
manifested in the way pagan names were changed and appropriated to reflect the
introduction of the new religion and even more specifically on how the temples

---

[39]  See Crouzet-Pavan, *Venice Triumphant*, 54: "[I]t tells us how Venetian maritime enterprises found
a privileged protector. As the ships made their way to Venice with their precious cargo, they were
saved from shipwreck by the personal intervention of the saint. In the decades that followed, the
holy relic was seen as committed to the protection of a city that was still far from being a major
power and had many enemies in the Adriatic. At the end of the tenth century the situation
gradually changed and Venice went on the offensive. Venetian forces won their first victories, and
the name of the Evangelist was connected with them." Also, Wills, *Venice: Lion City*, 33, remarks
that "Mark's body ordered the whole of society around itself."

[40]  Thomas E. A. Dale, "Stolen Property: St Mark's First Venetian Tomb and the Politics of Communal
Memory," *Memory and the Medieval Tomb*, eds. Elizabeth Valdez del Alamo and Carol Stamatis
Pendergast (Aldershot, England, and Brookfield, VT: Ashgate, 2000), 205–15; here 205.

[41]  Dale, "Stolen Property," 205.

[42]  Ruth Nisse, "'A Coroun Ful Riche': The Rule of History in *St Erkenwald*," *English Literary History*
65 (1998): 277–95; here 278.

[43]  Quotations taken from *Saint Erkenwald*, ed. Clifford Peterson (Philadelphia: University of
Pennsylvania Press, 1977). For studies of the legend of the saint, see Gordon Whatley, *The Saint
of London: The Life and Miracles of St. Erkenwald* (Binghamton, NY: Medieval & Renaissance Texts
& Studies, 1989) and "Heathens and Saints: St. *Erkenwald* in Its Legendary Context," *Speculum* 61.2
(1986): 330–63 as well as T. McAlindon, "Hagiography into Art: A Study of *St. Erkenwald*," *Studies
in Philology* 67 (1970): 472–94.

and people of pre-Christian London were converted.[44] Indeed, the pseudo-history of London is recounted throughout the course of the text—how Brutus founded the city and so forth—all of which is situated in chronological relationship with the life of Christ, the effect of which is to create a parallel timeline for the city. Furthermore, the more immediate setting of St. Paul's Cathedral emphasizes, as Lynn Staley remarks with reference to *Saint Erkenwald*, the work's particularly urban nature for "[t]he cathedral is at once the point of intercession for the lost, a sign of London's new identity, an exemplar for proper worship, a repository of learning, a site where classes come together in different labors, and the intersection of past and present."[45] In addition, D. Vance Smith has classified Saint Paul's Cathedral, mainly by citing the evidence of a public tablet crafted in 1346 that identified key dates in London history, as responsible for the "symbolic management of London time" and the "repository of memory and an historiography beyond human experience."[46]

Beyond the location of the story, the focus of the poem on the bishop, Saint Erkenwald, identifies it with the affairs of both London and St. Paul's. Patron saint of medieval London, Erkenwald himself is worthy of examination in a study of the juxtaposition of the dead and the city. The body of the bishop, the inspiration for a widespread cult, was interred for a long time in a prominent position behind the altar of the cathedral until it was moved in 1326 to a shrine in the chapel of St. Mary.[47] Although observance of rituals to the saint waned in the mid-fourteenth century, it was renewed after an influential 1386 decree by Bishop Braybroke. The history of Erkenwald's cult as well as of his ascension to popularity in London rituals provides much detail for consideration.[48] However, more to the point for this study, the importance of his relics in the late fourteenth century, during the time of the composition of the *Saint Erkenwald* poem, is evident. For example, in Richard Maidstone's *Concordia*, composed in 1392 in response to Richard II's return to London after an estrangement with the metropolis, he explicitly

---

[44]   Raymond P. Tripp, Jr., "*St.Erkenwald*: A Tale of Two Souls," *In Geardagum* 14 (1993): 89–110; here 94, states that "the poet's synopsis is less a history than a judgement of how Austyn went about his reforms, which he presents as hasty and shallow, little more than changing the signs on the door." Also see Patricia Price, "Integrating Time and Space: The Literary Geography of *Patience, Cleanness, The Siege of Jerusalem*, and *St. Erkenwald*," *Medieval Perspectives* 11 (1996): 234–50.

[45]   Lynn Staley, "The Man in Foul Clothes and a Late Fourteenth-Century Conversation about Sin," *Studies in the Age of Chaucer* 24 (2002): 1–47; here 23–24.

[46]   D. Vance Smith, "Crypt and Decryption: *Erkenwald* Terminable and Interminable," *New Medieval Literatures* 5 (2002): 59–85; here 63.

[47]   See Whatley, *The Saint of London*, especially 57–70.

[48]   For instance, Whatley, *The Saint of London*, 58, references an Anglo-Norman hagiographer, Hermann of Bury, from the eleventh century who talks about the fact that Londoners are saintless, even though the cult of Erkenwald was strong; Hermann's intention seems to have been to supplant the saint with his own choice of patron, St. Edmund.

mentions that the king's symbolic procession through the city included a visit to Erkenwald's tomb:

> Rex reginaque mox post hec pedites adierunt,
>   Sacra monasterii tunc visitare loca.
> O[c]currunt pariter primas et episcopus urbis;
>   Obviat et clerus illius ecclesie.
> Concomitantur eos, in cultu pontificali,
>   Ad Erkenwaldi sancta sepulcra simul.
> Quippe, deo precibus sanctoque datis venerato;
>   Concito scandit equm, qui fuit ante pedes.                    (343–50) [49]

> [Soon after this the king and queen went forth on foot
>   To pay a visit to the abbey's holy site.
> The primate and the city's bishop met them there;
> A cleric of that church came out to greet them too
>   These three, in bishop's robes, escort the king and queen
> Together, to the holy tomb of Erkenwald They pray to God and to the
>                                             saint they all revere;
>   He swiftly mounts the horse that stands before his feet.]

The fact Maidstone considers it necessary to include this representation in his work emphasizes the connection between the body of the holy bishop and the civic workings of the city.[50]

The *Saint Erkenwald* poem presents a nexus of these images—historical and contemporary London, St. Paul's Cathedral, and a saint with strong urban ties. Then, into this conceptual situation is brought the other main character of the text—the dead body of a virtuous pagan judge found in the foundations of the cathedral.[51] Miraculously, once discovered, the "dede body," the only name given to this figure and one that is frequently restated, is allowed to speak, but only to Erkenwald; in this dialogue, the judge's virtues in life as well as the current state of his corpse and soul are recounted in the hearing of the townspeople.[52] Eventually, when Erkenwald's tears fall on the judge, his soul is released and his body shows, for the first time, the ravages of decomposition. Given that the text depicts the bishop in the process of rebuilding St. Paul's, an exploit designed to

---

[49] Quotation from "De Concordia" taken from *Richard Maidstone: Concordia (The Reconciliation of Richard II with London)*, ed. David R. Carlson, trans. A. G. Rigg (Kalamazoo, MI: Medieval Institute Publications, 2003).

[50] See Nisse, "'A Coroun Ful Riche'," 279–80.

[51] For discussions of the body itself, see Siegfried Wenzel, "*St. Erkenwald* and the Uncorrupted Body," *Notes and Queries* 28.1 (1981): 13–14; Allen J. Frantzen, "*St. Erkenwald* and the Raising of Lazarus," *Mediaevalia* 7 (1981): 157–71;

[52] For a discussion of "the speaking dead," see Patricia Harkins, "St. Erkenwald and the Speaking Dead," *Publications of the Mississippi Philological Association* (1987): 96–105.

reinforce and continue the Christianization of England's capital,[53] the dead body seems to represent London's religious and legendary past, claiming as he does his relationship to the old city and its previous name of "New Troie." Despite the fact that it is a pagan time he is referring to, by establishing his own righteousness, he creates a "fundamentally virtuous history" for London.[54] Yet, at the same time, since he requires the intervention of Saint Erkenwald in order to achieve complete salvation, the bishop's work in advancing the Christian conversion Augustine began before him through the renovation of St. Paul's is validated and made even more sacred. As Monika Otter states, "Once communication with the dead man is established, the mysterious discovery can be made to work for Erkenwald's people, offering moral instruction, highlighting and reinforcing the changes that have taken place since the judge's death, and that are currently taking place under Erkenwald's leadership."[55] While London's past may be virtuous, its present is undeniably Christian, providing two-fold support, through the presence of the dead body, for the perception of London in the beginning of the text as the "mayster-toun."

## Conclusion

In the examples I've provided here, I have demonstrated the importance and the wide-ranging prevalence, across time, space, and genre, of the medieval relationship between death and the image of the city. It is a rich topic for discussion in medieval urban studies, as it takes into account a variety of perceptions and demands exploration of history, politics, literature, hagiography, and anthropology, among other fields. The particular cases that I have discussed here reveal how the dead and their bodies were manipulated in a variety of ways, both physically and fictionally, within representations of the city. Jean-Claude Schmitt has said that the "dead have no existence other than that which the living imagine for them."[56] Indeed, the people of medieval cities or those authors who

---

[53]  Monika Otter, "'New Werke': *St Erkenwald*, St Albans, and the Medieval Sense of the Past," *Journal of Medieval and Renaissance Studies* 24 (1994): 387–414; here 407: "[T]he poet stresses that London (then called New Troy) was the capital of pagan England, and that its new religious and civic prominence under Christian leadership is, again, both a complete change and a logical, organic continuation. Erkenwald is then introduced as Austyn's successor . . . and his 'New Werke,' the rebuilding and rededication of the chief pagan temple as St. Paul's cathedral, is seen in direct continuity with Austyn's Christianization of England. It is in the course of this work that the tomb is found and the events of the poem unfold."

[54]  Nisse, "'A Coroun Ful Riche'," 291.

[55]  Otter, "'New Werke'," 412.

[56]  Schmitt, *Ghosts in the Middle Ages*, 1.

created literary cities imagined a vital existence for their dead, but, even beyond that, the dead were real. They were active in urban politics, claimed their own spaces in city landscapes, and were energetic parts of literary narratives, establishing and emphasizing the complexities of urban concerns. The dead more than matched the physicality of their living counterparts.

Alan V. Murray

(University of Leeds)

# The Demographics of Urban Space in Crusade-Period Jerusalem (1099–1187)

## Introduction

On 15 July 1099, after a siege lasting just over five weeks, the armies of the First Crusade stormed the walls of the city of Jerusalem. The seizure of the Holy City from the Muslim Fātimid caliphate fulfilled the goal of an expedition that had been proclaimed three and a half years before by Pope Urban II at the council of Clermont, and laid the foundations for a Christian state, the kingdom of Jerusalem, in Palestine. On 2 October 1187, Jerusalem surrendered to Saladin, ruler of Egypt and Muslim Syria, whose forces had defeated the army of the kingdom in battle at the Horns of Hattin on 5 July of that same year. The time between these two events constituted the longest period of Christian rule of the Holy City from the time of its capture from the Byzantine empire by the caliph 'Umar in 638 right up to the present day.

These eighty-eight years were a period in which the Franks, as the Western settlers in Palestine came to be known to themselves and their Muslim enemies, engineered major changes in the character of the city and its population. The most visible and enduring development was the transformation of sacred architecture, occurring in three related phenomena: the rebuilding and decoration of existing Christian structures; the construction of new Latin churches and monastic institutions in a Western style; and, perhaps most strikingly, the identification of existing Islamic structures as Old Testament sites. The second main development was the alteration of the city's demographic composition by the Franks. Control of the Holy Places was the main determinant of the policies of both Christian and Muslim powers that sought to occupy Jerusalem during the period of the crusades. The demographic composition of the city was an essential factor in this control; for the city to be under secure Christian rule, it was necessary that its population should be made up of Franks or other nationalities who were supportive or sympathetic to them. The first of these two developments has left structures and stylistic features which are still noticeable in the urban landscape, and has been extensively studied by religious and art historians.[1] The effects of the second development were largely reversed in the course of Saladin's conquest in 1187 and almost completely obliterated when Frankish rule in the city, re-established by treaty in 1229, was finally extinguished in 1244. This essay will not aim to add to the extensive literature on the physical appearance of Jerusalem, but rather to study the human occupation of urban space, examining how the conquerors of the city in 1099 and 1187 manipulated its demographic composition, by both violent and peaceful means, in the interests of religious identity and military security.

## The Population of Jerusalem in 1099

The siege of Jerusalem by the Arabs under 'Umar, the second caliph, in 638 cost the lives of many of its Byzantine—at that time almost exclusively Christian—population, and on the city's surrender many of its surviving administrators, soldiers and clerics fled to Byzantine territory. These fugitives were replaced by Muslim immigrants from Arabia, as well as Jews (including members of the Samaritan and Karaite sects), since 'Umar appears to have revoked the Byzantine-period prohibition on Jews residing within the city.[2] Yet while the language of the city seems to have changed from Greek in favor of Arabic in the course of the next five centuries, the Muslim and Jewish immigrants and their descendants remained a minority within a population that was largely Christian; the majority of the Christians belonged to the Greek Orthodox church, but there were also numbers of the so-called Eastern or non-Chalcedonian churches: Syrian Orthodox (Jacobites), Armenians, and Copts. The eleventh-century Arab geographer al-Muqaddasī, himself a Jerusalemite by origin, sang the praises of "the most sublime of cities", but lamented that its population was still largely Christian, complaining that "the Christians and Jews are predominant here, and

---

[1]   On the sacred topography of Jerusalem in the Frankish period, see especially: T. S. R. Boase, "Ecclesiastical Art in the Crusader States in Palestine and Syria," *A History of the Crusades,* gen. ed. Kenneth M. Setton, 6 vols (Madison: University of Wisconsin Press, 1969–89), 4: 69–139; Bernard Hamilton, "Rebuilding Zion: The Holy Places of Jerusalem in the Twelfth Century," *Studies in Church History* 14 (1977): 105–16; Hamilton, "Ideals of Holiness: Crusaders, Contemplatives and Mendicants," *International History Review* 17 (1995), 693–712; Adrian J. Boas, *Jerusalem in the Time of the Crusades: Society, Landscape and Art in the Holy City under Frankish Rule* (London: Routledge, 2001). All dates cited in this essay refer to the Christian Era (C.E./A.D.).

[2]   Dan Bahat and Chaim T. Rubinstein, *The Illustrated Atlas of Jerusalem* (New York: Simon & Schuster, 1990), 68–89.

the mosque devoid of congregations and assemblies."[3] The demographic makeup of Jerusalem was not substantially altered after the Fātimid caliph al-Hākim bi-Amr Allāh started to persecute non-Muslim communities in 1009, although several of the Christian churches, notably the Holy Sepulchre, were demolished and eventually restored in rather inadequate fashion after al-Hākim abandoned his persecutions in 1020.

The Jerusalem that was conquered by the crusaders in the summer of 1099 essentially corresponded to the area of the present-day Old City. Its area was defined in a period of reconstruction following an earthquake occurring in 1033 or 1034, which destroyed many of the city's Byzantine-period fortifications. While the western, northern, and most of the eastern walls were rebuilt, it did not prove practical to restore the southern and south-eastern sections which had enclosed the spur containing the religious sites of Mount Zion as well as much of the terrain that sloped down to the east toward the Kidron valley as far as the springs of Siloam (mod. 'Ain Silwan). A new, shorter southern wall was constructed, leaving the city's defences in a roughly trapezoid form corresponding to the Ottoman-period walls that survive today.[4]

The process that led up to the rebuilding of Jerusalem's fortifications after the earthquake gives us the first reasonably detailed information on the contemporary composition of the city's population, which remained substantially unchanged until the arrival of the crusaders. The Fātimid caliph, Abū Tamīm Ma'add al-Mustansīr bi-llāh, ordered each religious community to defray the costs of reconstruction. The Christians found themselves unable to pay, and appealed to the Byzantine emperor for assistance. He diverted funds from the imperial revenues from Cyprus, but made the condition that only Christians would be allowed to live within the section of the city enclosed by the walls that he had paid for. The late twelfth-century historian William of Tyre, who carried out extensive research on the history of the north-western section of the city that formed the Patriarch's Quarter under Frankish rule, recorded that "until that day the Saracens had lived together with the faithful indiscriminately, but from that time, by order of the prince [i.e., the caliph] they were obliged to withdraw to other parts of the city, so that this quarter was now left to the faithful without dispute."[5] The

---

[3]    Al-Muqaddasi, *The Best Divisions for Knowledge of the Regions: A Translation of Ahsan al-Taqasim fi Ma'rifat al-Aqalim*, trans. Basil Anthony Collins (Reading: Garnet, 1994), 151–52.

[4]    Bahat and Rubinstein, *The Illustrated Atlas of Jerusalem*, 87–88. The new course of the southern and south-eastern walls left several important religious sites outside the fortified sites, including the churches of St Mary on Mount Zion and St Peter in Gallicantu and the Pool of Siloam.

[5]    Guillaume de Tyr, *Chronique*, ed. Robert B. C. Huygens, Corpus Christianorum, Continuatio Mediaevalis 63–63A, 2 vols. (Turnhout: Brepols, 1986), IX.16–18, 442–45; here 444: "Habitaverant sane usque ad illum diem promiscue cum fidelibus Sarraceni, sed ab ea hora, audita iussione principali, ad alias civitatis partes de necessitate se contulerunt, quarta predicta fidelibus sine

completion of the walls, which William dates to 1063, may have given a greater impetus to members of different religious communities to live together in proximity, as seems to have happened in the case of the north-western section.[6] However, it would be wrong to assume that this tendency brought about the formation of exclusive residential quarters; rather, there was a clustering around certain neighbourhoods. Since Christians still formed the majority of the population, as indicated by al-Muqaddasī, it would be unrealistic for all of them to be confined within what later became the Patriarch's Quarter. The Byzantine emperor regarded himself as protector of Greek Orthodox church, and it is likely that those who resided in the section whose fortifications he had financed were members of that confession, who were known as Melkites, literally 'imperialist' Christians.[7] After the Muslim conquest the Jews had mostly lived south of the Aqsā Mosque, but this area was left outside the city's limit after the construction of the new, shorter southern wall. They seem to have relocated to the north-eastern section, since this area, or at least part of it, was still sometimes referred to as the *Juiverie* (or Lat. *Juderia*) by the Franks.[8]

The basic demographic composition of Jerusalem can have been little altered by the seizure of the city, along with most of the interior of Palestine, by the Saljūq Turks in 1077. Fātimid rule was restored when an Egyptian army besieged and recaptured the city in the summer of 1098. When the armies of the First Crusade entered northern Syria, the Fātimids had made diplomatic overtures toward them, hoping for an alliance against the Turks. Yet once the crusaders entered Palestine, less than a year after Fātimid rule had been restored, it was clear that the Holy City

---

contradictione relicta." Translations from the chronicle of William of Tyre given in this essay are, unless indicated otherwise, by the author.

6   The precise chronology of the reconstruction is problematic. William of Tyre identifies the Byzantine emperor who provided funding as Constantine (IX) Monomachos (1042–55). However, he also dates the completion of the Christian section of walls very precisely to the year 1063, and to thirty-six years before the crusader liberation. There are two possibilities of reconciling this conflicting information. One is that Constantine IX provided funds, but that the work was not completed until at least a decade after his reign; the other is that William confused the name and reign of this emperor with that of Constantine X Doukas (1059–67), who was actually reigning at the time the walls were finished.

7   The term derived from the Arabic *malik*, "king, ruler," relating to the Byzantine *basileos*. Sidney H. Griffith, "The Church of Jerusalem and the 'Melkites': The Making of an 'Arab Orthodox' Identity in the World of Islam (750–1050 CE)," *Christians and Christianity in the Holy Land: From the Origins to the Latin Kingdoms*, ed. Ora Limor and Guy G. Stroumsa, Cultural Encounters in Late Antiquity and the Middle Ages, 5 (Turnhout: Brepols, 2006), 175–204.

8   *Chartes de Terre Sainte provenant de l'abbaye de N.-D. de Josaphat*, ed. Henri-François Delaborde (Paris: Ecoles Françaises d'Athènes et de Rome, 1880), 43–45; *Cartulaire du chapitre du Saint-Sépulcre de Sépulcre de Jérusalem*, ed. Geneviève Bresc-Bautier (Paris: Académie des Inscriptions et Belles-Lettres, 1984), no. 169; Joshua Prawer, *The History of the Jews in the Latin Kingdom of Jerusalem* (Oxford: Clarendon, 1988), 17–18, 22.

was their intended target. The city had only a small garrison, and so the Fātimid governor, Iftikhār al-Dawlah, would need to withstand the expected crusader siege until a relieving army arrived from Egypt. In the meantime, he attempted to improve the city's chances of resistance by restorting to some fairly drastic measures. He expelled the Christian inhabitants, fearing that they might collaborate with the crusaders.[9] Their place was taken by Muslims and Jews brought in from the surrounding villages; they, along with their co-religionists among the city's population, were expected to take an active part in its defence against the crusader onslaught.

## The Crusader Conquest

There is a broad agreement among Western, Armenian, Arabic and Hebrew sources that as soon as they had fought their way into Jerusalem on 15 July, the crusaders began a massacre of the city's Muslim and Jewish inhabitants, which was resumed the next day. Modern historians have been greatly affected by the descriptions of the contemporary Western sources which describe the killing in lurid and sometimes extensive terms.[10] Thus the southern French chronicler Raymond of Aguilers, himself an eyewitness, relates: "Some of the pagans were mercifully beheaded, others pierced by arrows plunged from towers, and yet others, tortured for a long time, were burned to death in searing flames. Piles of heads, hands, and feet lay in the houses and streets, and indeed there was a running to and fro of men and knights over the corpses."[11] It is noticeable that much of the imagery used to describe these events is Biblical in character; the books of Isaiah and Zechariah and the Revelation of the New Testament were employed to justify the liberation of Jerusalem and the slaughter of the Gentiles as having been divinely ordained.[12] Raymond goes on to state that on the Temple

---

[9] Guillaume de Tyr, *Chronique*, VII.23, 374–75.

[10] For a detailed analysis, see Benjamin Z. Kedar, "The Jerusalem Massacre of July 1099 in the Western Historiography of the Crusades," *Crusades* 3 (2004), 15–75, here 65.

[11] "Raimundi de Aguilers canonici Podiensis historia Francorum qui ceperunt Iherusalem," in *RHC Hist. Occ.* 3: 231–309, here 300: "Alii namque, quod levius erat, obtruncabantur capitibus; alii autem sagittati de turribus saltare cogebantur; alii vero diutissime torti et ignibus adusti flammeriebantur. Videbantur per vicos et plateas civitatis aggeres capitum et manuum atque pedum. Per cadavera vero publice, hominum et equitum discursus erat;" Raymond of Aguilers, *Historia Francorum qui ceperunt Iherusalem*, trans. John H. Hill and Laurita L. Hill. Memoirs of the American Philosophical Society, 71 (Philadelphia: American Philosophical Society, 1968), 127.

[12] Guibert of Nogent, "Historia quae dicitur Gesta Dei per Francos," *Recueil des Historiens des Croisades: Historiens Occidentaux* [henceforth cited as *RHC Hist. Occ.*], 5 vols (Paris: Académie des Inscriptions et Belles-Lettres, 1844–95), 4: 113–263; here 227–29, 237–38; Robert of Rheims, "Roberti Monachi historia Iherosolimitana," *RHC Hist. Occ.* 3: 717–882; here 868–82.

Mount the crusaders "rode in blood [up] to the knees and bridles of their horses."[13] This phrase can be identified as a reference to Revelation 14.20, which describes the vision of the winepress of the wrath of God, from which blood will flow up to the bridles of horses.[14] Fulcher of Chartres and Baldric of Dol describe how the Holy Sepulchre and the Temple had been cleansed of a contagion caused by pagan superstitions.[15] A problem of interpretation has been pointed out by Benjamin Kedar, who has undertaken the most exhaustive and nuanced investigation of the massacres: the adoption of such imagery does not in itself invalidate the descriptions given by Raymond and other chroniclers; slaughter remains slaughter, even if it is described in apocalyptic terms. Kedar's detailed diachronic study of the medieval and modern historiography concludes that the majority of the city's inhabitants were indeed killed, although numbers of both Muslims and Jews were able to escape or were ransomed.[16]

Another problematic issue in the interpretation of the Western accounts is that their extensive use of Biblical imagery seems more like a retrospective justification of the slaughter, and does not by itself necessarily explain why the crusaders embarked upon the massacre. In recent years some historians have argued that the massacre of both combatants and civilian population alike was the normal fate of any city taken by storm according to the conventions of warfare at the time, pointing to similar events where the defenders had refused to surrender.[17] Certainly the slaughter on the actual day of the capture, 15 July, can be explained as the effect of a bloodthirsty desire for revenge on the part of enraged crusaders;

---

13    "Raimundi de Aguilers ... historia Francorum," 300: "Sed tantum sufficiat, quod in templo et in porticu Salomonis equitabatur in sanguine usque ad genua, et usque ad frenos equorum. Justo nimirum judicio, ut locus idem eorum sanguinem exciperet, quorum blasphemias in Deum tam longo tempore pertulerat."; Raymond of Aguilers, *Liber*, ed. John H. Hill and Laurita L. Hill. Documents relatifs à l'histoire des croisades, 9 (Paris: Paul Geuthner, 1969), 150 n. 2; Raymond of Aguilers, *Historia Francorum qui ceperunt Iherusalem*, 128 n. 22.

14    *Biblia Sacra iuxta Vulgatam versionem*, ed. Robert Weber et al., 3rd edn (Stuttgart: Deutsche Bibelgesellschaft, 1969), 1896: "et calcatus est lacus extra civitatem et exivit sanguis de lacu usque ad frenos equorum per stadia mille sescenta." It is also noticeable that Raymond, unlike the other contemporary Western authors, seems to heighten the theological-apocalyptic dimensions of the slaughter by omitting any references to baser concerns such as the seizure of plunder and captives.

15    *Fulcheri Carnotensis Historia Hierosolymitana (1095–1127)*, ed. Heinrich Hagenmeyer (Heidelberg: Winter, 1913), I.xxxiii, 305–06; Baldric of Dol, "Baldrici episcopi Dolensis Historia Jerosolimitana," *RHC Hist. Occ* 4: 102–03.

16    Kedar, "The Jerusalem Massacre of July 1099 in the Western Historiography of the Crusades," 65.

17    John France, *Victory in the East: A Military History of the First Crusade* (Cambridge: Cambridge University Press, 1994), 355–56; Kaspar Elm, "Die Eroberung Jerusalems im Jahre 1099: Ihre Darstellung, Beurteilung und Deutung in den Quellen zur Geschichte des Ersten Kreuzzugs," *Jerusalem im Hoch- und Spätmittelalter: Konflikte und Konfliktbewältigung—Vorstellungen und Vergegenwärtigungen*, ed. Dieter Bauer, Klaus Herbers, and Nikolas Jaspert. Campus Historische Studien, 29 (Frankfurt am Main: Campus, 2001), 31–54.

as they climbed over the walls and fought their way through the unfamiliar narrow streets, it must have been difficult to distinguish between enemy soldiers and unarmed civilians, and in the heat of battle, as we know from numerous subsequent conflicts, soldiers have often been known to show a tendency to kill any potential opponents, whether armed or not. Yet these explanations are harder to sustain when we acknowledge that most sources agree that the slaughter continued the next day, 16 July, while once source, the Rhineland chronicler Albert of Aachen, states that the crusaders killed off the remaining Saracens on the third day, that is 17 July.[18]

One can believe that the desire to cleanse the holy sites of the gentile cult, which figured as one of the main themes of the Western chroniclers, may have motivated the clerical leadership of the crusades and possibly some of the more devout laity, but the descriptions of the sources are less convincing in explaining the actions of the majority of the rank-and-file crusaders. For weeks they had been short of food and water, and by this time they must have been physically exhausted by the exertions of the siege and the fighting that followed it within the city. Their most immediate concerns must have been their physical security and well-being, and food and water; beyond that, the desire to worship at the holy sites they had longed to see for so long, and conceivably, the wish to secure plunder and ransoms.

The slaughter of the first day may have been the result of the revenge-driven craze of battle, but we must assume that the majority of crusaders slept or at least rested on the following night. What was the situation that confronted the weary and blood-stained crusaders as the sun rose on the second day after the capture? By the time of the conquest crusader numbers had been reduced to about 10,000 fighters and non-combatants.[19] A small garrison had been left behind at Lydda, near the coast, but essentially the crusaders had no secure communications either with the West or with the pockets of Frankish-held territory far to the north at Antioch (modern Antakya, Turkey) and Edessa (Şanlıurfa, Turkey). The only ships that had joined the crusaders in Palestine had been dismantled and transported overland by their Genoese crews to provide wood for building siege engines at

---

[18] Albert of Aachen, *Historia Ierosolimitana: History of the Journey to Jerusalem*, ed. and trans. Susan B. Edgington, 2 vols. Oxford Medieval Texts (Oxford: Clarendon, 2007), 439–45. On the importance and accuracy of Albert's testimony, see especially: Peter Knoch, *Studien zu Albert von Aachen: Der erste Kreuzzug in der deutschen Chronistik*. Stuttgarter Beiträge zur Geschichte und Politik, 1 (Stuttgart: Klett, 1966); Susan B. Edgington, "The First Crusade: Reviewing the Evidence," *The First Crusade: Origins and Impact*, ed. Jonathan Phillips (Manchester: Manchester University Press, 1997), 57–77.

[19] France, *Victory in the East*, 131, gives this estimate for the crusader forces at the battle of Ascalon, fought by the crusaders against the Fātimid relieving army in August 1099; it thus provides an approximation for numbers which allows for crusader casualties at the siege of Jerusalem.

Jerusalem. The Fātimids controlled the port of Ascalon (mod. Tel Ashqelon, Israel), where relieving forces from Egypt were already concentrating. The only conceivable strategy for the crusaders was to secure Jerusalem as quickly as possible, and use it as a base to confront the Fātimid army in the coastal plain; in the event of a defeat they could retreat back into the fortified city and attempt to hold out there in the hope that some relief would arrive from the West in the form of later waves of the crusade.

Securing Jerusalem in these circumstances was by no means a foregone conclusion.[20] Even allowing for the previous expulsion of the Christian population and the casualties of 15 July, there were still a large number of Muslims and Jews left within the city. Not all of them were captives. Some had taken refuge on the Temple platform; others were hiding in houses or cellars; and finally, the Fātimid garrison and some civilians were still holding out in the Tower of David, the main fortification of the city, under the command of the governor. The crusaders had to man the city's walls and keep the Fātimid troops in the tower isolated, while also attempting to locate food supplies for the coming weeks; in the face of these tasks, they needed to control the surviving inhabitants inside the city, whose numbers may have been equal or possibly even greater than their own. They must have feared that these people might rise up against the crusaders as soon as the Fātimid relieving army approached the city.

The native inhabitants could have been ransomed or simply expelled *en masse*, but they would still present a major problem. Allowing large numbers of Muslims and Jews to leave would have simply increased the number of people competing for scarce resources of food and water in the environs of Jerusalem.[21] More dangerously, they could have provided a labor force that could be employed by the Fātimids in mounting a siege of the city. The chances of a successful assault would have been greatly improved by large numbers that could be used to construct and move siege engines, fill in ditches, and haul supplies of food and water. The thinking of the crusade leadership can be discerned in a passage given by Albert of Aachen, who derived his information from returning crusaders. Albert reports a speech which he attributes to the "greater and wiser men", a formulation that must mean the leaders of the crusade armies:

---

[20]   The population of Jerusalem before the siege has been estimated at around 20,000–30,000, see Joshua Prawer, *The Latin Kingdom of Jerusalem: European Colonialism in the Middle Ages* (London: Weidenfeld and Nicolson, 1972), 82. It has recently been shown that at the time of the conquest, the Tower of David did not yet have an associated citadel; the citadel that survives today probably originated in the early thirteenth century. See Ronnie Ellenblum, "Frankish Castles, Muslim Castles, and the Medieval Citadel of Jerusalem," *In Laudem Hierosolymitani: Studies in Crusades and Medieval Culture in Honour of Benjamin Z. Kedar*, ed. Iris Shagrir, Ronnie Ellenblum, and Jonathan Riley-Smith (Aldershot: Ashgate, 2007), 93–110.

[21]   On the problems of supply, especially the scarcity of water, see France, *Victory in the East*, 334–35.

Jerusalem, city of God on high, has been recovered, as you all know, with great difficulty and not without harm to our men, and today she has been restored to her own sons and delivered from the hands of the king of Egypt and the yoke of the Turks. But now we must be careful lest we lose it through avarice or sloth or the pity we have for our enemies, sparing prisoners and gentiles still left in the city. For if we were to be attacked in great strength by the king of Egypt we should be suddenly overcome from inside and outside the city, and in this way carried away into eternal exile. And so the most important and trustworthy advice seems to us that all the Saracens and gentiles who are held prisoner for ransoming with money, or already redeemed, should be put to the sword without delay, so that we shall not meet with any problem from their trickery or machinations.[22]

From these descriptions it would seem that considerable deliberation had already taken place. Most of the city's inhabitants were being held as captives for ransom, and arrangements may even have been in place for the release of many of them. Yet the crusader leaders were acutely aware of the twin dangers posed by internal and external enemies. The massacres of 16 and 17 July can be most plausibly understood as a calculated action carried out with the aim of removing this threat. The Fāṭimid garrison was still capable of offering serious resistance; it was therefore removed by being granted free passage to Ascalon.[23] The crusaders then turned to the remainder of the Muslim and Jewish inhabitants who were executed in the course of the next two days. The fact that so many crusaders postponed their plundering and did without ransoms in order to carry out executions is an indication of a slaughter that was as systematic as it was merciless. The captive inhabitants were split up into groups and systematically executed, while fugitives were hunted down so that, in the words of Albert of Aachen, "not only in the streets, houses and palaces, but even in places of desert solitude numbers of slain were to be found."[24] Some of the captives were spared to carry out the tasks of cleansing the city and dragging the bodies of the dead outside the walls for disposal, until they too, were slaughtered in their turn.[25] When the chronicler

---

[22]  Albert of Aachen, *Historia Ierosolimitana*, 440–41: "Ierusalem, ciuitas Dei excelsi, ut uniuersi nostis, magna difficultate, et non sine dampno nostrorum recuperata, propriis filiis hodie restituta est, et liberata de manu regis Babylonie et iugo Turcorum. Sed nunc cauendum est ne auaricia aut pigricia uel misericordia habita erga inimicos hanc amittamus, captiuis et adhuc residuis in urbe gentilibus parcentes. Nam si forte a rege Babylonie in fortitudine graui occupati fuerimus, subito ab intus et extra expugnabimur, et sic in perpetuum exilium transportabimur. Vnde primum et fidele consilium nobis uidetur quatenus universi Sarraceni et gentiles qui captiui tenentur pecunia redimendi aut redempti sine dilatione in gladio corruant, ne fraude aut ingeniis illorum nobis aliqua aduersa occurrant."

[23]  *Fulcheri Carnotensis Historia Hierosolymitana*, I.30, 308–09. As Kedar argues, it is likely that some of the civilians who had taken refuge in the Tower of David were able to leave with the garrison.

[24]  Albert of Aachen, *Historia Ierosolimitana*, 442–43.

[25]  'Historia quae dicitur Gesta Dei per Francos,' 228.

Fulcher of Chartres visited the city a year later, he was struck by the huge stench that arose from the rotting bodies of the defenders that still lay around the city walls.[26]

## Jerusalem and Its Population under Frankish Rule

The massacres of 1099 can be understood as a horrific, short-term solution to the strategic situation, which found its retrospective justification in religious idealism. It is even conceivable that some of the leaders were thinking of the longer-term security of the city. At any rate, the new demographic facts on the ground that were created by the slaughter were perpetuated for ideological reasons. After the immediate threat was averted, the Franks permanently enshrined the consequences of the massacre by enacting a law that no Muslims or Jews would be allowed to reside in the city. As it was expressed by the Frankish historian William of Tyre, "to allow anyone not belonging to the Christian faith to live in so venerated a place seemed like sacrilege to the leaders in their devotion to God."[27] Non-Christian merchants and pilgrims were allowed in, but only as temporary visitors; the rules eventually seem to have been relaxed to permit residence for a handful lucky enough to secure exemptions because they had necessary skills that could not be supplied by the Christian population, such as the Jewish dyers mentioned by Benjamin of Tudela in 1170.[28] However, the new capital did not attract large numbers of Franks. Neither did it attract Italian colonists, for unlike the kingdom's main ports such as Acre (mod. 'Akko, Israel) and Tyre (mod. Soûr, Lebanon), it had no significance in terms of long distance trade. Jerusalem in the Frankish period had two principal functions: it was the seat of the royal and ecclesiastical administrations, and it serviced an increasing pilgrim traffic which took off as a result of the establishment of Western access to the holy sites. It contained a relatively high proportion proportion of clerics, both secular and regular, because of the large number of holy sites now operated by the Latin church which catered to pilgrims from the West as well as to the Frankish population.

The Franks took over the church of the Holy Sepulchre, the principal religious site of the city, expelling its Greek clergy, and carried out a major renovation programme that was still going on when it was reconsecrated in 1149. The Franks established several completely new religious foundations, such as the abbey of St Mary in the Valley of Jehosaphat, built on the ruins of a Byzantine church outside the eastern walls, and the convent of St. Anne, sited just inside the Jehosaphat Gate

---

[26]   *Fulcheri Carnotensis Historia Hierosolymitana*, I.33, 332–33.
[27]   Guillaume de Tyr, *Chronique*, XI.27, 535–36.
[28]   Boas, *Jerusalem in the Time of the Crusades*, 40.

between the Sheep Pools. These various buildings were easily outshone by the towering magnificence of the Islamic structures on the Haram al-Sharif ("the noble sanctuary"), as the Temple Mount in the south-east of the city was known to Muslims. The Islamic sites there were reclaimed for the Christian faith by a process of what might be called creative re-identification by the Latin Church. The Dome of the Rock, situated at the centre of the Temple Mount, was identified as the ancient Jewish Temple (Lat. *Templum Domini*), and provided with Augustinian canons in 1112. The Aqsā Mosque situated to its south was identified as the Palace of Solomon (Latin *Templum Salomonis*) and in 1119 it was given to the newly founded military religious order of the Temple, which took its name from the building.[29] These two buildings were mosques constructed in a typical Islamic style, and so they were given a new, Christian appearance by the construction of new conventual and ancillary buildings and the addition of unambiguously Christian symbols and decorations, such as a large golden cross that was erected on top of the Dome of the Rock. The Temple Mount was far more prominent and splendid than the site of Christ's burial at the Holy Sepulchre, and could not be ignored, and so it was redefined as a group of Old Testament sites, which could thus be integrated into the liturgical life of the city along with the many New Testament sites.

The Temple Mount with its architectural grandeur and large open spaces contrasted with the crowded narrow streets that characterized the rest of the city. Its main function under Frankish rule was worship—as it had been under the Muslims—and until the number of pilgrims began to increase it must have often been fairly deserted. It had only a small resident population, consisting mainly of the Templars and their ancillary staff who were stationed along its southern side from 1119.[30] During the first two decades of the kingdom much of the remainder of the city's space was evidently unoccupied. The majority of crusaders returned to western Europe in the summer of 1099; William of Tyre later estimated that Godfrey of Bouillon, the first ruler of the kingdom, was left with only 300 knights and 2000 foot-soldiers.[31] To this number we should add dependents, together with clerics and other non-combatants, but even allowing for them, as well as native

[29]   John Wilkinson, *Jerusalem Pilgrimage 1099–1185*. Hakluyt Society Second Series, 167 (London: The Hakluyt Society, 1988), 28, points out that Greek *naos* and Latin *templum* both had the dual meanings of "temple" and "palace." Since the Dome of the Rock was seen as the Jewish Temple, the Aqsā mosque, despite being known as a *templum*, had to be identified as a building with a quite different character.

[30]   Templar houses in this area are mentioned by the pilgrim Theoderic who visited the city around 1170, see Wilkinson, *Jerusalem Pilgrimage 1099–1185*, 295.

[31]   Guillaume de Tyr, *Chronique*, IX.19, 445. For the relatively small numbers of fighting forces avaialble during the reign of Baldwin I, see Alan V. Murray, "The Origins of the Frankish Nobility of the Kingdom of Jerusalem, 1100–1118," *Mediterranean Historical Review* 4 (1989), 281–300.

Christians who returned to the city and other Franks who arrived in late 1100 with Godfrey's successor, King Baldwin I, the total population must have been substantially smaller than before the conquest. The problem of depopulation can be seen from the "Law of a Year and a Day", presumably enacted under Godfrey or Baldwin I, which recognized the rights of anyone who occupied any urban property if its owners were absent for this length of time. In effect, it was a measure to expropriate the property of non-residents.[32]

The small size of the population during the first two decades of the kingdom's existence meant that the security of the city was a major concern. The capital was less than 50 miles distant from the Fātimid forward base at Ascalon, and the caliphate proved capable of mounting invasions of the kingdom up until 1123. William of Tyre claims that "there was not sufficient population in the city to carry out the necessary business of the kingdom, or even to defend its gates, towers and ramparts against sudden enemy attacks."[33] He goes on to explain that at this time the Frankish population was scarcely numerous enough to fill a single *vicus* (i.e. quarter or district).[34] Prawer concluded that the Franks "doubtless settled in the north-western quarter of the city."[35] In many ways this would have been a logical development. This area was centred on the church of the Holy Sepulchre, which was the most important shrine of the city, and it enjoyed additional protection in the form of the Tower of David, situated close to the central point of the western wall; the two main exits of the north-western segment, the Jaffa Gate and St Stephen's Gate, gave access to the two main routes to Frankish settlements on the coast and to the north in Samaria and Galilee. Yet one wonders whether the settlement pattern was quite so drastic as Prawer assumes. The main gates on all four sides would be in regular use to bring in supplies of foodstuffs, livestock and firewood. Pilgrims returning from the Mount of Olives, Bethlehem or the Jordan and would presumably use the gates in the eastern and southern walls. All of these gates would need to be guarded, and so it would be reasonable to assume that

---

[32]  Guillaume de Tyr, *Chronique*, IX.19, 446.

[33]  Guillaume de Tyr, *Chronique*, XI.27, 535: "…ita ut eo ad cetera regni negocia de necessitate vocato non esset in civitate populus, qui saltem ad protegendos civitatis introitus et turres et menia contra repentinas hostium irruptiones munienda sifficeret…."

[34]  Guillaume de Tyr, *Chronique*, IX.19, 536: "Nostrates vero adeo pauci erant et inopes, ut vix unum de vicis possent incolere, Suriani autem, qui ab initio urbis cives extiterant, tempore hostilitatis per multas tribulationes et infinitas molestias adeo rari erant, ut quasi nullus eorum esset numerus." The translation by Emily Atwater Babcock and August C. Krey, *A History of Deeds Done Beyond the Sea by William Archbishop of Tyre*, 2 vols. Records of Civilization: Sources and Studies, 35 (New York: Columbia University Press, 1941), 1: 507 is surely mistaken in translating the word *vicus* in this context as "street," which would indicate a tiny number of Franks, even allowing for some rhetorical exaggeration.

[35]  Joshua Prawer, "The Settlement of the Latins in Jerusalem," *Speculum* 27 (1952), 490–503; here 493.

members of the garrison and possibly their families may have been billeted close to their stations, outside the north-western quadrant.

Around the year 1116, King Baldwin I took measures to increase the city's population by resettling Syrians from the Transjordan region south-east of the Dead Sea, who had been "living in villages under hard conditions of servitude and forced tribute."[36] The circumstance that the king resorted to importing complete families together with their herds and flocks from small villages into an unfamiliar, urban environment, is an indication of a certain desperation on the king's part. *Syri* or *Suriani* was the term used by the Franks for Arabic- or Syriac-speaking Christians; it could refer either to the Greek Orthodox (Melkites), who used Greek as their liturgical language, or to the Syrian Orthodox (Jacobites), whose liturgy was in Syriac. Modern historians have often assumed that the Syrians were settled in the north-eastern section of the city where the pre-Conquest *Juiverie* had been situated, and have thus used the designation "Syrian Quarter" for the entire area corresponding to the present-day Muslim Quarter.[37] In the Ottoman period the Old City outside the Haram al-Sharif was divided into four confessional quarters: Christian (north-west), Muslim (north-east), Armenian (south-west) and Jewish (south-central). However, we need to be careful not to exprapolate these conditions back hundreds of years to the time of the crusades.

This apparent agreement on the existence of a Syrian Quarter goes back to the work of Prawer, who in his study of Latin settlement in Jerusalem sought to connect the immigration of the Syrians around 1116 with evidence provided by a later Old French guide to the city of Jerusalem. This text, known by its modern editors as either *Estat de la cité de Iherusalem* or simply *Citez de Iherusalem*, survives in several different manuscripts of an early thirteenth-century compilation now known as the *Chronicle of Ernoul and Bernard le Tresorier*.[38] The whole transmission history of this compilation is complex, and it is difficult to date the Old French guide precisely. It may have been written between 1187 and 1229, since some phrasing seems to imply that the city had been captured by the Muslims when it

---

[36] Guillaume de Tyr, *Chronique*, XI.27, 535–36.

[37] Prawer, "The Settlement of the Latins in Jerusalem," 496; Prawer, *The Latin Kingdom of Jerusalem*, 40; Boas, *Jerusalem in the Time of the Crusades*, 88; Bahat and Rubinstein, *The Illustrated Atlas of Jerusalem*, 97. The "Syrian Quarter" is a commonplace in maps accompanying books on Jerusalem in the time of the crusades.

[38] Ernoul, "L'Estat de la cité de Iherusalem," *Itinéraires à Jérusalem et descriptions de la Terre Sainte rédigés en français aux XIe, XIIe et XIIIe siècles*, ed. Henri Michelant and Gaston Raynaud, Publications de la Société de l'Orient latin, Série géographique, 3 (Genève: Fick, 1882), 29–52; here 49. Confusingly, while this is the form of the title given in the contents of this collection and the first page of the edition, the running heads give the variant *La Citez de Iherusalem*. The latter is the form of the title used by Boas, *Jerusalem in the Time of the Crusades*. To further complicate matters, Micheland and Raynaud also used the title *Estat de la Cité de Iherusalem* to denote a shorter text transmitted in the work known as *Estoires d'Outremer et de la naissance Salahedin*.

was written down in its surviving form; however, it seems to have drawn on an earlier text or texts of a similar genre and thus gives detailed information on the topography of the city shortly before the conquest of 1187 .

The *Citez de Iherusalem* describes the area situated between the Street of Jehosaphat and the city walls: a number of streets here were known as the *Juiverie*, and this was where the greatest number of Syrians lived.[39] However, the wording at this point of text does not imply that the Syrians lived *exclusively* in this district, and indeed, it would seem that the area being discussed was a neighbourhood consisting of several streets around the Syrian Orthodox monastery of St Mary Magdalene, rather than the entire north-eastern quadrant. In any case, it would be unwise to assume that living patterns in the late twelfth century had remained unchanged since around 1116; all that it means is that by the later date, Syrians were to be found predominantly in the north-east. In fact William of Tyre, who is our principal source of information on the immigrant Syrians in the time of King Baldwin I, does not mention a specific location where they settled. He says only that the king "conferred upon them those parts of the city which most seemed to require such relief, and filled the houses with them."[40] This phrasing suggests that the immigrants were not confined to a single area, but settled in different neighbourhoods which were depopulated or needed economic regeneration. Considerations of security would also argue in favour of distributing population around the city, rather than imposing a block settlement in a single area which would leave other areas empty. Throughout history immigrants of distinct ethnicity or religious affiliations have often tended to congregate within urban environments, and so it is quite possible that *Citez de Iherusalem* simply reflects the result of gradual population movement over the course of the twelfth century rather than a situation which had remained unchanged since the settlement in the time of Baldwin I.

There is no reason to doubt that over time there was a high proportion of Syrian settlement in the north-eastern section of the city, but it would be wrong to imagine this as an exclusive ethnic or confessional area. It contained the Latin convent of St. Anne, and this institution presumably had servants living nearby as well as possibly Frankish tenants in the houses that it owned, while the *Citez de Iherusalem* itself indicates that Syrians also were to be found outside the *Juiverie*. There was a Syrian money exchange situated in the covered streets just south-east

---

[39]  Ernoul, "L'Estat de la cité de Iherusalem," 49: "Or revieng à le Rue de Iosaffas. Entre le Rue de Iosaffas & les murs de la cité, à main senestre, dusque à le Porte de Iosaffas, a rues ausi com une ville. Là manoient li plus des Suriiens de Iherusalem. Et ces rues apeloit on le Iuerie. En celle rue de Iuerie avoit .j. Moustier de Sainte Marie Madeleine. Et près de cel mostier avoit une posterne don't on ne pooit mie issir hors as cans, mais entre .ij. murs aloit on."

[40]  Guillaume de Tyr, *Chronique*, XI.27, 536: "Quibus rex eas civitatis partes, que magis hoc solatio videbantur indigere, conferens, eis domicilia replevit."

of the church of the Holy Sepulchre (a Latin, i.e., Frankish, money exchange was situated further south).[41] In this same central area there were also Syrian goldsmiths, while Syrian shopkeepers were to be found in the street known as the covered market, selling products as diverse as cloth and candles. Assuming that artisans and shopkeepers normally lived above their business premises, as was common in medieval urban society, there must have been a significant Syrian presence in the central commercial district.[42] Similarly, Armenians seem to have lived around around the nucleus of their cathedral of St James in the south-western section that forms the modern Armenian Quarter; yet Franks must have here too after a new royal palace was constructed here in the second half of the twelfth century.[43]

It would therefore seem that from evidence from the time of the crusades the city was not divided into exclusive residential quarters.[44] A more accurate use of the term "quarter" in this period would be to denote ownership rather than residence, as in the case of the Patriarch's Quarter, that is the north-western section which was owed by the patriarch of Jerusalem and the canons of the Holy Sepulchre,[45] and the neighbouring (but much smaller) Hospitallers' Quarter, which included churches, storehouses and the great hospital which provided lodging and medical care for pilgrims.[46]

Even after the settlement of Syrians there was evidently still considerable unoccupied space, since the city was regularly able to house and service a population of non-permanent residents, that is the pilgrims who arrived in the spring of every year and departed at the end of the summer; in some cases, they

---

[41] Ernoul, "L'Estat de la cité de Iherusalem," 42: "Ançois c'on viegne al Cange des Suriiens, a une rue à main diestre, c'on apiele le Rue del Sepulcre. Là est li Porte de maison del Sepulcre."

[42] Ernoul, "L'Estat de la cité de Iherusalem," 34: "A main diestre de cel marcié sont les escopes des orfevres Suriiens;" 42–43: "Quant on vient devant chel Cange, si treuve on, à main diestre, une rue couverte à volte, par ou on va al moustier del Sepulcre. En cele rue vendent li Suriien lor draperie, & s'i fait on les candelles de cire."

[43] Boas, *Jerusalem in the Time of the Crusades*, 80.

[44] One wonders whether Prawer's postulation of a Syrian Quarter was not influenced by his beliefs about wider relationships between the Franks and the native peoples. In his highly influential work, *The Latin Kingdom of Jerusalem*, Prawer describes this relationship as being characterized by exploitation of the native population as well as "political and social non-integration" (512) and even *apartheid* (524), in which "native Christians were treated no better than Moslems, Jews or Samaritans" (510). If this were true, then one could well imagine that non-integration would have been buttressed by physical separation. However, recent research by Ellenblum has shown that the Franks lived together with native Christians and had close relations with them in the countryside of Palestine. There is no reason to believe that such relations were not replicated in the city of Jerusalem. See Ronnie Ellenblum, *Frankish Rural Settlement in the Latin Kingdom of Jerusalem* (Cambridge: Cambridge University Press, 1998), esp. 119–44.

[45] Guillaume de Tyr, *Chronique*, IX.17–18, 442–45.

[46] Boas, *Jerusalem in the Time of the Crusades*, 85–88.

prolonged their stays into second or further years so that they might be considered as permanent residents. Much of the central and south-central sections of the city were devoted to support of pilgrims: a large number of communal institutions, such as hospices, were essential to coping with the large numbers, as were moneychangers, and even catering arrangements. Most of the shops in the city were situated centrally on the streets running north to south along the course of the ancient Roman thoroughfare known as the Cardo. Because of the shortage of wood around the city it was not possible for every household to keep its own oven, and so much of the cooking and baking was done in large communal ovens. Pilgrims were especially reliant on the services provided by the *Vicus Coquinatorum*; this was the burger strip of twelfth-century Jerusalem, which provided a large assortment of ready-cooked food; it was better known ironically in French as *Malquisinat*, that is the "Street of Bad Cooking."[47] It is also interesting to consider where much of this food came from. There was a cattle market and abbatoir situated just inside the southern wall to the west of the Temple Mount and a pig market (the *Porcharia patriarchalis*) in the south-west of the Patriarch's Quarter.[48] The latter facility is noteworthy because many of the non-Frankish Christians of Palestine, whether Melkite, Syrian Orthodox or Armenian, tended not to keep pigs or eat pork, as a result of centuries of Islamic influence. So the existence of the pig market is a clear indication of the heavy proportion of Western population, that is both Frankish residents and pilgrims.

## The Conquest by Saladin (1187)

On 20 September 1187, having overrun most of Palestine in the wake of his devastating victory over the army of the kingdom of Jerusalem in July, Saladin's army began to besiege the Holy City. Frankish refugees had flooded into Jerusalem from its environs, while others had fled from places further afield that had surrendered to Saladin. However, the city contained relatively few fighting men. Almost all of the kingdom's available forces had been put into the field, and the majority had been killed or captured at Hattin, although a few had managed to make their way back to Jerusalem.[49] The demographic situation of the city at this

47 Ernoul, "L'Estat de la cité de Iherusalem," 37–38: "Devant le Cange, venant à la Rue des Herbes, a une rue c'on apele Malquisinat. En celle rue cuisoit on le viande c'on vendoit as pelerins."
48 Boas, *Jerusalem in the Time of the Crusades*, 142–43.
49 *The Chronicle of the Third Crusade: The Itinerarium Peregrinorum et Gesta Regis Ricardi*, trans. Helen J. Nicholson (Aldershot: Ashgate, 1997), 38; Ibn al-Athīr, *The Chronicle of Ibn al-Athīr for the Crusading Period from al-Kāmil fi'l-ta'rīkh*, Part 2: *The Years 541–589/1146–1193. The Years of Nur al-Din and Saladin*, trans. D. S. Richards (Aldershot: Ashgate, 2007), 330–31.

moment, involving an almost exclusively Christian urban population, swollen by large numbers of refugees from the surrounding countryside, but containing a relatively small proportion of trained soldiers, was thus almost a mirror image of Muslim-held Jerusalem on the eve of the crusader conquest eighty-eight years before.

In terms of its effects on the besieged populace Saladin's conquest was radically different. At the beginning of the siege Saladin offered terms, which were rejected by the defenders. However, once his sappers had undermined a section of the northern walls, the Frankish commander, Balian of Ibelin, opened negotiations for surrender. Prevalent military custom dictated that since the defenders had rejected surrender terms when they had first been offered, and Saladin was under no further obligation to show any mercy; indeed, the Muslim clerics with his army had reminded him of the massacre carried out by the Christians in 1099, and were now urging him to avenge it by taking the city by storm. However, such an action would bring its own risks. According to the chronicler Ibn al-Athīr, Balian of Ibelin threatened to destroy the Dome of the Rock and the Aqsā Mosque and to kill several thousand Muslim prisoners who were being held within the city.[50]

The potentially damaging costs of taking the city by assault evidently persuaded Saladin to agree that the inhabitants should be allowed to purchase their freedom, and the city surrendered on 2 October. There is a fairly close agreement between Arabic and Western sources on the rates of ransom that were eventually concluded. Saladin had started off with relatively high demands, but eventually agreed to ten dinars (or "Saracen bezants" to the Franks) for a man, five for a woman and one for a child. A large number of indigent Christians could not raise their own ransoms, and so Saladin agreed to accept a lump sum in exchange for at least 7,000 of them. Since the defenders had now exhausted all available funds, including a large sum of money lodged with the Order of the Hospital by King Henry II of England, the remainder were enslaved, although Saladin and some of his officers freed many of these as an act of charity.[51]

The circumstances of the surrender of Jerusalem to Saladin have often been contrasted favourably with the massacres carried out after the capture of the city by the crusaders in 1099. By the time that the defenders of Jerusalem asked for terms, Saladin was in control of all of Palestine, save for the well fortified coastal

[50]    "The Old French Continuation of William of Tyre, 1184–97," *The Conquest of Jerusalem and the Third Crusade: Sources in Translation,* trans. Peter W. Edbury (Aldershot: Ashgate, 1998), 58.
[51]    "The Old French Continuation of William of Tyre," 60–63; Bahā' al-Dīn Ibn Shaddād, *The Rare and Excellent History of Saladin, or al-Nawādir al-Sultāniyya wa'l-Mahāsin al-Yūsufiyya,* trans. D. S. Richards (Aldershot: Ashgate, 2002), 78; 'Imâd ad-Dîn al-Isfahânî, *Conquête de la Syrie et de la Palestine par Saladin,* trans. Henri Massé, Documents relatifs à l'histoire des croisades, 10 (Paris: Paul Geuthner, 1972), 49. Ibn al-Athīr, *The Chronicle,* 332, diverges from the prices of ransom given by the *Continuation* and Ibn Shāddad only in specifying two dinars as the ransom for a child.

city of Tyre and some inland fortresses. He had campaigning still to do, but he was in a rather different situation from the crusaders of 1099, who, as we have seen, had been engaged in a race against time to seize the city before the arrival of a Fātimid army. A fight to the finish would have cost the lives of many of the soldiers (whether with his army or in captivity) who would be needed to besiege Tyre; if we are to believe the threats attributed to Balian of Ibelin, he would also be risking the destruction of the two great religious sites on the Haram al-Sharif and the adverse effect on Muslim public opinion that this would entail.

The surrender terms granted by Saladin were an effective means of gaining control of Jerusalem. His subsequent actions show that his immediate aim was to empty the city of its Frankish population, but they brought other advantages in his wider struggle to recover all of Palestine and Syria for Islam. There is a great divergence among the sources concerning the numbers of poor Franks who were released and those who were kept as prisoners, but it is clear that the entire Frankish population was removed from the city. They were sent under escort to Christian territory; most of them went to Tyre, while others went to the county of Tripoli, the Frankish principality to the north of the kingdom.[52] Yet only a minority of the fugitives were fighting men; the greater part were non-combatants, women and children. By having these people peaceably removed to Tyre and Tripoli, Saladin was adding to the number of mouths to be fed in these already overcrowded places that he would soon be attacking, thus placing an additional strain on their logistic resources without increasing their capacity for defense to any significant extent. Individual Franks were obliged to collect their own ransoms, often by selling valuables to Saladin's troops or native Christians at knockdown prices. This was a much more efficient means of securing the wealth of the city than would have been possible after a general assault, in which valuables would have been concealed by their owners or seized by Saladin's plundering soldiers, and it gave him the opportunity to systematically reward his followers and make benefactions to religious and charitable causes.[53]

The new identity of Jerusalem as a Muslim city was rapidly symbolized by a transformation of religious sites ordered by Saladin. The great golden cross on top of the Dome of the Rock was cast down, and the ancillary buildings built to service the Templar headquarters were demolished.[54] Other church buildings belonging to the Latin Church were confiscated to serve as Islamic religious foundations and charitable institutions. The church of St Anne was turned into a *madrasa* (religious

---

[52]   "The Old French Continuation of William of Tyre," 64–65; Bahā' al-Dīn Ibn Shaddād, *The Rare and Excellent History of Saladin*, 78.

[53]   'Imād ad-Dîn al-Isfahânî, *Conquête de la Syrie et de la Palestine par Saladin*, 61–62.

[54]   Bahā' al-Dīn Ibn Shaddād, *The Rare and Excellent History of Saladin*, 78; 'Imād ad-Dîn al-Isfahânî, *Conquête de la Syrie et de la Palestine par Saladin*, 51–59.

school), while a Sūfī convent was established in the patriarchal palace. These, and other foundations such as hospitals, were also given properties taken from the Latin Church to provide endowments.[55]

Saladin's new institutions were not only a sign of Jerusalem's new status as an Islamic city, but were intended to serve as focal points for Muslim immigrants. For the manipulation of the city's population was just as important in defining its identity, and even more so in guaranteeing its security. Jerusalem did not become an exclusively Muslim city, and it is doubtful whether Saladin could have made it so. However, he made significant changes. He revoked the Frankish prohibition on Jewish settlement, and the Jews retained a particularly positive memory of the sulatn because of his perceived benevolent policies toward them.[56] Armenians and Syrian Orthodox Christians were permitted to remain, and thrived. Their religious authorities resided at locations beyond Frankish control and Saladin evidently supposed that they had no particular reason to wish a reversal of the conquest. He was less generous to the Melkites, probably because of their allegiance to the Byzantine emperor. They retained their rights of residence, but with a less privileged status than the non-Chalcedonian churches: they were not permitted to replace the Latin patriarch with a Greek Orthodox one, as the Byzantine emperor had hoped.[57] The most significant effect of Saladin's conquest was that the entire Frankish population was removed. In terms of urban demography, Saladin's apparently merciful but pragmatic treatment of Jerusalem's population in 1187 brought about a similar consequence as the slaughter carried out as a result of a systematic policy of execution in 1099: the emptying of the Holy City of enemy inhabitants as defined by their religious affiliation.

## Conclusions

The slaughter that followed the crusader conquest of Jerusalem in 1099 was not primarily the result of the frenzy of battle, but the cold-blooded implementation of a phenomenon which has, inappropriately, become known as 'ethnic cleansing' in the modern world. It was an action which was by no means unique in its time, and in the course of the following decade the Western Christians who settled in

---

[55] Johannes Pahlitzsch, "The Transformation of Latin Religious Institutions into Islamic Endowments by Saladin in Jerusalem," *Governing the Holy City: The Interaction of Social Groups in Medieval Jerusalem*, ed. Lorenz Korn and Johannes Pahlitzsch (Wiesbaden: Reichert, 2004), 47–69.

[56] Prawer, *The History of the Jews in the Latin Kingdom of Jerusalem*, 64–75.

[57] Richard B. Rose, "The Native Christians of Jerusalem, 1187–1260," *The Horns of Hattin: Proceedings of the Second Conference of the Society for the Study of the Crusades and the Latin East, Jerusalem and Haifa, 2–6 July 1987*, ed. Benjamin Z. Kedar (Jerusalem: Yad Izhak Ben-Zvi, 1992), 239–49.

Palestine carried out similar massacres in the coastal cities they captured from
their Muslim rulers. In the strategic thinking of the Frankish Christians, the
security of their new kingdom required that the Muslim population of its main
cities be destroyed, expelled, or reduced to a small minority. However, the strict
demographic policies pursued by the Franks with regard to Jerusalem in the
following years show that the Holy City had a unique status within the states of
Outremer, and perhaps even within the whole of Christendom, and that these
policies had as much to do with religious identity as with security. After 1099 the
city could be—and was—marked out as Christian through the construction of new
religious buildings or, as in the case of the Temple, the appropriation of the cultic
sites of other faiths, but it was equally important to the new rulers that the city's
Christian identity was embodied in the makeup of its population. This
demographic manipulation represented a challenge to the powers of Islam that
meant that in 1187, the victorious Saladin had little choice but to reverse its
consequences, even though his actions were to prove markedly less bloody in their
realization.

Andreas Meyer

(Philipps-Universität Marburg, Germany)

# Hereditary Laws and City Topography: On the Development of the Italian Notarial Archives in the Late Middle Ages

At the beginning of the twelfth century, the rise of the notarial register, or cartulary, revolutionized the existing system of documentation, because with it ended the age of charters, and the age of administrative records began.

In the age of charters, two parties had reached a settlement before a notary, who then drew up a public instrument and handed it to the parties. The notary's sole function in this process was to execute the parchment. The document enjoyed general credibility as long as it met certain formal criteria. The fabrication of such a document was cumbersome and labor intensive, since the notary had to write a fair copy before the issuer and the witnesses of the proceedings could sign the document. This procedure originated in late antiquity, when charters in the form of sealed wax tablets were common. The term *tabellio* for a notary is a reminiscence of that time. When parchment charters began to replace wax tablets, the procedure did not change immediately, but the autographic signatures of the issuer and the witnesses soon disappeared because of these inconveniences.[1]

The notarial register developed from the notes that were originally taken by the notary in the presence of the contracting parties. From these notes, the charter could later be drawn up. Such provisional notes, which had no legal bearing, can be found until the middle of the twelfth century. But already at the beginning of that century notaries stopped taking notes on the back of future charters. Instead,

---

[1] The following abbreviations will be used: AAL = Archivio Arcivescovile di Lucca, ACL = Archivio Capitolare di Lucca, ASL = Archivio di Stato di Lucca, Dipl. = Diplomatico. Andreas Meyer, "Notar," *Der Neue Pauly: Enzyklopädie der Antike*, vol. 15/1: La–Ot (Stuttgart and Weimar: Verlag J. B. Metzler, 2001), col. 1088–101. I would like to express my gratitude to Rebekka Götting, Marburg, for the translation of my article into English.

they began to inscribe them more or less chronologically on special parchments or sheets of paper, which were then stored at the notary's house.

This change in the procedure brought a couple of advantages. First of all, the contracting parties could now abstain from having a charter dressed up on parchment, which was especially profitable for the short term transactions of trade and industry. In the thirteenth century, the percentage of engrossments on the basis of notarial registers has probably not risen above 15 to 20 percent.[2] This means that since the emergence of the notarial register, 80 per cent of the proceedings recorded by a notary have never existed outside his register. And because the number of registers surviving from the thirteenth century is very small,[3] those proceedings that have been dressed up on parchment represent a first selection of our source material.

Not only did this new way of proceeding rationalize the process, it also effected a reduction of costs. Entries into the notarial registers were much cheaper than a parchment charter since they required less time and material. At the same costs, one could now employ a notary far more often. The third improvement was the fact that a charter's authenticity could now be verified by comparing it with the register of the notary concerned. In short: The keeping of a register turned the notary into an archivist on behalf of his clients. Since there were always several notaries in every quarter of a town, they practically lived next door to their clients, and the archives were always within reach.

Registers were the property of the notary. They represented an additional source of income for him and his heirs since a parchment charter could also be dressed up a long time after the original entry of the proceedings into the register. The commission to prepare an engrossment (*commissio*) could either be included into the notary's last will, or else the competent judge of the municipality gave the respective order.

\* \* \*

However, the aforementioned advantages did not come for free. Since the cartulary served as an archive for the clients of the notary, its accessibility had to be warranted during the absences of the notary, and also after his death. I have now reached the center of my argument. In the following, I wish to demonstrate how the emergence of public notarial archives came to pass. Closely connected to this is a question that historians are keenly interested in: Why have so few

---

[2] Andreas Meyer, *Felix et inclitus notarius. Studien zum italienischen Notariat vom 7. bis zum 13. Jahrhundert.* Bibliothek des Deutschen Historischen Instituts in Rom, 92 (Tübingen: Max Niemeyer Verlag, 2000,) 294–95.

[3] Cf. Meyer, *Felix et inclitus notarius,* 179–222.

cartularies from the time before 1300 survived? Is this an accident of tradition, or are those losses due to structural circumstances?

It is surprising to us that the thirteenth-century *commissiones* seldom mention the exact position of the notarial register concerned.[4] This information was probably omitted because contemporaries knew where to find the respective registers,[5] and

---

[4]  In thirteenth-century Lucca such memoranda can paradoxically almost only be found if the notary Henricus Guercii (Meyer, Felix et inclitus notarius, no. 188) had stored the register in question, cf. AAL Archivio dei Beneficiati perg. M 136: the engrossing notary Velter quondam Albertini Veltri (no. 911) noted: "hec omnia fideliter sumens de rogito quondam Ingherrami Raggiosi notarii (no. 192) parabola et mandato Henrigi Guercii notarii, apud quem ipsius rogita inveni, ut in eo inveni, hic bona fide scripsi et meum singnum et nomen apposui" ASL Dipl. Archivio di Stato 1219.09.14: Aldebrandus qd. Dacti Maghenthie (no. 531) signed with "suprascripta omnia de libro qd. Rolandi notarii (no. 674) rogitorum fideliter summpens parabola et mandato Henrigi Guercii notarii, apud quem predictum liber rogitorum inveni, scripsi et meo signo et nomine publicavi," AAL Dipl. ††G 5: Bullione Pagani Cantonis (no. 601) noted: *de rogito Lucterii notarii* (no. 240) ". . . parabola et mandato Henrigi Guercii notarii, apud quem predicta rogita inveni, ... scripsi" etc.; AAL Dipl. †C 55: Aldibrandinus Jacobi Tadiccionis (no. 12) subscribed with "hec omnia de rogito Bonaventure Guercii notarii (no. 71) fideliter summpens parabola et mandato Henrigi Guercii eius filii, apud quem predicta inveni, scripsi et memorie causa meum signum et nomen apposui," ASL Dipl. S. Ponziano 1250.09.08, is an exception: Ricciardus Bonaventure Vecchii (no. 305) noted: "prout in rogitorum libro Jacobi Leccamolini notarii (no. 211) contineri inveni licentia et mandato Gerardini Malusi notarii germanis (sic) sui, cui predicti libri sint et lic[entiam] habet cartas faciendi per se et per alium, ita hic scripsi." The remaining pieces of evidence stem from the fourteenth century. Nicolaus Cecii Bonaiuncte von Lucca (no. 567) wrote: "de quodam libro rogitorum Guidi Caldovillani notarii (no. 166) ... de licentia et voluntate Percivallis Ricchomi Pagani de Luca notarii, qui dictos libros habet . . . ," ASL Dipl. Opera di S. Croce 1280.10.08; Ursus qd. Orlandini dictus de Vico *civis lucanus* wrote: "predicta omnia prout contineri inveni in libris rogitorum qd. ser Bonacursi Johannis de Valgiano notarii (no. 784) fideliter sumens ex licentia mihi concessa a qd. domino vicario qd. domini lucani potestatis hic exemplavi scripsi et publicavi et mei singnum et nomen apposui et qui liber remansit sub custodia Johannis filii qd. suprascripti Bonacursi," ASL Dipl. Ghivizzani 1296.11.19; the cartularies of Bellone (no. 43) in 1378 were situated "in custodia Dettori Lanfredi de Luca," ASL Dipl. Andreuccetti 1269.03.22. A charter from Tortona from 1255 bears the following signature: "Ego Guillelmus de Bagnolo notarius palatinus filius qd. domini Petri hanc cartam, quae imbreviavi per Rufinum de Cagnano notarium iussu Ariberti Suavis notarii, in quem ipsius imbreviature pervenerunt, auctoritate predicta scripsi," cf. *Documenti degli archivi tortonesi relativi alla storia di Voghera aggiuntevi le carte dell'Archivio della cattedrale di Voghera*, ed. by V. Legé e F. Gabotto. Biblioteca della Società storica subalpina, 39 (Pinerolo: Chiantore-Mascarelli, 1908), no. 108.

[5]  The Bergomasc statutes of 1264 compel notaries to hand back "ownerless notarial scripts" to their owners within three days, *Statuti notarili di Bergamo (secolo XIII)*, ed. Giuseppe Scarazzini. Fonti e strumenti per la storia del notariato italiano, 2 (Rome: Consiglio nazionale del notariato, 1977), 80 § 11 and 119 § 146. In Pavia each notary had to swear that he would not hide *breviaria* of other notaries, be they alive or dead, Renato Sóriga, "Statuta, decreta et ordinamenta societatis et collegii notariorum Papie reformata (1255–1274)," *Carte e statuti dell'Agro ticinese. Biblioteca della Società storica subalpina*, 129 (Torino: M. Gabetta 1933), 135–261; here 178, § 175. According to the statutes of Albenga (1288), the Podestà and his judge were compelled to find the notarial registers of deceased notaries: "Et si ipsa cartularia vel aliquod cartularium, quod fuerit quondam alicuius notarii publici, inventa vel inventum fuerit penes aliquem, qui non fuerit notarius, potestas et

notaries who worked in the same town knew each other well because they were joined in a college. The overview over the depositories of the cartularies of deceased notaries was also maintained by special location directories kept by the communes, respectively by the notary colleges. If I am not mistaken, this circumstance is first mentioned in a statute of 1264 from Bergamo:

> Et per consules illius collegii eligantur duo notarii pro qualibet porta civitatis Pergami, qui teneantur inquirere notarios defunctos a decem annis infra et qui sunt illi, qui habent et habere debent illorum imbreviaturas . . . . Et predicta scribantur in uno quaterno remansuro penes consules ipsius collegii.[6]

> [The consuls of the notary college should choose two notaries for every quarter of the town Bergamo that had to find out who stores the registers of the notaries that died less than ten years ago. And they should keep an index about it which is deposited with the consuls of this college].

Analogous arrangements can be documented for many upper Italian and Tuscan cities since the thirteenth century. For example, the statutes of the Lucchese commune of 1308 compelled notaries to create an index (*memoriale*) of their contracts (*contractus*) after 1240, a marginal note in the statute of 1331 specifies they must be *per alfabetum*. Furthermore, every new Podestà was obliged to convene all notaries during the first two months of his tenure, compelling them on oath to create a list of all the registers in their custody, including both their own registers and those of other notaries. Both lists served to help citizens locate their contracts.[7]

---

iudex teneantur ea dari facere seu poni in potestatem alicuius seu aliquorum notariorum electorum per heredes defuncti notarii, dummodo videantur boni et discreti" (And when registers which had belonged to a deceased notary are found with someone who is not a notary, the podestà or the judge must ensure that they are deposited with a notary who was chosen for this purpose by the successors, provided that he has a good reputation), quotation from Giorgio Costamagna, "La conservazione della documentazione notarile," *Archivi per la storia* 3 (1990): 7–20; here 8. Corrado Pecorella, *Studi sul notariato a Piacenza nel secolo XIII*. Università di Parma. Pubblicazioni della facoltà di giurisprudenza, 26 (Milan: A. Giuffrè 1968), 140, argues that the number of notaries in the Duecento had still been manageable, and that notaries had furthermore been bound to each other by friendly and family relations.

6   *Statuti notarili di Bergamo*, 118 § 141–42. The legislation was repeated and amended in 1281, ibid. 138–43 § 199–212. In Pavia control over the writings of deceased notaries lay with the notarial college, cf. Sóriga, Statuta 153 § 39–41, 159 § 56, and the index 158 nos. 58–60.

7   Arnaldo D'Addario, "La conservazione degli atti notarili negli ordinamenti della Repubblica lucchese," *Archivio storico italiano* 109 (1951) 193–226; here 195 and 220 (Statute of 1331). *Statutum lucani comunis* 108–09: "Et quislibet notarius lucane civitatis, burgorum et suburgorum et lucani districtus teneatur facere memoriale de omnibus contractibus, quos habet et fecit ab anno domini M.CC.XL citra et quos facturus est in antea. Et potestas lucanus infra duos menses sui introytus teneatur per se vel suum iudicem convocare vel convocari facere coram se omnes suprascriptos notarios et eis et cuique eorum imponere per novum iuramentum ab eis prestandum et percipere, quod de omnibus suprascriptis rogitis, tam de suis, quam de alteris, de quibus habet licentiam faciendi cartas, memoriale faciant; ita quod citius et levius contractus inveniri possint" (Each

Furthermore notaries were obliged to report foreign cartularies, which were given into their hands, to the municipal chamber within the period of a month. From these lists, two delegated notaries compiled indexes that were issued in book form.[8]

This regulation remained unaltered until 1448 when the Lucchese authorities issued new orders. From then on, heirs were compelled to deliver the documents of a deceased notary into the custody of the public archive within ten days. After they had been inventoried, the documents should then be placed in a *capsa* at the charge of the community.[9] This marked the creation of a communal notarial archive in Lucca. To sum up: Notarial archives developed in three phases. In the early days, from the middle of the twelfth until the middle of the thirteenth century, registers were stored exclusively by notaries and their heirs, which accorded with their very own interests.

But the number of notaries simultaneously working in the same place was rapidly increasing since 1250, which in turn necessitated a higher degree of regulation, since the accustomed way of proceeding threatened to become unmanageable. Owners of notarial registers were from then on obliged to create an index of all the volumes they stored, which would be publicly accessible, a

---

       notary of Lucca should produce an index of all contracts since 1240 which he stores. The podestà or his judge should convene all notaries within the first two months of his term of office and oblige them on oath to produce an index of all those registers out of which they are allowed to draw up charters so that the contracts can be found easier and faster).

[8]  *Statutum lucani comunis an. MCCCVIII* (Lucca: Maria Pacini Fazzi editore, 1991) (is a Reprint of *Statuto del comune di Lucca dell'anno MCCCVIII*. Memorie e documenti per servire alla storia di Lucca, 3/3 [Lucca: Tipografia Giusti, 1867]) 109–10: "Et quod omnes notarii lucane civitatis, districtus et sex miliariorum presentes et fucturi habentes libros aliquorum notariorum vel alicuius notarii teneantur et debeant denunptiare in camera lucani comunis, cuius et quorum notariorum habeant libros inter unum mensem post denuntiationem publice factam ex parte maioris lucani regiminis; quam denuntiationem lucanum regimen infra unum mensem a die sui introytus facere teneatur. Et Conte Clavarii (Meyer, *Felix et inclitus notarius*, no. 103) et Tedaldinus Lazarii Gay (no. 327) notarii et custodes librorum lucani comunis, et qui loco eorum fuerint subrogati vel positi, teneantur et debeant exinde unum librum facere, in quo predicta describant" (All notaries of Lucca who store cartularies of deceased notaries should declare, within one month after they were ordered to do so by the government, registers oif other notaries they own. The government should ask them to do this during the first month of their term of office; the notaries and the keepers of the municipal books, Conte Clavarii and Tedaldinus Lazarii Gay, or their substitutes should produce an index out of the informations obtained). Whoever disobeyed this directive had to pay the extraordinary high fee of a hundred pounds. But this was not a novelty of 1331, as D'Addario, "La conservazione," 196, claimed.

[9]  D'Addario, "La conservazione," 207 and 222 (Statute of 1448). In 1540 all owners of notarial registers were finally obliged to deliver them to the public record office, ibid. 211. The same wording of the statute of 1448 again in Vito Tirelli, "Il notariato a Lucca in epoca basso-medioevale," *Il notariato nella civiltà toscana*. Studi storici sul notariato italiano, 8 (Rome: Consiglio nazionale del notariato, 1985), 239–309; here 300–01, note 97.

compromise that both guaranteed the reservation of proprietary rights of notaries, and facilitated the locating of contracts. It was only around the middle of the fifteenth century that the obligation to deliver private registers into the care of an archive—controlled by the commune or the notary college—finally prevailed. From the creation of the first registers to the establishment of public notary archives, 300 years had passed.

\* \* \*

However, this long duration does not fully explain why so few registers from the early days have survived. In order to answer this question, I now want to present a source that has not been analyzed before. Not only does this source give us valuable information about the afterlife of the early registers, it also exemplarily shows why only a few registers were able to survive in this manner.

The oldest surviving catalogue of the locations of notary registers in Lucca opens in the year 1344.[10] In the following, let us have a closer look at the *denuntiationes* (declarations) of two notaries. On the 26th of January 1367, Johannes quondam Pieri Benetti de Luca,[11] who had been working as a notary since 1350, declared that he was in possession of several volumes by Ser Aldibrandinus Ghiandonis,[12] by Ser Ghiandone Gregorii[13] and by Ser Fava Beccafave,[14] "de quibus habet licentiam sumendi" (for which he has permission to draw them up) since July 30, 1361; by Ser Paganellus Ghiove, by Ser Rustichellus Ghiove[15] and by Ser Andreas Parenti,[16] "de quibus habet licentiam" (for which he has a permission) since May 7, 1354; by Ser Johannes Regabenis,[17] by Ser Tedicius Morlani,[18] by Ser Bonaventura Vecchii and by Ser Riccardus Vecchii, *de quibus habet licentiam* since December 1362;[19] by

---

10 ASL Archivi pubblici 13.
11 ASL Archivi pubblici 13 fol. 5rs.
12 Possibly identical with Aldebrandinus quondam Ghiandolfi Homodei, cf. Meyer, *Felix et inclitus notarius,* no. 11.
13 Meyer, *Felix et inclitus notarius,* no. 153. Probably working in the Contrada di San Matteo, cf. AAL Dipl. *C 70: [Luce] in dicta domo [quondam Venture quondam Advenantis in contrada sancti Mathei].
14 Meyer, *Felix et inclitus notarius,* no. 119.
15 Meyer, *Felix et inclitus notarius,* nos. 1303 and 646; the Ghiova probably worked in the Contrada di Santa Maria in Via. Some volumes of the Ghiova were stored in the house of Vannella filia quondam Ser Paganelli Ghiove *de Luca* in 1382, engrossing notary was Jacobus quondam Ser Nicola Domaschi, cf. ASL Archivi pubblici 30 fol. 133r.
16 Meyer, *Felix et inclitus notarius,* no. 20.
17 Meyer, *Felix et inclitus notarius,* no. 223.
18 Meyer, *Felix et inclitus notarius,* no. 329.
19 Meyer, *Felix et inclitus notarius,* nos. 721 and 305. The Vecchii worked in the quarter *(porta)* of San Donato, they also called themselves *de posterula fluminis,* which was situated at the church S. Tommaso, cf. ACL LL 17 fol. 66v, LL 21 fol. 76v: "Bartholomeus de contrata sancti Thomei de posterula fluminis quondam Angiori." This gate has been documented since the tenth century,

Ser Tomasus Leonis and by Ser Landus Leonis, "de quibus habet licentiam" since the 6th of March 1365;[20] by Ser Jacobus quondam Guilielmi Vecchii and by Ser Ghirardinus Ricciardi Vecchii, "de quibus non habet licentiam."[21] His collection of old cartularies, about the size of which Johannes's commentary is unfortunately very sparse (*quosdam libros*), was hence acquired within the period of eleven years, provided we only consider those names which are known to us by signatures from

---

cf. Isa Belli Barsali, "La topografia di Lucca nei secoli VIII–XI," *Atti del V congresso internazionale di studi sull'alto medioevo, Lucca 3–7 ottobre 1971* (Spoleto: Centro italiano di studi sull'alto medioevo, 1973), 461–555; here 476 and 547 (San Tommaso). The localistation of Giulio Ciampoltrini, "Archeologia lucchese d'età comunale: Le mura urbiche e le terre nuove," *Archeologia medievale* 29 (1997): 445–70; here 445–60, copied unseen by Guido Tigler, "Der Fall Lucca," *La bellezza della città: Stadtrecht und Stadtgestaltung im Italien des Mittelalters und der Renaissance*, ed. Michael Stolleis and Ruth Wolff (Tübingen: Max Niemeyer Verlag, 2004), 134–203; here 150–51, is incorrect. The evidence produced by Ciampoltrini (460, note 53) correctly reads: "ultra Lucam apud posterulam fluminis in domo suprascripti Lanberteschi notarii [quondam Guinithelli notarii]" (Meyer no. 228), while the area situated close to Fratta outside the city walls is described as "extra murum civitatis lucane iuxta pontem Fracte," ACL LL 31 fol. 37v. It belonged to the Contrada di San Pietro Somaldi: "Luce extra muros novos civitatis apud Fractam contrate sancti Petri Somaldi in domo, quam dicta Jacobina inhabitat, que est Johannis quondam Antelminelli Cornadoris," AAL Dipl. *M 76, respectivly "in dicta domo [prope muros lucane civitatis extra pontem de Fracta in contrata sancti Petri Somaldi]," ASL Archivi gentilizi De Nobili perg. n. 2B. *Flumen* of course stands for the Serchio, whose course was continually forced back from the city during the Middle Ages. Tigler's source (150) thus refers not to the part of the city wall that starts at the Hospital of San Giovanni in capite burgi and runs south, parallel to the modern Via di Santa Gemma Galgani, but to the part which runs from the former *Hospitale sancti Fridiani* to the west. Parts of it can still be detected in the present-day city wall, cf. Paolo Mencacci, Lucca:. Le mura romane. Accademia lucchese di scienze, lettere ed arti. Studi e testi, 67 (Lucca: Edizioni S. Marco Litotipo, 2001), Tables XXVII– XXVIII. The passage correctly reads: "Et a capite muri, quem prior sancti Fridiani fieri fecit novum pro muro civitatis ex parte septentrionis hospitalis usque ad turrem de posterula, ubi est modo platea fluminis ex parte civitatis, per amplum conservabo in validitatem civitatis et utilitatem lucani populi et comunis brachia 25 iuxta ipsum murum et de foris novos muros brachia 36, si tanta plagia et terrenum ibi est, sin autem usque ad id, quod modo ibi est, usque ad predictam mensuram, et ipsum terrenum sive plagias faciam terminatum permanere infra novum et veterem murum et, si aliqua persona ipsum aldium [sic, instead of alvium] imbrigaverit etc., disgomberari faciam etc. et tollam imbrigamentum et nullam foveam esse permittam inter ortos et ipsum aldium, nisi sepes est (?) ex parte vie seu aldii, ita quod fovea non separeretur de ipso aldio" (and from the wall which the prior of San Frediano had recently built as townwall north of the hospital up to the towngate (posterula), where the platform (platea fluminis) is situated for some little time now, I keep open a strip 25 arms wide towards town, and outside of the wall one strip 36 arms wide for the benefit of the town, provided that there is so much space, or as much space as there is open; and I have this terrain inside and outside of the townwall secured with boundary stones, and when somebody grabs it, I have it cleared; furthermore, I do not allow a ditch to be dug there), ASL Raccolte speciali G. B. Orsucci 40 fol. 38v.

20    Meyer, *Felix et inclitus notarius*, nos. 330 and 270: The Leoni owned a Bottega at the church of San Pietro in Cortina, on the present-day Piazza Napoleone.

21    Meyer, *Felix et inclitus notarius*, nos. 1107, 1016.

the Duecento. The bundles of documents that found their way into the hands of
Johannes often contained the papers of related notaries, as, for example, those of
the Ghiova, the Vecchii, or the Leonis. In most cases, Johannes was allowed to
execute from the registers stored in his care. It is noticeable that not a single one
of all these cartularies mentioned in the above source has survived. His complete
collection was lost at a later point in time.

The many registers that the notary Bernardus filius quondam Ser Bonacursi *de
Lanfredis* from the *contrada S. Petri Cigoli* stored at his place on the 27th of January
1367 suffered the same fate.[22] In his collection we can find not only the cartularies
of the Glandolfini,[23] who worked in the same quarter of the town in the duecento,
but also those of Gualtroctus de Quarto,[24] of Bellone,[25] of Nicolaus Jacobi
Gualistaffi,[26] of Perus Peri, and of several others.[27] The only registers that
Bernardus's son Dectorus explicitly declared in 1378 are those of late Ser Bellone,
and those of three members of the Glandolfini family.[28] The other volumes have
probably been lost in the meantime.

During the fourteenth century, one can perceive a slow, but constant
concentration of older registers in the hands of only a few notaries, who often
worked in the same quarter. Due to this development, a single catastrophe, a
single carelessness was often sufficient to delete irrevocably the complete
collection of registers of a whole group of notaries, simultaneously shaping, or
rather distorting, our historical knowledge.

---

[22]   ASL Archivi pubblici 13 fol. 12r–13r; cf. Meyer, *Felix et inclitus notarius*, 375. For the Lanfredi cf.
       Andreas Meyer, "Die ältesten Luccheser Imbreviaturen (1204) – eine bislang unbeachtete Quelle
       zur Handelsgeschichte," *Italia et Germania: Liber amicorum Arnold Esch*, ed. Hagen Keller, Werner
       Paravicini, and Wolfgang Schieder (Tübingen: Max Niemeyer Verlag, 2001), 563–82; here 570–71.
[23]   To this family cf. Meyer, *Felix et inclitus notarius*, 371–77 and Meyer, Luccheser Imbreviaturen,
       564–65.
[24]   Meyer, *Felix et inclitus notarius* no. 161; he had worked at San Michele *de Burghicciolo*.
[25]   Meyer, *Felix et inclitus notarius*, no. 43; his Bottega was probably situated in the Contrade of San
       Pietro Somaldi.
[26]   Meyer, *Felix et inclitus notarius*, no. 569.
[27]   Meyer, *Felix et inclitus notarius*, no. 801.
[28]   ASL Archivi pubblici 30 fol. 121v. This depository is also confirmed by the signature of Johannes
       quondam Ser Ursi Consilii olim de Decimo *civis lucanus*, cf. ASL Dipl. Andreuccetti 1269.03.22:
       "predicta omnia fideliter summens de libro rogitorum quondam Bellonis notarii existenti in
       custodia Dettori Lanfredi de Luca hic scripssi (!) et publicavi, prout in eo inter aliud contineri
       inveni, ex licentia mihi concessa a maiori lucano regimine per cartam publicam scriptam manu
       ser Federigi quondam ser Nicolai Pantasse de Luca notarii et custodis librorum cammere lucani
       comunis factam, anno nativitatis domini millesimo trecentesimo septuagesimo octavo, indictione
       prima, die decima octava mensis maii" (I have faithfully taken the aforesaid from the notarial
       register of the deceased Bellone which is stored with Dettorus Lanfredi of Lucca and I have
       published it here the way I found it inside it among other things, according to the permission of
       the government of Lucca which the notary and keeper of the municipal books, Federigus
       quondam Ser Nicolai Pantasse of Lucca, gave me on May 18, 1378).

* * *

Notaries were not always so brief when reporting the registers they stored. Detailed information in these declarations allow for an identification of several surviving volumes, even their location in the Trecento can be reconstructed. On the 22nd of January 1367, the notary Filippus Gangi owned, amongst others, "libros multos quorum primus est anni domini MCCLXX et primus contractus est quarto kalendas ianuarii" (many volumes of which the oldest goes back to the year 1270 and in which the first contract dates from December 29, 1269) Johannes Berald[29] "libros tres quorum primus est anni domini MCCLXXII et LXXIII" (three volumes of which the first dates from the years 1272 and 1273) by Paganellus de Fiandrada,[30] "librum unum pacium anni domini MCCC et CCCI" (one volume with peace treaties from the years 1300 and 1301) by Lambertus Sornachi,[31] and "libros tres, quorum primus est anni domini MCCLXXXIIII" (three volumes of which the first dates from the year 1284) by Nicolaus Chiavarii.[32] But of those many volumes, only four have survived.[33]

These stocklists also inform us about the fate of communal volumes of documents. The register of Lambertus Sornachi mentioned above contained only peace settlements (*pax*), it was hence written on communal order, and nevertheless found its way into the personal archive of the notary. A perusal of the mentioned inventories of the fourteenth century shows that the documents of the Lucchese law courts frequently remained with the respective notaries. Although the statutes of 1308 only compelled the *cancellarii comunis Lucani* to deliver their registers to the communal chamber once a year, it seems that this regulation quickly extended itself onto notaries working at court, as can be seen from the earliest inventory of the chamber in 1344.[34] Nevertheless, the declaration of possession by Gregorius

---

[29]    Meyer, *Felix et inclitus notarius,* no. 215; he lived in the Contrada di San Giusto, ASL Dipl. Miscellanee anno 1287. In the Middle Ages the new year began in Lucca at Christmas.
[30]    Meyer, *Felix et inclitus notarius,* no. 280; he worked in the Contrada di San Anastasio.
[31]    Meyer, *Felix et inclitus notarius,* no. 466.
[32]    Meyer, *Felix et inclitus notarius,* no. 468.
[33]    ASL Archivi pubblici 13 fol. 45rs; ASL Archivio dei notari parte prima filza 37 registro 1 (Johannes, from 1300), filza 12 registro 1 (Paganellus, from 1272–1273), filza 41 (Lambertus), filza 14 registro 2A (Nicolaus, from 1284). In the index that his son Johannes quondam Ser Filippi Ganghi *de Luca* submitted in 1383, the aformentioned volumes can no longer be found, with the exception of the one by Johannes, cf. ASL Archivi pubblici 30 fol. 136r.
[34]    Statutum lucani comunis 108: "Item quod omnes libri consiliorum et licterarum lucani comunis debeant deponi apud cameram lucani comunis per cancellarios eos habentes singulo anno infra octo dies cuiusque mensis Ianuarii iuramento preciso" (The chancellors should deposit all volumes of the councils and of the letters of the commune of Lucca which they store at their houses in the chamber of the commune of Lucca every year in the first week of January). The

*filius olim* Andreucci Arnaldi of the year 1389 contains a sum total of ten volumes "rogita Ser Jacobi Dardagnini de Luca," among them "unus liber testium examinatorum, unus liber insolutorum anni MCCCXLIIII cartarum duodecim, unus liber insolutorum curie domini potestatis manu dicti Ser Jacobi anni MCCCLI" [one volume with testimonies, one volume with assignments from 1344 containing 24 pages, one volume with assignments of the podestà's law court by the hand of the mentioned notary Jacobus from 1351].

The four communal registers that Gregorius kept in his care represented only a small part of his total store of volumes, which consisted of 66 registers from 14 different notaries. The oldest cartularies were five volumes "manu Ser Johannis notarii, non est prenomen," from 1245 to 1260.

* * *

The fact that volumes written by many different notaries accumulated in a private archive is not in itself extraordinary. In 1381, the *house* of Pina, headed by the widow of Ser Paulus quondam Ser Jacobini de Corelia *olim notarius*, held the production of no less than sixty notaries. Eleven of these notaries can be evidenced already in the Duecento, which proves that the collection had a considerable age.[35]

The Lucchese merchant and son of a notary Andreas quondam Ser Andree Domaschi[36] stored fifteen volumes of Alluminatus Jacobi and another notary in 1389, some of which have survived despite the conspicuous annotation "sunt ad pondus librarum LII" (weighing 52 pounds).[37] Maybe Andreas considered to

---

oldest surviving inventory of the Lucchese Chamber stems from 1344. It lists many volumes of the Lucchese law courts, cf. Antonio Romiti, "Archival inventorying in fourteenth-century Lucca: Methodologies, theories, and practises," *The "other" Tuscany. Essays in the Hhistory of Lucca, Pisa, and Siena Dduring the Tthirteenth, Ffourteenth, and Ffifteenth cCenturies*, ed. Thomas W. Blomquist and Maureen M. Mazzaoui. Studies in Medieval culture, 34 (Kalamazoo: Medieval Institute Publications, 1994), 83–109; here 85–86, with notes 9–13. At the latest from 1286, delivery was compulsory for chancellors, cf. ASL Archivio dei notari prima parte filza 5 p. 64/1, by the hand of Lambertus Rape *notarius et cancellarius* (Meyer no. 232): "Gerardectus de Chiatri notarius consignavit et dedit dompnis Nicolao et Filippo camerariis lucani comunis unum librum literarum conpositum et factum tempore domini Johannis Cencii Malabranche olim potestatis lucensis in anno domini MCCLXXX pro VI ultimis mensibus dicti anni" (The notary Gerardectus de Chiatri handed over to the cammerarii of Lucca, Nicolaus and Filippus, a volume of letters that have been written during the last six months of the year 1280 under the rule of the podestà at that time, Johannis Cencii Malabranche).

[35]   ASL Archivi pubblici 30 fol. 133r.
[36]   Meyer, *Felix et inclitus notarius,* no. 486.
[37]   Namely ASL Archivio dei Notari parte prima filza 17 registri 1–2, filza 18 registro 2, filza 19 registro 1.

recycle the volumes as waste paper when he had them weighed, since the register he described as "valde corruptum et distructum" today is missing.[38]

Storing the registers of their deceased colleagues was apparently interesting to notaries of the fourteenth century, especially if there had been a family relation, or else if they had worked in the same quarter of a town.[39] Since the older generation had themselves already collected documents from their predecessors, huge private archives were quickly accumulated through inheritance. The expenses of these archives were probably enormous, because they took up a lot of space. When the storage rooms became too narrow to hold the entire collection, very likely the oldest volumes of the stock were successively stored away in unfit adjoining rooms. There they mouldered away until they were discarded secretly, against the rules, at the next change of ownership. But this procedure often eliminated not only the production of a single notary or of a single family of notaries. – In the worst case, it also destroyed the production of a complete generation or of a group of notaries that had been working in the same quarter, with severe consequences to our historical knowledge.

* * *

Contemporaries were able to locate the registers of deceased notaries by the help of the aforementioned communal index volumes. The application of this solution

---

[38]   ASL Archivi pubblici 15 fol. 253r.

[39]   After the early death of Philippus quondam Specte, who had his office close to Santa Maria in Via, his cousin Ursus quondam Lamberti Armanni, who was a notary in faraway "capite Burgi sancti Fridiani," drew up 81 proceedings, Meyer, *Felix et inclitus notarius*, 292–94.

can be found in Piacenza,[40] Treviso,[41] Pisa,[42] Florence,[43] Pistoia,[44] and Siena[45] since the latter part of the thirteenth century. But this procedure, as mentioned above, did not fully secure the storage of the volumes through the centuries. Accordingly, in 1389 it was advised in Siena to store the cartularies of deceased notaries in the rooms of the notary college.[46] But it seems that this advice was not heeded in the following centuries because the two oldest surviving cartularies from Siena, stemming from the early thirteenth century, reached the Record Office of Siena

---

[40]   Pecorella, *Studi sul notariato*, 140.

[41]   Bianca Betto, *I collegi dei notai, dei giudici, dei medici e dei nobili in Treviso (secc. XIII–XVI). Storia e documenti.* Miscellanea di studi e memorie, 19 (Venice: Deputazione editrice, 1981), 120: "quando aliquis de confratribus dicti collegii decesserit, scribatur penes eius nomen millesimum indictio et dies sub quibus decesserit et etiam cui fuerint sue abreviationes conces‹s›e" (when a member of this college dies, the date of his death, strictly speaking the year, indiction and day, and the name of the one whom his registers were handed over to, should be written down next to the name).

[42]   *Statuti inediti della città di Pisa dal XII al XIV secolo*, ed. by Francesco Bonaini, 3 vols. (Florence: G. P. Viesseux, 1854–1870), vol. 1: 229: "Et heres cuiusque notarii teneatur post mortem notarii ipsa acta recomendare apud aliquem notarium cum conscientia iudicis de cancellaria" (The heir of a notary is ordered to deposit the records of the deceased with another notary with the approval of the judge of the chancellery), and vol. 3 794–95.

[43]   Since 1420, cf. Antonio Panella, "Le origini dell'archivio notarile di Firenze," *Archivio storico italiano* 92 (1934) 57–92; here 66. G. Biscione, "La conservazione delle scritture notarili a Firenze dal XII secolo all'istituzione del pubblico generale archivio dei contratti," *Dagli archivi all'archivio. Appunti di storia degli archivi fiorentini*, ed. by C. Vivoli (Florence: EDIFIR, 1991), 27–52, is of little value since it lacks references.

[44]   Ezelinda Altieri Magliozzi, "Protocolli notarili conservati nell'Archivio di Stato di Pistoia," *Bullettino storico pistoiese* 80 (1978): 121–33; here 121–23 (1332). The correlating Pistoiese register from 1466 according to prescriptions should contain: "a chui sono state commesse quelle scripture . . . e quanti libri sono et quando cominciarono le soprascritte scripture e quando finirono e quanti quaderni è il libro et quante charte: exemplo, "et cetera, le scritture di ser Taiuolo di Piero sono appresso a me ser Giovanni suo figliuolo e sono libri nove, el primo libro cominciò a dì 12 di gennaio 1450, finì a dì 6 d'ottobre 1457 et è quaderni XI e carte 160" "e chosì seguiti gl'altri libri" (at whose house the records are deposited . . . , how many volumes there are, when they start and when they end, which extent they have, for example: "the records of Ser Taiuolo di Piero are stored at my son's house, the notary Johannes, there are nine volumes, the first starting on January 12, 1450, and ending on October 6, 1457, there are nine books and 160 leaves" and so on for all the other volumes).

[45]   In 1351, Siena contented itself with the drawing up of a list of all those notarial registers of deceased notaries (and their location) that were still present in the city. Cartularies that had been handed over to the college were redistributed to trustworthy notaries. Nobody contemplated a central depository, cf. Giulio Prunai, "I notai senesi del XIII e XIV secolo e l'attuale riordinamento del loro archivio," *Bullettino senese di storia patria* 60 (1953): 78–109; here 103–09.

[46]   Archivio di Stato di Siena. L'archivio notarile (1221–1862). Inventario, ed. by Giuliano Catoni and Sonia Fineschi. Pubblicazioni degli archivi di Stato, 87 (Rome: Fratelli Palombi, 1975), 15–16

only through a purchase in 1908.[47] As a rule, public notary archives came into existence only in the fifteenth and sixteenth century.[48]

But there is an exception to that rule: Genoa apparently started building central depots for notarial scripts as early as the beginning of the fourteenth century. The Genuese commune paid the rent for two vaults in 1304, in which the registers of deceased notaries *deversus Burgum* respectively deversus Castrum were stored.[49] The place of activity of a notary hence determined to which depot his legacy was brought.

The two vaults, to which a third one was to be added in 1453 due to a lack of space, were in use until 1466, when they had to be cleaned out because the *Casa di San Giorgio*, who was then responsible for the rent, refused to pay any longer.[50]

---

[47] Dina Bizzarri, *Imbreviature notarili I, Liber imbreviaturarum Appulliesis notarii comunis Senarum MCCXXI–MCCXXIII*. Documenti e studi per la storia del commercio e del diritto commerciale italiano, 4 (Torino: S. Lattes e C^ie., 1934), IX. Without these two volumes, Siena's situation would be no better than that of Bologna, whose notarial archive was first established by Napoleon, cf. Giorgio Tamba, "Un archivio notarile? No, tuttavia," *Archivi per la storia. Rivista dell'Associazione nazionale archivistica italiana* 3 (1990): 41–96; here 41–42

[48] Cf. the relevant passages in *Guida generale degli Archivi di Stato italiani*, vol. I: A–E (Rome: Ministero per i beni culturali e ambientali. Ufficio centrale per i beni archivistici, 1981), vol. II: F–M (Rome: Ministero per . . ., 1983), vol. III: N–R (Rome: Ministero per . . . , 1986), vol. IV: S–Z (Rome: Ministero per . . ., 1994). That of Verona was founded in 1500, unfortunately, it burned down completely on the night of the 31st August 1723, cf. Giulio Sancassani, "Il collegio dei notai a Verona," *Il notariato veronese attraverso i secoli*, ed. Giulio Sancassani et al. (Verona: Collegio notarile, 1966), 1–24; here 18. Sixtus V. prompted the founding of notary archives in the Papal States (with the exception of Rome and Bologna) in 1588, cf. Giorgio Tamba, "La formazione del fondo notarile dell'Archivio di Stato di Bologna e la figura di Giovanni Masini," *Atti e memorie della Deputazione di storia patria per le province di Romagna* N.S. 37–41 (1987–1990), 41–66; here 47.

[49] *Leges Genuenses*, ed. C. Desimoni et al. Historiae Patriae Monumenta, 18 (Torino, apud fratres Bocca bibliopolas regis, 1901), col. 171: "Pro pensione volte, in qua reponuntur cartularia notariorum defunctorum de versus Burgum lib. VI. Pro pensione volte notariorum defunctorum versus Castrum lib. VIII." Giorgio Costamagna, *Il notaio a Genova tra prestigio e potere*. Studi storici sul notariato italiano, 1 (Roma: Consiglio nazionale del notariato, 1970) 219–220 points out that this solution can not stem from a time earlier than the second part of the thirteenth century. This is probably due to a printing error in Giorgio Costamagna, "La conservazione della documentazione notarile," *Archivi per la storia* 3 (1990): 7–20; here 7: "Proprio da un documento si ha notizia che già nel secolo XII [!] doveva esistere un luogo dove venivano raccolti e conservati documenti redatti da notai, in quanto vi si accenna alla conservazione 'cartulariorum posse'," since no furter references are given.

[50] The Casa di San Giorgio (founded in 1407) in Genua governed the municipal revenues of Gabelle, dues and custom duties. Elsewhere this was the task of the communal chamber, cf. A. Sciumé, "Casa di San Giorgio," *Lexikon des Mittelalters* vol. 2 (Munich and Zürich: Artemis Verlag, 1983), col. 1537–39. A petition of the notarial college to the doge of Venice, dated 6 October 1492 maintains that the commune had decided to rent two vaults for the storage of the registers at its own expense almost 400 years ago; after the foundation of the *Officium Sancti Georgii* this agency became responsible for the payments, but soon refused to pay the rent. "Ex quo secutum est, quod domini dictarum voltarum, non valentes solucionem suam consequi et habere de dictis

Around 1470, at the very latest, the cartularies of the late notaries were deposited in other buildings at the costs of the notary college. Until they were finally transferred to some vacant rooms in the archiepiscopal Palais, which the notary college had bought for this special purpose,[51] the volumes had been on a veritable odyssey. Unfortunately this very building was bombed on the 17th of May 1684, when the French laid siege on Genoa, which resulted in massive and deplorable losses of papers and documents.[52]

Now, what had been stored in the two Genoese vaults? A l l the cartularies of the deceased notaries? The answer is no. In 1358, the Vicar of the Podestà publicly announced that everybody was supposed to hand over the cartularies they stored *contra formam capituli*, to the two notaries that were charged with the custodia. In 1384, the command was repeated.[53] According to the notarial statutes of 1462, the obligation to deliver notarial scripts, and the prohibition to trade with them, should be made public once a year.[54] But the emendations to the aforementioned

---

pensionibus, scripturas ipsas sic repositas in dictis voltis partim vendiderunt, partim autem pro aliquali eorum satisfactione dictarum pensionum retinuerunt, partim autem scripture ipse ex dictis voltis subtracte et disperse fuere" (This proves that the owners of this vault, because of their incapacity to pay the rent, sold parts of the records deposited in these vaults, withheld other parts of them for the rentals, or the records were even removed from the vaults and got lost), cf. *Tra Siviglia e Genova. Notaio, documento e commercio nell'età colombiana:. Atti del Convegno internazionale di studi storici per le celebrazioni colombiane (Genova 12–14 marzo 1992)*, ed. Vito Piergiovanni. Per una storia del notariato nella civiltà europea, 2 (Milan: Dott. A. Giuffrè editore, 1994), 565–67.

[51]  Alfonso Assini, "L'Archivio del collegio notarile genovese e la conservazione degli atti tra quattro e cinquecento," *Tra Siviglia e Genova*, 213–28; here 223–25.

[52]  Marco Bologna, "1684 maggio 17. Le perdite dell'archivio del Collegio dei notai," *Atti della Società ligure di storia patria* N.S. 24 (1984), 267–90; here 273, by a comparison of the inventories of 1644, 1681, 1734 and 1984 arrives at the conclusion that no registers of notaries from the twelfth and thirteenth century were destroyed.

[53]  Assini, "Archivio del collegio notarile," 217: "contra formam capituli positi sub rubrica de duobus notariis eligendis et contra formam emendationis facte per capitulatores communis Ianue supra dictum capitulum" (against the wording of the article of "the two notaries to be elected" and against the wording of the addendum which the responsible persons of the commune of Genua enacted in addition to it). He assumes that this might refer to the codex of statutes in use since the end of the Duecento; the *emendationes* might stem from the time of Simone Boccanegra.

[54]  Puncuh, Gli statuti del collegio dei notai,  298 § 17: "Non debeat aliquis notarius, uxor, filius vel de familia sua vendere, lacerare vel aliter destruere aliquem librum, prothocollum vel foliacium publicum nec aliquam scripturam publicam nisi de consensu rectorum dicti collegii sub pena soldorum centum ianuinorum . . . . Nemo etiam possit emere, receptare nec destruere librum aliquem, prothocollum vel foliacium publicum nec aliquam scripturam publicam sub pena premissa: et si ad manus alicuius persona dicta pervenerint acta publica vel ipsorum aliquod, cito debeat id significare premissis rectoribus sub pena applicanda ut supra eorundem rectorum arbitrio. De quibus omnibus sindicatores civitatis Ianue per ipsam civitatem semel in anno preconium mittant cum per ipsos rectores facta fuerit requisitio de predictis" (No notary, nor his wife, his son or another member of the family should sell, mutilate or destroy a register or a public document without the permission of the rectors of the mentioned college, on a penalty of one hundred shillings ( . . . ). No one is allowed to buy, receive or destroy a notarial register or another

statutes, which became valid in 1470, reveal that the close relatives of a notary were not only allowed to store the scripts of the deceased at home, they could even fetch them back from the archive, provided they themselves were notaries. But this regulation did not create a new law, it only confirmed an entrenched habit explicitly.[55]

Next to the private cartularies of late notaries, volumes of documents written in the communal service were also stored in the vaults because the Genoese notaries, according to the statutes of 1462, were obliged to take these volumes home and to store them properly no later than a year after the expiration of their term of office.[56] After their death, the registers that had been written in communal service

---

public volume of records on the mentioned penalty; however, if someone gets hold of such records, he should notify the rectors of it as soon as possible, on a penalty measured by the rectors. The leaders of the commune should have these regulations proclaimed by the barker once a year, as soon as they were asked to do so by the rectors).

[55]   *Leges Genuenses*, col. 35 (a notarial subscription of 1364: "Ego Conradus Mazzurrus sacri Imperii notarius et cancellarius comunis Ianue, predictum instrumentum baylie et potestatis dicti domini ducis et dictorum sapientium ad dictum sacramentum extraxi et in hanc formam publicam redegi a cartulario instrumentorum compositorum manu condam Oberti Mazzurri notarii et cancellarii comunis Ianue, nihil addito vel diminuto, quod mutet sensum vel variet intellectum, nisi forte sillaba seu puncto abreviacionis causa. Habens ad hec, tamquam constitutus super custodiam cartulariorum defunctorum notariorum Ianue de quatuor compagnis deversus Burgum, *quam tamquam filius* dicti quondam Oberti, generale mandatum" (I, Conradus Mazzurrus, notary and chancellor of Genua, have copied the mentioned instrument from the records of the deceased notary and chancellor of Genua, Obertus Mazzurri, because of the permission of the Doge and the wise men. I have changed nothing about it that would alter the meaning, except, perhaps, an abbreviated syllable or a punctuation mark. I had a general permission to do this as the responsible keeper of the registers of the deceased notaries for the four companies towards the castle and also as the son of the deceased Obertus). The source provides no information about the location of this register; it was probably situated in the house of the executing notary. A statute of 1402 allows for exceptions from the general obligation to deliver registers, cf. *Leges genuenses*, col. 641 (from 1402): "Statuimus et ordinamus, quod omnis persona, cuiuscumque conditionis sit, penes quam fuisset reperta aliqua cartularia, protocola, manualia, sentencie vel processus aliquorum vel alicuius notarii de collegio defonctorum vel defoncti, teneantur et debeant ipsa consignare et ponere in virtute notariorum ad eorum custodiam deputatorum secundum formam alicuius capituli. Nisi esset persona cui, per formam alicuius capituli vel decreti, permissum esset retinere ipsa cartularia vel scripturas" (We prescribe that all who store the registers of deceased notaries with them are, according to the corresponding rule, ordered to hand over these volumes to the notaries responsible for the keeping, except for when it is exceptionally allowed to keep them oneself). Cf. also Giorgio Costamagna, *Il notaio a Genova tra prestigio e potere. Studi storici sul notariato italiano*, 1 (Rome: Consiglio nazionale del notariato, 1970), 223–24.

[56]   Dino Puncuh, "Gli statuti del collegio dei notai genovesi nel secolo XV," *Miscellanea di storia ligure in memoria di Giorgio Falco* (Genova: Tip. Ferrari, Occella e Cie., 1965), 267–310; here 298 § 17: "Quoniam etiam libri veteres cum aliis actibus publicis officiorum communis Ianue quandoque ex mala custodia videntur destructi et de ipsis pro capiendo papiro carte videntur ablate, non debeant notarii, per quos ipsi libri scripti fuerint in officiis predictis, libros ipsos dimittere nec alia ipsorum acta publica, nisi solum per annum unum postquam exiverint ab ipsis officiis; quo quidem anno finito, dictos libros et acta publica eorum domos apportent . . ." (As old volumes

were supposed to be transported to the two public vaults, together with their private cartularies.[57]

The story of the Genoese vaults reveals that it was not the 'Public Archive of Cartularies,' but rather a depository in which all the documents written by Genoese notaries, including communal documents and court papers, were stored. Especially the latter were probably the reason why the commune had initially paid the rent for the vaults, since as a rule the Italian communes were quick to archive their own documents.[58] But when in the fifteenth century people started to realize that the amount of private scripts surpassed the amount of public scripts by far, the depository of notarial books was privatized, and the rent was passed on to the notary college.[59]

It was hence the public interest in the municipal documents that induced the Genoese commune to rent two vaults, maybe as early as the late thirteenth century, but certainly since 1304, in order to store the registers of deceased notaries. Other Italian cities that differentiated very accurately between public and private notarial registers were quick to introduce a general obligation to deliver

---

with public documents of Genua's offices were already destroyed or paper was removed from within them, no notary who has set up such a volume in the mentioned offices should part with this volume, except during the first year after he retired from his office; when this year has passed, he should take these records home ...) Then follow arrangements in case of a temporary absence from Genoa. "Nec habeat tamen locum presens capitulum in actis curie dominorum consulum rationis nec etiam in actis curie maleficiorum Ianue, sed eadem acta serventur et servari debeant more solito penes notarium ad ipsorum custodiam deputatum seu per tempora deputandum" (This rule should neither apply to the records of the audit division of the consuls nor to the records of the criminal court, because these should be deposited, as usual, with the notaries assigned for this). The documents of the municipal chamber and those of the tribunal were apparently stored centrally by the Genoese commune. In Lucca all courtpapers had to be delivered to the municipal chamber after the expiration of the tenure of office.

[57] Assini, "Archivio del collegio notarile," 221-22; cf. also the source 36 in *Tra Siviglia e Genova*, 564.

[58] Cf. also Pietro Torelli, *Studi e ricerche di diplomatica comunale*. Studi storici sul notariato italiano, 5 (Rome: Consiglio nazionale del notariato, 1980) (this is a Reprint of the *Atti e memorie della R. Accademia Virgiliana di Mantova* N.S. 4 [1911], 5–99 and of *Pubblicazioni della R. Accademia Virgiliana di Mantova* vol. 1, Mantova 1915), 375–80; cf. for Bologna: Diana Tura, "La camera degli atti," *Camera actorum. L'Archivio del Comune di Bologna dal XIII al XVIII secolo*, ed. Massimo Giansante, Giorgio Tamba, Diana Tura. Deputazione di Storia patria per le province di Romagna. Documenti e studi, 36 (Bologna: Deputazione di storia patria, 2006), 3–36; Antonio Romiti, *L'Armarium comunis della camara actorum di Bologna:. L'inventariazione archivistica nel secolo XIII*. Pubblicazioni degli Archivi di Stato. Fonti, 19 (Roma: Ministero per i beni culturali e ambientali. Ufficio centrale per i beni archivistici, 1994), and for Pisa: Paola Vignoli, "La questione dei *Libri iurium* a Pisa: a proposito dell'interpretazione del termine ‚Pandette' usato in alcune fonti dei secoli XIII–XIV," *Bollettino storico pisano* 76 (2007): 57–72.

[59] Assini, "Archivio del collegio notarile," 221: "Possiamo perciò concludere situando nei due decenni tra il Cinquanta e il Sessanta del '400 la svolta che conduce alla 'privatizzazione' degli archivi" (We can therefore arrange the change which led to the privatization of the archives chronologically to the 50s and 60s of the fifteenth century).

communal registers, a decision which in the long run went at the expense of private cartularies. But Genoa in this way was able to save some volumes even from the twelfth century because the two vaults contained also those scripts that were the core of the communal archive in other cities, namely fiscal and financial papers as well as court papers.

* * *

Because of the late establishment of public notarial archives, it is not surprising that a great number of the cartularies surviving from the time before 1300 can not be found in the Public Record Offices, but in church archives.[60] However, even if cartularies quickly found their way into clerical archives, this was not a guarantee for their survival. Of the 53 volumes of the Lucchese notary Ciabattus that are listed in the inventory of the Lucchese chapter of the cathedral of 1315, only 30 have survived.[61]

Age was dangerous to the registers: the older they were, the less likely it was that an engrossment would be made from their pages. With the accrual of years, the chances of earning money with a register waned; instead, old cartularies became a burden to their owners by occupying precious space.[62] In a time devoid

---

[60]  To the situation of the Historical tradition cf. Meyer, *Felix et inclitus notarius*, 179–222.

[61]  The cartularies were situated in the sacristy of San Martino: "Quaterni de cartis montaninis XLV, extracti de libris rogitorum Bartholomei notarii de Boçano / Libri LI Ciabatti notarii contractuum et causarum / Libri VII causarum scripti manu quondam Leonardi notarii de Massagrosa / Liber unus causarum eiusdem Lunardi notarii / Liber alius causarum eiusdem notarii / Libri alii duo causarum eiusdem notarii / Libri causarum Orselli notarii A.D. MCCLXXI / Liber causarum scriptus manu Orlandi Ugolini notarii de Cardoso / Liber causarum et contractuum Benedicti notarii / Liber Anselmi notarii de terris et redditibus extractus de extimationibus sex Miliariorum et factus per Luc(anum) Comune / Liber causarum scriptus manu Francischi Bonsostegne notarii sub a. D. MCCLXXXI / Liber Armanni notarii de causis et aliis / Liber sex causarum scripti manu Viviani notarii de Luciano / Liber unus testium inter Capitulum ex una parte et nobiles et populares de Boçano ex alia / Libri duo causarum Bartholomei notarii de tempore domini Macaciori et domini Aldebrandini Tallialmeli rectorum terrarum Lucani Capituli pro Capitulo / Quaterni duo contractuum scriptorum manu Ciabatti notarii," cf. *Inventari del vescovato, della cattedrale e di altre chiese di Lucca*, ed. Pietro Guidi e E. Pellegrinetti. Studi e testi, 34 (Rome: Biblioteca Apostolica Vaticana, 1921), 205–06.

[62]  References to the usage of old cartularies are naturally sparse. Martin Bertram, "Bologneser Testamente, erster Teil: Die urkundliche Überlieferung," *Quellen und Forschungen aus italienischen Archiven und Bibliotheken* 70 (1990): 151–233; here 202–03, published one that might be record-breaking: 1368 the notary Guilielmus Petroboni de Bançis executed an act stemming from 1257 "ex rogationibus quondam domini Ysnardi Bonzohannini Rubei de Picholpilo notarii." An act of Paganellus Maconis (Meyer, *Felix et inclitus notarius*, no. 278) from 1247 was executed in Lucca in 1308, ASL Dipl. Certosa 1247.02.16; in 1378 a proceeding from 1269 was executed, ASL Dipl. Andreuccetti 1269.03.22. Two generations lie between the entry of ASL Dipl. Fregionaia 1223.01.26

of antiquarian tendencies, these volumes were regarded as useless ballast. Especially in the fourteenth century, hints at a careless handling of cartularies accumulate. In Siena, people complained that cartularies made of paper were sold to "salumieri ed altri bottegai."[63] Florence repeatedly prohibited the destruction and sale of registers.[64] And yet we learn from the *Libri di ricordi* of Orsanmichele that two cartularies from the early Duecento were on sale in 1357: "un libro d'inbreviature di carte pecora, cominciato nel 1213, un libro d'inbreviature di carte pecora, cominciato nel 1229" (one notarial register made of parchment that starts in 1213, one notarial register made of parchment that starts in 1229).[65] On the 9th of February 1389 the Lucchese *guardiano dei libri de la camera del comune* complained to his superiors about the great number of cartularies that had lately been sold to traders. He furthermore reported that of the registers of fifty notaries, which according to communal records should have been in the possession of a certain person, not a single one could be found.[66] On the other hand, in 1413 it was still allowed in Milan to sell the cartularies of deceased notaries to merchants as wrapping paper, provided one had the consent of the head of the notary college.[67]

---

into and its drawing up from the cartulary. In 1264 the commune of Savona asked the Vicar of Alba to dress up an act from 1192 from the "abbreviationibus Raymundi civis Albensis dicti Judicis notarii quondam," cf. *Documenti intorno alle relazioni fra Alba e Genova (1141–1270),* ed. Arturo Ferretto, 2 vols., Biblioteca della Società storica subalpina, vols. 23 and 50/1 (Pinerolo: Chiantore-Mascarelli, 1906–1910); here vol. 1: 259–61 no. 309. A Florentine charter of 1184 was copied to parchment only in 1259, cf. Robert Davidsohn, *Geschichte von Florenz,* 4 vols. (Berlin: Ernst Siegfried Mittler und Sohn, 1896–1927),vol. 1: 662–63. A Genoese charter of 1189 was engrossed in 1268, *Le Carte del monastero di San Venerio del Tino* vol. 1, ed. by Giorgio Falco. Biblioteca della Società storica subalpina, 91 (Torino: Tip. San Giuseppe, 1920), no. 71.

[63]   *Archivio di Stato di Siena. L'archivio notarile* 15.

[64]   Panella, Le origini dell'archivio notarile,  58 and 63.

[65]   Francesco Carabellese, "La Compagnia di Orsanmichele e il mercato dei libri in Firenze nel secolo XIV," *Archivio storico italiano* 5$^{\text{ta}}$ serie 16 (1895): 267–73; here 268–69.

[66]   D'Addario, Conservazione, 201–02; Tirelli, "Il notariato a Lucca," 298–99 with note 96: "... che di nuovo molti libri di rogiti et contracti di notari morti assai frescamente sono stati venduti a spetiali qua a Luca e di fuori, et maximamente a uno spetiale che ne comprò a un'ora libre cento, li quali perché ne fu ripreso à conservato et conserva in de la botega sua senza straciarli. (...) Sa bene che a questi giorni alcuno essendo ito per cercare a casa d'una persona di questa terra, la quale avea libri di cinquanta notari, o più come si trova per scripto in la Camera del comune predicto per mano di notaio publico, non si trovò neune di quei libri" (that recently here, in Lucca and its environs, registers of deceased notaries had again been sold to spice merchants, especially to one single, who had bought 100 pounds of it at once, but had stored them untorn in his bottega because he was caught doing this. [ . . . ] It was also known that, in the past days, somebody had been visiting a certain person, at whose house the registers of 50 notaries should have been stored according to the municipal indexes, but where no single volume had been found).

[67]   Alberto Liva, *Notariato e documento notarile a Milano dall'alto medioevo alla fine del settecento.* Studi storici sul notariato italiano, 4 (Rome: Consiglio nazionale del notariato, 1979), 116 quotes from a letter of Filippo Maria Visconti: "ut non sit aliquis spiziarius, formagiarius, luganegarius, venditor pissium, salsorum, carnium nec aliarum rerum qui emat nec recipiat aliquas

* * *

Although many things that we would hold dear today have been destroyed in that time, we should not be too harsh on the past. If a notary, great grandson of a dynasty of notaries, had really been asked to store the complete family production of cartularies, and all the registers of the notaries who had worked in the same quarter, which the commune had transferred to him for practical reasons, in his own house, and to keep this immense amount of volumes safe from mice, water and fire, it is easy to imagine that he would encounter a severe space problem.[68]

imbreviaturas notarii defuncti sine licentia Abbatum collegii Mediolani" (so that no spice, cheese or sausage merchant, no seller of fish, sauces, meat or other things might buy any registers of deceased notaries without the permission of the head of the notarial college of Milan). In Milan, the registries of a deceased notary were still deposited with other notaries in 1498, ibid. 112–13.

[68]  The Luchese notary Thomasus filius Orlandi Leonis (Meyer, *Felix et inclitus notarius*, no. 330), who worked in the second half of the Duecento, stored the *rogita* of his great grandfather of the year 1173 at his house, cf. *Regesto del capitolo di Lucca*, ed. by Pietro Guidi e Oreste Parenti, 4 vols. Regesta chartarum Italiae, 6, 9, 18 and 18bis (Rome: E. Loescher, 1910–1939); here vol. 2 no. 1310, note.

Britt C. L. Rothauser
(University of Connecticut)

# "A reuer . . . brighter þen boþe the sunne and mone": The Use of Water in the Medieval Consideration of Urban Space

When we, just as much as medieval authors, consider the nature of urban spaces, it is necessary for us to look at the city's most precious natural resource: water. Water is a preoccupying feature in urban spaces even as perfect as the divine city, as the use of a quotation from *Pearl* in the title of this paper suggests. And it is little wonder that medieval authors focused their attention to this geographical feature. Civilization cannot advance without a ready source of water to sustain the people. Most obviously, water is necessary for hydration and food production. Water, in the form of ground water, irrigation, and geographic water features sustains the crops that provide food. Additionally, water power facilitates the refinement of the raw materials grown, by turning mill wheels, for example.[1] It is no coincidence that water is an integral part of the planning and development of most major medieval urban centers.[2] In discussions of historical cities, such as London, fictitious ones, such as New Troy, and divine urban center, such as New Jerusalem, medieval English authors from William Fitz Stephen to John Lydgate

---

[1]  For further reading on the use of mills from antiquity through the Middle Ages, see Steven A. Walton's collection of eleven essays from the 2004 Pennsylvania State University conference, "Wind and Water: The Medieval Mill." This collection offers wide-ranging discussions on the uses of what we now consider "alternative energy" sources. While the first eight essays focus on the historical presence, use, and legalities of mills, the last three essays look at the use of mills in a literary context. *Wind and Water in the Middle Ages: Fluid Technologies from Antiquity to the Renaissance*, ed. Steven A. Walton. Medieval and Renaissance Texts and Studies, 322. Penn State Medieval Studies, 2 (Tempe: Arizona Center for Medieval and Renaissance Studies, 2006).

[2]  If we look at the major medieval urban centers, we find that each of them has proximity to water: London, Paris, Rome, Brussels, Florence, and Venice just to name a few of the European centers of trade and population.

and John Gower highlight the importance of water through their descriptions of the rivers, streams, wells, and fountains that surround and permeate the civic space. We find that this prominent consideration of water exists not only in terrestrial cities, but also in descriptions of the holy city of New Jerusalem, by authors such as the *Pearl* poet, and of more diabolical territory, such as Dante's *Inferno*.[3] Water acts as a focus for medieval authors not only because of its literal proximity to most major towns, but also because of its role in the literary conceptualization of the urban space. Medieval authors describe not only the presence of water near and in cities, but also the use of water by the citizens. We see water being used primarily in three roles in these texts: 1) a defining element; 2) a protective barrier; and 3) a cleansing agent. In depictions of historical or fictitious earthly cities, we see water used in these functions individually, or perhaps dually, suggesting an important topos for water, but not a formulaic use of it. When all of these roles appear in one description, we find the perfection that exists in the celestial city of *Pearl*. But when these roles are subverted, we see the apocalyptic nightmare of John Gower's London in *Vox Clamantis*. It is through the author's manipulation of water in these three roles that we can see how medieval authors may express their concept of the urban space.

Significant research has been done in recent years concerning the prevalence and need for water in cities from antiquity to the modern era. Much of this scholarship overlaps, thematically. For example, in the field of waste management in the urban environment, Michèle Dagenais uses the cleansing properties of water to discuss the dichotomy of civilized and wild, as well as the relationship of the individual to the group.[4] And while this topic is very close to my own section three of this paper, Dagenais's interest rests in twentieth-century Montreal, Canada. We can see similarities for the use of water in both modern Canada and medieval England, but the bureaucracies and environmental dilemmas that concern civic planners in Canada at the turn of the last century are not those of medieval London. For Dagenais, the manipulation of water and the creation of the city both "conquer[ed] the land" and "reform[ed] society's morals and behavior."[5] There is no indication that the civic planners of London hoped to reform anyone's "morals and behaviors" through their manipulation of waterways. There are, of course, articles on the medieval uses of water. Dolly Jørgensen examines the system by which

---

[3]    For this paper, I am limiting my discussion to a handful of authors from the fourteenth and fifteenth centuries. Although I will also consider William Fitz Stephen's twelfth century *Descriptio nobilissimæ civitatis Londoniæ* , the bulk of this paper focuses on the *Pearl* poet's *Pearl* and *St. Erkenwald* (for a discussion of the authorship of these works, please see note below), John Lydgate's *Troy Book*, and John Gower's *Mirrour de l'homme* and *Vox Clamantis*.

[4]    Michèle Dagenais, "Cleaning, Draining, and Sanitizing the City: Conceptions and Uses of Water in the Montreal Region," *The Canadian Historical Review* 87.4 (December 2006): 621–51.

[5]    Dagenais, "Cleaning, Draining, and Sanitizing the City," 621.

medieval drainage ditches and paved roads were maintained in late medieval England and Scandinavia, considering the complex relationship of government and citizen in the removal of household wastes from the city.[6] While fascinating, Jørgensen's purpose is not to consider how literary authors use the image of water to express their theoretical concept of urban space, but to consider the historical uses of water in medieval northern Europe.

There have also been many articles written on medieval cities, such as C. David Benson's "Some Poets' Tours of Medieval London: Varieties of Literary Urban Experience."[7] In this essay, Benson explores medieval London through the eyes of his "guides": William Fitz Stephen, Geoffrey Chaucer, John Gower, Thomas Hoccleve, John Lydgate, and the anonymous author of *London Lickpenny*. The resulting differences lead Benson to conclude, alongside Michel de Certeau, that depictions of the city are as different as the authors that compose them.[8] These poets, for Benson, give vivid descriptions of the city from, with the exception of William Fitz Stephen, roughly the same era. While our authors often intersect, and I am indeed indebted to David Benson for the genesis of my own article, his purpose is not to argue that the poets are creating their urban space through their literary use of water, as I hope to accomplish here.[9]

## I. Water as Definition

The first role of water is that of definition. It is not, however, typically, the first image that comes to the modern mind when the image of a medieval city is invoked. We often first envision the massive walls outlining the borders and keeping out the wilderness and unwanted people. Of course, completely walled cities were not the only urban spaces constructed during the Middle Ages; the image of the impregnable walls of a city such as Carcassonne, however, typifies the modern conception of the medieval urban space, reinforced by Hollywood's depiction of medieval and fantasy cities in movies such as *The 13th Warrior, Robin*

---

[6]    Dolly Jørgensen, "Cooperative Sanitation: Managing Streets and Gutters in Late Medieval England and Scandinavia," *Technology and Culture* 49.3 (July 2008): 547–67.

[7]    C. David Benson, "Some Poets' Tours of Medieval London: Varieties of Literary Urban Experience," *Essays in Medieval Studies* 24 (2007): 1–20.

[8]    Benson, "Some Poets' Tours of Medieval London," 2 and 17. Ultimately, Benson concludes that the medieval point of view on nearly every subject is as varied as the people under consideration: "These tours offer contemporary images of medieval London, and belie the idea that there is a single medieval view, even medieval literary view, about anything, especially anything as complex as a city like London" (17).

[9]    For a broader discussion of the many uses of water in an urban setting, see Albrecht Classen's introduction to this volume.

*Hood: Prince of Thieves*, or *The Crusades*.[10] Our imagined medieval city probably more closely resembles a walled garden, only on a much grander scale. In *La Roman de la Rose*, for example, the garden is completely surrounded by high walls, keeping out those who wish to enter the enclosure without permission. Manfred Kusch argues that gardens represent a "rationally controlled system surrounded by an often amorphous wilderness."[11] Although Kusch is discussing the enclosed garden within an urban setting, his arguments apply equally to the enclosed city surrounded by wilderness popular in the modern consciousness. Although the protective nature of walls is not lost on the medieval perception, a walled enclosure does not merely represent security. The garden, such as that in *La Roman de la Rose*, is considered by medieval authors to be "the locus of virtue, piety, harmony, lust, and gluttony, to mention but a few examples."[12] And we see these traits in medieval author's descriptions of cities as well. The holy city in *Pearl* highlights the virtuous piety of its citizens, those blessed dead who have found eternal reward for their pious lives. London for Fitz Stephen exists as the harmonious balance of rural and urban, its citizens cohabitating peacefully. But for John Gower, the urban becomes the site of the evils of civilization when it is forcibly invaded by the ravening hordes of peasants who, bestial in their nature, represent the basest elements.

John Scattergood, in "Misrepresenting the City," argues that authorial descriptions of the completely enclosing walls of a city represent the individual's view of perfection.[13] On the literal level, however, the city often manifests as a space demarcated by natural *and* constructed barriers. In the last quarter of the twelfth century, William Fitz Stephen, clerk to Thomas Becket and later his encomiast, describes the city of London in a work entitled *Descriptio nobilissimæ*

---

[10]   Although set in a fantasy world, *The Lord of the Rings* also helps promote the concept of the medieval walled city because of its portrayal of medieval-esque clothing, weaponry, and technology. While some of the cities portrayed by Hollywood, such as the city of Troy in *Troy*, may have indeed been encircled, the popular vision of a medieval city appears to be that they were all walled. To be fair to the popular view, many medieval towns were – but cities such as Venice apparently never had such fortifications, and some cities were first walled well after they were established urban communities (for example, Brussels, Belgium was not walled until the thirteenth century, but was inhabited continuously from the tenth century.)

[11]   Manfred Kusch, "The River and the Garden: Basic Spatial Models in *Candide* and *La Nouvelle Héloïse*," *Eighteenth-Century Studies* 12.1 (Autumn, 1978): 1–15; here 1. Although Kusch is discussing much later uses of gardens and the binary of inclusive/exclusive space, his comments here on the garden in art in literature apply to the use of enclosed garden spaces throughout literary history.

[12]   Kusch, "The River and the Garden," 1. See also the contributions to this volume by Jean E. Jost and Connie Scarborough.

[13]   John Scattergood, "Misrepresenting the City: Genre, Intertextuality and Fitz Stephen's *Description of London*," *Reading the Past: Essays on Medieval and Renaissance Literature* (Dublin: Four Courts Press, 1996), 15–36; here 19.

*civitatis Londoniæ*.[14] The text is variably dated to "sometime before 1183"[15] or "between 1173 and 1175"[16] and describes London, both in terms of its physical appearance, as well as its inhabitants and trades, in the vivid first-person detail of someone who knows the area well. After a brief description of the city's clean air, major churches, and the Tower of London, Fitz Stephen turns his attentions to the city's fortifications.[17] At some point in the past, from Fitz Stephen's perspective, London had been entirely enclosed by fortified towers connected by gated walls.[18] If, as John Scattergood suggests, the perfectly encircled city is necessary to fulfill the author's view of an ideal city, London once met those requirements. And Fitz Stephen's description of London, as noted by Scattergood, is exceedingly idealistic.[19] The ideal of a perfectly enclosed and defined city does not last however, as one of the walls falls to the inexorable force of the river:

> On the South, London was once walled and towered in the like fashion, but the Thames, that mighty river, teeming with fish, which runs on that side with the sea's ebb and flow, has in course of time washed away those bulwarks, undermined and cast them down.[20]

Scattergood argues that although London does not need to have a completed wall in Fitz Stephen's time to exist as his ideal, it must have been complete at some point in the past.[21] For Scattergood, Fitz Stephen cannot view a city as perfectly

---

[14]   The edition used here, the 1990 Italica Press printing, follows the translation of the text by H.E. Butler, originally published in 1934 by The Historical Association. The 1990 edition includes Frank M. Stenton's essay "Norman London," as well as an introduction by F. Donald Logan. The *Descriptio nobilissimæ civitatis Londoniæ* serves as the introductory preface to William Fitz Stephen's *Life of Thomas Becket*.

[15]   F. Donald Logan, "Introduction" in *Norman London* by William Fitz Stephen (New York: Italica Press, 1990), ix.

[16]   Scattergood, "Misrepresenting the City," 19.

[17]   "On the East stands the Palatine Citadel, exceeding great and strong, whose walls and bailey rise from very deep foundations, their mortar being mixed with the blood of beasts. On the West are two strongly fortified Castles, while thence there runs continuously a great wall and high, with seven double gates, and with towers along the North at intervals" (49).

[18]   Scattergood, "Misrepresenting the City," 49. In addition to the great height of the walls, with their "deep foundations (49), Fitz Stephen's walls are strengthened by the inclusion of "the blood of beasts" mixed into the mortar (49).

[19]   As Scattergood notes, Fitz Stephen does not comment on any of the more negative aspects of urban development (19); overcrowding, poverty, disease, waste contamination, and crime are all absent from Fitz Stephen's "description of the most noble city of London" (48). Just as the twelfth century author turns a blind eye to the flaws inherent to city life, he also must represent the fortifications of the city as ideal. However, he cannot conjure a physical edifice as easily as he an erase unwelcome segments of the population and so in his text Fitz Stephen addresses the missing wall on the south side of London.

[20]   William Fitz Stephen, *Norman London* (New York: Italica Press, 1990): 49.

[21]   Scattergood, "Misrepresenting the City," 19.

completed unless at some point in its history, it was totally encircled by a wall. This requirement for perfection, however, does not seem to fit Fitz Stephen's description of the wall in his own time. There is no sense of imperfection in Fitz Stephen's description of London. Instead, Fitz Stephen describes London as premier among cities, blessed in, among other things, "the strength of its bulwarks."[22] The Thames is equal to the wall in terms of satisfying his requirements for a civic boundary. The river is described as "mighty," able to "undermine and cast. . . down" the stalwart bulwarks.[23] Simply, the river is stronger than the wall. The failed wall is never replaced and so the river fulfills the role of the destroyed fortification in defining the physical composition of the city on its banks.

But the river does not act simply as an acceptable substitution for a failed wall. The presence of the river as the southern boundary of London predates the creation of the wall. The inhabitants of London must have used the river as a boundary marker even before they realized the need to enclose their civic space with walls. The southern wall of London fell to the Thames because the civic planners decided that the southern boundary of the city *was* the Thames. They placed their protective edifice within the natural boundary of the river. And when the force of the current undermined and eventually destroyed the bulwarks, civilization accepted the naturally occurring barrier as sufficient. Irrespective of a constructed boundary, it is the Thames that defines the southern edge of medieval London.

While the presence of the river creates a natural, physical boundary for London, separating the city from that which is *not* the city, water also works to define the city in the *Descriptio nobilissimæ civitatis Londoniæ* as the urban center as well as the surrounding countryside. In Fitz Stephen's time, the urban space of London must include the rural space outside the wall as integral to the continued habitability of the city. Jacques Le Goff notes that scholars since Karl Marx have seen the relationship between town and country as that of master and slave; but Le Goff argues instead for a sense of civic unity between the enclosed city and the countryside with freely occurring travel between the two.[24] In concert with this theory, Fitz Stephen's London is not only the physical structures and people contained within the wall, but it is also the surrounding area that supports the citizens of London: "On the North are pasture lands and a pleasant space of flat meadows, intersected by running waters, which turn revolving mill-wheels with

---

[22]   Fitz Stephen, *Norman London*, 48
[23]   Fitz Stephen, *Norman London*, 50.
[24]   Jacques Le Goff, "The Town as an Agent of Civilisation" in The Fontana Economic History of Europe ed.Carlo M. Cipolla (New York : Barnes & Noble by agreement with Fontana Books, 1976–1977), 77–106; here 92.

merry din."[25] Although there is significant travel between city and country, it is not the symbiotic relationship that le Goff envisions. Fitz Stephen does not expand the city's definition to include the rural peasantry; it is only their buildings, wells and running water, their "fresh air," and the products of their "merry" mills that appear in Fitz Stephen's description of the city of London. The movement is unidirectional. The urban citizens move out of the city, mingling with the physical essence of the countryside, but not her people, and then retreating within their fortifications.

The preferred unidirectional relationship of the city and the country is one that is shared among all the texts that I discuss here. In each, as I will describe, the city is the territory enclosed within the walls and the surrounding countryside is only part of the urban area in that it contains the methods of food production that people in the city need to survive. In the case of *Pearl*, the surrounding countryside does not even produce food for the inhabitants of New Jerusalem; the countryside there exists only as a further separation of the dreamer from the urban. This is a conception of the city supported by Isidore of Seville's discourse in the *Etymologiae*.[26] Isidore, with his typical correlation of name and thing represented, argues in book fifteen that a town is so called either because of the walls that surround it, the greed that sustains it, or the defenses that protect it.[27] It is important to note, however, that the examples I use here provide a literary vision of the city, not necessarily the reality of urban life. In reality, people moved into and out of the urban center: farmer's from the outlying areas brought produce to the markets in towns and individuals arrived looking for honest work, or perhaps less than honest opportunities.

As David Benson has noted, cities are not static entities: over the course of the fourteenth century, as nearly half of the population of London, originally as high as 100,000, died, immigrants from the outlying areas arrived.[28]

---

[25]   Fitz Stephen, *Norman London*, 49–50.

[26]   Isidore of Seville, *Etymologiae*, ed. Rudolph Beer (Leiden, The Netherlands: A. W. Sijthoff, 1909); particularly Book XV.

[27]   Isidore of Seville, *Etymologiae*, XV, ii, 5. Isidore continues to argue in lines eleven and sixteen, that the smaller villages are merely a collection of people, without the dignity commanded by a city and that the suburbs (or "under city") are the buildings around a city. Clearly there is a common theme in the Middle Ages that the physical property of the city is that which lies within the wall as well as the production of the lands surrounding it, but not necessarily the people. For a more thorough discussion of medieval concepts of the city, see Hartmut Kugler, *Die Vorstellung der Stadt in der Literatur des deutschen Mittelalters*. Münchener Texte und Untersuchungen zur deutschen Literatur des Mittelalters, 88 (Munich: Artemis, 1986). See also Albrecht Classen's Introduction to the present volume.

[28]   C. David Benson, "London," *Chaucer: An Oxford Guide*, ed. Steve Ellis (Oxford: Oxford University Press, 2005), 66–80; here 66.

But as much as the reality of London was one of fluctuating populations, the description of the idealized London appears remarkably urban-centric. At first, Fitz Stephen describes the palace of Westminster as a connection between the city and the "populous suburb."[29] However, this is not a population that we ever see in action. We know only that the royal palace is surrounded by the houses in which this unseen mass lives, and beyond those houses lie the fields that sustain life in the city: "On all sides, beyond the houses, lie the gardens of the citizens that dwell in the suburbs, planted with trees, spacious and fair, adjoining one another."[30] Instead of describing the people that inhabit this rural space, Fitz Stephen focuses on the trees and gardens. It is not the people that belong to the city of London; it is the productive lands. He further describes the pastures and meadows, giving us a more thorough description of the wild beasts that inhabit the space than the people:

> Hard by there stretches a great forest with wooded glades and lairs of wild beasts, deer both red and fallow, wild boars, and bulls. The corn-fields are not of barren gravel, but rich Asian plains such as 'make glad the crops' and fill the barns of their farmers 'with sheaves of Ceres' stalk.'[31]

The pastures and flat meadows, although presumably tended by the people, do not have people actively working them. The corn fields grow abundantly and fill the storage facilities of the farmers, but they do it apparently under their own power. Of course, Fitz Stephen understands that the land is actively tended by individuals. His description, however, focuses not on those people who grow the food necessary to support urban life, but rather on the remarkably fertile land and on the wild beasts that inhabit the forest.

In addition to the important production of grain and game animals, the countryside surrounding London is also the location of frivolity and games for the

---

[29]   Fitz Stephen, *Norman London*, 49.
[30]   Fitz Stephen, *Norman London*, 49.
[31]   Fitz Stephen, *Norman London*, 50.

inhabitants of the city.[32] The very first interaction Fitz Stephen describes between town and country, involves water:

> There are also round about London in the Suburbs most excellent wells, whose waters are sweet, wholesome and clear, and whose 'runnels ripple amid pebbles bright.' Among these Holywell, Clerkenwell and Saint Clement's Well are most famous and are visited by thicker throngs and greater multitudes of students from the school and of the young men of the City, who go out on summer evenings to take the air.[33]

It is quite clearly from the city and toward the rural environs that city-dwellers move to interact with water. The wells, sweet, clear, and famous, bring people into the countryside from the city. But while in the countryside, the urban citizens do not apparently meet with any rural inhabitants. Instead, they interact solely with the water that serves to tie the countryside to the city in a holistic definition. The uninhabited countryside acts as an extension of the city, a place of production where the city inhabitants visit, but surely belonging to the city itself. Water acts to tie the pastoral to the urban as a location for the citizens to visit as well as the means of producing, quite literally, their daily bread. In his holistic consideration of London, Fitz Stephen uses the image of water to define the city as both the urban setting and the countryside that supports it.

Water does not merely serve to define the limits of the city as a physical boundary or through inclusion with the countryside, however. In addition to this concrete definition created by the author's manipulation of waters in and around

---

[32]  It is important to note that the lack of people who apparently reside in the country does not stem from a general dearth of people described in the *Descriptio*. Fitz Stephen's text includes riotous stories of the pastimes and pleasures of all manner of people. These people, however, are all regularly described as coming from the city, citizens of London, or Londoners. Indeed, Fitz Stephen describes numerous frolics, games, and diversions in which the people of London partake that would require their departure from the city: "In winter on almost every feast-day before dinner either foaming boards and hogs, armed with 'tusks lightning-swift' themselves soon to be bacon, fight for their lives, or fat bulls with butting horns, or huge bears, do combat to the death against hounds let loose upon them" (58). Each week, horse traders bring their livestock to flat fields outside of London, bringing out the "Earls, Barons and Knights who are in the City, and with them many of the citizens" (53). He also describes the "great marsh" to the north of London that freezes in the winter, when "dense throngs of youths go forth to disport themselves upon the ice" (58). Furthermore, "Londoners" enjoy "taking their sport with birds of the air, merlins and falcons and the like, and with dogs that wage warfare in the woods. The citizens have the special privilege of hunting in Middlesex, Hertfordshire and all Chiltern and in Kent as far as the river Cray" (59). He tells of "all the youth of the City" going into the fields to play ball games (56.) We must note that each of these descriptions create the image of crowds of individuals leaving the walls of the city in order to play in the fields, woods, and waters of the countryside. There is no suggestion that the people involved in these games and hunts come from the countryside itself. For Fitz Stephen, the people involved in these pastimes are those who reside within the walls of London.

[33]  Fitz Stephen, *Norman London*, 50.

the city, there is a symbolic definition that water serves to create in our consideration of the city of London. Fitz Stephen describes the Thames as a river "teeming with fish, which runs on that side with the sea's ebb and flow . . . ."[34] The Thames is not simply a river that creates a barrier on the south side of London; it is an outlet to the ocean, and through this outlet, expands the scope of the city. London's trade is not limited to its immediate surroundings, but brings in people through its position on a major waterway to the ocean. London is, through its exportation of wool to the continent, an international city. The identification of London with this maritime trade also occurs in Robert of Gloucester's *Chronicles*, dated around 1300, where he identifies London with the presence of "ssipes" as the "mest" plentiful image, just as he identifies Canterbury with "fiss" and Winchester with "win."[35] This suggests that, like today, cities are equated symbolically to an image, role, or product. Cairo, for example, calls to mind the pyramids; Paris is the city of lovers; or Bruges is renowned for its lace. The identity of London as a maritime power, symbolically represented by Gloucester's "ssipes" (ships), obviously comes from its location near a water source, and through this definition London becomes an international city. Water, therefore, defines London on a metaphorical level as a center of maritime activity.

While the actual river and waterways around London work to define, somewhat ambiguously, either the divisive or inclusive relationship between the city and the countryside, the role of rivers becomes absolute in conjunction with the divine city in *Pearl*. Written in the late fourteenth century, *Pearl* forms part of a collection of poems all argued to have been written by one master of medieval alliterative poetry, the *Pearl* poet.[36] The *Pearl* poet treats the subject of water in conjunction with an urban center in many of the same ways that Fitz Stephen uses water in his description of London. As with the definition of the real city through its proximity to water sources, the river in *Pearl* defines New Jerusalem both in the literal sense

---

[34] Fitz Stephen, *Norman London*, 49.

[35] *The Metrical Chronicle of Robert of Gloucester*, ed. William Aldis Wright (London: Printed for H. M. Stationery off., by Eyre and Spottiswoode, 1887), lines 139–41.

[36] The *Pearl* poet is alternately known as the *Gawain* poet, after another of the well known texts attributed to the same artist, *Sir Gawain and the Green Knight*. Also presumed to be by the same author are *Cleanness, Patience*, and, perhaps, *St. Erkenwald*. For more on the debate concerning *St. Erkenwald's* authorship, see Larry D. Benson, "The Authorship of St. Erkenwald," *Journal of English and Germanic Philology* 64 (1965): 393–405; and C.J. Peterson, "Pearl and St. Erkenwald: Some Evidence for Authorship," *The Review of English Studies*, New Series 25.97 (Feb., 1974): 49–53. The preponderance of evidence, as suggested by Larry Benson, seems to exclude *St. Erkenwald* from the *Pearl* poet's collection, but as Peterson notes, "showing common authorship to be 'not proven is not the same as showing it to be impossible'" (4). For a discussion of the authorship of *Pearl*, see Barbara Nolan and David Farley-Hills, "The Authorship of Pearl: Two Notes," *The Review of English Studies*, New Series 22.87 (Aug., 1971): 295–302.

by revealing the city to the dreamer and in the metaphorical sense through its divine origin. As the narrator wanders through his dream vision, he catches a glimpse of a paradisiacal city: "Forþy I þo₃t that paradise/ Watz þer ouer gayn þo bonkez brade" ["Therefore, I thought that paradise was nearby over the broad banks"].[37]

As with London, the river outlines the boundary of the city's physical space, but in conjunction with the walls defines New Jerusalem as a city of exclusion. In *Pearl*, there is a redundancy of definition suggested by the river and the walls. The river offers a boundary over which the casual observer can view a city, whereas the walls block the specific joys of paradise from view. Sarah Stanbury argues in "*Pearl* and the Idea of Jerusalem" that the city represents the Christian's inability to reunite in the body of Christ until the Last Judgment, suggesting its "tantalizing yet ephemeral nature."[38] Because the river does not impede the dreamer's view, it does indeed "tantalize" the narrator with a glimpse of the heaven foretold by the Church. As a physical boundary, however, it marks the limit of where he may approach the manifestation of that theological theory. While the paradisiacal city exists as a tangible location in the context of the dream, it is beyond the reach of the dreamer as a living being. John Finlayson argues, in "*Pearl*: Landscape and Vision," that the elegiac nature of the poem and dream necessitates the progression of clarity allowed to the dreamer.[39] The city is available to the dreamer with no immediacy and no personal relationship, yet. It is only after he, like his daughter the Pearl maiden, dies that he will be allowed a personal relationship with the city he can only know through the mediation of the church in life. The river defines the city as a place the dreamer can "see" through his dream, but the walls define the city as a place of exclusion, whose joys are unavailable to the narrator even in a dream.

While on a literal level the river divides the physical locations in *Pearl* as inclusive or exclusive to the dreamer, it also works to define the city on a figurative level. The Thames figuratively defines London as a city of international commerce; the river in *Pearl* serves to highlight the inhuman and awesome qualities of the city. In an earthly city, such as London, the ability to manipulate the path of running water through the use of pipes and conduits highlights the civility of that urban center.[40] In the middle of the thirteenth century, for example,

---

37    *Pearl*, in *The Complete Works of the Pearl Poet*, ed. and trans. Casey Finch )Berkeley : University of California Press, c1993), 43–103; here lines 137–38. From this point, all references to *Pearl* will be to line numbers.

38    Sarah Stanbury, "*Pearl* and the Idea of Jerusalem," *Medevalia et Humanistica* 16 (1988): 117–31; here 118.

39    John Finlayson, "'Pearl': Landscape and Vision," *Studies in Philology*, 71.3 (Jul., 1974): 314–43; here 315.

40    For how the description of the city highlights the civility as well as engineering skills of the

the continued existence of numerous urban centers in Holland, Belgium, and Germany was possible through man's ability to alter the course of water.[41] As William H. TeBrake argues, the development of "one of the most densely populated and highly urbanized regions of Europe" occurs only because people began manipulating water flow away from human settlements.[42] In the same fashion, the paving of the celestial river in *Pearl* serves to highlight the divine civilization of New Jerusalem. This is not merely a naturally existing divine river; this is a river whose path is predetermined by divine will. Its course is dictated by paving stones.

In "The Imagery and Diction of *The Pearl*," Wendell Stacy Johnson argues that a celestial riverbed paved with gems is a metaphor for purity.[43] But waterways paved in gems also suggest a civilized setting. In *Pearl*, the human ability to control small amounts of water within the city is overwhelmed by the wealth and skill suggested by the divine ability not only to reinforce the river bed with "bonkez bene of beryl bry$_3$t" ["banks that were made of bright beryls (precious stones)][44] but also to control the depth and flow of the river itself by paving the bottom with "emerad, saffer, oþer gemme gente" [emeralds, sapphires, and other beautiful gems].[45] This is not a small amount of water navigated by the urban engineers, but rather an entire river whose course and purpose is created through a divine civilization paving with precious stones. At the time of *Pearl*'s composition, paving is not unknown in the urban centers of Europe: Paris was paved in 1184; London paved at the end of the thirteenth century; "in the fourteenth century, paving became general," according to Le Goff.[46] This is one more separation between the

---

inhabitants, even monstrous inhabitants, see Albrecht Classen's discussion of the description of Grippia in *Herzog Ernst* in the Introduction to this volume. The excesses in the construction of Grippia, while hardly realistic, suggest a fantastically advanced civilization. Indeed, Classen suggests that the description of running water used as baths and then as a cleansing agent fits more with an eighteenth-century city (or as I will argue below, the celestial city). While the waterways described in *Herzog Ernst* suggest civility, it is important to remember that the monstrous citizens are probably not meant to represent the pinnacle of civilization in ethical, moral, and religious terms.

[41]  William H. TeBrake, "Taming the Waterwolf: Hydraulic Engineering and Water Management in the Netherlands during the Middle Ages," *Technology and Culture* 43 (July 2002): 475–99; here 475.

[42]  TeBrake, "Taming the Waterwolf," 483.

[43]  Wendell Stacy Johnson, "The Imagery and Diction of The Pearl: Toward an Interpretation" in *Middle English Survey: Critical Essays*, ed. Edward Vasta (Notre Dame: University of Notre Dame Press, 1965), 161–80; here 168.

[44]  *Pearl*, 110.

[45]  *Pearl*, 118.

[46]  Jacques Le Goff, *The Medieval Imagination*, trans. Arthur Goldhammer (Chicago: University of Chicago Press, 1988), 89. Argues that although the Italian towns, even the smaller ones, paved their streets, the 1185 paving of Paris was for only the major roads and was "a novelty in the north" (Leopold Arnaud, "Medieval Towns," *The Journal of the American Society of Architectural*

civilization of man, and the cities he creates, and the wilderness that surrounds them. Feats of engineering such as paved streets and the manipulation of water sources divide the civilized culture from the beasts that wear paths through the wilderness simply by repeated use. Even in a description of the heavenly city, the *Pearl* poet reverts to images and phraseology that exist in realistic urban descriptions. The civic authority of London may not pave the Thames in precious gems, but both earthly and divine engineers use the river as a natural boundary for their city, allowing those not permitted through the barriers a glimpse of that which they cannot attain, access to the freedom of the city. In this way, the river in both London and *Pearl* works as a strong defining element.

Up to this point we have discussed the positive roles of water in the literal and figurative considerations of London and the heavenly city. John Gower, however, in the *Vox Clamantis* as well as in the *Mirour de l'Omme* manipulates the imagery of tranquil water to display the catastrophic power barely contained by a river's banks. Gower composed the *Vox Clamantis* as a reaction to the horrors he viewed and imagined occurring during the so-called Peasants' Revolt of 1381 when the inhabitants of the outlying areas of London, in a widespread reaction to the unusually high poll tax of 1380, invaded the city, burned John of Gaunt's palace, and murdered the Archbishop of Canterbury.[47]

To highlight the utter lack of civility during the four day uprising in June of that year, Gower juxtaposes the idyllic pre-riot interaction of town and country with a nightmarish description of the town during the period of unrest. Gower uses water imagery to suggest not the literal boundaries of the city, but rather a positive definition of his pastoral ideal before the 1381 rebellion; nature and the peasantry dwell in the countryside and grow the provisions required by the city. Water here, therefore, does not define the city itself, but rather Gower's preferred social hierarchy between city and country: the productive water, like the peasants that use it, can move unrestrained in the countryside. Water in the cities, however, much like the peasants that visit, must be constrained. Water must flow through designated channels and pipes; the peasantry must conform to the level of civility that Gower expects to see within an urban environment.

Le Goff, in *The Medieval Imagination*, argues that nature imagery in literature and art does not point to a contest between city and country, but rather to that which

---

*Historians*, 3.1/2 (Jan.-April, 1943): 30–35; here 31–33). For an opposing view on the prevalence of paved roads in medieval Europe, see Allison P. Coudert's contribution to this volume.

47  The purpose of this paper is not to investigate the events leading up to the riots of 1381, among which were the depopulation of the area due to the plague of 1348–1350, the attempt by the ruling classes to create a wage freeze and restricted movement for the peasantry, as well as a poll tax that was three times higher than the previous year. No instance of social unrest is as simple as this, but that is a matter for another paper.

is essential to each, an "opposition between what was built, cultivated, and inhabited (city, castle, village) and what was essentially wild (the ocean and forest, the western equivalents of the eastern desert)."[48] In a slight extension of Le Goff's argument, uncontrolled, or perhaps uncontrollable, water synonymously embodies that which is untamed and uncivilized. But uncontrolled water does not have to be a negative force, as long as it stays where it belongs. For Gower, water that flows freely through the countryside is not "wild water." It is water that is conforming to its natural place in a greater world order, as he understands it. Water flows in the fields and grows the things that the city-dwellers, and by extension Gower himself, like to eat. These bodies of water in the country do not act as the binary opposition to the essential qualities of a city; rather they are an extension of the civilization that creates the city or a locus of provision that allows the city to exist, much as we found in Fitz Stephen. The idyllic peace of Fitz Stephen, however, will not last in Gower's time. Water *will* become the binary opposition to the essential qualities of the city, the destructive force that undermines the creations of civilization.

Before the countryside overwhelms London in the *Vox Clamantis*, Gower describes his utopian setting:

> Est alter paradises ibi, nam quicquid habere
> Mens humana cupit, terra beata parit,
> Fontibus irriguis fecundus, semine plenus,
> Floribus insignis fructiferisque bonis.
>
> (*Vox Clamantis*, Liber Primus, ll. 79–82)[49]

[It was a second Paradise there, for whatever the human mind wished to have, the blessed earth brought forth. It was teeming with flowing fountains, filled with seeds, and marked with flowers and fruitful good things.][50]

This is not a pastoral setting inhabited by people, just as Fitz Stephen's depiction of the "most excellent" wells around London with their "sweet, wholesome and clear" waters.[51] Similar to Fitz Stephen's preface, where the young men leave London to cavort in the uninhabited countryside, Gower here describes a setting where, although filled with all manner of growing things, few people appear. Where the river absolutely defines the physical city in *Pearl*, rural waterways for both Fitz Stephen and Gower suggest a preferred natural social hierarchy where nature and the peasants who cultivate it remain in the countryside producing

---

[48]   Le Goff, *The Medieval Imagination*, 58.

[49]   Quoted from John Gower, *The Complete Works of John Gower*, ed. G. C. Macaulay (Oxford: Clarendon Press, 1902), here and throughout.

[50]   John Gower, *Vox Clamantis* in *The Major Latin Works of John Gower: The Voice of One Crying, and The Tripartite Chronicle*, ed. Eric W. Stockton (Seattle: University of Washington Press, 1962), 52.

[51]   Fitz Stephen, *Descriptio*, 50.

things the city-dwellers can use. But Fitz Stephen uses waterways to include the pastoral within his definition of the city, while Gower uses them to exclude. Fitz Stephen includes the countryside specifically in an encomium for the city itself and it is a location *to* which people travel to enjoy the country air.

Gower's countryside, significantly separate from the city, is a place *from* which people come only in an apocalyptic nightmare. There is a subtle difference in the distinctions between the two authors. Fitz Stephen's pastoral peasantry invisibly works in the fields, creating the things the city needs to survive, but staying in their place. Gower's country dwellers move into the urban space as an invading force. The idyllic peace of the country exists only as long as the unseen peasantry remains invisibly working in its rightful, as defined by Gower, pastoral place. As Barbara Hanawalt points out in her introduction to *Chaucer's England*, descriptions like Fitz Stephen's and Gower's, of the pastoral ideal which "could sanitize and tame the peasants,"[52] did not mask the real dangers present in the countryside. The city, for Gower, is that which the walls protect. Water defines the countryside as the peaceful locus of production for the city's consumption, nourishing the seeds and growing "flowers and fruitful good things,"[53] until the social hierarchy is inverted by the destructive 1381 riots and the tranquil setting is spoiled.

In the *Mirour de l'homme*, written sporadically over the third and fourth quarters of the fourteenth century, Gower explains expressly his fear of social disorder in his larger comparison of the courtly tradition of true love with spiritual morality.[54] Written during the period of social unrest that leads up to the 1381 riots, the *Mirour* briefly touches on Gower's views of a civil uprising. When the pastoral setting described in the *Vox Clamantis* deteriorates, Gower fears the resulting hierarchical inversion, which he describes first in the *Mirour*:

> Trois choses sont d'une covyne,
> Qui sanz mercy font la ravine
> En cas q'ils soient au dessus:
> L'un est de l'eaue la cretine,
> L'autre est du flamme la ravine,
> Et la tierce est des gens menuz
> La multitude q'est commuz:
> Car ja ne serront arrestuz
> Par resoun ne par discipline.                    (26497–505)

["There are three things with a single behavior that ravage mercilessly when they get the mastery. One is flood waters. Another is wild fire. The third is the multitude of

---

[52]   Barbara A. Hanawalt, *Chaucer's England: Literature in Historical Context* (Minneapolis: University of Minnesota Press, 1992), xxii.

[53]   Gower, *Vox Clamantis*, 52.

[54]   For the debate over Gower's date of work on the *Mirour*, please see R. F. Yeager, "Gower's French Audience: The *Mirour de l'Omme*," *The Chaucer Review* 41.2 (2006): 111–37.

little people when they are stirred up, for they will not be stopped by reason or by discipline."[55]]

In the *Mirour*, Gower predicts that the multitudes of "little people" will invert the social order, creating civic chaos in London. In the cited passage, Gower treats the mobs as senseless and destructive as wildfires and floodwaters, both of which can be seen with destructive force in the modern era. The direct parallel between rioting peasants and floods suggests a cataclysmic intersection between wilderness and city. Without the social hierarchy, the rural peasantry becomes as senseless as water and invades the city just as the Thames could flood the market streets of London or Southwark. For the civic entity of the city, an uprising, such as in 1381, represents a significant threat to the status quo, shattering this other Eden and inverting the roles water plays in the city.[56]

If Gower's first use of water in the *Vox Clamantis* is that of a positive demarcation between urban and rural, it quickly shifts to a negative representation with the approach of the rioting pastoral laborers: "Sic adeunt vrbem turbe violenter agrestes, / Et maris vt fluctus ingrediuntur eam (ll. 911-12; "And so the savage throngs approached the city like the waves of the sea and entered it by violence").[57] The physical definition of the city has failed, becoming increasingly swamped by the tide of "little people" who destroy the boundary between urban and rural by leaving their natural place in the social hierarchy and invading the city. Gower equates the invading peasantry with the uncontrollable ocean, leaving its natural place and overwhelming the boundaries of the city. If water in the form of rivers serves to delineate the boundaries of the city through their containment within their banks, then their overflow destroys the city's defining physicality.

## II. Water as Protective Barrier

The second role of water, in the form of a river, is to protect the city from outside forces. In "The Nature of the City," Max Weber argues that many cities, in the Middle Ages, are locations of fortresses, surrounded by walls and protecting the merchants and tradesmen.[58] Real rivers, however, are not easily defensible

---

[55]   The translation is taken from G. C. Coulton, *Social Life in Britain From the Conquest to the Reformation* (Cambridge: Cambridge University Press, 1919), 353.

[56]   For a further discussion of urban social unrest, see Lia B. Ross, "Anger and the City: Who Was in Charge of the Paris *Cabochien* Revolt of 1413?," in this volume.

[57]   Gower, *Vox Clamantis*, 70.

[58]   Max Weber, "The Nature of the City" in *Classic Essays on the Culture of Cities*, ed. Richard Sennett (New York: Appleton-Century-Crofts, 1969), 23–46; here 32–36. Originally published as "Die Stadt: Eine soziologische Untersuchung," *Archiv für Sozialwissenschaft und Sozialpolitik* 47 (1921):

fortifications. Contained within the fifty volume set of the *Calendar of Letter Books* is a detailed record of the civic concerns that faced London from 1275 to 1509. The entries catalog the recognizance of citizens for their neighbors, ordinances governing everything from murder to the proper weight of bread, and the fines leveled and paid for failure to comply with those rules. There is a definite concern regarding the defensibility of the Thames, as we read in the provisions for the protection of the city in the *Letter-Books*. The river needs constant vigilance because of the ease of crossing into the city undetected. At night, when no one should be entering or leaving the city, only two sleeping men monitor the gates, but the river has a larger, more active, patrol:

> The serjeants of Billingesgate and Queen Hythe are to see that all boats are moored on the City side at night, and are to have the names of all boats; and no one is to cross the Thames at night. And each serjeant must have his own boat with four men, to guard the water by night, on either side of the bridge.[59]

The gates, once shut, offer their own protection for the citizens of London and only require the attention of two somnolent guards, but the river requires the active patrol of a sergeant and four men. In other words, the only openings within the walls of the city, the gates, require only the most cursory of administration in order to fulfill its role as protection. The river requires a far more active guard, gathering all boats to ensure no late crossings and forcefully blocking trespassers. It is not an easily defensible location, and trespassers by way of water are a constant threat, if the concern in the *Letter-Books* is an indication. It is not the river itself that protects the worldly city; it is the men who patrol it. It is only the divine barriers, both in *Pearl* and *Saint Erkenwald*, which can act independently of a guard to protect the city.

If the river is an imperfect barrier suggesting a defensible fortification but failing to provide protection from boat invasion, or indeed from anyone who can swim, the river surrounding the city in *Pearl* perfects this defensive role, keeping the undeserving dreamer out of New Jerusalem. Maddened by his desire to be reunited with his daughter, the narrator rashly attempts to cross the river into New Jerusalem, in lines 1153–70. These actions, however, do not please the Prince of the city, Christ, and therefore win the dreamer exile not only from the city, but also from his dream. Reading *Pearl* through the imagery used in fifteenth century courtly love poetry, Maria Bullón-Fernández argues in ""By₃onde þe water": Courtly and Religious Desire in *Pearl*" that swimming the river in *Pearl* symbolizes

[59] 621–772.
*Calendar of Letter-books Preserved Among the Archives of the Corporation of the City of London at the Guildhall.* Vol. 1. ed. Reginald R. Sharpe (London: Printed by John Edward Francis, 1899), 21.

sexual activity culminating on the bank at the other side.[60] The poet's description of the river, however, suggests not physical intimacy between the dreamer and the maiden, but rather Christ's annoyance at the dreamer's attempts to enter the city unlawfully:

> When I schulde start in þe strem astraye,
> Out of þat caste I watz bycalt:
> Hit watz not at my Pryncez paye.
> Hit payed Hym no þat I so flonc
> Ouer meruelous merez, so mad arayd . . . .
> For ry₃t as I sparred unto þe bonc,
> þat brathþe out of my drem me brayed

> [When I wanted to leap astray into the stream
> Out of that dream I was summoned
> It was not at my Prince's pleasure
> It did not please Him that I rushed
> Over the marvelous waters, in such a frenzy . . . .
> Because just as I rushed to the bank,
> That impetuosity jerked me out of my dream].[61]

It is possible to read this passage as an exile from the dream as soon as the dreamer enters the water. The line "when I schulde start in þe strem astray" suggests that the dreamer is removed from the dream at the moment that he desires to swim across the river. But the passage continues that it is not until the dreamer has "sparred" [rushed] to the bank, after having "flonc ouer meruelous merez" [rushed over the marvelous waters].

As the he touches the opposite bank, the dreamer finds himself exiled by the river because of the Prince's displeasure. The river acts as an absolute guardian, upholding the laws of the city and the desires of its Lord by repelling the invasion of this unworthy foreigner. It is unlikely that the river is a metaphor for sexual activity, as swimming in water itself does not prompt any retaliation, but, as Sarah Stanbury argues, it is the dreamer's inability to enter the city as a living creature combined with his inability to understand God's ineffability, that prevents him from crossing the river.[62] The swimmer may spend as much time as he likes rushing through the water, an unlikely situation if swimming symbolizes sexual activity, but he may not remain in the vision once he attempts to enter the physical space of the city defined by the far bank. The river serves not only to defend the city from unwelcome foreign presences, but it also acts within the text of the poem

---

60 María Bullon-Fernandez, ""By₃onde Þe water": courtly and religious desire in Pearl," *Studies in Philology* 91.1 (1994): 35–49; here 47–49.
61 *Pearl* 1162–70.
62 Stanbury, "*Pearl* and the Idea of Jerusalem," 127.

to symbolize the Christian soul's attempt to understand his relationship to God. While the Christian may contemplate God's nature, or strive to cross the river, he may not fully interact with God, or enter the city in *Pearl*, until the moment of death.[63]

In my discussion of the redundancy of defining elements in *Pearl*, I noted that while the river defines the city limits, the walls also serve to define its physical area. Similarly, the walls and river perform redundant functions in protecting the city from foreign invasion. It is not, of course, the desire of the physical defenses of New Jerusalem that remove the dreamer from the dream in *Pearl*. Christ himself is the acting agent protecting New Jerusalem through sheer will. However, the poet represents this absolute defense of the city by two easily identifiable landmarks: the river and the walls. Should the river fail, the walls remain as an easily defended fortification. As with London, walls require less attentive guards because they are simply more difficult to breach. Should the river in *Pearl* fail to stop the dreamer's invasion, giving the human, or in this case divine, guards the opportunity to remove the offender, the walls of New Jerusalem will certainly succeed. But because of the divine setting, the river cannot fail to protect the city; this perfect city remains absolutely guarded by two infallible defenses.

The fourteenth-century *Pearl* poem serves my argument as a good example of the perfected role of water in the medieval consideration of the urban space, but it is not unique in its appropriation of this topological feature. Water serves to protect the divine city in the anonymous late fourteenth-century alliterative *Legend of Saint Erkenwald*, as well. Although firmly set in the real city of London, the *Legend* only refers to water in conjunction with the spiritual defense of the divine city, keeping the unbaptized soul from reaching the celestial paradise, "Quen we are dampnyd dulfully into the depe lake/ And exilid fro that soper so" (When we are sorrowfully condemned into the deep lake and therefore exiled from that supper).[64]

The soul, unable to attain the joys of Heaven because of its pagan state, is exiled from the supper served in heaven until baptized as a Christian by St. Erkenwald's tears. The lake replaces the river in *Pearl* and forms a natural and insurmountable barrier protecting heaven from the undeserving souls who are not welcome at the

---

[63] For further discussion on the imagery of New Jerusalem, see Ann R. Meyer, *Medieval Allegory and the Building of the New Jerusalem* (Rochester, New York: D.S. Brewer, 2003). See also J. Allan Mitchell, "The Middle English *Pearl*: Figuring the Unfigurable," *The Chaucer Review* 35.1 (2000): 86–111.

[64] *Saint Erkenwald*, ed. Clifford Peterson (Philadelphia : University of Pennsylvania Press, 1977), 302–03. For a discussion of *Saint Erkenwald* and the other *Pearl* poet's works as a social commentary on the state of religion and politics in London during the Ricardian era, see John M. Bowers, *The Politics of "Pearl": Court Poetry in the Age of Richard II* (Woodbridge, England, and Rochester, NY: Boydell and Brewer, 2001).

feast. Just as the living consciousness of the dreamer in *Pearl* suffers because the water blocks his entrance into the celestial city, so too does the pagan soul in *Erkenwald* lament because, while not precisely damned to hell, he cannot reach the tantalizingly visible paradise. It is not until the soul has been cleansed of its pagan taint that he is released from the deep lake and into the feast for which he pines.[65] If the Thames River is the human equivalent of a naturally occurring, but faulty, protective barrier, the river in *Pearl* and the lake in *Saint Erkenwald* are the ultimate expressions of celestially protective water. The Thames fails to protect the city, requiring the presence of guards, but the divinely created barriers protect New Jerusalem and the heavenly feast absolutely.

Where the Thames represents the imperfect, earthly barrier and the river in *Pearl* the divine perfection of that protection, Gower inverts the protective quality of water, highlighting its more destructive force. As we see above, Gower defines the invading peasantry as "the waves of the sea," entering the city "by violence" and destroying the walls of London. In Fitz Stephen, the destructive power of the Thames topples London's South wall, but replaces it, however imperfectly, as a natural barrier. In Gower's portrayal of violently destructive water, however, the

---

[65]   The image of the river is not uncommon in medieval literature. Rivers appear three times, at lines 160, 246, and 308, in *Sir Orfeo* as scenery in the forest through which Heurodis and later Orfeo himself must pass to get to the underwold. In lines 699–700, Sir Gawain crosses a river from Holyhead to Wirral, the "wyldernesse." The river here forms a boundary between the known and the unknown. In Canto III of Dante's *Inferno*, Dante sees a band of souls that pine to cross the river into Heaven:

> "Figliuol mio," disse 'l maestro cortese,
> "quelli che muoion ne l'ira di Dio,
> tutti convegnon qui d'ogne paese;
> e pronti sono a trapassar lo rio
> chè la divina giustizia li sprona
> sì che la tema si volve in disio.
> Quinci non passa mai anima buona;
> e però, se Caron di te si lagna,
> ben puoi sapere omai che 'l suo dir suona"

> ["My son," said the gentle master, "here are joined
> The souls of all who die in the wrath of God,
> From every country, all of them eager to find
> Their way across the water – for the good
> Never pass this way; therefore, if you hear
> Charon complaining at your presence, consider
> What that means."]

*The Inferno of Dante*, ed. and trans. Robert Pinsky (New York: Farrar, Strauss, and Giroux, 1994), III, 100–108. See also Charles Dahlberg, *The Literature of Unlikeness* (Hanover and London: University Press of New England, 1988).

tides remove any trace of the walls and render the gates useless[66]: "A dextrisque nouam me tunc vidisse putabam / Troiam, que vidue languid more fuit: / Que solet ex muris cingi patuit sine muro, / Nec potuit seras claudere porta suas (ll. 879–82; "On my right I then thought I saw New Troy, which was powerless as a widow. Ordinarily surrounded by walls, it lay exposed without any wall, and the city gate could not shut its bars").[67] Gower portrays London as a city that has lost the essential, immobile qualities of being a city. Robbed of their protective power by the destructive force of water, the walls vanish and the gate no longer works to keep the wildness of the country out of the city. This is not merely an imperfect barrier as we see in the *Letter-Books*. It is the full destructive force of people, symbolized as floodwaters, gaining a level of mastery not permitted by their social station and working to destroy the defenses and civilization of the city.

## III. Water as Cleansing Agent

The final way in which the urbanization of water expresses the extent of man's civilization is through its cleansing properties, both literal and spiritual. I wish to turn first to the literal importance of cleanliness in both terrestrial and celestial cities, and then consider the baptismal quality suggested by *Pearl* and *Saint Erkenwald*. The filth of city streets is a subject that frequently concerns medieval Londoners. In *Letter-Book A* of 1275 alone, the chronicler writes that neglectful owners forfeit any rubbish, useful item, or livestock found in the streets,[68] that the streets must be clean so that horsemen and pedestrians can pass unhindered,[69] that fish vendors may not throw refuse or water in the streets, but must carry it to the Thames,[70] and that "no one shall throw any filth into the highway, nor allow it to be raked in the time of rain, nor remove it so as to be a nuisance to neighbors."[71]

These entries in *Letter-Book A* suggest the high concern shown by urban authorities regarding the cleanliness of their streets. Further edicts from the king continue this concern for waste management. King Edward II appears preoccupied with the streets of London in his 1309 order dictating that the people of London need to stop throwing their trash into the street and return to their older practice of throwing it in the Thames, or "elsewhere out of the City, whither it used to be

---

[66] Ironically, despite the concerns of the *Letter-Books* and their river patrols, it is through the more easily defended gates, with their two sleeping guards, that the rioters flood—according to legend.
[67] Gower, *Vox Clamantis*, 70.
[68] *Calendar of Letter-Books*, Vol. A, 220.
[69] *Calendar of Letter-Books*, Vol. A, 218.
[70] *Calendar of Letter-Books*, Vol. A, 219.
[71] *Calendar of Letter-Books*, Vol. A, 219.

carried."[72] Before the plague of 1348–1350, the authorities focus on the physical obstacles posed by refuse as a "nuisance" and show little care for *where* the trash should go, so long as it is out of the streets. After the population of London has been decimated by the plague, Edward III declares that the citizens of London may no longer remove their trash, dirt or dung into the street, the Thames, or the outer walls of the city because of the "grievous and great abomination" that is "commonly inflicted upon all the great city."[73] Filth-strewn passages and waste management become a larger civic concern, as they contribute to the "grievous and great abomination," pestilence, which visits the city. Is it not entirely surprising, therefore, that authors after the plagues echo this civic concern for filth, contagion, and cleanliness.

The 1348–1350 Black Death that decimated the population of England was not the end of the plagues that frequented the island. For the remainder of the century and into the fifteenth century, the plague descended on the English population with frightening regularity, with other large outbreaks occurring in 1361, 1374, and 1390.[74] It is this repetition of plague and the still constant complaint of filth that echoes in John Lydgate's description of New Troy in his *Troy Book*, written in 1420. Lydgate, understandably, appears preoccupied with waste management in his literary urban creation. While Londoners hire rakers and scavengers to remove the refuse from the streets,[75] Lydgate's citizens of New Troy engineer waterways to remove the street debris to unknown locations.[76] It is through the use of water that

---

[72]   *Memorials of London and London Life*, H.T. Riley, ed. (London: Longmans, Green and Co., 1868), 67. This text includes excerpts from multiple *Letter Books*. The quotation here is found within the law codes of Edward II, found in *Letter-Book C*, fol. xcvi.

[73]   *Memorials*, 299. This text can also be found under the law codes of Edward III in *Letter-Book G*, fol. lxi.

[74]   For a more thorough description of the plague epidemics and the debate regarding the exact strain of plague, or even if the disease was *the* Plague, see John Theilmann and Frances Cate, 'A Plague of Plagues: The Problem of Plague Diagnosis in Medieval England," *Journal of Interdisciplinary History* 37.3 (Winter, 2007): 371–93.

[75]   Caroline M. Barron, "Lay Solidarities: the Wards of Medieval London." *Law, Laity and Solidarities: Essays in Honour of Susan Reynolds*, eds. Pauline Stafford, Janet L. Nelson and Jane Martindale (Manchester and New York: Manchester University Press, 2001), 218–33; here 230

[76]   John Lydgate, *Troy Book: Selections*, ed. Robert R. Edwards (Kalamazoo, MI: Medieval Institute Publications, 1998). All citations from this book will refer to line numbers in Book II:

> Thus river eke, of fysche ful plenteuous,
> Devided was by werkmen corious
> So craftily, through castyg severeyne,
> That in his course the stremys might atteyn
> For to areche, as Guydo doth conjecte,
> By archies atrong his cours for to refelcte
> Thorough condut pipis, large and wyde withal,
> By certeyn meatis articial,

the people of the city cleanse their environment and remove the filth that brings death, according to Lydgate:

> Wher-by the toun was outterly assured
> From engederyng of al corrupcioun,
> From wikked eyr & from infeccioun,
> That causyn ofte by her violence
> Mortalite and gret pestilence

> [By which means the town was utterly protected
> from the engendering of all corruption
> from wicked air and from infection,
> That, by great violence, often causes
> death and great pestilence].[77]

Lydgate, like Edward III, is keenly aware that the filth in the city streets adds to the risk of pestilence and death, therefore the crucial aspect of this feat of engineering is its ability to remove the waste products that, cause "mortalite and gret pestilence" [death and great pestilence].[78] It is uncertain what contaminants litter the street, given that the downspouts attached to each building remove "Voyding filþes low in-to þe grounde,/ þoru₃ gratis percid of yren percid rounde" [removing filth low into the ground through grates of pierced iron],[79] but Lydgate expresses the same concern over filth in the street that we find in the statutes of the *Letter-Books* of London and the royal proclamations. The ability in Lydgate's city for the contaminants to be removed without human intervention represents a high level of civic achievement. They eliminate the need for people to expose themselves to contagion and free all the citizens for productive work, perhaps in the guilds and trades he discusses earlier. In a city where people are removed from menial labor, the lowest social strata are raised from such unhealthy occupations

---

> That it made a ful purgacioyn
> Of al ordure and fylthes in the toun,
> Waschyng the stretys as thei stod a rowe
> And the goteris in the erthe lowe,
> That in the cite was no filthe sene;
> For the canel skoured was so clene
> And devoyded in so secre wyse
> That no man might espien nor devyse
> By what engyn the filthes, fer nor ner,
> Wern born awey by cours of the river –
> So covertly everything was cured.          (740–58)

77  Lydgate, *Troy Book*, 760–63.
78  Lydgate, *Troy Book*, 763.
79  Lydgate, *Troy Book*, 698–99.

to those of tradesmen or craftsmen. Additionally, by not leaving the job to human fallibility, but rather to the always-running water, Lydgate's citizens ensure that the streets are clean and that the debris is not removed in an unsuitable manner. Unlike the city of London, whose waste management is not always the most efficient as suggested by Edward III's proclamation, Lydgate's waterways act as automatic street sweepers, cleansing the roads of contagion causing debris.

While the earthly cities of London and New Troy recognize the dangers of street garbage and work, imperfectly as usual in the case of London, to cleanse their cities, *Pearl* again shows us the perfection of the divine city and its redundant systems. The *Pearl* poet, following the text of Apocalypse 22,[80] speaks of a river flowing from the throne of God and streaming throughout the streets of New Jerusalem. The Biblical text focuses on the miraculous and ineffable nature of this river; not only does it remarkably remain "clear as crystal,"[81] despite its travels through the streets, it also sustains the twelve trees whose fruits offer monthly healing for all nations. But rather than follow John's model exactly, the *Pearl* poet first considers the cleanliness of the streets, showing a concern for more mundane roles for the river, only returning to John's text fifteen lines later:

> A reuer of þe trone þer ran outryghte
> Watz brighter þen boþe the sunne and mone.
> Sunne ne mone schon neuer so swete
> As þat foysoun flode out of þat flet;
> Swyþe hit swange þurg uch a street
> Wiþouten fylþe oþer galle oþer glet
>
> [A river ran out from the throne
> that was brighter than both the sun and moon.
> Neither sun nor moon ever shone so purely
> As that copious river out of that city;
> Swiftly, it rushed through each street
> Without filth, bile, and slime].[82]

---

80  All references to Biblical texts are from *The Holy Bible Translated from the Latin Vulgate (Douay-Rheims Version)*, ed. and trans. Richard Challoner (London: Baronius Press, 2005).
     (1) And he shewed me a river of water of life, clear as crystal, proceeding from the throne of God and of the Lamb. (2) In the midst of the street thereof, and on both sides of the river, was the tree of life, bearing twelve fruits, yielding its fruits every month: the leaves of the tree for the healing of the nations. (3) And there shall be no curse any more: but the throne of God and of the Lamb shall be in it. And his servants shall serve him (Apocalypse 22: 1–3).

81  Apocalypse 22:1.
82  *Pearl*, 1055–60.

Like John's river, which flows "clear as crystal"[83] through the streets, the *Pearl* poet's water remains "brighter then bothe the sunne and mone,"[84] highlighting its divine nature. Although the divinity of God and New Jerusalem are, of course, predominant in this highly spiritual poem, there is a brief moment where the thoroughly terrestrial concern of waste management creeps into the poet's description of New Jerusalem. Immediately after considering the brightness of the river, the poet returns to more civic concerns and notes that the water flows through streets that are free of "fylthe other galle other glet" [filth, bile, and slime].[85] The role of this river cannot be to cleanse the street of debris. It is unlikely that the wide streets of the heavenly city, so clean that they do not at any point cloud the crystal waters of the river, are littered with refuse and slime. So, although the purpose of this river is not to clean the already spotless streets of New Jerusalem, the author still pauses in his retelling of the Biblical account to dwell on this cleanliness highlighting the water's ability to cleanse the streets, if the need existed. His vision of the perfect city is one whose streets, while already clean, are redundantly sluiced with crystal clear water to ensure absolute freedom from corruption. This betrays the author's human concern, not for the cleanliness of New Jerusalem which must by its divinity be free from all corruption, but rather for waste management in his own environment. This description of the holy city and the river suggests a preoccupation with the worldly that seeps into even the most divine revelation.

In "The Town as an Agent of Civilisation," Jacques Le Goff argues that urban fountains "were both necessary for hygiene, and aesthetically satisfying, show well the many-sided nature of medieval urbanism."[86] Fountains, much like the pipes and conduits which highlight man's mastery over his surroundings described above in Section I, act also to provide cleansing water throughout the city. But in *Vox Clamantis*, we again find that the normative functions collapse amid the social unrest of 1381. During the riots, the water that exists within the fountains no longer performs its cleansing functions and instead becomes a location of potential contamination: "Fons vbicumque tumet, sanguinitate rubet (l. 1172; "Wherever a fountain swelled, it became red with bloodiness").[87]

Just as the protective role of water as a natural barrier is inverted to emphasize the uncontrollable destructive capability of water in the *Vox Clamantis*, here too does the inversion of Gower's social norms deprive water of its positive urban role. No longer can fountains offer the London citizenry a place of hygiene and

---

83    Apocalypse 22:1.
84    *Pearl*, 1056.
85    *Pearl*, 1060.
86    Le Goff, "The Town as an Agent of Civilisation," 89.
87    Gower, *Vox Clamantis*, 75.

beauty, suggested by Le Goff. They now become the location of potential pestilence and horror. If refuse littering the streets, walls, and river of London concerns Edward III in 1358, the usually cleansing fountain waters, befouled with blood, must also be a concern to Gower. They have not only lost their ability to cleanse, they now offer a possible source of that "grievous and great abomination"[88] that ravaged London from 1348–1350 and prompted the social imbalance that ultimately sparked the subject of Gower's *Vox Clamantis*, the revolt of 1381.

# IV. Conclusion

If water acts as a cleansing agent in the literal sense, it also cleans figuratively as the baptismal medium, and is unsurprisingly found in urban spaces. It is the baptismal use of water that brings together all of the roles water holds in a quintessentially urban way. Christianity is a highly urban religion. Jennifer Summit, in her article ""Topography as Historiography: Petrarch, Chaucer, and the Making of Medieval Rome," argues that the conversion of Rome occurs when Christianity moved out of the suburbs, the site of their catacombs, and "into the central urban spaces formerly claimed by the pagan temples and monuments."[89] For Summit, the conversion of the medieval Christian city is specifically tied to its urbanization, an idea also highlighted by Le Goff. Because there is a higher population in cities, there are more people to hear preaching and consequently more sins to cleanse through baptism.[90] The cleansing of the citizens' sins, therefore, becomes crucial to the purifying role of water. It is through the use of water as a baptismal medium that medieval Christian's sought to identify their cities as the locus of Christian ideals, sought to protect their inhabitants from temptations, and sought to cleanse the urban space, at the individual level. In *Pearl*, baptismal water comes not from an earthly source, but rather in the form of Christ's bodily fluids. Wendell Stacy Johnson describes this water imagery as "a never-exhausted fountain . . . reinforced with the traditional symbols of the water and the blood."[91] If water is a means of definition, protection, and cleansing in an

---

[88]  *Memorials*, 33.
[89]  Jennifer Summit, "Topography as Historiography: Petrarch, Chaucer, and the Making of Medieval Rome," *Journal of Medieval and Early Modern Studies* 30.2 (2000): 211–46; here 237.
[90]  Le Goff, "The Town as an Agent of Civilisation," 78.
[91]  Wendell Stacy Johnson, "The Imagery and Diction of The Pearl: Toward an Interpretation," *Middle English Survey: Critical Essays*, ed. Edward Vasta (Notre Dame: University of Notre Dame Press,

urban context, highlighting man's achievements in civilization or failure in its absence, then the fountain as a metaphor for contained water expresses the highest level of that achievement. For the author of *Pearl*, the idea of perfectly contained fluids in a fountain appears to resound. The fluids that pour forth from the wounds of Christ and deliver mankind fromHell are divinely controlled torrents, presenting Christ's body, not as a river, but as a baptismal fountain:

> Innoghe ther wax out of that welle,
> Blod and water of brode wounde.
> The blod vus boght fro bale of helle,
> And delyuered vus of the deth secounde;
> The water is baptem, the soothe to telle,
> That fol₃ed the glayue so grimly grounde,
> That waschez away the gyltes felle
> That Adam with inne deth vus drounde

> [Enough grew out of that fountain,
> Blood and water from the broad wound.
> The blood bought us from the pain of hell,
> And delivered us from the second death;
> The water is baptism, to tell the truth,
> That accompanied the spear so grimly sharpened,
> That washes away the deadly guilt
> That Adam has drowned everyone in death].[92]

The fluids which flow forth from Christ's body during the crucifixion, the blood and the water, bathe the world in a baptismal medium, erasing the sins of Adam that had, until that point, drowned the inhabitants of the world. Much as the peasantry invading London in Gower's *Vox Clamantis* appear to drown civilization with the flood of their riotous behavior, so too does Adam drown mankind in the flood of his sinfulness. But Christ's sacrifice redeems mankind through baptism and Christocentrically defines the world. It purifies the sins of mankind and redefines them as "the saved." And it does this first and foremost, as Summit and Le Goff argue, in the cities.

Within a thoroughly urban text, the tears of the devout convert the individual pagan soul to Christianity's civility. In *Saint Erkenwald*, the London saint prays for baptismal water to release the soul of the noble pagan, but achieves that baptism with his own tears, "wyt the wordes and the water that weshe us of payne" [with the words and the water that wash us of pain].[93] Erkenwald's tears, the "water" that he "sheddes," bring the release of the unbaptized soul, cleansing

---

[92] 1965), 161–81; here 172
*Pearl*, 649–56.
[93] *St. Erkenwald*, 333.

him of his pagan taint and redefining the soul as Christian. While Christ accomplished baptism on a global scale, St. Erkenwald gives of his body, through tears, on an individual level, to the one noble pagan soul cleansing him of the sins of his birth.

Just as the water of divinity or of the devout have the ability to restore mankind to heaven, God's manipulation of water in Gower's *Vox Clamantis*, returns social order: "He [God] calmed the waters of the deep and established a boundary for them . . . . So the sea had a shore, and the riverbank held its full streams in check, and the roads were again open to law and order."[94] Here, we see an excess of water closely identified with the uncivilized countryside. As God restores the peace of London and reasserts the civic hierarchy, the water, just as the peasantry, is again put in its rightful, natural place. The water returns to its ocean or river to be confined, and literally defined, by its banks just as the peasantry returns to the countryside and its socially prescribed role as agricultural laborer. The return of order, then, is also a return to the three roles of water to define, protect, and cleanse, seen in its descriptions of London and New Troy, and perfected in the divinely redundant systems of New Jerusalem. It is the departure from Gower's preferred hierarchy, and therefore the positive roles of water, that brings about his apocalyptic vision. And it is through their descriptions and uses of water that each of these authors presents their vision, ideal or apocalyptic, of the urban space.

---

[94]    Gower, *Vox Clamantis*, 91.

Birgit Wiedl

(Institute for Jewish History in Austria)

# Jews and the City: Parameters of Jewish Urban Life in Late Medieval Austria[1]

In 1391, the municipal court of the Swiss town of Zurich was confronted with a series of charges brought in by several attendees of a wedding that had been hosted by the family of Vifli, one of the wealthiest and most prominent Jews of the town.[2] During the wedding, a long-pending quarrel between members of his and

---

[1] This article does not aim at providing an encompassing coverage of medieval Jewish urban life but rather at pointing out various aspects of Jewish existence in (Late) Medieval Austrian towns that may either correspond with general developments of Jewish urban life or differ from those due to circumstances particular to the countries that make up today's Austria. For a general overview over Austrian Jewish History, see *Geschichte der Juden in Österreich*, ed. Eveline Brugger, Christoph Lind, Albert Lichtblau, and Barbara Staudinger. Österreichische Geschichte, 15 (Vienna: Ueberreuter, 2006); on Jewish-Christian cohabitation, see now Jonathan Elukin, *Living Together, Living Apart: Rethinking Jewish-Christian Relations in the Middle Ages. Jews, Christians, and Muslims from the Ancient to the Modern World* (Princeton: Princeton University Press, 2007). For valuable comments and corrections, I would like to thank Albrecht Classen and Marilyn Sandidge. Furthermore, I would like to express my gratitude to Martha Keil, Hans-Jörg Gilomen, Gerd Mentgen, and Markus Wenninger for granting me access to galley proofs of their newest research publications.

[2] See Markus Wenninger, "Jüdische und jüdisch-christliche Netzwerke im spätmittelalterlichen Ostalpenraum," *Beziehungsnetze aschkenasischer Juden während des Mittelalters und der frühen Neuzeit*, ed. Jörg R. Müller. Forschungen zur Geschichte der Juden, Abteilung A, 20 (Hanover: Hahnsche Buchhandlung, 2008), 163–76; here 167; Markus Wenninger, "Nicht in einem Bett – aber doch auf einer Hochzeit. Zur Teilnahme von Christen an jüdischen Festen im Mittelalter," *Nicht in einem Bett: Juden und Christen in Mittelalter und Frühneuzeit*, ed. Institute for Jewish History in Austria (St. Pölten: Eigenverlag des Instituts, 2005); 10–17, here 13–14 (downloadable as pdf file here: http://www.injoest.ac.at/upload/JudeninME05_2_9-17.pdf; last accessed on April 8, 2009). Markus Wenninger is planning an extensive publication on the subject; id., "Von jüdischen Rittern und anderen waffentragenden Juden im mittelalterlichen Deutschland," *Aschkenas: Zeitschrift für Geschichte und Kultur der Juden* 13.1 (2003): 35–83; here 72–75. The incident has first been recounted by Augusta Weldler-Steinberg, *Intérieurs aus dem Leben der Zürcher Juden im 14. und 15. Jahrhundert*

274                                    Birgit Wiedl

other prominent Jewish families had obviously reached a crisis and had erupted
in first a vociferous argument, then in a brawl and had ended in several members
of the respective families facing each other with their swords drawn. The quite
detailed court records reveal astonishing facts: Not only did the Jews turn to the
Christian municipal court to settle their dispute, they were bearing arms and were
obviously accustomed to using them;[3] yet the probably most remarkable fact, as
Markus Wenninger has pointed out, was the quite high number of Christian
witnesses who gave testimony at court. Apart from those who had been hired as
servants or musicians, twelve Christians—hence about a third of the
witnesses—had clearly been present as guests, most of them being members of the
Zurich upper class: a knight, the former mayor, the town scribe; and at least five
of them lived in close vicinity, some even within the same lane, the Brunngasse,
which housed the majority of the Zurich Jewish population in the Middle Ages.[4]
Under penalty of excommunication, the synods at Wrocław (for the archbishopric
of Gniezno) and Vienna (for the ecclesiastical province of Salzburg, and city and
bishopric of Prague) had stated in 1267, Christians shall not invite Jews and
Jewesses as their dinner guests, or drink or eat with them, neither shall they dance
at their weddings or feasts.[5] This article was, in fact, an elaboration of the

---

(Zurich: Verlags- und Versandbuchhandlung 'Der Scheideweg', 1959), 22–24; for a focus on the
jurisdictional issues see the works by Susanna Burghartz, *Leib, Ehre und Gut: Delinquenz in Zürich
Ende des 14. Jahrhunderts* (Zurich: Chronos, 1990), and "Juden – eine Minderheit vor Gericht
(Zürich 1378–1436)," *Spannungen und Widersprüche. Gedenkschrift für František Graus*, ed. Susanna
Burghartz (Sigmaringen: Jan Thorbecke 1992), 229–44. On prominent Jews in Zurich, see *Germania
Judaica*, vol. III: *1350–1519*, part 2: *Mährisch Budwitz – Zwolle*, ed. Arye Maimon, Mordechai Breuer,
and Yacov Guggenheim (Tübingen: J. C. B. Mohr, 1995), 1733–34.

[3]  On the prohibition for Jews to bear arms and its 'reality,' see the articles by Wenninger, "Von
jüdischen Rittern," and Christine Magin, "'Waffenrecht' und 'Waffenverbot' für Juden im
Mittelalter – zu einem Mythos der Forschungsgeschichte," *Aschkenas: Zeitschrift für Geschichte und
Kultur der Juden* 13.1 (2003): 17–33; Markus Wenninger, "Bearing and Use of Weapons by Jews in
the (Late) Middle Ages," *Jewish Studies* 41 (2002, appeared in 2003): 83–92.

[4]  Wenninger, "Hochzeit," 13–14. On the location of Jewish households in Zurich in general, see
*Germania Judaica*, vol. II: *Von 1238 bis zur Mitte des 14. Jahrhunderts*, part 2: *Maastricht – Zwolle*, ed.
Zwi Avneri (Tübingen: J. C. B. Mohr 1968), 946 (up until 1350) and *Germania Judaica*, vol. III/2,
1726–27. A contrasting example, where Christians were punished for partaking in a Jewish
wedding feast, is given by Hans-Jörg Gilomen, "Kooperation und Konfrontation: Juden und
Christen in den spätmittelalterlichen Städten im Gebiet der heutigen Schweiz," *Juden in ihrer
Umwelt: Akkulturation des Judentums in Antike und Mittelalter*, ed. Matthias Konradt and Rainer
Christoph Schwinges (Basel: Schwabe, 2009), 157–227; here 176–77 (Zurich 1404).

[5]  See "Continuatio Vindobonensis a. 1267–1302, 1313–1327," ed. Wilhelm Wattenbach. Monumenta
Germaniae Historica Scriptores, vol. 9 (1851; Stuttgart: Anton Hiersemann, 1983), 698–722; here
699–702 (Vienna), the 1851 original ed. online (applies to all the MGH volumes quoted) here:
www.dmgh.de (last accessed on April 8, 2009). With respect to the articles concerning Jews, see
Heinz Schreckenberg, *Die christlichen Adversus-Judaeos-Texte und ihr literarisches und historisches
Umfeld (13.–20. Jh.)*. Europäische Hochschulschriften. Series XXIII: Theologie, 497 (Frankfurt a. M.,

regulations of the Fourth Lateran Council that had generally aimed at limiting the possibilities for Jews to take part in the everyday lives of their Christian neighbours, and vice versa.[6] The church authorities were, however, not oblivious to the impossibility of transferring these regulations into the reality of (inevitable) daily interaction between Jews and their next-door Christian neighbors; the lamentations and complaints of the Bishop of Olomouc and the provincial synod at Salzburg as early as 1273 and 1274 respectively about the 'persistent violation' of these regulations speak for themselves.[7] Tellingly, it was the breach of the 'safe conduct and peace' (*freies geleit und fried*) that the town of Zurich had promised the out-of-town visitors on Vifli's request that required an examination before the aldermen, the fisticuffs, the verbal and bodily assaults, and particularly the drawn

---

[6] Bern, New York, and Paris: Peter Lang, 1994), 224 (Wrocław) and 228 (Vienna, both German translation of the relevant articles); Solomon Grayzel, *The Church and the Jews*, vol. 2: *1254–1314*, ed. and completed Kenneth R. Stow (New York and Detroit: Wayne State University Press, 1989), 244–46, no. 6 (Wrocław), 247–48, 277, 290, no. 7 (Vienna); Eveline Brugger and Birgit Wiedl, *Regesten zur Geschichte der Juden in Österreich im Mittelalter*, vol. 1: *Von den Anfängen bis 1338* (Innsbruck, Vienna, and Bolzano: StudienVerlag, 2005), 59–61, no. 45 (Vienna); the whole book is downloadable as pdf-files in 3 parts here: http://www.injoest.ac.at/projekte/laufend/mittelalterliche_judenurkunden/index.php?lang=EN; last accessed on April 8, 2009). The second volume, forthcoming in 2009, will cover the time period from 1339 to 1365.

Fourth Lateran Council, Canon 67 *Quanto amplius*, quoted after the German rpt. of Giuseppe Alberigo, *Conciliorum oecumenicorum decreta* (Bologna 1973) by Josef Wolmuth (ed.), *Dekrete der ökumenischen Konzilien: Konzilien des Mittelalters vom ersten Laterankonzil (1123) bis zum fünften Laterankonzil (1512 – 1517)*, vol. 2 (Paderborn and Vienna: Ferdinand Schöningh, 2000), 265–66. With respect to the Jews, see Solomon Grayzel, *The Church and the Jews*, vol. 1: *1198–1254* (Philadelphia: Dropsie College, 1933; Sec. ed. New York: Hermon Press, 1966), 312–13, no. 13. Many of these regulations were adapted by legal codes like the Schwabenspiegel or Sachsenspiegel, which then in turn, due to their quick and wide circulation, had an impact on further secular and ecclesiastical legislation, see Klaus Lohrmann, "Die Rechtsstellung der Juden im Schwabenspiegel," *Die Legende vom Ritualmord: Zur Geschichte der Blutbeschuldigung gegen Juden*, ed. Rainer Erb (Berlin: Metropol-Verlag, 1993), 73–94. On the topic of Jews and Christians using the same baths, a particularly widely discussed issue which can be found in the 1267 ecclesiastical regulation as well as the Schwabenspiegel (among others), see latest Hans-Jörg Gilomen, "Jüdische Nutzung öffentlicher und privater Brunnen im Spätmittelalter," . . . zum allgemeinen statt nutzen. *Brunnen in der europäischen Stadtgeschichte*, ed. Dorothee Rippmann, Wolfgang Schmid, and Katharina Simon-Muscheid (Trier: Kliomedia, 2008), 133–45.

[7] Olomouc: *Constitutiones et acta publica imperatorum et regum*, vol. 3: *1273–1298*, ed. Jakob Schwalm. Monumenta Germaniae Historica Leges IV, Constitutiones, 3 (1904–1906; rpt. Hanover and Leipzig: Hahnsche Buchhandlung, 1980), 594, no. 620; Salzburg: Joannes Dominicus Mansi, *Sacrorum conciliorum nova et amplissima collectio*, vol. 24: *1269–1299* (1903 rpt.; Graz: Akademische Druck- und Verlagsanstalt, 1961), 136. In 1254, Pope Innocent IV had already complained that the Jews of the town and bishopric of Constance did not wear the mandatory attributes, see Shlomo Simonsohn, *The Apostolic See and the Jews: Documents 492–1404*. Studies and Texts (1988; Toronto: Pontifical Institute of Medieval Studies, 1991), 209, no. 203; Gilomen, "Kooperation und Konfrontation," 172–73, also on the (partial) enforcement of this regulation.

swords,[8] whereas the presence of Christians at what was clearly a 'Jewish feast' merely meant the interrogation of additional witnesses.

In whichever house the wedding took place, it must have been close to the house which once had belonged to the money-lender Minna,[9] widow of Menachem, who had lived in the same street in the first half of the fourteenth century with her sons Mordechai and Moshe.[10] She had the representative parts of her house decorated with what is today regarded as one of the most striking examples of cultural translation, having commissioned wall paintings the iconographic program of which were accessible to both Christians and Jews alike.[11] Some of the scenes,

---

[8]   Wenninger, "Von jüdischen Rittern," 73.

[9]   The role of Jewish women in the money-lending business is not to be underestimated, see the article of Rosa Alvarez Perez in this volume. Further, with particular but not exclusive regard to Austria, see the works of Martha Keil, latest "Business Success and Tax Debts: Jewish Women in Late Medieval Austrian Towns," Jewish Studies at the Central European University, vol. II (1999–2001), ed. András Kovács and Eszter Andor (Budapest: Central European University, 2002) 103–23; "Public Roles of Jewish Women in Fourteenth and Fifteenth-Century Ashkenaz: Business, Community, and Ritual," The Jews of Europe in the Middle Ages (Tenth to Fifteenth Centuries), ed. Christoph Cluse. Cultural Encounters in Late Antiquity and the Middle Ages, 4 (Turnhout: Brepols, 2004), 317–30; "Jüdinnen als Kategorie? Judinne in obrigkeitlichen Urkunden des deutschen Spätmittelalters," Räume und Wege: Jüdische Geschichte im Alten Reich 1300–1800, ed. Rolf Kießling, Peter Rauscher, Stefan Rohrbacher, and Barbara Staudinger. Colloquia Augustana, 25 (Berlin: Akademie Verlag, 2007), 335–61; "Mobilität und Sittsamkeit: Jüdische Frauen im Wirtschaftsleben des spätmittelalterlichen Aschkenas," Wirtschaftsgeschichte der mittelalterlichen Juden: Fragen und Einschätzungen, ed. Michael Toch. Schriften des Historischen Kollegs München, Kolloquien, 71 (Munich: Oldenbourg, 2008), 153–80.

[10]  Moshe was an acknowledged scholar, thus the family was "by far not at the brink of the baptismal font," as put by Martha Keil, "Lebensstil und Repräsentation. Jüdische Oberschicht im spätmittelalterlichen Aschkenas," Tres Culturas: Die drei Kulturen Europas zwischen Mittelalter und Neuzeit. Transkulturalität in der Ausgrenzung. Proceedings of the Conference in Vienna 2005, ed. Rudolf Karl and Hartmut Krones (Madrid [in print]), chapter 2; further Michael Toch, "Selbstdarstellung von mittelalterlichen Juden," Bild und Abbild des mittelalterlichen Menschen, ed. Elisabeth Vavra. Schriftenreihe der Akademie Friesach, 6 (Klagenfurt: Wieser, 1999), 178–83; here 181–82.

[11]  Frescoes in Zurich, Brunngasse 8. See Toch, "Selbstdarstellung," illustrations 185–91. Dölf Wild, "Bedeutende Zeugnisse jüdischer Wohnkultur in der Zürcher Altstadt entdeckt," Aschkenas: Zeitschrift für Geschichte und Kultur der Juden 7 (1997): 267–99; with a particular focus on the iconography, see Rudolf Böhmer, "Bogenschütze, Bauerntanz und Falkenjagd: Zur Ikonographie der Wandmalereien im Haus "Zum Brunnenhof" in Zürich," Literatur und Wandmalerei vol. I: Erscheinungsformen höfischer Kultur und ihre Träger im Mittelalter, ed. Eckart Conrad Lutz, Johanna Thali, and René Wetzel. Freiburger Colloquium 1998 (Tübingen: Niemeyer, 2002), 329–63; see further Edith Wenzel, "Ein neuer Fund: Mittelalterliche Wandmalereien in Zürich," Zeitschrift für deutsche Philologie 116 (1997): 417–26; Gilomen, "Kooperation und Konfrontation," 164–66; Harald Wolter-von dem Knesebeck, "Profane Wandmalerei in jüdischen Häusern des Mittelalters," Abstract of the third conference "Interdisziplinäres Forum Jüdische Geschichte und Kultur in der Frühen Neuzeit, " online here: http://www.forum-juedische-geschichte.de/2002Wolter.html (last accessed on April 8, 2009); Keil, "Lebensstil und Repräsentation," chapter 2; Wenninger, "Von jüdischen Rittern," 43–44; Edith Wenzel, "Alt-Jiddisch oder Mittelhochdeutsch?" Grenzen und Grenzüberschreitungen: Kulturelle Beziehungen zwischen Juden und Christen im Mittelalter, ed. id. Part

particularly the rural and somewhat rude dance scenes, greatly resemble the scenes described in the lyrics of the thirteenth-century Austrian poet Neidhart and could as well have been the decoration of a Christian household—like the 'Neidhart-frescoes' from around 1398 in the house of a wealthy Viennese citizen,[12] or the fourteenth century dance scenes a citizen of Regensburg had one of his representational rooms decorated with.[13] And like the Vienna (Christian) example, the decoration of the Zurich Jewish house also bears scenes that cater to a more noble audience—hunting scenes, particularly falconry, and as a special 'bonus' the coats of arms of Minna's noble guests (and quite probably debtors)[14] on a frieze running above the paintings and provided with a inscription of their names in Hebrew letters. The conclusion that intense cultural translation took place between the Jews and Christians of medieval Ashkenas and Sepharad in the areas of their lives they shared as well as those they lived separately, is most widely recognized by now.[15] However, it does not translate as assimilation but rather as transferring

---

of *Aschkenas: Zeitschrift für Geschichte und Kultur der Juden* 14.1 (2004): 31–50, 47–48, on the question of a Jewish-Christian audience.

[12] Frescoes in Vienna, Tuchlauben 19. Eva-Maria Höhle, *The Neidhart Frescoes, the oldest secular mural paintings in Vienna* (Vienna: Museums of the City of Vienna, 1984); Gertrud Blaschitz and Barbara Schedl, "Die Ausstattung eines Festsaales im mittelalterlichen Wien: Eine ikonologische und textkritische Untersuchung der Wandmalereien des Hauses 'Tuchlauben 19'," *Neidhartrezeption in Wort und Bild*, ed. Gertrud Blaschitz. Medium Aevum Quotidianum, Sonderband X (Krems: Medium Aevum Quotidianum, 2000), 84–111.

[13] Nikolaus Henkel, "Ein Neidharttanz des 14. Jahrhunderts in einem Regensburger Bürgerhaus," *Neidhartrezeption*, 53–70; for further examples on Neidhart motifs in wall paintings, see the other articles in this volume (Lake Constance, Matrei).

[14] Wenninger, "Jüdische und jüdisch-christliche Netzwerke," 166–67, calls the frieze a "reference list" of Minna's business partners.

[15] Thus explicitly put by Keil, "Lebensstil und Repräsentation," chapter 1. Just as explicit is Israel Jacob Yuval, *Two Nations in Your Womb: Perceptions of Jews and Christians in Late Antiquity and the Middle Ages*, trans. from the Hebrew by Barbara Harshav and Jonathan Chipman (2000; Berkeley, Los Angeles, and London: University of California Press, 2006), 206, on the question to what extent Jews were aware of Christian rituals. The phenomenon of cultural translation has been the central topic of many studies, most of which, however, focus on the Early Modern Period. For the specific topic of Jewish-Christian cultural translation in the Middle Ages, see the anthology by Wenzel, "Grenzen und Grenzüberschreitungen"; further, albeit with a focus on the nineteenth and twentieth centuries, *Kulturtransfer in der jüdischen Geschichte*, ed. Wolfgang Schmale and Martina Steer (Frankfurt a. M. and New York: Campus, 2006). For a methodological concept of cross-cultural translation in the European Middle Ages, see *Mittelalter im Labor: Die Mediävistik testet Wege zu einer transkulturellen Europawissenschaft*, ed. Michael Borgolte, Juliane Schiel, Bernd Schneidmüller, and Annette Seitz. Europa im Mittelalter, 10. Abhandlungen und Beiträge zur historischen Komparatistik (Berlin: Akademie Verlag, 2008), 195–209: part III: Arbeitsforum B: Kontakt und Austausch zwischen Kulturen im europäischen Mittelalter, followed by two case studies on Christian-Jewish cultural translation (Frederek Musall on Moshe ben Maimon, 209–28, and Rainer Barzen and Lennart Güntzel on the expulsion of the Jews in France and England and the perception of crisis, 228–51).

one's own culture into a new context,[16] as adapting personal tastes as well as general concepts of aesthetics that are shared by people of a comparable social status.[17] This shared taste extends to areas of life that remain more private, or at least representational within a smaller group of people. When, for example, Israel Isserl, *magister iudeorum* and one of the most prominent Jews of Vienna, commissioned a *Sefer Mordechai*, a collection of Rabbinical responsae by Mordechai bar Hillel from the late thirteenth century, to be written for him in 1371/1372, he had the manuscript decorated in what is known as *Niederösterreichischer Randleistenstil*, a particular style of book illumination that was quite widely used at that time; it was, for example, the style a missal of the Lower Austrian monastery of Klosterneuburg that originated from about the same time was adorned in (see Figure 5).[18] Despite the fact that Isserl's Hebrew codex would rather not, or at least not mainly, be used in the presence of Christians, he nevertheless had it decorated in what can be called the 'in-fashion' style of the time and region, Isserl's codex being but one example of Hebrew manuscripts the margins of which were decorated in that particular style.[19] Both Jews and Christian monks had acquired the same taste as far as book illumination was concerned, regarded the same style as beautiful and prestigious, and, probably, knew how to impress visitors with their gems.

However close though the cultural and social contacts to their Christian neighbors were, Jews remained in many respects a separate, if not homogenous, group within (or rather outside) the Christian society.[20] As far as the Christian

---

[16]  Raingard Eßer, "Migrationsgeschichte und Kulturtransferforschung," *Das eine Europa und die Vielfalt der Kulturen: Kulturtransfer in Europa 1500–1850*, ed. Thomas Fuchs and Sven Trakulhun (Berlin: Berliner Wissenschafts-Verlag, 2003), 69–82; here 73–74. On the medieval Ashkenasic Jews and their cultural and social identity in general, see Michael Toch, *Die Juden im mittelalterlichen Reich*. Sec. ed. Enzyklopädie deutscher Geschichte, 44 (1998; Munich: Oldenbourg, 2003), 33–34, on the intensified contacts to Christians in the Late Middle Ages as born out of necessity due to the (violently) reduced Jewish population, 38.

[17]  Keil, "Lebensstil und Repräsentation," on the example of luxury garments.

[18]  Andreas Fingernagel and Alois Haidinger, "Neue Zeugen des Niederösterreichischen Randleistenstils in hebräischen, deutschen und lateinischen Handschriften," *Codices Manuscripti* 39.40 (2002): 15–41; here 15–29. Martha Keil, "Gemeinde und Kultur – Die mittelalterlichen Grundlagen jüdischen Lebens in Österreich," *Geschichte der Juden in Österreich*, 15–122; here 28–29, illustration (*Sefer Mordechai* and missal from Klosterneuburg), 28.

[19]  Keil, "Gemeinde und Kultur," 29. See also Robert Suckale, "Über den Anteil christlicher Maler an der Ausmalung hebräischer Handschriften der Gotik in Bayern," *Geschichte und Kultur der Juden in Bayern (Aufsätze)*, ed. Manfred Treml and Josef Kirmeier. Veröffentlichungen zur Bayerischen Geschichte und Kultur 17.88, ed. Claus Grimm (Munich, New York, London, and Paris: K. G. Saur, 1988), 123–34.

[20]  On the highly problematic and widely discussed 'label' of Jews as a fringe group, see Frantisek Graus, "Randgruppen der städtischen Gesellschaft im Spätmittelalter," *Zeitschrift für historische Forschung* 8 (1981): 385–437; here particularly 396 on the definition of 'fringe group'; Gerd

secular authorities were concerned, the legal as well as the economic position of Jews, both as a group and as individuals, was generally defined by the ruler, in particular the Holy Roman Emperor who held the general sovereignty over all the Jews of the empire, counting them as a part of his treasure:[21] "the rulers' sole purpose is money," as Rabbi Jacob bar Jechiel phrased it clearly in mid-thirteenth century.[22] As early as the beginning of the thirteenth century, however, this sovereignty was reduced to a mere claim, the Imperial lordship weakening in the course of the transition of Imperial rights to the regional rulers, the right to the Jews (*Judenregal*) being but one among them.[23] In quite a number of German cities, their grip on the Jews dwelling within their realm tightened along with their rise to economical as well as political importance,[24] whereas in the region of modern-day Austria, both towns and Jews remained under the strong grip of the respective regional ruler, be he the Habsburg duke, the Archbishop of Salzburg, the Bishop of Bamberg, or a local nobleman.

---

Mentgen, "'Die Juden waren stets eine Randgruppe.' Über eine fragwürdige Prämisse der aktuellen Judenforschung," *Liber amicorum necnon et amicarum für Alfred Heit: Beiträge zur mittelalterlichen und geschichtlichen Landeskunde*, ed. Friedhelm Burgard, Christoph Cluse, and Alfred Haverkamp. Trierer Historische Forschungen, 28 (Trier: Verlag Trierer Historische Forschungen, 1996), 393–411; Anna Foa, "The Witch and the Jew. Two Alikes that Were Not the Same," *From Witness to Witchcraft. Jews and Judaism in Medieval Christian Thought*, ed. Jeremy Cohen. Wolfenbüttler Mittelalter-Studien, 11 (Wiesbaden: Harrassowitz, 1997), 361–74.

[21] First explicitly stated in the general Imperial privilege by Emperor Frederic II in 1236, *Constitutiones et acta publica imperatorum et regum*, vol. 2: *1198–1272*, ed. Ludwig Weiland. Monumenta Germaniae Historica Leges IV, Constitutiones, 2 (1896; Hanover: Hahnsche Buchhandlung, 1963), 274, no. 204. On the vast discussion on the Jews as *servites camere* ("servants of the treasure"), see the summary by Toch, "Juden im mittelalterlichen Reich," 48 and 102–10. For a similar development in France, see the contribution of Rosa Perez Alvarez in this volume.

[22] Martha Keil, "Nähe und Abgrenzung. Die mittelalterliche Stadt als Raum der Begegnung," *Nicht in einem Bett*, 2–8; here 4–5. The whole article is downloadable as a pdf file here: http://www.injoest.ac.at/upload/JudeninME05_1_1-8.pdf (last accessed on April 8, 2009).

[23] Generally see *Germania Judaica*, vol. III: *1350–1519*, part 3: *Gebietsartikel, Einleitungsartikel, Indices*, ed. Arye Maimon, Mordechai Breuer, and Yacov Guggenheim (Tübingen: J. C. B. Mohr, 2003), 2173–74; Toch, "Juden im mittelalterlichen Reich," 48–49.

[24] Still essential is Herbert Fischer (later Arye Maimon), *Die verfassungsrechtliche Stellung der Juden in den deutschen Städte während des dreizehnten Jahrhunderts*. Untersuchungen zur Deutschen Staats- und Rechtsgeschichte, 140 (1931; Aalen: Scientia-Verlag, 1969). Further see Toch, "Juden im mittelalterlichen Reich," 106–07; for a general summary of Jews and towns, see Alfred Haverkamp, "Jews and Urban Life: Bonds and Relationships," *Jews of Europe*, 55–69; on Imperial/regal rights and their relation to the Imperial cities, see *Germania Judaica*, vol. III/3, 2167, on cities and Jews, 2169–70, on Jews as citizens, 2181–87, on jurisdictional matters 2188–91; for regional examples, see Alfred Haverkamp, "Die Juden im Erzstift Trier," *Die Juden in ihrer mittelalterlichen Umwelt*, ed. Alfred Ebenbauer and Klaus Zatloukal (Vienna, Cologne, and Weimar: Böhlau, 1991), 67–89; Klaus Lohrmann, *Judenrecht und Judenpolitik im mittelalterlichen Österreich* (Vienna and Cologne: Böhlau, 1990), especially 146–66.

The first encompassing definition of the legal standing of the Austrian Jews was the quite comprehensive regulation which the Babenberg Duke Frederic II issued in 1244,[25] which remained the basis for further legislation within the duchy of Austria[26] and also served as a model for other rulers.[27] The rather detailed economic issues, mostly in favor of the Jews, and the quite wide-ranging protection suggest that Duke Frederic aimed at providing an incentive for Jews to settle down in Austria[28]—as part of his, and no longer the Emperor's, treasure. With regard to the towns, this also means that the ruler was determined not to lose his control over what he had just acquired[29] and regarded as his immediate property, a part of his treasure that he protected and/or exploited and utilized as he saw fit. It remained the rulers' sole prerogative to grant Jews the right to take their abode on his realm, their favorite financiers were given wide-ranging economic and legal privileges without as much as informing the cities. Only during the last decades of the fourteenth century, some Austrian cities were able

[25] Most recent edition by Brugger and Wiedl, *Regesten*, vol. 1, 35–38, no. 25. For an English translation, see http://www.fordham.edu/halsall/jewish/1244-jews-austria.html (last accessed on April 8, 2009), which is based on the (somewhat problematic) translation by Jacob Marcus, *The Jew in the Medieval World: A Sourcebook, 315–1791* (New York: JPS, 1938), 28–33.

[26] Re-issued *ad imitationem clare memorie quondam Friderici ducis Austrie et Stirie* by King Rudolf I in 1277 (Brugger and Wiedl, *Regesten*, vol. 1, 71–73, no. 56). The explicit reference to Duke Frederick II conveys a clear meaning—on the one hand, Rudolf's rival Přemysl Otakar, the (outlawed) duke of Austria, was being blatantly ignored, and on the other hand, by reverting to the ducal privilege of 1244, and not the Imperial one, Rudolf stressed his family's claim on the duchies of Austria and Styria (Eveline Brugger, "Von der Ansiedlung bis zur Vertreibung – Juden in Österreich im Mittelalter," *Geschichte der Juden in Österreich*, 123–228; here 142).

[27] Hungary: Bela IV, 1251 (*Monumenta Hungariae Judaica*, vol. 1: *1092–1539*, ed. Ármin Friss and Mór Weisz [Budapest: Magyar Izraeliták Országos, 1903], 23–30, no. 22); Bohemia and Moravia: Přemysl Otakar II, 1255, 1262, and 1268 (Brugger and Wiedl, *Regesten*, vol. 1, 45–48, no. 34, 51–54, no. 39 , and 62–65, no. 47, the first including Austria, the latter two Austria and Styria); Poland: Duke Boleslav, 1264 (*Juden in Europa: Ihre Geschichte in Quellen*, vol. 1: *Von den Anfängen bis zum späten Mittelalter*, ed. Julius Schoeps and Hiltrud Wallenborn [Darmstadt: Wissenschaftliche Buchgesellschaft, 2001], 139–43, no. 65); Bamberg: Bishops Henry II and Wulfing, between 1304 to 1328 (Brugger and Wiedl, *Regesten*, vol. 1, 255–57, no. 302). No privileges for the Styrian and Carinthian Jews have been transmitted, the later Habsburg privileges of the second half of the fourteenth century however include both these territories, referring to an 'older existing legislation' (see Lohrmann, *Judenrecht*, 182–89 [Carinthia], 200–06 [Styria], late Habsburg privileges 230–35).

[28] The Jewish immigration into the middle Danube area had already increased during the first half of the thirteenth century; at least for Vienna, an existing community can be proven for around 1200 (first mention of the Vienna Synagogue in 1204; see Brugger and Wiedl, *Regesten*, vol. 1, 18–19, no. 5), thus Frederic might also have reacted to the newly arisen need of regulating the Jewish life that had begun to flourish.

[29] In 1331, Emperor Louis IV officially enfeoffed the Austrian dukes with the right to the Jews (*Judenregal*), Brugger, "Ansiedlung," 143–44.

to gain at least partial control over the Jews, mainly focusing on jurisdictional and economic matters.[30]

Yet the seemingly undue preference accorded the Jews rankled with the citizens, causing the author of the Viennese *Stadtrechtsbuch* (a compendium of legal regulations from the end of the fourteenth century) to complain polemically about the "cursed Jews" having a better legal position against the Christians than the Christians against the Jews, directly referring to the 1244 regulations and blatantly ignoring the everyday reality that had by then long changed to the clear disadvantage of the Jews.[31]

Their increasing influence notwithstanding, Austrian cities remained for the most part powerless should the respective ruler, in whose official possession the Jews remained until the end of Jewish medieval settlement, decide to interfere. The Austrian dukes gave their Jews as fiefs to noblemen they wanted to particularly honor, reward, or bribe,[32] without as much as notifying the government of those cities where the Jews dwelled; should a Jew flee from a ruler's territory, the cities were neither involved in the ensuing trial nor did they participate in the sharing of the Jew's confiscated property.[33] This applies not only to towns that were under the rule of a powerful lord, like (partially) the Duke of Austria, but also to noblemen whose immediate rule extended to a considerably limited area managed to maintain a close grip on the Jews as an outstanding group. In 1350, the nobleman and chancellor of Styria, Rudolf Otto of Liechtenstein, granted the Jew Häslein, the wealthiest and most prominent Jew in the Carinthian/Styrian area at that time, the right to settle in his town of Murau, placing him and his family in a

---

[30]  See Birgit Wiedl, "Codifying Jews. Jews in Austrian Town Charters of the Late Middle Ages," *The Constructed Jew: Jews and Judaism through Medieval Christian Eyes*, ed. Kristine T. Utterback and Merrall L. Price (Turnhout: Brepols, forthcoming 2009).

[31]  Christine Magin, "*Wie es umb der iuden recht stet:*" *Der Status der Juden in spätmittelalterlichen deutschen Rechtsbüchern* (Göttingen: Wallenstein-Verlag, 1999), 103; Heinrich Maria Schuster, *Das Wiener Stadtrechts- und Weichbildbuch* (Vienna: Manz, 1973), 130–31; Lohrmann, *Judenrecht*, 161; id., *Die Wiener Juden im Mittelalter* (Berlin and Vienna: Philo, 2000), 36–37.

[32]  The most famous of these was the enfeoffment of the Counts of Cilli (today's Celje, Slovenia) with the Jew Chatschim and his family by duke Rudolf IV. Despite the fact that the towns Chatschim lived in were quite prosperous (Ljubljana, Celje, Trieste), there is no notion of any involvement of either of these towns. See *Germania Judaica*, vol. III/3, 209; Brugger, "Ansiedlung," 184–85; Lohrmann, *Judenrecht*, 206–07; Markus Wenninger, "Die Bedeutung jüdischer Financiers für die Grafen von Cilli und vice versa," *Celjski grofje, stara tema – nova spoznanja*, ed. Rolanda Fugger Germadnik (Celje: Pokrajinski Muzej, 1999), 143–64; here 151–52. On Jews between ruler and (Lower Austrian) nobility, see Eveline Brugger, *Adel und Juden im mittelalterlichen Niederösterreich.* Studien und Forschungen aus dem Niederösterreichischen Institut für Landeskunde, 38 (St. Pölten: Selbstverlag des Niederösterreichischen Instituts für Landeskunde, 2004).

[33]  For 'famous flights' of Jews see below; further Brugger, "Ansiedlung," 181–82 (Häslein) and 184–85 (Chatschim and Mosche); Lohrmann, *Judenrecht*, 218–20 (Häslein) and 225–30 (Chatschim and Mosche).

very privileged position with respect to both the Jewish community of Murau and the town itself.[34]

Although it is very likely that Rudolf Otto of Liechtenstein issued the privilege with ducal approval, there is no mention of any involvement whatsoever of the town of Murau — which, if nothing else, had to renounce any jurisdictional rights over Häslein who fell under the sole competence of Rudolf Otto himself. This example concurs with a general increase of personalized privileges in the second half of the fourteenth century,[35] privileges that granted a special status to an individual Jew or Jewess (usually including the entire family) and exempted them from the legal requirements of the town they lived in. When several years later, Häslein left his new abode in the ducal town of Judenburg without seeking permission beforehand and Duke Rudolph IV confiscated all his property and outstanding debts, neither of the towns he had lived in or had business contacts with was given a share.

The Austrian rulers' control even extended to Jewish geographical spaces within a city. The permission to erect or rebuild a synagogue, to establish or to enlarge a cemetery remained the right of the respective lord of the town,[36] leaving the town's administration with no say in the matter.[37] To the contrary, a ruler like the Bishop of Bamberg who owned the Carinthian town of Villach could even, after having granted the Jew Aschrok the right to erect a synagogue (in return for a payment of 200 pounds)[38], coerce his Christian subjects, in this case the mayor and council of Villach, into promising to protect the Jews should any "uprise" against them occur.[39] But even if reduced to the mere geographical space, to the public and

---

[34]   Brugger, "Ansiedlung," 181–82; Wilhelm Wadl, *Geschichte der Juden in Kärnten im Mittelalter: Mit einem Ausblick bis zum Jahre 1867*. Revised second ed. Das Kärntner Landesarchiv, 9 (Klagenfurt: Verlag des Kärntner Landesarchivs, 1992), 196–98.

[35]   Eveline Brugger and Birgit Wiedl, "'... und ander frume leute genuch, paide christen und juden.' Quellen zur christlich-jüdischen Interaktion im Spätmittelalter am Beispiel Österreichs," *Räume und Wege*, 286–305; here 288–89.

[36]   See for the similar French legislation the contribution of Rosa Alvarez Perez in this volume.

[37]   The Church, however, tried to gain control over the erection of new and the alteration of already existing synagogues. The provincial synagogue of Vienna in 1267 forbade the erection of new synagogues, while (re-)used existing ones were not to be made wider, higher nor more precious (latest print Brugger and Wiedl, *Regesten*, vol. 1, 59–61, no. 45; here 60).

[38]   State Archives of Bavaria, Bamberg, A 78 Lade 403 Nr. 4 (1510 May 4). Joseph Babad, "The Jews in Medieval Carinthia," *Historia Judaica* 7 (1945): 13–28 and 193–204; here 27; *Germania Judaica*, vol. III: *1350–1519*, part 1: *Aach - Lychen*, ed. Arye Maimon and Yacov Guggenheim (Tübingen: J. C. B. Mohr, 1987), 415; *Germania Judaica*, vol. III/2, 1533–34; *Germania Judaica*, vol. III/3, 1759; Wilhelm Neumann, "Die Juden in Villach," *Carinthia* I 155 (1965), 327–66; here 349–50; Wadl, *Juden Kärnten*, 166, 223.

[39]   Austrian State Archives Vienna, Haus-, Hof-, und Staatsarchiv, AUR Uk. 1359 IV 1. *Germania Judaica*, vol. III/2, 1534, *Germania Judaica*, vol. III/3, 1759; Lohrmann, *Judenrecht*, 163; Neumann, "Juden Villach," 342, 350; Johann Egid Scherer, *Die Rechtsverhältnisse der Juden in den deutsch-*

private places, a medieval town was a space of meeting for Jews and Christians.[40] They were living next door, and not only in these two streets in Zurich—in Vienna and Krems, in Wiener Neustadt and Graz, in the episcopal towns of Friesach, Villach and Wolfsberg in Carinthia and the then South-Styrian, now Slovenian Maribor and Ptuj, to name but the biggest of the Jewish communities, Jewish settlement might have been concentrated around central locations, in particular the synagogue(s), yet many members lived outside these parts of the city where Christians lived, as (not only) the Viennese sources call it, *under den Juden,* "among the Jews": thus, encounter was inevitable. Jews employed the services of Christian craftsmen as much as Christians called on Jewish services;[41] and, although frowned upon by the Church,[42] Christian servants to Jewish households were common, even essential: "he had servants and maids, non-Jewish and Jewish too," Ephraim bar Jacob wrote in his memorial book about the Jew Schlom, master of the ducal mint in Vienna around 1192, not finding this in the least peculiar.[43] On both sides, religious authorities were up in arms about Christian women engaging Jewish, and Jewesses engaging Christian wet nurses;[44] and the story told by the Carinthian Abbot and historiographer Johann of Viktring about a Christian wet nurse, who in 1343 abducted the daughter of her Jewish employers to have her baptized, may on the one hand confirm that the worries, at least on the Jewish side, weren't completely unfounded, but on the other hand gives evidence of the

---

österreichischen Ländern. Mit einer Einleitung über die Principien der Judengesetzgebung in Europa während des Mittelalters. Beiträge zur Geschichte des Judenrechtes im Mittelalter, 1 (Leipzig: Duncker & Humblot, 1901), 509; Wadl, *Juden Kärnten,* 162.

[40] Keil, "Nähe und Abgrenzung," 2–4; Haverkamp, "Jews and Urban Life," 62 and 65–66.

[41] Keil, "Nähe und Abgrenzung," 2.

[42] Whereas the synod at Wrocław, where the matter is addressed directly for the first time, does not forbid Christians to work as servants in Jewish households, but merely declares that they were not to stay there day and night (*die noctuque*), it is debated whether the wording of the Viennese synod (*die nocteve*) aims at prohibiting Christian servants at all. Grayzel, *Church and Jews,* vol. 2, 244–46, no. 6 (Wrocław); Brugger and Wiedl, *Regesten,* vol. 1," 59–61, no. 45 (Vienna), see above for further editions; Schreckenberg, *Adversus-Judaeos-Texte und ihr literarisches und historisches Umfeld* ( 13– 20. Jh.), 230. For the *schabbesgoj,* the ritually essential Christian servant, see Keil, "Gemeinde und Kultur," 76.

[43] Brugger and Wiedl, *Regesten,* vol. 1, 17–18, no. 4 (full text in Hebrew and German translation); Brugger, "Ansiedlung," 126.

[44] Martha Keil, "Lilith und Hollekreisch: Schwangerschaft, Geburt und Wochenbett im Judentum des deutschen Spätmittelalters," *Aller Anfang: Geburt, Birth, Naissance.* Tagungsband der 5. Wiener Gespräche zur Sozialgeschichte der Medizin, ed. Gabriele Dorffner and Sonia Horn (Vienna: Verlagshaus der Ärzte, 2004), 145–160; eadem, "Gemeinde und Kultur," 107; eadem, "Nähe und Abgrenzung," 7–8. On the topic of female interaction Elisheva Baumgarten, *Mothers and Children: Jewish Family Life in Medieval Europe* (Princeton: Princeton University Press, 2004), 119–53, particularly 135–44 on Christian wet nurses in Jewish households and vice versa. Baumgarten emphasizes the close relationship that must have existed between a Jewish and a Christian woman if one was to breast-feed the child of the other.

commonness of this practice (since Johann of Viktring interprets the abduction as remarkable, but not the employment itself).[45] There has been, and still is, a vast and vivid discussion on the topic of Jewish quarters, and whether their settlement was scattered or close-together within the city, and the most prominent public building within, the synagogue.[46]

In addition to being the center of Jewish life on many levels—the primary worship institution, the social center, a place of identification,[47] but also a place of

---

[45] Fedor Schneider (ed.), *Iohannis abbatis Victoriensis Liber certarum historiarum*. Monumenta Germaniae Historica Scriptores rerum Germanicarum in usum scholarum, 36.2 (Hanover and Leipzig: Hahnsche Buchhandlung, 1910); Keil, "Lilith und Hollekreisch," 151–52; *Germania Judaica*, vol. II: *Von 1238 bis zur Mitte des 14. Jahrhunderts*, part 1: *Aachen – Luzern*, ed. Zvi Avneri (Tübingen: J. C. B. Mohr, 1968), 265; *Germania Judaica*, vol. II/2, 786; Wadl, *Juden Kärnten*, 185.

[46] From the extensive literature on this subject, see the latest summary in *Germania Judaica*, vol. III/3, 2082–89. Further see *Jüdische Gemeinden und ihr christlicher Kontext in kulturräumlicher vergleichender Betrachtung: Von der Spätantike bis zum 18. Jahrhundert*, ed. Christoph Cluse, Alfred Haverkamp and Israel Jacob Yuval. Forschungen zur Geschichte der Juden, A 13 (Hanover: Hahnsche Buchhandlung, 2003); *In and Out of the Ghetto: Jewish-Gentile Relations in Late Medieval and Early Modern Germany*, ed. Hartmut Lehmann, R. Po-Chia Hsia, and David Lazar (Washington, DC: German Historical Institute, 1995), particularly the article by Alfred Haverkamp, "The Jewish Quarters in German Towns during the Late Middle Ages," 13–28; Simha Goldin, "The Synagogue in Medieval Jewish Communities as an Integral Institution," *Journal of Ritual Studies* 9.1 (1995): 15–39; Keil, "Lebensstil und Repräsentation," chapter 1; eadem, "Orte der Öffentlichkeit: Judenviertel, Synagoge, Friedhof," *Ein Thema – zwei Perspektiven: Juden und Christen in Mittelalter und Frühneuzeit*, ed. Eveline Brugger and Birgit Wiedl (Innsbruck, Vienna, and Bolzano: StudienVerlag, 2007), 170–86; eadem, "Bet ha Knesset, Judenschul: Die Synagoge als Gotteshaus, Amtsraum und Brennpunkt sozialen Lebens," *Wiener Jahrbuch für jüdische Geschichte, Kultur und Museumswesen* 4 (1999/2000): 71–90; Silvia Codreanu-Windauer, "Stadtviertel oder Ghetto? Das mittelalterliche Judenviertel Regensburgs," *Centre—Region—Periphery. Medieval Europe, Pre* printed Papers, 2 (Hertingen 2002), 316–21; id., "Regensburg: The Archaeology of the Medieval Jewish Quarter," and Pam Manix, "Oxford: Mapping the Medieval Jewry," both in *Jews of Europe*, 391–403, and 405–20, respectively; Paul Mitchell, "Synagoge und Jüdisches Viertel im mittelalterlichen Wien," *Synagogen, Mikwen, Siedlungen: Jüdisches Alltagsleben im Lichte neuer archäologischer Funde*, ed. Fritz Backhaus and Egon Wamers. Schriften des Archäologischen Museums Frankfurt, 19 (Frankfurt a. M.: Archäologisches Museum Frankfurt, 2004): 139–50; Markus Wenninger, "Grenzen in der Stadt? Zur Lage und Abgrenzung mittelalterlicher deutscher Judenviertel," *Aschkenas: Zeitschrift für Geschichte und Kultur der Juden* 14.1 (2004): 9–30; id., "Zur Topographie der Judenviertel in den mittelalterlichen deutschen Städten anhand österreichischer Beispiele," *Juden in der Stadt*, ed. Fritz Mayrhofer and Ferdinand Opll. Beiträge zur Geschichte der Städte Mitteleuropas, 15 (Linz: Österreichischer Arbeitskreis für Stadtgeschichtsforschung, 1999), 81–117. On the confined space of the *eruv chazerot* (the 'mixing, putting together of courtyards' to facilitate carrying objects from one domain to another on Sabbath, symbolized by a loaf of bread, see *Encyclopaedia Judaica*, sec. ed., vol. 6 [Detroit, New York, San Francisco, et al: Thomson Gale, 2007], 484–85), within a city, see Keil, "Gemeinde und Kultur," 75–76, further Yuval, *Two Nations*, 236–39 with particular, and intriguing, reference to the alleged host wafer accusations; also Gilomen, "Brunnen," 133–35. For a continuously updated bibliography on Jewish archeology in Europe see http://www.project-yesod.org/bibliography.html (last accessed on April 8, 2009).

[47] Mordechai Breuer, "Ausdrucksweisen aschkenasischer Frömmigkeit in Synagoge und Lehrhaus,"

flaunting one's social status[48] and the stage where sanctions of the internal Jewish jurisdiction were imposed publicly[49]—the synagogue was also perceived by Christians not as an "exclusively" Jewish space but as a public one they too had access to. In some towns, the Jews had to take their oaths in front of the synagogue,[50] and according to Austrian ducal legislation, the synagogue was the place to hold a court sitting if a Jew was somehow involved in the process.[51] Thus, the synagogue held a semi-legal function for Jews and Christians alike, in addition to providing a convenient and therefore common meeting place where business transactions were negotiated and concluded, goods delivered and the newest gossip discussed while its acoustic signals permeated into Christian space as much (if not as manifold) as church bells.[52]

Christians therefore showed no sign of hesitation, or repulsion, to use the synagogue as a meeting point and accept it as a place of public significance. In early November 1354, Nikolaus Petzolt, the town judge of the prospering southern Styrian (today's Slovenian) town of Maribor, which housed one of the largest Jewish communities of that region, was called on by messengers of the Counts of Pfannberg, a local noble family with considerable business contact to the Jews. They asked him to accompany them to the *shul*, the synagogue. Petzolt, the *iudex iudeorum* Wilhelm, and another citizens of Maribor, obliged, and having arrived at the synagogue, the messengers sent for the *shulklapper*[53] to ask around whether

---

[48] *Judentum im deutschen Sprachraum*, ed. Karl E. Grözinger (Frankfurt/Main: Suhrkamp, 1991), 103–16; here 105; Goldin, "Synagogue," 15–16; Keil, "Lebensstil und Repräsentation," chapter 1.

[49] *Germania Judaica*, vol. III/3, 2085; Goldin, "Synagogue," 22–23; Keil, "Lebensstil und Repräsentation," chapter 1.

Michael Toch, "Mit der Hand auf der Thora: Disziplinierung als internes und externes Problem in den jüdischen Gemeinden des Spätmittelalters," *Disziplinierung und Sachkultur in Mittelalter und Früher Neuzeit*, ed. Gerhard Jaritz. .Veröffentlichungen des Instituts für Realienkunde des Mittelalters und der Frühen Neuzeit, 17. Österreichische Akademie der Wissenschaften. Philosophisch-Historische Klasse, Sitzungsberichte, 669 (Vienna: Verlag der österreichischen Akademie der Wissenschaften, 1999), 155–68; here 161; Keil, "Orte der Öffentlichkeit," 175–77; *Germania Judaica*, vol. III/3, 2105–08; Goldin, "Synagogue," 23–24.

[50] The 'minor oath' of the Jews of the Lower Austrian town of Krems had to be taken in front of the synagogue, with the oath-taker's hand on the doorknob; see Brugger, "Ansiedlung," 151. According to ducal legislation, the Jews had to take their oath solely in front of the duke, which proved highly inexecutable, whereas humiliating rituals accompanying the oath (self-execration, standing on a sow's skin), as described in the Schwabenspiegel, are not recorded for Austria; see Hans Voltelini, "Der Wiener und Kremser Judeneid," *Mitteilungen des Vereins für Geschichte der Stadt Wien* 12 (1932): 64–70; here 69–70; Toch, "Hand auf der Thora," 162–67.

[51] Brugger and Wiedl, *Regesten*, vol. 1, 36, no. 25, § 30.

[52] On 'Jewish' sounds within a town, see Keil, "Orte der Öffentlichkeit," 172.

[53] The *shulklapper* (German *Schulklopfer*, in Christian documents—like in the charter quoted above—often called 'sacristan of the Jews', *judenmesner*) was responsible for calling the Jews to prayer; he served as a crier, and was involved in the collection of taxes, the taking of oaths, and in handling jurisdiction, see *Germania Judaica*, vol. III/3, 2092–93; *Encyclopaedia Judaica*, sec. ed., vol.

any of the Jews still held some debenture bonds of the Pfannberg family, and if so, to produce them at the synagogue in order that they could repay the debts. The Jews answered that none of them held any obligations; thus the messengers had the *shulklapper* declare that any bonds presented later on were to be considered null and void. The three citizens corroborated the charter issued on that occasion with their seals, declaring that they had been present at the synagogue along with 'other respectable people.'[54]

One of the main opportunities of contact and interaction remained the contact via business—and the close everyday contact and the interaction can easily be detected in items and activities of the daily business life. Business documents are one of the most extensively transmitted type of sources in Austria as far as Jewish-Christian interaction is concerned.[55]

From the financier of noblemen and rulers to the lowly pawn broker, their clientele was predominantly Christian and often recruited from their immediate surroundings, especially when it comes to small-scale pawning and loaning; whereas the noble clients, both secular and ecclesiastical, of financially stronger Jews usually came from a greater geographical area.[56] Jewish-Christian business interaction might evoke ideas of credit transactions and pawn-broking only, yet these are by far not the sole form of business that took place between Jews and their Christian neighbors. 'Classical' contracts like debenture bonds, pawn certificates, and charters for safeguarding the guarantor (*Schadlosbriefe*) are but a part of the vast amount of Jewish appearances in business documents. Jews appear in both ducal and municipal account books,[57] they were registered in rentals not only as pawn keepers but as regular land- and/or house-owners and appear in charters as such; when, e.g., the Styrian nobleman Poppo of Peggau bequeathed several of his estates to the Upper Austrian monastery of Reichersberg in 1235, he did so *aput Winnam in domo Techani iudei*, in Vienna, in the house of Teka the Jew, to whom, along with several Viennese citizens,[58] the estates had been pledged.

---

18 (Detroit, New York, San Francisco, et al.: Thomson Gale, 2007), 531.
54 Austrian State Archives Vienna, Haus-, Hof- und Staatsarchiv, AUR Uk. 1354 XI 4.
55 Brugger and Wiedl, "Christlich-jüdische Interaktion," 285.
56 See the survey by Eveline Brugger, "'Do musten da hin zue den iuden varn' – die Rolle(n) jüdischer Geldgeber im spätmittelalterlichen Österreich," *Ein Thema – zwei Perspektiven*, 122–38; for in-depth studies for Lower Austria and Carinthia, see Brugger, *Adel und Juden*, and Wadl, *Juden Kärnten*, 193–225, respectively.
57 Brugger and Wiedl, "Christlich-jüdische Interaktion," 292.
58 Apart from the aforementioned broad variety of other occupations Jews pursued, it is of great importance to stress that money-lending was at no time exclusively a 'Jewish trade'; see with respect to Jews the newest summary by Michael Toch, "Economic Activities of German Jews in the Middle Ages," *Wirtschaftsgeschichte der mittelalterlichen Juden*, 181–210; here 184–87 and 194–95; generally Joseph Shatzmiller, *Shylock Reconsidered. Jews, Moneylending, and Medieval Society* (Berkeley and Los Angeles: University of California Press, 1990); for a comparison of the different

Even more so, Teka did not only act as a host but was named as the intermediary of the entire transaction (*quo mediante et procurante hoc omnia facta sunt*).[59] Although Teka is to be considered a rather exceptional figure with close connections to the Hungarian king and the Austrian duke[60], quite casual references to Jews owning houses or plots of land are not exceptional, and often merely given to identify another—Christian-owned— house.[61]

However, it would most definitely be short-sighted to dismiss those business contracts as yielding merely information on matters of economy;[62] as objects of

---

forms of credit, see Hans-Jörg Gilomen, "Die ökonomischen Grundlagen des Kredits und die christlich-jüdische Konkurrenz im Spätmittelalter," *Ein Thema – zwei Perspektiven*, 139–69; further id., "Wucher und Wirtschaft im Mittelalter," *Historische Zeitschrift* 250 (1990): 265–301; id., "Kooperation und Konfrontation," 216–22, with statistics on Jewish and Lombard credits in fifteenth-century Zurich. As early as the thirteenth century, Lombards and Cahorsins appear in the Austrian region; Duke Rudolf IV bestowed himself with the right to "hold Jews and Cahorsins" (*tenere judeos et usurarios publicos, quos vulgus vocat gawertschin*) in the forged Privilegium Maius of around 1358. Particularly in the south of Austria, the Carinthian dukes and the nobility resorted to business companies from the Veneto-Friulanian area that included both Jews and Christians; see now the two articles by Wenninger, "Jüdische und jüdisch-christliche Netzwerke," and Gerd Mentgen, "Netzwerkbeziehungen bedeutender Cividaler Juden in der ersten Hälfte des 14. Jahrhunderts," *Beziehungsnetze aschkenasischer Juden*, 163–76 and 197–246 respectively, with further literature. See also Gerd Mentgen, *Studien zur Geschichte der Juden im mittelalterlichen Elsaß*. Forschungen zur Geschichte der Juden, Abteilung A, Abhandlungen, 2 (Hanover: Hahnsche Buchhandlung, 1995), 574–789, on the 'Jewish' Alsace vs. the 'Lombard' Lorraine as far as money-lending is concerned, with further literature. However, Christian participation in all kinds of money-based business is not reduced to these specific groups. Apart from (rather rare) open money-lending and pawn-broking, which was severely criticised by the contemporaries, Christians usually engaged themselves in more 'clandestine' transactions, like masking the pawning of a pledge, usually a plot of land, as selling and subsequently re-purchasing it after a predetermined time span, where only the final total was stated in the documents, usually already including the interest to be paid at the end; for Austrian examples, see Brugger, "Ansiedlung," 157.

59 Brugger and Wiedl, *Regesten*, vol. 1, 24–25, no. 11.

60 Probably the best example for this is the peace treaty of 1225 between King Andrew II and Duke Leopold VI, where Teka stands bail for the Austrian duke; a few years later, he is the *comes camere* (tax farmer) of the Hungarian king (Brugger and Wiedl, *Regesten*, vol. 1, 20–21, no. 7, 23, no. 10, with further literature).

61 From the vast amount of charters, see the arbitrament that settled a dispute between citizens of the Lower Austrian town of Klosterneuburg over several vineyards and houses, one of which was located *an dem nidern marcht ze nachst Steuzzen haus dez juden* ("at the lower market, next to the house of [David] Steuss the Jew," Archives of the Monastery of Klosterneuburg, Uk. 1364 X 31, facsimile online at: http://www.monasterium.net, sub archivio; last accessed on April 8, 2009).

62 On the broad variety of using charters as sources, see Paul Herold, "Schrift als Möglichkeit – Möglichkeiten von Schrift. Genese, Wirkungsweise und Verwendung von Schrift am Beispiel österreichischer Privaturkunden des 12. und 13. Jahrhunderts," *Text als Realie*, ed. Karl Brunner and Gerhard Jaritz. Veröffentlichungen des Instituts für Realienkunde des Mittelalters und der Frühen Neuzeit, 18. Österreichische Akademie der Wissenschaften. Philosophisch-historische Klasse, Sitzungsberichte, 704 (Vienna: Verlag der Österreichischen Akademie der Wissenschaften,

daily life, they give as much clear evidence of the mutual impact of the overlapping living spaces of Jews and Christians as any building, piece of cloth, or object of art. In everyday transactions, Jewish businessmen adjusted to the needs of their Christian clientele: documents they issued for their Christian partners were not only in either German[63] or (very rarely) in Latin,[64] they differ in no point to those issued by Christians—the formula commonly used by Christians is adopted word-for-word. Crucial dates like the due date of the debt or the date of issuance are rendered in the same way as in Christian charters, by usage of commonly known days of saints or feasts. As much as this is due to the fact that the Christian business partner had to understand the document as well, this also provides evidence of a firm knowledge (and usage) of the Christian calendar and certain 'key days' like the ever-popular pay days of St. Michael (September 29), St. Martin (November 11), and St. George (April 23/24).

Following the standard formulae, however, was not limited to documents issued by Jews for Christians; in the (rare) charters in Hebrew[65], which were either, in the majority of cases, issued as an additional confirmation of the transaction dealt with in the German one (see Figure 6)[66] or kept by the Jewish business partner, most of the common phrases (e.g., "of our own accord and with the approval of our heirs," the *Schadlosformel* that protects the business partner should a third party raise claims) were literally translated into Hebrew. In contrast, all the dates are stated according to the Jewish calendar, and the corroboration is exclusively given by signature. Quite telling is the only modification to one of the standard formulae—whereas the Christian version reads "all who see this letter or hear it being read" (*allen die diesen brief sehen oder hören lesen*), the Hebrew version is adapted as merely "all who see this letter," proceeding on the assumption that any Jew who sees the letter will be able to read it as well on his own.[67]

---

2003), 135–52.

[63] The question whether medieval Ashkenazic Jews spoke Middle High German or Old Yiddish, or regional dialects, has been a topic of academic literature since the nineteenth century, albeit with a clear focus on literary texts. The still ongoing discussion has been summed up and analyzed lately by Edith Wenzel, "Alt-Jiddisch oder Mittelhochdeutsch?" *Grenzen und Grenzüberschreitungen*, 31–50, with an extensive bibliography in the footnotes.

[64] The eldest Latin charter in the Austrian region is also the eldest one issued by a Jew altogether in this region: February 18, 1257, the two brothers Lublin and Nekelo, *comites camere* (tax farmers) of the Austrian duke and later Bohemian king Otakar Přemysl II, settled a dispute with Bishop Conrad I of Freising, which they corroborated with their shared (and, unfortunately, missing) seal, see Brugger and Wiedl, *Regesten*, vol. 1, 50–51, no. 38, with further literature.

[65] Brugger and Wiedl, "Christlich-jüdische Interaktion," 305, fig. 2.

[66] These Hebrew charters were often stitched, glued, or somehow else attached to the German document they correspond to (which was partially done centuries later); see the example from the monastery of Kremsmünster from 1305, Figure 6.

[67] See, e.g., the two eldest Hebrew charters from the Austrian region, both of them issued by the four

Jews do appear in other functions as well: should the need arise, they act as arbitrators together with Christians,[68] they corroborate Christian charters as witnesses even if they (or any Jews at all) are not involved in the transaction documented in the charter.[69] Jewish appearance as witnesses declines perceptibly from the last quarter of the thirteenth century onward, which precedes the general decrease in the usage of witnesses in favour of seals as the (almost) only means of authentication by only a few decades. Wealthy and prominent Jews, however, did adapt this custom, this 'new fashion article,'[70] and started using seals, albeit only for charters issued for Christian business partners.[71]

The common way of corroboration among Jews remained the aforementioned Hebrew signature that was used on both Hebrew and German documents,[72] partly announced with the same formula that would be used for announcing a seal: with the forumla *und umb taz pesser sicherhait bestett ich die obergeschrift mit meiner judischen hantgeschrift unden darunder* ("as an additional corroboration [as an additional insurance] I hereby confirm the above-written [text] with my Jewish

---

brothers Mosche, Mordechai, Isak and Pessach, sons of Schwärzlein/Asriel, and corroborated by their signatures and those of the Rabbis Chaim and Abraham, Brugger and Wiedl, *Regesten*, vol. 1, 119, no. 124 (April 29, 1305, see Figure 6), 167–68, no. 165 ([1309]), Hebrew and German translation.

68  E.g., the ducal cellarer Konrad von Kyburg and the Jew Marusch, who decided a dispute between the monastery of Heiligenkreuz and the Jew Mordechai over the postponed payment of duties (Brugger and Wiedl, *Regesten*, vol. 1, 203–04, no. 219).

69  E.g., the Jew Bibas who testified in a deed of suretyship which the (rather high-ranking) nobleman Albero von Kuenring and the citizens of the towns of Krems, Stein, and Linz issued for two other noblemen in 1247, assuring them of their standing surety. Bibas is listed as the last of the altogether 21 witnesses from Krems (Brugger and Wiedl, *Regesten*, vol. 1, 39, no. 28); a further example is the Jew Smoiel who acts as a witness in a sale charter of canon Irnfried of Passau in 1270 (Brugger and Wiedl, *Regesten*, vol. 1, 66–67, no. 49).

70  Heinrich Fichtenau, *Das Urkundenwesen in Österreich vom 8. bis zum frühen 13. Jahrhundert*. Mitteilungen des Instituts für Österreichische Geschichtsforschung, Ergänzungsband, 23 (Vienna and Graz: Böhlau, 1971), 238.

71  The eldest still existing Jewish seal in the German-speaking realm is the seal of Peter bar Mosche haLevi from Regensburg, attached to a charter issued by his sons Hatchim and Jacob in 1297 for Archbishop Conrad IV of Salzburg. It shows a cornuted hat with a bird on top, flanked by a crescent and a eight-pointed star, see Keil, Martha: "Ein Regensburger Judensiegel des 13. Jahrhunderts. Zur Interpretation des Siegels des Peter bar Mosche haLewi," *Aschkenas: Zeitschrift für Geschichte und Kultur der Juden* 1 (1991): 135–50; Brugger and Wiedl, *Regesten*, vol. 1, 97, no. 93; on seals of Austrian Jews in general, see Brugger, "Ansiedlung," 123–228. See also Daniel M. Friedenberg, *Medieval Jewish Seals from Europe* (Detroit: Wayne State University Press, 1987), unfortunately with serious mistakes and misunderstandings.

72  Keil, "Judensiegel," 135–36; eadem, "'Petachja, genannt Zecherl': Namen und Beinamen von Juden im deutschen Sprachraum des Spätmittelalters," *Personennamen und Identität. Namengebung und Namengebrauch als Anzeiger individueller Bestimmung und gruppenbezogener Zuordnung*, ed. Reinhard Härtel. Grazer Grundwissenschaftliche Forschungen, 3. Schriftenreihe der Akademie Friesach, 2 (Graz: Akademische Druck- und Verlagsanstalt, 1997), 119–46; here 138–41.

handwriting") the Jew Mosche from Herzogenburg announced his signature (*Mosche ben haKadosch Rabbi Izchak s.k.l.*, "Mosche, son of the martyr Rabbi Izchak, the memory of the martyr may be honored"), using the same 'keywords' of *pesser sicherheit* a Christian would herald their seal with.[73] Additional confirmatory signatures, often those of Rabbis, were introduced using of a wording similar to that Christians would introduce additional corroborators with.[74]

Town-dwelling Jews without a seal of their own often turned toward the particular Christian who at that time occupied the office of what was known as *iudex iudeorum*, an office quite unique to the eastern parts of modern-day Austria,[75] to witness and seal their documents.[76] Introduced in Duke Frederic II's 1244 privilege for the Austrian Jews and usually held by a member of a high-ranking family of the town, the principal duty of the *iudex iudeorum* was the settling of disputes between Jews and Christians;[77] furthermore, he had limited rights of control over the selling of unredeemed pledges and was entitled to a number of fines from both Jews and Christians, thus, participating at least marginally in the revenues of the ducal protection of the Jews. Despite the strong ties to the ruler which the *iudex iudeorum* could enjoy,[78] the towns were generally interested in

---

[73] Keil, "Namen und Beinamen," 138, sales deed from May 10, 1445.

[74] Brugger and Wiedl, "Christlich-jüdische Interaktion," 294–95.

[75] The first *iudex iudeorum* is mentioned in the lower Austrian town in 1264 of Krems (Brugger and Wiedl, *Regesten*, vol. 1, 56–57, no. 42.). It was to become a rather common office in both Austria and Styria, partly also in the Styrian and Carinthian enclaves of Salzburg, but was never introduced into other parts of the Holy Roman Empire save Bohemia and Moravia, where the 1244 privilege was introduced by King Přemysl Otakar II. For the few appearances outside these territories see *Germania Judaica*, vol. III/3, 2190.

[76] Having someone else seal a document was a common practise among Jews and Christians alike; if the issuer had no seal of their own, they asked for someone else to corroborate the charter with their seals (*Siegelbitte*), which was noted down separately in a particular formula together with the announcement of the seals. For the *iudex iudeorum* as corroborator for Jews, see also Keil, "Namen und Beinamen," 138.

[77] Little is known about the organization that is referred to as *Judengericht* (despite the literal translation "Jewish court" it is not to be confused with the internal court of the Jewish community, see Keil, "Gemeinde und Kultur," 40–41, 60–72). Its existence is first documented for the city of Vienna in 1361 (Lohrmann, *Wiener Juden*, 47; Brugger, "Ansiedlung," 150). In the course of a general court reform, Duke Rudolf IV decreed the continued existence of the Viennese *Judengericht*, yet specified neither its constitution nor its competence in detail. Presided over by the *iudex iudeorum*, its assessors consisted of delegates from the city and the Jewish community in equal representation. Its range of jurisdictional competence, however, can not be inferred from its only mention for Vienna or from the Styrian references of the fifteenth century (see Brugger, "Ansiedlung," 150), although it is very likely that the extent of empowerment mainly encompassed conflicts between Jews and Christians.

[78] E.g., all of the *iudicis iudeorum* of today's Upper Austria's capital of Linz were also caretakers of the castle of Linz, the residence of the ducal steward (Lohrmann, *Judenrecht*, 159). None of the legal documents refer to how the *iudex iudeorum* was to be appointed/elected; thus, an appointment by the ruler is at least possible, if not likely (at least as far as less influential towns are concerned).

strengthening his position as well as expanding his competences, gradually transforming the office into an at least partly municipal one.

With the growing claim of the towns on a more comprehensive jurisdictional and economic control of 'their' Jews, which, unsurprisingly, started shortly after the wide-ranging persecutions of 1338, the offices of the town judge and the *iudex iudeorum* were utilized to supervise the business activities of the Jews to a greater extent. Jews were obliged to produce their debt instruments to the town judge annually[79] or even thrice a year,[80] whereas pledges had to be presented to the *iudex iudeorum* on a regular, sometimes even weekly basis;[81] in some Styrian towns, the municipal control was expanded further by demanding that any debt instrument was to be sealed not by either but by both the town judge and the *iudex iudeorum*.[82] In the second half of the fourteenth century, cities tried to get organized when it came to keeping an eye on the Jews and their business transactions.

The increasing decline of the ducal protection offered considerable leeway for the towns to shift competences to their favor, allowing them to tighten their grip on the Jews perceptibly. Their aim of controlling and monitoring loans and pledges no longer merely encompassed the aforementioned producing, and certifying, of business documents but was extended to the many transactions concerning smaller amounts, most of which had heretoforth not been documented in writing at all. To establish this control, many towns set up what is known as *Judenbücher* ("codices for the Jews").[83] Sometimes included in the general *Satzbuch* of the respective town[84] and usually administered by the *iudex iudeorum*, the

---

[79] E.g., 1376 in the town charter of the Salzburg town of Ptuj, today in Slovenia, see Scherer, *Rechtsverhältnisse*, 549–50, Wadl, *Juden Kärnten*, 176–77.

[80] E.g., in the town charter of the Lower Austrian town of St. Pölten from 1338, granted by the Bishop of Passau who was the lord of the town; see Brugger and Wiedl, *Regesten*, vol. 1, 341, no. 444.

[81] Ptuj: Inanimate pledges (*Schreinpfand*, as opposed to *essendes Pfand*, "eating pledge," i.e., livestock) had to be presented to the *iudex iudeorum* every Thursday, Lohrmann, *Judenrecht*, 160; *Germania Judaica*, vol. III/2, 1100.

[82] Meir Wiener, *Regesten zur Geschichte der Juden in Deutschland während des Mittelalters*, vol. 1 (Hanover: Hahn'sche Hofbuchhandlung 1862), 236, no. 144 (Graz, Leoben); Lohrmann, *Judenrecht*, 160, incorrectly applies this regulation to the majority of Styrian towns.

[83] The setting up of *Judenbücher* was not exclusive to the cities —rulers as well as noble families and in the fifteenth century, also the Estates of Styria and Carinthia tried to keep track of their debts by establishing *Judenbücher* (Brugger, "Ansiedlung," 161–62). In some cases, it was the ruler who committed the town to set up a *Judenbuch* (e.g., Duke Albrecht III, who obliged the Lower Austrian town of Bruck a. d. Leitha to set up a *Judenbuch*, see Lohrmann, *Judenrecht*, 158). Most of the *Judenbücher* were lost during the persecutions of 1420/1421 that ended Jewish settlement in Lower Austria. As far as the general scholarly discussion on Judenbücher is concerned; for a recent discussion see Thomas Peter, "Judenbücher als Quellengattung und die Znaimer Judenbücher. Typologie und Forschungsstand," *Räume und Wege*, 307–34.

[84] The best documented examples within Austria are the "Judenbuch der Scheffstrasse" and the *Liber*

*Judenbuch* was the place where all the business transactions conducted by and with Jews had to be registered in (which also provided some protection for the Jews since the entry rendered it impossible for debtors to claim that the bonds the Jews presented were forgeries).

With the tightening grip of the cities on their Jews, the demand for them to partake in civic duties grew,[85] whilst in return, many German cities had taken to granting (partial) citizenships to Jews;[86] a right that had, for the most part, been transferred to them by the lord of the town.[87] In the territory of modern-day Austrian territory, both the dominating position of the ruler(s) and the lack of really powerful, important cities is most likely the reason for non-existing Jewish citizenship, the granting of settlement remaining exclusively in the hands of the rulers.[88] Information on Austrian Jews participating in urban duties is therefore

*Judeorum* of Wiener Neustadt. The Scheffstrasse, a small community right outside the Vienna city walls that was subject to the duchess of Austria, had its own register, kept by both ducal officers and representatives of the city of Vienna, which was a cadastral register as well as a book of loans. Whereas the second part was dedicated to loans among Christians, the third part is the "Judenbuch," entries of loans granted by Jews (Viennese as well as Lower Austrian and Bohemian Jews) to inhabitants of the Scheffstrasse. Since the majority of the inhabitants were small-scale craftsmen, most of the sums (a considerable number of which were granted by Jewesses) were rather small. Artur Goldmann, *Das Judenbuch der Scheffstrasse zu Wien (1389–1420)*. Quellen und Forschungen zur Geschichte der Juden in Deutsch-Österreich, 1 (Vienna and Leipzig: Wilhelm Braumüller, 1908). An older Judenbuch of the city of Vienna has been lost; see Artur Goldmann, "Das verschollene Wiener Judenbuch (1372–1420)," *Quellen und Forschungen zur Geschichte der Juden in Österreich*, 11: *Nachträge* (Vienna: Selbstverlag der Historischen Kommission, 1936), 1–14. For Wiener Neustadt, see Martha Keil, "Der Liber Judeorum von Wiener Neustadt 1453–1500. Edition," *Studien zur Geschichte der Juden in Österreich*, ed. eadem and Klaus Lohrmann (Vienna, Cologne, and Weimar: Böhlau, 1994), 41–99.

85   Wenninger, "Von jüdischen Rittern," 54–67, on Jews partaking in the military duties within a city.
86   Alfred Haverkamp, "'Concivilitas' von Christen und Juden in Aschkenas im Mittelalter," *Gemeinden, Gemeinschaften und Kommunikationsformen im hohen und späten Mittelalter*, ed. Friedhelm Burgard, Lukas Clemens and Michael Matheus (Trier: Kliomedia, 2002), 315–44 (rpt. of the article first published in *Jüdische Gemeinden und Organisationsformen von der Antike bis zur Gegenwart*, ed. Robert Jütte and Abraham P. Kustermann. *Aschkenas: Zeitschrift für Geschichte und Kultur der Juden*, Beiheft 3 [Vienna, Cologne, and Weimar: Böhlau, 1996]: 103–36); *Germania Judaica*, vol. III/3, 2181–87; Barbara Türke, "Anmerkungen zum Bürgerbegriff im Mittelalter: Das Beispiel christlicher und jüdischer Bürger der Reichsstadt Nördlingen im 15. Jahrhundert," *Inklusion/Exklusion: Studien zur Fremdheit und Armut von der Antike bis zur Gegenwart*, ed. Andreas Gestrich and Raphael Lutz. Second edition (2004; Frankfurt a. M. and Vienna: Peter Lang, 2008), 135–54; more generally, see Hans-Jörg Gilomen, "Städtische Sondergruppen im Bürgerrecht," *Neubürger im späten Mittelalter: Migration und Austausch in der Städtelandschaft des alten Reiches (1250–1550)*, ed. Rainer Christoph Schwinges. Zeitschrift für historische Forschung. Beiheft, 30 (Berlin: Duncker & Humblot, 2002), 125–67.
87   There are very few examples of cities (Worms, Prague) where this right to grant citizenship to Jews was independent from the concession of the ruler; see *Germania Judaica*, vol. III/3, 2169, 2181–82.
88   Klaus Lohrmann, "Bemerkungen zum Problem 'Jude und Bürger'," *Juden in der Stadt*, 145–66; here

scarce. Since the Jews were generally subjected to taxation to no one but the ruler, the towns strove either to charge additional taxes or at least partially to incorporate the Jews into the tax revenue of the town.[89] The earliest documented example in Austria, however, is remarkable in two respects: in 1277, King Rudolph I not only confirmed but also expanded the rights of the (small) town of Laa/Thaya (Lower Austria), amongst which he added the right to exclude 'their' Jews from the general Jewish tax and to include them into the citizens' tax revenue,[90] thus documenting not only the first exception to the general tax the Jews were paying directly into the treasury but the first mention of the 'Jewish tax' on Austrian territory at all.[91]

For more than a century, however, the rulers' claim to taxing the Jews remained widely unchallenged; only the late fourteenth century saw Austrian dukes yield to the pressure of both towns and the rising estates. In 1396, a large number of Styrian towns were allowed by the Dukes Albrecht IV and William to coerce the Jews owning houses and/or plots of land within the realm of the town either to sell these premises within a year or to participate henceforward in the tax revenue of the town.[92] The references to Jews partaking in other civic duties like the city

---

161–64. There is but one exception: the small town of Feldkirch in the utmost west of today's Austria which was under the rule of a local and not overly powerful noble family. Unlike in Austria, Jewish citizenship was fairly common especially in the area around Lake Constance, to which Feldkirch belonged both politically and culturally; see Karl Heinz Burmeister, *medinat bodase. Zur Geschichte der Juden am Bodensee*, vol. 1: *1200–1349* (CKonstancez: Universitätsverlag Konstanz, 1994), 40–42. However, Jewish citizens are only mentioned 'in theory' in the town charter of Feldkirch from the mid-fourteenth century, and no individuals possessing the status of citizens are known; Gerda Leipold-Schneider, "as mittelalterliche Stadtrecht von Feldkirch: Überlieferung und Edition," Ph.D. dissertation, University of Innsbruck, 2001, 236. See also Brugger, "Ansiedlung," 204.

[89] On the many 'stages' and compromises of taxation of Jews by cities, see *Germania Judaica*, vol. III/3, 2263–67.

[90] Brugger and Wiedl, *Regesten*, vol. 1, 74, no. 57. See also Lohrmann, *Judenrecht*, 113–14.

[91] Rudolph I was acting as King of the Romans and not as the duke of Austria (which he never was), preparing, however, the grounds for his sons to take over the duchy and thus trying to coax the—however small—towns into siding with him. Old, but still a work of reference is Thomas Michael Martin, *Die Städtepolitik Rudolfs von Habsburg*. Veröffentlichungen des Max-Planck-Instituts für Geschichte, 44 (Göttingen: Vandenhoeck & Ruprecht, 1976), with particular respect to this charter 75–78.

[92] Scherer, *Rechtsverhältnisse*, 403. There is a rather similar regulation noted down in the then Hungarian town of Eisenstadt; it is questionable though whether this town charter, which mentions the taxes of Jews living in- and outside the city walls, is authentic; see Harald Prickler, "Beiträge zur Geschichte der burgenländischen Judensiedlungen," *Juden im Grenzraum: Geschichte, Kultur und Lebenswelt der Juden im burgenländisch-westungarischen Raum und in den angrenzenden Regionen vom Mittelalter bis zur Gegenwart*, ed. Rudolf Kropf. Wissenschaftliche Arbeiten aus dem Burgenland, 92 (Eisenstadt: Burgenländisches Landesmuseum, 1993), 65–106; here 68–69.

watch, of which there is evidence in other regions,[93] are even rarer; there is but one example of the nowadays Italian town of Gorizia where in 1307, Jews and Christians alike were committed to watch duties.[94]

Faced with similar challenges, Jews and Christians often arrived at quite similar solutions. The organization of the Jewish community (*kehilla*) is in its main features rather uniform;[95] yet, it bears astonishing analogies to Christian organizations, particularly to those of craft guilds.[96] The contemporaries were not oblivious to this fact: in the Austrian region,[97] the Jewish community is quite commonly called *Judenzeche*, "Jewish guild," whereas their *parnass*, the head of the Jewish community, was referred to as *Zechmeister der Juden*, "guild master of the Jews."[98] The term was partly used as self-denomination by the Jews as well,[99] whereas the scribe of the Viennese *Eisenbuch*[100] translated the Hebrew expression into *sammung*, a word regularly used to describe conventual communities.[101] As diverging as the

---

[93]   Wenninger, "Von jüdischen Rittern," 54–67, who gives numerous examples from the late thirteenth century onwards. See also *Germania Judaica*, vol. III/3, 2181–82; Toch, *Juden im mittelalterlichen Reich*, 51–54; Magin, "'Waffenrecht'," 23–24; Haverkamp, "Concivilitas," 125–128; from a 'rabbinical perspective' Israel Jacob Yuval, "Das Thema Waffen aus der rabbinischen Perspektive," *Grenzen und Grenzüberschreitungen*, 13–16; here 15 (Jews participating in the defense of the city of Worms in 1201).

[94]   Brugger and Wiedl, *Regesten*, vol. 1, 160, no. 153. For Swiss examples, see Gilomen, "Kooperation und Konfrontation," 168–70, who discusses the question of Jews actually partaking in watch duties or merely paying their share in the charges and gives examples for both.

[95]   For a latest summary on the Jewish communities and their form of organization, see *Germania Judaica*, vol. III/3, 2080–2138; Yacov Guggenheim, "Jewish Community and Territorial Organization in Medieval Europe," *Jews of Europe*, 71–92, on the striking similarities of Jewish communities throughout medieval Europe 72–73, and with further literature.

[96]   See the two corresponding articles: Rainer Barzen, "'So haben wir verhängt und beschlossen ...' Takkanot im mittelalterlichen Aschkenas," 218–33, and Birgit Wiedl, "'Confraternitas eorum quod in vulgari dicitur zhunft': Wirtschaftliche, religiöse und soziale Aspekte von Handwerkszünften im Spiegel ihrer Ordnungen," 234–52 (both in *Ein Thema – zwei Perspektiven*).

[97]   *Germania Judaica*, vol. III/3, 2080, with the emphasis on this being an Austrian particularity.

[98]   E.g., in Krems: *zecha iudeorum* in a municipal rental from between 1350 and 1370, Leopold Moses, "Aus dem Kremser Stadtarchiv," *Jüdisches Archiv* Neue Folge 1, 3–4 (1928), 3–8; here 5; for further references, see *Germania Judaica*, vol. III/1, 678 (Krems), 1598 (Vienna), 1621 (Wiener Neustadt). See also Keil, "Gemeinde und Kultur," 39.

[99]   E.g., in the Sefer Terumat haDeschen (a collection of legal opinions) of the rabbi Israel Isserlein of the (then) Styrian town of Wiener Neustadt (ed. Shemuel Abitan, Jerusalem 1991), who uses the term quite frequently, see *Germania Judaica*, vol. III/2, 1621.

[100]  A collection of rights and liberties of the city of Vienna, kept from 1320 to 1819; see Ferdinand Opll, *Das große Wiener Stadtbuch, genannt "Eisenbuch." Inhaltliche Erschließung*. Veröffentlichungen des Wiener Stadt- und Landesarchivs. Reihe A: Archivinventar, Serie 3, Heft 4 (Vienna: Eigenverlag des Wiener Stadt- und Landesarchivs, 1999).

[101]  Brugger and Wiedl, *Regesten*, vol. 1, 33–338, nrr. 439 (Hebrew) and 440 (German), the Jewish community reducing their interest rate in 1338. The scribe who copied the Hebrew text into the Eisenbuch also provided a German translation, where he used the abovementioned expression. A depiction of the page can be found here:

'basic prerequisites' may have been, the similarities both in the general composition of the community as well as many details are striking: by demand of mandatory membership, the organization could not only offer extensive protection for, but also wield wide-ranging authority over the members, whilst the ban from the community, which posed a genuine threat to insubordinate members, was utilized to exert control. Social concerns like the care for widows, orphans and impoverished members were dealt with by, and through, the community by the institution of *Tzedakah* and the guilds' welfare system respectively, both of which were financed by regular contributions;[102] members who somehow offended against rules were put on trial at the internal court; premises of religious as well as secular denomination were owned in common; and generally, a code of conduct regulated (at least theoretically) many areas of life both public and private. Feasts that were celebrated together played an important role in creating a sense of identity, an identity that in fact went far beyond the local scope—itinerant craftsmen arriving in the town were taken care of by the guild which provided them with shelter, food and sometimes money, the same way as foreign Jewish students and/or paupers were looked after by the *kehilla*.[103]

Jews were participating in everyday activities at the cities' market(s), thus entering and sharing both social and economic space with their Christian neighbors.[104] Areas like markets, however, also provided convenient opportunities for exclusion and (physical) division. While thirteenth century towns were busy banning Jews from holding public offices[105], they generally strove to gain control

---

http://www.wien.gv.at/kultur/archiv/geschichte/zimelien/images/juden.jpg (last accessed on April 8, 2009).

[102]  For a summary of the academic discussion, see Rainer Barzen, "'Was der Arme benötigt, bis Du verpflichtet zu geben:' Forschungsansätze zur Armenfürsorge in Aschkenas im hohen und späten Mittelalter," *Wirtschaftsgeschichte der mittelalterlichen Juden*, 139–52; particularly 142–48.

[103]  On the similarities, see Birgit Wiedl, "Eine zünftige Gemeinde: Handwerkszünfte und jüdische Gemeindeorganisation im Vergleich," *Nicht in einem Bett*, 44–49, downloadable as pdf here: http://www.injoest.ac.at/upload/JudeninME05_4_43-49(1).pdf.

[104]  On the importance of markets as 'crucial elements of the medieval city,' the aspect of gender, and how market space can be utilized for in- and exclusion see the article by Shennan Hutton in this volume.

[105]  The prohibition goes back to canon 69 of the Fourth Lateran Council which in turn referred to canon 14 of the Third *Concilium Toletanum* of 589. It is, however, the only regulation from the Lateran IV that had made its way into secular legislation. From the vast literature on the topic, see Heinz Schreckenberg, *Die christlichen Adversus-Judaeos-Texte (11.-13. Jahrhundert): Mit einer Ikonographie des Judenthemas bis zum 4. Laterankonzil*. Europäische Hochschulschriften. Second edition. Reihe XXIII: Theologie, 335 (1988; Frankfurt a. M., Bern, New York, and Paris: Peter Lang, 1991), 425–26. Emperor Frederick II included this paragraph in the privilege he granted the city of Vienna in 1238 (for the latest edition, see Brugger and Wiedl, *Regesten*, vol. 1, 28–29, no. 17, with additional editions and literature). The ban was reconfirmed for Vienna in 1247 (by Emperor Frederick II) and 1278 (by King Rudolf I) and was also included in the privilege for the Styrian

over the legal status and to restrict, or at least monitor, the economic activities of
'their' Jews during the late thirteenth and fourteenth centuries[106]. Neither Jewish
landownership nor Jews being involved in wine-growing and -trade[107] were
uncommon, yet the range of professions the Jews could make a living with within
the towns' realms was being more and more limited. With the craft guilds gaining
importance, regulations that excluded Jews from specific professions[108] on behalf
of the respective guild appeared in town charters as well as guild articles. In
Austria, the Jews of one of the biggest and most important Jewish communities on
Habsburg territory, Wiener Neustadt, were prohibited the trading and selling of
cloth, presumably at the request of the guild;[109] but it was mainly professions
concerned with food that were blacklisted. For instance, professions such as the
brewing of beer (St. Veit, Carinthia)[110] or the trading as well as serving of wine at
a (local) bar (Ptuj, Lower Styria, Slovenia)[111] was not permitted to Jews, yet overall,
the butchering and selling of meat turned out to be the most disputed issue.

town of Wiener Neustadt, which allegedly predates the Viennese charter but is in fact a forgery
from the last third of the thirteenth century (Brugger and Wiedl, *Regesten*, vol. 1, 40, no. 29, 76, no.
60, 22–23, no. 9). For the whole complex of the Wiener Neustädter forgeries, see Peter Csendes,
"Die Wiener Neustädter Stadtrechtsfälschungen," *Fälschungen im Mittelalter*, vol. 3: *Diplomatische
Fälschungen* (part 1). Monumenta Germaniae Historica Schriften, 33.3 (Hanover: Hahnsche Buch-
handlung, 1988), 637–52; for this charter 646–47); on the factual validity of forged charters, see
Thomas Hildbrand, "Sisyphus und die Urkunden: Mediävistische Überlegungen zur semiotischen
Arbeit," *Text als Realie*, 183–92; here 186.

[106]  Wiedl, "Codifying Jews."
[107]  Haym Soloveitchik, "*Halakhah*, Taboo and the Origin of Jewish Moneylending in Germany," *Jews
of Europe*, 305–17, who, despite the title, examines Jewish wine growing and trading as well as
viticultural credits; further Toch, "Economic Activities," 205–06. For Austrian Jews, see Martha
Keil, "'Veltliner, Ausstich, Tribuswinkler': Zum Weingenuss österreichischer Juden im
Mittelalter," '*Und wenn schon, dann Bischof oder Abt': Im Gedenken an Günther Hödl (1941–2005)*, ed.
Christian Domenig and others (Klagenfurt: Kärntner Druck- und Verlagsgesellschaft, 2006), 53–72,
Brugger and Wiedl, "Christlich-jüdische Interaktion," 302–03.
[108]  For Jews as craftsmen, see Michael Toch, "Jüdische Geldleihe im Mittelalter," *Geschichte und Kultur
der Juden in Bayern*, ed. Manfred Treml and Josef Kirmeier (Munich, New York, London, and Paris:
K. G. Saur, 1988), 85–94; here 85–86; id., "Geldleiher und sonst nichts? Zur wirtschaftlichen
Tätigkeit der Juden im deutschen Sprachraum des Spätmittelalters," *Tel Aviver Jahrbuch für
deutsche Geschichte* 22 (1993): 117–26; id., "Economic Activities," 187, 204–10; Mentgen, *Juden im
mittelalterlichen Elsaß*, 579–85; *Germania Judaica*, vol. III/3, 2139–46.
[109]  Wiener Neustadt 1316, Brugger and Wiedl, *Regesten*, vol. 1, 195–96, no. 205. It is not quite clear
whether the regulation refers to cloth trade or tailoring, or both.
[110]  1297/1308, Brugger and Wiedl, *Regesten*, vol. 1, 99, no. 96, § 13.
[111]  Ptuj/Pettau 1376. Ferdinand Bischoff, "Das Pettauer Stadtrecht von 1376," *Sitzungsberichte der
Akademie der Wissenschaften, philosophisch-historische Klasse* 113 (1886), 695–744. The article (§ 18),
however, refers only to the retail trade within the city; the Jews of Pettau were far-distance traders
on a big scale, especially with wine and goods from Venetia. Wenninger, "Juden Salzburg,"753.

The Christian mistrust toward 'Jewish meat' had been clearly expressed at the provincial synods of Wrocław and Vienna in 1267, where in very clear words, Christians were cautioned against buying any nourishments from Jews lest these, who allegedly regarded the Christians as their enemies, poison them with their food (*nec christiani carnes venales seu alia cibaria a iudeis emant, ne forte per hoc iudei christianos, quos hostes reputant, fraudulenta machinatione venenent*).[112] The later adaptions in several town charters, however, hardly ever referred straightforwardly to any threat posed to Christians should they buy, or consume, meat (or, come to that, any other goods) of "Jewish origin." The first attempt at excluding Jews at least partially from that branch of business appeared as early as 1267 (!), when the butchers' guild of the Lower Austrian town of Tulln put additional charges on the fatstock that was bought by Jews. Considering that the Jews were most likely butchering the animals themselves to guarantee kosher slaughter, the sum the Jews had to pay was presumably intended as a kind of fine for the loss of income the craftsmen suffered since they could not charge them for their slaughtering service.[113]

Up until the fifteenth century, the main problem however remained that the Jews were not only doing the slaughtering themselves,[114] but were also selling meat to Christians; and that by doing so they entered the domain of the crafts guilds. The Christian authorities, partially at the instigation of the craft guilds, partially of their own volition, dealt with the issue in different ways, most of which went along with, or were expressed by, a physical separation. The "simplest" solution, chosen by the Carinthian town of St. Veit in the late thirteenth century, was to ban Jews from selling their meat publicly altogether. The Jews of this town were only allowed to butcher and sell their meat at home; according to the town's regulations, they not only remained without a possibility to participate in the public meat marked but were also being denied the right to own livestock (most likely for breeding purpose, since they were allowed to slaughter at home) and refused their share in the borough's common.[115]

---

[112] Brugger and Wiedl, *Regesten*, vol. 1, 59–61 (quote 59), no. 45.
[113] Brugger and Wiedl, *Regesten*, vol. 1, 61, no. 46. English translation (incorrectly dated 1237): http://www.fordham.edu/halsall/source/1237butchers-tuln.html (last accessed on April 8, 2009). *Germania Judaica*, vol. I: *Von den ältesten Zeiten bis 1238*, ed. I. Elbogen, A. Freimann, and H. Tykocinski (Tübingen: J. C. B. Mohr, 1963), 388–89.
[114] Jews were, however, not the only group of people medieval butchers had to concede the right to carry out slaughter on their own. Butchering within certain limits (*zur hausnotdurft* [for personal needs at home]) was regarded as the right of the citizens in many towns, and particular institutions like inns or taverns sometimes even had their own slaughterhouse and employed journeymen of the butchers' guilds.
[115] Brugger and Wiedl, *Regesten*, vol. 1, 99, no. 96, § 13.

This complete ban of Jews from the public (economic) sphere of market activities remained rather unique among the regulations of the thirteenth to fifteenth centuries. Commonly, Jews were allowed to sell their meat at the public market via a specific stall that was either directly administered by the municipal government or at least under their strict control. That stall was usually remote from those of the Christian butchers and quite often located at the fringe of the market place.[116] In addition to that, some towns demanded that the meat be presented 'in an unobtrusive way': not, as at the butchers' guild's booths, hooked-up and dangling from the ceiling or a pole, but placed on a stool.[117] That their meat was to be sold solely at this particular type of stall may thus be interpreted as placing the Jews at a mere economic disadvantage, yet in many of the regulations, additional specifications aimed at a segregation of the Jews that went further beyond a mere economic measure.

The municipal stall was usually the place where *pfinnig fleisch* was to be sold,[118] which meant foul (trichinous) meat as well as meat from sick or injured animals.[119]

---

[116]    An den endten ("at the sides") and not at the regular butchers' stalls shall the *judenfleisch* ("Jewish meat") be sold, where it has been sold *von allter* ("since time immemorial"), states the regulation the town of Judenburg issued for their butcher's guild in 1467; Fritz Popelka, *Schriftdenkmäler des steirischen Gewerbes*, vol. 1 (Graz: Eigenverlag des Wirtschaftsförderungsinstitutes der Kammer der gewerblichen Wirtschaft für Steiermark, 1950), 137–37, no. 104; *Germania Judaica*, vol. III/1, 594.

[117]    Liberties of the city of Salzburg, 1420: *Item, das judenfleisch und pfinnigs sol man vor dem schlätorr vaill haben auf einen stull und niet auffhahen.* Adolf Altmann, *Geschichte der Juden in Stadt und Land Salzburg von den frühesten Zeiten bis auf die Gegenwart.* Rpt. of the 1913 ed. and continued until 1988 by Günter Fellner and Helga Embacher (Salzburg: Otto Müller Verlag, 1990), 100–01.

[118]    Salzburg 1420 (see above), but the regulation dates back to the early fourteenth century: it appears as early as 1307 in the town charter of the Bavarian town Burghausen (1307, Christian Haeutle, "Einige altbayerische Stadtrechte," *Oberbayerisches Archiv für vaterländische Geschichte* 45 [1888/1889]: 163–262; here 183) and was adopted, often with a quite similar wording, in the town charters of Neuötting (1321, id., "Einige altbayerische Stadtrechte: Fortsetzung und Schluß," *Oberbayerisches Archiv für vaterländische Geschichte* 47 [1891/1892]: 18–124; here 29), Landshut (1344, *Germania Judaica*, vol. II/1, 467–68), and Schärding (1316, today Upper Austria, Brugger and Wiedl, *Regesten*, vol. 1, 194, no. 202). The inclusion of the article in the town privilege of Schärding, however, is the only indication of a Jewish settlement in this (rather small) town at all; and since the wording of the article in the town charters is rather similar, it might have merely been copied, perhaps as a kind of 'preventive measure' against potential future Jewish inhabitants. Further, e.g., *Germania Judaica*, vol. II/2, 557 and *Germania Judaica*, vol. III/2, 902 (Munich), 1500 (Ulm), *Germania Judaica*, vol. II/2, 946 (Zurich); Gilomen, "Kooperation und Konfrontation," 177.

[119]    According to the liberties of the town of Mühldorf (before 1360), *pfinichs flaischs, wolfpaizzichs flaischs und swaz der jud ersucht* (foul meat, meat that 'has been bitten by the wolf' and meat 'which the Jew desires'), should be sold by the butchers, but in front of and not inside their booths. Karl Theodor Heigel (ed.), "Mühldorfer Annalen 1313–1428," *Die Chroniken der baierischen Städte Regensburg, Landshut, Mühldorf, München*, ed. Historische Kommission bei der Bayerischen Akademie der Wissenschaften. Second edition. Die Chroniken der deutschen Städte vom 14. bis ins 16. Jahrhundert, 15 (1878; Göttingen: Vandenhoeck & Ruprecht, 1967), 369–410; here 396; Hans-Georg Herrmann, "Das Mühldorfer Stadtrecht im Spätmittelalter und in der Frühen

The additional association of Jews with the "rotten" and "foul" is therefore quite obvious, a connotation that was stressed even more when the meat had to be clearly tagged and/or the potential Christian customer had to be alerted to the fact that they were about to buy either foul or "Jewish meat."[120] In late fourteenth/ early fifteenth centuries, the idea of the well-poisoning Jews prevailing, many towns resorted to more drastic and encompassing measures by declaring any meat that had merely been touched by Jews as being in the same category, therefore considering it being of a lesser quality, or even unfit for Christian consumption. This often concurs with, or is included in, regulations which aim at a comprehensive control of the behavior of Jews at the market: instead of touching the goods, Jews were to point at those items, particularly victuals, they intended to buy, and should they happen to touch an item, they had to purchase it, often with a surcharge.[121]

Jewish existence within the space of cities was, to conclude, a risky one at all times. Schlom, the master of the ducal mint and the first Austrian Jew known by name, fell prey together with his family to crusaders in 1196;[122] some 100 years later, the first blood libels and accusations of alleged host wafer desecrations were launched on Austrian territory, claiming their victims among the Jews of Lower Austrian towns. Yet as much as these horrendous incidents are indicative of the at best fragile balance between Jews and their Christian surroundings, details still hint at

---

[120] Neuzeit," *Mühldorf am Inn: Salzburg in Bayern 935–1802–2002*. Begleitband zur gleichnamigen Ausstellung vom 8. Juni bis 27. Oktober 2002 (Mühldorf am Inn: Eigenverlag der Stadt, 2002), 36–47; here 36; Altmann, *Juden Salzburg*, 67–69.

[121] Liberties of the town of Mühldorf: (. . . ) *swer daz flaisch von in chauft, ez sei gast oder purger, dem sol er ez sagen, wie ez umb daz flaisch ste, pei 72 den* (whoever buys the meat, be they visitor or citizen, he [the butcher who sells the meat] shall tell them about the condition of the meat, at a penalty of 72 pence), Heigel, "Mühldorfer Annalen," 396; The *judenfleisch* has been frequently interpreted as "kosher meat" in general, whereas the fact that it was sold at the market to Christians suggests that the term refers to the parts of the kosherly slaughtered animals the Jews were not allowed to eat and thus sold via the municipal stall (which, in fact, might have also heightened the Christian suspicion that the Jews were selling them meat of low quality). The bigger Jewish communities usually owned a slaughterhouse and employed their own kosher butcher, e.g. Vienna; see Lohrmann, *Wiener Juden*, 55, 100, and 102.

[122] Town liberties of Bolzano (late fourteenth century, see *Germania Judaica*, vol. II/1, 99; pertaining to all kinds of goods), adapted the butchers' regulation; town liberties of Munich (fish), order of the municipal council of Ulm (1421, livestock, fish, meat, poultry, fruits), see Scherer, *Rechtsverhältnisse*, 577–78, with analogies to French legislation; whereas the city of Passau took a different (and quite intriguing) stance by forbidding their butchers to work for them, Municipal Archives of Passau III/22 (*Gemainer Statt Passau Recht und Freiheiten sambt alten und neuen Verträgen*). The 1424 dating in *Germania Judaica*, vol. III/2, 1089, is questionable: the butchers' regulation originates from 1432, and the paragraph containing the aforementioned sentence is an undated yet clearly later addition.

Brugger and Wiedl, *Regesten*, vol. 1, 17–18, no. 4 (Hebrew and German translation).

a in parts functioning Jewish-Christian coexistence. Schlom had his thievish Christian servant imprisoned, and only the strident complaints of the servant's wife in the nearest church alerted the crusaders; and when the accusation of a host wafer desecration was launched in the small Lower Austrian town of Korneuburg in 1305, the Jew Zerklin sought refuge at his Christian neighbor's house, who took him in willingly and tried to protect him from the enraged citizens, albeit in vain.[123]

The first overall shift to the worse came with the persecutions that followed another alleged host wafer desecration. Starting from Pulkau in 1338, thus almost parallel to the catastrophic "Armleder" persecutions that heavily affected the Jewish communities in Southern Germany,[124] this soon became the first wave of persecutions that went beyond the local scope, affecting over 30 towns in Austria, Bohemia, and Moravia.[125] While in Zurich, Minna and her sons fell prey to the pogroms accompanying the Black Plague[126] during the fatal years of 1348–1350, Duke Albrecht II still managed to hold a protective hand over most of the Austrian Jewish communities; his coming down heavily on the town of Krems that had persecuted their Jews on account of an alleged well poisoning earning him the

---

[123]  The whole incident is uniquely documented: a transcript of the interrogation of altogether 21 witnesses by the Cistercian monk Ambrosius of Heiligenkreuz, who carried out the investigation at the order of the Bishop of Passau, is transmitted (Brugger and Wiedl, *Regesten*, vol. 1, 125–42, no. 133), and from a later source we know that the bloodied wafer had been faked by a priest (Brugger and Wiedl, *Regesten*, vol. 1, 339–40, no. 442). See Eveline Brugger, "Korneuburg 1305 – eine blutige Hostie und die Folgen," *Nicht in einem Bett*, 20–26, down-loadable here: http://www.injoest.ac.at/upload/JudeninME05_2_19-26.pdf (last accessed on April 8, 2009); Miri Rubin, *Gentile Tales: The Narrative Assault on Late Medieval Jews* (New Haven and London: Yale University Press, 1999), 57–65; Winfried Stelzer, "Am Beispiel Korneuburg: Der angebliche Hostienfrevel österreichischer Juden von 1305 und seine Quellen," *Österreich im Mittelalter: Bausteine zu einer revidierten Gesamtdarstellung*, ed. Willibald Rosner. Studien und Forschungen aus dem Niederösterreichischen Institut für Landeskunde, 26 (St. Pölten: Selbstverlag des Niederösterreichischen Institut für Landeskunde, 1999), 309–48, on this source, particularly 312–28; Fritz Peter Knapp, *Die Literatur des Spätmittelalters in den Ländern Österreich, Steiermark, Kärnten, Salzburg und Tirol von 1273 bis 1439. Geschichte der Literatur in Österreich von den Anfängen bis zur Gegenwart*, vol. 2, part 1 (Graz: Akademische Druck- und Verlagsanstalt, 1999), 106–07; Brugger, "Ansiedlung," 211–26, all with further literature.

[124]  From the vast literature, see Friedrich Lotter, "Hostienfrevelvorwurf und Blutwunderfälschung bei den Judenverfolgungen von 1298 ('Rintfleisch') und 1336–1338 ('Armleder')," *Fälschungen im Mittelalter*, vol. 5: *Fingierte Briefe. Frömmigkeit und Fälschung. Realienfälschungen*. Monumenta Germaniae Historica Schriften, vol. 33.5 (Hanover: Hahnsche Buchhandlung, 1988), 533–83; Jörg R. Müller, "Erez gezerah – Land of Persecution: Pogroms Against the Jews in the regnum Teutonicorum From c. 1280 to 1350," *Jews of Europe*, 245–60.

[125]  Brugger, "Ansiedlung," 216–19; Rubin, *Gentile Tales*, 66–67.

[126]  Keil, "Lebensstil und Repräsentation," chapter 2; Toch, "Selbstdarstellung," 181–82; Böhmer, "Bogenschütze," 330–34.

insulting ephitet of *fautor iudeorum*, "Patron of the Jews," from the Church.[127] The traditional stereotype of the 'Wucherjude,' the rapacious Jewish usurer, was repeated in and permeated by literature and iconography alike,[128] posing a deathly threat together with the ideas of Jewish well-poisoning, the blood libel accusations and alleged host wafer desecrations. Although there were fewer persecutions in the second half of the fourteenth century than had been in the first half, the political and economic interests of rulers, estates and municipalities alike led to a considerable worsening of the overall situation of the Jews in the Austrian territories during the last decades. The rulers', noblemen's, and cities' ideas of profiting from prospering Jewish communities had changed from squeezing as much money as possible out of them to not needing them any further at all,[129] while the ecclesiastical climate had shifted from being at least ambiguous to clearly—and outspokenly—anti-Jewish, further fostering those sentiments within both authority and the populace. From the devastating Viennese Geserah in 1420/1421 that ended Jewish life in the duchy of Austria to the expulsion of the Jews of Salzburg in 1498,[130] Jewish existence was violently brought to an end in the Austrian territories in the course of the fifteenth century.

In the beautiful illumination of an early fourteenth century Mahzor, a woman and a man during a wedding scene are depicted (see Figure 4). The man, clad in a cloak of an offish white and dark green garments, wears a cornuted hat, and his hand reaches out towards his presumptive bride. It is the figure of the bride that is unusual—not the garments in reversed colors, the cloak brimmed with fur, and the hint at a throne which she is sitting on, but the a crown on her head and the blindfold across her eyes come as a surprise. The connection with the Christian iconography is clear, the reference to the numerous statues and depictions of

---

[127]   Wilhelm Wattenbach, ed., "Kalendarium Zwetlense a. 1243–1458," *Monumenta Germaniae Historica Scriptores*, vol. 9, ed. Georg Heinrich Pertz (1851; Stuttgart: Anton Hiersemann, 1983), 689–98; here 692; Brugger, "Ansiedlung," 173, 219; *Germania Judaica*, vol. II/1, 454; Alfred Haverkamp, "Die Judenverfolgungen zur Zeit des Schwarzen Todes," *Zur Geschichte der Juden im Deutschland des späten Mittelalters und der frühen Neuzeit*, ed. Alfred Haverkamp. Monographien zur Geschichte des Mittelalters, 24 (Stuttgart: Anton Hiersemann, 1981), 27–93; here 40, 46–47, and 60; Lohrmann, *Judenrecht*, 144.

[128]   See the contribution by Albrecht Classen in this volume, on the example of Hans Sachs; further see Christoph Cluse, "Zum Zusammenhang von Wuchervorwurf und Judenvertreibung im 13. Jahrhundert," *Judenvertreibungen in Mittelalter und früher Neuzeit*, ed. Friedhelm Burgard, Alfred Haverkamp, and Gerd Mentgen (Hanover: Hahnsche Buchhandlung, 1999), 135–64; see also the overview by Giacomo Todeschini, "Christian Perceptions of Jewish Economic Activity in the Middle Ages," *Wirtschaftsgeschichte der mittelalterlichen Juden*, 1–16.

[129]   With an emphasis on the financial aspect, see David Nirenberg, "Warum der König die Juden beschützen musste, und warum er sie verfolgen musste," *Die Macht des Königs: Herrschaft in Europa vom Frühmittelalter bis in die Neuzeit*, ed. Bernhard Jussen (Munich: C. H. Beck, 2005), 225–40 and 390–92.

[130]   Brugger, "Ansiedlung," 221–27, with reference to further literature.

Synagoga defeated with her blindfold, the broken staff and the crown slipping off her head, Ecclesia triumphant with her crowned head watching her often somewhat warily (see Figures 1, 2, and 3). Here, the roles are reversed, the Christian character sits with her eyes blindfolded and the Jewish one can see, yet both figures reach out for each other. Encounter, contact, and interaction were inevitable, neither Christian nor Jewish authorities being able to hamper Christians and Jews meeting on a daily basis in their shared living space of a medieval city. Neither group being a homogenous one, Jews and Christians also meet on several social levels, the personal meeting level often being more defined by belonging to a comparatively similar social class. The close contact allowed and facilitated the exchange of knowledge, the mutual translation of cultural goods and habits, and the general acquaintance with the respective other; but with changes in the economic, social, and ecclesiastical climate and by the will, or at least lack of interest, of the rulers, these neighborly relationships erupted into violence and expulsion.

While the academic focus has widened as far as Jewish history is concerned during the past decades to encompass broader, and more different, questions, it is, in many regards, still a desideratum for Jewish history to be fully integrated into the history of a region, city, or topic rather than to be treated in a footnote or, at the best, a separate chapter. Jews do play a role in urban history, claiming their spaces within medieval cities and interacting in many ways and on many levels, their history being, in the case dealt with here, as much urban as it is Austrian and Jewish.

Figure 1: Statue of Synagoga, Bamberg cathedral, ca. 1230

Figure 2: Statue of Synagoga, Strasbourg cathedral, ca. 1225

Figure 3: Statue of Ecclesia, Strasbourg cathedral, ca. 1225

Figure 4: Mahzor with a depiction of a bridal couple, the bride, with the typical
items of Ecclesia, has her eyes blindfolded, which, in Christian depictions, is the
distinctive feature for Synagoga, ca.1330,
(Staats- und Universitätsbibliothek Hamburg)

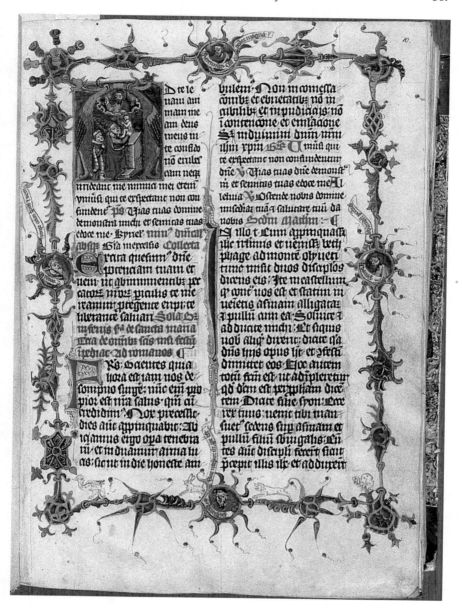

Figure 5: Decoration in the "Niederösterreichischen Randleistenstil," Missale, second half of fourteenth century (Stiftsbibliothek Klosterneuburg, Cod. 74)

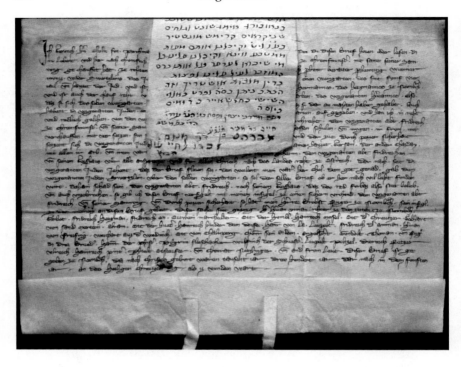

Figure 6: Sales deed of the monastery of Kremsmünster (Upper Austria) with the corresponding Hebrew charter attached to it (Stiftsarchiv Kremsmünster, 1305 April 29, Hebrew, and May 3, German)

Rosa Alvarez Perez

(Southern Utah University)

# Next-Door Neighbors: Aspects of Judeo-Christian Cohabitation in Medieval France

The complex relations Jews and Christians developed in Northern France between the eleventh and the fourteenth centuries prior to their final expulsion in 1394 reveal the distinct boundaries that mapped and demarcated the permissible zones of contact and interaction. Despite multiple restrictions, individuals from the two divergent communities did cross the real and virtual borders of social separation and created temporal 'pockets' of more viable relationships. If in general Jewish women's activities during that period affected mostly the local commerce, leaving minimal if any traces in the French archives, the few documents that remain do nevertheless attest to their involvement. This aspect of Judeo-Christian relations has often gone unnoticed until recently when Rebecca L. Winer and Elisheva Baumgarten began working respectively on Jewish women in Mediterranean France and Spain, and Germany.[1] While Winer focuses on the city of Perpignan, a Catalan city in the thirteenth century, I examine the Northern French Jewish communities, socially, linguistically, and culturally independent from those of the south, which are considered Ashkenazi since they shared similar traditions with German Jews,[2] and unlike their brethren in the South, these communities have not been as abundantly studied and documented.[3] They also offer an excellent basis for a study of the development of the economy and the establishment of numerous

---

[1]   Rebecca L. Winer, "Silent Partners? Women, Commerce, and the Family in Medieval Perpignan c. 1250–1300," Ph.D. diss., University of California Los Angeles, 1996; Elisheva Baumgarten, *Mothers and Children: Jewish Family Life in Medieval Europe* (Princeton, NJ: Princeton University Press, 2004); for more information on urban Jewish life in Germany, see also Birgit Wiedl's article in this volume.

[2]   See David Shohet, *The Jewish Court in the Middle Ages: Studies in Jewish Jurisprudence according to the Talmud, Geonic and Medieval German Responsa* (New York: Columbia University Press, 1931).

[3]   Eliakim Carmoly, *Bibliographie des Israélites de France* (Frankfurt a. M.: G. Hess, 1968), 7.

Jewish communities during that period. It is thus within a micro-context that I will explore interactions between the two communities that lived in such close proximity, and more particularly the recurrent exchanges between women of the two faiths.

Although the term "invisibility" is perhaps an overused cliché in relation to women, it remains relevant for medieval Jewish women who have been trapped for so long in a "fictional role," living in a society that highly valued spirituality and stressed male preeminence. The communities of Northern France were indeed renowned for their spiritual leaders in the fields of Talmudic studies, Biblical exegesis, and mystical speculations.[4] Women thus were instructed to comply with Biblical matriarchal models prescribed by *Halakha* (religious law). In such a fervent environment, the more ordinary aspects of everyday life were not considered worthy of being recorded; therefore, the social and economic impact of these women, more inclined to be involved in social life than the pious men of their communities, was often historically overlooked. In complying with the concept of *zahkor* (remembrance), a major tenet in traditional Jewish practices and teachings,[5] the recorders of Jewish events, in their own peculiar way, obliterated women and dissolved their past within the frame of the general historical discourse. The memory of things past was recombined to mirror the community's aspirations and struggles, and to recount mostly the dramatic moments lived by the communities. Jewish women's ability to maneuver thus fell between the cracks of social practices and religious obligations, and despite their recognized entrepreneurial abilities, they remained in a subservient position.

Undeniably, Jewish scholarship has remained predominantly the study of male Jews, considered the default-value of their culture. Within such a perspective, the central figure of the Jew could only be "the body with the circumcised penis — an image crucial to the very understanding of the Western image of the Jew at least since the advent of Christianity."[6] While Jewish Studies have taken a sharp turn in the past several decades with new research generating new perspectives that have greatly affected the outlook of this field of study, Jewish feminism only emerged as a new current in Jewish thought during the 1990s,[7] generating an

---

[4]   Robert Chazan, "Ephraim Ben Jacob's Compilation of Twelfth-Century Persecutions," *Jewish Quarterly Review* 84 (1993–94): 397–416, 397.

[5]   Sarah Silberstein Swartz and Margie Wolfe, ed., *From Memory to Transformation: Jewish Women's Voices* (Toronto: Second Story Press, 1998), 9.

[6]   Sander Gilman, *The Jew's Body* (New York and London: Routledge, 1991), 4–5.

[7]   See, to name a few, the contributions to *On Being a Jewish Feminist*, ed. Susannah Heschel (New York: Schocken Books, 1995); Paula Hyman, *Gender and Assimilation in Modern Jewish History: The Role and Representation of Women* (Seattle: University of Washington Press, 1995); Judith Baskin ed., *Jewish Women in Historical Perspective* (Detroit: Wayne State University Press, 1991); Bernadette

animated debate that re-contextualized the position and actual role of Jewish women within their own communities.

In medieval society, Jewish communities, shaped by social isolation, had come to inhabit an in-between space, a space that Elizabeth Grosz defines as a position of possible movement and development, but interestingly enough also as a space for contestation.[8] We might also call it a 'third space.' Indeed in the absence of legitimacy, Jewish appropriation of space, within the cities and towns, was a way of reclaiming space, both spatially and symbolically. But even this liminal presence was in itself a form of excess in the eye of Christian society, and the disruptive function of this excess significantly rendered these communities inassimilable. But in spite of the difficulties of coexistence, Jews nevertheless inhabited the margins of society, adding diversity to urban life in medieval France.

The assertion of the French *tosaphist*[9] R. Jacob Tam (d. 1171) that "less than ten years ago there were no *mezuzot* (*mezuzah* (sing.): encased parchment placed on the door post of Jewish homes) to be found in our kingdom"[10] is puzzling. Does this statement emphasize the rapid expansion of Jewish communities, or was the famous Rabbi strictly concerned with laxity in the application of this specific religious commandment, as some scholars have suggested? In any case, during that period of transition (tenth to the twelfth century), in the kingdom of France there was not only a rapid growth of the general population, but also the establishment of multiple Jewish communities.[11] Urbanization in Northern France was achieved more suddenly than in the South, and as a result, there were rapid adjustments that incorporated new social and economic realities.[12] The demographic explosion of the Jewish communities is to be viewed in parallel with the growth of the rest of the population. Moreover, in a relatively short period of time, the economic progress of the Jewish communities promoted a rapid advance in its intellectual endeavors, and by the second half of the twelfth century, there

---

Brooten, *Love Between Women: Early Christian Responses to Female Homoeroticism* (Chicago: University of Chicago Press, 1996); Aviva Cantor, *The Jewish Woman, 1900–1985: A Bibliography* (New York: Biblio Press, 1987); Judith Hauptman, *Rereading the Rabbis: A Woman's Voice* (Boulder: Westview Press, 1998); Rachel Biale, *Women and Jewish Law* (New York: Schocken Books, 1984).

[8] Elizabeth Grosz, *Architecture from the Outside: Essays on Virtual and Real Space* (Cambridge, MA: MIT, 2001), 92–93.

[9] The Tosaphists added comments to the work of Rashi on the Talmud.

[10] Elliot Horowitz, "The Way We Were: Jewish Life in the Middle Ages," *Jewish History* 1–3 (1986–1988): 75–90; here 77.

[11] Bernhard Blumenkranz, *Juifs et chrétiens dans le monde occidental (430–1096)*. Series Ecole Pratique des Hautes Études (France). Section des Sciences Economiques et Sociales. Études Juives, 2 (Paris: Mouton & Co, 1960).

[12] Robert Ian Moore, *The Formation of a Persecuting Society: Power and Deviance in Western Europe (950–1250)* (Oxford: Basil Blackwell, 1987), 60.

were at least fifteen important Rabbinical schools in France.[13] Yet, despite their growing renown as religious centers that exercised authority in matters of civil and ceremonial law, the communities of Northern France remained small entities independent of each other that managed to compensate for their isolation within a Christian majority through an important network of exchanges and an active correspondence.

While earlier Jews in France had been not only urban dwellers, but also rural landowners and wine producers, the situation started to change by the tenth century. In a movement of general defection, Jews progressively migrated to the growing towns, abandoning rural settlements. R. Joseph Bonfils, a well-known French scholar of the eleventh century, called it a justified change in a *responsum* addressed to the Jews of Troyes. He further explained that the possession of fields was less profitable than money invested in commerce, which brought great profits and could easily be withdrawn in times of crisis.[14] The sale contracts in which Jews had previously appeared as buyers of land showed them thereafter mostly as sellers, a change that accelerated between the eleventh and the twelfth centuries.[15]

The movement toward the cities and towns clearly appears in the examination of the topography of the cities of Paris, Sens, Troyes, Rouen, Senlis, Soissons, Auxerre, Chartres, Provins, Orléans, and Etampes, indicating that by the eleventh century a majority of the Jews lived near the royal or noble palaces.[16] But if the move was often motivated by economic reasons, ironically the city became later on for Jews a mandatory place of residence, sanctioned by the royal ordinance of April 1289. This additional regulation forbade Jews hereafter to settle in small towns and rural areas.[17]

The regrouping of Jews in administrative centers was certainly mandated by the desire to exercise a tighter control on these groups. If the serfs had been

---

[13]   Norman Golb, *The Jews in Medieval Normandy: A Social and Intellectual History* (Cambridge: Cambridge University Press, 1998), 174.

[14]   Jacob Mann, *The Responsa of the Babylonian Geonim as a Source of Jewish History* (Philadelphia: The Dropsie College for Hebrew and Cognate Learning, 1918), 319.

[15]   Siméon Luce, "Catalogue des documents du Trésor des Chartes," *Revue des Etudes Juives* 1–2 (1880–81): 15–72; here 62. After the expulsion of 1306, in 1309 Jews were still owning agricultural land in Champagne: ". . . heritages des Juifs d'Andelot sis à Andelot et au finage de cette ville, consistant en champs cultivés, prairies et vignobles . . .," 1309, 29 November, Paris (JJ 41, folio 91,92 no. 156).

[16]   Brigitte Bedos-Rezak, "The Confrontation of Orality and Textuality: Jewish and Christian Literacy in Eleventh and Twelfth-Century Northern France," Sed-Rajna, Gabrielle ed., *Rashi 1040–1090: Hommage à Ephraïm E. Urbach* (Paris: Editions du Cerf, 1993), 541–88; here 551.

[17]   Gustave Saige, *Les Juifs du Languedoc antérieurement au XIVe siècle* (Paris: A. Picard, 1881) 212, 223. Among other interdictions, Philip the Bold forbade Jews to live in small towns (Fonds Doat, tome XXXVII, folio 197); this decree was reiterated by Philip the Fair in April 1291 (Fonds Doat, tome XXXVII, folio 211).

emancipated on a large scale by the thirteenth century in the region of Paris,[18] Jews had become servants of the crown by the eleventh and twelfth centuries. They became the king's serfs, *servi camere, Judei nostri*, which was a special status, a social category in itself. But these different appellations convey the same meaning: in a position of subjected objects, Jews were politically and economically exploited. Jewish bodies had become the property either of the king or of feudal lords.[19]

The feudal system, a rigidly top-down structure, established between 950 and 1150,[20] resulted in the fragmentation of political authority.[21] The lack of centralized authority in medieval France gave Jews the opportunity to establish autonomous communal entities. Although Talmudic law enabled Jewish communal authorities to exercise social control with punitive measures for the suppression of crime,[22] they only imposed minor sentences like the "bastonnade" and turned to the secular authorities for the application of major punishments.[23] The period between the ninth and the eleventh centuries constitutes a comparatively lenient time in which the rules of segregation were not systematically enforced, and with only sporadic spurts of violence.[24]

The influence that Jewish leaders could exert is illustrated by the informative case of Lyons, a city that, during the Carolingian period (780–900), was an important commercial center at the crossroads of Italy, Spain, and Germany. Its weekly market, held on Saturdays, had barred Jews from participating in commercial transactions. This disadvantageous condition was overturned by the power of a royal decree of King Louis the Debonair (778–840). In these centuries preceding the slow centralization and strengthening of royal power, as Irving Agus asserts, Jews were in a stronger position to negotiate the terms and conditions of their settlement with the local ruling power.[25]

[18] Olivier Martin, *Histoire de la coutume de la prévôté et vicomté de Paris*, vol. 1 (Paris: Ernest Leroux, 1922), 21.

[19] *L'Histoire des Institutions et de la vie privée en Bourgogne*, ed. Jules Simonnet (Dijon: Imprimerie Rabutot, 1867), 399–400 (f. 338). One of the first mentions of a transaction in which a Jew was traded as an object occurred in 1196; a Jewish family was given as a donation to a certain Vigier, but more often Jews were the objects of profitable acts of sale.

[20] Robert Fossier, "Remarques sur l'étude des commotions sociales aux XIe et XIIe siècles," *Cahiers de Civilisation Médiévale* 16–1 (1973): 45–50; here 45.

[21] Olivier Martin, 42.

[22] *Rabbi Meir of Rothenburg: His Life and His Works as Sources for the Religious, Legal and Social History of Germany in the Thirteenth Century*, ed. Irving A. Agus (Philadelphia: Dropsie College, 1947), 55n (Responsum of R. Joseph Bonfils, L423).

[23] Simon Schwartzfuchs, *Kahal: La Communauté juive de l'Europe médiévale* (Paris: Maisonneuve et Larose, 1986), 105–06.

[24] Jacob Katz, *Exclusiveness and Tolerance: Studies in Jewish-Gentile Relations in Medieval and Modern Times* (Oxford: Oxford University Press, 1961), 9.

[25] Irving Abraham Agus, *Urban Civilization in Pre-Crusade Europe: A Study of Organized Town-Life in Northwestern Europe during the Tenth and Eleventh Centuries Based on the Responsa Literature* (New

Communities come into existence and find expression, as Elizabeth Grosz argues, not only through the recognition and establishment of common interests, values, and needs, but also through the marginal groups they reject.[26] The signs defining these 'others' strengthen the stability of the center. Christian society had circumscribed the integration of Jews to liminal spaces, to better insure their control. This held true even in the experience of daily life, in the mere act of living and moving across a city. As art historian Michael Camille astutely remarked, the medieval town's signs were not only cut in stone but also marked on bodies moving through space like the Jewish body with its yellow or red felt fabric,[27] the only piece of bright color it was allowed to wear. Jews were not the only individuals to harbor a sign of humiliation; prostitutes and lepers were also the bearers of signs that singularized them and set them apart from mainstream society. Another group also wore a temporary mark, a more positive sign, the one the pilgrims proudly displayed on their return from an arduous and dangerous journey to a holy place. But if for other groups the sign was the manifestation of an individual physical degradation or a sign of distinctiveness, the Jewish label was the outward mark of a rejected group.

Officially tolerated as witness of the faith, the disruptive and culturally marked category of Jews served as the catalyst for Christian cultural fears.[28] The Christian preponderant and central position in medieval society was certainly due to refusing and marginalizing Jewish presence. The anti-Jewish sentiments that were stirred up beginning with the First Crusade denote how medieval sensibility channeled by Church influence and pressure strongly reacted to and opposed diversity in all its manifestations. Coexistence with a cultural other constituted a challenge and a menace that compelled Christians to resort to violence as a radical way of negotiating difference.

Fear of Jewish pollution was a dominant concern for Christians, and it drove the authorities, secular and religious, to punish Jewish transgressors. As several Parliament records reveal, the population was eager to ensure that Jews did not commit infractions; for that matter individuals did not hesitate to take justice into their own hands and administer a prompt punishment by beating, for instance, Jewish women contravening the Christian interdiction of Jews bathing in rivers.[29]

---

York: Yeshiva University Press, 1965), 17.

26   Grosz, *Architecture from the Outside*, 152.

27   Michael Camille, "Signs of the City, Place, Power and Public Fantasy in Medieval Paris," *Medieval Practices of Space*, ed. Barbara A. Hanawalt and Michal Kobialka. Medieval Cultures, 23 (Minneapolis and London: University of Minnesota Press, 1999), 1–36; here 28.

28   Jeremy Cohen, *Living Letters of the Law: Ideas of the Jews in Medieval Christianity* (Berkeley, Los Angeles, and London: University of California Press, 1999).

29   See Léon Brunchwicg, "Les Juifs d'Angers et du pays angevin," *Revue des Etudes Juives* 28–29 (1894) : 229–44; here 239. Jews were forbidden to bathe in the river Maine; Georges, Pon, *Recueil*

This could happen in places where Jewish women in small communities lacking the necessary funds for the construction of a *mikveh* (ritual bathhouse) were compelled to resort to rivers for their monthly cleansing ritual to fulfill the religious commandment (*nidah*). What can be perceived, at first, as an unusual public activity for Jewish women was certainly not an uncommon practice, although it was strictly forbidden to Jews.

The Church, as the main controller of social homogenization, assumed an ambiguous and contradictory position regarding Jewish communities. Although in its official discourse the Church promoted tolerance toward a minority that was part of the 'symbolic order,' in reality there was not a definite sense of acceptance, and Jewish inclusion into society was limited. The first legal prescription imposing on Jews the wearing of a mark of recognition goes back to the Fourth Lateran decree of 1215.[30]

In the following years and decades, additional provincial synods, royal decrees, and town ordinances enforced this decree in a variety of modulations until their expulsion from the kingdom of France. However, it remains unclear in what precise periods, and to what extent in what cities and towns, this law was effectively imposed on the Jewish population. Quite a few cases in French official records attest to and document the violence Jews brought on themselves when they transgressed against this regulation, and according to these records, men rather than women were generally the ones subjected, to various degrees, to insult, assault, and theft by individuals if they were recognized as Jews[31] in the town's streets and not wearing the prescribed badge.[32] It is also true that in most cases a bearded appearance targeted more men to be subjected to an inquisitive gaze, to be singled out, and to be exposed to abuse and violence.

---

[30] *des documents de l'Abbaye de Fontaine-le-Comte: XIIe–XIIIe siècles* (Poitiers: Société des archives historiques du Poitou, 1982) T.25 : "she was bathing in the river Clain at Poitiers."
Charles Joseph Hefele, *Histoire des Conciles d'après les documents originaux* (Paris: Letouzey et Ané, 1913), vol. 5: Can. 68, 386; it is only from the council of Narbonne in 1227 that the *rouelle* became canonically a characteristic Jewish sign.

[31] Sara Lipton, *Images of Intolerance* (Berkeley: University of California Press, 1999). As she points out the use of the pointed hat and beards as attributes in medieval art dates back to the eleventh century and by the thirteenth was widespread and conventional, 16,19; see also Bernhard Blumenkranz, *Le Juif médiéval au miroir de l'art chrétien* (Paris: Etudes Augustiniennes, 1966); a rare instance of a mention "un habit juif" stolen by Vivant de Montréal in a letter of pardon after the revolt in Paris in 1380. Roger Kohn, *Les Juifs de la France du Nord*, 94.

[32] Jules Viard ed., *Les Journaux du Trésor de Philippe IV Le Bel* (Paris: Imprimerie Nationale, 1940), XVI. Jews were the property of the king. Saint Louis' Ordinance of 18 June 1269 prescribed Jews to wear a badge made of scarlet fabric or felt. If they were accused by a passerby, they could be fined up to 10 pounds and their (specified with a masculine pronoun) outer garment was confiscated and given to the denouncer.

Social separation between Christian and Jews was promoted and encouraged by the Church, but mandatory residence only became customary by the end of the thirteenth century. Wealthy Jewish families could still circumvent the interdiction and live among Christians if they paid an additional tax. Segregation varied in different periods and locations, but Jewish quarters were not exclusively populated by Jews; Christians lived in the same buildings, or on the same streets. An examination of the registers of the Châtelet for the period between 1389 and 1392 clearly attests to Jewish-Christian urban coexistence. In several instances, Christian individuals arrested for petty criminal offenses are described as living in or at the periphery of the Jewish quarter, as in the following:

> En Quareisme dernièrement passé volerent dans un hostel une paire de draps de lit ... les vendirent à Lorence la Picarde, demourant au bout de la rue aus Juifs.[33]

> [During Lenten season, they stole from an inn a pair of bed sheets . . . (and) sold them to Lorence the Picard, living at the end of the Jew's street]

In this apparently strictly informative narrative, the scribe juxtaposes the illicit activities of Lorence, a Christian woman, and urban space within the Jewish quarter. Intentional or not, the comment nevertheless suggestively establishes a link between the shady transactions and their place of occurrence. No accusation is made but the suspicion is aroused, and if Jewish individuals were indeed occasionally implicated in trafficking in stolen property,[34] it was generally understood by Christians that this practice was common.

Gilbert Dahan contends that there were no typical French Jewish quarters in medieval France towns and furthermore that there is no common history left for these quarters.[35] Permanence, a necessary factor to retrace culture, was for the Northern communities very limited, the Jewish inhabitants being easily uprooted by expulsions that brought in their wake a homogenous Christian identity. Nevertheless Jews, operating outside the social order, tended to congregate for religious purposes within a short distance of a synagogue and a *mikveh*. They followed the pattern of medieval urban occupation of space where streets typically regrouped the members of the same corporation or individuals sharing similar interests. The tax roll for the city of Paris for the year 1292 is a good index of this

---

[33]  Charles Lahure, ed., *Registre Criminel du Châtelet de Paris* (du 6 septembre 1389 au 18 mai 1392), 2 vols., (Paris: Charles Lahure, 1861) vol.1 377 (August 15 1390).
[34]  Edgard Boutaric, ed., *Actes du Parlement de Paris*. 2 vols. (Paris: Plon, 1863–1867), 2283 "Ordonnance défendant aux chrétiens et aux chrétiennes de demeurer dans les maisons des juifs pour les servir et aux juifs de les y garder" (*Olim* II fol. 50 ro).
[35]  Gilbert Dahan, "Quartier juif et rue des Juifs," *Art et archéologie des Juifs en France médiévale*, ed. Bernhard Blumenkranz (Toulouse: Privat, 1980), 15–32; 21–28.

phenomenon.[36] The Jewish taxpayers, listed in a separate section at the end of the roll, lived within the confines of a few streets of the city.

In a later depiction of Jewish communities' quarters, Nicolas Delamare gives us a description of medieval Paris, information he gathered from *The Chronicle of St. Denis*, known as *The Great Chronicle*.[37] He notes that Jews were housed in very limited quarters, in hastily built houses of poor quality, and in narrow and dark streets closed at night.[38] The reduced space available had in fact forced Jews to adopt a vertical distribution of dwellings. In Northern France, Germany, and England, most Jewish communities were very small in number and represented at most 1 or 2 % of a city's population.[39] Even though the percentage was small, the number of individuals and families authorized to reside in a town was limited and strictly regulated.[40] Each community was empowered to enforce these regulations, granting or denying permission to newcomers to settle.

Delamare's description of a medieval Jewish quarter does not differ much from descriptions of other populated quarters in any given town or city. Therefore, living in cramped quarters and dark narrow streets was commonplace, and the deplorable sanitary conditions of the cities were notorious. Philip Augustus was offended by the loathsome smell of the streets of Paris, which required every year a levy of a hundred thousand francs to remove the mud. They were "… noires, puantes d'une odeur insupportable aux étrangers, qui pique et ça fait sentir à 3 ou 4 lieues à la ronde." [black, smelling of an odor which is unbearable to foreigners, which offends and can be smelled up to 3 or 4 leagues.] The King ordered a certain number of streets to be paved to reduce the pestilence.[41]

The majority of Jews became town dwellers until their final expulsion, but frequently the only physical trace of Jewish presence left in any given town is a street harboring the name "rue aux juifs." The term *Vicus Judaeorum* that Romans used to designate the Jewish quarter was reduced in medieval times to *vicus* and the expression "settlement of the Jews" gradually came to be translated into "rue aux juifs," or simply "la Juiverie."[42] Every expulsion was accompanied by confiscation and resale of Jewish property, and with every departure another layer

[36] Hercule Géraud, *Paris sous Philippe le Bel: d'après un manuscrit contenant "le rôle de la taille" imposée sur les habitants de Paris en 1292* (Paris: Crapelet, 1837).

[37] Jules Viard, ed., *Les Grandes Chroniques de France*, 8 vols. (Paris: Société de l'Histoire de France, 1920).

[38] Nicolas Delamare, *Traité de Police*, 4 vols., (Paris: Michel Brunet, 1722), vol.1, 301.

[39] Salo W. Baron, "The Jewish Factor in Medieval Civilization," *Facets of Medieval Judaism*, ed. Seymour Sieggel (New York: Arno Press, 1973), 1–48; here 6.

[40] Edgard Boutaric, *Actes*, no. 1948.

[41] Henri Sauval, *Histoire et recherches: Les Antiquités de la ville de Paris*, 2 vols., (Paris: C. Moette, 1724), vol. 1, 187. For a further discussion of this topic from an early-modern perspective, see the contribution to this volume by Allison P. Coudert.

[42] Golb, *The Jews in Medieval Normandy*, 75.

of Jewish presence was scrapped, even erased. New occupants were installed, new activities followed, displacing Jewish memory. Thus, when Philip Augustus expelled the Jews in 1182, in Paris alone the synagogue and a total of forty-two houses, twenty-four in rue de la Pelleterie and eighteen in rue de la Vieille Draperie,[43] were confiscated by the royal officers and sold to merchants or donated as gifts by the king to the Church or to loyal royal officers.[44]

The political landscape of medieval France was far from homogeneous and its fragmentation caused Jews to live under different rules and regulations according to the authority in place. In a changed political and urban scene,[45] Jews were readmitted to Paris in 1198, but they were not allowed to reoccupy their ancient quarter in the heart of the city. This time, they were relegated to the new limits of the city close to the fortifications, even outside the walls, in a quarter named Les Champeaux. The decentralization of the Jewish habitat was in part compensated for by the fact that the expansion of the capital had prompted the development of new axes of trade. Re-established in Paris, Jews organized themselves in two separate communities: one more populated[46] and well oriented toward business on the right bank of the Seine; the other, on the left bank that was the domain of intellectuals where members of the school of Saint-Victor ventured to seek the *Hebraica veritas* from Jewish masters.[47]

In this more dispersed habitat, Jews had two synagogues, a mill, and two cemeteries.[48] This was a privileged situation, however, that soon would have to be forfeited. Indeed, in 1270, Philip the Bold forbade Jews, regardless of the size of their community, to have more than one synagogue and one cemetery per town.[49] Jews were also specifically forbidden to pray or sing in a loud manner during their services. This particular ordinance was enforced in the year 1288 in Paris, where

[43] Bernhard Blumenkranz, *Juifs en France, écrits dispersés* (Paris: Diffusion Belles Lettres, 1989), 104.

[44] Henri Gross, transl. Moïse Bloch, *Gallia Judaica. Dictionnaire géographique de la France d'après les sources rabbiniques* (Paris: Librairie Cerf, 1897), 501, Philip Augustus gave to his cup-bearer, Rainald, the halle au ble of the Jewish quarter; see also Léopold Delisle, *Catalogue des Actes de Philippe-Auguste* (Paris: Durand, 1856). Later in 1311, Philip the Fair gave to his coachman the schools rue de la Tacherie, see Henri Sauval, *Histoire et recherches: Les Antiquités de la ville de Paris*, vol. 1, 21.

[45] John W. Baldwin, "La Décennie décisive: les années 1190–1203 dans le règne de Philippe Auguste," *Revue Historique* 266 (1981): 311–37.

[46] Robert Anchel, *Les Juifs de France* (Paris: Janin, 1946), 65–66; A survey of the tax roll of 1292 clearly shows that the vast majority of the population in Paris lived on the right bank of the city.

[47] Isidore Loeb, "La Controverse de 1240 sur le Talmud," *Revue des Etudes Juives* 1–2 (1880–1881): 247–61; here 249.

[48] Aryeh Graboïs, "Un Centre intellectuel juif à Paris sur la rive gauche aux XIIe–XIIIe siècles?" *Revue des Etudes Juives* 131 (1972): 223–24.

[49] Michel Roblin, "Les Cimetières juifs de Paris au Moyen Age," *Paris et Ile-de-France Memoires* 4 (1952): 7–20.

the Jewish community was condemned to pay a fine of three hundred *parisi* pounds for breaking the regulation.[50]

The omnipresent and haunting figure of the moneylender and usurer appearing in Christian *exempla*[51] points to the means of employment that many Jews did indeed turn to since many other possible trades and occupations were forbidden to them. However, against the generally accepted assertion that Jews were not artisans, names of that period are often proof that they were borrowed from the profession these men were practicing, like Corrigarius (maker of straps or girdles), Vaginarius (gainier),[52] or Lotin (peddler).[53] With no access to the crafts that provided for a wider market protected by the powerful guilds,[54] they had therefore to rely on Christian artisans and workers for goods and services in which they held no mastery, such as masonry for the construction of houses and their upkeep.[55] Jewish craftsmen tended to supply for the internal needs of their communities in trades more related to religious regulations, like butchers, bakers, winemakers, barbers, soapmakers, embroiderers, *tallit* and *tzizit* weavers, scribes, and bookbinders.[56] Jewish communities were able to circumvent obstacles and managed to have an impact on city affairs.

Money lending and usury constitute the most widely known aspect of regular and repeated interactions between the Christian and Jewish communities of

---

[50] Théophile Cochard, *La Juiverie d'Orléans* (1895; Marseille: Laffitte Reprints, 1976), 115; (Baillie de Paris 1288: "De emendâ Judaeorum pro eo quod nimis alte cantaverunt, IIIe lib. Parisis"); apparently it was not an isolated complaint: the Precheurs Mineurs from Troyes complained to Philip the Long that Jews prayed in a loud voice in their synagogue and that they disturbed them. Frowald Gil Hüttenmeister, "Synagogues et cimetières en Champagne médiévale," *Rashi 1040–1990: Hommage à Ephraïm Urbach,* ed. Gabrielle Sed-Rajna (Paris: Les Editions du Cerf, 1993), 579–85; here 583.

[51] Jacques Le Goff, *La Bourse et la vie: économie et religion au moyen âge* (Paris: Hachette, 1986).

[52] Michel Roblin, "Les Cimetières juifs de Paris au moyen âge," *Paris et Ile-de-France (Mémoires)* 4 (1952): 7–20; here 14–15.

[53] P. Piétresson de Saint-Aubin, "Document inédit relatif aux juifs de Troyes," *Le Moyen Age* 31 (1920–1921): 84–86 ; here 85. (Arch. de l'Aube 7H.136 fo131, Helieus, filius Douceron la juyve).

[54] For protection against Jewish interference, see Etienne Boileau, *Le Livre des métiers*.: "Il est ordené que nule mestresse ne ouvrière du mestier ne peuvent acheter soie de juys, de fileresses, ne de nul autre,fors de marcheanz tant seulement . . . " [100; It is the law that no mistress, or female worker in the trade can buy silk from Jews, not from spinners, not from anyone else but, from merchants]; "Nos juyf de la vile de Paris ne peut ne ne doit acheter saie escrue ne tainte, qu'ele que ele soit, se ce n'est de marcheant convegnable et souffisant, ne que nui ne nule ne puisse acheter ne vendre bourree de soie, se ele n'est boulie" [378; Our Jews from the city of Paris cannot buy raw or dyed silk no matter which type except from a suitable and adequate merchant, nor can anyone buy or sell silk if it is not boiled].

[55] Aryeh Graboïs, "La Société urbaine chrétienne dans la France septentrionale du XIe siècle, vue à travers les Responsa de Rashi," *Revue historique* 296 (1996): 241–52; here 250.

[56] Mark Wischnitzer, *A History of Jewish Crafts and Guilds* (New York: Jonathan David Publishers, 1965), xx–xxi.

Northern France. Constant monetary demands from the twelfth century on were certainly one of the factors allowing numerous Jewish women the opportunity to participate alongside of Jewish men in the economic sphere of the region. For that matter, as Zeev Falk argues, Franco-Ashkenazi Jewish law accorded to business women the capacity to contract on their own behalf and to appear in court with or without representation. In a money-sparse economy, the inter-communal service that Jewish moneylenders provided to all groups in society was a valuable commodity; however, their position at "the complex intersection of temporal, cultural and social factors"[57] exposed them and all the members of the community to manipulation and exploitation. In other words, Jews, owned in their bodies and marked for recognition, were commodified by the political and social structures in place.[58]

Although rabbis argued in defense of money lending, the following exemplum still presents this activity as "ce qui était detestable."

> Une femme sortit de la synagogue avant que la communauté n'eut fini de prier. Elle envoya sa servante à son mari pour lui demander la clé. Lorsqu'il sortit à son tour de la synagogue, il demanda à son épouse pourquoi elle avait eu besoin des clés. Elle répondit que des chrétiennes étaient venues chercher leurs objets engagés parce qu'elles devaient aller à l'église. Le mari lui dit qu'elle avait eu tort de sortir de la synagogue et d'envoyer chercher les clés afin de leur remettre les objets engagés, avec lesquels elles iraient à l'église. Elle avait fait passer ce qui était détestable avant ce qui était sacré.[59]

> [A woman left the synagogue before the community had finished praying. She sent her servant to her husband to ask for the key. When he came out of the synagogue, he asked his wife why she had needed the keys. She answered that Christian women had come looking for their pledges because they had to go to church. The husband told her that she had been wrong to leave the synagogue and ask for the keys in order to return their pledges with which they would go to church. She had put that which is detestable before that which was sacred.]

Like his Christian contemporary, Caesarius of Heisterbach, Rabbi Jehudah the Hasid, in his *Sefer Hasidim*, used the exemplum for teaching, and often draws his tales from a common reservoir of Germanic and other folkloric tales. This exemplum serves to demonstrate the inability of women to separate material and

---

57  Arjun Appadurai, "Introduction: Commodities and the Politics of Value," *Commodities in Cultural Perspective*, ed. Arjun Appadurai (Cambridge: Cambridge University Press, 1986), 15.

58  Cf. Diane Peters Auslander, "Victims or Martyrs: Children, Anti-Semitism, and the Stress of Change in Medieval England," *Childhood in the Middle Ages and the Renaissance: The Results of a Paradigm Shift in the History of Mentality*, ed. Albrecht Classen (Berlin and New York: Walter de Gruyter, 2005), 105–34.

59  Judah ben Samuel, *Sefer Hassidim*, trans. Rabbi Edouard Gourévitch (Paris: Editions du Cerf, 1988), 332 (Pa. 465; Bol. 783).

spiritual matters. It reveals that because Jewish women are not time-bound for prayer as men are, and their participation in the liturgical ritual of the synagogue is limited to a more passive presence praying in silence, they are more likely to be aware of and accommodate to the needs of Christians borrowers. This woman is indeed more open to the pleas of Christian women, which might suggest that a certain complicity and understanding existed between women of different faiths working together on a daily basis.

The passage also reveals a very interesting perspective, the Jewish woman's willingness to return home and retrieve the pledges. Trust plays an important part since the pledges are returned to the borrowers for a short period of time with the expectation that they will be brought back. Trans-confessional communication only seems possible between women. The husband only intervenes to scold his wife for interrupting her prayers, showing total indifference to Christian women.

Arguments over high interest on money lending were certainly a contributing factor to urban violence and intensified conflicts between the two communities. In one of the rare recorded cases of a Jewish homicide that took place in Montargis (in the Orléanais region in late fourteenth century), a fight started between, on the one hand, two unnamed Jewish women mentioned as the wives of Eliot Salman and Moreau du Bourc, and Valenète, a Christian woman, on the other. When Moreau, one of the husbands, joined the fight, the disproportion between the two sides led to the death of Valenète. Homicide committed collectively by a group was frequent in medieval society, where the bonds of mutual dependence among family members and kin were strong. The three Jews were imprisoned and their belongings (as 'Jews of the king') immediately confiscated by royal officials.[60] The cause of the quarrel remains unknown, although the mention of "spouses of moneylenders" in the court statement might be an indication that money was the trigger.

Gérard Nahon[61] and William Chester Jordan, in his studies of Picard records from mid twelfth-century (*Supplementum: Queremoniae contra judaeos*), have emphasized the role of Jewish women in lending transactions. They affirmed that one third of the lending business in that region was in Jewish women's hands, thus putting them in close and daily contact with the Christian population.[62] With few exceptions, Jewish women moneylenders did not seem to have had contemporary

[60] Théophile Cochard, *La Juiverie d'Orléans du VIe au XVe siècles, son histoire et son organisation* (1895; Marseille: Laffitte Reprints, 1976), 149–50.
[61] See Gérard Nahon, "Le Crédit et les Juifs dans la France du XIIIe siècle," *Annales* (ESC) 24 (1969): 1121–48; "Pour une géographie administrative des juifs dans la France de Saint-Louis (1226–1270)," *Revue Historique* 253–254 (1975): 305–44.
[62] William Chester Jordan, "Jewish-Christian Relations in Mid-Thirteenth Century France: An Unpublished Enquete from Picardy," *Revue des Etudes Juives* 138 (1979): 47–55.

Christian counterparts,[63] and for unclear reasons, these medieval Jewish businesswomen left fewer contracts than men.[64]

As Roger Khon asserts, it is true that for the most part according to the documents women dealt with small loans, probably preferring pledges to contractual loans that necessitated notary fees. The borrowers—peasants, artisans, and workers—were often in need of small short-term funds, and the only possessions they could deposit as security were cooking vessels, bedding, and clothing items. In the recurrent pattern that emerged, Christians attempted on many occasions to reject and eliminate Jews only to discover that they were too dependent upon them. And when finally they decided to get rid of them in 1394, it was simply because the practice of money lending had been increasingly used by Christians no longer fearing the Church.[65]

This visible and documented aspect of Jewish participation in the economic sector concealed the role that Jewish women played. The tax roll of the city of Paris for the year 1292 lists a total of 125 Jewish taxpayers, one of the largest communities in the kingdom of France. Fifty-five are women, representing forty-four percent of the Jewish taxpayers. While a close look at these numbers reveals that sixteen percent of them were recorded in conjunction with their husbands and thus without any mention of their own names, twenty-five women are recorded alone. And, in a rare addition, two women are mentioned with a trade occupation, Joie la farinière (the miller) and Sarre la mirgesse (the physician).[66]

Violence was a common aspect of urban life at all levels of society, and within that frame, violence among Jews and Christians was not only triggered by religious resentments, but also through daily contacts.[67] Proximity and differences

---

[63] Kenneth R. Stow, *Alienated Minority: The Jews of Medieval Latin Europe* (Cambridge: Harvard University Press, 1992), 203.

[64] Roger Kohn, *Les Juifs de la France du Nord dans la seconde moitié du 14ème siècle* (Louvain: E. Peeters, 1988), 96.

[65] For German scholarship on Jewish communities, see Gerd Mentgen, Hans-Jörg Gilomen, Markus Wenninger and Michael Toch, *Die Juden im mittelalterlichen Reich.* Enzyklopädie deutscher Geschichte, 44 (Munich: R. Oldenbourg, 1998); Alfred Haverkamp, *Gemeinden, Gemeinschaften und Kommunikationsformen im hohen und späten Mittelalter: Festgabe zur Vollendung des 65. Lebensjahres,* ed. Friedhelm Burgard, Lukas Clemens, and Michael Matheus (Trier: Kliomedia, 2002); Robert Chazan, *Medieval Jewry in Northern France: A Political and Social History* (Baltimore: John Hopkins University Press, 1973). I am grateful to Birgit Wiedl for pointing out these studies to me; see also *The Jews of Medieval Western Christendom, 1000–1500* (Cambridge, UK, New York: Cambridge University Press, 2006); Joseph Shatzmiller, *Shylock Reconsidered: Jews, Moneylending and Medieval Society* (Berkeley: University of California Press, 1990). See also the contributions to *German Literature Between Faiths: Jew and Christian at Odds and in Harmony,* ed. Peter Meister. Studies in German Jewish History, 6 (Oxford, Bern, et al.: Peter Lang, 2004).

[66] Hercule Géraud, *Paris sous Philippe-le-Bel* (Paris: Crapelet, 1837), 178.

[67] For further studies on this topic, see the contributions to *Violence in Medieval Courtly Literature: A Casebook,* ed. Albrecht Classen. Routlededge Medieval Casebooks (New York and London:

sharpened grievances and resulted in frequent quarrels, as French records attest. Quarrelsome women squabbling with neighbors and susceptible to "chaude colle" were an urban reality. In one of the rare cases of recorded female violence, which took place in Dijon in August 1388, Pérenote, wife of Jacquot (or Perinot) le Pitoul, inflicted serious injury on a Jewish woman whose identity is reduced to the mention of her marital status. The violent gesture is vividly described, but the cause of the attack is left out:

> . . . qu'elle injurieusement gita plein une ponoicle de chaux touz chaux sur le visaige de la femme Saulemin le Juif dont ay eu et ay des empôles au visaige.[68]

> [. . . that she threw a handful of hot lime at the face of the wife of Saulemin the Jew injuring her, which she had and has blisters on her face.]

Pérenote was arrested and jailed. She was condemned to pay a fine of one franc, a sentence disproportionately low for such an injury. The fine is modest indeed, but the sentence had acknowledged that the woman was poor and that she had already spent three days in jail. As a common practice, violence between individuals that did not end in death was sanctioned by compensation or the payment of a fine. Medieval law applied harsher penalties only when private property was violated.

However, contrary to common belief, interactions were not always filled with violent acts. Women from both communities also shared a certain complicity in everyday life, often turning to each other for the help, assistance and exchange of services that Judith Bennett labeled as "female sociability."[69] For instance, on a regular basis female neighbors or domestic servants helped Jewish families to keep Shabbat observance. French rabbis, more lenient according to certain sources, permitted non-Jews to keep fires burning in Jewish houses during the cold winter months, an act that represented a Shabbat violation.[70] The employment of Christian servants and wet-nurses by Jewish families was a common practice in spite of the Church's interdiction, and it is an important area of interaction between women of the two communities. It opened, as Elisheva Baumgarten affirms, "a complex world of interactions," a subject she extensively develops in her study of Jewish family life in Northern Europe.[71]

---

[68] Routledge, 2004). See also the contribution by Birgit Wiedl in the present volume.
Roger Kohn, *Les Juifs de la France du Nord*, 178.

[69] Judith M. Bennett and Amy M. Froide, "A Singular Past," *Singlewomen in the European Past 1250–1800*, ed. Judith M. Bennett and Amy M. Froide (Philadelphia: University of Pennsylvania Press, 1999), 1–37; here 25.

[70] Jacob Katz, *The "Shabbes Goy": A Study in Halakhic Flexibility*, trans. Yoel Lerner (Philadelphia and New York: The Jewish Publication Society, 1989), 57–66.

[71] Elisheva Baumgarten, *Mother and Children: Jewish Family Life in Medieval Europe*, 2004.

A tale contained in a letter of pardon (dated April 1375) also illustrates female complicity. The well-anchored popular belief that Jews, men and women, with their knowledge of Hebrew, could cast magic spells and make amulets[72] encouraged a Christian woman abandoned by her husband, Adam Bigon d'Auxerre, to turn to a Jewish woman for help, hoping to bring back her husband with "poudres et charmes," but the scheme was uncovered and the two women were arrested and imprisoned. The bailiff of Sens, declaring that the spells were inoffensive and not "chose dont mors se peut ensuivre,"[73] dismissed the case and the two women were promptly released.

Cohabitation with Christians not only was a source of friction, tensions, and violence, but also presented a possibility of more intimate contacts between Jews and Christians. However, if interrelations were inevitable, sexual interrelations —the transgression par excellence—represented a social disruption that both communities condemned and tried to prevent with a series of punitive measures. In that social context the Jewish body was marked and forbidden, but at the same time the temptation of otherness exerted an attraction for Christians and created a nexus of conflicting desires that limits and prohibitions, often zones of fluid boundaries, could not contain.

In response to interfaith sexual relations, Christian punitive measures varied according to the place they occurred, the nature of the transgression and the social status of the perpetrator. Sexual relations between Jews and Christians were often punished by death in the region of Angers (thirteenth century). Christian men accused of sexual relationships with Jewish women were burned at the stake if they were convicted.[74] But on many occasions the sanction was indeed replaced by a fine. The Synod of Vienne (1267) applied a lighter punishment for sexual intercourse between Jews and Christians, declaring that the Jew who had fornicated with a Christian woman would be sentenced to pay a fine of 10 silver marks,[75] but the accused Christian woman was banished from the city after being flogged.[76] The sentence applied to the woman was much more severe since it severed her ties with her family and kin, abolishing her status in society, whereas the man was freed upon payment of a fine. It remains true that regardless of faith,

---

[72]    Susan L. Einbinder, Beautiful Death: Jewish Poetry and Martyrdom in Medieval France: Jews, Christians, and Moslems from the Ancient to the Modern World (Princeton, NJ: Princeton University Press, 2002), 160.

[73]    Roger Kohn, Les Juifs de la France du Nord, 84.

[74]    Léon Brunschvicg, "Les Juifs d'Anger et du pays angevin," Revue des Etudes Juives 29–30 (1894–1895): 229–44; here 239.

[75]    Gérard Nahon, "Le Crédit et les Juifs dans la France du XIIIe siècle," Annales (ESC) 24 (1969): 1121–48. This amount was equivalent, by the end of the thirteenth century, to two pounds, or 480 deniers. The daily living cost of a family of several children was 12 to 16 deniers.

[76]    Arthur Beugnot, Les Juifs d'Occident (Paris: Imprimerie de Lachevardière Fils, 1824), 24.

in the examination of cases of forbidden sexual crimes, criminal sentences often reveal unequal treatment of men and women.[77]

In 1397, a few years after the dismantling of the Jewish communities and their expulsion from the kingdom of France, the remaining Jews in the territory were either imprisoned or were itinerant merchants. In that year the Christian Petrus, alias Jean Hardy, was condemned by the Bailiff of Paris to be burned at the stake. The story is remarkable by all accounts: he was guilty, according to the historian Henri Sauval, for allowing the children he had with a Jewish woman to practice the religion of their mother.[78] Johannes Gallus, in his judicial chronicle of the period, insists on the sexual aspect of the relation between the Christian man and the Jewish woman, presenting her as a polluting agent. Gallus takes the Church prohibition a step further and presents the guilty relationship as a sexual deviance "contre nature," a bestial act punishable by burning at the stake:

> habere rem cum Judea, pro Christiano, est rem habere cum cane, juris interpretatione; sic comburi debet."[79]

> [to have relations with a Jewess, for a Christian, is like having relations with a dog, according to the interpretation of the law; therefore he should be burned.]

Equating Jews with animals was but one among many derogatory practices that dehumanized Jews, and in this precise case the popular condemnation is transposed into the judicial field and incorporated into the legal rhetoric.[80] This case indirectly informs us about the presence of crypto Jews in the city after their expulsion. In spite of the danger, this Jewish woman was most certainly still living in Paris and raising her children according to Jewish precepts. Had the father secretly converted to Judaism? The question remains unanswered and whether Jean Hardy was accused of apostasy remains unsaid. He nevertheless met his death at the stake like a heretic. We are left to surmise about the fate of the Jewish woman.

Willingly or not, numerous Jews succumbed to assimilation and conversion, but specific conversion numbers remain difficult to ascertain since reports on conversions from Christian and Jewish sources functioned to different ends. Elisheva Carlebach notes that the most frequent pattern, found in both Jewish and Christian literary sources, is that the husband initiated conversion while the wife

[77] Kathryn Gravdal, *Ravishing Maidens: Writing Rape in Medieval French Literature and Law*. New Cultural Studies Series (Philadelphia: University of Philadelphia Press, 1991), 130.

[78] Henri Sauval,*Histoire et recherches: Les Antiquités de la ville de Paris*, vol. 2, 510.

[79] Jean Le Coq, *Questiones Johannis Galli*, ed. Marguerite Boulet. Bibliothèque des Écoles Françaises d'Athènes et de Rome, Fasc. 156 (Paris: E. de Boccard, 1944), 481–82, q. 403 (folio 187).

[80] Esther Cohen, "Symbols of Culpability and the Universal Language of Justice: The Ritual of Public Executions in Late Medieval Europe," *History of European Ideas* 11 (1989): 407–16; here 411.

tended to resist.[81] The position of Christians toward Jewish women was more ambivalent. If they followed the postulate that by nature women are a commodity subject to transfer, then they could assume that Jewish women would be more receptive than men to Christian teachings and therefore accept conversion. But in reality this gendered assumption was challenged on many occasions by the fierce determination of Jewish women opposed to conversion, giving up their lives if necessary to remain faithful to their faith.

In Christian religious educational texts, Jewish men were seldom represented as willing converts to Christianity; however, Jewish women frequently appeared as more eager to embrace the Christian faith. In *The Dialogue on Miracles*, a series of exempla destined for the instruction of novices, Caesarius of Heisterbach manipulates Jewish women's visibility in narratives of attraction and conversion to Christianity. The clerical discourse on the attraction exerted by the Christian faith on Jewish women is rather evocative, depicting young Jewish girls more than anxious to convert.[82] Heisterbach offers us several portraits in which Jews are constructed through the repetitive use of the archetype of the young Jewish girl only to serve the ideological interests of the Church. In the exempla very young women are easily seduced and convinced to convert. Jewish men are presented as harmless and since their masculinity is questioned, there are no examples of Christian women seduced by Jews.

In one of Caesarius of Heisterbach's exempla of a converted Jewish girl, a curious story laden with elements of popular culture, the latrine becomes the focal element of a scatological ceremony performed by a Jewish mother. By submitting her daughter to a parody of Christian ritual, she attempts to annul her daughter's conversion by reversing the ritual of baptism with the following words:

> Ego, inquit Judaea, tribus vicibus te sursum traham per foramen latrinae, sicque remanebit ibi virtus baptismi tui.[83]

> [I would draw you three times through the opening of a latrine and thus the virtue of your baptism would be left behind.][84]

Men are not present in this tale where the connection between women and magic is particularly significant. According to Carmen Caballero-Navas, the ritual invocation must be made through maternal filiation, defying deeply-rooted

[81]   Elisheva Carlebach, *Divided Souls: Converts from Judaism in Germany, 1500–1750* (New Haven and London: Yale University Press, 2001), 31.

[82]   Caesarius of Heisterbach, *The Dialogue on Miracles*, trans. H. von E. Scott and C. Swinton Bland, 2 vols. (London: Routledge, 1929), 107–09.

[83]   Caesarii Heisterbacensis, *Dialogus Miraculorum*. J. M. Heberle, 2 vols. (1851; Ridgewood, N. J.: Gregg Press, 1966), 98–99.

[84]   Caesarius of Heisterbach, *The Dialogue on Miracles*, 109–110.

patriarchal principles.[85] The mother is presented as the desecrator of the sacrament of baptism, which she perceives as a polluting element that has to be physically ejected from the body. And according to a widespread folkloric belief, the defilement has to be expelled through the anus.[86] This exemplum emphasizes the power of Christianity against practices that are more associated with witchcraft; the mother-daughter confrontation will provide the opportunity to show the triumph of Christianity against such practices. The reference to profanation in the latrines by the Jews is also used in a letter of Innocent III of 1205 affirming that:

> Faciunt enim Christianas filiorum suorum nutrices, cum in die Ressurectionis Dominice illas recipere corpus et sanguinem Jesu Christ, contingit per triduum antequam eos lactent, lar effundere latrinam.

> [On the day of the Lord's Resurrection the Christian women who are nurses for the children of Jews, take in the body and blood of Jesus Christ. The Jews make these women pour their milk into the latrine for three days before they again give suck to the children.][87]

Cohabitation made Jews part of society, albeit a fragile part, and their incorporation and representation in literature produced a distorted view of them, as well as resentment and fantasies.[88] If we look in literature for glimpses of Jewish-Christian relations, we encounter mostly negative representations, reflections that carry all the prejudices and misconceptions about the decried group. Jews, close neighbors in life, become in fiction shadowy presences distilling hate and are held responsible for the devious behavior of a Christian character. In

---

[85]   Carmen Caballero-Navas, ed. and trans, *The Book of Women's Love and Jewish Medieval Literature on Women (Sefer Ahavat Nashim)* (London; New York; Bahrein: Kegan Paul Limited, 2004), 53; according to Abbaye's mother: "All incantations which are repeated several times must contain the name of the patient's mother." Talmud Shab. 66b.

[86]   See Claude Gaignebet and J. Dominique Lajoux, *Art profane et religion populaire au moyen âge* (Paris: PUF, 1985).

[87]   Solomon Grayzel, *The Church and the Jews in the XIII Century: A Study of their Relations During the Years 1198–1254 Based on the Papal Letters and the Conciliar Decrees of the Period* (New York: Hermon Press, 1966), 314–15 (July 15, 1205 Innocent III to the Archbishop of Sens and the Bishop of Paris).

[88]   See the following for a detailed analysis of the literary corpus: Gilbert Dahan, Ernest Renan, Bernhard Blumenkranz, Abraham E. Millgram, Charles Lehrmann, Manya Lifschitz-Golden, M. Steinschneider In the epics, representation is minimal: Jews are mostly reduced to epithets like *desfaez, tirant, félon, fals*. Jewish characters in these texts are often depictions of Jews living at the time of Christ or associated with Saracens. The largest representation of Jews in French literature occurs in religious plays; Heinz Pflaum, "Les Scènes de Juifs dans la littérature dramatique du moyen âge," *Revue des Etudes Juives* 89 (1930): 111–34. (From the twelfth century on, Jews are negatively represented, allowing the authors to introduce a comic element in the play, not possible otherwise with such a topic. They are given ridiculous names such as "Pinceguerre, Trinqua-la-Palha, Malenquarant, Cambafort (note 7 "Mal encarat (prov.) "à mine renfrognée [sullen face], Camba fort (prov.) cuisse, "quartier de porc [pork hind], or real names like Haquin, Vivant, Mousa, Marques . . . 113–15).

fact, the Jew who appeared upon the stage, in tales, chronicles, and in the moralized anecdotes or exempla of the preachers was not an individual but a type, the pattern after which the entire community was modeled. In these productions, the Jew often lacked a name, and rarely did he have personal characteristics.[89] In a more general sense, Jews were the stock liminal characters embodying evil and treason. The accusation of witchcraft practices in real life translated into the literary texts and vice versa.

The romance-epic *Li Roumans de Berte aus Grans pies* (late thirteenth century) is a good example of that conventional practice. There are no Jewish characters in the narration, but their hated practices become apparent in the discourse of two of the female characters. The author, Adenet le Roi, combines in his contemporaneous rendering of the story of Berthe, the future wife of Pepin the Brief, the historical and the folkloric elements that surrounded the obscure origins of this woman. Although the story originated in the eighth century, this "roumans" evolves in the midst of Louis IX's and Philip le Hardi's courts. In the plot that focuses almost exclusively on women, two of them, mother and daughter of serf origin, bring about an immediate change in their social status by substituting the bride during the nuptial night (a folklore-type motif). When the subterfuge is about to be uncovered, Margiste, the mother, is presented as a typological sorceress, a stock device in medieval literature. The mother reveals to her daughter that her knowledge of poisons was transmitted to her by a Jewish woman, another recurrent trope in French literature:

> A enherber m'aprist jadis une juise
> Mieus le sai ne set femme qui dusques en Frise
> Blancheflour traÿrai en poire ou en cerise
> Dou venin serai tost pourveüse et pourquise[90]

> [To make poisons a long time ago a Jewess taught me
> No woman knows how to better than me from here to Frise
> Blancheflour will turn into a pear or cherry
> Of venom I will soon be the purchaser and purveyor]

Adenet le Roi portrays these two women of lower social status in very negative terms. Though Christian, they exhibit all the ill sides of the decried group, insinuating that Jewish negative influence permeated the social fabric through women. While the mother indirectly stands as the stereotypical Jewess who is a brewer of poisons, Aliste, the daughter, represents another stereotypical aspect of

---

[89]  Joshua Trachtenberg, *The Devil and the Jews: The Medieval Conception of the Jew and Its Relation to Modern Antisemitism* (Philadelphia: Jewish Publication Society of America, 1983), 13.

[90]  Adenés Li Roi, *Li Roumans de Berte aus Grans pies*, ed. Auguste Scheler (Bruxelles: Closson, 1874), verses 1830–34.

Jews: usury and moneylending. This ambitious but more pragmatic character proposes an alternate lifestyle to her mother, denoting a Jewish influence: "De prester à usure très bien nous garirons"[91] [by usury lending very well we will be saved].

The "scaffolding," or series of invisible screens that Jewish communities had patiently erected for protection over centuries, was subjected to constant strains, and the fissures inflicted by repeated expulsions and setbacks since 1180 further exposed its vulnerability. With the final blow of 1394, the entire structure collapsed and the remaining Northern French Jews were sent once more into exile, scattered east, north, and south, closing a long chapter of cohabitation.

Fragility is the term that best summarizes the Judeo-Christian relations. However, despite being subjected to a formidable pressure and to an array of religious and secular interdictions, provisions and concessions made cohabitation possible although precarious. Jewish women, defined both in contrast and in relation to a male-centered society, have often emerged as silent figures thus cultivating persisting stereotypes. Nevertheless, in spite of the dearth of documentation and the difficult task of dissociating women's experiences from the collective identity, the available sources reveal that frequent exchanges between Jewish and Christian women took place and occasionally nurtured more positive interrelations.[92]

French Jewish culture vanished completely for several centuries.[93] And until their reinsertion in French society four centuries later, this group that had been socially peripheral proved to be symbolically much more important. Indeed, the vanished Jews left persistent traces, definite imprints on the French cultural landscape.

---

[91]  Adenés Li Roi, *Li Roumans de Berte aus Grans pies*, verse 1850.

[92]  A similarly complex situation emerges in medieval German literature where we come across numerous examples where Jews more often than not enjoy a rather positive reputation, see Albrecht Classen, "Jewish-Christian Relations in the German Middle Ages – the Exploration of Alternative Voices? The Deconstruction of a Myth or Factual History? Literary-Historical Investigations," *Amsterdamer Beiträge zur älteren Germanistik* 58 (2003): 123-49; id., "Jewish-Christian Relations in Medieval Literature," *German Literature Between Faiths: Jew and Christian at Odds and in Harmony*, ed. Peter Meister, 53-65.

[93]  Roger S. Kohn, "L'Expulsion des Juifs de France en 1394: Les Chemins de l'xil et les refuges," *Archives Juives* 28–1 (1995): 76–84; here 80.

Jeanette S. Zissell

(University of Connecticut)

# Universal Salvation in the Earthly City: *De Civitate Dei* and the Significance of the Hazelnut in Julian of Norwich's *Showings*[1]

In the medieval period, as now, urban space could define the identity of the individuals who dwelled within it. A London citizen could claim special rights and privileges within the city that all others could not.[2] Chaucer satirizes Londoners and city life in general throughout many of his tales, and Dante's souls in Hell are acutely aware of their city affiliations, even as they suffer eternal torments.[3] One's city shapes how one views the world, what one wears and eats, and who one's enemies may be. *Where* someone is, in a sense, defines *who* someone is.

This paper will consider how Julian of Norwich (born sometime in the years 1342 or 1343) adapts the medieval conception of urban space to a theological purpose. In doing so she followed a tradition that originates in the Bible, in the Book of Revelation's description of the heavenly city in which God will dwell among the souls of all the saved at the end of time. Augustine of Hippo uses this abstraction to describe the spiritual status of the whole of humanity. The Heavenly city, in this interpretation, is the eternal home of those who love God, and its enemy, the earthly city, is a temporary refuge of those who love only themselves. Citizenship in either city is defined by spiritual similarity rather than by any

---

[1] I would like to thank C. David Benson for reviewing previous drafts of this article.

[2] For example, the ability to participate in higher level city politics, and greater freedom to trade within the city. See Shannon McSheffrey, *Marriage, Sex, and Civic Culture in Late Medieval London* (Philadelphia: University of Pennsylvania Press, 2006), especially 10–11.

[3] For an in-depth review of Chaucer's relationship to London and literary depictions of cities, see *Chaucer and the City*, ed. Ardis Butterfield, Chaucer Studies, 37 (Cambridge: D. S. Brewer, 2006). To learn more about Dante's satire of contemporary Florence, see John M. Najemy, "Dante and Florence," *The Cambridge Companion to Dante*, ed. Rachel Jacoff (Cambridge: Cambridge University Press, 2007), 236–56. For the broader issue, the individual's identity with a city, see the contribution to this volume by Albrecht Classen.

connection with geographical location, culture, or time. The image is used in literature, such as the Middle English poem *The Pearl*,[4] and the works of other theologians such as Bernard of Clairvaux.[5] The design and ornamentation of churches were often intended to evoke the heavenly city to which parishioners believed that they really belonged.[6]

As anyone who studies Julian notes, little is known about her life. However, scholars nearly universally acknowledge the beauty, incisiveness, and theological complexity of her prose. As Rita Mary Bradley states, "Julian of Norwich is the first known woman of letters in English literature, and one is hard-put to find prose superior to hers in the Middle English period."[7] She produced two books in her lifetime, both describing a series of religious visions she experienced during a life-threatening illness in May of 1373 at the age of thirty and a half. The first book, known as the "short text," seems to have been written shortly after the visions took place, and the second, the "long text," was a more detailed adaptation of the first, written after at least twenty years of contemplation about the meaning of what she had seen. At some point in her life, probably after her visions had taken place, she was enclosed as an anchorite at the Church of St. Julian in Norwich.[8] The name of this church is the only name by which she is known. It is clear through the records of bequests given to her as anchorite of this church that she lived at least until the year 1416, but her exact date of death is unknown.[9]

---

[4]    The poem's description of the heavenly city may be found in lines 973–1092, *Pearl*, ed. Sarah Stanbury (Kalamazoo: Medieval Institute Publications, 2001). See also the contribution to this volume by Britt C. L. Rothauser.

[5]    For a brief summary of Bernard of Clairvaux's take on the heavenly city, see Adriaan H. Bredero, *Bernard of Clairvaux: Between Cult and History* (Grand Rapids: Eerdmans Publishing, 2001), especially 267–75.

[6]    Herbert L. Kessler, *Seeing Medieval Art* (Peterborough, Orchard Park: Broadview), 34.

[7]    Rita Mary Bradley, "Julian of Norwich: Writer and Mystic," *An Introduction to the Medieval Mystics of Europe: Fourteen Original Essays*, ed. Paul E. Szarmach (Albany: State University of New York Press, 1984), 195–216; here, 195.

[8]    For more information about medieval anchorites and anchoritic life, see F.A. Jones, "Anchorites and Hermits in Historical Context," *Approaching Medieval English Anchoritic and Mystical Texts*, ed. Dee Dyas, Valerie Edden and Roger Ellis, Christianity and Culture: Issues in Teaching and Research (Woodbridge and Rochester, NY: D. S. Brewer, 2005), 3–18.

[9]    Biographical information regarding Julian's life may be found in Mary R. Reichardt's *Exploring Catholic Literature: A Companion and Resource Guide* (Lanham: Rowman and Littlefield, 2003), especially 43–58, and also in John Jae-Nam Han's "Julian of Norwich," *Catholic Women Writers: A Bio-Bibliographical Sourcebook*, ed. Mary R. Reichardt (Westport: Greenwood, 2001), 187–92; see also Lisa Gaudet, "Julian of Norwich," *Women in the Middle Ages: An* Encyclopedia, ed. Katharina M. Wilson and Nadia Margolis, vol. I (Westport, CT, and London: Greenwood Press, 2004), 499–503.

Julian was enclosed within a vibrant city that had achieved a population of 25,000 people by 1330.[10] However, despite living in the heart of such a large town, Norwich itself is notably absent from her writing. In her account, Julian describes cities as theological abstractions, in the tradition rooted in Augustine's work. Julian, as an anchorite, was more interested in the heavenly city, and, as I will argue, in the earthly city, as she saw them reflected within her own spirit. She is not slavish in her adaptation of these images, and argues, against Augustine's prevailing model, that both cities are held equally in God's love. Her knowledge of the image, and her ability to adapt and change it to suit her own theology demonstrates the significance that urban space could have as a medieval model of spiritual identity.

The idea at the heart of Julian of Norwich's *Showings* has long been acknowledged as the transcendental power of divine love. This seemingly straightforward theme, however, raises more questions than it answers. What does love mean from the perspective of the divine? How far can that love extend to those who dwell in a sinful world? Julian's simple message of God's love required two texts, short and long, apparently written over the course of a lifetime to explore. Throughout her *Showings*, Julian attempts to push the limits of Christian theology outwards, to place God's love, rather than his omnipotence or judgment, at the center of all theological issues.

In my paper I intend to discuss the ways in which Julian of Norwich uses the image of the heavenly and earthly cities to explore the nature of God's love for mankind. Julian's reading forms a response to the predominant medieval understanding of the two cities, initially established by Augustine in *De civitate Dei*, nearly a thousand years before her visions took place. Augustine depicts the two cities as wholly separate, diametrically opposed entities. The heavenly city is eternal, but at the end of time the earthly city will be destroyed, and its citizens will be condemned to hell for their prideful self-love. To Augustine, the two cities symbolize separation and judgment.

To Julian, however, the two cities both equally represent the soul's union with God. I wish to argue that Julian's discussion of the heavenly and earthly cities centers largely on two sections of the text. The first is the passage regarding the hazelnut, found at the beginning of her visions, in which she describes the whole of the world as not larger than a hazelnut lying in the palm of her hand, and which, despite its smallness, will be forever held in God's love. I believe that this hazelnut represents Julian's reinterpretation of Augustine's earthly city. The second is the passage which closes the visions, where Julian describes her

---

[10]    Norman Tanner "Religious Practice," *Medieval Norwich*, ed. Carole Rawcliffe and Richard Wilson (London: Hambledon Continuum, 2006), 137–56; here, 141.

334 Jeannette S. Zissel

discovery of the heavenly city, and finds that it is nestled deeply into her own heart. Both depict the whole of human society in a microcosm, held in the body of the believer. Both are eternally preserved by God's love. In the similarity of the language and imagery used to describe them, they naturally evoke each other in the reader's minds.

Through her depiction of the earthly city, in the hazelnut passage, as a fundamentally good entity that is eternally preserved by God's love, she essentially equates its spiritual status with that of the heavenly city. In some sense, to Julian, the earthly and heavenly cities consist of the same spiritual space, located inside the believer. By so uniting earth and heaven, Julian raises the possibility of the universal salvation for all humanity. Where Augustine, in *De civitate Dei*, uses the prideful, fleeting nature of the earthly city to argue against Origen's argument for universal salvation, Julian inverts his strategy against itself, and uses the same image to explore the possibility of eternal redemption for all mankind.[11]

While Julian's depiction of the heavenly city has sometimes been compared with Augustine's, it is more often associated with the heavenly city as described in Revelation.[12] Christopher Abbot reads Julian's use of the heavenly city image as rooted partly in *De civitate Dei*, but does not relate the earthly city image with that of the hazelnut.[13] Overall, there seems to have been more discussion of an Augustinian influence on Julian through the *Confessiones* and *De Trinitate* than there has been through *De civitate Dei*.[14] The influence of *De civitate Dei* on Julian's

---

[11]  Peter Dinzelbacher, "Ekstatischer Flug und visionäre Weltschau im Mittelalter," id., *Von der Welt durch die Hölle zum Paradies—das mittelalterliche Jenseits* (Paderborn, Munich, et al.: Ferdinand Schöningh, 2007), 181–206; here 196, emphasizes the symbolic meaning of the hazelnut as an expression of the vanity and irrelevance of this material world in face of the macrocosm. According to Dinzelbacher, the hazelnut might be loved by God, but it still distracts from the true goal the human soul ought to pursue. In my paper I will offer the opposite reading.

[12]  Nicholas Watson and Jacqueline Jenkins, for instance, note that: "The city in the soul resembles the New Jerusalem of Rev. 21:1–27, as represented in art and poems such as *Pearl* or *The Pricke*." See *The Writings of Julian of Norwich: A Vision Showed to a Devout Woman and a Revelation of Love*, ed. Nicholas Watson and Jacqueline Jenkins (University Park: Pennsylvania University Press, 2006), 110. Quotations of Julian's *Showings* are from the version of the long text included in Watson and Jenkin's edition, unless the short text is specifically indicated.

[13]  See Christopher Abbot, *Julian of Norwich: Autobiography and Theology*. Studies in Medieval Mysticism, 2 (Cambridge: Brewer, 1999), 155.

[14]  Abbot has identified Augustine's *Confessiones* as an indirect model for Julian's autobiographical approach to writing her *Showings* (ibid., 10), and J. P. H. Clark believes there is evidence she may have known *De Trinitate* either directly or through other sources, such as Peter Lombard's *Sentences*. See J. P. H Clark, "Time and Eternity in Julian of Norwich," *Downside Review* 109 (1991): 259–76. Denise Baker also reads *De Trinitate* as a source for Julian's understanding of the structure of the soul. See "The Structure of the Soul and the "Godly Wylle" in Julian of Norwich's *Showings*," *The Medieval Mystical Tradition in England*, ed. E. A. Jones. Exeter Symposium, 7 (Cambridge: D. S. Brewer, 2004), 37–49; especially 37–38. Directly or indirectly, it would be

understanding of the heavenly and earthly cities warrants more investigation than it has yet received.

Julian is an independent thinker and writer, aware of but not constrained by the theological inheritance from Augustine. As J. P. H. Clark states, "Julian of Norwich seldom quotes authorities, but her creative insights can repeatedly be shown to be rooted in theological tradition," and also that "it is clear that she could grasp and express the commonplaces of theology, especially those of Augustinian theology."[15] While some see similarities in interpretation between Augustine's theology and Julian's,[16] most argue for some degree of divergence between the two. Those who argue for the strongest degree of separation between them, such as Kenneth Leech, Maria R. Lichtman, and Kevin J. Magill, tend to focus on their interpretations of the sinfulness of the body.[17] However, most view Julian's theology as divergent from Augustine's in the interpretation of specific doctrines, rather than through an overarching rejection of the theological tradition he established. For example, Denise Baker asserts that, in contrast with Walter Hilton's more standard recapitulation of Augustine's *De Trinitae*, Julian adapts his interpretation of the *imago Dei* in a way that is "so different from his more traditional recapitulation as to constitute an innovative contribution to late-medieval theology," and yet finds its conceptual basis in Augustine nonetheless.[18] J. P. H. Clark suggests that she reinterprets Augustine's assertion that God stands outside of time, stating that while "the emphasis on the timelessness of God's vision can claim affinities with Augustine, the manner in which it is applied nevertheless goes beyond him."[19]

It is in the same spirit that Julian reinterprets the heavenly and earthly cities to express the value of all life as it is held in the love of God. Julian's ideas may indeed be innovative, but in their innovation they do not completely reject

---

difficult for any serious religious thinker to avoid Augustine's pervasive influence on medieval thought.

[15] Clark, "Time and Eternity," 259.

[16] Abbot in particular identifies a "retrospectively discernable Augustinian paradigm operative within the text." See Abbot, *Autobiography and Theology*, 34.

[17] See Kenneth Leech, "Hazelnut Theology: Its Potential and Perils," *Julian Reconsidered*, ed. Kenneth Leech and Sr. Benedicta Ward, SLG (Oxford: SLG Press, 1988) 1–9; especially 3. See also Maria R. Lichtmann, "God fulfilled my bodye": Body, Self, and God in Julian of Norwich," *Gender and Text in the Later Middle Ages*, ed. Jane Chance (Gainesville, Tallahassee, et al.: University Press of Florida, 1996), 263–79, and Kevin J. Magill, *Julian of Norwich: Mystic or Visionary?* Routledge Studies in Medieval Religion and Culture (London and New York: Routledge, 2006), especially 116.

[18] Denise Baker, "The Image of God: Contrasting Configurations in Julian of Norwich's *Showings* and Walter Hilton's *Scale of Perfection*," *Julian of Norwich: A Book of Essays*, ed. Sandra J. McEntire. Garland Medieval Casebooks, 21 (New York and London: Garland, 1998), 35–60; here 35.

[19] J. P. H. Clark, "Predestination in Christ According to Julian of Norwich," *Downside Review* 100 (1982): 79–91; here, 83.

Augustine or the Augustinian tradition, but instead adapt his ideas to new purposes. Indeed, "Like a wise scribe, she brings out of her treasure things new as well as old, yet what is new has its roots in tradition."[20]

Before further exploring Julian's interpretation of the two cities, it is perhaps necessary to briefly explain Augustine's interpretation of them. The two cities discussed in *De civitate Dei* find their origin in Isaiah 65:17–19 and Revelation 21:1–4, both of which describe a heavenly Jerusalem, created when all former creations perished, and in which there will be no tears.[21] Augustine identifies all those who shall be saved as members of this heavenly city, and expands upon the Biblical passage to describe an opposing, earthly city, whose members will be damned at the end of time. To Augustine, the two cities represent "the most fundamental cleavage in humanity."[22] These two groups, divided against each other, represent the essential state of mankind, both in this world and after the final judgment.[23]

---

[20]  J. P. H. Clark, "Nature, Grace and the Trinity in Julian of Norwich," *Downside Review* 100 (1982): 203–20.

[21]  In the Douay Reims Bible, Isaiah 65:17–19, reads as follows: "For behold I create new heavens, and a new earth: and the former things shall not be in remembrance, and they shall not come upon the heart. But you shall be glad and rejoice for ever in these things, which I create: for behold I create Jerusalem a rejoicing, and the people thereof joy. And I will rejoice in Jerusalem, and joy in my people, and the voice of weeping shall no more be heard in her, nor the voice of crying." Augustine directly references this passage in book XX, Chapter 17 of *De civitate Dei*. Revelation 21:1–4 mirrors the Book of Isaiah's language: "And I saw a new heaven and a new earth. For the first heaven and the first earth was gone, and the sea is now no more. And I John saw the holy city, the new Jerusalem, coming down out of heaven from God, prepared as a bride adorned for her husband. And I heard a great voice from the throne, saying: Behold the tabernacle of God with men, and he will dwell with them. And they shall be his people; and God himself with them shall be their God. And God shall wipe away all tears from their eyes: and death shall be no more, nor mourning, nor crying, nor sorrow shall be any more, for the former things are passed away." All Bible passages are quoted from Douay Reims, as it is the standard English translation of the Latin Vulgate, and, as such, is perhaps the closest English approximation to the Bible as medieval thinkers would have experienced it. The passages quoted here are from *The Holy Bible: Douay Rheims Version*, ed. James Cardinal Gibbons (Rockford: Tan Books, 1989), 814.

[22]  Paul Weithman, "Augustine's Political Philosophy," *Cambridge Companion to Augustine*, ed. Eleaonore Stump and Norman Kretzmann (Cambridge: Cambridge University Press, 2001) 234–52; here, 235.

[23]  Augustine also had a practical purpose in making this distinction. As Gerald Bonner states, *De civitate Dei* is "designed to refute those pagans who claimed that Christianity had ruined the Roman Empire, and to reassure anxious Christians who could not understand why God had not protected Christian Rome against the Goths." See his "Augustine's Understanding of the Church as a Eucharistic Community," *Augustine the Bishop: A Book of Essays*, ed. Fannie LaMoine and Christopher Kleinhenz. Garland Medieval Casebooks, 9 (New York and London: Garland, 1994) 39–64; here, 39. By describing the city of God as distinct from the city of Rome, Augustine finds himself able "to answer the charge that the abandonment of the Roman deities for the God of

In discussing the two cities, Augustine focuses primarily on mankind and its attachment to God—or conversely, to its own, worldly pride. He therefore defines affiliation in either city by the nature of what the individual loves. Book Fourteen, Chapter Twenty-Eight explains this dichotomy:

> Fecerunt itaque civitates duas amores duo; terrenam scilicet amor sui usque ad contemptum Dei, coelestem vero amor Dei usque ad contemptum sui. Denique illa in se ipsa, haec in Domino gloriatur. Illa enim quaerit ab hominibus gloriam: huic autem Deus conscientiae testis maxima est gloria. (XIV.28)[24]

> [Two cities, then, have been created by two loves: that is, the earthly by love of self extending even to contempt of God, and the heavenly by love of God extending to contempt of self. The one, therefore, glories in itself, the other in the Lord; the one seeks glory from men, the other finds its highest glory in God, the Witness of our conscience.][25]

In his argument, Augustine particularly emphasizes human perspective, human love, and human society. Unlike Julian, as I will later demonstrate, Augustine is primarily interested in the social interactions of people in the world, in their loves, rather than God's love for them.[26] The cities are two distinct entities, living side-by-side in the same human society. The differences between them may not be apparent externally, but in reality they are entirely separate and opposed to each other.

If they are separate in the focus of their loves, the two cities are also separate in their eventual fates. Only the members of heavenly city will achieve salvation and be admitted into eternal life. The heavenly city is immortal and unending, and the earthly city, conversely, will fall. The earthly city is a temporary structure, which will cease to exist at the end of time: "Terrena porro civitas, quae sempiterna non erit (neque enim cum in extremo supplicio damnata fuerit, jam civitas erit)" (XV.4; But the earthly city will not be everlasting; for when it is condemned to that punishment which is its end, it will no longer be a city). The structure of the

---

Christianity was an injustice to the gods which had led to Rome's sack by the barbarians" See Weithman, "Political Philosophy," 241. Pagan religious practices were a potential threat to Augustine's belief system. He has a motivation Julian lacks, in the face of this perceived threat, to be divisive in his language and in his interpretation of God's judgment.

[24] All quotations from *De civitate Dei* are from volume 41 of Patrologia Latina.

[25] All English translations of *De civitate Dei* are from *The City of God Against the Pagans*, trans. R.W. Dyson. Cambridge Texts in the History of Political Thought (Cambridge: Cambridge University Press, 1998).

[26] For a detailed discussion of Augustine's social and political theories, see R.A. Markus, "De Civitate Dei: Pride and the Common Good," *Proceedings of the Patristic, Medieaval and Renaissance Conference* 12/13 (1997–1998), 1–16, and John M. Parrish, "Two Cities and Two Loves: Imitation in Augustine's Moral Psychology and Political Theory," *History of Political Thought* 26 (2005): 209–35.

earthly city will be destroyed when it is judged and damned to eternal torment. It is led by Satan, and will be condemned by Christ at the final judgment:

> Cum per Jesum Christum Dominum nostrum, judicem vivorum atque mortuorum, ad debitos fines ambae pervenerint civitates, quarum una est Dei, altera diaboli, cujusmodi supplicium sit futurum diaboli et omnium ad eum pertinentium, in hoc libro nobis, quantum ope divina valebimus, diligentius disputandum est. (XXI.1)

> [We come next to the nature of the punishment which is to be visited upon the devil and all who belong to him when the two cities—the City of God and the city of the devil—have reached their deserved ends through Jesus Christ our Lord, the Judge of the living and dead.]

The appropriate fate for the earthly city is utter annihilation, exacted through Christ's judgment. The earthly city is finite, and will be destroyed at the final judgment:

> Quod est autem de ista civitate mortali homines supplicio primae mortis, hoc est de civitate illa immortali homines supplicio secundae mortis auferre. Sicut enim non efficiunt leges hujus civitatis, ut in eam quisque revocetur occisus; sic nec illius, ut in vitam revocetur aeternam, secunda morte damnatus. (XXI.11)

> [And just as the punishment of the first death removes men from this mortal city, so does the punishment of the second death remove men from the immortal city. For as the laws of this mortal city have no power to call back one who has suffered death, so neither is he who is condemned to the second death recalled again to life eternal.]

Augustine is very clear about the utterly disparate natures of the two cities. They are completely, diametrically opposed to each other: one loves God, the other itself, one lasts forever, the other will perish, one is led by Satan, the other by God.

This binary opposition between the two cities paves the way for Augustine's argument against Origen's theory of universal salvation:

> Nunc jam cum misericordibus nostris agendum esse video, et pacifice disputandum, qui vel omnibus illis hominibus, quos justissimus Judex dignos gehennae supplicio judicabit, vel quibusdam eorum nolunt credere poenam sempiternam futuram, sed post certi temporis metas pro cujusque peccati quantitate longioris sive brevioris eos inde existimant liberandos. Qua in re misericordior profecto fuit Origenes, qui et ipsum diabolum atque angelos ejus post graviora pro meritis et diuturniora supplicia ex illis cruciatibus eruendos atque sociandos sanctis Angelis credidit. (XXI.17)

> [Certain merciful brethren of ours refuse to believe that any or all of those whom the most just Judge shall pronounce worthy of the punishment of hell will suffer eternally. They suppose that the damned are to be released after a fixed term of punishment, longer or shorter according to the amount of each man's sin. I see that I must now deal with these people and engage in peaceable debate with them. In this regard, Origen carried mercy to even greater lengths. For he believed that even the devil himself and

his angels, after suffering the more grievous and protracted punishments which their sins merit, will be released from their torments and united with the holy angels.]

While sympathetic to the desire to believe in the salvation of all mankind, Augustine wholly rejects the possibility that all men will be saved. Such a belief contradicts Augustine's understanding of God's justice. By associating it with the belief in the salvation of the devils, it seems that universalism, in his view, borders on the ridiculous. It is not merely ridiculous, however, but dangerous. He continues on to argue that a universal salvation is not merciful, but actually a cruelty, because it constitutes an injustice to the righteous:

> Sed illum et propter hoc et propter alia nonnulla et maxime propter alternantes sine cessatione beatitudines et miserias et statutis saeculorum interuallis ab istis ad illas atque ab illis ad istas itus ac reditus interminabiles non inmerito reprobauit ecclesia; quia et hoc, quod misericors uidebatur, amisit faciendo sanctis ueras miserias, quibus poenas luerent, et falsas beatitudines, in quibus uerum ac securum, hoc est sine timore certum, sempiterni boni gaudium non haberent.

> [But the Church has condemned Origen, and not without reason, because of this and several other errors. In particular, he suggests that there is a ceaseless alternation of blessedness and misery, and that the interminable transitions from the one state to the other occur at fixed ages. At this point, however, he loses even the mercy which he had seemed to display. For he assigns to the saints real miseries for the punishment of their sins, yet only false happiness, in which there is no true and certain joy in the fearless assurance of eternal goods.]

For Augustine, the heavenly and earthly cities are wholly separate, and to believe in an alteration of their spiritual status after the judgment is to negate the mercy and joy offered to the elect. Their happiness is false, to Augustine, when it is not secure—when it is not eternal and unchangeable. The heavenly city is eternal, and loves God in rejection of all worldly things. The temporal, fleeting earthly city, to its own detriment, loves only itself. To Augustine, only eternal damnation of the condemned and the eternal salvation of the elect can constitute just and thus truly compassionate action on the part of the judge.

Julian's reading of the two cities seems to be entirely opposed to Augustine's. Julian follows its outlines so closely, even while challenging its conclusions at every step, that it seems likely she may have directly or indirectly been aware of the text. It is impossible to know whether or not Julian had read *De civitate Dei* personally, but there is good reason to believe any serious fourteenth-century religious thinker would have been influenced by its interpretation of the heavenly and earthly cities. As M. W. F. Stone states, the text was available and widely used even in the thirteenth century, and his ideas were also known indirectly through other texts:

Thirteenth-century philosophers and theologians knew Augustine primarily through a few standards treatises—*Confessiones, De civitate Dei, De libero arbitrio, De doctrina chirstiana, De vera religione, and Ge Genesi ad litteram libri duodecim*—and through the abundant quotations that circulated under his name in *florilegia*, canon law, and Lombard's *Sententiae.*[27]

The fourteenth century, however, marked a resurgence of interest in Augustine's theology. His texts were more widely and accurately circulated. As Stone states:

> The fourteenth century can be said to have witnessed a profound change in the use and discussion of the works of Augustine by medieval philosophers. To begin with, one finds a greater variety of works being cited, accompanied by longer and more exact quotations. Further to this, there is an earnest effort on the part of scholars to maintain the highest standards of accuracy in their critical presentation of Augustine's views.[28]

This was the environment in which Julian wrote her *Showings*. The Augustinian influence on her text, long acknowledged by scholars, seems to include a reinterpretation of Augustine's theology of the heavenly and earthly cities. She inverts his argument, using the same imagery as a foundation from which to build an entirely different view of human salvation. Where Augustine's focus is on the division of mankind into insoluble categories based on what they love, one eternally saved and the other eternally damned, Julian focuses on what God loves, and what God's love means for believers on earth. As I will argue in the following section, God's love, to Julian, is so pervasive that it extends throughout the earth, to all that has been made, and will never be destroyed. To Julian, the earthly, as well as the heavenly city is held within God's love.

One of the most famous and memorable images in Julian's *Showings* is that of the hazelnut. Appearing in the fifth chapter of the Long Text, it is one of the first in the series of visions Julian relates. Julian describes seeing a little thing, shaped like a hazelnut, sitting in the palm of her hand. It is round, like a ball, and very small. She is told it is all that has ever been made, and she is amazed that creation can sustain itself, because she is aware, holding it in her hand, that it is so small and insignificant that it should hardly be able to exist at all. However, she is overcome at the same time by the assurance, provided for her, that its insignificance and unsustainability are irrelevant, because God's love will never leave it, and that love will allow it to last forever:

[27]   M. W. F. Stone, "Augustine and Medieval Philosophy," Cambridge Companion to Augustine, ed. Eleonore Stump and Norman Kretzmann (Cambridge: Cambridge University Press, 2001), 253–66; here, 255–56.
[28]   Stone, "Augustine and Medieval Philosophy," 259.

And in this, he shewed a little thing the quantity of an haselnot, lying in the palme of my hand as me semide, and it was as rounde as any balle. I looked theran with the eye of my understanding, and thought: "What may this be?" And it was answered generally thus: "It is all that is made." I marvayled how it might laste, for methought it might sodenly have fallen to nought for littlenes. And I was answered in my understanding: "It lasteth and ever shall, for God loveth it. And so hath all thing being by the love of God."

In this little thing I saw three propreties: the first is that God made it, the second is that God loveth it, the thirde is that God kepeth it. But what is that to me? Sothly, the maker, the keeper, the lover. For till I am substantially oned to him I may never have full reste ne very blisse: that is to say, that I be so fastned to him that ther be right nought that is made betweene my God and me. (5.7–18)

I believe that Julian's use of the hazelnut image provides a reinterpretation of Augustine's depiction of the earthly city. Like Augustine, Julian of Norwich presents her audience with an image of earthly creation, balanced with an image of Heaven. However, Julian employs these images to unite the heavenly and the earthly realm—to describe their similarities, rather than their differences.. The hazelnut image, in which Julian holds the whole of creation in her hand and is told that God will love it and preserve it forever, demonstrates an equation of the fates of the earthly city and heavenly city. Both are held equally in God's love. Julian's description of the heavenly city is consistent with her description of the hazelnut, often using the same language to make the same points. In contrast to Augustine's dominant view, Julian's heavenly and earthly cities are united in the believer—one held in the hand, the other in the heart.

Scholars have long acknowledged the hazelnut as an image of God's enduring love for his creation. Most view it as a positive assertion of man's union with God, despite mankind's apparent insignificance and the unworthiness of created creatures to engage in such a union. It has been generally accepted that, to Julian, God's love redeems and preserves the world. Examples of arguments centering on this interpretation of the hazelnut are nearly too numerous to note. Hugh Feiss suggests that:

> Julian's discussion of the littleness of the world is inseparable from the "homely loving" of Christ manifest in his coming to earth and in his suffering for humanity.[29]

The world is small, insignificant, but loved nonetheless. Charles Cummings makes a similar comment:

---

[29]  Hugh Feiss, "Dilation: God and the World in the Visions of Benedict and Julian of Norwich," *American Benedictine Review* 55 (2004): 55–74; here, 65.

Julian's thought is that God holds the whole universe in his loving hands, and though the whole may be as tiny as a hazel nut or a grain of sand yet it is precious in his sight. He made it all, out of his love, and he preserves it all "for tender love."[30]

Susan K. Hagen notes that the everyday familiarity of the hazelnut renders it "an effective and efficient mnemonic device for the remembrance of God's creative, loving, and sustaining power."[31] Kerrie Hide sees the hazelnut image as central to Julian's understanding of salvation, noting that the world, like the nut, is insignificant and small:

> It looks worthless, fragile, as if it could insignificantly fall into nothing, and yet creation is of inestimable value, is precious, and belongs to God. Creation is eternally enfolded in the love of God."[32]

Most scholars regard Julian's interpretation of the hazelnut as a dramatic divergence from Augustine and other medieval thinkers' understanding of God's relationship to his creation. This feeling is particularly strong among those scholars who make a case for Julian's positive understanding of the human body. Grace M. Jantzen sees the hazelnut image as part of the strategy through which Julian provides "a sharp challenge to the idea that chastity is essential for spirituality,"[33] and Zina Petersen agrees, stating that:

> She is gentler than most if not all of her past or contemporary Christian thinkers when discussing such topics as the human body, preferring to praise God for the body's functions rather than condemn the flesh as part of the mortal world to be subdued and cast off. When shown nothingness incomprehensible than "all of creation" as a tiny unit the size of a hazel nut, she at the same time perceives God's tremendous love for the thing as sustaining it.[34]

The hazelnut is the whole of creation, eternally preserved through God's love. In this it provides a striking counter argument to many more commonplace theological arguments, which interpreted creation as inherently flawed and corrupted.

---

[30] Charles Cummings, "God's Homely" Love in Julian of Norwich," *Cistercian Studies* 13 (1978): 68–74; here, 71.

[31] Susan K. Hagen, "St. Cecilia and St. John of Beverly: Julian of Norwich's Early Model and Late Affirmation," *Julian of Norwich: A Book of Essays*, ed. Sandra J. McEntire. Garland Medieval Casebooks, 21 (New York and London: Garland, 1998) 91–114; here, 106.

[32] Kerrie Hide, "Only in God do I Have All: The Soteriology of Julian of Norwich," *Downside Review* 122 (2004): 43–60; here, 51. Also of interest is Hide's *Gifted Origins to Graced Fulfillment: The Soteriology of Julian of Norwich* (Collegeville, MN: Order of St. Benedict, 2001).

[33] Grace M. Jantzen, *Power, Gender, and Christian Mysticism.* Cambridge Studies in Ideology and Religion, 8 (Cambridge: Cambridge University Press, 1995), 238.

[34] Zina Petersen, "Every Manner of Thing Shall be Well": Mirroring Serenity in the *Shewings* of Julian of Norwich," *Mystics Quarterly* 22 (1996): 91–101; here, 238.

Indeed, hazelnuts were closely associated with physicality, sexuality, and the body in medieval medicine and romance tales alike. Peter Dronke, in writing about medieval lyrics, notes "the age-old association of hazelnuts with fertility and erotic fulfillment."[35] To this he adds:

> It is under the hazelnut tree that love has the best chance of being returned, even by those who have shown no love elsewhere. In a wide range of proverbial expressions going into the hazelnut trees [...] is synonymous with love-making; already in the ancient world sterile women were beaten with hazel twigs to make them fertile, and hazelnuts were given to the bride and bridegroom on the wedding-night.[36]

Melitta Weiss Adamson notes that, among their other medical uses, hazelnuts were considered an aphrodisiac.[37] Hazelnuts and hazel trees also often figure in romance literature intimately associated with erotic experiences.[38]

This association with sex, love, and fertility has not gone unnoticed in its connection to Julian's imagery. Liz Herbert McAvoy believes the hazelnut stands as evidence of Julian's use of "gynaecentric imagery,"[39] and associates it with the nuts described in the Biblical Song of Songs:

> However, within the context of the Song of Songs the tiny nut of little value takes on inordinate significance in its association with the *hortus inclusus* which is also the location of sexual desire and its fulfillment.[40]

The earthly city's goodness, in Julian's hazelnut image, seems to be closely associated with erotic, material physicality. It is on earth, after all, that mankind was commanded to be fruitful and multiply. It is the means by which mankind participates in God's creation. The earthly city is a fertile city, bearing fruit like the hazel tree itself, growing like a garden even though Eden is lost.

---

[35] Peter Dronke, *The Medieval Lyric*, 3rd ed. (1968; Woodbridge and Rochester, NY: Boydell and Brewer, 1996), 194.

[36] Ibid., 194.

[37] Melitta Weiss Adamson, *Food in Medieval Times*. Food Through History (Westport: Greenwood, 2004), 25.

[38] For instance, see Karl P. Wentersdorf, "Pandarus's "haselwode": a comparative approach to a Chaucerian puzzle," *Studies in Philology* 89 (1992), 293–313. A hazel tree also figures largely in Tristan and Iseult's tryst, as described in Marie de France's *Chevrefoil*. See William Sayers, "Marie de France's *Chievrefoil*, hazel rods, and the Ogam letters Coll and Uillenn," *Arthuriana* 14 (2004), 3–16. For the iconographic meaning of nuts in general, see Gertraud Meinel, "Nuss, Nussbaum," *Enzyklopaedie des Marchens*, ed. Rolf Wilhelm Brednich, vol. 10.1 (Berlin and New York: Walter de Gruyter, 2000), 159–63.

[39] Liz Herbert McAvoy, *Authority and the Female Body in the Writings of Julian of Norwich and Margery Kempe* (Cambridge and Rochester, NY: Boydel and Brewer, 2004), 84.

[40] Ibid., 83.

Julian's hazelnut image parallels her image of the heavenly city, both in the language she employs and the meaning expressed in that language. The images bookend her visions, one appearing nearly at the beginning of the *Showings*, and the other at the end.

To Julian, the human soul is God's city, in which Christ sits enthroned. The heavenly city image emphasizes God's love for mankind, his union with the believer, and the eternal redemption of all who are united to him in love. This image of the heavenly city seems to be based in the same tradition as Augustine's, and yet responds to his interpretation with a new understanding of the image's significance. Julian relates the heavenly city to the earthly city, echoing the language used in the hazelnut passage to unite the two in the reader's mind.

The long text expands the use of the heavenly city image from the single passage present in the short text. However, all references seem to use the city for the same purpose: to describe the union of mankind with God.[41] In the last vision described in the *Showings*, Julian relates her discovery of the heavenly city in her own heart, in the final vision of the text:

> And then oure good lorde opened my gostely eye and shewde me my soule in the middes of my harte. I saw the soule so large as it were an endlesse warde, and also as it were a blissefull kingdom, and by the conditions that I saw therein I understode that it is a wurshipfulle citte. In middes of that citte sitteth oure lorde Jhesu, very God and very man: a fair person and of large stature, highest bishoppe, solempnest kinge, wurshipfullest lorde. And I saw him clothed solemply in wurshippes. He sitteth in the soule even righte in peas and rest, and he ruleth and yemeth heven and erth and all that is. (68.1–9)

The image of the "wurshipfulle cite" within the believer's soul naturally evokes the heavenly city of the Bible. As in Revelation, Christ dwells within it, in union with it. Both are described in the same terms: the city is "wurshipfulle" and Christ is "wurshipfullest lord," clothed in "wurshippes." It is a place where Christ is constantly loved and praised. In this it seems consistent with Augustine's reading of the heavenly city: it is the eternal dwelling place of those who love God. Julian

---

[41]  These passages, provided in Chapter Fifty-One's parable of the lord and servant, read as follows: "But his sitting on the erth, bareyn and desert, is thus to / mene: he made mannes soule to be his owne citte and his dwelling place, which is / most pleasing to him of all his workes" (51.123–25), and "Now sitteth the son, very God and very man, in his citte in / rest and in pees, which his fader hath dighte to him of endlesse purpose, and the / fader in the son, and the holy gost in the fader and in the son" (51.278–80). These passages all associate the heavenly city with the present world. As I will argue in this section, this seems to be a response to Augustine's reading of the heavenly city, by placing it in the same context as the earthly city, as depicted by the hazelnut. The world, to Julian, is also enclosed within the believer, and God's eternal preservation of both stand as tokens of his love. for all of mankind.

not only looks forward to another place or another time, but also looks within herself as she is now, on earth. The city is located within the believer's heart, in the created world, rather than in a more nebulous, invisible form, only awaiting the judgment to take its true shape. Unlike Augustine's heavenly city, Julian's heavenly city is victorious on earth, as it is in heaven.[42]

The text immediately turns to concerns about the nature of creation, and whether the substance of creation can be sustained forever: "The place that Jhesu taketh in oure soule he shall never remove it withouten / ende, as to my sight, for in us is his homeliest home and his endlesse wonning. And / in this he shewde the liking that he hath of the making of mannes soule" (68.12–14). Julian is assured Christ will never be removed from the soul, and that it is his home without end, just as the heavenly city, in Revelation and in Augustine, is God's eternal home.[43]

The beginning of the hazelnut passage uses precisely the same terms to establish its message. It presents a striking image of the earthly realm in relation to the individual believer: just as the heavenly city is described as enclosed in the believer's heart, the earthly city is enclosed in the believer's hand. Furthermore, it is described as eternal, a prominent divergence from Augustine's interpretation of the fate of the worldly realm:

> And in this, he shewed a little thing the quantity of an haselnot, lying in the Palme of my hand as me semide, and it was as rounde as any balle. I looked theran with the eye of my understanding, and thought: "What may this be?" And it was answered generally thus: "It is all that is made." I marvayled how it might laste, for methought it might sodenly have fallen to nought for littleness. And I was answered in my understanding: "It lasteth and ever shall, for God loveth it. And so Hath all thing being by the love of God." (5.7–13)

This passage bears some striking similarities to the image of the heavenly city provided in chapter sixty-eight. In both, Julian sees some aspect of God's creation in microcosm: the city of God in one instance, and the whole of creation, "all that is made," in the other. In both cases, the observed object rests within her: either enfolded in her grasp, or deep within her, in her heart and soul. In both instances, she is assured that the object will last forever because of its abiding connection to

---

[42] See Frederick Christian Bauerschmidt, *Julian of Norwich and the Mystical Body Politic of Christ.* Studies in Spirituality and Theology, 5 (Notre Dame and London: Notre Dame University Press, 1999), 182–83.

[43] Joan M. Nuth notes the Augustinian source of this image, among its other sources: "While Julian sometimes calls the soul without qualification the city of God, the fact that she often specifically designates sensuality as God's city shows that she was conscious of the historical and bodily implications of the term as employed by Augustine." It seems likely that the hazelnut, in its close association with the body, may also refer to Augustine's earthly city. See *Wisdom's Daughter: The Theology of Julian of Norwich* (New York: Crossroad, 1991), 113.

God. To state that the world "lasteth and ever shall, for God loveth it," is a startling contrast to Augustine's view of the temporary nature of the earthly realm.

As J. P. H. Clark states, regarding the hazelnut, "God's love is shown in conservation as well as in creation."[44] Augustine's interpretation of Heavenly City is also described in these terms. To Julian, God loves the earth as he loves heaven. Both earth and heaven are connected to the living body of the believer, within the world, and will never be destroyed. They are not only loved, but loved in the same way: eternally, within the believer.

In the heavenly city passage in chapter sixty-eight, Julian again refers to "all that is made," arguing creation's inherent connection to God, the believer, and the kingdom of heaven: "Al thing that he hath made sheweth his lordshippe—as understanding / was geven in the same time by example of a creature that is led to "se grete noblinesse / and kingdoms longing to a lorde" (68.19–21). The language used here, again referring to creation as "Al thing that he hath made," draws a parallel in this final vision with the image of the hazelnut depicted in the first. This balance between the two images perhaps reflects the Bible, beginning with Genesis and the creation of all things, and ending with Revelation, and its promise of the heavenly city's eternal reign. The two passages in some sense unite God's heavenly and earthly creations, giving them each equal value. Both "sheweth his lordshippe," and both are specifically described as kingdoms which belong to him. This depiction of the "kingdoms longing to a lorde" stands in contrast to Augustine's more traditional reading of the two cities. More than one kingdom belongs to this lord. Instead of one city ruled by Satan and the other by God, both belong to God.

Both passages reach the same conclusion regarding the importance of the earthly and heavenly realms: both are preserved by God for the express purpose that believers may be united with him. The earth does not provide rest and true security in itself, but it indicates God's love and is a means by which that love will be eternally expressed. The hazelnut passage states that:

> In this little thing I saw three propreties: the first is that God made it, the secund Is that God loveth it, the thirde is that God kepeth it. But what is that to me? Sothly the maker, the keper, the lover. For till I am substantially oned to him I may never have full reste ne very blisse: that is to say, that I be so fastned to him that ther be right nought that is made betweene my God and me. (5.14–17)

The sight of the hazelnut indicates, to Julian, that God is the creator, lover, and preserver of all creation. It is a sign of the believer's union with God that he preserves what he has made, and the lesser nature of earthly creation makes it

---

44    Clark, "Trinity," 203.

clear that "full reste" is impossible without the creator, lover, and preserver of all things.

The same point is made again in the heavenly city passage, this time employing God's heavenly creation as a sign of God's love and a means of union with him. The sight of heaven indicates the need to find rest in God. As Julian states, she comes to

> understonde sothly that oure soule may never have rest in thing that is beneth itselfe. And whan it cometh above alle creatures into itselfe, yet may it not abide in the beholding of itselfe, but alle the beholding is blissefully set in God, that is the maker, wonning therin. For in mannes soule is his very wonning. (68.24–26)

The heavenly city image has, for Julian, the same meaning as the hazelnut image: that mankind's only rest can be found in God. As Christopher Abbot notes, "The climactic sixteenth showing discloses the completion of a retrospectively discernible Augustinian paradigm operative within the text: Julian's concern is with the passage from knowledge and love of created things "wherin is no rest" to knowledge and love of God who is "the very rest."[45] If this is Augustinian in one sense, in that God is the only true source of human happiness, it also diverges from Augustine by the association of the hazelnut with the earthly city. Julian sees the earthly and heavenly cities as equal tokens of the love of God. God is present in both, in the world and in the believer as well as in the heaven that is to come.

Indeed, to Julian, the heavenly city is also not an end in itself, but instead "the highest / light and the brightest shining of the citte is the glorious love of oure / Lorde God, as to my sight" (68.27–29). It is not the city itself, but God's love that is significant. As Cynthea Masson states, "Besides her belief that God dwells within humankind, Julian also discusses the possibility of human entrance into the divine realm."[46] This is another divergence from Augustine's interpretation of the separation of the heavenly and earthly cities, which focused on mankind and mankind's loves. Julian inverts this structure and discusses the two cities in terms of God's love for man, instead of man's love for God.

Augustine defines the two cities in terms of what their members love. Julian responds to this interpretation by applying the same standard to God as Augustine applies to man. To Julian, the heavenly and earthly cities are both signs, indicating that God loves mankind without reservation, just as Augustine argues that mankind must love God beyond all else to warrant admittance to the heavenly

---

[45]  Abbot, *Autobiography and Theology*, 34.

[46]  Cynthea Masson, "The Point of Coincidence: Rhetoric and the Apophatic in Julian of Norwich's *Showings*" *Julian of Norwich: A Book of Essays*, ed. Sandra J. McEntire. Garland Medieval Casebooks, 21 (New York and London: Garland, 1998), 153–81; here 168.

city. The hazelnut, as a symbol of the world, alters Augustine's interpretation to explore new interpretations of the earthly city's significance. Julian transforms it from an impermanent, damned kingdom ruled by Satan, to a symbol and testament of God's love.

Julian's message is nearly universally acknowledged as one of the overpowering nature of God's love. Scholars repeatedly note Julian's positive understanding of man's relationship with God. Karl Tamburr states that "Julian proposes a vision of redemption that is ultimately more tolerant and universal,"[47] and Jay Gilchrist states that Julian's theology is a "theology of mercy."[48] Her text explores the outermost reaches of how God's love can function in a human life. Both in the passages discussed here and in her work as a whole, she experiments with how much and in how many ways God's love can affect men's hearts.[49]

Julian's interpretation of the heavenly and earthly cities suggests that God's love has no limits, and may have the ability to save all of mankind—all members of both cities— from their sins. If Julian is testing the borders of Christian experience, attempting to create a theology based wholly on God's love, then a universal salvation is perhaps the greatest expression of the far extent those borders can reach. Nicholas Watson, among others, proposes that a belief in universal salvation existed in Middle English theology in general, and Julian's *Showings* in particular.[50] He asserts that Julian and other English thinkers espoused "the idea—widely implied in early patristic thought and made explicit by Origen, but attacked in Augustine's *De civitate Dei*, and condemned at the Second Council of

---

[47]   Karl Tamburr, "Mystic Transformation: Julian's Version of the Harrowing of Hell," *Mystics Quarterly* 20 (1994): 60,67; here, 66.

[48]   See Jay Gilchrist, "Unfolding Enfolding Love in Julian of Norwich's Revelations," *Mystics Quarterly* 9 (1983): 67–88, 83.

[49]   This is not to say, however, that she does not discuss the nature evil in her work. See Brad Peters, "The Reality of Evil Within the Mystic Vision of Julian of Norwich," *Mystics Quarterly* 13 (1987): 195–202; and also Simon Tugwell, "Julian of Norwich as a Speculative Theologian," *Mystics Quarterly* 9 (1983): 199–209. Overall, Julian's discussion of evil seems to be separate from her discussion of the heavenly and earthly cities, which focuses on God's love for mankind, in response to the Augustinian interpretation. C. E. Banchich, however, argues that the hazelnut passage is an articulation of pious dread, because it makes Julian and the reader aware of the fragility of existence. See C. E. Banchich, "'A Heavynly Joy in a Dredfulle Soule': Julian of Norwich's Articulations of Dread," *Fear and its Representations in the Middle Ages and Renaissance*, ed. Anne Scott and Cynthia Kosso. Arizona Studies in Middle Ages and the Renaissance, 6 (Turnhout: Brepols, 2002), 311–40; especially 321.

[50]   Many scholars identify Julian's text as a positive assertion of universal salvation. Stephen Fanning also argues that "in the midst of the calamities and pessimism of her age, Julian's message overflows with optimism. Contrary to the prevailing spirit emphasizing the horrors of hell awaiting the unrighteous, Julian believed that Jesus had given her assurance of the universal salvation of humankind," in "Mitigations of the Fear of Hell and Purgatory in the Later Middle Ages: Julian of Norwich and Catherine of Genoa," *Fear and its Representations in the Middle Ages and Renaissance,*, 295–310.

Constantinople in 553—that all humanity will attain salvation."[51] Watson identifies Julian as one of the theologians who revived Origen's belief in a universal salvation for all mankind.[52] It is of particular relevance to this paper that *De civitate Dei* was at the heart of the early church's argument against universal salvation. Where Augustine condemns the members of the earthly city, rejecting Origen's arguments, Julian reshapes the very same image to explore the possibility of universal salvation.

Julian's famous passage, stating that "alle shalle be wele, and alle shalle be wele, and alle maner of thinge / shalle be wel" (27.10–11), may indicate that all people will be saved, just as the hazelnut image suggests the whole of the world will be preserved and never condemned. However, it leaves the mechanism at work vague. *How* will all be saved? If sin has no substance, as Julian suggests, the sinful may not be "things" to her—they may also be without substance, and would not be included in the promise that "all maner of thinge shalle be wel." Her statements may not be definitive. However, Julian in any case founds her understanding of God's interactions with his creation in terms of his overwhelming love for what he has made.

Julian uses the images Augustine used to refute universal salvation to explore its very possibility. She questions the permanent separation of the heavenly and earthly cities, uniting them in their function of indicating the power of God's love for all people.

This kind of depiction of the earthly city is perhaps possible because Julian's focus rests on the spiritual life of an individual believer. She is essentially secure in the knowledge of her salvation. In the first chapter of the short text, she assures her readers that "I trayste sothfastlye that I shulde be safe" (1.17–18). She is not, perhaps, a member, or even a pilgrim captive of the earthly city as Augustine sees it. As an anchorite, or simply even as a believer, she has, in some sense, removed herself from the world, and from anxiety over sin. As Maria R. Lichtmann observes:

> Julian, in her isolation from social structures of family, church, and even religious community, became liberated from some of their confining implications. Her anchorite existence freed her to accept uncommon insights into the spiritual significance of the body. Further, her trust in her own experience, sometimes at odds with the received

---

[51]   Nicholas Watson, "Visions of Inclusion: Universal Salvation and Vernacular Theology in Pre-Reformation England," *Journal of Medieval and Early Modern Studies* 27 (1997): 145–97.

[52]   Watson, "Visions of Inclusion," 162.

authority of the Church, enabled her to unshackle herself from the exclusively patriarchal tradition.[53]

Due to her position, Julian is freed from the burden of instructing an audience. In doing so, Julian embraces the theological traditions of the church in order to explore new ways of understanding those traditions. As we have discussed here, she adapts Augustine's reading of the heavenly and earthly cities to new purposes. She does not reject the imagery, but challenges the argument behind that imagery. In any case, her purpose is not didactic, or apologetic, as Augustine's is. The world, to her, as represented by the earthly city, can be used as a positive image of union with, not opposition to, God.

The heavenly city seems to evoke naturally a comparison with the hazelnut. They are both reduced in scale to depict better the intimate connection between the individual believer and God. They are rendered small enough to be held by one person. One is held in the hand, the other in the heart. Her experience of the heavenly and earthly cities appears to be deeply individual, deeply focused on the personal connection between the individual believer and God. In some sense, the heavenly and earthly cities seem to have a population of two: the individual believer and God. If an individual believer is saved, then, to that believer, *all* is saved: "For in this onehede stondeth / the life of alle mankind that shalle be saved" (9.8–9). All outside of their "onehede" is insignificant, and their "onehede" in turn comprises the whole of existence, through the eternal, unfailing power of divine love.

Julian of Norwich's understanding of the heavenly and earthly cities is part of a long theological tradition, in which urban space is used as a metaphor for spiritual identity. Medieval theologians used city imagery to explain the fundamental nature of humanity, to divide it into political entities directly opposed to each other, like two city-states at war. As one's residence within a real city would convey information about one's identity to the world, so affiliation with the heavenly or earthly city reveals one's inner nature. Julian of Norwich is unique in the way she adapts this imagery in order to explore God's love for mankind. Julian inhabits both the earthly and heavenly cities, and unites them within herself and within the love of the divine. They are no longer opposed, in her view, but instead find harmony within the believer. Julian uses the images to explore the identity of the soul who lives within them, and in whom, paradoxically, those cities in turn

---

[53]   Maria R. Lichtman, "God fulfilled my bodye": Body, Self, and God in Julian of Norwich," *Gender and Text in the Later Middle Ages*, ed. Jane Chance (Gainesville, Tallahassee, Tampa and Boca Raton: Florida University Press, 1996) 263–79; here, 263.

may also be found. The identity Julian finds there is that of God's beloved creation—a creation loved equally within the cities of heaven and earth.

Patricia Turning

(Arizona State University)

# "With Teeth Clenched and an Angry Face:"[1] Vengeance, Visitors and Judicial Power in Fourteenth-Century France

On a spring afternoon in 1332, a business lawyer named Bernardus de Bosto was just one of many individuals making his way through the busy streets of Toulouse toward the town hall. Like many medieval cities, the town hall was situated in a central location in the urban space, where administrators could meet the needs of their constituents in the courtroom, or rid the city of the malefactors locked away in the municipal jail.[2] The building also served as a symbol of civic pride and autonomy, and reportedly stored the trebuchet responsible for the fatal stone that killed Simon de Montfort during the Albigensian Crusade.[3] It is unclear what brought Bernardus de Bosto to the town hall on that specific day, but his presence must have been familiar enough among the people coming and going in the area that a group of men, armed with concealed swords and other weapons, lay in wait for his arrival. When the gang's lookout spotted Bernardus emerging from the crowd, he signaled the others into action. The men began to stalk the lawyer down the prominent Rue de Borbona, and without any words of warning, they withdrew their swords and struck him in the head.[4] Through their repeated blows, lawyer

---

[1]  Archives municipales de Toulouse – FF 57, 45: "cum vulto irata et dentibus fremens." Hereafter referenced as AMT.

[2]  Jules Chalande, *Histoire Monumentale de l'Hôtel de Ville de Toulouse* (Toulouse: Imprimerie St. Cyprien, 1922).

[3]  Henri Gilles, ed. *Les Coutumes de Toulouse (1286) et leur premier commentaire (1296)* (Toulouse: Imprimerie Maurice ESPIC, 1969), 163: "qui lapis fuit projectus per machinam cum quo dictus comes Montisfortis fuit percussus. Que machine est adhuc in palatio communi." For a description of this event, see, for example, William of Tudela and anonymous successor, *The Song of the Cathar Wars: A History of the Albigensian Crusade*, trans. Janet Shirley. Crusade Texts in Translation (Sydney: Ashgate Publishing Limited, 1996), 172.

[4]  AMT– FF57, 31.

Bernardus de Bosto suffered a "devastating and cruel" wound to his face that would leave him perpetually deformed, and bleeding profusely on the ground.[5] Due to the amount of blood, one of the thugs thought he had slit Bernardus' throat, but still decided to strike the lawyer one last time as he lay helpless in the street. Before any spectators could intervene, the men ran to the ancient church of the Daurade, where they assumed the protection of the ecclesiastical privilege of asylum.

It did not take long for Toulouse's twelve elected officials, the capitols, to learn about the dramatic ambush of the lawyer that transpired just steps away from the very building that served their constituents for matters of law and order. City representatives soon sought contact with the fugitives hiding inside the church. Once the assailants realized they were both identified and trapped, they began to reveal that the whole attack had been planned and commissioned by a citizen of the nearby village of Villamuro. They alleged that this man, named Stephanus Saletas, had been in Toulouse on multiple occasions and had promised to pay them handsomely if they "mutilated the lawyer in the face." Later, the attackers provided sworn statements against Saletas to Toulouse's court officials, and detailed his plan and motivation for the whole event. As the evidence mounted against Saletas, the capitols began to mobilize their administration toward preparation for a trial, so that the lawyer Bernardus de Bosto could receive justice for this public affront and his facial disfigurement. However, one significant problem emerged: the city officials of Villamuro claimed authority over the person of Stephanus Saletas and refused to extradite their citizen to Toulouse. It was only through intense negotiation and jurisdictional wrangling that Saletas came to stand trial in Toulouse for his role in the assault against the respected lawyer, Bernardus de Bosto.

Stephanus Saletas's case of conspiracy, mutilation, and the intensive debates concerning extradition was recorded in a notary's register from 1332, found today in the municipal archives of Toulouse. The document as a whole contains the trial transcripts, copies of appeal letters (*papira cedula*), and the capitols' legal correspondence for fifty-two separate cases heard between the months of April and October. Verdicts, unfortunately, do not appear that often in the register. The trials themselves took place in the town hall's courtroom, where the capitols presided over the hearings and handled the many lawyers, jurists, medical experts, defendants, and witnesses who stood before them. So far, historians have only really exploited the transcript of one trial that resulted in the execution of a university student's squire.[6] The rest of the legal proceedings recorded in the

---

5    Ibid., 48.
6    Dubbed by modern scholars as the "Aimery Berenger Affair," this case provoked years of debate
     in the 1330s between the king, pope, and capitols concerning the extent of royal jurisdiction over

register concerned accusations of various violent crimes such as rape, kidnapping, and physical assaults that involved a wide range of weapons. The cases are certainly not representative of all of the criminal activity in Toulouse. If a clerk committed an infraction, for example, he would be tried in an ecclesiastical court. Aside from jurisdictional limitations to the number of cases heard by the capitols, many lesser offences were never recorded or even made it to trial. As the political capital of Languedoc with a population somewhere between 30,000 to 40,000 residents, there is little doubt that, like Paris, the city had its share of unemployed transients who had to steal or resort to violence to survive.[7] But for lesser offenses, perhaps the capitols' notary did not take the time to record the details of the case or to conduct an extensive investigation into the matter. The overwhelming majority of the victims or defendants who came to court were well established in the community; they had permanent residents in Toulouse, and they had extensive social and occupational contacts that provided financial and emotional support in court.[8] So in many respects, the function of the judicial process was not to

---

[7] university students' servants. The original notarial trial transcript is in AMT–FF57, 1–30. The entire case is copied by a different notary's hand in register AMT–FF 58. Fragments of the case have been transcribed in a variety of locations. An abbreviated version of the accusation and some of the witness testimony is copied in AMT–AA6, fol. 23. The archivist Ernest Roschach summarized this document in French in *Ville de Toulouse – Inventaire des Archives Communales Intérieurs à 1790* (Toulouse: Édouard Privat, 1891), 107.–Marcel Fournier published Roschach's version of the trial, and several letters between the King, archbishop of Toulouse, and the capitols from the Vatican archives in *Les Statuts et privilèges des universités françaises, depuis leur fondation jusqu'en 1789*, vol. 1 (Aalen, Germany: Scientia Verlag, 1970), nos. 563–89.

The population estimation is found in Jean-Nöel Biraben, "La Population de Toulouse au XIVe et XVe siècles," *Journal des Savants* (1964): 285–300. Toulouse seems to be a contrast to Paris, where scholars argue that the poor and marginal figures living in the Capetian capital committed most of the criminal offenses. Much of this is linked to the events of the fourteenth century, which led to a displaced population that fled to the capital city of Paris. Jacqueline Misraki, "Criminalité et pauvreté en France à l'époque de la Guerre de Cent Ans," *Études sur l'histoire de la pauvreté*, vol. 2, *Moyen Age – XVIe siècle*, ed. Michel Mollat (Paris: Publications de la Sorbonne, 1974), 535–46. Bronisław Geremek, *The Margins of Society in Late Medieval Paris*, trans. Jean Birrell. Past and Present Publications (1971; Cambridge: Cambridge University Press, 1987), 6–43. Most examinations of Parisian crime come from the only extant criminal register from the Châtelet of Paris dating from 1389 to 1392. From this register, containing one hundred and seven trials involving one hundred and twenty eight defendants, the majority of offenders were amongst the poorest inhabitants of Paris who had no permanent residences or possessions in the city, and had committed theft of some sort. *Registre criminel du Châtelet de Paris du 6 Septembre 1389 au 18 Mai 1392*, ed. M. Henri Duplès-Agier (Paris: Imprimer par C. Lahure, 1861–1864). See, Esther Cohen, "Patterns of Crime in Fourteenth-Century Paris," *French Historical Studies* 11 (1980): 307–27; Claude Gauvard, "La Criminalité parisienne à la fin du Moyen Âge: une criminalité ordinaire?" *Villes, bonnes villes, cités et capitales: Études d'histoire urbaine (XIIe–XVIIIe siècle) offertes à Bernard Chevalier*, ed. Monique Bourin (Caen: Paradigme, 1993), 361–70.

[8] For example, the criminal register AMT, FF–57 from 1332 contains over seventy named primary defendants, of which only three, including Stephanus Saletas, were not residents of Toulouse.

prosecute transient thieves who lurked on the margins of the city, preying upon unsuspecting citizens. Instead, the criminal proceedings allowed the capitols and their officers to resolve conflicts between neighbors and to demonstrate their authority by passing judgment upon their constituents caught, or suspected of, breaking municipal laws. The municipal court then became a forum in which the public and the civic leaders negotiated and solidified notions of inclusion in and exclusion from their constructed lawful society.

The trial of Stephanus Saletas, then, proves to be something of an exception to this rule. He was not a citizen of Toulouse, but he also was not a roaming bandit. His crime was not a spontaneous, emotional attack, but a cold, calculated assault that took months of coordination to unfold finally. Through a close examination of the whole affair using spatial theory as an analytical tool, this article will analyze the points of contact between the "insiders" of Toulouse and "outsiders," and will explore how justice (interpersonal and judicial) was performed in the urban space. Stephanus Saletas's case works on two different levels: the local arena, in which Saletas plotted to disfigure Bernardus de Bosto in order to display his vengeance in a symbolic location in the city; and in the larger regional theater, in which the two urban administrations struggled to demonstrate power by protecting their respective citizens. I will argue that because the infraction transpired in the public space of Toulouse, and involved the humiliation of a celebrated lawyer by the symbolic location of the town hall, the capitols had to go to great lengths to bring the perpetrator back to stand trial in their courtroom, to show that their city space and their citizens were protected, and law and order was maintained.

In order to tease out this interpretation, this article will follow the tradition of recent historians who have borrowed the notions of spatial theory in order to understand judicial trials as a performance, or ritual, of justice. Until recently, geographers were the most interested in applying social theories to constructs of space. They argued that because people need space in which to interact, and act a certain way because of their surroundings, understandings of spatial and social processes are inseparable concepts. In other words, trying to "explain why something occurs is to explain why it occurs where it does."[9] Whereas the discipline of geography urged historians to think more critically about space, Henri Lefebvre's work, *La Production de l'espace*, originally published in 1974, has been extremely influential also in driving scholars to unravel how space is

9     Robert David Sack, *Conceptions of Space in Social Thought: A Geographic Perspective* (Minneapolis: University of Minnesota Press, 1980), 70. Other geographers have incorporated sociological perspectives to emphasize how geographical planning, or proximity, and social relationships are interrelated, and interdependent forces. For urban planning, see David Harvey, *Social Justice and the City* (Baltimore: Johns Hopkins University Press, 1973).—

perceived, conceived, and lived.[10] Having accepted that the concept of space entailed more than mere geometrical confines, theorists, such as Michel Foucault and Pierre Bourdieu, described space as a contested geography and territory, over which groups and individuals try to exert power and control.

In *Power/Knowledge*, Foucault argued that, "a whole history remains to be written of spaces — which would at the same time be the history of powers . . . from the great strategies of geo-politics to the little tactics of the habitat."[11] Bourdieu came to a similar conclusion through his observation's of the Berber group, asserting that the power of a society's dominant group lay in its ability to control the constructions of reality that reinforce its own status, so that subordinate groups accept the social order, and their own place in it.[12] To maintain their advantages, any powerful group must create an ordering of space for subservient groups through symbolic rituals, laws, or the regulation of habitation and work opportunities. However, the power of a dominant group's power over space is not permanent. In her study of the male use of spatial power to subordinate women, Daphne Spain revealed that the "reciprocity between space and status arises from the constant renegotiation and re-creation of the existing stratification system."[13] At all levels of the social hierarchy and socialization process, powerful and less-powerful groups are continually vying to assert, or maintain their power over space.

Over the past few years, medieval historians have begun to examine the various ways in which monarchs, municipal governments, and the common man manipulated, perceived, and lived in their urban space in light of spatial theory. As the editors of *City and Spectacle* acknowledge, "to medieval urban inhabitants, space was not neutral. Selection of particular spaces for events speaks to exclusion of some urban inhabitants as well as inclusion of others."[14] On a large scale, people living in medieval cities recognized the symbolic meanings behind civic rituals and ceremonies which were enacted throughout the streets in order to assert municipal authority, legitimize a new monarch, or celebrate pride in a guild's history or achievements. Spectacle used space to show, or refuse, a realignment of power and control, and social cohesion.[15] Beyond royal and religious processions,

---

[10]   Henri Lefebvre, *Production de l'espace* (Paris: Éditions Anthropos, 1974).

[11]   Michel Foucault, *Power/Knowledge: Selected Interviews and Other Writings, 1972–1977*, ed. and trans. Colin Gordon, et al. (New York: Pantheon, 1980), 149.

[12]   Pierre Bourdieu, *Outline of a Theory of Practice*, trans. Richard Nice. Cambridge Studies in Social Anthropology, 16 (1972; Cambridge and New York: Cambridge University Press, 1977), 90–91, 160–63.

[13]   Daphne Spain, *Gendered Spaces* (Chapel Hill: The University of North Carolina Press, 1992), 17.

[14]   Barbara A. Hanawalt and Kathryn L. Reyerson, introduction to *City and Spectacle in Medieval Europe*, ed. Barbara A. Hanawalt and Kathryn L. Reyerson. Medieval Studies at Minnesota, 6 (Minneapolis: University of Minnesota Press, 1994), ix–xviii.

[15]   Mervyn James, "Ritual, Drama and Social Body in the Late Medieval English Town," *Past and*

the residents of medieval cities also witnessed a copious number of public executions and punishments. Through the gory disfigurement and symbolic sentencing of criminals, which took place in various parts of the city, the urban crowd could witness the power of the municipal jurisdiction and the return of civic order.[16]

From these early efforts to explain how a well-orchestrated spectacle reinforced the sovereignty of the centralized authority, more historians have begun to unpack trials themselves as a civic ritual of justice performed throughout the city space. Robert Bartlett, for example, argues that the trials should be interpreted as windows into greater meanings of the interaction within social communities and concepts of crimes.[17] In other words, the trial itself served as a "staged event" in which the criminal proceedings were a play of a real life drama.[18] The "tales" that are told in the court records bring to light the values of the judges and the judged, and establish the society's system of rules of behavior.[19] Thus, the notary's description of crimes and the witness testimony reveal to historians the boundaries of good and bad behavior, and decided who was included in and excluded from an ordered society.[20] Michel de Certeau asserts that trials are "spatial" stories in

*Present* 98 (February 1983): 3–29.

[16] Joëlle Rollo-Koster, "The Politics of Body Parts: Contested Topographies in Late-Medieval Avignon," *Speculum* 78 (January 2003): 66–98. Mitchel B. Merback, *The Thief, The Cross and the Wheel: Pain and the Spectacle of Punishment in Medieval and Renaissance Europe* (London: Reaktion Books, 1999). Esther Cohen, "'To Die a Criminal for the Public Good': The Execution Ritual in Late Medieval Paris," *Law, Custom, and the Social Fabric in Medieval Europe: Essays in Honor of Bryce Lyon*, ed. Bernard S. Bachrach and David Nicholas. Studies in Medieval Culture, XXVIII (Kalamazoo, MI: Medieval Institute Publications, 1990), 285–304. Walter Prevenier, "Violence Against Women in a Medieval Metropolis: Paris Around 1400" *Law, Custom, and the Social Fabric*, 263–84. Claude Gauvard, "Pendre et dépendre à la fin du Moyen Âge: les exigences d'un rituel judiciaire," *Riti e rituali nella società medievali*, ed. Jacques Chiffoleau, Lauro Martines, and A. Paravicini Bagliani (Spoleto: Centro italiano di studi sull'alto medioevo, 1994), 191–214. Guido Ruggiero, "Constructing Civic Morality, Deconstructing the Body: Civic Rituals of Punishment in Renaissance Venice," *Riti e rituali nelle società medievali*, 175–90.–

[17] See, Robert Bartlett, *The Hanged Man: A Story of Miracle, Memory, and Colonialism in the Middle Ages* (Princeton: University of Princeton Press, 2004).

[18] Antoine Garapon, *Bien Juger: Essai sur le rituel judiciaire* (Paris: Odile Jacob, 1997). Andrée Courtemanche divides one trial into literary categories such as "protagonists" and the "plot" in "The Judge, The Doctor, and the Prisoner: Medical Expertise in Manosquin Judicial Rituals at the End of the Fourteenth Century," *Medieval and Early Modern Ritual: Formalized Behavior in Europe, China, and Japan*, ed. Joëlle Rollo-Koster. Cultures, Beliefs, and Traditions, 13 (Leiden and Boston: Brill, 2002), 105–23.

[19] Daniel Lord Smail, "Telling Tales in Angevin Courts," *French Historical Studies* 20 (1997): 183–215. Natalie Zemon Davis, *Fiction in the Archives: Pardon Tales and their Tellers in Sixteenth-Century France*. The Harry Camp Lectures at Stanford University (Stanford, CA: Stanford University Press, 1987).

[20] For example, B. Ann Tlusty examines witness testimony in early modern Augsburg in order to argue that the society had varying levels and standards of acceptable violence, particularly among

a sense, drawing both literal and figurative borders in the city: restrictions of acceptable behavior, communal obligations of conduct, as well as physical boundaries of social interaction in neighborhoods and city streets.[21] The litigants who brought cases before the capitols did not necessarily consider the outcome of the trial as the most important factor of the dispute. Instead, the public nature of the accusation and the spectacle of the social drama involved in taking an enemy to court were just as significant.[22] Medieval people invested in pressing charges against their enemy, not necessarily for the financial outcome, but because they could defame an opponent, or give legitimacy to the hatred or anger they may possess. So for both the capitols and the litigants there was more at stake then just an outcome of the trial. The citizens received an audience for their grievance, and the administrators could establish their sovereignty.

This essay attempts to situate the trial of Stephanus Saletas within the historiography of spatial theory by accepting urban space as a contested topography over which different groups struggle to maintain dominance through displays and negotiations of power. In other words, the city streets and public squares, buildings, and landmarks of Toulouse served as a forum for the residents and the administration to "perform" their status, to suppress a rival, or to seek restitution for some perceived injustice. To accentuate this point, my analysis of the case will be divided into two parts. The first portion will explore the planned assault against Bernardus de Bosto. The court records reveal that after a business transaction went awry between Stephanus Saletas and the lawyer, Saletas vowed to avenge this dishonor through the spectacle of mutilation. Even though he was a citizen of Villamuro, and thus an outsider to the social hierarchy of Toulouse, he still aspired to have this retaliation take place in public. But instead of playing a leading role, he was content to work through his personal connections in the city to orchestrate the event from a distance. In the second portion of the case, the struggle for jurisdiction over Saletas, the capitols utilized this interpersonal crime to display and solidify their jurisdictional sovereignty both within the city limits and beyond. This case was an opportunity for social and judicial power structures to be negotiated, and legitimized, within a public urban sphere.

---

the artisans who frequented taverns. "Violence and Urban Identity in Early Modern Augsburg: Communication Strategies Between Authorities and Citizens in the Adjudication of Fights," *Cultures of Communication from Reformation to Enlightenment: Constructing Publics in the Early Modern German Lands*, ed. James Van Horn Melton. St. Andrews Studies in Reformation History (Aldershot, Hants, England, and Burlington, VT: Ashgate Publishing Company, 2002), 10–23

[21] Michel de Certeau, *The Practice of Everyday Life*, trans. Steven Rendall (Berkeley: The University of California Press, 1984), 123.

[22] Daniel Lord Smail, *The Consumption of Justice: Emotions, Publicity, and Legal Culture in Marseille, 1264–1423*. Conjunctions of Religion and Power in the Medieval Past (Ithaca, NY: Cornell University Press, 2003), 23.

Due to the nature of the extant archival sources, it is difficult to offer any
accurate assessment of the social composition of Toulouse, or to gain any real
knowledge of the movement of people in and out of the city.[23] But we do know
that by the fourteenth century, the city of Toulouse played a pivotal role in the
political and legal network of southern France. After the French king conquered
the region and ended the Albigensian Crusade in 1229, Toulouse became the
region's headquarters for royal officials sent to protect the interests of the king,
and for the Dominican friars sent by the pope to combat the Cathar heresy.
Between 1280 and 1320, the King Philip the Fair sent large numbers of officers
trained in Roman law to serve in the royal administration in Languedoc as judges,
or as royal procurers.[24] In addition, the region was integrated into the royal judicial
hierarchy by being divided into regions, *sénéchaussées*; each administered by a
seneschal, a royal officer, who had a judicial court, which served as the last court
of appeals in matters before the parlement in Paris.[25] The *sénéchaussées* were then

---

[23]  For the most part, scholars have concentrated on the city's political transition into the royal
kingdom during the thirteenth century. Beyond the copious publications of John Hine Mundy,
the most recent study is Christopher Gardner, "Negotiating Lordship: Efforts of the Consulat of
Toulouse to Retain Autonomy under Capetian Rule (ca. 1229–1315)," Ph.D. dissertation, Johns
Hopkins University, 2002. Historians interested in the city beyond political issues have consulted
tax records, guild statutes, and various ecclesiastical documents in order to ascertain standards
of living, means of economic production, and family structures. For example, in 1335, the capitols
began to gather a census of the taxable wealth of each head of household, either male or female.
Philippe Wolff has worked with these documents extensively from the later fourteenth- and
fifteenth-century in *Les "estimes" Toulousaines des XIVe et XVe siècles* (Toulouse: Centre National
de la Recherche Scientifique, 1956); *Commerces et Marchands de Toulouse (vers 1350–1450)* (Paris:
Librairie Pilon, 1954); and "Toulouse vers 1400: Répartition topographique des fortunes et des
professions," *Regards sur le midi* (Toulouse: Édouard Private, 1978), 269–78. For a discussion of the
available guild records, see Sister Mary Ambrose Mulholland, *Early Guild Records of Toulouse* (New
York: Columbia University Press, 1941). See also her "Statutes on Clothmaking: Toulouse, 1227"
*Essays in Medieval Life and Thought: Presented in Honor of Austin Patterson Evans*, ed. John H. Mundy,
Richard W. Emery, and Benjamin N. Nelson (New York: Columbia University Press, 1955),
167–80. Beyond that documents from the Dominican inquisitors, stationed in Toulouse as early
as 1233, have been exhaustively mined by scholars of heresy and the mechanisms of church
repression, partly because inquisitors such as Bernard Gui kept fastidious records of the penalties
that they administered to the convicted heretics. See, for example, Célestin Douais, ed. *Documents
pour servir à l'histoire de l'inquisition dans le Languedoc* (Paris: H. Champion, 1977); and Walter L.
Wakefield, *Heresy, Crusade and Inquisition in Southern France* (Berkeley: University of California
Press, 1974).

[24]  Joseph R. Strayer, *Les Gens de Justice du Languedoc sous Philippe le Bel* (Toulouse: Association Marc
Bloch, 1970), and *The Reign of Philip the Fair* (Princeton, NJ: Princeton University Press, 1980).
Marie-Martin Chague, "Contribution à l'étude du recrutement des agents royaux en Languedoc
aux XIVe et XVe siècles," *France du Nord et France du Midi: Contacts et influences réciproques*, vol. 1,
*Actes du congrès national des sociétés savantes. Section de philologie et d'histoire jusqu'à 1610* (Paris:
Bibliothèque Nationale, 1971), 359–78.

[25]  This political organization of France is best described in John W. Baldwin, *The Government of Philip
Augustus: Foundations of French Royal Power in the Middle Ages* (Berkeley: The University of

further subdivided into *viguerie*, or *jugerie*, with a royal vicar presiding over a court with a variety of lesser officers and bureaucrats.

Most of these royal officials resided and worked in the Chateau Narbonnais in the southern portion of Toulouse. The newly instituted University of Toulouse also provided the city with a body of professional lawyers and jurists trained in Roman law.[26] The friars resided in various locations throughout the city, but they conducted their trials in the Jacobins monastery, where they standardized and institutionalized the practices of inquest to eliminate heresy. The Dominicans had at their disposal groups of notaries and soldiers who would summon or force suspects into the city of Toulouse to stand trial for their beliefs, or to suffer the consequences of their condemnation. Many of their officers, especially notaries, cruelly extorted money from the people they encountered, and, worse, captured and tortured men and women until they secured confessions.[27] The overlapping jurisdictions of the municipal, royal and ecclesiastical officials in the city led to frequent disputes and confusion, but they also ensured that Toulouse became a fundamental location for the significant legal concerns of the residents of Languedoc.

The municipal court structure of Toulouse dramatically changed due to the presence of these two new influences. All judicial systems, including that of the capitols, benefited from the Dominicans' perfection of the inquisitorial method.[28] In this new process, the authorities no longer had to wait for accusations against malefactors to be brought to their attention; instead, they could actively pursue and prosecute suspects or other deviants by the power of their office. The Dominicans also proved to be tremendously effective in formulating methods of interrogation and ways to extract confessions from people in their custody. As more men were trained in canon and civil law at the universities of Europe, many

---

California Press, 1986), and more recently, Elizabeth M. Hallam, *Capetian France, 987–1328* (New York: Longman, 2001).

[26] A general history of the University of Toulouse may be found in Cyril Eugene Smith, *The University of Toulouse in the Middle Ages: Its Origins and Growth to 1500 A.D.* (Milwaukee, Wisconsin: The Marquette University Press, 1958). Eduard Maurits Meijers has published the debates of the professors of law at the University of Toulouse concerning canonical and civil legal matters from hypothetical situations, and a list of the faculty during the late thirteenth and early fourteenth century, in *Responsa doctorum tholosanorum* (Haarlem: H. D. Tjeenk Willink & Zoon, 1938).

[27] Menet de Robécourt is the best example of a notary who exploited and violently persecuted the inhabitants of Carcassone. See Jean-Marie Vidal, "Menet de Robécourt, commissaire de l'inquisition de Carcassone," *Moyen Âge* 16 (1903): 425–49; James B. Given, *Inquisition in Medieval Society: Power, Discipline and Resistance in Languedoc* (Ithaca: Cornell University Press, 1997), 145–46.

[28] The Fourth Lateran Council in 1215 forbade the use of ordeals in ecclesiastical courts, and systematically outlined provisions of an inquisitorial procedure in tribunals to prosecute suspects. Given, *Inquisition in Medieval Society*, 13–22.

of these techniques of the inquisition carried over into the civic judicial procedures in France. [29]

So the capitols had adopted the mechanisms to investigate allegations of crimes through questioning, detainment, and in some circumstances, torture. But at the same time that the capitols acquired the inquisitorial method, the integration into the royal court hierarchy threatened many of the privileges and customs of the municipal judicial system. The capitols did negotiate with the king in order to preserve some of their traditional legal privileges and laws (which were either accepted or rejected by the king).[30] One of the most contested issues for the capitols concerned who had legitimate custody of the town, and who held jurisdiction over its inhabitants.[31] In October, 1283, Philip III addressed this debate and worked out a compromise between the capitols and the royal vicar.[32]

Most significantly to this essay was the royal proclamation that granted the capitols the right to hear all criminal cases for offenses committed in Toulouse and the surrounding vicariate of Languedoc, either brought to their attention in the form of an official complaint, or if municipal sergeants seized the defendant in the process of committing the crime. During the trial, the vicar or his lieutenant would sit in on the proceedings, and approve the capitols' recommendation for corporal sentences. With this royal mandate, the capitols continued in the role as the first resource for justice for the people of Toulouse, enforcing the customary law of their predecessors. In the subsequent years, the municipal officials would fight ardently to protect this right against the competing administrations, and to maintain a position of relevance and authority for their constituents.

It is into this environment, then, that we begin the story of Stephanus Saletas and Bernardus de Bosto. Like many other citizens of a smaller city, Saletas came to Toulouse for the services of de Bosto, a business lawyer (*advocatus negotiaris*). More specifically, Saletas needed to purchase the official seal of Toulouse for a document

---

[29]    A. Esmein, *A History of Continental Criminal Procedure with Special Reference to France*, trans. John Simpson. The Continental Legal History Series [V] (Boston: Little, Brown, 1913), 88–93.

[30]    Many of the exchanges and rejected statutes are preserved in AMT–AA3:2, from 1274–1275, and ATM–AA3:3, lists the ones that are rejected. The codification of the customary law is preserved in a variety of locations, including a manuscript at the Bibliothèque Nationale, man. lat. 9187. This has been analyzed and discussed in great detail by Gilles, *Les coutumes de Toulouse.*

[31]    Claude Devic and Joseph Vaissètte, *Histoire générale du Languedoc*, ed. Auguste Molinier (Toulouse: Privat, 1872–1904), X, doc. 26, art. IV, col. 154. "Item super eo, quod dicti consules supplicabant quod inhiberetur dicto vicario, ne de cetero villam Tholose custodiat, set permittat dicte ville custodiam dictis consulibus, cum ad eos solos, ut dicunt, spectet dicta custodia, quod eis negatur per vicarium, ut eis contrarium asseratur. Responsum est, quod dicti consules custodiant villam, prout consueverunt, et nichilominus vicarius vel subvicarius et servientes ipsorum eam custodiant, cum viderint expedire."

[32]    AMT–AA3:4 and AMT AA4:1, dated October 1283.

that was being held by another Master Petrus de Erto. When de Bosto informed Saletas that the asking price was twenty six *sol tols*, Saletas became agitated and, with an "angry expression, said that he did not owe Master Bernardus money or love."[33] Upon hearing this explosive response, Bernardus de Bosto refused to deal any further with the client. According to witness testimony, Stephanus left the lawyer's office and began to complain bitterly to his friends that the price had changed. He claimed that they had previously agreed upon a specific payment, and they had sworn an oath confirming the deal. Stephan believed that Bernardus had broken this promise, and had changed the price at the last minute. The next day, Stephanus asked his first cousin (*consobrinus*) to confront the lawyer in the streets before the Château Narbonnais.[34]

After several verbal exchanges and grudging negotiations between the two, Bernardus de Bosto agreed to meet with Saletas once again, and to involve another legal official to resolve the dispute. Unfortunately for Stephanus Saletas, this meeting with a third party also proved unsatisfactory, as he now owed in additional sixteen *sols tols* to the notary for his mediating services.[35] What had begun as a simple transaction between a lawyer and a client had escalated into widespread debacle that left Stephanus Saletas feeling frustrated and cheated by the legal system that brought him to Toulouse in the first place.

It did not take long for this aggravation to manifest itself in a dramatic fashion. From the day after the dispute with Bernardus de Bosto and into the next, Saletas started making verbal threats that very soon he would get his revenge. He informed numerous people that an "evil punishment" was coming to the lawyer. Witnesses remarked that he became so infuriated that he bore an "angry expression and clenched teeth,"[36] or that he maintained a "raging and angry face."[37] In most criminal records, the mention of a defendant's emotion, or "ira," at the time of a crime was indicative of an act driven by passion or an irrational impulse. But in this case, it seems to serve a couple of different functions. To begin with, it was a way in which Saletas "performed" his fury to an audience that reinforced his sentiment toward the lawyer and the whole ordeal. He announced his hostility and his criminal intentions, and made it known that he would not tolerate this perceived injustice. From a practical and litigious perspective, the witnesses provided a rhetoric that clearly implicated Saletas in the crime. If Saletas

---

[33] AMT–FF57, 44: "tunc respondit irato animo et dixit pro sibi magistro bernardo non debebat pecuniam nec amorem."

[34] Ibid.: "Raymundus Jordani qui dicitur consobrinus dictum Stephanum."

[35] Ibid., 45.

[36] Ibid.: "cum vultu irato existens et dentibus fremens."

[37] Ibid.: "vultu furibando et irato."

proclaimed innocence during his trial, his facial expressions and vocalization were specific indicators that established a connection and motivation for the attack.

Stephanus Saletas devised a calculated and symbolic payback against Bernardus de Bosto. He hired some men he knew through his social networks in the city to stalk and attack the attorney, and enact his vengeance. A close friend, named Petrus Cortesii, coordinated a meeting with two men willing to accept money for the assault. When the conspirators met for the first time, Saletas informed them that, "a certain lawyer called Master Bernardus de Bosto has done me wrong; I want vindication, and so I am asking you to wound him so badly in the face that he will be deformed for the rest of his life."[38] The act of mutilating a foe as a form of vengeance can be found in several medieval records.[39] Perhaps the best known example is the story of Peter Abelard, who was castrated by his lover Heloise's vengeful uncle who "cut off the parts of my [Abelard's] body whereby I had committed the wrong of which they complained."[40] The German historian Valentin Groebner argues that the concentration on the face, or the severing of a nose, signified an assault against the honor of an individual, both in criminal punishments sanctioned by the municipal governments, and through duels fought between rivals. A husband, for example, could punish his wife for infidelity by cutting off her nose.[41] We even find an example of this action in Marie de France's story of the werewolf Bisclavret, who bit off the nose from his scheming wife's face.[42] But an officer wounded or mutilated indicated a real vulnerability of commune's control of a city.[43] It represented the powerful group's lack of control over the subservient population. In some fights, men carry wounds proudly as badges of a toughly fought battle.[44] In this instance, Bernardus de Bosto was mutilated to the point where he was no longer able to perform his duty either as a man, or as a contributing member of the social hierarchy. By explicitly

---

[38] Ibid.: "bacallaris in legibus vocatus Magister Bernardus de Bosto fecit michi aliquas injurias ita pro modis omnibus volo ipsos vendicari et ipsos rogano instanter ut dictum Magistrum Bernardum taliter in facie vulnerarent pro totaliter vita sua esset defformatus."

[39] For example, in several cases of vengeance from fourteenth-century Avignon, the records record acts such as blinding an enemy, or severing of the lips, nose and feet. Jacques Chiffoleau, "La Violence au quotidian: Avignon au XIV siecle d'apres les registres de la cour temporelle, " *Melanges de l'Ecole Francaises de Rome* (Moyen Age) 92 (1980): 354.

[40] *The Letters of Abelard and Heloise*, trans. Betty Radice (New York: Penguin Books, 1974), 75.

[41] Valentin Groebner, "Losing Face, Saving Face: Noses and Honour in the Late Medieval Town," trans. Pamela Selwyn, *History Workshop Journal* 40 (1995): 1–15.

[42] Marie de France, "Bisclavret," *The Lais of Marie de France*, trans. Glyn S. Burgess and Keith Busby (New York: Penguin Books, 2003), 68–72.

[43] Guido Ruggiero, *Violence in Early Renaissance Venice*. Crime, Law, and Deviance Series (New Brunswick, NJ: Rutgers University Press, 1980), 140–43.

[44] Robert C. Davis, *The War of the Fists: Popular Culture and Public Violence in late Renaissance Venice* (New York: Oxford University Press, 1994), 87.

instructing the men to leave Bernardus de Bosto facially deformed, Saletas aimed to leave his mark, and to render him impotent as a respected professional and member of the community. The lawyer was meant to suffer this public humiliation, so that anyone who looked at him could see that he was dishonored. Because Saletas had expressed his plan for vengeance to an audience, people would be able to make the connection, and know that even though Saletas did not commit the act himself, his honor and dominance over de Bosto were restored through this maiming.

After they agreed upon the payment of one hundred *sols tols* for the attack, Saletas left Toulouse to await word that his revenge had been carried out by his mercenaries. This suggests that non-citizens had mobility in and out of the city limits, and that there was some network of communication. It also becomes clear from the court records that the plan was not a private or concealed affair. Instead, as the days progressed, more people became entangled in the plot that continued to unfold in various public spaces of Toulouse. For example, when no notice of the attack arrived, Saletas came back to the city on numerous occasions to speed things along with promises of additional money. He met with the hired thugs in crowded taverns or in the houses of his friends.[45] But the organization of the assault does not appear to have been the most sophisticated, because suspicious neighbors kept questioning the intentions of the men when they congregated. The conspirators all hid in the same home with their wives and prostitutes, gathering weapons and their courage for months.[46] In one instance, all of the men were fully armed and exited the home they used as a headquarters for their operation. When a couple who lived close by interrogated the home owner, a friend of Stephanus Saletas, he explained that the men intended to take a long journey, and were not a threat to the security to the neighborhood.[47] So Stephanus Saletas had allies within the city of Toulouse willing to lie on his behalf and to house the men paid to mutilate Bernardus de Bosto. But this activity did not go unnoticed: neighbors stepped forward to ensure that illicit activities were questioned, and that their community remained safe.

---

[45] AMT–FF57, 46–47. In the medieval city, taverns served as a public environment where social and professional activities could transpire. B. Ann Tlusty, *Bacchus and Civil Order: The Culture of Drink in Early Modern Germany.* Studies in Early Modern German History (Charlottesville: University Press of Virgina, 2001), 158–82. Barbara A. Hanawalt, "The Host, the Law and the Ambiguous Space of Medieval London Taverns," *'Of Good and Ill Repute:' Gender and Social Control in Medieval England* (Oxford: Oxford University Press, 1998), 104–23. Nicole Gonthier, *Cris de haines et rites d'unité: la violence dans les villes, XIIIe–XVIe siècle.* Collection Violence et Société (Turnhout: Brepols, 1992), 111–49.

[46] AMT–FF57, 46–47.

[47] Ibid., 46.

When the men finally felt secure enough in their preparation and in Saletas's promises of payment to launch the attack, the spectacle transpired in significant portions of the city space. Stephanus Saletas's trusted accomplice, Petrus Cortesii, received a tip from an informant that Bernardus de Bosto was heading toward the town hall for work. The men gathered their arms and headed to the center of the city. Much like today, the courtyard around the town hall would have been bustling with city administrators and lawyers, pilgrims passing through on their way to visit the great basilica of Saint Sernin, university students heading to class, and merchants selling their wares to eager customers. Why, then, did the conspirators choose this moment, at this location to attack the lawyer? Although the records are silent, we may speculate that perhaps they hoped that the crowd would conceal their attack and enable them to catch Bernardus de Bosto off his guard. Or, they may have chosen this spot for a symbolic purpose, to reinforce the initial complaints of Stephanus Saletas.

There needed to be an audience of Bernardus de Bosto's peers in order to properly defame and disgrace the lawyer. But in many respects, the town hall represented the legal system that had failed Saletas, had humiliated him among his friends and family. It was only fitting, then, that the assault should not only bring down one of the city's respected lawyers, but also signal a warning to the capitols and their administration as well. It may also have been a means to demonstrate that justice had been served outside of the judicial system of the municipal authority of Toulouse. To add further insult to injury, the perpetrators fled the scene of the crime to a church where they took advantage of ecclesiastical jurisdiction.

According to the canonical law of asylum, anyone seeking refuge from a public authority could be protected in any church or monastery, where they could not be removed. This was an issue that had been hotly debated between the capitols and the king, as they tried to establish their own privilege to make sure that the interests of the Toulousains were protected.[48] The notion of asylum was important to the church, as it was a means of continuing a physical presence and authority in the secular legal component of Toulouse: the ecclesiastical authorities wanted to keep churches as recognizably protected spaces in order to maintain power in municipal jurisdiction.[49] The capitols and their officers challenged this stipulation in 1288, which caused the archbishop of Toulouse to issue a complaint to King

---

[48]    AMT–AA1: 4 (1152). Limouzin-Lamothe, *La Commune de Toulouse*, 267–68.

[49]    See, for example, an example of the negotiations between the church and municipal authorities in Montpellier in 1332, in Katheryn L. Reyerson's "Flight from Prosecution: The Search for Religious Asylum in Medieval Montpellier," *French Historical Studies* 17 (Spring 1992): 603–26; J. Charles Cox, *The Sanctuaries and Sanctuary Seekers in Mediaeval England* (London: G. Allen and Sons, 1911).

Philip IV.[50] Earlier that year, a criminal had fled from the capitols to the church of Nazareth, immediately evoking the privilege of asylum. A messenger of the capitols disregarded the safeguard of the religious site, broke into the church and dragged the accused to the town hall. Horrified to learn that capitols submitted the man to interrogation and the torture of "questioning" in order to hear a confession, the archbishop beseeched the king to enforce the protection of the church's sacred space. The royal *parlement* ordered the capitols to return the prisoner to the church, thus continuing the tradition of asylum for the church and rendering the capitols impotent against the royal protection of the church.

Even though the assailants remained protected from secular authority in the confines of the church, six days passed, and their sponsor's silence became all too disturbing. The most daring of the bunch crept out of the church and fled Toulouse in the middle of the night and located Stephanus Saletas at a small nearby location of Boudigos.[51] The unnamed man described the attack to Saletas, and ceremoniously handed over the sword that had wounded Bernardus de Bosto as he proclaimed "this sword has done great things."[52] This was the moment that Saletas was expected to fulfill his promise, and pay the one hundred *sols tols*. If he had, maybe his role in the attack would never have been revealed to Toulouse's authorities. But Stephan Saletas handed over only twenty-five *sols tols* to this representative of the attackers. It did not take long for this fact to make its way back to Toulouse as Saletas retired to his native city of Villamuro. Within days, the men from inside the church of the Daurade began to negotiate with the capitols of Toulouse. Even Petrus Cortesii, once Saletas most trusted comrade, offered a sworn statement and confession about the whole conspiracy to the capitols.[53] As the men who attacked Bernardus de Bosto walked out of the church and into the custody of the jail in the town hall, the capitols may have perceived the physical assault as an attempt for an "outsider," a non-citizen, trying to exert his own power into the streets by disregarding the *capitoul's* authority over urban space, and proclaiming it his own. The trial of Stephanus Saletas would signal the restoration of the power structure through the utilization of city space to display the municipal government's authority.

It became crucial, then, for the capitols and their officers to ensure that Saletas was tried within their courtroom in the town hall of Toulouse for a couple of reasons. From a legal perspective, the capitols had gained jurisdiction over the surrounding territory when they were assimilated into the royal judicial system, and they could extradite defendants to stand trial for crimes committed in

---

50    Archives départmentales de la Haute Garonne – 1 G 345, fol. 42–43.

51    AMT–FF57, 50.

52    Ibid.

53    AMT–FF57, 51.

Toulouse. In September, 1291, the capitols contacted the authorities of
Castelnaudry (40 kilometers to the southeast), to capture and hand over a certain
Raymundus Furutrii, so he could be held responsible and punished for his
"excesses and crimes" committed in Toulouse.[54] But from a symbolic perspective,
the courtroom was not only a location for accusations of criminal offenses to be
recorded and to be considered by the capitols, but it also became a forum for
establishing the cycles of inclusion and exclusion within the community.[55] The
authorities had to conduct the trial in a public and formalized manner, so that the
urban residents could witness that the capitols and their officers delivered justice
for the victim. And much like the attack against Bernardus de Bosto was a
spectacle intended for a specific audience, the trial and legal proceedings were also
a performance of justice that involved a variety of participants.

The twelve capitols ruled over the court proceedings, but many other "good
men" were also present, including bureaucrats and legal advisors such as notaries
and jurists. In addition, dozens of professional attorneys and notaries were
recorded as witnesses, which is not surprising considering the attack took place
close to the busy and bureaucratic town hall. In total, the notary recorded one
hundred and thirty-four names of witnesses who came to the courtroom, including
a fisherman, a tavern owner, a silversmith, a barber, a tailor, several wives
(unattended by their husbands), a female servant (*ancilla*) and a notary
accompanied by his trainee.[56] Clearly, this was a case that transcended beyond an
interpersonal conflict between Stephanus Saletas and Bernardus de Bosto: this was
a public affair that affected many levels of the social hierarchy.

As stated earlier in this paper, the criminal register included copies of the
capitols' correspondence to the officials of Villlamuro and the regional seneschal
concerning the extradition of Stephanus Saletas to the city of Toulouse. From these
records, we are able to gain some insight into the capitols' jurisdictional strategies
and ways in which they negotiated with smaller administrations within
Languedoc. In their first official letter, the capitols informed the consuls of
Villamuro that they had sworn confessions from Bernardus de Bosto's assailants

---

[54]    AMT, layettes II, carton 84. September 21, 1291. "Ex parte domini nostri regis Francie et nostra
        voca requirimus ac Rogamus quathinus Ramundum Furutrii quem lator seu latores sub fida
        custodia transmittatis inquirendum et puniendum super quibusdam excessibus et criminibus per
        eundem Ramundum in Tholosa et sub iurisdictione nostra comissia taliter super his vos habentes
        ut vos valeatis noci facturos."
[55]    For example, if someone was falsely accused of a crime, his honor had to be restored in the public
        opinion through a ritual cleansing of the defamation by bringing the accuser to court. The judicial
        trial became a "trial of transformation" for an accused or slandered individual to be reinstated
        among the respectable people of the society. Courtemanche, "Medical Expertise," 123.
[56]    AMT– FF57, 104: "Magister Petrus de Hertia notaire et eius discipulus."

(who were in their custody in the municipal jail), and that the men had specifically implicated Stephanus Saletas in the crime.[57]

The capitols requested that the consuls and bailiff of Villamuro surrender Satelas into their custody, and to cease the protection and the concealment of their resident. The letters promised that they would give Saletas a fair trial, and that he would be treated well. When this written reassurance failed to yield a result, the capitols of Toulouse deployed three municipal sergeants, a notary, and several jurists to Villamuro on multiple occasions to convince the administration that the capitols' had proper jurisdiction in the matter because the crime had taken place in Toulouse.[58] Apparently the presence of Toulouse's officials did not intimidate the consuls of Villamuro either, so the capitols drew from their royal privileges and appealed to the court of the seneschal of Languedoc.[59] They argued that even though Saletas was not in Toulouse when the crime took place, he should be held responsible because Saletas had orchestrated and paid for the attack. Although the records do not contain the responses of Villamuro's officials, the issue of contention between the two administrations seems to have been surrounding whether or not conspiracy to commit a crime warranted an extradition.

As the correspondence and political wrangling for Stephanus Saletas dragged on for weeks without any results, the capitols began to release new charges against Saletas. It seems as though they were absolutely determined to have Stephanus Saletas come back to Toulouse to stand trial, regardless of the offense. It also demonstrates the capitols' firm belief that they had to take active steps toward achieving justice both to satisfy their constituents and to maintain their place in the local and region judicial hierarchy. The capitols revealed to the consuls of Villamuro that Stephanus Saletas had also terrorized some local land holding families around Toulouse. For example, he had robbed several families with weapons, and he had struck one man in the face with his fist and a sword.[60] The star witness for the prosecution, Petrus Cortesii, also told the capitols that during Stephanus Saletas's reign of terror against Bernardus de Bosto, Saletas set fire to a large pile of the lawyer's wood that was situated outside of the walls of Toulouse. It took several hundred men to extinguish the fire with water and to make sure that the city and its inhabitants were safe.[61] By adding these new offenses to their initial charges against Saletas, the capitols were perhaps trying to establish that he was a threat to the community at large; Bernardus de Bosto was

---

[57] Ibid., 32.
[58] Ibid., 33–5.
[59] Ibid., 36.
[60] Ibid., 52.
[61] Ibid.

not the only victim of Saletas's evil intentions, but anyone in Languedoc was vulnerable to his manipulation or outright violence.

In the example of Stephanus Saletas, royal intervention worked on the behalf of the capitols. Pressured by the authority of the royal seneschal, the consuls of Villamuro handed Saletas into the custody of the capitols' officials. The city sergeants escorted the prisoner back into the city space that he had violated to be held accountable for his crimes. Despite all of the promises of Toulouse's capitols, it was very unlikely that had a fair trial. Stephanus Saletas always maintained his innocence in the case. He insisted that he barely knew the men involved in the attack against Bernardus de Bosto and that he had no involvement in the attack.[62] But Saletas was submitted to the torture of the "question," even though his attorneys protested that this violated their jurisdiction.[63] Torture (*quaestio* or *tormentum* in the documents), was considered part of the legal process in the thirteenth and fourteenth centuries, and another element of jurisdiction that had been secured as a legal privilege by the administrations of Toulouse.[64] Unfortunately, this is as much information that the records contain. The archives of Toulouse do not provide any indication as to whether or not Saletas was found guilty, and if he was convicted, what was the designated punishment for his role in the attack that left a prestigious lawyer in mortal peril and perpetually deformed in the face. Nor do we know the fate of the men who actually performed the deed.

But even though we are left with more questions than answers in the resolution of this dramatic case, the extant records establish the importance of utilizing city space to perform justice. Stephanus Saletas had come into Toulouse to take advantage of the legal system that Toulouse provided as the capital of Languedoc. When he believed that Bernardus de Bosto had failed him, he sought vengeance through a spectacle that transpired by the town hall of Toulouse. This offered a blow against the honor of de Bosto and the whole judicial structure of Toulouse. After Saletas fled to his home in Villamuro, the capitols mobilized their administration to bring him back to Toulouse where the attack occurred, so that they could display their sovereignty and authority. The capitols used the trial to demonstrate to their constituents that they had restored order to the community, and that they had dominance over the smaller municipal jurisdictions in the region of Languedoc. The trial of Stephanus Saletas, then reveals much more than a

---

[62]  Ibid., 41–42.

[63]  Ibid., 56.

[64]  Edward Peters, *Torture* (New York: Basil Blackwell, 1985), 40–73. Historians debate how often torture was administered in secular cases. For example, Kenneth Pennington believes that torture was not practiced as often during the thirteenth and fourteenth centuries as previously suspected. *The Prince and the Law, 1200–1600: Sovereignty and Rights in the Western Legal Tradition*. A Centennial Book (Berkeley and Los Angeles: University of California Press, 1993), 42–4, 157–60.

random act of medieval violence: it is a sublime example of the negotiation of urban space and power.

Jean E. Jost
(Bradley University, Peoria, IL)

# Urban and Liminal Space in Chaucer's *Knight's Tale:* Perilous or Protective?

Barbara A. Hanawalt and Michael Kobialka have eloquently defined the new postmodern concept of space within literary contexts:

> Ever since the word "space" lost its strictly geometrical meaning, it has acquired and been accompanied by numerous adjectives or nouns that defined its "new" use and attributes. Mental space, ideological space, literary space, the space of the imagination, the space of the dreams, utopian space, imaginary space, technological space, cultural space, and social space are some of the terms that have emerged alongside the Euclidian, isotropic, or absolute space. . . . the possibility that space can be produced altered how one talks about and envisions that which used to be an empty area.[1]

The method of utilizing space reveals much about how authors conceptualize, design, and execute their literary art, as well as shape the meaning and significance of their artifact. In particular, space within both fictive and real cities offers uniquely effective landscapes on which to scribe the literal and fictive human story. As Michael Camille points out, "Many historians of the city, as a mode of experience as well as an architectural site, have described how urban life puts more emphasis upon visual recognition, and the importance of visual signs certainly suggests another kind of quotidian literacy, based not upon textual learning but another system of understood symbols and structure."[2] That series of

---

[1]  *Medieval Practices of Space,* ed. Barbara A. Hanawalt and Michael Kobialka. Medieval Culture Series, 23 (London and Minneapolis: University of Minnesota Press, 2000), Introduction, ix.

[2]  Michael Camille, "Signs of the City," in *Medieval Practices of Space,* ed. Barbara A. Hanawalt and Michael Kobialka. Medieval Culture Series, 23 (London and Minneapolis: University of Minnesota Press, 2000), 1–36; here 9. Unfortunately fewer literary studies have considered the role of urban space within specific literature. Some of the most interesting include David Wallace, "Chaucer and the Absent City" in *Chaucer's England: Literature in Historical Contexts,* expanded in his *Chaucerian Polity: Absolutist Lineages and Associational Forms in England and Italy* (Stanford: Stanford University Press, 1997); Craig Bertholet, "Urban Poetry in the Parliament of Fowles," *Studies in Philology* 93.4(1996): 365–89; John. H. Fisher, "City and Country in the Fabliaux," *Medieval Perspectives* 1

visual signs reveals and is part of the broader spatial landscape of the medieval city, and its meaning. Camille claims, "Signs are indicators of lived social place, not disembodied abstract space."[3] In fact, according to Edward S. Casey, medieval society was concerned only with place, not the abstract, postmedieval, expanded category of space—mental, ideological, literary, imaginative, dream, utopian, technological, cultural, and social space—[4] mentioned above by Hanawalt and Kobialka. Nevertheless, modern concepts of space can be applied to literature of the Middle Ages, whether the writers called their setting "space" or "place." As David Nichols indicates,

> the physiognomy and spatial distribution of urban life in modern Europe were fixed essentially during the Middle Ages .... English is the only west European language that distinguishes "town" from "city" functionally, although "city" in French may refer only to the area enclosed by the late Roman wall while the rest of the settlement is the "town." German scholars in particular have used an all-embracing definition of urbanisation that lumps together as "towns" everything from the great metropolises to the tiniest of settlements that had charters of privilege .... The city-town distinction is admittedly arbitrary and depends to a great degree on the level of regional urbanisation.[5]

John Micheal Crafton recognizes these overlapping usages, claiming "the words *city* and *town*, used almost completely synonymously, appear most often in Troilus and second most in the *Knight's Tale*."[6] With this caveat of the arbitrariness of the city-town distinction in mind, we will consider the urban spatial arrangement of Chaucer's *Knight's Tale*, in the ancient city-states of Thebes and Athens, as carefully delineated loci with aspects both perilous and protective. The fictive nature of the tale, or fiction in general, usually follows the actual layout of real cities, and in fact, medieval authors may even have experience of those real cities from which they may draw their design.

David Wallace points out that "Chaucer's *Canterbury Tales* does not begin in London: it begins south of the Thames in Southwark and moves us steadily away from the city walls."[7] The body of fictive tales and its fictive construct of pilgrimage is meant to be liminal, spanning the distance between London and

---

(1986): 1–15; *City and Spectacle in Medieval Europe*, ed. Barbara Hanawalt and Kathryn L. Reyerson. Medieval Studies at Minnesota Series, 6 (Minneapolis: University of Michigan Press, 1994); John Micheal Crafton, "Chaucer and the City," *Medieval Perspectives* 17.2 (2002): 51–67.
3    Camille, "Signs of the City," 9.
4    Edward S. Casey, *The Fate of Place: A Philosophical History* (Berkeley: University of California Press, 1997), 103–15.
5    David Nichols, *The Growth of the Medieval City From Late Antiquity to the Early Fourteenth Century. A History of Urban Society in Europe*, 4. (New York and London: Longman, 1997), Preface, xiv, xv.
6    Crafton, "Chaucer and the City," 52.
7    Wallace, "Chaucer and the Absent City," 59.

Canterbury; most tales describe spaces which are not London, but represent a wide array of places. Wallace continues, describing the significance of beginning the venture in this liminal suburb of London:

> The choice of a Southwark tavern as the gathering place for Chaucer's pilgrimage is at once realistically plausible and arrestingly eccentric. Pilgrims from London to Canterbury often spent the night in Southwark so that they could begin their journey before the city gates were opened for the day . . . . The effect of assembling at Southwark is to emphasize the randomness of this encounter. . . . [Further,] Southwark functioned as a dumping ground and exclusion zone for early modern London: messy or marginal trades such as lime burning, tanning, dying brewing, innkeeping, and prostitution flourished there; criminals fleeing London courts and aliens working around London trade regulations found a home . . . . The name of Southwark, in short, identifies governance as a problematic issue, takes the issue out of the city, and yet cannot quite leave the city behind.[8]

Both appropriately and ironically in this raucous and subversive liminal space, a ragtag assembly gather together and tell their equally unconventional tales. In this unruly place, the rules of tale-telling are established, themselves to be both disordered and broken; here the tales of game and earnest, solas and sentence, will be set and interrupted. Here the sacred and profane adventure begins, but does not end. Here, the condition of peril is as prominent as that of protection. The act of pilgrimaging itself consists of moving from one urban space, through liminal rural space,[9] to the next urban space with an ever-fluctuating series of events and narratives punctuating those spaces. The goal of pilgrimaging may well be a religious or spiritual space at its conclusion, and reflect a psychological progression of the spirit, in yet another kind of emotional space.

But what happens, fictively and literarily in those intermediate liminal spaces are the real object of the poet's scrutiny. Here, Tellers from varied cultural and hierarchical loci compete for the space to tell their tales of solas and sentence and win the prize. Crafton interestingly contends that "Chaucer places the problem of the city as a problem of margins, not a marginal problem but margins that set out, that frame, the spaces of inscription;"[10] the pilgrimage frames Chaucer's narrative spaces, highlighting the importance of those liminal material border spaces as well

---

[8]   Wallace, "Chaucer and the Absent City," 60, 61. Wallace also notes that "Such a detailed concern with the regulation and division of time and space in the city is a constant feature of the Letter Books. . . . these records attest to a sophisticated understanding of the functioning and governance of urban space; they suggest, in short, an urban consciousness " (64, 65) The Letter Books are found in H. T. Ridley, ed. *Memorials of London and London Life in the XIIIth, IVXth, and XVth Centuries, AD 1276–1419* (London: Longmans, Green and Co., 1868), 492.

[9]   The Italian word *contado* signifies "surrounding countryside;" *captains* (or greater knights) and *valvasours* (or their vassals) are the two levels of urban and rural nobility. See David Nichols, *Growth of the Medieval City*, 117–20 and 282–86, for further discussion.

[10]  Crafton, "Chaucer and the City," 65.

as the literary links connecting tales. These spaces protect the integrity of the Tales and the composite, despite its fragmented nature.[11]

Within the fictive *Canterbury Tales'* pilgrimage, material, emotional, and psychological space may expand, limit, define, contrast, evoke, give meaning to, and diminish narrative situations. The evolving setting of *The Knight's Tale* alternates between large city, small village, uninhabited forest, and near environs of each, with concomitant emotional volatility. It encompasses battlefields, gardens, towers, groves, castles, and chambers within. As V. A. Kolve points out, "Chaucer's subject [in the *Knight's Tale*] is nothing less than the pagan past at its most noble and dignified, imagined from within."[12] That noble, pagan past offers rich and varied loci, each with its own challenges.

The space of the city, imagined from within that city and without, both indoor and outdoor, artificial and natural, and even on the borders spanning both, is thus public and private, democratic and autocratic, military and inclusive, personal and intimate. But the question narratively linking them all remains: "Are those loci perilous or protective?" And "Can they be made more or less so?" Outdoor spaces indeed appear the most perilous and pitiful, for there battles and tournaments are fought, there sorrowing widows bemoan their losses, there suppliants pray at temples, there internment for unfortunate events occurs. But inside city spaces, such as prison towers, death-bed rooms, and internal psychological places may confine and debilitate as well. Conversely, within external spaces of gardens and groves, nature rules beneficently, freedom beckons, and joy appears possible.

The entire complex structure of the *Knight's Tale* in particular hangs on its multiple loci, revealing both their physical and emotional significance, interspersing political, legal, and personal landscapes to deepen their impact. Additionally, human events occurring within these spaces may change the nature of their protection or preservation, as new emotional perspectives modify those sites of Nature. Thus the Knight offers a complex pattern of sites to explore persistence, ritual, and finally resolution, all predicated on the relative uses of multiple types of space.

The tale begins as Duke Theseus journeys on a secular pilgrimage from the now-conquered "reign of Femenye"[13] to his native Athens. As John H. Fisher notes

---

[11]   Chaucer's *Canterbury Tales* are divided into ten fragments, assembled after his death according to various editorial principles. Those Tales with links to prior or subsequent Tales are put together into a fragment. Those Tales lacking links comprise their own fragment, and are placed into the whole based on an editor's sense of where they belong.

[12]   V. A. Kolve, *Chaucer and the Imagery of Narrative: The First Five Canterbury Tales* (Stanford, California: Stanford University Press, 1984), 86.

[13]   John H. Fisher suggests the place name of the home of Amazons, in the "regne of Femenye" (from Lat. *femina*, woman), was evidently invented by Chaucer. [Boccaccio's *Teseida*] makes Teseo's war against the Amazons a 'purgation' of their 'sin' of feminism" (*The Complete Poetry and Prose of Geoffrey Chaucer*, ed. John H. Fisher (New York, Chicago, et al.: Holt, Rinehart and Winston, 1977),

"Medieval people looked upon Athens as the fountainhead of secular social and political theory;"[14] perhaps Chaucer is juxtaposing a medieval conception of illegitimate or unnatural lawlessness—rule by women—with orderly law by Theseus, which nevertheless ultimately brings peril and disaster. The Duke rejoices in his victory and his upcoming marriage to Ypolyta, Queen of the defeated Amazons. The site of battle has treated him kindly. However, we have no evidence of her desire to be dethroned from power, to belong to Theseus, or to be moved from her city into his. For Ypolyta, the city-space has proven perilous, in that she has unwillingly lost her liberty and independence through Theseus's conquest of her lands. As Laura Kendrick sees it, "Theseus curtails and represses outrageous, unlawful, erotic and aggressive desires: first, he conquers the Amazons and turns their Queen, Ypolyta, into his obedient wife."[15] If the proof is in the pudding, we might ask, does Theseus's reign finally prove protective, or perilous, lawful and peaceable, or militaristic and deadly, to his citizens? We do know Ypolyta's sister Emily's desire: she wants no part of marriage, as one would expect from an Amazonian; presumably she and Ypolyta would prefer to remain in their own queendom. Nevertheless, from a perspective outside the tale, the voiceless Ypolyta is forced to leave her habitat behind, accompany her imposed husband to her new city. Both external urban spaces, "Amazonia" and Athens bring Theseus joy, however, despite his Queen's perilous exile.

On the outskirts of Athens, however, Duke Theseus is met by his initial provocation. "Whan he was come almoost unto the toun,"[16] keening widows in black garb who "biseken mercy and succor" (918) present his first difficulty. They are in a miserable emotional space. Beseeching his help, they place him in a similar, empathetic position, on the edge of their pain. A repeated pattern of complication emerges in which the most evocative and emotional events occur on the brink of, but not in the heart of a putatively well-governed city. The liminal space between the outskirts and the city should protect the community and ensure urban harmony is not disturbed by the disharmony of its inhabitants. In these border spaces, conflict is acknowledged, negotiated, and perhaps resolved, protecting the city at large from involvement. The locus of these keening widows, formerly powerful Queens, suffering battle scars and emotional trauma, is a physically and emotionally desperate place. Kneeling abjectly at the feet of a powerful figure to beg reprisal for their husbands' deaths, and needing a new

---

[14]  25, note to l. 866. Chaucer has not fully removed the stigma of that site for Theseus's conquest is accepted as legitimate while ignoring the reasons for doing so.
Fisher, *Complete Poetry and Prose*, 25, note to ll. 860–61.

[15]  Laura Kendrick, *Chaucerian Play: Comedy and Control in the Canterbury Tales* (Berkeley and Los Angeles: University of California Press, 1988), 118.

[16]  *Riverside Chaucer*, ed. Larry D. Benson (Boston, MA: Houghton Mifflin, 1987), I.894. This and subsequent quotations are taken from this edition.

social order for a safer future, these weak and vulnerable women are a visual representation of their plight in their own city. Their situation recapitulates the military and amatory experience Theseus has just completed: in militarily overcoming and emotionally wooing Ypolita in that land of Femenye, and now, in seeking a new inclusive social organization at his court. Theseus is in charge in all three places.

If one Chaucerian motif here is the value of a stable society run by a wise and astute ruler, his physical reign, particularly its urban space, must exemplify that excellent governance soon to be prized in Renaissance "Rules for Princes" Handbooks. Such urban space, then, must eschew unstable brawling and out-of-control excess which plagues the widow-Queens, relegating such abominations to other, more sub-urban regions, there to be resolved. But enemy cities such as Femenye seem not always to fall within Theseus's protective purview.

These prostrate widows beg a reprieve; Theseus politely dismounts and raises them up into his royal space, gently lifting them from the earth into his domain where they belong by birth. He leaves his elevated place astride his horse, and "in his armes he hem alle up hente/ And hem conforteth in ful good entente" (I A.957–58). Jill Mann brilliantly reveals the meaning of the carefully arranged iconography: "Chaucer places his Theseus on horseback and makes him instantly dismount under his 'pitous' impulse, so as to illustrate dramatically the levelling of conqueror with victims, the abandonment of his triumph for identification with their grief."[17] This is most appropriate, for Theseus has, after all, conquered Femenye, just as Creon has conquered Athens, albeit with less cruelty we assume. The Duke's elevation of the Queens to his more comfortable space of dignity and respect foreshadows the care and healing action he will soon perform on their behalf, in the space of their city, as he will attempt later in Thebes.

This liminal space outside the city is a safe place, where the sovereign is not symbolically and literally above them, but is in their space, to effect their business. The black-garbed mourners on the "heighe weye" (1.897) represent deprivation, injustice, and violation: 1) deprivation of husbandly support, wise governance, opportunity to leave the past behind and move on to the present; 2) injustice in unfair treatment against them, for Creon has not only killed their husbands in this locus, but has left them unburied carrion for the birds and roaming dogs, a very bad locus for the dead; and 3) violation, in denying them their burial practices and rituals, their proper place as mourners and Queens, thus disrespecting their cultural mores and desecrating victims' afterlives. The unconfined environs of the road neither frees nor protects the widows, humbly kneeling on the ground. But it offers them Theseus's gesture of pity, and hope of reparation and regeneration.

---

[17]    Jill Mann, *Feminizing Chaucer*. Chaucer Studies, 30 (1991; Woodbridge, UK, and Rochester, NY: D. S. Brewer, 2002), 135.

Duke Theseus, always the sage problem-solver, vows vengeance on Creon, and moves into the city confines of Athens, into a site of prior killing, to unseat and destroy that reigning tyrant. For Creon, the space of his own domain has become dangerous, not protective, as retribution is established with his death. A rebuilding or restructuring is only possible after the razing of the prior urban space, its confines, and its psychic identity. For those allied with Creon and currently within the city, the space is indeed perilous. In a field, "He faught, and slough [Creon] manly as a knyght / In pleyn bataille, and putte the folk to flyght" (987–88). For the Queens outside the city, their rights to their domain, their ability to offer burial rites, and their protection to fulfill custom's rituals have been reinstated. Here, on the site of the demolition, Theseus chooses to remain the night: "Still in that feeld he took al nyght hys reste" (1003) thus reinforcing his claim to power and assuring his dominance in the urban space of Thebes. No comment is made about the future of this now-demolished space, its empty vacuity speaking volumes about the prior criminality of its leader Creon.

After the Athenian siege of Thebes, ransackers find two half-dead cousins piled on a heap of corpses "liggynge by and by, / Bothe in oon armes" (1.1011–12) intertwined with each other on the grounds of the battlefield. They even share the same familial DNA, as we would say today, and hierarchical place in society. Their physical proximity confirms their intertwined future, in spaces both amicable and hostile to each other, albeit in ways neither could immediately envision. This external locus of near-death, in a field just outside the city and castle, exemplifies their tragic status: once high-born knights, now fallen, literally and metaphorically, to the depths of despair and bare physical existence. Their proximity to each other establishes their relationship, both straight and ironic, within the tale. Saved from extinction on the edge of one defeated city, they are moved to the internal prison of another which traps their minds, and the external prison which traps their bodies, high in the Athenian tower "in angwisse and in wo" (1.1030). This contrasts the winning position of Theseus in Athens: "With lauer crowned as a conquerour / And ther he lyveth in joye and in honour / Terme of his lyf" (1.1027–29). While the city may protect Theseus, it merely deadens the defeated–Creon's soldiers and survivors. Gerhard Joseph's excellent visualization of space here accurately summarizes the space divisions:

> The *Knight's Tale* moves through four earthly enclosures that give way to one another as the locales of significant action: the prison tower in which Palamon and Arcite contend verbally for the right to Emilye, with whom they have both fallen in love (Part I); the grove in which Palamon and Arcite come upon one another and in which they try to slaughter each other before the intercession of Theseus (Part II); the temples of Venus, Mars, and Diana within the amphitheatre that Theseus has built for the clash

of two hundred worthies (Part III); and the the arena itself in which the climactic tournament takes place (Part IV). The tale is thus organized scenically.[18]

The young knights are thus only marginally better for their change of place. While they are out of physically fatal peril for the moment, they have lost control and power over their existence: no mental freedom of movement, action, choice, location. V. A. Kolve claims Chaucer

> communicates his vision of the pagan past most powerfully through two great images central to the narrative, the prison / garden and the tournament amphitheatre . . . . The action requires that the garden be within sight of the prison tower, but Chaucer (following his original the *Teseida* of Boccaccio) goes beyond that, to insist on their architectural contiguity. He joins them in an emblematic way . . . . In this striking juxtaposition of structures, the prison and garden are "evene joynt": they share a common wall.[19]

Nevertheless, they are nothing alike—one representing Nature, freedom, openness to the sky, the other representing man-made artifice, confinement, darkness without sky. Kolve enumerates Chaucer's repeated use of the verb "to roam," as Palamon "romed in a chambre on heigh" (1.1065), Emily "romed up and doun"(1.1069), Palamon "Goth in the chambre romynge to and fro" (1.1071), Emily "romed to and fro" and "rometh in the yonder place" (1.1119);[20] this insistence on physical movement through the space highlights their varied experience of uncomfortable confinement or freedom. Ironically, these two spaces are integrally connected, architecturally sharing the same wall:

> The grete tour, that was so thikke and stroong,
> Which of the castel was the chief dongeoun
> (Ther as the knyghtes weren in prisoun
> Of which I tolde yow and tellen shal),
> Was evene joynant to the gardyn wal
> Ther as this Emelye hadde hir pleyynge.             (1056–61)

Speaking of the walls in *Troilus and Criseyde*, Crafton contends they "provide a number of narrative arrangements, but they are connoted ambiguously as freedom or enclosure, protection or threat, and finally unity or fragmentation,"[21] an observation equally true of the *Knight's Tale's* walls. One might conclude that the fates of the characters on each side of the wall, the good and ill of life experiences,

[18] Gerhard Joseph, "Chaucerian 'Game'–'Earnest' and the 'Argument of Herbergage' in *The Canterbury Tales*," *Chaucer Review* (1970): 83–96; here 84.
[19] Kolve, *Chaucer and the Imagery of Narrative*, 86, 87.
[20] Kolve, *Chaucer and the Imagery of Narrative*, 88, 89.
[21] Crafton, "Chaucer and the City," 61.

are represented as inextricably bound to each other, and form the matter of this tale. Any change of locus would dramatically alter the course of events.

One day, outside the prison-tower walls, steps bright, shining May roaming through Nature's locus, the garden of flowers rivaling her beauty. Palamon, roaming about high in the man-made tower is instantly captivated by the unavailable maiden he spies through his excluding thick-barred window—too far from him in distance and social rank. Arcite soon discovers his cousin's obsession, and joins him in love-longing. The two knights are caught in a new space, the imprisonment of their infatuation. Kolve recounts how one artist, the Master of René of Anjou, depicts this tableau:

> Emilia in the pleasure garden, sitting on a turfed bench, and weaving a garland of flowers, while the two knights look out upon her through the bars of their prison window. The room beyond them is in darkness, whereas the garden, delicate in its colors and open to the heavens, is washed by the light of spring. The double setting immediately establishes the *ethos* of the action, the themes the action will explore . . . . The contrast between these two places, for these artists as well, serves as an entry into the meaning of the event . . . the first in a series of transformations he would work upon this image—a new approach to the young knights' discovery of passionate love.[22]

The effect of space on emotion is palpable. As Henry Ansgar Kelly points out, "Palamon's joy, though briefly told, makes life's prison noticeably less foul."[23] An emotional place of happiness can thus temporarily mitigate distance to some degree, lessen the pain that Emily is not in the knights' place. Palamon would penetrate into the locus of Emily's heart. Arcite is similarly wounded by her beauty; however, he sees Emily as the locus of social and political capital to be won, and triumphant winning as the place of successful achievement more than appreciation of woman's love. He would penetrate the locus of her body only.

Her exploration and roaming freely about in the space of the flowering garden highlights the knights' caged, spatial confinement apart from nature, and apart from the object of their desire. They have no power, no ability to communicate, no freedom to act. But her place of freedom motivates their escape. Here in Part I, the complication of the story is clearly set: the conquest of spatial and emotional places is the goal sought through the Knight's carefully established architectural pattern. Lee Patterson reminds us that

> the *Knight's Tale* is a tableau, a frieze, a set of static images, a pageant; at its most dynamic, a procession . . . . The events of the narratives are so patterned that what we have seen we will see again . . . three scenes of spring observances: Emily's in the garden is followed by Arcite's 'observaunce to May' in the grove and then, most

22 Kolve *Chaucer and the Imagery of Narrative*, 87.
23 Henry Ansgar Kelly, *Chaucerian Tragedy* (1997; Cambridge: D. S. Brewer, 2000), 86.

tellingly, by Theseus's hunt 'at the grete herte in May.' The argument in the prison becomes the battle in the grove and then the tournament in the amphitheater.[24]

This triple tableau reinforces the Knight's nature: conservative, traditional, patterned, expected–all according to design in the right place. Patterson concludes: when "all narrative actions assume the same configuration . . . [the narrative] perfectly expresses both the self-congratulation of chivalric ideology and the inconclusiveness of chivalric practice."[25] The two-fold configuration of order and expansion parallel the Knight's, and his hero Theseus's order-loving, ritual-seeking nature. Speaking of spatial progression, Joseph notes:

> . . . while both the prison and the grove are merely functional and neutral spaces unconsecrated by any conscious ritual, Theseus goes to elaborate lengths to dignify the tournament in his amphitheatre, to give it the widest possible metaphysical significance . . . The point of such gradual widening is clear: the larger the arena in which violent passions can play themselves out, the less destructive and the more susceptible to ritual they become. Mere decorative elaboration makes for order, a fact that Theseus surely understands. It is for this reason that he moves the combat from the grove into the massive arena with its temples; it is for this reason that he dispenses the single combat between the enraged Palamon and Arcite over a company of two hundred knights. If spatial expansion becomes a process which can mitigate the fury of the passions, the Tale's insistence upon expansiveness of time reinforces such a movement towards order. . . . It is through such a continuing consecration, via expansion, of both space and time that Theseus attempts to bring a temporary, a limited perfection into the confusion of this life.[26]

Thus, the handling of space in repetitive patterns based on the fear and insecurity of Teller (Knight) and character (Theseus) seeking order through expansiveness is congruent to Chaucer's depiction of the Teller's psyche, a careful man used to military order, as this discussion suggests.

Ultimately, the loss of Emilye supplants the loss of freedom and power, for the small joy of seeing her cannot wipe out the anguish of prison. Laura Kendrick sees it this way:

> These two heroes, confined to their prison tower, are powerless, conflicted child figures par excellence. They are subject not only to fate and Theseus but also to their own emotions and desires–to love and hate. When they see Emelye walking in the garden below their prison, both of them fall in love with her instantly and completely, and "sibling" rivalry begins for the right to possess the female love object, which is unattainable not only because Emelye "belongs" to Theseus, her sister's husband, who has the paternal authority–and the right of the conqueror–to dispose of her person.

24  Lee Patterson, *Chaucer and the Subject of History* (Madison, WI: University of Wisconsin Press, 1991), 209.
25  Patterson, *Chaucer and the Subject of History*, 209.
26  Joseph, "Chaucerian Game," 84–85.

Instead of openly expressing their resentment at Theseus for preventing fulfillment of their desires, the two young men turn their anger against each other . . . in relatively genteel, sublimated forms such as verbal dispute and, later, in formalized, secret battle to the death for the love object.[27]

The lovers are in a place of impotence, tied to the physical tower and frustrated by their desire, and inability to move. That these knights are stripped of their maturity and independence in the face of this love object exacerbates their dissatisfaction with place. Kolve suggests an emotional change of place as well, in that

> Chaucer shows a deeper movement of the spirit as well—a compulsion not comic, arbitrary, or trivial . . . [they] fall in love with Emelye for her beauty, unmistakably, but the beauty of her freedom most of all . . . . From within prison they fall in love with a creature who seems to incarnate a condition the exact opposite of their own[28]

—able to choose her own space. Her entrance into the garden and the tale establishes a distance, an emotional rift between the cousins, now political rivals for possession of her charms, however differently conceived. It also transforms

> a formal architectural tableau . . . [into an] animated opening out into a realm of contingency and change. Perotheus obtains Arcite's freedom, Palamon escapes, and the opening icon of the prison / garden-now left behind as a literal place . . . is redefined through a series of metaphors and used to illuminate the significance of the action.[29]

In other words, Emily's locus of freedom generates a second kind of locus for the desirous young men. Little does Arcite realize that exile to an alien place bereft of his beloved will in fact be a worse locus of imprisonment.

When Perotheus, mutual friend of Theseus and Arcite, visits Athens, he arranges to free the latter on condition of his removal, his exile from that place. But for Arcite, one freedom in Athens leads to another bondage out of it—deprived of the sight of his beloved in Thebes: "Nought in purgatorie but in helle" (l.1226), low on Fortune's wheel, does he think himself now, envisioning the confining tower as paradise. After six months of agonizing, Arcite breaks his promise, and returns to Athens, near but not with his beloved; here he languishes for a year or two and finally, incognito, becomes "Philostrate," Emily's page. Despite his diminished social status, his locus is now ideal! For the Knight, then, freedom is more than liberty to act at will, however and wherever one chooses. Perhaps the Knight fears

---

[27]   Kendrick, *Chaucerian Play*, 119.
[28]   Kolve, *Chaucer and the Imagery of Narrative*, 90.
[29]   Kolve, *Chaucer and the Imagery of Narrative*, 91.

the languishing, impotent, inactivity Arcite agonizingly endures, and hence rushes to the pilgrimage at his first chance.

Yet another transformation enacted here is the move from relative stasis, two knights imprisoned within a tower watching a maid walking in a confined garden, to relative activity and animation in the tournament, in a city within the city, "opening out into a realm of contingency and change."[30] But as Jill Mann points out, first "Palamon goes to the grove to hide himself, and 'by aventure' (1506) Arcite makes for the same place . . . he wanders into the very path by whose side Palamon lies hidden."[31] They first began in the same locus, separate temporarily, and seven years later by chance come back together, now with a deadly agenda, making the terrain itself dangerous as we shall see. They are further in a new emotional locus of desire and competition, threatening and perilous.

Thus after those painful years in the Athenian prison-tower, Palamon, berating Dame Fortuna, Saturn, and Juno, determines to escape his "cage." Here, in an outdoor grove on the outskirts of Athens, in a marginal space neither urban nor rural which might well be more dangerous than his interior protective prison, Palamon the new escapee hides in his exterior place of exile; while preserved from legal imprisonment in his hideout, he is confined to secret isolation, away from physical protection, and deprived of human interaction. Who, including the Knight, would not fear a place of such isolation?

By "aventure," in this same grove as noted above, Arcite has chosen to make his May obeisances. Also emotionally imprisoned behind his masquerade in a protective feigned identity, and located in the body of the squire he calls "Philostrate" in order to protect his life and be near Emilye, he seeks this salvific refuge as an escape. Both knights are in danger. Their common physical locus, outdoors in nature, ironically what Arlyn Diamond rightly calls "the traditional refuge of lovers"[32]—but without their lover. Palamon hiding in the bushes and Arcite hiding in a feigned body—initiates a minor climax: hostile single combat over possession of the beloved, who is not even "possessable." Perhaps this evidence of fear and frustration marks the Knight as well. Kolve finds that the grove "encounter is described in language that recalls their former incarceration: Palamon hides in a bush while Arcite 'rometh up and doun' (I.1515). Even outside

---

[30]   Kolve, *Chaucer and the Imagery of Narrative*, 91.

[31]   Jill Mann, "Chance and Destiny in *Troilus and Criseyde* and the *Knight's Tale*," *The Cambridge Companion to Chaucer*, ed. Piero Boitani and Jill Mann (Cambridge: Cambridge University Press, 1986, 2003), 106.

[32]   Arlyn Diamond, "Sir Degrevant: What Lovers Want," *Pulp Fictions of Medieval England: Essays in Popular Romance*, ed. Nicola McDonald. (Manchester and New York: Manchester University Press, 2004), 82–101; here 86.

the prison tower, their experience is characterized as captivity and constraint"[33] regardless of physical locus.

In this benign natural orchard, removed from urban eyes, three forces converge: while two cousins engage in their physical contest, "Up to the ancle foghte they in blood" (1.1660), by happenstance, the third, father-figure Theseus, will soon go hunting in the same grove! And, as Ansgar Kelly points out in speaking of narrative and thematic circuit breaks, "we can cite the grove first destroyed by Theseus in constructing his Colosseum and then used as the site of Arcite's exequies"[34] as an instance of mutated construction. A place of potential peril between two knights becomes a place of actual peril between two hundred, which ultimately, perhaps inevitably, will become a fatal place of burial.

Confined to the safe space back in his room apart from the dangerous action, but clad in riding clothes in preparation for some event, Theseus is at first oblivious to the devastation. When he rides out, the confluence of the three, the symbolic father reigning in his two sons, meeting in one external locus, initiates a major conflict which only maternal, feminine intercession can mollify. Thus, following his sources, the Knight must create a separate terrain, albeit on the same spot, specifically to resolve the Emily-rivalry, she being the symbolic and literal prize and the locus of the romance. Her free, social self is a seductive conduit to her emotional and military stability. On that terrain, of Emilye and the grove where her lovers contend, is the site on which the next part of the narrative is played out.

Although Theseus would kill the vow-breaking knights for their infidelity on the spot, one for breaking prison and the other for breaking exile by returning to the city of Athens, his weeping Queen Ypolyta, her sister Emelye, and her Ladies would mark this terrain, affect this situation by their placement and actions as well. They piteously beg:

> "Have mercy, Lord, upon us wommen alle!"
> And on hir bare knees adoun they falle
> And wolde have kist his feet ther as he stood.          (1757–59)

As Mann points out, "It is Chaucer who introduces this second set of kneeling women into the narrative; Boccaccio's Teseo feels only a momentary anger that passes of its own accord (V 88), so that there is no need for the women to intervene. Again the visual image points up the feminine nature of pity, the 'verray wommanhede' that prompts it."[35] This external tableau on the field parallels that of the Amazonian women whom Theseus found on the highway,

---

[33]   Kolve, *Chaucer and the Imagery of Narrative*, 91.
[34]   Ansgar Kelly, *Chaucerian Tragedy*, 224.
[35]   Mann, *Feminizing Chaucer*, 136.

two of whom were the very Queen Ypolyta and Emelye now pitying the young knights. Happily, "what goes around comes around" or in Chaucerian idiom, "pitee renneth soone in gentil herte" (1761) as empathy links the two vignettes.

The climax one year hence, a proper, safe, controlled, compassionate tournament will be fought with one hundred warriors per side in that exact locale where Palamon and Arcite were found. Mann finds Theseus "provides a civilized context within which [the contest] can operate."[36] Unlike the vicious, personal one-on-one battle of the combatants alone in the grove, this public contest and its displays of strength by professionals is controlled by rules and regulations designed to win without death rather than with it. Although certain danger of individual conflict to the death in the outdoor grove is replaced by potential danger in controlled group battle in the same grove-cum-arena, both activities create a perilous environment.

The outcome at that grove, the most consistent and unifying space in the romance, determines the resolution of the tale, Emily's final locus, and the political locus of the knights. As Julian Wasserman suggests,

> Interestingly enough, the knights first set forth their conflicting views in a tower—Chaucer's addition to the poem—reminiscent of Boethius's metaphor of the "heye towre of [God's] purveaunce" (iv, prose vi, 219) in which oppositions are held "to-hepe althoghe that thei ben diverse." When the oppositions are no longer held in dynamic harmony, the two knights leave the tower and fight out the conflict in the world of "moveable" things as symbolized by the arena with its carvings that emphasize the worldly manifestations of the three separate deific principles to whom the protagonists pray.[37]

Part Three of the tale, then, narrates those prayers and its results; it creates an artificial, outdoor, triple-templed space, open to the sky, but contained by walls as is a stadium, full of craft and artifice worthy of the dignified events to be enacted. Ironically, the Colosseum abutting the temples is also an artistic construct on which are crafted loci of varied descriptions creating a kind of religio-historical art-museum at the edge of the arena, within the city of Athens.

Albrecht Classen notes the growth of thirteenth-century cities in his article in this collection, and that "the increase of power accumulated by cities grew at an astounding rate, which found fascinating expression in a wide variety of urban art,

---

[36]   Mann, "Chance and Destiny," 107.

[37]   Julian Wasserman, "Both Fixed and Free: Language and Destiny in Chaucer's *Knight's Tale* and *Troilus and Criseyde*," *Sign, Sentence, Discourse: Language in Medieval Thought and Literature*, ed. id. and Lois Roney (Syracuse, NY: Syracuse University Press, 1989), 194–222; here 208. For an opposing view, see Henry Ansgar Kelly, "Chaucer's Art and Our Art," *New Perspectives in Chaucer Criticism*, ed. Donald M. Rose (Norman, Oklahoma: Pilgrim Books, 1981), 107–20, who maintains "The same conclusions of muddlement and inattention to the visual arts must be drawn for Chaucer's depiction of the three temples in *The Knight's Tale*" (114).

whether we think of cathedrals and churches, city halls, urban houses, libraries, or splendid city walls as part of the fortification system."[38] Within this classical setting, that expression would be manifested as temples and Coliseum. It is not surprising that Theseus's creative structure would be artistically expressive. It is liminal, neither exclusively city nor country, but an appendage of both, bridging the two loci. This "noble theatre" (1.1885),

> The circuit a myle was about,
> Walled of stoon, and dyched al withoute
> Round was the shap, in manere of compas,
> . . . Swich a place
> Was noon on erthe, as in so litel space.          (1.1887–89; 1895–96)

Interestingly, the walled boundary around this city wall is spatially represented allegorically as a mini-globe, "in manere of compas," with opposing posts in the Eastern (honoring Venus), Western (honoring Mars), and Northern (honoring Diana) domains: a microcosm of a world of contrasting religious ideals. It is carefully and appropriately designed, with order and reason. Theseus's artists fabricate graffiti on this wall reflecting an artificial, unnatural nature on the wall placard, itself placed within nature. The space of Venus's Eastern wall is a garden setting painted on white marble depicting broken sleeps, sacred tears, and fiery strokes of desire on its face, a telling cuckoo on her hand and a fragrant rose garland on her head. The space is seductive. Mars's Western wall of gold copies the temple of Mars in Thrace (Greece), not a garden but a cold, frosty forest of barren trees with a stormy wind blowing through, a space under a grassy hill. The ghastly burnished steel temple and the gate shaken by a blast are anti-natural. The space is brutal. The Northern wall of alabaster, white and coral red, protects an oratory to the chaste Diane. Here artificial illumination mimicking a window's light reveals the hardest, strongest stones bound with iron both crosswise and endwise to uphold its barrel-sized pillars. The space is firm and determined.

Each locus can easily be identified with the deity in whose honor it was created. Further, space is demarcated, divided into discrete units, organizing, ordering, prioritizing, and hierarchizing to emphasize additional points of his narrative. As Patterson suggests,

> one of the Knight's most common strategies of narrative containment is, literally, to build containers: it will help us to see how his version of narrative is in fact anti-narrative by thinking of it as construction, as architectonics. Each narrative event is carefully sealed off from the others with a statement of finality . . . [seen in] the large number of transitional passages that staple the narrative together."[39]

---

[38]  Albrecht Classen, Hans Sachs and his Encomia Songs," in this volume, 568.
[39]  Patterson, *Chaucer and the Subject of History*, 210–11.

Three such evident demarcations can be seen in the following: "Suffiseth heere ensamples oon or two, / And though I koude rekene a thousand mo" (1953–54); "Suffiseth oon ensample in stories olde; / I may nat rekene hem alle though I wolde" (2038–39); and "Now wol I stynten of the goddes above, Of Mars, and of Venus, goddesse of love, And telle yow as pleynly as I kan / The grete effect, for which that I bygan" (2479–82). Each of these divisions forms a compartment unique and separable from the whole. The style of discrete units amply reflects Theseus's patterned behavior and organizational mode of governing and the Knight's patterned thought process and mode of narration. In fact, John V. Fleming would expand that observation, based on the General Prologue narratives, claiming "in the portraits of the Prologue Chaucer's 'sense of an ending' is strong and active, and that what we might call his 'last liners' in particular enjoy a certain pride of place . . . the descriptions of the Pilgrims usually conclude with a flourish of thematic wit or an emphatic statement of summary character."[40] The same tone is evident in the material art of the Coliseum walls. Ambiguous at best, this theatre of death and beauty just outside the civilized city is miraculously arrayed with pictures, paintings, artistic designs, statues, and elaborately crafted altars to Mars, Venus and Diana. Allegorical representations of Plesaunce, Hope, Desire, Foolhardiness, Youth, Baudry, Riches, Felony, Ire, Dread, Madness, Outrage, Conquest, Diana, Pluto, Calistope, and others line the walls; they signify sources of power and association with Venus, Mars, and Diana, Love, War and Chastity, Arcite, Palamon, and Emily respectively.

Fleming suggests that "Decorative design and pictorial representation was everywhere in Chaucer's world, in the consecrated spaces of the churches and in the banquet halls of the City . . . from the modest decorations of ivy leaf or zigzag to complex history executed in continuous narration."[41] The walls of this amphitheater represent such fictive history, although they are deceptively painted, ambiguously placed both inside and outside of the city, both interior and exterior; while they create a contained space, the scenes they depict are of uncontained, uncontrolled nature: a forest, a garden, the cold frosty region of Thrace, a hill, hunting grounds, and Pluto's dark region. Although they are beautiful, they are also the backdrop of vice, from dark Felonie to cruel Ire, red as glowing coal, to smiling Knife-murderer, to treasonous Killer-in-bed, the bleeding of open War, to gaping-mouthed cold Death, to name a few. No doubt the Knight himself witnessed such atrocities which still burn in his consciousness.

The visions represent places and means of death in actual life, fitting since here will be located the deadly tournament. The space, the concrete tournament theatre, then becomes an amalgam of nature and artifice, beauty and destruction; it unifies

---

[40]   John V. Fleming, "Chaucer and the Visual Arts of His Time," *New Perspectives in Chaucer Criticism*, ed. Donald M. Rose (Norman, OK: Pilgrim Books, 1981), 121–36; here 132–33.

[41]   Fleming, "Chaucer and the Visual Arts," 124.

the three ideological positions of the gods, as well as the personae they reflect, through imitation and delineation of their deific patrons, and the contenders each represents. And yet it is also a place of death, and a tomb site. The characters the Knight chooses to depict have ironic relevance to this tale of love, reinforcing the text. He instantiates the many themes of love and conflict, self and other, subtly pervading the text throughout; he publicly announces Theseus's identity, values, and great learning in the images by giving the subjects of Theseus's imagination a concrete locus on the walls. The splendid, dramatic presentation threatens to steal the show, the actual physical contest for a place in the heart of Emily.

The entourages of Palamon and Arcite arriving the night before the tournament are presented in a spatial dimension. Palamon is paired with Lygurge, King of Thrace, carried "ful hye upon a chaar of gold" (2138); Arcite is paired with Emetreus, King of India, riding high "Upon a steede bay trapped in steel" (2157). The host Duke Theseus ushers in parades of combatants hierarchically, according to their degree of power; they are placed in orderly spaces within his opulent internal palace within his city, resplendent with luxury and regulated with fine precision, rank after rank in proper order.

> This Theseus, this duc, this worthy knyght,
> Whan he had broght hem into his citee,
> And inned hem, everich at his degree,
> He fested hem, and dooth so greet labour
> To esen hem and do hem al honour
> That yet men wenen that no mannes wit
> Of noon estaat ne koude amenden it.          (2190–96)

This internal space is perfect! They are seated for dinner according to rank, in perfectly protected, controlled order. Here, finally, is the safety and security upon which both Theseus and the Knight can rely. At least until the games begin.

When all retire for the night, the three principles in this prayer-fest visit their shrine of choice. First Palamon arises to visit Venus "And in hir houre he walketh forth a pas / Unto the lystes there hire temple was" (2217–18). Here, humbly on his knees, he begs "to have fully possessioun / Of Emilye . . . So that I have my lady in [the space of] myn armes" (2242–43, 2247). He vows the place of "Thy temple wol I worshipe everemo, /And on thyn auter, where I ride or go, / I wol do sacrifice and fires beete" (2251–53). Recalling her status as goddess who rose from the sea at the island of Cythera further creates a mental construct by which to know her. This sacred space of her oratory as well as her historic origins he will honor with his everlasting sacrifice and fires. But then this place is deified with the presence of Venus herself, since "atte laste the statue of Venus shook, / And made a signe" (2265–66) thus transforming it into a miraculous site.

Next, "up roos Emyle, / And to the temple of Dyane gan hye" (2273–75), to her place of worship where she lights fires, burns incense, and sacrifices clothes and all the rest that sacrifice entails. Noting her three-fold role of goddess of the hunt, of the moon, and of the underworld, Emily prays "O chaste goddesse of the wodes grene, / To whom both hevene and erthe and see is sene, / Queen of the regne of Pluto derk and lowe, / Goddesse of maydens, that myn herte hast knowe" (2297–2300) and beats two fires on her altar. She then explains her own place as a maid who loves hunting and venery, and to walk the wild woods, not to be a wife with child, and begs this virginal life. She wishes love and peace between Palamon and Arcite, "And fro me turne awey hir hertes so" (2318) to another place.

The tears streaming down her cheeks demarcate her place of sorrow. The goddess's response physically shakes up the site when "oon of the fyres queynte / And quyked agayn" (2334–35), flickering out and back on again as winds roar around. When Diana appears in person as huntress with bow in hand and arrows clattering, the goddess creates the site of a miracle to prophesy and reassure the fearful maid.

Finally, Arcite walks into fierce Mars's sovereign temple, the god honored in the cold regions of Thrace who "hast in every regne and every lond / Of armes al the brydel [reins] in thyn hond" (2375–76), a place of power and strength. This place he will "moost honoren / Of any place . . . In thy temple I wol my baner honge" (2406–07, 2410). Thus the space of the temple becomes the space of Arcite as well as of Mars, a sharing of values and commitment. Arcite will ever burn fires to Mars, binding his beard and hair to the god. The response elicits clattering of rings and doors of the temple, a sweet aroma from the fires, a ringing of his hauberk, and a low murmuring "Victory" from Mars's statue. The scene now moves to a new non-urban setting: "in the hevene above" (2439) the place of power where Father Saturn who dwells "in the signe of the leoun" (2462) utters the final decision and consoles each contestant.

Thus, early morning before the tourney begins, both opponents and Emily kneel in place before the altars at the temples of their respective deities, as much the place of determination of the outcome as the combat zone itself. Seemingly an extension of the theatre, at this site they beg their mentors for their desired outcomes, and are promised fulfillment, an unlikely foreshadowing of the outcome, given the contradictory nature of the desires. Isolated in the sacred oratories of the deities, Emelye weepingly begs her patroness Diana exemption from unwanted marriage; Palamon entreats Venus for his true love; Arcite prays to Mars for victory.

The setting then switches to the sacred space of heaven where the gods negotiate, and Saturn reassures Venus "I wol thy lust fulfille" (1.2478). Mann contends that "It is because Saturn's sphere is the outermost in the planetary order (his course thus being widest of all) that his influence dominates the planets beneath him."[42] Being furthest away from earth, and offering the greatest perspective, the all-seeing locus of the gods reinforces their great authority. Here the Knight uses the authority of the gods' celestial locus to tantalize the audience: how can all three wishes be fulfilled? Only with their intervention. As the morning of the tourney breaks, Theseus's guests roam the palace, predicting the day's outcome. They are indoors, personally safe, and removed from perilous external influence. True to form, the noble Theseus "Heeld yet the chambre of his paleys riche / Til that the Thebane knyghtes, both yliche / Honoured, were into the paleys fet" [fetched] (1.252–27). By remaining confined in his room, not stealing the show, and allowing the knights their respect, Theseus proves himself honorable, thoughtful, and sensitive. His gesture is also a reminder that the combatants have no leisure to do the same. They must exit the protective space of the castle, and battle in the grove, now remade into a formalized place of death. Theseus sits at a window on a throne like a god, removed from combat danger as the throngs below press toward him. Perhaps the Knight identifies with him here, powerful and safe. As the ceremonies begin, his place is high on a horse, leading the contestants into battle. "Tho were the gates shet" (1.2597), their clang creating a closed system, an internal, controlled arena in which uncontrolled actions will be perpetrated.

Let the games begin in the new city-within-the-city. The two hundred warriors who enter Theseus's prefabricated enclosure are only marginally safer than Palamon and Arcite who contended in wide-open spaces one year before on the same spot. Although Theseus orders his "lysts" to protect unnecessary loss of life, and follows proscribed tournament protocol, danger still prevails in this ambiguously designed indoor-outdoor space of conflict. The Duke escorts warriors of each knight from his perfect palace where they rested the night into his war-theatre with honor and dignity befitting their kingly status.

After fierce fighting and great losses on the battlefield by each side outside the city, Palamon is vanquished. Indeed, he loses the battle. But as the victor, Arcite, rides about the stadium accepting congratulations, the place over which he rides is disrupted by Pluto at Saturn's request: "Out of the ground a furie infernal sterte" (1.2684); it becomes the locus of his death. After Arcite's incident outdoors, he is brought inside, into a place of rest in Theseus's castle, in a futile attempt to save him. But removing the danger of battle does not ameliorate the wound. Thus, a supernatural miracle must generate a natural effect in this liminal space bridging war and peace, an internal-external environment. He has won the battle, but loses the prize by his death. Great funeral rituals and observances follow until Theseus must determine a locus for the body. In a structurally perfect circular ending, the

---

42 Mann, "Chaucer and Destiny," 107.

Duke chooses the very place where he and Arcite first fought, the very place where Arcite won the contest, and the very place where he lost his life.

Ansgar Kelly recalls this pattern, noting, "The grove first destroyed by Theseus in constructing his coliseum [is] then used as the site of Arcite's exequies."[43] But no matter how appropriate, the fearful attitude pervades the grove / arena. Further, as H. Marshall Leicester, Jr. claims,

> there is a momentary atmosphere of something genuinely ghastly here that echoes the landscape of the temple of Mars with its broken trees "in which ther dwelleth neither man ne best" (1976). The hyperbolic destruction of the grove has interesting and disturbing implications for the symbolic topography of the poem. At the end of Part II Theseus says, "The lystes shal I maken in this place" (1862), a detail not found in Boccaccio, where the arena predates the quarrel between Palamon and Arcite. Chaucer's alteration thus makes the lists more of an ad hoc institution created for a specific occasion and thus stresses more pointedly the power and energy of human making. But in the description of the funeral the Knight makes the destruction of the grove sound so total that we may wonder whether the lists that Theseus built on its site go up in flames too. Certainly it seems appropriate to his mood here that he should leave the possibility hanging: more than wood is being burned in his mind.[44]

It is the end of an era which marked the ground on which the tourney was held, just as the arena itself marked the narrative. The place will always connote the dangerous locus of battle between cousins for love and honor. But that narrative is not yet over. Years later, Theseus calls the Parliament into session; then he summons Palamon, and finally Emily to convene at a place where he lays out their future. The wise ruler points out the time elapsed, and suggests the pair cease mourning, and they concur. Both Emily and Palamon have lived their lives in separate spaces, alone and lonely. Now, Theseus suggests, they shall be united. Thus in solemn, dignified ritual, Theseus weds them: "Bitwixen hem was maad anon the bond / That highte matrimoigne or mariage" (1.3094–95). This deferred winning of the prize has moved Palamon from locus to locus: from the pile of corpses on the Theban battlefield, to the confusing tower and the desires it generates, to the city of Athens' borders, to the interior of Theseus's ritualized theatre, to the battlefield itself, to his domicile, a temporary state of limbo, and finally to Theseus's conference to receive the amatory prize of union with his beloved. However, description of the intimate space of the bedchamber common in many romances is withheld by a Knightly Teller, perhaps more political than amatory. Theseus's bestowal of Emily also occurs in the liminal space between public and private—not on a grand scale in the stadium before thousands of

---

[43]  Ansgar Kelly, *Chaucerian Tragedy*, 224.
[44]  H. Marshall Leicester, Jr., *The Disenchanted Self: Representing the Subject in the Canterbury Tales* (Berkeley, Los Angeles, and Oxford: University of California Press, 1990), 355.

adulating fans, but in the confined quarters of the wise Duke who will no doubt give it some public notice.

In discussing Boccaccio's function of city-space, Crafton posits "representatives of two very different social classes developing a bond as citizens ready to defend the city against external threat."[45] Often Chaucer's citizens likewise unite to protect their political and material space. Chaucerian pilgrim-Tellers and their characters recognize "alle in their companye," but in the *Knight's Tale*, agonistic competition rather than cooperation or bonding is the order of the day for Palamon and Arcite. Rather than supporting their blood relatives, in a kind of inversion, each is the cause of danger to the other.

Interestingly, each knight's wish is fully granted from their respective deities; but the Amazonian Emily receives merely a partial reprieve from the marriage she does not want, from the marital peril she does not choose. Unlike the determined, strong-willed Melidor in *Sir Degrevant*, whose political powers equal those of her suitors, Emily, a century before, is more docile, accepting of her circumstances, and less combative. Although she would not be a wife, she accepts the role if Diana demands. For her, the city is relatively safe while she is a maid, until Theseus determines her new uxorious station. The function of this fringe area in which she resides for many years, the liminal space between the confinement posed by human habitation and marriage, and the freedom from interference, is both a perilous and protective one.

In this domain, embodying the best-and-worst of both worlds, she is free, but uncertain and insecure that her status will not soon change. City trespassers are temporarily accorded human intercourse and safety when traveling to a nearby city; but ironically they may also encounter their greatest danger, or experience their greatest turmoil without protection in a city not desiring their presence. These complex, even ambivalent loci add human drama, a sense of narrative evolution, and emotional punctuation to this drawn-out excursion into the romance of love and war in city and rural spaces.

The public face of chivalry precludes a place of reflection and the merely personal which defines the Knight of the *General Prologue*, "released from his formulaic enclosure into the unstable territory where questions are asked—into the problematic of self-definition that motivates the *Canterbury* Tales,"[46] as Patterson suggests. In this new locus of open exploration and self-understanding, the Knight emerges, not surprisingly, as Chaucer's first, and one of his finest Tellers of city tales. The domain of knights in general is somewhat liminal, traveling as they do through dangerous terrain from urban court to rural battlefield and back. It is

---

[45]   Crafton, "Chaucer and the City," 52.

[46]   Patterson, *Chaucer and the Subject of History*, 168–69.

somewhat ironic, then, that Chaucer's Knight who has battled throughout the world, in cities and countrysides, has chosen to tell a spatially based Tale so heavily focused on the city. In fact, it can be said that Theseus, the Knight's surrogate, has created urban space by extending its protective boundaries to shield and preserve those in its previously liminal spaces of the dangerous rural grove. Rather than seeking dangerous "aventure," he would privilege wise and secure terrain. Fleming reminds us of "the great pictorial riches that would have surrounded Chaucer in the more cosmopolitan world of the City, in the churches and private palaces of Thames-side . . . we must not forget that Chaucer was a Londoner, and his poetic urbanity is the sophistication of a cultural capital."[47] In this first *Canterbury Tale*, Chaucer sets the tone and place of urbane gentility while rehearsing all manner of urban spaces, public and personal, protective and perilous, in his narrative. Perhaps the most intimidating locus, however, is the internal one, the place of self, the seat of identity, the space of order and public refinement, which the Knight has successfully captured and resolved, perhaps both for himself and in the person of Theseus, by the end of his tale.

---

[47]    Fleming, "Chaucer and the Visual Arts," 125.

Daniel F. Pigg

(The University of Tennessee at Martin)

# Imagining Urban Life and Its Discontents: Chaucer's *Cook's Tale* and Masculine Identity

Depictions of contemporary, medieval London, a city growing as a mercantile center in the fourteenth century, show it to be a place of problems almost in a stereotypical way. By medieval standards, London was a significant city. As David Wallace has observed, the 1377 poll tax returns show London to be twice the size of cities such as York or Bristol.[1] It was a city with clear rivalries among various guilds, and as it is depicted in civic records, it was a place where the typical temptations and vices might be found. Examination of the London *Letter Books* reveals a world where a common standard of justice in terms of punishments for crimes was lacking, but one in which the "masculine oligarchy" is clearly operating in an urban space to support and benefit the group in power.[2] Since the people who rose to power in London in the post-Plague period were often themselves members of guilds—an aspect that Chaucer himself observed in his portraits of the guildsmen in the *General Prologue* to the *Canterbury Tales*—Chaucer's depiction of life in the city was structured around the material successes of the guilds.

Anyone who challenged these powerful men would fall under the judgment of the city they controlled. Male authority represented in the guise of the ruling class seemed particularly keen on defining for other males aspiring to the status of

---

[1]  David Wallace, "Chaucer and the Absent City," *Chaucer's England: Literature in Historical Context*, ed. Barbara Hanawalt, Medieval Studies at Minnesota, 4 (Minneapolis and London: University of Minnesota Press, 1992), 61–64.

[2]  Wallace, "Chaucer and the Absent City," 63–64. For a study of the implications of guild life in the city of York, particularly the way in which masculine authority and power are connected with the guilds' role in the production of the Corpus Christi cycle plays, see Christina Marie Fitzgerald, *The Drama of Masculinity and Medieval English Guild Culture*. The New Middle Ages (New York and London: Palgrave/Macmillan, 2007).

"citizen" what acceptable behavior was. To challenge or break that image meant certain ostracism, if not being labeled as criminal activity. As Jacques Rosssiaud has noted, such associations within an urban space such as London brought people together with the kinds of association where a man .might "fraternize with people without risking his honor."[3] The entire social organization of the city was thus reaffirmed as a symbolic and literal system.

Chaucer Cook's Tale provides the audience with the seemingly most apparent depiction of that London life, even with the location of "Chepe" (4377) in the text.[4] In fact, the Cook's Tale is unique in the Canterbury Tales with its setting in an English city, as opposed to a town or village. The Cook's Tale also provides us a window onto the construction of masculinity within the context of a mercantile economy by showing us the boundaries of acceptable male behavior in that city. Apprenticeship was undertaken by both males and females in post-plague London, but the Cook focuses his attention directly on the particular challenges to males. David Wallace has investigated this tale from the perspective of contemporary history, but I would like to examine it from the grounds of the social history and in light of a system of thinking intended to generate social structures that affirm the strictures present around medieval anxiety about property, wealth, and the protection of guild authority.[5] The medieval city of London is built within the social anxieties implicit in this unique Chaucerian tale. Those anxieties particularly concern the production of capital for the marketplace through hard work. The very life of the city depends on a reading of the social circumstances in a way that puts Perkyn Revelour in his place. He may be the proverbial "life of the party," but he represents a challenge to the various systems through which he is being compelled to make his behavior conform to a highly ritualized pattern of life.

Clearly the point that the Cook intends to show is that Perkyn Revelour, the foot-loose and fancy-free singer and dancer, disregards the systemic building of male character through a legal contract of service, a legal contract almost feudal in character and practice.[6] Although the tale has typically been regarded as incomplete, its state is certainly sufficient to show how failure to follow the strictures of a mercantile-based masculinity leads to a path of dubious moral

[3]   Jacques Roussiaud, "The City-Dweller and Life in Cities and Towns," Medieval Callings, ed. Jacques Le Goff, trans. Lydia G. Cochrane (Chicago and London: The University of Chicago Press, 1990), 162.

[4]   Geoffrey Chaucer, "The Cook's Tale," The Riverside Chaucer, 3rd ed., ed. Larry Benson (Boston: Houghton Mifflin, 1987), 84–86. All references to the text of the tale are to this edition. "Chepe" refers to Cheapside.

[5]   David Wallace, Chaucerian Polity: Absolutist Lineages and Associational Forms in England and Italy, Figurae: Reading Medieval Culture Series (Stanford: Stanford University Press, 1997), 156–81.

[6]   Wallace, Chaucerian Polity, 168.

associations as well as to the development of a metaphoric thinking to remove all who violate those norms. At the same time, however, this tale seems to lack the moral imperatives found in other tales of Fragment I, at least from a medieval Christian perspective. This lack of moral imperative, as Daniel Pinti observes, led the fifteenth-century scribe of Bodley 686 to add to the tale with additional text to support the theme of governance,[7] a theme that I argue is already implicit in Chaucer's original tale. In typical fashion, Chaucer allows his tellers and characters a free reign to do what they will, even to succumb to implicit self-critique. Investigating Perkyn Revelour within the context of the mercantile-based vision of masculinity helps make better sense of a tale that after we see the course of action that Perkyn takes, there is little point in continuing a story where a vision of male behavior and responsibility has passed. In this sense, the *Cook's Tale* is certainly complete—"there is no more to say," as E. G. Stanley once observed.[8] In a more recent study, Jim Casey contends that texual aspects such as the placement of the *Cook's Tale* in Fragment I and its description of a failed apprentice seem to have authorial intention, "since the tale appears to inform later conversation and interaction between his pilgrims."[9] Both of these studies rely on textual evidence. This article argues from a position inside the fiction of the text itself with respect to the importance of the ideas themselves. There is an implicit text logic for the state of the tale. Chaucer may have intended to leave the tale incomplete for a reason.

# I

The difficulty of understanding Perkyn Revelour in this tale is made more problematic by the conflicting social discourses present in the late fourteenth century surrounding performative masculinity and its constraints in the world of apprenticeship. In essence, the questions "What did it mean to be male?," and "What did it mean to be an apprentice?" must be reconciled according to social standards. From the start, the name "Perkyn Revelour," a name assigned by the Cook, makes him an "identifiable literary type."[10] But as Earl Lyon notes, Chaucer is probably drawing on London life less than on a literary depiction that he might

---

[7]   Daniel Pinti, "Governance in the "Cook's Tale' in Bodley 686," *Chaucer Review* 19.1 (1996): 379–88.
[8]   E. G. Stanley, "Of This Cokes Tale Maked Chaucer Na Moore," *Poetica* 5 (1976): 36–59.
[9]   Jim Casey, "Unfinished Business: The Termination of the 'Cook's Tale,'" *Chaucer Review* 41.2 (2006): 185–96.
[10]   V. J. Scattergood, "Perkyn Revelour and the 'Cook's Tale,'" *Chaucer Review* 19.1 (1984): 14–23; here 21.

have found somewhere else.[11] Some London records regarding the interactions of masters and apprentices, for instance, might easily have been transformed into a work of fiction as they seem close to that genre as well. Chaucer's original audience might have had difficulty separating the Cook's fiction from an all too present reality.

To suggest that the representation of masculinity was anxious during the Middle Ages and also the subject of Chaucerian comedy is perhaps a commonplace that seems so obvious that it needs not be explored. Yet it is specifically the world of "pryvetee"—a term used several times in the Fragment I—that must be disclosed if we seek to understand the unspoken secrets that underlie Chaucer's texts as well as the quest for control in the growing London middle class.

Late-medieval society inherited a philosophical position that biology equals destiny. Drawing on classical medical sources, medieval philosophers and theologians affirmed male superiority on biological grounds and reasoned those foundations to extend to psychological and mental capacities as well. Yet physical form alone did not grant an individual a position as fully functional. As Vern L. Bullough notes, manhood was defined as "impregnating women, protecting dependents, and serving as provider to one's family."[12] Masculinity was thus defined in terms of performance. Thus impotence threatened the existence of that world, and frequently became the source of comedy in medieval texts just as it provided the status of perpetual virginity for Mary. That it was the potential source of annulment of a marriage suggests how significant male performance was to the social fabric.

As scholars have noted, in this biological-based construction of masculinity, the presence of the feminine was negative. As Bullough and Sponsler note, cross-dressing, for example, except during carnival settings, was inappropriate to the hegemonic paradigm of maleness.[13] Love itself was considered a feminization of the male. The desire of lovesickness was overcome by recourse to sexual intercourse with women, preferably with multiple partners to avoid any amorous attachment to one.[14] Perhaps Perkyn is following that advice in the line "Wel was the wenche with hym myghte meete" (4374; fortunate was the woman who might meet him). The fiction, however, does not enlarge upon his sexual prowess, and

[11]   Earl D. Lyons, "Roger De Ware, Cook," *Modern Language Notes* 52.7 (1937): 491–93.
[12]   Vern L. Bullough, "On Being a Male in the Middle Ages," *Medieval Masculinities: Regarding Men in the Middle Ages*, ed. Clare A. Lees, Thelma Fenster, and Jo Ann McNamara. Medieval Cultures, 7 (Minneapolis and London: University of Minnesota Press, 1994), 31–45; here 34.
[13]   Bullough, "One Being Male in the Middle Ages," 33–35; Claire Sponsler, "Outlaw Masculinities: Drag, Blackface, and Late Medieval Laboring-Class Festivals," *Becoming Male in the Middle Ages*, ed. Jeffrey Jerome Cohen and Bonnie Wheeler. The New Middle Ages, 4 (New York and London: Garland Publishing, 1997), 321–47.
[14]   Bullough, "On Being Male in the Middle Ages," 33–35.

such excess would put in difficulty his vocation. The fiction merely attests to the obvious potential with its similes and larger controlling metaphors. The intent of certain love therapies was to rid the male of non-male qualities.

The late fourteenth century witnessed the further development of cities and civic responsibility and the importance of craft guilds to both the literal and symbolic fabric of a city. In that world, masculinity was formed, nurtured, and controlled as a series of obligations. From the fourteenth through the fifteenth century, guilds were coming to dominate the economic and governmental life of the city. Economically healthy guilds were important to a city's fortunes. Keeping that strength meant keeping apprentices of worth and social class equivalent to those who were training them.[15] City governments, realizing this fact, often placed tough restrictions on them and all but prohibited foreign competition in the city.[16] As Sylvia Thrupp has noted, these rules extended into the relationship between master and apprentice.[17] The goal of apprenticeship was to be sponsored by the master into the freedom of the city.[18] The process required between three to seven years and sometimes as many as ten, and sometimes provided for a small stipend.[19] Kowaleski calls apprenticeship a "means of social mobility for many young men" within certain bounds.[20] They come from all over England to the city of London to seek their fortunes, but they often lacked discipline, coming to London around age fourteen.[21] Apprenticeship provided for that discipline and training. They were often carefully chosen; a connection with crime or vice would have certainly prohibited an affiliation.[22]

Given that an apprentice became a member of a master craftsman's family in some material way, great care was often exercised in choice, training, and discipline.[23] Dissolving the bond was not only problematic, perhaps a source of shame and the recognition of misjudgment, but could also bring the wrath of the city and other guild members upon the master of the craft.[24] The master of craft

---

[15] Ruth Mazzo Karras, *From Boys to Men: Formations of Masculinity in Late Medieval Europe*. The Middle Ages Series (Philadelphia: University of Pennsylvania Press, 2003), 119–20.

[16] Maryanne Kowaleski, *Local Markets and Regional Trade in Medieval Exeter* (Cambridge: Cambridge University Press, 1995), 100.

[17] Sylvia Thrupp, *The Merchant Class of Medieval London 1300–1500* (Chicago: University of Chicago Press, 1948), 215–20.

[18] Kowaleski, *Local Markets and Regional Trade in Medieval Exeter*, 169.

[19] Kowaleski, *Local Markets and Regional Trade in Medieval Exeter*, 170.

[20] Kowaleski, *Local Markets and Regional Trade in Medieval Exeter*, 170.

[21] Barbara A. Hanawalt, *Growing Up in Medieval London: The Experience of Childhood in History* (New York and Oxford: Oxford University Press, 1993), 135.

[22] Thrupp, *The Merchant Class of Medieval London, 1300–1500*, 217.

[23] Shannon McSheffrey, *Marriage, Sex, and Civic Culture in Late Medieval London*, The Middle Ages Series (Philadelphia: University of Pennsylvania Press, 2006), 84; Karras, *From Boys to Men*, 121–23.

[24] Karras, *From Boys to Men*, 123.

might even use imprisonment as a means of instructing his apprentice, but clearly if events reached this stage, it was beyond hope. In her study of guild relations during apprenticeship periods, Barbara Hanawalt has observed that whenever there was a conflict between the master and an apprentice, there was typically a kind of compromise that would solve the problem of severing the relationship.[25]

One specific area that the institution of apprenticeship sought to control was marriage and sexual relations during the period of service. For the period of service, marriage was most often prohibited by contract. Given that this practice continued beyond the fourteenth and fifteenth centuries into the sixteenth, one scholar notes that it often led to overt immorality of a sexual nature among apprentices.[26] Breaking the contract by way of illegal marriage of make one "libel to arrest on a warrant of trespass."[27] At the same time, sexual activity was only frowned upon but subject to punishment. Indentures generally prohibited an apprentice from having sexual relations either on or off the master's property. In one instance, a draper punished his erring apprentice with a "ceremonial flogging in the company hall, inflicted by masked men."[28] The point could hardly be clearer: a violation was a violation against one's profession, guild status, and citizenship, not against one's master alone. A guilty apprentice was disciplined by men in front of men to uphold the status of men. Of course, penalties do not suggest that all male apprentices were sexual profligates, but there would not be such rules if there were no problems in this area.

From these two intersecting planes, we can understand the difficulties of the Cook's Tale. At once, male power manifested sexually and sublimated through male competition was to be turned into the making of capital and reputation, usually among one's male peers and superiors. Transgressions of that method of symbolic and material development were regarded as violations of the world of business, where human labor is quantified and rewarded with social status. The apprentice could marry after being admitted to the city freedom, and his wife would bring to the marriage her own capital to contribute to the household. The theory seems too neat, and is the stuff of literary fiction that Thomas Deloney was to make fashionable in the sixteenth century and which Beaumont and Fletcher were to ridicule in The Knight of the Burning Pestle. The world of the private threatened to undermine its very public manifestation of male power in Chaucer's

[25] Hanawalt, Growing Up in Medieval London, 166–67.
[26] McSheffrey, Marriage, Sex, and Civic Culture in Late Medieval London, 84.
[27] Thrupp, The Merchant Class of Medieval London, 1300–1500, 192. For further examination of the role of sexuality in the Late Middle Ages and Renaissance, see Sexuality in the Middle Ages and Early Modern Times: New Approaches to a Fundamental Cultural-Historical and Literary-Anthropological Theme, ed. Albrecht Classen. Fundamentals of Medieval and Early Modern Culture, 3 (Berlin and New York: Walter de Gruyter, 2008).
[28] Thrupp, The Merchant Class of Medieval London, 1300–1500, 169.

world. Human desire often grows around social constraints, and that has been the message of Fragment I, particularly in the tales of the Miller and Reeve. Here the Cook merely makes public the all-too-latent desire of the country and village in a city swarming with apprentices, all bent on the management of desire, even through subterfuge as Perkyn's friend has dissembled.

## II

The Prologue to the *Cook's Tale* provides an interesting link between the *Reeve's Tale* and a warning that brings together the competing discourses of performative masculinity and mercantile-controlled masculinity. Roger Hogge of Ware claws the Reeve on the back in appreciation of the Miller's being tricked in the *Reeve's Tale*. He notes:

> Wel seyde Salomon in his langage,
> 'Ne bryng nat every man into thyn hous,'
> For herberwynge by nyghte is perilous.
> Wel oghte a man avysed for to be
> Whom that he broghte into his pryvette.          (4330–34)

> [Well said Solomon in his language
> Do not being every man into your house
> For harboring by night is perilous.
> Well out a man to be advised
> Whom he brings into his secret counsel.]

The Cook clearly sees the crime against the Miller as a violation of property, of goods—the rape of the wife and daughter. Working or improving on the Reeve, he says: "But God forbede that we stynte heere" (But God forbid that we should stop here) (4339). The violation of property is similar to the theft of the craftsman's goods he will tell about. The Miller is defeated by the power of male performance by the two Solar Hall scholars, but the Cook, most certainly a member of a guild, sees the violence directed primarily against the Miller on purely mercantile grounds. Everything has monetary worth, and male power is defined by the control and circulation of capital. In some medieval English cities, cooks were among the poorest in the food industry; their economic fortunes were often in jeopardy.[29] Thus his attention to the Miller's loss of goods becomes even more telling. Economic ruin equals the loss of male power in his world. This image is reopened again in the prologue with the Host's comments about the quality of Roger's food. The Host would be at the top of the same industry as the Cook. His

---

[29] Kowaleski, *Local Markets and Regional Trade in Medieval Exeter*, 141–42.

fortunes, however, have proven him to be the "better man." The contest here is more than meets the eye and is deeply hidden in "pryvetee."

The struggle between the Host and Roger of Ware in the *Cook's Prologue* requires a deeper analysis. The conflict between these two men in similar, supporting professions, but operationalized by competing guilds brings their contempt for each other to the surface. Constance B. Hieatt suggests that the charges leveled by the Host concerning the Cook's using meat in pastries that has become dangerous for others to eat are designed to expose the Cook as a charlatan. He would have been a rival to innkeepers and tavern-keepers, all of whom were in an industry that served the public.[30] That city ordinances were written against false advertising about the meat ingredients in pies and about the cleanliness of the workers in cook shops suggests that there was a great deal of fear about the nature of food services in the medieval city.[31] The challenges regarding food preparation continued long after Chaucer's Cook as the essay by Allison Coudert in this collection shows. Getting even after such accusations seems to be on the mind of Roger, whose name has been linked historically with a "nightwalker" of London streets and whose reputation is associated with the kinds of activities of theft and prostitution that readers discover in the tale itself.[32] The Cook says that he could indeed tell a tale of a "hostileer" (4360), yet he decided, "But natheless I wol nat tell it yit; / But er we parte, ywis, thou shalt be quit" (4361–62; But nonetheless I will not tell it yet, but before we part company, certainly, you shall be quited; ).

Tison Pugh suggests that the Cook's locating the tale in Eastcheap, near the location of the Host's inn, and perceiving the Host as the companion of Perkyn Revelour may be a way of getting even with the Host. In this sense, it should be noted that the wife of Perkyn's friend is operating a shop of prostitution.[33] In a very symbolic way—as in real life—the fortunes of cooks and innkeeper are connected. That we might read Roger's own situation as Perkyn's in some measure through his tale deepens the anxieties about social disintegration within the guild structure that must have been at the heart of the late-medieval city. While modern scholarship has certainly uncovered a range of attitudes toward prostitution, even its vital existence as an urban institution particularly associated with "women's work,"[34] the teller of this Chaucerian tale considers the associations as negative.

---

[30]  Constance B. Hieatt, "A Cook They Had with Hem for the Nones," *Chaucer's Pilgrims: An Historical Guide to the Pilgrims in 'The Canterbury Tales*, ed. Laura C. Lambdin and Robert T. Lambdin (Westport, CT, and London: Greenwood Press, 1996), 201–02.

[31]  Hieatt, "A Cook They Had with Hem for the Nones," 201–04.

[32]  Hieatt, "A Cook They Had with Hem for the Nones," 203.

[33]  Tison Pugh, *Sexuality and its Queer Discontents in Middle English Literature*, The New Middle Ages (New York and London: Palgrave Macmillan, 2008), 60–61.

[34]  Ruth Mazo Karras, "Prostitution in Medieval Europe," *Handbook of Medieval Sexuality*, ed. Vern L. Bullough and James A. Brundage. Garland Reference Library of the Humanities, 1696 (New

The tale itself introduces us to one of Chaucer's most foot-loose and fancy-free characters, and yet at the same time one of the most unproductive male figures in terms of masculine performance and mercantile masculinity. Typical of Chaucer's method in the fabliau, we receive details about Perkyn's description that connect him to the natural world. He is merry as a "goldfynch in the shawe" (4367; goldfinch in a wood and "Broun as a berye" (4368; brown [in his skin] as a berry). He "was as ful of love and paramour / As is the hyve ful of hony swete" (4372–73; was as full of love and sexual desire as is the hive full of sweet honey). What seems ironic about this aspect is that the animal imagery in Chaucer's other fabliau is associated with female characters such as the description of Alisoun in the *Miller's Tale*. Clearly, the import in the imagery is to show energy, life, and vitality, with the last detail having sexual potential. William F. Woods sees similar potentials in the description of Perkyn's dancing, hoping, and leaping.[35] According to Joyce E. Salisbury, medieval medical and theological texts located male sexuality in the thighs. They "represented strength, musculature, power, and activity."[36] Strong thighs would be necessary for that leaping and dancing. None of these actions is, however, productive for mercantile masculinity; none involves conversion of energy into productive economic capital. In fact, these actions are more connected with Perkyn's theft of goods.

While typical statements of initiation into apprenticeship required that the person should be "without deformities," there were also requirements relating to reading and writing.[37] The comment that he "loved bet the taverne than the shoppe" (4376; he loved better the tavern than the workplace) indicates none of those abilities, however. In a sense, Perkyn loves the world where the goods that he traffics in are sold and reinvested in business, yet it is not his own productivity that is being earned but a passive one in which money is being exacted from him. In cultural terms, according to the patriarchal paradigm, he is engaging in a socially feminine act; thus it should not surprise us that his activity on the literal level, too, is somewhat feminized. To further emphasize his non-productive male status, the Cook notes that he sings and dances at wedding parties, collects like-

---

York and London: Garland Publishing, 1996), 243–60. See also Gertrud Blaschitz, "Das Freudenhaus im Mittlealter (The Brothel in the Middle Ages], *Sexuality in the Middle Ages and the Early Modern Times: New Approaches to a Fundamental Cultural-Historical and Literary-Anthropological Theme*, ed. Albrecht Classen, Fundamentals of Medieval and Early Modern Culture, 3 (Berlin and New York: Walter de Gruyter, 2008), 715–50.

[35] William F. Woods, "Society and Nature in the 'Cook's Tale,'" *Papers on Language and Literature* 32 (1996): 189–205.

[36] Joyce E. Salisbury, "Gendered Sexuality," *Handbook of Medieval Sexuality*, ed. Vern L. Bullough and James A. Brundage. Garland Reference Library of the Humanities, 1696 (New York and London: Garland Publishing, 1996), 85.

[37] Hanawalt, *Growing Up in Medieval London*, 139.

minded gamesters around him, and conducts his affairs in "pryvette" (4388). Mercantile-based masculinity was clearly oriented toward a meticulous counting of goods as is seen in the *Shipman's Tale*, but clearly not in the private world of Perkyn that silently undermines the very outward substance of business. The master's "box" (4390) is empty! Unlike the merchant of the *Shipman's Tale*, however, Perkyn has nothing to show for his activity.

The master of the victuallers discovers that his goods are being stolen and that he must take action against Perkyn. At the same time, this master must tolerate a certain amount of Perkyn's behavior, given that he has a "papir" (4404) or contract with him. Many crafts prohibited certain actions, but it is not clear that "mynstralcye" (4394) was among them, except for the fact that some associated minstrels with vagabonds and with theft and brawl. Maria Dobozy has made similar associations in her study of minstrels in medieval German literature.[38] Such behaviors might include statements about "drinking, gaming and going to theaters."[39] William Langland in *Piers Plowman* connected them with faulty speech and called them children of Judas because they denatured language.[40] Here the import is that it takes Perkyn not only away from work by leaving the shop at many times during the day to see street activities and to engage in gaming, but the lifestyle also leads him to prison, even "Newegate" (4402).

At the end of the apprenticeship period, the master does not recommend him to be offered freedom of the city and instead dismisses him. If the frequent charges against masters was that they did not educate their apprentices,[41] it is also fair to say in this setting that the master "snybbed bothe erly and late" (rebuked him both early and late) (4401); he was, after all, a member of his own family in a sense. There is a clear contrast created here between the frivolous nature of Perkyn and the steady nature of the master. He simply does not want the influence of Perkyn to ruin any of the other apprentices. By dismissing him, he asserts his own authority, shows that recommendation to city freedom is not automatic, and so demonstrates that unproductive masculinity can yield a metaphor of rotten apples. Thus the initial images of life, vitality, and male sexuality are charted as a loss of productivity. The image is clearly not an accidental one.

What happens next is just as significant as the dismissal in illustrating unproductive masculinity. Roger narrates:

---

[38] Maria Dobozy, *Remembering the Present: The Medieval Poet-Minstrel in Cultural Context*. Disputato, 6 (Turnhout, Belgium: Brepols, 2005)

[39] Hanawalt, *Growing Up in Medieval London*, 135.

[40] William Langland, *Piers Plowman: The B Version*, rev. ed., ed. George Kane and E. Talbot Donaldson (Berkeley: University of California Press, 1988), Prologue, 35–39.

[41] Hanawalt, *Growing Up in Medieval London*, 157–59.

> And for ther is no theef withoute a lowke,
> That helpeth hym to wasten and to sowke
> Of that he brybe kan or borwe may,
> Anon he sente his bed and his array
> Unto a compeer of his owene sort,
> That lovede dys, and revel, and disport,
> And hadde a wyf that heeld for contenance
> A shoppe, and swyved for hir sustenance.          (4415–22)

> [And because there is no thief without a helper
> That helps him to waste and to spend
> Of that he can steal and may borrow
> Soon he sent his bed and his things
> To a companion of his own kind,
> That loved dicing, and reveling and pleasure
> And [he] had a wife that held for appearance
> A shop and prostituted herself for their substance.]

Perkyn forms another association, again locked in "pryvetee"—one with an outward appearance of business. The text is not clear about Perkyn's place in this world, other than that he lives there. For Roger, guilt by association is more than enough evidence of activity. The world is one of prostitution, of goods delivered, and money obtained; yet it is also a world of unproductive performative masculinity as well as unproductive mercantile masculinity. Perkyn in a metaphorical sense is here the prostitute; whether he himself is directly connected with prostitution is unclear. If so, he would be the only male prostitute in Chaucer's works, but male prostitution is such a cultural taboo that it would not likely rise to the surface in Middle English texts. At the very least, he is moved into a passive position, being the recipient of wealth through feminine business practices. By associating with his friend and his friend's wife, he has finally come into contact with the life he has lived with in his private life while still living the world of mercantile productivity in the master's shop.

At the end of the story, Perkyn has lost out on interconnected and competing images of masculinity that we have been considering. There is indeed "no more for him to say on the subject,"[42] not because of moral outrage, lack of plot, or a too obvious plot. Looking at the Fragment I as a concentrated study on masculinity, it is clear that Perkyn has moved out of the world of male productivity. In this world, there is no humor. From this world, there is no return. Whether we consider the image on the basis of medieval Christian morality or mercantile values, Perkyn has failed. Masculinity no longer exists in its socially constructed

---

[42]   Stanley, "Of This Cokes Tale Maked Chaucer Na Moore," 55.

version for Perkyn. He simply represents a threat that the forces of power have excluded.

Seen in this way, the Cook has pushed the argument of the anxiety of masculine performance in the *Reeve's Tale* to the ultimate. In his story the Cook describes a masculinity that from his mercantile perspective is no longer a viable option for Perkyn, at least based on his choice. London with its appeal, its promise, perhaps even more telling in the late fourteenth century after the Black Death, has become a place of corruption for a person like Perkyn who gets caught up in the performance in the world of "pryvetee" in a profession that expects anything but that kind of world. Built into that world was a series of obligations, training, fees, and responsibilities. Perkyn squandered many chances, and he has fallen victim to what must have been a reality for many who were caught up in the aspects of city life. It was a long way from the guild hall or the Lord Mayor's residence to Newgate and to the illicit shop of prostitution. Perkyn may be amusing, and we may be fooled by his foot-loose and fancy-free behavior, but for the world of Roger and the guildsmen, this man represents sheer trouble as he threatens the fabric of their existence in the sense that if everyone followed the lead of Perkyn—something that the master himself fears—the neatly balanced ideology of how masculinity is contructed in the guild world would be compromised. It is no wonder that Roger speaks in contempt of him. There is truly "no more to say"—Perkyn had it, squandered it, lost it, and now the world has lost him.

Yet at the same time, we should ask, "Has the Cook become both the witting and unwitting subject of the tale?" At least on the surface, the answer must be "no." Clearly, he condemns the actions of Perkyn, even at the same time that the language of the text is associated with the world of carnival. At a deeper level, however, given the later deceptions of this same Cook in the prologue to the *Manciple's Tale*, whose "cursed breeth infecte wole us alle" (IX. 39; accursed breath would infect all of us), readers can likely answer "yes." In Susan Sontag's *Illness as Metaphor*, the idea arises that with diseases, a whole battery of language develops in order to isolate the disease and destroy it and that a kind of metaphorical thinking is the means by which that illness is controlled.[43] In a direct way, allowing Roger of Ware to tell a tale—however incomplete that tale might be—allows for the linguistic forces of male mercantile behavior to critique and eliminate those elements that strain its production. It might indeed not be too much of a stretch to say that the master's eliminating Perkyn from his shop of food preparation is the means by which unproductive masculinity is subsequently eliminated. "Pryvetee" at some level is maintained through the action, and the

---

[43]    Susan Sontag, *Illness as Metaphor* (New York: Farrar, Straus, and Giroux, 1978), 1–15.

larger structure of London public life is protected. For Perkyn Revelour, the city of London offered the potential of economic stability within the domains of a mercantile-based masculinity, but at the same time it offered the world of vice in which the allures of a debased masculinity, perhaps tinged with a nascent anti-feminism and an unbridled feminine desire that come to mark his future existence. He is now free to move beyond the mercantile-based radar screen to become part of the social fabric of corruption that dots the pages of the London register.

If we posed the question about whether Perkyn is typical or atypical, then we look at the world from the vantage point of the social historian whose understanding of truth is adjudicated by statistics. Certainly the notion behind the *Canterbury Tales* from the perspective of the tale telling contest which the Host himself at the conclusion of the *General Prologue* sets up as a motivating force for the fiction would suggest that the *Cook's Tale* is meant to present merriment to its hearers. At the same time, the social anxieties that are generated by the potential for waste in monetary funds expended by guildsmen and the families of apprentices over degenerate apprentices would be enough to power a work of fiction whose potential for blurring the distinction between the world of fiction and the world of the London marketplace could only be seen by a person such a the Cook. He is deeply enmeshed in the system he critiques. The Cook, the Host, and Perkyn Revelour are implicated together in that nexus between fiction and reality, the nebulous space between *ernest* and *game* that underlies Chaucerian myth-making.

Shennan Hutton

(Independent Scholar, Napa, CA)

# Women, Men, and Markets: The Gendering of Market Space in Late Medieval Ghent

One of the most crucial elements of the medieval city was its indoor and outdoor marketplaces, as sites for the commerce which provided the city's wealth and supplied the provisions necessary for its existence.[1] Outdoor market squares were also the sites for the deployment and display of political power and cultural hegemony.[2] In Ghent, a city that had grown large and prosperous through the production and marketing of wool cloth, certain market spaces served not only

---

[1]   The research on which this article is based was funded by a Fulbright grant and conducted at the City Archives of Ghent (Stadsarchief Gent). Many thanks to Joan Cadden, Patricia Turning, Marc Boone, Jelle Haemers, Jan Dumolyn, and Albrecht Classen for their assistance and comments on earlier versions of this article.

[2]   Marc Boone, "Urban Space and Political Conflict in Late Medieval Flanders," *Journal of Interdisciplinary History* 32, 4 (2002): 621–40; Peter Stabel, "Marketing Cloth in the Low Countries: Manufacturers, Brokers and Merchants (14th–16th centuries)," *International Trade in the Low Countries (14th–16th Centuries): Merchants, Organisation, Infrastructure: Proceedings of the International Conference Ghent-Antwerp, 12th–13th January 1997*, ed. Peter Stabel, Bruno Blondé, and Anke Greve. Studies in Urban Social, Economic, and Political History of the Medieval and Modern Low Countries, 10 (Leuven-Apeldoorn: Garant, 2000), 15–36; and "Women at the Market: Gender and Retail in the Towns of Late Medieval Flanders," *Secretum Scriptorum: Liber alumnorum Walter Prevenier*, ed. Wim Blockmans, Marc Boone, and Thérèse de Hemptinne (Leuven-Apeldoorn: Garant, 1999) 259–76; Donatella Calabi, *The Market and the City: Square, Street and Architecture in Early Modern Europe*, trans. Marlene Klein (Aldershot: Ashgate, 2004); James M. Murray, *Bruges: Cradle of Capitalism 1280–1390* (Cambridge: Cambridge University Press, 2005), 63–81; Christopher Dyer, "The Consumer and the Market in the Later Middle Ages," *Economic History Review* 43 (1989): 305–27; David Nicholas, *The Later Medieval City 1300–1500*. A History of Urban Society in Europe (New York: Longman, 1997); *Medieval Practices of Space*, ed. Barbara A. Hanawalt and Michal Kobialka. Medieval Cultures, 23 (Minneapolis and London: University of Minnesota, 2000); Peter Arnade, Martha Howell, and Walter Simons, "Fertile Spaces: The Productivity of Urban Space in Northern Europe," *Journal of Interdisciplinary History* 32, 4 (2002): 515–48. .

local and regional trade networks, but international commerce as well. Although the highest echelon of sales was dominated by elite men, Ghent women had access to some market spaces and the opportunity to function as legitimate market sellers in their own right in specific niches. As a result, numerous women could attain a middling level of prosperity, instead of being confined to the lowest-paid, least-respected markets. Gender difference also helped structure each of the city's major markets—the Cloth Hall, the Meat Hall, the Corn Market and the Friday Market. Market rules or strategies often partitioned market space by gender (women can go here, but not there) in a way that has been interpreted as the limitation of women's access to the guild or trade which occupied that market space.[3] However, after analyzing records of actual practice, judgments and contracts from the annual registers of the aldermen who ruled Ghent, I argue that some women market sellers may have experienced the partition of market spaces as a bridge rather than a barrier to prosperity. Women market sellers built on the legitimacy of their presence in the market space to enhance their profits, actually cooperating with male merchants rather than merely obeying them. Their everyday practices helped structure those market spaces as well.

This paper explores the gender constructions of these fourteenth-century markets through the lens of spatial theory, particularly Michel de Certeau's definition of space as a practiced place.[4] Certeau's ideas offer a way to look at fragmentary sources of actual practice in relation to normative sources, such as market or guild regulations, which he identifies as strategies. He claimed that a place, which is the combination of a physical location and strategies, was transformed into a space by the operations and everyday tactics of historical subjects. A few of their stories, or traces of these operations on places, can be found in court decisions and contracts, like those preserved in the registers of the aldermen of the *Keure*, the premier board of aldermen in Ghent.[5] The texts of the aldermen's judgments and the negotiated agreements and contracts which they confirmed by affixing their seal, contain fragments of stories, remnants of orality, fitted together in a bricolage to found and articulate the space of each market. These stories reveal the usually invisible operations of women and men, which together with official strategies, founded the space of each market. Spaces are also articulated by partitioning and marking boundaries. The partition is a boundary, but also a bridge which actors in the market space can exploit to their advantage.

[3]   David Nicholas, *The Domestic Life of a Medieval City: Women, Children, and the Family in Fourteenth-Century Ghent* (Lincoln and London: University of Nebraska Press, 1985), 102–03.

[4]   Michel de Certeau, *The Practice of Everyday Life*, trans. Steven Rendall (1980; Berkeley, Los Angeles, London: University of California Press, 1984), 125–30.

[5]   Annual Registers of the Aldermen of the *Keure* (*Schepenen van de Keure: Jaarregisters*), City Archives of Ghent (*Stadsarchief Gent*) (hereafter SAG), series 301, nos. 1 and 2.

The stories about gender in the Ghent market spaces are particularly significant because Ghent was an exceptionally large, wealthy, and powerful city in medieval northern Europe. In addition, its stories about market space illuminate the operations of market spaces in towns across a broad swath of continental Europe from Paris through Germany. In accordance with the customary gender relations in these towns, many women performed economic activities and interacted with male and female business persons and customers in central, public spaces.

In the mid-fourteenth century, Ghent had a population of approximately 64,000 people, making it a large metropolis by medieval standards.[6] In northern Europe, only Paris and perhaps London were larger. Ghent was the most powerful of the semi-autonomous cities in the highly urbanized county of Flanders, and closely tied into the international networks of trade focused in nearby Bruges. From the eleventh through the thirteenth centuries, Ghent's merchants grew extremely wealthy from wool cloth production and trade, and thousands poured into the city to work in the drapery or wool cloth industry. In the huge indoor market called the *Lakenhalle* or *Wolhuis* (Cloth Hall), brokers and merchants arranged deals with international merchants for wool and finished cloth, and local merchants, market sellers, and drapers bought and sold wool, thread, and cloth in numerous grades and stages of production. Ghent and other Flemish cities actually built their fortunes on production of cheaper grades of wool cloth for export to markets all over Europe.

In the late thirteenth century, a series of developments—loss of the Mediterranean markets for cheap cloth, increased competition from other cities and rural producers, rising wool prices, and wool embargoes—challenged the traditional drapery industry of Ghent. In response to these pressures, the city's producers focused increasingly on high-quality cloth made exclusively with wool imported from England, because it was the most profitable product for a changing market.[7]

---

[6]  Most historians estimate that the population of Ghent was between 55,000 and 64,000 in 1356 through 1358; Walter Prevenier and Marc Boone, "The 'City-State' Dream, 1300–1500," *Ghent: In Defence of a Rebellious City: History, Art, Culture*, ed. Johan Decavele (Antwerp: MercatorFonds, 1989), 81–105, here 81; Wim P. Blockmans, G. Pieters, Walter Prevenier, and R. W. M. van Schaik, "Tussen crisis en welvaart: Sociale veranderingen 1300–1500," *Algemene Geschiedenis der Nederlanden: Middeleeuwen: sociaal-economische geschiedenis 1300–1482, politieke ontwikkeling, instellingen en recht 1384–1482, socioculturele en intellectuele ontwikkeling 1384–1520, kerkelijk en godsdienstig leven 1384–1520*, vol. 4 (Haarlem: Fibula-Van Dishoeck, 1980), 42–86. But also see David Nicholas, *The Metamorphosis of a Medieval City: Ghent in the Age of the Arteveldes, 1302–1390* (Lincoln and London: University of Nebraska Press, 1987), 37.

[7]  From the extensive literature on this topic, here are a few key works: Henri Pirenne, *Les Villes et les institutions urbaines*, vol. 1 (Paris and Brussels: Librairie Felix Alean, 1939), 143–301; J. A. Van Houtte, *An Economic History of the Low Countries 800–1800* (New York: St. Martin's Press, 1977); Patrick Chorley, "The Cloth Exports of Flanders and Northern France During the Thirteenth

A shrinking cloth market and increased competition forced changes in cloth production and marketing as well. In the thirteenth century and perhaps earlier, drapers (including many women) managed and supervised the cloth-making process, but the real profits went to the long-distance (mostly male) brokers and wholesalers.[8] By the fifteenth century, historians have argued, most of those dominant merchants were limited to a small, wealthy elite at the top of the weavers' guild. These elite weaver-drapers controlled both the supply of wool to their fellow guildsmen and the sale of finished cloth.[9] By the sixteenth century, women had almost no role in the Ghent wool cloth trade beyond the lowest-paid occupations of spinning, carding, and combing.[10]

Economic pressures on the wool cloth industry also forced changes in the ranking of the city's markets and the access of women to economic opportunities. Although Ghent did not suffer from as deep a depression as was once thought, the

---

Century: A Luxury Trade?" *Economic History Review* 40 (1987), 349–79; *La Draperie ancienne des Pays-Bas: Débouchés et stratégies de survie (14e–16e siècles) Actes du colloque tenu à Gand le 28 avril 1992/Drapery Production in the Late Medieval Low Countries: Markets and Strategies for Survival (14th–16th Centuries): Proceedings of the Colloquium Ghent, April 28th 1992*, ed. Marc Boone and Walter Prevenier. Studies in Urban Social, Economic, and Political History of the Medieval and Modern Low Countries (Leuven-Apeldoorn: Garant, 1993); John Munro, "The Symbiosis of Towns and Textiles: Urban Institutions and the Changing Fortunes of Cloth Manufacturing in the Low Countries and England, 1270–1570," *Journal of Early Modern History* 3 .1 (Feb. 1999): 1–74, as well as many other works; Marc Boone, "L'Industrie textile à Gand au bas moyen âge ou les resurrections successives d'une activité réputée moribonde," *La Draperie ancienne*, ed. Boone and Prevenier, 15–62; Stabel, "Marketing Cloth," 15–36.

[8] Alain Derville, "Les Draperies flamandes et artésiennes vers 1250–1350: quelques considerations critiques et problematiques," *Revue du Nord* 54.215 (1972): 353–70; Hans Van Werveke, "De koopman-ondernemer en de ondernemer in de Vlaamse lakennijverheid van de middeleeuwen," *Mededelingen van de koninklijke Vlaamse academie voor wetenschappen, letteren en schone kunsten van België, klasse de letteren* 8 (1946), 5–26; Boone, "L'Industrie textile à Gand," 16–17. Women worked as drapers in Douai and Ghent in the thirteenth century, and as drapers in Leiden in the fifteenth century. Martha C. Howell, *Women, Production, and Patriarchy in Late Medieval Cities* (Chicago: University of Chicago Press, 1986); Ellen E. Kittell, "The Construction of Women's Social Identity in Medieval Douai: Evidence from Identifying Epithets," *Journal of Medieval History* 25,3 (1999): 215–27; Marc Boone, Thérèse De Hemptinne, and Walter Prevenier, "Gender and Early Emancipation in the Low Countries in the Late Middle Ages and Early Modern Period," *Gender, Power and Privilege in Early Modern Europe*, ed. Jessica Munns and Penny Richards (Harlow and London: Pearson Education Limited, 2003), 21–39.

[9] Marc Boone, *Gent en de Bourgondische hertogen ca. 1384–ca. 1453. Een sociaal-politieke studie van een staatsvormingproces*. Verhandelingen van de koninklijke academie voor wetenschappen, letteren en schone kunsten van België, 133 (Brussels: Paleis der Academiën, 1990); Martha Howell and Marc Boone, "Becoming Early Modern in the Late Medieval Low Countries," *Urban History* 23, 3 (1996): 320–21.

[10] Stabel, "Women at the Market," 22. The exception to this was the right of guildmembers' widows to carry on their deceased husbands' crafts. Marianne Danneel, *Weduwen en wezen in het laat-middeleeuwse Gent*. Studies in Urban Social, Economic and Political History of the Medieval and Modern Low Countries, 3 (Leuven-Appeldoorn: Garant, 1995), 344–86.

city gradually lost its predominance as an international powerhouse of the cloth trade.[11] The city's salvation was the development of a grain staple, which gave Ghent control over crucial imports of grain from northern France, and tax revenues from the reshipment of grain to the rest of northern Flanders. The staple, which increased in importance after 1357 to be firmly established by the end of the century, augmented the power and importance of the provisioning guilds, which also controlled the local and regional provisioning markets.[12] The spatial and economic dominance of the Cloth Hall gradually shifted to the *Koornmarkt* (Corn Market), the outdoor market for grain imports and exports, and the *Vleeshuis* (Meat Hall), the indoor market hall of the butchers, as well as other provisioning markets. The butchers, fishmongers, shippers, and brewers were the first Ghent guilds to restrict their membership to sons of previous masters. None admitted women. These guilds, which were all connected to provisioning or the grain staple, were also among the most powerful and influential in city government. The highest officials of these guilds belonged to a close-knit oligarchy that controlled Ghent both politically and economically, passing public offices, leases for tax-farming (collecting indirect taxes,) and provisioning contracts around among their (male) membership.[13] While women had never had equal economic opportunities to men in this patriarchal society, the economic shift from wool cloth production to regional provisioning tended to marginalize women by excluding them from the middling positions some had formerly held and confining them to the lowest-paid occupations.

In addition to the economic challenges of the period, Ghent was also engaged in a long-term struggle to remain semi-autonomous (as opposed to independent) from Flemish counts, French kings, and Burgundian dukes.[14] Although the Ghent burghers never tried to supplant the counts themselves, the cities frequently rose in revolt against comital policies that threatened urban interests. The city was governed by two boards of aldermen: the aldermen of the *Keure*, who issued ordinances, administered justice, and sealed contracts, and the aldermen of the *Gedele*, who supervised guardianship of orphans, inheritance, and resolution of

---

[11] Boone, "L'Industrie textile à Gand," 15–7 and 50–51.

[12] Nicholas, *Metamorphosis*, 250, 291–92; Howell and Boone, "Becoming Early Modern," p. 321.

[13] Boone, *Gent en de Bourgondische hertogen*, 79; Peter Stabel, "Guilds in Late Medieval Flanders: Myths and Realities of Guild Life in an Export-Oriented Environment," *Journal of Medieval History* 30, 2 (2004): 187–212.

[14] Although Flanders was technically a province of France, French kings were only sporadically able to enforce their hegemony over the county. The counts of Flanders had similar problems with the powerful cities of Ghent, Bruges, and Ypres. After 1384, the county of Flanders passed to the rule of the dukes of Burgundy, see Prevenier and Boone, "The 'City-State' Dream"; Maurice Vandermaesen, "Vlaanderen en Henegouwen onder het huis van Dampierre 1244–1384," *Algemene Geschiedenis der Nederlanden* (Haarlem: Fibula-Van Dishoeck, 1982), 2: 399–440; David Nicholas, *Medieval Flanders* (London and New York: Longman, 1992).

feuds. The city's law was a combination of written privileges from the Flemish counts and unwritten custom, interpreted by the aldermen. In a process that was often contested in the mid-fourteenth century, aldermen were chosen from the patrician elite and leadership of the most prominent guilds.

The city's guilds provided the militias that fought in revolts and wars, and often amongst themselves for dominance of city government. Some Ghent guilds did admit women, and allowed them opportunities to grow prosperous in the trade. However, because women were rigidly excluded from the political and military functions of the guilds, they were significantly marginalized within those guilds that did admit them.[15] The gendered boundary around political activity resonated throughout the city's market spaces. During almost every year in the fourteenth century, Ghent experienced war, revolt, or significant internal violence, as the city was torn by intertwining conflicts at the local, regional, and international levels.[16] Much of the political conflict was acted out in the Friday Market square. This market square, like large outdoor market squares in other medieval cities, shared a multiplicity of functions—political gatherings, official pronouncements, assembling of militia, guild demonstrations, riots, punishment, and religious processions.[17] The market function of this space was marked off from the political and religious uses of the same space by temporal boundaries, not physical ones. One of the sharpest contrasts which occurred in the Friday Market square was its transition from a market space, with sellers and buyers of both genders, to a site for political demonstrations, official proclamations, and even battles, all of which excluded women (at least officially).

Before delving into the gendering of market space in this turbulent era, one further issue needs to be addressed—the lack of sources, especially for the earliest period of Ghent's history. There are only scattered references to women in the wool cloth production, or to any details about wool cloth production and marketing in Ghent, before 1349. Few guild records from Ghent are extant, and the earliest systematic written records which survive are the annual registers of the

---

[15]  Marc Boone, "Les Métiers dans les villes flamandes au bas moyen âge (XIVe – XVIe siècles): Images normatives, réalités socio-politiques et économiques," *Les Métiers au moyen âge: Aspects économiques et sociaux: Actes du colloque international de Louvain-la-Neuve 7–9 octobre 1993*, ed. Pascale Lambrechts and Jean-Pierre Sosson. Publications de l'Institut d'études médiévales.Textes, études, congrès, 15 (Louvain-la-Neuve: Université Catholique de Louvain, 1994), 1–21; here 6–15.

[16]  Jan Dumolyn and Jelle Haemers, "Patterns of Urban Rebellion in Medieval Flanders," *Journal of Medieval History* 31, 4 (2005): 369–93; Raymond van Uytven, "Het stedelijke leven 11de–14de eeuw: Stadsgeschiedenis in het Noorden en Zuiden," *Algemene Geschiedenis der Nederlanden* 2:187–245; Vandermaesen, "Vlaanderen."

[17]  Boone, "Urban Space and Political Conflict," 622–23.

aldermen of the *Keure* and *Gedele*, which begin in the mid-fourteenth century.[18] In Flemish courts, legal acts were written out on pieces of parchment, called chirographs, and a copy was given to each principal. For an extra charge, the clerk would also record the act in the aldermen's registers. Practice in Ghent and other Flemish cities was therefore quite distinct from notarial practice, analyzed in Andreas Meyer's piece in this volume, because the legal instrument was the (highly perishable) chirograph, rather than the register.

The Ghent aldermen's registers only contain a fraction of contracts and disputes in the city. Many acts were oral and there were other courts and corporate bodies that performed these functions. The Cloth Hall, for example, had its own officials who adjudicated disputes, authorized contracts, and kept records of activity. None of those records survive today. In addition, the annual registers include only a fraction of the acts heard before the aldermen, because copying the act into the register cost extra money. The contracts and judgments in the aldermen's registers are biased towards wealthy elites, and are fragmentary, terse, and often oblique.

Since records from the fifteenth and sixteenth centuries are much more lengthy, informative, and complete, the temptation is to read back on earlier centuries what is true in the later period, and to supplement with what is known about other cities (often from England, for example). In this paper, I am attempting to use the mid-fourteenth century evidence about market space to strip away the changes which occurred over the fifteenth and sixteenth centuries, but at the same time, not to superimpose mid-fourteenth-century conditions on the Ghent markets of the twelfth and thirteenth centuries. The evidence in this paper largely comes from the period when the wool cloth production had been under pressure for more than eighty years, and many years after each of these market spaces had been founded. Certeau's theories about space are particularly useful in this context, as he offers strategies for partially reconstructing lost oral practice from fragments in the surviving sources.

The surviving sources show us that women and men interacted in different roles and patterns within specific market places, which were shaped by different discourses and had distinct functions, sellers, clienteles, and gender boundaries. The two largest open markets, held in physical marketplaces of the same name, the Corn Market and the Friday Market, represent opposite poles; the former was

[18] The aldermen kept annual registers in the thirteenth and early fourteenth centuries, but none have survived. The earliest surviving registers of the aldermen of the *Gedele* begin in 1349 (SAG, series 330.) The earliest surviving registers of the aldermen of the *Keure* are fragments from 1339–1340, 1343–1344, and 1345, followed by four complete year registers, from 1349–1350, 1353–1354, 1357–1358, and 1360–1361 (SAG, series 301). Some of the city accounts survive from the early and mid-fourteenth century as well. The guild records were destroyed on the orders of Emperor Charles V, after he had defeated a rebellion of the city in 1540. Howell and Boone, "Becoming Early Modern," 310.

configured as male space, while the latter was the site of considerable intermixing of men and women in all roles. In the Cloth Hall, men dominated the most important and profitable roles in sales, while women had subordinate roles, but the two co-existed in the same space and sometimes cooperated. In the Meat Hall only men could sell, and women could only be present as customers. Each of these market spaces had its own gender boundaries and discourses; taken together, they define the contours of gender in the Ghent marketplace.

In three Ghent market spaces—the Cloth Hall, the Meat Hall, and the Corn Market—official strategies partitioned space in terms of gender difference. As the relative status of these market spaces changed over time, the impact of that gender difference shifted as well. In mid-fourteenth-century Ghent, access of women to the city's premier market space, the Cloth Hall, allowed women stallholders to attain middling status and prosperity as sellers of wool and cloth. Their status as mercers and spice merchants with shops and booths in the Friday Market put many of them in the middle range of prosperity as well. Other fourteenth-century market spaces, like the Meat Hall and the Corn Market, marginalized and excluded women. As these markets became more important than the older cloth trade, the male grain merchants and butchers who controlled these market spaces became the dominant elites. In the same time period, Ghent women had lost much of their access to middling-status market selling. The following analysis of the four major market spaces through the lenses of gender and spatial theory aims to recreate the stories and the operations on places which founded and sustained Ghent market space.

*The Cloth Hall*
Ghent's traditional source of wealth was woolen cloth, which had enriched the city's producers and sellers for centuries. By the mid-fourteenth century, the date of the earliest surviving records of actual practice, the cloth trade was already in decline, after being hit hard by wool embargoes and competition. The center of wool and cloth sales was the Cloth Hall, a large multi-story building along the city's wealthiest street, the Hoogpoort, a spatial confirmation of the importance of wool cloth production to the city.[19] Sales of wool, yarn, and cloth probably also took place outside of this hall. The aldermen made many attempts to confine sales to the hall, but the repetition of ordinances suggests that they were not particularly

---

[19]    The fourteenth-century Cloth Hall was located between the city hall and the Belfry tower, about two blocks away from the Corn Market. It was located to the north of the present cloth hall, which was constructed in the mid-fifteenth century. Frans De Potter, *Gent van de oudsten tijd tot heden: geschiedkundige beschrijving der stad* (1883; rpt. Ghent: Familia et Patria Handzame, 1969), 2:104–07.

successful.[20] Nevertheless, the aldermen, and the elites whose views they promoted, envisioned the physical space of the Cloth Hall as the legitimate center of the wool and cloth trade. The building itself was larger than the city hall and had two stories and cellar. The cellar contained scales for weighing wool and cloth, and the two upper floors contained large open halls, with the top floor reserved for the highest grades of luxury cloth.[21] On the lower floor, cheaper grades of cloth, known as white and blue cloth, were sold, along with wool and possibly yarn.[22] Along the walls of each floor were either stalls or benches, assigned to specific women for their lifetime use. The Cloth Hall was therefore partitioned by either table or counter structures. Women stallholders sat or stood behind the counters, while male brokers and wholesalers made deals with foreign merchants (almost exclusively male) in the open center of the room.[23]

The cloth trade was controlled by brokers and cloth wholesalers, who handled large transactions with foreign merchants. Most of them belonged to a small elite group within the weavers' guild, and they also profited from supplying imported raw materials to their poorer fellow weavers.[24] In one ordinance from 1338, the brokers appear as the persons in charge of the Cloth Hall when they "agreed that the women should be allowed to sell their white and blue cloth," referring to the cheaper grades of cloth sold in the lower hall.[25] The brokers also agreed that "the women" were allowed to buy up to fifteen stones of wool, equivalent to ninety pounds. If a female market seller brought more than fifteen stones of wool, the sale had to go to a broker who would receive half of the profit. This ordinance clearly limits women from large wholesale deals.

---

[20] For example, in 1374, the aldermen ordered that "no foreign man or foreign woman should sell any wool within Ghent except at the woolhouse," Napoléon De Pauw, *De Voorgeboden der stad Gent in de XIVe eeuw (1337–1382)* (Ghent: C. Annoot-Braeckman, Ad. Hoste: 1885), 131.

[21] Cloth for local consumption was sold in the Friday Market.

[22] White (*witte*) and blue (*blauwe*) wool textiles were varieties of cheaper grades of fabric, known as "sayes," or "worsted" in England. Guy De Poerck, *La Draperie médiévale en Flandre et en Artois: Technique et terminologie* (Bruges: Rijksuniversiteit te Gent, 1951), 1:227.

[23] One act refers to benches along one side of the hall. SAG, series 301, no. 2, f. 28v, act no. 3, 14 July 1362.

[24] Stabel, "Marketing Cloth in the Low Countries." Many of these men sold cloth to the city for uniforms, aldermen's robes and festival costumes, and a few bought tax farms. Along with the hostellers, they also sold large lots of cloth to foreign merchants. Boone, "L'Industrie textile à Gand." For the influential position of the weavers in the social structure of late-medieval cities, see also the contribution to this volume by Fabian Alfie.

[25] 1338 Ordinance entitled "Van den makeleren": "*Voert, so hebben de makeleeren gheconsentert dat de vrouwen zullen moghen vercoepen hare witte lakene ende haer blaeuwe, ende voert zullen de vrouwen moghen coepen 15 steene wullen ende niet daerboven . . . .*" De Pauw, *Voorgeboden*, 29; also transcribed in *Recueil de documents relatifs à l'histoire de l'industrie drapière en Flandre. Première partie: des origines à l'époque bourguignonne*, ed. Georges Espinas and Henri Pirennne (Brussels: P. Imbreghts, 1909), n. 432, item 5, 2: 431.

However, most small drapers who managed the production of individual lengths of wool cloth purchased wool in lots of less than ninety pounds. For example, after a married couple, Wouter and Aechte van Vinderhoute, died suddenly in 1360 (probably from the plague), the inventory of their estate included four entries for wool in lots of eighteen to thirty-five pounds.[26] The couple probably worked together as drapers because the list of their debts included purchases on credit for wool and cloth-producing services.[27] Aechte contracted several purchases on credit by herself, in addition to other debts and purchases made by Wouter alone and the couple together. Whether this couple purchased the wool lots in the Cloth Hall is unknown, but the estate inventory clearly shows that wool was regularly sold in small quantities to small drapers. The women wool sellers in the Cloth Hall could make a tidy living from selling wool in these smaller quantities, while the brokers and wholesalers may not have been as interested in breaking up large shipments of wool into these smaller lots. The women stallholders thus constituted a middle layer in the wool distribution system. Brokers purchased wool in bulk, and sold it in sacks to the stallholders in the Cloth Hall, who then divided the wool into smaller lots and sold it to individual drapers.

These women occupied a crucial central niche in the sales and distribution of wool, thread, and cloth. At the same time, women sellers had to defer to male brokers when sales reached a certain volume. The text of the ordinance narrates that elite men controlled the space, allocated resources, and thus apportioned income, but allowed women into that space to perform auxiliary roles. Beneath the text may be an older existing spatial practice in which women stallholders had been selling wool, thread, and cloth in the Cloth Hall perhaps far back into the undocumented cloth production and trade in the city stretching back to the eleventh century.

This ordinance is also an acknowledgement of women's and men's practice—their tactics and everyday actions—inscribed on the place of the Cloth Hall. The ordinance shows that women had been selling cloth and wool in that space for some time. Merchants, brokers, drapers, and cloth wholesalers

---

[26] SAG, series 301, no. 1, loose chirograph numbered 215.1, 21 Aug 1360. The inventory reads:
"Item, V ½ steen wollen, XL gt. den steen (5–1/2 stones of wool, at 40 d. groot per stone)
Item, VII steen wollen, II p. g. den steen (7 stones of wool, at 2 lbs. groot per stone)
Item, III steen wollen 1 pont min blaus, XVIII gt. den steen (3 stones less 1 pound of blue? wool, at 18 d. groot per stone)
Item, III steen ende I pont, VIII gt. den steen." (3 stones and 1 pound, at 8 d. groot per stone.) The weight used for wool was the stone (steen), in fourteenth-century Flanders usually equivalent to six modern pounds.
[27] The couple contracted nine debts together, and each contracted two debts alone. Two of their creditors were women, one was a husband-and-wife partnership, and two were mothers working with sons. SAG, series 301, no. 1, loose chirograph 215.1.

conducted much of their business in the open floor space around the stalls, if not at the stalls themselves. Seated or standing behind tables covered with wares, the women visibly contrasted with men circulating on foot in the center of the hall. The space of the Cloth Hall was partitioned either by tables or the front counters of stalls. A partition structures the space, according to Certeau, and functions both as a frontier and a bridge. The strategy of the Cloth Hall (the regulations and ordinances) designated the open area for male merchants, brokers, and cloth wholesalers. The table or stall counter was a barrier dividing the sellers by gender.

But in practice, how could a merchant show a piece of cloth to a potential buyer without laying it out on a table? Probably a broker used a female stallholder's table to lay out a cloth, an action that would have transformed the partition into a bridge. The structure of space actually encouraged the cooperation of brokers and stallholders, and it is likely that they referred customers to each other. What the ordinance depicts as a liability for the women stallholders was probably a more equitable, cooperative, and long-standing practice.

Furthermore, allocation of the stalls in the Cloth Hall was controlled at least in part by women. Two stories surviving from documents in the aldermen's registers indicate that women held the stalls for their lifetimes, and passed those stalls on to other women or to female family members. One story was told to the aldermen by Simeon van Aelst, himself a former aldermen. He testified that his late wife, Aechte, had appeared before a previous board of aldermen to transfer her stall in the Cloth Hall to a woman named Bette van den Wijngaerde. On the basis of Simeon's testimony, "the aldermen transferred that stall back to Bette to use for her lifetime."[28] The initial transfer took place between the women, followed by the aldermen's official grant of the stall to Bette van den Wijngaerde. The aldermen's right to grant stalls to women is likely a graft onto older oral practice, a way of emphasizing their control by approving a long-standing customary practice. It is also noteworthy that Aechte, the original holder of the stall, was the wife of an aldermen, meaning that she was at least of middling status.[29]

---

[28] SAG, series 301, no. 1, f. 27r, act no. 3, 5 Sept. 1349: "... *so hebben wij scepenen, Gillis Rijnvisch ende sijne ghezellen, mids de vors. informatie dit vors. stal ghegheven en gheven der vors. Betten dat soet paisivelike en rustelijc moghe ghebruken alse langhe alse leven sal zonder yemens calaenge.*"

[29] Simeon van Aelst held the ninth seat on the bench of the aldermen of the *Gedele* for the year 1346–7. (The aldermen served for one-year terms, beginning on 15 August.) The *Gedele* bench was less powerful than the *Keure* bench, and the ninth seat held much less power than the first or second seat. In addition, in 1346, Ghent guilds and factions were struggling over power, meaning that there might have been an opportunity for lesser craftsmen to win seats in city government. Since Simeon does not appear again in the surviving lists of city officials, it is likely that he was either not a member of the city's elite, or that he lacked sufficient standing in any of the city's factions, *De Rekeningen der Stad Gent. Tijdvak van Jacob van Artevelde 1339–1349*, ed. Napoléon De Pauw and Julius Vuylsteke. Maatschappij van Nederlandsche letterkunde en geschiedenis (Ghent: Ad. Hoste, 1874–1885), 3:1; Boone, *Gent en de bourgondische hertogen*, 33–39.

The second story makes the theory that the aldermen were imposing their control over a long-standing customary practice among women even more likely. In a decision from 1362, the aldermen granted a stall to the minor daughters of a deceased stallholder, and charged her widower to maintain the stall for the young girls:

> Kenlic sij etc. dat her Jacob Willebaerd, her Lievin vanden Hole ende hare gezellen scepenen van der Keure in Ghend hebben ghegheven en gheven Betkine ende Kallekine Heinrics Gheilards kindren die hij hadde bij Mergriete Koens siin wijf was, de zelve stede ende banc in de neder halle witte ende blaeuwe lakine up te vercoppene die Mergriete harer beeder moeder vors. uter ghiften van scepenen die doe waren haudende was. Ende dese banc zal van der vors. kindre weghe ghevoedt ende ghemainteniert moeten zijn ghelijc datter toe behoert.[30]

> [Be it known that Heer Jacob Willebaerd, Heer Lievin vanden Hole and their fellow aldermen of the Keure in Ghent have given and give to Betkine (Betty) and Kallekine (Kathy), children of Heinric Gheilards whom he had by his late wife Mergriete Koens, the same place and bench in the lower hall to sell white and blue wool cloth that Mergriete their mother was holding (had, had been keeping) as a gift from the aldermen [of that time?]. And on behalf of the children this bench must be paid for and maintained just as it should be.]

While the aldermen claimed that they gave this selling "place" to Mergriete and then to her young female children as a "gift," it was much more likely that the daughters were actually inheriting the selling space.[31] If the aldermen were freely granting market stalls, they could surely have found an adult to receive this favor. Giving the selling space to minors with the expectation that their father and guardian would have to maintain it for the children's benefit does not seem in the city's best interests.

These stories suggest that the gendered practices—that stalls were passed from woman to woman—of the Cloth Hall predated the aldermen's control. The women who held stalls and/or selling places in the Cloth Hall had hereditary rights, at least in part. As Certeau argues, stories go before social practices to create a theater of actions.[32] Judicial decisions can only manipulate and reaffirm this theater. In the Cloth Hall marketspace, women stallholders by custom passed their stalls on to other women, and the aldermen were confirming this practice, and manipulating it to enhance their own authority. The Cloth Hall space had been partially founded by women stallholders.

---

[30] SAG, series 301, no. 2, f. 28v, act no. 3, 14 July 1362.
[31] The difference in terminology is also interesting. Aechte held a stall (*stal*) and Mergriete held a place (*stede*) on a bench (*banc*). Perhaps these were different arrangements for the upper and lower halls?
[32] Certeau, *Practice of Everyday Life*, 125.

The presence of women sellers in the Cloth Hall and in the acts from the aldermen's registers also complicate the received generalization that male weaver-drapers, brokers, and wholesalers monopolized the sales of wool and cloth. Restrictions on the quantities of wool and types of cloth women could sell has to be balanced against the legitimacy of their presence in the Cloth Hall and the profit potential of their deals.[33] Women cloth sellers were sometimes entrepreneurs, not at the highest levels, but at the level of middling, local, or retail sales. They occupied an important niche in the distribution system of raw materials and finished cloth for the city's drapery production. The space of Cloth Hall, partitioned by the tables or counters of the stalls, was created by practices which privileged male brokers, but included female stallholders, and encouraged cooperation across the gendered partition of the market space.

However, wool cloth production in Ghent was not as profitable as it had once been, and there was widespread unemployment at points in the mid-fourteenth century. In this environment of economic pressure and declining profitability, women drapers and wool sellers would have been vulnerable to attacks from male guildsmen, and the access of women to middling positions in the textile industry declined. In addition, the status and importance of wool cloth production, once the dominant industry that had made Ghent wealthy, declined over the course of the fourteenth and fifteenth centuries. It was increasingly replaced by the provisioning trades, led by the butchers' guild, which also partitioned its market space with gender boundaries, but in a very different way.

## The Meat Hall

In the mid-fourteenth century, the Ghent butchers' guild was already on its way to becoming one of the most influential, powerful, and exclusive guilds in the city. After the weavers, the butchers' guild was perhaps the most powerful guild in mid-fourteenth century Ghent, and it would soon surpass the weavers. It was also one of the first guilds in Ghent to restrict membership to the sons of masters.[34] The guild excluded all women, including daughters of masters.[35] In 1377, the butchers'

---

[33]  There are additional archival sources which indicate that women and husband-and-wife partnerships sold wool and cloth. SAG, series 301, no. 1, f. 48r, act no. 1, 1 Feb. 1350 (n.s.); f. 14v, act no. 4, 14 June 1344; f. 19r, act no. 2 and 3, 27 Oct. 1345; f. 117v, act no. 1; undated, f. 225v, act no. 2, 19 Dec. 1360. Eighteen women sold cloth to the city from 1339 to 1361, compared to 166 men. De Pauw and Vuylsteke, *Rekeningen;* and Alfons Van Werveke, ed., *Gentse Stads- en Baljuws-rekeningen (1351–1364)* (Brussels: Paleis der Academiën, 1970).

[34]  Hans Van Werveke, "De Gentse Vleeshouwers onder het Oud Regime: Demografische studie over een gesloten en erfelijk ambachtsgild," *Handelingen der maatschappij voor geschiedenis en oudheidkunde te Gent* 3 (1948): 3–32.

[35]  Danneel, *Weduwen en wezen,* 357; De Potter, *Gent,* 2: 366–67.

guild replaced their original indoor marketplace, the Meat Hall (*Vleeshuis*), with a large wooden hall beside the Leie River, and in 1407 built the magnificent stone Meat Hall which stands there still. The rapid upgrading of facilities is a testament to the growing power and wealth of the butchers' guild over the second half of the fourteenth century. Individual butchers sold their meat from stalls which lined the walls of the hall, partitioning, and therefore founding, the space of this market. By the fifteenth century, this partition became a gendered boundary as well. A draconian ordinance ordered that:

> Voort dat gheen vleeshauwers wijf noch joncwijf enne comme in veertich voeten na den vleeschuuse, up den dach dat men vleesch vercoopt, up de mesdaet van III pond. . . .[36]

> [Henceforth no butcher's wife or maid may come within forty feet of the Meat Hall on the day that meat is sold, on the penalty of three pounds.]"

Women from the butcher's households were excluded from the market, even from the space occupied by customers. While the ordinance was probably never effectively enforced, it is evidence of the desire of the butchers to mark off their hall as male space. Women apparently continued to violate these rules, however. A later ordinance specified that "*van nu vortan gheen vrauwen ter banck staen en zullen omme vleesch te vercoopene*. . . (from now on no woman can stand at a stall in order to sell meat)."[37] The butchers could not eliminate women sellers, but they could marginalize women and cast them as interlopers and illegitimate participants.

   The partition of the stall front counters divided male butchers from female and male customers. The strategies of the butchers to restrict their craft's membership included eliminating even the presence of their own family women from the privileged space behind the table or counter. These women had no rights, no countering story to justify their transgression of the partition of Meat Hall space. The rigidity of the written guild regulations cut across whatever flexible oral practice had gone before. The nature of the work done by the butchers' guild, dealing with large animals and heavy carcasses, suggests that the trade was always predominantly male, but such a consideration would not preclude wives, daughters, or female servants from serving customers and collecting money. The guild leadership was taking aim at a practice which had existed, but perhaps only on the margins of acceptability.

---

[36]   Statutes of Vleeschouwers, undated, c. 15th century, De Potter, *Gent*, 2: 554.
[37]   Ordinance of 1541, De Potter, *Gent*, 2: 559.

*The Corn Market*

A different kind of gender boundary marked off the Corn Market. Market regulations excluded women, even as customers. In addition, everyday practices within the market space marked it out as male space. The Corn Market square (*Koornmarkt*) was an open triangular area at foot of St. Michael's bridge, separated by a row of buildings from the famous *Koornlei* (Corn Wharf) and *Graslei* (Hay Wharf) along the Leie River in the city center. These wharfs, now at the heart of the tourist district, mark the site at which boats carrying grain from northern France unloaded their cargoes. Large grain warehouses along the wharf provided space for storage.[38] Other ships visited this site as well, but those carrying grain to the city were the most important. Ghent was dependent on imports of grain to feed itself, because the demand for food exceeded Flemish agricultural productive capacity from the twelfth century onwards.[39] The fields of Picardy and Artois in nearby northern France produced a surplus of grain, which merchants shipped down the Scheldt and Leie rivers to feed the Flemish cities. In the 1330s through the 1350s, Ghent, like other Flemish cities, suffered intermittent shortages of grain, which caused periods of crisis.[40] Ghent claimed a staple on grain which its elites were able to strengthen and increase in the second half of the century. By the 1370s and 1380s, Ghent had secured the exclusive right to import grain and to re-export it to other Flemish cities, most notably (and profitably) Bruges. Grain was not only vitally important to feed the city, but also provided a major source of income for the city's elite after the decline of the wool cloth trade.

The Corn Market square itself was an open space, bordered by the church of St. Niklaas on the west, and lined with inns and the houses of important patrician families. These were often one and the same, because members of many patrician families worked as hostellers, brokers and wholesalers, providing financial and merchandising services to foreign merchants. Moneychangers' booths, food markets, and the city's wealthiest neighborhoods were located on the streets leading into the open marketplace.[41] The Corn Market square, ordinarily open to foot traffic, was configured as male space on the three days of the week designated as market days.[42] On those days, the open area would have been filled with wagons, carts, merchants, shippers, brokers, and grain-buyers from the smaller cities of Flanders, along with their porters, dockworkers and waggoneers.[43] Women appeared only as customers, and illegal ones at that. Four ordinances from

---

[38]  One of these, *De Spijker*, still survives on the *Koornlei*.
[39]  David Nicholas, "Of Poverty and Primacy: Demand, Liquidity, and the Flemish Economic Miracle, 1050–1200," *American Historical Review* 96, 1 (1991): 17–41.
[40]  Boone, *Gent en de Bourgondische hertogen*, 21–23.
[41]  Nicholas, *Metamorphosis*, 118.
[42]  De Pauw, *Voorgeboden*, 2.
[43]  De Pauw, *Voorgeboden*, 2.

the mid-fourteenth century forbade women to buy grain at the Corn Market on market days.[44] In 1338 women were forbidden to buy at the market, on penalty of a 3-lb. fine, the same fine which was levied on bakers who bought more than a set quantity of grain.[45] In 1343, an ordinance specified that "no man or woman [should] buy more than one halster of grain in the [Corn] Market on market day."[46] Evidently the previous ordinance had lapsed, and some women were now buying grain, or perhaps had always continued to buy grain. In 1350, women were forbidden "to come into the Corn Market on market days to buy grain," on penalty of losing "her best dress."[47] Some of these ordinances were promulgated in times of extreme grain shortage, and provisions against women buyers appeared among provisions against hoarding. The extremity of the provisions, as well as the repetition, suggest that the ordinances were only enforced temporarily, and that women did normally buy at that market. But they evidently did not sell grain in this market, and every reference to them casts them as illegal interlopers in a male space of economic activity.

The movements of vehicles, male porters, merchants, and sailors through the Corn Market also made the space hostile to women. It was crowded with wagons, horses, and carts. Foreign merchants lined up to buy from the grain merchants, and since distribution took place in the same area, they must have brought with them their porters, waggoners, and other laborers, who stood around waiting to load up the grain. Shippers off-loaded the grain on the wharf nearby, and sailors mingled with the crowds. Dockworkers passed through sweating under the burden of heavy bales and swearing at those who blocked their passage through the crowd. Women stood a good chance of being jostled, pushed, ogled, insulted, and propositioned by an assortment of unsavory characters. Despite the ease with which Ghent women seemed to operate in public, few women from the middling and elite groups would have wanted to go into the Corn Market. A woman who entered the Corn Market risked her reputation and her social status, and by extension, the reputation of her family. It is no coincidence that the punishment for a woman buying grain at the Corn Market—confiscation of her best dress—was the same punishment meted out to a prostitute caught hanging around the wharfs.[48] Women who penetrated this male space were morally suspect—and also too poor to pay a fine. However, even the poorest woman would have a dress

---

[44] Ordinances from 1338, 1350, and 1366. De Pauw, *Voorgeboden*, 7, 37, 48–49, 95. Nicholas identified one widow who sold grain in 1377, Nicholas, *Metamorphosis*, 333.
[45] De Pauw, *Voorgeboden*, 7.
[46] De Pauw, *Voorgeboden*, 37.
[47] De Pauw, *Voorgeboden*, 48–49.
[48] An ordinance also forbade prostitutes to "wander in the evening in the square in front of the [Cloth] Hall or in front of the *Spijker* [the grain warehouse on the Corn Market wharf] at the Vee bridge, on penalty of losing her best dress. . . .," De Pauw, *Voorgeboden*, 44 (1349)

that the authorities could confiscate. Only desperately poor women or those with no reputation to lose would violate this male space, which was founded by strategies delimiting it (the aldermen's ordinances and exclusion of women from the profitable international grain trade) and by the social practices of the male merchants, porters, and sailors.[49]

The gender boundary drawn around the physical and temporal space of the Corn Market did not enclose the houses and inns around it, or St. Niklaas church, or the smaller food markets, shops, booths, and moneychangers' tables within a one-block radius. Space outside of the Corn Market was much more amorphously constructed, and similarly, the Ghentenars involved in international trade were a mixed and amorphous group. The hostellers and brokers, the organizers of international trade, were a group of professionals who operated in and between the Corn Market, the Cloth Hall, the inns and money exchanges. They arranged, expedited, and profited from import and export deals with foreign merchants, principally in grain, wool and cloth. Their versatile and multifaceted interests preclude their classification into a single marketplace. The heart of their activities was, however, in the inns of the hostellers lining the edges of the Corn Market.

This group of brokers, shippers, hostellers, grain measurers, and cloth wholesalers did not confine themselves to a single trade, but instead often changed occupational labels, or cooperated with family members in different occupations.[50] Hostellers, or their family members, were often cloth wholesalers as well.[51] Shippers were also heavily involved in making deals for grain import and export.[52] The city promulgated numerous ordinances designed to keep drapers, weavers, brokers, wholesalers, and hostellers in tightly defined and mutually exclusive categories, but their efforts were largely unsuccessful.[53] Members of this elite group provided a full range of services for the merchants who came to the city to buy and sell grain, cloth, wool, and other imported goods. Hostellers not only provided lodging and meals, but also acted as sureties for foreign merchants so that these merchants could purchase cloth in the Cloth Hall, and make financial arrangements in the local markets.[54] Brokers arranged purchases and financing, and hostellers provided banking services for merchants, either personally, or

---

[49]   Nicholas, *Metamorphosis*, 118.
[50]   Nicholas, *Metamorphosis*, 144–47, 183.
[51]   Nicholas, *Metamorphosis*, 144–48.
[52]   One small and very wealthy guild, the grain measurers, regulated the grain trade, and they doubled sometimes as innkeepers providing housing for French grain merchants.
[53]   A sampling: 1349: drapers and weavers could do no other trade other than "woolwork." 1353: hostellers and brokers could not make cloth or have cloth made, or sell wool. 1360: hostellers could not be brokers for their own goods. 1374: brokers could not make cloth or have it made. De Pauw, *Voorgeboden*, 45, 64, 79, 144.
[54]   Murray, *Bruges*, 87–118 describes a more sophisticated version of this for the city of Bruges.

through their accounts with moneychangers.[55] This group was dominated by elite males, and many belonged to patrician families. Together with the elites from the weavers and the provisioning guilds, they extracted the largest amount of profit from international trade, and they dominated Ghent, politically, economically and socially.

Women were excluded from this group, just as they were excluded from the Corn Market, although wives of brokers and hostellers were sometimes involved in international trade because the activity took place in inns. Hostellers' wives probably contributed significantly to their husbands' innkeeping businesses, just as they did in Bruges.[56] Before the death of her hosteller husband, Soete van Ghend forced Wouter Scoiart to acknowledge that he owed her more than twelve shillings groot for "food and drink and money loaned [to him.]"[57] While her husband Gillis was on a trip to England, Soetin Naes posted a two-thousand-pound bond to act as a hosteller with official privileges to trade at the Cloth Hall.[58] Hostellers, brokers, and wholesalers brokered deals in the Cloth Hall and the Corn Market, they traded in imported dyes, they lodged, fed and entertained foreign merchants and their local clients in their inns, which were also their households. Having a wife to manage the domestic side of innkeeping was necessary, and by extension, wives of hostellers and brokers could handle sales that took place within the inns.[59] The aldermen recognized this in a 1369 ordinance in which they required hostellers' and brokers' wives to swear along with their husbands that they would not buy and sell madder (a dye-stuff) if it was stored in their residences.[60]

In addition, while women were not allowed in the exterior space of the Corn Market, in the interior space of the inns, women probably provided the majority of services for foreign merchants. Hundreds of women must have made their living as barmaids, servers, cooks, laundresses, and servants in the inns on the

---

[55]   Foreigners could buy grain from the grain measurers, hostellers, bakers or brewers. Nicholas, *Metamorphosis*, 245–47.

[56]   Murray, *Bruges*, 318–21.

[57]   SAG, series 301, no. 1, 62v, act no. 5, 16 April 1350. The other debtor, Jan van Expoele, owed her eight shillings for food and drink, f. 63r, act no. 2, 22 April 1350. Philip van Ghend, Soete's husband, seems to have been alive on 24 July 1350, but was definitely dead by 9 Dec. 1350. I suspect that he was already ill in April, and as a result, Soete took the more active role. f. 93v, act no. 7, 24 July; series 330, no. 11, f. 19r, acts no. 1 and 2, 9 Dec. 1350.

[58]   SAG, series 301, no. 1, f. 97r, 1349–50. She had to post a bond of 2,000 pounds parisis, as did the other thirteen hostellers, all of whom were male. Philip de Pape, a prominent tax farmer, was her surety "until Gillis Naes comes from England (*Philip de Pape tote Gillis Naes ute Ingheland comt.*)" See also f. 35v, act no. 1, 15 Dec. 1349. Nicholas found that there were numerous female hostellers in the 1370s through the 1390s, Nicholas, *Domestic Life*, 87–89.

[59]   De Pauw, *Voorgeboden*, 104.

[60]   Although most ordinances referred to brokers with just the male form of the word, one ordinance from 1378 specified both a male broker (*saemcoepre*) and a female broker (*saemcoepericghe*.) De Pauw, *Voorgeboden*, 131.

Corn Market. Prostitutes clustered around the warehouses and in the square in front of the Cloth Hall.[61] These women made a meager living providing services to the men who profited from international trade. The heart of the Corn Market was an exclusively male space, and women operated only at its fringes.

As the provisioning guilds became the most profitable and dominant economic institutions in Ghent, their market spaces, such as the Meat Hall and the Corn Market, grew in importance. There was no space in either of these markets for women to occupy as legitimate market sellers. Even if they belonged to the families of guildsmen, they could only operate on the fringes of the spaces that were produced and reproduced by movements of male merchants, market sellers, and transporters. As these markets bypassed the Cloth Hall in importance, women's access to middling-status positions suffered as well, with the eclipse of the traditional cloth industry which had allowed them a legitimate and profitable middling role.

### The Friday Market

The Friday Market square (*Vrijdagmarkt*) lies three city blocks away from the Corn Market, on a large open space next to St. Jacob's Church. It was the largest open space in the city during the fourteenth century. Surrounded on four sides by household shops, it stood on the dividing line between the wealthy central neighborhood and the poorer neighborhoods of artisans and laborers on the north side of the city.[62] Shops and perhaps some booths were open every day, but one of the major functions of the space was (and still is) a large open-air market on Fridays. Merchants sold a wide array of products for local consumption at the Friday Market, with the exception of most food items, which were sold in their own marketplaces. It was not a market for large merchants involved in import and export of bulk merchandise, although these merchants may have sold items at retail from booths there. On Fridays many craftsmen and women would set up booths or tables in order to sell their wares, and thousands of Ghentenars and people from surrounding villages came to the market to buy household goods, shoes, clothing, tools, and other everyday necessities of life. While other market spaces catered to international trade, or specialized in one type of product, the Friday Market specialized in local retail sales of a large variety of wares. The Friday Market space was founded and organized with boundaries that were easy to penetrate and friendly to shoppers of both genders.

Women were ubiquitous in the Friday Market, as customers and as market sellers. In this market, women were rarely among the richest merchants, but many

---

[61]   De Pauw, *Voorgeboden*, 44.

[62]   Nicholas, *Metamorphosis*, 118.

attained a level of prosperity in the middle niche of small merchandising and retail sales. Several lesser merchant guilds—such as the mercers and spice merchants—allowed women members.[63] Spice merchants (*kruideniers*) also sold soap, oils, ash, minerals, some wines, and many other imported goods, and one story of practice suggests that women spice merchants were common. In 1360, Clais de Ruddre applied for membership in the spice merchants' guild, on the basis of his wife's rights as the daughter of guildmember.[64] The guild leadership decided to grant her the freedom of the guild for a payment of twenty pennies groot and a jug of wine, and ordered Clais to serve a four-year apprenticeship with her in order to be admitted to the freedom of the guild. The spice merchants recognized the right of daughters to practice their fathers' trade, and saw no difficulty with allowing a married woman to practice their craft and to train her husband formally. Their difficulty was rather with the husband's lack of training. Women's access to freedom in this guild in their own right was an opportunity for relative prosperity and middling economic and social status.

The mercers' guild offered women the same opportunity.[65] Mercers sold items like combs, nails, locks, tin and copper cookware, leather bags and gloves, and paternosters. They also catered to an elite clientele by selling luxury items: fine imported fabrics, like silk, satin, velvet, cotton, and embroidered cloth, and fashion accessories, such as hoods, girdles, belts, caps, and hair coverings. The most expensive items they offered for sale were wines and luxury goods decorated with gold and silver. Most of the items sold by mercers were imported, bought at the yearly fairs in Ghent and nearby towns.

Some women mercers were quite prosperous. In 1360, the mercer Lisbette van den Conkele sued Jan Bollaerd for debts he and his late wife owed to her.[66] Those debts amounted to two pounds groot, enough to support a well-to-do orphan for one year. The mid-fifteenth-century mercers' guild statutes mention female mercers prominent enough to own their own shops.[67] Mercers sold out of shops and also from temporary booths (*kramen*) set up on the Friday Market itself. These shops were located on the sides of the open space of the Friday Market square,

---

Nicholas, *Metamorphosis*, 254.

[64] SAG, series 156, no. 1, f. 20r, June 1360; transcribed by Marc Boone.

[65] E. Van der Hellen, "Het Gentse meerseniersambacht (1305–1540)," *Handelingen der maatschappij voor geschiedenis en oudheidkunde te Gent* 31 (1977): 77–149.

[66] This act contains a rare identification of profession. SAG, series 301, no. 1, f. 223v, act no. 3, 5 Dec. 1360.

[67] The 1456 guild privilege of the mercers' guild: "*Item dat elc mersenier of mersenierigghe sal moghen hauden binnen sijnen huuse ende binnen zijnen winkele een dienst joncwijf omme zijnen huerbuer to doene, sonder meer* (Item, that each mercer (male) or mercer (female) will be allowed to keep within their house and within their shop one maid servant to do their work, and no more.)" De Potter, *Gent* 6, 555.

along the Lange Munt street that runs between the Corn Market square and the Friday Market square, and along the Veldstraat, that runs south from the Corn Market square.[68] The mercers had a designated spot for booths on the Friday Market square in front of a certain house.[69] Because mercers offered both household necessities and small luxury items, their booths in the Friday Market and their shops along the neighboring streets offered medieval consumers a true shopping experience—a customer who stopped in to buy a pot could also gaze at the fine fabrics, accessories and unique items that a crafty mercer would display prominently. The Friday Market was huge and diversified, but the booths and shops in and around it also produced small intimate spaces where buyers and sellers interacted.

The Friday Market and the shops that surrounded it included many women who sold a wide variety of products, and the presence of large numbers of female market sellers is a characteristic Ghent shares with most of the towns of northern Europe. In Ghent and the Low Countries in general, these women were not marginal figures. The mid-fourteenth-century French-Flemish language manual, the *Livre des Mestiers*, written in Bruges, features a number of female market sellers, including one who sold parchment, and includes a dialogue simulating a spirited bargaining session between a French merchant and Bruges market woman.[70] Women second-hand dealers (*huutdraeghsterighen*) routinely bought used clothing and household furnishings to resell.[71] The Friday Market square was open to women, not only as the poorest market sellers or as saleswomen for their husbands' products, but also as middling merchants operating their own businesses.

The real gender boundary around the Friday Market was drawn when the square was used for political purposes. Guilds in Ghent had a crucial political function, both for city government and the organization of the city militia. In this most rebellious of Flemish cities, when the guilds called out their membership for street action, the assembly took place on Friday Market square.[72] The ringing of the bell calling the guild members to assemble must also have been the signal for women to close up their booths and vacate the marketplace. The practice of political action was the province of men. When the Friday Market square transformed into political space, the boundaries marginalized women.

Female market sellers worked in every medieval town. There were perhaps more women selling in public in Ghent than there were in many other areas of

---

[68]   These streets are, incidentally, still the main shopping streets in the city center.
[69]   Van der Hellen, "Het Gentse meerseniersambacht."
[70]   Stabel, "Women at the Market," 265.
[71]   Danneel, *Weduwen en wezen*, 380.
[72]   Dumolyn and Haemers, "Patterns of Urban Rebellion."

medieval Europe, and perhaps those women were freer, less deferential, and more assertive in their interactions with men, but what was really different about Ghent was that some women possessed legitimate, accepted access to market-selling positions at the middle level of local retail sales in the Friday Market, or in smaller, intermediary sales in the Cloth Hall. Women market sellers owned and operated their own businesses and possessed a space in some markets in their own right, perhaps through their family connections, but not by virtue of their husbands, deceased or otherwise. Women stallholders in the Cloth Hall even had a measure of control in handing down their stalls to other women, a right which probably survived from oral custom.

The space of the Cloth Hall was articulated by the partition of the booth counter. It was simultaneously a gendered boundary which restricted women market sellers from making the largest sales, and also a bridge which connected women stallholders and male brokers who cooperated for their mutual profit. Their stories are evidence of operations and everyday practices which are as important to the founding of market space as the strategies of the male officials expressed in the written ordinances. In other market spaces, the Meat Hall and the Corn Market, strategies and everyday tactics marginalized women market sellers. And these market spaces were the wave of the future, in gender relations, in economic preeminence, and in political power. Just as the wool cloth trade declined in prestige compared to the butchers and other provisioning guilds from the fourteenth to the sixteenth centuries, women's access to economic opportunities within the city's marketplaces declined from the Middle Ages to the early modern period.

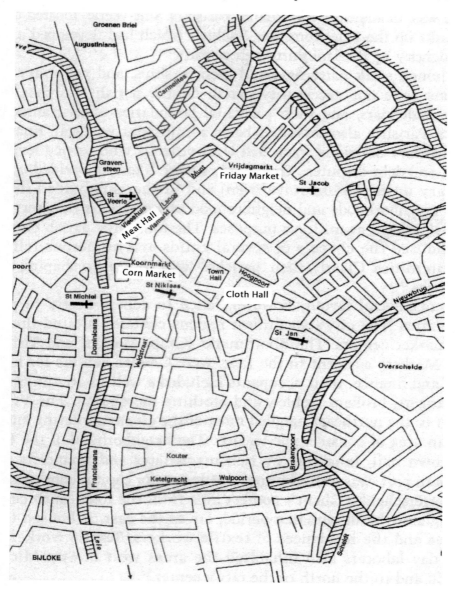

Figure 1: Map of Ghent in the fifteenth century. Taken from Marc Boone, *Gent en de Bourgondische hertogen, ca. 1384–ca. 1453. Een sociaal-politieke studie van een staatsvormingsproces.* Courtesy of the author.

Lia B. Ross

(University of New Mexico)

# Anger and the City: Who Was in Charge of the Paris *cabochien* Revolt of 1413?

The so-called *cabochien* revolt that took place in Paris in the Spring and Ssummer of 1413, and that was named after one of its popular leaders, has failed to make an impression on modern historians. More often than not it is dismissed as a minor episode of the long civil war that followed the murder of the duke of Orléans, the powerful brother of the mad king Charles VI, by order of his rival John the Fearless, duke of Burgundy, in 1407.[1] Yet at least five contemporary sources report it as a significant event in its own merit, even as the politically charged background of this event influences their viewpoint, and adds a cautionary note to the interpretation of their stories. Michel Pintoin, the Religieux of Saint-Denis, follows the respected tradition of Dionysian historiography, which would be expected to be impartial and yet leaning heavily toward respect for royalty and "due process" of law. His narrative is the most coherent and detailed as he dedicates to it the greater part of Book Thirty-Four of his *Chronicles of Charles VI*,

---

[1] For example, Richard Vaughan dismisses it in barely three pages in his biography of John the Fearless, where he summarizes it as a couple of serious riots that provoked the death of ten people and the temporary arrest of less than fifty. He concludes that its role in the duke's fortunes "has been much exaggerated." Richard Vaughan, *John the Fearless: the Growth of Burgundian Power* (1966; Woodbridge: The Boydell Press, 2002), 99–101, Bernard Guenée barely mentions it in a chapter dedicated to the conflicts of the years 1413–16. See also Bernard Guenée, *Un Meurtre, une société: l'assassinat du duc d'Orléans, 23 novembre 1407* (Paris: Gallimand, 1992); R. C. Famiglietti describes some salient episodes, taken from the Religieux, in ten pages, but without much analysis, as his focus in on the king's illness. R. C. Famiglietti, *Royal Intrigue: Crisis at the Court of Charles VI 1392–1420* (New York: AMS Press, 1984), 117–27; and David Nicholas dedicates less than a page to it in a work on late medieval revolts. David Nicholas, *The Later Medieval City 1300–1500* (London: Longman, 1997), 139. Even works of sociology that examine social movements from a historical perspective move directly from medieval peasant revolts to the Reformation. See, for example, Sidney Tarrow, *Power in Movement* (Cambridge: Cambridge University Press, 1994), 32–33.

a work that has been hailed as one of the most original and thoughtful histories of the later Middle Ages.[2] His account is particularly enlightening because despite an obvious anti-populist bias, he examines the actions (if not the motives) of all parties involved. The chronicler Enguerran de Monstrelet gives a more succinct but equally dramatic version of the events. A member of the gentry, he is definitely critical of the entire episode and of the misalliance between a peer of the realm and what he perceives as a mob. In fact, the portion of his *Chronique* that deals with the brief insurrection is one of the very few in which this usually imperturbable writer gives vent to emotion; still, as his custom, he backs his opinions with an abundance of facts.

Jean-Juvénal des Ursins, bishop, diplomat, historian, and son of the homonymous royal magistrate, is clearly averse to mob rule, albeit sympathetic toward reforms, and predictably offers a version of facts that reflects the views of the royal court. Still, his narrative has the quality of being enlivened by tidbits of privileged recollections as his father found himself in the thick of events, and reveals some aspect of princely personalities and policies that were not available to other authors. An anonymous Burgundian sympathizer includes the revolt in his brief chronicle of the reign of Charles VI in a much-abbreviated form. The last author of the list, the anonymous diarist known as the Bourgeois of Paris, was probably a clerk or a doctor of the University, and his account is particularly significant because it is the only one to reflect the "view from the street," with all its contradictions. Unfortunately this is also its drawback as this opinionated author, who does not hide strong Burgundian sympathies, often confuses the facts and presents the reader with an incongruous narrative, in part at least because of the private and informal nature of his writing, and in part probably because of his position as outsider.[3]

The most intriguing aspect of the episode to emerge from those narratives is its apparent dual nature, part urban insurrection and part courtly coup, and yet both aspects are amply described but inadequately explained by those sources, leaving

---

[2]  For a discussion of the merits of Michel Pintoin as historiographer, see Bernard Guenée, *L'Opinion publique à la fin du Moyen Âge d'après la "Chronique de Charles VI" du Religieux de Saint-Denis* (Paris: Perrin, 2002).

[3]  Religieux de Saint-Denis, *Chronique du Religieux de Saint-Denis contenant le règne de Charles VI de 1380 à 1422*, trans. M. L. Bellaguet. 6 vols. (1842; Paris: Éditions du Comité des travaux historiques et scientifiques, 1994), vol. 5, 2–182; Enguerran De Monstrelet, *La Chronique d'Enguerran de Monstrelet*, ed. L. Douët-D'Arcq (please check this name again). 6 vols. (Paris: Jules Renouard, 1857–1863), vol. 2, 343–98; Jean-Juvénal des Ursins, *Histoire de Charles VI, roy de France*. Choix de chroniques et mémoires sur l'histoire de France, ed. J. A. C. Bouchon (Paris: Auguste Desrez, 1838), 477–87; *Extrait d'une chronique anonyme pour le règne de Charles VI 1400-142: La chronique d'Enguerran de Monstrelet*, ed. Louise-Claude Douët-D'Arcq. 6 vols. (Paris: Jules Renouard, 1857-1863), vol. 6, 217-19; *Journal d'un bourgeois de Paris: 1405-1449*, ed. Colette Beaune (Paris: Livre de poche, 1990), 56–71.

the reader with unanswered questions about the potentially common motives of such diverse parties. In this essay, after a synopsis of the events, I plan to discuss precisely those tantalizing but neglected topics, and for this I will resort to the aid of modern sociology.

The tangled background of the episode reveals in itself a mixture of motives, and goes as far back as 1404, with the accession of John the Fearless to the duchy of Burgundy, when his cousin Louis, duke of Orléans was still living and contending with him for preeminence at court. Their rivalry was certainly personal: John believed that closeness to the king was his rightful place as he was son and heir of Philip the Bold, the influential statesman and uncle of the king who had often held the reins of power during his nephew's episodes of madness. And Louis of Orléans, once reaching adulthood, demanded the privilege for himself as he was the king's only brother. The personalities of the rivals may also have played a part. The Religieux affirms that Orléans was proud, arrogant, and headstrong. For example, in 1402, no sooner had the king named him regent during his times of illness that the latter imposed a large tax on commoners and clergy alike to the chagrin of his uncles, the dukes of Burgundy and Berry, and of the duke of Bourbon. Once the king had regained his sanity they protested that Louis was too young to be regent (he was then thirty, having been born in 1372!) and succeeded in having him stripped of the title and replaced by Philip of Burgundy, father of John the Fearless.[4]

But the rivalry transcended personality to touch on issues of policy: Orléans represented the "aristocratic" party, generally perceived as indifferent to the people's needs and always ready to raise taxes, while Philip and later his heir John seem to have leant toward a more populist direction. Likely because of this different attitude toward public opinion, propaganda seems to have been more active on the Burgundian side, and to have resulted in various pamphlets that criticized waste at court and the scandalous behavior of princes wallowing in luxury while the king lived in a perpetual state of poverty and neglect. The main targets of their attacks, aside from the duke of Orléans, were the duke of Berry, the only surviving uncle of Charles VI, and the count of Foix, all standing accused of having exploited the king's mental illness for personal advantage. Significantly, however, the most hated figure was not a prince, but the grand master of the

---

4    *Is arrogans preterea et neminem pre se ducens hominem, alio inconsulto cuncta pro suo disponere volebat arbitrio*. Religieux, *Chronique*, vol. 3, 12. See also Jean-Juvénal, *Histoire*, 412. He adds, *Histoire*, 425–26, that by 1405 the people openly accused Orléans and the queen of being responsible for the onerous *tailles* and *aides*.

436 Lia B. Ross

king's hotel Jean de Montaigu, a favorite of the dukes of Berry and Orléans, who had amassed a large fortune apparently through dubious channels.[5]

It is hard to tell how deeply John the Fearless was personally involved in the dissemination of anti-court propaganda, but as early as 1405, according to the Religieux and Jean-Juvénal, on at least one occasion he tried to destroy his adversary by exploiting popular discontent and through a popular movement, as he came to Paris to harangue publicly the leading citizens. Like any good politician he started out by affirming that he was motivated not by private interests but by concern for the kingdom that was burdened by intolerable taxes. He added that if Orléans was allowed to continue with "his designs" (he did not specify what these designs might be) the country would never be safe, and concluded by asking the Parisians to follow him in arms under his banner to "reestablish peace." Paris, that had been rocked by several tax riots in the preceding century, the most famous being the revolt of the *Maillotins* of 1382, had since lost many privileges, which might have rendered its citizens less willing to risk the ire of the court.[6]

Therefore the burghers replied (wisely) that they were grateful for the duke's efforts on their behalf, but were afraid to take arms for fear of revenge on the part of Orléans once peace among princes would return. But they added diplomatically that if the king or the dauphin would issue orders to mobilize, they would obey.[7] At this the duke might have realized that the next move was entirely up to him, and concluded that the populace would follow only if orders came from the legitimate authority, the king (in his moments of sanity) or the dauphin. Since the sixteen-year-old dauphin Louis, duke of Guyenne, was married to one of John's daughters, the young prince might have seemed the most amenable to being manipulated. But, as will become apparent, the fact that legitimacy rested exclusively with the unpredictable young prince would later turn to John's disadvantage.

Ideological motives, then, blended with personal ones when on the evening of 23 November 1407 John the Fearless sent assassins to kill Louis of Orléans as the latter rode peacefully though the streets of Paris.[8] After a hasty confession followed by a swift exit from the city, John opted for a brazen defense that was presented to the assembled court in 1410 by a University doctor, Master Jean Petit. Through his words the murderer justified the deed on altruistic grounds, claiming that he had to intervene to save the king and his sons from repeated murderous

---

[5] These concepts are expressed in the *Songe véritable* (1406), a long poem by an anonymous clerk of Paris. Guenée, *Un Meurtre*, 173–75, and Jacques Lemaire, *Les Visions de la vie de cour dans la littérature française de la fin du Moyen Âge* (Paris: Klincksieck, 1994), 292.

[6] Nicholas, *Medieval City*, 128.

[7] Religieux, *Chronique*, vol. 3, 340, and Jean-Juvénal, *Histoire*, 429.

[8] The famous event is in Monstrelet, *Chronique*, vol. 1, 154–66, Jean-Juvénal, *Histoire*, 437, and Religieux, *Chronique*, vol. 3, 730–44.

attempts by the tyrannical Orléans, and refused to ask forgiveness for the crime. While this harangue has rightly been called "one of the most insolent pieces of political chicanery and theological casuistry in all history," it seems to have cemented the public image of John the Fearless as the rescuer of the helpless royal family and of the people.[9] At any rate the murder, which aristocratic chroniclers in the tradition of Froissart record in horrified tones, seems to have made relatively little impression on the population. On the contrary, if we have to believe the anonymous writer of the chronicle mentioned earlier and the author of the *Livre des trahisons,* a pro-Burgundian manifesto dressed up as chronicle, commoners secretly welcomed the news with relief.[10] For them the victim had been an object of hatred, the symbol of courtly waste and corruption, so that they immediately dressed up with normative values the cowardly and illegal act that they might have condemned under different circumstances.

The king's feeblemindedness and John's military strength helped also to cement the latter's standing at court, while a determined Orléanist opposition party was hampered by the youth of its leader Duke Charles, son of the murdered Louis. Not only was the crime not punished, but after several failed attempts at mediation between the factions, by 1413 civil war between Burgundians and Orléanists had been raging with no end in sight, in a vicious cycle of skirmishes, mutual destruction of property, and general brutalization of the population. At the time Duke John resided in Paris where he exerted control over the court, easily dominating both the weak and mad king and the adolescent dauphin. But his power did not go unchallenged. While Charles of Orléans and his confederates surrounded and threatened the city with their marauding armies, inside Paris

---

9
   The quote is from Vaughan, *John the Fearless,* 70. The allegorical poem *Le Pastoralet,* a piece of Burgundian propaganda which was written probably around 1423, repeats the same themes and adds the gossip that Orléans and the queen might have had an illicit affair. *Le pastoralet,* ed. Joel Blanchard (Paris: Presses Universitaires de France, 1983), 15–17. The feeble-minded king seems to have accepted the explanation that his brother had coveted the crown for himself and plotted to murder him and his children and was easily convinced that his cousin had to bring about his death for the "seureté et préservacion de nous et de nostre dite lignée" (safety and preservation of ourselves and our line). *Chronique Anonyme,* 197–98.

10
   *Le Livre des trahisons de France envers la maison de Bourgogne.* Chroniques relatives a' l'histoire de la Belgique sous la domination des ducs de Bourgogne, ed. Kervyn de Lettenhove (Brussels: Commission Royale d'Histoire, 1870–1876), 20–21. Incidentally, the work completely skips the *cabochien* revolt, and only hints at its conclusion when Duke John felt threatened in Paris and left for Flanders. *Livre des trahisons,* 22, 25. The *Chronique Anonyme,* 195 says of the murder, "De celle mort fut le commun peuple moult joyeulx, car ledit duc d'Orléans leur faisoit souffrir moult de maux par les grandes tailles et aides que il faisoit souvent ceuillir et mectre sus, el nom du Roy, et tout retournoit à son seul singulier plaisir et fourfit" (The common people were joyous for that death as the duke of Orléans caused them much suffering because of the high taxes and *aides* that he often imposed on them in the king's name, but which were entirely for his own personal profit and enjoyment). Jean-Juvénal, *Histoire,* 438, states that the people openly cheered Burgundy.

prominent members of the royal family and of the bourgeoisie were either neutral or outright their sympathizers, in particular, the dukes of Bar and of Bavaria and the count of Vertus, brother of Charles of Orléans.[11] The writers inform us that John had forged an alliance with the powerful Paris butchers' guild, perhaps (we may guess) because his position with princes was so tenuous, but they skim over the actual arrangements. Jean-Juvénal is the most specific in categorizing the situation: he states that during Burgundy's intermittent absences from the city in 1411 his vassal the count of Saint-Pol was left in charge and that he, in turn, "sousleva et mit sus les bouchers de Paris" (roused and raised the butchers of Paris) on the duke's behalf.

He then supplies a few details about them: the Legoix, a father and three sons, were a successful family of masters at the slaughterhouse and meat market (*boucherie*) of Sainte-Geneviève; the Saint-Yons and the Thiberts, apparently the better off of the group, owned the big *boucherie* near the Châtelet, and attracted to their cause members of various arts (*mestiers*) such as the surgeon Master Jean de Troyes, a man known for his eloquence. Other adherents were tanners (*pelletiers*) and sewers (*cousturiers*) and a skinner (*écorcheur*) called Caboche who worked at the *boucherie* of the Hotel-Dieu near Notre-Dame, and "toutes gens pauvres, et meschans desirans piller et disrober estoient avec eux" (all the poor people and bad types eager to steal and rob were with them). The writer appears to associate the worst elements with the humble skinner, and since Caboche himself will not have a preponderant part in the accounts of rebellious action, the reader may conclude that the butchers' party and the eponymous revolt took their name from the lowliest of the lot, just as the Burgundian party referred to the Orléanists as "Armagnacs" after their lowest-ranking leader, the count of Armagnac.[12] From the accounts of Jean-Juvénal and the Religieux the butchers seem not to have quite held the reins of the city but rather to have mainly filled security functions as captains of bridges.[13] Additionally, three of the four elected aldermen (*échevins*), Garnier de Saint-Yon, Robert de Belloy, and Jean de Troyes (the latter also surgeon and caretaker of the Palais), were *cabochiens*.[14]

---

[11]  Monstrelet, *Chronique*, vol. 2, 335.

[12]  Jean-Juvénal, *Histoire*, 461. Later on, *Histoire*, 482, he refers to the rebels as "ceux qu'on nommoit cabochiens" (those who were called *cabochiens*).

[13]  Beaune, *Journal*, 63 (the author specifies that Denisot de Chaumont was captain of the bridge of Saint-Cloud and Simon Caboche of that of Charenton and de Troyes a "mire juré," or licensed surgeon. Jean-Juvénal, *Histoire*, 461, 479 confirms all this and adds that Hélion de Jacqueville, a knight at John's service, was captain of the city and effectively ruled it. The Religieux, *Chronique*, vol. 5, 36, states that Caboche and de Chaumont were given captaincies of bridges after the start of the revolt to prevent the passage of political adversaries.

[14]  Beaune, *Journal*, 66, note no. 70.

Given that the butchers and their protector John the Fearless enjoyed a period of ascendancy in the local political arena, why then did they start a revolt? Sources agree that the spark that ignited it was a controversy surrounding some high court officials whom the University accused of corruption, chief among them the provost of Paris Pierre des Essarts. He had been a Burgundian favorite and a popular magistrate with both "roi et commun" (king and populace) and in 1409 had been instrumental in procuring the execution of the hated Montaigu. But within a couple of years he had in turn been involved in a corruption scandal, as he was also in charge of royal finances "et ne s'en estoit point bien acquittés, si comme ilz disorient" (and, as the rumor went, had not acquitted himself well at all).[15] Forced to defend himself from the accusation that he had squandered the royal treasury, he implicated John the Fearless, claiming that he had been forced by a royal order to give the duke two million francs (or two thousand *lyons*), for which he could produce a receipt. According to the Religieux, this statement assured him the gratitude of the dauphin, but also the hatred of his former protector.[16] And to the reader it also suggests that the young dauphin was beginning to shake off the yoke of his father-in-law and to pursue, or to attempt to pursue, an independent policy. Des Essarts was subsequently dismissed and banished from the city under unclear circumstances.[17] Inexplicably, however, he returned to Paris (apparently invited by the dauphin, but the reasons are unconvincing), and together with his brother Antoine took residence in the well-fortified Bastille Saint-Antoine. At this point some Parisians became convinced that he and his sympathizers had plotted to remove forcibly the king and the dauphin, and then to turn the city over to the Orléanists during the upcoming wedding of the duke of Bavaria, brother of the queen, who had come to Paris for the occasion.[18]

---

[15] *Chronique Anonyme*, 216. Also Jean-Juvénal, *Histoire*, 477, Monstrelet, *Chronique*, vol. 2, 343, and Beaune, *Journal*, 56, where the Bourgeois specifies that he had enjoyed "grande grace" (great favor) more than any other provost in a century.

[16] Religieux, *Chronique*, vol. 5, 6, and Jean-Juvénal, *Histoire*, 477 (he puts the amount at two thousand *lyons*).

[17] He had been appointed provost for the first time in 1408, during a temporary ascent of the Burgundian party in Paris, displacing the favorite candidate Guillaume de Tignonville, who had been a retainer of the late Orléans. He was replaced by another Burgundian favorite, Le Borgne de la Heuse. Jean-Juvénal, *Histoire*, 439, 477.

[18] Religieux, *Chronique*, vol. 5, 9, and Beaune, *Journal*, 57. The Bourgeois adds that the University "tout savait" (knew everything) of the plot.

Fig.1: The Bastille before the Revolution

The Religieux affirms that the rumor originated with the butchers, and that as a consequence on April 28 a crowd of thousands of Parisians led by Élyon de Jacqueville, a chamberlain of John the Fearless, and by two other knights of the duke's household, marched in arms on the Bastille to demand the rendition of the des Essarts brothers.[19] In vain the ex-provost tried to appease the furious mob and pleaded from a high window to be allowed to leave the city once again in safety. An attack on the fortress was deflected only when John the Fearless intervened in person to mediate a surrender of des Essarts, which took effect a few days later and that would lead to his execution within two months.[20] Soon afterwards, from six-thousand to twenty-thousand citizens (depending on the source) marched to the hotel of the young dauphin, led by the same de Jacqueville, who now was joined by a group of butchers and skinners: the Legoix brothers, Denisot de Chaumont, and Simon Caboche, and also the surgeon Jean de Troyes, who would become the spokesman of the movement as the best educated of the lot.[21] There they burst into the dauphin's private apartment and demanded that he hand over fifteen or so "traitors," among whom the duke of Bar and the dauphin's chancellor

---

[19] Religieux, *Chronique*, vol. 5, 8 and Monstrelet, *Chronique*, vol. 1, 344 (he mentions Charles de Lens as the third knight). Jean-Juvénal, *Histoire*, 477, talks only of one other leader beside de Jacqueville, Robert de Mailly, and states that the mob was three-thousand strong.

[20] His brother Antoine was also sentenced to death, but escaped execution with the end of the revolt. *Chronique Anonyme*, 216. The easy surrender appears strange, but because Duke John had promised his protection, apparently des Essarts believed until the last moment in a reprieve, and even went to his execution smiling happily. Religieux, *Chronique*, vol. 5, 14, 24, 74–76 and Jean-Juvénal, *Histoire*, 477, 481. The Bourgeois, *in describing the execution*, Beaune, *Journal*, 60, returns to his "grand orgueil" (great pride) and alleged plots to destroy the very city whose inhabitants "tant l'aimaient loyalement" (loved him so loyally).

[21] Religieux, *Chronique*, vol. 5, 16–18 and Jean-Juvénal, *Histoire*, 477. Both bring the number to twenty-thousand, while Monstrelet, *Chronique*, vol. 2, 344–45, brings the crowd to six thousand, omits mention of the Legoix, adds that "many more" armed men from Burgundy's hotel participated in this new attack, and gives Caboche's first name as Jehanninot.

Jean de Vailly.[22] Over the young prince's furious protests, and in Duke John's presence, they seized their victims by force and dragged them to prison. A valet was yanked from the very arms of the dauphin's wife, who was trying in vain to protect him. During the violent irruption a secretary of the king was fatally wounded by the mob and then thrown into the Seine, and two artisans were also killed, apparently for their Orléanist sympathies.[23] The obvious question that arises at this point is, who supplied the list to the insurgents and what was their criterion for determining treason. Most chroniclers do not say, but Monstrelet hints obliquely at responsibility as he has the dauphin angrily accuse his father-in-law of having caused the arrests.[24]

After this violent opening, the insurgency seems to have refocused on a bizarre pedagogical goal: the rescue of the adolescent dauphin from the influence of "bad" servants who indulged him in his debaucheries and love of late night parties, which, they feared, would cause his vulnerable mind to become afflicted by the same illness as his father's. The University once again stepped into the middle of things, as one of its doctors, Master Jean de Pavilly, delivered a sermon in front of the assembled court and of the dauphin himself, scolding the prince for his loose lifestyle and cautioning him against disobeying his worried mother. Then the armed mob forced him to dwell with his father at the hotel Saint-Pol ostensibly "pour sa correction" (for his correction), but also to save on unneeded expenses, and for good measure placed guards both at the royal palace and at the city gates lest the prince escape to join the Orléanist confederates.[25] The correctional theme is not incidental, but rather central to most contemporary narratives, which concur in the portrait of the dauphin as a rebellious adolescent.[26] For example, a revealing episode occurred in July at the height of the *cabochien* rule. Late one evening, toward midnight, the already-mentioned Élyon de Jacqueville, by then promoted

---

[22] Another victim was the chamberlain Jacques e la Rivière, who later was found dead in prison under suspicious circumstances. Jean-Juvénal, *Histoire*, 477, Monstrelet, *Chronique*, vol. 2, 345. The Bourgeois, Beaune, *Journal*, 58, condenses this one and a subsequent irruption into the palace in one page.

[23] They were a *tapissier* (textile worker) according to Monstrelet or *menestrier* (musician) according to Jean-Juvénal and a *cannonier* (gunsmith) according to Monstrelet or a maker of siege engines according to Jean-Juvénal. Monstrelet, *Chronique*, vol. 2, 346, Jean-Juvénal, *Histoire*, 477, and Religieux, *Chronique*, vol. 5, 20–22.

[24] He records the dauphin's angry words and John's sheepish reply that they should talk it over once the dauphin was calmer. Monstrelet, *Chronique*, vol. 2, 345–46. Famiglietti, *Royal Intrigue*, 118, openly accuses Burgundy of bad faith in his "mediation" attempts.

[25] Monstrelet, *Chronique*, vol. 2, 346. See also Religieux, *Chronique*, vol. 5, 28, 30.

[26] Religieux, vol. 5, 18. He confirms this moral portrait after the prince's premature death in 1415. Religieux, vol. 5, 586–88. Monstrelet, *Chronique*, vol. 2, 346, says of him that "il estoit de jeune aage et ne povoit souffrir estre redargué de quelque personne" (he was young and could not tolerate being contradicted by anyone). The Bourgeois, *Journal*, 65, says that he "ouvrait à volonté" (acted willfully).

to captain of the city, burst into the dauphin's hotel during a ball and rebuked him for improper behavior. The irate youth stabbed the intruder repeatedly in the chest, but the other was wearing a breastplate and received no damage. Then the lord de La Tremoïlle, another chamberlain like de Jacqueville and apparently his rival, intervened to defend the young prince, and a scuffle ensued, joined by the *cabochien* guards, and only quelled when the duke of Burgundy intervened in person. The dauphin was so incensed by the intrusion that he spat blood for three days.[27]

While pushing reforms of princely mores, the city government seems to have become progressively more controlling, and life under mob rule may strike a chord with those familiar with more recent revolutions. Thousands of Parisians took to wearing white hooded hats (*chaperons*), a symbol of Flemish urban autonomy adopted in solidarity with Flemish revolts.[28] Here it signified adherence to the *cabochien* movement, and as such it was forced on nobles, prelates, and later even the king. Jean-Juvénal regales the reader with an unwittingly comical scene when he recalls a visit of his father to the old duke of Berry, who at the time was lodged in the cloister of Notre Dame. The magistrate found the old prince helplessly fretting over the abuses of the mob while dutifully wearing his white *chaperon*![29] More ominously, against royal orders the *cabochiens* prowled the city in arms and arrested about sixty prominent citizens and merchants who had refused to back their insurrection.[30]

On May 22, as an armed crowd accompanied as usual the king to his apartment at the hotel Saint-Pol, Duke John himself pleaded with them to withdraw their watch that could upset the feeble monarch. They refused, and demanded that he hand over a number of people listed in a "roll of traitors," among whom were the duke of Bavaria and several more household knights and servants. Curiously, the

---

[27]  Religieux, vol. 5, 78, 80 and Jean-Juvénal, *Histoire*, 481 (he states that de Jacqueville and his men planned to kill de la Tremoïlle on the following day but Burgundy talked them out of it).

[28]  Religieux, *Chronique*, vol. 5, 26, 38, Monstrelet, *Chronique*, vol. 2, 349. The Bourgeois, *Journal*, 59, states that in May three-thousand to four-thousand *chaperons* were made. Jean-Juvénal, *Histoire*, 478–79, adds a detail that confirms the dauphin's rebellious nature: he was spotted wearing the hat with the white hood across his chest in the guise of a band, the Armagnac symbol, which irked the butchers. For echoes of the riots at the Tuileries in 1792 when the royal family was forced to wear the Cap of Liberty, see George Rudé, *The Crowd in the French Revolution* (Oxford: Clarendon Press, 1959), 100.

[29]  Jean-Juvénal, *Histoire*, 482.

[30]  Religieux, *Chronique*, vol. 5, 34, and Jean-Juvénal, *Histoire*, 478 (he adds that the prowling thugs neglected their trade and robbed with impunity). Monstrelet, *Chronique*, vol. 2, 346, laments that "c'estoit lors piteuse chose de veoir le règne desdictes communes et comment ilz se conduisoient dedens Paris, tant envers le Roy comme envers les autres seigneurs" (it was then a pity to see the reign of these vulgar people and their behavior within Paris both toward the king and the other lords).

roll also included the names of about a dozen ladies-in-waiting of Queen Isabeau. In vain the queen tearfully begged reprieve for few days, while the dauphin, helpless to intervene on her behalf, retired to a private room where he burst into tears. The insurgents refused to relent, even as the duke of Bavaria volunteered to offer himself alone to their judgment and promised, if freed, never to return to France. The terrified ladies, who had scattered throughout the royal apartments, were captured and carted away, tied in pairs on horseback (or in boats on the Seine, according to other sources), followed by an armed crowd. Soon the dauphin's pro-Burgundian chancellor, who had previously been dismissed, was reinstated, and a commission of inquiry was set up to examine the crimes of the prisoners and determine their punishment.[31] Once again there seems to be a correlation between a violent popular eruption and a power shift inside the court in a direction favorable to Burgundy.

Fig. 2: Butchers' arms

The insurrection seems to have produced at least one positive result, however, when late in May its leaders presented to the assembled court a draft of a long document that would become known as the *Ordonnance cabochienne*. This was a list of two-hundred and fifty-eight articles outlining an ambitious program of administrative reform (for example, reduction of the royal council, suspension of the sale of offices and gifts to royal secretaries, tighter control over the personnel of the royal treasury).

---

31    Religieux, *Chronique*, vol. 5, 42–46, Monstrelet, *Chronique*, vol. 2, 353–55 (he gives the list of prisoners at p. 353), Beaune, *Journal*, 58 (the Bourgeois skims over the episode in one sentence). Jean-Juvénal, *Histoire*, 479, says that fourteen or fifteen ladies were taken to the *concièrgerie* of the Palais. The reason for the arrest of the ladies remains a mystery also because, once freed, they were forbidden from talking about their experience. Religieux, *Chronique*, vol. 5, 90.

There is nothing revolutionary about this sensible document and it is not surprising that it won praise from even the two most conservative authors, the Religieux and Jean-Juvénal.[32] But at the same time the nobility had started a stealthy exodus from Paris, to avoid the fate of some prisoners, women included, who some writers claim were drowned in mass without trial.[33] Particularly damaging for the insurgents and John was the fact that the count of Vertus, who was an intimate of the dauphin, fled to his brother Charles of Orléans to give a harrowing account of events inside the city.[34] Charles sent a letter to the city leaders demanding the release of the two dukes of Bar and Bavaria and freedom of movement for the royal family, and threatened reprisals. But at court, except for the ineffectual duke of Berry and the helpless dauphin, only Burgundian partisans were left, and the king was cajoled into issuing an edict in which he outlawed the armed congregation of princes outside the city, and denied that the dauphin had any intelligence with them.[35]

Eventually, however, the threat posed by the princely armies became too much to ignore, and just when the revolt seemed unstoppable it started unraveling. According to Monstrelet, the leaders of the insurrection feared having gone too far in incurring the ire of the princes and, to cover all eventualities, demanded a royal pardon, which resulted in a curious document full of quibbles and disclaimers that the writer reproduces in full.[36] Soon they submitted a petition to the University to obtain approval of their actions, in particular the arrests, but now that authoritative body refused to be implicated. On the contrary, it proposed that all prisoners should be set free and the *cabochien* leaders excluded from any peace

---

[32] Religieux, *Chronique*, vol. 5, 48–52, praises it and Jean-Juvénal, *Histoire*, 479, 486, while not covering its content in details, regrets its abolition after the failure of the revolt. The text of the provisions is in Alfred Coville, *L'Ordonnance cabochienne 26–27 mai 1413* (Paris: A. Picard, 1891), 4–181.

[33] Monstrelet, *Chronique*, vol. 2, 361–62. One documented murder of a prisoner was that of de le Rivière, who was allegedly killed by de Jacqueville with a blow to the head. His lifeless body was beheaded on the following day. Jean-Juvénal, *Histoire*, 479–80. The Religieux, *Chronique*, vol. 5, 260, reduces the number of victims to a few as he states that the insurgents had "et ex eis aliquos secrete interfecerunt, submerserunt vel ad redempcionem peccunialem et importabilem posuerunt" (even slaughtered or drowned some in secret, and forced others to pay exorbitant ransoms). Jean-Juvénal, *Histoire*, 486, reports that after the fall of the *cabochiens* a list was found with the names of people destined to be drowned. The reference to mass executions is in the royal edict that accompanied the restoration of Orléanist princes, and may well be an exaggeration. See Monstrelet, *Chronique*, vol. 2, 445. Vaughan, *John the Fearless*, 100, does not believe it.

[34] Jean-Juvénal, *Histoire*, 479, Monstrelet, *Chronique*, vol. 2, 361, and Religieux, *Chronique*, vol. 5, 32.

[35] The text of the edict is in Monstralet, *Chronique*, vol. 2, 347–48. For the demands of the princes, see Religieux, *Chronique*, vol. 5, 88. The Bourgeois, *Journal*, 61, jumps from the execution of des Essarts (July 1) to the negotiations with the princes that will lead to the peace of Pontoise (latter half of July).

[36] Monstrelet, *Chronique*, vol. 2, 356–60.

with the Orléanists, even as the previously-mentioned doctor Eustache de Pavilly, "qui tendoit fort au profit de sa bourse" (who was quite mindful of his own profit) according to Jean-Juvénal, had an understanding with the Legoix and the Saint-Yons and argued in favor of the arrests.[37] This unexpected about-face of the University angered the Bourgeois diarist, yet from the start this institution appears less interested in revolutions than in orderly reforms, and even less in creating a populist commune.[38]

At the same time the mood within the city shifted in favor of peace with the Orléanists. While until this point the only popular party seems to have been that of the *cabochiens*, and the only policy one of resistance to the princely armies, now a true "peace party" seems to emerge from the ranks of the bourgeoisie. The course of internal reconciliation was rendered even more urgent as Henry V of England was starting to exploit the disarray of the French and organize an expedition in Normandy. In fact, the sudden unpopularity of the *cabochiens* was helped by a fiscal initiative imposed by them for an expedition against the English.[39] Some pro-peace merchants and the district captains (*quarteniers*) secretly contacted the dauphin and Berry, who by then was meeting regularly with Jean-Juvénal Sr., to obtain their support and thus legitimize their "counterrevolution." Together they formulated a plan to seize control of the situation counting on a majority vote for peace once the citizens were allowed to vote by district.[40]

While the writers generally attribute the new turn of events to the initiative of the dauphin alone, Jean-Juvénal supplies additional details of the counter-insurgency as the only one with inside information supplied by his father. He relates that the *cabochiens*, fearing that power was slipping from them, tried everything to prevent a vote for peace. During a tumultuous session at City Hall, attended by a thousand people, the peace proposals drafted by the king and the dauphin were put forward for a vote, after apparently being approved by the provost of merchants and by the *échevins*. Suddenly Jean de Troyes, Caboche, the Legoix and the Saint-Yons irrupted into the hall demanding that the vote be postponed, but were overrun by shouts of "Par les quartiers!" (By districts!). One

---

[37] Jean-Juvénal, *Histoire*, 479.

[38] The Bourgeois, *Journal*, 62–63, is angry and confused at this and states that the University doctors acted "comme si le diable les eût conseillés" (as if advised by the devil).

[39] The money was to be given to the lord of Heilly to fight the English in Guyenne, but he was captured by the enemy and the expedition aborted. The *cabochiens* also extorted money from Jean-Juvénal Sr. under threat of arrest, but allowed him to pay in installments (!). Then they ransacked the house of the University chancellor Jean Gerson, who had resisted the tax. Jean-Juvénal, *Histoire*, 480. See also Religieux, *Chronique*, vol. 5, 60–62.

[40] Jean-Juvénal, *Histoire*, 482. He adds that at first Berry was unsure of how many Parisians would side with them. The bourgeois *quarteniers* in the plot were two drapers, Etienne d'Ancenne and Gervaisot de Merilles. For the functions of the *quarteniers*, see Religieux, *Chronique*, vol. 5, 86.

of the Legoix, who was armed, challenged anyone who was for peace to show up in person at the assembly, but then a *quartenier*, Guillaume Cirace, carpenter of the graveyard of Saint-Jean, stood up and bravely declared that the majority wanted to vote by districts and that if the *cabochiens* tried to prevent this vote they might find that in Paris there were just as many tool smiths as butchers. At this the others quieted down.[41]

On the following morning, during an exchange between Jean-Juvénal Sr. and Jean de Troyes, the old surgeon tried to convince the magistrate to side with the "war party" and accept an open letter that accused the Armagnacs of treason. But the other, now safe behind royal authority, denounced (albeit politely) the document as seditious, at which point someone grabbed it from de Troyes and tore it in a hundred pieces.[42] The *cabochiens* attempted to play a last card and assembled a crowd at Place de Grève, but found the place already filled with a rival crowd clamoring for peace. When a public vote was taken by dividing the assembly in two groups, all moved to the right, signifying that they were for peace.[43] After the results of the dramatic gathering became known, an emboldened Jean-Juvénal Sr. led thirty prominent citizens to the king, as he was sitting in council attended, among others, by Duke John. Suddenly the *quartieniers* interrupted the meeting demanding peace and that the dauphin would lead them to release the prisoners. The group marched under the dauphin's window as planned (*accordé*) and he grandly consented to the crowd's request. The ubiquitous Jean-Juvénal Sr. appears at this point to take the leading role in coordinating action, as he instructed the irresolute Berry to accompany the dauphin to the Louvre and deliver the two imprisoned dukes of Bar and of Bavaria.[44]

Throughout the scene, which appears a well-choreographed charade, John the Fearless seemed overtaken by the events and voiced only a cautious protest, while the dauphin, suddenly metamorphosed from hedonist into warrior, and wearing armor under the silk robe, rode at the head of a large militia and a huge crowd to free Bar and Bavaria among celebratory ringing of bells, and then the rest of the prisoners. At this point the revolt quickly imploded, and its leaders, Caboche included, slipped away unnoticed during the demonstration and sought refuge in Flanders.[45]

---

[41] *autant de frappeurs de coignées, que de assommeurs de bœufs, ou vaches.* Jean-Juvénal, *Histoire*, 483. The Religieux, *Chronique*, vol. 5, 120–22, gives a similar, but much abbreviated version of the meeting.

[42] Jean-Juvénal, *Histoire*, 483–84.

[43] Beaune, *Journal*, 63–64. The Bourgeois makes the *cabochiens'* argument against trusting the princes appear reasonable, while the proponents of peace are a fanatical mob shouting "peace!"

[44] Jean-Juvénal, *Histoire*, 484–85.

[45] The Religieux, *Chronique*, vol. 5, 90, 128, states that the ladies had been previously released. This last group included the male prisoners, among whom Antoine des Essarts, who thus escaped execution. The Bourgeois, *Journal*, 64, is sarcastic about the liberation of the two dukes and

The story has a predictable epilogue. Berry was soon made captain of Paris, Bar of the Louvre, and Bavaria lieutenant of the Bastille (the very castles where they had been imprisoned), and other posts were doled out among Armagnac supporters.[46] Peace was proclaimed on August 6, preempting some half-hearted attempts of John at playing mediator between the parties. Seeing himself outmaneuvered, finally he quietly planned his own escape: during a hunt late in August, he quickly took leave of the king and raced homeward to Lille.[47] The princes reentered Paris in great pomp and reoccupied their various hotels. The royal council met to issue yet a new edict, reversing all previous ones, which (naturally) presented the Orléanists as the true supporters of legitimacy.[48] Useless to say, the *Ordonnance cabochienne* was repealed, and the city fell into a long period of brutal repression, which may explain the explosion of popular fury that accompanied its reoccupation by the Burgundians five years later in 1418.[49]

---

describes their triumphal progress beside the dauphin, "comme s'ils vinssent de faire le plus bel fait qu' homme pût faire en ce monde de sarrasinemie" (as if just returned from the most glorious enterprise against the Saracens). As for the flight of the *cabochiens*, Jean-Juvénal, *Histoire*, 485, states that his father ordered to leave the city gates open to let them go and thus avoid bloody reprisals.

[46] Beaune, *Journal*, 65–66. According to the version of Jean-Juvénal, *Histoire*, 485, his father took charge of the confused situation: it was he who advised the dauphin to replace the two pro-Burgundian *échevins* de Troyes and du Belloy with the loyal Guillaume Cirace and Gervaisot de Merilles, give the captaincy of Paris to Berry, take over the Bastille (with Bavaria as his second-in-command), make Bar captain of the Louvre, and Tanneguy du Chastel provost of Paris. The Religieux, *Chronique*, vol. 5, 130, inverts the roles of Bar and Bavaria.

[47] Jean-Juvénal, *Histoire*, 485–86, Beaune, *Journal*, 69. The Religieux, *Chronique*, vol. 5, 124–26, mentions that the duke had talked in secret with the *cabochiens* before their flight.

[48] For the full text see Additions in Monstrelet, *Chronique*, vol. 6, 113–23. Also Religieux, *Chronique*, vol. 5, 258–61.

[49] The hostility of the princes toward the city was well known: they had even refused to meet the king there during the peace talks, but were persuaded to relent by the king himself. They remained resentful, however, because previously Burgundy had been allowed to enter the city "in apparatu bellico" (in war gear) but they had to leave their arms behind. Religieux, *Chronique*, vol. 5, 82, 138–40. For the Burgundian reoccupation of 1418 and anti-Armagnac violence see Beaune, *Journal*, 110–20 and *Chronique Anonyme*, 258–60.

Fig. 3: John the Fearless

What to make of this abundant but ambiguous material? As mentioned before, contemporary narratives are rich in facts, and for the most part cogent when analyzing the behavior of the princely parties, such as the weak but well-meaning Berry, the impulsive dauphin, or the indignant Orléans. In particular, albeit without explicitly making this point, they seem to suggest through their narratives that this was a palace coup by other means rather than a spontaneous popular movement. The most obvious clue is that John the Fearless was constantly on scene, miraculously showing up at the climactic moment of various crises, and casting a presence that is generally more felt, it may be noted, than that of Caboche, who lent his name to the revolt. Thus he arrived in the nick of time at the Bastille to protect the royal fortress and convince des Essarts to surrender, falsely promising his protection; he was present during the two irruptions into the dauphin's apartments, where he played once again the part of mediator in convincing the prince to content the mob (and it may be recalled that the dauphin openly accused him of collusion with the invaders); and he quelled the altercation between de Jacqueville and La Tremoïlle.

Another noteworthy clue to his role is that each act of popular violence seems to have favored his plans, as it was immediately followed by measures against those hostile to himself or his favorites. For example, the Parisians turned "nunc nescio quo ducta spiritu" (inexplicably) in the Religieux's words, against des Essarts just after he fell from grace with the duke; the attack on the Bastille was led by some of his retainers notoriously hostile to des Essarts; and the second irruption into the dauphin's palace was followed by a replacement of his chancellor.[50] Further, only by attributing the initiative to John can we make sense of the "pedagogical" goals of the mob to replace the dauphin's entourage, a purpose that otherwise seem bizarre and useless in furthering the butchers' interests.

Not only that, but there is a noticeable fading of John from the scene once the opposition assumes the initiative: as his allies lose control of the game he becomes suddenly a diminished presence, if not a passive observer of events.[51] And lastly, an examination of the most concrete result of the revolt, the *Ordonnance cabochienne*, reveals exclusively concern with organization of the royal household and the general administration of justice, and not at all with civic privileges: not only is it formulated in terms of royal decree, but it also fails to mention the topics usually brought up in treaties between urban leaders and princely rulers, such as elective rights of guilds, use of civic banners, or limitation of powers for court officials.[52]

However, when it comes to the role and aims of the urban insurgents, whom the writers despise, they leave the reader quite in the dark. In particular, it is almost impossible from their accounts to pinpoint exactly who organized the insurrection and how close was the butchers' understanding with John the Fearless. After the revolt was over, it was easier to see what the powerful backing of Burgundy had brought about and the reaction taken away. The street chains, a sign of trust in the citizenry and a cherished measure for their safety, were locked away in the Bastille; the populace was disarmed to the point that even possession of a knife was deemed illegal, a measure that left them helpless; and the butchers lost their choice market place and were forced to wander from one location to the other to sell meat.[53]

---

[50] Religieux, *Chronique*, vol. 5, 6, 12, 34. Vaughan, *John the Fearless*, 186, also raises the hypothesis that the duke had influenced the redaction of the *Ordonnance cabochienne*, which reveals intimate knowledge of court finances.

[51] For example, he meekly reprimands Jean-Juvénal at the dramatic meeting of the royal council that votes for peace; he follows the dauphin to free the imprisoned dukes; and later he accompanies the dauphin and Berry to a meeting with the assembled University. Jean-Juvénal, *Histoire*, 484–85 and Religieux, *Chronique*, vol. 5, 132.

[52] Purely local topics dominate, for example, the demands of the Ghenters upon their new duke Charles the Bold in 1467. Georges Chastellain, *Chroniques. Œuvres*, ed. Kervyn de Lettenhove, 8 vols. (1863–1866; Geneva: Slatkine, 1971), vol. 5, VII: 271–78.

[53] This is precisely the list of privileges that the *cabochiens* claimed would be threatened if the city fell under the princes' yoke. Religieux, *Chronique*, vol. 5, 84. Guenée, *Un Meurtre*, 171, states that John the Fearless allowed the Parisians to put chains on streets, a privilege lost after the 1382 revolt. But after Burgundy left the city in August 1413 the new provost of Paris Tanneguy du Chastel was ordered by Berry and Orléans to remove all the chains at the road crossings in the city and lock them in the Bastille or the Louvre. According to Monstrelet, *Chronique*, vol. 2, 457–58, the citizens were "moult troublez et ennuyeux au cuer, quant ilz virent qu'on tenoit telles manières contre eulx. Et y en avoit plusieurs qui moult se repentoient de ce qu'ilz s'estoient mis en la

What is less clear is whether these privileges (except for the street chains that had been abolished since the previous century) were so threatened before the insurrection that the citizens were at risk of losing them, or whether they hoped to achieve some other goal beyond the retention of existing rights. Did they really think that the court was to be permanently a ward of the self-appointed rescuers? Did they believe that the duke wished to perpetuate a government "by the people"? The butchers and their followers apparently felt confident of the duke's tacit consent to their acts of violence, but to the reader some of those very acts appear as planned personal vendettas of individuals connected with rival parties at court.[54] Episodes like the altercation between the two chamberlains at the dauphin's ball illustrate a state of unchecked personal animosity among courtiers, with the *cabochien* guards playing the part of stooges for Duke John and his entourage, so that it is legitimate to question how much power the rebels actually did yield, and, more generally, who was in charge during the entire affair.

Here modern sociology may prove more helpful than medieval historiography, at least in identifying the mechanics of the movement. First, it can help find out what kind of people were the insurgents and offer some insight into their views. It appears that the participants in the brief insurrection, both *cabochien* and anti-*cabochien* (the presence of the latter illustrated by the dramatic exchange between de Troyes and Guillaume Cirace), were for the most part the precursors of the *sans-culottes* studied by George Rudé, workshop masters, craftsmen, wage-earners, shopkeepers, and petty traders, but not vagrants or criminals.[55]

---

subjeccion des adversaries du duc de Bourgongne, mais semblant n'en osoient faire" (quite upset and vexed when they saw how badly they were treated. And several amongst them regretted allowing themselves to fall under the adversaries of the duke of Burgundy, but did not dare show it). Other measures were: two city gates were immured and a new uniform was introduced consisting of a violet jacket bearing a white band with the slogan "le droit chemin" (the right way). Even children were roughed up if caught singing pro-Burgundian songs. Beaune, *Journal*, 68–70. For specific measures against the butchers see Beaune, *Journal*, 94–96. For the social significance of choice market places, see the contribution of Shennan Hutton, "Women, Men, and Markets: The Gendering of Market Space in Late Medieval Ghent," in this volume.

[54] The Religieux, *Chronique*, vol. 5, 16, states that they were "inducti"(led) by some (unnamed) powerful figure to invade the dauphin's apartment, and later, *in Chronique*, vol. 5, 46, he relates the butchers' confidence in the duke's tacit approval.

[55] George Rudé, *The Crowd in History* (New York: John Wiley & Sons, Inc., 1964), 199–205 and Rudé, *French Revolution*, 178. Rudé also notices the "sustained militancy" of members of certain trades: the most militant were the locksmiths, cabinet-makers, shoe-makers, and tailors. These were followed by stone-masons, hairdressers, and engravers, wine-merchants, water-carriers, porters, cooks, and domestic servants, while those employed in manufacturing (textiles, glass, tobacco, tapestries, porcelain) played a relatively minor part. Rudé, *French Revolution*, 185. Evidently, by the late eighteenth century butchers were no longer the instigators of revolts. Jean-Juvénal, *Histoire*, 477, makes a statement that seems to challenge the assumption that the criminal element was absent: "se mirent sus plus fort que devant meschantes gens, trippiers, bouchers, et escorcheurs, pelletiers, cousturiers, et autres pauvres gens de bas estat, qui faisoient de très-

This fact points to a remarkable consistency in the composition of revolutionary crowds, at least in France. As to their views, some of their actions (for example, respect for the dauphin even during the invasion of his apartment, or requesting the king's written pardon) reveal dramatically their helplessness vis-à-vis the monarchy, a finding that fits Eric Hobsbawm's classical portrait of pre-industrial metropolis, symbiotically tied to a court and looking upon its rulers as providers. In such an environment angry riots were endemic, in fact, the accepted language of political dialogue. This was facilitated by the proximity of the houses of the rich to those of the poor, a situation that instilled in the populace alternately a feeling of entitlement over the activities of the princely courts (for example, determining the dauphin's bedtime) and of betrayal when the latter showed themselves unresponsive to their needs.[56]

Fig. 4: Map of old Paris
The left arrow points to the approximate location of the hotel of Burgundy and the right arrow to the market of Les Halles

inhumaines, detestables, et deshonnestes besongnes" (some riff-raff rose higher than before, tripe-sellers, butchers, skinners, tanners, sewers, and other poor people of low condition, who committed inhuman, detestable, and illegal acts). But deprecatory comments about the poor are more likely a reflection of class prejudice than a definite indication of the presence of criminals among the insurgents.

[56] Eric J. Hobsbawm, *Primitive Rebels: a Study in Archaic Forms of Social Movement in the 19th and 20th Centuries* (New York: Norton, 1965), 114–15. For example, the hotel of Burgundy was close to the market of Les Halles, whence the derogatory anti-Burgundian expression "vous puez les harengs" (you stink of herrings) mentioned by Chastellain, *Chronique*, vol. 5, VI: 74.

The dependence upon the court was reflected in the very political structure of the city, as after the failed revolts of the fourteenth century its only municipality consisted of the provost, a royal appointee, while the council of four elected aldermen (*échevins*) had only recently been restored.[57] The Bourgeois diarist exemplifies this schizophrenic relationship: he repeatedly turns to the nobility to solve all problems, from law and order to the economy, and repeatedly lashes out in anger and spite at various princes who came and went without doing "any good" for the city, often referring contemptuously to their agents as "robbers" (*larrons*). Yet, even after blatant evidence of ineffectual government, he cannot help but partake in the general feeling of abandonment at the death of Charles VI, or lament the long periods of absence of Philip the Good of Burgundy, despite his low opinion of the new duke, and even display frustration whenever the English regent the duke of Bedford would leave town to reside in his own country.[58]

The attitude of the Bourgeois is intriguing also because of his ties to the University. Albeit sympathetic toward the mob, he attributes the initiative of the movement to his own institution, which he claims was animated by love for king and people.[59] Others share somewhat his belief but react to it in a different manner. For example the Religieux concurs in attributing to the University a central role in denouncing corruption at court and proposing reforms, but does so sarcastically, as he turns to the reader with a derisive aside and asks rhetorically how a gathering of scholars, removed from daily affairs, could presume to fix social problems.[60] In between the lines the reader may also detect a certain disunity

---

[57] Jean-Juvénal, *Histoire*, 445, is not sure whether the *échevinage* was restored in 1409 or later, but mentions no activity by the *échevins* prior to the revolt.

[58] He sprinkles the journal with numerous examples of his mixed feelings toward princes. For example, in *Journal*, 193, he has the city lament the beloved Charles VI with, "Maudite soit la mort! jamais n'aurons que guerre, puisque tu nous as laissés" (Damned be death! Now we will have nothing but war since you left us) and adds that the king has gone in peace and abandoned his subjects in grief like the children of Israel in Babylon. In *Journal*, 163, 375, he declares in frustration that royal visits only caused prices to increase, and as prices soared "ni roi, ni duc, ni comte, ni prévot, ni capitaine n'en tenait compte" (no king, duke, count, provost, or captain cared). In *Journal*, 228, 326, 332, he laments the long absence of Philip the Good and of the duke of Bedford, as if dead. In *Journal*, 362, 376, 405, he complains that Charles VII, after the reoccupation of the city "ne fit quelque bien" (did no good) for it, and that he came back in June 1441 "comme un homme étranger" (like a foreigner) to lodge with the dauphin near the castle Saint-Antoine (the same that had housed des Essarts) "comme s'ils eussent paour qu'on leur fît aucun grief, dont on n'avait talent, ni volonté" (as if fearing that someone would do them some harm, something for which they [the Parisians] had no means nor inclination).

[59] The University, "moult aimait le roi et le commun" (much loved king and people). Beaune, *Journal*, 56.

[60] *libricole et speculacioni dediti*. Religieux, *Chronique*, vol. 5, 4. In this he echoes the dismissive remark uttered by Louis of Orléans in 1405 that the University should not meddle in reforms of the kingdom but leave those to princes of the blood. Monstrelet, *Chronique*, vol.1, 122.

within the University ranks: as mentioned before, Jean-Juvénal suggests that Master de Pavilly was ready to harangue against the dauphin and justify the worst deeds of the *cabochiens* to fatten his own purse, a not-too-subtle hint that money was involved, while the Religieux affirms that its very chancellor Jean Gerson was punished for his opposition to the *cabochiens* by having his house ransacked. In general, during the entire episode the University acted less like a party to the action than like the modern-day media, that is, ostensibly limiting itself to an educated commentary on events, but in reality influencing their outcome through subtle intervention (for example, by denouncing certain actors but not others), and in so doing elicited ambiguous reactions from the authors. Throughout the revolt the University doctors shared with the populace a close interest in maintaining relations with the court, and the Religieux records their delight when, after the flight of the *cabochiens*, the dauphin paid them an unexpected visit to flatter that illustrious body.[61]

Paris was indeed exceptional in its obsessive dependence on a court, an attitude that is much less evident when examining the relations between other late-medieval urban communities and their princes. It is well known that the fifteenth century, like the preceding one, was rife with conflicts, riots, and open rebellions of the great cities of Flanders, in particular Ghent and Bruges, against the dukes of Burgundy and their successor Maximilian of Austria. The actions of their citizens during various confrontations included the creation (or restoration) of autochthonous civic institutions, the employ of a third party such as the king of France as mediator (as in the wars between Ghent and Philip the Good in 1451–1453), open defiance of ducal requests for subsidies and troops (witnessed by the testy exchanges between the Estates of Flanders and Philip's successor Charles the Bold), and even imprisonment of the duke and his servants (as the guilds of Bruges did with Maximilian, whose authority they considered illegitimate).[62] Notwithstanding the sentimental statements of Burgundian courtly

---

61  Religieux, *Chronique*, vol. 5, 30, 40, 132–36. At times, the University was sought after by the court precisely for its role in disseminating propaganda. For example, in 1411 it was asked to help the king's cause against the rebellious Armagnacs. On this occasion the University was instrumental in circulating a papal bull that excommunicated the rebels. Jean-Juvénal, *Histoire*, 465.

62  For an account of the revolt of Ghent, see Chastellain, vol. 2, III: 221–378. His subsequent statement, vol. 3, IV: 399–400, that Ghent was "broullant en amour" (burning with love) for Philip the Good after its defeat is belied by the insurgents' behavior and appears exaggerated even if he meant to apply it only to the upper bourgeoisie who had sided with the duke. See also Mathieu d'Escouchy, *Chronique*, ed. G. du Fresne de Beaucourt. 3 vols. (Paris: Jules Renouard, 1863), vol. 1, 368–423, 443–51, vol. 2, 1–27, 80–111. The revolt of Bruges against Maximilian is in Jean Molinet, *Chroniques*, ed. Georges Doutrepont and Omer Jodogne. 3 vols. (Brussels: Palais des académies, 1935–1937), vol. 2, I: 583–642. The difficult relationship between the Flemish cities and Charles the Bold is amply documented in L. P. Gachard, *Collection de documens inédits concernant l'histoire de la Belgique*. 3 vols. (Brussels: Louis Hauman et comp. libraires, 1833), 128–31, 172–74, 216–24, and

chroniclers like Chastellain, who only acknowledges the opinions of the upper bourgeoisie, Flemish cities appeared to perceive the Burgundian dukes as equal partners in a contract and, while tolerating their authority as counts of Flanders, always maintained consciousness of their own economic independence from the court, and in fact, of the dukes' very reliance on the revenues generated by them. An extreme example of this contractual attitude is an episode that took place in 1411 at the height of the civil war between John and the Orléanists, and that is recorded by both Monstrelet and the anonymous chronicler. Informed that the enemies were approaching his camp near Montdidier, John the Fearless was confident that battle could be engaged within a week, but the contract binding his urban Flemish troops was expiring and they started to decamp. He rode hastily out there, accompanied by his brother the duke of Brabant, to beg them hat in hand to delay their departure for a few days, but in answer they showed him the contract and threatened to cut into pieces his son (who resided in Ghent) if he did not abide by it. He had no choice but to let them go.[63]

Even London, which like Paris was a royal capital, yet enjoyed its own independent wealth being a commercial center in its own right, displayed a measured deference tinged with pride toward its sovereign. The Burgundian courtier and memoirist Olivier de la Marche illustrates this attitude in an episode that he witnessed while visiting London on behalf of his master Philip the Good in 1467. At a tournament hosted by King Edward IV, after the king and dignitaries had seated themselves, the mayor of London made his entry with his sword carried in front of him as a sign of authority. He quickly knelt to the king with the sword pointed downward out of respect, then just as quickly stood up and went to his seat with his sword still in front of him.[64] Unlike other northern cities, Paris (or at least a significant portion of its permanent residents) seems to have derived

---

especially 249–70.

A similar stance is conveyed by the anonymous Flemish text contained in *Flandria Generosa* that narrates the revolt of Bruges of 1436–1438 against Philip the Good. In it the dominant feeling is shame for the collective loss of honor when Ghent abandoned the duke at the siege of Calais of 1436, but also hostility between Bruges and Sluis caused by economic rivalry. Jan Dumolyn and Elodie Lecuppre-Desjardin, *Propagande et sensibilité: la fibre émotionnelle au cœur des luttes politiques et sociales dans les villes des anciens Pays-Bas bourguignons. L'exemple de la révolte brugeoise de 1436–1438*. Emotions in the Heart of the City (14th–16th century) ed. Elodie Lecuppre-Desjardin and Anne-Laure Van Bruaene (Turnhout, Belgium: Brepols, 2005), 44–53.

[63] Monstrelet, *Chronique*, vol. 2, 182–85, and *Chronique Anonyme*, 211.

[64] Olivier de La Marche, *Mémoires d'Olivier de la Marche*, ed. Henri Beaune et J. d'Arbaumont. 4 vols. (Paris: Librairie Renouard, 1883), vol. 3, I: 50–51. In another episode that took place in 1465 during the king's absence, the mayor of London appeared at a feast offered by the royal sergeants, but finding his place occupied left the room with all the city notables and held a rival banquet in his own home. William Gregory, "Chronicle of London," *The Historical Collection of a Citizen of London in the Fifteenth Century*, ed. James Gairdner (London: Camden Society, 1876), 142.

its self-image almost exclusively from the court, to the extent that its artisans regarded asserting control over court expenditures and daily routine as worthy enough a goal to risk an insurrection.

Another question not adequately satisfied by contemporary writers is what prompted the violent explosion. The topic of collective movements has interested sociologists since Emile Durkheim in the nineteenth century, and up to the 1960s the classical "strain and breakdown theory" dominated the field and was particularly popular with European theorists.[65] According to this view violent collective behavior is triggered by the breakdown of normal social routines. As it posits a pre-existing integrated society, this theory implicitly paints rebellion in negative colors as an anomaly, and places emphasis on its irrational, spontaneous, and unstructured nature. Neil Smelser, in his encyclopedic *Theory of Collective Behavior* (1962) offers a more structural version of breakdown theory. He adds other components that are necessary to precipitate collective action, such as the presence of (irrational) generalized beliefs among the crowd and structural strain that may be caused by conflicting directives from ossified or ineffectual authority. He also makes the important observation that the partial decay of normative order, rather than the unfairness of the norms themselves, causes the greatest likelihood of outbursts.[66] This concept applies very closely to fifteenth-century Paris, a city that since the closing of the previous century had felt heavily the normative strain caused by a weak but legitimate monarchy that left room for alternate, yet unsanctioned, sources of power.

A second and more recent paradigm, developed between the 1970s and 1980s, has attempted to replace breakdown theories with those of "resource mobilization," which view insurrections as part of the normal political process, thus marginalizing the role of causal strain in favor of the rationality and

---

[65] A discussion of various scholarly currents on this topic is found in Steven M. Buechler, *Social Strain, Structural Breakdown, Political Opportunity, and Collective Action,* Sociology Compass 2/3 (2008), 1031–44. My succinct overview is largely based on Buechler's article. For a more in-depth analysis of political opportunities that affect reform or revolutionary movements, see Doug McAdam, "Conceptual Origins, Current Problems, Future Directions," *Comparative Perspectives on Social Movements,* ed. Doug McAdam, John D. McCarthy, and Mayer N. Zald. Cambridge Studies in Comparative Politics (Cambridge and New York: Cambridge University Press, 1996), 23–40.

[66] The author cites several examples, the earliest being that of German society on the eve of the Reformation. His most interesting example of normative strain is taken from Tocqueville's characterization of the relations between peasants and aristocracy before the French Revolution. Tocqueville had noted that the greatest revolutionary fervor occurred in areas of the country in which the persistence of feudal taxes, dues, and other traditional obligations of the peasants coexisted with the simultaneous decline of the feudal responsibilities of the nobility. On the other hand, in areas where feudal institutions were still vital the revolutionary spirit was relatively weak. Neil J. Smelser, *Theory of Collective Behavior* (New York: The Free Press of Glencoe, 1963), 28, 59–61.

purposefulness of the rebellion, which they also dissociate from more ephemeral manifestations like crazes, panics, or fads. These newer theories are also significant to the present discussion because they claim that the perpetrators of collective violence seldom are uprooted and marginal elements of society, a finding that agrees with the point made earlier about the social composition of the Parisian crowd. In Steven Buechler's words, "this new perspective advocated a shift away from a deterministic collective behavior paradigm (with strain and breakdown as major determinants) to an agency-oriented resource mobilization paradigm in which actors' purposes, interests, and goals are foremost. The insistence that collective action was political foreclosed questions about the subjective states of participants and the role of strain."[67] The mobilization model also offers a basis for evaluating the behavior of the most unlikely partner in the revolt. Usually sociologists do not think of princes as leaders of insurrections, yet this revolt and its antecedents offer evidence of this possibility.[68] Just as in 1407 John had acted against the law by killing his rival to reach the goals that his defense of 1410 claimed to be legitimate, so now his servants joined and even organized a mob. The duke kept a certain distance from the action, but apparently he was not fooling anyone, nor was he trying very hard to do so. The sociologist Charles Tilly affirms that opportunity for violent action comes about when a contender for power makes other coalition members more vulnerable to his own claims.[69] John's actions provided the butchers with just such an opportunity, and everywhere his intervention deflected, at least in part, the emotional and spontaneous revolt to redirect it toward his own "more rational calculus of costs and benefits."[70]

Since the 1990s, however, strain theories have staged a comeback and have been co-opted into a new syncretism that recognizes the value of opportunity and organization in collective movements, while still acknowledging the fact that they

---

[67] Buechler, *Social Strain*, 1035.
[68] Donald M. Taylor and Fathali M. Moghaddam come close to acknowledging this. They observe that it is possible for collective action of a disadvantaged group to be led by "disenchanted members of the advantaged group," for example, modern revolutionary leaders such as Mao, Gandhi, and Castro. Donald M. Taylor, Fathali M. Moghaddam, *Theories of Intergroup Relations*, 2nd ed. (1987; Westport, CT, and London: Praeger Publishers, 1994), 155.
[69] Charles Tilly, *From Mobilization to Revolution* (Reading, MA: Addison-Wesley, 1978), 141. Also cited in Buechler, *Social Strain*, 1039. Sidney Tarrow, *Power in Movement*, 2, links social strain to opportunity in similar terms: "contentions politics occurs when ordinary people, often in league with more influential citizens, join forces in confrontation with elites [It] is triggered when changing political opportunities and constraints create incentives for social actors who lack resources of their own.."
[70] Buechler, *Social Strain*, 1040.

are triggered by anomalies and decay within the existing system.[71] For example, David Snow and others have located social decay and its link to rebellions in the disruption of everyday life with its "routinized expectations" caused by accidents that create "suddenly imposed grievances," such as "intrusions or violations of community space, [...] changes in taken-for-granted subsistence routines, and [...] dramatic changes in structures of social control." They add that for collective action to occur the "disruption must be experienced collectively, and it must not have a normal, institutional resolution."

While these authors do not invoke late medieval models, some of their examples of disruptions find parallels in the present context, for example in the removal of the street chains. True to the new syncretism, they also note that the breakdown of everyday routines does not preclude the existence of solidarity between individuals; in fact, the combination of the two is most likely to produce a collective movement (and here we may acknowledge the contribution of guild structure to the organization of the revolt).[72]

In general, the new theories concede Smelser's point that normative strain alone is not sufficient to cause an outburst, and that what is needed is also the belief that established ways of relieving the strain are not available, thus severely limiting "the actor's opportunities and limitation of the environment, and the actor's ability to influence the same."[73] Thus the *cabochien* movement, brewing in an ambiguous atmosphere of decaying power, needed a contingency to be set in motion: the intolerable fiscal situation brought about by a combination of high taxes and out-of-control expenditures that failed to provide any benefits to the taxpayers, a situation that lent credibility to conspiracy theories. Finally, the frustration spilled over in 1407 with the murder of Orléans, and by 1413 had affected a wider public,

---

[71]    For example, Jack Goldstone has posited that the breakdown of the state is caused by a combination of popular distress and alienation and infighting of the elite (both evident in the *cabochien* case). Jack A. Goldstone, *Revolution and Rebellion in the Early Modern World* (Berkeley: University of California Press, 1991), 10. Also cited in Buechler, *Social Strain*, 1036. And Frances Fox Piven and Richard A. Cloward *have recently formulated a defense of breakdown theories by affirming that "malintegration" of hierarchical social structures is critical to collective movements. They also de-emphasize the necessity of a network (a cornerstone of mobilization theory) by claiming that all that is needed for an insurgency to occur is a collective perception of injustice: even previously unconnected people will then participate. Frances Fox Piven, and Richard A. Cloward, "Normalizing Collective Protest," Frontiers in Social Movement Theory*, ed. Aldon Morris and Carol McClurgMueller (New Haven, CT: Yale University Press,1992), 310.

[72]    David Snow, Daniel M. Cress, Liam Downey and Andrew W. Jones, "Disrupting the 'Quotidian': Reconceptualizing the Relationship between Breakdown and the Emergence of Collective Action," *Mobilization* 3 (1998): 8, 17–19. Also cited in Buechler, *Social Strain*, 1037–38.

[73]    Smelser, *Collective Behavior*, 28.

458 Lia B. Ross

namely the guild of wealthy but hitherto politically marginal butchers and also the University.[74]

The two (no longer so diverging) paradigms on the nature of insurrections are reflected in the versions of the *cabochien* revolt that came to us from two different groups of writers. Those (more numerous) who represented royal authority viewed social control in a positive light and the rebels as deviants, much like modern social breakdown theorists; while the opposite is true of the Bourgeois, who in fact attributed the initiative for action to his beloved University, a fitting example of organizational resource to the aid of mobilization. Bringing together both views, we could say that the state breakdown was precipitated by the king's madness in the absence of sanctioned alternatives to royal authority, which opened the door to rivalry amongst the princes, and in turn reflected institutional weakness on a populace exceptionally attuned to courtly affairs and whose well-established guild system provided an adequate network for mobilization.

Motivational analysis helps also in deciphering what is perhaps the most puzzling aspect of the insurrection, the strong bond between butchers and duke. For John the revolt of 1413 could well be the realization of his dreams of 1405 and the vindication of his rash action of 1407. This prince, who had his own reasons for dissatisfaction, as he saw himself unjustly (in his view) alienated from his peers after murdering his rival, now leaned on a population that had almost no indigenous power structure and assumed its informal leadership. His improbable but inspirational direction of the movement reflects Rudé's findings that the crowd may create a "hero" outside the rebels' social environment and who becomes almost reluctantly a symbol of their cause.[75] And for his part, John certainly helped his heroic standing among Parisians with his unusual habit of

---

[74] The ambiguous perception of butchers in late-medieval writings is intriguing. For example, Elisabeth von Nassau-Saarbrücken (after 1393–1456), who translated into German prose the fourteenth-century French poem *Hugues Capet*, presented (like her source) the founder of the Capetian dynasty as the grandson of a vile butcher, who ascended to power thanks to a less-than-exemplary behavior that put him on a level with the nobility: dueling, warfare, murder and seductions. Was the writer mindful of the 1413 *cabochien* revolt? Elisabeth von Nassau-Saarbrücken, *Hug Schapler*. Volksbücher vom sterbenden Rittertum, Heinz Kindermann ed., Entwicklungsreihen, Reihe: Volks-und Schwankbücher, 1 (Weimar and Leipzig: Böhlau, 1928), 23–114; Albrecht Classen, "Elisabeth von Nassau-Saarbrücken," *German Writers of the Renaissance and Reformation: 1280–1580*, ed. James Hardin and Max Reinhart. Dictionary of Literary Biography, 179 (Detroit, Washington, DC, and London: Gale Research, 1997), 42–47. See also the contributions to *Zwischen Deutschland und Frankreich: Elisabeth von Lothringen, Gräfin von Nassau-Saarbrücken*, ed. Wolfgang Haubrichs and Hans-Walter Herrmann, together with Gerhard Sauder. Veröffentlichungen der Kommission für Saarländische Landesgeschichte und Volksforschung e. V. (St. Ingbert: Röhrig Universitätsverlag, 2002)

[75] Rudé, *Crowd in History*, 247–48 and *French Revolution*, 199.

paying for supplies and keeping his troops from pillaging.[76] To our eyes the unexpected alliance between urban commoners and an alienated member of the upper nobility appears one of convenience, with the duke aiming at ruling the court, the butchers at keeping local control, and the poor at fiscal relief.[77]

Still, contemporary sources seem to challenge this skeptical assumption. For example, the *Livre des trahisons* paints the bond between John and the Parisian butchers in strong personal terms. In its version of the previously-mentioned episode in which John was abandoned by his Flemish troops, the anonymous author states that the duke's adversaries took the occasion to spread the rumor that he had been routed. The duke hastened to send a reassuring letter to his supporters in Paris: his messenger reached the butcher Guillaume Legoix and one of his sons on the day before an anti-Burgundian rally had been convoked by the authorities. In this account the butcher hugs the duke's messenger addressing him as "my friend," then tearfully kisses the letter and places it reverently inside his jacket. His son in turn proposes to read the letter aloud to the assembly on the following day, in order to unmask the false Orléanist report, and declares himself ready to die fighting for "droit et justice" (right and justice).[78] This grandiloquent declaration seems to suggest a life-and-death struggle of opposing ideologies, and sits oddly with a civil war that originated from a personal rivalry between two princes, even if one of the two was unpopular. It is possible, however, that some alienated princes could feel kinship with artisans, who, like them, were also trying to hang on to threatened rights.

This paradoxical identification may also explain why John the Fearless and his successor Philip the Good assumed "working class" tools as their personal devices, respectively the plane and the flint. In support of this hypothesis, Jean-Juvénal mentions that in 1411 John the Fearless had attended the extravagant funeral of the butcher Thomas Legoix, and that when the writer's father met with the duke on behalf of the Burgundian nobility to try to convince him to abandon his unseemly

[76] Beaune, *Journal*, 29, 34. Religieux, *Chronique*, vol. 5, 332–34.
[77] Having so far avoided the term "class" as anachronistic, the issue of how to label the butchers in contemporary society is far from easy. Nicholas, *Medieval City*, 123 refers to them as "solidly middle class," and the *Livre des trahisons*, 106–07, quotes a Legoix as stating that, "nous avons une grande partie de la ville de Paris en nostre gouvernement, et sy avons moult grand plenté de riches et puissans parens" (we rule a large part of the city of Paris, and are well endowed with wealth and powerful relatives). But all chroniclers refer to them as "vile." Probably the assumption closest to the truth is that of Colette Beaune, *Journal*, 63, note no. 53, who states that they enjoyed wealth but resented not having the social status that went with it.
[78] *Livre des trahisons*, 106–08. The episode, minus the sentimental outpourings is confirmed by Jean-Juvénal, *Histoire*, 463.

alliance with butchers, the latter categorically refused.[79] While the leadership of urban revolts was at times assumed by local nobles (like the lord of Heers in Liège in the 1460s or the count of Montfoort in Utrecht in the 1480s), identification of an urban insurgency with a member of the royal family was rare. But this pattern did reemerge in other revolts (for example that of Jack Cade in England in 1450) and therefore we cannot exclude some underlying commonality of motives, if not outright ideological affinity.[80]

The third issue that is inadequately addressed by medieval authors is how did the insurgents select the victims of their anger and what did they hope to achieve by attacking them. What seems clear is that whatever the understanding between duke and butchers, the targets of their violence, both during the *cabochien* revolt and in the earlier murder of Orléans, were quite specific, and pursued only when both Parisian commoners and the powerful but outcast prince saw other avenues for redress against them blocked.[81] The weak but unchallenged authority of the king, flanked by his favorites, precluded any other means for rectifying perceived injustices, a pattern that will be repeated in the Wars of the Roses in England a generation later. Smelser observers that:

> The closing of means of protest is always relative to existing expectations. For example, if nobles who previously had had close access to a king in his deliberations are suddenly excluded from his councils, this constitutes a closing of avenues of protest relative to their expectations. On an absolute basis, however, they may still have greater influence than other groups in the population, e.g., peasants. Because the latter do not entertain such expectations, however, their sense of exclusion is not so great.[82]

---

[79]  Jean-Juvénal, *Histoire*, 468, 476–77. The alliance apparently left even his supporters uneasy. For example, *Le Pastoralet*, 18–19, only obliquely hints at the episode by mentioning in allegorical terms the triumphal entry of Léonet (John) into Paris welcomed by the shepherds (the citizens, with no reference to the butchers as a separate group). Then Léonet is advised of a mysterious treason and leaves the gathering immediately for his own pastures.

[80]  For the rebellion of Liège, see de la Marche, *Mémoires*, vol. 1, I: 125–29, Chastellain, *Chronique*, vol. 5, VI: 217, VII: 423–32, and Philippe de Commynes, *Mémoires*, ed. Joseph Calmette (Paris: Société d'édition "les Belles lettres", 1965), II: 441–57. For that of Utrecht, see Thomas Basin, *Histoire de Louis XI*, trans. and ed. Charles Samaran and M.C. Garand. 3 vols. Les classiques de l'histoire de France au Moyen Age, 26–27, 30 (Paris: Les Belles Lettres, 1963–1972), vol. 3, VI: 127–217, VII: 237–81. For a discussion of Jack Cade's rebellion and its possible link to Yorkist politics, see John Gillingham, *The Wars of the Roses* (Baton Rouge: Louisiana State University Press, 1981), 67–68, and P.A. Johnson, *Duke Richard of York 1411–1460*. Oxford Historical Monographs (Oxford: Clarendon Press; New York: Oxford University Press, 1988), 79. The role of butchers could be even closer than ideological affinity.

[81]  As posited by the "resource mobilization" theory that defends the rationality of rioters. For this point see Buechler, *Social Strain*, 1034 and Rudé, *Crowd in History*, 253. For a similar view but from a medievalist's perspective, see Steven Justice, *Writing and Rebellion: England in 1381* (Berkeley: University of California Press, 1994).

[82]  Smelser, *Collective Behavior*, 334.

This statement, which refers to more recent history, is quite applicable to a late-medieval prince such as John the Fearless, and from contemporary narrative it is not difficult to conclude that both commoners and disaffected lords resented successful courtiers and royal agents (such as Montaigu, des Essarts, and the dauphin's chancellor), and judged their authority illegitimate and odious.[83] In 1409 the scapegoat for popular fury had been Montaigu, and in 1413 des Essarts, whose secretive return to the city with the complicity of the court and ominous residence in a fortress initiated the unstoppable chain reaction.[84]

However, as events unfolded, this purpose became blurred, as, to quote again Smelser, collective behavior "involves generalization to a high-level component of action." Attacks on specific scapegoats lost their immediate vengeful nature, and the insurgents might even have forsaken their true interests in the name of "higher goals." Apparently the rebels' grievance, that initially seems to have stemmed from the purely contingent and material motivation of the return of the disgraced provost, in the course of riots became elevated to a higher and more generalized one of reforming the court by ridding it of "traitors," and in so doing colluded with John's interests.[85]

As for their specific goals, it appears that the *cabochien* revolt, like other late-medieval protests and riots, aimed at the preservation of past rights, not at the addition of new ones or at changes in political structure. It seems to fit somewhere between the spontaneous "food riots" described by Rudé and what Smelser calls "norm-oriented movements," which are set off by events that threaten the existing normative order (a new tax imposed by outsiders, a limitation of civic autonomies, an alien magistracy).[86] Neither the citizens nor their leaders envisioned themselves as revolutionists, but as guardians of established norms based on a pre-existing contract between themselves and their lord, which was threatened from the

---

[83] The dauphin's reinstated chancellor Jean de Nieles had angered the rebels by roughly refusing some of their requests. Religieux, *Chronique*, vol. 5, 50.

[84] For the phenomenon of "scapegoating" in hostile outbursts, see Smelser, *Collective Behavior*, 101, 250–51.

[85] Smelser, *Collective Behavior*, 71. Tilly, *Mobilization*, 14, makes a similar observation in arguing against Marx's interpretation of the 1848 French Revolution..

[86] Rudé, *Crowd in History*, 4. To avoid possible confusion, it may be necessary to emphasize the difference between "normative movement" and "norm-oriented movement." Piven and Cloward, "Collective Protest," 306, apply the first term to legally-sanctioned collective mobilization, such as electoral rallies. They specify that "norms change over time [. . . Forms of collective action impermissible in one period may be permissible in another, or the reverse. [. . .] normative collective actions occur much more frequently than nonnormative" ones in modern periods with the spreading of political rights. Smelser, *Collective Behavior*, 109, 120, 284–88, applies the second to the *goals* of the collective movement, and distinguishes normative goals from those (for example) of a value-based revolution, which aims at modification of base concepts related to man's place in nature.

outside, and that they tried to restore through the *Ordonnance cabochienne*.[87] Jacques Lemaire in his vast work on political and social literature of the period *Les visions de la vie de cour*, places this revolt in the same context of spontaneous popular movements as its fourteenth-century precursors, mere outbursts against fiscal oppression, and not proper bourgeois revolutions with a program of changing the political landscape. In his view, intellectuals had not yet developed a concept of class and so they could and would not yet influence insurrections.[88] While this is certainly true, I would not discount the possibility that a medieval civic group could be sensitive to normative principles; in fact, it is evidenced by the bizarre relationship that developed during *cabochien* rule between royal family and mob. While the former (except, perhaps, the king) was horror-struck at the forced familiarity, the latter stepped exuberantly into the role of protectors of their rulers against the "traitors," and therefore as the ultimate repository of legitimacy, a situation familiar to students of the French Revolution.

In conclusion, the little-known *cabochien* revolt of 1413 that came in the wake of anti-government rumblings and of the shocking murder of the duke of Orléans, has so far defied interpretation thanks to its dual nature, part spontaneous urban uprising and part princely coup. Its ambiguous reputation has been (perhaps unwittingly) helped by its very chroniclers who on the one hand have overwhelmed the reader with the irrational violence of the Parisian crowd through episodes that ominously anticipate accounts of a later revolution (the gathering of the crowd at the Bastille, the irruption on the palace, the self-righteous mob rule over the court's daily life as barriers between public space and princely living quarters were broken), and on the other hand have suggested the ever-lurking presence of princely rivalries in the background, as John exploited popular furor to effectuate a purge of his rivals.

Still, this event has the potential to go beyond a well-documented mystery. Despite its tortuous unfolding and the ambiguities generated by the social difference of its perpetrators, the revolt shares basic characteristics with more recent and better understood insurrections, in particular as to crowd composition and behavior. And as such it offers an intriguing glimpse into the mechanics of late-medieval collective movements, inter-class relationships, and urban self-perception.

---

[87]   The crowd could even believe that the king, a father figure, was so concerned about justice that riots would be led in his name. Rudé, *Crowd in History*, 228–31.

[88]   Jacques Lemaire, *Les Visions*, 287.

Fabian Alfie

(University of Arizona)

# "The Merchants of My Florence": A Socio-Political Complaint from 1457[1]

Although Benedetto Croce characterized the period between 1375 and 1475 with the popular designation as the "century without poetry," it is probably better to describe it as the "century of Burchiello."[2] In Florence the figure who predominated the literature of the early fifteenth century is the poet-barber of the Calimala district, Domenico di Giovanni, nicknamed il Burchiello (b. ca. 1390–1400; d. ca. 1448). Burchiello enjoyed great fame at the time, inspiring ranks of imitators of his bizarre nonsensical style. His renown was not limited to the *literati*; despite Burchiello's anti-Medici stance, Cosimo's son Giovanni so appreciated his work that he invited the poet to entertain him at the sulfur baths at Pietrolo.[3] The author of numerous lyrics, Burchiello was thoroughly immersed in the comic-realistic verse of Tuscany of the *Duecento* and *Trecento*.[4] He was knowledgeable of the poetry by such writers as Franco Sacchetti, Orcagna, and Pieraccio Tedaldi,[5] and went so far as to rewrite a sonnet by Cecco Angiolieri.[6]

---

[1]   I would like to acknowledge the receipt of a Small Grant from the Office of the Vice President for Research and Graduate Studies at the University of Arizona, which allowed me to study on site the manuscripts at the Biblioteca Nazionale Centrale of Florence in March 2004.

[2]   Emilio Pasquini, "Il 'secolo senza poesia' e il crocevia di Burchiello," *Le botteghe della poesia: studi sul Tre-Quattrocento italiano* (Bologna: Il Mulino, 1991), 25–86; here 35.

[3]   Christopher Hibbert, *The House of Medici: Its Rise and Fall* (New York: Perennial Press, 1980), 95.

[4]   Antonio Piromalli, "Aspetti della cultura e della poesia giocosa in Toscana nel Quattrocento," *Dal Quattrocento al Novecento: Saggi critici*, Biblioteca dell' "Archivium Romanicum," vol. 76 (Florence: Olschki, 1965), 1–10; here 4.

[5]   Achille Tartaro, "Burchiello, dell'immaginazione grottesca," *Il manifesto di Guittone e altri studi fra Due e Quattrocento* (Rome: Bulzoni, 1974), 139–53; here 143–44.

[6]   For analysis of Burchiello's rewriting of Angiolieri's sonnet, see Fabian Alfie, "'I' son sì magro che quasi traluco': Inspiration and Indebtedness among Cecco Angiolieri, Meo dei Tolomei and Il Burchiello," *Italian Quarterly* 35 (1998): 5–28.

Thanks to his popularity at the time, Burchiello may have been responsible for a reawakening of interest in comic poetry during the early *Quattrocento.*[7]

Fortunately, scholars have investigated more thoroughly the poetry of the early fifteenth century in the decades since Croce passed his severe pronouncement.[8] Nevertheless, much of the poetry of that period remains unpublished and unstudied. There are, of course, many reasons for such a critical oversight, but one factor is that it is highly municipal in nature. That is, rather than dealing with universal topics, it frequently addresses the specific political, social and cultural concerns of the day in the city of its author. Nowhere is that more evident than in the sonnet which shall form the focus of this study, an unedited anonymous complaint against the merchants of Florence. I will analyze the sonnet in the light of its philological information, as well as its historical context.

As is well known, the complaint against the merchants was a common topos of the period throughout all of Europe.[9] Yet it would be mistaken to read satiric texts as mere literary exercises devoid of real-world historical importance. Rather, they illustrate the internal tensions of the cities caused by the economic boom of the Renaissance. Although the development of Italian cities followed its own unique trajectory, certain constants are found among the European writers of the late Middle Ages and early modern period. Alongside the numerous urban encomia poets expressed rather strong ambivalence toward the growth of the cities and the ascendency of the merchant classes. The wealth generated by trade brought with it social changes that are reflected in such artifacts as the anonymous sonnet below. Commerce enriched the city, it is true to say, but it also ennobled non-aristocratic individuals. This is not to read the socio-economic changes strictly through the lens of class conflict, or as a group of insiders resentful of upwardly mobile newcomers; instead, economic success often depended on attitudes antithetical to those of the stereotypical medieval aristocracy still prevalent in early Renaissance society. In short, while this sonnet is indicative of the society of

---

[7]   Renee Watkins, "Il Burchiello (1404–1448). Poverty, Politics, and Poetry," *Italian Quarterly* 14 (1970): 21–57; here 22.

[8]   See, for instance, Antonio Lanza, *Polemiche e berte letterarie nella Firenze del primo quattrocento* (Rome: Bulzoni, 1972); and *Lirici toscani del quattrocento*, ed., Antonio Lanza, 2 vols. (Roma: Bulzoni, 1973–75).

[9]   Mario Marti emphasized the pan-European nature of medieval satiric poetry; see Mario Marti, "Europeismo dell'antica letteratura giocosa" *Cultura e stile nei poeti giocosi del tempo di Dante* (Pisa: Nistri-Lischi, 1953), 1–40. For examples of the anti-mercantile topos in German, see Heinrich der Teichner. For analyses of Heinrich's satires, see Albrecht Classen, "Heinrich der Teichner: The Didactic Poet as a Troublemaker, Whistle-Blower, and Social Rebel," *Medievalia et Humanistica* 32 (2007): 63–81; and id., "Heinrich der Teichner: Commentator and Critic of the Worlds of the Court and the Aristocracy," *Orbis Litterarum* 63. 3 (2008): 237–61. See also his comments on the treatment of merchants in medieval discourse in the introduction to this volume.

Florence in the 1450s, it has implications for understanding the development of the cities throughout the continent.

Perhaps the most important edition of Burchiello's works was published in 1757 in Lucca (although the title-page says London).[10] Until very recently, despite its occasional drawbacks it formed the basis for the critical editions of Burchiello's works.[11] In the third section of the 1757 edition, a portion of the volume dedicated to the sonnets of dubious attribution, appears an invective against the Florentine merchants (186–87).[12]

---

[10] Burchiello, *Sonetti del Burchiello, del Bellincioni e d'altri poeti fiorentini alla burchiellesca* ( Londra [but actually Lucca]: n.p., 1757).

[11] In 2000, Michelangelo Zaccarello published the most recent critical edition of Burchiello, and based it not on the London 1757 volume, but on the numerous extant fifteenth-century manuscripts. See *I sonetti del Burchiello*, ed., Michelangelo Zaccarello (Bologna: Commissione per i testi di lingua, 2000). For an example of an earlier edition of Burchiello's works based upon the 1757 edition, see *Burchiello: I sonetti*, ed., Alberto Viviani (Milan: Bietti, 1940).

[12] The version published in 1757 reads as follows (186–87): "I mercatanti della mia Fiorenza / Son fatti trecchi, cuochi, e calzolai, / Panattieri, Vinattieri, e Mugnai, / Così Cristo ne spenga la semenza. / Proprio del Lupo è la lor coscienza, / Che l'altrui stiman poco, e 'l loro assai, / E 'l merito che danno a' mercennai / Per pagamento, abbiate pazienza. / Oh Dio, come sostien tu tanto male? / Ov'è la tua potenza, il tuo furore? / Ha la giustizia tua sì rotte l'ale? / Porgi le orecchie all'orfaneo languore, / Vedi la crudeltà quanto l'assale? / Morta c'è la tua fede, ed ogni amore. / Adunque, o buon Signore, / Fa piover al terrestre tanti morbi / Che la lor sepoltura sieno i corbi."

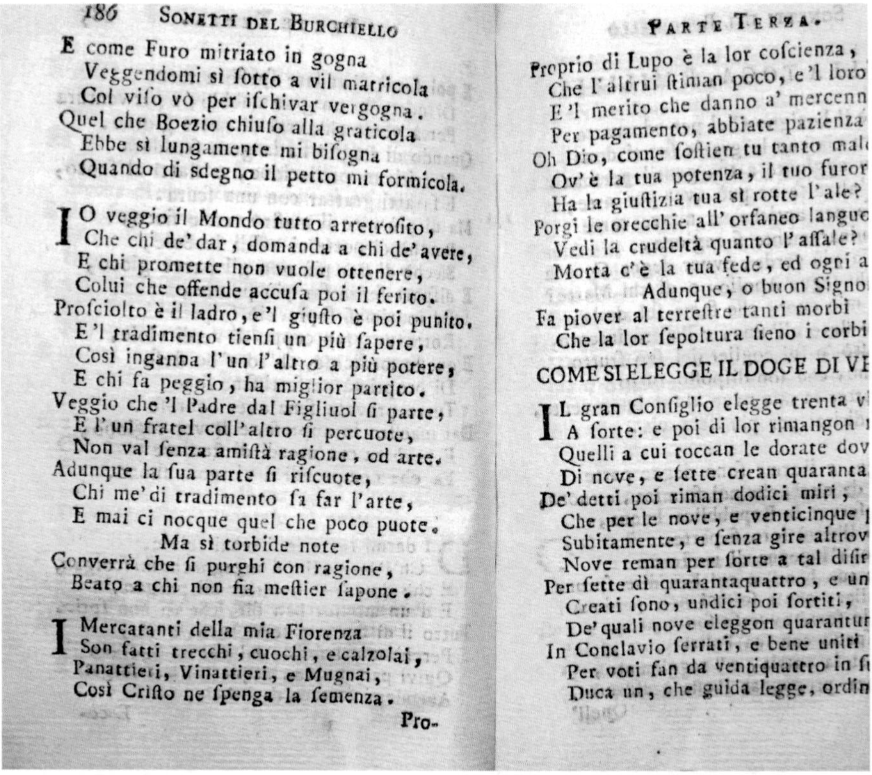

*186*  SONETTI DEL BURCHIELLO

E come Furo mitriato in gogna
  Veggendomi sì fotto a vil matricola
  Col vifo vò per ifchivar vergogna.
Quel che Boezio chiufo alla graticola
  Ebbe sì lungamente mi bifogna
  Quando di sdegno il petto mi formicola.

IO veggio il Mondo tutto arretrofito,
  Che chi de' dar, domanda a chi de' avere,
E chi promette non vuole ottenere,
Colui che offende accufa poi il ferito.
Profciolto è il ladro, e 'l giufto è poi punito.
  E 'l tradimento tienfi un più fapere,
  Così inganna l'un l'altro a più potere,
  E chi fa peggio, ha miglior partito.
Veggio che 'l Padre dal Figliuol fi parte,
  E l'un fratel coll'altro fi percuote,
Non val fenza amiftà ragione, od arte.
Adunque la fua parte fi rifcuote,
  Chi me' di tradimento fa far l'arte,
  E mai ci nocque quel che poco puote.
    Ma sì torbide note
Converrà che fi purghi con ragione,
Beato a chi non fia meftier fapone.

I Mercatanti della mia Fiorenza
  Son fatti trecchi, cuochi, e calzolai,
Panattieri, Vinattieri, e Mugnai,
Così Crifto ne fpenga la femenza.
                                    Pro-

PARTE TERZA.

Proprio di Lupo è la lor cofcienza,
  Che l'altrui ftiman poco, e 'l loro
E 'l merito che danno a' mercenn
Per pagamento, abbiate pazienza
Oh Dio, come foftien tu tanto mali
Ov' è la tua potenza, il tuo furor
Ha la giuftizia tua sì rotte l'ale?
Porgi le orecchie all'orfaneo langue
Vedi la crudeltà quanto l'affale?
Morta c'è la tua fede, ed ogni a
                    Adunque, o buon Signo
Fa piover al terreftre tanti morbi
Che la lor fepoltura fieno i corbi

COME SI ELEGGE IL DOGE DI VE

IL gran Configlio elegge trenta v
  A forte: e poi di lor rimangon
Quelli a cui toccan le dorate dov
Di nove, e fette crean quaranta
De' detti poi riman dodici miri,
  Che per le nove, e venticinque
Subitamente, e fenza gire altrov
Nove reman per forte a tal difir
Per fette dì quarantaquattro, e un
Creati fono, undici poi fortiti,
De' quali nove eleggon quarantur
In Conclavio ferrati, e bene uniti
Per voti fan da ventiquattro in fi
Duca un, che guida legge, ordin

Figure 1: Burchiello 1757 edition

Because of its inclusion in the London volume, other subsequent editors of Burchiello also accepted the tirade as possibly authentic. Given the state of the information at the time, the view of the sonnet as possibly Burchiello's is not unreasonable; after all, Burchiello capitalized on his real-world role as a barber in his verse, giving voice to the class of urban laborers and craftsmen.[13] The extremely scant criticism of the satiric sonnet consists of commentaries on it in relationship to Burchiello's literary corpus. In 1949 Eugenio Giovannetti described it as an imprecation against the Florentine merchants ("imprecando ai mercanti fiorentini") and in 1972 Antonio Lanza categorized it as an example of the "gnomic

---

[13]    Antonio Toscano, "Il polisenso della parola nel Burchiello," *Forum Italicum* 10 (1976): 360–76; here 312.

[i.e., sententious] genre" ("di genere gnomico").[14] However, according to the *Incipitario unificato della poesia italiana,* a research tool that lists the incipit verses of all the known Italian manuscripts, two fifteenth-century codices also carry the sonnet.[15] Those codices have not been consulted in relationship to the sonnet. Unlike the 1757 edition, the manuscripts provide important information about its author and the date of its composition. They also supply data to interpret the sonnet in a manner more subtly than has been previously published.

The two codices in question, Firenze II iv 250 (FI) and Magliabechiano VII 1168 (MG), are both housed in the Biblioteca Nazionale Centrale of Florence. The former manuscript (FI) was transcribed in the fifteenth century, while the latter (MG) was compiled in the sixteenth; both are compendia of the poetry of Burchiello and the *burchiellisti.*[16] The rubrics of the two manuscripts are similar to one another. The ascription in FI reads diplomatically: "Sonetto si dicie aver fatto un battjlana co(n)tro a ma paghamenti fa(n)no oggi j merchatanti delle loro manj fature 1457" ("Sonnet said to have been made by a wool-beater against evil payments. Today the merchants make the receipts themselves with their own hands, 1457"). The rubric in MG appears to be a simplification the attribution of FI: "S$^{to}$ fatto p(er) j battilana di fire(n)ze" ("Sonnet made by a wool-beater of Florence"). More shall be said below about the attributions and their impact on the interpretation of the sonnet. For now suffice it to say that both codices ascribe it to an anonymous wool worker, and the earlier manuscript dates it to 1457, roughly a decade after Burchiello's death. The sonnet, then, probably does not belong to the poet-barber, but to one of his many imitators.

---

[14] *Antologia burchiellesca,* ed., Eugenio Giovannetti (Rome: Colombo, 1949), 205; and Antonio Lanza, *Polemiche e berte letterarie nella Firenze del primo quattrocento* (Rome: Bulzoni, 1972), 211. It should also be noted that simply situating the sonnet into Burchiello's corpus comprises a type of critical commentary on it; see, for instance, Alberto Viviani, ed., *Burchiello: I sonetti* (Milan: Bietti, 1940), 278; and Eugenio Giovannetti, *Antologia burchiellesca* (Rome: Colombo, 1949), 142.

[15] The incipit verse of the sonnet in question is listed in *Incipitario unificato della poesia italiana,* ed. Marco Santagata. Vol. 1 (Modena: Edizioni Panini, 1988), 738.

[16] For codicological information about Firenze II iv 250, see Giuseppe Mazzatinti, *Inventari dei manoscritti delle biblioteche d'Italia,* vol. 10 (Forlì: Casa Editrice Luigi Bordandini, 1900), 165–91. For codicological information about Magliabechiano VII 1168, see Domenico de Robertis, "Censimento dei manoscritti di rime di Dante, I," *Studi danteschi* 37 (1960): 141–273; here 218–19.

Before continuing, the textual form of the sonnet should be established. Happily, the two manuscript versions do not differ greatly from one another,[17] nor from that published in the 1757 edition of Burchiello's verse (BU).

---

[17]    The version of the sonnet in FI reads diplomatically as follows (f. 194r): "E merchatanti della mia fiorenza / son fatti chuochi treche et chalzolai / panattierj vinattieri et mugnai / chosj xpo ne spengha la semenza / propio dellupo e la loro choscienza / chellaltruj stima(n) pocho elloro assai / et merito che da(n)no a mercienai / p(er) paghamento abjate pazienza / o dio chome sostientu ta(n)to male / ove la tua potenza et tuo furore / a la giustizia tua si rotte lale / porgi gli orechi allor fanco languore / vedj la crudelta qua(n)tella sale / morta e la fede tua et ogngj amore / (et) dunque o buo(n) signore / fa piovere atterrestra tanti morbj / chella loro sepoltura sjano j chorbj." The version of the sonnet in MG reads diplomatically as follows: "E mercatanti della mia fiorenza / son facti chuochi trecche e calzolaj / panattierj uinattierj e mugniaj / cosj xpo ne spengha la semenza / Propio del lupo e la loro coscienza / che laltruj stiman poco elloro assaj / el merito che danno amerciennaj / p(er) pagamento abbiate pacienza / O dio come sostienj tutanto male / oue la tua potenzia el tuo furore / ala giustizia tua si rotte lale / Porgi li orecchj allor franco langore / uedj la crudelta quantella sale / morta e la fede tua e ognj amore / Adunque o buon signiore / fa piouere alla terresta tanti morbj / chellalor sepoltura sieno e corbj." For comparison with the version in BU, see note 9.

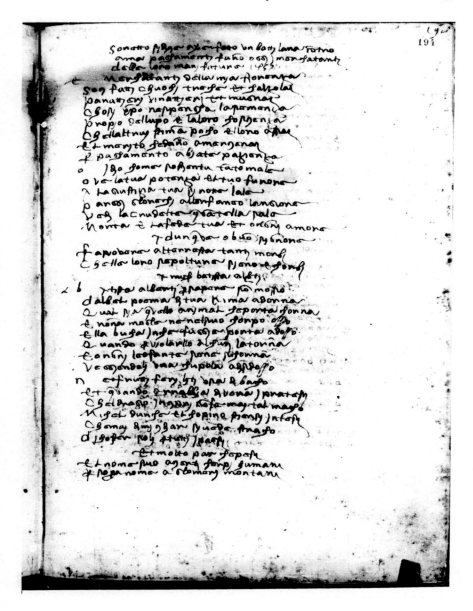

Figure 2: Firenze II iv 250 (f. 194r)

For the sake of simplicity, the variations of the three versions will be compared in the chart below; the items in bold indicate similarities between two of the three versions:

| MG | FI | BU |
|---|---|---|
| v. 1: **E mercatanti** | E mercatanti | I mercatanti |
| v. 2: **trecche** | treche | trecchi |
| v. 2: **chuochi trecche** | **chuochi treche** | trecchi, cuochi |
| v. 5: **Propio** | **propio** | Proprio |
| v. 9: sostienj tu | sostientu | **sostien tu** |
| v. 12: **li orecchi** | **gli orechi** | le orecchie |
| v. 12: allor franco | allor fanco | all' orfaneo |
| v. 13: **ella sale** | **ella sale** | l'assale |

Most of the traits held in common between FI and MG are preferable to those in BU. In fifteenth-century Florentine, the masculine plural definite article was commonly rendered as "e", "trecca" was a feminine noun, and "propio" was typically spelled without a second "r."[18] Furthermore, "assale" ("assaults" or "assails") in the thirteenth verse of BU depends upon the interpretation of the twelfth; more shall be said below about the *lectio* in BU for that line. Leaving aside the differences in spelling, which are typical for handwritten materials of this time (e.g., treche / trecche, gli orecchi / li orechi), most of the characteristics demonstrate the derivation of MG from FI.

At the same time, there are also indications of the relationship of BU to the handwritten codices. The one key similarity between FI and the BU occurs in verse nine ("sostientu"; "sostien tu"); the complete form of the verb in MG results in a hypermetric verse ("sostienj tu"). Yet the difficulty appears in verse twelve, where all three sources differ ("allor franco"; "allor fanco"; "all'orfaneo"). In terms of denotation, the reading that makes the most sense appears in BU. In it the wool-beater asks God to look at the weakness of orphans; in the following verse in BU, the author seemingly asks the reader to see how the merchants' cruelty assaults the disadvantaged. The problem is that the lexeme of BU's verse twelve,

---

[18] Regarding the fifteenth-century definite article as "e," see Bruno Migliorini, *Storia della lingua italiana* (Florence: Sansoni, 1963), 288. Regarding the lexeme "trecca," see *Vocabolario degli Accademici della Crusca*, vol. 6 (Verona: Dalla stamperìa di Dionigi Ramanzini, 1806), 530. Regarding the lexeme "propio," see *Vocabolario degli Accademici della Crusca*, vol. 5 (Verona: Dalla stamperìa di Dionigi Ramanzini, 1806), 233.

"orfaneo," apparently an adjective related to "orfano," is unattested anywhere else in the Italian language.[19] So too the term in FI, "fanco," means nothing.[20] Of the three versions, only "franco" in MG represents a genuine Italian lexeme; sadly, "franco" ("frank") makes little sense in the greater context of the verse. Yet the problematic verse also suggests the relationships between the three versions. Perhaps the scribes of FI, or those of its sources, garbled another term into "fanco." The scribes of MI and BU attempted to correct "fanco" into more recognizable words.[21] Put simply, along with the variations in the other lines, the twelfth verse demonstrates that MG and BU are both derived, whether directly or indirectly, from FI.

Having thus established FI as the best version, the sonnet can now be presented. In the *lectio* that follows, I have retained most of the spellings from FI. I have merely added punctuation and separated words where appropriate. The sonnet reads:

Sonetto si dicie aver fatto un battjlana contro a ma' paghamenti. Fanno oggi j merchatanti delle loro manj fature, 1457

> E merchatanti della mia Fiorenza
> son fatti chuochi, treche, et chalzolai,
> panattierj, vinattieri et mugnai:
> chosj Cristo ne spengha la semenza!
> Propio del lupo è la loro choscienza
> che 'll'altruj stiman pocho e 'l loro assai,
> et merito che danno a' mercienai
> per paghamento—abjate pazienza!
>     O Dio, chome sostien tu tanto male?
> Ov'è la tua potenza et tuo furore?
> À la giustizia tua sì rotte l'ale?
> Porgi gli orechi allor fanco [sic] languore:
> vedj la crudeltà quant'ella sale:
> morta è la fede tua et ogngj amore
>     et dunque, o buon Signore,

---

19   See the *Lessico Universale Italiano*, vol. 15 (Rome: Istituto della Enciclopedia Italiana, 1975), 450. See also the *Vocabolario degli Accademici della Crusca*, vol. 4 (Verona: Dalla stamperìa di Dionigi Ramanzini, 1806), 332. No such term as "orfaneo" appears therein.

20   See the *Lessico Universale Italiano*, vol. 7 (Rome: Istituto della Enciclopedia Italiana, 1975), 458. See also the *Vocabolario degli Accademici della Crusca*, vol. 3 (Verona: Dalla stamperìa di Dionigi Ramanzini, 1806), 72. No such term as "fanco" appears therein.

21   I will not conjecture as to what the original term might have been. Given the similarity between "f" and "s" in the fifteenth-century hand, was it perhaps "stanco" ("tired")? Or was it perhaps an odd spelling for "fango" ("mud")? The problem is, like "franco," "stanco" and "fango" make little sense in the context of the verse.

fa piovere a ·tterrestra tanti morbj
che ·lla loro sepoltura sjano j chorbj.

[Sonnet said to have been made by a wool-beater against evil payments. Today the merchants make the receipts themselves with their own hands, 1457

The merchants of my Florence
are made from cooks, peddlers, and cobblers,
bakers, vintners and millers:
thus may Christ extinguish their seed!
Their conscience is like the wolves',
for they value the property of others very little, their
          own property much;
and the interest they give to mercenary people[22]
as payment—have patience!
    Oh God, how do You endure such evil?
Where is Your power and Your fury?
Does Your justice have broken wings?
Turn Your ears to [allor fanco] weakness;
see how much their cruelty increases;
faith in You is dead, as is all love.
    Therefore, oh Good Lord,
make so many plagues rain on this Earth
that crows will be their tombs!]

Before beginning the analysis of the sonnet, comment should first be made about the purported author of the work. Traditionally, Florence's wealth derived from the wool industry,[23] although the economy had certainly diversified by the fifteenth century. Still, the wool workers were legally considered among the lowest ranks of the urban population, even though economically speaking a number of them had attained a level on a par with other shopkeepers.[24] In addition, in 1457 the mention of a wool-beater certainly evoked memories of the popular uprising of the Florentine "ciompi" in 1378. At that time, the wool-workers, along with the other laborers, revolted in response to their poor wages and the abuses of the

[22] In Renaissance Italian, "mercennaio" meant "mercenary" in its etymological sense as a person who behaves immorally in pursuit of money. It did not mean "mercenary" as in a soldier-of-hire. See *Vocabolario degli Accademici della Crusca*, vol. 4 (Verona: Dalla stamperìa di Dionigi Ramanzini, 1806), 167. The English adjective "mercenary" can mean the former, but in order to distinguish it from the latter denotation I rendered the verse as "the mercenary people."

[23] Ernesto Sestan, "Il comune fiorentino nel Duecento," *Italia medievale* (Naples: Edizioni scientifiche italiane 1968), 224–49; here 227. See also the contribution to this volume by Lia B. Ross.

[24] Gene A. Brucker, "The Ciompi Revolution," *Florentine Studies: Politics and Society in Renaissance Florence*, ed. Nicolai Rubinstein (London: Faber and Faber, 1968), 314–56; here, 319. For urban revolts in the late Middle Ages, see also Lia R. Ross's contribution to this volume.

magnates.[25] Salvestro de' Medici, ancestor to Cosimo, exploited the situation of the 1370s to challenge the oligarchy in the city government, and the eventual failure of the "ciompi" regime led to his political demise; for decades thereafter, the name of the Medici was associated with the party of the people.[26] Assuming the ascription is not pseudonymous, the wool-beater, like the poet-barber Burchiello, foregrounds his social class as a common urban laborer.

Whatever the biographical status of the sonnet's author might have been, he or she clearly possessed knowledge of Florentine literature. After all, the two manuscripts are dedicated to the poetry of the *burchiellisti*, a group to which the wool-beater belonged. In keeping with the sonnet's derisive subject matter, the poet employs a recognizably satiric style. The author creates a harsh sound in the sonnet, emphasizing voiceless stops (e.g., *chuochi, treche, et chalzolai,"* 2), and geminate consonants (e.g., "pana*tt*ierj, vina*tt*ieri et mu*gn*ai," 3). The wool-beater constructs consonantal rhymes (A: -E*NZA*, E: -O*RBI*) and a complex vocalic B-rhyme (-AI). These are all phonological traits that diminish the melodiousness of the verses. Furthermore, in the sonnet's quatrains the writer oscillates between traditional hendecasyllable (1, 4, 5, 8) and a truncated ten-syllabic verse (2, 3, 6, 7). The poet, therefore, understood the expectations of fifteenth-century derogatory verse and composed the lyric accordingly.

The subject matter too demonstrates the author's knowledge of Italian poetry. The sonnet is based upon a traditional literary topos, the complaint against the merchants. In Italy and throughout Europe, as the Middle Ages came to a close, the traditional negative stereotypes of the third estate now fell upon the mercantile classes.[27] For example, the thirteenth-century Sienese poet Bindo Bonichi satirizes

---

[25] For other overviews of the revolt of the "Ciompi," see Gene A. Brucker, "The Demise of the Regime," *Florentine Politics and Society 1343–1378* (Princeton: Princeton University Press, 1962), 336–96; Gene Brucker, "Corporate Values and the Aristocratic Ethos of Trecento Florence," *The Civic World of Early Renaissance Florence* (Princeton: Princeton University Press, 1977), 14–59; and Samuel K. Cohn Jr., trans. "The Revolt of the Ciompi, 1378–1382," *Popular Protest in Late Medieval Europe: Italy, France, and Flanders,* selected, trans. and annotated id. Manchester Medieval Sources Series (Manchester and New York: Manchester University Press, 2004), 201–60.

[26] Gene A. Brucker, "The Demise of the Regime," *Florentine Politics and Society 1348–1378* (Princeton: Princeton University Press, 1962), 363–64; see also Christopher Hibbert, *The House of Medici: Its Rise and Fall* (1974; New York: Perennial Press, 1980), 31.

[27] For an Italian perspective, see Philip Jones, *The Italian City-State: From Commune to Signoria* (Oxford and New York: Clarendon Press, 1997), 325. For a broader European perspective, see Johan Huizinga, *The Autumn of the Middle Ages,* trans., Rodney J. Payton and Ulrich Mammitzsch (1919; Chicago: University of Chicago Press, 1996), 63–64. One example of the traditional slander of the third estate—in this case, the peasantry—is the poem *De natura rusticorum,* found in the sixteenth-century codex Marciano I, 66. One stanza of the poem suffices to illustrate the denigration of the peasants: "Rusticani sunt fallaces,/ sunt immundi, sunt mendaces,/ et in cunctis contumaces/ et in vitiis pertinaces:/ adsit his penuria!" ( 56–60). The poem *De natura rusticorum* is cited from Francesco Novati, *Carmina Medii Aevii* (Florence: alla Libreria Dante, 1883). Carmelo Previtera also

the merchants in his sonnets, in one instance claiming that the asses of the world are themselves traders ("Gli asin del mondo sono i mercatanti").[28] Perhaps the most famous author of Italy to upbraid the merchants was Dante, who considered them as peasant upstarts in a refined urban environment (e.g., *Inferno* XVI, 73–75). Clearly, the wool-beater treats the fifteenth-century traders in a similar manner in the opening quatrain of the poem.

The author updates the literary trope to an urban environment, equating the vendors not with the rural peasantry but with the manual laborers of the city. Indeed, the sonneteer does not proclaim that they are *equivalent* to the workers, but instead that they *are* enriched laborers ( 2–3). In this respect, the wool-beater makes a historically accurate statement. For centuries Florence was dominated by the wealthy urban merchants, many of whom were of non-noble status, but they co-mingled with the aristocracy and took on the trappings of nobility.[29] Increasingly, this mixed mercantile class was the driving force behind the historical and cultural developments.[30] Hence, the lyric comments on the socio-cultural evolution of the Republic.

Furthermore, it is possible that the poem can be interpreted politically. Cosimo de' Medici, whose own non-noble origins were well known and who in the 1450s reached a low-point in his influence, championed the non-nobility, at least as a political tactic. He obliterated the distinction between *grandi* and *popolani*, essentially making everyone *popolani*, thereby restoring the rights of citizenship to the *grandi*; and then made all *popolani* dependent on his patronage.[31] And, of course, the term "battilana" evoked memories of Cosimo's ancestor, Salvestro, and his involvement with the "Ciompi" revolt. In other words, the sonnet may have been read at the time as derisive of specific political actors in Florence. Yet if that was the intention of the wool-beater, the sonnet shows almost no textual traces directly connecting it to the Medici, nor to any other powerful non-noble family of the age.

The poet closes the first quatrain by calling on God to extinguish the mercantile families (4), thus anticipating the violent language of the final verses. In the process, the wool-beater injects into the sonnet an element of the ideology of nobility. The discourse of lineage ("semenza") recalls the bloodlines of the ancient

---

describes the vituperation of the peasant entitled "Detto del Villano." See Carmelo Previtera, "Primordi di poesia giocosa," *La poesia giocosa e l'umorismo*. Storia dei generi letterari italiani, 1 (Milan: Vallardi, 1939), 97–141; here 133.

[28] Bindo Bonichi is cited from Bindo Bonichi, *Rime di Bindo Bonichi da Siena edite ed inedite*, ed., Francesco Zambrini (Bologna: Commissione per i testi di lingua, 1977).

[29] Philip Jones, *The Italian City-State: From Commune to Signoria* (Oxford: Clarendon Press, 1997), 318.

[30] Luisa Avellini, "Metafora 'regressiva' e degradazione comica nei sonetti del Burchiello," *Lingua e stile* 8 (1973): 291–319; here 292.

[31] K. Dorothea Ewart, *Cosimo de' Medici* (1899; Port Washington NY: Kennikat Press, 1970), 141–42.

families and therefore ties in with the literary tradition of anti-mercantile complaints. Typically, the writers who decried the upstart merchants were themselves aristocrats, upset that the ignoble traders were usurping their role and power in the society. In the second quatrain, the poet elaborates on this perspective by enumerating the merchants' moral failings. Rapacious like wolves, they are greedy and disrespectful of others ( 5–6). They charge interest, which they give to other avaricious individuals (7–8). In the eighth verse, he uses the term "mercenary" ("mercenai"), which indicated a person motivated only by base monetary considerations. Unlike the cities of Northern Europe, which have been described as islands of non-feudalism in a sea of feudalism, the communes of Italy developed around the urban nobility; therefore they were steeped in the mentality of the medieval aristocracy.[32] Physical labor, trade, greed, and the lending at interest were all values considered antithetical to the ethos of nobility.[33] The poet recollects the aristocratic ideology to cast the powerful sellers now in charge of Florence as unworthy of their rank and status.

In the sextet, the "battilana" changes direction, moving from a third-person characterization of the merchants to a second-person discourse with God. The poet asks how He can endure their cruelty (9), and invokes the Lord's justice upon them (10–11). In the second tercet, the writer creates a parallel, calling upon God first to hear of their iniquity, and then to see Himself how their cruelty ever increases (12–13). The poet's statement in the thirteenth line that God should turn His ears to the merchants' failings—this is, it will be recalled, the unresolved verse—may be based upon a proverbial statement at the time. The expression "the merchant's ear" ("far orecchio di mercatante") meant to feign not hearing something.[34] It appears that God needs not to give "the merchant's ear" to the socio-economic situation in Florence, according to the author.

The sonneteer constructs the poem's sextet around intertextual references to other literary diatribes. The poet opens the tercets by recollecting Dante's *Commedia*. In *Paradiso* 21, the blessed soul of Peter Damiani decries the excesses of modern-day prelates, whose sumptuous clothing requires four attendants when they ride. Damiani then proclaims: "oh paz¨ienza che tanto sostieni!" ("O patience, what a heavy load you bear!").[35] Verses seven and eight of the anonymous sonnet

---

[32] Philip Jones, "Economia e società nell'Italia medievale: la leggenda della borghesia," *Storia d'Italia: Annali*, vol. 1, *Dal feudalismo al capitalismo*, ed., Giulio Einaudi (Turin: Einaudi, 1978), 185–372; here 197.

[33] Philip Jones, *The Italian City-State: From Commune to Signoria*, 199–200.

[34] *Vocabolario degli Accademici della Crusca*, vol. 4 (Verona: Dalla stamperìa di Dionigi Ramanzini, 1806) 331.

[35] Dante's *Paradiso* and its translation are cited from *Paradiso*, ed. and trans. Robert and Jean Hollander (New York: Doubleday, 2008). Dante's *Purgatorio* and its translation are cited from Robert M. Durling, ed. and trans., *The Divine Comedy of Dante Alighieri*, vol. 2, *Purgatorio* (Oxford:

echo Dante's work rather closely: "abjate pazienza! / O Dio, chome sostien tu tanto male?" Interestingly, the wool-beater also includes another allusion to Dante's great work in the two tercets. The sonneteer evokes Dante's invective in the sixth canto of *Purgatorio* by requesting that God turn His ears to the situation. In that passage Dante decries the political situation in Italy; specifically, he condemns the Emperor's disregard for the peninsula, which has resulted in civic strife throughout the communes. At a key instance, Dante writes:

> E se licito m'è, o sommo Giove
> che fosti in tera per noi crucifisso,
> son li giusti occhi tuoir rivolti altrove?
> O è preparazione che ne l'abisso
> del tuo consiglio fai per alcun bene
> in tutto de l'accorger scisso?                                    (118–23)

[And if it is permitted me, O highest Jove, who were crucified on earth for us, are your just eyes turned elsewhere? Or, is it a preparation that in the abyss of your counsel you are making, for some good utterly severed from our perception?]

Like Dante, the author of the sonnet wonders about God's apparent lack of interest in the current terrible situation, as if His attention were directed elsewhere. But the wool-beater calls on God to hear, rather than see, the depraved conditions.

The tercets close with the statement that all faith in God and love of neighbors has died (14). The last verse of the sextet evokes another traditional topos of Tuscan comic verse, that of decrying the corrupted social order. Based upon the older trope of *contemptus mundi*, early fourteenth-century poets such as Folgòre da San Gimignano, Pieraccio Tedaldi, and Dante complained about the loss of noble values, the destruction of Christian virtue, and the rejection of agape as a result of the flourishing economies.[36] Indeed, the wool-beater seems to echo deliberately the incipit verse of another example of that commonplace, Cecco Angiolieri's "Egli è sì poco di fede e d'amore" ("There is so little faith and love"). The *burchiellista* adapts the traditional lament to his dialogue with God, proclaiming that faith in

---

Oxford University Press, 2003).

[36] See Folgòre da San Gimignano's sonnet "Cortesia cortesia cortesia chiamo" in which he writes: "Avarizia le gente ha prese a l'amo / ed ogne grazia distrugge e confonde" ("The people have taken the bait of avarice, and it destroys and confuses all grace," 391). See also Pieraccio Tedaldi's sonnet "El mondo vile è oggi a tal condotto." In *Purgatorio*, Dante similarly writes: "Lo mondo è ben così tutto diserto / d'ogne virtute come tu mi sone, / e di malizia gravido e coverto" ("The world is surely barren of every virtue as you say, pregnant with malice and covered with it," XVI, 58–60). Folgòre, Pieraccio, and Cecco Angiolieri are cited from Mario Marti, ed., *Poeti giocosi del tempo di Dante* (Milan: Rizzoli, 1956); the translations of those three poets are mine. Of course, statements about the degeneration brought about by mercantile activities are not limited to Italian poets, but again are found in social critiques throughout Europe.

Him has died ("la fede *tua*"). As before, the poet demonstrates awareness of the Florentine literary tradition and composes the sonnet in line with it.

In keeping with the fifteenth-century practices of insulting poetry, the wool-beater attaches a three-verse *coda* to the end of the sonnet. In it, the writer begs God to send plagues to Earth so that the bellies of crows might serve as the merchants' cemeteries (15–17). The violent language of the *coda* itself recollects another, unexpected aspect of the literary tradition. To be sure, violent language does occur in satiric poetry of the Italian Middle Ages and Renaissance,[37] but it is typically not found in political[38] or social harangues.[39] Such violent language is absent from most anti-merchant or anti-peasant diatribes. It sometimes shows up in insulting verse of an interpersonal nature, but again it is uncommon.[40]

---

[37] See, for instance, Dante's *Inferno* XXV ( 10–12), in which the poet asks why the city of Pistoia does not immolate itself out of shame of the actions of Vanni Fucci; see also *Inferno* XXXIII ( 79–81), in which he calls on the mountains of Capraia and Gorgona to block the mouth of the Arno and thereby flood Pisa for its treatment of Count Ugolino's sons. The violent language appears related primarily to the misdeeds of the respective communes' citizens, and only marginally to a social or political agenda.

[38] For an example of such violent language in a political invective, see the anonymous fourteenth-century sonnet "Nati di pescatori, o gente bretta." Written after Venice did not assist Florence in her war against Mastino II della Scala of 1338—assistance Venice had promised in a treaty—the sonnet proclaims: "Io ti fare' parer la mosca un baco / e de la carne tua fare' tonnina / e del tuo propio sangue un largo laco" ("I would make the fly seem like a worm, and I would make a salami of your flesh, and a large lake of your blood," 12–14). "Nati di pescatori, o gente bretta" is cited from Giuseppe Corsi, ed., *Rimatori del Trecento* (Torino: UTET, 1969), 936–37; the translation of "Nati di pescatori, o gente bretta" is mine.

[39] For examples of violent language in social satires, see two sonnets by the fifteenth-century poet Francesco Scambrilla. In a complaint against the ill-living thieves and gamblers of the Sant'Ambrogio neighborhood, "Chi vuol di ladroncelli una chiassata," he hopes that the political authorities will execute them all: "Rettor, fate pensieri, / po' che vivono al mondo come diavoli, / di farne una piantata come cavoli!" ("Rectors, give thought—since they live like devils in the world—to plant them in the ground like cabbages!" 15–17). In another sonnet, "O teste bugie, o mercennai sciocchi," which decries numerous categories of evil-doers, Francesco expresses his hopes that they will be destroyed: "Così fussi voi strutti, / come per voi s'aspetta!" ("Thus were you destroyed as you deserve," 15–16). Similarly, in the sonnet, "O triunfal Fiorenza, fatten bella," Antonio di Meglio anticipates Florence's destruction of her political enemies: "e' tuoi inimici stermina e dirupa" ("exterminate and root out your enemies," 12). Francesco Scambrilla and Antonio di Meglio are cited from Antonio Lanza, ed., *Lirici toscani del quattrocento*, vol. 2 (Roma: Bulzoni, 1975); the translations are mine.

[40] For exceptions to this, see Cecco Angiolieri's "Io non vi miro perzar, morditori," in which he writes: "ma 'l me' ch' i' ho e che miglior mi pare, / si è 'l veder di vo' che ciascun muore" ("but the best that I can have, and the best that seems to me is that of seeing that all of you die," 12–13). In the fifteenth century, see Niccolò Cieco's sonnet "O ignorante plebe, o turba stolta," a complaint against gossips, in which the poet writes: "quando la bocca per mal dire aprite /vi sie la lingua della strozza tolta" ("but when you open you mouth to speak ill, may your tongue be cut out," 7–8).

Yet it is extremely common in a particular topos of invective, *vituperatio vetulae* or the derision of the stereotyped old woman.[41] A few examples will suffice to demonstrate the connection. In one of the earliest instances of the trope, the thirteenth-century Bolognese poet Guido Guinizzelli hopes that a whirlwind will carry the old woman off, or that heaven will strike her down, and then concludes that the vultures will not devour her because her flesh is too tough.[42] The fourteenth-century Florentine author Franco Sacchetti portrays a battle between the beautiful ladies and the ugly old women of Florence; as the young women triumph, he describes the carrion-eaters picking over the remains of the defeated.[43]

In the fifteenth century, Rosello Roselli seems to rewrite Guinizzelli's sonnet, again calling on heaven to rain misfortunes on the old woman's head.[44] And Burchiello himself opens a sonnet by proclaiming: "May fire burn you, smelly old woman!"[45] Like the poets of *vituperatio vetulae*, the wool-beater not only prays on God to destroy the cause of indignation, but to utterly obliterate them and scatter their remains into the bellies of scavengers. By linking aggressiveness to the

---

[41]   The topos of *vituperatio vetulae* is itself a long-standing trope found throughout Europe and not just in Italy. For an overview of the tradition, see *Woman Defamed and Woman Defended: An Anthology of Medieval Texts*, ed., Alcuin Blamires (Oxford: Oxford University Press, 1992). For representative analyses of the tradition, particularly as it relates to the vernacular literatures, see Gretchen Mieszkowski, "Old Age and Medieval Misogyny: The Old Woman," *Old Age in the Middle Ages and the Renaissance: Interdisciplinary Approaches to a Neglected Topos*, ed., Albrecht Classen. Fundamentals of Medieval and Early Modern Culture, 2 (Berlin and New York: De Gruyter, 2007), 299–319; and id., *Medieval Go-Betweens and Chaucer's Pandarus* (New York: Palgrave MacMillan, 2006); Karent Pratt, "*De vetula*: The Figure of the Old Woman in Medieval French Literature," *Old Age in the Middle Ages and the Renaissance*, 321–42; see also Simonetta Mazzoni Peruzzi, *Medioevo francese nel "Corbaccio"* (Florence: Le lettere, 2001).

[42]   See Guido Guinizzelli, "Volvol te levi, vecchia ra<b>bïosa." Cited from Guido Guinizzelli, *Rime*, ed., Luciano Rossi (Turin: Einaudi, 2002).

[43]   See Franco Sacchetti, *La battaglia delle belle donne di Firenze*, ed. Sara Esposito (Rome: Zauli editore, 1996). The particular language used by Sacchetti is worth reading. He describes the scene at the end of the battle: "Non truovan [le belle donne] più le spade che ferire, / ed è la terra piena di carogne; / quivi molti moscon' si fan sentire, / nibbi, cornacchie, corvi e gran' cicogne: / chi con budella fugge, a non mentire, / chi li lor membri portan per le fogne; / i teschi e l'ossa i lupi divoraro, / le mosche il sangue tutto consumaro" ("The beautiful women cannot find more swords to strike them, and the earth is full of carrion; here, many flies are heard, as well as buzzards, ravens, crows and great storks. Some flee with guts, to tell the truth, others carry off their members to the pits; the wolves devoured their skulls and bones and the flies consumed all their blood," IV, 44, 1–8; the translation is mine).

[44]   See Rosello Roselli, who writes: "Piovi dal cielo una crudel tempesta / sopra di te [...] O giustizia di Dio, vòltati un poco / in ver costei" ("May a cruel storm rain down upon you out of the sky... O Divine Justice, turn a little towards her," 1–2, 9–10; the translation is mine). Rosello Roselli is cited from *Lirici toscani del quattrocento*, ed., Antonio Lanza, vol. 2 (Rome: Bulzoni, 1975).

[45]   Burchiello writes: "Ardati il fuoco, vecchia puzzolente" ( 1). Burchiello is cited from *I sonetti del Burchiello*, ed., Michelangelo Zaccarello. Collezione di opere inedite o rare, 155 (Bologna: Commissione per i testi di lingua, 2000).

discussion of carrion-eaters, the echo of *vituperatio vetulae* is unmistakable. The "battilana" seemingly transposes the violent poetic language from the insult of the old woman to the socio-political denigration of the Florentine merchants.

Analysis of *vituperatio vetulae* reveals more fully the wool-beater's intentions. Recently, Patrizia Bettella charted the history of the insulting motif, and illustrated that in the thirteenth century it was primarily employed as a *dissuasio amoris*, while in the fourteenth the poets portrayed the old woman as the repository of vice.[46] The authors who decried the old woman did not merely engage in an empty literary exercise, but employed the trope as a means to reprehend sin. Since the wool-beater represents the Florentine merchants as similarly corrupt, the recollection of *vituperatio vetulae* is not unmotivated. Nor is the "battilana" the first poet to conflate the abuse of the old woman with a socio-political message. The great lyric poet, Francis Petrarch, in the first of his three complaints against the Papal Court in Avignon, personifies the city as the Whore of Babylon, writing: "May fire from Heaven rain down on your tresses, wicked one."[47] In short, by 1457, the *vituperatio vetulae* trope did not express a univocal denotation, but could be used to convey multiple meanings. The wool-beater simply co-opts some of its vocabulary in composing the socio-political satire.

To conclude, if the poet of this sonnet was truly a wool-beater, he or she also possessed intimate knowledge of Florentine literature of the fourteenth and fifteenth centuries. The poem recollects other, more noted examples of derogatory verse such as Dante, Cecco Angiolieri, and the authors of the *vituperatio vetulae* topos. We should also not forget the importance of invective among erudite humanistic writers as well.[48] But we should be careful not to interpret the sonnet

---

[46] Patrizia Bettella, *The Ugly Woman: Transgressive Aesthetic Models in Italian Poetry from the Middle Ages to the Baroque*. Toronto Italian Studies (Toronto, Buffalo, and London: University of Toronto Press, 2005), 17–66.

[47] Petrarch writes: "Fiamma dal Ciel su le tue treccie piova." As an aside comment, I cannot but help to see a similarity between Petrarch's incipit verse and Guinizzelli's sonnet. Yet scholarship has yet to associate the anti-Avignon invective with the *vituperatio vetulae* topos. Rather Gianfranco Contini writes that Petrarch refused or ignored the lessons of the realistic tradition ("egli rifiuta o piuttosto ignora la tradizione detta realistica"); and Paolo Trovato elaborates on Contini, claiming that the comic tradition is far from Petrarch's intentions and sensibilities ("il comico allo stato puro ripugna alle intenzioni e alle sensibilità petrarchesche"). See Gianfranco Contini, "Preliminari sulla lingua di Petrarca," *Varianti e altra linguistica. Una raccolta di saggi (1938–1968)* (Turin: Einaudi, 1970), 169–92; here 178. See also Paolo Trovato, *Dante in Petrarca. Per un inventario dei dantismi nei "Rerum vulgarium fragmenta."* Biblioteca dell'Archivium Romanicum: Serie 1, Storia, Letteratura, Paleografia, 149 (Florence: L. S. Olschki, 1979), 13. Petrarch's verse and translation are both cited from Robert M. Durling, trans. and ed., *Petrarch's Lyric Poems: The Rime Sparse and Other Lyrics* (Cambridge, MA, and London: Harvard University Press, 1996).

[48] For a general overview of invectives among the humanists, see Ennio I. Rao, *Curmudgeons in High Dudgeon: 101 Years of Invectives (1352–1453)* (Messina: A. Sfameni, 2007).

as mere rhetoric. Whether inspired or not by specific events or individuals, it clearly comments on developments in Florentine society in the 1450s.

One of the most interesting aspects of the sonnet has only been slightly touched upon, however—its rubric. As mentioned previously, complaints against the merchants were typically composed by members of the nobility. Aristocratic writers of anti-mercantile verse conflated the traders with the peasantry, even when the vendors outranked them in terms of money and prestige. This sonnet, on the other hand, is assigned to a wool-beater, a status among the lowest in fifteenth-century Florentine society. The poet does not distinguish the merchants from him- or herself, as might a nobleman. On the contrary, the "battilana" affirms that they are no different from her- or himself (3–4).

Readers of the sonnet in the twenty-first century, seeing it ascribed to a wool worker, might expect it to exalt the socio-economic mobility in fifteenth-century Florence; but its author absolutely condemns the upward mobility of the merchants. Instead, the poet seemingly posits a static view of social organization where non-noble workers should remain on their respective lower levels while the community is run by those born to the upper echelons. Perhaps for this reason the poet includes traces of aristocratic ideology throughout the lyric. In contrast to the social and economic evolution of fifteenth-century Florence, the writer apparently endorses the conservative political agenda of rule by the nobility.

The sonnet demonstrates *in nuce* that the evolution of the European cities at the end of the Middle Ages did not consist of a smooth linear transition. Instead, elements throughout the culture in the early Renaissance clung to the mentality of feudal social structures, even though the economy and society had rendered such an organization to society as obsolete.

Jan Hirschbiegel and Gabriel Zeilinger
(Christian-Albrechts-Universität zu Kiel)

# Urban Space Divided?
# The Encounter of Civic and Courtly Spheres in
# Late-Medieval Towns

Studies explicitly dealing with the encounters between civic and courtly cultures in the urban spaces of premodern Europe without displaying the usual inclination of separating these two spheres are scarce. This lack is a symptom of a perceivable shadow in research—cast both by the Urban History and the Court History communities. Only recently has there been a tendency to change perspectives and to pursue a new paradigm regarding this matter that might eventually close this gap. Some efforts pointing in this direction have recently been or are about to be published[1] —aiming at analyzing the various aspects and forms of cooperation and confrontation between two social systems that were supposedly both heterogenous and antagonistic: the corporate communes vs. the hierarchical court

---

[1]   See, e.g., Matthias Meinhardt, *Dresden im Wandel: Raum und Bevölkerung der Stadt im Residenzbildungsprozeß des 15. und 16. Jahrhunderts.* Hallische Beiträge zur Geschichte des Mittelalters und der Frühen Neuzeit, 3 (Berlin: Akademie-Verlag, 2008); and forthcoming: *Symbolische Interaktion in der Residenzstadt des späten Mittelalters,* ed. Gerrit Deutschländer, Marc von der Höh, and Andreas Ranft; cf. Thomas Zotz, "Informelle Zusammenhänge zwischen Hof und Stadt," and Stephan Müller, "Im Rücken der Repräsentation: Eine Skizze zur Informalität in der höfischen Literatur des Mittelalters am Beispiel des 'Guoten Gêrhart' Rudolfs von Ems," *Informelle Strukturen bei Hof: Dresdener Gespräche III zur Theorie des Hofes,* ed. Reinhardt Butz and Jan Hirschbiegel. Vita Curialis, 2 (Berlin and Münster: LIT, 2009), 157–68, 169–70. See also the introduction to this volume by Albrecht Classen, notably "The City and the Courtly World," 33–60. The authors would like to thank cordially Professor Dr. Gerhard Fouquet (Kiel), Dr. Reinhardt Butz (Dresden), Dr. Matthias Steinbink (Munich), Kathrin Zickermann, M.A. (St. Andrews), Prof. Dr. Albrecht Classen (Tucson, AZ), and Prof. Dr. Marilyn Sandidge (Westfield, MA) for their valuable advice on this paper.

society rotating around the prince.[2] In light of recent research it is rather questionable still to claim that court and city, lordship and commune, courtly and civic cultures were indeed adversarial in nature and behavior. After all, the roots of both spheres lay in the feudal structures of the Early and High Middle Ages.[3] The above observed "shadow" has its origin in the very setup of two well-established and prolific fields of research: The historical as well as the interdisciplinary analysis of urban settlements and urban landscapes ("Städtelandschaften"), for instance in the Holy Roman Empire, has a long tradition with numerous "classics"[4] and an abundance of current research,[5] in many cases

---

[2]    This is the way Andreas Ranft, "Adel, Hof und Residenz im späten Mittelalter," *Archiv für Kulturgeschichte* 89 (2007): 69–81, has phrased it in a programmatic layout for converging the two spheres.

[3]    See, e.g., Franz Irsigler, "Zur wirtschaftlichen Bedeutung der frühen Grundherrschaft," *Strukturen und Wandlungen der ländlichen Herrschaftsformen vom 10. zum 13. Jahrhundert: Deutschland und Italien im Vergleich*, ed. Gerhard Dilcher and Cinzio Violante. Schriften des Italienisch-Deutschen Historischen Instituts in Trient, 14 (Berlin: Duncker & Humblot, 2000), 165–87; *Grundherrschaft und Stadtentstehung am Niederrhein*. Referate der 6. Niederrhein-Tagung des Arbeitskreises niederrheinischer Kommunalarchive für Regionalgeschichte, ed. Klaus Flink and Wilhelm Janssen. Klever Archiv, 9 (Kleve: Stadtarchiv, 1989); *Burgen, Märkte, kleine Städte: Mittelalterliche Herrschaftsbildung am südlichen Oberrhein*, ed. Ursula Huggle and Thomas Zotz. Das Markgräflerland, 2 (Schopfheim: Geschichtsverein Markgräflerland, 2003).

[4]    See, for instance, Edith Ennen, *Frühgeschichte der europäischen Stadt* (Bonn: Röhrscheid, 1953); Hans Planitz, *Die deutsche Stadt im Mittelalter: Von der Römerzeit bis zu den Zunftkämpfen* (Graz and Cologne: Böhlau, 1954); Edith Ennen, *Die europäische Stadt des Mittelalters* (Göttingen: Vandenhoeck & Ruprecht, 1972); Eberhard Isenmann, *Die deutsche Stadt im Mittelalter 1250–1500: Stadtgestalt, Recht, Stadtregiment, Kirche, Gesellschaft, Wirtschaft* (Stuttgart: Ulmer, 1988); focusing on Northwestern Europe: *The Cambridge Urban History of Britain. Vol. 1: 600–1540*, ed. David Michael Pallister (Cambridge and New York: Cambridge University Press, 2000); David Nicholas, *The Growth of the Medieval City* and *The Later Medieval City. A History of Urban Society in Europe* (London and New York: Longman, 1997).

[5]    For a short list of recent publications, see: *Vielerlei Städte: Der Stadtbegriff*, ed. Peter Johanek and Franz Joseph Post. Städteforschung. Reihe A: Darstellungen, 61 (Cologne, Weimar, and Vienna: Böhlau, 2004); *Städtelandschaft—Städtenetz—zentralörtliches Gefüge: Ansätze und Befunde zur Geschichte der Städte im hohen und späten Mittelalter*, ed. Monika Escher, Alfred Haverkamp, and Frank G. Hirschmann. Trierer historische Forschungen, 43 (Mainz: Zabern, 2000); *Städtelandschaft: Städte im regionalen Kontext in Spätmittelalter und Früher Neuzeit = Réseau urbain = Urban network*, ed. Holger Th. Gräf, and Katrin Keller. Städteforschung. Reihe A: Darstellungen, 62 (Cologne, Weimar, and Vienna: Böhlau, 2004); *Die urbanen Zentren des hohen und späteren Mittelalters: Vergleichende Untersuchungen zu Städten und Städtelandschaften im Westen des Reiches und in Ostfrankreich*, 3 vol., ed. Monika Escher and Frank G. Hirschmann. Trierer Historische Forschungen, 50/1–3 (Trier: Kliomedia, 2005). Cf. Gabriel Zeilinger, "Das Netz wird dichter: Neue Forschungen zu alteuropäischen Städtelandschaften," *Jahrbuch für Regionalgeschichte* 25 (2007): 89–99. For the spatial concept, see, e.g., *Landschaften im Mittelalter*, ed. Karl-Heinz Spieß (Stuttgart: Steiner, 2006).

developed at the "Institut für vergleichende Städtegeschichte" in Münster.[6] In recent times research especially on the Urban History of Western and Central Europe has increasingly turned its attention to the processes of premodern urbanization from the perspective of Social History.[7] In the course of this research it has become even more evident that it was the small or even minimal towns[8]—among those quite a few with princely residences[9]—which were formative for the urban structure of, for example, the Holy Roman Empire. The relatively autonomous imperial cities were comparatively big in size, but few in numbers.[10] Yet they have dominated the research focus for many decades, even

---

[6]   Cf. the Institute's internet-presentation: http://www.uni-muenster.de/Staedtegeschichte/Publikationen.shtml, and the associated "International Commission for the History of Towns" at http://www.historiaurbium.org/ (both last accessed on April 6, 2009).

[7]   See, among others: Monika Escher-Apsner, *Stadt und Stift: Studien zur Geschichte Münstermaifelds im hohen und späteren Mittelalter*. Trierer Historische Forschungen, 53 (Trier: Kliomedia, 2004); Bernhard Brenner, *Ludwig der Bayer—ein Motor für die Urbanisierung Ostschwabens? Zu den Auswirkungen herrscherlicher Städtepolitik auf die Entwicklung der schwäbischen Städtelandschaft im ausgehenden Mittelalter*. Materialien zur Geschichte des Bayerischen Schwaben, 27 (Augsburg: Wißner, 2005); *Die Urbanisierung Europas von der Antike bis in die Moderne*, ed. Gerhard Fouquet and Gabriel Zeilinger. Kieler Werkstücke. Reihe E: Beiträge zur Wirtschafts- und Sozialgeschichte, 7 (Frankfurt a. M., Berlin, et al.: Peter Lang, 2009).

[8]   See, e.g., Martina Stercken, *Städte der Herrschaft: Kleinstadtgenese im habsburgischen Herrschaftsraum des 13. und 14. Jahrhunderts*. Städteforschung. Reihe A: Darstellungen, 68 (Cologne, Weimar, and Vienna: Böhlau, 2006); Katrin Keller, *Kleinstädte in Kursachsen. Wandlungen einer Städtelandschaft zwischen Dreißigjährigem Krieg und Industrialisierung*. Städteforschung. Reihe A: Darstellungen, 55 (Cologne, Weimar, and Vienna: Böhlau, 2001); Oliver Auge, "Stadtwerdung in Tirol: Ansätze, Ergebnisse und Perspektiven vergleichender Stadtgeschichtsforschung," *König, Kirche, Adel—Herrschaftsstrukturen im mittleren Alpenraum und angrenzenden Gebieten (6.–13. Jahrhundert)*, ed. Rainer Loose and Sönke Lorenz (Lana: Tappeiner, 1999), 307–64; *Kleine Städte im neuzeitlichen Europa*, ed. Holger Th. Gräf. Innovationen, 6 (Berlin: Berlin-Verlag Spitz, 1997). Pathbreaking in modern research of small towns of the German Southwest: Gerhard Fouquet, "Stadt, Herrschaft und Territorium: Ritterschaftliche Kleinstädte am Beispiel Südwestdeutschlands an der Wende vom Mittelalter zur Neuzeit," *Zeitschrift zur Geschichte des Oberrheins* 41 (1993): 70–120.

[9]   See the compilation of this type of towns between 1200 until 1650 in: *Höfe und Residenzen im spätmittelalterlichen Reich: Ein dynastisch-topographisches Handbuch*, ed. Werner Paravicini, assembled by Jan Hirschbiegel and Jörg Wettlaufer, 1: *Dynastien und Höfe*. 2: *Residenzen*. Residenzenforschung, 15, I, 1–2 (Ostfildern: Thorbecke, 2003), especially vol. 2.

[10]   See the cities within the "Reichsmatrikel" (Imperial Register), e.g., of 1521, numbering 85: "Übersicht über die Reichsstände: I. Die Reichsstände nach der Matrikel von 1521 mit vergleichenden Angaben nach der Matrikel von 1755," ed. Gerhard Oestreich and E. Holzer. *Handbuch der deutschen Geschichte*, ed. Herbert Grundmann (orig. ed. by Gebhardt), vol. 2: *Von der Reformation bis zum Ende des Absolutismus*, bearbeitet von Max Braubach, Walther Peter Fuchs, Gerhard Oestreich, Walter Schlesinger, Wilhelm Treue, Friedrich Uhlhorn, and Ernst Walter Zeeden, 9th, newly arranged edition (Stuttgart: Klett-Cotta, 1970), 769–84; *Quellen zum Verfassungsorganismus des Heiligen römischen Reiches deutscher Nation: 1495–1815*, ed. Hanns Hubert Hofmann. Ausgewählte Quellen zur deutschen Geschichte der Neuzeit, 13 (Darmstadt: Wissenschaftliche Buchgesellschaft, 1976), for the Imperial Estates, see XVIII–XXII and 40–51: "Die

being considered the paradigm for the medieval and early modern city.[11] On the other hand, researchers on courts and residences of the Ancien Régime have certainly examined urban structures around royal or princely residences—notably those scholars affiliated with the "Residenzen-Kommission" of the Göttingen Academy of Sciences covered related topics.[12] But from that point of view towns were often interpreted mainly as the mere location of the formation of princely residences[13] as they emerged around 1500; or they were looked at as auxiliary

---

'allzeit neueste Matrikel' von 1521." The feasible scope of political action for imperial cities is described by Gerhard Fouquet, "Lübeck als Reichsstadt—die Zeit Friedrichs III.," *Von Menschen, Ländern, Meeren: Festschrift für Thomas Riis zum 65. Geburtstag*, ed. Gerhard Fouquet, Mareike Hansen, Carsten Jahnke, and Jan Schlürmann (Tönning: Der Andere Verlag, 2006), 277–305.

[11]   Cf., for instance, Felicitas Schmieder, *Die mittelalterliche Stadt* (Darmstadt: Wissenschaftliche Buchgesellschaft, 2005); notably 86–96, once more underestimating the small towns. Counterpoints—and splendid surveys of the subject—are given by Tom Scott, *Society and Economy in Germany 1300–1600*. European Studies Series (Basingstoke, Hampshire, and New York: Palgrave Macmillan, 2002), 32–37, 132–52 et passim; and Ulf Dirlmeier, Gerhard Fouquet, and Bernd Fuhrmann, *Europa im Spätmittelalter 1215–1378*. Oldenbourg Grundriss der Geschichte, 8 (Munich: Oldenbourg, 2003), in particular 68–77.

[12]   See http://resikom.adw-goettingen.gwdg.de/index.php (last accessed on April 6th 2009). An outline of the research on the Court History of the Holy Roman Empire is offered by Jan Hirschbiegel, "Fürstliche Höfe und Residenzen im spätmittelalterlichen Reich: Ein Projekt der Residenzen-Kommission der Akademie der Wissenschaften zu Göttingen," *Jahrbuch der historischen Forschung in der Bundesrepublik Deutschland: Berichtsjahr 2001*, ed. Arbeitsgemeinschaft außeruniversitärer historischer Forschungseinrichtungen in der Bundesrepublik Deutschland (Munich: Oldenbourg, 2002), 15–23; Werner Paravicini, "Les Cours et les résidences du Moyen Âge tardif: Un Quart de siècle de recherches allemandes," *Les Tendances actuelles de l'histoire du Moyen Âge en France et en Allemagne: Actes des colloques de Sèvres (1997) et Göttingen (1998)*, ed. Jean-Claude Schmitt and Otto Gerhard Oexle. Histoire ancienne et médiévale, 66 (Paris: Publications de la Sorbonne, 2002), 327–50; Pierre Monnet, "Cours et résidences dans l'Empire et en Europe: une commission, des colloques, des publications," *Bulletin d'information de la Mission Historique Française en Allemagne* 41 (2005): 167–73; Jan Hirschbiegel, *Die Residenzen-Kommission der Akademie der Wissenschaften zu Göttingen*, http://www.histosem.uni-kiel.de/Lehrstuehle/wirtschaft/VorstellungResiKom2006AKTUELL.pdf [last accessed on April 6, 2009). Even more recent and programmatic not only by title is Andreas Bihrer, "Curia non sufficit: Vergangene, aktuelle und zukünftige Wege der Erforschung von Höfen im Mittelalter und in der Frühen Neuzeit," *Zeitschrift für historische Forschung* 35 (2008): 237–72; Gerhard Fouquet, "Stadt und Residenz im 12.–16. Jahrhundert—ein Widerspruch?," *Stadt, Handwerk, Armut: Eine kommentierte Quellensammlung zur Geschichte der Frühen Neuzeit: Helmut Bräuer zum 70. Geburtstag zugeeignet*, ed. Katrin Keller, Gabriele Viertel, and Gerald Diesener (Leipzig: Universitätsverlag, 2008), 164–85; Werner Paravicini, "Die Gesellschaft, der Ort, die Zeichen: Aus der Arbeit der Residenzen-Kommission der Akademie der Wissenschaften zu Göttingen," *Spätmittelalterliche Residenzbildung in geistlichen Territorien Mittel- und Nordostdeutschlands*, ed. Klaus Neitmann and Heinz-Dieter Heimann (Berlin: Lukas-Verlag, 2009), 15–40.

[13]   Hans Patze, "Die Bildung der landesherrlichen Residenzen im Reich während des 14. Jahrhunderts," *Stadt und Stadtherr im 14. Jahrhundert: Entwicklungen und Funktionen*, ed. Wilhelm Rausch. Beiträge zur Geschichte der Städte Mitteleuropas, 2 (Linz: Österreichischer Arbeitskreis für Stadtgeschichtsforschung, 1972), 1–54. An excellent case study is presented, e.g., by Johannes Kolb, *Heidelberg: Die Entstehung einer landesherrlichen Residenz im 14. Jahrhundert*. Residenzen-

institutions for appraising and supplying the adjacent court, not as social and
political entities on their own.[14] It is this shift of the paradigm toward a more town-
oriented perspective that we would like to focus on by way of combining the
research on Urban and Court History on an equal footing.[15] So far there seems to
be no sustainable juncture of the two on an institutional level. Thus, the above
mentioned supposed antagonisms of the two spheres appear to persist even in
today's research—in spite of the claims to consider not only distinctive but also
integrative aspects of city and court.[16] In the course of this paper the interchange
between city and court will be demonstrated in an exemplary fashion. Festivities
as highly condensed communicative events—with the respective historiographical
tradition—are particularly useful for this purpose. By concentrating on the social
implications of symbolic actions displayed during premodern festivals, one may
still capture or at least sense some of the economic, political, religious, cultural and
even legal aspects.[17] Festivals are determined by community, occasion, and
appearance[18] as well as by their deliberate interruption of everyday life.[19] They

---

forschung, 8 (Sigmaringen: Thorbecke, 1999).

[14] Accordingly Bihrer, "Curia non sufficit," 271, who is urging to consider the external contexts and
references of the premodern courts more intensely: "Die Konzentration der Forschung allein auf
den Hof [. . .] sollte der Vergangenheit angehören, [. . .] das Forschungsfeld muß eine Ausweitung
erfahren [um die] Kontakte und Bezüge der Höfe nach außen. Die [. . .] Erforschung von Höfen
muß kontextualisiert werden. [. . . ] Es gilt, die Höfe in einem Spannungsfeld mit ihren äußeren
Bezügen zu sehen." Yet, Werner Paravicini, "Vom sozialen zum realen Raum: Hof und Residenz
in Alteuropa. Vortrag der öffentlichen Sitzung am 12. Dezember 2003," *Jahrbuch der Akademie der
Wissenschaften zu Göttingen 2003* (2004): 128–45, has observed—once more looking from the court
to the town—an aristocratic alignment of the urban space that is both interfering with and going
beyond the town walls ("in die Stadt eingreifende und über sie hinausgreifende Ordnung des
realen Raumes," 139). Fouquet, "Stadt und Residenz," emphasizes the importance of small towns
with princely residences both for urban history and court history.

[15] See the preliminary steps in that direction by Peter Johanek, "Residenzbildung und Stadt bei
geistlichen und weltlichen Fürsten im Nordwesten Deutschlands," *Historia Urbana* 5 (1997, publ.
2000): 91–108; and the volumes: *Ein zweigeteilter Ort? Hof und Stadt in der Frühen Neuzeit,* ed.
Susanne C. Pils and Jan Paul Niederkorn. Forschungen und Beiträge zur Wiener Stadtgeschichte,
44 (Innsbruck, Vienna, and Bozen: Studien-Verlag, 2005); and *Der Hof und die Stadt. Konfrontation,
Koexistenz und Integration in Spätmittelalter und Früher Neuzeit,* ed. Werner Paravicini and Jörg
Wettlaufer. Residenzforschung, 20 (Ostfildern: Thorbecke, 2006).

[16] Compare the preceding notes and Ulrich Rosseaux, "Das Vogelschießen und die Vogelwiese in
Dresden: Ständetranszendenz und gesellschaftliche Integration in einer frühneuzeitlichen
Residenzstadt," *Stadtgemeinde und Ständegesellschaft: Formen der Integration und Distinktion in der
frühneuzeitlichen Stadt,* ed. Patrick Schmidt and Horst Carl. Geschichte, Forschung und
Wissenschaft, 2 (Berlin, Münster: LIT, 2007), 56–71; especially 58.

[17] For fifteenth-century court festivals, see Gabriel Zeilinger, *Die Uracher Hochzeit 1474: Form und
Funktion eines höfischen Festes im 15. Jahrhundert.* Kieler Werkstücke. Reihe E: Beiträge zur Sozial-
und Wirtschaftsgeschichte, 2 (Frankfurt a. M., Berlin, et al.: Peter Lang, 2003).

[18] Lars Deile, "Feste—eine Definition," *Das Fest: Beiträge zu seiner Theorie und Systematik,* ed. Michael
Maurer (Cologne, Weimar, and Vienna: Böhlau, 2004), 1–17; here 9. For an outline on the research
tradition, see Michael Maurer, "Feste und Feiern als historischer Forschungsgegenstand,"

offer a rhythmic structure within time by their very occurrence and/or by their festive structure.[20] This applies also to medieval festivals that were specifically organized to provide identity and a forum for integration—at least for the participants[21]—and which were characterized by a (partially) public dimension[22] offering an example of symbolic communication.[23] In recent times medievalists have intensely worked on the subject of festivals in history[24] and in particular on court festivals.[25] Yet Gert Melville's statement of 1997 still holds true that a fundamental analysis of late-medieval court festivals is a desideratum,[26] although various studies have been presented.[27]The same observation can be made for civic

*Historische Zeitschrift* 253 (1991): 101–30.

[19] Michael Maurer, "Prolegomena zu einer Theorie des Festes," *Das Fest*, ed. Maurer, 19–54; here 23–26.

[20] Maurer, "Prolegomena," 26–31.

[21] See, e.g., Peter Johanek, "Fest und Integration," *Feste und Feiern im Mittelalter*, ed. Detlef Altenburg, Jörg Jarnut, and Hans-Hugo Steinhoff (Sigmaringen: Thorbecke, 1991), 525–40.

[22] On the problem of the 'public' in the Middle Ages, see Peter von Moos, '*Öffentlich' und 'privat' im Mittelalter: Zu einem Problem historischer Begriffsbildung, vorgetragen am 22.6.1996* (Heidelberg: Winter, 2004). Cf. Alfred Haverkamp, " . . . an die große Glocke hängen: Über Öffentlichkeit im Mittelalter," *Jahrbuch des Historischen Kollegs* 1995 (1996): 71–112.

[23] Barbara Stollberg-Rilinger, "Symbolische Kommunikation in der Vormoderne: Begriffe—Forschungsperspektiven—Thesen," *Zeitschrift für historische Forschung* 31 (2004): 489–527; and earlier William Roosen, "Early Modern Diplomatic Ceremonial: A Systems Approach," *Journal of Modern History* 52 (1980): 452–76. Cf. André Krischer, *Reichsstädte in der Fürstengesellschaft: Politischer Zeichengebrauch in der Frühen Neuzeit.* Symbolische Kommunikation in der Vormoderne. Studien zur Geschichte, Literatur und Kunst (Darmstadt: Wissenschaftliche Buchgesellschaft, 2006), substantiating that the adaption of the semiotic and symbolic conduct of emperors and princes by the urban elites of the imperial cities was the basis for their cultural and political participation.

[24] See, e.g., *Feste und Feiern im Mittelalter*, and Jacques Heers, *Vom Mummenschanz zum Machttheater: Europäische Festkultur im Mittelalter.* Transl. by Grete Osterwald (Frankfurt a. M.: Fischer, 1986); Christian Rohr, *Festkultur des Mittelalters* (Graz: Akademische Druck- und Verlagsanstalt, 2002).

[25] Gerhard Fouquet, Harm von Seggern, Gabriel Zeilinger, "Höfische Feste im Spätmittelalter: Eine Einleitung," *Höfische Feste im Spätmittelalter*, ed. Gerhard Fouquet, Harm von Seggern, and Gabriel Zeilinger. Mitteilungen der Residenzen-Kommission. Sonderheft 6 (Kiel: Vervielfältigungsstelle der Christian Albrechts-Universität zu Kiel, 2003), 9–18, including a detailed research review.

[26] Gert Melville, "Rituelle Ostentation und pragmatische Inquisition: Zur Institutionalität des Ordens vom Goldenen Vließ," *Im Spannungsfeld von Recht und Ritual: Soziale Kommunikation in Mittelalter und Früher Neuzeit*, ed. Heinz Duchhardt and Gert Melville (Cologne, Weimar, and Vienna: Böhlau, 1997), 215–71; here 238, note 78. Cf. Jörg Jochen Berns, "Die Festkultur der deutschen Höfe zwischen 1580 und 1730: Eine Problemskizze in typologischer Ansicht," *Germanisch-Romanische Monatsschrift* 34 (1984): 295–311; here 295. He also observes this deficiency in research.

[27] See note 25 and recently Michail A. Bojcov, "Höfische Feste und ihr Schrifttum: Ordnungen, Berichte, Korrespondenzen," *Höfe und Residenzen im spätmittelalterlichen Reich: Hof und Schrift*, ed. Werner Paravicini, assembled by Jan Hirschbiegel and Jörg Wettlaufer. Residenzenforschung, 15, III (Ostfildern: Thorbecke, 2007), 179–84, especially the bibliography 183–84.

festivals of that period,[28] while many case studies have been produced on that matter as well.[29]Bridging those thematic fields are the works on monarchs' meetings,[30] and coronations within cities.[31]

The prospects of the outlined integrative analysis of the two spheres of city and court, of commune and lordship in the Late Middle Ages will be demonstrated in the following focusing on one of the mega-events of fifteenth-century Europe: the Council of Constance, 1414–1418. By looking closely at the proceedings of the festive royal entry into the city—according to contemporary tradition—we want to observe the convergence of the courtly and the civic spheres in the urban space[32] of a city that was in some ways both an episcopal residence and an imperial city.[33]

When King Sigismund entered Constance on Christmas Eve in 1414, it happened indeed within a festive frame culminating in a holy mass at the cathedral. The report by the local chronicler Ulrich Richental is not the only one, but certainly the

---

[28] Rohr, *Festkultur*, 62–63, covers only those two pages on cities and festival. An overview is offered by Ludwig Schmugge, "Feste feiern wie sie fallen—Das Fest als Lebensrhythmus im Mittelalter," *Stadt und Fest: Zu Geschichte und Gegenwart europäischer Festkultur: Festschrift der Philosophischen Fakultät I der Universität Zürich zum 2000-Jahr-Jubiläum der Stadt Zürich*, ed. Paul Hugger in collaboration with Walter Burkert and Ernst Lichtenhahn (Unterägeri: W & H Verlag, 1987), 61–87. Cf. for the early-modern history, see Ruth-E. Mohrmann, "Fest und Alltag in der Frühen Neuzeit—Rituale als Ordnungs- und Handlungsmuster," *Niedersächsisches Jahrbuch für Landesgeschichte* 72 (2000): 1–10; here 6.

[29] For a selection, see Juliane Kümmel, "Alltag und Festtag spätmittelalterlicher Handwerker," *Mentalität und Alltag im Spätmittelalter*, ed. Cord Meckseper and Elisabeth Schraut. Kleine Vandenhoeck-Reihe, 1511 (Göttingen: Vandenhoeck & Ruprecht, 1985), 76–96; Klaus Tenfelde, "Die fürstliche Einholung als städtisches Fest," *Stadt und Fest*, 45–87; Thomas Zotz, "Die Stadtgesellschaft und ihre Feste," *Feste und Feiern im Mittelalter*, 201–13; Gerhard Fouquet, "Das Festmahl in den oberdeutschen Städten des Spätmittelalters: Zu Form, Funktion und Bedeutung des öffentlichen Konsums," *Archiv für Kulturgeschichte* 74 (1992): 83–123; *City and Spectacle in Medieval Europe*, ed. Barbara A. Hanawalt and Kathryn L. Reyerson. Medieval Studies at Minnesota, 6 (Minneapolis and London: University of Minnesota Press, 1994).

[30] See, e.g., Gerald Schwedler, *Herrschertreffen des Spätmittelalters: Formen – Rituale – Wirkungen*. Mittelalter-Forschungen, 21 (Ostfildern: Thorbecke, 2008).

[31] See, e.g., *Krönungen: Könige in Aachen—Geschichte und Mythos*. Ausstellungskatalog, ed. Mario Kramp, 2 vols. (Mainz: Philipp von Zabern, 2000).

[32] Here in a broader sense of "spatial turn," cf., among others, Doris Bachmann-Medick, "Spatial Turn," Doris Bachmann-Medick, *Cultural Turns: Neuorientierungen in den Kulturwissenschaften*, 2nd ed. (Reinbek: Rowohlt, 2006), 284–328; Christian Hochmuth, Susanne Rau, "Stadt— Macht —Räume: Eine Einführung," *Machträume der frühneuzeitlichen Stadt*, ed. Christian Hochmuth and Susanne Rau. Konflikte und Kultur—Historische Perspektiven, 13 (Constance: UKV Verlagsgesellschaft, 2006), 13–40; Martina Löw, *Raumsoziologie* (Frankfurt a. M.: Suhrkamp, 2001).

[33] The central political places of the late medieval Holy Roman Empire are outlined by Gerhard Fouquet, "Hauptorte—Metropolen—Haupt- und Residenzstädte im Reich (13. - beginnendes 17. Jh.)," *Ein dynastisch-topographisches Handbuch*; here vol. 1: 1–15.

most renowned one.[34] According to his account, the king and Queen Barbara, accompanied by noblemen and servants, arrived from Überlingen two hours after mid-night. First the group went to the chambers of the city council to warm up for about an hour. From there they went to the cathedral to attend the mass—sheltered by pieces of cloth that were kept around and above the nobility (Figure 1).

---

[34]   Ulrich Richental, *Das Konzil zu Konstanz MCDXIV–MCDXVIII*. 1: *Faksimileausgabe*. 2: *Kommentar und Text*, ed. Otto Feger (Starnberg, Sigmaringen: Keller, Thorbecke, 1964); here vol. 2: 149–278, the following on 169–71. Cf. *Ulrichs von Richental Chronik des Constanzer Concils 1414 bis 1418*, ed. Michael Richard Buck. Bibliothek des litterarischen Vereins in Stuttgart, 158 (1882; Hildesheim: Olms, 1962], 35–36. For the written sources of that event, see Hermann Heimpel, "Königlicher Weihnachtsdienst auf den Konzilen von Konstanz und Basel," *Tradition als historische Kraft: Interdisziplinäre Forschungen zur Geschichte des früheren Mittelalters: Karl Hauck zum 21.12.1981 gewidmet*, ed. Norbert Kamp and Joachim Wollasch, with contributions by Manfred Balzer, Karl Heinrich Krüger, and Lutz von Padberg (Berlin and New York: Walter de Gruyter, 1982), 388–411; here 390, and notes 11–20.

Figure 1: King Sigismund on the way to the cathedral of Constance, December 1414

(Richental, *Konzil*, 1: *Faksimileausgabe,* fol. 19v)

The cathedral was supposedly decorated with so many lit candles that Richental thought it looked like a burning house. Pope John XXIII, who had been in town for some time, was dressed in precious garments and had a golden crown although apparently not wearing it. After the singing of "Dominus dixit ad me," it was time for the Gospel to be read, so the king ascended the pulpit and delivered the "Exiit edictum."[35] During that lecture the Duke of Saxony is reported having raised a sword above the king—its tip pointing right toward the king's head.[36] The scepter and the crown were held by Hungarian noblemen instead of the designated Elector Palatine and the Margrave of Brandenburg who had not arrived yet:

> "Und man sang 'Dominus dixit ad me' Und do es kam zů dem ewangeli, do gieng der Romsch küng mit vil brinenden kertzen uff die kantzel und sang das ewangelium 'Exiit edictum' Und die will er das sang, stůnd der hertzog von Saxen ob im und hat ain bloß schwert in der hand, und hub das hoch uff und stackt den spitz gen des kaisers hopt; und hůb im das zepter vor ain her von Unger an stat des pfaltzgraven, und die kron och ainer von Unger anstat des marggrafen von Brandenburg, wann die dennocht nit kommen waren"(Figure 2).[37]

[For a paraphrase in English, see above]

---

[35]  For this ceremonial aspect, see Heimpel, "Königlicher Weihnachtsdienst," and Hermann Heimpel, "Königlicher Weihnachtsdienst im späteren Mittelalter," *Deutsches Archiv für Erforschung des Mittelalters* 39 (1983): 131–206; for this incident particularly 169–73; Hermann Heimpel, "Königliche Evangeliumslesung bei königlicher Krönung," *Aus Kirche und Reich: Studien zu Theologie, Politik und Recht im Mittelalter: Festschrift für Friedrich Kempf zu seinem fünfundsiebzigsten Geburtstag und fünfzigjährigen Doktorjubiläum,* ed. Hubert Mordek (Sigmaringen: Thorbecke, 1983), 447–59.

[36]  On the phenomenon of the "sword in the crown," see Werner Paravicini, "Das Schwert in der Krone," *Festschrift Gert Melville* (2009) [in preparation].

[37]  Richental, *Konzil,* 2: *Kommentar und Text,*169– 171.

Figure 2: King Sigismund in the cathedral of Constance Christmas 1414
(Richental, *Konzil*, 1: *Faksimileausgabe*, fol. 20r[38])

---

[38] According to the editorial note the king—dressed in a deacon's robe—is reading the Christmas Gospel [*lectio septima*, Luke 2,1, Richental, *Konzil*, 2: *Kommentar und Text*, 170, its note 2 referring to §48], while two Hungarian knights stand on both sides of the pulpit with the imperial insignia,

After the mass the "Laudes" were sung until daybreak. The following prayers lasted until eleven o'clock. At the end of those ceremonies the Pope gave his blessing and everyone went to his home or his hostel.[39]

So, at first glance, the royal *introitus* into the city appears to have been dominated largely by the courtly sphere. But this labeling demands a closer look: Having received notice of the king's approach, the city council had sent ships and staff to Überlingen to carry and escort the royal entourage over that stretch of Lake Constance (Figure 3).[40]

---

behind the king the Duke of Saxony with the raised sword, behind him two clerical dignitaries and then secular candle-bearers (seen from right to left), Richental, *Konzil*, 2: *Kommentar und Text*, 170, and Heimpel, "Königlicher Weihnachtsdienst," 399.

[39]   For the proceedings, see Heimpel, "Königlicher Weihnachtsdienst," 391–96. Cf. Walter Brandmüller, *Das Konzil von Konstanz 1414–1418*, 1: *Bis zur Abreise Sigismunds nach Narbonne.* Konziliengeschichte. Reihe A: Darstellungen (Paderborn, Munich, Vienna, Zurich: Schöningh, 1991), 178–79; Alois Niederstätter, *Ante Portas: Herrscherbesuche am Bodensee 839–1507* (Konstanz: Universitäts-Verlag Konstanz, 1993), 126–31 (and the respective notes 203 and 204); Achim Thomas Hack, *Das Empfangszeremoniell bei mittelalterlichen Papst-Kaiser-Treffen.* Forschungen zur Kaiser- und Papstgeschichte des Mittelalters. Beihefte zu J. F. Böhmer. Regesta Imperii, 18 (Cologne, Weimar, and Vienna: Böhlau, 1999), 563–69; Jörg K. Hoensch, *Kaiser Sigismund: Herrscher an der Schwelle zur Neuzeit, 1368–1437* (Munich: Beck, 1996), 194–96. For a comprehensive analysis, see Gerrit Jasper Schenk, "Sehen und gesehen werden: Der Einzug König Sigismunds zum Konstanzer Konzil 1414 im Wandel von Wahrnehmung und Überlieferung (am Beispiel von Handschriften und frühen Augsburger Drucken der Richental-Chronik)," *Medien und Weltbilder im Wandel der Frühen Neuzeit*, ed. Franz Mauelshagen and Bendikt Mauer. Documenta Augustana, 4 (Augsburg: Wißner, 2000), 71–106.

[40]   Richental, *Konzil*, 2: *Kommentar und Text*, 169, cf. Heimpel, "Königlicher Weihnachtsdienst," 391. For the "adventus" by ship cf. Gerrit Jasper Schenk, *Zeremoniell und Politik: Herrschereinzüge im spätmittelalterlichen Reich: Forschungen zur Kaiser- und Papstgeschichte des Mittelalters.* Beihefte zu J. F. Böhmer. Regesta Imperii, 21 (Cologne, Weimar, and Vienna: Böhlau, 2003), 276.

Figure 3: King Sigismund is escorted over Lake Constance, here in January 1417
*Die Schweiz im Mittelalter in Diebold Schillings Spiezer Bilderchronik*, ed. Hans
Haeberli and Christoph von Steiger. Studienausg. zur Faks.-Ed. der Hs. Mss.

hist. helv. I. 16 d. Burgerbibliothek Bern (Luzern: Faksimile-Verlag, 1991), 392,
based on the Spiezer Bilderchronik, 609
(as in Schenk, *Zeremoniell und Politik*, Figure 13)

In the well-prepared and warm chambers of the city hall[41] the royal guests met
with several representatives of the citizenry, who offered Sigismund and Barbara
a drink of malmsey and bestowed two pieces of gilded cloth on them.[42] Eight
distinguished citizens of Constance—noted by name in Richental's chronicle[43]
—then carried the canopies, while representatives of the city's guilds were bearing
candles—a visualization of the civic order (see Figure 1).[44] Again in the cathedral,
with pope and king present, civic, secular-courtly and clerical-courtly groups met
in a religious ceremony that was part of a royal entry into a city.[45] The general
public ("Volk") of Richental's report may have been to some degree excluded from
active participation,[46] but played a role at least as audience for the staging of
festive splendor. The social elite of Constance, on the other hand, was not limited
to a passive part in the ceremonies; the urban aristocracy had the semiotic and
communicative knowledge to interact with the landed nobility and the high
clergy.[47] Thus, not only were city and court facing each other on that occasion, but
the partially congruent circles of the city's council, citizenry, and other city-
dwellers also present an embodiment of its social ensemble.[48]

---

[41] Richental, *Konzil*, 2: *Kommentar und Text*, 169: [...] *und hieß man die ratstuben wol wermen, wenn sy
kamen, das sy sich warmten, als och beschach.*

[42] Richental, *Konzil*, 2: *Kommentar und Text*, 170; cf. Heimpel, "Königlicher Weihnachtsdienst," 391.

[43] Richental, *Konzil*, 2: *Kommentar und Text*, 170.

[44] Richental, *Konzil*, 2: *Kommentar und Text*, 170: *Und giengen also in das Münster mit allen zunftkertzen
und sust mit vil kertzen* [...], cf. Heimpel, "Königlicher Weihnachtsdienst," 395.

[45] For an essential analysis on this form of festival, see Schenk, *Zeremoniell und Politik*, see also Gerrit
Jasper Schenk, "(Reichsstädtische) Einzugsordnungen und Einzugsberichte," *Hof und Schrift*,
161–77; and Michail A. Bojcov, "Einzug," *Hof und Schrift*, 232–41.

[46] Cf. Schenk, *Zeremoniell und Politik*, 339–40.

[47] Cf. Richard Alewyn and Karl Sälzle, *Das große Welttheater: Die Epoche der höfischen Feste in
Dokument und Deutung*. Rowohlts deutsche Enzyklopädie, 92 (Hamburg: Rowohlt, 1959), 23–26
[2nd, expanded ed. (Munich: Beck, 1985), 28–31]; Vera Jung, *Körperlust und Disziplin: Studien zur
Fest- und Tanzkultur im 16. und 17. Jahrhundert* (Cologne, Weimar, and Vienna: Böhlau, 2001), here
specifically 217–22; Werner Paravicini, *Die ritterlich-höfische Kultur des Mittelalters*. Enzyklopädie
deutscher Geschichte, 32 (Munich: Oldenbourg, 1994), 50–53, already questioning a genuinely
civic form of life within the urban elites; for Lübeck, see recently Fouquet, "Lübeck als
Reichsstadt."

[48] Membership in Constance's confraternal society "Zur Katz" was open to remarkably many social
groups in town, which contributed to a lessening of social tensions, see Christoph Heiermann: *Die
Gesellschaft "Zur Katz" in Konstanz: Ein Beitrag zur Geschichte der Geschlechtergesellschaften in
Spätmittelalter und früher Neuzeit*. Konstanzer Geschichts- und Rechtsquellen, 37 (Stuttgart:
Thorbecke, 1999); cf. *Geschlechtergesellschaften, Zunft-Trinkstuben und Bruderschaften in spätmittel-
alterlichen und frühneuzeitlichen Städten*, ed. Gerhard Fouquet, Matthias Steinbrink, and Gabriel
Zeilinger. Stadt in der Geschichte, 30 (Ostfildern: Thorbecke, 2003).

Richental is not very specific about the lower ranks of the court society present, but is all the more loquacious on the high aristocracy—not just in the context of the mass. The respective corteges are listed in numbers, as he reports on the arrivals of various princes: there were many clerical and secular lords,[49] many knights and squires,[50] along with, for one instance, 60 horses and as many people,[51] and so forth. The names of the city's elite appear repeatedly as hosts of specified noble guests—as Richental had been himself.[52] The Council of Constance as a great medieval festival offered numerous opportunities for encounters between city and court(s).

Constance itself was—as pointed out before—an episcopal see in spite of considerable setbacks in the bishop's dominion over the city in the centuries before the council. At the same time, the citizens' turning to the king as overlord and subsequent royal grants had made Constance at least a semi-imperial city. The convergence or even clash of civic and courtly life forms was therefore also an everyday experience within and around the city walls—often enough in conflicting ways, as Andreas Bihrer has shown for fourteenth-century Constance,[53]and as other authors have for different times and places.[54] But was the Council of Constance then a distinctively urban event at all? Helmut Maurer has affirmed that concept maintaining that its publicly conspicuous rituals embraced the entire population of the city as a "Sakralgemeinschaft" (sacred community)—including the cathedral chapter. Thereby, rituals and ceremonies during the Council were embedded into the city's habitual custom. He claims that only in such a place—the city of a bishop and a chapter—could a chronicler like Richental, with links both to the commune and to the clergy, form the notion of the Council as a highly

---

[49] Richental, *Konzil*, 2: *Kommentar und Text*, 168 (accompanying four cardinals).
[50] Richental, *Konzil*, 2: *Kommentar und Text*, 180 (in the cortege of Duke Ludwig of Bavaria).
[51] Richental, *Konzil*, 2: *Kommentar und Text*, 178 (in the company of the bishop of Passau).
[52] Richental, *Konzil*, 2: *Kommentar und Text*, pass. The problem of accomodations in a midsize imperial city is now described by Ansgar Frenken, "Wohnraumbewirtschaftung und Versorgungsdeckung beim Konstanzer Konzil (1414–1418): Zur logistischen Bewältigung eines Großereignisses im Spätmittelalter," *Zeitschrift für die Geschichte des Oberrheins* 156 (2008): 109–46; cf. Albrecht Classen's introduction to this volume for Oswald von Wolkenstein's literary account on the situation in Constance during the Council, 74–76.
[53] Andreas Bihrer, *Der Konstanzer Bischofshof im 14. Jahrhundert: Herrschaftliche, soziale und kommunikative Aspekte*. Residenzenforschung, 18 (Ostfildern: Thorbecke, 2005); notably 80–96, and the chapter on "Feste und Rituale," 451–61. Cf. Kurt Andermann, "Das schwierige Verhältnis zur Kathedralstadt: Ausweichresidenzen südwestdeutscher Bischöfe im späten Mittelalter," *Spätmittelalterliche Residenzbildung*, 113–31; Kolb, *Heidelberg*; Meinhardt, *Dresden im Wandel*.
[54] See, e.g., Michael Scholz, *Residenz, Hof und Verwaltung der Erzbischöfe von Halle in der ersten Hälfte des 16. Jahrhunderts*. Residenzenforschung, 7 (Sigmaringen: Thorbecke, 1998). Cf. also the preliminary overview by Jörg Wettlaufer, "Zwischen Konflikt und Symbiose: Überregionale Aspekte der spannungsreichen Beziehung zwischen Fürstenhof und Stadt im späten Mittelalter und in der frühen Neuzeit," *Der Hof und die Stadt*, 19–33.

integrative urban event.[55] With all social groups in town purportedly participating, the concept of a local identity was even more impressive at a time when the parties struggling for dominance in the city were forced to withdraw from that internal fight for the moment—although redeploying after the end of the Council.[56] In the example[57] considered here, we have shown within an urban space the integration of differing social spheres; we will next analyze the reported occurrences around Christmas Eve in 1414 and discuss their individual participants.[58]

Ulrich Richental,[59] born around the middle of the fourteenth century, deceased in 1436/1437, was the son of the citizen and city clerk of Constance, Johannes Richental, and thus a contemporary witness of the Council. His chronicle was probably written without official assignment[60] around 1420. It discloses many

---

[55]   Helmut Maurer, "Das Konstanzer Konzil als städtisches Ereignis," *Die Konzilien von Pisa (1409), Konstanz (1414–1418) und Basel (1431–1449): Institutionen und Personen,* ed. Heribert Müller and Johannes Helmrath. Vorträge und Forschungen, 67 (Ostfildern: Thorbecke, 2007), 149–72; here 172.

[56]   Klaus D. Bechtold, *Zunftbürgerschaft und Patriziat: Studien zur Sozialgeschichte der Stadt Konstanz im 14. und 15. Jahrhundert.* Konstanzer Geschichts- und Rechtsquellen, 26 (Sigmaringen: Thorbecke, 1981), 133.

[57]   For a research report, see Remigius Bäumer, "Die Erforschung des Konstanzer Konzils," *Das Konstanzer Konzil,* ed. Remigius Bäumer. Wege der Forschung, 415 (Darmstadt: Wissenschaftliche Buchgemeinschaft, 1977), 3–34, as well as Ansgar Frenken, *Die Erforschung des Konstanzer Konzils (1414–1418) in den letzten 100 Jahren.* Annuarium Historiae Conciliorum, 25,1–2 (Paderborn: Schöningh, 1993). The variation of results in examining court and city is demstrated, e.g., by Gerhard Fouquet, "'Geschichts-Bilder' in einer Reichs- und Hansestadt —Christian von Geren und seine Chronik der Lübecker Bergenfahrer (ca. 1425–1486)," *Das Gedächtnis der Hansestadt Lübeck: Festschrift für Antjekathrin Graßmann zum 65. Geburtstag,* ed. Rolf Hammel-Kiesow and Michael Hundt (Lübeck: Schmidt-Römhild, 2005), 113–25.

[58]   For an outline of the sources, see Heimpel, "Königlicher Weihnachtsdienst"; cf. Bojcov, "Höfische Feste," summarizing on 226–27 the account by Richental, *Konzil,* 2: *Kommentar und Text,* 169–71.

[59]   For his biography, see *Ulrichs von Richental Chronik,* ed. Buck, 9–12; Eduard Heyck, "Richental, Ulrich von," *Allgemeine Deutsche Biographie* XXVIII, 1889, 433–35; Konrad Beyerle, "Ulrich von Richental," *Zeitschrift für Geschichte des Oberrheins* NF 14 (1899): 13–27; Otto Feger, "Zur Konzilchronik des Ulrich von Richental," Richental, *Konzil,* 2: *Kommentar und Text,* 21–36; here especially 22–25; Dieter Mertens, "Ulrich Richental," *Verfasserlexikon* VIII, 1992, 55–60; Wilhelm Matthiessen, "U. (v.) Richental," *Lexikon des Mittelalters* VIII, 1997, 1201–02.

[60]   For a contrastive viewpoint, see Maurer, "Das Konstanzer Konzil als städtisches Ereignis," 160. As to the chronicle itself, see Feger, "Konzilchronik"; Stefan Weinfurter, "Zum Gestaltungsprinzip der Chronik des Ulrich Richental," *Freiburger Diözesan-Archiv* 94 (1974): 517–31; Wilhelm Matthiessen, "Ulrich Richentals Chronik des Konstanzer Konzels: Studien zur Behandlung eines universalen Großereignisses durch die bürgerliche Chronistik," *Annuarium Historiae Conciliorum* 17 (1985): 71–192, 323–455. Cf. Gisela Wacker, "Ulrich Richentals Chronik des Konstanzer Konzils und ihre Funktionalisierung im 15. und 16. Jahrhundert," Ph.D. diss. University of Tübingen, 2001, vol. 1: http://w210.ub.uni-tuebingen.de/dbt/volltexte/2002/520/pdf/Band_1.pdf; vol. 2: http://w210.ub.uni-tuebingen.de/volltexte/2002/520/pdf/Band_2_low.pdf) (last accessed on April 6, 2009). Schenk argues convincingly for the illustrations as being close to reality, "Der Einzug König Sigismunds;" cf. Lilli Fischel, "Kunstgeschichtliche Bemerkungen zu Ulrich Richentals Chronik des Konstanzer Konzils," *Zeitschrift für die Geschichte des Oberrheins* 68 (1959): 321–37; Lilli Fischel, "Die Bilderfolge der Richental-Chronik, besonders der Konstanzer Handschrift,"

aspects of the time and the region of its origin, but definitely contains a specific urban-civic point of view toward the events as they evolved in front of his eyes—or "Wirklichkeitssicht,"[61] as Wilhelm Matthiessen has termed it. It does not belong to the specific type of conciliar chronicles but rather represents urban historiography.[62] Ulrich refers to himself in the beginning of his work: "das alles ich Uolrich Richental zesammenbracht hab, und es eigentlich von hus ze hus erfaren hab, wann ich burger und seßhaft ze Costentz was, (. . .) erkannt was, das mir gaistlich und och weltlich herren saiten, wes ich se dann ye frauget"[63] (as a citizen and resident of Constance, I, Ulrich Richenthal, have assembled all of this. I have either directly witnessed or have been told of the reported events by clergy and by laymen).

Consequently, his narrative cannot simply be categorized as historiography, but in addition shows elements of what has been called an ego-document,[64] expressing a subjectively true reality that can be tested for plausibility solely by comparison with corresponding sources.[65] Richental names the participants in the royal entry either by name or by their respective social group: The following of King Sigismund and Queen Barbara consisted of the queen's sister queen Anna of Bosnia, the elector Rudolf III. of Saxony (Sachsen-Wittenberg), and Sigismund's niece, the countess Elisabeth of Württemberg; furthermore two high-ranking Turkish prisoners-of-war, "quorum unus erat rex et alius dux" (one of them was a king, the other one a duke),[66] and the accompanying servants.[67] The citizens of Constance had made the preparations mentioned above, sent out ships and heated

61 Richental, *Konzil*, 2: *Kommentar und Text*, 37–55.
62 Matthiessen, "U. (v.) Richental," 1202. Schenk, "Der Einzug König Sigismunds," 96, writes of it as a class-specific perception ("schichtspezifischen Wahrnehmung").
See Maurer, "Das Konstanzer Konzil als städtisches Ereignis," 152–53; Cf. in general *Städtische Geschichtsschreibung im Spätmittelalter und in der frühen Neuzeit*, ed. Peter Johanek. Städteforschung. Reihe A: Darstellungen, 47 (Cologne, Weimar, and Vienna: Böhlau, 2000).
63 *Ulrichs von Richental Chronik*, ed. Buck, 13.
64 Cf. Benigna von Krusenstjern, "Was sind Selbstzeugnisse? Begriffskritische und quellenkundliche Überlegungen anhand von Beispielen aus dem 17. Jahrhundert," *Historische Anthropologie* 2 (1994): 462–71; *Egodocuments and History: Autobiographical Writing in its Social Context Since the Middle Ages*, ed. Rudolf Dekker. Publicaties van de Faculteit der Historische en Kunstwetenschappen, 38 (Hilversum: Verloren 2002).
65 For the problem of objectivity—merely understood as verifiable, even if conveyed information—see, e.g., Detlef Junker, "Objektivität/Parteilichkeit," Lexikon Geschichtswissenschaft. Hundert Grundbegriffe, ed. Stefan Jordan (Stuttgart: Reclam, 2003), 227–31.
66 *Der Liber gestorum des Jacobus Cerretanus*, ed. *Acta Concilii Constanciensis*, ed. Heinrich Finke, vol. 2: *Konzilstagebücher, Sermones, Reform- und Verfassungsakten*, ed. Heinrich Finke in cooperation with Johannes Hollnsteiner (Münster: Regensberg, 1923), 171–348; here 200.
67 Richental, *Konzil*, 2: *Kommentar und Text*, 169–70; cf. Heimpel, "Königlicher Weihnachtsdienst," 391; Niederstätter, *Ante portas*, 128; Hack, *Empfangszeremoniell*, 564–55; Schenk, "Der Einzug König Sigismunds," 79.

the council chambers in the city hall,[68] which would doubtless be welcome after a lake passage by night in cargo vessels in late December. It may have been three o'clock in the morning when the royal passengers reached the harbor and were guided to the city hall.[69]

By Richental's lists of names and by the heraldic information on the bearers of the canopy in the chronicle's illustration, one can partially identify the townsmen escorting the king and his entourage from the St. Konradsbrücke[70] to the city hall on the fish market[71] via the Konradstor or Fischbrucktor[72] and later on to the cathedral through the Blattengasse[73]: "Hainrich von Ulm, Hainrich Schiltar, Hanns Hagen, Hainrich Ehinger" *were the bearers of the royal canopy*; "Conrat Mangolt, Conrad in der Bünd, Caspar Gumpost," and "Hainrich von Tettikoven" held the canopy for the two queens.[74] It is more than likely that the city's former mayor, "Hanns Swartzach,"[75] who had just completed his term,[76] was also present on the way as well as his successor in office, Heinrich von Ulm.[77] Gerrit Jasper Schenk assumes that three-fourths of the canopy-bearers were patricians, among them the reeve and other office holders.[78]

This social group was at that time allotted only one-third of the posts in the municipal government, but nevertheless could argue two cases on that occasion—in front of the city public and in front of the king's eyes[79]: their outstanding position as urban elite[80] and the presentation of the commune's civic order, which was to be manifested in the entering ceremony.[81] "Hainrich von Ulm, Hainrich Schiltar, Conrat Mangolt," and "Hainrich von Tettikoven" were among

---

[68]   Richental, *Konzil*, 2: *Kommentar und Text*, 169; cf. Heimpel, "Königlicher Weihnachtsdienst," 391; Hack, *Empfangszeremoniell*, 565, argues conclusively that a delegation of the Constance city council went out to Überlingen to greet the king and returned with him.

[69]   Heimpel, "Königlicher Weihnachtsdienst," 392–93.

[70]   Heimpel, "Königlicher Weihnachtsdienst," 392 with note 25; Schenk, "Der Einzug König Sigismunds," 80; cf. Helmut Maurer, *Konstanz im Mittelalter*, 2 vols. Geschichte der Stadt Konstanz, 2; Konstanz im Mittelalter, 2 (Constance: Stadler, 1989); here vol. 2, 18 and 36–37.

[71]   Hack, *Empfangszeremoniell*, 565.

[72]   Schenk, "Der Einzug König Sigismunds," 80.

[73]   Schenk, "Der Einzug König Sigismunds," 80.

[74]   Richental, *Konzil*, 2: *Kommentar und Text*, 170.

[75]   Richental, *Konzil*, 2: *Kommentar und Text*, 169.

[76]   Richental, *Konzil*, 2: *Kommentar und Text*, 167.

[77]   Schenk, "Der Einzug König Sigismunds," 86 with note 64.

[78]   Cf. Schenk, *Zeremoniell und Politik*, 467 with note 1130, and Matthiessen, "Ulrich Richentals Chronik," 146–48, 186–88; Schenk, "Der Einzug König Sigismunds," 86, 89.

[79]   For the problem of the public sphere in this case, see Schenk, "Der Einzug König Sigismunds," 72–73.

[80]   Schenk, *Zeremoniell und Politik*, 223, note 694.

[81]   Schenk, *Zeremoniell und Politik*, 223. Schenk, "Der Einzug König Sigismunds," 82, follows Weinfurter, "Gestaltungsprinzip," in pointing out that Richental may have used his chronicle to portray his own idea of public order.

the wealthiest citizens according to the tax roll of 1425, as was a member of the In der Bünd family.[82] Konrad Mangold—covered exemplarily by Klaus D. Bechtold in his study on the social history of Constance—was mayor, deputy mayor, and member of the city council,[83] besides being married to Barbara, the sister of Konrad In der Bünd.[84] Bechtold has analyzed an abundance of connections within the citizenry of Constance: Heinrich Schilter and Heinrich von Ulm, e.g., were members of a faction of 23 persons, who had to pay taxes for movable values of more than 5000 lb hl in the year 1418.[85] Members of the Ehinger family held the offices of mayor, deputy mayor, and others frequently; Heinrich was sheriff at the time of Sigismund's entry.[86] Heinrich Tettikoven was mayor in 1413, Caspar Gumpost was presiding mayor in 1418, following mayor 1423, and sat in the city council in the meantime;[87] Hans Hagen was reeve in 1414.[88]

Other personnel are also depicted in the illustrations of the Richental chronicle—not the least clerics: Another source emphasizes, viewing it from a papal background, the attendance of the local bishop[89] and clergy[90] in certain ceremonies. The clearly visible law enforcement staff hints at the actual presence of the masses, which were welcome as a cheering crowd but had to be contained from shoving and bothering the processions.[91] Certainly, male servants and maidservants were needed in great numbers to guarantee the convenience of the dignitaries—even if they were not considered dignified enough to appear in the illustration.

Surely, a festive entry was no singularity in late-medieval Constance; it was an element of the ceremonial repertoire of the city.[92] However, in this case, among other things, the travelling speed of the approaching king was quite unusual. After his coronation in Aachen in November Sigismund rushed south not merely to reach the recently opened council, whose patron he was. He obviously wanted to

---

[82]   Bechtold, *Zunftbürgerschaft*, 29–30.
[83]   Bechtold, *Zunftbürgerschaft*, 32–33 with note 31.
[84]   Bechtold, *Zunftbürgerschaft*, 33.
[85]   Bechtold, *Zunftbürgerschaft*, 86.
[86]   Bechtold, *Zunftbürgerschaft*, 142.
[87]   Bechtold, *Zunftbürgerschaft*, 137, note 231.
[88]   Schenk, "Der Einzug König Sigismunds," 86. For the above mentioned person, cf. *Die Konstanzer Ratslisten des Mittelalters*, ed. Konrad Beyerle (Heidelberg: Winter, 1898).
[89]   At that time Otto III, Margrave of Hachberg-Rötteln, cf. "Otto von Hachberg," *Die Bischöfe des Heiligen Römischen Reiches: ein biographisches Lexikon*, ed. Erwin Gatz and Clemens Brodkorb (Berlin: Duncker & Humblot, 2001), 298. For an overview on the bishop's court, see Andreas Bihrer, "Konstanz, Bf.e von," *Ein dynastisch-topographisches Handbuch*; here vol. 1: 548–51.
[90]   This is according to Hack, *Empfangszeremoniell*, 566 and note 89. He refers to the above mentioned *Liber gestorum* of the curial Jacobus Cerretanus as in note 65; here 199–200.
[91]   Schenk, *Zeremoniell und Politik*, 343. These guards may even symbolize the dividing line between urban elite and urban underclass implying also a cultural barrier.
[92]   Hack, *Empfangszeremoniell*, 565.

fill his prominent role in the liturgy of the mass on Christmas Eve, which his father had helped to establish for the Holy Roman kings and emperors.[93] As things were, that agenda made a nocturnal entry necessary.[94] And the very combination of royal entry and royal lecture on the Gospel on Christmas Eve was another exceptional incident, even though no coincidence.[95] At this point, we leave the much observed setting of Christmas Eve in 1414 and turn to another aspect of social spatiality during the Council.

The lodging of the high nobility and the courtiers generated at least a spatial closeness of the social spheres. Richental reports in detail about the accommodations of the high-ranking guests in his city: "Glich nachdem do zoch unser her der küng mit der künginen und mit der von Wirtemberg zu der Laiter vor sant Steffan, das dozem l was Conrats in der Bünd genant Rüll, und belibent darin dry tag und nacht"[96] (Immediately thereafter the king and the queen and the lord of Württemberg moved to the house known as "Zur Leiter" belonging to Konrad In der Bünd and stayed there for three days and nights). Afterwards the princes moved to the near-by Petershausen Abbey. The Duke of Saxony, e.g., was housed in a priest's home in the city center.[97] As was customary, the coats of arms of guests were transfixed on their hosts' houses—rendering that building almost some sort of extraterritorial status[98] and at the same time leaving some of the hosts, we may assume, ambivalent about that occupancy given the high consumptive expectations of noblemen.

Even if there is no distinctly court-based source reporting at great length about the happenings of the Council, it can be suggested that the festive entry of King Sigismund into Constance in 1414 was a multi-media event, a cultural enactment, and a communicative process between monarch, pope, delegates of the Council, and citizens.[99] By looking closely at this communicative-interactive process we come to the conclusion that the civic-courtly encounters in the topographical as well as in the socially relational spaces of the city[100] were vested with the

---

[93] In detail, Heimpel, "Königlicher Weihnachtsdienst," specifically 395–96.

[94] Schenk points to the "adventus" by night as a rare exception, Schenk, *Zeremoniell und Politik*, 218–19.

[95] Schenk, *Zeremoniell und Politik*, 379; Schenk, "Der Einzug König Sigismunds," 80–81.

[96] Richental, *Konzil*, 2: *Kommentar und Text*, 171. For Konrad, see Elfriede Kleß, "Das Konstanzer Patriziergeschlecht in der Bünd," *Schriften des Vereins für Geschichte des Bodensees und seiner Umgebung* 108 (1989): 13–67; here 40–42 and 57 Nr. A30. On the house "Zur Leiter," see Fritz Hirsch, *Bauwesen und Häuserbau*. Konstanzer Häuserbuch, 1 (Heidelberg: Winter, 1906), 281.

[97] Richental, *Konzil*, 2: *Kommentar und Text*, 171.

[98] Schenk, *Zeremoniell und Politik*, 255 with its note 83.

[99] This is the way how Schenk, "Der Einzug König Sigismunds," 96, puts it.

[100] See, e.g., Martina Löw, "Raum—topologische Dimensionen der Kultur," *Handbuch der Kulturwissenschaften: Grundlagen und Schlüsselbegriffe*, vol. 1, ed. Friedrich Jäger and Burkhard Liebsch (Stuttgart and Weimar: Metzler, 2004); here vol. 1: 46–59; *Sozialstruktur und Sozialtopographie vorindustrieller Städte: Beiträge eines Workshops am Institut für Geschichte der Martin-*

ceremonial procedures described above. Yet, the intertwining of ceremonial prescriptions, of courtly and civic participation along with the claims of both social reference systems to occupy symbolically the urban space during the Council generated, because of the specifics of occasion and situation, a social space that included both spheres, both sets of values and both concepts of social order. This integrative dynamic may not be easily attributed strictly to one sphere or the other.

The possible ramifications of such a perception for the analysis of the social constitution of courts and cities needs to be studied far more intensely for socially, geographically, and chronologically varying situations. Such an analytical framework would be necessary to get from question to hypothesis and finally to substantiated thesis on whether there was at all a self-contained urban-civic culture and society in premodern Europe.

After all, the tremendous social change from the court-centered societies of the Ancien Régime toward the civically dominated societies of modern times figuratively and factually 'caught fire' in the eighteenth century, but had its base and origin in the fourteenth through eighteenth centuries. The theoretical and methodological approach that we have proposed for future research on that topic still harbors a lot more research potential.

In closing we want to cast a few spotlights on other fields of research that are thematically adjacent to the panorama presented thus far: While the sources of information about the Council of Constance are primarily local, i.e., urban sources on the non-canonical events, other fifteenth-century court festivals are documented mainly from a courtly perspective. This is evident in three highly renowned princely weddings of the years 1474/1475 in Amberg, Urach, and Landshut, which were celebrated in indeed small territorial towns with palaces, but still could offer all the richness and refinement demanded of a contemporary court festival. Again, even on a much smaller scale, the townfolks were to provide supplies and lodge guests as well as to serve as audience and witnesses of the princely pomp.[101] Even there we see the formation of

---

Luther-Universität Halle-Wittenberg am 27. und 28. Januar 2000, ed. Matthias Meinhardt and Andreas Ranft. Hallische Beiträge zur Geschichte des Mittelalters und der Frühen Neuzeit, 1 (Berlin: Akademie Verlag, 2005).

[101] Zeilinger, *Uracher Hochzeit*; Karl-Heinz Spieß, "'So sie gecleydet wird nach deutschen sitten, so wirt sie ein wolgeschicktes fuerstin': Internationale Fürstenheiraten im Spätmittelalter," *Universität und Staat—Autonomie oder Abhängigkeit: 42. Jahrestagung der Universitätskanzler Greifswald 1999*, ed. Jürgen Kohler. Greifswalder Universitätsreden. NF, 94 (Greifswald: Ernst-Moritz-Arndt-Universität, 2000), 30–42; Karl-Heinz Spieß, "Fremdheit und Integration der ausländischen Ehefrau und ihres Gefolges bei internationalen Fürstenheiraten," *Fürstenhöfe und ihre Außenwelt: Aspekte gesellschaftlicher und kultureller Identität im deutschen Spätmittelalter*, ed. Thomas Zotz. Identitäten und Alteritäten, 16 (Würzburg: Ergon-Verlag, 2004), 267–90. Karl-Heinz Spieß, "Europa heiratet: Kommunikation und Kulturtransfer im Kontext europäischer

"Anwesenheitsgesellschaften," or communities established by those living concretely together irrespective of the social class differences.[102] For Rudolf Schlögl those social spaces are crucial in the building of social orders and allow a junction of micro-history with macro-history.

If one takes that notion one step further from the singular—if not recurring—situation of festivals with their extraordinary tradition to an analysis of everyday experience of the encounter between city and court, it is essential, first, to acknowledge that festivals did not socially suspend everyday life, but rather exalted or transposed it.[103] Of course, we will always have to cope with the scarcity of sources regarding quotidian contexts, that is, the everyday-life situation. Therefore, as many archaeological and historical sources as possible have to be considered to get in-depth results. It is quite significant in this context that Martina Stercken has also examined coins and seals in the chapter of her remarkable monograph *Städte der Herrschaft*, dealing with "Visuelle Präsenz von Herrschaft im Alltag" (visual presence of governmental power in everyday life).[104] The relationship between commune and lordship can be described in much greater detail by including, for example, seigneurial as well as municipal account books and ordinances, corpora of correspondences in the data base—especially when it comes to (small) towns of the late Middle Ages and early modern times.[105] For the

Königsheiraten des Spätmittelalters," *Europa im späten Mittelalter: Politik—Gesellschaft—Kultur*, ed. Rainer C. Schwinges, Christian Hesse and Peter Moraw. Historische Zeitschrift. Beiheft 40 (Munich: Oldenbourg, 2006), 435–64.

[102]  Rudolf Schlögl, *Der Raum als "Universalmedium" in der frühneuzeitlichen Stadt*: http://www.uni-konstanz.de/FuF/Philo/Geschichte/Schloegl/Schloegl/RaumalsUniversalmedium03.pdf; alternatively: http://74.125.113.132/search?q=cache:JTDlXjd57HgJ:www.uni-konstanz.de/FuF/Philo/Geschich te/Schloegl/Schloegl/RaumalsUniversalmedium03.pdf+%22Der+Raum+als+%E2%80%9CUnive rsalmedium&cd=1&hl=en&ct=clnk&gl=us&client=firefox-a (last accessed on April 6, 2009); cf. Rudolf Schlögl, "Kommunikation und Vergesellschaftung unter Anwesenden: Formen des Sozialen und ihre Transformation in der Frühen Neuzeit," *Geschichte und Gesellschaft* 34.2 (2008): 155–224; cf. the assumption by Schlögl according to which the pre-modern public space was transferred from the court to the city, Rudolf Schlögl, "Politik beobachten: Öffentlichkeit und Medien in der Frühen Neuzeit," *Zeitschrift für historische Forschung* 35 (2008): 581–616.

[103]  Cf. Werner Paravicini, "Alltag bei Hofe," *Alltag bei Hofe*, ed. Werner Paravicini. Residenzenforschung, 5 (Sigmaringen: Thorbecke, 1995), 9–30; Zeilinger, *Uracher Hochzeit*, 18.

[104]  Stercken, *Städte der Herrschaft*, 184–88. For the non-feudal, civic-courtly relations between two eminent members of the Holy Roman Empire around 1500, the Elector of Saxony and the imperial city Nuremberg, see Sina Westphal, "Briefe und Macht: Die Reichsstadt Nürnberg, Kursachsen und das Reich um 1500," Ph.D. diss. Kiel 2009.

[105]  Christian Schneider, *Hovezuht: Literarische Hofkultur und höfisches Lebensideal um Herzog Albrecht III. von Österreich und Erzbischof Pilgrim II. von Salzburg (1365–1396)*. Beiträge zur älteren Literaturgeschichte (Heidelberg: Winter, 2008), examines the interaction of courtly and civic societies on the basis of courtly behavioral patterns according to literary tradition; see particularly the chapter on "Adelsgesellschaften und Bürgerschichten," 50–58.

early period of European urbanization in the Middle Ages, i.e., mainly the twelfth and thirteenth centuries, it would be well worth the effort also to reevaluate the diplomatic and urbarial tradition from the perspective of an integrating focus on city and court.

Klaus Amann and Max Siller

(University of Innsbruck, Austria)

# Urban Literary Entertainment in the Middle Ages and the Early Modern Age: The Example of Tyrol[1]

## Preliminaries

Looking at "Urban Literary Entertainment in the Middle Ages and the Early Modern Age," we restrict ourselves to a certain geographical area and this, as we think, for good reason. Speaking, as it is, about the "city" in the Middle Ages and the Early Modern Age, we face a huge historical-sociological complex, even if we just take Central Europe into account. This complex ranges from the great imperial and residential cities to the smaller ones founded by regional princes, down to the towns of petty local and patrimonial rulers. Only the privilege of holding a town charter distinguishes the latter ones from the market towns, which are often much larger.[2] Whereas the population of the great cities is very heterogeneous, that of the smaller towns is comparatively homogenous, and, like the population of the surrounding areas, lives off crop farming and livestock breeding.

Cologne, with its 40,000 inhabitants by far the largest German city at the end of the Middle Ages, a city with a history reaching back to the times when it served as the official residence of a Roman governor, cannot be compared to the town of Glurns, founded at the end of the thirteenth century by the Count of Tyrol, where until to this very day one can see the manure heaps in the streets — or can it? One of the smallest towns of the Alpine region, even Glurns is situated on a spot which has been a traffic junction since Roman times. This — in one way or another — very

---

[1]    We would like to express our gratitude to Marilyn Sandidge and Albrecht Classen for their thorough revision of this article and for their many helpful suggestions, which we greatly appreciate.

[2]    Cf. Heinz Dopsch, "Epoche – sozialgeschichtlicher Abriß," *Von der Handschrift zum Buchdruck: Spätmittelalter, Reformation, Humanismus. 1320–1572*, ed. Ingrid Bennewitz and Ulrich Müller. Deutsche Literatur: Eine Sozialgeschichte, 2. (Reinbek bei Hamburg: Rowohlt, 1991), 9–31.

central situation is crucial for an urban settlement and it is also the prerequisite for its development not only when we speak of economy and trade, but equally so when we think about the arts, culture, and education. Exchanging goods and ideas is the fundamental element which leads to new ways of living and new standards of civilization in the late-medieval "age of the city."

If we now turn to the analysis of literature that was produced and/or received in any given city, we first of all would like to point out that we must aim at a sound founding of the subject on a basis of local history. Not only the Cologne area, but all areas surrounding greater urban centers, perhaps those around cities with more than 20,000 inhabitants,[3] should be explored according to their sometimes very different premises: "Die deutsche Städtelandschaft bietet an der Wende zur Neuzeit ein buntes Bild"[4] (The overall picture of the German city during the transition from the Middle Ages to the Early Modern Age is quite colorful).

We have chosen the example of Tyrol, because it is very suitable as a heuristic area given the fact that it has been a realigned territory since the late thirteenth century.[5] The area ranged from the Salurn ravine (including some single extensions into the Veronese and Tridentine areas) to the Zillertal valley, where it overlapped with the archdiocese of Salzburg. It had approximately the same western borders as nowadays, and from 1271 onwards, the Mühlbach ravine formed the Eastern border with the county of Görz in the Pustertal valley.

---

[3]   Augsburg, Gdansk, Lübeck, Magdeburg, Metz, Nuremberg, and Strasbourg could be mentioned here, but also the increasingly important imperial residential cities Prague and Vienna. Cf. Dopsch, "Epoche – sozialgeschichtlicher Abriß," 21–22.

[4]   Dopsch, "Epoche – sozialgeschichtlicher Abriß," 21.

[5]   Cf. especially Josef Riedmann, "Das Mittelalter," Von den Anfängen bis 1490: Geschichte des Landes Tirol. Vol. 1, ed. Josef Fontana, Peter W. Haider, Walter Leitner, Georg Mühlberger, Rudolf Palme, Othmar Parteli, and Josef Riedmann (Bozen, Innsbruck, and Vienna: Athesia-Tyrolia, 1985), 265–661; here 399–410; 481–86. Tyrol can serve as an example in case for a paradigmatic discussion of "Methoden, Aufgaben und Möglichkeiten einer territorialen Literaturgeschichtsschreibung des Mittelalters und der Frühneuzeit" (methods, tasks, and possibilities of writing the literary history of a medieval and early modern territory). See: Max Siller, "Territorium und Literatur: Überlegungen zu Methoden, Aufgaben und Möglichkeiten einer territorialen Literaturgeschichtsschreibung des Mittelalters und der Frühneuzeit," Geschichte und Region / Storia e regione 1,2 (1992), 39–84. Cf. also id., Literatur – Sprache – Territorium: Methoden, Aufgaben und Möglichkeiten einer regionalen Literaturgeschichtsschreibung des Mittelalters. 3 Vols. (Innsbruck: Institut für Germanistik, 1991), Vol. 1, 8–45.

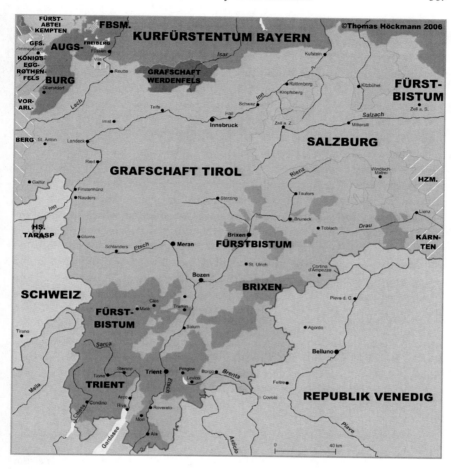

Figure 1: Tyrol in 1766 (http://hoeckmann.de/deutschland/tirol.htm)

## History of Literature: Some Introductory Remarks

Looking at the geopolitical situation of Tyrol and at the small web of its towns and their connections to other territories allows for following possible "literary routes"[6] quite exactly. It can be shown that literature written in medieval Tyrol is not necessarily restricted to its cities, but there is a constant interaction between the towns and the surrounding rural areas. The bishop of Brixen, Ulrich Putsch, for example, wrote *Das liecht der sel* (*The Light of the Soul*), his well-known translation of the *Lumen Animae*, in 1426,[7] when he was a parish priest in Dorf Tirol (the village of Tirol near Meran, which gave its name to the whole territory), as the acrostic of the rhymed prologue shows. It seems that he found time for his translation activities thanks to the leisurely lifestyle of a rural priest. It may well be that Hans Vintler found himself in a similar situation when he wrote his *Blumen der Tugend* (*Flowers of Virtue*) in 1411. Maybe only in the rural seclusion of his office as a "Hawptmann Vnd phleger auf dem Stain An dem Ritten"[8] (captain and governor of Stein castle in Ritten) it was possible for him to translate and revise the more than 10,000 verses of the Italian *Fiore di Virtù*. Oswald von Wolkenstein obviously also composed parts of his oeuvre in the solitude of the woods around his Hauenstein castle: "Auff ainem runden kofel smal, mit dickem wald umbfangen" (Kl. 44, 22–23;[9] on a round and narrow mountain top, surrounded by deep woods), where he was accompanied by "neur kelber, gaiss, böck, rinder und knospot leut, swarz, hässeleich" (Kl. 44, 46–47; only calves, goats, bucks, cattle, and coarse people, black, ugly).

---

[6]   Horst Wenzel, "Zentralität und Regionalität: Zur Vernetzung mittelalterlicher Kommunikationszentren in Raum und Zeit," *Bildungsexklusivität und volkssprachliche Literatur. Literatur vor Lessing – nur für Experten?*, ed. Klaus Grubmüller. Kontroversen, alte und neue. Akten des VII. Internationalen Germanisten-Kongresses Göttingen 1985, Vol. 7 (Tübingen: Niemeyer, 1986), 14–26; here 26.

[7]   Now, thanks to Nigel Harris there is a bilingual edition: *The Light of the Soul: The 'Lumen anime C' and Ulrich Putsch's 'Das liecht der sel'. Critical edition with introduction*, ed. Nigel Harris (Oxford, Vienna, et al.: Lang, 2007).

[8]   Cf. Max Siller, "Die Standesqualität der Vintler von Bozen zu Beginn des 15. Jahrhunderts. Prolegomena zu einer Interpretation von Hans Vintlers 'Blumen der Tugend' (1411)," *Durch aubenteuer muess man wagen vil: Festschrift Anton Schwob*, ed. Wernfried Hofmeister and Bernd Steinbauer. Innsbrucker Beiträge zur Kulturwissenschaft. Germanistische Reihe, 57 (Innsbruck: Institut für Germanistik, 1997), 447–62; here 456–57.

[9]   *Die Lieder Oswalds von Wolkenstein*, ed. Karl Kurt Klein. 3rd edition, ed. Hans Moser, Norbert Richard Wolf, and Notburga Wolf. Altdeutsche Textbibliothek, 55 (1962; Tübingen: Niemeyer, 1987). The songs in this edition will hence be referred to as Kl. Now there is an English translation: Albrecht Classen, *The Poems of Oswald von Wolkenstein. An English Translation of the Complete Works (1376/77–1445)*. The New Middle Ages (New York: Palgrave, 2008). The translations used in this paper are our own.

Things may be different with the literature of the mendicants. Even if they were partly begging for their living in rural areas, their "home" was and has always been the city. In Bozen, Heinrich von Burgeis,[10] born perhaps in the 2nd decade of the thirteenth century in Trent, founded the Dominican monastery between the years 1272 and 1275, and here he wrote his didactic confessional tractate *Seelenrat* (*Counsel of the Soul*), which shows a high socio-political ethos.

## Songwriting in the City: The *Sterzing Miscellanea Manuscript* (*Sterzinger Miszellaneenhandschrift*)

Lays or songs meet the needs of urban literary entertainment very well.[11] Even if the *Gesellschaftslied* and the folk song, which developed in the late Middle Ages, very often emerged from the sphere of the gentry, and even if the texts were spread among and recorded by the noble classes, by far the bigger part of the songs originated from the cities.[12] The famous *Sterzing Miscellanea Manuscript*, dating back to the early fifteenth century (now preserved in the Sterzing municipal archives),[13] seems to show very well the change from courtly love poetry to late-medieval popular poetry. In this collection of songs, authentic and 'apocryphal' Neidhart-songs from the thirteenth century and songs from a courtly

---

[10] For Heinrich von Burgeis, see: Max Siller, "Der Südtiroler Dichter Heinrich von Burgeis und die Entstehung des Bozner Dominikanerklosters (1272–1276)," *Bozen – Von den Anfängen bis zur Schleifung der Stadtmauer: Berichte über die internationale Studientagung, veranstaltet vom Assessorat für Kultur der Stadtgemeinde Bozen, Schloß Maretsch – April 1989* (Bozen: Athesia, 1991), 223–31; Max Siller, "Der Tiroler Dichter Heinrich von Burgeis und die Politik seiner Zeit (13. Jahrhundert)," *Der Vinschgau und seine Nachbarräume: Vorträge des landeskundlichen Symposiums veranstaltet vom Südtiroler Kulturinstitut in Verbindung mit dem Bildungshaus Schloß Goldrain. Schloß Goldrain, 27. bis 30. Juni 1991*, ed. Rainer Loose. Schriftenreihe des Südtiroler Kulturinstitutes, 18 (Bozen: Athesia, 1993), 165–79.

[11] Cf. Thomas Cramer, *Geschichte der deutschen Literatur im späten Mittelalter*. Geschichte der deutschen Literatur im Mittelalter, 3 (Munich: dtv, 2000), 312.

[12] Cf. Cramer, *Geschichte der deutschen Literatur im späten Mittelalter*, 312.

[13] For the *Sterzing Miscellanea Manuscript*, see Manfred Zimmermann, *Die Sterzinger Miszellaneen-Handschrift: Kommentierte Edition der deutschen Dichtungen*. Innsbrucker Beiträge zur Kulturwissenschaft. Germanistische Reihe, 8 (Innsbruck: Institut für Germanistik, 1980). Cf. also: Max Siller, "Wo und wann ist die Sterzinger Miszellaneen-Handschrift entstanden?" *Entstehung und Typen mittelalterlicher Lyrikhandschriften: Akten des Grazer Symposiums, 13.–17. Oktober 1999*, ed. Anton Schwob and András Vizkelety in collaboration with Andrea Hofmeister-Winter. Jahrbuch für Internationale Germanistik. Reihe A: Kongressberichte, 52 (Bern, Vienna, et al.: Lang, 2001), 255–80; Manfred Zimmermann, "Vigil Raber und die 'Sterzinger Miszellaneen-Handschrift,'" *Vigil Raber: Zur 450. Wiederkehr seines Todesjahres. Akten des 4. Symposiums der Sterzinger Osterspiele (25.–27.3.2002)*, ed. Michael Gebhardt and Max Siller. Schlern-Schriften, 326 (Innsbruck: Wagner, 2004), 269–74.

tradition of love-poetry,[14] e.g., no. 27: "Trostlicher trost, mein hochstes hail" (Comforting consolation, my greatest happiness) are recorded next to Neidhart-stories: nos. 24 and 34: *Awenttawr der weiz ich vil, da von ich nw euch sagen wil* (I know a lot of adventures, of which I shall now talk to you), *Veilchenschwank* (Violet jest narrative) A and B, and no. 40, the so-called *Chanterelle and Ointment*, which is preserved only in the Sterzing manuscript. These 'Neidhartiana' became immensely popular from the fourteenth century onwards and can be found next to bawdy songs about women, like no. 17: "Von Prag ein hawpt aus Pehamerlant" (A head from Prague in Bohemia). Refrain-songs like no. 12, "Was sol ich furbaz fahen an" (What am I supposed to do in the future?), by Herman Smid are probably taken from the sphere of the popular drinking song.[15]

---

[14]  Cf. Cramer, *Geschichte der deutschen Literatur im späten Mittelalter*, 314–15.
[15]  Cf. Cramer, *Geschichte der deutschen Literatur im späten Mittelalter*, 315.

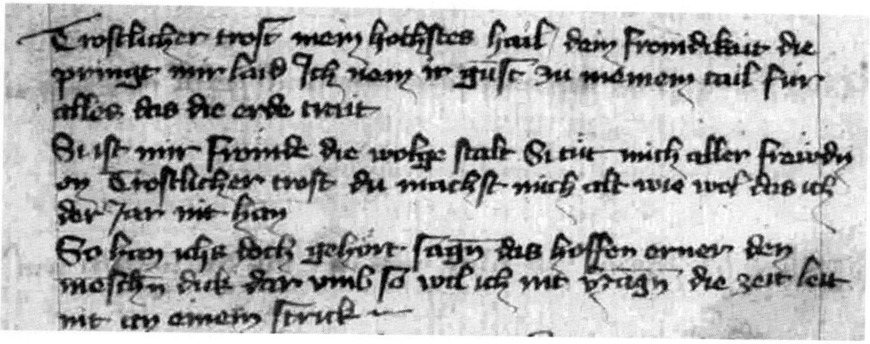

Figure 2: *Sterzing Miscellanea Manuscript,* fol. 42r (detail)

## [Anonymous] *Trostlicher trost, mein hochstes hail*[16]

| I. | Trostlicher trost, mein hochstes hail, |
| | dein fromdikait die pringt mir laid. |
| | jch nem ir gunst zu meinem tail |
| | für alles, das die erde trait. |

| II. | Si ist mir frömde, die wolgestalt, |
| | si tut mich aller frewdn on. |
| | trostlicher trost, du machst mich alt, |
| | wie wol das ich der jar nit han. |

| III. | So han ichs doch gehört sagen, |
| | das hoffen erner den menschen dick. |
| | dar vmb so wil ich nit verzagen, |
| | die zeit leit nit an einem strick. |

| [I. | Comforting consolation, my greatest happiness! |
| | It is painful for me that you avoid me. |
| | I, for my part, would prefer her grace |
| | over anything else in the world. |

| II. | The beauty avoids me. |
| | Thus, she takes away every joy from me. |
| | Comforting consolation! You make me old, |
| | even though I am still young. |

| III. | Yet they say that hope |
| | often saves man. |
| | Therefore, I do not want to lose courage. |
| | Time is not tied with a rope.] |

Also, the mixture of German and Latin texts in the *Sterzing Miscellanea Manuscript* hints at its overall "urban character"; it may very well be that a grammar school teacher or another educated person has written it.

## The 'Innsbruck Song'

However, the small Tyrolean urban settlements completely lacked the scholarly air of a university city. Most Tyroleans gained their higher education in Vienna or Padua. And yet, the inhabitants of Tyrolean cities may not have needed collegiate tutelage or literary traditions in order to get to know carousals and

---

[16]　　Zimmermann, *Die Sterzinger Miszellaneen-Handschrift*, No. 27 (153).

nightly "courting." Especially the burghers in their parlors probably fostered collective music-making and singing, as we can see on a woodcut in the *Ambras Songbook*[17] from 1582.

---

[17] The *Ambras Songbook*, formerly from Ambras castle near Innsbruck, library of Ferdinand II (1529–1595), contains 260 songs. *Das Ambraser Liederbuch vom Jahre 1582*, ed. Joseph Bergmann. Bibliothek des literarischen Vereins in Stuttgart, 12 (Stuttgart: Literarischer Verein, 1845). Albrecht Classen, *Deutsche Liederbücher des 15. und 16. Jahrhunderts*. Volksliedstudien, 1 (Münster, New York, et al.: Waxmann, 2001).

Figure 3: *Ambras Songbook,* front page (detail)

In any case, songs were sung in the Tyrolean towns, like the touching farewell-
and love-song "Isbruck, ich mus dich lassen" (Innsbruck, I Must Leave You),
which Heinrich Isaac (1450–1517) set to music and which has been handed down
through many manuscripts and prints. The content of the song shows the
important role the city plays in the first stanza of the poem. Being the residence
of the loved one, it serves as a metaphor for the beloved woman herself.

I
    Isbruck ich mus dich lassen,
    ich fahr dahin mein strassen,
    in frembde land da hin,
    Mein freud ist mir genommen,
    die ich nit kan bekommen,
    wo ich im elend bin.

II
    Gros leid mus ich jetzt tragen,
    das ich allein thu klagen,
    dem liebsten bulen mein,
    Ach lieb nun las mich armen,
    im hertzen dein erbarmen,
    das ich mus von dannen sein.

III
    Ach frewlein du solt nit weinen,
    du bist doch nit alleine,
    nim dir einen ringen mut,
    Ich wil dich nit auffgeben,
    dieweil ich hab das leben,
    hett ich des keysers gut.

IV
    Mein trost ob allen weiben,
    dein thu ich ewig bleiben,
    steht trew der ehren fromb,
    Nun mus dich Gott bewaren,
    in aller tugendt sparen,
    bis das ich wider kom          (*Ambras Songbook*, no. CLXXXVIII).

[I
    Innsbruck, I must leave you
    I travel along my way
    To foreign lands
    My joy is taken away from me
    Which I cannot get back again
    In an alien country.

II
    Now I have to bear great sorrows
    Which I only lament
    To my loved one
    Oh love, have pity for poor me

In your heart
That I must travel from thence.

III  Oh lady, do not cry,
For you are not alone.
Stay in a light mood!
I shall not abandon you
As long as I am alive,
Even if I had the emperor's riches.

IV  My consolation above all women!
I shall always be yours,
Faithful to you, full of honor.
Now God shall protect you,
Keep you all virtuous,
Until I shall come back!]

## The 'Glurns Song'

Whereas the people of Innsbruck still like to sing their 'Innsbruck song,' the song of yet another town has probably been belted out only by its enemies: the so-called 'Glurns song.' In the year of 1499, the Swiss, together with the peasants of Grisons, defeated King Maximilian's Tyrolean army in a disastrous battle—the so-called Calven-battle—near the town of Glurns. This devastating defeat of the Tyroleans was celebrated by the victorious adversaries in a few historio-political songs. The triumphalistic 'Glurns song' "So will ich aber singen, Singen ein nüws gedicht"[18] (I want to sing again, sing a new song) can undoubtedly be counted among the most impressive examples of contemporary political songwriting. Because of this battle near Glurns, the town gained some notoriety and the description of the stampede of the royal troops, written down by a Tyrolean historian a century later, is comical and shocking at the same time: "Die Tyroller nemen iren weeg nacher Glurns, fliechen zu einem thor ein, zum anndern wider aus, mit grosser eil der statt Meran zue" (the Tyroleans take to Glurns, they enter the town on one side, leave it on the other and with great speed hasten toward the city of Meran). This city wasn't far away and for many inhabitants of the town the

---

18  Cf. Max Siller, "Die Calvenschlacht (1499) in der Dichtung: das Bündner oder Glurnser Lied," *Calven 1499–1999: Bündnerisch-Tirolische Nachbarschaft. Vorträge der wissenschaftlichen Tagung im Rathaus Glurns vom 8. bis 11. September 1999 anläßlich des 500-Jahr-Gedenkens der Calvenschlacht,* ed. Josef Riedmann (Lana: Tappeiner, 2001), 263–86 (edition of the song 284–86) .

flight ended tragically, when the bridge over the river Etsch collapsed. The next day, Glurns was burning.[19]

## Drama

The literature we have mentioned so far had its greatest impact certainly in the city and only to a lesser extent in rural areas or on the castles of the gentry. Medieval plays, however, almost exclusively belong to the city. This applies, above all, to the religious play in its extended versions which lasted for a few days. This "cycle" of plays from Tyrol, which consists of three parts and is closely linked to the ecclesiastical rites before and on Easter day, has been referred to as *Tyrolean Passion Play* ever since Josef Eduard Wackernell first edited it in such a masterly way.[20] On Maundy Thursday, on Good Friday, and on Holy Saturday, or on Easter Sunday, a play of the Last Supper, a Passion Play, and an Easter Play were staged in the Tyrolean towns of Bozen, Brixen, Sterzing, and Hall. This thematic range of the Passion Play was extended by plays of Christ's entombment and Mary's Lament. Plays of the walk to Emmaus, the Ascension, and other plays going along with the liturgical calendar year were added. This tradition of religious plays, by the way, reached well into the modern era, when also rural communities started to stage plays.[21] Like the religious plays, the secular plays were also restricted to a particular time of the year, depending on the liturgical year: carnival.

---

[19] Cf. Siller, "Calvenschlacht."

[20] *Altdeutsche Passionsspiele aus Tirol: Mit Abhandlungen über ihre Entwicklung, Composition, Quellen, Aufführungen und literarhistorische Stellung*, ed. Josef Eduard Wackernell. Quellen und Forschungen zur Geschichte, Litteratur und Sprache Österreichs und seiner Kronländer, 1 (Graz: Styria, 1897). Cf. the overview in: Hansjürgen Linke, "Die Osterspiele des Debs-Codex," *Zeitschrift für deutsche Philologie* 104 (1985): 104–29.

[21] Wackernell, *Altdeutsche Passionsspiele aus Tirol*, CC–CCI; Anton Dörrer, "Passionsspiele, Tiroler," *Die deutsche Literatur des Mittelalters – Verfasserlexikon*, ed. Wolfgang Stammler and Karl Langosch. 1st ed., Vol. 3 (Berlin: de Gruyter, 1943), 742–835; here 769–71; Norbert Hölzl, *Theatergeschichte des östlichen Tirol: Vom Mittelalter bis zur Gegenwart*. 2 Vols. Theatergeschichte Österreichs, Band II: Tirol 2, 1/2 (Vienna, Graz, et al.: Böhlau, 1966–1967); Ekkehard Schönwiese, *Das Volksschauspiel im nördlichen Tirol: Renaissance und Barock*. Theatergeschichte Österreichs, Band II: Tirol 3 (Vienna: Verlag der Österreichischen Akademie der Wissenschaften, 1975). As one example among many, we would like to mention the *Sillian Passion Play* from eighteenth-century East Tyrol which has been handed down in a few versions (Hölzl, *Theatergeschichte des östlichen Tirol*, 17–164). The Passion Plays from Erl and Thiersee are based on a younger Oberammergau tradition (Schönwiese, *Das Volksschauspiel im nördlichen Tirol*, 28–29).

## Benedikt Debs and Vigil Raber[22]

We have to mention mainly two persons when we talk about Tyrolean drama in the Middle Ages and the Early Modern Era: Benedikt Debs and Vigil Raber. We know about the first one only that he was originally from Ingolstadt, that he worked as a grammar school teacher in Bozen, and that he was a passionate collector of drama texts.

At the beginning of the modern era, a remarkable figure emerges in Tyrol's literary history: Vigil Raber. He descends from a family who had been Sterzing residents since 1420, and he was probably born in the years around 1480. He died in 1552, in the middle of December, and was buried in Sterzing.[23] He was a painter by trade—there is evidence of his smaller works—and his achievements as a painter of coats of arms are quite impressive (Weimar, Brixen, and Neustift heraldic books); he may also have worked as a painter of panels.[24] His invaluable contribution to European culture, though, is his collection of manuscripts recording medieval religious and secular plays, the largest one in the German speaking world. On February 3rd, 1510, we meet him for the first time, as he starts to copy two secular plays (*Rumpold und Mareth III* and *Das Chorgericht II*); in 1539 he wrote down his last play, the (religious) *Tiroler Spiel vom reichen Mann und Lazarus* (*Tyrolean Play of the Rich Man and Lazarus*). All in all, he copied 40 plays in these 30 years, 15 religious and 25 secular ones.[25] The drama texts in his collection which were not copied by himself are of no lesser importance; among them is the well-known 'Debs Codex' containing the oldest stock of religious plays. The *Sterzing Miscellanea Manuscript* probably was among those manuscripts that were bought by Raber. This large collection of texts together with the stage props was sold for six florins to the city of Sterzing by his widow, *Virgili Räberin* already within a year after his death. Today, the Raber manuscripts are preserved in the Vigil-Raber-archives, a part of the Sterzing municipal archives.

---

[22]  Cf. Max Siller, "*Es mag auch chainer chain reichtum han, es mües ain ander mit armuet stan*: Tirolische Literatur des Mittelalters und der Frühneuzeit in ihrer europäischen Dimension," forthcoming 2009.

[23]  For details and further literature, see: *Vigil Raber: Zur 450. Wiederkehr seines Todesjahres. Akten des 4. Symposiums der Sterzinger Osterspiele (25.–27.3.2002)*, ed. Michael Gebhardt and Max Siller. Schlern-Schriften, 326 (Innsbruck: Wagner, 2004).

[24]  Cf. Harwick W. Arch, "Der Heraldiker Vigil Raber," *Vigil Raber*, ed. Michael Gebhardt and Max Siller, 33–43, and Leo Andergassen, "Vigil Raber als Tafelmaler," *Vigil Raber*, ed. Michael Gebhardt and Max Siller, 21–32.

[25]  For details, see: Hansjürgen Linke, "Vigil Raber als Schreiber," *Vigil Raber*, ed. Michael Gebhardt and Max Siller, 117–46; Eckehard Simon, "Die Fastnachtspielhefte: Vigil Raber als Schreiber, Textbearbeiter, Dramaturg und Spielleiter," *Vigil Raber*, ed. Michael Gebhardt and Max Siller, 213–33. Linke provides an accurate list of the plays copied by Raber, their chronological order, and the editions which have been published up to now.

For many Raber texts, 'models' or parallel versions have been found, which sometimes differ greatly from each other. Twelve of the 25 secular plays show, for example, a Nuremberg model. Earlier scholars tended to see Vigil Raber's "historical" achievements in his collecting activities and in his promotion of the local and regional theater-life, whereas nowadays we esteem Raber at least partly as the editor of his texts, too.[26] There is, for example, a version of a Nuremberg play, written probably by Hans Folz, called *Ein Faßnachtspil von einem Artzt vnd einem Krancken* (*A Shrovetide-Play about a Doctor and His Patient*), which was edited by Raber, in whose collection it is called *der scheissennd* (*the shitting* [*person*]).[27] Not only is the small river Fischbach, which runs through Nuremberg and is mentioned at the end of Folz's play, 'translocated' to the Bozen equivalent Talfer, but there are also remarkable linguistic and thus sociological changes: In Raber's version, the patient and his company, including the precursor, are German-speaking peasants, while the doctor is Italian and only speaks broken German.[28] This holds an enormous potential of additional comedy: There are the funniest misunderstandings between the farmers speaking their rural vernacular and the Italian doctor. In literary terms, the Raber version has undoubtedly to be preferred over the Nuremberg version.

It would be interesting to know more about Vigil Raber's political positions in his own restless times. Where was he, what did he do, for instance, during the Tyrolean peasants' uprising, when his slightly younger compatriot Michael Gaismair from Sterzing (born around 1491/1492, murdered on April 15th, 1532) took the lead in this movement? Raber knew Gaismair's family, not least because they also took part in theater performances. And what was his attitude toward the emerging Protestant Reformation, which found many followers in Sterzing? Can we deduce his political and religious positions from his repertoire of plays? When,

---

[26] "Raber hat offenbar alle von ihm aufgezeichneten Spiele bearbeitet. Sein Anteil an der Texterung – Zusatzverse, Solostücke, Pro- und Epiloge, 'abendfüllende' Doppelspielfassungen, ein neu aufgefundener "Beschluss" – war größer als die Forschung wahrgenommen hat." (Raber obviously also edited all plays he copied. The quota of his changing the texts—additional verses, solo parts, prologues, epilogues, 'feature-length' double versions, a newly discovered "conclusion"—was greater than scholars have hitherto assumed.) Simon, "Die Fastnachtspielhefte," 231. A similar statement is provided by Linke, "Vigil Raber als Schreiber," 144: "[E]r hat beim Abschreiben die Spiele zugleich auch bearbeitet." (By copying the texts, he [i.e., Raber] changed them at the same time.)

[27] A critical parallel edition is provided by: Max Siller, "Textkritische Paralleledition des Nürnberger Fastnachtspiels [Hans Folz], 'Ein Faßnachtspil von einem Artzt vnd einem Krancken' und des Sterzinger Fastnachtspiels 'der scheissennd'," *Fastnachtspiel – Commedia dell'arte. Gemeinsamkeiten – Gegensätze. Akten des 1. Symposiums der Sterzinger Osterspiele (31.3.–3.4.1991)*, ed. Max Siller. Schlern-Schriften, 290 (Innsbruck: Wagner, 1992), 161–98.

[28] For details, see: Max Siller, "Ausgewählte Aspekte des Fastnachtspiels im Hinblick auf die Aufführung des Sterzinger Spiels 'der scheissend'," *Fastnachtspiel – Commedia dell'arte*, ed. Max Siller, 147–59; here 151–54.

in any case, King Ferdinand's I repressions reached their peak in Tyrol around 1532, when anti-Catholic opinions were punished with fire and sword and when censorship and interior espionage threatened even the freedom of thought, when Michael Gaismair was stabbed by paid killers of the country's ruler near Padua and when Anabaptists were killed by the hundreds either with the executioner's ax or at the stake, the Shrovetide-play *Die zwen Stenndt* (*The Two Orders*) circulated in Tyrol. The play, which was probably written by Christoph Kefer, a grammar school teacher from Meran who was educated at the university of Vienna, shows a clear pro-Reformation tendency and it has survived only thanks to Vigil Raber, who copied it twice: once around 1533 and the second time in 1535.[29] What is even more important with regard to literary sociology and religious politics: Raber not only copied this drama twice—which is unheard of in his collection—he also staged it; we have proof of a performance in Sterzing in 1533, but it was probably played more often and possibly also in other Tyrolean towns.

## Sociological Aspects of Urban Drama

### a. Religious Plays

In addition to discussing problems of reconstructing a given text's historical situation of production and reception, questions about material culture and social relations have become more and more important over the past few years. Such research has to start in small geographical and social milieus,[30] and it is only possible, if—in addition to the texts—concrete contemporary notes about performances are preserved. "The social character of the actors," which "is formally sensed with their distinguished names and functions from the urbane [sic!] upper strata or from emphasized social elite groups"[31] can be pinpointed with the help of lists recording the actors' names of the Bozen[32] and Sterzing[33]

---

[29]  For the play's origins, performances, and author, see: Siller, *Literatur – Sprache – Territorium*, 375–87; 498–511; and most recently (summing up): Max Siller, "Die Lokalisierung der mittelalterlichen Spiele mit Hilfe der (historischen) Dialektologie," *Ritual und Inszenierung: Geistliches und weltliches Drama des Mittelalters*, ed. Hans-Joachim Ziegeler (Tübingen: Niemeyer, 2004), 247–54; here 251–54.

[30]  Wenzel, "Zentralität und Regionalität," 16.

[31]  Hannes Obermair, "Die soziale Bühne der Stadt: Vigil Raber und der Spielbetrieb in Bozen um 1500 – eine sozialhistorische Skizze," *Vigil Raber*, ed. Michael Gebhardt and Max Siller, 147–59. An English version of this article was published also in 2004: Hannes Obermair, "The Social Stages of the City: Vigil Raber and Performance Direction in Bozen/Bolzano (Northern Italy) – a Socio-historical Outline," *Concilium medii aevi* 7 (2004), 193–208; here 195. Citations are taken from this version.

[32]  The casting lists of the *Bozen Passion Play* from 1495 and 1514 are published in: *Bozner Passion 1495:*

plays performed during the decades before and after 1500. And indeed, the casting seems to reflect a city's social structure. Obermair's analysis of the casting list of the 1495 *Bozen Passion Play*[34] suggests that plays were "a strong cultural and symbolic capital, that were effective both horizontally and vertically in the context of interaction between people, and in particular between both those who were present and those who were not present."[35] Mainly "representatives of the top professions of the city from the artisan or upper class sectors [...] mayors, merchants, and church provosts, directors of hospitals and schools, tax and duties collectors, elite professions (cobblers, saddlers, and coopers), and monopolistic supply professions (bakers, butchers)"[36] act on stage, just as on the "stage" of the political and social urban life. Just how "exclusive" the character of the urban drama was can be demonstrated not only by the fact that women were absent and the lower classes were excluded. But it is also true, surprisingly, that there are no members of the nobility mentioned, even though they had their representatives in the Bozen city council. What we have here, obviously, is a "corporative connection of the play direction": The conditions for participation in playing were full citizens' rights, real estate property, and eligibility for the council ("part of the social insignias of the city's caste society"), but also participation in the urban "service sector,"[37] which possibly excluded the nobility from participation.

The example of Sterzing shows most distinctly that play culture was "an affirmative consensus model for the urban public that stabilized social relations."[38] The casting lists of the Passion-Play-performances in 1489, 1496, and 1503 are yet

---

*Die Spielhandschriften A und B*, ed. Bruno Klammer. Mittlere deutsche Literatur in Neu- und Nachdrucken, 20. (Bern, Frankfurt, and New York: Lang, 1986), 173–74; 349–50; 366–69; and Bernd Neumann, *Geistliches Schauspiel im Zeugnis der Zeit: Zur Aufführung mittelalterlicher religiöser Dramen im deutschen Sprachgebiet.* 2 Vols. Münchener Texte und Untersuchungen zur deutschen Literatur des Mittelalters, 84–85 (Munich: Artemis, 1987), Vol. 1, 143–56; 190–203.

[33] The casting lists of the Sterzing plays of 1489, 1496, and 1534 are described in: Rolf Bergmann, *Katalog der deutschsprachigen geistlichen Spiele und Marienklagen des Mittelalters.* Veröffentlichungen der Kommission für deutsche Literatur des Mittelalters der Bayerischen Akademie der Wissenschaften (Munich: Beck, 1986), 320–22 (no. 144). They are published in: Neumann, *Geistliches Schauspiel im Zeugnis der Zeit*, 647–56; *Die geistlichen Spiele des Sterzinger Spielarchivs*, ed. Walther Lipphardt and Hans-Gert Roloff. Vol. 4. Mittlere Deutsche Literatur in Neu- und Nachdrucken, 17 (Bern et al.: Lang, 1990), 180. The lists of the 1503 performance are published in: *Die geistlichen Spiele des Sterzinger Spielarchivs*, ed. Walther Lipphardt and Hans-Gert Roloff. Vol. 2. Mittlere Deutsche Literatur in Neu- und Nachdrucken, 15 (Bern et al.: Lang, 1988), 374–75. For this play, see also: Bergmann, *Katalog*, 296–99 (no. 135).

[34] Obermair, "The Social Stages of the City."

[35] Obermair, "The Social Stages of the City," 195.

[36] Obermair, "The Social Stages of the City," 198.

[37] Obermair, "The Social Stages of the City," 199. Obermair is right when he puns that the *dramatis personae* were at the same time the *civitatis personae* (201) referring to the urban dignitaries and elites.

[38] Obermair, "The Social Stages of the City," 203.

to be thoroughly examined, but for the time being Josef Eduard Wackernell's analysis shows clearly that the town's "oberster Beamter sowie die geistige und finanzielle Blüte der Bürgerschaft"[39] (top official and the intellectual and economic prime citizens) carried out the performances. About five members of the well-respected Köchel family, a dynasty of master builders, played a role in these plays, Caspar Köchel played the Savior twice. Also in Sterzing, the clergy is completely absent as well as the nobility, and here, too, female characters are played by (young) men.[40] A certain Aichler, for example, took on the role of the *Ancilla hostiaria* (the usher's maid) and had to crow as the cock in Peter's denial scene (*et gallus*).[41] It becomes evident that the play reflected real social relations, when Wolfgang Scherer plays *Longinus*, and *sein knecht Ulreich* (his servant Ulrich) takes on the role of the *servus Longini* (the servant of Longinus).[42] As a curiosity we may mention that a certain *Gaismair* played the *Falsus testis* (false witness) in the 1503 *Play of the Last Supper*, and in the Passion Play he was cast as the *Latro a sinistris Gesmas* (Gesmas, the thief on the left).[43]

The earliest recordings of performances come from the city of Hall: From 1430 onwards,[44] in intervals over the course of a century, we encounter notes which record expenses for the *osterspil* (Easter Play) or *zum passion* (for the Passion Play)

---

[39]   Wackernell, *Altdeutsche Passionsspiele aus Tirol*, LIII.

[40]   Cf. Wackernell, *Altdeutsche Passionsspiele aus Tirol*, LII–LVI. The first name *Martine* with Kelderer (*Martine Keldrer gab die Maria Cleophe* [Martine Keldrer played Maria Cleophe]) does not "suggest a woman" (ibid., LV). *Martine* was (like *Heinrice* and others) the 'humanistic scholarly' form derived from the Latin vocative. The dialect form of the name is *Mártl*.

[41]   Cf. Neumann, *Geistliches Schauspiel im Zeugnis der Zeit*, 650 and footnote 22; Wackernell, *Altdeutsche Passionsspiele aus Tirol*, LV.

[42]   Wackernell, *Altdeutsche Passionsspiele aus Tirol*, LIII–LIV; cf. Neumann, *Geistliches Schauspiel im Zeugnis der Zeit*, 652. Here, we can see clearly the "solidification of societal-social roles through their representation" in drama performances that Obermair ("The Social Stages of the City," 203) suggests.

[43]   Cf. Neumann, *Geistliches Schauspiel im Zeugnis der Zeit*, 655–56. According to Wackernell (*Altdeutsche Passionsspiele aus Tirol*, LIV), it was "vermutlich derselbe Gaismair, der später in den Bauernkriegen nicht viel schönere Rollen gespielt hat" (probably the very same Gaismair, who didn't play more beautiful roles later in the peasants' revolt). It is undoubtedly wrong that we have the same Michael Gaismair, the leader of the peasants' war of 1525/1526 before us, because he was born around 1491/1492, see: Angelika Bischoff-Urack, *Michael Gaismair: Ein Beitrag zur Sozialgeschichte des Bauernkrieges. Vergleichende Gesellschaftsgeschichte und politische Ideengeschichte der Neuzeit*, 4 (Innsbruck: Inn-Verlag, 1983), 67. In any case, Wackernell's evaluation of the Sterzing peasants' leader clearly shows traits of nineteenth-century attitudes.

[44]   Neumann (*Geistliches Schauspiel im Zeugnis der Zeit*, 389, note for no. 1868) is right when he considers linking certain recordings from 1430 (nos. 1866–1868) to the performance of a Shrovetide Play. Similarly: Eckehard Simon, *Die Anfänge des weltlichen deutschen Schauspiels 1370–1530: Untersuchung und Dokumentation*. Münchener Texte und Untersuchungen zur deutschen Literatur des Mittelalters, 124 (Tübingen: Niemeyer, 2003), 390.

in urban account books.[45] The grandest performance of a Passion Play, which was extended by a Palm Sunday Play, was staged here in 1511. We don't have casting lists from Hall, but a reference  in a chronicle shows that the socio-political background of these performances is the same as in Bozen and Sterzing:

> Anno domini 1511 hat man zue Hall ghalten ain trefflichs spil, nemlichen den passion Christi, darin vil namhafter leit und anseliche perschonen seind gewesen, haben auf iren aignen kosten vil darüber lassen geen.[46]

> [A.D. 1511 a splendid play was performed in Hall, namely the passion of Christ, wherein many renowned people and respected persons have taken part, and they have spent a large sum from their own money for that purpose.]

Bozen wanted to catch up with Hall at least. The patrician Lienhard Hiertmair, provost of the church in Bozen, had a meeting with Benedikt Debs and Vigil Raber in 1514, where they decided to plan for the play to last seven days.[47]

In Brixen, we have notes on plays performed there from around 1522, the first performance of an Easter Play took place in 1544, and also the manuscript of a *Brixen Passion Play* has been preserved.[48] This play was performed in the cathedral and we have accurate recordings of the duties of the cathedral sexton (written down between 1555 and 1558 by Veit Feichter): "so man das oster spil will halten nach der metten"[49] (when the Easter play is to be performed after matins), the sexton had to prepare the stage props on the evening before. These instructions paint a very vivid picture of early-modern theater performances, when we learn for instance that the Savior is clad all in red, St. Peter in white, or that the gardener carries as a sign of his office: "ain Eýssen Schaúffl"[50] (an iron shovel) in his hands. Moreover, we are told that the urban audiences did not always observe law and order. Veit Feichter, for instance, complains that people stood—rather near the

---

[45]  In many cases, these notes are about building up and dismantling the stages. See: Neumann, *Geistliches Schauspiel im Zeugnis der Zeit*, 389–400. Cf. Wackernell, *Altdeutsche Passionsspiele aus Tirol*, CCXXIX–CCXXXV; Monika Fink, "Geistliche Spiele in Hall im 15. und 16. Jahrhundert," *Literatur und Sprache in Tirol von den Anfängen bis zum 16. Jahrhundert: Akten des 3. Symposiums der Sterzinger Osterspiele (10.–12. April 1995)*, ed. Michael Gebhardt and Max Siller. Schlern-Schriften, 301 (Innsbruck: Wagner, 1996), 231–37; here 232–35.

[46]  Neumann, *Geistliches Schauspiel im Zeugnis der Zeit*, 394, No. 1896; cf. Wackernell, *Altdeutsche Passionsspiele aus Tirol*, CCXXXIII.

[47]  Neumann, *Geistliches Schauspiel im Zeugnis der Zeit*, 203–204, No. 545; cf. Wackernell, *Altdeutsche Passionsspiele aus Tirol*, CCXXXVI–CCXXXVII.

[48]  Neumann, *Geistliches Schauspiel im Zeugnis der Zeit*, 247–48, No. 545; cf. Wackernell, *Altdeutsche Passionsspiele aus Tirol*, CCLVII–CCLXXXVII; 351–431 (edition).

[49]  Neumann, *Geistliches Schauspiel im Zeugnis der Zeit*, 249–51; *Veit Feichter. Das Brixner Dommesnerbuch. Mit elektronischer Rohtextversion und digitalem Vollfaksimile auf CD-ROM*, ed. Andrea Hofmeister-Winter. Innsbrucker Beiträge zur Kulturwissenschaft. Germanistische Reihe, 63. (Innsbruck: Institut für Germanistik, 2001), 281–82; 285–87.

[50]  Hofmeister-Winter, *Das Brixner Dommesnerbuch*, 282.

stage! — on carpets that covered two benches serving as the seat of the Apostles in
the washing of the feet and he advises the sexton to take all candles out of the
candlesticks, otherwise they may be broken, "dan das volckh Ist vnzogen"[51]
(because people have bad manners). These remarks suggest that religious plays
were highly popular and people were pressed around the 'stage' in order to see
all of the play.

In the sixteenth century, the citizens of Bruneck seemed to have been especially
keen on performing plays. We have registers from 1532 until 1598 recording the
town's expenses not only "zu dem Passion" (for the Passion Play, 1550 and 1577),
but also for numerous other plays during the year.[52] In Meran, too, the tradition
of the Easter play, the first recordings of which go back to around 1519, seems to
have been replaced by other types of religious plays — in 1570 the council and the
mayor approved of a Play of the Last Judgment.[53] It seems that the performance
of an Easter Play in Innsbruck by a certain schoolteacher *Udalricus* in 1494[54] could
not establish a real tradition.

It is remarkable that the 'devil's play,'[55] a scene, which appears right after the
'Harrowing-of-Hell'-scene in the *Innsbruck (Thuringian) Easter Play*[56] of 1391, also
turns up in the younger Tyrolean versions of the Passion Play (*Hall Passion Play*
of 1514 and *Brixen Passion Play* of 1551) right after the guard-scene, which has been
interpreted very early as a "bürgerliche Satire gegen das herabgekommene Rittertum"[57] (bourgeois satire against the declining chivalry). After Christ has liberated
the patriarchs and prophets from hell, Lucifer orders the devils to fill up his
kingdom with evil souls once again:

> Sy seyen edl, glert, reich oder arem,
> (So habt uber sy kain erparem)
> Es seien hantbercher guet oder schlecht,
> Die maister mit sampt dem knecht,
> Di frauen mit sampt der diern:
> Di all sollt ir zu mir her fiern![58]

> [May they be noble, learned, rich or poor
> (Don't have mercy upon them)

---

[51]   Hofmeister-Winter, *Das Brixner Dommesnerbuch*, 286.
[52]   Neumann, *Geistliches Schauspiel im Zeugnis der Zeit*, 252–55.
[53]   Cf. Neumann, *Geistliches Schauspiel im Zeugnis der Zeit*, 592–93.
[54]   Cf. Neumann, *Geistliches Schauspiel im Zeugnis der Zeit*, 412.
[55]   According to Wackernell, *Hall Passion Play, Altdeutsche Passionsspiele aus Tirol*, 341, v. 1555–1560.
[56]   Innsbruck University Library, Cod. 960, fol. 35v–50r. Edition: *Das Innsbrucker Osterspiel. Das
       Osterspiel von Muri. Mittelhochdeutsch und Neuhochdeutsch*, edited, translated, annotated, and with
       an afterword by Rudolf Meier. Reclams Universal-Bibliothek, 8660 (Stuttgart: Reclam, 1962).
[57]   Wackernell, *Altdeutsche Passionsspiele aus Tirol*, CLXXXV.
[58]   *Hall Passion Play*, Wackernell, *Altdeutsche Passionsspiele aus Tirol*, 341, v. 1555–1560.

May they be masterly or poor craftsmen,
The masters together with the servants,

The ladies together with their maids:
Lead all of them to me!]

This tormenting scene[59] is of course a great basis for a class satire. Because mainly urban professions—ranging from the steward (*procurator*), miller, shoemaker, and baker to the tailor and the blacksmith—are satirized, one has the impression that the urban government takes the opportunity here to stage a haunting sermon for the urban classes.

## b. The Secular Play

The class satire of the religious devil's play shows a certain relationship with the secular "courting play," like the Sterzing *Venus Play*;[60] it even forms the humorous equivalent to the gruesome hell scene. It was copied by Vigil Raber in 1511, significantly in the same year in which the Passion Play with this hell scene at the end was performed in Hall.[61] All trades come off badly in the *Venus Play*, and also a violent knight and a primitive peasant are made to look like fools who exit the stage in humiliation. The ore miner[62] (*Arczknapp*, v. 134), of course, could not be neglected in the mining city of Sterzing.[63]

---

[59] According to Wackernell (*Altdeutsche Passionsspiele aus Tirol*, CLXXXVIII–CXCIV) the devil's scene is the 2nd part of the 3rd play of the *Tyrolean Passion Play*. Texts (ed. Wackernell): *Hall Passion Play*, 340–349, *Brixen Passion Play*, 426–431.

[60] *Sterzinger Spiele. Die weltlichen Spiele des Sterzinger Spielarchivs nach den Originalhandschriften (1510–1535) von Vigil Raber und nach der Ausgabe Oswald Zingerles (1886)*, ed. Werner M. Bauer. Wiener Neudrucke, 6 (Vienna: Österreichischer Bundesverlag, 1982), 206–236.

[61] Cf. Wackernell, *Altdeutsche Passionsspiele aus Tirol*, CLXXXIII.

[62] In 1509, master Matheis Stöberl depicted two miners on the (carved) high altar of the St. Magdalena Chapel of Ridnaun, near Sterzing. Cf. Josef Weingartner, *Die Kunstdenkmäler Südtirols. I. Band: Eisacktal, Pustertal. Ladinien*. 6th edition, edited by Josef Stadlhuber (Innsbruck, Vienna: Tyrolia, 1977), 191. The fact that *M. Stöberle* played the *Diabolus* in the *Sterzing Passion Play* of 1503 shows the close relationship between the playing community and this artist, too. Cf. *Die geistlichen Spiele des Sterzinger Spielarchivs*, ed. Walther Lipphardt and Hans-Gert Roloff. Vol. 2. Mittlere Deutsche Literatur in Neu- und Nachdrucken, 15 (Bern et al.: Lang, 1988), 374–75.

[63] For the Sterzing mining jurisdiction see Georg Mutschlechner, "Das Berggericht Sterzing," *Sterzinger Heimatbuch*. Ed. and collected by Anselm Sparber and collaborators. Schlern-Schriften, 232 (Innsbruck: Wagner, 1965), 95–148.

Figure 4: Depiction of miners in the St. Magdalena chapel of Ridnaun (near Sterzing). Master Matheis Stöberl, 1509 (photograph: Max Siller)

Above all, though, the burgher is also rejected by Venus, although he introduces himself as "ain purger also reich, / Das man hart in einer stat / mein geleichn gesechn hat" (v. 83–85; such a rich burgher / that you can hardly find someone like me / in any city). There is certainly a grain of self-irony or even a ribald side-swing by the play's author, obviously a scholar, when the townsman is judged and rejected by Venus: "Mein hercz kains guecz nicht pegert, / darum pistu vor mier vnberdt!" (v. 96–97; My heart doesn't long for goods / therefore you are unworthy in my eyes!). The author lets the university student (*Schreiber*), who has studied theology "auf den hohn schueln der vnifersitet" (v. 806; at the university colleges), gain the lovely lady's hand. Many a contemporary citizen may have felt concerned; others may have winked at one other about similar figures.

It is maybe only a coincidence that the oldest records of secular plays come from Hall, the Tyrolean center of salt production. We don't know which plays were actually performed, but we know from archive files that the community spent 7 pounds and 6 pence for the construction and subsequent dismantling "von zwein pünn vnd gerüsten ze zwain Spiln ze vasnacht"[64] (of two stages and scaffolds for two Shrovetide Plays) in 1426. In 1430, we find a similar reference to a performance; after that date the urban account books fall silent. So, this sole evidence of a performance in Hall represents "ein Vorspiel ohne Hauptaktion"[65] (a prelude without the main action). We find only scattered notes on Shrovetide Plays from 1503 in Innsbruck and from 1522 in Bozen and Meran.[66]

The first evidence from Sterzing is amazing.[67] In the accounts (*Bürgermeisteramtsreitung*) of the Sterzing mayor Jörg Artzperger from 1527, we find the following entry:

> A[nno] d[omin]j am 6 tag marczj dem Stoffl schopher gebn das er das spil auf dem Rathaús hat ghaltn aús beúelch der Herrnn—tút 5 ph[und].
>
> [A.D. on the sixth day of March, Stoffl Schopfer was given 5 pounds, because he has performed the play in the town hall according to the aldermen's orders.]

There is evidence that this Stoffl (Christoph) Schopfer, who was the first director of a Sterzing Shrovetide Play on March 6th, 1527 (Ash Wednesday!), which was performed in the town hall,[68] was in fact a peasant from the nearby village of

---

64     Simon, *Die Anfänge*, 142–43 and 390.

65     Simon, *Die Anfänge*, 143; cf. also 179.

66     Simon, *Die Anfänge*, 143.

67     For the following cf. Siller, *Literatur – Sprache – Territorium*, 378–380. Cf. now Simon, *Die Anfänge*, 171–72.

68     "Ihrem Existenzgrund entsprechend dokumentieren Tiroler Spielzeugnisse fast ausnahmslos Aufführungen im Rathaus." (According to their raison d'être, Tyrolean recordings of plays almost always document performances in the town hall.) Simon, *Die Anfänge*, 174; cf. Simon, "Die Fastnachtspielhefte," 231.

Mareit. He was part of the *Ehrbarkeit* or respected class, i.e., the rural class of proprietors. He was related to Ulrich Haimbuecher, an influential citizen and, in 1530, mayor of Sterzing, which probably made contacts with the urban society easier. We don't know which play he directed with what cast. It was probably a rural ensemble, in which the director himself may have taken part, as well as some of his seven children whom we know by name.[69] We don't know anything about his education either, but we may infer that he could read.

This performance of 1527 was not to remain the only interaction of city and country in the Sterzing theater culture. A play with a *dörperlich* (rustic) company around carnival time was performed in the town hall as early as the following year. This time, the actors came from the nearby mining village of Gossensaß.[70] This 'rustic import' is all the more surprising when we know that by the middle of the fifteenth century Vigil Raber's ancestors owned the *Vasnachts haus* (Shrovetide house), a fact which seems to suggest that the Raber family, who had been in Sterzing since 1420, took pride in carnival traditions, and Hans, grandfather of our Vigil, may have organized carnival diversions such as parades. Michael, Hans's son may have inherited the fostering of these traditions, and under these circumstances the grandson's, Vigil's, interest in texts associated with urban religious and secular traditions isn't astonishing at all.[71] His 24 (or perhaps 25) small manuscripts recording Shrovetide Plays represent "ein in der frühen europäischen Spielüberlieferung einmaliges Repertorium von Aufführungs-skripten"[72] (a repertory of scenarios unmatched in the early European theater tradition).

In the *Venus Play*, we have observed a certain reflection of urban social life and culture. We find this in other Tyrolean Shrovetide Plays, too, as for example in the *recken spil*[73] (*Play of the Warriors*). This dramatization of the Dietrich-epic *Der*

---

[69]  A roaming troupe of actors consisting of peasants from Wattens performed, for example, in Hall in 1549. Walter Senn, *Aus dem Kulturleben einer süddeutschen Kleinstadt: Musik, Schule und Theater der Stadt Hall in Tirol in der Zeit vom 15. bis zum 19. Jahrhundert* (Innsbruck, Vienna: Tyrolia 1938), 121; 127; 611, No. 84.

[70]  Mayor Hans Selauer recorded the spending for 1528: *Mer Aûsgeben den spill Leitn von gossnsass Aûf peûelch der herrn/ Alls sy daß spill Aûfm Rathaûß gehabt haben — Thûet 0 m[arck] 3 ph[und] 0 k[reuczer] 0 flierer]* (More [was] spent for the actors from Gossensaß according to the councillors when they performed the play in the town hall—0 marks, 3 pounds, 0 kreutzers, 0 fours). Siller, *Literatur – Sprache – Territorium*, 380. There is evidence of a company from Gossensaß in Sterzing in 1544, 1549, and 1575. Cf. Conrad Fischnaler, "Die Volksschauspiele zu Sterzing im XV. und XVI. Jahrhundert," *Zeitschrift des Ferdinandeums* 3 (1891), 23–382; here 375–76. Cf. now Simon, *Die Anfänge*, 173–74.

[71]  Cf. Michael Gebhardt and Max Siller, "Vigil Raber in alter und neuer Sicht," *Vigil Raber*, ed. Michael Gebhardt and Max Siller, 7–20; here 7–8.

[72]  Simon, *Die Anfänge*, 180.

[73]  The caption in the codex reads: "Ain vasnacht spill von den risn oder reckhn etc." (lines 3–4; A Shrovetide Play about Giants or Warriors etc.), Bauer, *Sterzinger Spiele*, 9–26.

*Rosengarten zu Worms* (*The Rose Garden of Worms*), copied down by Vigil Raber in 1511, is about the duels between the warriors of Dietrich von Bern on the one side and those of Kriemhild on the other. Thus the play offers an opportunity for fencers to demonstrate their skills on stage.

Figure 5: Hans Thalhofer, *Fechtbuch von 1476*, Bayerische Staatsbibliothek München, Cod.icon. 394a, fol. 7v (Internet: http://daten.digitale-sammlungen.de/~db/0002/bsb00020451/images/index.html?id=00020451&native no=7v

Figure 6: Hans Thalhofer, *Fechtbuch von 1476*, Bayerische Staatsbibliothek München, Cod.icon. 394a, fol. 86v (Internet:http://daten.digitale-sammlungen.de/~db/0002/bsb00020451/images/index.html?id=00020451&native no=86v)

The actors undoubtedly hoped for the admiration of the present women, who are explicitly addressed by the precursor:

> Ir frauen sollet auch nit erschrickn,
> wan ir dy schbert wert sechn plickhen,
> Dan es gar schimpflichn zuegat,
> wie woll es yederman ernstlich anstat. (v. 30–33)

> [Oh, you ladies, don't be startled
> When you see the swords on display,
> For we don't play for real, even though
> It looks as if everybody plays in earnest]

The protagonists "vechten vmb ain krenczelein" (v. 27; fight for a little wreath) or, as the hero Wittich in his fight against the giant Asprian puts it: "Durch got vnd schoner frauenn" (v. 285; for the sake of God and beautiful ladies). In Dietleib's words:

> zu gefallen aller schonen weib
> Vnd zu lieb dem liebstn puelen mein
> mueß es gar ritterlich gestritn sein.                    (v. 405–407)

> [for the grace of all beautiful women
> and for the love of my mistress
> we must fight gallantly.]

Figure 7: Runkelstein Castle, Tournament Hall, southern wall: joust, ball
games, round dance. *Schloss Runkelstein. Die Bilderburg*, ed. André Bechtold
(Bozen: Athesia, 2000), figure 114

Figure 8: Runkelstein Castle, Tournament Hall, southern wall: joust (detail: female spectators). *Schloss Runkelstein. Die Bilderburg*, ed. André Bechtold (Bozen: Athesia, 2000), figure 118

Not only courtly literature and heroic epics are imitated—partly in a satirizing way[74]—on an urban stage, but also noble martial arts games, like the joust and tournament, are represented in the bourgeois variation of sportive stage fencing. The magnificent noble tournaments like the ones that took place in Innsbruck and the ones arranged just outside Runkelstein castle near Bozen already around 1400, appear in an artistic or even in a deliberately clumsy parody on the urban stages, as even the carnival herald announces:

> Ruckht auß dem weg stuell vnd penckh,
> der hirnen seyfrid ist gar vngelenckh                          (v. 40–41)

> [Move away all chairs and benches
> the horny skinned Seyfried is very awkward]

This 'awkwardly' horny skinned Seyfrid once was *Sîfrit*, the courtly knight par excellence; yet on the urban stage around 1500 he epitomizes the noble 'loser.'[75] The victorious old Hildebrand (*Hilprant*) dryly commands *Frau krimhild* (lady Kriemhild), the noble queen, to put the wreath on his gray head ("Secz mir den krancz auff meinen graen kopf!" v. 505), but he rejects the other prize for his victory indignantly, as if he was a *frum* (pious) burgher created by the Nuremberg mastersinger Hans Sachs:[76]

> Ich aht eurs halsn vnd kussn nit,
> verfluecht sey eur hoffsit!
> Das halsn will ich sparn meiner fraen,
> dy sich in ern alleczeyt last schauen.                        (v. 514–517)

> [I scorn your embracing and kissing
> Cursed be your courtly fashion
> I save my embraces for my wife
> Who always walks in great honor.]

What is talked about and is shown on stage "nur In Schalatz weiß"[77] (only in a jocular way), tells a lot about the historical social and communicative reality. In Tyrol as well, the feudal nobility was the real enemy of the rural and urban population. From the fourteenth century onwards, the cities of southern Germany had to defend themselves against the extortion of protection money by the knightly mobs.[78] Enviously and covetously the knights were looking at the urban

---

[74]    Cf. Bauer, *Sterzinger Spiele*, 482.

[75]    Cf. Albrecht Classen, "Hans Sachs's Reception of the Medieval Heroic Tradition: Social Criticism in the Cloak of Nibelungenlied Source Material," *Parergon: Journal of the Australian and New Zealand Association for Medieval and Early Modern Studies* 23 (2006), 93–117.

[76]    See also the contribution to this volume by Albrecht Classen.

[77]    *Sterzinger Spiele*, v.10, v. 753 (452).

[78]    Cf. Dopsch, "Epoche – sozialgeschichtlicher Abriß," 21–22.

population who had become wealthy through trade, industriousness, and work. Oswald von Wolkenstein shows the conflict between knights and burghers in a poem (Kl. 25) already at the beginning of the fifteenth century. He lets two people—"Ain burger und ain hofman"—(v. 1; a burgher and a nobleman) "tispietiern, welcher bas möcht geben / den freulin hohen muet" (v. 2; 5–6; discuss who can better put the ladies in a high state of mind). The judge, a procuress from Brixen called Diemuet (Humbleness), unequivocally decides in favor of the burgher. The defeated nobleman resorts to violence just like the knight in the *Venus Play* almost would have done. Where, like in the drama, only the commoners express themselves, the knights are depicted as they have probably often been seen in reality. In their utter uselessness and their parasitism they, in the eyes of the urban population, resemble the guards of the Holy Sepulchre[79] in many Easter Plays, who brag about their bravery as they go to secure the grave and are reduced to a bunch of cowards when the angel comes and raises Jesus from the dead.

## Concluding Remarks

Within the sphere of literary entertainment found in Tyrol, we can explicitly see the development of a 'civic' urban culture from the late Middle Ages onwards. This culture had already won the battle against church and nobility who had dominated cultural life until then. Untouched by all that, a royal nostalgic, Emperor Maximilian, ordered his toll keeper Hans Ried to collect and to copy courtly epics of the thirteenth century as late as in the early sixteenth: This is how the *Ambraser Heldenbuch* came into being between 1504 and 1516, written upon royal orders and on precious parchment—while at the same time burghers were writing their plays on simple paper. As dust jackets they often used old parchment folios which were sorted out because they were of no use anymore, at least at that time.

---

[79]  Cf. the Bible: Mt 27, 62–66; 28, 3–4

Connie L. Scarborough

(University of Cincinnati)

# Urban Spaces in the *Tragicomedia de Calisto y Melibea*

The work, commonly known today by its popular title, *Celestina*, exists in two versions with two different original titles, both of which are usually attributed to Fernando de Rojas. The sixteen-act *Comedia de Calisto y Melibea* was published in Burgos in 1499 and the expanded version in twenty-one acts, the *Tragicomedia de Calisto y Melibea,* some three years later. To avoid confusion with the name of the main character, Celestina, in this essay, I will refer to the work as the *Tragicomedia,* i.e., the longer of two versions. Although both versions of the work are divided into *Autos* (Acts) and the text is composed entirely in dialogue without recourse to a narrative voice, the *Tragicomedia* is not a play in the traditional sense. It is too long to be performed in its entirety and it lacks any sort of directorial notes; most critics refer to it as a hybrid genre or a novel in dialogue. Although the work defies conventional genre classification its plot is relatively simple: an upper-class youth, Calisto, is smitten by a lovely young lady, Melibea, and in order to win her favors, enlists the aid of Celestina, a worldly-wise go-between, known in Spanish an *alcahueta*. Celestina is a procuress, a madam, a maker of love potions and other remedies, restorer of lost maidenheads and facilitator of illicit love affairs—all for a price, of course.[1] Mid-plot, Calisto's servants murder Celestina in a fit of greedy rage and are summarily decapitated for her murder. Despite these tragedies, the young lovers, Calisto and Melibea, consummate their affair only to have their happiness cut short when Calisto dies as the result of a fall from the ladder which he had used to scale the wall of Melibea's garden. Melibea, in response to the loss of her lover, commits suicide by throwing herself from a high tower.

---

[1] Gretchen Mieszkowski, *Medieval Go-Betweens and Chaucer's* Pandarus. The New Middle Ages (Houndmills, Basingstoke, Hampshire, and New York: Palgrave Macmillan, 2006).

The town where these events take place is never identified and critics have spilled gallons of ink arguing for one setting over another.[2] While their efforts are interesting, the exact city where the action takes place is not as important as what Patrizia Botta has called "the idea of the city"[3] and how that idea affects the characters' realities and the decisions they make. The configurations of the city and its neighborhoods, the noble houses of Calisto and Melibea, the *putería* or designated brothel zone, the church, the plaza, Celestina's house on the outskirts of town are all significant to the plot development and without these geographical and societal markers, the work could not exist in its present form. In addition, much of the action and key points of dialogue occur in the streets, while the characters are either en route to a destination or hurrying to some activity or errand that advances the plot. Spaces within this fictitious city can be classified as public or private even though this distinction is, at times, porous as we shall see.

In an important article published in 1994, "Itinerarios urbanos en la *Celestina* de Fernando de Rojas" ("Urban Itineraries in the *Celestina* of Fernando de Rojas"), Botta establishes the centrality of an urban setting for all the action and interactions that take place in the *Tragicomedia*. Botta states that in this work the city is not just a backdrop against which the plot unfolds:

> muchas de las escenas se dan directamente en la calle, o delante de una iglesia, o detrás de una puerta. Sus espacios reales sirven a la acción del drama, son necesarios para que los acontecimientos preparen o incluso ocurran"
>
> ["Many of the scenes take place in the street or in front of the church or behind a door. These real spaces serve the action of the drama, they are necessary to prepare for events or for their actual occurrence."][4]

In fact, the place most often identified in the *Tragicomedia* is the street itself. There are a total of 27 scenes which take place in the street, as characters are en route or returning from meetings or related tasks. Botta has noted that these

---

2   For examples see the following: Theodore S. Beardsley, Jr., "The House and Gravesite of Celestina," *Celestinesca* 24 (2000): 123–30; Stephen Gilman, *The Spain of Fernando de Rojas*, (Princeton: Princeton University Press, 1962), see especially, Chapter 6, "Salamanca" ( 267–353); María Rosa Lida de Malkiel, *La originalidad artística de La Celestina* (Buenos Aires: Editorial Universitaria de Buenos Aire, 1962), see especially the section, "El Lugar"; Francisco Maldonado de Guevara, "La casa de Celestina," *Anales Cervantinos* 7 (1958): 287–89; Francisco Márquez Villanueva. *Orígenes y sociología del tema celestinesco*, (Barcelona: Anthropos, 1993); Higinio Ruiz y Carmen Bravo-Villasante, "Talavera de la Reina (1479–98), ¿lugar de acción de *La Celestina*?," *Anuario de Estudios Medievales* 3 (1966): 553–62; Dorothy S. Severin and Joseph T. Snow, "La casa de Pleberio en Salamanca," *Celestinesca* 12,1 (1988): 55–58.

3   Patrizia Botta, "Itinerarios urbanos en la *Celestina* de Fernando de Rojas," *Celestinesca* 18.2 (1994): 113-31; here 123.

4   Botta, "Itinerarios urbanos en la *Celestina* de Fernando de Rojas," 114. This and all other translations throughout are my own.

"street scenes" are scattered throughout the work and there are only five of the 21 acts which do not include a street scene.[5] Key for a work without a narrative voice is the characters' monologues in which they reveal their desires, fears, anxieties, and frustrations. Many of these monologues take place as a character is on his/her way in the street. Perhaps one of the most famous is that of Celestina at the beginning of Act Four. She has agreed to help Calisto in his bid to win Melibea and while on her way to the young woman's home she speaks very openly about the task she is about to undertake and expresses second thoughts about the risks involved. Celestina regrets having taken on this dangerous mission in which she may be denounced or punished by Melibea's family if they find out the real purpose of her visit. But she is even more concerned about what Calisto and his servants will think of her if she abandons the mission after having so confidently taken it on. She is torn and in frustration she exclaims:

> "¡Pues triste yo, mal acá, mal acullá, pena en ambas partes! Quando a los estremos falta el medio, arrimarse el hombre al más sano es discreción."

> ["Oh, woe is me, evil on the one hand, evil on the other, sorrow on all sides! When between two extremes, there exists no middle ground, sticking to the safest path is the wisest choice."][6]

She decides to pursue her mission to Melibea rather than be accused of being a coward and to reassure herself about this decision, she notes that all the omens for good fortune have been in her favor during her walk:

> "Todos los agüeros se adereçan favorables, o yo no sé nada desta arte: quatro hombres que he topado, a los tres llaman Juanes y los dos son cornudos. La primera palabra que oý por la calle fue de achaque de amores; nunca he tropeçado como otras vezes. Las piedras parece que se apartan y me hazen lugar que passe; ni me estorvan las haldas, ni siento cansación en andar; todos me saludan. Ni perro me ha ladrado ni ave negra he visto, tordo ni cuervo ni otras noturnas." (150)

> ["All the omens have been favorable or I don't know anything about this art. Of the four men I've run into, three are named John and two are cuckolds. The first word I heard in the street was about the aches and pains of love. I haven't stumbled at all as I have other times. The stones seem to move out of my way and give me room to pass. My skirts haven't gotten in my way and I don't feel tired from walking. Everybody greets me. No dog has barked at me and I've seen no black birds, neither thrush nor crow nor any other nocturnal ones."][7]

---

5   Botta, "Itinerarios urbanos . . . ," 115.
6   This and all subsequent quotes from the *Tragicomedia* are from the edition of *La Celestina*, ed. Dorothy S. Severin. 3rd ed. Letras Hispánicos, 4 (Madrid: Ediciones Cátedra, 1989), here 150.
7   All translations are mine.

For me, the most interesting detail in Celestina's monologue is her reference to not stumbling in the street; she mentions that at times her skirts are a hindrance or there are stones in her path. Through her comments we have a vivid mental picture of uneven, cobbled streets where a long skirt which one would most probably try to hold above the muck could prove hazardous, especially for a woman of advanced years. She returns to the image of her skirts being a hindrance as she travels the city streets on other occasions. When she is walking from Melibea's house to meet Calisto after her first meeting with the young woman to report to him the outcome, she curses the skirts which impede her progress: "¡O malditas haldas, prolixas y largas, cómo me estorváys de allegar adonde han de reposar mis nuevas!" (171; "Oh you cursed skirts, cumbersome and long, how you hinder my arrival where I will make my report.") And later, in Act Eleven, when she is trying to catch up with Calisto's servants, Sempronio and Pármeno, in the streets she again blames her long skirts for slowing her down: "Toda la calle del Arcediano vengo a más andar tras vosotros por alcançaros, y jamás he podido con mi luengas haldas" (249; "All down the street of the Archdeacon, I been trying to catch up to you, but I never could because of these long skirts of mine.")

There are many other references to the city streets. For example, when Sempronio and Pármeno are standing guard outside Melibea's house where their master is secretly meeting with his lover, Sempronio fears that street by which they had come might be blocked by her father's guards should they need to make a hasty retreat:

> Sempronio: Dios nos libre de traydores; no nos ayan tomado la calle por do tenemos que huyr, que de otra cosa no tengo temor. (259)

> [Sempronio: God keep us from traitors; I only hope they haven't occupied the street by which we could flee, that's the only thing that has me worried.]

There are also references to more specific dangers in the streets at night. On Calisto's first visit to Melibea's house, arranged to take place at midnight, he and his servants make special preparations before venturing into the dark and deserted streets. Calisto puts on his cuirass and he tells his servants to arm themselves. Before they leave the safety of the house Calisto asks if there is anyone outside in the streets.

And his servant, Sempronio, replies that it is so dark that it makes it almost impossible to tell if anyone is lurking about:

> Sempronio: Señor, ninguna gente pareçe y aunque la oviesse, la mucha escuridad privaría el viso y conoscimiento a los que nos encontrassen.
> Calisto: Pues andemos por esta calle, aunque se rodee alguna cosa, porque más encobiertos vamos." (256)

[Sempronio: Sir, nobody is about and even if they were, the utter darkness would make it impossible to see them or recognize anyone we might run into.

Calisto: Let's go down this street, even though it's a bit out of the way, because we're less likely to be seen.]

Hoping to pass undetected, the men are armed and vigilant when they venture into the dark streets. They carry weapons in case they are attacked or forced to confront servants or guards at Melibea's house should their presence be detected there. The realities of unlighted streets at night pose a danger both of physical accident and potential assault as we see in this scene.[8]

There are other references, too, to the danger in the streets at night. After Celestina comes to Calisto's house to tell him about her first meeting with Melibea, Calisto insists that his servants accompany her home to safeguard her. While this could be viewed as a simple courtesy, other allusions to the possibility of assaults in the streets are frequent. For example, Celestina recalls that in her younger days, her clients always sent their "escuderos y moços" (236; "squires and servants") to accompany her in her comings and goings to protect her. When Celestina arrives home after bringing news to Calisto that Melibea has agreed to speak with him at midnight, Elicia, the young prostitute that lives with her scolds her for being out so late:

Elicia: ¿Cómo vienes tan tarde? No lo deves hazer, que eres vieja; tropeçarás donde caygas y mueras. (254)

[Elicia: What is this coming home so late? You shouldn't do that since you are old; you might stumble, fall in the street and die right there.][9]

Celestina answers her objections by saying that she knows well how to navigate the streets at night:

"No temo esso, que de día me aviso por do venga de noche que jamás me subo por poyo ni calçada sino por medio de la calle. Porque como dizen, no da passo seguro quien corre por el muro, y que aquel va más sano que anda por llano. Más quiero ensuziar mis çapatos con el lodo que ensangrentar las tocas y los cantos." (254)

["You shouldn't worry because during the day I take note of where I'll be at night and I never go along by the stone benches or on the shoulder but right in the middle of the street. Because, as they say, he who goes along the wall never takes a sure step and he who goes down the middle travels most safely. I'd rather get my shoes dirty with mud than bloody my head scarf and hems."]

---

[8]  See also the contribution to this volume by Patricia Turning.

[9]  This and other frequent references to death foreshadow the imminent deaths of not only Celestina but also of the servants, Sempronio and Pármeno, as well as of the protagonists, Calisto and Melibea.

Deborah Ellis remarks that "Celestina has an ambivalent relation to street-life, yet on balance her attitude towards the street is one of more security than her attitude towards her own house."[10] As we shall see later the relative comfort that Celestina feels when she is out and about has to do with the need to conduct the business of her house with caution whereas in the street she is literally a free agent.

Melibea is greatly distressed that some evil has befallen Calisto in the dangerous streets at night when she is waiting for him to arrive for their first rendezvous in her garden. She imagines that he may have run into trouble with the night watchmen, or have been bitten by wild dogs who freely wander the streets at night, or they he may have fallen into some hole or gully and injured himself.[11] Obviously, the thought of her beloved in the urban streets at night is enough to conjure up any number of possible disasters he could have encountered.

Pleberio, Melibea's father, also sees the streets as sites of potential disaster. When he addresses fortune in his last speech following Melibea's suicide he alludes to those who blithefully wander the streets without fear of assault:

> "Pues agora sin temor, como quien no tiene qué perder, como aquel a quien tu compañía es ya enojosa, como caminante pobre que sin temor de los crueles salteadores va cantando en alta boz." (338)

> ["Now like one without fear who has nothing to lose, like one for whom your company is now tiresome, like a poor traveler (on foot) who without fear of cruel assailants goes along his way singing in a loud voice."]

Just as city streets are frequently referred to in the *Tragicomedia*, another feature of urban life is which also occupies the characters' attention is the city clock. By the time that Rojas is writing the *Tragicomedia* activities are associated with specific times of the day or night as dictated by the city clock. This essentially urban and public device was a central feature of towns in the late fifteenth and early sixteenth centuries. Maravall states that:

> "el reloj es típicamente un instrumento de la vida burguesa. En los siglos XIV y XV, se instalan relojes comunales en las ciudades . . . . De aquí, en éstas, se convierta en un elemento común de la arquitectura pública, de la misma manera que se generaliza en la vida privada de sus moradores. De esta última forma, lo descubrimos rigiendo cronológicamente la existencia de nuestros personajes."[12]

---

[10] Deborah Ellis, "'¡Adios paredes!': The Image of the House in *Celestina*," *Celestinesca* 5, 1 (1981): 1–17; here 5.

[11] "¿Quién sabe si él con voluntad de venir al prometido plazo en la forma que los tales mançebos a las tales horas suelen andar, fue topado de los alguaziles nocturnos, y sin le conoçer le han acometido, el qual por se defender los offendió o es dellos offendido? ¿O si por caso los ladradores perros con sus crueles dientes que ninguna differencia saben hazer ni acatamiento de personas, le ayan mordido; o si ha caýdo en alguna calçada o hoyo donde algún daño le viniesse? (P. 283)

[12] José Antonio Maravall, *El mundo social de "La Celestina."* 3rd ed. Biblioteca Románica Hispánia, II.

["the clock is a typical instrument of town life. In the fourteenth and fifteenth centuries, public clocks were installed in the cities . . . . From that time on, these clocks became a common element of urban architecture and they began to form an essential part of life for urban dwellers. In this way, we find it chronologically dictating the lives of our characters."]

When Celestina speaks to Sempronio about young women when they are in love she alludes to their impatience with the dictates of time as determined by the hour hands of the clock: "Si de noche caminan, nunca querrían que amanesciesse; maldizen los gallos porque anuncian el día, y el relox porque da tan apriessa" (144; "If they are about at night, they never want the sun to rise; they curse the roosters who announce the day and the clock because it runs too fast.") In a similar vein, when Pármeno complains about the litany of laudatory superlatives that Calisto always uses when talking about Melibea, he compares his master's long-winded praises to a watch which is stuck on sounding twelve o'clock: "Nunca da menos de doze; siempre está hecho relox de mediodía" (180; "He never gives less than twelve; his clock is always sounding noon.") The precise hour of twelve noon is also invoked when Pármeno invites Areúsa to dine with him at Celestina's house (212). And, when Celestina announces to Calisto that she has arranged for him to speak to Melibea that evening at her door, he immediately asks the specific time at which he should arrive. The bawd tells him to be there at the stroke of midnight (247). The pivotal Act Twelve in which Sempronio and Pármeno kill Celestina opens with Calisto expressing impatience for the appointed hour of midnight to sound so that he can keep his meeting with Melibea:

> Calisto: Moços, ¿qué hora da el relox?
> Sempronio: Las diez.
> Calisto: . . . O Cuytado de mí, si por caso me oviera dormido y colgara mi pregunta de la respuesta de Sempronio para hazer[me] de onze diez, y assí de doze onze, saliera Melibea, yo no fuera ydo, tornárase; de manera que ni mi mal oviera fin ni mi desseo execución. (255–56)

> [Calisto: Lads, what time is it by the clock?
> Sempronio: Ten o'clock.
> Calisto: Oh woe is me if perchance I have been asleep and my question hung on the reply of Sempronio who might say that eleven was ten, and thus twelve, eleven when Melibea will come to meet me and if she goes back in [because I don't appear on time] my torment will have no end nor will my desire be satisfied.]

And later, after Sempronio and Pármeno have been executed for Celestina's murder, he continues to complain that the appointed hour of midnight for his next meeting with Melibea is slow in coming. He curses the clock:

"O spacioso relox, aún te vea yo arder en bivo huego de amor, que si tú esperasses lo que yo quando des doze, jamás estarías arrendado a la voluntad del maestre que te conpuso." (292)

["Oh great clock, if you were like me burning alive with desire and if what awaited me at twelve awaited you, you would not be tied to the will of the clockmaker who created you."]

Sosia becomes worried when Calisto has not yet awakened by four o'clock in the afternoon after his visit the previous night with Melibea: " . . . ya son las quarto de la tarde y no nos ha llamado ni á comido" (293; " . . . it's already four in the afternoon and he still hasn't called for us and he hasn't eaten anything at all.")

After their first sexual encounter in Melibea's garden, Calisto curses when he hears the clock striking three in the morning saying that it seems like he has only been with Melibea for an hour: "Ya quiere amaneçer, ¿qué es esto? No [me] pareçe que ha una hora que estamos aquí y da el relox las tres" (287; "Now it is almost dawn, how could that be? It doesn't seem like we have been here even an hour and now the clock is chiming three o'clock"). [13] These references attest to the fact that urban dwellers' activities are arranged by specific times which would have been difficult to pinpoint if not for the presence of the town clock which had become an essential element of early-modern city architecture.

Sosia warns Calisto's other servant, Tristán, not to tarry near Melibea's house in the early morning hours when the city comes alive with activity and their presence there at that hour would arouse suspicion:

" . . . devemos yr muy callando, porque suelen levantarse a esta hora los ricos, los cobdiciosos de temporarles bienes,[14] los devotos de templos, monasterios y yglesias, los enamorados como nuestro amo, los trabajadores de los campos y labranças, y los pastores que en este tiempo traen las ovejas a estos apriscos a ordeñar . . . ." (287)

[" . . . we should go our way very quietly, because at these hours rich people get up and those who are greedy for material rewards; the faithful are on their way to temples, monasteries and churches and lovers, such as our master, are waking up; the workers are coming in from the fields and farms, and the shepherds at this hour bring their flocks in to me milked . . . "]

In this brief passage, Sosia paints a vivid portrait of a bustling city in the early morning, populated by farmers and shepherds coming to town to sell their products, enterprising businessmen, and the faithful attending morning services. Another example of the bustle of the city during the busy hours of the day is found

---

[13]   The motif of cursing the dawn is, of course, a familiar motif in late medieval and early modern poetry.

[14]   An elegant rephrasing of "the early bird gets the worm."

in Pármeno's description of Celestina as a "puta vieja" or "old whore." He defends his use of this term to his master explaining that she is known by that title throughout the city. In a long litany of those who refer to Celestina as the "puta vieja":

> "Si va [Celestina] entre los herreros, aquello dizen sus matrillos; carpinteros y armeros, herradores, caldereros, arcadores, todo officio de instrumento forma en el ayre su nombre. Cántanla los carpinteros, péynanla los penadores, texedores . . . ." (109)

> ["If she goes among the blacksmiths, that's what their hammers say; carpenters and arms makers, farriers, boilermakers, tinkers, and wool makers, every worker's instrument sounds out her name. The carpenters sing it, hairdressers comb it, the weavers weave it . . . ."]

The city square or *plaza* is the most public space in the city.[15] When citizens in the city of the *Tragicomedia* want to hide their activities, they fear that these may become common knowledge in the *plaza*. The *plaza* is the repository for gossip which can ruin one's reputation. Calisto openly violates the appropriate behavior for a courtly love who is bound to keep his lady's identity a secret when he wants to rush into the street and proclaim the his good fortune in the *plaza* when he receives a token gift from Melibea. He wants to make his prize, and by extension, the prize of Melibea herself, part of the public knowledge: "déxame salir por las calles con esta joya, por que los que me vienen sepan que no ay más bienandante hombre que yo" (189; "let me go out into the streets with this jewel, so that all who see me will know that I am the most fortunate man of all"). Melibea, on the other hand, specifically requests that Celestina not publicize the affair. Melibea's mother, too late, warns her daughter that Celestina's coming and goings to their house may engender suspicion and gossip: " . . . a tres veces que entra en una casa, engendra sospecha" (248; " . . . after she has entered a house three times, gossip starts".) When Sempronio and Pármeno confront Celestina demanding their share of her earnings she insists that they quiet down, so as not to alert the neighbors and make their private business known in the *plaza*: " . . . no dé bozes; no allegue la vezindad. No me hagáys salir de seso; no queráys que salgan a la plaça las cosas de Calisto y vuestras" (274; "Don't shout; don't let him [Pármeno] attract the attention of the neighbors. Don't make me lose my patience; you don't want your secret and Calisto's aired in the *plaza*.") Punishment is meted out in the *plaza* so that all will be aware of the consequences of criminal activity. When Celestina reminds Pármeno that his mother had followed the same professions as she, she tells him that his mother was arrested no less than four times and punished in the *plaza*. On one occasion she was accused of being a witch:

---

15   Even in Spanish cities today the *plaza* remains the he center of public life and the site of important events and spectacles.

" . . . aun la una le levantaron que era bruxa, porque la hallaron de noche con unas cadelillas cojendo tierra de una encruçijada, y la tovieron medio día en la plaça puesta, uno como rocadero pintado en la cabeza." (198)

[" . . . one time they arrested her and charged her with being a witch, because they found her at night with some candles digging up some soil at a crossroads, and they displayed her for half a day in the *plaza* on a scaffold with a penitent's cap on her head."]

When Tristán, another of Calisto's servants, hears shouting in the market (usually located in the central *plaza*) at an early morning hour he immediately suspects either an act of public punishment or a bullfight: ("¿O qué grita suena en el mercado; qué es esto? Alguna justicia se haze o madrugaron a correr toros") (277; "What's all that shouting in the market, what is this? They must be carrying out some punishment or they got up early to fight bulls.) Tristán does not have to wonder for long what is causing the uproar because Sosia soon arrives with the news that the commotion is none other then the public beheading of Sempronio and Pármeno in the *plaza*. And, with the public revelation of their crime, Calisto and the whole of his household are implicated and their affairs are now public knowledge. As Sosia explains: " . . . Sempronio y Pármeno quedan descabeçados en la plaça como públicos malhechores, con pregones que manifestavan su delito" (278; "Sempronio and Pármeno have been beheaded in the *plaza* like common criminals, and there has been a public proclamation of their crimes"). Calisto fears for his reputation because his servants' crime has been revealed, and punished, in public, thus implicating him in a relationship facilitated by the victim, i.e., Celestina. He exclaims: "¡O mis secretos más secretos, quán públicos andarés por las plaças y mercados!" (280–81; Oh my deepest, darkest secrets, now openly revealed and discussed in the *plazas* and the markets!").[16]

Another feature of urban space which has drawn considerable scholarly attention is the garden where the first scene in the *Tragicomedia* occurs. Calisto enters a garden in search of his hunting falcon and encounters Melibea there. Whether the escaped bird is a pretext for the encounter or the actual reason for his entrance into the garden is debatable. Chance meeting or not, the young people address each other as familiars, using first names:

---

[16]     Churches, too, are a place of common movement and activities there are also likely to enter into public knowledge. For this reason, Sempronio tries to persuade Calisto to leave the church of the Magdalena where his fervent prayers (to win Melibea) are causing people to talk: "Si passión tienes, súfrela en tu casa; no te sienta la tierra; no descubras tu pena a los estraños, pues está en manos el pandero que le sabrá bien tañer" (249; "If you are suffering from passion, do it at home; not out here in front of everyone; don't reveal your pain to strangers; the matter is in capable hands.")

Calisto: En esto veo, Melibea, la grandeza de Dios.
Melibea: ¿En qué, Calisto? (85)

[Calisto: Melibea, in this I see the greatness of God.
Melibea: In what, Calisto?]

While some scholars assume that the garden Calisto enters is that of Melibea's home, this is not necessarily the case. Alfredo Sosa Velasco has pointed out that this could be any urban garden. Sosa believes that, given the social realities of Castilian cities in the fifteenth and sixteenth centuries, the two young people may have known each other's name without having had a previous relationship.[17] The critical debate about whether the garden where Melibea and Calisto have their first "chance" meeting is the same one where the lovers eventually have their rendezvous has waged for decades.[18] One important fact we must keep in mind is that the garden in Act One is one that Calisto enters freely; there is no mention of high walls around the garden or any other obstacle to entering it at will. By contrast, the garden of Melibea's home is enclosed by very high walls and one cannot enter it "by accident." Thus we can assume that the garden of Act One is indeed a public space where the meeting of Melibea and Calisto sets the plot of the *Tragicomedia* in action.

The houses which make up the city delineate essentially private spaces among the public areas of the urban landscape as described in the *Tragicomedia*. The noble houses, those of Calisto and Melibea, are key locales which are described in some detail. For example, we know that Calisto's house has stables and that he spends much of his time, isolated in his bedroom. Ellis points out that "The identification between Calisto and his house is developed with simple irony. Calisto is always withdrawn into his bedroom, where he sets up elaborate scenes to express his lovelorn state."[19] When he enlists Celestina's aid in trying to win Melibea, he

---

[17]  Alfredo Sosa Velasco, "El huerto de Melibea: Parodia y subversión de un topos medieval," *Celestinesca* 27 (2003): 125–48; here 131.

[18]  Among the many articles on this subject, the following are especially important to the development of theories about the garden in the *Tragicomedia*:
Donald McGrady, "Entrando Calisto una huerta ... and Other Textual Problems in the *Celestina*," *Hispanic Review* 63 (1995): 433–40; Emilio Orozco Díaz, "El huerto de Melibea (Para el estudio del tema del jardín en la poesía del siglo XV)," *Paisaje y sentimiento de la naturaleza en la poesía española* (Madrid: Ediciones del Centro,1974), 63–76; George A. Shipley, "*Non era hic locus;* the Disconcerted Reader in Melibea's Garden," *Romance Philology* 27 (1974): 286–303; James R. Stamm, "De 'huerta' a 'huerto', elementos líricos-bucólicos en *La Celestina*," *La Celestina y su contorno social: Actas del 1 Congreso Internacional sobre La Celestina* (Barcelona: Borrás Ediciones, 1977), 81–88; William D. Truesdell, "The *Hortus Conclusus* Tradition and the Implications of its Absence in The *Celestina*," *Kentucky Romance Quarterly* 20 (1973): 257–77.

[19]  Deborah Ellis, "'Adios Paredes!': The Image of the Home in *Celestina*," *Celestinesca* 5.2 (1981): 1–17; here 9.

makes her an initial down payment of a hundred gold coins. We know that he keeps his treasure in a special store place under lock and key because he leaves Celestina alone with Pármeno while he goes off with Sempronio to another part of the house to unlock the storeroom:

> Calisto: Pues ven conmigo; trae las llaves, que yo sanaré su dubda.
> Sempronio: Bien harás, y luego vamos, que no se deve dexar crescer la yerva entre los panes, no la sospecha en los coraçones de los amigos . . . . (117)

> [Calisto: Come with me; bring the keys, and I will cure her doubts (doubts expressed by Celestina when Calisto delays in offering her payment).
> Sempronio: You do well; let's go because one shouldn't let grass grow among the bread loaves nor suspicion in the hearts of friends.]

Melibea's home appears to have a receiving room, or parlor similar to the one in Calisto's house.[20] Melibea and her mother, Alisa, first meet Celestina in the parlor when she appears at the young woman's home on the pretext of selling thread. It is precisely in this room where Alisa leaves Melibea alone with Celestina when she is suddenly called away to visit her sick sister. We can assume that the sister lives in somewhat close vicinity for she does not anticipate a long absence from home. Alisa's departure gives Celestina time to speak to Melibea at some length about the true nature of her visit. Much of their conversation is overheard by Lucrecia, the only servant to whom we have reference in Melibea's house. For Itziar Michelena the mention of only one servant in Melibea's home, as well as other details in the description of this dwelling, are evidence that Melibea's family may have been of more humble circumstances than we are to believe by textual references to her grand lineage and nobility. For example, Michelena notes that when Celestina makes her first visit to Melibea's home there are is no physical separation between the servant who answers the door and the living room where Melibea and Alisa receives Celestina: "La criada, que entra y sale de la abierta vivienda, avisa al ama de quién es la vieja, y sin necesidad de atravesar cámaras o depositar la demanda en manos de distintos servidores . . . ."[21] ("The maid, who enters and leaves the open household, tells her mistress who the old lady is

---

[20] There are also references to Melibea's bedroom. She speaks clandestinely there with Celestina when she asks the bawd to cure her "love sickness" and she returns to her bedroom after her midnight meetings with Calisto. The bedroom is referred to as "cámara" or "retraymiento". See pp. 266, 328 and 340 for appearances of these terms in the *Tragicomedia*. Michelena also discusses the use of these terms on p. 191 of his article, "El humilde condición de Melibea . . . ."

[21] Itziar Michelena, "La humilde condición de Melibea y su familia," *Tras los pasos de "La Celestina,"* Eds. Patricia Botta, Fernando Cantalapiedra, Kart Reichenberger and Joseph T. Snow. Estudios de Literatura, 67 (Kassel: Edition Reichenberger, 2001), 183–201; here 186.

without need to pass through antechambers or to give the message to other household servants . . . ." )[22]

Michelena also notes that Melibea's mother does not take a servant to accompany her on her visit to her ill sister's home as one would have expected.[23] However, other textual details about Melibea's household seem to contradict Michelena's assessment that hers is not a grand house. Sempronio tells Celestina that she is taking great risks in entering Pleberio's (Melibea's father) home because he is very noble and powerful (145). Also we know that the house has a high-walled garden as well as a tower, both of which suggest certain grandeur to the house. This fortress-like description of the house is noteworthy since it appears designed to keep the outside world at bay. But Celestina first and, later, Calisto invade the household, thus proving its vulnerability and eventual demise. Ellis states that "Melibea destroys her home by destroying her parents, and her father's loss in particular is in turn expressed through the image of the destroyed house."[24] The doors to Melibea's house figure prominently as a feature designed to control ingress to the house. In their first rendezvous the young lovers are physically separated by these doors. Both Calisto and Melibea make specific references to that fact that the doors represent, figuratively and literally, a barrier to their union:

> Melibea: . . . Las puertas impiden nuestro gozo, las quales yo maldigo y sus fuertes cerrojos y mas flacas fuerças, que ni tú estarías quexoso ni yo descontenta.
> Calisto: . . . ¡O molestas y enojasas puertas, ruego a Dios que tal huego os abrase como a mí da guerra, que con la tercia partes seríades en un punto quemadas! Pues por dios, señora mía, permite que llame a mis criados para que las quiebren. (262)

> [Melibea: . . . The doors prevent our enjoyment and I curse them for it. Their strong bolts are too much for my weak strength but if I could break them open then you would have nothing to complain about nor would I be left discontented.
> Calisto: . . . Oh these bothersome and onerous doors, I pray to God that such a fire might burn them as if in a war so that a mere third of the flames would be enough to destroy them. For God's sake, my lady, let me call my servants to break them down.]

A number of important factors arise in this brief exchange between Calisto and Melibea. The most infamous feature is perhaps Melibea's open acknowledgement of her carnal desires. It is she who first curses the doors that impede their physical

---

[22] Michelena also sees in the fact that Lucrecia, the servant in Melibea's home, is the cousin of Elicia, the young prostitute who lives with Celestina, as a sign that the servant is from a disreputable family (185). However, as I point out later, the path of either prostitute or household servant, was one of the few open to unmarried women of the lower classes in the urban environment.

[23] Michelena, "La humilde condición de Melibea . . .," 186.

[24] Ellis, "'¡Adiós paredes!' . . .," 14.

coupling and speaks of her own sexual frustration. Calisto prays to God to bring down fire and brimstone upon the doors of the house. His language conjures up pictures of a wrathful God who, in this instance, would destroy the doors so that Calisto's desires could be immediately fulfilled. While this seems like a petty petition in the extreme, the fact that God, fire, and the image of war are all brought to bear on this situation speaks not only to Calisto's desperation but to the fact that his desires have been elevated to near Biblical proportions—a continuation of the heresy theme initiated in the first act when Calisto denies being a Christian saying that he has now a "Melibean."[25] When the servants hear themselves invoked to break down the doors, Pármeno's initial reaction is to flee the scene rather than to attack Melibea's home—a crime that would certainly not go unnoticed or unpunished.[26] But he and Sempronio overhear Melibea's rebuttal of this idea and also the invitation that she extends to Calisto to come see her clandestinely the next evening in her garden. She, like Calisto's servants, knows that breaking down the doors of her home would not go undetected and news of it would spread throughout the city:

> Melibea: . . . Que si agora quebrasses las crueles puertas, aunque al presente no fuéssemos sentidos, amanescería en casa de mi padre terrible sospecha de mi yerro. Y pues sabes que tanto mayor es el yerro quanto mayor es el que yerra, en un punto será por la ciudad publicada. (262–63)

> [Melibea: . . . Even if you break down these cruel doors and even it were not immediately detected, tomorrow morning all my father's house would suspect my misbehavior. And you know that the degree of misconduct is proportionate to the importance of the one who errs, and in a thrice it would be public knowledge throughout the city.]

Melibea is aware that she must be discreet even though she is planning to breech the security of her father's home in the near future. Her immediate concern is to keep her sin out of public knowledge and arrange a way that the two may enjoy each other without creating a scandal. When Calisto's servants hear a noise in the streets they are poised to flee from Melibea's house, intending to go directly to

---

[25]    Sempronio: ¿Tú no eres christiano?
         Calisto: ¿Yo? Melibeo só, y a Melibea adoro, y en Melibea creo, y a Melibea amo (93).
         [Sempronio: Aren't you a Christian?
         Calisto: Me? I'm a Melibean and I adore Melibea and I believe in Melibea and I love Melibea.]

[26]    Later, on this point, Pármeno remarks, " . . .quiere quebrar las puertas, y no avrá dado el primer golpe quando sea sentido y tomado por los criados de su padre, que duermen cerca" (263). (" . . .he wants to break down the doors, and we wouldn't have struck the first blow when we would be perceived and caught by her father's servants who are sleeping nearby.") Pármeno also alludes to the fierceness of Pleberio's guards: "Estos scuderos de Pleberio son locos; no dessean tanto comer ni dormir como cuestiones y ruydos" (263; "Those squires of Pleberio are crazy; they prefer quarreling and troublemaking to eating and sleeping").

Celestina's house rather than to Calisto's where they may be found and apprehended later. But they are relieved to find out that the noise that aroused them was only the mayor's night patrol passing by.[27] The fact that there are men patrolling the city streets at night attest to an organized urban peacekeeping force as well as to a perception that such guards are necessary to protect the townspeople.

The doors, as well as the walls to Melibea's garden, are parts of the urban landscape and serve as obstacles to be overcome so that the lovers may consummate their passion. The doors prove to be an unbreechable deterrent in the first meeting between the lovers but the walls of the garden eventually will be scaled and Melibea's home invaded by Calisto. The symbolic importance of these obstacles, these physical boundaries which delineate space with the purpose of allowing for the entrance of some and the exclusion of others, help to create what Stephen Gilman has called the "ficticia ciudad de *La Celestina*" ("the fictitious city of *Celestina*"). On this point, Gilman states: " . . .cuando surgen obstáculos (muro, puertas, etc.), lo son en efecto para los deseos de los personajes y no simple decorado o mero juego de detalle escénico"[28] (" . . .when obstacles emerge (walls, doors, etc.), they are in effect obstacles to the desires of the characters and not simple decoration or a mere whim of scenic detail.")

The garden of Melibea's home plays a central rôle because it is where the relationship between the two is sexually consummated. The *huerto* (garden) in Melibea's home is surrounded by high walls. When Calisto first scales them with a ladder in order to gain access, Melibea expresses fear when he jumps down into the garden from such a great height: "O mi señor, no saltes de tan alto, que me morré en verlo; baxa, baxa poco a poco por el scala . . ." (284; "O my lord, don't jump from so high up; it scares me to death; climb down carefully little by little using the ladder . . ..")[29] Once having entered the garden, there are abundant references to deflowering, obviously related to the Calisto's deflowering of the virginal Melibea within its grounds. Calisto equates Melibea's garden to a "paraýso dulce"[30] (292; "sweet paradise"), where he enjoys the sweet delights of

---

[27]   See the interchange between Pármeno and Sempronio on pp. 263–64.

[28]   Stephen Gilman. *La Celestina: Arte y estructura,* trad. Margit Frenk de Alatorre (Madrid: Taurus, 1974), 368.

[29]   The reference to the high walls and dying of fright are, of course, precursors to Calisto's final mortal fall from these same walls. There are numerous other references throughout the *Tragicomedia* to fall from high places, fall from grace, falling on hard times, etc.—all pointing too Calisto's eventual end.

[30]   On linking Melibea's garden with the image of the Garden of Eden, Sosa observes, "Solamente los personajes malvados como, por ejemplo, la serpiente en el paraíso terrenal, son capaces de violar este espacio, o bien de apoderarse de él, tal y como aquí sucede con el mismo Calisto ("El huerto de Melibea . . .,"134.) ("Only wicked characters such as, for example, the serpent in the earthly paradise, are capable of violating this space, or to take possession of it, just as happens

his lover "entre aquellas suaves plantas y fresca verdura" (292; "among those gentle plants and fresh greenery.") On Calisto's last, fatal rendezvous with Melibea in the garden, Melibea sees the garden as a living participant in their sexual delights. She tells Calisto:

> "Oye la corriente agua desta fontesica, quanto más suave murmurio y zurrío lleva por entre las frescas yervas. Escucha los altos cipresses, cómo se dan paz unos ramos con otros por intercessión de un templadico viento que los meanea. Mira sus quietas sombras, quán escuras y aparejadas están para encobrir nuestro deleyte." (323)[31]

> ["Listen to the running water of that little fountain, how sweetly it murmurs and whispers among the fresh grasses. Listen to the tall cypress trees as their branches blow in the gentle breeze and bring a feeling of peace. Look at the quiet shadows that give us darkness where we might hide and take our delight."][32]

The garden environs become both witness and participant in the lovers' sexual enjoyment. It is a kind of urban oasis where, clandestinely, the lovers hope to avoid any public knowledge of their affair.

The garden represents an artificial transplantation of a pastoral environment into the urban landscape and becomes the place where love flowers among the stone and brick of the city.[33] Also, this "rural" space is where the lovers come to escape the ever-present gaze of other urban dwellers who live in close proximity one to another. The fact that Calisto has invaded both the house of Pleberio as well as Melibea's body both constitute breeches to the social fabric/façade. When Melibea loses her virginity in the garden she admits to having brought shame and dishonor on his household: "¡O mi padre honrado, cómo he dañado tu fama y dado causa y lugar a quebrantar tu casa!" (286; "Oh my honorable father, how I have damaged your reputation and enabled your house to be ravished!') The invasion of Pleberio's home is also a metaphor for the ravishing of Melibea's body—the proverbial flower in the center of garden who Calisto has deflowered.

The tower from which Melibea throws herself after witnessing Calisto's death is also an important feature of her house which has been the source of several critical studies. Michelena finds discrepancy in the fact that Melibea first refers to

---

with Calisto.")

[31] The uses of diminutives, such as *fontesica* and *templadito* add to the idealized description.

[32] Severin notes that the mention of giving peace links sexual love to religious and that the cypress trees symbolically foreshadow Calisto's death (323, fn 8).

[33] Sosa sees Melibea's garden as both a public and private space within the city: "Si [el huerto] forma parte de la vida privada porque pertenece a la estructura espacial del hogar, se constituye también como componente de la vida pública al permitir la entrada a otros individuos provenientes de esa misma esfera, como es el caso de un Calisto que llega del exterior" ("If it [the garden] forms part of private lands because it belongs to the spatial structure of the home, it also constitutes a component of public life because it permits the entrance of people from the vicinity to enter from outside, such as is the case with Calisto.") ("El huerto de Melibea . . .," 138).

it as an "açutea", i.e., terrace or flat roof , but when she climbs to the roof she calls it a high tower.[34] He sees some ambiguity of terminology which could lead the reader to believe that it is not the lofty tower of a grand town house. However, the presence of the tower is viewed by José Antonio Maravall, María Rosa Lida de Malkiel,[35] and Angel Gómez Moreno as part of the "idea" of urban landscape which Rojas had gleaned from the visual arts and from literary sources. Maravall suggests that Rojas was influenced by "el modelo de esas ciudades de ficción que eran frecuentes en la pintura flamenco-castellana de la época, estampas de ciudades en las que se contemplan todos los elementos de paisaje urbano que en *La Celestina* se combinan . . . ."[36] ("the model of these fictional cities was frequently found in the Flemish-Castilian paintings of the period, illustrations of cities in which all the elements of the urban environment of *La Celestina* can be seen.") Gómez Moreno fully develops this thesis citing not only paintings but the idea of the city, and particularly the prominence of towers, in the depiction of great cities from the earliest descriptions of Rome to modern cinematic representations of great cities.[37] He also identifies a number of literary descriptions of cities which could have influenced Rojas as well as the use of the tower as symbol of the fall from grace by Biblical writers on.[38]

The tower of Pleberio's home figures very prominently in the last two acts of the *Tragicomedia*. In Act Twenty, Melibea is despondent after Calisto's death and her father, although initially unaware of the cause of his daughter's distress, proposes that she take some fresh air. Melibea gladly accepts his idea and suggests that they go up to the terrace of the house to enjoy the view of the ships in harbor. She sends her father for some musical instruments so that she can play and calm her nerves. She seizes this moment of her father's absence to climb the tower of the house and bolt the door behind her. When her father sees her in the tower alone, he wants to climb up after her but she insists that he remain at the foot of the tower so that she may tell him the reason for her impending suicide. She begins her speech by calling Pleberio's attention to the signs of mourning evident throughout the city:

"Bien ves y oyes este triste y doloroso sentimiento que toda la cibdad haze. Bien oyes este clamor de campanas, este alarido de gentes, este aullido de canes, este [grande]

---

[34] Michelena, "La humilde condición de Melibea . . . ." 191. Melibea calls the place *torre* (tower) and even remarks "muy alto es esto" (331; "this is very high up").

[35] See her book, *La originalidad artística de La Celestina*, 2nd ed. (Buenos Aires: Editorial Universitaria de Buenos Aires, 1970).

[36] Maravall, *El mundo social de "La Celestina,"* 72.

[37] Gómez Moreno, "La torre de Pleberio y la ciudad de *La Celestina* (un mosaico de intertextualidades artístico-literarias . . .y algo más," *El mundo social y cultural de* La Celestina: *Actas del Congreso Internacional, Universidad de Navarra, junio, 2001*, ed. Ignacio Arellano and Jesús M. Usunáriz. (Madrid: Iberoamericana and Frankfurt: Vervuert, 2003), 211–36; here 216.

[38] See especially 226–28 of "La torre de Pleberio . . . ."

strépito de armas. De todo esto fue yo [la] causa. Yo cobrí de luto y xergas en este día quasi la mayor parte de la cibdadana cavallería; yo dexé [hoy] muchos sirvientes descubiertos de señor . . . ." (333)

["You can plainly see and hear the sad and mournful feeling that pervades the whole city. Surely you hear the pealing of bells, people shrieking, dogs howling, and the great clamor of arms. Of all this I was the cause. I caused all the gentlemen of the city to dress in mourning and put on sackcloth today; I left many servants deprived of a master . . . ."]

From this part of Melibea's speech we learn that Calisto had been an important personage of the city since his untimely death has thrown the entire populace into mourning. Also Melibea blames herself not only for his death but for how his death will impact Calisto's peers and servants. The death of Calisto, according to Melibea, has been not only a personal tragedy for her but one shared by the entire city.

From the high tower, Melibea continues her confession to her father, revealing, without guile, the fact that she had had a clandestine affair with Calisto and that their coupling had taken place within the grounds of her father's home: "Vencida de su amor, dile entada en tu casa. Quebrantó con scalas las paredes de tu huerto; quebrantó mi propósito; perdí mi virginidad" (334; "Conquered by his love, I gave him entrance to your home. He scaled the walls of your garden with a ladder; he broke down my resistance; I lost my virginity.") Gerli has studied Calisto's invasion of Pleberio garden and concludes "The incursion into Pleberio's physical space negotiated by Celestina and her confederates constitutes the disintegration of the illusionary walls of class and identity erected by Pleberio to keep the two worlds apart."[39] But, as we have seen, the lower class represented by Celestina and the servants and the upper class do not remain separated in this city and Melibea tells her father, in no uncertain terms, that his efforts to protect her with walls and towers have been unsuccessful. Just before she throws herself from the tower, Melibea requests her father to bury her and Calisto together. Their tomb will thus stand as part of the monumental architecture of the city and a testament to the love they had so briefly enjoyed.

The tower of Pleberio's home also figures in the last act of the *Tragicomedia* which is largely given over to the *planctus* or lament of the father after he witnesses his daughter's suicide. When he realizes that his only child and sole inheritor of his fortune is gone he rhetorically asks: "¿Para quién edifiqué torres; para quién adquirí honrras; para quién planté árboles, para quién fabriqué navíos?" (337; "For whom did I build towers; for whom did I acquire honors; for whom did I plant

---

39    Gerli, "Precincts of Contention . . .," 73.

trees; for whom did I build ships?").[40] This litany of the inheritance he had prepared for his daughter would seem to point to Pleberio as a man of wealth. He has a fine home in the urban center (with its prominent tower or towers), he is well known in the town, he owns property (owing to the mention of planting trees), and appears to be a businessman or investor in industry. He then rails against fortune saying that he would rather that fate had destroyed his wealth, burned his house, and devastated his properties than have taken away his only child.[41] He is without an inheritor and all his accumulated wealth, his fine home, and his hard work now seem meaningless. He dismisses the deaths of Celestina, Sempronio, and Pármeno as deserved, given the unscrupulous nature of their "business." Calisto's death resulted from as an accident. But he finds no explanation for the loss of his daughter and blames love itself, whom he accuses of being "enemigo de toda razón" (342; "enemy of all reason").

Perhaps the most important house in the city is Celestina's. It is, literally, the base of operations for the missions she performs throughout the city. In her home, she repairs lost maidenheads, makes love potions, conjures spirits to help her in her intrigues, receives guests, maintains the young prostitute, Elicia, and rests after her numerous comings and goings as a panderess. Michael Gerli has discussed the complex imagery evoked by Celestina's abode: " . . .Celestina's house . . . is used to express a sense of ownership, group solidarity, and radical insouciance at the thought of ill-gotten wealth. Her house . . . stands as an arresting image of both group identity and unprincipled ambition."[42]

I agree that Celestina is greedy and ambitious and that her house provides the physical space for these "vices" to flourish. Her home also has political implications for the city and "stands as a monument to the craving for personal empowerment through the ownership and dominion of possession—as a fantasy of stability and legitimacy that lies at the center of proletarian illusions."[43] Since wealth was becoming the determinant factor for social mobility and the cities allowed mercantile ambitions to flourish, conflicting ideas of social status played themselves out in Celestina's activities both inside and outside her home. Inside her home, she receives errant women, their lovers, and, at times, parents who wish to remedy a daughters's fallen state. Pármeno describes the importance of Celestina's home for those who patronize it: "Muchas encubiertas vi entrar en su casa; tras ella hombres descalços, contritos y reboçados, desatacados, que entravan

---

40  Severin cites various interpretations of these lines which seem to point to a similar passage in Petrach's *De remediis*, I, 90 even though that passage makes no reference to ships (337).

41  "¿Por qué no destruýste mi patrimonio; por qué no quemaste mi morada; por qué no asolaste mis grandes heredamientos?" ( 338).

42  Gerli, "Precincts of Contention . . .," 69.

43  Gerli, "Precincts of Contention . . .," 69.

allí a llorar sus peccados" (110–11; "I saw many veiled women enter her house, and after them men barefoot, contrite and hooded, unbuttoned that entered there to cry over their sins"). The veiled women in this quote do not necessarily refer to nuns (though nuns were not unknown clients in Celestina's home) but rather to those who enter her home wishing to disguise their identity. Similarly the men following behind them who are described as barefooted, contrite and hooded could be religious, but they could also be any man keen to hide his identity as he entrusts to Celestina's ministrations the woman he had deflowered or gotten pregnant. The reference to unbuttoned men conjures up allusions of passions, the results of which have brought customers to Celestina's door.

In the course of the plot, we learn that Celestina's house has a large dining area, a type of laboratory or dispensary where she mixes her potions, and an upper floor where Elicia entertains her customers.. Her house is located on the outskirts of town, near the tanneries. As we shall see, legislation regarding the regulation of prostitution to certain defined areas, may have occasioned Celestina's move to this non-central location.[44] Gerli notes that "the peripheral location of Celestina's house may . . . be viewed in terms of the social stratification expressed through the spatial segregation of classes which began to appear in cities at the end of the fifteenth century."[45] Thus, not only is Celestina's home marginalized because of the activities related to prostitution which occur there but also because, although intrinsically linked to the workings of the society, she is, nevertheless, a member of a non-privileged socio-economic class whose lodging must be physically separated from those of the "respectable" citizenry.[46] Even after Celestina's death her house remains almost as a living museum with her protégée, Elicia, as its sole inhabitant. Areúsa invites Elicia to come and live with her in her house after the loss of Celestina but Elicia insists on staying on in Celestina's house:

> " . . .allí, hermana, soy conocida, allí estoy aparrochiada; jamás perderá aquella casa el nombre de Celestina . . . . Y también esos pocos amigos que me quedan no me saben otra morada." (300)

---

[44] On the location of Celestina's home, see P.E. Russell, "Why did Celestina Move House?" *The Age of the Catholic Monarchs 1474–1516. Literary Studies in Memory of Keith Whinnom,* ed. Alan Deyermond and Ian Macpherson (Liverpool: Liverpool University Press, 1989); 155–61.

[45] Gerli, "Precincts of Contention . . .," 72.

[46] On this point, Gerli states that "Celestina did not just move house: she was compelled to do so by community forces which sought to isolate not just prostitutes and beggars but all the other members of the lower classes" ("Precincts of Contention . . .," 72). It is also worth noting that Celestina's previous home had been near the home of Melibea. Her former location, near a rich household, reflects the mixing of social classes within the old medieval city, whereas, now at the end of the fifteenth century, the classes are beginning to congregate and become physically isolated one from another.

[" . . .there, sister, I am known, it's my neighborhood; that house will never lose the name of Celestina . . . . And also the few clients that I have left don't know any other place to find me."]

Alan Deyermond calls Elicia "Celestina's heir"[47] and proposes that Celestina's "line of succession" will continue and her house will remain an essential and well-known part of the urban landscape.[48]

The location of the houses in "Celestina's city," the identification of specific neighborhoods, and relationships between neighbors were influenced, in part, by the laws regulating prostitution. María Eugenia Lacarra has written extensively on prostitution at the end of the fifteenth and beginning of the sixteenth century in Castile and its relationship to the urban society portrayed in the *Tragicomedia*.[49] Lacarra explains that although the statutory penalties for prostitutes were severe, the repeated efforts to legislate the practice indicate that it was difficult to eradicate due largely to the profits that others made from the prostitutes:

" . . .uno de los problemas con los que se enfrentaba el legislador es que con frecuencia eran los padres, madres o señores quienes obligaban a sus hijas, siervas o criadas, a prostituirse para obtener ganancia de ellas. Más grave todavía era la corrupción de jueces y oficiales, quienes en lugar de indagar estos delitos y castigarlos toleraban su actividad e incluso la impulsaban."[50]

["One of the problems which confronted lawmakers was the frequency with which fathers, mothers, or masters obliged their daughters, servants or maids, to prostitute themselves to earn money for them. Even more serious was the corruption of judges

---

[47]   Alan Deyermond, "Female Societies in 'Celestina,'" *Fernando de Rojas and Celestina: Approaching the Fifth Century,* eds. Ivey A. Corfis and Joseph T. Snow (Madison: Hispanic Seminary of Medieval Studies, 1993): 1–31; here, 18.

[48]   Deyermond further proposes that what Rojas is actually portraying with the inheritance of Elicia is a kind of matrilineal succession since we know that Celestina had learned much of arts from Claudina, Pármeno's mother, and that is was none other than Elicia's own grandmother who had taught Celestina how to repair lost maidenheads. ("Female Societies in 'Celestina,'" 18.)

[49]   "La evolución de la prostitución en la Castilla del siglo XV y la mancebía de Salamanca en tiempos de Fernando de Rojas," in *Fernando de Rojas and* Celestina: *Approaching the Fifth Century*, 33–78. Lacarra recognizes that the representation of prostitution in literature does not necessarily reflect the realities of legal or social practice. Therefore, she bases her study primarily on municipal ordinances, royal legislation, and even some police records of the period, all of which seem to corroborate much of the information about the lives of prostitutes who inhabit the world of the *Tragicomedia.*

[50]   María Eugenia Lacarra, "La evolución de la prostitución en la Castilla del siglo XV y la mancebía de Salamanca en tiempos de Fernando de Rojas," *Fernando Rojas and Celestina: Approaching the Fifth Century: Proceedings of An International Conference in Commemoration of the 450th Anniversary of the Death of Fernando de Rojas, Purdue University, West Lafayette, Indiana, 21–24 November 1991*, eds. Ivy A. Corfis and Joseph T. Snow (Madison: Hispanic Seminary of Medieval Studies, 1993), 33–60; here, 34.

and officials who, instead of investigating and punishing these crimes, tolerated this activity and even promoted it."]

Lacarra cites Alfonso X's important law code, the *Siete Partidas*, as an example of the punishments meted out to *alcahuetes* or *alcahuetas*, i.e, men and women who worked as pimps for the prostitutes. Among the different categories of pimps, the law code recognizes go-betweens who induce honorable women into unsanctioned sexual relationships. Thus, Celestina's doubts and concerns about the true purpose of her visits to Melibea's house are well-founded in the knowledge that she is acting illegally. Also applicable to the world of prostitution as presented in the *Tragicomedia* is the distinction the law makes between prostitutes considered "públicas", i.e., those that live and work in an assigned neighborhood of the city known as the *putería*, and those who ply their trade clandestinely, i.e. outside the confines of the *putería* and without regard to restrictions. The "prostitutas públics", i.e., those sanctioned prostitutes who lived and worked in the official brothel zone, paid a tribute to local authorities. Many women tried to avoid this payment by working outside the boundaries of the law, risking both economic and corporal punishment should they be discovered.[51]

A prime example of this clandestine type of prostitute is Areúsa who works out of her own house, choosing her clients and exacting what payments in money, goods, or protection she is able to negotiate. In the *Tragicomedia* she is the lover of Pármeno, the younger of Calisto's two servants. We learn that before her relationship with Pármeno she had had a steady companion, a soldier now gone off to war. The absence of this steady client opens the door for Pármeno to become her lover. But she is very circumspect when Celestina first proposes him as her next partner. She is especially concerned that the neighbors will see his comings and goings and inculpate her:

> Areúsa: Tengo vezinas embdiosas; luego lo dirán . . ..
> Celestina: Esso que temes yo lo proveý primero, que muy passo entramos.
> Areúsa: No lo digo por esta noche, sino por otras muchas. (205)

> [Areúsa: I have envious [female] neighbors, later they will talk . . .
> Celestina: I've already thought about what worries you, so we entered very quietly.
> Areúsa: I don't just mean tonight, but all the other times.]

---

[51]  " . . .muchas mujeres siguieron ejerciendo la prostitución, a espaldas, o con la connivencia, de la justicia, en mesones, ventas, casas de alcahuetas [como la de Celestina ], e incluso en sus propias casas si tenían mayores ganancias y/o gozaban de mejor protección" (Lacarra, 44) ("many women continued o work as prostitutes on the sly or in collusion with the justice system in taverns, inns, pimps' home [like that of Celestina], and even en their own houses if they could earn more there and/or enjoy greater protection).

Celestina is aware of Areúsa's fears and has taken the precaution to arrive undetected. As Lacarra points out, the Catholic Kings, Fernando and Isabel, offered generous rewards to those who turned unsanctioned prostitutes or pimps over to the law.[52] Areúsa's fears that her neighbors might become aware of her activities and denounce her are firmly rooted in her knowledge that these neighbors would stand to profit financially from denouncing her.[53]

Celestina, herself, had been forced to move her house and its operations to the outskirts of the city. In a famous speech in Act Nine, Celestina reminisces about her "glory days" when she had run a successful and lively house of prostitution on her own terms. At the time of the events in the *Tragicomedia*, she has been reduced in circumstance and lives in a small house near the tanneries with but one woman, Elicia, in residence. Celestina explains to Lucrecia what life had been like for her in the past:

> "Yo vi, mi amor, a esta mesa donde agarra están tus primas assentadas, nueve moças de tus días, que la mayor no passava de deziocho años, y ninguna avía menos de quatorze.... Cavalleros, viejos [y] moços, abades de todas dignidades, desde obispos hasta sacristanes. En entrando por la yglesia vía derrocar bonetes de mi honor como si yo fuera una duquesa .... Allí se me offrescían dineros, allí promessas, allí otras dádivas, besando el cabo de mi manto, y aun algunos en la cara por me tener más contenta." (234–35)

> ["I saw, my dear, at this very table where your cousins are now seated, nine young girls of about your age, the oldest was no more than eighteen and none was younger than fourteen . . ... Noblemen, old and young, clergymen of every distinction, from bishops to sacristans. When I entered the church, hats were removed in my honor as if I were a duchess . . ..Over there they showered me with money, over there with promises, over there with gifts, kissing the hem of my cape and some even kissing me on the cheek just to keep me happy."]

Although lengthy, even after severe editing, I have quoted this speech of Celestina because, rather than simply being a rhetorical *ubi sunt*, it reveals a number of facets about the urban environment where Celestina lives and works. She alludes to greater relative freedom and respect that she had enjoyed in the city in years past. Also, among her important clients are members of the clergy, an unvarnished allusion to the sexual practices of even the highest echelons of church hierarchy. She is generously rewarded by all for her services. These memories are in contrast to the more secretive and less lucrative circumstances in which she now finds herself as result, in part, to enhanced regulations on one of her primary modes of income—trafficking in prostitutes. We learn, too, that Celestina had once lived in

---

[52]  See especially pp. 44–45 of the above-cited article.

[53]  On this point, see also David Hook's article, "Areúsa and the Neighbors," *Celestinesca* 23, 1–2 (1999): 17–20.

the *putería*, before establishing her own house. When she is arguing with
Sempronio over his request that she hand over part of her payment from Calisto
to him, she responds with a "who do you think you are?": "¿Quitásteme de la
putería?" (273; "Was it you who got me out of the prostitution quarter?")

Areúsa explains her decisions to pursue her "profession" as a clandestine
prostitute rather than live in the *putería* or work as a servant in a rich household.
She prefers her life, although potentially dangerous and technically illegal, to the
life of a servant, the only other possibility of employment for a woman of her
social status. After a long diatribe about the mistreatment that servants receive at
the hands of their masters, Areúsa declares: " . . . me he querido más bivir en mi
pequeña casa, esenta y señora, que no en sus ricos palacios sojuzgada y cativa"
(233; "I've preferred to live in my own little house, my own mistress, not obligated
to anyone, than in rich palaces, subjugated and captive").

This allusion to the conditions of servitude in the new, monied economy refers
to a situation in which service to the upper classes was based purely on
considerations of financial remuneration rather than on any sort of feudal or
familial loyalty. Maravall sees a close relationship between money as a new form
of social distinction and the urban society. Whereas, social distinction based on
hereditary nobility was the norm during the Middle Ages, on the eve of the
Renaissance, precisely at the time when Rojas is penning the *Tragicomedia*, one is
now valued by the ability to amass wealth. Maravall states "Del desarrollo del
dinero como medio de cálculo económico y medio de pago y atesoramiento,
venían causándose, en gran parte, las transformaciones sociales de la época" ("
Along with the development of money as the means of economic calculation,
method of payment, and accumulation of wealth came many of the social
transformations of the age").[54] This transformation is especially apparent in the
comments of Calisto's servants, particularly those of Sempronio. A desire for
financial reward has completely replaced, and indeed undermined, any sense of
familial loyalty betweens servants and masters. Sempronio, from his first
appearance in the work, makes it clear that his service to Calisto, especially his
help in arranging a meeting with Celestina, is predicated on the rewards his
master will give him for securing the go-between to help in his affair with Melibea.
When Calisto promises his servant a brocaded doublet as payment for his entreaty
to Celestina, Sempronio responds:

> "Prospérete Dios por éste" and then whispers, in an aside: "(y por muchos más
> que me darás. De la burla yo me llevo lo mejor; con todo, si destos aguijones me
> da, traérgela he hasta la cama. Bueno ando; házelo esto que me dio mi amo, que
> sin merced, imposible es obrarse bien ninguna cosa)." (103)

[54] José Antonio Maravall, *El mundo social de 'La Celestina'*, 3rd edition revised. Biblioteca Románica
Hispánica, II Estudios y ensayos, 80 (Madrid: Editorial Gredos, S.A., 1972), 69.

["May God reward you for this (and for everything else you'll give me. From this joke, I'll get the best of him. If he gives me more things like this, I'll even bring her into his bed. I'm doing well; spurred on by what my master gives me, for without reward, it's impossible for anything to work out well.)"]

In fact, both Sempronio and Pármeno had worked for other masters before coming to serve in Calisto's house. Pármeno alludes to his previous employment saying that he had had several posts including services to the friars of Guadalupe where he admits to getting into a number of violent skirmishes (264–65). Sempronio enumerates his various previous jobs including serving the priest of San Miguel, the innkeeper on the *plaza*, and a farmer named Mollejas. Like Pármeno, he had been known to have run-ins with trouble makers in his previous jobs (265). When Celestina speaks alone with Pármeno, see counsels him to plan for his future when he will not be forced to serve in the houses of other. She tells him that he must take hold of every opportunity to earn more and to become financially independent: "Hijo, a bivir por ti, a no andar por casas ajenas; lo qual siempre andarás mientra no te supieres aprovechar de tu servicio . . . .") (195; "Son, live for yourself, not working in others' homes which you'll always be doing if you don't learn how to take advantage of your master.") Sempronio echoes this same idea when he excuses himself with Elicia for arriving late to lunch. His excuse is simply "quien a otro sirve no es libre" (224; "he who serves another is not free."). And Areúsa states that Lucrecia, Melibea's maid, and others like her in domestic service to the upper classes are missing out on the joys of youth: " . . . éstas que sirven a señoras ni gozan deleyte ni conocen los dulces premios de amor. Nunca tratan con parientes, con yguales a quien pueden hablar tú por tú . . ." (232; " . . . these that serve ladies never enjoy pleasure nor know the sweet delights of love. They never get to be with their relatives nor with their peers, people they can talk to as familiars . . . ."). Celestina preaches against blind loyalty to one's masters because a servant can never enjoy a relationship of equals with them because of the clear distinction in their respective social rank. She warns Pármeno not to consider Calisto his friend: "con él no pienses tener amistad, como por la diferencia de los estados o condiciones pocas vezes contezca" (122; "don't think about being friends with him because friendships between those of different social status and condition is very rare.") Just as masters will look out for their own interests over those of their servants, the servants too must find ways to fend for themselves.

Again, Celestina warns Pármeno to look out for number one: "dexa los vanos prometimientos de los señores, los quales deshechan la sustancia de sus sirvientes como huecos y vanos prometimientos" (122; "don't count on vain promises from masters who will undermine the well-being of their servants with empty and futile promises"). We also learn that some members of the serving class previously lived in the country but have moved to the city for more opportunity. For example, Tristán speaks of Sosia's rural background before coming to serve in the house of Calisto; he describes Sosia as "naçido y criado en una aldea quebrando terrones con un arado" (319; "born and raised in a village breaking up the earth with a plow").

As Maravall emphasizes, services in the *Tragicomedia* are exchanged for very specific and quantified amounts of money or the equivalent in valuable goods.[55] Money is specifically mentioned throughout the work. For example Calisto gives Celestina 100 gold coins on their first meeting to ensure that she will plead his case with Melibea. And, in the Act Three, Sempronio, in an aside, complains of Celestina's tardiness in carrying out her mission when he says, "A dineros pagados, braços quebrados" (138), an old proverb that roughly translates, "Once paid, slow to act." When Celestina speaks of her former companion (and Pármeno's deceased mother), Claudina, she talks about their relationship in terms of sharing everything, including the money they earned: "Nunca blanca gané en que no toviesse su mitad" (142; "I never earned a dime without giving her half of it."). In this same Act, Celestina utters her most frank statement regarding money: "Todo lo puede el dinero" (143; "Money can do anything.")[56] Celestina first gains entry to Melibea's house on the pretext of selling some thread; she has had to resort to this type of commerce because of a lack of money: "Con mis fortunas adversas otras, me sobrevino mengua de dinero . . ." (153; "Among my many adversities, I find myself in need of money"). And when negotiating the price for this thread, Celestina quotes its market value in terms of coinage; "tres monedas me davan ayer por la onça') (153; "They gave me three coins per once yesterday.") And although the *alcahueta* bemoans her poverty, she tells Melibea that by the grace of God, "jamás me faltó . . . una blanca para pan y un quarto para vino" (159; "I never lacked for a penny to buy bread nor a quarter for wine"). She is excited about what she might eventually earn from her mission to win Melibea and is confident that Calisto will pay her more for this one enterprise than what she makes by repairing fifteen "virgins."[57] When Celestina comes to report to Calisto the outcome of her first meeting with Melibea, both Sempronio and Pármeno realize that in her greed, she will not share her earnings with them, despite their

---

[55]  "Ahora reduzcámonos a observar que con el empleo del dinero, la contrapartida del servicio personal, que cada vez más se convierte en relación de puro contenido económico, se calcula y se agota en el pago de una cantidad determinada" ("We can summarize by observing that the use of money, as opposed to personal service, produced relationships based on purely economic concern, calculated and paid by means of specific quantities") (*El mundo social de 'La Celestina'*, 70).

[56]  After this broad statement, Celestina launches into a litany of difficulties that can be overcome by money: money can break rocks, cross rivers on dry land, a donkey burdened by gold can climb the highest peek, etc. (143–44).

[57]  "Pues alégrate, vieja, que más sacarás deste pleyto que de quinze virgos que renovaras" (171).

cooperation in the endeavor. Pármeno clearly states that the *alcahueta* will not ask for her reward in money, precisely because it can be divided and shared: "verás como no quiere pedir dinero, porque es divisible" (177; "you'll see that she won't ask for money because it can be divided.")

The newly coined word, "salario" ("salary"), which first appeared in Castilian in the fifteenth century is used in the *Tragicomedia*..[58] For example, Celestina states in Act Three in response to Sempronio's worries that this undertaking may be dangerous: "Siquiera por los presentes que lo vieren no digan que se gana holgando el salario" (141; "Let all those present observe that no one earns a salary by loafing.") In Act Twelve, when Sempronio and Pármeno confront Celestina and insist that she share a portion of the 100 gold coins and the gold chain she had received from Calisto with them, she refuses, using the word "salary": "¿Qué tiene que hazer tu galardón con mi salario, tu soldada con mis mercedes?" (270; "What does your reward have to do with my salary, your stipends with my benefits?") She further argues that the services she provides are her sole source of income whereas Sempronio and Pármeno have participated in the Melibea affair as a great lark. She has risked more, invested more, and thus deserves to enjoy all the salary for herself (271). Sempronio responds by calling Celestina greedy for money: "O vieja avarienta, [garganta] muerta de sed por dinero . . ." (274; "Oh you avaricious old woman, with an unquenchable thirst for money").

Money is directly associated with class standing in this society. Nobility of birth as the sole entrée into the upper class is being eroded by the new mercantile class who rose to prominence by virtue of their possession of wealth and property in the city.[59] And conflicts between social classes began to be debated in economic terms. When Elicia debates the "gentility" of Melibea with Sempronio, she sees Melibea's position and appearance as properties she literally had bought in the market: "Aquella hermosua por una moneda se compra de la tienda" (226; "That kind of beauty can be bought for money in a shop.") And she goes on to say that there are many of other women more beautiful and gentile in the city than Melibea who

---

[58]  On this point, Maravall states "La palabra 'salario' apareció en el vulgar castellano en ese siglo XV; se encuentra en el vocabulario de Alonso de Palencia, lo interesante es que en *La Celestina* se revela ya como habitual en el lenguaje hablado, en correspondencia con la rápida transformación de las relaciones entre amos y criados que se opera en la época, a causa de las nuevas formas económicas que esas relaciones asumen" (70; "The word 'salary' appeared in popular Castilian in the fifteenth century; it is found in the vocabulary of Alonso de Palencia and it is interesting that its use in *La Celestina* reveals that it was now common in the spoken language corresponding to the rapid transformation in the relationships between masters and servants that resulted from the new economic nature that these relationships assumed.")

[59]  On this point, see Maravall especially chapter two: "La transformación social de la clase ociosa y la alta burguesía. Las figuras de Calisto y Pleberio" (32–58; "The Social Transformation of the Idle Class and the Upper Bureaucracy. The Figures of Calisto and Pleberio").

earns such regard merely due to her ostentatious manner of dress.[60] Areúsa's is even harsher in her criticism of Melibea and her supposed "beauty" than was Elicia:

> "Las riquezas las hazen a éstas hermosas y ser alabadas, que no las gracias de su cuerpo, que assí goze de mí, unas tetas tiene para ser donzella como si tres vezes oviesse parido; no parescen sino dos grandes calabaças. El vientre no se le he viso, pero juzgando por lo otro creo que le tiene tan floxo como vieja de cincuenta años." (226–28)

> ["Riches make her type beautiful and highly praised but not because of the loveliness of her body, of which I am blessed. Her breasts appear to be those of a woman who has given birth three times; they look like two big squashes. And, even though, I haven't seen her belly, judging by the rest of her it must be as flabby as that of a fifty-year old woman."]

The animosity felt by members of the lower classes is also revealed in their opinions about the idea of what constitutes nobility. They question whether it is simply a matter of birth or a quality of spirit which can be possessed by anyone regardless of his/her social status. In the Spain of Fernando de Rojas the Catholic Kings, Fernando and Isabel, found their strongest allies in those of the lesser nobility, i.e. the "cavalleros" and "hijosdalgos" who earned their titles primarily through service or economic success. Many of the older and powerful noble families whose titles were earned through inheritance were constantly asserting their rights against those of the crown. It is important to note that the wealth of these older noble families was usually rural in origin, stemming from large grants of lands, monasteries, and even townships under their control whereas members of the lesser nobility usually settled in the urban areas where they built their homes and exercised substantial economic clout in the cities. The advent of this new upper class brought into question the age-old notion of access to nobility merely by chances of birth. Also the increasing obsession with proving that one was a "cristiano viejo" or "old Christian," i.e., not a Jew who had converted to Christianity, revealed a society steeped in hypocrisy,[61] unwilling to play on an even field and fully accept the "conversos" despite that fact that many of these so-

---

[60] "Por cierto que conosco yo en la calle donde ella [Melibea] bive, quatro doncellas en quien Dios más repartió su gracia que no en Melibea, que si algo tiene de hermosura es por buenos atavíos que trae. Ponedlos a un palo, tanbién dirés que es gentil" (226).

[61] On this point, Sosa states: "... mientras los mismos cristianos viejos promulgaban unos principios que había que seguir, éstos al momento de practicarlos los ignoraban. Y si la enseñanza cristiana era la de 'predicar con el ejemplo' es bastante acertado afirmar que en la práctica esto no se daba y que Rojas como converso fue consciente de ello" ("El huerto de Melibea . . ." ( 139; " . . . while the old Christians preached certain principals to followed, in their actions they ignored these principals. And if the Christian teaching was 'preach by example' then it is quite right to assert that this teaching was not followed in practice and Rojas, as a convert, was fully aware of it.")

called new Christians were economically powerful. For example, in Act Four, Celestina speaks of Calisto as of "noble sangre" (167; "noble blood") and, later in Act Twelve Calisto refers to Melibea's "limpieza de sangre"[62] (261; "cleanliness of blood"). In turn, Melibea refers to Calisto's "alto nasciemiento" (262) or "high birth."

The debate between nobility of birth versus nobility of character is front and center in the *Tragicomedia*. When Sempronio speaks of the high linage by birth of Melibea and Calisto, Areúsa immediately strikes back arguing that:

" . . . las obras hazen linaje, que al fin todos somos hijos de Adam y Eva. Procure de ser cada uno bueno por sí, y no vaya a buscar en la nobleza de sus passados la virtud." (229)

[" . . . one's works determines one's linage because in the end we are all sons of Adam and Eve. Just try to do good and don't go looking for virtue in the nobility of your ancestors."][63]

Areúsa repeats this same idea later in the work when she is planning to revenge the loss of Sempronio and Pármeno. She says that she cares nothing for "linaje ni hazañas viejas"[64] ("linage or past famous deeds.")

Despite these debates about what constitutes nobility, the reality of the urban environment presented in the *Tragicomedia* is one divided by considerations of class. Calisto, Melibea and her parents, Alisa and Pleberio represent the upper strata of the town, while Celestina, Calisto's servants, and the prostitutes, Elicia

---

[62]  This reference to blood as well as others to "limpieza" ("cleanliness") of blood have to do with the post-expulsion Spanish preoccupation with "cristianos nuevos" or "new Christians" and "cristianos viejos" or Old Christians. The former implied that one had converted from Judaism to Christianity to avoid the expulsion of 1492. When someone wanted to assert his rights of nobility, the most often cited entitlement was that he/she was an Old Christian with clean blood, i.e., without any trace of Jewish ancestry.

[63]  Marqués Villanueva has pointed out that such expressions of equality of linage despite circumstance os birth were common among *conversos*. On this point see his book, "*Orígenes y sociología del tema celestinesco.*" Colección Hispanistas, Creación, Pensamiento, Sociedad, 2 (Barcelona: Editorial Anthropos, 1993), especially 141–42. Since we know that Rojas was from a family of *conversos* it is not at all unusual that one of his characters voice this opinion. But we should note that Rojas himself never had any conflict with Inquisition. His father-in-law was arrested twice by the Inquisition, there seems to be no supporting evidence that Rojas himself suffered at their hands. In fact, he rose to the post of mayor of Talavera and his estate included vineyards, beehives, houses, and rental properties. See Peter E. Russell, ed. *Comedia o Tragicomedia de Calisto y Melibea.* Clásicos Castalia, 191(Madrid: Editorial Castalia, 1991), especially 31–37.

[64]  316. Admittedly here the use of this phrase is somewhat ironic because Areúsa utters it in reply to the gangster, Centurio, who she hopes to enlist as agent of her revenge. She questions the origin of his name and asks if it means he had once been a captain for a hundred men. Centurio replies that the name actually originated because he had been the scoundrel for a hundred women. In reply, Areúsa states that she isn't interested in his linage or famous deeds of the past.

and Areúsa represent the lower strata. True to her station in this society, Melibea, in spite of her own carnal interest in Calisto, can not merely capitulate to his wishes, even if she shares them. She must be persuaded by that linchpin around which this society functions—Celestina. The *alcahueta* has access to all the social classes and is not bound by the sharp distinctions that keep the worlds of the servants and masters largely separate. It is Celestina who allows this city to maintain the outward appearance of morality and honor; Celestina repairs lost maidenheads so that the upper-class families may make good marriages for their "virgin" daughters; she arranges secret trysts for laymen and cleric alike who thus maintain a façade of fidelity while at the same time assuring that the bonds of either matrimony or vows of celibacy do not become too repressive; and, she moves freely about the city disguising her true missions by clever ruses. Celestina not only has the run of the city but she runs the city of secrets behind the metropolitan façade of respectability. She invades spaces previously considered exclusively private, such as Melibea's home and garden. She essentially shatters the borders between public and private space as well as those that historically separated the noble class from the poor and the mercantile classes.

The involvement of Celestina in the love affair between two members of the urban upper class, the new economy based on the exchange of money for goods and services, the clock as arbiter of the town's activities, the idea of personal advancement for members of the lower classes are all essential elements in the early modern city life portrayed in the *Tragicomedia*. The urban spaces where these phenomena emerge and develop are more than mere backdrop for the story. The municipality and the activities of the city are requisite for the plot of the *Tragicomedia* as it unfolds in Rojas work.[65] For Rojas the confluence of socio-economic classes, access to places and people to fulfill illicit desires, and economic opportunities which exist only in an urban environment are essential for the development of both plot and character. In the *Tragicomedia*, the spatial and economic realities of the early modern city become in a sense co-protagonists with Celestina, the young lovers, Calisto and Melibea, town officials, servants, prostitutes, and ruffians who inhabit it.

---

[65]   On this point, Michael Gerli states, "descriptions of [urban] locations and settings are almost imperceptively embedded in the characters' speeches and become integral parts of the narrative fabric of the work, complements of what the characters do, say and believe." "Precincts of Contention: Urban Places and the Ideology of Space in *Celestina*," *Celestinesca* 21.1–2 (1997): 65–77; here 65.

Albrecht Classen

(University of Arizona)

# Hans Sachs and his Encomia Songs on German Cities: Zooming Into and Out of Urban Space from a Poetic Perspective. With a Consideration of Hartmann Schedel's *Liber Chronicarum (1493)*[1]

It would be tantamount to a commonplace by now to claim that the late Middle Ages and early modern age witnessed a most robust growth of cities all over Europe that ultimately served as the catalyst to shed the last vestiges of the medieval culture.[2] Despite the Black Death in the middle of the fourteenth century with its devastating impact on the population, with estimates of up to thirty percent of the populace having succumbed to the plague around 1347 to 1351, and many times thereafter in ever returning epidemic waves,[3] urban development witnessed an unforeseen and amazing flowering since the thirteenth century,[4]

---

[1]   I would like to express my gratitude to Marilyn Sandidge for her critical reading of my article and the many good suggestions.

[2]   See the vintage study, for instance, by Henri Pirenne, *Medieval Cities: Their Origins and the Revival of Trade*, trans. from the French by Frank D. Halsey (1925; Princeton: Princeton University Press, 1952). His thesis was criticized from many sides; see, for instance, *The Pirenne Thesis: Analysis, Criticism, and Revision*, ed. Alfred F. Havighurst. Problems in European Civilization (Boston: Health, 1958). Now see David Nicholas, *The Growth of the Medieval City: From Late Antiquity to the Early Fourteenth Century*. A History of Urban Society in Europe (London and New York: Longman, 2001); Keith D. Lilley, *Urban Life in the Middle Ages: 1000–1450*. European Culture and Society (Houndmills, Basingstoke, Hampshire, and New York: Palgrave 2002). The list of related studies is legion. See also my introduction to this volume.

[3]   Joseph P. Byrne, *The Black Death*. Greenwood Guides to Historic Events of the Medieval World (Westport, CT, and London: Greenwood, 2004); much more detailed and thorough in their investigations prove to be the contributions to *Pest: Die Geschichte eines Menschheitstraumas*, ed. Mischa Meier (Stuttgart: Klett-Cotta, 2005).

[4]   George Huppert, *After the Black Death: A Social History of Early Modern Europe*. Sec. ed. Interdisciplinary Studies in History (1986; Bloomington and Indianapolis: Indiana University Press, 1998), 14–40.

whether we think of many new foundations or the significant growth of heretofore rather small urban centers.[5] One of the best Italian Renaissance artists reflecting upon this phenomenon, Ambrogio Lorenzetti (ca. late thirteenth century, active ca. 1319, d. ca. 1348) created marvelous frescoes of cityscapes showing us the city of Siena, its environs, and, above all, its citizens. Not by accident has Lorenzo Ghiberti identified him as "il famosissimo e singolarissimo" artist of his hometown,[6] most poignantly referring to his frescoes of *Good and Bad Government* in the Palazzo Pubblico, Siena.[7] The sheer volume of written records produced in cities all over Europe exploded exponentially at least since the thirteenth century,[8] and the increase of power accumulated by cities grew at an astounding rate, which found fascinating expression in a wide variety of urban art, whether we think of cathedrals and churches, city halls, urban houses, libraries, or splendid city walls as part of the fortification system.[9]

Every aspect of human life was affected and influenced, if not determined, by the conditions that dominated in the city at least since the eleventh and twelfth centuries, whether we think of architecture, craftsmanship, industrial production, literature, music, politics, the military, or religion.[10] Naturally, that development only increased by the late Middle Ages. Of course, the nobility still maintained its palaces and castles, country estates, palazzi, and so forth, but most of them also

---

[5]   There are countless studies focusing on the economic and cultural conditions in late-medieval cities, see, for instance, Evamaria Engel, *Die deutsche Stadt des* Mittelalters (Munich: Beck, 1993); *Dortmund und Conrad von Soest im spätmittelalterlichen Europa*, ed. Thomas Schilp and Barbara Welzel. Dortmunder Mittelalter-Forschungen, 3 (Bielefeld: Verlag für Regionalgeschichte, 2004); Günther Binding, *Als die Kathedralen in den Himmel wuchsen: Bauen im Mittelalter* (Darmstadt: Primus, 2006); Keith D. Lilley, *Urban Life in the Middle Ages: 1000–1450*. European Culture and Society (Houndmills, Basingstoke, Hampshire, and New York: Palgrave, 2002).

[6]   George Rowley, *Ambrogio Lorenzetti* (Princeton: Princeton University Press, 1958), 3.

[7]   Rowley, *Ambrogio Lorenzetti*, 99–122; now see also *Ambrogio Lorenzetti: La vita del Trecento in Siena e nel contado senese nelle committenze istoriate pubbliche e private. Guida al buon governo*, a cura di Alberto Colli, introduzione di Mario Ascheri (Siena: n.p., 2004).

[8]   See, for instance, Andreas Meyer, *Felix et inclitus notarius: Studien zum italienischen Notariat vom 7. bis zum 13. Jahrhundert*. Bibliothek des Deutschen Historischen Instituts in Rom, 92 (Tübingen: Niemeyer, 2000); Eliassen Finn-Einar and Geir Atle Ersland, *Power, Profit, and Urban Land: Landownership in Medieval and Early Modern Northern European Towns* (Aldershot, England: Scolar Press; Brookfield, VT: Ashgate, 1996).

[9]   See, for example, the excellent selection of primary sources: *The Towns of Italy in the Later Middle Ages*, trans. and annotated by Trevor Dean. Manchester Medieval Sources Series (Manchester and New York: Manchester University Press, 2000); see also Chiara Frugoni, *A Distant City: Images of Urban Experience in the Medieval World*, trans. William McCuaig (1983; Princeton: Princeton University Press, 1991).

[10]  *Das Leben in der Stadt des Spätmittelalters: Internationaler Kongress Krems an der Donau 20. bis 23. September 1976*. Österreichische Akademie der Wissenschaften. Philosophisch-historische Klasse, Sitzungsberichte, 325. Veröffentlichungen des Instituts für mittelalterliche Realienkunde Österreichs, 2 (Vienna: Verlag der Österreichischen Akademie der Wissenschaften, 1980).

lived in the city for a greater part of their time, which quickly led to a most fascinating mingling of social classes, religious groups, artists, and professions in the urban centers.[11]

This most impressive shift in focus on the city finds its stunning and impressive documentation in the extraordinary, basically since then unmatched production of the famous *Nuremberg Chronicle*, the *Liber chronicarum*, or *World Chronicle* by the medical doctor and humanist Hartmann Schedel (1440–1514) that appeared in print in Nuremberg in 1493, first in its Latin, and a few months later in its German version. Schedel did not only write a history of the world from the time of Genesis to his present, but he also asked many famous artists to contribute a large number of woodcuts, many of which have as their theme (city) vedutas, clearly signaling Schedel's primary interest in urban life where the economy, the arts, literature, and architecture developed more than anywhere else.

But the city as the focal point of early-modern culture also found expression in numerous literary texts starting already from the twelfth and thirteenth century,[12] whether we think of the anonymous goliardic narrative *Herzog Ernst* (Ms. B. ca. 1220/1230),[13] the courtly romance *Partonopier und Meliur* by Konrad von Würzburg (ca. 1270), the poems by Oswald von Wolkenstein (1376/1377–1445), or those by the Nuremberg poet Hans Rosenplüt (ca. 1400/1405–ca. 1460). Some of the most interesting city encomias, however, can first be discovered in the poetic œuvre by the Nuremberg mastersinger poet Hans Sachs (1494–1576) who was one of earliest

---

[11]  *Living in the City: Elites and Their Residences, 1500–1900*, ed. John Dunne and Paul Janssens. Studies in Early Urban History, 12 (Turnhout: Brepols, 2008). See also Jacob Wisse, *City Painters in the Burgundian Netherlands*. Art History Series, 6 (Turnhout: Brepols, 2008). Fabian Alfie's contribution to this volume confirms this observation with a focus on a rather bizarre sonnet by a Florentine poet, probably an imitator of Burchiello.

[12]  Ursula Peters, *Literatur in der Stadt: Studien zu den sozialen Voraussetzungen und kulturellen Organisationsformen städtischer Literatur im 13. und 14. Jahrhundert*. Studien und Texte zur Sozialgeschichte der Literatur, 7 (Tübingen: Niemeyer, 1983); Erich Kleinschmidt, *Stadt und Literatur in der Frühen Neuzeit: Voraussetzungen und Entfaltung im südwestdeutschen, elsässischen und schweizerischen Städteraum*. Literatur und Leben, Neue Folge, 22 (Cologne and Vienna: Böhlau, 1982), focuses above all on the urban space as the place for education, for religious practices, economy, and communality, as expressed in literary texts; see also *Literatur in der Stadt: Bedingungen und Beispiele städtischer Literatur des 15. bis 17. Jahrhunderts*, ed. Horst Brunner. Göppinger Arbeiten zur Germanistik, 343 (Göppingen: Kümmerle, 1982); see also the contributions to the *Jahrbuch der Oswald von Wolkenstein Gesellschaft* 7 (1992/1993) that had been delivered at the symposium "Literatur und Stadtkultur im späten Mittelalter und in der frühen Neuzeit," Basel 1991. For an intensive discussion of German literature and the urban space since the late sixteenth, but primarily since the seventeenth century, see *Stadt und Literatur im deutschen Sprachraum der Frühen Neuzeit*, ed. Klaus Garber, together with Stefan Anders and Thomas Elsmann. 2 vols. (Tübingen: Niemeyer, 1998); see particularly Garber's introductory article, "Stadt und Literatur im alten deutschen Sprachraum: Umrisse der Forschung – Regionale Literaturgeschichte und kommunale Ikonographie – Nürnberg als Paradigma," 3–89.

[13]  See my comments on *Herzog Ernst* in the Introduction to this volume.

poets to develop this genre extensively, though certainly not systematically. In his effort to praise Nuremberg, above all, he had some predecessors, such as Hans Rosenplüt (1447), Enea Silvio Piccolomini, who was later elected as Pope Pius II (in Latin, ca. 1455), Augustinus Patricius (in Latin, 1471), Sigismund Meisterlin (ca. 1485), Kunz Has (ca. 1490/1492), and Conrad Celtis (in Latin, 1492).[14] Nevertheless, Sachs did not content himself with an encomium on his home city; instead he cast his poetic net very wide and dedicated numerous poems to a variety of cities in Northern, Central, and Southern Germany, obviously reflecting upon his years as a journeyman, traveling from city to city as part of his training program.

For the purpose of this paper I will not endeavor a direct comparison between Schedel's monumental work (text and images) and Sachs's sporadic poems created a whole generation later, but the common interest in the city as the major icon of the time still deserves to be noted by itself, particularly because the literary genre of the city encomium had, in its earliest stages, developed already in the high Middle Ages, based on rich classical-antique roots.[15] To be sure, medieval chronicle literature contains numerous descriptions of cities, which probably had a considerable influence on fictional strategies in that regard.[16] But the publication of the famous *Nuremberg Chronicle* in 1493, and then the series of poetic city encomia by Sachs represent, together, a significant step forward in the idealization of the early-modern city.

The enormous publicity and respect that Schedel's *Liber chronicarum* enjoyed probably carried over for decades, and we might imagine that Sachs, also a citizen of Nuremberg, tried to follow that model somewhat by his own means. If we can trust the entry in his own list of books that he owned put together in 1562, he might even have possessed a copy of Schedel's work, since one entry states: "Cronica der der [so] Nürnberger gros Kobergers" (The Great Nuremberg Chronicle by Koberger).[17]

---

14  Hartmut Kugler, *Die Vorstellung der Stadt in der Literatur des deutschen Mittelalters*. Münchener Texte und Untersuchungen zur deutschen Literatur des Mittelalters, 88 (Munich: Artemis Verlag, 1986), 254–55.

15  Paul Gerhard Schmidt, "Mittelalterliches und humanistisches Städtelob," *Die Rezeption der Antike: Zum Problem der Kontinuität zwischen Mittelalter und Renaissance: Vorträge gehalten anläßlich des ersten Kongresses des Wolfenbütteler Arbeitskreises für Renaissanceforschung in der Herzog August Bibliothek Wolfenbüttel vom 2. bis 5. September 1978,* ed. August Buck. Wolfenbütteler Abhandlungen zur Renaissanceforschung, 1 (Hamburg: Dr. Ernst Hauswedell, 1981), 119–28.

16  John Kennth Hyde, "Medieval Descriptions of Cities," *Bulletin of the John Rylands Library* 48 (1966): 308–40; rpt. in id., *Literacy and Its Uses: Studies on Late Medieval Italy* (Manchester and New York: Manchester University Press, 1993), 1–32.

17  Hans Sachs, ed. A[delbert]. v[on]. Keller and E. Goetze. Bibliothek des Litterarischen Vereins in Stuttgart, CCL (Tübingen: Litterarische Verein, 1908), vol. 26, ed. E. Goetze, 152 (for later quotations I will resort to the modern reprint of Sachs's work; see below).

He was, as we will see later, an attentive observer of urban art and literature during his years as a traveling journeyman, including major bibliophile treasures kept at various monasteries, so it would seem self-evident that he also took note of the famous world chronicle produced in his own city of Nuremberg. At any rate, the discourse on and about the city had gained tremendous momentum since the late fifteenth century, as the publication of Schedel's world chronicle confirms, which I will discuss first at some length, before I turn to Sachs's poetic contributions. Those deserve our particular attention in this context because Sachs was regarded as one of the major voices in late-medieval German literature, producing an enormous number of literary texts of different kinds and deeply influencing his contemporaries, at least in Nuremberg and other South-German cities.[18]

Schedel's work belongs to the outstanding treasures of bibliophile art from the *incunabulum* period, that is, the early time of the printing press until 1500.[19] The Latin version consists of 326 leaves, the German of 297 leaves, which makes themtwo heavy tomes simply in terms of weight. A whole team of experts in craftsmanship, printing, and the arts, writers, and the necessary financial sponsors got together twenty years prior to 1493 and began working on his unique and massive book project that appeared in the printing house of famous Anton Koberger (ca 1440/1445–1513). Schedel himself, who had received a solid and broad education in the liberal arts, was a medical doctor by profession, but he is best known today for his world chronicle, a profound expression of his deep humanistic interests, which he supported with a vast library that would ultimately form, several generations later, the basis for the future royal library in Munich (today: *Staatsbibliothek München*).[20]

The *Liber chronicarum* could be the topic of a completely independent study, and scholarship has not been amiss in turning its attention to this masterpiece of late-medieval chronicle literature.[21] After all, major artists such as Michel Wolgemut (1434/37–1519), Wilhelm Pleydenwurff (d. 1494), probably also Albrecht Dürer (1471–1528) during his years as an apprentice in Wolgemut's workshop, as well as

[18]    Maria Galvez, "1515, Ash Wednesday," [Hans Sachs] *A New History of German Literature*, ed. David El Wellbery and Judith Ryan (Cambridge, MA, and London: The Belknap Press of Harvard University Press, 2004), 215–19.

[19]    Hartmann Schedel, *Weltchronik:Nachdruck [der] kolorierten Gesamtausgabe von 1493*. Einleitung und Kommentar von Stephan Füssel (Augsburg: Weltbild, 2004).

[20]    For biographical information, see Martin Kirnbauer, *Hartmann Schedel und sein "'Liederbuch": Studien zu einer spätmittelalterlichen Musikhandschrift (Bayerische Staatsbibliothek München, Cgm 810) und ihrem Kontext*. Publikationen der Schweizerischen Musikforschenden Gesellschaft. Serie II, 42 (Bern, Berlin, et al.: Peter Lang, 2001), 72–93.

[21]    Elisabeth Rücker, *Hartmann Schedels Weltchronik: Das größte Buchunternehmen der Dürer-Zeit* (Munich: Prestel-Verlag, 1988).

various print technicians, scholars such as Hieronymus Münzer (some texts and the famous map of Germany), and others contributed in significant ways to this massive enterprise.[22] The chronicle contains altogether 1,809 woodcuts from 645 woodblocks and thus was, at its time, the one printed book in the entire world with the most illustrations.[23] The images closely interact with the texts and are lavishly arranged on ca. 600 pages throughout the entire book. No other book printer or publisher was ever daring enough after Schedel's 1493 world chronicle had appeared to carry out a similarly ambitious project, although a few cheaper and less elaborate pirated versions were also printed.[24]

One of the most stunning features of the *Liber chronicarum* proves to be the large number of city vedute, or cityscapes, many of which depict specific cities in astounding accuracy, but some of them are of a rather fictional character. These vedute do not only give us a general idea of what a city might have looked like, with its distinctive city wall structures, the major churches, and perhaps a castle in the middle. The eye of the spectator is regularly, actually consistently invited to wander over a large canvas which shows the city in its larger context, providing us with a sense of the natural setting, such as rivers, mountains, forests, bridges, tributaries, fields, roads, etc. In other words, here we come across the typically Renaissance perspective of what constitutes, at least conceptually, a true city as imported from Italy north across the Alps and enthusiastically welcomed and adopted by German artists, writers, and poets.[25]

Of course, lines of traditions can be traced back at least to the twelfth century, if we think of William Fitzstephen's description of London from ca. 1180, Fra Bonvesin della Riva's *De magnalibus urbis Mediolani* (1288), Jean de Jandun's *Tractatus de laudibus Parisius* (1323), and then the description of Rome by John Caballinus (*Polihistoria*, 1320), and the description of Pavia by Opicino de Canistris

---

[22]  *The Nuremberg Chronicle: A Facsimile of Hartmann Schedel's Buch der Chroniken* Printed by Anton Koberger (New York: Landmark Press, 1979).

[23]  Hartmann Schedel, *Weltchronik: Nachdruck [der] kolorierten Gesamtausgabe von 1493.* Einleitung und Kommentar von Stephan Füssel (Augsburg: Weltbild, 2004); *500 Jahre Schedelsche Weltchronik: Akten des Interdisziplinären Symposions vom 23./24. April 1993 in Nürnberg,* ed. Stephan Füssel. Pirckheimer-Jahrbuch, 9 (Nürnberg: Carl, 1994); Stephan Füssel: *Die Welt im Buch: buchkünstlerischer und humanistischer Kontext der Schedelschen Weltchronik von 1493.* Kleiner Druck der Gutenberg-Gesellschaft, 111 (Mainz: Gutenberg-Gesellschaft, 1996).

[24]  Rücker, *Hartmann Schedels Weltchronik,* 8.

[25]  Hartmut Kugler, *Die Vorstellung der Stadt in der Literatur des deutschen Mittelalters,* 188–210; see also Paul Gerhard Schmidt, "Mittelalterliches und humanistische Städtelob," *Die Rezeption der Antike: zum Problem der Kontinuität zwischen Mittelalter und Renaissance: Vorträge gehalten anlässlich des ersten Kongresses des Wolfenbütteler Arbeitskreises für Renaissanceforschung in der Herzog August Bibliothek Wolfenbüttel vom 2. bis 5. September 1978,* ed. August Buck. Wolfenbütteler Abhandlungen zur Renaissanceforschung, 1 (Hamburg: Hauswedel, 1981), 119–28.

(*Liber de laudibus civitatis Ticinensis*, ca. 1329/1330).[26] Nevertheless, Schedel's chronicle clearly signals the rise of a new time in which urban pride extended even beyond the narrow city walls and included all the lands in the near-by environs.[27] One of the most triumphant images of civic glory can be easily identified as the one of Nuremberg itself, significantly right on page 100 in the chronicle, one of the richest and most important cities in late-medieval and early-modern Germany.[28] Not only do we clearly recognize the famous castle in the top center where traditionally the royal jewels were kept, but also many of the major churches that are identified by name. Two gates open the city to the outside world, the left one leading to the fields, the right one to the paper mill, one of the earliest in Germany. Remarkably, this is a double-fold colored woodcut, an extremely expensive artwork which strongly signals the pride which the author, the artists, and the various collaborators all had in their own city. Some of the vedute were probably created on the basis of personal observations, such as in the case of Nuremberg; others were most likely drawn from drafts supplied by friends, colleagues, and journeymen who had practiced their art while traveling by drawing cityscapes. Finally, many other city woodcuts were, as we can assume, based on fictional images and simply followed model images, but they all certainly reflect the mental concept burghers living in these late-medieval urban centers had of the cities as such, the most stunning icons of their time.[29]

Both Schedel and the artists expressed interest in cities wherever they could be found and wherever they might have played a significant role in world history. So the vedute include images of many German, Austrian, and Swiss cities, such as Augsburg, Basel, Eichstätt, Erfurt, Cologne, Constance, Lübeck, Magdeburg, Munich, Passau, Regensburg, Salzburg, Strasbourg, Ulm, Vienna and Würzburg. But other major cities beyond those borders also figure prominently, such as Venice, Constantinople, Jerusalem, Genoa, Cracow, Florence, and Prague. Surprisingly, cities in Western and Southwestern Europe, such as in Spain or England, do not seem to have interested the artists, the author, or the patrons. But it would seem unlikely that those, if they had also been considered, would have revealed remarkably different features because the focus always rests on the same ensemble of elements: the city wall and gates, the churches, the core of the city with densely packed houses, at times a castle on top of a hill (such as in the case

---

26 Kugler, *Die Vorstellung*, 148. See also the contribution to this volume by C. David Benson.
27 Norman Pounds, *The Medieval City*. Greenwood Guides to Historic Events of the Medieval World (Westport, CT, and London: Greenwood Press, 2005), 161.
28 Ludwig Veit, *Handel und Wandel mit aller Welt: aus Nürnbergs großer Zeit*. Bibliothek des Germanischen Nationalmuseums Nürnberg zur deutschen Kunst- und Kulturgeschichte, 14 (Munich: Prestel, 1960); Dieter Wuttke, *Nuremberg: Focal Point of German Culture and History*. Gratia, 16 (Bamberg: S. Wendel Verlag, 1988).
29 Rücker, *Hartmann Schedels Weltchronik*, 115–17.

of Nuremberg and Würzburg), then some of the surrounding areas, mostly hilly, though without much forestation, apart from a few trees. If a river runs by a city, the artist made sure to direct the viewer's attention to the bridges or ships anchored outside of the wall. Hardly any of the city vedute show any people, animals, or any signs of human activities, although the city gates are open, the harbors are ready to receive the ships, and the roads leading to the cities are clear (see, e.g., Munich, CCXXVv–CCXXVIr).

Most significantly, for Schedel and his team of collaborators the cities were the critical hubs of the entire empire, as a double-page image on fol CLXXXIVv to CLXXXVr shows. Although here the cities themselves are only indicated through a few buildings—Salzburg, for instance, at the bottom right, seems to be nothing but a small farm, whereas Lübeck on the top right register is shown with an extensive city wall, one church, but practically no houses—the artists clearly related their sense of the cities representing the most powerful and important entities in the political arena. And for that reason it also makes sense that every city is portrayed in its wider context, mostly hills, fields, sometimes rivers, or smaller settlements and buildings, whether that environ proves to be an accurate depiction of the landscape surrounding a city, or whether the artists simply followed a specific matrix to provide a sense of the city in a quasi-natural setting.

To be a member of an urban class offered many privileges, such as easy access to advanced learning, highly developed craftsmanship and the arts, many travel possibilities, proximity to political power, and economic prosperity. In general, living conditions in the city were considerably more pleasant and secure than elsewhere. This finds its perhaps best expression not only in the many public buildings in the Nuremberg plate, particularly the churches, but also in the double city wall and the density and large number of urban houses. Indeed, as we may deduce from this incredible woodcut, to be a citizen of Nuremberg elevated the individual, at least in the artist's perspective, out of the mundane and connected him/her with the international world, though not quite comparable to Paris, London, or Rome because it was not a capital city in the literal sense of the word.[30]

Now let us turn to late-medieval or early-modern poetic reflections upon the city to grasp how writers responded to this new and exciting phenomenon. One of the best known Nuremberg poets, the shoemaker, or cobbler, Hans Sachs, demonstrated a strong sense of self-identification with this home city in several of his poems. Moreover, he also reflected a strong interest in city life as such, and created numerous poems dedicated to various cities all over Germany, praising them for their glorious history, their beautiful churches and squares, and giving

---

[30] *Nürnberg—Geschichte einer europäischen Stadt*, ed. Gerhard Pfeiffer (Munich: Beck, 1971).

more or less detailed information about major features of each individual city. These poetic encomia promise to be of great significance in our context of 'urban space' as a metaphor for an intriguing and powerful aspect of late-medieval and early-modern history, culture, and mentality.

Many scholars have carefully examined the rise of the late-medieval city from an economic, political, military, and religious perspective. And Sachs, though in previous years commonly disregarded as a prolific but not necessarily qualitative poet, has regained much appreciation insofar as his diverse work consisting of Shrovetide, or carnival, plays, other types of entertaining plays (comedies and tragedies), lyrical poems, dialogic poems, etc., has been recognized as a valuable testimony of sixteenth-century mentality.[31] Sachs himself enjoys considerable respect as an influential contributor to the dissemination of Reformation ideas by way of his verses, and as an important cultural figure in Nuremberg, conveying much knowledge of ancient-classical literature, the Bible, but also of medieval and Renaissance literature that he freely adapted and remodeled for his own purposes.[32]

Surprisingly, despite the huge output of literary works, Sachs did not travel much outside of the city after having settled there and enjoyed a rather tranquil life in Nuremberg until his death, which certainly contributed significantly to his literary creativity and productivity. Born on November 5, 1494, as the son of the tailor Jörg Sachs, he attended the Latin school from 1501 to 1509, learned the craft

---

[31] Hans Sachs, *Meisterlieder, Spruchgedichte, Fastnachtspiele: Auswahl*. Eingeleitet und erläutert von Hartmut Kugler (Stuttgart: Reclam, 2003), 7–17.

[32] Eckhard Bernstein, *Hans Sachs* (Reinbek bei Hamburg: Rowohlt, 1993); *Hans Sachs und Nürnberg: Bedingungen und Probleme reichsstädtischer Literatur. Hans Sachs zum 400. Todestag am 19. Januar 1976*, ed. Horst Brunner, Gerhard Hirschmann, Fritz Schnelbögl (Nuremberg: Selbstverlag des Vereins für Geschichte der Stadt Nürnberg, 1976); still proves to be very valuable until today, Rudolph Genée, *Hans Sachs und seine Zeit: Ein Lebens- und Kulturbild aus der Zeit der Reformation*. Rpt. (1894; Niederwalluf bei Wiesbaden: Martin Sändig, 1971); Horst Brunner, "Hans Sachs – sein Bild nach 500 Jahren," id., *Annäherungen: Studien zur deutschen Literatur des Mittelalters und der Frühen Neuzeit*. Philologische Studien und Quellen, 210 (Berlin: Erich Schmidt, 2008, orig. 1994), 350–65. See also my recent essays on Sachs: "Der verkannte Meister? Eine Schlüsselfigur des 16. Jahrhunderts im Kreuzfeuer der Kritik. Die Darstellung von Frauen im Werk von Hans Sachs," *Etudes Germaniques* 59 (2004): 5–39; "Women, Wives, and Marriage in the World of Hans Sachs," *Daphnis* 32, 3–4 (2003): 491–521; "Mittelalterliche Chronistik und Literatur im Werk von Hans Sachs: Rezeptionshistorische Perspektiven im 16. Jahrhundert," *Colloquia Germanica* 37, 1 (2004): 1–25; "Hans Sachs's Reception of the Medieval Heroic Tradition: Social Criticism in the Cloak of *Nibelungenlied* Source Material," in *Parergon* 23, 1 (2006): 93–117; "Poetische Proteste gegen den Krieg: Der Meistersänger Hans Sachs als früher Kriegsgegner im 16. Jahrhundert," *Amsterdamer Beiträge zur älteren Germanistik* 63 (2007): 235–56. For Sachs's reception and adaptation of medieval literature, see also Winfried Neumann, *Zeitenwechsel: Weltliche Stoffe des 12. bis 14. Jahrhunderts in Meisterliedern und motivverwandten Dichtungen des Hans Sachs*. Jenaer Germanistische Forschungen. Neue Folge, 19 (Heidelberg: Universitätsverlag Winter, 2005).

of shoemaking until 1511, and embarked on his travels as a journeyman from 1511
to 1516, visiting one city after another:

> Erstlich gen Regnspurg und Braunaw,
> Gen Saltzburg, Hall und gen Passaw,
> Gen Wels, Münichen und Landshut,
> Gen Oeting und Burgkhausen gut,
> Gen Würtzburg und Franckfurt, hernach
> Gen Coblentz, Cölen und gen Ach.[33]

> [First from Regensburg and Braunau
> To Salzburg, Hall, and Passau,
> To Wels, Munich, and Landshut,
> To Oeting and nice Burghausen,
> To Würzburg and Frankfurt, afterwards
> to Koblenz, Cologne, and Aachen.]

Having returned in 1516, he opened his own workshop and married Kunigunde
Kreuzer in 1519. In the meantime, the Protestant Reformation had begun and the
news of it had also reached Nuremberg, where Sachs quickly turned into a
passionate adherent and supporter, though he had always to be careful not to
transgress the censure laws of the city that tried to control the political opinions
of its inhabitants out of fear that too radical statements either regarding one of the
two churches or regarding a political or military leader could endanger the city's
economic well-being, such as cutting off trade routes, besieging the city itself, or
imposing prohibitive tolls for its products. In 1560, Kunigunde died, and one year
later Sachs married his second wife, Barbara Harscher. In 1567 he created a second
(the first he had written in 1556), more complete and most noteworthy *Summa* of
all of his poems, and on January 19, 1576 he died in Nuremberg.[34]

Not surprisingly, Sachs also composed an encomium on Nuremberg, his
*Lobspruch der statt Nürnberg*, in 1530, but scholars have mostly dismissed it as

---

[33]   Hans Sachs, "Summa all meiner gedicht vom MDXIIII jar an biß ins 1567 jar," Hans Sachs, ed. A.
       v. Keller and E. Goetze. vol. 21 (1892; Hildesheim: Georg Olms, 1964), 337–44; here 338, vv. 7–12.
[34]   Bernstein, *Hans Sachs*, 140–42; ibid., "Hans Sachs," *German Writers of the Renaissance and
       Reformation 1280–1580*, ed. James Hardin and Max Reinhart. Dictionary of Literary Biography, 179
       (Detroit, Washington, DC, and London: Gale Research, 1997), 241–52; see also Hans-Joachim Behr,
       "Hans Sachs – Handwerker, Dichter, Stadtbürger: Versuch einer Würdigung anläßlich der 500.
       Wiederkehr seines Geburtstages," *500 Jahre Hans Sachs: Handwerker, Dichter, Stadtbürger*.
       Ausstellungskataloge der Herzog August Bibliothek, 72 (Wiesbaden: Harrassowitz, 1995), 9–16;
       and Irene Stahl, "Hans Sachs (1494–1576): Eine biographische Skizze," ibid., 25–32. See also
       Wilhelm Richard Berger, *Hans Sachs: Schuhmacher und Poet* (Frankfurt a. M. : Societäts-Verlag,
       1994); *500 Jahre Hans Sachs: Handwerker, Dichter, Stadtbürger*, ed. Dieter Merzbacher and Hans-
       Joachim Behr (Wiesbaden: Harrassowitz, 1994).

highly traditional, without any clear sensitivity for the new ways that Italian Renaissance poets, but also German writers, had developed this literary genre, regularly situating the city in its wider context, thereby allowing the eye to roam freely and the mind to comprehend the larger framework supporting a city, including its *hinterland*. He never would have stood, as Hartmut Kugler opined, the comparison with such intellectual minds as Conrad Celtis who had composed in Latin a similar text, his *Norimberga*.[35] But such a comparison itself would not be fair, considering the totally different cultural and educational backgrounds and intentions, Sachs belonging to the class of craftsmen, Celtis being a representative of the German Renaissance elite, himself the first poet laureate in Germany (crowned on April 18, 1487).[36] And as Kugler himself admits, Sachs focuses in great detail on the interior structure of the beloved city and counts everything that might be countable to impress his audience with the considerable wealth and richness of Nuremberg. He obviously followed the model by his predecessors, such as Hans Rosenplüt, and he seems to have achieved his goal of appealing with his poem both to the populace and to the city government. It deserves to be noted that Celtis's first version from 1495 did not find the approval of the city government, so he was forced to revise it considerably and to add, just as Sachs does, details about the city in much more specific terms.[37]

The purpose here will therefore not be to compare and contrast Sachs's encomiastic poems with those by contemporary Renaissance writers and to examine where he might have failed to achieve the same goals as they did, or have superseded them. It would also be inappropriate to set his songs side by side with the fairly large corpus of Latin *laudes urbium* from the twelfth through the sixteenth century because we could not really expect common elements or direct connections among these very different strands of literary traditions.[38] After all, the

---

[35]  Kugler, *Die Vorstellung der Stadt*, 212–14; Jean Lebau, "L'Éloge de Nuremberg dans la tradition populaire et la littérature humaniste de 1447 à 1532," *Hommage à Dürer: Strasbourg et Nuremberg dans la première moitié du XVIe siècle: Actes du Colloque de Strasbourg (19–20 novembre 1971)* (Strasbourg: Istra, 1972), 15–35; see also Hartmut Kugler, "Die Stadt im Wald: Zur Stadtbeschreibung bei Hans Sachs," *Hans Sachs – Studien zur frühbürgerlichen Literatur im 16. Jahrhundert*, ed. Thomas Cramer and Erika Kartschoke. Beiträge zur Älteren Deutschen Literaturgeschichte, 3 (Bern and Las Vegas: Peter Lang, 1978), 83–103.

[36]  Dieter Wuttke, "Conradus Celtis Protucius," *Deutsche Dichter der frühen Neuzeit (1450–1600): Ihr Leben und Werk*, ed. Stephan Füssel (Berlin: Erich Schmidt Verlag, 1993), 173–99.

[37]  Albert Werminghoff, *Conrad Celtis und sein Buch über Nürnberg* (Freiburg i. Br.: J. Boltze, 1921), 46–47; Kugler, *Die Vorstellung der Stadt*, 215.

[38]  Carl Joachim Classen, *Die Stadt im Spiegel der Descriptiones und Laudes urbium in der antiken und mittelalterlichen Literatur bis zum Ende des zwölften Jahrhunderts*. Beiträge zur Altertumswissenschaft, 2 (Hildesheim and New York: Georg Olms, 1980); Nikolaus Thurn, "Deutsche Neulateinische Städtelobgedichte: ein Vergleich ausgewählter Beispiele des 16. Jahrhunderts," *Neulateinisches Jahrbuch– Journal of Neo-Latin Language and Literature* 4 (2002): 253–70.

early-modern city had grown so much in importance all over Europe that it was
regularly on people's mind, as reflected by poetry, the visual arts, even music,
pageantry, and various types of writing, so Sachs can be credited for having
responded to his own observations, though he obviously also studied a variety of
relevant sources for each city.

The economic centers were all located in cities, where the most money was
accumulated, which in turn allowed the building of new churches, city palaces,
walls, and other constructions. Not surprisingly, the creation of encomia on cities
both south and north of the Alps became a central interest for city rulers, the upper
urban class of administrators, but then also for the members of the guilds, the
intelligentsia, poets and artists alike.[39] After all, as Sebastian Münster observed in
the prologue to his *Cosmographey* from 1544, the world had been transformed
because of the tremendous growth of cities: "Nimm für dich vnser Tevtsch Landt
/ so wirst du finden / das zu vnsern zeiten gar viel ein andere gestalt hat / weder
es vor zwölff hundert jaren gehabt . . . . Dann dazumal hat man kein vmbmawrte
Statt darinn gefunden . . . " (Take into view our Germany, then you will find that
our times have assumed quite a different shape, very different from what the
world was like twelve hundred years ago. At that time there were no cities with
a wall around them . . .).[40]

Sachs lived in Nuremberg most of his life and was a keen observer, as the many
successful Shrovetide plays indicate in which people's individual shortcomings
and weaknesses are profiled and ridiculed.[41] In his poems he treated, for instance,
the ancient gender conflict, poverty, the role of money, marriage, the role of wine,
the value of good health, podagra, distrust, bickering, love, changing of heart and
mind, *memento mori*, etc. The same wide range of themes can be observed in his
many Shrovetide plays, and Sachs never seems to have rested in his attempts to

---

[39]  Nils Büttner, "*Johannes arte secundus?* Oder: Wer signierte den Genter Altar?," *Dortmund und
      Conrad von Soest im spätmittelalterlichen Europa*, ed. Thomas Schilp and Barbara Welzel.
      Dortmunder Mittelalter-Forschunten, 3 (Bielefeld: Verlag für Regionalgeschichte, 2004), 179–200;
      here 187–88; Henk Th. van Veen, *Cosimo I de' Medici and His Self-Representation in Florentine Art and
      Culture*, trans. Andrew P. McCormick (1998; Cambridge, New York, et al.: Cambridge University
      Press, 2006), ch. 9, 148–59.

[40]  Quoted from Kugler, *Die Vorstellung*, 226. See also Klaus Arnold, "Städtelob und
      Stadtbeschreibung im späteren Mittelalter und in der frühen Neuzeit," *Städtische Geschichts-
      schreibung im Spätmittelalter und in der frühen Neuzeit*, ed. Peter Johanek. Städteforschung. Reihe
      A: Darstellungen, 47 (Cologne, Weimar, and Vienna: Böhlau, 2000), 247–68, who traces the history
      of Latin *laudes urbium* from the high to the late Middle Ages, but also touches, every so briefly, on
      the work by Hartmann Schedel and the city encomia by Hans Sachs without particular comments
      or any comparative evaluation.

[41]  See the various contributions to *Hans Sachs und Nürnberg: Bedingungen und Probleme
      reichsstädtischer Literatur. Hans Sachs zum 400. Todestag am 19. Januar 1976*, ed. Horst Brunner,
      Gerhard Hirschmann, and Fritz Schnelbögl (Nuremberg: Verein für Geschichte der Stadt
      Nürnberg, 1976).

focus on whatever was on people's minds and what was discussed in public, thereby making himself the literary spokesperson for the entire city.

On February 20, 1530, he composed his well-known *Ein lobspruch der statt Nürnberg*, apparently with the specific intention to test the city government's willingness to drop a ban on his writing issued on March 27, 1527, which had seemed to them to threaten the internal peace, the good relationships with external powers, and the fragile stable conditions in the world beyond the city wall after the crushing defeat of the peasant revolt in 1525.[42] Sachs, however, was not the man to be hushed into silence, as the more than 300 mastersongs (*Meisterlieder*) indicate that he composed between 1527 and 1529 in gnomic stanzas, taking positions regarding larger political, religious, and military issues that affected both Germany at large and Nuremberg in particular.[43] In the "lobspruch der statt Nürnberg" all critical comments have disappeared, and instead the poet presents to us a most glowing image of this imperial city in all its industry, wealth, virtues, honor, and civic pride.[44]

Although the "lobspruch" begins with an allegorical-topical setting, with the poet wandering around in a forest until he comes across an opening with a fountain, where he lies down and falls asleep, the focus really rests on the city itself, which he first takes into view from the distance before he turns to details. But in his subsequent dream vision, a trope commonly used in medieval literature (see, for example, Guillaume de Lorris's *Roman de la rose*),[45] he observes a mighty eagle, the traditional bird of coats of arms and seals, being attacked by other birds and animals, but it knows how to defend itself energetically with its claws. Soon after, the poet is awakened by an old herald who takes him to a site where he can witness with his own eyes the materialization of his dream vision, that is, the city of Nuremberg where the black eagle is flying in the city's banner: "die selb ein schwartzen adler füret" (191, 28). At first they visit the castle itself, hovering high above the city, ennobled by being one of the central points where the German emperor visits regularly. Afterwards, they go to an outlook and take into view the splendor of the city: "Do sach ich ein unzelich zal / Heuser gepawen hoch und nieder / In dieser state hin und wieder" (192, 14–16; I saw in immeasurable number houses built high and low in this city up and down). For him this is an "edel schatz" (12; a noble treasure) that is worth his personal admiration. He notices, above all, the delicate precaution the builders have taken to protect the houses from fire, and their deliberate attempt to introduce the Italian style, which seems

---

[42]  Bernstein, *Hans Sachs*, 51–53.

[43]  Bernstein, *Hans Sachs*, 54–66.

[44]  Hans Sachs, ed. Adelbert von Keller. Vol. 4 (1870; Hildesheim: Georg Olms, 1964), 189–99.

[45]  The classical study on this topic continues to be C. S. Lewis, *The Allegory of Love: A Study in Medieval Tradition* (1936; London, Oxford, and New York: Oxford University Press, 1977).

to transform the entire city into a princely palace (23). From here his eyes wander through all the streets and squares, and he begins his enumeration of the narrow streets, the public fountains, the church bells, the city gates, the bridges made out of stone, the market squares, bathhouses, churches, and watermills. Amazed at this splendid assembly, the narrator asks his guide about the city and its inhabitants and is immediately informed: "Ein embsig volck, reich und sehr mechtig, / Gescheyd, geschicket und fürtrechtig. / Ein grosser thayl treybt kauffmanns-handel. / In alle landt hat es sein wandel / Mit specerey und aller wahr" (193, 18–22; An industrious people, rich and very powerful, intelligent, clever, and circumspect. Many of them are merchants and do business in many different countries with spices and all kinds of goods).[46]

Being a craftsman himself, Sachs, not surprisingly, emphasizes the dominant role of craftsmen in the city: "Der maist thail sich mit hand-werck nert" (193, 25; the greatest part makes a living through working with their hands). But he does not ignore the important printers and painters, among many other types of professionals who all excel in their work and can pride themselves in being some of the very best in the entire world: "Der-gleich man find in keynen reichen, / Die ihrer arbeyt thun geleichen" (193, 38–39; You do not find anyone in other kingdoms who do such good work as they do). Whatever aspect of human activity it might be, one could always find the best representation in Nuremberg, whether physical labor or the arts, fencing, singing, or playing a music instrument (194, 5).[47]

Next he turns to the city government and openly sings a song of praise about it without daring to let a strain of criticism enter his discourse: "Ein fürsichtiger weiser rat" (194, 16; a careful, wise council). The poet is full of praise of the councilors' wisdom that can orderly and wisely direct the entire populace to its best goals, supported by a whole army of subordinate administrators responsible for ever smaller neighborly units, and all that sustained by a sound legal system and a city constitution that protects everyone from the dangers resulting from tyranny because a well thought-out system of rules and laws prevents all transgressions (195, 4–5).[48]

---

[46] Walter Tauber, *Der Wortschatz des Hans Sachs*. Vol. 1: *Untersuchungen*. Vol. 2: *Wörterbuch* (Berlin and New York: de Gruyter, 1983). The text is partially also available online at: http://books.google.com/books?id=KY6rbtj7b3QC&dq=f%C3%BCrtrechtig&source=gbs_summ ary_s&cad=0 (last accessed on March 9, 2008).

[47] Jörn Reichel, "Handwerkerleben und Handwerkerdichtung im spätmittelalterlichen Nürnberg: Hans Rosenplüt genannt Schnepper," *Literatur in der Stadt: Bedingungen und Beispiele städtischer Literatur des 15. bis 17. Jahrhunderts*, ed. Horst Brunner. Göppinger Arbeiten zur Germanistik, 343 (Göppingen: Kümmerle, 1982), 115–42.

[48] For the discourse on, or rather against, tyranny in the Middle Ages, see Albrecht Classen, The People Rise Up against the Tyrants in the Courtly World: John of Salisbury's *Policraticus*, the *Fables* by Marie de France and the Anonymous *Mai und Beaflor*," *Neohelicon* XXXV, 1 (2008): 17–29. Hans Sachs repeatedly voiced his explicit opposition against tyrants, see his poem "Gesprech von der

More important, however, proves to be the harmony between the city population and the city council: "Einhellig und einmütig sein" (195, 13; in agreement and in unison), which results in an advantage for everyone and the growth of public wealth (195, 15). To underscore the extraordinarily positive situation for Nuremberg, the poet further explains his dream allegory, identifying the hostile birds that attacked the eagle as all those envious of the imperial city, which is protected, however, by four allegorical figures, the lady of wisdom, the lady of justice, the lady of truth, and the lady of self-protection, involving the 'Gewalt, macht, reichthumb, krafft und sterck" (197, 15; Authority, power, wealth, might, and strength).[49]

Just as in Schedel's *Nuremberg Chronicle*, Sachs emphasizes the double ring wall around the city, the large number of towers (a total of 183), and then also artillery, gun powder, weapons, stored food, and urban troops, which all guarantee that the city is being protected at day and at night (197). But instead of going into many further details, the herald recommends the poet spend his life there and experience the city himself which would confirm his concluding comment: "Darmit sie reichlich ist gezieret, / Gekrönet unnd geblesenieret" (198, 15–16; it is richly decorated, crowned and blessed).

Switching from the allegorical speech to an autobiographical reflection, Sachs turns to the city itself and reflects upon the positive experiences that he has had there, emphasizing the harmony between city council and the populace (198, 30), the orderliness of the estates (198, 31), and the praiseworthiness of the government (198, 32). It is obviously a flattering poem intended to ingratiate the poet with the authorities after he has suffered from their censure for so long. But we also get a remarkable sense of civic pride that pervades the entire poem, especially because he identifies Nuremberg as his "vatterland" (198, 37; fatherland) that he equates with a blooming rose garden that is taken care of by God Himself. Inasmuch as Sachs apparently tried to ingratiate himself with the city leaders when he wrote this poem, he still granted his audience a remarkable overview of the entire city both in its physical structure and in its social system, with a non-tyrannical

---

himelfart margraff Albrechtz anno 1557," vol. 23, 113–21. For urban revolts and protests against princely rulers in the late Middle Ages, see the contributions to this volume by Britt C. L. Rothauser and Lia Ross. Cf. also Knut Schulz, "*Denn sie lieben die Freiheit so sehr . . .*": *Kommunale Aufstände und Entstehung des europäischen Bürgertums im Hochmittelalter* (Darmstadt: Wissenschaftliche Buchgesellschaft, 1992); Paul Burgard, *Tagebuch einer Revolte: ein städtischer Aufstand während des Bauernkrieges 1525*. Historische Studien, 20 (Frankfurt a. M. and New York: Campus, 1998). See also the contributions to *Emotions in the Heart of the City (14th-16th Century)*, ed. Elodie Lecuppre-Desjardin and Anne-Laure Van Bruaene. Studies in European Urban History (1100–1800) (Turnhout: Brepols, 2005), in Part I: The Politics of Emotion in Urban Revolts.

[49] The social stability within the city was of greatest importance for all late-medieval urban poets and chroniclers, see Hans-Christoph Rublack, "Grundwerte in der Reichsstadt im Spätmittelalter und in der frühen Neuzeit," *Literatur in der Stadt*, 9–36.

government (whatever that might mean in this context) and a population that fully embraced the authorities and subscribed to the ideal of the urban commonwealth. He did not limit his perspective to his own social class, the craftsmen; instead he also discussed the merchants, the artists, and the judges, although women, children, and other minorities find no mention at all.

Undoubtedly, there is a heavy emphasis on quantification, insofar as Sachs, full of admiration, emphasizes the large number of streets, workshops, fountains, bells, etc. At the same time he does not neglect to mention the Italian architecture that has had some influence on Nuremberg (192, 22), the markets, the churches, and also the river that runs through the city (193). In other words, he combines the economic with the cultural, the religious, and the political to paint the image of an ideal city, strong on the inside because of a solid cohesion among the population, and strong on the outside because of its double defense wall, the well-stocked artillery, stored food, and trained soldiers.

No wonder that Kugler could recognize many similarities with medieval urban encomia because the focus never rests on the outside world, rather the emphasis is placed on the internal cohesion and stability within.[50] But Sachs was a life-long inhabitant of this city, whereas Celtis, as a learned scholar, only passed through and had entirely different interests when he composed his Latin *Norimberga*.[51] Sachs tried to get back on a good footing with the city council, whereas Celtis tried to use the poem he was commissioned to write for pay to secure also their support, in his case for the appointment to the faculty at a planned humanist school, though ultimately to no avail.[52]

Leaving the differences aside, we can determine at least that the development of urban life had reached such a point by the first third of the sixteenth century that it seemed most appropriate for Hans Sachs to regain the city council's favor by composing such a detailed praise poem on the entire city with which he himself identified thoroughly, irrespective of his open attempt to flatter the authorities. For him, after all, Nuremberg was his home and he regarded himself as an intimate member of the larger urban community that prospered so well and enjoyed justice and peace because it was dominated by a corporate mentality specifically opposed to "aygen-nutz" (selfishness).[53]

---

[50]   Kugler, *Die Vorstellung der Stadt*, 214–15.
[51]   Kugler, "Die Stadt im Wald." See also Klaus Arnold, "Konrad Celtis und sein Buch über Nürnberg," *Acta Conventus Neo-Latini Guelpherbytani: Proceedings of Sixth International Congress of Neo-Latin Studies, Wolfenbüttel 12 August to 16 August 1985*, ed. Stella P. Revard, Fidel Rädle, and Mario A. Di Cesare. Medieval & Renaissance Texts & Studies, 53 (Binghamton: Medieval & Renaissance Texts & Studies, 1988), 7–15.
[52]   David Price, "Conrad Celtis," *German Writers of the Renaissance and Reformation*, 23–33; here 28.
[53]   Rüdiger Brandt, "*Von wegen ewerß aygen-nutz*: Städtische Ordnungsvorstellungen als religiöse Argumentationshilfe bei Hans Sachs im Spruchgedicht KG XXIII, 505ff," *Jahrbuch der Oswald von*

But we would miss a great opportunity to study the new relevance of urban life in the sixteenth century if we ignored Sachs's numerous other encomia, such as his song "Lobspruech der statt München in Payern," composed on September 11, 1565. Whereas Oswald von Wolkenstein (1376/77–1445) had previously turned his attention to cities as part of his mental horizon, though certainly with a lot of hesitation and doubts about the market conditions there, leaving him no chance of competing with his traditional skills and abilities,[54] Sachs composes his texts from the complete opposite perspective insofar as he writes from within the city as a proud burgher who adulates his community and intends to glorify the city poetically to the best of his abilities. Moreover, Sachs embraces the concept of the city completely, as a whole series of other urban encomias indicate, to which I'll turn next.

Very different from his praise poem on Nuremberg, here the poetic view assumes the bird's-eye perspective, first describing the location of Munich next to the river Isar, then determining the date of its origin in 962 and its founder, Duke Henry, who erected first a bridge over the river.[55] Under Emperor Otto I a little city was built next to it, which led, however, to conflicts with the local bishops who were competing for the road toll. In fact, the major portion of this poem is dedicated to the historical account, taking us through the entire Middle Ages. But Sachs also emphasizes here the major role played by the citizenry who are doing mostly merchant business, whereas others work as craftsmen and artists (265, 26–28). Next his attention turns to the architecture, and again it is the global, aerial perspective that determines the description: "Darinn sind auch herlich und weit gassen / Und schöne heuser ubermassen, / Die gotsheuser wol geziert und gros / Und auch ein wolgebawtes schloß" (265, 29–32; Therein are also splendid and wide streets and unbelievably many beautiful houses. The churches are wonderfully decorated and large, and there is also a well-built castle).

Like a regular tourist of today, he reflects upon the most impressive churches, the ducal palace with its host of particular rooms, cellars, office space, etc., and the lion park, without, however, going into further details. In fact, this is more an encomium on the Bavarian ducal family and its history in briefest form, than an encomium on the city, as the epimythion indicates: "Der durchleuchtig hertzog Albrecht / Mit seinem adel, from und grecht, . . . / Das dem fürsten grün, plüe und

54  *Wolkenstein Gesellschaft* 7 (1992/1993): 75-101.
    *Die Lieder Oswalds von Wolkenstein*, ed. Karl Kurt Klein. 3rd, revised and expanded ed., ed. Hans Moser, Norbert Richard Wolf and Notburga Wolf. Altdeutsche Textbibliothek, 55 (1962; Tübingen: Niemeyer, 1987), Kl. 86, Kl. 98, Kl. 99, Kl. 104, Kl. 122, and Kl 123. For an excellent commentary, see Werner Marold, *Kommentar zu den Liedern Oswalds von Wolkenstein*, revised and ed. Alan Robertshaw. Innsbrucker Beiträge zur Kulturwissenschaft. Germanistische Reihe, 52 (1926; Innsbruck: Institut für Germanistik, 1995).

55  Hans Sachs, Vol. 23, 264–66.

wachs / Sein fürstlich lob, wünscht Hans Sachs" (266, 1–6; To the illuminated Duke Albrecht, with his nobility, virtue, and justice, . . . I, Hans Sachs, am wishing this duke that everything will grow green, bloom, and grow). Nevertheless, despite the quick historical survey we gain a good idea of the slow yet steady growth of Munich, involving the division into two parishes, the expansion of the city wall to enclose further quarters, and the erection of monasteries by the Friars and the Augustinians.

Perhaps most interesting is that Sachs alerts us to the fact that the streets in Munich are impressively wide and beautifully maintained (265, 29). The poet actually manages to balance the report about the various professions pursued in the city with his accolades of the ducal palace, apparently the triumph of the entire city, especially because he has great respect for Duke Albrecht who goes so far, as Sachs comments, to maintain the roads well in his own country: "Da im land alle straß gemein / Werden gehalten sauber und rein" (266, 3–4; In that country all roads are kept clean and tidy).

More than two years later, Sachs composed an encomium on the imperial city Vienna (Dec. 1, 1567),[56] which had apparently impressed him even more for its metropolitan character, hence its large size, which required massive defense systems, both a wall and a trench. He pays great homage to the capital, as he calls it ("haubtstat," 304, 3) and identifies it as the most noble city among all those that are situated on the banks of the Danube. Although Sachs tries to give an etymological explanation of Vienna's name (304, 11–16), he is not really successful in that, but in this effort he even adds further information about the geographic setting of this city, referring to another river near by. The poet notices with great astonishment the use of stones to stabilize the streets within the city (304, 25–26) and in the construction of the houses (305, 2–3), both very expensive processes. The extensive range of cellar space underneath the houses makes him think that there might be more buildings underground than above ground (305, 11–14).

As is always the case, he pays close attention to the various churches, especially the cathedral St. Stephan, "Das in ganczem Deutschland hat rum" (305, 25; which is famous all over Germany). But then he also mentions the highly reputable Viennese university where many students are enrolled from Hungary and Germany (305, 27–32). For Sachs, however, the most important feature seems to be, as was also the case in his encomium on Nuremberg, the election of a city council and of a supreme judge who govern exceedingly well and fairly, exuding a sense of confidence in their work.

---

[56]   Hans Sachs, Vol. 23, 304–08.

From here Sachs turns to the wine production, which was of greatest importance for Vienne, also considering its location and position as a major wine exporter, as we can learn from Sachs brief comments: "Den maisten wein, den fürt man naw / Mit pferdn in schaiffn rawff die Thonaw" (306, 14–15; Most of the wine is transported away on ships pulled by horses upstream), sending it as far away as to Bavaria and Swabia. Whereas in his encomium on Nuremberg Sachs had contented himself with a rather myopic perspective, here he describes Vienna as the center of a vast export business, being connected with towns as far away as in southwest Germany and elsewhere.[57]

Then the poet offers some historical tidbits, such as the city's conquest by the Hungarian King Matthew in 1477, its liberation by the Hapsburgian Emperor Frederick III on behalf of his son Maximilian, then its being besieged by the Turks in 1529 (306–307), who robbed and burned the entire land around the city, raped the women and impaled the children (307, 4–8), a typical condemnation of all Eastern enemies that have ever attacked Europe.[58] Very briefly, without full understanding of the background, Sachs outlines the events during the siege and the final retreat by the Turks, which makes him jubilate: "Doch war aus gotlichen genaden / Wien, die gros stat, erettet frey / Vons Tüercken mort und thiranney" (307, 40–41 – 308, 1; Through divine grace, the great city Vienna was liberated of the Turks murdering and tyranny). The poet limits himself subsequently to final comments about the reconstruction of the defense system and about the absolute need to trust in God (308).

On September 29, 1568, Sachs created an encomium on Frankfurt, "Ain lobspruech der stat Franckfurt,"[59] combined with a praise on the suburb Sachsenhausen on the other side of the Main river, but connected by a bridge made out of stone, as he emphasizes full of admiration. Again, though much earlier than in the previous poems, Sachs underscores the successes of the laudable city government, based on a good justice system and the courts (399, 9). The poet's interest rests, as usual, on the economic conditions that made this city so rich, referring his audience to the major fairs that take place twice a year in Frankfurt. These fairs fascinate him because, already being aware of the international connections necessary for a major business center like Nuremberg, they attract customers from all over Europe: "Werden pesucht durch gancz Deutschland, / Engeland und Ytalia, /

---

[57]     Hartmut Kugler, "Die Stadt im Wald," 103, concludes that the space outside of the city of Nuremberg plays no role for Sachs, but this does not apply to this and other poems. The real question would rather be why Sachs focuses on the core of Nuremberg to the exclusion of the world outside of the city walls whereas he does not follow that model in other cases.

[58]     Bernstein, *Hans Sachs*, 55, woodcut by Erhard Schön for Sachs's poem "Türkische tyranney" from ca. 1529/1530.

[59]     Hans Sachs, Vol. 23, 399–402.

Poland, Holand und Gallia, / Von kramern, hendlern und kauffhern" (399, 21–19;
they are attended by visitors from all over Germany, from England, Italy, Poland,
the Netherlands, and France, by haberdashers, traders, and merchants).

Realizing that these fairs represent the major points of attraction of Frankfurt,
Sachs does not even bother to inform us further about the city; instead he provides
an intriguingly impressionistic description of the hustle and bustle of the market,
with all kinds of wares exhibited, and vendors and purchasers dealing with each
other: "Drey dag, die nacht oft pis an morgen, / Ein lauffen, gen, schlauffen und
faren" (400, 8–9; lasting three days, often until late at night, everyone running,
walking, moving around and driving). Again, given the purpose of such an
encomium, the poet praises the city government for taking care of everyone,
keeping good law and order (400, 12–14).

As he had done in his encomium on Vienna, Sachs then provides a relatively
detailed outline of the history of Frankfurt, highlighting major events and
mentioning some of the most famous rulers who had stayed there. He is
particularly interested in the recent decades in which the religious wars had
broken out, affecting also cities like Nuremberg and Frankfurt, discussing various
sieges of the city by the Duke Moriz of Saxony and the Margrave Albrecht (401,
36–39). But Sachs quickly concludes his text by highlighting Frankfurt's resolute
resistance and subsequent liberation when the enemies left without having
achieved their goals.

Apart from the reference to the bridge out of stone, the two sections of the city
on both sides of the river, and to the good city council we learn nothing concrete
about Frankfurt because the emphasis on the two fairs and on the history of the
city keeps Sachs completely occupied. Nevertheless, here as well, the position of
Frankfurt at the center of an international trading network proves to be most
remarkable, situating these cities in a global grid that far extends beyond the
borders of Germany.

When we turn to his "Lobspruech der reichstat Nörlingen in Schwaben,"[60] which
was composed on November 20, 1568, the last traces of interest in the urban space
and the structure of the city have disappeared. Instead, here the historical aspect
dominates entirely insofar as Sachs relates exclusively how the city was founded
by the Roman Emperor Nero in the year 20 B.C.E. when he was still a major in the
army. From then on the city underwent a constant series of fortunes and
misfortunes, as it once burned down, but then was rebuilt again, and suffered
from the alleged usury of the Jews who were therefore subjugated to a terrible
pogrom in which several hundred of them were killed. Sachs naively repeats the

---

[60]    Hans Sachs, Vol. 23, 412–14.

traditional stereotype of Jewish practices as usurers for which they deserved to be punished, although, as thirteenth-century preachers such as Berthold von Regensburg had already observed, greed and capitalistic abuse were common in all of society.[61] At any rate, the encomium here is entirely drawn from historical knowledge and disregards a view of the city as such, not even considering, as is usually the case with Sachs, the wise and considerate city government. However, still deeply concerned about the well-being of the people, he concludes with comments on the suffering the city had to go through during the Schmalkaldic War: "Auch etlich dausent menschen sturben, / An leib und guet elent verdurben" (414, 21–22; Also, several thousand people died and lost their life and property).

By contrast, his encomium on Regensburg, composed on February 19, 1569,[62] demonstrates radically different features, probably because the poet was personally familiar with this city and could add many details that he had observed himself during his years as a journeyman. Although Sachs introduces the urban history once again, tracing it back to the time of the Roman Empire, this has specific bearing on the city structure as it still can be observed within the extant remains of the ancient fortress, as he comments, "Wie man hinter sant Jacob schawt" (325, 20; if you look behind St. Jacob). For him the wide streets and tall buildings leave the most positive impression on the visitor, and so also the large market squares, all of them revealing part of a glorious past (326, 1–5). For the first time he also turns his poetic eye toward the economic side of a city, referring his audience/readers to the harbor along the Danube: "Darauff die flös und auch die schieff / Auf- und ab-gen mit kaufmans-war" (326, 9–10; on which the rafts and boats travel up and down loaded with merchants' goods). For him the bridge out of stone, built in 1115—more likely constructed over a longer period of time,

---

[61] For Berthold's sermon 'On Peace" where he deals also with this topic (vol. 1, no. 17), see *Berthold von Regensburg*: Vollständige Ausgabe seiner deutschen Predigten mit Einleitungen und Anmerkungen von Franz Pfeiffer und Joseph Strobl. Mit einer Bibliographie und einem überlieferungsgeschichtlichen Beitrag von Kurt Ruh. Deutsche Neudrucke. Reihe: Texte des Mittelalters (Berlin: de Gruyter, 1965). For the association of Jews with usury in the Middle Ages, see Markus J. Wenninger, "Juden und Christen als Geldgeber im hohen und späten Mittelalter," *Die Juden in ihrer mittelalterlichen Umwelt*, ed. Alfred Ebenbauer and Klaus Zatloukal (Vienna, Cologne, and Weimar: Böhlau, 1991), 281–99; Winfried Frey, "*zehen tunne goldes*: Zum Bild des 'Wucherjuden' in deutschen Texten des späten Mittelalters und der frühen Neuzeit," *Sô wold ich in fröiden singen: Festgabe für Anthonius H. Touber zum 65. Geburtstag*, ed. Carla Dauven-van Knippenberg and Helmut Birkhan. Amsterdamer Beiträge zur älteren Germanistik 43–44 (1995): 177–94; id., "Der 'Wucherjude' als Karikatur christlicher Praxis," *Das Mittelalter* 10 (2005): 126–35. See also Hans-Jörg Gilomen, "Wucher und Wirtschaft im Mittelalter," *Historische Zeitschrift* 250 (1990): 265–301.

[62] Hans Sachs, Vol. 23, 325–27.

probably around 1135 to 1146[63]—represents a masterpiece of medieval masonry for which there is no match anywhere in Germany: "Der prueck gleicht kaine in Deutschland" (326, 18; There is no bridge like that in Germany). Again, the reference to the Danube indicates how much Sachs was inclined to perceive the various cities in their global environment, especially as far as trade was concerned: "Dardurch die Thonaw schnel hin-schewst, / Auf Ostereich und Ungern flewst" (326, 16–17; under which the Danube rushes through flowing toward Austria and Hungary).

Next Sachs turns to some early history of Regensburg, which also involves the foundation of a bishopric there which had proven to be superior to all the others in Bavaria (326, 39), a comment that sounds rather curious coming from a devout Protestant, unless we remember that this is an encomium through which the poet tries to appeal to a specific audience to achieve an individual purpose. More than ever before does the poet identify the various churches in the city by name and mentions the large number of chapels, endowments, and priests (327, 1–8). St. Emmeram receives particular attention as one of the monasteries that was incorporated into the city when the city wall was expanded at the time of Emperor Arnolphus, or Arnolf (327, 9–13), who had been crowned in 887 and died in 899. Amazingly, Sachs even knows of a major medieval manuscript held in the monastic library granted by the Emperor: "Mit eim puech des ewangelium, / Geschrieben mit guelden puchstaben, / Ains grosen schacz wert, det ers pegaben" (327, 16–18; donated a book with the Gospel, written in golden letters, which was worth as much as a great treasure).

It might well be that Sachs had in mind the so-called *Uta Codex*, an illustrated Gospel lectionary produced locally around 1025 at the behest of Uta, abbess of the Niedermünster nunnery, since she was closely associated with St. Emmeram—she is mentioned in one of their necrologies. Or, more likely, he might have had the opportunity to look at the *Codex Aureus* of Charles the Bald, a ninth-century manuscript, perhaps even more splendid in its appearance and embellishments, today in the Bayerische Staatsbibliothek Munich, clm 14000.[64] At any rate, this is the first time that a German poet references a medieval manuscript and employs it as an instrument to increase the praise that he can heap on the city as a whole

[63] For many more technical details, see: http://de.wikipedia.org/wiki/Steinerne_Br%C3%BCcke; see also: http://www.baufachinformation.de/denkmalpflege.jsp?md=1988017185558 (both websites last accessed on Sept. 20, 2008).

[64] Adam S. Cohen, *The Uta Codex: Art, Philosophy, and Reform in Eleventh-Century Germany* (University Park: The Pennsylvania State University Press, 2000), 4–23. For an illustration of the cover for the *Codex Aureus*, see online at: http://www.cushnieent.force9.co.uk/WebSitePhotoGallery/CodexAureus.htm (last accessed on Sept. 25, 2008). See also Paul Gichtel, *Der Codex Aureus von S[ank]t Emmeram: Die Restaurierung des Cod. lat. 14000 der Bayerischen Staatsbibliothek München* (Munich: G. D. W. Callwey, 1971).

because it holds such enormous treasures as this most valuable Gospel book created for a Carolingian emperor.

But insofar as Sachs immediately turns away from such artistic details to discuss, as so often in his previous encomia, military history, such as a battle that once took place outside of Regensburg, he reveals how limited his concept is of how to develop a clear presentation of a city and to evaluate the relative importance of the arts versus buildings, the economy, the government, and the citizenry. He feels daunted in the face of the massive constructions from the past, the wide open spaces, and splendid streets: "Darpey man wol ist yngedechtig, / Das vor alter zeit in der stat / Mechtig herschaft gewonet hat" (326, 1–3; In the face of it one realizes that a long time ago a mighty dynasty had ruled in the city).

His focus concentrates on individual objects such as the mighty bridge, then he moves away again to assume a bird's-eye perspective, then he turns to a historical account, which allows him to mention the various churches and their treasures, including those in the library, and then he quickly reaches his conclusion, and we are left with a *bricolage* of disparate narrative pieces. It is an encomium, and we gain some impressions of the central features of this city, but in sum there is no cohesion or any sense of a holistic ensemble. Sachs was certainly impressed by Regensburg and leaves the impression that this city deserves to be admired, but ultimately the poem does not serve the city well enough and leaves us wondering how his audience might have reacted to it. Nevertheless, Sachs relates more information about Regensburg than about all the other previous cities, including Nuremberg, though his poem would be a far cry from the artistic representation of Regensburg in Hartmann Schedel's *Liber Chronicarum*, if such a comparison would be fair in the first place considering the entirely different media. He combines significant details, such as the stone bridge, with bibliophile masterpieces, adds historical background and offers a sketchy bird's-eye view of the city focusing on the streets and squares. It remains a *bricolage*, but it offers a wide variety of information about the city and clearly reflects the poet's considerable interest in Regensburg, its history, and artworks.

It seems surprising that Sachs also turned his attention to the urban world far in the north of Germany, when he composed his encomium on Lüneburg on March 17, 1569,[65] but it had simply been one of the stations during his lengthy period as a traveling journeyman, as he claims in his autobiographical poem.[66] Here he also begins with a historical account concerning the original date of the city's

---

[65]   Hans Sachs, Vol. 23, 445–47.

[66]   Hans Sachs, Vol. 21, 336. See also Bernstein, *Hans Sachs*, 24–26. Friedrich Windolph, "Der Reiseweg Hans Sachsens in seiner Handwerksburschenzeit nach seinen eigenen Dichtungen," D.Phil. Greifswald 1911.

foundation, and it is interesting to note that he learned this information from a medieval chronicle: "Der Sachsen kronic dut offen-waren . . . " (445, 6; the Saxons' chronicle reveals that . . . ). Then Sachs outlines the actual size of the city, providing us with exact measurements: "Virzehundert schrit lang iczund, / 900 schrit lang in die preit" (445, 10–11; one thousand four hundred steps in length, 900 steps in the width), which he either might have counted himself or read in his source, as he indicates subsequently in a different context: "Von der stat nam schreiben die alten" (445, 15; the ancient authors write about the meaning of the city's name), then even naming the chronicler, Albertus Krancz (445, 21).

It is also worth noting that here Sachs makes an attempt to give his readers/listeners a sense of geographical direction by indicating where the women's convent is located (445, 23–24) and where an open field extends outside of the city wall (445, 25–27). His attention then rests on the churches and monasteries in the city, and again on some of their collected items in their treasure: "Darunter ein daffel, vor vil tagen / Mit arabischem gold peschlagen, / Daran die pild kostlich formirt" (446, 23–25; among them a tablet that a long time ago had been ornated with Arabian gold and preciously designed decoration). He knows about it because the monastery had displayed this valuable piece in an exhibition, like a modern-day museum: "Die lest man schawen, wers pegert" (446, 28; they let it be seen to those who are interested). His curiosity was also awakened by the existence of two retirement communities for old and sick people ("siechewsser," 446, 30; homes for sick people), which obviously appealed to him considerably, though he does not provide specific information on this institution, except that the inhabitants receive food and medication.

Further, the city's intensive trade with salt also plays a major role in this encomium, especially because here Sachs goes into extensive detail; describing how the salt is produced, how many salt workshops there are, how many fireplaces are used to boil the water and to crystallize the salt out of it through a condensation process, etc. But not satisfied with that, the poet also reflects upon the trade in salt that is exported to Hamburg and Lübeck, and from there to other places, which connects Lüneburg with the rest of the world—quite similar to the case of Regensburg and other cities which Sachs regularly describes in terms of their international and national trade. After all, as he knows only too well from Nuremberg, this type of business yields much profit and increases the city's reputation and power: "Mit dem salcz-handel hat aufgenumen / Die stat in er, gwalt und reichtumen / Ie lenger mer in kurczen jaren" (447, 18–20; With the trade in salt the city has gained in honor, power, and wealth, and this increasingly over few years).

The encomium on Lübeck, written just four days later than the previous one on Lüneburg, that is, on March 21, 1569, follows a different path insofar as here the interest in history dominates entirely.[67] We learn only that it is a famous city, located in Saxony, or rather in Holstein, as Sachs corrects himself, and then the poem limits itself entirely to the historical events concerning Lübeck, especially concerning the introduction of the Protestant Reformation through Johann Bugenhagen in 1530. With the establishment of the new Church, two women's convents were transformed into secular institutions, the first, Burgkloster, into a hospital, the second, Katharinenkloster, into a school (452). Sachs concludes with some comments on the wealth that the city has acquired since the last war by way of its trading, though he also warns of the dangers that result from the jealousy and envy felt by those who are less fortunate and begrudge the successful rise of Lübeck to its present position: "Weil doch glueck al-zeit has und neit / Al-mal pey iren nachtpaurn hat" (452. 33–34; because fortune always finds hatred and jealousy with its neighbors).

When he subsequently pays respect to Hamburg in his encomium from April 30, 1569, the history of its foundation and the early account of the city reenter the center stage, without us gaining a clear notion of what truly constitutes the city in its urban space, structure, and essence.[68] The poet briefly highlights some of the major events in the church history prior to the Reformation, without mentioning the latter with one word. Although intended as a "Contrafactur," or portrait of Hamburg, as he usually calls his city poems, Sachs offers more of a chronicle poem without mentioning any details or taking into view the city overall. However, even here we get a sense of close inspection by the poet because at one point he mentions the ancient and strong foundation upon which one church was built: "Da fund man in dem fundament / Manch alt gepew, gros, starck und weit" (465, 32–34; they discovered in the foundation many old structures, large, strong, and wide). Yet then he is immediately distracted again and relays more of the urban history without following a consistent time frame, concluding, according to his usual pattern, with best wishes for the social peace and harmony in the city: "Auch gueten frid und ainikeit / Und beschüecz sie zu aller zeit / Vor krig und alleß ungemachs" (467, 9–11; [and give it] also good peace and unity and protect it all the time from war and all other trouble).[69]

---

[67] Hans Sachs, Vol. 23, 450–52.

[68] Hans Sachs, Vol. 23, 464–67.

[69] For a contemporary, Latin, encomium on Hamburg, see Walther Ludwig, "'Multa importari, multa exportarier inde': Ein humanistisches Loblied auf Hamburg aus dem Jahre 1573," *Humanistica Lovanensia: Journal of Neo-Latin Studies* XXXII (1983): 289–308. Arnold, "Städtelob und Stadtbeschreibung," 264–66, discusses the encomium on Hamburg by Johannes Freder(us) Pomeranus (1537).

But we would not do full justice to Sachs's literary skills and interests if we ignored that he also pursued a very different type of urban encomium, as illustrated by his poem dedicated to Salzburg that he had written already on April 9, 1549.[70] Surprisingly, here he begins with a brief discussion of the most characteristic new profession representative of the early-modern age, the book printer whose work is, of course, situated in the city.[71] However, instead of describing the actual activities by a printer, Sachs focuses on the dissemination of the technique and know-how all over Europe, pretending that he himself traveled to those various countries: "Zog ich auch hin in Engelant; / Der-gleich in Franckreich an vertries, / Gen Leon und auch gen Paris, / Dieser kunst ich zw eren kom, / Auch in Italia gen Rom" (479, 9–13; I went to England, then to France without any grudge, to Leon-Castile and Paris; through this art I achieve honor, and then I went to Rome in Italy). Because of the vagaries brought about by war, the poetic voice, a printer, finally ends up in Salzburg, which then initiates the actual encomium.[72]

Arriving at the city gate after having walked through the mountains, he inquires of an old black Moor about the situation of the city, and is then thoroughly instructed about its ancient history. These details do not interest us here, though they still prove to be remarkable regarding Sachs's degree of learning and apparently thorough study of the sources.[73] Although certainly not a Renaissance thinker, the poet still reflects his great fascination with the ancient ruins and sculptures that were found at the site where Salzburg had been settled: "Wie wir vor kurzer zeit noch haben / Mancherley pildwercks aus-gegraben" (481, 33–34; as we have excavated only recently so many a sculpture). The Moor points out the various buildings, such as the cathedral and the castles, and admonishes the listener, hence also us, to look for himself and admire the beautiful buildings (483, 14). Then he emphasizes the impressive houses in the city, directing our view both to the outside and the inside, paying particular attention to the many floors, the cellars, wells, and iron window shutters (484, 3–6).

---

[70]   Hans Sachs, Vol. 22, 479–86.

[71]   Albrecht Classen, "Buchdrucker und das Druckerwesen als literarisches Motiv im Spätmittelalter und der Frühneuzeit. Miszelle zu einem weltbewegenden Thema," *Gutenberg-Jahrbuch* 83 (2008): 128–40.I had not yet been aware of this poem by Hans Sachs when I wrote that previous article, but the evidence provided by Sachs's poem only underscores and strengthens my findings.

[72]   See also the vintage biography by Rudolph Genée, *Hans Sachs und seine Zeit: Ein Lebens- und Kulturbild aus der Zeit der Reformation* (1894; Niederwalluf bei Wiesbaden: Dr. Martin Sändig, 1971), 60–64. Though often lacking in a critical perspective, Genée has assembled most valuable biographical information and historical data concerning Hans Sachs and Nuremberg.

[73]   This finds its confirmation also in his considerable familiarity with medieval chronicles and medieval literature, irrespective of what channels he learned them from, see Classen, "Mittelalterliche Chronistik und Literatur im Werk von Hans Sachs."

But the narrative focus zooms in and out, as is typical of Sachs's encomias, as he turns in his description to the ruling bishop and his government in Salzburg, the churches, the schools, and the social welfare system, and evaluates it all with great approval and admiration: "Ich sprach: 'Selig ist diese stat, / Die ein solchen regirer hat" (484, 28–29; I said: "Blessed this city that has such a ruler"). Subsequently the poetic voice inquires about the economic base of the city and is informed about the intensive trading that takes place in Salzburg, the craftsmen, and the textile industry. Most noticeably, already here in this early work Sachs takes pains to situate the city as the center of an extensive trading network, connecting it with different regions and countries: "Aus dem pirg pringt man keß und schmalz, / Aus dem Welschlant mancherley wein, / Vom Necker, Franckenlant und Rein" (485, 10–12; From the mountains they bring cheese and lard; from Italy all kinds of wine, and so from the Neckar, Franconia, and the Rhine).

Once the narrator has been sufficiently instructed about the nature and features of Salzburg, he enters the city and studies it thoroughly, finding it much to his liking because: "Da all ding war so wol ornirt / Und so vürsichticlich regirt, / Das volck so ghorsam untertenig / Und all ding umb ein ringen pfening" (485, 33–36; all things were beautifully decorated, the city was carefully governed, the people were obedient, and everything was affordable). Subsequently he settles there and pursues his job as a book printer in the service of the bishop.

As an encomium this poem must have fulfilled its purpose, addressing both the history of the city and describing some of its outstanding features, heaping praise on the city as a whole, including the bishop and the people. In terms of specific descriptions of how the city is arranged, however, we would be rather disappointed. Nevertheless, Sachs has at least provided information about Salzburg's specific location within a mountainous terrain and focused even on the inside of some of the houses, which he would never do again in the future. But his attention to the economic basis for the city, its trade in salt and many other products, and the importation of goods from many distant countries, allows him to define Salzburg in more global terms, as he was to do also for Regensburg and Nuremberg.

To conclude, altogether, Sachs created a considerable corpus of encomia poems dedicated to many different cities in Germany, offering much local history, but also various insights into specific economic aspects, studying buildings, especially churches, and at times also a major bridge, and thereby he conveyed a fairly good sense of what these cities were like from the perspective of a craftsman who had passed through them during his young years as a journeyman.[74] For Sachs, the

---

[74] See also W. W. Finlator, Jr., "The City in Germany's Literature of the Fifteenth Through Seventeenth Centuries," Ph.D. thesis, Yale University, 1979, 14ff.; here cited from Arnold,

history of those cities was at times more important than any of the buildings, squares, or streets. Nevertheless, he made a comprehensive, though not always consistent, effort to capture both historical and concrete, physical highlights of each city through his encomiastic poetry. The woodcuts in Schedel's *Liber chronicarum* naturally provide much more information because of their visual nature, but these are also not necessarily all correct and tend to follow artistic patterns, often resembling more *vedute ideata* than *vedute realistica*.

Nevertheless, taken together, both Schedel and Sachs approached their task with great diligence and attention to details, and both contributed thereby to the further development of the discourse on the city and urban space in early-modern German culture. Both artist and poet expressed a deep sense of identity with Nuremberg and projected it as the ideal urban entity where the government and the people collaborated harmoniously and in agreement with each other. Moreover, both Schedel and Sachs regarded the city itself with the greatest respect and presented it not only in its architectural setting. Rather, we discover throughout a great concern to situate each city in a wider geophysical, economic, political, and cultural context, indicating the connections with the external world and outlining the trade and commerce with far-away places all over Europe. Not only had the city emerged as a central institution at the latest by the fifteenth and sixteenth century, it also offered a new sense of identity. Neither Sachs nor Schedel can be simply compared to Ambrogio Lorenzetti, and it would be difficult to identify these two German intellectuals as members of the Renaissance in the narrow sense of the word. But their fascinating approach to and explicit intrigue with urban space as the most important stage of human activities still closely relates them to Lorenzetti and other Italian Renaissance thinkers.

---

"Städtelob und Stadtbeschreibung," 248–49, notes 5 and 6.

Marilyn Sandidge

(Westfield State College)

# Urban Space as Social Conscience in Isabella Whitney's "Wyll and Testament"

When Isabella Whitney lists her bequests in her "Wyll and Testament," we learn of her views on the city of London in 1573— its wealth, its neighborhoods, and its social problems. As she moves across the environs of the old city of London, we tour the city from the perspective of an observant woman in the late sixteenth century writing before the division of London into upper- and lower-class neighborhoods that takes place in the early seventeenth century. On the surface her "Wyll and Testament" reads as a lively catalogue of features found in early modern London; however, the institutions, streets, and goods take on symbolic value, first evoking promises of wealth and plenty and then evincing the reality of poverty and injustice. Although Robert Shoemaker states, "There is little direct evidence of how the vast majority of Londoners thought about their city, and this applies particularly to female Londoners," Whitney's work makes her thoughts on London quite clear.[1]

As Danielle Clarke states in the introduction to her edition of the *Nosgay*, despite the brimming descriptions of prosperity throughout the poem, "commercial power," "financial rapaciousness," and "lack of charity" define London for Whitney.[2] Starting from the narrow subjective point of view of one individual in the city, the poem almost immediately extends its perspective to encompass a

---

[1]  Robert Shoemaker, "Gendered Spaces: Patterns of Mobility and Perceptions of London's Geography, 1660–1750," *Imagining Early Modern London*, ed. J. F. Merritt (Cambridge and New York: Cambridge University Press, 2001), 144–65; here 147–148. Shoemaker argues that literary passages don't show people's real thoughts about the city.

[2]  *Isabella Whitney, Mary Sidney and Aemilia Lanyer: Renaissance Women Poets*, ed. Danielle Clarke. Penguin Classics (London, New York, and Toronto: Penguin Books, 2000), xiv.

shared experience of urban life — the events, perceptions, and views that Whitney's persona records become those of the average London citizen in the early 1570s.

Since little is known about Isabella Whitney's life, scholars have debated her economic and social status based on the biographical information she gives us in her second published work, *A Sweet Nosgay or Pleasant Posy: Containing a Hundred and Ten Philosophical Flowers*, printed by Richard Jones in 1573.[3] Because she describes herself in *Nosgay* as having previously been in service to a lady, some critics such as Danielle Clarke have assumed that she was a member of the lower-middle class or the poor: "Not only is Whitney a woman, rare for venturing into print at this period, but she is also lower-middle class" (xiii). Using as the cultural context in which to understand Whitney's poem the Mother B figure, a repulsive old bawd accused by the Elizabethan moralist Edward Hake of turning unemployed maidservants into streetwalkers, Patricia Phillippy states that Whitney's "treatment of service and the household inscribes and gives voice to the concerns and experiences of a large population of illiterate, lower-class women . . ."[4]

After referring to her as the "mid-Tudor poet and maidservant," Laurie Ellinghausen argues that Whitney's poetic persona places her on par with London's prostitutes: "When Whitney fashions herself as an unemployed maidservant, she specifically aligns herself with a group that was prone to prostitution in cultural imagination as well as in fact."[5] Since service in Elizabethan England, however, could apply to young people of any rank in that even the children of aristocrats were at times sent to other households to serve for a period of time, it is not at all clear that Whitney and/or her persona is a member of the lower class.[6]

I want to argue instead that we have to see Whitney as a representative of the middle class in London and not of the poor and not a "vagrant nightwalker." Her indictment of London is much sharper if we envision its effects not only on those

---

[3]   Isabella Whitney. *Isabella Whitney, Mary Sidney and Aemilia Lanyer: Renaissance Women Poets,* Danielle Clarke, ed. 3–43. All quotes from Whitney will be taken from this edition. Betty Travitsky, "The 'Wyll and Testament' of Isabella Whitney," *English Literary Renaissance* 10 (1980): 76–94 first brought Whitney's poem to most current readers' attention. See R. J. Fehrenbach, "Isabella Whitney, Sir Hugh Plat, Geoffrey Whitney, and 'Sister Eldershae,'" *English Language Notes* 21.1 (Sept. 1983): 7–11, for the possibility that Whitney later married to become Isabella Eldershae.

[4]   "The Maid's Lawful Liberty: Service, the Household, and 'Mother B' in Isabella Whitney's *A Sweet Nosegay,"* *Modern Philology* 95 (1998): 439–61; here 442.

[5]   "Literary Property and the Single Woman in Isabella Whitney's *A Sweet Nosgay." Studies in English Literature* 45.1 (2005): 1–22; here 1, 3.

[6]   See Phillippy, "Maid's Lawful," 443.

who are born into poverty and crime, but also on those who start out as law-abiding, middle-class, educated citizens, or even as "minor gentry."[7]

The information we gain from a series of verse epistles preceding the "Wyll and Testament" in *Nosgay*, written to family members and friends, underscores her earlier comfortable background as she tells us why she is writing from the country. In the first verse epistle, she addresses her brother Geoffrey Whitney, a court figure frequently listed as receiving bequests from Queen Elizabeth and best known for writing *Choice of Emblems* dedicated to the Earl of Leicester. She reminds him that she has lost her position in service to a "vertuous Ladye," and now must remain at the family home dependent on the favors of friends and her parents.[8] The opening dedication of *Nosgay* to George Mainwaring, a prominent figure in Shropshire who owned much property, calls him her chief friend and asks him to accept the work as a present to repay him for the things he has done for her in the past.[9] In Wendy Wall's words, Isabella Whitney doesn't come from an aristocratic family herself, but is "socially connected with aristocratic households."[10] Although Whitney, in the voice of her fictional persona, claims to be dependent on friends and family, this cannot be taken as evidence of actual poverty since almost all women in England were dependent on others then, and the people she is dependent on are not poor or even lower-middle class. The letter to her two younger sisters, giving practical advice on how to succeed in service in London, is meant to prepare them, she says, to "wealth posses, and quietnesse of mynde."[11] She advises them to please their employers because experience has taught her that "fleetyng is a foe" and warns them not to abuse the night when their employers are in bed:

> See Dores & Windowes bolted fast
> for feare of any wrack.
> Then help yf neede ther bee,
> to doo some housholde thing:
> Yf not to bed, referring you,
> unto the heavenly King.          (33, 42–44)

Whitney wants to be sure that her sisters do not adopt the behaviors of the underclass in London that social critics such as Hake complained about.

---

[7] Linda Gregerson, "Life among Others," *Virginia Quarterly Review* 83.1 (Winter 2007): 204–17; here 204.

[8] Whitney, "To her Brother. G. W.," *Nosgay*, 8–9.

[9] Whitney, "To the worshipfull and right vertuous yong Gentylman, George Mainwaring Esquier: IS. W. wisheth happye health with good successe in all his godly affayres," *Nosgay*, 3–4.

[10] "Isabella Whitney and the Female Legacy," *English Literary History* 58.1 (Spring 1991): 35–62; here 47. Wall's article makes many good points about the context in which Whitney was writing.

[11] Whitney, "A modest meane for Maides In order prescribed, by Is. W. to two of her yonger Sisters servinge in London," *Nosgay*, 10–11.

Furthermore, Whitney's decision to print her poetry has added to the debate over her social status. Wendy Wall notes that it was especially troubling for a woman to take part in this "lower class activity" of having a printer sell her work publicly.[12] Since the works of authors as well as the authors themselves who engaged in the commercial print culture of the early modern period are seen as inferior, Whitney scholars point to her use of letters in *Nosgay* as a way to "imitate the dynamics of manuscript culture . . . to offset the potential opprobrium which might attach to Whitney as a writer circulating without check throughout a wider interpretive community."[13] If we look at her printer, though, Richard Jones, we see that he is noted for his role in the printing of poetry collections that suddenly became popular with a wide readership in the mid-1570s. Originally a publisher of "ballads and works of a popular character," he became an active participant in what Kirk Melnikoff calls the "more elite markets for poetry collections and courtesy manuals from the mid-1570s until the end of his career."[14] As a prolific publisher of collected vernacular poetry, Jones put out at least eleven collections of poetry, and Whitney's *Nosgay* is the first of these: *A SweetNosgay, or Pleasant Posye* (1573), *A Smale Handfull of Fragrant Flowers* (1575), *The Paradise of Daynty Deuices* (1576), Nicholas Breton's *A Floorish vpon Fancie* (1577), *A Gorgious Gallery of Gallant Inuentions*(1578), WilliamAverell's *A Speciall Remedie against the Furious Force of Lawlesse Love* (1579), *A Poore Knight his Pallace of Priuate Pleasures* (1579), *A Handefull of Pleasant Delites* (1584), *Brittons Bowre of Delights* (1591), *The Arbor of Amorous Deuices* (1597), and *Pans Pipe* (1595).[15]

In his study of early modern women writers, Randall Martin points out that "by the standards of the day her writing is intelligently conceived, artfully varied, and even fashionable," and Ann Rosalind Jones argues in *The Currency of Eros* that Jones's willingness to publish her second work, *Nosgay*, six years after publishing her first work, *The Copy of a Letter* in 1567, shows the popularity of her first venture into print.[16] Several times in "Wyll and Testament," Whitney encourages Londoners to buy books at St. Paul's to help her printer prosper; she obviously sees herself as a part of an exciting new commercial literary world in London of

---

[12]   Wall, "Female Legacy," 35.

[13]   Clarke xvi; Wall, "Female Legacy."

[14]   Kirk Melnikoff, "Jones's Pen and Marlowe's Socks: Richard Jones, Print Culture, and the Beginnings of English Dramatic Literature," *Studies in Philology* 102.2 (Spring 2005): 184–209; here 208.

[15]   Collections that Jones entered in the Stationers' Register that are no longer extant are *Lusus Pastorales Newly Compiled* (1566), Breton's *The Payne of Pleasur* (1578), and Richard Edwards's *The Mansion of Myrthe* (1582), Melnikoff, " Jones's Pen," 196, n. 34.

[16]   Randall Martin, *Women Writers in Renaissance England* (London and New York: Longman, 1997), 279–310; here 279; Ann Rosalind Jones, *The Currency of Eros: Women's Love Lyric in Europe, 1540–1620* (Bloomington: Indiana University Press, 1990), 47.

the late sixteenth century and hopes to succeed there. Ellinghausen argues that since Whitney would have gotten only a small flat fee from her printer, her championing of printers, that is, those who would profit from her works, points ironically to herself as an economic outsider in early-modern London (18). In a similar way, Ann Rosalind Jones sees Whitney's writing in terms of the out-of-work domestic servant who has "appropriated bourgeois gender discourse for her own profit."[17] It is possible, however, to view Whitney's publication as something more than just a desperate woman's commercial venture; the positive attention she gives to books, printers, and readers throughout her "Wyll" suggests the cultural value she places on literature. When she tells us in "The Auctor to the Reader" that she turned away from reading scripture, history, and classical writers to draw instead on *The Floures of Philosophie* (1572), Hugh Plat's popular aphorisms, she is showing her support for the contemporary literature of her time. In the same way that Whitney has reversed gender expectations in the poetic conventions she employs, for example by writing a will when no women except widows were legally able to, and by using a Petrarchan blazon to describe London as her undeserving male lover, she has also reversed gender expectations in offering her poetry publicly for sale in the masculine medium of print.

We draw from these details in Whitney's poems and from their context the picture of a young woman from a good, though not wealthy family, who hopes to use not only her influential friends and family members, but also her writing talent to achieve security.[18] Though not a part of the aristocratic, manuscript-based literary circles that welcomed women like the Countess of Pembroke, Whitney is not a part of the other extreme either, a poor working-class servant declaring her poverty publicly in print to gain economically. Whitney and her persona were in a better position to get along in London than most other single women were. Despite this, however, the "Wyll and Testament" makes it clear that even the advantages of coming from a firmly middle-class family, literate and healthy, with some social connections cannot guarantee security in London in the 1570s—for men or women.

Recent social and economic studies give us data on the young people found in London then. At a time when less than one half of London-born children lived to marriageable age, migrants filled out the population.[19] Since death rates were

---

[17] Ann Rosalind Jones, "Nets and Bridles: Early Modern Conduct Books and Sixteenth-Century Women's Lyrics," *The Ideology of Conduct: Essays on Literature and the History of Sexuality*, ed. Nancy Armstrong and Leonard Tennenhouse (New York: Methuen, 1987), 39–72; here 64.

[18] In her attempt to support herself through her writing, Whitney follows in the tradition of Christine de Pizan, usually considered the first professional woman writer. See Charity Cannon Willard, *Christine de Pizan: Her Life and Works* (New York: Persea Books, 1984).

[19] A. L. Beier and Roger Finlay, ed., Introduction to *London 1500–1700: The Making of the Metropolis*, (London and New York: Longman, 1986), 50.

frequently affected by diseases such as plague, as when nearly a quarter of the city's inhabitants died of plague in 1563,[20] the city needed young migrants to sustain its population, and according to A. L. Beier, about 5,600 of them entered the city a year from 1560 on.[21] Since apprentices and servants made up roughly half (54.7%) of laborers inside the city walls and the 100-plus guilds that controlled most trade and manufacturing there required that young apprentices work seven years before being free to work on their own and to marry, most of these young workers were single.[22] Although called servants and apprentices at the time, recent studies suggest that few of the newcomers who came into the city had been members of the poorer classes in Britain and that most people living in London in the late sixteenth century were "of the middle station."[23] It is estimated that only 23% of London's apprentices in the sixteenth century were sons of yeomen.[24] Moreover, Boulton reminds us that London's exceptional literacy rate at this time was probably caused by the literate migrants, having been educated in the rural provinces, moving to the city for employment (344). Finally, John Stow, in his famous *Survey of London* in 1598, claims that one of London's strengths is that it "consisteth not in the extremes, but in a very mediocrity of wealth and riches."[25] In a city that will grow from ca. 75,000 in 1550 to 200,000 in 1600, these are the people Whitney envisions around her.[26]

If we turn to the poem itself, the conventions of the will and testament format allow Whitney to appropriate urban space rhetorically. At the same time that she "construes her departure from the city as a kind of social death," she takes ownership of the cityscape, and the subversive act of writing a will and displaying her knowledge of London's commercial and seedy side is tempered by her adopting the voice of a social and moral satirist.[27] In Wall's words:

---

[20]  Paul Slack, "Metropolitan Government in Crisis: the Response to Plague," *London 1500–1700*, 60–81; here 61.

[21]  A. L. Beier, "Social Problems in Elizabethan England," *Journal of Interdisciplinary History* 9.2 (August 1978): 203–221; here 205.

[22]  A. L. Beier, "Engine of Manufacture: the Trades of London," *London 1500–1700*, 141–67; here 154.

[23]  Jeremy Boulton, "London 1540–1700," *The Cambridge Urban History of Britain*, vol. 2, *1540–1840*, ed. Peter Clark, (Cambridge: Cambridge University Press, 2000), 315–346; here 329. See also Christopher Brooks, "Apprenticeship, Social Mobility and the Middling Sort, 1550–1880," *The Middling Sort of People: Culture, Society and Politics in England, 1550–1800*, ed. Jonathon Barry and Christopher Brooks (New York: St. Martin's Press, 1994), 52–83. Also Ian W. Archer, *Pursuit of Stability: Social Relations in Elizabethan London* (Cambridge and New York: Cambridge University Press, 1991), 13.

[24]  Barbara A. Hanawalt, *"Of Good and Ill Repute": Gender and Social Control in Medieval England* (Oxford: Oxford University Press, 1998), 192.

[25]  John Stow and Henry Benjamin Wheatley, *Stow's Survey of London* (London: Dent; New York: E. P. Dutton, 1956), 490.

[26]  Boulton, "London 1540–1700," *The Cambridge Urban History of Britain*, 316.

[27]  Gregerson, "Life Among Others," 205, 207.

The speaker becomes empowered specifically by her role as social commentator.

Because her leave-taking constitutes a stroll through London's streets, it serves to display her knowledge of urban life. Like the travel literature of the time that exuberantly staged the exotic, her inventory of London reveals her mastery of a public world often denied to more privatized aristocratic women. Men may have had to travel to the New World to discover an exciting new life, but women could still marvel at the somewhat forbidden public world outside their door. Whitney's "Wyll" thus grants to her the privileged vantage point of social and moral satirist seen in popular poetic and prose works . . . .[28]

Instead of beginning the will in the conventional way by bequeathing her soul to God, Whitney commends not only her soul, but her "Body eke: / to God the Father and the Son, / so long as I can speak" (6–8). Given her familiarity with the conventions of contemporary wills and testaments evident in the rest of the work, this change of emphasis to ask God to care for her body must be intentional. Most sixteenth-century wills follow the pattern of "Annys Borde of the pariche of Seynt Myhelles in Woodstrett in London [who] made her testamentt and last wyll in thys maner, first sche bequethyd her soull to Allmyghty God, to Owr Lady Sentt Mary and to all the seynttes in hevyn, and her body to be beryyd in Crystyn berryall," so that the body is firmly buried, often in a specific church yard.[29] Whitney does request that her body be buried, but only after she can no longer speak and just until all rise again for judgment when she hopes her body and soul will meet again to live in joy. This careful attention to the treatment of her body in a poem written in the standard ballad form of popular verse highlights her focus on material considerations during life.[30] Furthermore, as Jill P. Ingram argues, Whitney's "Wyll and Testament" is a mock testament, sharing the genre's intention of entertaining while offering subtle social criticism and her tone throughout conveys these two aims.[31]

Although Whitney personifies the city as her own cruel lover who has refused to offer her the credit she needs to continue to live there, this personal economic and social distress simply prefigures the expanding lists of those victimized by the same circumstances which we encounter while moving geographically through the city. Admonishing London to "see that none you do deceive / of that I leave them

[28]   *The Imprint of Gender: Authorship and Publication in the English Renaissance* (Ithaca and London: Cornell University Press, 1993), 289–90.

[29]   "Separate Wills: 1544–47 nos. 200–45," *London Consistory Court Wills 1492–1547: London Record Society* 3 (1967), 125–150; here 125., http://www.british-history.ac.uk/report.aspx?compid=64538 (last accessed on November 19, 2008).

[30]   In this way I differ from Wall, who in "Female Legacy" argues the poem is an indictment of spiritual sickness, too.

[31]   "A Case for Credit: Isabella Whitney's 'Wyll and Testament' and the Mock Testament Tradition," *Early Modern Culture* 5 (Fall 2005): 1–21; here 8, http://emc.eserver.org/1-5/ingram.html (last accessed on Feb. 1, 2009).

till," the last line in the opening "Communication" section clearly shows Whitney's distrust of the city's treatment of the young workers living there (35–36).

In a complex set of associations that shifts as the poem progresses, London, paradoxically, is the main recipient of the things she "dispose[s]" of as well as the collective name for the places and items bequeathed (21). Even though her first bequest is to give London its own buildings, said to be "brave buildings rare, of Churches store, / and Pauls to the head" (27–28), the poem all but ignores the important spiritual or aristocratic structures we expect in city encomiums or travel literature. Despite the conventional placement of St. Paul's Cathedral at the beginning of her lists, she says nothing else about religious institutions anywhere in her poem. She makes two references to churches later on as landmarks to point to the tailors or bookbinders nearby. According to Patrick Collinson, John Stow blames the "end of citizenship and community" on the changes brought about by the Reformation earlier in the century, and his work is peppered with nostalgia for the Catholic institutions now gone.[32] Whitney, on the other hand, seems indifferent to the practices of religious figures or institutions in London.[33]

Moreover, in a similar way, she also avoids any mention of London's historic past or ancient ruins, ignoring the ancient monumental buildings that Henri Lefebvre argues carried social meaning in medieval communities.[34] Places in her poem do convey meaning, but this meaning is determined only by what these places have to offer London's citizens. Arthur B. Ferguson says that the antiquarian movement of the 1570s and 1580s changed the concept of history to incorporate at that time a dynamic social perspective: "It involved an ability to think of people in terms of their collective relationships rather than of their acts and their moral responsibility as individuals."[35] This description might also apply to Whitney's perspective on London in the 1570s as she examines the social dynamics of contemporary London. As fitting for someone who says she herself has no property or wealth, Whitney directs our attention to public sights: scenes of alluring merchandise, public buildings and streets, and the ordinary people that interact there every day.

---

[32]   "John Stow and Nostalgic Antiquarianism," *Imagining*, 27–51; here 37.

[33]   In her emphasis on the robust secular city, Whitney is working in the tradition of William FitzStephen's 12th-century poem "A Description of London." See C. David Benson, "Some Poets' Tours of Medieval London: Varieties of Literary Urban Experience," *Essays in Medieval Studies* 24 (2007): 1–20, for a discussion of FitzStephen's poem.

[34]   *The Production of Space*, trans. Donald Nicholson-Smith (Oxford: Blackwell, 1991), 53. For a discussion of medieval urban memory, as in the case of travelogues or pilgrimage accounts focusing on ancient and Christian Rome, see the contribution to this volume by C. David Benson.

[35]   Arthur B. Ferguson, *Clio Unbound: Perception of the Social and Cultural Past in Renaissance England* (Durham, NC: Duke University Press, 1979), 79.

Whitney's view of London differs in several other key ways from that of conventional works of this type as described by Gail Kern Paster in *The Idea of the City in the Age of Shakespeare*.[36] Although ambivalence pervades both traditional views of the city and Whitney's poem, different areas of concern are highlighted in hers. In the traditional views, praise for a city's variety, experiences, and social community is juxtaposed with complaints over noise, crowding, dirty conditions, and constant change—in other words, the city's inadequate structural resources. Moreover, in the conventional tropes, Fortune rules the city, which is constantly buffeted by change. The repeated references in Whitney's poem to misfortune, however, allude to its effect on people, not on the city itself, to their unemployment and poverty resulting from misfortune.

Danielle Clarke has criticized the poem for lacking a clear organization in its lists and catalogues: "Her listing of places, persons, professions and commodities reinforces a sense of chaos and disorder, and she swings from area to area, and trade to trade, without any apparent sense of connection: in fact, the only connecting thread is Whitney's self-representation in terms of exclusion from the abundance that she describes."[37] In the descriptions of the people, places, and goods she bequeaths to London, however, her organization actually reflects the needs of its citizens, starting with essentials and then moving to luxuries. Her pattern of organization reflects the social message underlying the poem's use of catalogues and lists. In order for London to provide its citizens with food, her first bequests are made up of the streets where butchers, brewers, bakers, and fish sellers can be found, all within several blocks of the old market area of Cheapside.[38] Running roughly parallel to and a block south of Cheap Street, the next two streets mentioned, Watlyng and Canwyck, interestingly intersect with the street on which she lived at that time, Abchurche Lane.[39] Whitney says these streets can provide "wollen," and she promises "linnen store" on "Friday Streete," which intersects with Watling (42–43). Her first bequests, therefore, drawn from a neighborhood she knows firsthand, provide the basics of food, bread, meat, fish, and beer, and wool and linen clothing for those who need them, presumably from the poorest to the wealthiest citizens.

---

[36] *The Idea of the City in the Age of Shakespeare* (Athens, GA: University of Georgia Press, 1985), 4–5.

[37] *Isabella Whitney*, xv.

[38] In *A New History of London: Including Westminster and Southwark*, book 2, ch. 13 (1773), 576, the eighteenth-century historian John Noorthouck says the EastCheap market may be the oldest one in London with its easy access to the "Roman trajectus" over the Thames, http://www.british-history.ac.uk/report.aspx?compid=46756&strquery=butchers (last accessed on Feb. 1, 2009).For a careful analysis of public spaces, including markets, where both men and women could pursue their businesses and crafts, as in Ghent, see the contribution to this volume by Shennon Hutton.

[39] *Nosgay*, 4.

Following this are goods for "those which are of callyng such, / that costlier they require," clearly more fashionable goods aimed at a class of people who want to look prosperous (45–46). Within this same market area, the poem lists the merchants or artisans who provide these more costly goods, the mercers selling silk, goldsmiths, hat makers, and shoemakers. In providing for those whose occupations, or "callying[s]," require the look of prosperity, these businesses serve the middle ranks of those employed in the city, neither the unemployed poor nor those with inherited wealth.

For her next grouping of merchandise, items offered for sale in the pawn, she moves a few blocks east to the upper walk of the Royal Exchange, built only a few years earlier, and to Birchin Lane, St. Martins, and the Stocks, where a boy will "aske you what you lack" (68). With mention of the "boy," a worker employed to help bring in customers but not a customer himself, the poem has clearly established a social division among Londoners. In the description of the fancier clothing available in this area for London's citizens, Whitney points to French fashions such as "French Ruffes, high Purles, Gorgets" and men's trunks of "Gascon guise" (63, 72). After the 1560s London merchants earned most of their profits from imported goods, and it was not just fashionable clothing that was imported for London's stores; wine, soap, hats, pins, and mirrors were brought in, too.[40]

Although earlier buyers of expensive items considered luxury goods in London had been wealthy aristocrats and the royal court, in the last quarter of the sixteenth century, according to Beier, these goods were being merchandised to the other socio/economic groups as well.[41] Whitney's lists of goods available, therefore, might reflect the new appetites of young workers with perhaps some disposable income while also documenting the spending habits of London's more affluent citizens. Even if they could not afford such goods, the young workers would desire the goods being marketed in these more upscale shops. Despite sumptuary laws such as one prohibiting those below the level of magistrates of corporations from "ornamenting their apparel with silk," London's markets catered to all classes.[42] In fact, most offenders brought before magistrates by watchmen appointed to enforce Elizabethan sumptuary laws in the 1560s and 1570s were apprentices and servants.[43]

---

[40]  Jeremy Boulton, "London 1540–1700," in *The Cambridge Urban History,* 322.

[41]  Beier, "Engine of Manufacture," 152.

[42]  John Noorthouck, "Edward VI and Mary," in *A New History of London: Including Westminster and Southwark* book 1, ch. 8 (1773), 122–30,
http://www.british-history.ac.uk/report.aspx?compid=46725 (last accessed on Nov. 21, 2008).

[43]  Wilfred Hooper, "Tudor Sumptuary Laws," *English Historical Review* 30 (1915): 433–35; qtd. in Randall Martin, "Whitney's 'Lamentation Upon the Death of William Gruffith,'" *Early Modern Literary Studies* 3.1 (1997): 1–15; here 6–7.

Moving associatively from men's clothing to weaponry, Whitney bequeaths London's citizens the sites where weapons can be obtained across the expanse of the old city from artillery at Temple Bar, to pistols at Tower Hill, with swords in between on Fleet—to end this section with goods that assure London's citizens' safekeeping. She herself summarizes the whole first section of bequests at this point by saying, "Now when thy folk are fed and clad," confirming her intention to focus on the items most people need, or think they need, first (89).

After this, the temper of the poem starts to change. The first set of bequests, medical care given by apothecaries, physicians, and surgeons, carries a more ominous tone. People have weak stomachs and diseases, and roisterers' quarrels lead to life-threatening injuries that surgeons must fix so that ruffians won't hang and quiet people won't die. Then she believes she must offer money from the Mint in case the merchants who store what she has freely given in her will demand payment, suggesting that London's markets demand ever more money for goods from people unable to pay for them. Next, she moves us south to the Steelyard, a dock area controlled by Hanseatic merchants who sell wine to "glad[en]" "dulled minds," suggesting weariness in the lives of London's citizens (114). The people she points to here are handsome apprentices who, she reminds us, are prevented by law to wed, and thus seek girls "that neede compels, or lucre lures" (119).

Whether motivated by need or monetary gain in a city filled with enticing goods, these "proper Gyrles," not the professional prostitutes, called "single women," usually found on Clerkenwell and Turnmill Streets or in the stews across the river from London, may engage in casual prostitution meant to supplement their incomes, the most frequent form of prostitution in England up through the sixteenth century.[44] Near these wine merchants and "Gyrles," Whitney leaves bath houses, which she says are to prevent infection and to trim those up on Saturdays "which all the weeke doo drug" (126). Although the prostitutes and apprentices in the Steelyard and public baths of Queenshyth and Broken Wharf seem worlds apart from the displays of wealth and merchandise cited earlier, Whitney locates them only a few blocks away. By the end of the sixteenth century, Londoners will have segregated themselves into rich and poor neighborhoods, but Whitney's text points to quite different classes of people and commodities intermingling in the heart of the city. This juxtaposition of wealth with poverty in her text makes the injustices described even more disturbing.

---

[44] Ruth Mazo Karras, *Common Women: Prostitution and Sexuality in Medieval England* (Oxford: Oxford University Press, 1996), 52–53; Paul Griffiths, "Structure of Prostitution in Elizabethan London," *Continuity and Change* 8 (1993): 39–63. For a literary-historical analysis of prostitution in the late Middle Ages, see Gertrud Blaschitz, "Das Freudenhaus im Mittelalter [The Brothel in the Middle Ages]: In der stat was gesessen ain unrainer pulian," *Sexuality in the Middle Ages and Early Modern Times*, ed. Albrecht Classen. Fundamentals of Medieval and Early Modern Culture 3 (Berlin and New York: Walter de Gruyter, 2008), 715–50.

As she turns from acclaiming London's well-stocked markets to recounting the conditions in its prisons, she reminds London that she has taken nothing from it, as if she has to be careful herself not to be accused of theft, and then explicitly links poverty with imprisonment: "And that the poor, when I am gone, / have cause for me to pray, / I will to prisons portions leave" (135–37). Jill Ingram points to the contrasts between these and her earlier scenes: "Exposing the city's landscape of prisons and punishment through rhetorical amplification, the speaker foregrounds market failure. The satire excoriates not only the prodigality that sends debtors to prison, but also the exclusivity of parts of the London economy that offer such abundance, an exclusive club she nonetheless craves."[45] The bleak details that emerge from her bequests to the Counter, or Compter, Newgate, Fleet, and Ludgate prisons show a justice system inadequate to handle the large numbers of people caught up in debt. Although she speaks of other types of criminals at Newgate, to whom she leaves a monthly sessions, since prisoners there seldom received court hearings, and an old horse to quickly draw those to be executed up Holborn Hill, most of her attention is given to those imprisoned for poverty and debt.

Instead of using the infamous underground cells in the Counter for dangerous prisoners, she leaves the hole to people who will not lend their friends the money they need to get out of prison. Whereas court sessions in Newgate, she says, might lessen the overcrowding that spreads the plague, they will also, ironically, allow some people to be able to beg for their discharge fees. Historical records and commentaries frequently speak of the inadequate number of court sessions held in Newgate. From 1475 on, five court sessions a year were to be held, instead of just two a year, but these were hardly adequate, and a new building in which to hold sessions was erected in 1539 at the Old Bailey because judges had refused to enter the prison itself out of fear of sickness.[46]

To the Fleet, Whitney leaves an old papist to help prop up the roof and a collection box for the poor. With approximately 285 seminary priests imprisoned in jails for long years during Elizabeth's reign, it was in the prisons that English Catholics gathered most frequently in the late sixteenth century; lay Catholics came and went in the prisons as the priests ministered to them freely.[47] The jailers, unpaid by the government, were interested only in receiving the Catholics' payments for food and upkeep.[48] No matter what Whitney's religious beliefs may have been, her phrasing when she offers "some Papist olde / to underprop [the

---

[45]   "A Case for Credit," 9.

[46]   Margery Bassett, "Newgate Prison in the Middle Ages," *Speculum* 18.2 (1943): 233–46; here 243–44.

[47]   Lisa McClain, "Without Church, Cathedral, or Shrine: The Search for Religious Space among Catholics in England, 1559–1625," *Sixteenth Century Journal* 33.2 (2002): 381–99; here 386–87.

[48]   Ibid., 387.

Fleet's] roofe" implies she recognizes the absurdity of jailing an old Catholic for loyalty to his religion (169–70).

Whitney's leaving a collection box for the poor at a prison is not unusual since many wills in medieval and early modern England leave bequests for both the poor and prisoners, showing the association in people's minds between the groups. Encouraged originally as a way for Catholics to acquire good deeds before Judgment Day, the practice of leaving money to feed the poor or to help prisoners did continue after the Reformation though in a less structured way. Instead of paying for prayers in chantries, after the Reformation Protestant congregations were urged, in fact, to give more to charity.[49] John Stow, however, laments that the rich are giving less to hospitals and other institutions for the poor since the Reformation and that daily food offerings to the poor, such as that given earlier by Thomas Cromwell's men, have ended. He blames the worsening conditions of the poor in the late sixteenth century on the problems he sees in the English church and its mission at that time.[50] It was in fact a particularly hard time for many people then because food prices soared during this period and wages did not keep up, leading to much poverty for those in certain occupations, according to Lawrence Stone.[51]

A. L. Beier notes that most people arrested for vagrancy during the Tudor period were children, adolescents, and young adults: "Keeping the young at labour was clearly a major social problem of this period."[52] Noting the lack of resources to handle these people, he argues that the late Elizabethan period's social problems had their origins in "massive immigration, which a backward economic and social system was unable to absorb into the regular workforce."[53] Noting that the unemployed were frequently the targets of social critics, Lawrence Manley's chapter on Tudor social complaints points to the "displaced, wandering hordes of More's *Utopia* and Tudor complaint [that] thus mark the advent of a major transition in the socio-economic order."[54] Many of those making up the poor in Whitney's world were, therefore, these same young men who flocked to London

---

[49]  Ian W. Archer, "The Arts and Acts of Memorialization in Early Modern London," in *Imagining*, 89–116; here 95. See also Eamon Duffy, *The Stripping of the Altars: Traditional Religion in England 1400–1580* (New Haven: Yale University Press, 1992).

[50]  Patrick Collinson, "John Stow and Nostalgic Antiquarianism," *Imagining*, 27–51; here 33, 29.

[51]  Lawrence Stone, "Social Mobility in England, 1500–1700," *Past and Present* 33 (1966): 16–55; here 42.

[52]  A. L. Beier, "Vagrants and the Social Order in Elizabethan England," *Past and Present* 64 (1974): 3–29; here 9.

[53]  A. L. Beier, "Social Problems in London," *Journal of Interdisciplinary History* 9:2 (1978): 203–221; here 217.

[54]  Lawrence Manley, *Literature and Culture in Early Modern London* (Cambridge and New York: Cambridge University Press, 1995), 63–122; here 68. Manley's work is helpful for understanding the conditions leading to the economic crisis and unemployment during the Tudor reigns.

for employment. She, however, unlike the typical author of Tudor social criticism, treats the people who were the subjects of these complaints with great sympathy.

To Ludgate, the chief debtor's prison, Whitney says she originally meant to leave nothing because she had intended to flee there herself as a debtor: "To shroud myself amongst the rest / that choose to die in debt / Rather than any creditor should money from them get" (185–88). Ironically, though, no one, she says, will lend her money to put her in debt; therefore, she will leave Ludgate some "Banckrupts," a term that came into use in England only in the sixteenth century (192). First begun in the later thirteenth century, imprisoning people for debt was originally meant to deter careless borrowing and to lead to repayment as the debtor would get family or friends to procure the money for release.[55] By the late sixteenth century, however, a growing capitalist economy was making borrowing and debt widespread.

With catalogues of merchandise for sale in London preceding scenes highlighting credit and debt, the connection between the arrays of goods available and overspending is obvious. While the borrowing of late sixteenth-century aristocrats is legendary, the other classes in London borrowed money heavily as well. According to Lawrence Stone, English aristocrats borrowed roughly 100,000 pounds a year during the last few years of the sixteenth century, and two thirds of the earls and barons were in terrible financial trouble during the last years of Elizabeth's reign.[56] Jeremy Boulton states, "Increasingly sophisticated credit and banking arrangements, run initially by the London goldsmiths, further increased purchasing power" at this time.[57] Whitney, however, points to the trouble with these new arrangements for many Londoners who found themselves in Ludgate with little hope for release. She does not call for ending London's current credit arrangements; instead, as Ingram says, "Her critique, less than assailing a failed system, more urgently asks of London's citizens a certain civic responsibility."[58]

The last institution she cites for the poor, Bridewell, will receive beadles and matrons from her to ensure that work continue at the poor house. In the decade after Whitney's poem was published, John Howes laments that "all London is but an hospitall"; "the very name of Brydewell is in the eares of the people so odyous tha it kylleth the creadit for ever"; "a thousande to one if ever he or shee comme to any preferment, having tasted of that soyle"; "nothing is to be learned but

---

55   James R. Hertzler, "The Abuse and outlawing of Sanctuary for Debt in Seventeenth-Century England," *The Historical Journal* 14.3 (1971): 467–477; here 467, no. 1.
56   "Social Mobility," 38, 40.
57   "London 1540–1770," 325. See Frederick J. Fisher, "The Development of London as a Centre of Conspicuous Consumption in the Sixteenth and Seventeenth Centuries," Frederick J. Fisher and Penelope J. Corfield, *London and the English Economy* (London: Hambledon Press, 1990), 105–18.
58   Ingram, "A Case for Credit," 13.

lewdenes amoungest that generacion."[59] Given to the city to administer by Henry VIII, Bridewell was founded with the good intentions of relieving and reforming the poor as well as removing them from the streets, but there was simply never enough financing or adequate administration to meet the needs of the growing numbers of vagrants.[60] According to Boulton, in the 1570s about the same time that Whitney was writing, a special movement was begun at Bridewell to suppress prostitution, but this was unsuccessful.[61]

Whitney's listing of these buildings, the Counter, Newgate, Fleet, Ludgate, and Bridewell, makes clear her views on contemporary London's treatment of the poor. She also, however, makes bequests to St. Bartholomew's hospital and Bedlam, places where she says live those "blind and lame" or "that out of tune do talk," showing her views on London's treatment of the disabled and mentally ill, too (223, 228). That the institutions for the poor and ill existed at all is due to the efforts of ordinary people. After the breakdown of the charity systems and healthcare brought on by the Reformation, London's citizens petitioned Henry VIII for the grant of four hospitals, St. Thomas's in Southwark and St. Bartholomew's, Bedlam, and Bridewell, which he agreed to turn over to the city. Funding was, however, never adequate, and Paul Slack notes that collecting rates for hospitals and poor relief was especially difficult in the 1570s when Whitney was writing.[62]

Although centralization of parish poor relief was being established in other English towns then, this was not the case in London since the individual parishes there demanded independence.[63] With the exception of the Counter, the prisons discussed earlier and hospitals are all located on the city's outer walls or outside of the walls themselves. Although the spaces in and around the city of London were not as socially segregated as they would become in the seventeenth century, already the "less well off and really poor were concentrated, as one would expect, in the suburbs to the north and east, notably in Whitechapel and Shoreditch, and along riverside parishes on both banks of the Thames," which is where these institutions were located.[64]

---

[59] John Howes, Tudor Economic Documents, III, 431, 439. Quoted in Beier "Social Problems in London," 217.

[60] Beier, "Social Problems in London," 218–219.

[61] Boulton, "London 1540–1700," 337.

[62] Paul Slack, "Metropolitan Government in Crisis: the Response to Plague," London 1500–1700, 60–81; here 67.

[63] Ibid., 68.

[64] Jeremy Boulton, London 1540–1700, 328. Boulton also notes that the city's parishes routinely made payments for poor relief to the parishes in the suburbs. J. F. Merritt argues that London was "becoming increasingly fragmented culturally, socially, and economically in this period, with its different areas characterized by distinctive living patterns, health, social structure, household size, and social dynamics," Imagining, 11–12.

Also outside of the city walls but quite different in makeup, the last places Whitney cites are the Inns of Court and Chanceries, where she says lawyers will take the causes of those who want houses or land.[65] Driven by the incredible turnover of land caused by the seizing of lands during the English Reformation as well as the selling of Crown property to pay for war, an estimated 25% to 30% of land in the country was put up for public sale between 1534 and 1660, and these sales increased litigation enormously.[66] The numbers of law students at these inns increased considerably in the second half of the sixteenth century when, Wilfred Prest argues, "residence for a year or so at one of the Inns was considered an integral part of the normal gentlemanly education. . . . to cope with the suits of avaricious neighbours and troublesome tenants."[67] A 1574 Privy Council Census found 759 men at the Inns of Court, and Whitney says she will leave at each inn or chancery a youthful crowd of active young men.[68] To these young men, she then leaves stalls of books, tennis courts, dancing schools, fencing schools, and every Sunday at least players "to make them sport" (250).[69]

This final space with its relatively well-off young men raises questions about Whitney's intentions at the end of her bequests. Why has she taken us from the center of commercial activity in the old markets of London, to the prisons and hospitals on the outer edges of the city, to the Inns of Court completely outside of London at that time? Is she showing her readers the differences in the lives of young men based on social class or is she bringing up the possibility of educating a new generation of more socially conscious leaders at the law schools? The fifteenth-century ballad "London Lackpenny," originally attributed to John Lydgate, was cited by John Stow in his *Survey* in 1598, suggesting that Whitney, fond of the ballad form herself, could also have known the work in the 1570s.

As the poem's persona travels to London to complain to men of law about being cheated out of his money, he portrays the various courts and law figures, including the clerks at the chancery, as indifferent to those without money.[70]

---

[65]   Interestingly, the environs of the Inns of Court and the Temple Church at Whitefriars were considered debtors' sanctuaries. See James R. Hertzler, "The Abuse and Outlawing of Sanctuary for Debt in Seventeenth-Century England," *The Historical Journal* 14.3 (Sept. 1971): 467–77; here 468.

[66]   Stone, "Social Mobility," 42–43.

[67]   "Legal Education of the Gentry at the Inns of Court, 1560–1640," *Past and Present* 38 (1967): 20–39; here 23.

[68]   R. M. Fisher, "Reform, Repression and Unrest at the Inns of Court, 1518–1558," *Historical Journal* 20:4 (1977): 783–801; here 796, no. 52.

[69]   Stow, *Survey*, 244, 246, notes that in 1574, the year following Whitney's publication, an Act of Common Council prevented players from acting on Sundays and otherwise corrupting youth. Also, those receiving licenses to perform plays must pay agreed upon sums to the poor in hospitals.

[70]   "London Lyckpeny," British History Online, book 2, ch. 13. See Benson, "Some Poets' Tours of

Furthermore, he describes the many goods for sale in the same London markets that Whitney takes us to, Cheap, Candlewick, Eastcheap, and Cornhill, before ending with a plea for true lawyers in London to help those without money. Charges of corruption, according to Jill Mann, were the most frequent stereotypes associated with lawyers in the medieval estates satires of writers like Gower and Langland, but this fifteenth-century author can envision the possibility for change.[71] Perhaps in a way similar to this author's, Whitney is using the lawyers both to point to social injustices and to call for help for the poor. These well-off young men with their books and entertainment are shown in dramatic contrast to the poor and sick locked up within the city. Since the law students, however, like the figures in "London Lackpenny," will someday make and enforce the law, it is possible that Whitney wants her bequests *of* young men to the Inns of Court and *to* the young men in the Inns of Court to strengthen the legal system in early modern London.

A major difference between "London Lackpenny" and "Will and Testament," however, is the circumstances that led to the narrator's poverty. Whereas the fifteenth-century narrator says he had been cheated out of his money while in the country and then is robbed of his hood while in London, Whitney's persona states that "my luck which ever was too bad" led to her poverty (303–304). Furthermore, the way she describes the people in trouble in London—the people in the Counter as "some Coggers, and some honest men," the people in the Fleet as Papists and the poor, and those in Ludgate as bankrupts who choose to die in debt—suggests that things beyond their control, simply bad luck, and not criminal behavior, put them behind bars (143). Although the lawyers and courts in "London Lackpenny" are just as corrupt as the villains in the streets and market places, Whitney's poem may see promise for the future in courts populated by the young men now studying to be lawyers. This corner of urban space can perhaps offer relief to the others.

In the final section of the poem, when she tells London that she has "dispersed round about / Such needful things as they should have / here left now unto thee" (256–58), her "Wyll and Testament" is an act of generous charity on her part. Since, however, she also tells London to remind those who mourn her leaving that they could have helped her out earlier, the work is at the same time an indictment of those who allow others to go without the basics in life. She ends the poem on line 364, one line short of a year, completely alone.

With several different personae forming the narrative perspective in "Wyll and Testament," including the lover jilted by London, the out-of-work female

---

Medieval London," for a discussion of the cynical account of London in the poem.

71    Jill Mann, *Chaucer and Medieval Estates Satire: The Literature of Social Classes and the General Prologue to the Canterbury Tale* (Cambridge and London: Cambridge University Press, 1973), 89.

companion, and the caring older sister, in addition to the poor poet who is also the generous benefactor, the poem obviously has several types of audiences as well. Her primary audience, though, not unlike the audiences of other medieval and early-modern authors in this volume, such as Hans Sachs as discussed in the article by Albrecht Classen, is the urban middle class. Although the audience addressed directly in "Wyll and Testament" is the personified city of London, outside of this fictional frame in which a generous benefactor makes series after series of bequests, other intended readers become apparent. In her bid for literary success, she is appealing to the large number of middle-class readers who made it profitable for London's printers to publish popular literature; however, at the same time, her choice of subject matter is clearly aimed at those in the city who could bring about change, those within city government, social institutions, and the justice systems who needed to sharpen their social consciences.

In writers who follow her, such as Bacon, Wotton, and Donne, the city "came to signal the privileges and challenges opened up by urban mobility," and London in its post-Calvinist role was said to be the new Jerusalem, "the basic framework for life on earth."[72] For her, though, compressed within this narrow urban space, the streets and buildings of early modern London reflect the desires and despair of those who live there. At once both an inventory of items bequeathed in a will and a map of social and economic space, Whitney's poem is a testament to the paradox of poverty occasioned by plenty and despair brought on by earlier opportunity.

A few years later, Thomas Lupton's *Sivqila: Too Good, to be True* (1580), posits a utopia in which merchants' wealth provides ample charity for a long list of needy persons, including widows, prisoners, poor apprentices, servants, and debtors.[73] In 1573, however, Whitney surveys the number of desperate people and the social institutions in place to handle poverty in early-modern London and finds them in great need of bequests. Ultimately, Whitney is an intelligent middle-class woman who, during Queen Elizabeth's reign, can walk freely throughout the city of London, observing the range of interactions in its public spaces, wary but not afraid, ambivalent about parts of the city's makeup, but not a prophet of future doom. Her insights into the human character, whether it be about the ruffians who quarrel for no reason or the Saturday bathers who want to look good in church on Sunday, give us a more balanced view of early-modern London than either the scripted acclamations of praise found in the lord mayors' pageants or the scathing sermons and popular pamphlets that demonized the city.[74]

---

[72]   Manley, *Literature and Culture*, 112–13.
[73]   Quoted in Manley, *Literature and Culture*, 117.
[74]   J. F. Merritt, *Imagining*, 14–16.

In the introduction to this volume, Albrecht Classen notes that "urban space became increasingly the critical setting for people's emotions to be acted out, performed, ritualized, and staged," and Whitney would appear to agree.

Michael E. Bonine

(The University of Arizona, Tucson)

# *Waqf* and its Influence on the Built Environment in the *Medina* of the Islamic Middle Eastern City[1]

Cities in the Middle East have a long heritage, for the urban centers since the ancient period were the foci for empires and local elites as well as being central places for their surrounding hinterlands. While the majority of the population would certainly still have been peasants in the countryside, it is the cities that were the centers of power, prestige, and religion. The traditional city during the Muslim period (from the mid-seventh century onwards) was called the *medina* in Arabic (and *shahr* or *shahristan* in the Iranian world and Central Asia.). Many of the traditions, values, and even much of the specific built environment were inherited from the ancient (pre-Islamic) Middle East by the cities of the Muslim period. Nevertheless, the city in the Islamic Middle East, along with Muslim society in general, was administered by *shari'a* (Islamic law), in combination with local customary law (*urf*), which created its own specific dynamic for the urban environment. One institution which was particularly important for Muslim society (and especially for the cities), was *waqf* or religiously endowed property. This institution not only supported the principal religious buildings such as the mosques, religious schools, and shrines, but it had also a most significant social role in supporting various charitable needs of the city, such as providing food for the poor, drinking water to neighborhoods, or funding particular religious

---

[1] This present work is a revised and updated paper first presented at the Congresos Internacionales "La Ciudad en el Occidente Islámico Medieval," 4th *Congreso: "La Medina en Proceso de saturación,"* *Granada, Spain, May 10–13, 2006.* I thank Julio Navarro Palazón, the organizer of that conference, as well as comments and suggestions from several participants. Also, thanks to my colleague Albrecht Classen, The University of Arizona, for his comments, suggestions, and the organization of the conference on Urban Space on which this volume is based.

gatherings and festivals. *Waqf* was one of the principal institutions that enabled cities (and urban societies) to function effectively during the Muslim period.

This paper specifically examines the role of *waqf* on the built environment of the city in the Middle East. The focus is particularly on how this institution may have promoted the increase in the density of the built environment of the *medina* — or, on the other hand, how *waqf* may have been a factor in slowing that process, and hence might have contributed to a decrease in the density. Perhaps *waqf* property sometimes promoted increasing the density of buildings, but, then, in other instances, it might have inhibited urban development. Can we identify when and why it is one or the other? Are there, then, predominant, recognizable patterns of the influence of *waqf* on the urban built environment in the cities of the Middle East, and can we come up with generalizations about the significance of *waqf* related to the density of the urban fabric?

These are the principal questions which will be addressed in this paper and it will provide at least some initial insights and partial answers. After first discussing the concept of the Islamic city and the context and role which *waqf* plays in the urban environment, I will then examine the various types of *waqf* to show how endowed property might be exchanged, sold, or otherwise used. There is a view that *waqf*, since it is mortmain property (an inalienable possession, endowed in perpetuity), is basically static and hence taken out of the fluid economic, urban system. However, this is not necessarily the case, as will be shown in this paper. The institution of *waqf* was part of a very dynamic social and economic system, and one that had a number of options for its use — even if some uses were not legal in the strictest interpretation. A number of case studies from the available literature will be used to illustrate these patterns.

## The Islamic City in the Middle East

The idea or concept of an Islamic City has a rather tortuous and controversial legacy, one which can only be touched upon here. First, why do (or did) we talk about the Islamic City, when we don't discuss such (religious) typologies as the Christian City or the Buddhist City, for instance. Yes, we do talk about European cities and Chinese cities — as there are also Middle Eastern cities. The concept that there is an Islamic City had its origins among western Orientalists, among whom it was believed that the religion and culture of Islam pervaded all aspects of Muslim society, including the built environment. Abu-Lughod traces this *isnad* (chain of transmission); how it emerged beginning in the late 1920s from the work of several French scholars in particular, including William Marçais and his brother Georges Marçais, culminating in the 1955 article by Gustave von Grunebaum entitled "The Structure of the Muslim Town."[2] Several major workshops or conferences focused on Islamic and Middle Eastern cities over the next several decades where, besides discussing aspects of the model of the Islamic city, individual city studies or particular topics related to the Islamic city were presented.[3] As Abu-Lughod discusses, the model of the Islamic city began to be evaluated more and more critically, questioning the assumptions and the *isnad* upon which it was built. By the 1990s fewer and fewer scholars addressed the model of the Islamic City, and the concept continued to be highly criticized.[4] As one Japanese scholar has commented, "the concept of the 'Islamic city,' which developed from an Orientalist base, has not a great deal of possibility. No longer should we need adhere to the framework of that well-worn theory."[5]

In fact, the studies of the "Islamic City" have become much more sophisticated, and now are focused on a much deeper understanding of Middle Eastern (and Muslim) societies. A greater understanding of the role of *shari'a* or Islamic law is

---

[2]    Janet L. Abu-Lughod, "The Islamic City—Historic Myth, Islamic Essence, and Contemporary Relevance," *International Journal of Middle East Studies* 19 (1987): 155–76. Some of the principal works related to this *isnad*, include, for instance: William Marçais, "L'Islamisme et la vie urbaine," *L'Académie des Inscriptions et Belles-Lêttres, Comptes Rendus* (1928): 86–100; Georges Marçais, "L'Urbanisme musulman," *5e Congrès de la Fédération des Sociétés savants de l'Afrique du Nord* (Algiers, 1940), 13–34; Georges Marçais, "La Conception des villes dans l'Islam," *Revue d'Alger* 2 (1945): 517–33; Robert Brunschvig, "Urbanisme médiéval et droit musulman," *Revue des Études Islamiques* 15 (1947): 127–55; Gustav von Grunebaum, "Die islamische Stadt," *Saeculum* 6 (1955): 138–53; also published as "The Structure of the Muslim Town," id., *Islam: Essays in the Nature and Growth of a Cultural Tradition*. Comparative Studies of Cultures and Civilizations, 4. Memoirs of the American Anthropological Association 81 (1955): 141–58; published also as Gustav von Grunebaum, *Islam: Essays in the Nature and Growth of a Cultural Tradition* (London: Routledge and Kegan Paul, 1955), 141–58.

[3]    The principal collections resulting from these early gatherings, include *Middle Eastern Cities: A Symposium on Ancient, Islamic, and Contemporary Middle Eastern Urbanism*, ed. Ira M. Lapidus (Berkeley and Los Angeles: University of California Press, 1969); *The Islamic City: A Colloquium*, ed. A. H. Hourani and S. M. Stern (Oxford: Bruno Cassirer and University of Pennsylvania Press, Papers on Islamic History I. Published under the auspices of the Near Eastern History Group, Oxford, and the Near East Center, University of Pennsylvania, 1970); *From Madina to Metropolis: Heritage and Change in the Near Eastern City*, ed. L. Carl Brown (Princeton, NJ: The Darwin Press, Princeton Studies on the Near East, 1973).

[4]    For example, see André Raymond, "Islamic City, Arab City: Orientalist Myths and Recent Views," *British Journal of Middle Eastern Studies* 21.1 (1994): 3–18.

[5]    Masashi Haneda, "Introduction: An Interpretation of the Concept of the 'Islamic City,'" *Islamic Urban Studies: Historical Review and Perspectives*, ed. Masashi Haneda and Toru Miura (London and New York: Kegan Paul International, 1994), 1–10; here 9. An excellent recent discussion and criticism of the Islamic city model can also be found in Giulia Annalinda Neglia, "Some Historiographical Notes on the Islamic City with Particular References to the Visual Representation of the Built City," *The City in the Islamic World*, vol. 1, ed. Salma K. Jayyusi, Renata Holod, Attilio Petruccioli, and André Raymond (Leiden and Boston: Brill, 2008), 3–46. This two volume work in fact has 46 articles which represent some of the latest research and ideas related to "the city in the Islamic world."

being used to understand urban society and the built environment.[6] More documents, such as court records, are being used to reconstruct urban histories and better understand urban society. One institution which is beginning to be perceived as more and more important for the city and urban society in the Islamic Middle East, is *waqf*—which is the focus of this paper, and which we will now address.

## The Institution of *Waqf*

*Waqf* (pl. *awqaf*; Persian *vaqf* or Turkish *vakif*, and in the Maghreb or Northwest Africa *hubs*—or French *habous*) is property or an object that is endowed permanently for a charitable or pious purpose, which often was a mosque or other religious institutions, such as a *madrasa* (religious school).[7] The ultimate purpose for every *waqf* had to be something pleasing to God. *Waqf* could also be for the public good, such as supporting a public fountain, or it could be in support of certain religious ceremonies, such as, among the Shi'a, for Imam Hussain, meaning support of the mourning ritual ceremonies commemorating the death of the third Imam during the month of Muharram. The traditional legal definition of *waqf* has been discussed in the context of Islamic law rather extensively in the past,[8] and the standard concept of this institution is that "waqf property is totally withdrawn from commercial circulation and therefore can hinder economic development and land reform."[9] However, the significance of *waqf* for the urban environment and as a dynamic instrument for the changing social and economic life of Islamic society has only more recently become evident, as more and more scholarship and studies have been conducted.[10] Richard van Leeuwen, for instance, has provided

---

[6]    For instance, see Basim Selim Hakim, *Arabic-Islamic Cities: Building and Planning Principles* (London: KPI Ltd., 1986). Other newer developments in urban studies in the Middle East can be found in Michael E. Bonine, "Islamic Urbanism, Urbanites and the Middle Eastern City," *Blackwell's Companion to the History of the Middle East* ed. Youssef Choueire (London: Blackwell Publishers, 2005), 393–406, 534–81 (comprehensive bibliography for the volume).

[7]    In my discussion of *waqf* I will be using the Arabic *waqf* even when referring to the institution in Iran or Turkey, and instead of using the Arabic plural of *oaqaf* I will use *waqfs*. Such convention is used by many scholars when discussing the institution in general; however for quotes from articles focusing on Turkey (*vakif*) and Iran (*vaqf*) their spellings will be as used by those authors.

[8]    For instance, see N. J. Coulson, *A History of Islamic Law* (Edinburgh: Edinburgh University Press, 1964); Joseph Schacht, *An Introduction to Islamic Law* (Oxford: Clarendon Press, 1964).

[9]    David S. Powers, "Waqf," *Dictionary of the Middle Ages*, vol. 12 (New York: Scribner, 1982–1989), 543–44; here 544.

[10]   Bonine, "Islamic Urbanism, Urbanites and the Middle Eastern City;" Randi Deguilhem, "The Waqf in the City," *The City in the Islamic World*, Vol. 2, ed Salma K. Jayyusi, Renata Holod, Attilio Petruccioli, and André Raymond (Leiden and Boston: Brill, 2008), 923–50.

an important analysis of *waqf* in the urban context, noting that "the legal approach to waqfs has usually been ahistorical and concentrated on an ideal type of waqf."[11] In his work he argues that the traditional (legal) view of waqf "is not only inconsistent with recent approaches to historical processes, but also too narrow, neglecting some essential characteristics of the institution."[12]

The intentions of the founder (*waqif*) and the purpose of the endowment is spelled out in a written document, the foundation deed, a *waqfiyya* (Persian *vaqfnameh*, Turkish *vakifname*), which details what was endowed, who benefited, and how the proceeds of payments are to be distributed. As Powers has noted:

> The accepted definition of *waqf*, according to the Hanafite school, is "the detention of the corpus from the ownership of any person and the gift of its income or usufruct, either presently or in the future, to some charitable purpose." To create a *waqf*, an owner must make an oral declaration permanently reserving the income of the property for a specific purpose. Once this declaration has been made, the property may not be transferred or alienated by the founder, the administrator, or the beneficiaries, and it cannot be inherited by the founder's heirs.[13]

These foundation deeds often have been the main source of information of *waqfs*, although more recently other documents, such as court records (*sijills*), various written agreements or statements about *waqf* as in *farmans*, and accounts in chroniclers and histories of a particular ruler or city, have been used to tell us more details on what has happened to specific *waqf* property (including its disappearance).

*Waqf* is overseen or supervised by an administrator (*mutawalli, nazir*), who is mandated to carry out the provisions of the endowment. The *mutawalli* distributes the income to the various beneficiaries as well as maintains the upkeep of the property. The administrator usually gets 10 percent of the income for this task, although in some instances it may be only 5 percent or as much as 20 percent (or some other percentage in between).

There are two major types of *waqf*: public *waqf* (*waqf-i khayri* or '*amm*), sometimes called charitable *waqf*, and family or private *waqf* (*waqf-i ahli* or *khass, dhurri, auladeh*). Family *waqf* uses the benefits or income of the property for the founder himself (or herself) and the *waqif*'s own children and their descendants. The difference between the two types, however, is not always clear, because even for private or family *waqf*, there must an ultimate religious, charitable purpose for the benefit of God. This means that even if the *waqf* is for the benefit of the donor's family and family members, if for some reason and at some point in time there are

---

[11] Richard van Leeuwen, *Waqfs and Urban Structures: The Case of Ottoman Damascus* (Leiden, Boston, and Cologne: Brill, 1999), here 10.

[12] Ibid., 13.

[13] Powers, "Waqf," 543.

no more designated heirs, the endowed property will revert to a religious institution, the poor or other charitable purpose. On the other hand, for many public *waqfs* substantial support for the founder and his family and descendents may be included in the deed, from being the administrator of the *waqf* to being readers of the Qur'an in the mosque (or elsewhere) on particular occasions—with payments from the *waqf* for all these positions and activities. Although not common, there could also be a mixed *waqf*, called *mushtarak*, with a combination of both public and private recipients.

Most *waqf*, however, is public *waqf* and it is often endowed for a mosque or other religious building, as well as supporting many public services that today are often seen as the purview of the government or the state, such as water fountains (and even the water supply), bathhouses, hospitals, guesthouses, food kitchens, caravanserais, and bazaars. Whereas agricultural land and even irrigation water shares from the rural areas often supported buildings or religious activities in the city, within the urban area the *waqf* often consisted of commercial structures, which would generate a rental income in support of the designated endowment.[14] Other urban property, such as houses or even urban gardens, might also be *waqf* (paying rent), but, in general, this was not as common as commercial property. The objective of the endowments, for example, a mosque or religious school, was also *waqf*. Hence, within the urban environment there was considerable property which was *waqf*. How that might influence the actual built environment, promoting or inhibiting development, is what remains to be evaluated in this paper. Various case studies are used to show how *waqf* was functionalized in the urban environment, leading to preliminary generalizations and conclusions how *waqf* affected the density of the city.

*Waqf* also must be placed in the context of the ownership of property in general. Some of the basic principles that affected building and planning in the traditional Middle Eastern and North African city have been outlined, for instance, by Besim Hakim.[15] There were various guidelines that had to be followed which were sanctioned by *shari'a* (Islamic law) or sometimes even by *urf* (local customary law). Although basing his information on Maliki law and *qadi* records mainly from late-thirteenth- and early-fourteenth-century Tunis, Basim provides us with principles including not causing harm to others, the right of privacy, the rights of prior usage and ownership, the respect for the property of others, the rights and obligations

---

14    For example, for the irrigation shares endowed for the city of Yazd, Iran, see Abd al-Vahhad Taraz, "Ketabcheh-ye Mouqufat-e Yazd [Small Book of the Yazd Endowments]," Text of 1257/1841–1842, ed. Iraj Afshar, *Farhang-e Iran Zamin* 10 (1962–1963), 5–123 (in Persian); Michael E. Bonine, "Islam and Commerce: Waqf and the Bazaar of Yazd, Iran," *Erdkunde* 41 (1987): 182–96.

15    Hakim, *Arabic-Islamic Cities*, chapter 1: "Islamic Law and Neighbourhood Building Guidelines," 15–54.

of neighbors, and other guidelines, such as the width of streets, heights of buildings, use of excess water, or how to handle activities that might generate unpleasant smells or loud noises.[16] *Waqf* property also had to fit into this framework of building principles. It also should be stressed that within Islamic law (*shari'a*) private property is particularly important and sacrosanct. Hence, the attempt to establish *waqf* property was sometimes limited by the fact that it was privately owned (instead of state property, for instance). As we will see, this also means that *waqf* often became private property over time—both legally and illegally.

The transformation of *waqf* property into private property—or other *waqf*—or the use of *waqf* for purposes other than what the endower had intended, enabled this type of property to be much more fluid and dynamic than the legal definitions would imply. Some of the ways endowed property was changed or used differently, and how that might have affected the urban fabric and density, will be brought out in some of the case studies. At this point, some of the methods for this transformation or other use will be explained briefly. For instance, *istibdal* was the exchange of an unprofitable *waqf* property for another piece of property, because the original *waqf* property was in decline or even dilapidated. Besides actual exchange, this also might entail the selling of the *waqf* property and the purchase of another property in its place as *waqf*. The *mutawalli* or administrator of the *waqf* is seen to have this right, recognized by *shari'a*, because the original purpose of the *waqf* could not be fulfilled because of the deteriorated condition of the property. This also might occur, for instance, when major repairs are needed for a building and the *waqf* does not have the funds.

Other devices were used to circumvent specifically the restrictions imposed on *waqf* by Islamic law. One of these was the *mursad*, which was found, for instance, in Ottoman Damascus and "was a loan contract arranged between a waqf administrator and a lender to finance repairs on any waqf structure which had fallen into ruin or disrepair in the event that waqf revenues themselves could not cover repair costs,"[17] The *mutawalli*, after approval by the *qadi*, could negotiate such a loan to repair a damaged *waqf* property. As Deguilhem-Schoem notes:

> In return [for financing the repairs], a contract for long-term rent would usually be offered on the grounds that the waqf structure had deteriorated to an extent that no one could be found to rent it on an annual or other short-term basis. Only a long-term

---

[16]    See ibid., Chap. 1, for details of these guidelines.

[17]    Randi Geguilhem-Schoem, "The Loan of Mursad on Waqf Properties," *A Way Prepared: Essays on Islamic Culture in Honor of Richard Bayly Winder*, ed. Farhad Kazemi and R. D. McChesney (New York: New York University Press, 1988), 68–79; here 69.

renter would be interested in repairing damaged waqf property and investing his own funds and time in them to render them productive again.[18]

Often it was the tenant or renter of the *waqf* property who would request such a loan, because of needed repairs, and if there were insufficient funds for such repairs, then a *mursad* loan would be possible. A lease might be several three-year terms or other periods, and even as many as 99 years in some instances. Repayments might be a specific percentage of the income of the *waqf*, a reduction in the rent paid by the lessee, or part of the rent of a subtenant of the *waqf*. A *mursad* lender could also sell the loan to another person, which required permission of the *mutawalli*. In some cases, a *waqfiyya* forbid *mursad*, which for instance, was, in the *waqf* of Muhammad Bey Abu al-Dhahab in Cairo, one of the case studies examined below. (Muhammad Bey's *waqf* also forbad *istibdal*, the exchange of *waqf* property.)[19] McChesney has also noted that the *mursad* was redeemable by the *waqf* administration at any time, which was unlike the sale of development rights (see below). But he recognizes that "it is clear that, as time passed, property deteriorated, and repair costs mounted, the mursad liens could eventually exceed the value of the original waqf property, at which point there was de facto divestment"[20]

Similar to the *mursad* was the *ijaratayn*, a "double rent" permitted on *waqf* property by the Hanafi school. As McChesney explains: "a large advance payment was made in exchange for a long-term, below-market-rent lease. The large advance payment, like 'key money' or 'furnishings and fixtures money,' was recoverable by the tenant by 'sale' to a new tenant."[21] This enabled the lessor to receive a large payment and not lose the property, while the tenant had a favorable long-term rent. The same as *mursad*, the double rent also "removed control of the property from the lessor and . . . established a kind of quasi-lien against the property in the form of the advance, which gave the lessee a claim."[22]

Another way in which *waqf* is used differently than what had been intended—or for different beneficiaries than designated—is the use of *hikr*. This was, again, a type of rent or lien for the use—or usufruct—of the *waqf* and, hence, is similar to *mursad* or *ijaratayn*. The *hikr* was an "effective sale of development rights" to a tenant who wanted to make improvements on property which was *waqf*. A higher rent was negotiated (with the approval of the *mutawalli* or even the *qadi*). The improvement, such as a building constructed on *waqf* land, "became the property

---

[18]   Ibid.
[19]   Ibid., 71.
[20]   R[obert] D. McChesney, *Waqf in Central Asia: Four Hundred Years in the History of a Muslim Shirne, 1480–1889* (Princeton: Princeton University Press, 1991), 287.
[21]   Ibid., 285.
[22]   Ibid.

of the tenant and could be rented, sold, given away (as *waqf*, for instance), or left as part of the owner's estate"[23] Like *mursad* or *ijaratayn*, *hikr* also was a device that gave greater control and "ownership" of the property to the tenant, effectively leading to the status of private property over time in many instances: "The mutawalli may have retained certain preemptive rights (right of first refusal on a sale, for example), but if a new use was established with the improvement (for example, a caravansary where there had once been an orchard), the mutawalli's control of the *waqf* property for intents and purposes disappeared."[24]

Finally, a device that was similar to the above examples, was *khulu*, which Gabriel Baer discusses as one of the principal ways for the "dismemberment" of *waqf* in nineteenth-century Jerusalem.[25] For a *khulu* to take place, the *waqf* property had to be in need of repair and did not have the required funds, and so when this building condition was verified by the chief architect (*mi'mar basi*) and approved by the *qadi*, the *mutawalli* could enter into such an agreement. This would, again, be a situation where the tenant (or third party) would perform the restoration or repair of the *waqf* property, and in return receive a lower, viable rent. The Hanafi and Shaf'i schools have slightly different procedures; for instance, the Shaf'i law school:

> permitted the *mutawalli* to let the property to a certain tenant for a long period (*ijara twaila*), generally of ninety years (or rather thirty *'uqud* of three years each). The total rent, calculated for the whole period, would then be divided into two parts: one part to be paid immediately (*mu'ajjal*) to the *mutawalli* (in some cases to liquidate the debt of the *waqf*), and the other part would be left in the hands of the tenant in order to carry out the repairs. Any additional sum spent by the tenant for repairs or restoration would become his *khula*.[26]

Baer further emphasizes that the *khulu* arrangements in nineteenth-century Palestine are principally: "private investment in the restoration of deteriorated *waqf* property creating private property rights or claims in the *waqf* in addition to long-term leases of the *waqf* property for a fixed low rent."[27]

---

[23] Ibid., 286.
[24] Ibid.
[25] Gabriel Baer, "The Dismemberment of Awqaf in Early Nineteenth-Century Jerusalem," *Asian and African Affairs: Journal of the Israel Oriental Society* 13 (1979): 220–41
[26] Ibid., 221–22.
[27] Ibid., 222.

## Case Studies: *Waqf* in the Ottoman World

## Ottoman Istanbul

Perhaps the most dramatic instances of large urban *waqf* have been the major foundations and urban developments established by various rulers, the sultans and shahs of the Middle East. For instance, Inalcik (1990) provides an excellent account of how principally Christian Constantinople was transformed into an Islamic city by Mehmed II after he conquered the Byzantine capital in 1453.[28] *Waqf* property was critical in this metamorphosis of that urban environment. As Inalcik asserts:

> The world view of Islam determined the physical and social landscape of the city [Istanbul] which was prepared as a space where the prescriptions of the Islamic religion could be observed properly and in their entirety. The basic objective in the expansion of Islam was to acquire political control over an area and establish the symbols of Islamic sovereignty.[29]

Within Istanbul, many of the churches were turned into mosques. A citadel, royal palace, and the central bazaar complex—the *bedestan*—were priority constructions. The main urban developments, however, were based upon the *waqf-'imaret* system, a planned complex of religious and non-religious buildings, which included a mosque, religious school (*madrasa*), hospice, and often such other structures as a hospital, library, dervish convent, Qur'an school for children, and a fountain for ablutions. These complexes were also called a *külliye* and they were founded in various established or new districts, and they provided the nexus for the development of Muslim neighborhoods. *Waqf* property, particularly *bedestans* or bazaar complexes, were endowed to support the new developments. For instance, the Great Carsi, the main bazaar, was endowed for the newly converted Aya-Sofya (Hagia Sophia) mosque. In the case of the newly established Ottoman capital, "the main urban functions were viewed as being complementary to or extensions of the religious establishment or the imperial palace."[30]

Pınar Kayaalp also has examined how the *külliye* mosque complex was instrumental in creating new neighborhoods on the Anatolian shore of Istanbul in the sixteenth century.[31] She examines three major congregational mosques and

---

28    Halil Inalcik, "Istanbul: An Islamic City," *Journal of Islamic Studies* 1 (1990): 1–23.
29    Ibid., 6.
30    Ibid., 13
31    Pınar Kayaalp, "The Role of Imperial Mosque Complexes (1543–1583) in the Urbanization of

notes that "Üsküdar's stride toward urbanization was hastened by the construction of three imperial *külliyes* between 1453 and 1553."[32] Although she does not focus on the *waqf* per se, several references to the endowment deeds indicate that these complexes were indeed *waqf*. Whereas two of the *külliyes* were situated on the waterfront, but still created neighborhoods around them, the third mosque complex was inland and on a hilltop. As Kayaalp notes, this complex was built on an empty plot of land and "the primary function [of the mosque complex] was to create a large urban quarter (*mahalle*) in the hitherto unpopulated hilltop of Üsküdar."[33]

Other Ottoman cities, such as Bursa or towns in the Balkans, also were subjected to the *waqf-'imaret* or *külliye* system to develop them as Muslim cities. In any case, it was the *waqf* property itself—"the revenue-producing commercial installations . . . [which] was the key institution in creating a typical Ottoman-Islamic urban structure."[34] Istanbul, however, is perhaps a special case—partly because it was the Ottoman capital and also because much of the city had been abandoned by the former inhabitants when it was conquered in 1453. So we have a case in which much urban land and housing had been abandoned and the *waqf* system enabled the city to be repopulated—and rebuilt. Also, because of the (Muslim) Ottoman conquest, the land could be confiscated and hence turned into the *imaret* complexes and *waqf* commercial land.[35]

Another example of the possible influence of *waqf* by Ottoman sultans and pashas is Mauice Cerasi's fascinating study of the Divanyolu in Istanbul.[36] Although its meaning was sometimes more broadly and variously used, the Divanyolu basically meant the main avenue and the various ensembles of monuments along the avenue from the Topkapi Palace-Ayasofya complex (the latter the principal mosque of the Ottoman capital) westwards to Beyazit and then the Fatih mosque. During some time periods parts of the "avenue" were actually two parallel streets. As Cerasi notes, "It is a common view that the Divanyolu was so named because of the processional traffic of pashas and their crowded retinues back and forth between the Divan and their *konaks* (mansions). In actuality, the main streets that channeled the sultan's processions and military parades even where the transit to and from the pashas' *konaks* was rare have been called

---

[32]  Üsküdar" (in this volume).

[33]  Ibid., 650.

[34]  Ibid., 654.

[35]  Inalcik, "Istanbul: An Islamic City," 19

      However, Inalcik does not elaborate on the process of acquiring the land for the *waqf* or the building complexes.

[36]  Maurice Cerasi, "The Urban and Architectural Evolution of the Istanbul Divanyolu: Urban Aesthetics and Ideology in Ottoman Town Building," *Muqarnas* 22 (2005): 189–232. The road of the Divan means the route used for the sultan's and other officials' stately processions.

'Divanyolu.'"[37] Many mosques and other religious and public buildings were established along the Divanyolu. Some of the buildings were for the local neighborhood (*mahalle*), but others were "sultanic Friday mosques or connected to some non-local institution, [and] did not serve the local residential community."[38] There were many *konaks* (mansions of the pashas and elites) which were sometimes free-standing structures within a garden and enclosed by high walls that were on the street, or they were the typical wooden Ottoman house, which would be aligned with the streets. The mix of housing and gardens was still evident in many areas of Istanbul even in the 1920s, as evidenced by many of the fire insurance maps of Jacques Pervititch.[39]

The typical urban density is explained by Cerasi as follows:

> On the whole, building density was low, in the nature of the very loose Ottoman urban fabric; gardens and voids were woven into the built-up areas, and buildings were not tall. This was even characteristic of the monumental building of the [Divanyolu] axis: their typological categories differed in a certain measure from those of other quarters of Istanbul. While the Divan route led to the districts in which were sited some of the most important sultanic complexes, its architectural space included only four royal mosques: Fatih, Sehzade, Beyazit, and Mehrimah Sultan . . . .[And] Ayasofya is not quite on the axis.[40]

The Divanyolu actually had many other monumental buildings along its axis, including many local *mahalleh* mosques, Quran schools (*sibyan mektebi*), fountains, and libraries, although Cerasi stresses that these features "were not much more frequent on the axis than on other thoroughfares."[41] What does characterize the Divanyolu, however, is the greater occurrence of *medrese-turbe* complexes. At the end of the nineteenth century there were 63 of these religious school-tomb complexes along the axis (out of a total of 166 *medreses* in Istanbul—and Üskudar). *Sebils* or fountains were often found with the *medrese-turbe* complex as well. The importance of *waq*f for the buildings along the Divanyolu is also apparent:

> [T]he axis in some stretches acquired architectural coherence beyond single architectural units only thanks to individual pashas' donations in the late seventeenth and eighteenth centuries. Small and medium *vakif* [*waqf*] complexes, whose accessory elements—*turbes*, *hazires* (mosque-associated cemeteries), walls, *sebils*—were inserted into the urban scene along with libraries and schools donated both by pashas and by

---

37  Ibid., 189.
38  Ibid., 197
39  Jacques Pervititch, *Sogorta Hiritalarinda Istanbul / Istanbul in the Insurance Maps of Jaques Pervititch* (Istanbul: Axa Oyak, with the Tarih Vakfi tarafindan hazirlanmistir [History Foundation of Turkey], n.d.).
40  Cerasi, "The Urban and Architectural Evolution of the Istanbul Divanyolu," 199.
41  Ibid.

court officials, contained elements that were the basis for a coherent street architecture even though they were all individually planned.[42]

Cerasi does note that for the *vakif* endowments, there were major differences between periods. No major mosques were built along the axis after the fifteenth and sixteenth centuries. By contrast, mostly small neighborhood mosques (*mescits*) were built (or restored) after this period, as well many *medrese* complexes were endowed, as previously mentioned. They did establish many mausoleums (*turbe*), surrounded by the *hazire* or family cemetery areas. In fact, these buildings with their *hazires* become quite significant for the urban space:

> [The pashas'] mausoleums, surrounded by *hazires* for their families and followers, were the main feature of street architecture. The sites most visible from the street were allotted to prominent persons; of the 106 documented Sadrazam tombs, twenty-five were concentrated on the eastern tract of the Divan axis between Firuz Aga and Aksaray. The *hazire* walls show maximum transparency and the epitaphs maximum visibility from the street. The considerable number of nineteenth-century tombstones replacing earlier ones points to the continuing competition by a changing patronage for best placement.[43]

So, the question for this paper, is: did the patronage and building along the Divanyolu axis, much of it evidently *waqf*, promote increasing the density of the built environment—or did it do the opposite? Even though it is rather speculative to come to any final conclusions, perhaps some trends are apparent nevertheless. The difficulty in coming up with any simple answer is brought out by the dynamic nature of the urban environment of Istanbul, which Cerasi characterizes well:

> The pattern of historical change is . . . complex and at first sight duplicitous. No general principles of growth and expansion can be perceived; many factors had a determinant effect of the structure of the Divan axis and its mutations; the loose, open-space typology of Ottoman architectural complexes and housing, catastrophic fires, the decay or abandonment of many *vakif* buildings, the renovation of others where patrons saw fit, the existence and even prevalence since late Byzantine times of semi-rural voids in the city fabric, and the transient tenure of palaces and *konaks* [mansions], including the reduction of their sizes.[44]

Numerous pashas endowed considerable numbers of monuments over time, and this *wafq* was significant in establishing a newly built environment in Istanbul. Yet, this was not just a continuous one-way path to a greater density of buildings. Destruction of buildings as well as renewed and new structures were all part of a dynamic urban fabric. All along the Divanyolu different sections might have more

---

[42]  Ibid., 203.
[43]  Ibid., 203–04.
[44]  Ibid., 210–11.

construction activity at a specific period, which "explains why almost any part of even this vital thoroughfare—central or marginal, minor or monumental—could at different times be a sequence of void and built-up spaces."[45] It is obvious that *waqf* property was a major player in this process. What we do not find out from Cerasi's study is whether or not mostly vacant land (such as gardens—or dilapidated buildings) is being endowed as *waqf*, or whether or not existing structures, such as houses, are being destroyed in order to establish monumental buildings—and even the family cemeteries. If the former, the *waqf* would certainly have been promoting a great density of buildings (even if not population), while, if the latter, then the establishment of *waqf* property would have even been causing less density of population in the city. Cerasi, however, does mention that many of the tombs and cemeteries were being reused (at least after 1800), and hence many of these are not always new constructions.[46]

Although we certainly do not have a definite answer to the question of the influence of *waqf* in the case of the Divanyolu, since it consisted of buildings along one (or more) of the principal avenues, we can assume that perhaps there was decreasing "open space" along these streets even as early as the sixteenth century. Cerasi seems to imply that particularly in the seventeenth and eighteenth centuries, "refoundations" were the pattern, and this rebuilding was often done as endowed property.[47] *Waqf* property was also contributing toward a greater density of buildings: "The continuous trend—probably starting early—to relatively higher densities, smaller *vakif* buildings, and new functional building types such as single-class schools brought about façade continuity on the street front, in combination with the basically open and low-density Ottoman housing and public-use archetypes."[48]

## Ottoman Aleppo and Cairo

André Raymond writes about "les grands waqfs" of Ottoman Aleppo and Cairo, where he shows considerable *waqf* construction in each of these cities in the sixteenth and seventeenth centuries.[49] He points out that the establishment of *waqf* was a substitute for the lack of an effective urban administration and management,

---

[45]   Ibid., 211.
[46]   Ibid., 229, fn. 58.
[47]   Ibid., 215.
[48]   Ibid., 217. Cerasi also mentions that the Devanyolu and Divan axis no longer exists, and that no one has studied the destruction of the axis; 231, fn 91.
[49]   André Raymond, "Les Grands waqfs et l'organisation de l'espace urbain a Alep et au Caire a l'epoque ottomane (XIV—XVII siecles)," *Bulletin d'etudes orientales* 31 (1979): 113–28.

and that there is not any overall central urban planning. Major urban endowments become part of the principal (partially) planned areas of the city. For instance, in Aleppo various mosque complexes were founded with considerable numbers of shops (*suqs*) endowed to support these structures. In terms of urban density, it is relevant to note that many of the major endowments of sixteenth-century Aleppo were founded in the newer, western part of the city, in what was evidently open and vacant land. In fact, as newer (*waqf*) buildings were established, they continued to be built in the more western suburbs of the city, creating a moving frontier of the built environment.

Abraham Marcus also includes an examination of *waqf* property in Aleppo in the eighteenth century.[50] He shows how *waqf* was extensive in the city and that it was a significant institution for the support of religious structures as well as the social services of the city. He notes that:

> In the absence of any comprehensive figures the financial records of the charitable foundations provide a sense of the magnitude of investment in the maintenance of public buildings and rental real estate. Deterioration and decay haunted the administrators without respite. On the average, one-quarter to one-third of the annual rental income they collected was eaten up by outlays on renovation and repairs, and even that level of expenditure often proved inadequate. Many of the foundations found themselves in deficit, reduced to borrowing hundreds of piastres from private individuals to finance urgent construction work.[51]

Marcus emphasizes that the state (government) invested very little in the city, and, hence, most all the housing and commercial projects were funded either by *waqf* or private individuals.

Marcus provides us with an account of considerable detail on the specifics of the urban *waqf* of Aleppo. For instance, for 98 *waqfs* from 1751–1753, which included mosques, *madrasas*, and fountains, there were 1,337 separate properties:

> Half of the total income of the foundations came from commercial real estate—stores, workshops, bath houses, coffee houses, oil presses, and caravanserais—located in neighborhood markets and the central bazaar area. Endowed houses were far less numerous and yielded a smaller share of the income. Fields and orchards on the outskirts and in the countryside contributed almost a quarter of the revenues; they were twice as productive as urban properties. At the other end of the scale stood the least lucrative—plots of urban land. These were the site of former waqf buildings that had fallen into ruin.[52]

---

[50]    Abraham Marcus, *The Middle East on the Eve of Modernity: Aleppo in the Eighteenth Century* (New York: Columbia University Press, 1989).

[51]    Ibid., 292.

[52]    Ibid., 307.

Many of these ruined areas, in fact, were leased on *hikr* agreements. Also, Marcus notes that 45 of the 98 *waqfs* ended their audited year with a deficit, and 13 had a zero balance. Only one *waqf* of the 98 purchased any additional real estate to increase its income.[53]

For Cairo, Raymond discusses the major *waqf* foundations of Ridwan Bey, established in the southern part of the city (south of Bab Zuwaila), which included mosques, caravanserais (*wakalas* or *hans*), *rabs* (see below), *hammans*, *sabils*, houses and shops. *Waqf* property also replaced tanning shops, which were moved farther south in Cairo, out of the area of the Ridwan Bey complex.[54] Raymond also has written about the *rab'*, a type of collective multi-level housing found in Cairo during the Ottoman period.[55] He indicates that many of these complexes were in the commercial areas and particularly inhabited by merchants. Although some *rab'* were privately owned, many were *waqf* (and much of the information on this housing, in fact, comes from the *waqfiyya* deed documents). It may be that the *waqf* played an important, critical role in promoting the establishment of this collective housing—which also would be a step toward a greater density of population.

Daniel Crecelius also focuses on Cairo, where he has examined the *waqf* of Muhammad Bey Abu al-Dhahab, the Mamluk *shaykh al-balad* who in 1774 constructed a large mosque-*madrasa-takiyya* complex in the center of the city, next to al-Azhar.[56]

Both agricultural lands and urban properties were endowed to build the complex as well as for its maintenance and the support of the personnel stipulated in the *waqfiyya*. What is particularly relevant for this paper, is Crecelius's account of how the property was acquired for building the complex. Most of the urban properties were already encumbered in various *waqfs*, and they were converted to support the new endowment. As Crecelius notes: "The waqfiyya itself states only that the various properties were acquired through purchase (*tabayu'*), exchange (*istibdal*), and the relinquishing of rights (*isqat*) by the previous owners or those such as beneficiaries and *nazirs* having rights to the usufruct of the property."[57] Hence, we have a situation where there is the transfer of *waqf* properties, including "the acquisition and destruction of buildings that were already encumbered in previous waqfs . . . ."[58] The building of this complex and the use of *waqf*, as

---

[53]   Ibid., 307–08.

[54]   Raymond, "Les Grands waqfs."

[55]   André Raymond, "The Rab': A Type of Collective Housing in Cairo during the Ottoman Period," *Architecture as Symbol and Self-Identity* (Cambridge, MA: Agha Khan Award for Architecture, Seminar Four, 1980), 55–62.

[56]   Daniel Crecelius, "The Waqf of Muhammad Bey Abu al-Dhahab in Historical Perspective," *International Journal of Middle East Studies* 23.1 (1991): 57–81.

[57]   Ibid., 59.

[58]   Ibid.

Crecelius points out, "demonstrates the broad range of commercial practices in use in 18th-century waqf law, particularly concerning the exchange or recirculation of properties supposedly endowed in perpetuity. Sixty-four court documents and several firmans and *taqsits* are cited in the waqfiyya as giving evidence of exclusive ownership and/or rights to the usufruct of properties Muhammad Bey endowed in his waqf."[59]

Crecelius provides information on the finances of the Muhammad Bey *waqf* as well as the number of personnel it supported. This included, for instance, for the *madrasa*, stipends for 16 *shaykhs* (representing three different law schools, the Hanafi, Malaki, and Shafi'i *madhhabs*), 18 assistants to read lessons, and 164 students. Each of these individuals received a daily stipend and an annual allotment of grain. Support also went to the *shaykh* in charge of the *takiyya*, as well as for 53 Turkish students residing there. Disbursements for the mosque and *takiyya* also included stipends and grain for doormen, janitors, water carriers, lamp lighters, (blind) *muezzins*, and many others. The *nazir* (*mutawalli*) of the *waqf* was Muhammad Bey himself, for which he received a considerable sum. He also donated his private library, more than 2,000 volumes, as part of the *waqf*. The total expenditures for the personnel amounted to 1,666.180 *nisf fiddas* annually.

This large complex built by Muhammad Bey shows us the considerable impact that *waqf* can have on the urban fabric—and hence density. It appears that this construction, which constituted about a city block, would also have been a most positive development for the city of Cairo. But Muhammad Bey died in 1775, a year after the complex was completed. What then occurred shows how *waqf* can be a detriment instead of an asset for the urban environment (and, in this instance, how quickly). As Crecelius notes: "None of Muhammad Bey's efforts to protect his waqf from violation achieved its purpose, for the greater portion of the waqf's revenues were diverted from their pious purposes within one year of the donor's death and the large madrasa-*takiyya* quickly fell into virtual disuse"[60] Several of Muhammad Bey's personal mamluks apportioned most of the revenues among themselves, as well as soon fighting among themselves. Very soon the doors of the mosque closed and most payments ceased. Documents in 1777 also show that the Egyptian (Ottoman) courts made rulings to legitimize the seizure of the *waqf*. For example, a *diwan* of assembled *amirs* certified that Muhammad Bey had illegally acquired *hikr* rents from certain rural properties and that they should resume to be applied to their former *waqf*—which was controlled by another mamluk (Isma'il Bey). By the nineteenth century there are several references to only a few services, such as the fountain, and to a few payments. "There is evidence . . . to suggest that the waqf was passed on to Muhammad Ali Pasha in a battered state minus the

---

59    Ibid.

60    Ibid., 71.

revenues of its agricultural lands and that it was unable to support its extensive educational and devotional functions from its remaining income."[61]

## Ottoman Damascus

For Ottoman Damascus, as previously mentioned, Deguilhem-Schoem discusses the use of *mursad* loans for urban *waqf* property.[62] A few examples of these give us a glimpse of how they might have impacted the urban environment. In 1791 a *mursad* was arranged for a house (*dar*) of the *waqf* of Kamal ad-Din Hamzah Zadeh, located in the an-Nahhasin neighborhood of the al-'Amarh district of Damascus. The tenants loaned the *waqf* funds to cover the costs of repairs, which was to be repaid by a reduction in rent. When concluded, the tenants paid only 2.08 percent of their former rent, and had "another 56 years" to repay their loan, in effect having a rent-free house in exchange for their loan. In another instance in 1797–1798, a *mursad* loan was used for the *waqf* of the al-Usqifah Mosque. To repair the wooden ceiling, the tenants of a three-storied building (which was *waqf* for the mosque) gave a loan, which was to be repaid by a sublease of the building in a period of six years. In another case, a house (*dar*), which was *waqf*, needed repairs; but in this case the loan was made by one of the higher *waqf* administrators (the *muwakkil*). The loan was to be repaid by a percentage of the rent, in five periods of three years each.

What Deguilhem-Schoem also points out, is that there is considerable evidence that many of the *mursad* loans were ways that the *waqf* administrators gained control over *waqf* revenues. As she notes: "It is difficult to believe that all of these mursads were genuine and that so many awqaf were bereft of necessary funds to repair their properties."[63] Citing the study by Baer for nearby Ottoman Jerusalem,[64] Deguilhem-Schoem stresses that these long-term contracts were a way that individuals established private rights and assets on *waqf* property, which then became private property over time. (And the fact that some *mursad* loans were arranged on *waqf* of newly constructed buildings in Jerusalem, shows that no repairs were really needed!)

The extensive use of *mursad* loans for *waqf* property, at least in some of the Arab Ottoman provinces of the late eighteenth and nineteenth centuries, needs to be evaluated for the theme of this paper. *Waqf* property is sometimes considered to deteriorate more rapidly than private property, because there are insufficient

---

[61]  Ibid., 74.
[62]  Deguilhem-Schoem, "The Loan of Mursad on Waqf Properties."
[63]  Ibid., 74.
[64]  Baer, "The Dismemberment of Awqaf in Early Nineteenth-Century Jerusalem."

funds or lack of desire for the upkeep of this mortmain property. By using *mursad* loans, *waqf* urban property was better supported, and, along with its transformation into private property, was supposed to facilitate preventing the deterioration of the urban fabric—which would be a factor for at least sustaining the density of built environment if that were happening. Damascus also grew and developed considerably because of *waqf*. For instance, Kana'an, quoting Weber, states that in the sixteenth century "the development of the Darwishiyya Street to the west of the old city . . . was the result of a series of great waqfs supporting both religious and commercial institutions established under the patronage of successive Ottoman governors . . . ."[65]

## Ottoman Jaffa

In 1812 the Mahmudi Mosque or the Abu Nabbut Mosque, known as the Great Mosque, was built in Jaffa by the acting governor of Jaffa, Muhammad Aga Abu Nubbut (r. 1803–1819).[66] There was a *madrasa* and two *sabils* (fountains) associated with the mosque, and to support these, Abu Nabbut endowed bazaars, khans, and many shops. Abu Nabbut, among his many duties as acting governor, was also the *i'mar al-bilad*, the person overseeing construction and urban development; then in 1807 he became the main administrator of the *waqf* of Jaffa. The city was still recovering from Napoleon's destruction at the end of the eighteenth century, and so "between 1810 and 1816, Abu Nabbut engaged in an energetic program of reconstruction that led to the rebuilding of the city's center and the restorations of its fortifications"[67] He developed as *waqf* a vast complex of about 2.5 hectares in the northeastern corner of the city, which consisted of "the Great Mosque, three sabils, two khans, two markets, sixty-seven shops, and several stores, houses, and light industries"[68] What is particularly relevant for this paper, is the statement by Kana'an that Abu Nabbut "was continuously trying to concentrate his waqf property within the area in the city surrounding his waqf property."[69] He notes that the accumulation of property lasted from 1806 until 1816. The construction began in about 1810, and:

---

[65]   Ruba Kana'an, "Waqf, Architecture, and Political Self-Fashioning: The Construction of the Great Mosque of Jaffa by Muhammad Aga Abu Nabbut," *Muqarnas* 18 (2001): 120–40; here 135; Stefan Weber, "Architecture and Urban Development of Damascus in the 16th and 17th Centuries," *Aram* 10 (1998): 431–71.

[66]   Kana'an, "Waqf, Architecture, and Political Self-Fashioning."

[67]   Ibid., 134.

[68]   Ibid.

[69]   Ibid.

the morphology of the buildings also suggests that the waqf increased the density of land use in the area, and this is corroborated by information derived from property transactions in the Islamic court which confirms that before 1810 the northern and eastern part of the city comprised a number of gardens and empty plots of land that were bought, built over, or filled in by Abu Nabbut's waqf complex.[70]

In some cases open space for new construction was created by the demolition of older buildings. In one instance Abu Nabbut demolished a ruined *khan* (caravanserai) and built a courtyard-type market of 36 shops with an elaborate *sabil*.

## Case Studies: Waqf in the Persian Realm

### Safavid Isfahan

When Isfahan became the new capital of the Safavid state, it was specifically developed to be a proper center for the regime by Shah Abbas, where, as the Iranians say, it then became "*Isfahan nesfi Jahan*" [Isfahan is half the world]. Robert McChesney has examined the *waqfs* of Shah Abbas (for Mashad as well as Isfahan) as an instrument of public policy—and we will see a somewhat different situation for Isfahan compared to the Ottoman capital, for instance.[71] Mashad was also another most significant town of this Shi'i state, and as the locus of the tomb of Imam Reza, the Eighth Imam, Shah Abbas was keen on helping insure its importance. Abbas endowed considerable rural property as *waqf* to support his construction activities—although some of this support may also have been certain fees and tax rights (converted to *waqf*) on property and ownership. Quoting a history of the *waqf* of Isfahan by Abd al-Husayn Sipanta, McChesney notes that in the endowments of 1604 there was:

> "an entire undivided half" of properties either 'at the shah's legal disposal' . . . or which had come 'into his personal ownership by valid contract . . . .' Here we see an important distinction drawn between rights such as fee and tax rights on property and actual ownership. The properties included . . . were khans, their fixtures and furnishings (*muttasilat*), lands, gardens, mills, and various types of irrigation channels . . . in Isfahan and elsewhere.[72]

---

[70]   Ibid., 134, my emphasis.
[71]   Robert D. McChesney, "Waqf and Public Policy: The Waqfs of Shah 'Abbas, 1011–1023/1602–14," *Asian and African Studies* 15.2 (1981): 165–90.
[72]   Ibid., 171.

In the winter of 1607–1608, Abbas placed into *waqf* all of his personal estates—which he had acquired legally over the years—as an endowment for the Fourteen Immaculate Ones (i.e., the Twelve Imams, plus Muhammad and Fatima).

In Isfahan, Shah Abbas sponsored considerable construction, much of which was endowed as *waqf*. This included the major, huge square, the Maydan-i Shah, as well as a caravanserai, a *qaysariya* (enclosed bazaar), the entire bazaar around the *maydan*, and a large public bath (*hammam*). Much of the rental income from this *waqf* was endowed to support stipends (*wazifa*) and living allowances (*madad-i ma'ash*) for Hussain (i.e. Shi'i *sayyids* and *sayyidas* living in Medina or in Najaf. However, before any of the funds were given to the specified beneficiaries, the "maintenance and capital needs of the income-producing properties had to be met."[73]

Many of Shah Abbas's endowments were from the rural areas in order to support urban structures and individuals. Whereas we usually think of rural *waqf* as endowed agricultural land or water shares, McChesney shows examples of *waqf* being the tax revenues and other fees that were owed to the Shah. Hence, there was a distinction between the actual ownership of private property and the rights to certain revenues by legal contract. McChesney notes that this is an unresolved legal issue, a situation where something is being converted into *waqf* which is actually not one's own property. As he speculates: "Without access to legal challenges and *fatwa*-judgements on the matter it is useless to speculate on the question of legality. It is enough . . . to note that granting of tax rights as waqf seems to have been practised and accepted."[74]

In 1602–1603 Shah Abbas also had made major endowments to the Shrine of Imam Reza in Mashad. McChesney quotes (translates) a work by Mustawfi Hamadani: "Abbas donated 'all the improved land of the Sacred Threshold around the Pure Sepulchre and Sacred Courtyard and the land around the Blessed Foot and around the Sacred Courtyard . . . .'"[75] As McChesney notes, "The object of the waqf was to provide more cemetery space for those who wished to be buried near the Eighth Imam in the shrine precincts. The stipulations of the waqf set the distance from the Imam's grave as which people could be buried as well as the fees to be charged and the precedence given to those wanting burial there."[76] The burial fees (*haqq al-ard*) were used for repairs and upkeep of the buildings related to the shrine. Although it is not entirely clear how Abbas might have acquired the land around the shrine for the endowment, McChesney asserts that "Shah Abbas appears to be making waqf here not of the land at the shrine but

---

73  Ibid., 172.
74  Ibid., 177.
75  Ibid., 169.
76  Ibid.

rather of the right of the shrine administration to institute and control the systematic collection of interment fees."[77] Most interesting for us, nevertheless, proves to be the point that the *waqf* was providing for more cemetery space. Whether this meant the clearing of existing buildings and housing to make this space, or whether it is just insuring that such space was available, we seem to have a case here where *waqf* is promoting less dense use of urban space (for live individuals, anyway!).

In a *waqf* of 1607–1609 for the town of Ardabil there were considerable "movables" endowed, including jewelry, copperware, carpets, livestock, and even china. In the *waqf* deeds there was the typical "admonition against the purchase or leasing of any of *mawqufat* [*waqf*] lest the usufruct be diverted to others."[78] A further key point, and one that we need to be very aware as to how *waqf* property might affect the built environment, is that "the *mutawalli* was always to administer the *waqf*'in accordance with the requirements of the time (*bi-maslahat-i waqt*).' That is, if at some future time it seemed proper to sell or lease the properties, the *mutawalli* was presumably not restrained from doing so."[79] It is this flexibility that must be understood if we are to understand fully how *waqf* might have affected the built environment, and hence the urban density.

Shah Abbas is best known for the construction of the new square or *maydan* (Maydan-i Shah), with its bazaar and mosque complex (Masjid-i Shah) in Isfahan. That rebuilding was used to transform the city into the proper, beautiful capital of Safavid Iran. There were many gardens, orchards, agricultural lands, and commercial establishments endowed for this construction. The limits placed on Shah Abbas's ability to build whatever and wherever he might please, however, are also brought out by the construction and *waqf* in Isfahan. Shah Abbas had originally wanted to renovate and refurbish the older bazaar and *maydan* complex around the old Seljuq Friday Mosque, north of Maydan-i Shah. However, the merchants of Isfahan refused to allow him to redevelop this area, and so Abbas built commercial shops around the Maydan-i Shah instead, which had been built a few years earlier. A new, large mosque, Masjed-i Shah, was also built on the *maydan*, part of the motivation being an incentive to draw merchants and customers away from the older bazaar and the Congregation (Friday) Mosque. All of the newly constructed buildings were *waqf*. McChesney also speculates that as *waqf*, the new retail establishments could be more attractive than the older shops because "it seems fairly clear that the [*mutawalli*] could offer the shops at competitive if not under-market rents. There is little in the waqf material . . . that suggests that the principal aim of the *mutawalli* was to get a high yield for the

---

[77]   Ibid., 169–70.

[78]   Ibid., 173.

[79]   Ibid.

beneficiaries. To the contrary [the *waqf* document] stresses the necessity of re-investment before any payment of stipends"[80] (188–89).

## Afghanistan

McChesney provides other examples for this paper, the *waqf* of the Khwaja Abu Nasr Parsa Shrine in Balk, Afghanistan as well as his (already) classic work on the *waqf* of the 'Alid shrine at Balk, which becomes the kernel for the development of the town of Mazar-i Sharif in northern Afghanistan.[81] The shrine or tomb (*mazar*) of Khwaja Abu Nasr Parsa commemorated a fifteenth-century Naqshbandi sufi. There also was a *madrasa* connected to the shrine as well as a cemetery, and soon over time other shrines, which "in all probability . . . included the tombs of the three or four generations of Khwaja Abu Nasr Parsa's descendants . . . interred there as well as others for whom burial within the charismatic range of Abu Nasr Parsa was deemed desirable."[82] At least six large *madrasas* were also built next to the shrine. As a large, prestigious mausoleum complex, would this *waqf* actually have prevented the establishment of houses, and hence inhibited a denser development of Balk—or would this endowed property have attracted people to build near the buildings—and so promoted the intensification of the use of urban land? Although, there is no definite answer to that question, McChesney does point out that "the late sixteenth and early seventeenth centuries saw the transformation of the area surrounding the Parsa complex with the creation of a large educational and residential district."[83] I should also mention that Balk had an inner city within its old walls, while the Parsa shrine and new neighborhoods were all outside that city but within another set of (new) walls built by the Timurids.[84] By the eighteenth century many of the *madrasas* were collapsing and disappearing, but the shrine complex itself was maintained, continuing to be supported as *waqf*. What was the situation of the residential areas by the eighteenth century would be quite interesting to know of course.

Concerning the 'Alid shrine for which McChesney documents the *waqf* for a four hundred year period, the main (and very extensive) endowments were particularly agricultural land and irrigation water in the nearby, surrounding area

---

[80]  Ibid., 188–89.

[81]  McChesney, *Waqf in Central Asia*; "Architecture and Narrative: The Khwaja Abu Nasr Parsa Shrine: Part I: Constructing the Complex and its Meaning, 1469–1696," *Muqarnas* 18 (2001): 94–119.

[82]  Ibid., 100.

[83]  Ibid., 109, my emphasis.

[84]  See ibid., 100, fig. 3: Balkh, ca. 1690.

of the shrine and along the main irrigation canals.[85] Obviously, the great amount
of rural *waqf* enabled the shrine to continue to be supported over this very long
period of time, although McChesney notes how the amount of endowed irrigated
agricultural land diminished considerably from the seventeenth to the nineteenth
century. In any case, an important source of *waqf* revenue was from rents and fees
collected from urban properties. One reason for the reduction of the rural,
agricultural *waqf* was actually the expansion of the city of Mazar-i Sharif around
the shrine:

> What seems to have happened [for the reduction of rural waqf] . . . is linked to the
> overall transformation of the shrine into the main urban center of the old Balkh
> appanage under Afghan hegemony. With the urbanization of Mazar-i Sharif, the need
> for a permanent bazaar, and the creation of all the ancillary institutions to which a
> bazaar gives rise, the commercial pressure on the agricultural waqf immediately
> adjacent to the shrine must have increased . . . . [I]f the bulk of the land was held in
> waqf or controlled by the shrine, then it was the waqf land, we have every reason to
> believe, that was transformed by these pressures.[86]

Even though McChesney does not have any direct evidence for how *waqf* urban
property might have been transformed into private land, he certainly suspects that
a number of the "legal devices" played a role, as outlined in the beginning of this
paper:

> Our indirect evidence . . . suggests very strongly that some . . . legal devices were
> helping shape property tenure in nineteenth-century Mazar-i Sharif. The farman of
> 1889, by classifying income to the shrine from commercial property in the city as
> distinct from the waqf income, is almost prima facie evidence that a process of
> divestment had been going on for a long time.[87]

McChesney also discusses the contents of a *waqfnameh* by Muhammad 'Alam Khan
that was issued in 1873, which actually discloses the great amount of private
property (*milk-i khalis*), particularly shops, around the shrine, including
considerable property owned by Muhammad 'Alam himself.[88] (Some of the urban
private property is discerned by the fact that each of the *waqf* properties is
described by listing the adjacent properties.) Nevertheless, the urban commercial
(*waqf*) income for the shrine was probably still quite large, despite the
transformations into private property. In fact, it appears that some of this now
private land still brought income to the shrine, particularly in the form of fees to

---

[85]  McChesney, *Waqf in Central Asia*. Although a theme addressed throughout the book, see esp. the
      section called "Land Use and the 'Alid Waqf," 276–92.
[86]  Ibid., 284.
[87]  Ibid., 287.
[88]  Ibid., 289–90.

use the land. In an 1889 *farman* of 'Abd al-Rahman Khan, the Amir of Afghanistan, these fees are designated as *tahja'i*, a fee for a place to trade in the bazaar, and *girayah-i dukkanha*, which was a rental income from shops (which probably had been *waqf* originally, then transformed into private property leased by the shrine). What was the difference between *waqf* and private property here (as defined by the late nineteenth-century Kabul central government) is not clear. But the transformation is quite dramatic, as McChesney asserts:

> Under the Tuqay-Timurids, fiscal prerogatives on the land under the shrine's jurisdiction were all or mostly ceded to it as "waqf." But the superseding of the shrine-state by the Afghan state removed those fiscal prerogatives from the mutawalli's account books. 'Abd al-Rahman's [1889] farman is unambiguous proof of the process, for nowhere in it do we find mention either of the right of the shrine to certain tax fees or of the exemption of shrine properties, whether classified as waqf or not, from taxation.[89]

This is also the result of the transformation of a shrine-state to a state shrine, which is what McChesney's monograph on the 'Alid shrine documents over the span of four centuries.

## Qajar Tabriz

Christoph Werner has provided us with an in-depth analysis of the social and economic history of the Iranian city of Tabriz at the end of the Zand and early Qajar periods (1747–1848).[90] Tabriz, located in Azerbaijan, northwestern Iran, was founded during Abbasid times and has been an important city throughout the Islamic period (and even being the capital under the Mongols in the thirteenth and fourteenth centuries). By the early Qajar period in the early nineteenth century the city began to grow considerably and the urban fabric expanded beyond its original city walls: "Soon, former quarters of the town that had been deserted and lay outside the walls, were now reincorporated again into the understanding of the town Tabriz. The area inside the walls now formed the centre of the city, composed predominantly of the large bazaar district and the princely residence and its administration [the palace and the *divankhana*]"[91] This inner city was sometimes referred to as the *qal'a* in the Qajar period, and European visitors often called the surrounding neighborhoods or quarters the "suburbs" or "*faubourgs*."

---

[89]   Ibid., 292.

[90]   Christoph Werner, *An Iranian Town in Transition: A Social and Economic History of the Elites of Tabriz, 1747–1848*. Documenta Iranica et Islamica, 1 (Wiesbaden: Harrassowitz Verlag, 2000).

[91]   Ibid., 72.

The city also had suffered with the fall of the Safavids and the occupation of Azerbaijan by the Ottomans in the eighteenth century, and then much of the town was destroyed in a strong earthquake in January 1780, so the rapid growth of the city thereafter represented a substantial rebuilding effort.

Tabriz was rebuilt and redeveloped with both *waqf* and private property. The bazaar was rebuilt as a new complex and numerous new, but smaller mosques, were constructed. There were many small *waqfs* established in the early Qajar period, which also included endowed shares of water from *qanats*. In fact, of 71 *qanats* that came to Tabriz in this period, many were newly built or renovated: As Werner notes:

> The majority of the qanats appear to have been newly built or completely renovated in the nineteenth century, responding to both the damages wrecked by the quake of 1780 and the growing need for water, both inside the city and in its more rural suburbs. Whereas qanats designed primarily for the irrigation of the orchards and fields around Tabriz were often held in joint ownership with shares linked to the possession of land, those providing water for the residential areas of the town display more complex patterns of ownership. Some of the older and traditional qanats supplying water to specific areas of the town were held as communal property of the respective quarter, the use of their water was free and maintenance was financed by fees paid by the households.[92]

Many of these *qanats* were financed by private individuals (and sometimes endowed as *waqf*), but not usually by officials of the state (such as the governor). The supply of water was obviously important for enabling various neighborhoods to be established and maintained, although, the rather hilly typography of Tabriz did not result in the qanat-influenced morphology and pattern of the Iranian city as I have documented for Yazd and other Iranian cities.[93] There was, however, considerable building construction by government officials, particularly 'Abbas Mirza in the early decades of the nineteenth century. Werner reminds us that it is difficult to separate private from public in such cases, and that "'Abbas Mirza actually had to buy real-estate in respectable quantities, instead of simply seizing it and expropriating their owners without compensation. We can not exclude a certain amount of coercion exercised against proprietors unwilling to sell, but at least in the documents there is nothing to indicate shady legal procedures or unrealistic prices."[94] 'Abbas Mirza acquired 38 properties from 1809 to 1826, most of them in the inner quarters, including in Chahar-Minar, the old city quarter. They included mostly houses, but also a caravanserai, a huge garden south of the

---

[92]  Ibid., 77.

[93]  Michael E. Bonine, "The Morphogenesis of Iranian Cities," *Annals of the Association of American Geographers* 69.2 (1979): 208–24.

[94]  Werner, *An Iranian Town in Transition*, 86.

Chahar-Minar, shops, smaller gardens, and shares of two *qanats*. As for the garden, it was probably purchased to enlarge 'Abbas Mirza's residence in the center of the city.[95]

One of the major insights from Werner's work is that it shows how *waqf* property was transformed in Tabriz during the Qajar period, indicating how endowments were altered and how Qajar elites incorporated the institution into a changing social and economic system. As Werner notes:

> Control of the vaqf, especially a strong grip on its properties and the distribution of its income, was the central issue in the vaqf's history in Qajar times. Primarily, this meant access to the position of mutavalli, as the official administrator of the foundation, but . . . there rarely existed an unchallenged mutavalli—quite often there was even more than one at the same time.[96]

In some instances no *mutawalli* is mentioned in the documents, and such an administrator simply appears from among the descendants who are supposed to be the beneficiaries of a *waqf*. A person who is one of the descendants or inheritors (*vurras*) of the founder may act as the representative or agent of the property. "This is also a first sign that vaqf-property was increasingly considered as inherited personal property jointly held by a community of inheritors instead of being in the inalienable possession of the endowments."[97] There may be several lineages of descendants competing with one another, which could even lead to law suits in the courts.

Using the Zahiriya endowment (*mauqufat-i Zahiriya*) as one of his main examples, Werner shows how this *waqf*, founded by the Safavid *vazir* of Azerbaijan in Tabriz in 1679–1680 in Safavid times, was transformed in Qajar times into rather different ownership.[98] The *waqf* complex was built around the shrine or tomb of Sayyid Hamza, and included a mosque, *madrasa*, and other buildings, such as a pharmacy (*dar al-shifa*). It was endowed with considerable *waqf* property. Although half of the revenues were to go for the upkeep of the complex, by Qajar times, even though the complex existed, there does not seem to be any evidence of such revenues. What happened to the *waqf*'s funds? As Werner observes, "[I]t is quite safe to assume that the vaqf was gradually transformed from a 'mixed' vaqf to a pure, private family vaqf, with the descendants regarding the vaqf's holdings and their income as their inherited property."[99] The *mutawalli* often made individual contracts with the representatives of the lineage descendents, and property was

---

[95]    See the discussion in ibid., 86–88.
[96]    Ibid., 103.
[97]    Ibid.
[98]    See the discussion in ibid., 99–117.
[99]    Ibid., 110.

lent out to third parties. In some cases the *mutawalli* had to take his case to the court to try and regain *waqf* property. As Werner elucidates:

> [I]t was not so much a question of guarding vaqf properties, but rather a sometimes desperate attempt to fight against the constantly occurring acts of usurpation and losses threatening the existence of the vaqf as a whole. How successful the respective mutavallis were in this fight is difficult to decide, but probably a clear distinction evolved between vaqf properties held and controlled directly by the descendants, which even if disputed among the heirs themselves, remained at least secure inside the foundation itself, and contested properties in the actual possession (*tasarruf*) of strangers.[100]

By the mid and late nineteenth century the Zahiriya *waqf* had been totally transformed from a charitable and public endowment to a purely family *waqf*, with many of the descendants (the beneficiaries) far from Tabriz. "[T]he original primary aim of the vaqf, which was the upkeep of the complex around the shrine of Sayyid Hamza with its mosque and madrasa, seems to have been forgotten completely."[101] By the end of the nineteenth century the shrine complex was in ruins (and it was even used as a place for the storage of corpses!). In fact, throughout the Qajar period, in contrast to the large Safavid endowments, there were few newly constructed buildings founded and supported by *waqf* in Tabriz in the nineteenth century; endowments hence played a minimal role in the rebuilding and expansion of the city following the earthquake of 1780.


## Conclusion: The Role of *Waqf* in the Density of the Built Environment

We return to our initial question: how did *waqf* influence the built environment, and more specifically, the density of the *medina*? Obviously, endowed property was extremely important as both a social and economic institution within Middle Eastern and North African Muslim society, an understanding that is only beginning to emerge with many new in-depth studies from the last several decades.[102] But *waqf* property, obviously, did have a potential negative side effect. As McChesney asserts: "Waqf proved remarkably durable as a way in which to

---

[100]  Ibid., 116.

[101]  Ibid., 117.

[102]  Besides the works cited above, more recent studies that have put *waqf* in its wider social and economic contexts include Siraj Sait and Hilary Lim, *Land, Law and Islam: Property and Human Rights in the Muslim World* (London and New York: Zed Books, 2006), see Chap. 7, "The Waqf (Endowment) and Islamic Philanthropy," 147–73; and Amy Singer, *Charity in Islamic Societies* (Cambridge: Cambridge University Press, 2008).

maintain capital. An inherent contradiction in the institution, the irreconcilability of the legal notion of waqf as permanent and immutable with the impermanent nature of all material things, always had to be overcome."[103] But we also need to recognize, as Werner notes, that "like all aspects of Islamic law in practice, it [*waqf*] was much more subject to change and transformation than hitherto assumed. Vaqf [*waqf*] as a popular institution in 'use' was continuously modified and adapted according to the needs, wishes and ideas of the people involved with it."[104] Baer has also realized that "throughout Islamic history *awqaf* have been undergoing a perpetual process of dismemberment."[105] Furthermore, we have also seen with the brief example from Marcus how the *waqf* urban property of Aleppo tended to be rather less productive than private land in the city.[106]

Was *wafq* property positive or negative for the process of increasing the density of the urban environment—the *medina*? This is a question that cannot be simply answered. Certainly, many of the larger (*les grandes)* waqfs contributed to important and significant urban construction, both for major religious structures, such as mosques or *madrasas*, as well as for the urban property endowed for such structures—particularly bazaars and commercial shops. What happens to urban *waqf* certainly differs from period to period, as well as varies from one region or one city to another. In some instances, particularly, when there was a strong, powerful ruler/governor or other such official, *waqf* might have been an instrument that turned gardens and orchards—and vacant land—into urban structures. Endowed buildings themselves might have been large structures (and taking up a lot of urban space), and they might have stimulated residential areas in their vicinity, as well as having substantial commercial property (as in bazaars) built to endow them. The examples for Istanbul as analyzed by Inalcik and Kayaalp are good illustrations of this pattern.[107] Hence, we can say that this type of *waqf* was certainly promoting the density of the *medina* in these situations.

However, as we have seen, *waqf* property in the city was often not generating sufficient—or any—income and was even in decline. We have seen how considerable *waqf* urban property was dilapidated or in ruins, and that many ways were used to lease that land to attempt to make it productive (or repaired)—and that these devices often led to the transformation of *waqf* into private property. In these cases, we would have to speculate that *waqf* property is causing a decline in the density of the urban environment. On the other hand, since *waqf* property, even when dilapidated, is often transformed into private property—perhaps in the

---

103    McChesney, *Waqf in Central Asia*, 317.
104    Werner, *An Iranian Town in Transition*, 97.
105    Baer, "The Dismemberment of Awqaf in Early Nineteenth-Century Jerusalem," 220.
106    Marcus, *The Middle East on the Eve of Modernity.*
107    Inalcik, "Istanbul: An Islamic City;" Kayaalp, "The Role of Imperial Mosque Complexes."

long-run the *waqf* property was contributing to an increase of intensity of land use and hence to an increase in the density of the built environment of the city.

In the final analysis we have to say that *waqf* might in some instances have been promoting the increase of the density of the *medina*—while in other cases we see that it was an influential factor for the decrease in that density. However, when we take into consideration the founding of large complexes of buildings and the commercial establishments to support them, with the resulting impact on residential areas, we probably would lean toward saying that *waqf* was indeed contributing to the expansion and density of the urban environment in the early modern period. Yet, more studies and analyses are needed before we can characterize in more subtle detail these two somewhat rather contradictory influences of *waqf* on the density of the built environment of the traditional Middle Eastern / North African *medina*.

Pınar Kayaalp

(Ramapo College of New Jersey)

# The Role of Imperial Mosque Complexes (1543-1583) in the Urbanization of Üsküdar

In 1543, when the ground was broken for Mihrümah's mosque complex (*külliye*) in the district of Üsküdar, the city of Istanbul across the Bosphorus was the most heavily populated urban center in the European continent, with a population between 410,000 and 520,000.[1] The city's resident population had grown fivefold to 500,000 from the year of its conquest by Mehmed II (1453) to the year Selim II ascended the throne (1566).[2] The great number of civic and religious edifices, private palaces and mansions, ordinary dwellings, and business structures constructed during this period had given the capital city the characteristics of a true metropolis which even impressed Christian travelers from as far away as northwestern Europe. As Doğan Kuban vividly describes, most dwellers lived in gardened abodes, with Christian and Jewish populations concentrating in Eminönü, Samatya, Kumkapı, and Fener; the streets were lined with wooden stalls and shops, with an occasional covered market (*bedesten*) or inn (*han*) built in brick

---

[1] Robert Mantran, translated by Mehmet Ali Kılıçbay and Enver Özcan, *17. Yüzyılın İkinci Yarısında Istanbul: Kurumsal, İktisadi, Toplumsal Tarih Denemesi I* (Ankara: Türk Tarih Kurumu Basımevi, 1990), 45. The presence of permanent embassies in Constantinople from the mid-sixteenth century onward, along with their establishment in Western capitals, shows that in diplomatic terms this city was part of Europe, a door in the wall between Islam and Christianity, the 'seat of the Caliphate' as well as the 'system of Europe.' See Philip Mansel, *Constantinople: City of the World's Desire, 1453-1924* (New York: St. Martin's Griffin 1998), 189 and 415. I would like to express my gratitude to Albrecht Classen, Linda Darling, and Marilyn Sandidge for their critical reading of my article and their many valuable comments. I would also like to thank Gülru Necipoğlu for granting me permission to reproduce images from her *The Age of Sinan: Architectural Culture in the Ottoman Empire,* (London: Reaktion Books, 2005).

[2] Enrico Guidoni, "Sinan's Construction of the Urban Panorama," *Environmental Design* 5/6 (1987): 20-32; here 22. Hans G. Egli puts the figure at 600,000. See Hans G. Egli, *Sinan: An Interpretation,* (Istanbul: Ege Yayınları, 1997), 140.

or stone; hawkers carried their wares on animals of burden; porters, cavalry troops, Janissaries, seamen strolled in public areas and markets; the harbor was covered with galleons, galleys, sailboats, and caïques.[3] Of the many public structures dotting the city, the ones built for charity (*hayrats* or *vakıfs*) were greatly venerated, as even a small public fountain with fresh water and a drinking pot would be construed as a major act of magnanimity, a virtuous deed that evoked a heartfelt blessing from those who partook of its bounty.[4]

At the midpoint of the sixteenth century, the two choicest districts of the capital were Istanbul proper (*nefs-i İstanbul*) and Eyüb. Galata, on the northeastern tip of the Golden Horn, was virtually a foreign land, populated exclusively by Europeans. As for Üsküdar, a minor suburb encircled by meadows and vineyards,[5] it was little more than a military and trading junction. Mehmed II, Selim I, and Süleyman I had used Üsküdar mostly as a gathering place for their armies setting out on campaigns into Anatolia. Üsküdar also served as the unloading site of considerable amounts of goods and people that flowed from the opposite direction, especially at the end of victorious military operations. As such, Üsküdar was a halting station, a gateway to the capital, with a minuscule resident population dwelling mostly in the villages on the hilltop or in the settlements around the jetty. The former were normally engaged in horticulture and the latter in fishing and seamanship.[6] Yet, fifty years later, Üsküdar materializes as a vibrant urban center, guarded by a permanent Janissary regiment and boasting a bustling bazaar with myriad shops and warehouses. This previously inconsequential suburb of the capital had progressed administratively as well, emerging as a full-fledged district (*kaza*), under the tutelage of a high-ranking judge (*kadı*), district superintendent (*kaymakam*), and police chief (*subaşı*).[7] Though deprived of a harbor and at the mercy of capricious northerly and southerly winds, it was closely connected to Istanbul by means of a brisk sea traffic,[8] moving not only Üsküdar's

3    Doğan Kuban, *Sinan's Art and Selimiye* (Istanbul: The Economic and Social History Foundation of Turkey, 1997), 22.

4    Kuban, *Sinan's Art*, 22.

5    Stephan Yerasimos, "Üsküdār," *Encyclopaedia of Islam*, 2nd edition (Leiden and London: Brill 1986-2002), 10, 924, referring to a (privy) register of 1498.

6    Mantran, *Istanbul*, vol. 1, 82.

7    Evliya Çelebi specifies that the *kadı* of Üsküdar would have to be a highly learned scholar of Muslim law, worthy of a salary of five hundred *akçe*, and the *kaymakam* would have to be chosen from among "the highly notable (*nakībü'l-eşrāf*)." See *Evliya Çelebi Seyahatnamesi 1: Istanbul*, ed. Orhan Saik Gökyay (Istanbul: Yapı Kredi Yayınları, 1996), fol. 141b.

8    Guidoni, "Urban Panorama," 23, referring to Robert Mantran's *La Vie quotidienne a Constantinople au temps de Soliman le Magnifique et ses successeurs, XVIe et XVIIe siecles* (Paris: Hachette, 1965), remarks that the crossing was provided in the seventeenth century by some 15,000 boats. Actually, Mantran's data refer to the sea traffic between the two sides of the Golden Horn rather than the

urban residents across the Bosphorus to pay a visit or to run an errand, but also people from across the water to partake of the district's substantial religious, social, commercial, military, and educational amenities.

When Evliya Çelebi, the famous seventeenth-century Ottoman traveler, surveyed Üsküdar a hundred years after the construction of the first of the three imperial *vakıfs*, he described a sprawling urban community accommodating seventy Muslim quarters, eleven Greek and Armenian quarters, and one Jewish quarter. The traveler reports that the imperial bazaar (*esvak-ı sultani*) of Üsküdar contained 2060 shops, 11 caravansaries, and 105 *hans* with 40 to 50 cells in each.[9] Evidently, Üsküdar, notwithstanding the bustling commercial activity that took place on its square abutting the jetty, had retained its rural character on the hilltop, as evidenced by Evliya's trademark hyperbole that "'aded-i bāğ-ı engūr dörd bindir . . . ve 'aded bostān-ı gülistān üç yüzdür ve bunların her birinde niçe elvān-ı şükūfe ve ezhārat hāsıl olur kim rāyıhasından ādemin dimāğı muattar olur"[10] (there are four thousand vineyards . . . and three hundred rose gardens producing many thousands flowers and blossoms of different color, from whose aroma a person's brain gets fragrant). He goes on to intimate that this "Şehr-i 'azām ve bilādı kadīm bender-ābād Üsküdār"[11] (glorious city, the ancient town, and prosperous abode of Üsküdar) had bolstered rather than shed its military legacy in that it now contained a permanent Janissary barrack and the offices of the colonel of the local cavalry bodies (*sipahi kethüdayeri*) as well as the chiefs of both the local armory and the artillery (*cebeci ve topçu ihtiyarları*).[12] Üsküdar had not entirely outgrown its old role as the pulsating terminus of the overland route

---

9 Bosphorus. See Mantran, *Istanbul*, vol. 1, 71. Still, a good portion of this traffic must have taken place between Üsküdar and Istanbul or Galata.
*Seyahatname*, fol. 143a and b. In spite of this claim, Evliya Çelebi lists only three caravansaries—that of Mihrümah, Nurbanu, and Kösem (143a). As for Evliya's assertion that there were 105 *hans* frequented by merchants and travelers, he lists only two—Nısf Pasha and At Pazarı (143a). It is a small wonder how the bazaar, squeezed between the Mihrümah Mosque and the jetty, could accommodate 2060 shops. Impervious to such considerations, Evliya accentuates the vastness of the marketplace, noting that there were "even two tanneries in two separate locations, a well as a covered Sipahi Mall with two doors on opposite sides," *Seyahatname*, fol. 143b. However, considering that this mall "lack[ed] a *bedesten*," *Seyahatname*, fol. 143b, it could not be a venue of great consequence. Yet, much of the statistics provided by Evliya has often been taken by authors at face value. See Al-Ayvansarayi, Hafız Hüseyin, *Hadikat al-Cevami*, ed. and trans. into English by Howard Crane as *The Garden of the Mosques: Hafız Hüseyin Al-Ayvansarayî's Guide to the Muslim Monuments of Ottoman Istanbul* (Leiden: E. J. Brill, 2000), for instance, in which Crane, referring to another edition of Evliya Çelebi, states that there existed not 105, but 500 *hans* in the same marketplace (489, note 3411).

10 *Seyahatname*, fol. 143b.
11 *Seyahatname*, fol. 142b.
12 *Seyahatname*, fol. 141b.

through Anatolia, either. Evliya's description of Üsküdar strongly reflects the vestiges of the transient and heterogeneous spirit of the old military and trading junction that still hovered above its urbanized neighborhoods:

> Ahālī-i Üsküdār [çok] fırkadır. Bir fırkası 'askerī tāifesinin a'yān u eşraflarıdir kim günā-gün akmişe-i fāhire giyerler ve bir fırkası bağbāndır ve bir fırkası 'ulemā ve sulehādır ve bir fırkası fakr u faka kanā'at itmiş Giysüdār Mehmed Efendi fukarālarıdır kim haddeden bīrūndur. Ve bir fırkası keştibān ve kayıkçıyāndır ve bir zümresi esnāf-ı tüccārān ehl-i sanāyi'ātdır. Bu kavmīn libāsları iktidārlarına gore kapama ve çuha dolama ve ferāce giyerler. Bu halkın ekseri Anadolı diyārı halkı olmağıla lehçe-i mahsūsaları Etrāk lisānıdır ammā şehrinde hāsıl olan çelebileri fesāhat u belāgat üzre tekellüm idüp 'ulemāsı ve şu'arāsı vardır.[13]

> [Üsküdar's population is made up of (many) classes. One class is that of the chiefs and notables of military troops wearing their splendid raiment each and every day. Other classes comprise the viticulturists, the ulema, the pious, and the myriad dervishes of Giysüdar Mehmed Efendi. Still another class comprises sailors and boatmen, and yet another merchants and artisans. The clothes of these people, depending on their [economic] capacity, can be the cloaks fastened in front, broadcloth wrap-arounds, and cloaks worn by the ulema. Since most of these people come from the provinces of Anatolia, their proper dialect is Anatolian Turkish; only the educated gentlemen, having grown up in this city, converse with clarity and eloquence. (Yet,) it has (its own) poets and men of learning.]

One may conclude from the above excerpt that Üsküdar had not only shorn up its military and, by extrapolation, commercial foundation, but also supplemented them with a thick religious and mystical overlay. Indeed, the relatively small district came to accommodate a disproportionate number of mosques and dervish lodges vis-à-vis the larger districts of the capital.[14] Hundreds of sufi dervishes dwelled in numerous lodges (*tekkes* or *rıbats*), performing "sonorous rites at the end of the Friday prayer, intoxicating the nearby residents with their sweet cadence and lilt."[15] The transformation of Üsküdar from a site of sporadic army movement and trading activity into an urban hub with military, commercial, and spiritual overtones paralleled substantial public and private construction activity. As for the latter, Üsküdar had been chosen by many members of the royal household and high-ranking officials as the site for their summer palaces (*sarays*) and mansions (*kasırs*). These individuals evidently sought the serenity of Üsküdar's coastline, excursion spots (*mesires*), and promenades (*seyrangahs*), as

---

13  *Seyahatname*, fol. 144a.
14  Specifically, Al-Ayvansarayi lists 77 mosques in the district. See *Hadikat al-Cevami*, 489-537; Evliya Çelebi reports a total of 47 of dervish lodges in Üsküdar, the largest being the Halveti *tekke* of Mahmud Efendi. See *Seyahatname*, fol. 142b.
15  Evliya, *Seyahatname*, fol. 142b, adds that there were 300 dervishes living in the Mahmud Efendi *Tekke* alone.

well as the plentitude of the hunting grounds in its hinterland. At the time
Nurbanu ordered the construction of her mosque complex in 1571, four famed
viziers—Sokollu Mehmed, Rüstem, Koca Mehmed, and Şemsi—had already built
opulent palaces in the district.[16]

The Ayazma Palace was the first Ottoman imperial construction in Üsküdar, built
by Mehmed II. It was constructed immediately after the conquest of Constantinople in 1453 upon the foundations of the Scutarion, the ancient palace that lent its
name to this former suburb of Chalcedon.[17] Imperial pious architecture also began
with Mehmed II, who commissioned the small Fatih Mosque (Mosque of the
Conqueror) in the Salacak Quarter in Üsküdar.[18] The honor of erecting the first
post-conquest mosque complex in the suburb, however, is ascribed to Rum
Mehmed Pasha, who briefly served as Mehmed II's grand vizier (1467-1470). His
mosque complex (külliye), abutting the gardens of the Ayazma Palace, was erected
in 1469.[19] It comprised an "unpretentiously built ... congregational mosque, [with]
a divinity school (medrese) and, nearby it, a bath-house (hamam), a large ablution
fountain (şadırvan), and other necessities ... [as well as] a quarter (mahalle)."[20] Four
other congregational mosques were also in operation in Üsküdar in the middle of
the sixteenth century. They were the Hamza Fakih/Kapudan Pasha (1499-1500),

---

16  Seyahatname, fol. 143a. According to Sai Mustafa Çelebi, an apprentice of Sinan and the compiler
of the architect's works, Sinan built a total of five palaces for Sokollu (in Kadırga, Ayasofya,
Halkalı and Üsküdar, all in and around Istanbul, and the fifth in Bosnia) and three for Rüstem
(two in Istanbul proper and the third in Üsküdar). See Section 11 of Sai Mustafa Çelebi's,
Tezkiretü'l-Bünyan ve Tezkiretü'l-Ebniye in Hayati Develi and Samih Rıfat (eds.), Yapılar Kitabı:
Tezkiretü'l-Bünyan ve Tezkiretü'l-Ebniye (Istanbul: Koçbank, 2002). Incidentally, a number of
prominent royal women also had palaces in this district. Süleyman's daughter, Mihrümah, had
one built on the shore near her mosque complex, as did Nurbanu, the wife of Selim II and mother
of Sultan Murad III. For detailed information on Mihrümah's palace, see Cavid Baysun, "Mihr-ü-
Mâh Sultan," İslam Ansiklopedisi: İslam Alemi Tarih, Coğrafya, Etnografya ve Biyografya Lugatı
(Istanbul: Milli Eğitim Basımevi 1940-1994), 8, 308 (hereafter İA). As for Nurbanu's saray, Evliya
Çelebi cites it in his enumeration of important palaces in Üsküdar. See Seyahatname, fol. 141b.
Tezkiretü'l-Ebniye does not list this palace while noting Sinan's renovation of Nurbanu's palace in
Yenikapı. This may indicate that Nurbanu's Üsküdar palace was either not built by Sinan or, more
likely, was subsumed within the Atik Valide külliye's framework. The same inference seems
applicable to the Mihrümah Palace, which also is not listed in Tezkiretü'l-Ebniye.

17  This palace was later renovated by Sinan for Süleyman the Magnificent at the onset of the Sultan's
Nakhichevan campaign and Süleyman spent the month of August 1555 there upon his victorious
return.

18  Al-Ayvansarayi, Hadikat al-Cevami, 522.

19  Yerasimos gives the completion date as 876/1471-72. See "Üsküdār," 924. The same date is also
noted in Al-Ayvansarayi, Hadikat al-Cevami, 498. Goodwin remarks that the date of completion
should be 874/1469, as discerned by the mosque's chronogram. See Godfrey Goodwin, A History
of Ottoman Architecture (New York: Thames on Hudson,1987), 114 and note 126.

20  Al-Ayvansarayi, Hadikat al-Cevami, 498. The külliye also contained Rum Mehmed Pasha's türbe.

Davud Pasha (1505-1506), Babüssaade Ağası (1506), and Taşçılar (1548-1549) mosques.[21] Each of these houses of worship had its own urban quarter (*mahalle*), and contained its endower's mausoleum (*türbe*). In addition, four lesser, non-congregational mosques (*mescids*), were located in Üsküdar proper. They were, in the chronological order of their completion, the *mescid* of Fatih, mentioned earlier, and those of Takiyeci (1537-1538), Arakiyeci (1543-1544), and Ahmed Çelebi (1567-1568). A good number of large and small sufi lodges (*tekkes*), fountains (*sebils*), and inns (*hans*) were also in operation in the district.[22] As an example, the expansive Şah Kulu *Tekke* was in such good repair that Süleyman the Magnificent housed in it the Safavid envoys who arrived in Üsküdar in August 1555 at the conclusion of his Nakhichevan campaign.[23] Similarly, the Rüstem Pasha Fountain built in 1545-1546 was fully functioning.[24] There were also a great number of mausoleums *türbes* in Üsküdar, including that of the revered Şüca Baba, the famed companion of Battal Gazi, and Asumani Dede, a favorite of Sultan Selim I. Üsküdar's stride toward urbanization was hastened by the construction of three imperial *külliyes* between 1543 and 1583, all planned and overseen by Sinan, who held the position of chief imperial architect from 1539 to1588. He was the spearhead of an architectural movement toward the sea, and it was the district of Üsküdar in which Sinan introduced this tradition.[25] The trend continued well into the nineteenth century and flourished especially in the eighteenth, during which period more and more mosques came to adorn both sides of the Bosphorus.[26]

The first seaside imperial mosque complex built in Üsküdar by Sinan, the Mihrümah, was also the first to spur the transformation of the district into a major urban community. The Mihrümah *Külliye*, commissioned by Süleyman the

---

21    The Hamza Fakih Mosque was rebuilt in the 1720's by *Kapudan* (Grand Admiral) Kaymak Mustafa Pasha, the son-in-law of Maktul İbrahim Pasha. It came to be known in later times as the Kaptan Pasha or Kaymak Mustafa Pasha Mosque. Davud Pasha was the Imperial Seal Keeper (*Nişancı*) to Mehmed II and Bayezid II. This mosque, dubbed Üsküdar Ayasofyası, contained a children's school (*mekteb*). The Babüssaade Ağası Mosque was built by a certain Süleyman, who served Bayezid II in that capacity. This mosque is also referred to as the Selman Agha or, alternatively, the Horhor Mosque. As for the Taşçılar Mosque, it was built by Mehmed Agha, the *bina emini* (superintendent of constructions) of the Mihrümah *Külliye*. (Information culled from Howard Crane's notes in Al-Ayvansarayi, *Hadikat al-Cevami*, 3641, 3499, 3497, and 3605, respectively.)

22    *Seyahatname*, fol. 141a-144b.

23    Tahsin Yazıcı, "Üsküdar," *İA* 13, 28.

24    Yazıcı, "Üsküdar," 13. Many more instances of predating architectural works can be culled from İsmail Hakkı Konyalı, *Üsküdar Tarihi*, 1 and 2 (Istanbul: Ahmet Sait Matbaası, 1976).

25    The Mihrümah, Rüstem Pasha, Sinan Pasha, Kılıç Ali Pasha, and Şemsi Pasha *külliyes* were all set either on the shores of the Bosphorus or very close to it.

26    İnci N. Aslanoğlu, "Siting of Sinan's Külliyes in Istanbul," *Environmental Design* 5.6 (1987): 192-197; here 193.

Magnificent for his daughter, was completed in the year 1543-44.[27] Mihrümah was the only daughter of the Sultan and Hürrem, his legally wedded wife. Süleyman commissioned the *külliye* when the princess was in her twenties, soon after her husband, Rüstem Pasha, had risen to the rank of grand vizier.[28] Sinan was confronted with a severe challenge with respect to the location of the project: there was simply not enough room at the spot where the endower wanted a sprawling *külliye* to be built. How would it be possible for Sinan to position a majestic mosque, a 16-cell *medrese*, an 8-room hospice (*tabhane*), a caravansary, a storehouse (*ardiye*), and a pantry (*kiler*) in a narrow site tucked between the shoreline and steep hills behind (Figures 1 and 2)?[29]

Sinan rose to the challenge by resting the mosque on a high platform (Figure 3). The grand mosque, aptly dubbed as *"İskele Camii* (Jetty Mosque)" because of its proximity to the boat landing, boasted two single-balconied minarets and a solid marble *şadırvan* with twenty spigots set prominently in the elevated portico that doubled as the mosque's courtyard (Figure 4). As such, Sinan had transformed a severe topographic liability into an aesthetically pleasing and functionally effective asset. The setting of Mihrümah's monument on a high platform rendered it at once eminently visible to those approaching the jetty from afar and easily accessible to the merchants, shoppers, and soldiers filling the square immediately below.[30] The location of Mihrümah's monument must have been of great importance to Süleyman, who commissioned the *külliye* on his daughter's behalf. The spacious portico accommodating the massive *şadırvan* would allow large numbers of his soldiers to perform their ablutions and have some rest before setting out on the long march to Anatolia. Similarly, the traders would use the square to unload and unpack their goods before apportioning them for retailers across the Bosphorus. Toward the evening, the travelers and merchants would partake of the amenities provided by the caravansary and the adjacent storehouse. The caravansary was

---

27 Parts of the *külliye* were built later, in 1548. See Gülru Necipoğlu, *The Age of Sinan*, 301.

28 Necipoğlu, *Age of Sinan*, 296.

29 Konyalı *Üsküdar Tarihi* I, 214. Note that Konyalı, who keenly scrutinized Mihrümah's deed of endowment (*vakfiye*), did not find a record of a soup kitchen and caravansary. These amenities were added to the *külliye*'s flanks soon afterwards. Necipoğlu reports on an updated version of the *vakfiye* drawn up in 1558 that also lists an elementary school (*mekteb*), *Age of Sinan*, 302.

30 Accordingly, the Mihrümah Mosque set an example for the Rüstem Pasha Mosque in Tahtakale, which Sinan completed in 1557. Each mosque was built on a high platform to afford it high visibility from the shore, the Golden Horn and Bosphorus, respectively. Since neither mosque had sufficient room for a courtyard, none had a *şadırvan* erected in its conventional location. Mihrümah Mosque's terrace was more spacious vis-à-vis her husband's, so Sinan accommodated the huge *şadırvan* loggia in its front. As for Rüstem Pasha's mosque, Sinan solved the problem by building a smaller *şadırvan* below the east stairs. For more detail on this point, refer to Necipoğlu, *Age of Sinan*, 321-31.

amply equipped to accomplish this task. It flanked both sides of the mosque, boasting, according to Evliya Çelebi, 100 cells for travelers and room for 100 horses on each wing.[31]

The construction of the Mihrümah *Külliye* initiated the transformation of the district from a junction of transient traders, travelers, and soldiers into a venue of local merchants and residents. The elementary school (*mekteb*) and soup kitchen (*imaret*), which were later added to the original collection of buildings, afforded to the markets and residential neighborhoods that formed around the *külliye* a steadier existence. These local people, along with the Janissaries stationed in regular barracks, would have become frequent beneficiaries of the religious and social services provided by the *külliye*. The urbanization of Üsküdar had thus started, from the jetty toward the hills, with Mihrümah's *külliye* figuring centrally in this progression.

The second imperial mosque complex built in Üsküdar was Şemsi Pasha's. It was completed in the year 1580-1581, the year the Pasha died. Taken into the inner imperial palace (*enderun*) as a boy, Şemsi Ahmet was appointed by Süleyman, progressively, as chief hunter of the court (*avcıbaşı*), lieutenant commander of paid cavalry (*bölükağası*), commander of landed cavalry (*sipahiler ağası*), governor of Damascus, governor-general (*beylerbeyi*) of Anatolia, and finally of Rumelia.[32] Şemsi Pasha was ordered to retire at the beginning of Selim II's reign (1567-1568), but was allowed to retain his honorary title as vizier and serve the new Sultan as a gentleman-in-waiting (*müsahib*). Eventually he endeared himself to Selim to such extent that the Sultan often came as a guest to the fabulous palace Şemsi built on the shore of Üsküdar.[33] Later on, when the Sultan fell ill, Şemsi "presented the palace as a gift to Selim, who sought to escape his doctors' strict orders"[34] to quit drinking. Even more intensely favored by Selim's son, Murad III (1574-1595), Şemsi Pasha proceeded to construct a *külliye* incorporating a mosque, *medrese*, and *türbe* in the site next to the palace that he had transferred to Murad's father.[35] The construction plot was highly visible from across the Bosphorus, immediately to the north of the jetty "teeming with those passing to and from Anatolia."[36] The Pasha's *külliye* faced a topographic challenge similar to Mihrümah's: the tiny building site was severely constrained by the sea. Sinan was quick to come up with a remedy.

---

[31]   *Seyahatname*, fol. 143a.
[32]   Al-Ayvansarayi, *Hadikat al-Cevami*, 496, note 3450.
[33]   Konyalı, *Üsküdar Tarihi*, 1, 292.
[34]   Konyalı, *Üsküdar Tarihi* I, 292.
[35]   Al-Ayvansarayi, *Hadikat al-Cevami*, 497.
[36]   Necipoğlu, *Age of Sinan*, 496, quoting Mustafa Ali, Nuruosmaniye Library, Ms. 3409, fol. 133r.

It consisted of rotating the *medrese* around the mosque's Kaaba axis (*kıble*), setting its long flank parallel to the quay rather than the mosque (Figures 5 and 6). Thus, Sinan again turned a physical limitation challenging a major architectural undertaking into an aesthetic opportunity. The novel layout plan served to highlight rather than dampen the mosque's presence versus the *medrese*. This feat of design allowed Sinan to permit visitors to gaze at the sea from the courtyard through a series of square openings set at eye level on the courtyard's wall so that visitors could catch a glimpse of the Bosphorus through the openings as if they were looking at a collection of seascapes (Figure 7).

The Şemsi Pasha *Külliye* was known to have drawn a great number of people because of its "charm" and its resemblance to a "decorated pavilion."[37] Evliya Çelebi describes the mosque's dome as a "bubble on the lip of the sea" and each of its marble panels as "world-illuminating mirrors of the eight paradises."[38] Şemsi Pasha was conscious of the jewel-like beauty of his pious architecture, which he devoted to "the Community of Lovers" in the hope that the affiliates of that community, "when they pass along this shore, may… remember him with a prayer."[39] The endower's exhortation evidently took hold, considering Evliya Çelebi's remark that "bunda dahı cümle 'āşıkān ba'de'l-'asr gelüp āyende ve revende kayıkları temāşā idüp kesb [ü] hevā iderler"[40] [all lovers linger in this pleasure spot after the hour of afternoon service to have an airing and to watch the caïques coming and going by].

The double impact of the Mihrümah and Şemsi Mosque Complexes greatly added to Üsküdar's development on the waterfront. The district now boasted two charitable complexes around which two separate neighborhoods (*mahalles*) began to take shape. Şemsi Pasha had speculated correctly that while his monument was located in the periphery rather than in one of the preferred wards of *nefs-i İstanbul*, the fledgling *kaza* of Üsküdar would eventually become a choice district. In fact, Şemsi Pasha's retort to those who scoffed at the relative stature of his intended construction site was that Üsküdar was the gateway to the glorious capital, or, as he put it, "a way-station of mankind, a place where countless people come with business from the lands of Anatolia, Damascus, Aleppo, and especially Egypt and Iraq."[41]

---

37  Necipoğlu, *Age of Sinan*, 495-496, quoting Evliya Çelebi, *Seyahatname* (1896-1938), 1: 474.
38  Ibid.
39  Al-Ayvansarayi, *Hadikat al-Cevami*, 497, citing the inscriptions on Şemsi Pasha's mosque and *türbe*.
40  *Seyahatname*, fol. 143b.
41  Necipoğlu, *Age of Sinan*, 494, quoting Mustafa Ali, Ms. 3409, folio 133r, Nuruosmaniye Library, 2:97-98, 227.

The third mosque complex built in Üsküdar was the Atik Valide. Its construction began in 1571 and took twelve years to complete.[42] The project was commissioned by Nurbanu, one of the most ambitious female patrons of Ottoman pious architecture.[43] Her political career began as early as 1542, when she was chosen as the favorite (*haseki*) of the crown prince (*şehzade*) Selim II, who waited in his provincial governorate of Manisa for the day when he would inherit the throne. Nurbanu's considerable authority was amplified after 1562, when her young son Murad III was singled out as the next *şehzade*, and further still, after 1571, when she became the legal wife (*zevce*) of Sultan Selim II. In 1574, when Murad III inherited the throne, Nurbanu officially took on the title of Queen Mother (*Valide Sultan*), holding the highest station in the hierarchy of the imperial harem until her death in 1583.

The site Nurbanu chose for her *külliye* was not along the shore, but on the hilltop, affording superlative topographic features such as visibility, spaciousness, and rich foliage (Figure 8). Unlike the previous two imperial *külliyes,* Sinan was not constrained by the topography since the monument was to be built on an empty plot of land. The primary function of the Atik Valide Mosque Complex was to create a large urban quarter (*mahalle*) in the hitherto unpopulated hilltop of Üsküdar. This intention is evidenced by the wide array of religious, educational, and social facilities incorporated in the layout of the *külliye*. Extending over a 200-meter axis, this collection of buildings was designed to sustain the needs of a sizeable urban neighborhood, which immediately formed about the mosque complex. The Atik Valide was conceived to surpass those of Mihrümah and Şemsi Pasha not only in scale, but also in the number and extent of services it would provide. Evliya Çelebi described the Atik Valide as *"öyle büyük hayrattır ki tabir olunmaz"*[44] [such a grand pious work that defies description], clearly impressed by the *külliye*'s sprawling layout, consisting of two huge ensembles (Figure 9). The first was devoted to the promotion of social and benevolent services, incorporating a caravansary, *imaret*, hospital (*darüşşifa*), *tabhane*, and *mekteb*. The second was the mosque/*medrese* ensemble devoted to contribute to the religious and spiritual enhancement of the pious. This ensemble incorporated a Koran recitation-school (*darülkurra*), a hadith school (*darülhadis*), and a sufi convent (*rıbat*).

---

[42]  Certain expansions were carried out between the years 1584 and 1585-86, very much like in the case of the Mihrümah. See Necipoğlu, *Age of Sinan*, 285-87.

[43]  For detailed information on the political, diplomatic and building career of Nurbanu, see Pinar Kayaalp-Aktan, *The Atik Valide Mosque Complex: A Testament of Nurbanu's Prestige, Power and Piety*, unpublished PhD Dissertation, Harvard University, 2005.

[44]  *Seyahatname*, fol. 142a.

Eventually, the siting of the Atik Valide Mosque Complex fulfilled its intended purpose to create a *mahalle* in the vastly underpopulated space between the marketplace on the shores of the Bosphorus and the hilltop. Üsküdar's residents drew upon the *külliye*'s religious, educational, and social resources, and the meadows surrounding it soon turned into a halting station for caravans coming from or leaving for Anatolia. Evliya Çelebi reports that the *Valide* caravansary accommodated upwards of 1000 horses, not counting camels, which were housed in a separate enclosure.[45] Along with the two previously built imperial *külliyes*, Nurbanu's huge mosque complex deeply altered Üsküdar's economic and social structure. Mention already has been made of the role the Mihrümah *Külliye* played with respect to the transformation of the square between the jetty and the hilltop from a venue of sporadic movement of soldiers and traders into a settled venue of military and commercial activity. Nurbanu's *külliye* made even deeper changes in the urban fabric of the district. It provided extensive services not only to travelers, visitors, merchants, and other transients passing through the hills, but also to the residents who settled in the new *mahalle*, as well as the students of its superlative *darülhadis* and *darülkurra*.

As is generally the case, the physical and organizational features of the *külliyes* of Mihrümah, Şemsi Pasha, and Atik Valide were altered by the economic and political contingencies that prevailed in future centuries. In other words, as much as *külliyes* affected the lives of all those who benefited from its services, they were, in turn, affected by those whom they sustained and provided for. As for the Atik Valide, it eventually took on a sufi character, as the serene, distant hilltop became particularly amenable to mystics of various orders.[46] The *külliye*'s *rıbat*, sequestered from the bustle of the commercial and residential space around, nourished mystic spirituality and enlightenment, permitting the members of the Halveti order to practice their rites undisturbed. Finally, the Atik Valide increasingly committed itself to the social mission of improving the lives of the resident community that formed around it, as it catered more and more keenly to educating the children, treating the sick, and feeding the hungry of its *mahalle*.

The charitable projects undertaken in the period 1543-1583 collectively culminated in the anchoring of Üsküdar as a permanent component of *bilad-ı selase*.[47] The

---

45 *Seyahatname*, fol. 143a.

46 Al-Ayvansarayi's account of the Atik Valide Mosque Complex is indicative of the increased sufi influences on this outwardly orthodox structure. Sheikh Abdülkadir al-Hüseyni, the head of the dervish order of Kadiriye, claiming that he saw the apparition of Hızır, on the right side of the covered portico (*son cemaat yeri*) in 1730's hung on its wall a huge inscription full of sufi tropes and metaphors. See Al-Ayvansarayi, *Hadikat al-Cevami*, 489-490 for the full text.

47 This is the Ottoman term for the three choicest districts in the Empire, which are, in order of

*külliyes* of Mihrümah and Nurbanu especially became two benchmarks for subsequent female members of Ottoman royal family to reach and surpass in charitable monument building. Üsküdar was now the preferred locale for imperial women wishing to anchor their names in perpetuity. The Çinili Mosque Complex, located near the Atik Valide, was built in 1640-1641 by Mahpeyker Kösem, widow of Ahmed I (1603-1617) and mother of the Sultans Murad IV (r. 1623-1640) and Ibrahim I (r. 1640-1648).[48] In the century that followed, two Sultans who wished to elevate the names of their mothers to that of Mihrümah, Nurbanu, and Kösem commissioned mosques to be built in Üsküdar in their *valides'* names: Ahmed III (r. 1703-1730) built the *Yeni* (New) *Valide Sultan* mosque in the name of his mother, Gülnüş Emetullah, and Mustafa III (r. 1757-1774) built the Ayazma mosque for his *valide*, Mihrişah Emine.[49]

To sum up, the three imperial mosque complexes laid the foundation for a series of neighborhoods that sprang up in Üsküdar. These *külliyes* reached and touched the lives of all who partook of Ottoman imperial beneficence—the local worshipers who filled the prayer halls of the mosques, the needy who frequented the soup kitchens, the infirm or elderly seeking solace in their hospital wards, the disciples who pursued wisdom, not to mention a steady income once they graduated from their *medreses*, the dervishes who searched for spiritual enlightenment in the convents, the travelers looking for a room and a warm meal in the *tabhanes*, and the the youths who learned their alphabet in the *mektebs*. In addition, numerous employees who drew their salaries from the endowments of these *külliyes'* owed their livelihoods to these pious institutions. New quarters sprang up around these religious and social institutions as the old ones expanded; hence, larger and larger numbers of residents benefited from the services provided by these *külliyes*. Thus, the building of these charitable monuments in the mid-sixteenth century marked the beginning of Üsküdar's transformation into a choice urban district of the Ottoman capital.

Charitable building activity largely contributed to the urbanization of Ottoman provinces. *Vakıfs* erected in the Balkans gave newly acquired regions the typical characteristics of an Islamic community.[50] *Vakıfs* abundantly raised throughout the Muslim regions, alternatively, projected the personal aspirations and affirmations

---

[48]  importance: Istanbul, Eyüp and Üsküdar.
The Çinili *Külliye* is best known for its large *şadırvan* under a flamboyant hood roof and the fine blue and gray tiles lining the interior walls of its small mosque. See Goodwin, *Ottoman Architecture*, 351.

[49]  Goodwin, *Ottoman Architecture*, 125, 160, and 387.

[50]  See Randi Deguilhem, ed., *Le Waqf dans l'espace Islamique outil de povoir socio-politique* (Damascus: Institut français de Damas, 1995).

of their sponsors in the eyes of their co-religionists. In either case, *vakıfs* substantially contributed to Ottoman cities' socio-economic infrastructure, and imperial *külliyes* figured centrally in this effort. Indeed, these multi-purpose facilities served many segments of the local beneficiaries (the needy, the pious, the scholarly) as well as the transitory ones (the traveling, the trading, the preaching), many of the latter taking root in the newly developed community around the mosque, *imaret*, *medrese*, hospital, caravansary, *mekteb*, and *han* bearing the name of an imperial benefactor.

Figure 1: Axonometric projection of the Mihrümah Sultan Mosque Complex.
Üsküdar. Source: Necipoğlu, *Age of Sinan*, 300, F. 280

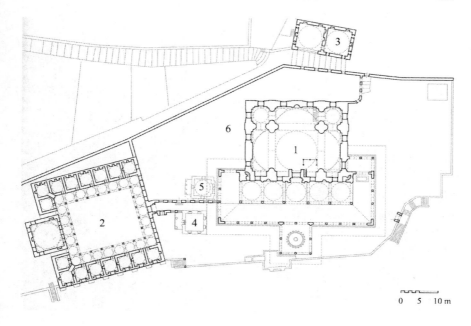

Figure 2: Plan of the Mihrümah Sultan Mosque Complex. Üsküdar: 1. mosque;
2. medrese; 3. elementary school; 4. mausoleum of Cigalizade Sinan Pasha (d.
1605); 5. mausoleum of Edhem Pasha (1892–1893); 6. cemetery garden. Source:
Necipoğlu, *Age of Sinan*, 299, F. 279

Figure 3: Mihrümah Sultan Mosque Complex in Üsküdar from the south.
Source: Necipoğlu, *Age of Sinan*, 302, F. 283

Figure 4: Mihrümah Sultan Mosque Complex, Üsküdar, double portico with projecting ablution fountain. Source: Necipoğlu, *Age of Sinan*, 302, F. 282

Figure 5: Axonometric projection of the Şemsi Pasha Mosque Complex,
Üsküdar. Source: Necipoğlu, *Age of Sinan*, 403, F. 518

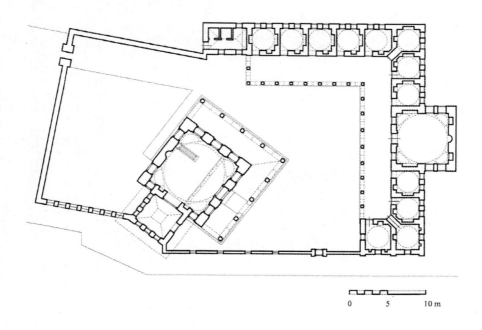

Figure 6: Plan of the Şemsi Pasha Mosque Complex, Üsküdar. Source:
Necipoğlu, *Age of Sinan*, 493, F. 517

Figure 7: Arial view of the Şemsi Pasha Mosque Complex, Üsküdar.  Source:
Necipoğlu, *Age of Sinan*, 495, F. 520

Figure 8: Louis-Francois Cassas, Sketch of the Atik Valide Mosque Complex,
Üsküdar ('Escki Validé, vielle mère à Scutari'), ca. 1786, pencil on paper.
Source: Necipoğlu, *Age of Sinan*, 289, F. 268

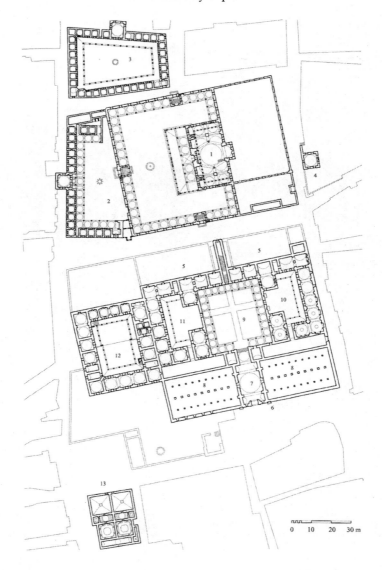

Figure 9: Plan of the Atik Valide Mosque Complex, Üsküdar, with a hypothetical reconstruction of its hospice-caravansary-hospital block: 1. mosque; 2. medrese; 3. Sufi convent; 4. elementary school; 5. Hadith school; 6. fountain of Hasan Çavuş; 7. vestibule; 8. double caravansary with stables; 9. hospice kitchens; 10. guest rooms; 11. hospital; 12. double bath. Source: Necipoğlu, *Age of Sinan*, 282, F. 261

Martha Moffitt Peacock

(Brigham Young University, Provo, Utah)

# Early Modern Dutch Women in the City: The Imaging of Economic Agency and Power

Most discussions of Netherlandish women and the urban environment would have us believe that these early modern women were restricted to the home and would not have dared venture forth into the "dangerous" streets of the city. Such arguments employ popular moralists of the day and their Biblically-oriented admonitions directed at women to leave the outside world to their husbands and to remain humbly situated at home fulfilling appropriately-ordained household tasks. In support of this hypothesis, scholars refer to the numerous domestic scenes created during this era as evidence of the success of this type of moralizing propaganda. This approach contends that the purpose of domestic images was to encourage the moral behavior of women in fulfilling prescribed female roles. Consequently, such interpretations have also been linked to feminist claims that Dutch genre imagery primarily attempted to inculcate attitudes of modesty and deference in women. Thus, Dutch art has been accused of aiding a patriarchal agenda to keep women in positions of low status and minimal power in this seventeenth-century culture. This stance, though prevalent, has largely neglected the numerous images of Dutch cityscapes, markets, and commercial enterprises that consistently portray women out in the urban environment where they participate in the economic activities of the city. Such images of public commerce frequently emphasize the economic significance of women as capable producers and merchants as well as shrewd consumers. In this article, I contend that an alternate approach to examining images of seventeenth-century Dutch women will yield a new and meaningful understanding of contemporary attitudes regarding female roles in the city. Specifically, an analysis of images of commerce from a lived female perspective will reveal the empowering aspects of these works for contemporary women in the public urban domain.

## Patriarchy in Dutch Art

The moralizing, patriarchal approach to Dutch genre imagery was given a strong foundation in the 1960s as Eddy de Jongh began to associate seventeenth-century domestic scenes with illustrated texts, such as those by the popular moralist, Jacob Cats.[1] In interpreting household scenes, de Jongh employed Cats's advice to women to remain situated at home fulfilling domestic duties, while admonishing husbands to go out on the city streets to conduct business:

> De man moet op de straet om sijnen handel gaen;
> Het wijf moet in het huys de keucken gade slaen.
> Men vint een seldsaem lant, daer slechts alleen de wijven
> Oock met het buyte volck den gantschen handel drijven;
> De man die broeyt in huys, en moeyt hem met het kint,
> De man let of de meyt eenprigh garen spint
> Daer zijn oock vlecken selfs in onse kust gelegen,
> Daer vrouwen handel doen en groote saecken plegen;
> Jae reysen over al, terwijle dat de man
> Sit ledigh, sit en troest ontrent een volle kan.[2]

> [The husband must conduct his business in the street,
> The wife must look after the kitchen of the house.
> One finds a country strange,
> Where only women conduct business with people outside.
> The husband broods in the house and busies himself with the child.
> The husband makes sure the maid is spinning uniform threads. There
> are also blots even here on our shores,
> Where women do business and carry out great affairs.
> Yes, traveling all over while the husband sits idle,
> Sits and consoles himself with a full jug.]

It is important to realize, however, that stereotypical directives for women to remain indoors and away from the contamination and dangers of the street were certainly not new with the Dutch moralists. They were simply repeating centuries-old patriarchal tropes used in most western European cultures. As such advice

---

[1] For early examples of this iconological method, see Eddy de Jongh, *Zinne- en Minnebeelden in de Schilderkunst van de Zeventiende Eeuw* (Amsterdam: Nederlands Stichting Openbaar Kunstbezit, 1967). For later works influenced by de Jongh's methods see *Tot Lering en Vermaak. Betekenissen van Hollandse Genrevoorstellingen uit de Zeventiende Eeuw* (Amsterdam: Rijksmuseum, 1976); and Peter Sutton et. al., *Masters of Seventeenth-Century Dutch Genre Painting* (Philadelphia: Philadelphia Museum of Art, 1984).

[2] Jacob Cats, *Dichterlijke Werken van Jacob Cats,* ed. Pieter Gerardus Witsen Geysbeek (Amsterdam: Gebroeder Diederichs, 1828), 1:288.

was not singular to seventeenth-century Dutch society, its use as the primary interpretive tool for their art is problematic.

In spite of this, the publication of two texts in the 1990's helped cement this moralizing paradigm for Dutch domestic imagery. Sylvia Jakel-Scheglmann argued that domestic images stemmed from religious subjects relating primarily to the Holy Family, thus giving these roles for women divinely-ordained sanction. Contemporary texts were also employed by Jakel-Scheglmann to provide evidence of attitudes regarding the virtue of and compulsion for women in domestic roles.[3] The publication of Wayne Franits's *Paragons of Virtue* further elaborated on the connection between female imagery and the advice of "father Cats." To emphasize this connection, he adopted the female-life-stages divisions found in Cats' text *Houwelyck* [*Marriage*] to similarly organize these images and their purportedly visual admonitions to women.[4] He also emphasized that women were required to stay at home and to not venture out onto the streets. The continued development of this attitude towards the insulation of women within the home was discussed in two texts initiated by Arthur Wheelock and published in 2000: the exhibition catalog, *The Public and the Private in the Age of Vermeer*, and an anthology of papers presented at a 1993 symposium entitled *The Public and Private in Dutch Culture of the Golden Age*.[5] Once again, in both texts, the moralizing directives of Dutch domestic imagery were stressed as they related to the prescribed private roles for women in this society. Another exhibition catalog, *Art and Home: Dutch Interiors in the Age of Rembrandt* organized by Mariët Westermann in 2001 primarily considered the domestic in Dutch art and culture. Once again, the catalog reviews the moralizing injunctions regarding the home as being particularly appointed to women with a strict demarcation from the perilous outside world inhabited by men.[6] In 2002, Martha Hollander's text *An Entrance for the Eyes: Space and Meaning in Seventeenth-Century Dutch Art* also lays out the division between public and private space, reiterating the moral restrictions on women to remain at home while men went out into the public streets. Although she is willing to allow that the public and private spheres are linked in purpose, namely that the familial order in the home reflected the greater social order of the urban environment, she still

---

3    Sylvia Jakel-Scheglmann, *Zum Lobe der Frauen: Untersuchungen zum Bild der Frau in der niederländischen Genremalerei des 17. Jahrhunderts* (Munich: Scaneg, 1994).

4    Wayne Franits, *Paragons of Virtue: Women and Domesticity in Seventeenth-Century Dutch Art* (New York: Cambridge, 1993).

5    *The Public and Private in Dutch Culture of the Golden Age*, ed. Arthur K. Wheelock (London: Associated University Presses, 2000); Arthur K. Wheelock et. al., *The Public and the Private in the Age of Vermeer* (London: P. Wilson, 2000).

6    Mariët Westermann et. al., *Art & Home: Dutch Interiors in the Age of Rembrandt* (Zwolle: Waanders Publishers, 2001).

ascribes moral danger to the outside world which, if allowed to penetrate into the domestic, might contaminate the virtue of the woman and the home environment.[7]

Because this moralizing and male-centered perspective on Dutch art has prevailed, discussions of female imagery are typically centered on the patriarchal attitudes of men toward women. Women in art are viewed as mere puppets at the whim of misogynist agendas, leading to the assertion that domestic scenes "do not portray women's self image."[8] Franits, for example, employs an image of a *Lacemaker* by Caspar Netscher, 1662, as a primary example of this type of moralizing propaganda, in that the woman modestly turns away from the viewer while concentrating on her virtuous domestic task (Figure 1). Another object of appropriate female labor, the broom, lies nearby. He asserts that her shoes are removed to indicate that she never leaves the home, but remains indoors fulfilling her assigned role.[9] In this way, most scholarly opinion regarding Dutch women suffers from a debilitating patriarchal viewpoint that allows women little power or freedom within the public space of the urban environment.

If, however, one attempts to understand this painting from a seventeenth-century female perspective, rather than a Catsian one, an altered view emerges. For instance, it is important to note that the composition of this painting did stem from a female perspective, that of the artist Geertruydt Roghman, ca. 1650 (Figure 2). Her *Spinner* was one scene in a series she completed that stressed individual women intently involved in various pursuits. All of these women are self-possessed subjects, whose averted gazes suggest that they do not work for the approval of male spectators. Instead, the back and profile views allow these women to go about their consequential daily work without becoming patriarchal symbols or allegories. As the woman directs her concentrated attention toward her work in both of these images, the viewer's gaze follows. Thus, this gaze gives visibility, and thereby economic importance, to the work performed. For those women familiar with the particular skill, it was a matter of common experience, thereby giving attention and assigning significance to the female viewer's work as well.[10] Women's work, such as producing textiles, was not an insignificant financial contribution to the Dutch economy. In some cases, these women were able to work outside the regulations of the guild, while

---

7      Martha Hollander, *An Entrance for the Eyes : Space and Meaning in Seventeenth-Century Dutch Art* (Berkeley: University of California Press, 2002).

8      Rudolf Dekker, "Getting to the Source. Women in the Medieval and Early Modern Netherlands," *Journal of Women's History* 10 (1998): 165–88; 176.

9      Franits, *Paragons*, 76–80.

10      For further discussion of this important print series see Martha Moffitt Peacock, "Domesticity in the Public Sphere," *Saints, Sinners, and Sisters. Gender and Northern Art in Medieval and Early Modern Europe*, ed. Jane Carroll and Alison Stewart (Burlington: Ashgate, 2003), 44–68; and eadem, "Geertruydt Roghman and the Female Perspective in Seventeenth-Century Dutch Genre Imagery," *Woman's Art Journal* 14. 2 (1993–1994): 3–10.

others formed their own subdivision of male guilds. Indeed, what the woman produced in the home often significantly contributed to the family economy. It is therefore important to recognize that even domestic labor had its public economic corollary.[11]

## Women and Textile Production

A realization of female economic significance in relation to textile production is witnessed in an anonymous Netherlandish allegorical painting from the first half of the seventeenth century entitled the *Struggle for Daily Bread*, where women with distaffs compete with men wielding the tools of blacksmiths, fishermen, soldiers, cobblers, tailors, bakers, etc. for their portion of economic prosperity, symbolized by bread in a large sack (Figure 3).

Furthermore, during the economic growth of the seventeenth century, greater numbers of women began to participate more publicly in the textile industry as guild members. Indeed, research indicates that during the seventeenth century there were no formal prohibitions to women joining guilds and thus working in professions.[12] Women's participation in industry was particularly significant in the case of Leiden, a city which became the world's largest textile producer during the first half of the seventeenth century. Furthermore, historians have begun observing that the large economic boom of the Dutch golden age was greatly enhanced by the labor contribution of women.[13] Reciprocally, it has been noted that women were significantly aided economically and in terms of job opportunities by this prosperity.[14] Thus, the number of women working in public mills, such as the Leiden Lakenhal, significantly increased during this era. Indeed, Isaac Claesz van Swanenburgh's turn of the seventeenth-century painting of Leiden spinners and weavers relates directly to these actual historical developments, as the artist monumentalizes and idealizes these strong female workers, thereby assigning value to their rigorous industry (Figure 4). Thus, the women approach an equality with the male textile workers

---

[11] Bibi Sara Panhuysen, *Maatwerk: Kleermakers, Naaisters, Oudkleerkopers en de gilden (1500–1800)* (Utrecht: University of Utrecht, 2000).

[12] Ariadne Schmidt, "Gilden en de Toegang van Vrouwen tot de Arbeidsmarkt in Holland in de Vroegmoderne Tijd," *De Zeventiende Eeuw* 23.2 (2007): 160–78.

[13] Leo Noordegraff and Jan Luiten van Zanden. "Early Modern Economic Growth and the Standard of Living: Did Labor Benefit from Holland's Golden Age?," *A Miracle Mirrored : the Dutch Republic in European Perspective*, ed. C.A. Davids and Jan Lucassen (Cambridge: Cambridge University Press, 1995), 410–37; 426.

[14] Elise van Nederveen Meerkerk, "Segmentation in the Pre-Industrial Labor Market: Women's Work in the Dutch Textile Industry, 1581–1810," *International Review of Social History* 51.2 (2006): 189–216.

represented in another van Swanenburg painting. Moreover, the painting situates the women looking out over a cityscape that makes them very much part of the public economic sphere, where other women mingle in the crowd as customers and merchants.

## The Marketplace

As a point of fact, women are consistently presented conducting business in seventeenth-century paintings of Dutch cityscapes—whether they carry shopping buckets or baskets as they go to market or whether they are shown selling and carting goods within the marketplace. Most commentators on Dutch female imagery, however, ignore scenes of women in the urban marketplace, with the exception of Elizabeth Honig.[15] In an attempt to reconcile these images with predominating scholarship, she suggests that such license was only allowed to women because the market was seen as an extension of the domestic realm. Otherwise, she agrees that the public domain would have been viewed as an inappropriate and perilous environment for women. She particularly illustrates her argument with a few market images in which male poultry sellers offer birds to women. The erotic innuendo of such scenes stems from a play on the word *vogel* or bird, as the verb *vogelen* was a crude euphemism for sexual intercourse.[16] Thus, for Honig, all market scenes display a sort of tension between the woman being out in the public sphere where she was not allowed, but where she also needed to attend to her shopping in order to fulfill her duly assigned domestic task of caring for the household. She asserts, therefore, that market scenes generally convey a sense of the woman on display, as if she is one of the goods for sell to a male audience. In her opinion, it makes no difference whether the market scenes contain men or any sexually symbolic metaphors—just the mere presence of women in the urban public sphere in the seventeenth century was problematic enough to put them under threat of being associated with prostitutes who were consistently coupled with the streets.

The point of the present article is not to insist that all such readings of market imagery are wrong or impossible; instead I would like to suggest that there were alternatives to these patriarchal, Calvinist, lustful or misogynist gazes.[17] Indeed, art

---

[15] Elizabeth Alice Honig, "Desire and Domestic Economy," *Art Bulletin* 83.2 (June 2001): 294–315.

[16] Eddy de Jongh, "Erotica in Vogelperspectief: De dubbelzinnigheid van een reeks 17de eeuwse Genrevoorstellingen," *Simiolus* 3.1 (1968–1969): 22–74.

[17] Attempts to theorize the gaze began with Laura Mulvey's recognition in 1975 of two separate fields of vision that were centered on gender and based on Freudian analysis in "Visual Pleasure and Narrative Cinema," *Screen* 16 (1975): 6–18. Mulvey's essentialist view asserted that the determinizing active, or male gaze, as opposed to the passive, female gaze, shaped the view of the female figure according to male sexual fantasy. In an attempt to escape such biological

historical studies on the Dutch golden age have become mired in these male perspectives. What did these market scenes mean for women? Important to this question is the fact that, during the course of the seventeenth century, a remarkable feminization of the market scene transpired.[18] In the sixteenth century, Netherlandish market scenes displayed males and females in abundance, but increasingly during the seventeenth century this gave way to a concentration on female merchants and female consumers, as is seen in the *Vegetable Market* painting by Hendrick Martensz Sorgh, c. 1662 (Figure 5). It is important to question why this was the case. First, as Honig rightly asserts, it would seem that the practice of consuming was progressively more associated with women. Cats and other moralists even advocated relinquishing the finances of the home to wives for prudent purchasing.[19] So we may theorize that the feminization of the market scene had something to do with this space being designated as a female domain in reality. This would certainly explain the emphasis on female customers, but what about the female traders? Why did they also become the standard in these images when clearly there were numerous male merchants in the seventeenth century? Firstly, it must have assuaged the sexual or dangerous implications that might have been otherwise absorbed from the images. The absence of a male gaze within the painting excludes a licentious interpretation, unless it is projected onto the painting by the male viewer. Secondly, as I will discuss below, recent research suggests that there were many more women in business in the seventeenth-century Dutch Republic than has been previously recognized. Thus, the actual visibility of women in the urban public sphere contradicts to a certain extent both the moralizing and lustful interpretations asserted by contemporary writers and modern scholarship.

In light of such evidence, it is essential to consider market paintings within the context of lived experience. This is not to suggest that the images are exact duplications of real events, but that they relate to the actual lives of female producers and consumers in this culture. Linda Stone-Ferrier has already set a precedent for this type of methodological practice in her research on market scenes.[20] She asserts the "real" character of Gabriel Metsu's *Vegetable Market at*

---

determinism, Griselda Pollock located the gaze historically, emphasizing societal and cultural influences as determinants of separate, gendered gazes in *Vision and Difference. Femininity, Feminism and the Histories of Art*, London, 1988.

[18]    Honig discusses this and possible reasons for it in "Desire."

[19]    Donald Haks draws upon the advice of several seventeenth-century moralists when discussing this admonition in *Huwelijk en Gezin in Holland in de 17de en 18de eeuw* (Assen: Van Gorcum's Historische Bibliotheek, 1982), including: Jacob Cats, *Alle de Wercken* (Amsterdam and The Hague 1726); G. Udemans, Practycke, dat is werckelijcke oeffeningen van de Christelycke hooftdeughtden...(Dordrecht, 1640); P. Wittewrongel, Oeconomia christiana ofte christelicke huyhoudinghe . . . ( Amsterdam, 1661).

[20]    Linda Stone-Ferrier, "Gabriel Metsu's Vegetable Market at Amsterdam: Seventeenth-Century Dutch Market Paintings and Horticulture," *Art Bulletin* 71.3 (September 1989): 428–52.

*Amsterdam* (ca. 1661–1662) by first locating and associating the pictured market with a precise one on a street near Metsu's home. Thus, it must have been a market space that he encountered regularly. Second, she demonstrates that the depicted produce found in these scenes relates to the actuality of Dutch horticultural interests, which had gained international acclaim during the seventeenth century. Thus, she asserts that the images symbolized the reality of Dutch civic pride. Similarly, I would suggest that the purposes and understandings of market scenes can be expanded when considering the actuality of seventeenth-century Dutch lives, but from a different perspective—that of women.

## Early Developments

As will be seen, the social and legal situation in the Dutch Republic greatly facilitated women to engage in business pursuits. During earlier centuries in the Netherlands, however, women had already begun to interject themselves into the male domain.[21] They began to be educated and became increasingly involved in the public, professional world, engaging in trade and the running of businesses.[22] This was particularly true in the arena of second-hand dealers, where almost all members of the profession were women before and into the seventeenth century.[23]

Consequently, as early as the sixteenth century in Antwerp, a new category of painting developed involving female figures, the market scene. The artists Pieter Aertsen and Joachim Beuckelaer first started including market views with subsidiary Biblical scenes, such as the themes of *Ecce Homo* or *Christ in the House of Mary and Martha*. At times, however, market women became justification enough in themselves as subject matter, and their appearance was often competent and formidable, as in a painting by Beuckelaer in the Kunsthistorisches Museum, Vienna, 1561. Not surprisingly the remarks of travelers to the Netherlands correspond rather directly to these images in paint. Shocked foreigners often recorded the frequency of women participating in the public economic sphere. They note with either dismay or admiration their encounters with overbearing or intelligent female merchants.

---

[21]  Herman Pleij, "Wie wordt er bang voor het boze wijf," *De Revisor* 4.6 (1977): 41–42.

[22]  For further information on Netherlandish women in the marketplace during the late-medieval era, see Shennan Hutton's contribution to this volume.

[23]  Isabella van Eeghen, "Haes Paradijs en de Uitdraagsters," *Jaarboek voor Vrouwengeschiedenis* 8 (1987): 125–33.

As early as in 1517, Antonio de Beatis, secretary to the Cardinal of Aragon, commented on the skill of Netherlandish women in business:

> The inns are very well kept and the women that manage them are so capable in keeping the accounts and doing all. The same goes for the buying in the places for the sale of merchandise. In the public exercise of trade, the women are as well employed as the men.[24]

Juan Luis Vives, a Spanish scholar in the Netherlands from 1512 on, also notes the participation of women in trade. Even though he is known for his encouraging views regarding women and education, he condemns Dutch women for taking over the husband's rightful position as breadwinner:

> In Hollande, women do exercise merchandise and the men do geue themselues to quaffing, the which customes and maners I alowe not, for thei agre not with nature, ye which hath geuen unto man a noble, a high & a diligent minde to be busye and occupied abroad, to gayne & to bring home to their viues & families to rule them and their children, . . . and to ye woman nature hath geuen a feareful, a couetous & an humble mind to be subject unto man, & to kepe yt he doeth gayne.[25]

The Italian traveler Guicciardini, writing in the sixteenth century, also reluctantly admits to the great skill of Dutch women in business:

> The women of Holland are verie faire, wise, paynfull, and so practiced in affaires of the world, that they occupie theselves in most part of mens exercises, especially in marchandize.[26]

## The Seventeenth Century: Dutch Women and Trade

During the seventeenth century, images of the marketplace became even more descriptive and less tied to a religious or moralizing tradition, as in prints of specific Amsterdam markets by Claes Jansz. Visscher and Jan van de Velde, 1616 (Figure 6). As a matter of fact, several market scenes during the century are depicted in recognizable urban locations. Emanuel de Witte's painting of the *Old Fish Market on the Dam*, c. 1650, in Amsterdam is one such example (Figure 7).

---

[24] Don Antonio de Beatis, *Voyage du Cardinal D'Aragon: en Allemagne, Hollande, Belgique, France et Italie (1517–1518)*, ed. Madeleine Havard de la Montagne (Paris: Librarie Academique Perrin, 1913), 122–23.

[25] Vives is translated and quoted in Alice Carter, *Working Life of Women in the Seventeenth Century* (London: Routlegde and Kegan Paul, 1982), 37.

[26] Ludovico Guicciardini, *The Description of the Low Countreys* (Norwood: Walter J. Johnson, 1976), 71.

These scenes abound with women intent on buying and selling in surroundings that would have been familiar to the female viewer.

Another aspect of seventeenth-century images of trade is the cooperative practices between husbands and wives, as in this Sybrand van Beest painting of a pig market, c. 1650, where husbands and wives of various classes both sell and buy together (Figure 8). Cornelis Beelt's mid-century painting of a weaver also demonstrates cooperation between husbands and wives, as the woman assists the man at his loom while another woman spins nearby (Figure 9). That this was a real and not simply a constructed aspect of Dutch culture seems apparent in portraits such as one attributed to Quirijn Gerritsz. van Brekelenkam of an apothecary in his shop with his wife seated sewing behind the counter (Figure 10). The workspaces of husbands and wives were much more intertwined in the seventeenth century, and it has been noted that many women appear to have taken up secondary professions related to their husbands' work.[27] This was particularly the case in Amsterdam, where shopkeeping became the most significant way in which women contributed to the family economy. Nevertheless, economic historians conclude that throughout the Republic, "women were an independent presence in the economic life."[28] Another example of the cooperative business couple is seen in Jan Steen's portrait of the baker Arend Oostwaert and his wife Catharina Keyzerswaert, ca. 1658 (Figure 11). Of importance in this regard is the development of the nuclear family in relation to the new Dutch middle class. It has been asserted that this change made the woman more of an equal, rather than a subordinate, partner in marriage. An increased emphasis on maintaining a harmonious and orderly family life was incompatible with a husband's tyrannizing over his wife. It is evident that many women assisted in their husbands' trades or took over for them while they were gone from home, which was frequently the case in this overseas merchant economy.[29]

Also, it has been suggested that a change in the marriage pattern during these years contributed to a more independent spirit among women. While women had previously entered marriage in their early twenties, they were increasingly delaying marriage until a later age (late twenties). In relation to this, many women were going into service before marriage, thus putting many young, unwed women in the marketplace.[30] This may be related to the frequency of imaging young women in trade and service, such as the many mid-century milk maid and

---

27    De Vries and van der Woude, *Modern Economy,* 599–603.
28    Ibid., 600.
29    Ibid., 602.
30    J. Hajnal, "European Marriage Patterns in Perspective," *Population in History: Essays in Historical Demography,* eds. D.V. Glass and D.E.C. Eversley (London: Edward Arnold Publishers, 1965), 101–41.

vegetable seller paintings of Nicolaes Maes and Reinier Covijn (Figure 12). In another change from the past, when these women finally did marry, they often married men their same age or even younger. Certainly then, women were entering marriage with a greater degree of independence and were probably in more equal positions of authority with their young spouses.[31]

Furthermore, historians have demonstrated that women in the Dutch Republic enjoyed more rights than women elsewhere in Europe. Importantly, because they had the right to make commercial contracts, they could more easily engage in business. Dutch wives also had the right to inherit property, and they could own property while their husbands were alive. And when the husband's bad judgment in business matters threatened to bring the family to ruin, the wife could appeal to the law.[32] In addition, sociological historian Ad van der Woude has noted that in a comparative study of Holland and England in the seventeenth and eighteenth centuries, there is a marked difference in the proportion of households headed by single females. The ratio of such cases is three times as great in Holland as in England.[33] Whatever the reasons for these conditions, they are yet one more indicator of the independent and more dominant nature of Dutch women in the seventeenth century.

There are several important historical factors related to the rise of women in commerce during the Dutch golden age. It was a period marked by high urbanization with almost half the population living in towns. Trade was essential to the Dutch economy, and it was therefore necessary for women to have the legal capabilities, the education, and the training to conduct business independently while their husbands were away. Also, it was necessary for single and widowed women to be able to support themselves through these same advantages. Thus, it is no surprise that research indicates a high degree of literacy among women in the Dutch Republic compared to surrounding countries. This was particularly true of women in the cities; in Amsterdam, for example, nearly half the women were literate.[34] In addition, it appears that many women received training for various professions by working in family businesses. It is, therefore, difficult to precisely

---

31   Ibid.

32   Simon Schama, "Wives and Wantons: Versions of Womanhood in Seventeenth-Century Dutch Art," *The Oxford Art Journal* 3.1 (April 1980): 5–13; 9; and Simon Schama, *The Embarrassment of Riches* (New York: Knopf, 1987), 384–91; Alice Carter, "Marriage counseling in the early seventeenth century: England and the Netherlands compared," *Ten Studies in Anglo-Dutch Relations*, Jan van Dorsten, ed. (Leiden and London: University Press and Oxford University Press, 1974), 94–127.

33   A. M. van der Woude, "Variations in the size and structure of the household in the United Provinces of the Netherlands in the seventeenth and eighteenth centuries," in *Household and Family in Past Time*, ed. Peter Laslett (Cambridge: Cambridge University Press, 1972), 299–318; 311–12.

34   Erika Kuijpers, "Lezen en schrijven. Onderzoek naar het alfabetiseringsniveau in zeventiende-eeuws Amsterdam," *Tijdschrift voor sociale geschiedenis* 23 (1997): 490–522; 507.

assess how much of a female labor force there was in the seventeenth century, as many female contributions to the family economy were not registered.

Recently, however, Danielle van den Heuvel has discussed in particular the special status of married women who had the legal right to act as independent traders.[35] Again, this was a legal advantage not enjoyed by women in other countries. It is also of relevance to this discussion to note that in Amsterdam when there was a woman head of the household, she was most often engaged in some sort of commerce. For these independent women, retail appears to have been a socially acceptable profession. In reviewing contemporary opinion as well as the legal and educational status of women during this era, van den Heuvel concludes that women's capabilities to work in commerce were favorably enhanced. She then elaborates on the specific ways in which women engaged in trade, from peddlers, to shopkeepers, to international traders, and from different urban environments within the Republic.

These historical indicators that reveal Dutch women as self-sufficient and assertive are again supported by the continuing remarks of foreigners throughout the seventeenth century. Fynes Moryson, an English traveler who visited the Netherlands during the last decade of the sixteenth century recorded:

> Agayne it is generally obserued that as the wemen of these Provinces overtops the men in number (which I formerly shewed) so they commonly rule theire famylyes. In the morning they giue theire husbandes drincking mony in their pursses, who goe abroade to be merry where they list, leaving theire wyues to keepe the shop and sell all thinges.[36]

In addition, his comments regarding why the women so frequently took charge of business correspond rather directly to the social/historical research of van der Woude:

> the watery Provinces breed flegmaticke humors, which together with the mens excessive drinking, may disable them to beget Males; or that the Women (as I have heard some Hollanders confesse) not easily finding a Husband, in respect of this disparity of the Sexes in number, commonly live unmarried till they be thirty yeeres old, and as commonly take Husbands of twenty yeeres age, which must needs make the Women more powerfull in generation. And the Women not onely take young men to their Husbands, but those also which are most simple and tractable: so as by the foresaid priviledge of Wives to dispose goods by their last will, and by the contracts in respect of their Dowry, (which to the same end use to be warily drawne,) they keepe

---

35  Danielle van den Heuvel, *Women and Entrepreneurship: Female Traders in the Northern Netherlands, c. 1580–1815* (Amsterdam: Aksant, 2007).

36  Fynes Moryson, *Shakespeare's Europe: A Survey of the Condition of Europe at the end of the 16th Century, Being unpublished chapters of Fynes Moryson's Itinerary*, ed. Charles Hughes (New York: Benjamin Blom, 1967), 382.

their Husbands in a kind of awe, and almost alone, without their Husbands intermedling, not onely keepe their shops at home, but exercise trafficke abroade.[37]

He claims that the women traveled as far as Hamburg and England in order to conduct trade.

James Howell, who visited the Netherlands in 1642, comments on the intelligence, education, and business expertise of Dutch housewives:

> There is no part of Europe so haunted with all sorts of Foreigners as the Netherlands, which makes the Inhabitants, as well Women as Men, so well vers'd in all sorts of Languages, so that in Exchange-time one may hear seven or eight sorts of Tongues spoken upon their Bourses: nor are the Men only expert herein, but the Women and Maids also in their common Hostries; and in Holland the Wives are so well vers'd in Bargaining, Cyphering, and Writing, that in the absence of their Husbands in long Sea-voyages they beat the Trade at home, and their Words will pass in equal Credit:These Women are wonderfully sober, tho' their Husbands make commonly their Bargains in drink.[38]

Indeed, as mentioned earlier, men are frequently absent from shop or market scenes altogether, as in the painting of a *Bakery Shop*, ca. 1680, by Job Berckheyde (Figure 13). In other instances, the male figures are represented as irrelevant to the commercial transaction taking place, as in Gerard Dou's painting of a *Grocer*, 1647 (Figure 14).

Sir Josiah Child, an Englishman writing in 1668, asserts that because Dutch girls received an education it enabled the women to transact business capably:

> . . . the education of their Children as well Daughters as Sons; all which, be they of never so great quality or estate, they always take care to bring up to write perfect good Hands, and to have the full knowledge and use of Arithmetick and Merchant Accounts, . . . the well understanding and practise whereof doth strangely infuse into most that are the owners of that Quality, of either Sex, not only an Ability for Commerce of all kinds, but a strong aptitude, love and delight in it; and in regard the women are as knowing therein as the Men.[39]

At the end of the century, Sir William Montague also remarks on the large numbers of women engaged in trade in Amsterdam. He compliments both their skill and intelligence:

> 't is very observable here, more women are found in the shops and business in general than men; they have the conduct of the purse and commerce, and manage it rarely

[37]   Fynes Moryson, *An Itinerary* (Glasgow: James MacLehose and Sons, 1908), 4:469

[38]   James Howell, *Epistolae Ho-Elingae: The Familiar Letters of James Howell*, ed. Joseph Jacobs (London: David Nutt, 1890), vol. 1, section 2:128.

[39]   William Letwin, *Sir Josiah Child, Merchant Economist with a reprint of Brief Observations Concerning trade and interest of money (1668)* (Cambridge: Harvard University, 1959), 42–43.

well, they are careful and diligent, capable of affairs (besides domestik), having an education suitable, and a genius wholly adapted to it.[40]

Particularly popular were scenes of women selling fish as in mid-seventeenth-century paintings by van Brekelenkam, Hendrik Martensz. Sorgh, and Adriaen van Ostade, 1673 (Figure 15). Indeed, in 1614, an English fisherman expressed surprise at the number of Dutch women involved in this trade:

> At Ostend, Newport, and Dunkirk, where, and when, the Holland pinks come in, there daily the Merchants, that be but Women (but not such Women as the Fishwives of Billingsgate; for these Netherland Women do lade many Waggons with fresh Fish daily, some for Bruges, and some for Brussels etc., etc.) I have seen these Women-merchants I say, have their Aprons full of nothing but *English Jacobuses*, to make all their Payment of.[41]

Clearly, there is significant evidence of women involved in the public sphere of business, and thus many of them regularly inhabited the urban domain.[42] Consequently, the feminization of market scenes must have been related to some degree to the actual number of women out in the streets conducting business. From a female perspective, therefore, one can understand these images as a reflection of women's capabilities and of their freedom to engage in trade on the streets or even to set up a shop in the public sphere without damaging their reputations.

As already noted, Cats's comments do acknowledge that a number of Dutch women were engaged in trade. And at times, he softens his patriarchal tone by noting that while men were primarily the responsible breadwinners, wives should help their husbands to carry this burden.[43] Even more revolutionary and liberated, however, are the views of a seventeenth-century Dutch doctor and writer by the name of Johann van Beverwijck. He was much more sympathetic in his attitude toward women's abilities to participate in the public sphere than Cats. His surprisingly pro-female text, *Van de Wtnementheyt des Vrouwelicken Geslachts* [*On the Excellence of the Female Sex*], published in 1639 with another edition in 1643, defends the courage and intelligence of women and argues that women are superior to men. Beverwijk lauds the famous female scholars, writers, artists, and heroines of his era. Importantly, for this discussion, he also praises ordinary women and extols their

---

[40] William Montague, *The delights of Holland; or, a three months travel about that and the other provinces* (London, 1696), 183.

[41] Carter, *Working Life*, 36.

[42] While there have been criticisms regarding the reliability of foreigners' comments due to common stereotypes, I agree with van den Heuvel that many of these journals should be given credence as they relate such specific anecdotal information, *Entrepreneurship*, 19–20.

[43] Manon van der Heijden discusses this advice in *Huwelijk in Holland. Stedelijk rechtspraak en kerkelijk tucht (1550–1700)* (Amsterdam: Bert Bakker, 1998), 224.

contribution to the Republic in governing their homes. He immediately follows this discussion with a denial that his praise of the housewife is a means to restrict women to the domestic realm. He relates that many women are able to engage in trade and business without neglecting their homes, while other women practice arts and learning. Finally, he claims that if more women were allowed such opportunities, they would be found capable of all things.[44]

Thus, a more careful examination of market scenes suggests that the numerous depictions of women buyers and sellers points to the reality of women in the streets and to their actual presence in the public sphere. Undeniably, many women do appear to be astute merchants in market scenes. Some of the women peddlers are characterized by their dress and stalls as coming from the lower classes, such as in Figure 15. Other female figures, however, wear middle class clothing and are situated in affluent looking shops, such as in Figure 13. Thus, women of varied economic and social status are generally represented in a respectful manner. There is little in market images that could be deemed demeaning toward the women, in terms of their status, their wealth, or of their location in the urban domain. The viewer's attention is directed toward the focus of the depicted female merchant's and customer's attention—that is the act of a judicious consumer negotiating with a knowledgeable business woman. Significance is attached to both roles and to the independence and intelligence of women generally in the public sphere, thus closely mirroring the reactions of foreigners.

Recent research has begun to uncover a few women who engaged in trade during the seventeenth century. However, this type of research is difficult unless there was some specific reason for an archival entry. There is, for instance, the example of a woman who appears to have made a living on her own as a shopkeeper, Griete Pietersdochter. She was at a rather low point on the social scale, when, as a widow with four illiterate children, she married an entrepreneurial husband. He elevated his status from salt refiner's assistant to merchant. Similarly, she left a personal estate of 9,000 guilders from the operation of her own shop, although there are no details about her business enterprise.[45]

Women also appear to have been successful second-hand dealers from the late sixteenth through the seventeenth centuries; indeed, they dominated the trade. One woman in particular, Barber Jacobs, had a successful trade in Amsterdam.

---

[44] Johan van Beverwijk, *Wtnementheyt Des Vrouwelicken Geslachts* (Dordrecht, 1643), 2:209–211. Hugo de Groot shares this opinion when in c. 1603 he praises Dutch women as being adept in helping their husbands with trade, while at the same time managing their households in *Vergelijking der gemeenebesten*, 2:142–44; this example is pointed out in van den Heuvel, *Entrepreneurship*, 20.

[45] De Vries and van der Woude, *Modern Economy*, 599.

Even after she became a widow, she continued her trade and at her death in 1624, her estate was estimated at being over 22,000 guilders.[46]

Another impressive example of an entrepreneurial woman is Elisabeth Bas. She and her husband, Jochem Heijndricksz Swartenhondt, set up a tavern known as the Prince of Orange, in the city center. After Jochem's death in 1627, Elisabeth continued the business for several years. She appears to have done so very successfully because at her death in 1649, Elisabeth Bas's estate was valued at over 28,000 guilders.[47]

That women wanted to show themselves as competent business women is demonstrated to a certain extent in portraits of regentesses who oversaw charitable institutions, such as Michiel van Musscher's portrait of *Sara Antheunis*, 1671 (Figure 16). She sits surrounded by the evidence of her management skills: account books and papers, a purse and coins, writing implements. A portrait such as this demands a reconsideration of the numerous scenes of women keeping accounts and weighing coins in the home, such as those by Nicolaes Maes and Pieter de Hooch, ca. 1664 (Figure 17). Frequently, these scenes have been identified as allegories of avarice.[48] That a woman should choose, however, to portray herself with such implements in a portrait suggests that women associated with financial signifiers could instead convey positive attributes, such as intelligence and skill.

Indeed, these associations must have been positive ones for some women, indicating the industry and business acumen of an increasingly large number of female entrepreneurs far into the eighteenth century.[49] None of this is to suggest that women had equal opportunities to males in business. Nevertheless, for a seventeenth-century culture, the Dutch Republic increasingly appears to have constructed a more encouraging set of traditions and laws, as well as economic and business structures that did not prohibit and at times did encourage more female participation in the public urban sphere. Consequently, the visibility of women in this sphere also seems to have inspired their active representation in numerous images of the city.

---

[46]   Hilde van Wijngaarden, "Barber Jacobs en andere uitdraagsters. Werkende vrouwen in Amsterdam in de zestiende en zeventiende eeuw," *Tijdschrift voor Vrouwenstudies* 63 (1995): 334–47.

[47]   Els Kloek, *Instituut voor Nederlandse Geschiedenis, Digitaal Vrouwenlexicon van Nederland* (http://www.inghist.nl/Onderzoek/Projecten/DVN/, last accessed on Feb. 6, 2009).

[48]   Eddy De Jongh, "Vermommingen van *Vrouw Wereld* in de 17de eeuw," J. Bruyn et. al., *Album amicorum J.G. van Gelder* (The Hague: Nijhoff, 1973), 198–206.

[49]   Van den Heuvel's text *Entrepreneurship* discusses how the number of female entrepreneurs became even greater into the eighteenth century.

## The Seventeenth Century: Dutch Women and Consumption

Finally, it is essential to turn to the figure of the female consumer in market imagery, who is as critical as the vendor in terms of significance and meaning. She similarly contributes to engaging our attention in the all important transaction of commerce. Indeed, female consumers are frequently made the central focus in market scenes through the elements of light and composition. In this regard, the paintings of Emmanuel de Witte, who completed several scenes of the new fish market in Amsterdam during the 1660s, are enlightening. But it is in relation to a particular painting that the power of the female consumer is particularly emphasized, a portrait of *Adriana van Heusden and Her Daughter*, ca. 1662 (Figure 18). De Witte painted the work, and others, in payment for his room, board, and past debts while living with Adriana van Heusden and her husband, Joris de Wijs. When de Witte left their household, he took this painting and a few others with him. Later, Adriana hunted him down and sued to get the paintings back, even after the death of Joris de Wijs. The judgment went in her favor, and it appears that eventually she re-obtained the portrait.[50]

The setting for this portrait is unusual in that she is situated as a customer in the marketplace. It seems important, therefore, to ask why she desired to have herself represented in this remarkable fashion. This question can partly be answered simply by analyzing the manner in which she is characterized. Once again, women dominate the market space in the painting, and the formidable figure of van Heusden herself conveys the female power associated with this domain. Her authoritative position and gesture give significance to her skills as an astute and commanding buyer. Such is hardly the representation of the weaker sex acting in humble obedience to prescribed patriarchal dictums. Nor is it the timidity of a woman fearful of tarnishing her reputation out in the public streets by attracting a voyeuristic male gaze. This impressive woman displays her wealth and her capability to buy via her fur-trimmed jacket. She appears discriminating and expert in her taste as she instructs her daughter in consuming practices. The female vendor is also presented as proficient and skilled in the way she gestures toward the marvelous arrangement of fish. Nearby, another woman vendor glances over at the commercial transaction taking place, while numerous female customers freely meander through the stalls, constantly interfacing with other women in an unthreatening environment as they examine the various commodities. Thus, the women are all in the process of constantly observing one another in this consumerist space of interaction and display. Why should van

---

[50]    Neil MacLaren and Christopher Brown, *The Dutch School, 1600–1900*(London: National Gallery, 1991), 1:489–90. I am grateful for the discussions I had with my graduate student Stacey Lau in regards to this painting and to market scenes generally while she was working on her thesis.

Heusden choose this public urban space for her self-representation? Undoubtedly, she made this choice because it was a unique space where her wealth, her skills, her independence, her taste, and her power as a consumer could all be on display for a multitude of viewers. The portrait certainly conveys the sense of the forceful woman who independently insisted that her legal rights and complaints against the artist de Witte be upheld.

In this same manner, one could say that every time a woman shopped, her consumer tactics, her taste, her wealth, and her independence were all on view by other women. This is the realization in a multitude of female-dominated market scenes by de Witte, Sorgh, van Brekelenkam, and other artists. Such display and examination are clearly the point of van Brekelenkam's *Market Scene*, c. 1665 (Figure 19). The mother's skills as a consumer who carefully counts out coins are the focus of the observant daughter who holds out her hand in order to pay the similarly watchful vendor. A woman in the background ignores the man standing in front of her, as she also scrutinizes the female consumer with a side-long stare. Socially, the emphasis placed on women customers forcefully enhanced women's ability to influence consumer demand. Consequently, while women augmented their reputations via the goods that they acquired, they also influenced the objects bought by their neighbors and thus the commodities selected by merchants.

The power engendered through the woman's increasingly powerful position as an active consumer also encouraged her rights to be a discriminating and demanding customer. Such negotiations seem to be the subject of several market and shop scenes such as in a van Brekelenkam painting depicting a *Tailor's Shop*, 1661 (Figure 20). The dominant female customer in the foreground appears to be instructing the annoyed-looking tailor in his work.

An assessment of the female consumer's role in market scenes must entail some discussion of the plethora of consumerism studies across a wide variety of disciplines that have been conducted in the last few decades. One thing that has become abundantly clear through these discussions is that consumerism must not only be considered as the mere act of purchasing and obtaining goods. Indeed, it involves a whole range of socially discursive practices involving class, power, and particularly for this article, gender. While the neoclassical view of capitalism and the consumer essentially posits a "natural" process by which the needs of the buyer shape and determine the market, the Marxist critique instead indicts the market as exploitative of productive labor by capitalists.

For generations, this debate between neoclassical and Marxist economics overshadowed any significant theorizing of the consumer. During the latter half of the twentieth century, however, more and more attention was paid to the consumer. Particularly crucial were those theorists like Michel de Certeau who began trying to extricate the consumer from her/his exploited position to one of greater agency and power. In the supposedly trivial act of consuming, Certeau locates an ability to shape and determine social and cultural structures. Instead of assigning all power to the forces of production, he elevates the shopper as an individual who can resist or reconstitute seemingly hegemonic influences.[51]

More specifically, feminists have also begun to recognize the significance attached to the act of consuming. This step has been critical for later feminist studies in their attempt to assign greater female power and influence to women in the shaping of culture, due to the fact that earlier feminist studies had constantly critiqued the (male) capitalist system and its domination and manipulation of the female consumer. Thus, women, through the act of shopping, have begun to take on the active role of "consuming subjects."[52] And alternatively, this role is now seen as a powerful one in which female consumers can influence and affect social, cultural, and political ideologies.[53]

So, returning to the Dutch Republic and what some have labeled the "first modern economy," it is important to reevaluate the significance of market scenes and what they imply about women in the public urban domain. When looking at the consuming women in Dutch imagery, they generally lack the timidity and modesty generally assigned to them in much of the scholarship. Nor do they seem threatened in any way in this environment. As mentioned earlier, they don't really risk becoming objects of consumption or of being commodified because male voyeurs are usually absent. There are most often women merchants and women consumers, and neither become objects of male exchange. Instead, these female consumers boldly buy. They are aggressive in bargaining and the serious business

---

[51]  Michel de Certeau, "The Practice of Everyday Life," *The Consumption Reader*, eds. David B. Clarke, Marcus A. Doel and Kate M.L. Housiaux (London and New York: Routledge, 2003), 259–66. Other essays in this volume also discuss the position of consumer as one of power.

[52]  This phrase was borrowed from Elizabeth Kowaleski-Wallace, *Consuming Subjects: Women, Shopping, and Business in the Eighteenth Century* (New York: Columbia University Press, 1997). Although she pinpoints the eighteenth century as the founding moment for the development of the female consumer, I would argue that the subjectivity of the modern female shopper was already being shaped in the seventeenth-century Dutch Republic, if not earlier. Importantly, the seventeenth century was also a period during which the female consumer was less defined and therefore had greater agency, power, and mobility than was the case in eighteenth-century England.

[53]  Many feminist consumer studies have appeared in the last few decades including: *All the World and Her Husband: Women in Twentieth-Century Consumer Culture*, ed. Maggie Andrews and Mary M. Talbot (London and New York: Cassell, 2000); *Gender and Consumption: Domestic Cultures and the Commercialization of Everyday Life*, ed. Emma Casey and Lydia Martens (Aldershot: Ashgate, 2007); Kowaleski-Wallace, *Consuming Subjects*; Krista Lysack, *Come buy, come buy: Shopping and the Culture of Consumption in Victorian Women's Writing* (Athens: Ohio University, 2008); Morag Shiach, ed. *Feminism and Cultural Studies* (New York: Oxford University Press, 1999).

being transacted becomes the focus of the images. This is exemplified in a Nicolaes Maes painting of a *Poultry Shop,* ca. 1659, where the woman customer, bucket in hand, holds out a bird presumably to bargain the price with the female vendor still in the process of plucking in the foreground (Figure 21). The role of the male figure carrying more produce in the background is negligible compared to the dominant women and their economic transaction. Thus, the market became a public space in which women could transgress the boundaries predominantly prescribed for them by moralists. It was a place in the urban environment where women could disrupt and reshape standards of feminine propriety for themselves. And even more importantly, they could alter the understanding of female roles within this new modern economy.

In this vein, it is important to examine why finely dressed women, who could obviously afford to pay servants to do their shopping, should be portrayed going to market at all. Indeed, there are many images of well-to-do mistresses in the home instructing their maid servants as they prepare to go out shopping. Obviously, the market images displaying richly dressed females represent something about the power of women to transgress gender boundaries and to insert themselves in the public economic sphere as mentioned. But these images also seem to imply something even broader and more self-congratulatory about the Dutch Republic itself.

The image of the well-to-do woman buying expensive goods also describes something more generally about the power of the Dutch economy. Indeed, the luxury goods imported into the Republic were the subject of amazement and envy to foreigners. The economic strength of the Dutch resulted in whole new significations with the act of shopping. This era witnessed an astonishing expansion of the middle classes with their exceptional access to expendable income. Furthermore, due to large scale international trade, there was a remarkable increase in the flow of capital.[54] Indeed, Netherlandish cities truly witnessed a burgeoning of capitalist demand for everything from exotic fruits and flowers to Oriental porcelains and rugs to decorate the home. As mentioned, women were given the primary responsibility of picking and choosing among these goods. Shopping was no longer a question of daily survival, it related to setting standards of luxury consumption with a woman able to display her taste and her ability to acquire. That taste in turn influenced the market, which increasingly provided luxury goods for the female consumer.

In important ways, the female consumer became an important, albeit more realistic, substitute for the former "Dutch Maid." This allegorical figure found in

---

[54]   *A Miracle Mirrored : the Dutch Republic in European Perspective*, ed. C.A. Davids and Jan Lucassen (Cambridge: Cambridge University Press, 1995); Schama, *Embarrassment;* De Vries and van der Woude, *Modern Economy.*

early seventeenth-century Dutch prints was a patriotic symbol of the divinely blessed and economically powerful new Republic.[55] The Dutch Maid was depicted seated in a fertile garden that was enclosed and guarded by a watchful lion. The abundant produce of her garden symbolized Dutch prosperity, which needed constant protection from envious outsiders. Later, however, it was the real, everyday housewife and her power as a consumer that symbolized the economic might of the Dutch Republic. Certainly, the wealth of the Dutch was gauged by what they were able to consume. Thus, women played an important role in displaying the economic success of the Republic.

However, even though the female consumer in a market scene certainly must have signified such powerfully patriotic messages, she was also a reflection of the actualities of lived experience by women in the Republic. She embodied the economic power and freedom of women specifically to act publicly in the urban environment and to influence the economics of the public sphere through her consumer demands. Thus, these images elevated the seemingly trivial, common activity of shopping, to which all women could relate, to an act of conscious autonomy and power. Shopping is no longer pictured as only a chore to which any maid servant could be assigned; it is something one does actively, with purpose and with agency. The actions of a discriminating buyer in a public space are powerfully presented to the viewer.

The urban marketplace was clearly displayed as a public space—beyond the physical boundaries of the home and the quiet ordinariness of the domestic chores performed there. Shopping took housewives out into the urban environment, where they became part of the din, rush, and clatter of the streets. In cities like Amsterdam, it must have been a very lively environment where a great deal of commerce was conducted; where foreign languages were spoken; where there were interactions with people of various classes, ages, sexes; where new products were on display including the unusual and the exotic. Thus, the market became a physical space of female enjoyment, variety, and excitement, not just dreary utility.

The market was also importantly a place of public display for the consumer, as seems so evident in many of the images. It was a place in which through one's dress or the objects one chose a woman could display her taste, her judgment, and her ability to buy. Women's choices must have inevitably influenced the choices of merchants. The mobility and independence allowed women in this public space could be used as a tactical practice to enable women indeed to help construct the culture around them.

---

[55]   Schama discusses this allegory in *Embarrassment*, 70–71.

Through these spectacles of serious consumer power, there is a further enhancing of these women's reputations. In this way, the women resist the associations that might otherwise be assigned to women on the street. They are not mere objects on display like the commodities around them; they are active agents who, in the very process of consuming, are able to disrupt traditional notions of proper femininity and spheres of influence. As mentioned, artists generally ensure these types of positive associations by eliminating male voyeuristic possibilities in the images. The paintings create a female-dominated space that encourages a different discourse from that of the moralists. Again, it is important to remember the archaic origins of the moralists's stereotypical rhetoric and to remember that they were less inspired by contemporary lived experience in their injunction against women leaving the home. In contrast, the paintings portray the market spaces with which seventeenth-century Dutch women were familiar. It was a modern art form that positively celebrated the public participation of women in the abundance and autonomy of the current golden age.

In this way one can talk about market imagery revealing the subjectivity of women during this era. As women and their common pursuits are the focus of so many of these scenes, it is reasonable to assume that they frequently appealed to female consumers who could insert themselves into the pictured roles. They portrayed actions common to other women, and they also assigned cultural importance to those actions. Such images must have encouraged the assignation of consequence and power to the role of consumer, thereby transferring those status-enhancing significations to the consumer herself. In addition, the market scene could become a pleasurable reminder of the female consumer's own delight in her freedom, mobility, power, and ability to display in the urban domain. It was a public space to which women could lay claim as they became part of a female consumer community.

In this regard, it appears from all accounts that Dutch housewives could be very demanding customers, and collectively their consumer unhappiness could be catastrophic for the person to blame, as is so terrifyingly depicted in an illustration from J. S. Gottfried's *Historische Chronyck*, 1660, of a Delft riot (Figure 22).[56] Indeed, this riot of 1616 was labeled "the women's revolt of Delft." Reportedly, the women in protest of high grain prices shouted "Support our children, and give us bread!" The armed men in the print stand by helplessly watching as the women storm the city hall and beat the tax official with their spindles, brooms, key bundles, and other domestic objects. Rudolph Dekker has uncovered the existence of many

---

[56] I am grateful for the information given me about this print in a letter from John Vrouwenfelder, curator at the Belasting and Douane Museum. He states that the illustration comes from J. L. Gottfried's *Historische Chronyck*. The Dutch editions of this text were printed in 1660, 1698, and 1702. The engravings were done by Jacob van Meurs.

female-led and instigated riots in the Netherlands. Many food riots, as one would guess, broke out in marketplaces and near shops or mills where women assembled. It is also not surprising, therefore, that the powerful fish and fruit sellers were often the leaders of these riots. Women would gather other females from their neighborhoods, where together they would beat their pots, tie their aprons to poles, and march in military style against the powers that be. Thus, women of all types, both merchants and consumers, would transgress their ordained spheres and move out into the public space of the liberating market to exceed the bounds of feminine propriety and do battle against the male powers of the urban domain. Men appear to have been intimidated by these women en masse, and thus market images generally could have been distressing reminders to patriarchal authorities of the uncomfortably powerful and public display of women collectives in the market. Indeed, such paranoia regarding uncontrolled women freed from the confines of the domestic sphere may well have continued to inspire the dictums of Dutch moralists.

An awareness of the associations between public urban space and the power of women expands our understanding of meaning and interpretation in urban marketplace imagery. Undoubtedly, these scenes could signify relationships between women and authority in Dutch culture, due to the evidence of women as important conduits for both the influencing and satisfying of market demands. Depicted female merchants displayed an ability to transact business, to negotiate and to calculate price, while representations of female consumers displayed economic power as well as an ability to discriminate and to demand quality. Through an understanding of the power signified in images of women buying and selling in Dutch paintings, one must certainly call into question the harsh patriarchy so consistently ascribed to this culture and its depictions of women. Instead, it becomes clear that these images must have further enhanced the significant role already played by women in influencing the economic developments of their society and also in shaping the middle class modern urban market environment more generally. Again, it was a situation of common experience in which women could relate to the depicted actions of female merchants and consumers. As a result, Dutch urban marketplace imagery established a visual culture that was empowering for women through its encouragement of and approbation for women's public participation in the city.

Figure 1: Caspar Netscher, *The Lacemaker*, Wallace Collection, London, *The Wallace Collection: A Complete Catalogue*, Stephen Duffy and Jo Hedley (London: Unicorn Press and Lindsay Fine Art), 301

Figure 2: Geertruydt Roghman, *Spinner*, Rijksprentenkabinet, Amsterdam,
"Geertruydt Roghman and the Female Perspective in Seventeenth-Century Dutch
Genre Imagery," *Woman's Art Journal* 14. 2 (1993–1994): 5

Figure 3: Anonymous, *The Struggle for Daily Bread*, Historisch Museum, Amsterdam, *Ingelijst Werk, De verbeelding van arbeid en beroep in de vroegmoderne Nederlanden*, Annette de Vries (Zwolle: Waanders, 2004), 231

Figure 4: Isaac Claesz. Van Swanenburgh, *The Spinning, Reeling, Warping, and Weaving of Wool* Stedelijk Museum De Lakenhal, Leiden, *Ingelijst Werk, De verbeelding van arbeid en beroep in de vroegmoderne Nederlanden,* Annette de Vries (Zwolle: Waanders, 2004), 212

Figure 5: Hendrick Martensz. Sorgh, *Vegetable Market*, Rijksmuseum,
Amsterdam, *Rembrandt and the Golden Age of Dutch Art: Treasures from the
Rijksmuseum, Amsterdam*, Ruud Priem, ed. Penelope Hunter-Steibel (Dayton Art
Institute, Ohio, Phoenix Art Museum, Arizona, Portland Art Museum, Oregon,
in Association with The Rijksmuseum, Amsterdam, 2006), 63

Figure 6: Jan van de Velde, *Market,*Rijksprentenkabinet, Amsterdam, Elizabeth
Alice Honig, "Desire and Domestic Economy," *Art Bulletin* 83.2 (June 2001): 302

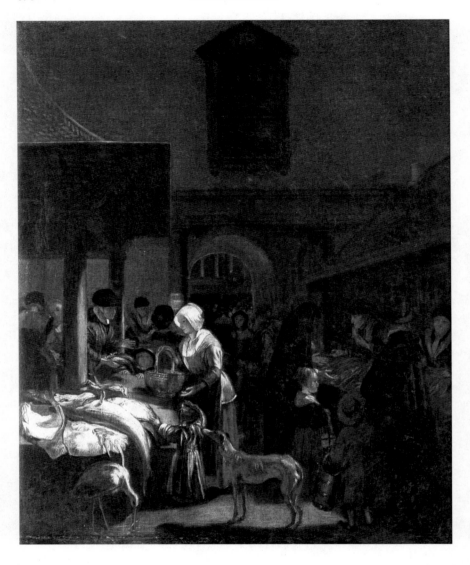

Figure 7: Emanuel de Witte, *Old Market on the Dam*, Museo Thyssen-
Bornemisza, Madrid,*The Thyssen-Bornemisza Collection: Seventeenth-Century
Dutch and Flemish Painting*, Ivan Gaskell, General Editor Simon de Pury
(London: Sotheby's Publications, 1990), 281

Figure 8: Sybrand van Beest, *The Pig Market in the Hague*, Bredius Museum, The Hague, *Museum Bredius: Catalogus van de schlderijen en tekeningen*, Albert Blankert (Zwolle: Waanders, 1991), 47

Figure 9: Cornelis Beelt, *Weaver's Workshop*, Bredius Museum, The Hague,
*Ingelijst Werk, De verbeelding van arbeid en beroep in de vroegmoderne Nederlanden*,
Annette de Vries (Zwolle: Waanders, 2004), 222

Figure 10: "Quirijn Gerritsz. van Brekelenkam," *Portrait of Apothecary and His Wife,* Present Location Unknown, Rijksbureau voor Kunsthistorische Documentatie

Figure 11: Jan Steen, Baker Arend Oostwaert and his wife Catharina
Keyzerswaert, Rijksmuseum, Amsterdam, *The Amusements of Jan Steen: Comic
Painting in the Seventeenth Century*, Mariët Westermann
(Zwolle: Waanders, 1997), 189

Figure 12: Reinier Covijn, *Milkmaid*, Bredius Museum, The Hague, *Museum Bredius: Catalogus van de schilderijen en tekeningen*, Albert Blankert (Zwolle: Waanders, 1991), 67

Figure 13: Job Berckheyde, *The Bakery Shop*, Allen Memorial Art Museum,
Oberlin, *The Golden Age, Dutch Painters of the Seventeenth Century*, Bob Haak
(New York: Harry N. Abrams, 1984), 392

Figure 14: Gerard Dou, *Grocer*, Louvre, Paris, *An Entrance for the Eyes: Space and Meaning in Seventheenth-Century Dutch Art*, Martha Hollander (Berkeley: University of California Press, 2002), 59

Figure 15: Adriaen van Ostade, *Fishwife*, Rijksmuseum, Amsterdam, *Masters of Seventeenth-Century Dutch Genre Painting*, Peter C. Sutton, ed. Jane Iandola Watkins (Philadelphia: Philadelphia Museum of Art, 1984), 30

Figure 16: Michiel van Musscher, *Sara Antheunis*, Present location unknown,
Rijksbureau voor Kunsthistorische Documentatie

Figure 17: Pieter de Hooch, *Woman Weighing Coins,* Gemäldegalerie, Berlin,
*Pieter de Hooch: 1629-1684,* Peter C. Sutton
(New Haven: Yale University Press, 1998), 55

Figure 18: Emanuel de Witte, *Adriana van Heusden and her Daughter*, The
National Gallery, London, *The Dutch School: 1600-1900*, Volume 2, *Plates and
Signatures*, Neil MacLaren. Revised and Expanded by Christopher Brown
(London: National Gallery, 1991), 412

Figure 19: Quirijn Gerritsz. van Brekelenkam, *Market Scene* (detail), Suermondt-
Ludwig-Museum, Aachen, Quiringh Van Brekelenkam, Angelika Lasius,
(Doornspijk: Davaco, 1992), 58

Figure 20: Quiringh Gerritsz. van Brekelenkam, *The Tailor's Workshop*,
Rijksmuseum, Amsterdam, *Leidse Fijnschilders: Van Gerrit Dou tot Frans van
Mieris de Jonge: 1630-1760*, Eric J. Sluijter, Marlies Enklaar, Paul Nieuwenhuizen
(Zwolle: Waanders, 1988), 88

Figure 21: Nicolaes Maes, *The Poultry Shop,* Courtesy by Douwes Fine Art,
Amsterdam

Figure 22: Jacob van Meurs, *Women's Revolt in Delft, 1616,*Courtesy by
Belasting & Douane Museum, Rotterdam

Allison P. Coudert

(University of California at Davis)

# Sewers, Cesspools, and Privies: Waste as Reality and Metaphor in Pre-modern European Cities

On October 20, 1660 Samuel Pepys stepped into a "great heap of turds" that had escaped from his neighbor's privy, landing in his cellar. Pepys unpleasant experience was not unusual for urban dwellers in early modern Europe, where solid and liquid waste from houses, dyers, butchers, builders, tanners, tailors, soap-boilers, and tallow-chandlers mingled in noxious and toxic streams that ran freely down the gutters of city streets. But while waste was a constant and real problem in urban areas, urban filth provided a rich source for metaphors in the "urban apocalypses" that stirred the anxious imaginations of Pepys's contemporaries and those of preceding and succeeding generations. City sewers and cesspools were even worse, for they represented an invisible, chaotic subterranean world where the indiscriminate mixing of opposites obliterated any kind of hierarchy and broke down all distinctions. To quote Victor Hugo:

> . . . the spittle of Caiaphas encounters the vomit of Falstaff, the gold piece from the gaming house rattles against the nail from which the suicide hung, a livid foetus is wrapped in the spangles, which last Shrove Tuesday danced at the Opera, a wig which passed judgment on men wallows near the decay which was the skirt of Margoton. It is more than fraternity, it is close intimacy.

Hugo described the sewer as "the conscience of the town, where all things converge and clash." For him it contains the "truth" that reveals the illusory nature of civilization:

> There is darkness here, but no secrets . . . . No false appearances, no white-washing, is possible; filth strips off its shirt and utter starkness, all illusions and mirages scattered, nothing left except what is, showing the ugly face of what ends.[1]

---

[1]     Victor Hugo *Les Misérables*, trans. Norman Denny (Harmondsworth: Penguin, 1980), II, 369.

In this passage the sewer takes on a physical presence. It is a teeming, seething, festering underworld—the urban equivalent of the Freudian unconscious—that threatens to irrupt and engulf the structures of the urban landscape above.

Hugo was, of course, writing in the nineteenth century, but the horror of mixing things indiscriminately was of great concern in early modern Europe as well.[2] In his biography of Calvin, William Bouwsma writes that Calvin "abominated" mixture, and that the very word was "one of the most pejorative terms in his vocabulary."[3] For Calvin mixture was synonymous with "adulteration," and "promiscuity," and ultimately with the disorder and confusion that he saw all around him and tried to remedy, if only symbolically, by establishing clear boundaries both physically and conceptually. Calvin anticipated Descartes in craving clear and distinct ideas. Bouswma attributes the clarity of his style to this concern: "he stabilized the meanings of words . . . but therefore also the structure of the universe he inhabited, by such linguistic devices as frugality in the use of adjectives."[4]

Calvin condemned curiosity precisely because it encouraged men to "greedily overstep their boundaries to inquire into the truth."[5] In the same way that God had established boundaries to knowledge, so had he established boundaries between peoples: "Just as there are in a military camp separate lines for each platoon and section, men are place on the earth so that each nation may be content with its own boundaries."[6] Calvin approved of land surveys because they ensured that "each one has his rights and things are not confused." But he disliked Gothic churches because the walls were broken up by broad windows. Gender boundaries were of particular importance to Calvin. Men who were effeminate and women who affected "manliness in their dress and gestures" were a disgrace. A particular target of his ire were women who resembled "lansquenets," German mercenary soldiers, and who aspired to shoot "as boldly as a man."

These women were "monsters so scandalous that one ought not only to spit at meeting one but pick up some piece of filth to throw at them for so audaciously perverting the order of nature."[7] Throwing excrement at these women indicates

---

2    On the anxiety aroused by mixture in the early modern period and the attempt to divide everything into neat binaries, see Jonas Barish, *The Antitheatrical Prejudice* (Berkeley: University of California Press, 1980); Stuart Clark, *Thinking with Demons: The Idea of Witchcraft in Early Modern Europe* (Oxford: Clarendon Press, 1997).

3    William J. Bouwsma, *John Calvin: A Sixteenth Century Portrait* (New York and Oxford: Oxford University Press, 1988), 34.

4    Ibid. Cf. Francis M. Higman, *Style of Calvin in his French Polemical Treatises* (London: Oxford University Press, 1967).

5    Bouwsma, *Calvin*, 39.

6    Ibid.

7    Ibid.

the depth of Calvin's dislike, for, as Bouwsma points out, excrement represented to Calvin the horror of everything that was unformed or without limits and, by extension, the void, nothingness, and the disintegration of the self: "Excrement, for Calvin, was not simply matter out of place: as an image for formlessness, that is of chaos, it stirred up his deepest horror of nonbeing."[8] Calvin associated excrement with impurity, pollution, and contagion, all of which were summed up by sin.

Inasmuch as humans are innately and ineradicably sinful, Calvin claimed that "We take nothing from the womb but pure filth . . . it is certain that there is no one who is not covered with infinite filth." The doctrines of Rome were nothing less than "stinking excrement."[9] While not unique in the sixteenth century, Calvin's emotionally charged references to excrement as both a reality and a metaphor became increasingly common in the next two centuries primarily as a result of urban growth and the social, political, and practical problems this involved and as a new theory of disease took hold, the miasma theory, which located the source of illness in foul odors.

But to understand fully how excrement and the sewers through which it ran came to assume such apocalyptic significance it is useful to turn to Norbert Elias and Mary Douglas. Both have provided insights into the connection between dirt and power. Elias correlates new concepts of personal hygiene in the early-modern period with changing political and social structures that placed increasing psychological and social constraints on individuals.[10] Douglas takes a more theoretical view of the relationship between dirt and power, first, by emphasizing the important role pollution plays in maintaining social structures by dividing social life into two basic categories, the acceptable and the unacceptable, and, second, showing that where there is dirt there is a system in which impurity is synonymous with danger and danger with potentially threatening forms of power.[11] In *The Politics and Poetics of Transgression* Peter Stallybrass and Allon White add a further dimension to Elias's and Douglas's insights by demonstrating

---

8  Bouwsma, *Calvin*, 46.

9  Ibid., 36.

10  Norbert Elia, *The Civilizing Process: Sociogentic and Psychogenetic Investigations*, trans. Edmund Jephcott. Revised Edition edited by Eric Dunning, Johan Goudsblom, and Stephen Mennell (Oxford: Blackwell Publishing, 2000). For an insightful discussion of Elias, see Abrecht Classen in the introduction to *Sexuality in the Middle Ages and Early Modern Times: New Approaches to a Fundamental Cultural-Historical and Literary-Anthropological Theme*, ed. Albrecht Classen. Fundamentals of Medieval and Early Modern Culture, 3 (Berlin and New York: Walter de Gruyter, 2008), 74–82, 84, 91–92, et passim; see also Classen's contribution to this volume, "Naked Men in Medieval German Literature and Art: Anthropological, Cultural-Historical, and Mental-Historical Investigations," 143–69.

11  Mary Douglas, *Purity and Danger: An Analysis of the Concepts of Pollution and Taboo* (London and New York: Routledge, 1966).

the way culturally constituted distinctions between "high" and "low" involve not only value judgments but also issues of power and pollution, and they show that the distinction between "high" and "low" applies equally well to four different domains: the human psyche, the human body, geographical space, and the social order. But as essential as these formulations are for understanding the real and imaginary significance of sewers in pre-modern cities and pre-modern minds, one very important factor has been left out, and that is the impact of changing medical and scientific ideas.

The sensualist theory of human perception and cognition formulated by Locke, developed and expanded by Maubec and Hartley, and transformed into a logical system by Condillac in the mid-eighteenth century[12] contributed to a heightened awareness of the sense of smell—in short, to an "olfactory revolution"—and this, in turn, led to the connection between noxious odors, illness, and epidemics.[13] What came to be described as the "miasma" theory of disease fostered a hypersensitivity toward excrement that led members of the aristocracy and upper bourgeoisie to express increasing disgust, distress, and even horror at the presence of human waste in urban environments. And this provided an incentive for individuals, institutions, and governmental agencies to take action to eliminate such waste on both a conscious and unconscious level.

The history of early modern sewers and the management or mismanagement of waste is an essential but generally overlooked part of the history of western subjectivity and burgeoning individualism. It is also an example of the increasing application of repressive power to unruly bodies, minds, spaces, and classes and thus an integral part of Europe's domestic, colonial, and imperial history. The new olfactory sensibility in regard to excrement transformed the environment in terms of domestic architecture, furnishings, public building, and public spaces. Even more importantly, by establishing a chasm between the so-called "washed" and "unwashed," it created a new boundary separating the "civilized" European body from lower class and foreign bodies alike. But as Stallybrass and White point out, separation is an intrinsic aspect of desire; as much as the "high" attempts to banish the "low" —or, as one might say, sweep the dirt under the rug—the "low" returns: "Repugnance and fascination are the twin poles of the process in which a *political* imperative to reject and eliminate the debasing "low" conflicts powerfully and unpredictably with a desire for this other."[14] As middle and upper-class Europeans

---

12    *Essai sur l'origine des connaissances humaines* (1746) and *Traité des Sensations* (1754)
13    Alain Corbin, *The Foul and the Fragrant: Odor and the French Social Imagination* (Leamington Spa, Hamburg, and New York: Berg Publishers 1986 [French 1982]).
14    Peter Stallybrass and Allon White, *The Politics and Poetics of Transgression* (London: Methuen, 1986), 5. See, however, the contribution to this volume by Britt C. L. Rothauser, who focuses on the cleansing function of rivers for late-medieval urban spaces in concrete historical and also metaphorical terms, indicating thereby how much the pollution of urban space was regarded as

became increasingly alienated from their own "low" bodily wastes and odors, they projected their disgust onto the bodies of lower class and foreign "others" and became obsessed with isolating and protecting the boundaries of their physical selves from the contagious miasma of their inferiors. At the same time, however, they exhibited a fascination with this "lowly" other. The conflation of the individual human body with the body politic led to the conviction that, like the human body, society itself could only be kept alive by constantly draining and flushing the alien and contagious bodies threatening to penetrate it.[15] And, in this regard, no substance was considered more dangerous than excrement. As David Inglis has argued, "The ruling classes were obsessed with excretion":

> Faecal matter was an irrefutable product of the physiology that the bourgeois strove to deny. Its implacable reoccurrence haunted the imagination; it gainsaid attempts at decorporalisation; it provided a link with organic life . . . . The bourgeois rejected onto the poor what he was trying to repress in himself. His image of the masses was constructed in terms of filth. The fetid animal, crouched in dung in its own den, formed the stereotype.[16]

This extreme, one might even say paranoid, attitude toward fecal matter and those associated with it had not always been the norm as we know from reading Bakhtin and Elias. In early-medieval towns, for example, waste was not the problem that it became as urban populations grew and density increased. In fact the chemicals dumped into rivers by tanners and dyers acted as purifying agents but were too diluted to kill fish. Skinners, glove makers, and curriers often worked downstream from dyers to take advantage of the alum they flushed into the river. Human feces was also viewed positively as a source of fertilizer for backyard gardens, while the garbage thrown into the street provided fodder for pigs.[17] Excreting and urinating

---

a great nuisance already in the fourteenth century. However, her literary examples mostly indicate a great concern with the embellishment and sophistication of urban architecture, not with the olfactory experience of dirt and excrement.

15   Catherine Gallagher makes this point brilliantly, but while she claims this concern with protecting the integrity of individual bodies largely through medical interventions marks a definite break between Victorian and earlier European thought, I argue that the issue of preserving boundaries between bodies emerged in the eighteenth century. Catherine Gallagher, "The Body Versus the Social Body in the works of Thomas Malthus and Henry Mayhew," *The Making of the Modern Body: Sexuality and Society in the Nineteenth Century,* ed. Catherine Gallagher and Thomas Laqueur (Berkeley and Los Angeles: University of California Press, 1987), 83–106.

16   David Inglis, "Sewers and Sensibilities: The Bourgeois Faecal Experience in the Nineteenth-century City," *The City and the Senses: Urban Culture Since 1500.* Ed. Alexander Cowan and Jill Steward (Aldershot and Burlington, VT: Ashgate, 2007), 118.

17   Donald Reid, *Paris Sewers and Sewermen: Realities and Representations* (Cambridge and London: Harvard University Press, 1991), 9–10. Jean-Pierre Leguay, *La Rue au Moyen Age* (Rennes: Presses Universitaire de Rennes, 1984); Goronwy Tidy Salusbury-Jones, *Street Life in Medieval England.* 2nd ed. (1st ed.; Susssex: Hassocks, 1975); Ernest L. Sabine, "Latrines and Cesspools of Medieval

in public was, as we might say, "no big deal," and if public privies existed, they were often located in public spaces overhanging rivers or streams.[18]

Such a relatively relaxed attitude toward public defecation was matched by equally relaxed views concerning verbal exchanges dealing with excrement. Rabelais provides a case in point with his "bathroom humor" manifested in the search for the perfect "asswipe" and Panurge's outrageous pranks involving body fluids and excrement. But even "serious' authors like Luther astonish us with their scatological humor and invective. As Persels points out, a great deal of early-modern vernacular art and literature is "disorderly" and "unclean" and "in need of the neo-classical bath it will receive in subsequent centuries."[19] Renée Balibar and Dominique Laporte describe the way the Académie Royale edited out excremental language from French vocabulary in the late eighteenth century.[20] The same kind of linguistic sanitizing occurred across Europe, reaching a height of inanity in Thomas Bowdler's (1754–1825) 1818 expurgated edition of William Shakespeare, deemed suitable for women and children.

The scatological language and humor of the early modern period went hand in hand with what we would consider elementary notions of personal hygiene. While people were expected to wash their hands and face, clean their teeth, and comb their hair in the morning and wash their hands before and after meals, a full bath was generally viewed with suspicion or apprehension as either a form of sensual indulgence or some kind of medical procedure.[21] In his article on standards of cleanliness in the early modern period, Keith Thomas quotes a popular proverb: "Wash thy hands often, they feete seldome, but thy head never," and he comments that "the normal toilet was a dry one: brushing or rubbing down with towels and changing clothes next to the skin."[22] What was most visible—for example, collars

---

London," *Speculum* 9 (1934): 303–21.

[18]  See Daniel Furrer, *Wasserthron und Donnerbalken: Eine kleine Kulturgeschichte des stillen Örtchens* (Darmstadt: Primus, 2004).

[19]  Jeff Persels and Russell Ganim, ed. *Fecal Matters in Early Modern Literature and Art: Studies in Scatology* (Aldershot and Burlington, VT: Ashgat, 2004), xvi.

[20]  Renée Balibar et Dominque Laporte, *Le Français National: Politique et Pratiques de la Langue Nationale sous la Revolution Français* (Paris: Hachette Littérature, 1974).

[21]  As Keith Thomas points out, there was probably less bathing in the early modern period than in the Middle Ages since the public baths had largely disappeared in response to the fear of plague and syphilis and their connection with prostitution. There was also undoubtedly a Protestant component to the idea that baths represented a suspicious form of indulgence. See Keith Thomas, "Cleanliness and Godliness in Early Modern England," *Religion, Culture and Society in Early Modern Britain: Essays in Honor of Patrick Collinson,* ed. Anthony Fletcher and Peter Roberts (Cambridge: Cambridge University Press, 1994), 56–83.

[22]  Ibid., 59. Editor's note: The whole issue would require, of course, a much broader cultural-historical critical perspective which is not the purpose of the present contribution; see, for instance, the contributions to *Wind & Water in the Middle Ages: Fluid Technoilogies from Antiquity to the* Renaissance, ed. Steven A. Walton. Medieval and Renaissance Texts and Studies, 322

and cuffs—were what was most important to keep clean. Appearance was what counted, and the motivating factor in keeping clean was to avoid making a bad impression. This is "why," as Thomas says, "even the most elegant gentlemen could be extremely filthy once they were off-stage."[23] The problem was that given the primitive nature of existing sanitary facilities even royalty had a difficult time getting off stage to take care of their bodily needs.[24] In a letter dated Oct. 9, 1694 to her Aunt, Sophie, Duchess of Hannover, Elizabeth Charlotte, Princess of the Palatine and Duchess of Orléans, complains about conditions at Fontainebleau and laments the fact that she is forced to defecate in public:

> Vous êtes bien heureuse d'aller chier quand vous voulez; chiez donc tout votre chien de soûl. Nous n'en sommes pas de même ici, où je suis obligée de garder mon étron pour le soir; il n'y a point de frottoir aux maisons du côté de la forêt. J'ai le malheur d'en habiter une, et par consequent le chagrin d'aller chier dehors, ce qui me fâche, parce que j'aime à chier à mon aise, et je ne chie pas à mon aise quand mon cul ne porte sur rien. Item, tout le monde nous voit chier; il y passé des homes, des femmes, des filles, des garçons, des abbés et des suisses. Vous voyez par là que nul plaisir sans peine, et que, si on ne chiait point, je serais à Fontainebleau comme le poisson dans l'eau.[25]

> [You are indeed fortunate to shit whenever you may please and to do so to your heart's content! We are not so lucky here. I have to hold my turd until evening: the houses next to the forest are not at all equipped with facilities. I have the misfortune of inhabiting one and consequently the displeasure of having to shit outside, which irritates me because I like to shit at my ease, and I cannot shit at my ease when my bum has no support. Item all manner of people can see us shitting: there are men who walk by, women, girls, boys, abbeys, and Swiss guards. As you can see, there is no pleasure without pain, and if we did not have to shit, I would be happy as a fish in water here at Fontainbleau.[26]]

---

(Tempe: Arizona Center for Medieval and Renaissance Studies, 2006); and cf. the studies collected in *The Nature and Function of Water, Baths, Bathing and Hygiene from Antiquity Through the Renaissance*, ed. Cynthia Kosso and Anne Scott. Technology and Change in History, 11 (Leiden: Brill, 2008).

[23] Thomas "Cleanliness," 71.

[24] While this essay is primarily devoted to the problem of waste management (or mismanagement) in urban areas, I include references to various European courts because they were themselves small cities in terms of the number of inhabitants both in the courts proper and the communities that grew up around them.

[25] *Madame Palatine. Lettres françaises.* Éditées, présentées et annotées par Dirk Van der Cruysse. Ouvrage publié avec le concours du Centre national des Lettres (Paris: Fayard, 1989), 126–27.

[26] Dominique Laporte, *History of Shit*, trans. Nadia Benabid and Rudolphe el-Khoury with an introduction by Rudolphe el-Khoury (1978; Cambridge, MA: MIT Press, 2000), 150–51, n. 11. I have slightly modified the translation.

The superficial nature of early-modern hygiene and the lack of private facilities even among the upper classes provides strong evidence that the sense of smell and the revulsion at public acts of defecation were not yet developed to the extent they would among elites in the following century. Consequently, body odors were not yet perceived as social markers. Given the lack of products for personal hygiene and the fact that soap was probably rarely used since it was made from rancid fats and alkaline matter irritating to the skin, a popular maxim rings true: "one is not smelt, where all stink."[27]

This began to change, however, in the eighteenth century as a new set of spoken and unspoken rules emerged as to where excretion could legitimately occur and how it should be discussed and as a new and positive view of bathing and personal hygiene caught on. Defecation became an increasingly private matter and references to it increasingly indirect. In London these changes were encouraged by the Great Fire of 1666. Before that catastrophic event, narrow streets, cramped housing, spouting gutters without downpipes, and the practice of dumping chamber pots directly into the "kennels," or gutters, that ran down the center of streets and often overflowed made life hazardous for pedestrians. After the fire, the London Building Act (1667) regulated the materials, designs, and standards used in construction to ensure that new houses were built of brick or stone and had tiled rather than thatched roofs. Gables or overhangs were prohibited; downpipes were mandated; and ordinances were passed directing householders to deposit their waste in places from which it could be removed by scavengers and rakers known as "Gounge fermours" (gunge farmers). According to one ordinance, Londoners were advised not to leave

> Any seacole ashes, oyster-shells, bones, horns, tops of turneps or carrets, the shell or husks of any Peas or Beans, nor any dead Dogs or Cats, offal of Beasts, nor any other carion or putrid matter or thing, nor any ordure or Excrements of Mankind or Beasts, nor any manner of Rubbish, dust, Dirt, Soile, Filth, nor any other filthy or noysome thing whatsoever" in front of their dwellings.[28]

This was clearly a largely unenforceable wish list since some seventy years later, in 1721, the Grand Jury of the City of London was still warning constables and watchmen to beware of the "quantities of soil cast into the streets in the night time," a practice recorded by William Hogarth in his engraving "Night" (1738). But it may have comforted some pedestrians to know that if the contents of a chamber pot did land on their heads, "the party . . . [shall] have a lawful

---

27    Emily Cockayne, *Hubbub: Filth, Noise & Stench in England, 1600–1770* (New Haven: Yale University Press, 2007), 54. This amusing and informative book provides material for anything one might want to know about physical life in early modern England under such telling chapter headings as: "Ugly," "Itchy," "Moudly," "Noisy," Grotty," "Dirty," and "Gloomy."
28    Ibid.,186.

recompense if he have hurt thereby." A guide for Justices of the Peace offered advice about how to deal with "one that shall cast down Chamber pots on men . . . of purpose to spoil, or do mischief."[29]

---

[29] Ibid., 79. Even though focusing on a slightly different approach, see also Peter J. Smith, "'The Wronged Breeches': Cavalier Scatology," *Fecal Matters in Early Modern Literature and Art*, 154–72; Furrer, *Wasserthron und Donnerbalken*, 65–82, discusses the technological development of water closets in the eighteenth and nineteenth centuries.

Figure 1: William Hogarth, "Night" (1738) from the series
"Four Times of the Day

But Hogarth's reality apparently trumped judicial activism. As Carole Fabricant observes in her insightful book on Jonathan Swift, most people's daily existence was literally engulfed in excrement, either because they lived in poverty or because they cleaned the houses of the more prosperous, taking care of their dirt as well as their own. [30]

Swift is a vocal witness to the excremental reality of urban life in the eighteenth century, too vocal for many people's taste. Middleton Murray excoriated Swift for his "excremental vision," a vision that led the psychoanalyist Ferenczi to declare Swift a neurotic with "an inhibition of normal potency" (1926).[31] But as Fabricant points out, such a diagnosis ignores the fact that Swift lived his adult life near St. Patrick's Cathedral in the oldest, poorest, and lowest part of Dublin known as "The Liberties." This impoverished area was subject to frequent flooding from the river Liffey and from the open sewer near the Cathedral that arose from the underground river known as the Poddle. Excrement and filth were an unavoidable part of Swift's life. As he says of Dublin city streets, "every person who walks the streets must needs observe the immense number of human excrements at the doors and steps of waste houses, and at the sides of every dead wall." In "A Description of a City Shower," he catalogs the detritus routinely flooding his neighborhood: "Filths of all hues and odours . . . . Sweepings from butchers' stalls, dung, guts, and blood. / Drowed puppies, stinking sprats, all drenched in mud,/ Dead cats and turniptops come tumbling down the flood." Swift's vision of city life was similar to Hogarth's in many respects, and Swift recognized this. As he wrote in a bit of doggerel, "How I want thee, humourous *Hogart*? / Thou I hear, a pleasant Rogue art; / Were but you and I acquainted, / Every Monster should be painted . . . ."[32] In colonized, exploited, and impoverished Dublin, Swift was far more likely to see the down and out types inhabiting Hogarth's monstrous "Gin Lane" than their more prosperous neighbors in "Beer Street."

Defoe dubbed London "the monstrous city," a sentiment echoed by Smollet's fictional character Matt Bramble when he declared that the "The Capital is become an overgrown monster which, like a dropsical head, will in time leave the body and extremities without nourishment and support."[33] London appears here as a

---

[30]   Carole Fabricant, *Swift's Landscape* (Baltimore and London: The Johns Hopkins University Press, 1982).

[31]   This diagnosis is taken several steps further by Karpman when he described Swift as "a neurotic who exhibited psychosexual infantilism, with a particular showing of coprophilia, associated with misogyny, misanthropy, mysophlia, and mysophobia." Cited in Norman O. Brown, *Life Against Death: The Psychoanalytical Meaning of History* (Middletown, CT: Wesleyan University Press, 1959; London: Sphere, 1968), 182.

[32]   Swift, "A Character, Panegyric, and Description of the Legion Club." Cited in Fabricant, *Swift's Landscape*, 14.

[33]   Roy Porter, "Cleaning up the Great Wen: Public Health in Eighteenth-Century London," *Living*

threatening vampire sucking the wealth and blood out of the countryside, a kind of huge hell's mouth devouring its inhabitants. In the nineteenth century William Cobbett simply referred to it as "the great wen," or sewer.[34] If we are to believe Lord Tyrconnel, London life was so corrupting and debilitating that anyone viewing its denizens would consider them degenerate savages,

> a herd of barbarians, or a colony of hottentots, The most disgusting part of the character given by travellers, of the most savage nations, is their neglect of cleanliness, of which, perhaps, no part of the World affords more proofs than the streets of London . . . [the city] abounds with such heaps of filth . . . as a savage would look on with amazement.[35]

In 1813 the situation seemed so grave to the radical thinker Richard Phillips that he predicted London's eventual obliteration:

> London will increase, . . . [but] the houses will become too numerous for the inhabitants, and certain districts will be occupied by beggary and vice, or become depopulated. This disease will spread like an atrophy in the human body, and ruin will follow ruin, till the entire city is disgusting to the remnant of the inhabitants; at length the whole becomes a heap of ruins: such have been the causes of decay of all overgrown cities. Ninevah, Babylon, Antioch, and Thebes are become heaps of ruins. Rome, Delphi, and Alexandria, are partaking the same inevitable fate; and London must some time, from similar causes, succumb under the destiny of every thing human.[36]

London was not alone is getting a bad press for its appalling filth. Describing his travels through France and Italy in 1766 Tobias Smollet reveals a similar disgust at the excrement that continually accosted his senses in public places. As he says,

> There are certain mortifying views of human nature, which undoubtedly ought to be concealed as much as possible, in order to prevent giving offense: and nothing can be more absurd, than to plead the difference of custom in different countries, in defense of those usages which cannot fail giving disgust to the organs and senses of all mankind.[37]

He singled out Rome and its Piazza Navona for special opprobrium:

> A great plenty of water has not induced the Romans to be cleanly. Their streets, and its even their palaces, are disgraced with filth. The noble Piazza Navona is adorned with three or four fountains, and all of them notwithstanding this provision, the Piazza

---

*and Dying in London*, ed. Ed. W. F. Bynum and Roy Porter. Medical History, Supplement No. 11. (London: Wellcome Institute for the History of Medicine, 1991), 61–75.

[34]    Ibid., 61–2.

[35]    Cockayne, *Hubbub*, 181.

[36]    Porter, "Cleaning up the Great Wen," 63.

[37]    Tobias Smollet, *Travels through France and Italy* (1766; Oxford: Oxford University Press, 1992), 33.

is almost as dirty as West Smithfield, where cattle are sold in London. The corridors, arcades, and even staircases of their most elegant palaces, are depositories of nastiness, and indeed in summer smell as strong as spirit of hatshorne. I have a great notion that their ancestors were not much ore cleanly.[38]

Johann Wolfgang Goethe registered the same distress on his travels through Italy when he noted the way locals defecated and urinated in public places.[39] An Italian contemporary describes his horrified reaction to the streets of Modena: "Upon corner stone / Untidy and scattered mounds of old manure / . . . Odorous turds and heaps of chamber pots upset and scattered about and lurid torrents / of urine and rank and foul-smelling broth / that you can not walk without boots."[40] The same indictment appears in a description of the stench emanating from the palace at Versailles:

> The unpleasant odors in the park, gardens, even the Chateau, make one's gorge rise. The communicating passages, courtyards, buildings in the wings, corridors are full of urine and feces; a pork butcher actually sticks and roast his pigs at the bottom of the ministers' wing every morning; the avenue of Saint-Cloud is covered with stagnant water and dead cats.[41]

In his *Essai sur la propreté de Paris* (1797) Pierre Chauvet complains that in the Palais de Justice, the Louvre, the Tuileries, the Museum, and the Opera "one is pursued by the unpleasant odor and infection from the places of ease [latrines]." Paris, he laments may be the "center of science, arts, fashion, and taste," but it is also the "center of stench."[42] Upper class noses had become so sensitive on the eve of the French Revolution that Arthur Young drew a map of urban stenches in Rouen, Bordeaux, Pamiers, and Clermont, all of which he described as making him choke. Clermont was especially bad.

> Clermont is in the midst of a most curious country, all volcanic; and is built and paved with lava: much of it forms one of the worst built, dirtiest, and most stinking places I have met with. There are many streets that can, for blackness, dirt, and ill scents, only be represented by narrow channels cut in a night dunghill. The contention of nauseous savours, with which the air is impregnated; when brisk mountain gales do not

---

38   Alexander G. McKay, "Piranesi's Impressions of Rome," *City & Society in the 18th Century*, ed. Paul Fritz and David William. Publications of the McMaster University Association for 18th-Century Studies, 3 (Toronto: Hakkert, 1973), 39–58; here 43.

39   Johann Wolfgang Goethe, *Italian Journey (1786–1788)*, trans. W.H. Auden and Elizabeth Mayer (Harmandsworth: Penguin, 1970 [1962]), 62, 64.

40   Piero Camporesi, *The Incorruptible Flesh: Bodily Mutilation and Mortification in Religion and Folklore*, trans. Tania Croft-Murray (Cambridge: Cambridge University Press, 1988), 186.

41   Cited in Corbin, *The Foul and the Fragrant*, 27.

42   Ibid., 27.

ventilate these excrementitious lanes, made me envy the nerves of the good people
who, for what I know, may be happy in them.[43]

To the evident distress of witnesses like these, public defecation continued to be
an acceptable fact of life in many parts of eighteenth-century Europe, even among
the upper classes. Visitors to the Louvre and to the Palais de Justice during the
reign of Louis XVI, for example, urinated publicly in these buildings without
condemnation.[44] At Frederick the Great's palace Sanssouci in Potsdam (west of
Berlin) things were a little better. A public notice asked courtiers not to urinate on
the stairs, but with how much success we do not know.[45]

It would be wrong, however, to take these disgusting descriptions of urban
spaces and urban living as fact pure and simple. Although they were surely that,
it is important to recognize that they were also indicative of a profound change in
sensibilities. They marked a new hypersensitivity toward human waste among the
upper echelons of society, a hypersensitivity that was accompanied by a growing
preoccupation with hygiene and repugnance for body odors, especially of others
but also of one's own. To quote Matt Bramble once again as he describes the
potpourri of foul odors that accosted his sensitive nostrils at a high society ball:

> Imagine to yourself a high exalted essence of mingled odours, arising from putrid
> gums, imposthumated lungs, sour flatulencies, rank armpits, sweating feet, running
> sores and issues, plasters, assafoetida drops, musk, hartshorn and sal volatile; besides
> a thousand frowzy streams, which I could not analyse (I, 135).

During the eighteenth century increasing numbers of people began to be repulsed
by aromas their ancestors had found quite tolerable, and this new olfactory
intolerance fostered a new kind of subjectivity as the individual self emerged from
the crowd to monitor his own smells in relation to those of others. The individual
bed and the individual tomb came into fashion in the eighteenth century and both
were examples of the kind of new boundaries that were being erected to separate
and isolate individuals from one another. As Laporte succinctly says, "To each his
cesspool and to each his grave."[46]

In his groundbreaking book *The Foul and the Fragrant*, Alain Corbin describes the
"perceptual revolution" that occurred in the eighteenth century when smell
usurped sight as the preeminent sense. Corbin connects this revolution with the
experimental work on air that began with Boyle in the seventeenth century and
continued in the work of Lavoisier and Priestly. The growing realization that the

---

[43]  Arthur Young, *Travels in France and Italy during the Years 1787, 1788, and 1789*, 185. Eighteenth-
      century E-texts (http://socserv2.mcmaster.ca)
[44]  Inglis, "Sewers and Sensibilities," 112.
[45]  Ibid., 112.
[46]  Laporte, *History of Shit*, xi.

air was not a homogeneous substance but a mixture of gases and a carrier of all kinds of chemical and organic substances ushered in what Corbin describes as the "Golden Age of Osphresiology," or, to put it less grandly, the science of smells.

This new sensitivity to smell reflected the "miasma" theory of disease that drew a direct connection between foul odors, illness, and epidemics. Thomas Tryon (1643–1703), an English autodidact and polymath who in many respects anticipated the broad interests and practical bent of Benjamin Franklin, was an early convert to the idea that noxious odors caused disease. In *Wisdom Dictates* (1691) he advised his readers to avoid privies because of the possibility of infection. He recommended defecating in a vessel and then emptying it into a privy or cesspool. For Tryon, as for so many others, the senses, and especially the sense of smell, were avenues into the inner body, from which the body often needed protection. As Corbin demonstrates, "degenerated air," mephitism, or foul odors, especially those emanating from the earth, and the "morbific vapors" arising from putrefaction became a central concern among scientists and elites alike, generating essays and enormous tomes describing experiments and observations devoted to smells. Mme Thiroux d'Arconville, for example, wrote a 600 page book, *Essais pour servir à histoire de la putréfaction* (1766), in which she records her experiments on more than 300 substances in order to study how putrefaction could be controlled. As a result of experimental work on the emanations arising from stagnant water, J.-B. Théodore Baumes demanded that agricultural workers be prevented from sleeping with their noses to the soil, something it is hard to imagine they actually did.[47] These are just a few of the examples given by Corbin to illustrate the fascination with smells, especially foul and putrid ones, that gripped the minds and imaginations of eighteenth-century Europeans. As Corbin says "Putrefaction was a time machine" because the putrid molecules emanating from decomposing bodies created an "aerial miasma" that not only threatened living organisms but could even corrupt butcher's meat laid out on slabs in the market as well as the knives that cut it. In short, foul smells were not simply disgusting they "provoked panic" because they could kill.[48]

The growing body of beliefs connecting foul odors with disease "engendered an obsession with fissures, faults, and imperfect joinings."[49] Cracked cesspools, badly joined floor boards, unsealed vaults and cisterns, scavenger carts that were improperly caulked, irregular paving stones—in sum faulty constructions of any sort—were considered potential sites of dangerous emissions. The idea of monitoring and securing boundaries that is central to Mary Douglas' analysis of purity and pollution became a fixation. This applied to the boundaries separating

---

[47] Corbin, *The Foul and the Fragrant*, 23

[48] Ibid., 21.

[49] Ibid., 23.

human bodies as well and explains the increased vigilance over body odors. Belches, farts, colic, wind, fetid breath, sweat, and bowel movements were carefully monitored for possible signs of disease, decay, and approaching death. The eighteenth century was an age of statistics and calculations, and a new calculus developed measuring degrees of internal body decay based on the odor of bodily waste.

As Corbin comments, this led to "astonishing excremental vigilance,"[50] which, in turn, intensified the growing obsession with the individual self. While encouraging higher standards of personal hygiene among the upper classes, such "excremental vigilance" fueled the fire of social and sanitary reform. It was no longer the case that "one is not smelt, where all stink." Body odor became a social marker that allowed newly deodorized elites not only to distinguish themselves from the stinking masses at home and abroad but also to justify their wretched treatment of them. As Mme de Giradin proclaimed in a letter of October 21, 1837, there is an unbridgeable chasm that separates the washed and the unwashed:

> Those who do not wash their hands will always hate those who wash their hands. You will never be able to bring them together . . . because there is one thing which can not be overcome and that is disgust; because here is another thing that can not be tolerated, and that is humiliation.[51]

Charles Leonard Pfeiffer has shown how Balzac uses smells as the basis for the social gradations that distinguish between the bourgeois, petit-bourgeois, peasants, and courtesans who appear in the novels in La Comédie humaine.[52] Delicacy of smell was a sign of social status, and one that, for example, distinguished naval officers from the common seamen under their command. In Les Paysans (1844) Balzac describes a scene in a dining room in which an aristocratic woman is almost forced to leave before finishing her meal:

> The strong, savage odor of the two habitués of the highway made the dining room stink so much that it offended Madame de Montcornet's delicate senses and she would have been forced to leave if Mouche and Fourchon had stayed any longer.[53]

Here is a clear example of the way delicacy of smell became a distinguishing sign of class; but it should also be pointed out that it was a gender marker as well. According to one nasologist, George Jabef, even Mme Montcornet nasal fastidiousness was no match for that of any male member of her class; for just as women body and brains were smaller than men's, so too were their nasal

---

50   Corbin, The Foul and the Fragrant, 20
51   Ibid., 270, n. 4.
52   Charles Leonard Pfeiffer, Taste and Smell in Balzac's Novels (Tucson: University of Arizona Humanities Bulletin. 6.1, 1949).
53   Cited in Corbin, The Foul and the Fragrant, 155.

appendages, and this put them at a distinct disadvantage in terms of olfactory sensitivity and intelligence:

> Whatever the cause, it is almost indisputable that women's characters are generally less developed than those of men; and this fact accurately accords with the usual development of their Noses. But for a small hiatus in the prosody, Pope's line would read equally well thus: —
>
> "most women have no Noses at all."
>
> Not, of course, that the nasal appendage is wanting, any more than Pope intended by the original line that women's characteristics were wholly negative; but like their characters, their Noses are, for the most part cast in a smaller and less developed mould than the Nose masculine.[54]

As we can see, the "civilized" nose had become the organ best able the sniff out and monitor the "civilized" body, which was well-washed and well-groomed with its boundaries carefully guarded and cordoned off from odoriferous "others." In this respect the "civilized" nose and body were wholly different from the uncivilized noses and bodies of the poor, whose boundaries were porous to such an extent that they were virtually indistinguishable from beasts. Even that great champion of the poor and crusader against inequality, Friedrich Engels, had absorbed this way of thinking as we can see from his description of the Irish sharing lodgings with their pigs:

> The Irishman allows the pig to share his own living quarters. This new, abnormal method of rearing livestock in the large towns is entirely of the Irish origin . . . The Irishman lives and sleeps with the pig, the children play with the pig, ride on its back, and roll about in the filth with it.[55]

For those acquainted with the long history of Christian anti-Semitism, Engels's statement brings to mind the disgusting motif of the "Judensau," which demeaned Jews by depicting them eating pig excrement and sucking at the teats of sows[56]. Eighteenth- and nineteenth-century upper and middle class Europeans may have been more fastidious than their ancestors when it came to olfactory sensitivity, but the practice of dehumanizing groups by associating them with animals would appear to be as old as human history.[57] And eating excrement was the ultimate image of an individual and a world gone to Hell.

---

[54] George Jabet, *Notes on Noses* (1848; London: Richard Bentley, 1852), 110.

[55] Cited in Stalleybrass and White, *The Politics and Poetics of Transgression*, 132.

[56] Editor's note: see the excellent study on this topic by Alexandra Cuffel, *Gendering Disgust in Medieval Religious Polemic* (Notre Dame, IN: University of Notre Dame Press, 2007); see my review in *Mediaevistik*, forthcoming.

[57] Isaiah Shachar, *The Judensau: a Medieval Anti-Jewish Motif and its History*. Warburg Institute Surveys, 5 (London: The Warburg Institute, 1974).

The moral dimensions of hygiene are increasingly highlighted in the eighteenth and nineteenth centuries. Foul odors had, of course, been associated with evil and the demonic from time immemorial. The Assyrian and Babylonian demon Pazuzu, source of disease and death, stank as a result of his rotting genitals. The stench of Hell is a common Christian motif, the reverse side of "the odor of sanctity," which was taken as a sign of saintliness in the medieval Church. However, in the eighteenth and nineteenth centuries the religious dimensions of smell were secularized to register poor hygiene as a new boundary marker separating rich and poor. In addition to being a sign of godliness, cleanliness was now the cause as well as the sign of an industrious, law-abiding, and prosperous citizenry. Bishop Berkeley drew this connection in his critique of the Irish:

> A little washing, scrubbing and rubbing, bestowed on their persons and houses would introduce a sort of industry, and industry in any one kind is apt to beget it in another . . . . You shall not find a clean house inhabited by clean people, and yet wanting in necessaries; the same spirit of industry that keeps folk clean being sufficient to keep them also in food and raiment.[58]

William Hazlitt (1778–1830) drew a similar correlation between cleanliness and industry: "a people that are remarkable for cleanliness will be so for industry, for honesty, for avarice." But he goes even farther in equating good, capitalist mores with morality:

> The more any one finds himself clinging to material objects for existence or gratification, the more he will take a personal interest in them, and the more will he clean, repair, polish, scrub, scour, and tug at them without end, as if it were his own soul that he was keeping clean from spot or blemish.[59]

Edwin Chadwick (1800–1890), one of the fiercest proponents of the miasma theory of disease and a leading British exponent of "the sanitary idea," drew a correlation between physical and moral depravity:

> how much of rebellion, of moral depravity and of crime has its root in physical disorder and depravity . . . . [the fever] nests and seats of physical depravity are also the seats of moral depravity, disorder, and crime with which the police have most to do.[60]

Such a statement anticipates the rhetoric of Social Darwinism.

---

[58] Cited in Thomas, "Cleanliness," 80.
[59] William Hazlitt, *The Collected Works of William Hazlitt*, ed. Alfred R. Waller Arnold Glover (London: J. M Dent & Co, 1903), vii, 176–77.
[60] Cited in Stalleybrass and White, *The Politics and Poetics of Transgression*, 131.

As Mary Douglas and other scholars have argued, every society's cosmology includes some kind symbolic connection between dirt and danger along with injunctions about how to eliminate both and restore purity. Even such mundane things as spring cleaning represents an attempt on a personal scale to re-order the environment by exposing and eliminating the dirt that is literally under the rug.[61] On a cosmic scale sacrifice has been one of the most prevalent ways to restore purity and rid the environment of disorder and the dangers it unleashes. In early-modern Europe heretics and witches were forced to assume the role of the sacrificial scapegoats, whose elimination would restore social equilibrium and eradicate pollution. Heretics and witches represented the demonic forces—which equals Stallybrass's and White's "low"—who threatened to erupt from the underworld engulfing those on "high" ground. In the increasingly secularized eighteenth and nineteenth centuries this underworld was more apt to be associated with the poor, the criminal, and the foreign, in short, with those social groups deemed socially unacceptable.

This is where the metaphor of the sewer as a threat to civilization became increasingly apt as in the description from Victor Hugo's Les Misérables with which this paper began. Sewers called to mind the diverse threats presented to society by a shady underworld inhabited by criminals, where all kinds of disreputable acts occurred beyond the gaze of law and order. As Inglis suggests, the task of mapping the Parisian sewers undertaken in the nineteenth century had implications far beyond the mundane goal of establishing a more rational system of waste collection and disposal. Mapping the existing sewer system "brought them into the light of day, allowing the gaze of the bourgeois state to penetrate into their deepest recess."[62] Mapping the sewers was part of the larger endeavor to control the irrational and the subversive, which by definition was also the feminine:

> The sewers of early nineteenth-century Paris were understood by the contemporary bourgeoisie to be 'feminine' in nature, for they were under the influence of Nature rather than Reason, and thus full of potentially subversive threats. Conversely, the sewers constructed by the State in the Haussmann period and after exhibited a

---

[61] Douglas categorically rejects the idea that we clean up our mess and dirt purely for hygienic reasons, while "primitives" avoid dirt out of irrational superstition and religious fears. As she says, "In chasing dirt, papering, decorating, tidying we are not governed by anxiety to escape disease, but are positively re-ordering our environment, making it conform to an idea. There is nothing fearful or unreasoning in our dirt-avoidance: it is a creative movement, an attempt to relate form to function, to make unity of experience. If this is so with our separating, tidying and purifying, we should interpret primitive purifications and prophylaxis in the same light" (Purity and Danger, 2).

[62] Inglis, "Sewers and Sensibilities," 124.

'masculine' rationality, allowing a predictable uniformity where Nature was harnassed rather than in control.[63]

The attempt to illuminate the dark underworld of sewer systems in Europe went hand in hand with schemes to reform and refashion prisons and hospitals. All such schemes were predicated on the increasingly prevalent assumption that cleanliness was a sine qua non moral probity. Dutch prisons became models of personal hygiene, in which each inmate had his own room, wooden bed, and straw mattress all in the interest of moral rehabilitation. John Howard (1726–1790), the father of prison reform in England, worked diligently to inculcate habits of cleanliness among prisoners because he believed that such habits were an essential aspect of honesty and decency. Deploring the crowded and unsanitary conditions in a prison ship anchored off Plymouth, he remarked:

> I could wish that the whole of Saturday were appropriated to cleanliness, viz., bathing, washing and mending their clothes, shaving, cleaning themselves and every part of the ship, and beating and airing their bedding. Thus endeavouring to introduce habits of cleanliness is an object of great importance as many officers have observed 'that the most cleanly ones are always the most decent and most honest, and the most slovenly and dirty are the most vicious and irregular.'[64]

Regardless of all the work of reformers like Howard and the innumerable sanitary engineers and scientists who tried to protect the elite members of society from the contagion emanating from their inferiors, the boundary separating rich and poor in terms of odor was decidedly porous. For at the heart of middle and upper class households were the lower class females who were increasingly entrusted with attending to the bodily needs of their employers as wives and daughters regarded such ministrations with growing disgust. This asymmetry between the upper and lower classes played out in a peculiar way, in what Gail Marshall has described as the "Galatea-aesthetic." Artists, writers, and males from all walks of middle and upper class life sought out working-class women as companions, models, lovers, and even wives, desiring them for their difference, yet attempting to transform them into more socially acceptable beings who would bridge the gap between lower-class physicality and bourgeois sensitivity.[65]

The fusion of power, fear, and desire involved in such attempts created a psychological dependence on precisely those aspects of dirt and disorder to be rejected and excluded. Thus the repressed returned with a vengeance, or to quote

---

[63]  Ibid.

[64]  Cited in Corbin, *The Foul and the Fragrant*, 108–09.

[65]  Gail Marshall, *Actresses on the Victorian Stage: Feminine Performance and the Galatea Myth* (Oxford: Oxford University Press, 1994); M. A. Danahay, "Mirrors of Masculine Desire: Narcissus and Pygmalion in Victoria Representation," *Victorian Poetry* 32 (1994): 35–53.

Stallybrass and White, "It is for this reason that what is socially peripheral is so frequently *symbolically* central . . . . ."[66]

This essay provides a lot, perhaps too much, information about the unpleasant fecal matters that dogged the footsteps and obsessed the minds of pre-modern urban dwellers, especially during the eighteenth century. They reveal how discordant actual life was from the idealization of that life that was such a part of contemporary aesthetic theory, neoclassical paining, pastoral poetry, and idyllic descriptions of country house living. In the sanitized depictions of life presented by Fragonard, Boucher, Poussin and Claude Lorraine, not to mention Gainsborough and Reynolds, as well as by the authors of pastoral poetry, the excremental reality in which the vast majority of people lived is utterly absent or repressed.[67] But for all the idealization that one finds in neo-classical art and eighteenth-century literature, it is not accurate to say that upper class elites lived in ivory towers and used art as an escape from the realities of daily life.

Although much of eighteenth-century art and literature ignores the urban realities I have described, the aim of this art was to improve, even perfect, nature. The wish to change and improve was precisely what motivated scientists and sanitary reformers in their efforts to locate and confine excremental filth on both a literal and figurative level to its proper place. While this had negative effects in terms of curtailing individual freedoms, as Foucault and others have emphasized, it also led to the concepts of city planning and public welfare we are used to today, however imperfect both have proven to be. In the course of doing this, a new kind of subjective sensibility emerged. While this had the immediate effect of erecting new barriers between classes and ethnic groups, in the long term it undermined these barriers as the more equitable distribution of wealth allowed increasing numbers of people to accommodate to the new standards of hygiene put in place by the olfactory revolution of the eighteenth century.

---

[66] Stallybrass and White, *The Politics and Poetics of Transgression*, 5.
[67] Frabricant, *Swift's Landscapes*, 18, 42.

# Illustrations

Illustrations for Albrecht Classen's "Introduction":

Figure 1: *Luttrell Psalter: A Facsimile*, commentary by Michelle P. Brown (London: The British Library, 2006), fol. 164 verso
Figure 2: Poznań City Hall
(http://image46.webshots.com/47/7/75/21/2992775210090122875XVvqUI_ph.jpg)


Illustrations for C. David Benson's article "The Dead and the Living: Some Medieval Descriptions of the Ruins and Relics of Rome Known to the English" (all @ C. David Benson):

Figure 1: Castel S. Angelo (Hadrian's Sepulchre)
Figure 2: Obelisk at St. Peter's (Caesar's Pillar or Needle)
Figure 3: Fresco of Equestrian Statue before Lateran (by Filippino Lippi at S. Maria sopra Minerva)
Figure 4: Copy of Equestrian Statue (Marcus Aurelius) on Capitoline Hill
Figure 5: Colosseum
Figure 6: Head, Hand, and Sphere of Emperor (Idol of Sun)
Figure 7: Tomb of Saints Lawrence and Stephen (under high altar of Saint Lawrence)
Figure 8: Capitoline Venus
Figure 9: Original Equestrian Statue (Marcus Aurelius)
Figure 10: Stone Thrown at St. Dominic by Devil (S. Sabina)
Figure 11: Site of Well of Oil at Christ's Birth (S. Maria Trastevere)
Figure 12: Altar in Octavian's Vision (S. Maria in Aracoeli)

Illustration for Shennan Hutton's article "Women, Men, and Markets: The Gendering of Market Space in Late Medieval Ghent":

Figure 1: Map of Ghent in the fifteenth century. Taken from Marc Boone, *Gent en de Bourgondische hertogen, ca. 1384–ca. 1453. Een sociaal-politieke studie van een staatsvormingsproces.* Courtesy of the author.

Illustrations for Lia B. Ross's article "Anger and the City: Who Was in Charge of the Paris *cabochien* Revolt of 1413?":

Figure 1: The Bastille before the Revolution (http://en.wikipedia.org/wiki/Bastille)
Figure 2: Butchers' arms (http://www.france-pittoresque.com/metiers/46.htm)
Figure 3: John the Fearless
    (http://www.wga.hu/frames-e.html?/html/m/master/zunk_fl/15_paint/1/12 john_f.html
Figure 4: Map of old Paris
    (http://employees.oneonta.edu/farberas/arth/arth214_folder/paris_maps.htm; map is edited by author, with addition of arrows)

Illustrations for Klaus Amann's and Max Siller's article "Urban Literary Entertainment in the Middle Ages and the Early Modern Age: The Example of Tyrol":

Figure 1: Tyrol in 1766 (http://hoeckmann.de/deutschland/tirol.htm)
Figure 2: Sterzing Miscellanea Manuscript, Sterzing Municipal Archives, no signature, fol. 42r. Digitized: http://alo.uibk.ac.at/webinterface/library/ALO-BOOK_V01?objid=14101&page=48&zoom=1&ocr=; fol. 42r (detail)
Figure 3: *Das Ambraser Liederbuch vom Jahre 1582*, ed. Joseph Bergmann (Stuttgart: Literarischer Verein, 1845), V, front page (detail)
Figure 4: Depiction of miners in the St. Magdalena chapel of Ridnaun (near Sterzing). Master Matheis Stöberl, 1509 (photograph: Max Siller)
Figure 5: Hans Thalhofer, *Fechtbuch von 1476*, Bayerische Staatsbibliothek München, Cod.icon. 394a, fol. 7v (Internet:
    http://mdzx.bib-bvb.de/codicon/Blatt_bsb00020451,00016.html)
Figure 6: Hans Thalhofer, *Fechtbuch von 1476*, Bayerische Staatsbibliothek München, Cod.icon. 394a, fol. 86v (Internet:
    http://mdzx.bib-bvb.de/codicon/Blatt_bsb00020451,00174.html)
Figure 7: Runkelstein Castle, Tournament Hall, southern wall: joust, ball games,

round dance. *Schloss Runkelstein. Die Bilderburg*, ed. André Bechtold (Bozen: Athesia, 2000), figure 114

Figure 8: Runkelstein Castle, Tournament Hall, southern wall: joust (detail: female spectators). *Schloss Runkelstein. Die Bilderburg*, ed. André Bechtold (Bozen: Athesia, 2000), figure 118

Illustrations for Fabian Alfie's article "'The Merchants of My Florence': A Socio-Political Complaint from 1457":

Figure 1: Burchiello 1757 edition, *Sonetti del Burchiello, del Bellincioni e d'altri poeti fiorentini alla burchiellesca*, [n.p.]: Londra [Lucca], 1757 (@ Fabian Alfie)

Figure 2: Firenze II iv 250 (f. 194r), codex Firenze II.IV.250 su concessione del *Ministero per i Beni e le Attività Culturali della Repubblica Italiana / Biblioteca Nazionale Centrale di Firenze*" (further reproductions are not permitted)

Illustrations for Birgit Wiedl's article "Jews and the City: Parameters of Jewish Urban Life in Late-Medieval Austria":

Figure 1: Statue of Synagoga, Bamberg cathedral, ca. 1230 (@ Birgit Wiedl)

Figure 2: Statue of Synagoga, Strasbourg cathedral, ca. 1225 (@ Birgit Wiedl)

Figure 3: Statue of Ecclesia, Strasbourg cathedral, ca. 1225 (@ Birgit Wiedl)

Figure 4: Mahzor with a depiction of a bridal couple, the bride, with the typical items of Ecclesia, has her eyes blindfolded, which, in Christian depictions, is the distinctive feature for Synagoga, ca.1330 (Staats- und Universitätsbibliothek Hamburg)

Figure 5: Decoration in the "Niederösterreichischen Randleistenstil," Missale, second half of fourteenth century (Stiftsbibliothek Klosterneuburg, Cod. 74)

Figure 6: Sales deed of the monastery of Kremsmünster (Upper Austria) with the corresponding Hebrew charter attached to it (Stiftsarchiv Kremsmünster, 1305 April 29, Hebrew, and May 3, German)

Illustrations for Jan Hirschbiegel's and Gabriel Zeilinger's article "Urban Space Divided? The Encounter of Civic and Courtly Spheres in Late-Medieval Towns":

Figure 1: King Sigismund on his way to the Cathedral of Constance, December 1414 (Richental, *Konzil*, 1: *Faksimileausgabe*, fol. 19v)

Figure 2: King Sigismund in the Cathedral of Constance, Christmas 1414 (Richental, *Konzil*, 1: *Faksimileausgabe*, fol. 20r)

Figure 3: King Sigismund is escorted over the Lake of Constance, here in January 1417 (*Die Schweiz im Mittelalter in Diebold Schillings Spiezer Bilderchronik*, ed. Hans Haeberli and Christoph von Steiger. Studienausgabe zur Faksimile-Edition der Hs. Mss. hist. helv. I. 16 d. Burgerbibliothek Bern [Lucerne: Faksimile-Verlag, 1991], 392, based on the *Spiezer Bilderchronik*, 609 [as in Schenk, *Zeremoniell und Politik*, Figure 13])

Illustrations for Pınar Kayaalp's article "The Role of Imperial Mosque Complexes (1543-1583) in the Urbanization of Üsküdar ":

Figure 1: Axonometric projection of the Mihrümah Sultan Mosque Complex. Üsküdar. Source: Necipoğlu, *Age of Sinan*, 300, F. 280

Figure 2: Plan of the Mihrümah Sultan Mosque Complex. Üsküdar: 1. mosque; 2. medrese; 3. elementary school; 4. mausoleum of Cigalizade Sinan Pasha (d. 1605); 5. mausoleum of Edhem Pasha (1892–1893); 6. cemetery garden. Source: Necipoğlu, *Age of Sinan*, 299, F. 279

Figure 3: Mihrümah Sultan Mosque Complex in Üsküdar from the south. Source: Necipoğlu, *Age of Sinan*, 302, F. 283

Figure 4: Mihrümah Sultan Mosque Complex, Üsküdar, double portico with projecting ablution fountain. Source: Necipoğlu, *Age of Sinan*, 302, F. 282

Figure 5: Axonometric projection of the Şemsi Pasha Mosque Complex, Üsküdar. Source: Necipoğlu, *Age of Sinan*, 403, F. 518

Figure 6: Plan of the Şemsi Pasha Mosque Complex, Üsküdar. Source: Necipoğlu, *Age of Sinan*, 493, F. 517

Figure 7: Arial view of the Şemsi Pasha Mosque Complex, Üsküdar. Source: Necipoğlu, *Age of Sinan*, 495, F. 520

Figure 8: Louis-Francois Cassas, Sketch of the Atik Valide Mosque Complex, Üsküdar ('Escki Validé, vielle mère à Scutari'), ca. 1786, pencil on paper. Source: Necipoğlu, *Age of Sinan*, 289, F. 268

Figure 9: Plan of the Atik Valide Mosque Complex, Üsküdar, with a hypothetical reconstruction of its hospice-caravansary-hospital block: 1. mosque; 2. medrese; 3. Sufi convent; 4. elementary school; 5. Hadith school; 6. fountain of Hasan Çavuş; 7. vestibule; 8. double caravansary with stables; 9. hospice kitchens; 10. guest rooms; 11. hospital; 12. double bath. Source: Necipoğlu, *Age of Sinan*, 282, F. 261

Illustrations for Martha Moffitt Peacock's article "Early Modern Dutch Women in the City: The Imaging of Economic Agency and Power":

Figure 1: Caspar Netscher, *The Lacemaker*, Wallace Collection, London, *The Wallace Collection: A Complete Catalogue*, Stephen Duffy and Jo Hedley (London: Unicorn Press and Lindsay Fine Art), 301

Figure 2: Geertruydt Roghman, *Spinner*, Rijksprentenkabinet, Amsterdam, "Geertruydt Roghman and the Female Perspective in Seventeenth-Century Dutch Genre Imagery," *Woman's Art Journal* 14. 2 (1993–1994): 5

Figure 3: Anonymous, *The Struggle for Daily Bread*, Historisch Museum, Amsterdam, *Ingelijst Werk, De verbeelding van arbeid en beroep in de vroegmoderne Nederlanden*, Annette de Vries (Zwolle: Waanders, 2004), 231.

Figure 4: Isaac Claesz. Van Swanenburgh, *The Spinning, Reeling, Warping, and Weaving of Wool*, Stedelijk Museum De Lakenhal, Leiden, *Ingelijst Werk, De verbeelding van arbeid en beroep in de vroegmoderne Nederlanden*, Annette de Vries (Zwolle: Waanders, 2004), 212

Figure 5: Hendrick Martensz. Sorgh, *Vegetable Market*, Rijksmuseum, Amsterdam, *Rembrandt and the Golden Age of Dutch Art: Treasures from the Rijksmuseum, Amsterdam*, Ruud Priem, ed. Penelope Hunter-Steibel (Dayton Art Institute, Ohio, Phoenix Art Museum, Arizona, Portland Art Museum, Oregon in Association with The Rijksmuseum, Amsterdam, 2006), 63

Figure 6: Jan van de Velde, *Market*, Rijksprentenkabinet, Amsterdam, Elizabeth Alice Honig, "Desire and Domestic Economy," *Art Bulletin* 83.2 (June 2001): 302

Figure 7: Emanuel de Witte, *Old Market on the Dam*, Museo Thyssen-Bornemisza, Madrid, *The Thyssen-Bornemisza Collection: Seventeenth-Century Dutch and Flemish Painting*, Ivan Gaskell, General Editor Simon de Pury (London: Sotheby's Publications, 1990), 281

Figure 8: Sybrand van Beest, *The Pig Market in the Hague*, Bredius Museum, The Hague, *Museum Bredius: Catalogus van de schilderijen en tekeningen*, Albert Blankert (Zwolle: Waanders, 1991,) 47

Figure 9: Cornelis Beelt, *Weaver's Workshop*, Bredius Museum, The Hague, *Ingelijst Werk, De verbeelding van arbeid en beroep in de vroegmoderne Nederlanden*, Annette de Vries (Zwolle: Waanders, 2004), 222

Figure 10: "Quirijn Gerritsz. van Brekelenkam," *Portrait of Apothecary and His Wife*, Present Location Unknown, Rijksbureau voor Kunsthistorische Documentatie.

Figure 11: Jan Steen, *Baker Arend Oostwaert and his wife Catharina Keyzerswaert*, Rijksmuseum, Amsterdam, *The Amusements of Jan Steen: Comic Painting in the Seventeenth Century*, Mariët Westermann (Zwolle: Waanders, 1997), 189

## Illustration for Allison P. Coudert's article Sewers, Cesspools, and Privies: Waste as Reality and Metaphor in Pre-modern European Cities":

# Contributors

FABIAN ALFIE is Associate Professor of Italian at the University of Arizona. He got his PhD from the University of Wisconsin, Madison in 1995 with a specialization in the Middle Ages. His field of research focuses on the comic literature of the thirteenth and fourteenth centuries, and in particular on insulting poetry. In 2001, he published his first book, *Comedy and Culture: Cecco Angiolieri and Late Medieval Society* (Leeds, UK: Northern Universities Press). He has published several articles on Cecco Angiolieri and his circle, including Rustico Filippi, Meo dei Tolomei and Pietro dei Faitinelli. For the past several years, he has been working on a monograph on Dante's insulting correspondence with Forese Donati.

ROSA ALVAREZ PEREZ got her Ph.D. at CUNY (City University of New York) in 2005 and so far has published five entries: "The Biblical Judith;" "Jewish Tradition, Gender and Women;" "Rabelais;" "Judaism;" "Jewish Women's League" in the *Encyclopedia of Sex and Gender*, Editor-in-Chief Fedwa Malti Douglas (Farmington Hills, MI: MacMillan, 2007). She is currently preparing an article temporarily titled "Porous Boundaries: Crisscrossing Networks between Jewish and Christian Women" for a special issue of *Women in French Studies*, titled *Rivalry, Cooperation, Conspiracy, and Patronage: Studies in the Dynamics of Women's Interaction in French Literature and Culture*, ed. by Julia Simms Holderness and Laurence M. Porter. She currently holds the position of an Assistant Professor of French at Southern Utah University.

KLAUS AMANN received his Ph.D. from the University of Innsbruck, Austria, in 2006 with a critical edition, commentary, and interpretation of *Das Pfäferser Passionsspielfragment. Edition, Untersuchung, Kommentar* (Innsbruck: Innsbruck University Press, forthcoming May 2009). Between 2002 and 2006 he was Lecturer at the "Institut für deutsche Sprache, Literatur und Literaturkritik" at the University of Innsbruck, and since 2006 he has been Lecturer in the Department of German at the same university. He has co-edited with Max Siller the conference proceedings of the fifth symposium on the *Sterzinger Osterspiele* that took place in 2004 (2008), and is currently preparing the proceedings of a symposium dedicated to Hugo von Montfort that took place in 2007.

C. DAVID BENSON is a professor of English and Medieval Studies at the University of Connecticut. He has also taught at Columbia, Colorado, Virginia, and Harvard. He has published books on Troy, Chaucer, and Langland, such as *The History of Troy in Middle English Literature* (1980), *Chaucer's Drama of Style* (1986), *Chaucer's Troilus and Criseyde* (1990), *Public Piers Plowman: Modern Scholarship and Late Medieval English Culture* (2004), and co-edited a collection of essays on *Chaucer's Religious Tales* (ed., with Elizabeth Ann Robertson, 1990), and a text of Mandeville's Travels (*The Book of John Mandeville*, ed., together with Tamarah Kohanski, 2007).

MICHAEL E. BONINE is Professor of Geography and Professor and Head of the Department of Near Eastern Studies at the University of Arizona, where he has been since 1975. He received his Ph.D. in Geography in 1975 from the University of Texas at Austin, completing a dissertation on city-hinterland relationships based upon two years of field work in Yazd and central Iran. He was Executive Director of the Middle East Studies Association of North America (MESA) from 1982 to 1989. He has served on the Board of Directors of the American Institute of Maghribi Studies, the American Institute of Yemeni Studies, the Society for Gulf Arab Studies, and the American Institute for Iranian Studies (and serving as President for three years). Dr. Bonine's research has focused on urbanism and urbanization in the Middle East, and besides his earlier work in Iran he has conducted research in Morocco, Tunisia, Egypt, Yemen, United Arab Emirates, and Turkey—and he has made extensive travels in many other Middle East and Muslim countries. He is the author of numerous articles as well as the author or editor of several books, including *Modern Iran: Dialectics of Continuity and Change* (1981), *Middle Eastern Cities and Islamic Urbanism* (1994), and *Population, Poverty, and Politics in Middle East Cities* (1997). He has just recently been asked to be the organizer and editor for a *Handbook on Middle Eastern Cities* for Routledge Press, and he is working on a textbook manuscript called *The Geography of Islam.*

ALBRECHT CLASSEN is University Distinguished Professor of German Studies at the University of Arizona. He has published numerous books and articles on German and European literature from the early Middle Ages to the seventeenth and eighteenth centuries. Most recently, he published *Meeting the Foreign in the Middle Ages* (2002); *Verzweiflung und Hoffnung* (2002; a study on communication in the Middle Ages); *Violence in Medieval Courtly Literature* (2004); *Childhood in the Middle Ages and the Renaissance* (2005); *Der Liebes- und Ehediskurs vom hohen Mittelalter bis zum frühen 17. Jahrhundert* (2005; Discourse on Love and Marriage from the high Middle Ages to the Early Seventeenth Century); and *The Medieval Chastity Belt: A Myth Making Process* (2007). His latest monograph, *The Woman's Voice in Medieval Literature* (2007) appeared with de Gruyter, for which he also serves as editor of the book series "Fundamentals of Medieval and Early Modern Culture (FMC). Dr. Classen is the editor of *Tristania* and co-editor of *Mediaevistik*. In 2004 the German government awarded him with the *Bundesverdienstkreuz am Band* (Order of Merit) in recognition of his contributions to the dissemination of German culture, language, and literature. In 2006 he received the AATG Outstanding German Educator Award and Checkpoint Charlie Foundation Scholarship (College-University Level), in 2007 the Southeastern Medieval Association Outstanding Scholarly Achievement Award, and in 2008 the *Henry & Phyllis Koffler Prize for Outstanding Accomplishments in Research* from the University of Arizona. In 2009 he was the recipient of the Five Star Faculty Award (student-only nomination). His English translation of the complete works of Oswald von Wolkenstein (1376/77–1445) appeared in 2008, and a book on sixteenth-century German jest narratives is forthcoming.

ALLISON P. COUDERT received her PhD from the Warburg Institute, University of London. She is currently the Paul and Marie Castelfranco Chair in the Religious Studies Program at the University of California at Davis. Her published books include *Leibniz and the Kabbalah* (Dordrecht: Kluwer, 1995) and *The Impact of the Kabbalah in the 17thCentury: The Life and Thought of Francis Mercury van Helmont, 1614–1698* (Leiden and Boston: Brill, 1999). Among her recent articles are, "Ange du foyer ou idole de perversité: ésotérisme au feminine au XIXe siècle," Politica Hermetica 20 (2006): 29–47 and "The Sulzbach Jubilee: Old Age in Early Modern Europe and America," Old Age in the Middle Ages and the Renaissance: Interdisciplinary Approaches to a Neglected Topic, ed. Albrecht Classen (Berlin and New York: Walter de Gruyter, 2005), 389–413. She is also represented in the new volume, *History of Sexuality in the Middle Ages and the Early Modern Age*, ed. Albrecht Classen (Berlin and New York: de Gruyter, 2008), with a study on "From the Clitoris to the Breast: The Eclipse of the Female Libido in Early Modern Art, Literature, and Philosophy."

JAN HIRSCHBIEGEL, studied Ancient, Medieval, and Early Modern history as well as European Ethnology and received his M.A. in History from the Christian-Albrechts-University of Kiel in 1993. In 1998 he was awarded a doctorate in History from the same university, his thesis dealing with gift-giving at the French courts in the later Middle Ages: *Étrennes. Untersuchungen zum höfischen Geschenkverkehr im spätmittelalterlichen Frankreich der Zeit König Karls VI. (1380–1422)* ( 2003). Since 1995 he has been working as a research assistant for the *Residenzen-Kommission*, a research-group of the *Academy of Sciences in Göttingen*. Currently he is working on a habilitation titled: "Manifestations of Trust? Close Relations at Princely Courts in the Later Middle Ages."

SHENNAN HUTTON is an independent scholar/adjunct lecturer who received a Ph.D. in medieval European history in 2006 from the University of California, Davis. She entered graduate school after many years of teaching world history and women's history to high school students. The author of two articles on women's economic activities in late medieval Ghent, she also has a strong interest in effective teaching of history at all levels, as she has organized and conducted institutes on world history for K–12 teachers as well as winning an Outstanding Graduate Student Teaching Award at UC Davis. She is currently making revisions on a book manuscript, provisionally titled "In Her Own Name: Women and Economic Activities in Late Medieval Ghent." This project, a reworking of the doctoral dissertation she wrote under the direction of Professor Joan Cadden, examines gendered divisions in craft production, property transactions, and credit markets.

JEAN E. JOST is Professor of English at Bradley University where she teaches graduate and undergraduate courses on Chaucer, Arthurian Literature, Old and Middle English surveys, Medieval Drama, and Middle English romance. She has published *Ten Middle English Arthurian Romances; A Reference Guide* and edited a collection called *Chaucer's Humor: Critical Essays*. Currently she is editing the *Southern Recension of the Pricke of Conscience*. Her articles have considered Chaucer's Performative Criseyde, masculinities in the Friar's and Summoner's Tales, various Middle English romances (*Amis and Amiloun, Awntyrs off Arthur at the Terne Wathelyne, The Turke and Gowin,* and *Tristan and Isolt*), the poetics of sexual desire in the Merchant's Tale, The Un-Chaucerian *Tale of Beryn*, The Gawain-Poet, and several articles published by Albrecht Classen. Her last NEH on the Old French Fabliaux has provided a new interest which she is pursuing.

PINAR KAYAALP holds a Ph.D. from Harvard University and is currently Assistant Professor of Islamic and Middle Eastern Studies at Ramapo College, New Jersey. Her interests lie in Ottoman women's history, art history, urban history, and poor relief. She is currently working on a history of health and welfare in the Ottoman Empire in the sixteenth and seventeenth centuries. Her most recent work includes: "The Atik Valide's Endowment Deed: A Textual Analysis," *Feeding People, Feeding Power: Imarets in the Ottoman Empire,* ed. Amy Singer and Christoph Neumann (Istanbul: Eren, 2007), 261–73; "Circumcision." *Encyclopedia of the Modern World,* ed. Peter N. Steams (2008), 179–181; "Bosphorus Strait," *Seas and Waterways of the World: An Encylcopedia of History, Uses, and Issues,* ed. John Zumerchick and Steven Danver (forthcoming); and "Foucault on the Diffusion of Power," *Introduction to Classical and Contemporary Social Theory,* ed. Berch Berberoğlu (forthcoming).

ANDREAS MEYER received his Ph.D. in 1984, and his Habilitation in 1993, both at the University of Zurich. Between 1989 and 1996 he carried out research in Rome, and since 2001 he has been Professor of History at the University of Marburg, Germany. His Habilitation appeared in print under the title *Felix et inclitus notarius. Studien zum italienischen Notariat vom 7.bis 13. Jahrhundert* (2000). Since then he has published *Ser Ciabattus. Regesti di imbreviature lucchesi del Duecento*, vol. I: *anni 1222–1232* (2005), and a number of articles on the "Volto Santo" in the thirteenth-century Lucca community (2005), on organized beggar business and other financial operations by the hospital in Altopascio (2007), on leprosy and medical examinations of this sickness in thirteenth-century Lucca (2007), and on marriage contracts, also in Lucca (2007).

ALAN V. MURRAY studied Medieval History, German, and Folk Studies at the universities of St Andrews, Salzburg, and Freiburg. He received his Ph.D. from St. Andrews in 1988. He is currently Senior Lecturer in Medieval Studies at the University of Leeds and Editor of the *International Medieval Bibliography*. He has written numerous studies on the crusades and the Latin states of Outremer, medieval chronicles, and Middle High German literature. His publications include the monograph *The Crusader Kingdom of Jerusalem: A Dynastic History, 1099–1125* (2000), the collection *Crusade and Conversion on the Baltic Frontier* (2001), and the 4-volume reference work *The Crusades: An Encyclopedia* (2006). His most recent work has been on the logistics and practical dimensions of how major military expeditions functioned in the central Middle Ages, as well as on chronicles of the Baltic Crusades.

MARTHA MOFFITT PEACOCK is Professor of Art History at Brigham Young University. She received her Ph.D. from The Ohio State University in 1989, specializing in the history of seventeenth-century Dutch art. Her research has particularly centered on the relationship of art to the lives of women—both as artists and subjects in art—in the Dutch Republic. She has published a number of articles and essays in both international and national art historical journals and books including: "Compatible Characters in Contrasting Cultures: Hieronymus Bosch and Jacopo Bellini," *Nord/Sud II*, University of Padua, to be published in 2009; "Hoorndragers and Hennetasters: The Old Impotent Cuckold as Other in Netherlandish Art and Farce," *Old Age in the Middle Ages and Renaissance*, ed. Albrecht Classen, 2007; and "Domesticity in the Public Sphere," *Saints, Sinners, and Sisters. Gender and Northern Art in Medieval and Early Modern Europe*, ed. Jane Carroll and Alison Stewart, 2003. Currently, she is working on a book, *Heroines, Harpies and Housewives: Women of Consequence in the Dutch Golden Age*.

DANIEL F. PIGG is a Professor of English at The University of Tennessee at

Martin. He teaches courses on Chaucer and medieval British literature in addition to courses on the History of the English Language and Restoration and Eighteenth-Century British literature. He has published widely on a variety of medieval British literature, including *Beowulf*, the *Canterbury Tale*, *Piers Plowman*, and medieval romance materials in *Athelston* and Malory's "Tale of Sir Gareth." He has presented papers on old age in *Piers Plowman* and sexuality surrounding the representation of Sir Gareth in *Malory's Le Morte D'Arthur* at previous International Symposia sponsored by the University of Arizona, subsequently published. A particular area of specialization is the representation of masculinity in medieval literature. He is completing a research survey for the *Handbook of Medieval Studies* on that topic.

LIA B. ROSS holds a Ph.D. in European History (Medieval & Early Modern) from the University of New Mexico where she works full-time as a computer analyst and part-time as a history instructor. She has specialized in studies of fifteenth-century France, Burgundy, and England and is an active member of the *Centre européen d'études bourguignonnes*. In between other publications she is working on a book version of her dissertation, which examines the behavior of people in groups as narrated by French and Burgundian late-medieval chroniclers. The current piece was inspired by a chapter that deals with urban revolts.

BRITT C. L. ROTHAUSER is a Ph.D. student at the University of Connecticut and a full-time visiting professor at Eastern Connecticut State University. She holds a B.A. in Medieval Studies from the University of Connecticut and a M.A. in English from the University of Maryland. Her major interests are Anglo-Saxon language, literature, history, and paleography. Previously, she published "Winter in Heorot: Looking at Anglo-Saxon Perceptions of Age and Kingship through the Character of Hrothgar" with this series in the volume entitled *Old Age in the Middle Ages and the Renaissance*. Her dissertation explores the Anglo-Saxon perception of age and the place of the elderly within that society.

MARILYN SANDIDGE's recent scholarship has included papers and articles in medieval and early modern English literature. She is the director of  the MA program in English at Westfield State College, where she is a  professor of English. Along with Albrecht Classen, she co-edits the  Fundamentals of Medieval and Early Modern Culture series of books  published by Walter de Gruyter Press. Her publications on the roles of women or family relationships in medieval and early modern literature include "Changing Contexts of Infanticide in Medieval English Texts" in *Childhood in the Middle Ages and the Renaissance* (Berlin and New York: de Gruyter, 2005) and "Constructing New Women in Early Modern English Literature" in *Discourses on Love, Marriage, and Transgression in Medieval and Early*

*Modern Literature* (Tempe, AZ: Center for Medieval and Renaissance Studies, 2004).

CONNIE L. SCARBOROUGH is Professor of Romance Languages and Literatures at the University of Cincinnati. Her books include *Women in Thirteenth Century Spain as Portrayed in the Cantigas de Santa Maria*, a critical edition of the *Libro de los exenplos por a.b.c.*, and *Text and Concordance of Castigos y dotrinas que un sabio daba a sus hijas: Escorial MS. a.IV.5*. She has published numerous articles on Alfonso X's *Cantigas de Santa Maria* as well as on *La vida de Santa Maria Egipciaca, Celestina, and El libro de buen amor*. Her latest book, *A Holy Alliance: Alfonso X's use of Religious Verse for Political Purposes*, appeared in 2008. She currently serves as Executive Editor of the *Cincinnati Romance Review* and the *Bulletin of the Cantigueiros de Santa Maria*. In Fall of 2009 she is joining the faculty at Texas Tech University.

MAX SILLER is Professor of Older German Language and Literature at the University of Innsbruck, Austria. He received his Ph.D. in 1974, and his Habilitation in 1991 ("Literatur – Sprache – Territorium: Methoden, Aufgaben und Möglichkeiten einer regionalen Literaturgeschichtsschreibung des Mittelalters," 3 vols.). His book publications include an edition of *Das Evangelium Nicodemi in spätmittelalterlicher Prosa* (1981), several edited volumes with conference proceedings drawn from the symposia dedicated to the *Sterzinger Osterspiele* (1992, 1994, 1996, 2004, and 2008), and an edition of Martin Wild's *Ridnauner Dialektwörterbuch* (2005).

KISHA TRACY is a Ph.D. student in the Medieval Studies Program at the University of Connecticut. She earned her M.A. in Medieval Studies from the University of Connecticut in 2004 and her B.A. in English Literature from the University of Evansville in 2002. Currently, she is finishing up her dissertation, which is entitled "Writing Memory: Reinvention and the Tradition of Confession in Middle English Literature;" this study is focused on how the influential practice of confession is manifested through the widespread juxtaposition of confession and memory in Middle English literary texts and how this concept permeated other representations of memory as written by authors in a variety of genres. Her article "Character Memory and Reinvention of the Past in Béroul's *Roman de Tristan*" appeared in the 2006 issue of *Tristania*. Also, her study of the multicultural medieval representations of the Fisher King is forthcoming in a collection of essays concerned with the emerging field of medieval disability studies.

PATRICIA TURNING graduated, after having received her Bachelor's and Master's degree from the University of Akron, a Ph.D. from the University of California, Davis, in 2007. In 2005, the Medieval Academy of America granted her the first Birgit Baldwin Fellowship, which allowed her to spend extensive time in the archives of southern France. This experience provided her with the bulk of the sources that fuel her subsequent research projects. She is currently working on a monograph that examines how the urban public not only shaped political and judicial policies, but also participated in constructing the notions of law, order and justice that played out in their community. She has recently completed an article on the importance of public punishments in the city of Toulouse (forthcoming in the *French History Journal*), and a second piece that analyzes the role of policing forces in the urban realm. She is currently a Visiting Assistant Professor at Arizona State University, where she teaches courses on the Middle Ages and the Early Modern History.

BIRGIT WIEDL studied History, German, and Russian Philology at the University of Salzburg where she received her Magister and Ph.D., focusing on the late medieval and early modern periods, economic history, especially crafts and craftsmen, and urban history. She was employed as an archivist for the *MuseumsQuartier Vienna* from 1998 to 2001; since 2000 she has been working at the Institute for Jewish History in Austria on the project "Documents on Jewish History in Medieval Austria," funded by the Austrian Science Fund (FWF), that aims at the establishment of an encompassing collection of charters, historiographical and literary documents that bear reference to Austrian Jews. She has published two books: *Regesten zur Geschichte der Juden in Österreich im Mittelalter*. Vol 1: *Von den Anfängen bis 1338* (2005), together with Eveline Brugger; and *Alltag und Recht im Handwerk der Frühen Neuzeit* (2006), as well as a number of articles, such as "'Damit man müg sprechen, das ainer gelebt hat': Der lange Weg zur modernen Autobiographie," *Jüdische Lebensgeschichten: Erinnertes Leben – erzähltes Gedächtnis*, ed. Eleonore Lappin (2006), 2-9; and: "'. . . und ander frume leute genuch, paide christen und juden': Quellen zur christlich-jüdischen Interaktion im Spätmittelalter," *Räume und Wege: Jüdische Geschichte im Alten Reich 1300-1800*, ed. Rolf Kießling, Peter Rauscher, Stefan Rohrbacher, and Barbara Staudinger (2007), 285-305. From 2001 to 2008, she was a guest lecturer for the American Heritage Association/University of Portland, Oregon, at Vienna, teaching medieval and early modern history.

GABRIEL ZEILINGER studied History as well as Scandinavian Languages and Literature in Kiel, Germany, and Oslo, Norway, graduating in 2002 with a Master's thesis on court festivals in fifteenth-century Württemberg (published as *Die Uracher Hochzeit 1474: Form und Funktion eines höfischen Festes im 15. Jahrhundert*, 2003). In 2006 he received his Ph.D from the Christian-Albrechts-Universität zu Kiel, with a dissertation on every-day life in late-medieval wars (published as *Lebensformen im Krieg: Eine Alltags- und Erfahrungsgeschichte des süddeutschen Städtekriegs 1449/50*, 2007). He is currently Lecturer for Medieval Economic and

Social History at the Department of History in Kiel with a research emphasis on the social history of medieval cities and of the late medieval nobility.

JEANETTE ZISSELL is a Ph.D. student at the University of Connecticut. She received a B.A. in English from the University of Massachusetts, and an M.A. in Medieval Studies at the University of Connecticut. Her interests include Middle English vernacular theology and poetry. She hopes to focus her dissertation on the theme of friendship in *Piers Plowman*.

# Index